Edition

An

Argument

Rhetoric

and

Reader

dialogues

Gary Goshgarian
Northeastern University

Kathleen Krueger

Janet Barnett Minc
University of Akron-Wayne College

An imprint of Addison Wesley Longman, Inc.

New York • Reading, Massachusetts • Menlo Park, California • Harlow, England
Don Mills, Ontario • Sydney • Mexico City • Madrid • Amsterdam

Publishing Partner: Anne Elizabeth Smith
Sponsoring Development Manager: Arlene Bessenoff
Developmental Editor: Leslie Taggart
Marketing Manager: Renée Ortbals
Supplements Editor: Donna Campion
Full Service Production Manager: Mark Naccarelli
Project Coordination, Text Design, and Electronic Page Makeup: Nesbitt Graphics, Inc.
Cover Designer/Manager: Nancy Danahy
Photo Researcher: Mira Schachne
Senior Print Buyer: Hugh Crawford
Printer and Binder: The Maple-Vail Book Manufacturing Group
Cover Printer: Coral Graphic Services, Inc.

For permission to use copyrighted material, grateful acknowledgment is made to the copyright holders on pages 764–770, which are hereby made part of this copyright page.

Library of Congress Cataloging-in-Publication Data
Dialogues : an argument rhetoric and reader / [edited by] Gary
  Goshgarian, Kathleen Krueger, Janet Barnett Minc. — 3rd ed.
        p.   cm.
    Rev. ed. of: Crossfire. 2nd ed. c1997.
    Includes index.
    ISBN 0-321-02399-4
      1. English language—Rhetoric.   2. Persuasion (Rhetoric).
  3. College readers.   I. Goshgarian, Gary.   II. Krueger, Kathleen.
  III. Minc, Janet Barnett.   IV. Crossfire.
  PE1431.C76   2000
  808'.0427—dc21   99-36123
                                                                                CIP

Please visit our website at http://www.awlonline.com/goshgarian

ISBN 0-321-02399-4

2345678910—MA—02010099

brief contents

detailed contents

"Something dramatic happens to girls in early adolescence. Just as planes and ships disappear mysteriously into the Bermuda Triangle, so do the selves of girls go down in droves. They crash and burn in a social and developmental Bermuda Triangle."

"Seen from the outside, my life is the model of modern female independence. I live alone, pay my own bills, and fix my stereo when it breaks down. But it sometimes seems like my independence is in part an elaborately constructed facade that hides a more traditional feminine desire to be protected and provided for."

"It isn't height or weight or strength that makes women easy targets; from infancy women are taught to be self-sacrificing, passive victims."

"While it may still seem like a 'man's world' from the perspective of power and wealth in adult society, on the whole, boys are falling terribly behind in our schools."

preface

Dialogues: *An Argument Rhetoric and Reader* (formerly *Crossfire*) embodies a new approach to reading and writing arguments. It moves students away from the traditional combative model of argument in which writers take opposing stances and attempt to defeat all viewpoints other than their own. Instead, students are encouraged to explore multiple perspectives on a particular topic before forming their own opinions and writing their own arguments. Through a process of debate, dialogue, and deliberation, students learn to investigate diverse opinions, synthesize and respond to the views of others, and carefully evaluate evidence to arrive at an informed position on a particular issue. Students are encouraged to abandon a pro/con, adversarial stance in favor of negotiation and the discovery of shared values among opponents. While we are well aware that not all arguments can be resolved to everyone's satisfaction, we believe that the power of argument can be used most productively when arguers actually listen to the voices of others and respond to them in a thoughtful way. In this book we provide a structure for this dialogue to take place.

Organization of the Book

As the title indicates, the book is divided into two parts. The rhetoric section consists of eight chapters explaining the strategies of reading and writing arguments. The reader section consists of 9 thematic units containing 90 essays—a challenging collection of thought-provoking contemporary and historical arguments.

Part I: Strategies for Reading and Writing Arguments

Our overall goal is to involve students in the process of writing arguments, a multifaceted activity involving careful reading, critical thinking, skillful writing, and thorough research. To this purpose we have organized the first eight chapters to guide students through the stages of argument writing, beginning with an explanation of what an argument is and progressing to the final argument essay. Throughout Part 1 we have included short arguments—20 essays in all—by professional and student writers to illustrate each chapter's focus and provide opportunities to apply, analyze, and synthesize the major ideas in the chapter. In some chapters, several essays on a particular issue demonstrate diverse ways of writing and thinking about a single topic. Exercises in each chapter reinforce concepts with immediate, hands-on practice.

Chapter 1 offers an overview of argumentation, clarifies key terminology, and introduces the processes of debate, dialogue, and deliberation. Chapter 2 focuses on critical reading, presenting a series of activities designed to help students evaluate arguments and recognize their primary components. An extensive section on testing arguments for logical fallacies ends the chapter. Chapter 3 discusses how to begin writing arguments. It helps students find worthwhile and interesting topics to write about by demonstrating techniques for brainstorming, limiting topics, and formulating claims. Chapter 4 examines the presence of audience, encouraging students to think about the different kinds of readers they may have to address. This chapter suggests ways to evaluate the audience's concerns and strategies to reach different audiences.

Chapter 5 focuses on the organization of the argument essay by analyzing two basic types of arguments—positions and proposals. Outlining is reviewed as a tool to ensure effective organization. Chapter 6 considers the importance of evidence. We demonstrate that the effectiveness of a writer's argument largely depends on how well evidence—facts, testimony, statistics, and observations—is employed to support the writer's ideas. Chapter 7 introduces the socially constructed Toulmin model of logic as a way of testing the premises of the writer's argument. Chapter 8 discusses research strategies, including locating and evaluating print and electronic sources, note-taking tips, and drafting and revising argument essays. The Documentation Guide provides documentation formats for both MLA and APA styles, and two annotated sample student research papers, one in MLA style and the other in APA style.

Part 2: Dialogues

The 90 contemporary and historical essays in the reader offer a wide range of provocative and stimulating selections to get students thinking about controversies that affect their lives, and make them aware of the diversity and complexity of argument. We expect that these readings will generate lively class discussion through shared debate and dialogue.

Seventy-eight of the essays are organized into seven broad thematic chapters: "Gender Matters," "Race and Ethnicity," "Freedom of Expression," "Media Influence," "Individual Rights," "Regulating Relationships," and "The Black Freedom Struggle." Each of these chapters is divided into three or four specific topics whose readings demonstrate both different viewpoints and shared concerns. While most of the readings deal with current controversies, Chapter 17 on the civil rights movement, "The Black Freedom Struggle," presents historical arguments that substantially altered twentieth century American history. In three sections, the chapter examines the controversies surrounding education, violence and nonviolence, and equal opportunity during the civil rights era; a fourth section reflects back from contemporary points of view on the gains and losses of the struggle for African American rights. From the formality of the Supreme Court decision in *Brown v. Board of Education of Topeka* to the eloquence of James Baldwin to the riveting passion of Malcolm X, the arguments here should inspire students' interest and challenge their assumptions about this important period of American political history.

Twelve readings comprise our casebooks on juvenile crime and teen parents, two subjects of particular interest to college students. Each casebook provides students with the opportunity to explore the subject in depth through extensive readings, discussion questions, collaborative exercises, writing assignments, and research opportunities. Many suggestions for using Web resources help ensure that students have access to the most current information about these rapidly evolving issues.

Study Apparatus

To help students become actively engaged with the readings and the issues, we have included a variety of apparatus throughout the text. Each chapter in Part 2 opens with an introduction explaining the chapter theme and underscoring the importance of the essays and the rationale behind their selection. An introduction to each essay provides a context for the reading and pertinent biographical information about the writer. "Before You Read" and "As You Read" questions guide students before and during the actual reading process. Following each essay are "For Analysis and Discussion" questions designed to stimulate thinking about the content, logic, and organization of the essay and the strategies of the writer. At the end of each section of readings, several writing assignments encourage students to synthesize their ideas about the essays, deliberate about their own ideas, and undertake further research and writing. In the casebooks on juvenile crime and teen parenting, each reading is also followed by more extensive opportunities to explore the topic by conducting interviews and surveys, visiting both Web sites and community facilities, and investigating additional reference sources. Finally, the Glossary of Rhetorical Terms defines terminology used throughout the text.

New to This Edition

While the second edition of *Crossfire* was a successful text, we knew that it was time for a change if we wanted our book to reflect the most current research being done in composition studies. To do this, we invited a new author on board, Janet Barnett Minc, a professor of English at The University of Akron-Wayne College, who brought her extensive teaching experience and research in the fields of composition and argument to the task of revision. As a result of her work, *Crossfire* shifted its emphasis away from a pro/con model to a new paradigm that acknowledges more effectively the complexity of argument. The revisions were so dramatic that the former title was no longer relevant to the text. *Dialogues* tells the story of our new focus on finding common ground, listening and responding to those who hold different views, and carefully deliberating about these multiple perspectives before arriving at a position.

This third edition also reflects the insights and suggestions of many of the instructors and students who used the second edition of *Crossfire*. We have left those features that people found most useful unchanged, and we have tried to make careful revisions where improvement was needed. Here are some of the major changes in this new edition:

The Rhetoric

- "Debate, dialogue, and deliberation" is presented as a process for evaluating and building arguments through comparing and synthesizing diverse viewpoints. This approach emphasizes listening and responding to the arguments of others and investigating multiple perspectives on an issue to arrive at an informed position.
- New Chapter 2, "Reading Arguments: Thinking like a Critic," takes students step by step through the process of critical reading and reflection, from pre-

viewing and skimming a reading, through annotating and summarizing, to analyzing, evaluating, and arguing with a reading.
- The coverage of logical fallacies has been expanded, making it an essential part of Chapter 2 on critical reading and integrating it throughout the rest of the rhetoric.
- The number of readings in the rhetoric has doubled. Twenty sample arguments—18 of them new—provide examples of important strategies in argument writing and give students practice in analyzing arguments. In addition, thematically connected essays allow students to compare different strategies and approaches to the same topic.
- Chapter 7, "Establishing Claims: Thinking like a Skeptic" has been revised to clarify the Toulmin model and to provide more effective examples for class discussion and analysis.
- New sections on using Internet sources in Chapter 8, "Researching Arguments: Thinking like an Investigator," detail specific information and examples of searching for, locating, and evaluating relevant electronic sources. Three Web sites are analyzed and compared to demonstrate how to determine the research value of information found on the Web.
- Examples of documentation using electronic sources have been updated and expanded in the "Documentation Guide: MLA and APA," which follows Chapter 8.
- The "Documentation Guide" now includes new sample student research papers in MLA and APA styles, annotated to highlight important documentation issues.

The Reader

- Part Two now includes 90 readings (increased from 69 in our second edition) with 81 essays new to this edition.
- Four new major themes include topics of current national interest as well as examples of classic arguments:

    "Media Influence" includes subthemes on the persuasive language of advertising (including three sample advertisements), the credibility of TV news, and movie and TV violence.

    "Individual Rights" examines physician-assisted suicide, the right to privacy, and drug testing of students.

    "Regulating Relationships" discusses same-sex marriage, sexual harassment, and adoption.

    "The Black Freedom Struggle" includes arguments on four themes: education, violence and nonviolence, equal opportunity, and contemporary reflections on the civil rights movement.
- Two new casebooks—"Juvenile Crime, Adult Punishment?" and "Teen Parents: Children Having Children?"—provide students with the opportunity to explore the issues in depth through research, class activities, and writing assignments.
- Suggestions for writing assignments follow each section of essays, helping students synthesize their own and the authors' ideas and directing them toward further research, including sources on the Internet.

Acknowledgments

It is with pleasure that we acknowledge the contributions of individuals who contributed invaluable advice and guidance on this project: Gary Bays, Elys Kettling, Mary Tohill, Lisa Simons, and Paul Weinstein, all of The University of Akron—Wayne College, and Joe Straw of The University of Akron Library. We would also like to thank those instructors who answered lengthy questionnaires about the second edition and who supplied many helpful comments and suggestions for the third: Mark Amsler, University of Delaware; Virginia Anderson, Indiana University Southwest; J. Robert Baker, Fairmont State College; Larry Beason, Eastern Washington University; James Boehnlein, University of Dayton; Eleanor Bowie, Penn Valley Community College; Robert Boyer, Columbus Community College; Sherry Dunlop, California State University, San Bernadino; David Elias, Eastern Kentucky University; Elizabeth Elchlepp, Santiago Canyon Community College; Julia Gergits, Youngstown State University; Maria Gillombardo, University of Illinois, Urbana; John Hanes, Duquesne University; Steve Hecox, University of Nevada, Reno; Dan Holt, Lansing Community College; Rebecca Moore Howard, Texas Christian University; Steve Kirby, York College of Pennsylvania; Catherine Carr Lee, University of Texas, Dallas; Tim McGee, The College of New Jersey; Susan Kelley, Fairmont State College; Nancy Kephart, Columbus State Community College; Deborah Kirkman, University of Kentucky; William Provost, University of Georgia; Jan Rainbird, California State University, Fullerton; Jamie Signorino, The University of Akron; Thomas Tobin, Duquesne University; Anne Turner, University of Kansas; Karen Waters, Marymount University; Lance Wilder, University of Georgia.

A special thanks goes to Kathryn Goodfellow, who created the study apparatus and introductory notes to the Part Two essays, as well as the answers for the Instructor's Manual. Her thoughtful and creative questions as well as her vast knowledge of Internet resources will no doubt produce stimulating classroom discussion and meaningful written responses.

We would also like to express our appreciation for the efforts of a number of people at Addison Wesley Longman, especially Leslie Taggart, our development editor, whose tireless energy and remarkable organization guided us through this process; Anne Smith, Arlene Bessenoff, and Lynn Huddon, our three English editors who contributed to the development of this edition from first inspiration to final copy; Robyn Renahan, our permissions editor; Mira Schachne, our photo editor; Mark Naccarelli, our production manager; and Tom Conville, our project manager at Nesbitt Graphics.

Finally, Janet expresses her heartfelt gratitude to Betty and Raymond Barnett for their encouragement and to David C. Minc for his endless support.

Gary Goshgarian
Kathleen Krueger
Janet Barnett Minc

the supplements package

Dialogues on the Web

Dialogues on the Web <http://www.awlonline.com/goshgarian> is a Web site specifically designed for instructors and students using *Dialogues: An Argument Rhetoric and Reader, 3/e.* It features numerous reading, writing, and research activities for students to complete as they visit a diverse collection of Web sites.

Daedalus Online

Daedalus® Online is the next generation of the well received and highly awarded Daedalus Integrated Writing Environment (DIWE). Developed by top composition scholars, Daedalus Online employs standard Web-based utilities to facilitate a shared writing process among students using any word processing program from any computer that connects to the Internet, with secure, 24-hour availability. Students using Daedalus Online can now easily explore online composition resources, employ prewriting strategies, partake in computer-mediated real-time conferencing, and post feedback to an asynchronous discussion board. They can use these features to sharpen meaning, style, and expression in their writing. Daedalus Online offers a comprehensive suite of online course management tools, which allow you, the instructor, to:

- Effortlessly create and post assignments
- Link these assignments to online educational resources
- Tie these lessons to integrated top-selling Longman textbooks
- Customize materials to fit with any instructional preference

Researching Online, 3/e

Researching Online is an indispensable media companion that helps students navigate the Internet. This print supplement includes detailed information on:

- Internet resources such as e-mail, listservs, Usenet newsgroups, IRCs, MU*s, Gopher, and the World Wide Web.
- Search engines and advanced search techniques.
- Assessing the validity of an electronic source as well as links to Internet resources that expand on this coverage.
- How to create and post Web pages using HTML.

English Pages

The English Pages <http://www.longman.awl.com/englishpages> is a Web site that provides professors and students with continuously updated resources for reading, writing, and research practice in four areas: composition, literature, technical writing, and basic skills. Features include:

- "Simulated Searches" show the process of finding and evaluating information on the WWW. Students visit "sources" and decipher whether they are legitimate, unbiased, and appropriate for use in a class writing assignment. This activity also walks students through the process of generating a bibliography using correct electronic citation style.
- "The Faces of Composition" presents first-person essays that show students how everyday men and women have applied what they learned in composition—investigation, collaboration, inquiry, and debate—to a wide variety of situations.
- Annotated "Links" give access to a wide variety of sites, from an online library to scholarly manuscripts, providing the best information on writing issues and research topics.

Penguin Program

In conjunction with our sister company, Penguin Putnam, Inc., Longman is proud to offer a variety of Penguin titles at a significant discount when packaged with any Longman title. We offer, for example, both of Mike Rose's books, *Possible Lives* and *Lives on the Boundary,* and Neil Postman's book, *Amusing Ourselves to Death,* when bundled with *Dialogues.* For a full listing of all Penguin titles available with Longman texts, please consult your local representative.

The Longman Guide to Columbia Online Style

The Longman Guide to Columbia Online Style is a 32-page booklet that includes an overview of Columbia Online Style, guidelines for finding and evaluating electronic sources, and examples for citing electronic sources. Columbia Online Style (COS) is a documentation style developed specifically for citing sources obtained in electronic form and either read online or printed out from the World Wide Web or Internet. It is intended for use in combination with MLA (Modern Language Association), APA (American Psychological Association), CMS (Chicago Manual of Style), CBE (Council of Biology Editors), or other documentation styles used in the humanities and sciences. *The Longman Guide to Columbia Online Style* is free when packaged with any Longman text. For special ISBN ordering information, please consult your local representative.

The Essential Research Guide

The Essential Research Guide is a handy two-page laminated card that features guidelines for evaluating print and online sources, including aspects such as the source's purpose, audience, and language; a reference list of editing and proofreading symbols; and a web guide to resources in fields such as history, arts and literature, and science. *The Essential Research Guide* is available free to students when bundled with *Dialogues.* Please consult your local representative for special ISBN ordering information.

The Instructor's Manual

The Instructor's Manual features answers to every question in Parts One and Two of *Dialogues,* and includes a sample syllabus using the third edition.

part one

STRATEGIES
FOR READING
AND WRITING
ARGUMENTS

chapter 1

UNDERSTANDING PERSUASION

Thinking like a Negotiator

Think of all of the times in the course of a week when someone tries to convince you of something. You listen to the radio on the way to school or work and are relentlessly bombarded by advertisements urging you to buy vitamins, watch a particular television show, or eat at the new Mexican restaurant in town. You open a newspaper and read about the latest proposals to lower the drinking age, to raise the age for retirement, and to provide tax relief for the poor. The phone rings and the caller tries to sell you a magazine subscription or to convince you to vote for candidate X. There's a knock on your bedroom door and your sister wants to borrow a CD and the keys to your car. Whether the issue is as small as a CD or as important as taxes, everywhere you turn you find yourself called on to make a decision and to exercise a choice.

If you think about all these instances, you'll discover that each decision you finally do make is heavily influenced by the ability of others to persuade you. People who have mastered the art of argument are able to influence others to do what they want. Your ability to understand how argument works and how to use it effectively will help you become aware of the ways in which you are influenced by the arguments of others, as well as become more persuasive yourself. Anyone can learn to argue effectively by learning the techniques needed to create successful arguments.

This book is designed to help you to achieve two goals: (1) to think critically about the power of other people's arguments and (2) to become persuasive in your own arguments.

Argument

Broadly speaking, *persuasion* means influencing someone to do something. It can take many forms: fast-paced glittering ads, high-flying promises from salespeople, emotional appeals from charity groups—even physical threats. What will concern us in this book is *argument*—the form of persuasion that relies on reasoning and logical thought to convince people. While glitter, promises, emotional appeals, and even veiled threats may work, the real power of argument comes from the arguer's ability to convince others through language.

3

Because this is a book about writing, we will concentrate on the aspects of persuasion that most apply in writing, as opposed to those that work best in other forms (advertisements or oral appeals, for instance). Although written arguments can be passionate, emotional, or even hurtful, a good one demonstrates a firm foundation of clear thinking, logical development, and solid supporting evidence to persuade a reader that the view expressed is worth hearing. The ultimate goal might be to convince readers to change their thinking on an issue, but that does not always happen. A more realistic goal might be to have your listeners seriously consider your point of view and to win their respect through the logic and skill of your argument.

Most of what you write in college and beyond will attempt to persuade someone that what you have to say is worthy of consideration, whether it's a paper stating your views on immigration laws, an analysis of "madness" in *King Lear,* a letter to the editor of your school newspaper regarding women's varsity basketball, or a lab report on the solubility of salt. The same demands of persuasion and argument will carry over into your professional life. Such writing might be in the form of progress reports on students or colleagues, legal briefs, business reports, medical evaluations, memos to colleagues, results of a technical study or scientific experiment, proposals, maybe even a sales speech. In searching for a job or career, you might have to sell yourself in letters of inquiry.

The success or failure of those attempts will strongly depend on how well you argue your case. Therefore, it's important that as a college student you learn the skills of writing persuasive arguments. Even if you never write another argument, you will read, hear, and make them the rest of your life.

What Makes an Argument?

Arguments, in a sense, underlie nearly all forms of writing. Whenever you express ideas, you are attempting to persuade somebody to agree with you. However, not every matter can be formally argued. Nor are some things worth the effort. So, before we go on to discuss the different strategies, we should make clear which subjects do and do not lend themselves to argument.

Facts Are Not Arguable

Because facts are readily verifiable, they can't be argued. Of course, people might dispute a fact. For instance, you might disagree with a friend's claim that Thomas Jefferson was the second president of the United States. But to settle your dispute, all you have to do is consult an encyclopedia. What makes a fact a fact and, thus, inarguable, is that it has only one answer. It occurs in time and space and cannot be disputed. A fact either *is* or *is not* something. Thomas Jefferson was the third president of the United States, not the second. John Adams was the second. Those are facts. So are the following statements:

* The distance between Boston and New York City is 214 miles.
* Martin Luther King, Jr.'s birthday is now celebrated in all 50 states.

- I got a 91 on my math test.
- The Washington Monument is 555 feet high.
- The Japanese smoke more cigarettes per capita than any other people on earth.
- My dog Fred died a year ago.
- Canada borders the United States to the north.

All that is required to prove or disprove any of these statements is to check with some authority for the right answer. Sometimes facts are not easily verifiable, for instance, "Yesterday, 1,212,031 babies were born in the world" or "More people have black hair than any other color." These statements may be true, but it would be a daunting, if not impossible, challenge to prove them. And what would be the point?

Opinions Based on Personal Taste or Preference Are Not Arguable

Differing opinions are the basis of all argument. However, you must be careful to distinguish between opinions based on personal taste and opinions based on judgments. Someone who asks your "opinion" about which color shoes to buy is simply seeking your color preference—black versus brown, say. If someone asks your "opinion" of a certain movie, the matter could be more complicated.

Beyond whether or not you liked it, what might be sought is your aesthetic evaluation of the film: a judgment about the quality of acting, directing, cinematography, set design—all measured by critical standards you've developed over years of moviegoing. Should you be asked your "opinion" of voluntary euthanasia, your response would probably focus on moral and ethical questions: Is the quality of life more important than the duration of life? What, if any, circumstances justify the taking of a life? Who should make so weighty a decision—the patient, the patient's family, the attending physician, a health team?

The word *opinion* is commonly used to mean different things. As just illustrated, depending on the context, opinion can refer to personal preference, a reaction to or analysis of something, or an evaluation, belief, or judgment, all of which are different. In this text we categorize all these different possibilities as either opinions of taste or opinions of judgment.

Opinions of taste come down to personal preferences, based on subjective and, ultimately, unverifiable judgments. Each of the following statements is an opinion of taste:

- George looks good in blue.
- Pizza is my favorite food.
- Brian May of the group Queen is the greatest living rock guitarist.
- Video games are a waste of time.

Each of these statements is inarguable. Let's consider the first: "George looks good in blue." Is it a fact? Not really, since there is no objective way to measure its validity. You might like George in blue, whereas someone else might prefer him in red. Is the statement then debatable? No. Even if someone retorts, "George does *not* look good in blue," what would be the basis of argument but personal preference? And where would the counterargument go? Nowhere.

Even if a particular preference were backed by strong feelings, it would not be worth debating, nor might you sway someone to your opinion. For instance, let's say you make the statement that you never eat hamburger. You offer the following as reasons:

1. You're disgusted by the sight of ground-up red meat.
2. When the meat is cooked, its smell disgusts you.
3. Hamburgers remind you of the terrible argument that broke out at a family barbecue some years ago.
4. You once got very sick after eating meatloaf.
5. You think beef cattle are the dirtiest of farm animals.

Even with all these "reasons" to support your point of view, you have not constructed an argument that goes beyond your own personal preference. In fact, the "reasons" you cite are themselves grounded in personal preferences. They amount to explanations rather than an argument. The same is true of the statements about pizza, musicians, and video games.

Opinions Based on Judgments Are Arguable

An *opinion of judgment* is one that weighs the pros and cons of an issue and determines their relative worth. That "something" might be a book, a song, or a public issue, such as capital punishment. Such an opinion represents a position on an issue that is measured against standards other than those of personal taste—standards that are rooted in values and beliefs of our culture: what's true and false, right and wrong, good and bad, better and worse. Consequently, such an opinion is arguable.

In other words, personal opinions or personal preferences can be transformed into bona fide arguments. Let's return to the example of hamburger. Suppose you want to turn your own dislike for ground meat into a paper persuading others to give up eating beef. You can take several approaches to make a convincing argument. For one, you can take a health slant, arguing that vegetarians have lower mortality rates than people whose diets are high in animal fat and cholesterol; or that the ingestion of all the hormones in beef increases the risks of cancer. You might even take an environmental approach, pointing out that the more beef we eat, the more we encourage the conversion of woodlands and rain forests into grazing land, thus destroying countless animals and their habitats. You can even take an ethical stand, arguing from an animal-rights point of view that intensive farming practices create inhumane treatment of animals—that is, crowding, force-feeding, and force-breeding. You might also argue that the killing of animals is morally wrong.

The point is that personal opinions can be starting points for viable arguments. But those opinions must be developed according to recognized standards of values and beliefs.

The Uses of Argument

Many arguments center on issues that are controversial. Controversial issues, by definition, create disagreement and debate because people hold opposing positions about them. And, most of the time, there are more than two sides. Depending on the issue, there may be multiple opinions and perspectives. Because these views are often strongly held, we tend to view argument only in the form of a *debate,* an encounter between two or more adversaries who battle with each other over who is right. The media does much to contribute to the way we picture argument, particularly in the area of politics.

Every four years or so the image returns to our television screens. Two candidates, dark suited and conservatively dressed, hands tightly gripping their respective podiums, face off for all of America to watch. Each argues passionately for his or her solution to poverty, educational failings, high taxes, and countless other social and economic problems. Each tries desperately to undermine the arguments of the opponent in an effort to capture the votes of those watching. It's a winner-take-all debate, and it's often the image we see in our minds when we think of argument.

Argument *is* a form of persuasion that seeks to convince others to do what the arguer wants. Argument allows us to present our views and the reasons behind those views clearly and strongly. Yet argument can serve more productive purposes than the above illustration. Although argument can be a debate between two or more opponents who will never see eye-to-eye, in the world outside presidential debates and television sound bites argument can also begin a *dialogue* among opposing sides. It can enable them to listen to each others' concerns and to respond to them in a thoughtful way. Rather than attempt to demolish their opponents' arguments, these negotiators can often arrive at positions that are more valuable because they try to reconcile conflicting viewpoints by understanding and dealing directly with their opponents' concerns. Through the practice of *debate, dialogue,* and *deliberation,* real change can happen. In this chapter we explore these three essential elements of argument and explain how they will enable you to be more effective when you write to persuade others.

Debate

Think for a moment of all the associations the word *debate* suggests to you: winning, losing, taking sides, opposition, and competition. Debate is how we traditionally think of argument. It is a situation in which individuals or groups present their views as forcefully and persuasively as possible, often referring to their opponents' arguments only to attack or deride them. Practiced with just this goal in mind, debate can serve the purpose of presenting your position clearly in contrast to your opposition's, but it does little to resolve controversial issues. Focusing too much on the adversarial qualities of debate can prevent you from listening and considering other viewpoints. You can become so preoccupied with defeating opposing arguments that you fail to recognize the legitimacy of other opinions. This may lead you to ignore them as you fashion your own argument.

Consider the last time you debated an issue with someone. Perhaps it was an informal occasion in which you attempted to convince the other person of your point of view. It may have been about a job opportunity or the best place to spend spring break or what movie to see next weekend. Your aim was to persuade the other person to "see it your way," and, if it was a typical debate, you were successful only if the other individual acquiesced. Debates are traditionally won or lost, and losers often feel frustrated and disappointed. Even more important, reasonable concerns on the losing side are often overlooked or not addressed. Debate does not provide a mechanism for compromise. It is not intended to provide a path toward common ground or a resolution in which all parties achieve a degree of success and positive change is made. Although some issues are so highly contentious that true consensus can never be achieved, an effective argument must acknowledge and respond to opposition in a thoughtful and productive manner.

But debate is an important way to develop your arguments because it allows you to explore their strengths and weaknesses. It can be a starting point for argument rather than a conclusion. Debate contains some of the essential elements of argument: Someone with a strong opinion tries to demonstrate the effectiveness of that view, hoping to persuade others to change positions or to take a particular course of action. When we debate we have two objectives: to state our views clearly and persuasively and to distinguish our views from those of our opponents. Debate can help us develop our arguments because it encourages us to *formulate* a *claim, create reasons to support it,* and *anticipate opposition.*

Formulating Claims

The claim is the heart of your argument. Whether you hope to protest a decision, change your readers' minds, or motivate your audience to take action, somewhere in your argument must be the assertion you hope to prove. In an argument essay this assertion or claim functions as the *thesis* of the paper, and it is vital to the argument. The claim states precisely what you believe. It is the *position* or opinion you want your readers to accept or the action you want them to take. Thus, it's very important to state your claim as clearly as possible. It will form the basis for the rest of your argument.

Claims often take the form of a single declarative statement. For example, a claim in an argument essay about homelessness might look like this:

> If we look further into the causes of homelessness, we will discover that in many cases it is not the homeless individual who is at fault but rather conditions that exist in our society that victimize certain individuals.

A claim for an essay about teen pregnancy might be stated even more simply:

> The current rhetoric that maintains that the sexual references in the lyrics of popular music are to blame for the rise in teenage parenthood in the United States ignores several crucial realities.

Sometimes writers signal their claims to their readers by certain words: *therefore, consequently, the real question is, the point is, it follows that, my suggestion is.* Here's an example:

Therefore, I believe that scientists can find other effective ways to test new medicines and surgical techniques other than relying on helpless laboratory animals.

Because some arguments make recommendations for solving problems, your claim might be framed as a conditional statement that indicates both the problem and the solution. This can be accomplished with split phrases such as *either . . . or, neither . . . nor, if . . . then.* For example,

> If we continue to support a system of welfare that discourages its recipients from finding employment, the result will be a permanent class of unemployed citizens who lack the skills and incentives to participate fully for their own economic benefit.

Claims must have support to convince a reader, so they are often followed by "because" statements—that is, statements that justify a claim by explaining why something is true or recommended or beneficial:

> Outlawing assisted suicide is wrong because it deprives individuals of their basic human right to die with dignity.

Formulating your claim when you debate is a first step for three basic reasons:

1. It establishes the subject of your argument.
2. It solidifies your own stand or position about the issue.
3. It sets up a strategy on which your argument can be structured.

There are no hard-and-fast rules for the location of your claim. It can appear anywhere in your essay: as your opening sentence, in the middle, or as your conclusion. However, many writers state their claim early in the essay to let their readers know their position and to use it as a basis for all the supporting reasons that follow. In later chapters we will look at strategies for arriving at a claim and ways to organize your reasons to effectively support it.

Creating Reasons

We have all seen a building under construction. Before the roof can be laid or the walls painted or the flooring installed, the support beams must be carefully placed and stabilized. Reasons are the support beams of an argument essay. Whether your claim will be considered correct, insightful, or reasonable will depend on the strength and persuasiveness of your reasons.

Reasons answer some basic questions about your claim:

> Why do you believe your claim to be true?
>
> On what information or assumptions do you base your claim?
>
> What evidence can you supply to support your claim?
>
> Do any authorities or experts concur with your claim?

You can derive reasons from personal experience, readings, and research. Your choices will depend on your claim and the information and evidence you need to make your reasons convincing. Let's use one of the examples from our discussion about claims to demonstrate what we mean:

> **Your Claim:** Outlawing assisted suicide is wrong because it deprives individuals of the basic human right to die with dignity.
>
> **Question 1:** Why do you believe your claim to be true?
>
> **Response:** When individuals are terminally ill, they suffer many indignities: they can lose control of their bodily functions and must be dependent on others for their care. A prolonged illness with no hope of recovery causes the individual and family members to suffer needlessly. When death is imminent anyway, individuals should be given the right to decide when and how to end their lives.
>
> **Question 2:** On what information or assumptions do you base your claim?
>
> **Response:** I believe that no individual wants to suffer more than necessary. No one wants to lose his or her independence and have to rely on others. Everyone wants to be remembered as a whole human being, not as a dying invalid.
>
> **Question 3:** What evidence can you supply to support your claim?
>
> **Response:** This is based on personal examples and on readings about how terminal illness is dealt with in hospitals and clinics.
>
> **Question 4:** Do any authorities or experts concur with your claim?
>
> **Response:** Yes, many authorities in the field of medicine agree with my claim. I can use their statements and research to support it.

By examining the responses to the questions, you can see how reasons can be created to support your claim. The answer to the first question suggests several reasons why you might be opposed to outlawing assisted suicide: the indignities suffered by the terminally ill, unnecessary suffering, the right to control one's own fate. Question 2 explores your assumptions about what the terminally ill might experience and provides additional reasons to support your claim. The third and fourth questions suggest ways to support your claim through personal examples, references to ideas and examples found in readings related to your topic, and the support of experts in the field.

Credibility is an essential element in creating reasons. To be a successful debater you must be believable; you must convince your audience that you are knowledgeable about your subject and that the facts, statistics, anecdotes, and whatever else you use to support your reasons are accurate and up-to-date. This means constructing your reasons through research and careful analysis of all the information available. For example, if you argue in an essay that there are better ways to run the U.S. welfare system, you will need to understand and explain how the current system operates. You can use the facts and statistics that you uncover in your research to analyze existing problems and to support your ideas for change. Being thoroughly informed helps you present and use your knowledge persuasively. Acquainting yourself with the information necessary for convincing reasons will make you appear believable and competent. In later chapters we will discuss how to formulate reasons to support your claim and how to evaluate evidence and use it effectively.

Another way to achieve credibility is to avoid logical fallacies, which will undermine the logic or persuasiveness of your argument. *Logical fallacies,* a term derived from the Latin *fallere* meaning "to deceive," are unintentional errors in logic or deliberate attempts to mislead the reader by exaggerating evidence or using methods of argument that appeal to prejudice or bias. In Chapter 2, we will review the most common forms of logical fallacies so you can recognize them in the arguments of others and avoid them in your own writing.

Anticipating Opposition

Because debate anticipates opposition, you need to be certain that your reasons can withstand the challenges that are sure to come. Your goal as a successful debater is not only to present your reasons clearly and persuasively, but also to be prepared for the ways in which those individuals holding other views will respond to them. For instance, in an essay on discrimination in women's collegiate sports, you may state that the operating budget of the women's varsity basketball team at your school is a fraction of that for the men's team. As evidence you might point to the comparative lack of advertising, lower attendance at games, and lesser coverage than for the men's team. Unless you anticipate other perspectives on your issue, however, your argument could fall apart should someone suggest that women's basketball teams have lower budgets simply because they have smaller paying audiences. Not anticipating such a rebuttal would weaken your position. Had you been prepared, you could have acknowledged that opposing point and then responded to it by reasoning that the low budget is the cause of the problem, not the result of it. Putting more money into advertising and coverage could boost attendance and, thus, revenue.

In short, it is not enough to simply present your own reasons, no matter how effectively you support them. Unless you are aware of and familiar with opposing reasons, you leave yourself open to being undermined. To make your case as effective as possible, you must acknowledge and respond to the strongest reasons that challenge your own. To present only the weakest points of those who disagree with you or to do so in a poor light would likely backfire on your own credibility.

The following are strategies we recommend to help you become more aware of views that are different from your own and ways you might respond to them.

"Yes, but . . ." Exchanges

One way to be aware of the reasons on the other side is to study and research your topic carefully. After you've done some reading, a useful method to explore the way others might respond to your ideas is to engage in a "Yes, but . . . " exchange. Imagine you are face to face with someone holding a different position and, as you run down the list of your own reasons, his or her response is "Yes, but . . . [something]."

What might that "something" be? Your task is first to acknowledge the validity of the other individual's viewpoint, and then to respond to that idea with reasons of your own. Consider, for instance, how a debate about affirmative action programs might proceed. You begin:

> Affirmative action programs discriminate against white males by denying them employment for which they are qualified.

From what you've heard and read, your opponent might respond this way:

> Yes, there are probably instances in which white males have lost employment opportunities because of affirmative action programs, but without these programs minority candidates would never be considered for some job openings regardless of their qualifications.

Another reason might be:

> Race and gender should not be a consideration when hiring an applicant for a job.

From your readings, you may uncover this opposing reason:

> Yes, in an ideal society race and gender would never be a factor for employers, but since we don't live in such a society, affirmative action programs ensure that race and gender don't become negative considerations when an individual applies for a job.

Imagining your debate in a "Yes, but . . ." exchange will help you work through a number of possibilities to strengthen your reasons in the light of opposition and to become more aware of other viewpoints.

Pro/Con Checklists

Another method to help you become more aware of opposing viewpoints is to create a pro/con checklist. Making a pro/con checklist is useful for several reasons. First, it helps you solidify your own stand on the issue. It puts you in the position of having to formulate points on which to construct an argument. Second, by anticipating counterpoints you can better test the validity and strength of your points. By listing potential resistance you can determine the weak spots in your argument. Third, tabulating your own points will help you decide how to organize your reasons—which points to put at the beginning of your paper and which to put in the conclusion. Depending on the issue, you may decide, for the sake of impact, to begin with the strongest point and end with the weakest. This is the strategy of most advertisers—hitting the potential customer right off with the biggest sales pitch. Or you may decide to use a climactic effect by beginning with the weakest point and building to the strongest and most dramatic. Last, by ordering your key points you can create a potential framework for constructing your argument. Here's an example of a pro/con checklist:

Sample Pro/Con Checklist

CLAIM: Human cloning should be outlawed because it is unnecessary and unethical.

PRO	CON
Human cloning is unnecessary because we have better ways to treat infertility.	Current fertility treatments are very expensive and are often unsuccessful.
Because we have too many unwanted children in the world already, we should not create more.	People have a right to have their own children.
Cloning is an unnatural process.	It is no more unnatural than many of the ways we currently treat infertility.
Human cloning will devalue the uniqueness of each individual.	A clone will still be a unique and separate human being.

Moving from Debate to Dialogue

"conflicting issues that lie at the heart

Debate is an important step in constructing an argument. It propels us to find a strong position and to argue that position as effectively as possible. But if we define argument as only debate, we limit the potential power of argument in our society. One common misconception is that all arguments are won or lost. This may be true in formalized debates, but in real life few arguments are decided so clearly, and when they are, the conflicting issues that lie at the heart of the debate can persist and continue to create dissension among individuals and groups. The prolonged tensions and sometimes violent confrontations that surround the issue of abortion may be the outcome of a debate that supposedly was resolved by a Supreme Court decision, *Roe v. Wade,* but remains a continuing problem because the debate did not engender a dialogue in which conflicting sides listened to each other and reconsidered their views from a more informed perspective. Argument must do more than provide an opportunity to present one's views against those of an opponent. We need to use it as a vehicle to explore other views as well and to help us shape a process in which change can happen and endure.

Dialogue

Take another moment to consider words that come to mind when you think of *dialogue:* discussion, listening, interaction, and understanding. By definition a dialogue includes more than one voice, and those voices are responsive to each other. When we have a dialogue with someone, we don't simply present our own views.

We may disagree, but we take turns so that no one voice monopolizes the conversation. The object of a dialogue is not to win or lose; the object is to communicate our ideas and to listen to what the other person has to say in response.

For example, you may find a policy in a particular class regarding make-ups unfair. Since your instructor seems to be a reasonable person, you visit her office to discuss your objections. Your dialogue might proceed like this:

> **You:** Professor, your syllabus states that if a student misses a test, there are no make-ups. I think that this is unfair because if a student is genuinely ill or has an important conflict, the student will be penalized.
>
> **Professor:** I can understand your concern, but I have that policy because some students use make-ups to gain extra time to study. And, by asking other students about the questions on the test, they gain an advantage over students who take the test when it's scheduled. I don't think that's fair.
>
> **You:** I hadn't thought of that. That's a good reason, but I'm still worried that even if I have a legitimate excuse for missing a test, my grade in the course will suffer. What can I do if that happens?
>
> **Professor:** Let me think about your problem. Perhaps there's a way that I can be fair to you and still not jeopardize the integrity of my exams.
>
> **You:** What if a student provides a physician's note in case of illness or a few day's advance notice in case of a conflict? Would you be able to provide an alternative testing day if that should happen?
>
> **Professor:** That might be a good way to deal with the problem, as long as the make-up could be scheduled soon after. I'm going to give this more thought before I decide. I appreciate your suggestions. Stop by tomorrow and we can come to an agreement.

This hypothetical dialogue works because each participant listens and responds to the ideas of the other. Each has an important stake in the issue, but both focus on finding constructive ways to deal with it rather than trying to prove that the other is wrong. As a result, a compromise can be reached, and each person will have made a contribution to the solution.

When we move from debate to dialogue, we move from an arbitrary stance to one that allows for change and modification. Dialogue requires that both sides of the debate do more than simply present and react to each other's views in an adversarial fashion; it demands that each side respond to the other's points by attempting to understand them and the concerns they express. Often it is difficult for those participating in a debate to take this important step. In such cases it will be your task, as a student of argument, to create the dialogue between opposing sides that will enable you to recognize common concerns and, if possible, to achieve a middle ground.

Creating a dialogue between two arguments involves identifying the writers' claims and key reasons. This is a skill we discuss in Chapter 2, when we look at strategies for reading and analyzing argument essays.

Deliberation

Deliberate is a verb that we don't use very much and we probably don't practice enough. It means to carefully and fully consider our reasons for and against something before making up our minds. We often speak of a jury deliberating about its verdict. Jury members must methodically weigh all the evidence and testimony that have been presented and then reach a judgment. Deliberation is not a quick process. It takes time to become informed, to explore all the alternatives, and to feel comfortable with a decision.

Deliberation plays an important part in the process of developing arguments. *Debate* focuses our attention on opposition and the points on which we disagree. *Dialogue* creates an opportunity to listen and explore the arguments that conflict with our own. Deliberation, the careful consideration of all that we have learned through debate and dialogue, enables us to reach our own informed position on the conflict. Because we have participated in both debate and dialogue, we have a more complete understanding of the opposing arguments, as well as the common ground they may share. We are able to take the concerns of all sides into account.

Deliberation does not always resolve an issue in a way that is pleasing to all sides. Some issues remain contentious and irreconcilable, so that the parties are unable to move beyond debate. And, just as a jury sometimes reaches a verdict that is not what either the defense or the prosecution desires, deliberation does not ensure that all concerns or arguments will be considered equally valid. However, deliberation does ensure that you have given the arguments of all sides careful attention. And, unlike a jury, you have much broader parameters to determine your position. You do not have to decide *for* or *against* one side or the other. Your deliberations may result in an entirely new way of viewing a particular issue or of solving a problem.

Consider, for example, a debate about whether a new football stadium should be built in a city experiencing economic problems, such as high unemployment and a failing public school system. One side of the debate may argue that a new stadium would result in additional jobs and revenue for the city from the influx of people who would come to watch the games. Another side may argue that the millions of dollars intended to subsidize a new stadium would be better spent creating job-training programs and promoting remedial education for schoolchildren. Your deliberation would involve several steps:

1. Becoming informed about the issue by reading and researching the information available
2. Creating a dialogue by listening to the arguments of all sides in the debate and trying to understand the reasons behind their claims
3. Carefully weighing all the arguments and information
4. Determining your own position on the issue

Your position might agree with one side or the other, or it might propose an entirely different response to the situation—say, a smaller stadium with the extra funds available to the schools, or a delay in the construction of a stadium until the unemployment problem is solved, or an additional tax to fund both, and so on. It would then be your task to convince all sides of the value of your position.

Deliberation enables you to use argument productively. It allows you to consider all sides of a problem or issue and to use your own critical analysis to find a way to respond.

As you learn more about writing your own arguments, you'll find that debate, dialogue, and deliberation can help you identify different perspectives, search for shared concerns, and develop your own position on an issue.

Review: Basic Terminology

Argument Essay	An essay that attempts to convince or persuade others through reason, logic, and evidence to do what the writer wants or believe as the writer wishes.
Claim	The statement in your essay that expresses your position or stand on a particular issue. The claim states precisely what you believe. It is the viewpoint you want your readers to accept or the action you want them to take.
Reasons	The explanation or justification behind your claim. To be effective, reasons must be supported by evidence and examples.
Debate	The act of presenting your claim and reasons and challenging and being challenged by someone who holds a different viewpoint. Debate often focuses on differences between opponents rather than shared concerns and values.
Dialogue	The act of listening and responding to those who hold viewpoints that are different from your own on a particular issue. The object of a dialogue is to find common ground by trying to understand other viewpoints while sharing your own. It is intended to reduce conflict rather than promote it.
Deliberation	The careful and informed consideration of all sides of an issue before reaching a conclusion or position on it. Deliberation can result in the resolution of a contentious issue.

Taking a "War of Words" Too Literally
Deborah Tannen

The following essay provides important insights into the ways in which we often approach argument in our society. The article by Deborah Tannen appeared in the weekly edition of the *Washington Post* on March 23, 1998. It is adapted from her current book, *The Argument Culture: Moving from Debate to Dialogue,* which explores how U.S. culture promotes a war-like, adversarial approach to problemsolving. Tannen is a professor of linguistics at Georgetown University. She is the author of the bestsellers *You Just Don't Understand: Women and Men in Conversation* and *Talking from 9 to 5: Women and Men in the Workplace.* As you read Tannen's article, think about whether you have had experiences similar to those Tannen describes, when disagreements could have been settled more successfully through dialogue and thoughtful deliberation rather than conflict.

1   I was waiting to go on a television talk show a few years ago for a discussion about how men and women communicate, when a man walked in wearing a shirt and tie and a floor-length skirt, the top of which was brushed by his waistlength red hair. He politely introduced himself and told me that he'd read and liked my book "You Just Don't Understand," which had just been published. Then he added, "When I get out there, I'm going to attack you. But don't take it personally. That's why they invite me on, so that's what I'm going to do."

2   We went on the set and the show began. I had hardly managed to finish a sentence or two before the man threw his arms out in gestures of anger, and began shrieking—briefly hurling accusations at me, and then railing at length against women. The strangest thing about his hysterical outburst was how the studio audience reacted: They turned vicious—not attacking me (I hadn't said anything substantive yet) or him (who wants to tangle with someone who screams at you?) but the other guests: women who had come to talk about problems they had communicating with their spouses.

3   My antagonist was nothing more than a dependable provocateur, brought on to ensure a lively show. The incident has stayed with me not because it was typical of the talk shows I have appeared on—it wasn't, I'm happy to say—but because it exemplifies the ritual nature of much of the opposition that pervades our public dialogue.

4   Everywhere we turn, there is evidence that, in public discourse, we prize contentiousness and aggression more than cooperation and conciliation. Headlines blare about the Starr Wars, the Mommy Wars, the Baby Wars, the Mammography Wars; everything is posed in terms of battles and duels, winners and losers, conflicts and disputes. Biographies have metamorphosed into demonographies whose authors don't just portray their subjects warts and all, but set out to dig up as much dirt as possible, as if the story of a person's life is contained in the warts, only the warts, and nothing but the warts.

5   It's all part of what I call the argument culture, which rests on the assumption that opposition is the best way to get anything done: The best way to dis-

cuss an idea is to set up a debate. The best way to cover news is to find people who express the most extreme views and present them as "both sides." The best way to begin an essay is to attack someone. The best way to show you're really thoughtful is to criticize. The best way to settle disputes is to litigate them.

Is she attacking or criticizing these views.

6   It is the automatic nature of this response that I am calling into question. This is not to say that passionate opposition and strong verbal attacks are never appropriate. In the words of Yugoslavian-born poet Charles Simic, "There are moments in life when true invective is called for, when it becomes an absolute necessity, out of a deep sense of justice, to denounce, mock, vituperate, lash out, in the strongest possible language." What I'm questioning is the ubiquity, the knee-jerk nature of approaching almost any issue, problem or public person in an adversarial way.

7   Smashing heads does not open minds. In this as in so many things, results are also causes, looping back and entrapping us. The pervasiveness of warlike formats and language grows out of, but also gives rise to, an ethic of aggression: We come to value aggressive tactics for their own sake—for the sake of argument. Compromise becomes a dirty word, and we often feel guilty if we are conciliatory rather than confrontational—even if we achieve the result we're seeking.

8   Here's one example. A woman called another talk show on which I was a guest. She told the following story: "I was in a place where a man was smoking, and there was a no-smoking sign. Instead of saying 'You aren't allowed to smoke in here. Put that out!' I said, 'I'm awfully sorry, but I have asthma, so your smoking makes it hard for me to breathe. Would you mind terribly not smoking?' When I said this, the man was extremely polite and solicitous, and he put his cigarette out, and I said, 'Oh, thank you, thank you!' as if he'd done a wonderful thing for me. Why did I do that?"

9   I think the woman expected me—the communications expert—to say she needs assertiveness training to confront smokers in a more aggressive manner. Instead, I told her that her approach was just fine. If she had tried to alter his behavior by reminding him of the rules, he might well have rebelled: "Who made you the enforcer? Mind your own business!" She had given the smoker a face-saving way of doing what she wanted, one that allowed him to feel chivalrous rather than chastised. This was kinder to him, but it was also kinder to herself, since it was more likely to lead to the result she desired.

10   Another caller disagreed with me, saying the first caller's style was "self-abasing." I persisted: There was nothing necessarily destructive about the way the woman handled the smoker. The mistake the second caller was making—a mistake many of us make—was to confuse ritual self-effacement with the literal kind. All human relations require us to find ways to get what we want from others without seeming to dominate them.

11   The opinions expressed by the two callers encapsulate the ethic of aggression that has us by our throats, particularly in public arenas such as politics and law. Issues are routinely approached by having two sides stake out opposing positions and do battle. This sometimes drives people to take positions that are

more adversarial than they feel—and can get in the way of reaching a possible resolution. . . .

12   The same spirit drives the public discourse of politics and the press, which are increasingly being given over to ritual attacks. On Jan. 18, 1994, retired admiral Bobby Ray Inman withdrew as nominee for Secretary of Defense after several news stories raised questions about his business dealings and his finances. Inman, who had held high public office in both Democratic and Republican administrations, explained that he did not wish to serve again because of changes in the political climate—changes that resulted in public figures being subjected to relentless attack. Inman said he was told by one editor, "Bobby, you've just got to get thicker skin. We have to write a bad story about you every day. That's our job."

13   Everyone seemed to agree that Inman would have been confirmed. The news accounts about his withdrawal used words such as "bizarre," "mystified" and "extraordinary." A New York Times editorial reflected the news media's befuddlement: "In fact, with the exception of a few columns, . . . a few editorials and one or two news stories, the selection of Mr. Inman had been unusually well received in Washington." This evaluation dramatizes how run-of-the-mill systematic attacks have become. With a wave of a subordinate clause ("a few editorials . . . "), attacking someone personally and (from his point of view) distorting his record are dismissed as so insignificant as to be unworthy of notice.

14   The idea that all public figures should expect to be criticized ruthlessly testifies to the ritualized nature of such attack: It is not sparked by specific wrongdoing but is triggered automatically.

15   I once asked a reporter about the common journalistic practice of challenging interviewees by repeating criticism to them. She told me it was the hardest part of her job. "It makes me uncomfortable," she said. "I tell myself I'm someone else and force myself to do it." But, she said she had no trouble being combative if she felt someone was guilty of behavior she considered wrong. And that is the crucial difference between ritual fighting and literal fighting: opposition of the heart.

16   It is easy to find examples throughout history of journalistic attacks that make today's rhetoric seem tame. But in the past such vituperation was motivated by true political passion, in contrast with today's automatic, ritualized attacks—which seem to grow out of a belief that conflict is high-minded and good, a required and superior form of discourse.

17   The roots of our love for ritualized opposition lie in the educational system that we all pass through.

18   Here's a typical scene: The teacher sits at the head of the classroom, pleased with herself and her class. The students are engaged in a heated debate. The very noise level reassures the teacher that the students are participating. Learning is going on. The class is a success.

19   But look again, cautions Patricia Rosof, a high school history teacher who admits to having experienced just such a wave of satisfaction. On closer inspection, you notice that only a few students are participating in the debate; the

majority of the class is sitting silently. And the students who are arguing are not addressing subtleties, nuances or complexities of the points they are making or disputing. They don't have that luxury because they want to win the argument—so they must go for the most dramatic statements they can muster. They will not concede an opponent's point—even if they see its validity—because that would weaken their position.

20   This aggressive intellectual style is cultivated and rewarded in our colleges and universities. The standard way to write an academic paper is to position your work in opposition to someone else's. This creates a need to prove others wrong, which is quite different from reading something with an open mind and discovering that you disagree with it. Graduate students learn that they must disprove others' arguments in order to be original, make a contribution and demonstrate intellectual ability. The temptation is great to oversimplify at best, and at worst to distort or even misrepresent other positions, the better to refute them.

21   I caught a glimpse of this when I put the question to someone who I felt had misrepresented my own work: "Why do you need to make others wrong for you to be right?" Her response: "It's an argument!" Aha, I thought, that explains it. If you're having an argument, you use every tactic you can think of—including distorting what your opponent just said—in order to win.

22   Staging everything in terms of polarized opposition limits the information we get rather than broadening it.

23   For one thing, when a certain kind of interaction is the norm, those who feel comfortable with that type of interaction are drawn to participate, and those who do not feel comfortable with it recoil and go elsewhere. If public discourse included a broad range of types, we would be making room for individuals with different temperaments. But when opposition and fights overwhelmingly predominate, only those who enjoy verbal sparring are likely to take part. Those who cannot comfortably take part in oppositional discourse—or choose not to—are likely to opt out.

24   But perhaps the most dangerous harvest of the ethic of aggression and ritual fighting is—as with the audience response to the screaming man on the television talk show—an atmosphere of animosity that spreads like a fever. In extreme forms, it rears its head in road rage and workplace shooting sprees. In more common forms, it leads to what is being decried everywhere as a lack of civility. It erodes our sense of human connection to those in public life—and to the strangers who cross our paths and people our private lives.

QUESTIONS FOR DISCUSSION AND WRITING

1. Do you agree with Tannen's assertion that our public discussions about controversial issues have been turned into "battles and duels" by the media? Explain why or why not. Look through several current newspapers or newsmagazines to see if you can find evidence of this trend. Do other forms of media, such as television and radio, also encourage this outlook?

2. How has the "argument culture" affected our ability to resolve controversial issues? Can you think of any examples of current controversies that have been negatively affected by the tendency of those involved to defend their own "turf" rather than listen and respond constructively to the ideas of others who hold differing views?

3. Tannen cites the example of a woman who called in to a talk show and questioned whether her conciliatory approach to a potential conflict was the best course of action (paragraphs 8 and 9). In your journal, discuss some of your own experiences in confronting someone else about behavior you find unacceptable. What approaches have been successful for you? Do you agree with Tannen that the woman was wise to avoid conflict?

4. In your own experience, have you found that schools and teachers promote and reward students who engage in heated debate with other students, as Tannen contends in paragraphs 18 to 20? Do you think this style of communication discourages students who may not be as comfortable with this confrontational behavior? Have you found that a "winner-take-all" approach to argument is a productive way to solve problems or disagreements? What problems can arise from this approach? Are there any benefits?

Sample Arguments for Analysis

Read the following two essays to find the basic components in writing arguments and to practice debate, dialogue, and deliberation. After you have read each essay carefully, respond to these questions about them:

1. Identify each writer's claim and restate it in your own words. What do you think is the writer's purpose in writing the essay?

2. What reasons does each writer use to support his claim? Make a list of the reasons you find in each essay. Are the reasons convincing?

3. Find examples of the ways each writer supports those reasons. How convincing is the evidence he presents? Is it pertinent? reliable? sufficient? Is it slanted or biased?

4. Does the writer acknowledge views about the subject that are different from his own? Where does he do this? What is the writer's attitude toward those who hold different views? Does he try to understand those views or does he respond only negatively toward them?

5. Using debate, dialogue, and deliberation, complete the following activities individually or in small groups:
   a. To become acquainted with opposing reasons, write a "yes, but . . ." exchange or a pro/con checklist.
   b. Using your checklist or exchange, create a dialogue between two or more opposing sides on the issue that attempts to find points of disagreement as well

as common ground or shared concerns among them. Look for opportunities for each side to listen and respond constructively to the other.

c. Deliberate. Review the reasons and examples from a number of perspectives. What reasons on either side do you find the most compelling? What concerns have particular merit? How can you balance the interests of all sides of the issue? Formulate a claim that takes into account what you have learned from listening and considering several perspectives and provide reasons to support it.

The Case Against Tipping
Michael Lewis

Many people have strong views about tipping. Some consider it an optional act of kindness to express appreciation for good service, an additional expense over what they have already paid. For others it is an essential part of their day's wages, and thus their income. The following essay by Michael Lewis explores this dichotomy. Lewis, a journalist, writes about economics, politics, international economic relations, and society. As you read this article which appeared in the *New York Times Magazine* on September 23, 1997, think about your own attitudes toward the practice of tipping. What motivates a tip? If you have ever been on the receiving end, did you find that relying on others' generosity for your income left you vulnerable to their whims?

Thesis No lawful behavior in the marketplace is as disturbing to me as the growing appeals for gratuities. Every gentle consumer of cappuccinos will know what I'm getting at: Just as you hand your money over to the man behind the counter, you notice a plastic beggar's cup beside the cash register. "We Appreciate Your Tips," it reads in blue ink scrawled across the side with calculated indifference. The young man or woman behind the counter has performed no especially noteworthy service. He or she has merely handed you a $2 muffin and perhaps a ruinous cup of coffee and then rung them up on the register. Yet the plastic cup waits impatiently for an expression of your gratitude. A dollar bill or two juts suggestively over the rim—no doubt placed there by the person behind the counter. Who would tip someone a dollar or more for pouring them a cup of coffee? But you can never be sure. The greenbacks might have been placed there by people who are more generous than yourself. People whose hearts are not made of flint.

2   If you are like most people (or at any rate like me), you are of two minds about this plastic cup. On the one hand, you do grasp the notion that people who serve you are more likely to do it well and promptly if they believe they will be rewarded for it. The prospect of a tip is, in theory at least, an important incentive for the person working behind the counter of the coffee bar. Surely, you don't want to be one of those people who benefit from the certain hop to the worker's step that the prospect of a tip has arguably induced without paying

your fair share of the cost. You do not wish to be thought of as not doing your share, you cheapskate.

3   And these feelings of guilt are only compounded by the niggling suspicion that the men who run the corporation that runs the coffee shops might be figuring on a certain level of tipping per hour when they decide how generous a wage they should extend to the folks toiling at the counters. That is, if you fail to tip the person getting you that coffee, you may be directing and even substantially affecting that person's level of income.

4   That said, we are talking here about someone who has spent all of 40 seconds retrieving for you a hot drink and a muffin. When you agreed to buy the drink and the muffin you did not take into account the plastic-cup shakedown. In short, you can't help but feel you are being had.

5   There in a nutshell is the first problem with tipping: the more discretion you have in the matter the more unpleasant it is. Tipping is an aristocratic conceit—"There you go, my good man, buy your starving family a loaf"—best left to an aristocratic age. The practicing democrat would rather be told what he owes right up front. Offensively rich people may delight in peeling off hundred-dollar bills and tossing them out to groveling servants. But no sane, well-adjusted human being cares to sit around and evaluate the performance of some beleaguered coffee vendor.

6   This admirable reticence means that, in our democratic age at least, gratuities are inexorably transformed into something else. On most occasions where they might be conferred—at restaurants, hotels and the like—tips are as good as obligatory. "Tipping is customary," reads the sign in the back of a New York City taxi, and if anything, that is an understatement. Once, a long time ago, I tried to penalize a cabdriver for bad service and he rolled alongside me for two crowded city blocks, shouting obscenities through his car window. A friend of mine who undertipped had the message drummed home more perfectly: a few seconds after she stepped out of the cab, the cab knocked her over. She suffered a fracture in her right leg. But it could have been worse. She could have been killed for . . . undertipping! (The driver claimed it was an accident. Sure it was.)

7   There, in a nutshell, is the second problem with tipping: the less discretion you have in the matter, the more useless it is as an economic incentive. Our natural and admirable reluctance to enter into the spirit of the thing causes the thing to lose whatever value it had in the first place. It is no accident that the rudest and most inept service people in America—New York City cabdrivers—are also those most likely to receive their full 15 percent. A tip that isn't a sure thing is socially awkward. But a tip that is a sure thing is no longer a tip really. It's more like a tax.

8   Once you understand the impossibility of tipping in our culture, the plastic cup on the coffee-bar counter can be seen for what it is: a custom in the making. How long can it be before the side of the coffee cup reads "Tipping Is Customary"? I called Starbucks to talk this over, and a pleasant spokeswoman told me that this chain of coffee bars, at least, has no such designs on American

mores. The official Starbucks line on their Plexiglas container is that it wasn't their idea but that of their customers. "People were leaving loose change on the counter to show their gratitude," she said. "And so in 1990 it was decided to put a tasteful and discreet cup on the counter. It's a way for our customers to say thanks to our partners." (Partners are what Starbucks calls its employees.)

9   Perhaps. But you can be sure that our society will not long tolerate the uncertainty of the cup. People will demand to know what is expected of them, one way or the other. Either the dollar in the cup will become a routine that all civilized coffee buyers will endure. Or the tasteful and discreet cup will disappear altogether, in deference to the straightforward price hike.

10   A small matter, you might say. But if the person at the coffee-bar counter feels entitled to a tip for grabbing you a coffee and muffin, who won't eventually? I feel we are creeping slowly toward a kind of baksheesh economy in which everyone expects to be showered with coins simply for doing what they've already been paid to do. Let's band together and ignore the cup. And who knows? Someday, we may live in a world where a New York cabdriver simply thanks you for paying what it says on the meter.

QUESTIONS FOR DISCUSSION AND WRITING

1. Do you think Lewis has had much experience in a job that relies on tips? What evidence can you find to demonstrate this?
2. Do you agree with Lewis? In your journal, respond to Lewis's ideas by exploring your own views on tipping. What is your position on this topic? What experiences have you had that support your own view?

The Consequences of "Carnage as Entertainment"
John Ellis

Television has been blamed for a multitude of social problems: Johnny does poorly in school because he watches too much television. Families are falling apart because instead of communicating with each other, they spend their time in front of the TV. Violent and overt sexual behavior is also blamed on television. The following article by John Ellis probes this controversy. Ellis is a columnist for the *Boston Globe,* in which this article appeared on May 23, 1998. As you read Ellis's essay, reflect on your own television viewing habits. Do you believe people imitate what they see on television? Are children especially vulnerable to television's influence?

1   Read the roll, as compiled by the Associated Press.

2   On Oct. 1, 1997, a 16-year-old student in Pearl, Miss., allegedly killed his mother, then went to his high school and shot nine students, two of them dead.

3   On March 24, 1998, an 11-year-old boy and his 13-year-old friend allegedly opened fire on classmates at a middle school in Jonesboro, Ark. Four schoolchildren and a teacher were killed in the hail of gunfire. Ten more were wounded.

4   On April 24, 1998, a 14-year-old boy went to his eighth-grade graduation dance in Edinboro, Pa. He allegedly opened fire on the festivities almost immediately thereafter, killing one teacher and wounding another. Two classmates were also injured in the shooting spree.

5   On May 19, 1998, a high school senior allegedly shot and killed a classmate in the parking lot of their Fayetteville, Tenn., school. Authorities said they had argued about a girl.

6   On May 21, 1998—the day before yesterday—a 15-year-old student allegedly opened fire in the Thurston High School cafeteria in Springfield, Ore., killing two, critically wounding eight others and injuring 14 more. Earlier in the day, the suspect allegedly shot and killed his parents. After the melee had ended, the suspect was quoted as saying: "Just shoot me, shoot me now."

7   We are inheriting a whirlwind. Television violence has come home to roost. Thirty years ago, Kipland Kinkel, the 15-year-old suspect in the Thurston High School massacre, would have been just another juvenile delinquent in need of counseling. It would never have occurred to him that he could walk into his high school's cafeteria with a semi-automatic weapon and start squeezing off rounds.   } thesis

8   These days, children like Kinkel have seen this kind of violent behavior on television countless times. They know that if someone shoots up his school, he will become a celebrity. News media will want to interview him. Talk show hosts will want to have him on their shows. Network correspondents will vie for the "exclusive" rights to his "story."

9   By the end of next week, more people will know Kinkel's name than will know the names of the doctors at Harvard who are gaining on a cure for cancer. To say that our media culture is sick is to vastly understate the dimensions of the virus. Consider the following dispatch from the April 16 edition of The Washington Post.

10   "Researchers at four universities who examined 9,000 hours of TV programming found that the overall level of violence on broadcast and cable television has held steady over the three years of their study. In all, they found that 61 percent of the programs examined last year contained some violence, roughly the same as the preceding two years."

11   "67 percent of the programs carried by the broadcast networks in prime
support time and 64 percent of prime-time shows on basic cable contained violence during the 1996–97 season, according to the study. For "premium" cable networks such as HBO and Showtime, which tend to air uncut theatrical movies, 87 percent of programs had violence."

12   More important, the violence depicted on television and in the movies escalates with each passing year, as audiences grow inured to "routine" violence. According to the American Medical Association, "TV portrays violence in a way that increases the risk of learning aggressive attitudes. The AMA considers violence to be a major national health problem, and television to be an important contributing factor."

13   Sissela Bok, in her new book "Mayhem," argues that media violence ("carnage as entertainment" as she calls it) is especially harmful to children, leading

to "increased fearfulness, progressive desensitization, greater appetite for more frequent and more violent programming, and higher levels of aggression."

14 Incredibly, the entertainment industry continues to maintain that there is no correlation between violence as depicted in the media and violence in American life. Jack Valenti, president of the Motion Picture Association of America, which represents major TV producers as well as Hollywood studios, blasted the study cited above as "unwarranted assumptions jumping to a pre-conceived conclusion. These are blurred and ephemeral numbers."

15 This is irresponsible nonsense. We are at a crossroads here. The fact is that school massacres in America this spring are running at the rate of one a month. If the violence continues, then a minor massacre at some middle school in Massachusetts won't even be a news story in three or four years. In the not dis-tant future, it is possible that someone will have to wipe out a whole class of kids to make the network news.

16 We can either do something about the excessive, gratuitous violence that permeates our national media or surrender a civilized society. The stakes are just that. What was once alarming is now chilling. Carnage as entertainment has consequences. The people of Springfield, Ore., can tell you that.

QUESTIONS FOR DISCUSSION AND WRITING

1. What are your own views about the effects of media violence on the actions of children and teenagers? Do you agree with Ellis's position?
2. How do you think our society could respond constructively to Ellis's concerns? Would simply cutting back on the amount of time children watch television have a significant impact on the problem of child violence? In your journal, suggest several ways this problem could be addressed.
3. In paragraph 16 Ellis states, "We can either do something about the excessive, gratuitous violence that permeates our national media or surrender a civilized society." Do you think these are two reasonable choices? In Chapter 2 we discuss a logical fallacy called a *false dilemma* in which the writer over-states the consequences of inaction or disagreement with his or her position. The reader is given a dramatic and often exaggerated choice. Do you think Ellis is guilty of this logical fallacy? If so, how would you restate his choices to avoid it?

EXERCISES

1. Try to determine from the following list which subjects are arguable and which are not.
   a. Letter grades in all college courses should be replaced by pass/fail grades.
   b. Capital punishment is no deterrent to crime.
   c. Lobster is my favorite seafood.
   d. Professor Greene is one of the best professors on campus.
   e. The university should install condom machines in all dormitories.
   f. Pornography poses a threat to women.

g. Minorities make up only 9 percent of the upper management positions in corporate America.

h. The earth's population will be 7.3 billion by the year 2010.

i. Juveniles who commit serious crimes should be sent to adult prisons.

j. Last night's sunset over the mountains was spectacular.

k. Advertisers often mislead the public about the benefits of their products.

l. AIDS testing for health care workers should be mandatory.

m. Bilingual education programs fail to help non–English-speaking children become part of mainstream society.

n. Abortion is a decision that should be left up to women, not the courts.

o. I think women are better listeners than men.

p. Couples should have to get a license before having children.

q. Given all the billions of galaxies and billions of stars in each galaxy, there must be life elsewhere.

r. Secondhand smoke causes cancer.

2. In your argument notebook, create a pro/con checklist for the following topics. Make two columns: pro on one side, con on the other. If possible, team up with other students to brainstorm opposing points on each issue. Try to come up with five or six solid points and counterpoints.

   a. I think women are better listeners than men.

   b. Capital punishment is no deterrent to crime.

   c. "Hard" sciences such as math are more difficult than "soft" sciences such as sociology.

   d. The production and sale of cigarettes must be outlawed for the health of the American public.

   e. The university should reduce tuition for those students who maintained an A average during the previous year.

3. Use one of these topics to construct a dialogue in which the object is not to oppose the other side but to respond constructively to its concerns. As a first step, analyze the reasons provided by both sides and make a list of their concerns, noting whether any are shared. Then create a dialogue that might take place between the two.

4. Write about a recent experience in which you tried to convince someone of something. What reasons did you use to make your claim convincing? Which were most successful? What were the opposing reasons? How did you respond?

chapter 2

READING ARGUMENTS

Thinking like a Critic

We read for a variety of purposes. Sometimes it's to find information about whether a particular event will take place or to check on the progress of a political candidate or to learn how to assemble a piece of furniture. Other times we read to be entertained by a favorite newspaper columnist or to discover the secrets behind making a pot of really good chili. But if you've ever picked up a book, a magazine article, a newspaper editorial, or a piece of advertising and found yourself questioning the ideas and claims of the authors, then you've engaged in a special kind of reading called *critical reading*. When you look beyond the surface of words and thoughts to think about the ideas and their meaning and significance, you are reading critically.

Critical reading is active reading. It involves asking questions and not necessarily accepting the writer's statements at face value. Critical readers ask questions of authors such as these:

- What do you mean by that phrase?
- Can you support that statement?
- How do you define that term?
- Why is this observation important?
- How did you arrive at that conclusion?
- Do other experts agree with you?
- Is this evidence up-to-date?

By asking such questions you are weighing the writer's claims, asking for definitions, evaluating information, looking for proof, questioning assumptions, and making judgments. In short, you are actively engaged in thinking like a critic.

Why Read Critically?

When you read critically, you think critically. Instead of passively accepting what's written on a page, you separate yourself from the text and decide what is convincing to you and what is not. Critical reading is a process of discovery. You discover where an author stands on an issue, and you discover the strengths and weaknesses of an author's argument. The result is that you have a better understanding of the issue. By asking questions of the author, by analyzing where the author stands with respect to others' views on the issue, you become more knowledgeable about the issue and more able to develop your own informed viewpoint on the subject.

Critical reading not only sharpens your focus on an issue. It also heightens your ability to construct and evaluate your own arguments. That will lead you to become a better writer because critical reading is the first step to critical writing. Good writers look at the written word the way a carpenter looks at a house—they study the fine details and how those details connect to create the whole. It's the same with critical reading. The better you become at analyzing and reacting to another's written work, the better you are at analyzing and reacting to your own: Is it logical? Are my points clearly stated? Do my examples really support my ideas? Have I explained this term clearly? Is my conclusion persuasive? In other words, critical reading will help you use that same critical eye with your own writing, making you both a better reader and a better writer.

Even though you may already employ many of the strategies of critical reading, we'd like to offer some suggestions and techniques to make you an even better critical reader.

Preview the Reading

Even before you begin reading you can look for clues that may reveal valuable information about the subject of the article, the writer's attitude about the subject, the audience the writer is addressing, and the purpose of the article. As a prereading strategy, try to answer the following questions:

1. *Who is the writer?* Information about the writer is sometimes provided in a short biographical note on the first or last page of the reading. The writer's age, education, current profession, and professional background can tell you about his or her experience and perspective on the subject. For instance, a physician who is writing about assisted suicide may have a very different attitude toward that subject than an individual who has a degree in divinity. A writer who has held a high-ranking position in a government agency or a political appointment will bring that experience to bear in a discussion of a political issue. A writer's background and professional training can provide knowledge and credibility; you may be more inclined to believe an expert in a field than someone with little or no experience. However, direct experience can also limit the writer's perspective. A review of this information before you read can help you better evaluate the writer as an authority.

2. *Where was the article originally published?* Often the publication in which the article originally appeared will indicate the writer's audience and purpose. Some publications, such as scholarly journals, are intended to be read by other professionals in a particular field. Writers for such a journal assume that readers are familiar with the terminology of that profession and possess a certain level

of education and experience. For example, an author writing about cancer research in a scholarly medical journal such as the *Journal of the American Medical Association (JAMA)* would assume a high degree of medical expertise on the part of the readers. An author writing about the same cancer research in *Newsweek* would provide a greatly simplified version with little medical terminology. Popular magazines you see at newsstands are designed to communicate to a larger, more general audience. Writers make an effort to explain difficult concepts in terms an inexperienced reader can understand. Knowing where the article was originally published will prepare you for the demands of the reading. It may also prepare you for the writer's point of view. Publications are usually designed for a specific audience. The *Wall Street Journal*, for example, has a readership largely comprising people interested in the economy, business, or investments. The articles in it reflect the concerns and interests of the business community. On the other hand, an article appearing in *High Times*, a publication that endorses the use and legalization of marijuana, has a very different set of readers. By familiarizing yourself with the publication in which the article originally appeared, you can learn much about the writer's likely political and professional opinions, knowledge you can use to judge the credibility of his or her argument.

3. *When was the article originally published?* The date of publication can also provide background about what was happening when the article was published. It will indicate factors that might have influenced the writer and whether the evidence used in the reading is current or historical. For instance, an article written about the economy during an earlier time of economic recession would be strongly influenced by factors of high unemployment and business failures. The writer's argument might not be as convincing during a period of growth and stability. Some readings are timeless in their consideration of basic truths about people and life; others can be challenged about whether their arguments can still be applied to current circumstances.

4. *What does the title reveal about the subject and the author's attitude toward it?* The title of an article often indicates both the subject of the article and the writer's attitude toward it. After you have identified the subject, look carefully at the words the writer has used to describe it. Are their connotations negative or positive? What other words do you associate with them? Does the title make reference to another written work or to a well-known slogan or familiar saying? Sometimes writers use their titles to suggest a parallel between their subject and a similar situation in recent times or a particular event in history. An article about the possibility of an annihilating nuclear attack in 2020 might be titled "Hiroshima in the Twenty-First Century." These choices are deliberate ways to inform readers about a writer's views and ideas on a subject. By considering the language in the title, you will be more aware of the writer's intent.

Let's try a preview of the first reading in this chapter. By carefully reading the introductory paragraph you can learn the following information:

Preview Question 1: Who is the writer? As the introduction tells us, Henry Wechsler is the director of the College Alcohol Studies Program at the Harvard University School of Public Health. His professional title suggests that he is knowledgeable about alcohol use, particularly at the college level, because he directs a program that studies this area. You are about to read an essay, then, written by an expert in the field of alcohol research.

Preview Question 2: Where was the article originally published? By reading further in the paragraph you find that the article was originally published in the *Boston Globe.* This is a widely circulated newspaper located in a major American city. The writer would expect the article to be read by a large cross-section of people with diverse economic and educational backgrounds. Because Boston is the city where Harvard and many other colleges are located, readers might have a special interest in issues that affect the college community.

Preview Question 3: When was the article originally published? The introduction tells you that the article first appeared on October 2, 1997. This is a fairly recent article, which makes it likely that it will be up-to-date and relevant to current concerns.

Preview Question 4: What does the title reveal about the subject and the author's attitude toward it? The title of the article, "Binge Drinking Must Be Stopped," suggests an emphatic and nonnegotiable attitude on the part of the author.

As you can see, your preview of the article has provided much valuable information that will help prepare you to begin the critical reading process.

Skim the Reading

Just as an athlete would never participate in a competitive event without first stretching his or her muscles and thoroughly warming up, you will find that successful critical reading is a process that benefits from a series of activities aimed at increasing your understanding of the writer's ideas. The first time through you may wish to skim the reading to get a general idea of its subject and intent. Further readings should be slower and more thoughtful so that each reason presented can be analyzed and evaluated and each idea judged and considered. Now that you have previewed the material about the author, the original publication and date, and the title, you are ready to skim the reading to find its basic features.

When you skim a reading, you are trying to discover the topic and the claim. Start by reading the first one or two paragraphs and the last paragraph. If the reading is a relatively short newspaper article, such as the following sample essay, this may be enough to give you a general idea of the writer's topic and point of view. If the reading is longer and more complex, you will also need to examine the first sentence or two of each paragraph to get a better sense of the writer's ideas.

Sample Argument for Analysis

For practice, let's skim the first reading in this chapter. To organize your impressions from skimming the reading, it's a good idea to write some of them down in your journal.

Binge Drinking Must Be Stopped
Henry Wechsler

"Binge" drinking is a problem on many college campuses. Away from home for the first time, many freshmen celebrate their new freedom by abusing alcohol at parties. But this behavior is not only confined to freshmen, as Henry Wechsler's research indicates. Henry Wechsler is the director of the College Alcohol Studies Program at the Harvard School of Public Health. He completed a survey focusing on the "binge" drinking practices of students at 140 colleges and universities. The survey revealed a high rate of binge drinking and a wide range of problems associated with this behavior, especially when connected to fraternity life. He wrote the following article in response to the death of MIT freshman Scott Krueger who died of alcohol poisoning after participating in binge drinking during a fraternity party. This essay was published in the *Boston Globe* on October 2, 1997.

1   We should be saddened and outraged by the tragic death of a young man just starting to fulfill his life promise.

2   This week's death from alcohol overdose of Scott Krueger, a freshman at the Massachusetts Institute of Technology, is an extreme and unfortunate consequence of a style of drinking that is deeply entrenched and widespread at American colleges. Binge drinking is a reality of college life in America and perhaps the central focus of fraternity-house life.

3   Since the Harvard School of Public Health study on college binge drinking was released almost three years ago, colleges have been deluged with reports on alcohol abuse. Even before our results became public, it was inconceivable that college administrators were unaware of the existence of alcohol problems at their institutions.

4   A quick ride in a security van on a Thursday, Friday, or Saturday night could provide all the information needed. A conversation with the chief of security could easily reveal where the binge drinking takes place and which students, fraternities, and alcohol outlets are violating college rules or local ordinances.

5   An incoming freshman learns during the first week of school where the alcohol and parties are and often has a binge drinking experience even before purchasing a text book. If students can find it so easily, so can college administrators. It is not that complicated: Drunken parties are usually at certain frater-

nity houses and housing complexes just off campus. The heaviest drinking most likely takes place in a few bars near campus where large quantities of alcohol are sold cheaply.

6   If we know so much about the problem, why is it that we have not been able to do much about it? First, because colleges, like problem drinkers, do not recognize that they have a problem. It has been there for so long that they have adapted to it. They are lulled into complacency as long as the problem does not seem to increase or a tragedy does not occur.

7   Second, the solutions that are offered are usually only partial: a lecture, an awareness day, a new regulation in the dorms. The root of the problem is seldom touched. The supply of large quantities of cheap alcohol is viewed as outside the purview of college officials. "It's off campus" is a euphemism for "that's not my job." The bar or liquor store may be off campus, but it is controlled by licensing boards that city officials and colleges can substantially influence. The fraternity house may be off campus and not owned by the college, but it is affiliated with and depends on the college for its existence. Many colleges and universities simply wink at the activities of the fraternities and claim no responsibility.

8   Third, when new policies are established, they are often assumed to be in effect without proper verification. It is easy to say there is no drinking allowed in a dormitory or a fraternity, but enforcement is necessary to put the policy into effect. Legally, no alcohol can be sold to people under age 21, but 86 percent of college students drink.

9   We can no longer be shocked at what is happening on many college campuses and in many fraternities. This is no longer a time merely to form a committee to study the situation. It is time to act.

10   Action needs to be taken on many fronts: the college president's office, the fraternity and sorority system, the athletics department, community licensing boards and, foremost, those students who are sick of the drinking they see around them.

11   Parents who pay for college tuitions should demand a safe environment for their children. Binge drinking need not remain an integral part of college life. University presidents must make it their responsibility to produce change.

After skimming "Binge Drinking Must Be Stopped," you might record the following (we indicate in parentheses the paragraphs in which we found our ideas):

Wechsler starts off with a reference to a young man who died from an alcohol overdose. He says we should be saddened and outraged by this. Then he suggests that binge drinking has become very common on college campuses, particularly in fraternities *(paragraphs 1 and 2)*. Wechsler believes parents should insist that colleges provide a safe environment for their children by finding solutions for binge drinking. University presidents must take responsibility for solving this problem *(paragraph 11)*.

By skimming the article you now have some sense of what the reading will be about and the writer's position. Before beginning a closer reading of the text, you will want to take one additional step to prepare yourself to be an active and responsive reader: Consider your experience with the topic.

Consider Your Own Experience

Your next step in the reading process is to consider your own experience. Critical reading brings your own perspective, experience, education, and personal values to your reading. Sometimes you begin with very little knowledge about the subject of your reading. It may be a topic that you haven't given much thought or one that is unfamiliar and new. Other times you may start with some of your own ideas and opinions about the subject. By taking the time to consider what you know and how your own experiences and values relate to the author's ideas, you can add a dimension to your reading that enables you to question, analyze, and understand the writer's ideas more effectively. You will be a more active critical reader because you can respond to the writer's ideas with ideas of your own.

Before beginning a close reading, take the time to reflect on these questions:

- What do I know about this subject?
- What have I heard or read about it recently?
- What attitudes or opinions do I have about the subject?

Exploring what you already know or think about a subject can have several benefits: You can use your knowledge to better understand the situation or issue described in the reading; you can compare your own experience with that of the writer; you can formulate questions to keep in mind as you read; and you can become more aware of your own opinions about the subject. For instance, you may be reading an article about the benefits of the proposed plan for improving your state's welfare system. If you have some knowledge about this proposal from reading news stories or hearing discussions about it, you will begin your reading with some understanding of the issue. If you have had actual experience with the welfare system or know of others' experiences, you can provide examples of your own to challenge or support those of the writer. If you have taken the time to consider questions you have about the proposed plan, you will be actively seeking answers as you read. And, by exploring your own views on the subject before you read, you will find that the ideas in the article will enrich, inform, and possibly change your opinion.

After previewing and skimming the reading, John, a freshman composition student, wrote the following reflection on the topic of binge drinking in his journal:

> It would be hard to be a student at college and not notice the heavy drinking that goes on every weekend. Some people just can't have fun unless they drink too much. It's a fact of college life—for some people. And if you live in a small college community, sometimes that's all there is to do on Saturday night. I've seen some kids really ruin their lives with too much partying. They forget why

they came to college in the first place—or maybe that is why they came. But not everybody drinks to excess. Most of us just like to get a little buzz and socialize and have fun. Most of us will just go just so far and stop, but there's always a few who can't seem to stop until they pass out or puke their guts out on the sidewalk. Yeah, we've all been told the dangers of drinking too much, but some people aren't mature enough to see that they're hurting themselves. Binge drinking happens every weekend around here. It's not a pretty sight, but I'm not sure how the college president or anybody else could stop it. College students have always partied to relieve tension and to socialize. It's been going on for years. Why is college drinking suddenly such a big issue? And, if the drinking takes place outside of campus, how can the college stop it? If students want to get alcohol, even if they're underage, they'll find a way. Why should the college tell us whether we can drink or not?

John clearly has considerable experience with the topic and some strong opinions of his own. By considering them before he begins a close reading of the article, he is ready to explore and challenge the ideas he encounters in the reading.

Annotate the Reading

Annotating the text is the next stage of critical reading to help you become a thoughtful and careful reader. *Annotating* is responding to the ideas in the reading right on the pages of your text. (If you don't own the publication the essay appears in, make a photocopy.) There are many different ways to annotate a reading, but many readers use the following methods:

* Highlight or underline passages that you consider significant.
* Write questions in the margins that respond to the writer's ideas or that you wish to follow up with further investigation.
* Circle words or phrases that need to be defined or made clearer.
* Add comments or brief examples of your own that support or challenge the writer's.
* Draw lines between related ideas.
* Note the writer's use of transitions and qualifiers which subtly shade meaning.
* Point out with arrows or asterisks particularly persuasive examples.
* Mark difficult-to-understand sections of the text that need a closer look.

Annotation is a way to create an active dialogue between you and the writer by responding in writing to individual points in the reading. Your annotations become a personal record of your thoughts, questions, objections, comments, and agreement with the writer. Annotation can help you read like a critic because it makes you slow down and pay attention to each idea as you read. As an additional benefit, your written comments in the margin will serve as a reminder of your response to the ideas in the essay when you read it again. Figure 2.1 is an example of some of the ways you might annotate "Binge Drinking Must Be Stopped."

BINGE DRINKING MUST BE STOPPED

1   We should be saddened and outraged by the tragic death of a young man just starting to fulfill his life promise.

2   This week's death from alcohol overdose of Scott Krueger, a freshman at the Massachusetts Institute of Technology, is an extreme and unfortunate consequence of a style of drinking that is deeply entrenched and widespread in American colleges. Binge drinking is a reality of college life in America and perhaps the central focus of fraternity house life.

Does everyone at college drink?

claim

3   Since the Harvard School of Public Health study on college binge drinking was released almost three years ago, colleges have been deluged with reports on alcohol abuse. Even before our results became public, it was inconceivable that college administrators were unaware of the existence of alcohol problems at their institutions.

find out more info on this

flooded

4   A quick ride in a security van on a Thursday, Friday, or Saturday night could provide all the information needed. A conversation with the chief of security could easily reveal where the binge drinking takes place and which students, fraternities, and alcohol outlets are violating college rules or local ordinances.

Is this the job of college administrators?

5   An incoming freshman learns during the first week of school where the alcohol and parties are and often has a binge drinking experience even before purchasing a textbook. If students can find it so easily, so can college administrators. It is not that complicated: Drunken parties are usually at certain fraternity houses and housing complexes just off campus. The heaviest drinking most likely takes place in a few bars near campus where large quantities of alcohol are sold cheaply.

qualifier

How does he know this?

qualifier

who is "we"?

6   If we know so much about the problem, why is it that we have not been able to do much about it? First, because colleges, like problem drinkers, do not recognize that they have a problem. It has been there for so long that they have adapted to it. They are lulled into complacency as long as the problem does not seem to increase or a tragedy does not occur.

Is this contradicted by the next ¶? Don't colleges try to do something about binge drinking?

smug self-satisfaction

Figure 2.1

7   Second, the solutions that are offered are usually *Agreed. These don't change behavior much*
only partial: a lecture, an awareness day, a new regula-
tion in the dorms. The root of the problem is seldom
touched. The supply of large quantities of cheap alcohol
is viewed as outside the purview of college officials. "It's *less offensive substitute word*
off campus" is a euphemism for "that's not my job." The
bar or liquor store may be off campus, but it is controlled by licensing boards that city officials and colleges can
substantially influence. The fraternity house may be off
campus and not owned by the college, but it is affiliated
with and depends on the college for its existence. Many
colleges and universities simply wink at the activities of
the fraternities and claim no responsibility. *— What does he mean?*

8   Third, when new policies are established, they are *Proven to be true.*
often assumed to be in effect without proper verification.
It is easy to say there is no drinking allowed in a dormitory or fraternity, but enforcement is necessary to put
the policy into effect. Legally, no alcohol can be sold to *Impressive statistic*
people under age 21, but 86 percent of college students
drink.

9   We can no longer be shocked at what is happening *Who is "we"? Has it changed?*
on many college campuses and in many fraternities. This
is no longer a time merely to form a committee to study
the situation. It is time to act.

10   Action needs to be taken on many fronts: the col- *his solution What should they do?*
lege president's office, the fraternity and sorority system,
the athletics department, community licencing boards,
and foremost, those students who are sick of the drinking they see around them.

11   Parents who pay for college tuitions should demand *Who is responsible? Don't the drinkers have some responsibility?*
a safe environment for their children. Binge drinking
need not remain an integral part of college life. University presidents must make it their responsibility to produce change.   *essential*   *Are college students "children"?*

Journal

Summarize the Reading

Before you can begin to analyze and evaluate what you read, it's important to clearly understand what the writer is saying. *Summarizing* is a type of writing used to capture the essential meaning of a reading by focusing only on the writer's main points. When you summarize you "tell back," in a straightforward way, the writer's main ideas. Although summaries can vary in length depending on the length of the original reading, all summaries share these qualities:

- *A summary is considerably shorter than the original.* Because a summary is concerned only with the writer's main ideas, supporting details and examples are usually omitted. The length of a summary will vary depending on your purpose and the length and content of the original.
- *A summary is written in your own words.* Although it may be necessary to use certain of the writer's words for which there are no substitutes, a summary is written in your own words. If you find it necessary to include a short phrase from the original, then quotation marks must be used to set it off. (In Chapter 8, we discuss ways to use summary in a researched argument paper and the need to document the ideas in your summary with a citation.)
- *A summary is objective.* When you summarize, your job is to "tell back" the writer's main ideas with no comments or personal opinions of your own. Of course, once you have completed your summary you are free to respond to it in any way you wish.
- *A summary is accurate.* It's a good idea to reread several times before you attempt to summarize a reading because it's important that you truly understand what the writer means. Sometimes it takes many tries to capture that exact meaning.
- *A summary is thorough.* Even though a summary is, as we've explained, much shorter than the original, a good summary contains each of the writer's main points.

Summarizing is an important step in critical reading because you need to thoroughly understand a writer's ideas before you can explain them, in writing, to others. Don't be discouraged when you first try to summarize a reading. Over time and with practice you will feel more comfortable writing summaries.

A good method to begin summarizing a reading is to write a one-sentence summary of the ideas in each paragraph. (Brief paragraphs that elaborate the same point can be summarized together.) By considering each paragraph separately, you will be sure to cover all the main ideas in the reading and be able to see at a glance how the ideas in the essay are connected to each other and how the writer has chosen to sequence them.

Let's go back to the essay "Binge Drinking Must Be Stopped" and try a one-sentence summary of each paragraph (we combine short paragraphs that are about the same idea):

> *Paragraphs 1 and 2:* The recent death of an MIT student was a terrible event that was caused by excessive drinking practices that are common on college campuses.

Paragraph 3: Colleges should be aware of the problem of excessive drinking among their students because studies have been released about it.

Paragraph 4: By speaking with law enforcement professionals in their own communities, colleges could become aware of where alcohol laws are being broken.

Paragraph 5: Freshmen learn where to find alcohol when they first arrive on campus: fraternities, student housing, and bars close to campus.

Paragraph 6: Colleges aren't doing anything about the problem because they have accepted it and don't want to admit it exists.

Paragraph 7: Because the cause of the problem is the availability of alcohol off campus, colleges don't think it is their responsibility to act even though they could exercise a strong influence over the places that sell alcohol to students.

Paragraph 8: Colleges don't check to see whether their own alcohol policies are being enforced.

Paragraphs 9 and 10: Rather than just talk about this problem, we need to do something about it at many different levels within the college and the community.

Paragraph 11: College presidents need to take responsibility for reducing the practice of excessive drinking at their colleges to provide a safe place for students.

Your one-sentence summary of each paragraph should reveal the essential parts of the essay: the claim and the main reasons the writer uses to support the claim. Once you have identified these important elements, you are ready to begin your summary. It might look something like this (note that we've added the name of the writer and the title of the article):

In his essay "Binge Drinking Must Be Stopped" Henry Wechsler expresses his concern about the common practice of excessive drinking on college campuses. He suggests that colleges are failing in their responsibility to deal with this problem adequately. Although colleges should be informed about the problem, they won't acknowledge its seriousness. Because it doesn't happen on their campuses, they don't feel that it is their responsibility. Wechsler thinks that colleges could exercise their influence off campus in ways that would help to solve the problem. And, even when colleges do have alcohol policies to restrict drinking, they don't check to see if their policies are being enforced. The problem of binge drinking needs to be dealt with now at many different levels within the college and the community. Wechsler thinks that college presidents need to take responsibility for dealing with binge drinking so that it is no longer an important part of college life.

In looking over this summary, you'll notice that we begin with a general sentence that presents the writer's topic and claim. Then, after reviewing our one-sentence paragraph summaries, we have chosen the writer's main reasons to include in the rest of our paragraph. We have tried to eliminate any ideas that are repeated in more than one paragraph, so we can focus on only the major points.

Summarizing a reading means taking all the separate ideas the writer presents, deciding which ones are important, and weaving them together to create a whole. Our next step in the critical reading process is to consider the ways in which the writer has presented those ideas.

Analyze and Evaluate the Reading

To *analyze* something means to break it down into its separate parts, examine those parts closely, and evaluate their significance and how they work together as a whole. You already began this process when you summarized the main idea in each paragraph of your reading. But analysis goes beyond identifying the ideas in the essay. When we analyze, we consider how each part of the essay functions. We are discovering and evaluating the assumptions and intentions of the writer, which lie below the surface of the writing and which we consider separately from the meaning of the essay itself. Analysis helps us consider how successfully and effectively the writer has argued.

Although there is no set formula for analyzing an argument, we can offer some specific questions you should explore when reading an essay that is meant to persuade you:

- What are the writer's assumptions? What does the writer take for granted about the readers' values, beliefs, or knowledge? What does the writer assume about the subject of the essay or the facts involved?
- What kind of audience is the writer addressing?
- What are the writer's purpose and intention?
- How well does the writer accomplish those purposes?
- What kinds of evidence has the writer used—personal experience or scientific data or outside authorities?
- How convincing is the evidence presented? Is it relevant? Is it reliable? Is it specific enough? Is it sufficient? Is it slanted or dated?
- Does the writer's logic seem reasonable?
- Did the writer address opposing views?
- Is the writer persuasive?

For the sake of illustration, let's apply these questions to our reading:

- *What are the writer's assumptions?*
  The writer assumes that the death of the MIT student indicates a widespread problem of binge drinking on college campuses. He thinks that colleges have a responsibility to control the behavior of their students. He assumes that college students will continue to binge drink without any such controls.

Journal

- *What kind of audience is the writer addressing?*

    He seems to be addressing college administrators, parents of college students, and readers who have a special interest in college life.

- *What are the writer's purpose and intention?*

    He wants to make his readers aware that a problem exists and that colleges are not effectively dealing with it.

- *How well does the writer accomplish this purpose?*

    He makes a strong argument that colleges refuse to acknowledge that there's a problem.

- *What kinds of evidence has the writer used?*

    He refers to a study by the Harvard School of Public Health and uses examples of student hangouts that he has heard about but not experienced personally. He seems familiar with college programs on alcohol awareness. He implies that he consulted with the campus security chief for some of his information.

- *How convincing is the evidence?*

    Wechsler mentions a scientific study in paragraph 3 but never offers any details from it. Wechsler could provide more solid evidence that the problem is widespread. His examples of places where students can find alcohol seem convincing.

- *Does the writer's logic seem reasonable?*

    Wechsler effectively links the evidence he presents to his claim that excessive drinking on college campuses is being ignored by college administrators.

- *Did the writer address opposing views?*

    No. We never hear how college administrators respond to this criticism. We also don't know if college students agree with the description of their behavior.

- *Is the writer persuasive?*

    The writer is persuasive if we assume that the problem is widespread and that colleges can have a major impact on students' behavior when they are not on campus.

Argue with the Reading

Asking questions and challenging assumptions are important ways to read critically. Although you may not feel qualified to pass judgment on a writer's views, especially if the writer is a professional or an expert on a particular subject, you should keep in mind that as a part of the writer's audience, you have every right to determine whether an argument is sound, logical, and convincing. Your questions about and objections to the writer's ideas will help you evaluate the effectiveness of his or her argument and form your own judgment about the issue.

You may wish to record some of these thoughts in your annotations in the margins of the text. However, a good strategy for beginning writers, is to respond at greater length in a journal. You might start by jotting down any points in the essay that contradict your own experience or personal views. Note anything you are skeptical about. Write down any questions you have about the claims, reasons, or evidence. If some point or conclusion seems forced or unfounded, record it and briefly explain why. The more skeptical and questioning you are, the more closely you are reading the text and analyzing its ideas. In particular, be on the lookout for logical fallacies, those instances in which the writer—whether unintentionally or purposefully—distorts or exaggerates evidence or relies on faulty logic to make a point. We discuss these fallacies extensively later in this chapter.

Likewise, make note of the features of the text that impress you—powerful points, interesting wording, original insights, clever or amusing phrases or allusions, well-chosen references, or the general structure of the essay. If you have heard or read different views on the issue, you might wish to record them as well.

As an example, let's consider some questions, challenges, and features that might have impressed you in our sample essay:

- Wechsler claims that binge drinking is a common practice at colleges across America. Is that true? Does binge drinking take place at all colleges or only on certain campuses? Do all students engage in this practice, or is it more common among certain age groups, gender, fraternity members as opposed to nonmembers, residential students? Do college students drink more than noncollege students in the same age group?
- The statistic about the percentage of college students who drink (paragraph 8) is convincing.
- Colleges exist to educate students. Are they responsible for monitoring students' behavior when they are not attending classes or socializing off-campus? Is it realistic to expect colleges to do this?
- Are colleges really denying that the problem exists? Don't they have counseling services to help students with drinking problems? What else can they do?
- Wechsler's points about the influence that colleges have in their communities (paragraph 7) are persuasive.
- Mentioning the concerns of students who don't drink and the parents of college students is a clever strategy Wechsler uses to expand his audience and pressure colleges to act.

Create a Debate and Dialogue Between Two or More Readings

Few of us would expect to be experts on tennis or golf after watching one match or tournament. We know that it takes time and effort to really begin to understand even the fundamentals of a sport. Reading a single article on a particular subject is the first step in becoming educated about the issues at stake, but a single essay provides us with only one perspective on that subject. As we continue to read about the subject, each new article will offer a new perspective and new evidence to support that view. The more we read, the more complex and thorough our knowledge about the subject becomes. Creating a dialogue between two or more readings is the next step in the process of critical reading.

When you annotate a reading in the earlier stages of critical reading, you begin a dialogue between yourself and the writer. When you create a dialogue between two or more readings, you go one step further: You look at the ideas you find in them to see how they compare and contrast with each other, how they are interrelated, and how the information from one reading informs you as you read the next. By creating a dialogue between the ideas you encounter in several readings, you will be able to consider multiple viewpoints about the same subject.

Sample Argument for Analysis

Begin reading this second selection on binge drinking by following the steps we've outlined in this chapter:

1. Preview the information about the author, where the article first appeared, the date of publication, and the title.
2. Skim the reading to discover the writer's topic and claim.
3. Consider your own experience, values, and knowledge about the subject.
4. Annotate the reading.
5. Summarize the essay.
6. Analyze and evaluate the effectiveness of the reading.
7. Argue with the reading

Child Care For College Students
Froma Harrop

Froma Harrop presents another viewpoint on the subject of binge drinking and college students in her essay "Child Care for College Students," which appeared in the *Tampa Tribune* on October 8, 1997. Harrop, an editorial writer and columnist for the *Providence Journal,* argues that college students should be the ones held responsible for their behavior, not businesses and educational institutions.

1 Anyone suspicious that the American university experience has become a four-year extension of childhood need look no farther than the colleges' latest response to the binge-drinking "problem." Now, in a grown-up world, college administrators would tell students who down four or five stiff drinks in a row that they are jerks.

2 If they commit violent acts as a result, the police get called. If they drive after drinking, they go to the slammer. If they die from alcohol poisoning, they have nothing but their own stupidity to blame.

3   But if they can drink responsibly, then let them have a good time.

4   Forget about hearing any such counsel, for that would turn students into self-directing adults. Better to blame the problem on all-purpose "cultural attitudes" and "societal pressures" abetted by the villainous alcohol industry.

5   Thus, demands grow for better policing of off-campus liquor outlets. That is, turn local businesses into babysitters. There are calls to ban sponsorship of college events by companies selling alcohol or the marketing of such beverages on campus. That is, protect their charges from evil influences and trample on free speech. (What should colleges do with the frequent references in Western literature to the glories of drink? Rabelais, for example, said, "There are more old drunkards than old physicians.")

6   One former college official has suggested that universities stop serving champagne at parents' weekend brunches or at fundraising events. Remove the bad example for the sake of the children. (Somehow it is hard to believe that a college with any sense of self-preservation would insist that its big-check writers remain cold sober.)

7   The truth is, most Americans can drink without problem. Careful use of alcohol relaxes and warms the drinker with a sense of well-being. Winston Churchill and Franklin Roosevelt saved Western civilization without ever missing a cocktail hour. Students have long enjoyed their own drinking traditions. Brahms' Academic Overture, the stately piece heard over and over again at college commencements, took its melody from a student drinking song.

8   Where is there a campus drinking crisis, anyway? Six college students have supposedly died this year from excessive drinking. These cases are lamentable, but many more college students died from sports-related injuries or car accidents.

9   An even more interesting question is: How many noncollege people in their late teens or early 20s have died from alcohol poisoning? Take note that no one is memorizing this particular statistic—even though the majority of high school students do not go on to college. That number is not etched on our national worry list for the following strange reason: Our society considers the 19-year-old who has a job an adult, while universities see the 19-year-old pre-law student as a child. Working people who cause trouble because they drink are punished. College students are given others to blame.

10   College administrators should know that, from a purely practical point of view, playing hide-the-bottle does no good when dealing with an alcoholic. Indeed, anyone who has hung around Alcoholics Anonymous or Al-Anon can immediately identify such behavior as "enabling." Rather than allow the problem drinker to sink into the mire of his addiction until he can no longer stand it and takes steps to straighten out, the enabler tries to save him. Rest assured that students interested in getting smashed for the night will find the booze.

11   Let us end here with yet another proposition: that binge drinking is more about binge than drinking. It would seem that someone who gulps five glasses of Jim Beam in five minutes is not looking for a pleasant high. Binge drinking is

a stunt that has more in common with diving off bridges or swallowing goldfish than the quest for inebriation.

12   What any increase in binge drinking probably indicates is that the students really don't know how to drink. Binging may just be the latest evidence of decline in our nation's table arts. Instead of savoring wine and spirits in the course of a civilized meal, young people are administering them. The colleges' response is to put condoms on bottles.

Construct a Debate

Now that you have a good understanding of Froma Harrop's views on binge drinking by college students, you are ready to consider the ideas in both the essays you read. Our first step will be to consider the differences between these two writers by constructing a debate. From your summaries of the readings, select the main ideas that seem directly opposed to each other. To highlight those differences create two columns, one for each writer. Here are a few of the ideas Wechsler and Harrop debate in their essays:

Wechsler	*Harrop*
Binge drinking is a major problem on college campuses: a student has died.	Binge drinking is not a major problem on campuses: few students have died.
Colleges have a responsibility to take action about this problem.	Students are responsible for their own drinking.
Colleges should prevent off-campus suppliers of alcohol from giving it to college students.	Colleges should not "police" off-campus suppliers of alcohol.
Colleges should provide a safe environment for students.	College students are adults and should take care of themselves.
Binge drinking continues because colleges aren't treating it as an important problem.	Binge drinking happens because some college students haven't learned to drink responsibly.

These are just a sampling of the many ideas that might be debated by these writers. You should be able to come up with several more.

By considering differences you can see at a glance the ways in which these writers oppose each other. Your next step is to find the ideas they have in common. This may take more searching, but it's an important step in creating a dialogue between them. To get you started we'll list a few of the ideas we found. See if you can come up with a few more:

1. Both writers acknowledge that drinking takes place on college campuses.
2. Both writers indicate that binge drinking can be a problem and that students have died as a result.
3. Both writers agree that colleges are aware that binge drinking takes place off campus.

Now that you have found both differences and common ideas, you are ready to create a dialogue. When you create a dialogue between two readings, you find ways for the writers to speak to each other that recognize their differences and points of agreement.

Your dialogue will reveal how the ideas in both readings interrelate. Let's try to create a dialogue using some of the ideas we found:

> **Wechsler:** Binge drinking is a serious problem on college campuses. It's an activity that has become commonplace.
>
> **Harrop:** I agree that college students engage in binge drinking, but six deaths this year don't necessarily indicate that this is a crisis.
>
> **Wechsler:** Just because more students haven't died doesn't mean that it isn't a dangerous activity and should be ignored. Colleges need to take steps to ensure that more students aren't harmed by this common practice.
>
> **Harrop:** It's unfortunate that students have died, but why should we think it is the college's responsibility to police student drinking? College students are adults and should suffer the consequences of their behavior. It's their choice whether to drink and how much.
>
> **Wechsler:** Colleges are responsible for their students. They need to find ways to prevent students from getting alcohol. They are responsible to the parents who pay the tuition and to the other students who have to tolerate excessive drinking among their peers.
>
> **Harrop:** Practically speaking, colleges can't prevent students from drinking. Students who want to drink will find a way because they are adults with drinking problems, not children in need of supervision.

Complete this dialogue by finding additional ways in which the writers' ideas speak to each other.

As you can see, the dialogue helps us explore the readings in far greater depth than if we had read both essays in isolation. Each writer's ideas help us to evaluate the ideas of the other. By interrelating them in a dialogue, we can better appreciate how the perspective of each writer changes the way similar facts and information are interpreted. For instance, Henry Wechsler is outraged by the death of one MIT student from a binge-drinking episode; on the other hand, Froma Harrop does not find the deaths of six college students from excessive drinking an alarming statistic when she compares it to the number of college students who have died from other accidental causes. It is up to us as readers to decide which writer's interpretation is more persuasive.

Sample Arguments for Analysis

To practice creating your own dialogue between readings, read the following two letters to the editor, which appeared in two newspapers before and after Henry

Wechsler's article. Read them critically, going through the steps we outlined in this chapter, and add them to the dialogue already created between Wechsler and Harrop. We think you'll find that your understanding of the issue will increase and that you'll feel more confident about forming your own position on the question of college binge drinking.

Letter from the *Washington Post,* October 5, 1996

To the Editor:

1   When we saw the headline "Party Hardly" and the revolting picture of four bare-chested, probably underage fraternity brothers guzzling cheap beer, we thought, "Finally! Your paper is tackling an issue that affects every college student." Much to our chagrin, however, the article wasted two pages of newsprint glorifying drunkenness and poor study habits.

2   Perhaps you need to be aware of some ugly facts before your next article on college drinking: One out of every four student deaths is related to alcohol use (research shows that as many as 360,000 of the nation's 12 million undergraduates will die as a result of alcohol abuse); alcohol is a factor in 66 percent of student suicides and 60 percent of all sexually transmitted diseases; studies show that between 33 percent and 59 percent of drinking college students drive while intoxicated at least once a year (with as many as 30 percent driving impaired three to 10 times per year); and alcohol consumption was a factor in at least half of the cases of a study of college women who had been raped by an acquaintance.

3   Alcohol affects not only those who drink it: Those students who do not drink are affected by their classmates or roommates who do. Students at schools with high levels of binge drinking are three times more likely to be pushed, hit or sexually assaulted than are students at schools with less drinking. Students who live with people who drink heavily often are kept awake by obnoxious behavior or the sound of their roommates vomiting in the trash can.

4   The shame does not lie solely with your paper, however. The Princeton Review, which ranks "party schools" based on how much students use alcohol and drugs, how few hours students study every day and the popularity of fraternities and sororities, should focus on what most feel is the real purpose of a college education: to learn—not to learn how to party.

Kathryn Stewart
Corina Sole

Letter from the *Times-Picayune,* October 24, 1997

To the Editor:

1   The entire nation is justifiably concerned about recent tragic deaths caused by alcohol abuse on our college campuses. College students everywhere know where to procure alcohol and where to consume it without being "hassled."

2   Public dialogue asks if institutions are doing enough to control the situation. Unfortunately, it must be stated that colleges and universities are doing all they can.

3   A typical university fosters an alcohol awareness program, provides the services of a substance abuse coordinator, disciplines students for infractions and provides an atmosphere in which young people can grow responsibly.

4   There is more that must be done. Parents at one time held their sons and daughters accountable for the company they kept. A student who deliberately associates with a group known for its excesses, or who joins an organization suspended or expelled by the institution, is choosing bad company. Peer pressure does the rest.

5   The courts restrict the ability of colleges to discipline students for off-campus behavior unless the activity in question has a fairly direct relationship with institutional mission.

6   They require due process, including confrontation by witnesses, for any disciplinary action. Peer pressures in the college-age group are so strong that testimony of witnesses is frequently difficult to obtain.

7   Until we return to a system in which colleges can function, at least in part, in loco parentis (in place of the parent), other agencies of society will have to step in.

8   To be fully effective, a college would need the ability to impose severe sanctions, including dismissal, on the base of reasonable proof of misbehavior or association with bad elements. Advocates of unrestrained constitutional rights will have difficulty with this, but the student enters a contractual relationship with a college to pursue an education.

9   The educators, not the legal system, should do the educating. Colleges exist to form good citizens, conscious of their own rights and the rights of others. Colleges and universities should be evaluated on the basis of the results of their educational work.

James C. Carter, S.J.
Chancellor,
Loyola University
New Orleans

Deliberate About the Readings

As we explained in Chapter 1, deliberation is a way to arrive at your own position on a particular issue. You can't begin deliberation until you have really listened to and reflected on the complexities each issue involves. Once you have engaged in all the steps in the process of critical reading, you are ready to deliberate.

In your deliberation, first consider each of the writer's claims and main points. Then, thinking like a critic, find a way to respond that defines your own position on the issue. Using the four readings in this chapter, a deliberation in your journal about college binge drinking might look like this:

All the writers see binge drinking as a problem, although they differ about where they place the blame and how they plan to solve the problem. Wechsler thinks that binge drinking among college students occurs because colleges are indifferent to it and refuse to recognize its seriousness. He urges colleges to use their influence and power to prevent students from obtaining alcohol. He doesn't seem to think that the students who engage in binge drinking have a lot of control over their behavior. Carter, Sole, and Stewart all agree with Wechsler about the seriousness of the problem; however, they disagree about where to place the blame. Carter thinks that colleges are doing all they can and should be given more legal power to discipline students who binge drink. Sole and Stewart suggest that the media is to blame by endorsing values that encourage students to drink and party rather than concentrate on their studies. Only Harrop places the blame squarely on the shoulders of the binge drinkers themselves. She feels strongly that students need to be treated as adults with drinking problems and suffer the consequences of their actions.

After reading these writings, I am convinced that binge drinking is a problem worthy of our attention. The statistics that Wechsler, Stewart, and Sole cite are convincing and impressive. I also know from my own experience that many students drink excessively, and I think that six deaths are too many for us to ignore. I also think that binge drinking is a problem that affects the entire college community, not just the drinkers, as Stewart and Sole point out. However, I tend to agree with Harrop that students must be held responsible for their own actions. I disagree with Carter that schools should act like parents. College is about becoming an adult in all areas of our lives, not just academics.

Any solution to the problem of binge drinking needs to include the students who abuse alcohol. Unless those students also see their drinking habits as a problem, nothing the college or legal system can impose will affect their behavior. Perhaps a combination of actions, including broader and stronger efforts to educate students about alcohol abuse, greater enforcement and harsher penalties for underage drinking by the legal system, and efforts by colleges to restrict alcohol availability in the community and on the campus, would make a significant dent in this problem.

Now try writing your own deliberation, in which you consider the points you find most important in each reading to arrive at your own position on the issue of binge drinking.

Look for Logical Fallacies

When you read the arguments of others, you need to pay attention to the writer's strategies, assertions, and logic to decide if the argument is reasonable. Like the cross-examining attorney in a court case, you must examine the logical connections among the claim, the reasons, and the evidence to reveal the strengths and weaknesses of the writer's argument.

Sometimes writers make errors in logic. Such errors are called **logical fallacies,** a term derived from the Latin *fallere,* meaning "to deceive." Used unintentionally, these fallacies deceive writers into feeling that their arguments are more persuasive than they are. Even though an argument may be well-developed and contain convincing evidence, a fallacy creates a flaw in the logic of an argument, thereby weakening its structure and persuasiveness.

Not all logical fallacies are unintentional. Sometimes a fallacy is deliberately employed—for example, when the writer's goal has more to do with persuading than with arriving at the truth. Every day we are confronted with fallacies in media commercials and advertisements. Likewise, every election year the airwaves are full of candidates' bloated claims and pronouncements rife with logical fallacies of all kinds.

Recognizing logical fallacies when they occur in a reading is an important step in assessing the effectiveness of the writer's argument. This final section of our chapter will acquaint you with some of the most common logical fallacies.

Preview: Logical Fallacies

- Ad hominem argument
- Ad misericordiam argument
- Ad populum argument
- Bandwagon appeal
- Begging the question
- Circular reasoning
- False analogy
- False dilemma
- Faulty use of authority
- Hasty generalization
- Non sequitur
- Post hoc, ergo propter hoc
- Red herring
- Slippery slope
- Stacking the deck

Ad Hominem Argument

From the Latin "to the man," the **ad hominem** argument is a personal attack on an opponent rather than on the opponent's views. Certainly the integrity of an opponent may be important to readers. Nonetheless, writers are usually more persuasive and credible when they focus on issues rather than character flaws. If, for instance, you are reading a paper against the use of animals in medical research and the writer refers to the opposition as "cold-hearted scientists only interested in fame and fortune," you might question whether the writer objects to the scientists' views or to their personal prosperity. Name-calling and character assassination should make you suspicious of the writer's real motives or balanced judgment. Personal criticisms, even if true can be overemphasized and therefore, undercut the writer's credibility.

However, there may be cases in which an ad hominem argument is a legitimate rhetorical tool. When the special interests or associations of an individual or group appear to have a direct impact on their position on an issue, it is fair to raise questions about their lack of objectivity on that basis. For example, the organizer of a petition to build a state-supported recycling center may seem reasonably suspect if it is revealed that he owns the land on which the proposed recycling center would be built. While the property owner may be motivated by sincere environmental concerns, the direct relationship between his position and his personal life makes this fair game for a challenge.

Examples of Ad Hominem Arguments

- How could Tom accuse her of being careless? He's such a slob.
- Of course Helen claimed that O. J. Simpson was innocent. She is black, after all.
- We cannot expect Ms. Lucas to know what it means to feel oppressed; she is the president of a large bank.

Ad Misericordium Argument

Its name also derived from Latin, the **ad misericordiam** argument is the appeal "to pity." This appeal to our emotions need not be fallacious or faulty. A writer, having argued several solid points logically, may make an emotional appeal for extra support. Your local humane society, for instance, might ask you to donate money so it can expand its facilities for abandoned animals. To convince you the society might point out how, over the last few years, the number of strays and unwanted pets has tripled. And because of budget constraints, the society has been forced to appeal to the public. It may claim that a donation of $25 would house and feed a stray animal for a month. Any amount you give, they explain, will ultimately aid the construction of a new pet "dormitory" wing. To bolster the appeal, the humane society literature might then describe how the adorable puppy and kitten in the enclosed photo will have to be put to death unless the overcrowding of the society's facilities is relieved by donations such as yours.

When an argument is based solely on the exploitation of the reader's pity, however, the issue gets lost. There's an old joke about a man who murdered his parents and appealed to the court for leniency because he was an orphan. It's funny because it ludicrously illustrates how pity has nothing to do with murder. Let's take a more realistic example. If you were a lawyer whose client was charged with bank embezzlement, you would not get very far basing your defense solely on the fact that the defendant was abused as a child. Yes, you may touch the hearts of the jurors, even move them to pity. Yet that would not exonerate your client. The abuse the defendant suffered as a child, as woeful as it is, has nothing to do with his or her crime as an adult. Any intelligent prosecutor would point out the attempt to manipulate the court with a sob story while distracting it from more important factors such as justice.

Examples of Ad Misericordiam Arguments

- It makes no difference if he was guilty of Nazi war crimes. The man is eighty years old and in frail health, so he should not be made to stand trial.
- Paula is 14 years old and lives on welfare with her mother; she suffers serious depression and functions like a child half her age. She should not be sent to adult court, where she will be tried for armed robbery, so she can spend her formative years behind bars.

Ad Populum Argument

From the Latin "to the people," an **ad populum** argument is just that—an argument aimed at appealing to the supposed prejudices and emotions of the masses. Writers attempt to manipulate readers by using emotional and provocative language to add appeal to their claims. The problem with the ad populum argument, however, is that such language sometimes functions as a smoke screen hiding the lack of ideas in the argument. You'll find examples of this fallacy on the editorial pages of your local newspaper—for example, the letter from parents raising a furor because they don't want their child or the children of their friends and neighbors taught by teachers with foreign accents; or the columnist who makes the ad populum case against capital punishment by inflating the number of innocent people wrongfully executed by the state; or the writer who argues that if gays and lesbians are allowed to serve in the military, our national defense will be jeopardized by "sex maniacs."

Examples of Ad Populum Arguments

- High school students don't learn anything these days. Today's teachers are academically underprepared.
- If you want to see the crime rate drop, tell Hollywood to stop making movies that glorify violence.
- Doctors oppose health reform because it will reduce their large incomes.

The Bandwagon Appeal

This familiar strategy makes the claim that everybody is doing this and thinking that. If we don't want to be left out, we had better get on the **bandwagon** and do and think the same things. The basic appeal in this argument is that of belonging to the group, behaving like the majority. It plays on our fears of being different, of being excluded. Of course, the appeal is fallacious inasmuch as we are asked to "get with it" without weighing the evidence of what is being promoted: "Smart shoppers shop at Sears"; "America reads Stephen King."

Examples of Bandwagon Appeals

- Everybody's going to the Smashing Pumpkins concert.
- Nobody will go along with that proposal.
- The majority of the American people want a constitutional amendment outlawing flag burning.

Begging the Question

Similar to circular reasoning, **begging the question** passes off as true an assumption that needs to be proven. For instance, to say that the defendant is innocent because he passed a polygraph test begs the question: Does passing a polygraph test mean somebody is innocent? Sometimes the begged question is itself loaded in a bigger question: "Are you ever going to act like you are equal and pay for one of our dates?" The begged question here is whether paying the costs of a date is a measure of sexual equality.

Examples of Begging the Question

- That foolish law should be repealed.
- She is compassionate because she's a woman.
- If you haven't written short stories, you shouldn't be criticizing them.

Circular Reasoning

Circular reasoning is another common fallacy into which many writers fall. In it, the conclusion of a deductive argument is hidden in the premise of that argument. Thus, the argument goes around in a circle. For instance: "Steroids are dangerous because they ruin your health." This translates: Steroids are dangerous because they are dangerous. Sometimes the circularity gets camouflaged in a tangle of words: "The high cost of living in today's America is a direct consequence of the exorbitant prices manufacturers and retailers are placing on their products and services." Cut away the excess, and this translates: The high cost of living is due to the high cost of living. Repetition of key terms or ideas is not evidence. Nor does it prove anything. Instead of simply restating your premise, find solid evidence to support it.

Examples of Circular Reasoning

- People who are happy with their work are cheerful because they enjoy what they're doing.
- Only a welfare mother can appreciate the plight of welfare mothers.
- Bank robbers should be punished because they broke the law.

False Analogy

An analogy compares two things that are alike in one or more ways. In any form of writing analogies are very useful, as they expand meaning and demonstrate imagination. In arguments they can be wonderful tools for persuasion. Unfortunately, they can also lead the writer astray and make his or her argument vulnerable to attack.

The problem with **false analogies** arises when the two things compared do not match up feature for feature, and ideas being compared do not logically connect or are pressed beyond legitimacy. The result is a false analogy. For instance, a candidate for a high-powered job may ask to be employed because of his extraordinary heroics during the Persian Gulf War. He may even claim that being a CEO is like fighting a battle: He needs to be brave, tough in mind and body, and willing to take and deal out punishment. Although the argument might sound appealing, running a company involves more than combat skills. Certainly it is important for a corporate executive to be strong and tough-minded. However, an office full of five-star generals might not be expert at dealing with economic recession or product liability. The fallacy is that the analogy is imperfect. Business and soldiering overlap minimally.

A sound analogy will clarify a difficult or unfamiliar concept by comparing it with something easily understood or familiar.

Examples of False Analogy

- The Ship of State is about to wreck on the rocks of recession; we need a new pilot.
- This whole gun control issue is polarizing the nation the way slavery did people living above and below the Mason-Dixon line. Do we want another Civil War?
- Letting emerging nations have nuclear weapons is like giving loaded guns to children.

False Dilemma

A **false dilemma** involves the simplification of complex issues into an either/or choice. For example, "Either we legalize abortion or we send young women to back-alley butchers," "Love America or leave it," "Either we keep gun ownership legal or only criminals will have guns." Such sloganizing ultimatums, although full of dramatic impact, unfortunately appeal to people's ignorance and prejudices.

Examples of False Dilemma

- English should be the official language of the United States, and anybody who doesn't like it can leave.
- Movies today are full of either violence or sex.
- Either we put warning labels on records and compact discs, or we'll see more and more teenage girls having babies.

Faulty Use of Authority

The **faulty use of authority** occurs when someone who is an expert in one area is used as an authority for another unrelated area. For instance, the opinions of a four-star general about the use of force against an uncooperative foreign tyrant carry great weight in a discussion of U.S. foreign policy options. However, the opinions of that same individual about the Supreme Court's ruling on the question of assisted suicide are less compelling. His military expertise does not guarantee that his views on euthanasia are particularly valuable.

Advertisers frequently resort to the faulty use of authority to promote their products. Celebrities are asked to endorse products they may have no special knowledge about or any interest in aside from the sizable check they will receive for their services. Another example occurs when well-known popular figures rely on their achievements in one area to lend credibility to their views in another. For instance, the late Benjamin Spock, famous for his work on child development, became a spokesperson for the nuclear disarmament movement. Because of his reputation, people were willing to listen more closely to his views than to others who were less well-known, yet his expertise in child-rearing gave him no more authority in this area than any other well-educated person. While Dr. Spock may, indeed, have been knowledgeable about nuclear arms, his expertise in that area would have to be demonstrated before he could be used as an effective authority on the subject.

Examples of Faulty Use of Authority

- You should buy these vitamins because Cindy Crawford recommended them on television last night.
- The American Bar Association states that second-hand smoke is a serious cancer threat to non-smokers.
- Americans shouldn't find hunting objectionable because one of our most popular presidents, Theodore Roosevelt, was an avid hunter.

Hasty Generalization

As the name indicates, the **hasty generalization** occurs when a writer arrives at a conclusion based on too little evidence. It's one of the most frequently found fallacies. If the local newspaper's restaurant critic is served underdone chicken at Buster's Diner during her first and only visit, she would be making a hasty generalization to conclude that Buster's serves terrible food. Although this may be true, one visit is not enough to draw that conclusion. If, however, after three visits she is still dissatisfied with the food, she is entitled to warn her readers about eating at Buster's.

Hasty generalizations can also occur when the writer relies on evidence that is not factual or substantiated. A generalization can only be as sound as its supporting evidence. Writers should provide multiple and credible examples to support their points. Be wary of sweeping, uncritical statements and words such as *always, all, none, never, only,* and *most.* Note whether the writer qualifies the claim with words that are limiting, such as *many, some, often* and *seldom.*

Examples of Hasty Generalizations

- That shopping mall is unsafe because there was a robbery there two weeks ago.
- I'm failing organic chemistry because the teaching assistant doesn't speak English well.
- This book was written by a Harvard professor, so it must be good.

Non Sequitur

From the Latin for "does not follow," a **non sequitur** draws a conclusion that does not follow logically from the premise. For instance, suppose you heard a classmate make the following claim: "Ms. Marshall is such a good teacher; it's hard to believe she wears such ugly clothes." The statement would be fallacious because the ability to teach has nothing to do with taste in clothing. Some of the worst teachers might be the best dressers. Although you might want to believe a good teacher would be a good dresser, there is no reason to think so. Writers must establish a clear connection between the premise and the conclusion. And unless one is made through well-reasoned explanations, readers will not accept the cause-and-effect relationship.

Political campaigns are notorious for non sequiturs: "Candidate Jones will be a great senator because she's been married for twenty years." Or, "Don't vote for Candidate Jones because she is rich and lives in an expensive neighborhood." Whether the voters decide to vote for Candidate Jones or not should not depend on the length of her marriage or the neighborhood in which she lives—neither qualifies or disqualifies her from public office. The non sequiturs attempt to suggest a relationship between her ability to be a successful senator and unrelated facts about her life.

Examples of Non Sequiturs

- Mr. Thompson has such bad breath that it's a wonder he sings so well.
- She's so pretty; she must not be smart.
- I supported his candidacy for president because his campaign was so efficiently run.

Post Hoc, Ergo Propter Hoc

The Latin **post hoc, ergo propter hoc** is translated as "after this, therefore because of this." A post hoc, ergo propter hoc argument is one that establishes a questionable cause-and-effect relationship between events. In other words, because event Y follows event X, event X causes event Y. For instance, you would be making a post hoc argument if you claimed, "Every time my brother Bill accompanies me to Jacob's Field, the Cleveland Indians lose." The reasoning here is fallacious because we all know that although the Indians lose whenever Bill joins you at Jacob's Field, his presence does not cause the team to lose. Experience tells us that there simply is no link between the two events. The only explanation is coincidence.

Our conversations are littered with these dubious claims: "Every time I plan a pool party, it rains"; "Whenever I drive to Chicago, I get a flat tire." "Every movie that Harry recommends turns out to be a dud." What they underscore is our pessimism or dismay, rather than any belief in the truth of such statements.

It's not surprising that post hoc reasoning is often found in arguments made by people prone to superstition—people looking for big, simple explanations. You would be committing such a fallacy if, for instance, you claimed that you got a C on your math test because a black cat crossed your path that morning or because you broke a mirror the night before. Post hoc fallacies are also practiced by those bent on proving conspiracies. Following the assassination of President Kennedy in 1963 there was considerable effort by some to link the deaths of many people involved in the investigation to a government cover-up, even though the evidence was scanty. Today we hear Democrats protest that America goes to war every time Republicans are in office and Republicans protest that America gets poorer when Democrats are in office.

You might also have heard people argue that since the women's liberation movement, the number of latchkey children has risen sharply. The claim essentially says that the women's movement is directly responsible for the rise in working mothers over the last 25 years. While it is true that the women's movement has made it more acceptable for mothers to return to the workforce, the prime reason is particular to the individual. For some it is simple economics; for others, personal fulfillment; for others still, a combination of the two. The feminist movement is one among many factors linked with women in the workforce and the consequent rise in latchkey children.

Examples of Post Hoc, Ergo Propter Hoc Arguments

- Just two weeks after they raised the speed limit, three people were killed on that road.
- I saw Ralph in the courthouse; he must have been arrested.
- It's no wonder the crime rate has shot up. The state legislature voted to lower the drinking age.

Red Herring

A **red herring,** as the name suggests, is evidence that is fallaciously used to distract the audience from the true issues of an argument. The term is derived from the practice of using the scent of a red herring to throw hunting dogs off the trail of their real prey. In modern life this fallacy is more often used to confuse the audience by providing irrelevant information or evidence. For instance, when the head coach of a major league team was accused of using team funds on personal expenses, he defended himself by pointing to the team's winning record under his leadership. While the team had undeniably performed well during this period, his response was irrelevant to the charges made against him. He had hoped to distract his accusers from the real issue, which involved his lack of honesty and abuse of power. A red herring may distract the audience momentarily, but once it is discovered it indicates that the individual has little or no effective reasons or evidence to support his or her position.

Examples of Red Herring

- Even though that hockey player was convicted of vehicular homicide, he shouldn't go to jail because he is such a great athlete.
- Susan didn't hire John for the job because his wife is always late for meetings.
- The teacher gave me an F in the course because she doesn't like me.

Slippery Slope

The **slippery slope** presumes one event will inevitably lead to a chain of other events that end in a catastrophe—as one slip on a mountain top will cause a climber to tumble down and bring with him or her all those in tow. This domino-effect reasoning is fallacious because it depends more on presumption than hard evidence: "Censorship of obscene material will spell the end to freedom of the press"; "A ban on ethnic slurs will mean no more freedom of speech"; "If assault rifles are outlawed, handguns will be next." America's involvement in Vietnam was the result of a slippery slope argument: "If Vietnam falls to the Communists, all of Southeast Asia, and eventually India and its neighbors, will fall under the sway of communism." Even though Vietnam did fall, the result has not been the widespread rise of communism in the region; on the contrary, communism has fallen on hard times.

Examples of Slippery Slope Arguments

- Legalized abortion is a step toward creating an antilife society.
- A ban on ethnic slurs will mean no more freedom of speech.
- If we let them build those condos, the lake will end up polluted, the wildlife will die off, and the landscape will be scarred forever.

Stacking the Deck

When writers give only the evidence that supports their premise, while disregarding or withholding contrary evidence, they are **stacking the deck**. (Science students may know this as "data beautification," the habit of recording only those results that match what an experiment is expected to predict.) A meat-packing manufacturer may advertise that its all-beef hot dogs "now contain 10 percent less fat." Although that may sound like good news, what we are not being told is that the hot dogs still contain 30 percent fat.

This stacking-the-deck fallacy is common not only in advertising but also in debates of controversial matters. The faculty of a college, for instance, may petition for the firing of its president for failing to grant needed raises while an expensive new football stadium is being built. The complaint would not be fair, however, if the faculty ignored mentioning that the stadium funds were specifically earmarked for athletic improvement by the billionaire benefactor. Also, if the complaint left unrecognized the many accomplishments of the president, such as the successful capital campaign, the plans for a new library, and the influx of notable scholars, it would be an example of stacking the deck.

Examples of Stacking the Deck

- Parents should realize that private schools simply encourage elitism in young people.
- We cannot take four more years of her in office, given the way she voted against the death penalty.
- Dickens's *Bleak House* is six hundred pages of boring prose.

As you progress through the chapters in this book, you will find that thinking like a critic is the key to understanding and responding to argument. It will make you a stronger reader and a more effective writer. In the next chapter we explore ways that you can think like a writer to find and develop topics for your own argument essays.

EXERCISES

1. In your journal, list examples of logical fallacies you find in essays, news articles, editorials, advertising, junk mail, and other persuasive materials that you confront on a daily basis. Based on the information you and other group members collect, draw some hypotheses about which fallacies are most prevalent today and why. If your instructor asks you to do so, convert those hypotheses into an outline of an argument essay for your campus newspaper.

2. Explain the faulty logic of the following statements. Of what fallacy (or fallacies) is each an example?
   a. When did you stop hiring other people to take your exams for you?
   b. He's too smart to play football; besides he broke his leg ten years ago.
   c. If we don't stop the publication of this x-rated material now, it won't be long before our children will be reading it at school.
   d. Karen must be depressed; she wore dark clothes all weekend.
   e. How can you accuse me of being late? You're such a slowpoke.
   f. Rap music isn't music because it's just noise and words.
   g. He's at least 6 feet 6 inches tall, so he must be a terrific basketball player.
   h. WGBB is the most popular radio station on campus because it has more listeners than any other station.
   i. Indians living on reservations get the necessities of life at government expense, so they have no worries.
   j. Take Tummy Tops laxatives instead of Mellow Malt, because Tummy Tops contains calcium while Mellow Malt has aluminum and magnesium.
   k. Lite Cheese Popcorn contains 34 percent fewer calories!
   l. Any decent person will agree that Nazism has no place in modern society.

chapter 3

FINDING ARGUMENTS

Thinking like a Writer

When confronted with an issue we feel strongly about, most of us have no trouble offering an energetically delivered opinion. Yet when we're asked to *write* an argument, we feel paralyzed. To express our ideas in written form forces us to commit ourselves to some position or to endorse a particular action. We have to take a risk and make a public statement about what we think and feel and believe. Our written words can be scrutinized. That makes us vulnerable, and nobody likes to feel exposed.

It is helpful to think of writing an argument as one way to explore our ideas about a subject or issue. As such, writing can be a means of growth and discovery. Exploring new ideas can be intimidating, but it's also challenging. Who doesn't secretly want to be Indiana Jones, at least once in a while? This chapter will demonstrate how writers begin the process of exploring their ideas to write argument essays. As novelist E. M. Forster explained, "How will I know what I think until I've seen what I've said?"

Exploration, of course, takes time. We're not recommending a writing process that begins an hour before a paper is due; rather, we're recommending what successful writers do: take time to think your writing through. This means starting assignments early, working through all the stages, and allowing time to revise and polish your work before you submit it. Learning to write well is the same as learning to perform any other skilled activity. You have to practice your strokes or your scales to be a good tennis player or pianist; likewise, you have to practice your craft to be a good writer. As you gain more experience, some of the stages of the writing process will go more quickly for you on most projects. Even when you become a polished logician, however, you may find yourself writing about a topic that requires you to work out the assumptions in your argument slowly and painstakingly. That's okay. All writers do that. Welcome to the club.

The Writing Process

Many rhetorical theorists have tried to describe the writing process, but that's a little like describing snowflakes: each one is different. Each person has a different way of writing, especially depending on the job. Think about it. You can dash off a note to your roommate in a second; if you're writing a job application letter you'll probably take a great deal more time. If you have only twenty minutes to answer an essay question on a history exam, you'll get it done somehow; but give you an entire semester to write a term paper on the same subject, and you'll probably spend several weeks (if not months) doing the job. The scope and length of the assignment dictate a different writing process.

What most people studying the writing process agree on is that almost everyone goes through four distinct stages when writing: incubating, framing, reshaping, and polishing.

Incubating

When something prompts you to write (your boss tells you to write a report, you get an assignment, a letter requires an answer, you feel strongly about a controversy and want to write a letter to the editor), you spend time either mentally or physically preparing to respond. You may make notes, go to the library, or stare out the window. You're *incubating* the ideas you'll use to respond to the writing stimulus. In this chapter we provide strategies you can use to make this early stage of writing work for you.

Framing

In the second stage you begin, however haltingly, to put words to paper. Some people make an outline; others write a bare-bones rough draft in an attempt to get some ideas down on paper. Many people like to start by sketching out their conclusions so that they can see where their writing must take them. Others prefer the linear, start-with-the-introduction system that moves them through the task. The first goal in the framing stage, as in building a house, is to get the framework of the writing in place so you can start adding material to fill it out. At some point in the framing process you also take your potential readers into account in order to get some idea of their expectations and receptivity.

Reshaping

Once you have a draft framed, you're ready to do the hard work of writing: *rewriting*. At this stage you may move parts of your paper around, or make a new outline, or add or cut material to fill in gaps or eliminate imbalances. You'll have your readers much more clearly in mind because your goal is to persuade them; what you know about their background, experiences, and values will help you decide on a final shape for your paper, even if it means throwing away nearly everything you have framed. (A bad paper that's finished is still a bad paper; that's why you need to allow time for flexibility. Writers who are pressed for time sometimes have to polish something that's not good and hope their readers won't notice, a technique that doesn't usually work.) At the reshaping stage most good writers like to get feedback from other writers to get a sense of what their prospective readers will think of their writing; in a classroom situation this practice usually involves exchanging drafts with classmates or having conferences with your instructor.

Polishing

To have the greatest chance of persuading your readers to consider your point of view, your writing needs to be as readable as possible. That's why, after you've re-shaped it, you need to work on your sentence structure so that words "flow" for your readers. Or you may need to change words here and there to heighten their impact. If others have read your paper and offered feedback, you may wish to act on some of their suggestions for improvement. You always need to edit and proof-read what you've written so that no careless errors distract your readers from getting the message you're trying to convey. And you have to produce a copy, whether by handwriting it, typing it, or convincing your computer printer to spit it out.

In a nutshell, that's the writing process. Now let's look at how you might ex-ploit the features of that process when you start writing arguments.

Finding Topics to Argue

Every writer knows the experience of being blocked, or of having a topic but not knowing what to say about it, or of having only one point to make about an issue. To help generate more ideas, writers need to tap both internal and external re-sources.

In Your Immediate Vicinity

The world around you is full of arguments; you just need to take a moment to see them. Look at the front page and editorial pages of your campus newspaper, for in-stance. What's going on? Look at billboards and bulletin boards. What are people having meetings about? What changes are coming up? Listen to the conversations of people on the bus, or waiting in line at the bookstore, or in the library. What's up? What have you been reading for a class that gets you thinking? You might want to know how a theory for the origin of the universe was derived, or what the results of a recent study of employment success for former welfare recipients were based on, or even why two experts in the field of early childhood learning draw different conclusions from the same evidence. The reading you do for your own enjoyment may also provide some interesting ideas. A science fiction novel may make you wonder about the plausibility of alien life. Reading a murder mystery may make you think about the value of forensic anthropology. Look through the magazines in your room, or at the ads on television, or at the junk mail that fills your mailbox. Even casually reading magazines and newspapers on a daily or weekly basis will turn up issues and controversies. What claims are people making? What are people ask-ing you to do, or think, or wear, or look like, or support? These are sources of po-tential arguments; all you have to do is become aware of them. As Thoreau put it, "Only that day dawns to which we are awake."

In Your Larger Worlds

Don't limit yourself to campus. Often there are debates and discussions going on in your workplace, in your place of worship, on your block, in your town. You belong to a number of communities; each has its issues of interest, and in those issues you can find plenty to write about. And those environments aren't the only places you'll find sources for arguments; the world turns on proposals, positions, and controversies. It's almost impossible to turn on the radio or television today without seeing someone presenting an opinion. Your computer (or the one available on your campus) can connect you to a global community engaged in debate and dialogue on every issue imaginable. On the Internet you can participate in a number of discussions about controversial issues through listservs, Usenet newsgroups, and chat rooms. Make a list of the issues that interest you. What are the headlines in the newspaper? What's Congress voting on? What are the hot spots around the globe (or in the larger universe)? Don't stick to the familiar; there is all experimental territory just waiting to be explored.

Keeping a Journal

You've probably noticed that we encourage recording ideas and observations in a journal, a technique used by many professional writers. The journal doesn't have to be fancy; the cheap supermarket variety works just as well as the $4,000 portable color computer. (If you're comfortable at a keyboard, a computer disk makes a great notebook and fits in your shirt pocket, too—although you might want to keep a backup copy.)

Writers use journals as portable file cabinets of ideas. In a journal we record anything in language that interests us, not just materials for current projects. We may copy down a word or phrase or sentence we hear that we like, or photocopy and staple in a piece by a writer we admire, or even add things that infuriate or amuse us. Not only does a journal become a supermarket of ideas and strategies, but there's something very positive about the simple act of copying words. Somehow, physically writing or typing them makes them yours; you learn something about technique in doing the physical work. (That's why we don't recommend making too many photocopies; you don't mentally store the information in the same way you do when you copy a passage yourself.)

For the beginning argument writer, a journal is invaluable. You can use yours to include notes on possible topics; examples of good introductions and conclusions; catchy words, phrases, and titles; examples of logical fallacies—just about anything a writer might need. A journal is also particularly helpful for creating *dialogues*, the voices and opinions of others who may hold views that are different from your own on particular issues. By keeping a record or notes on what people have to say in newspapers, magazine articles, television talk shows, and casual conversation about various controversial issues, you'll have a ready resource to consult when you begin to deliberate about your position on a particular issue.

When you begin keeping the journal, set yourself a formal goal: for example, adding 100 words a day or writing five days out of the week. Then *stick to it*. Journals don't fill themselves. It takes discipline to keep a journal, and discipline is a characteristic of good writers. If you don't do the groundwork, your creativity won't break through. Throughout this text we've scattered suggestions and exercises for using journals; if you want to fully master the power of argument, we encourage you to *do* the exercises. Don't just read them; write!

Developing Argumentative Topics

Topics alone aren't arguments, and many inexperienced writers have trouble making the jump from subject to argument. For example, you may be interested in heavy metal music. That's a subject—a big one. What can you argue about it? You could ask yourself, "What are the facts about heavy metal? When did it start? How can it be defined? What differentiates it from the mainstream rock played on most commercial radio stations? Why are some groups played, it seems, once an hour, and others almost totally ignored?" You can ask functional questions, such as "Who is the most influential figure in heavy metal music? Is heavy metal more relevant than, say, techno music?" You might ask aesthetic questions about the importance of melody or lyrics or harmony, or ethical questions such as whether the industry should put parental advisory labels on albums. You could even consider moral questions such as whether heavy metal music videos encourage sexism or violence. In recognizing the multiple possibilities of issues, you may find you have more to say on a topic than you think.

Getting Started

Sometimes getting started can be the most difficult step in the writing process. Where do I begin? What should I include? What ideas will work best? How shall I organize it all? You may have a hundred ideas in your head about the topic or— even worse—none at all. When this happens there are a number of tried-and-true techniques that professional writers use to redirect those anxious questions and concerns into productive writing. While you may not need to use all the strategies each time you begin to write, you'll find that trying out each one of them will help you discover what works best for you.

Brainstorming

Brainstorming can help you get your ideas on paper in an informal and unstructured way. When you brainstorm you write down as many ideas as you can about your subject, usually in short phrases, questions, or single words. Don't worry about placing them in any special order or even about making complete sense. The one rule to observe while you're brainstorming is not to judge the ideas that pop into your head and spill out onto your paper. When you give yourself permission to write down anything that seems related to your subject, you'll be surprised at the number of ideas that will occur to you. By not rejecting anything, you'll find that one idea will naturally lead to another. Even an idea that you may throw out later can lead you to an idea that may be a real gem. And the more ideas you record in your brainstorm, the more choices you will have to consider later as you sift through this record of your thoughts and decide what is and is not useful.

After critically reading the essays in Chapter 2 of this text, John, our first-year composition student, decided to write his first paper on college binge drinking. He began his writing preparation by brainstorming about the subject. Here's what he came up with:

binge drinking	why drink to excess?
drinking until you feel sick	want to forget all about the week
getting together with friends for a good time	makes us feel grown up
partying after a tough week at school	nothing better to do on Sat. night
so many bars, so little time	why does the college care?
half the people underage	people can really hurt themselves
whose responsibility is it?	prevention—how?
nobody checks anyway	part of the college experience
feeling terrible the next morning	ignore it—will it go away?
smelling like a beer can	trying to act cool
role of the college administration	what starts as fun can lead to death
rite of passage	definition of an adult
impact of peer pressure	do other cultures experience this?

As you can see, John had many different ideas about binge drinking, and the more he brainstormed, the more he discovered what they were. After looking over his brainstorm, John chose a few of the ideas that especially interested him to explore further.

John was lucky to have a subject already chosen before he began his brainstorm. But what happens if your instructor doesn't assign a particular topic for your paper and you are left to choose one for yourself? You may find it difficult to come up with a topic. You're not alone. Students often comment that the hardest part of writing is deciding what to write about. To ease the selection task, we suggest a brainstorming strategy. Take out a piece of paper and jot down whatever comes to mind in response to these questions:

- What issues in print or TV news interest you?
- What issues make you angry?
- What problems in your dorm/on campus/in your town/in your country concern you?
- What political issue concerns you most?
- What aspects about the environment worry you?
- If you were professor/dean/college president/mayor/governor/senator/president, what would be the first thing you'd do?
- What policies/practices/regulations/laws would you like to see changed?
- What do you talk about or argue over with friends or classmates?
- What ideas from books or articles have challenged your thinking?

- What books/movies/music/fashions/art do you like, and why?
- What books/movies/music/fashions/art do you hate, and why?
- What personalities in politics/show business/the media/academia do you have strong feelings about?

Here's a quick brainstorming list one student developed:

Issues That Interest Me
1. Whether welfare reform has been effective.
2. Excessive salaries for athletes.
3. People who protest movie violence but oppose bans on assault rifles.
4. The reasons behind eco-terrorism.
5. College campus speech codes.

Once you have brainstormed a list, organize the issues according to categories—for example, political, social, environmental, educational issues, and so on. Then transfer the list to your journal. Now, whenever an assignment comes up, you'll have a database of ideas to consult.

Clustering

Some writers find that visualizing their ideas on a page helps them explore their subject in new ways. Clustering* is a technique you can use to do that. It involves choosing a key word, phrase, or even a short sentence, and placing it in the center of a blank page with a circle around it. Next you try to think of ideas, words, or other short phrases that you can associate or relate to your key word or phrase. As you do, write them in the blank area surrounding the center and circle them and draw lines linking them to your center circled word or phrase. As you accumulate more and more clusters, the words and phrases within them will generate ideas on their own; these can be linked to the words that inspired them. When you have exhausted your cluster, you will have a complex network of ideas that should provide many ways to begin to explore your subject. By choosing any one or a combination of these words or ideas as a starting point, you can move to freewriting to find ways of developing these ideas further.

Figure 3.1 on page 68 shows how Rebecca, another student, used clustering to find new ways of thinking about assisted suicide, a topic she had chosen for her paper. When Rebecca examined her cluster she found a map of the many ideas she might explore further:

- What role should family play in this decision?
- Will the cost of medical care affect the patient's decision?
- If pain can be controlled, will the patient be less inclined to seek this alternative?

---

*Clustering is a technique explored by Gabriele L. Rico in her book *Writing the Natural Way: Using Right Brain Techniques to Release Your Expressive Powers* (J.P. Tarcher: Los Angeles, 1983).

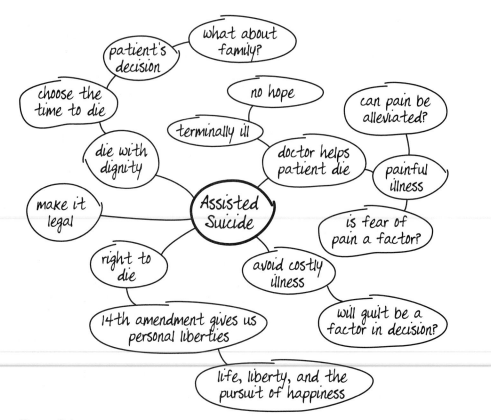

Figure 3.1

- Should assisted suicide be legalized?
- Does the right to die with dignity exist?

Her cluster revealed the complexity of the issue and became a starting point for Rebecca to investigate the subject in greater depth.

Freewriting

Freewriting goes one step beyond brainstorming. Instead of simply listing phrases, questions, and words related to your subject, freewriting involves writing freely, and without stopping, whatever thoughts and ideas you have about your subject, without worrying about sentence structure, spelling, or grammar. As in brainstorming, when you freewrite, it's important not to censor your ideas. Your aim is to discover what you know about your subject, and the best way you can do that is by giving your mind permission to go wherever it pleases. Freewriting isn't intended to be a finished part of your paper; instead, it's a way to generate the ideas and focus that you can use later as you begin to draft the paper itself.

Freewriting can begin with anything: your topic, a particularly interesting idea you've read about, or an experience that you can connect with your subject. If you have used brainstorming or clustering before freewriting, these activities can provide you with a key word or phrase to get you started. For instance, John found a good idea from his brainstorm to begin his freewrite:

> Getting together with friends for a good time. That's what everyone looks forward to every weekend. Throw away the books, get out of the dorm and party. Four, five, sometimes more drinks. Feeling no pain. Binge drinking just seems to happen. It isn't something you plan to do. When you're having a good time, you don't think about how terrible you're going to feel the next day or about all the stupid things you're doing. It's easy to get alcohol in town. Nobody ever checks for proof and if they do, you just go to another place down the street. It's so easy to get phony proof anyway. And the crowds are so large, no one looks so carefully. If college students want to drink, who's to say they can't? We're old enough to vote, die for our country, sign a contract. Why not drinking? And how are you ever going to learn to drink if you don't? College students drink for lots of reasons. Why? Well, it gets them in a party mood. It's fun. It makes us feel like adults. It's so cool. Everyone does it. There's nothing wrong with drinking, but is it a problem if you drink too much? Every weekend. I've heard about students who have died. They let it get out of control. Drunk driving, alcohol poisoning, stupid accidents. Binge drinking is drinking gone overboard. Guess that's all I can think of right now.

John used his freewriting to think on paper. While he didn't come up with any conclusions about how he felt about binge drinking, he did produce a number of ideas that he explored later, when he worked on the first draft of his paper:

- College students binge drink for many reasons.
- Binge drinking can be a problem.
- Drinking is related to feeling adult.
- Binge drinking is not a planned behavior, but it can get to be a habit.

One of the best reasons for using freewriting before you begin the first draft of your paper is to avoid the most intimidating sight a writer can see: a blank page. Unfortunately, sometimes that blank page is the result of a blank mind and an over-concern about how your writing and ideas will appear to others. When you freewrite, you write for yourself alone. It is a way to make your ideas flow. Freewriting generates ideas that will help you begin to think about your subject before worrying about polishing your writing for an audience.

Asking Questions

Once you have a subject in mind, a good strategy for generating ideas is to make a list of questions you have about the subject. Your questions can cover areas in which you need more information, as well as questions you might like to answer as you think and write about your topic. For instance, John tried this strategy for his topic of college binge drinking and came up with the following questions:

> Why do college students binge drink?
>
> How many college students actually binge drink?

Is binge drinking a result of peer pressure?

Do students binge drink to show they are adults?

Do most college students find binge drinking acceptable?

Is binge drinking strictly a college student activity or do other age and economic groups do this as well?

Do college students stop binge drinking once they leave college?

Who should be responsible for binge drinking? the drinkers? the college? the law?

Why do college administrations feel that they must respond to the problem of drinking if it's off campus?

Do colleges have a legal responsibility to protect their students?

Are the alcohol prevention programs on campus effective?

It's easy to see how one question can lead to another. By choosing one question or several related ones John had real direction for exploring his topic and focusing his paper as he began his research and his first draft.

Engaging in Dialogue with Others

Talking to other people is a great source of ideas. None of the techniques we've discussed so far have to be lonely activities. You can brainstorm with others, read your freewriting to a friend and listen to the response, or interview classmates to find out their questions and concerns about your subject. By sharing your ideas and listening to the responses of others you will find a wealth of new ideas and perspectives. In fact, you'll be engaging in the kind of *dialogue* we discussed in Chapter 1. You can do this in a number of ways: participate in either small peer groups in your class or larger class discussions; speak individually with your instructor; seek out members of your community, on campus or outside your school; share ideas with others electronically through Internet chat rooms, e-mail, or listservs; or talk with family and friends. As Larry King and other talk show hosts prove every day, people love to talk. So, take advantage of it—and take notes.

Refining Topics

Once you have found—through the strategies we've discussed—subjects that strike you as interesting, you have to begin narrowing down your topic to a manageable size. The next step, then, is to look over your list and reduce it to those topics that are legitimately arguable. (See Chapter 1 for a refresher.)

Reducing Your Options

Your first step is to determine whether your subject is manageable. You don't want a subject that is too broad or unwieldy or that requires prohibitive amounts of research. For example, you would not want to argue that "women have always been discriminated against in sports." You could write a book about that if you had time to do all the research. To write a short paper, you have to narrow your subject. "The

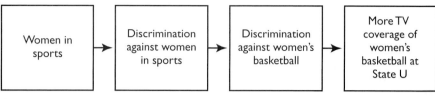

Figure 3.2

women's basketball team at State U. should get more television coverage" is a manageable reduction of your first idea, and one that you can handle in an average-length paper (see Figure 3.2). The more narrow your topic, the more you restrict your research and tighten the focus of your argument.

Avoiding Overspecialized Topics

On the other hand, don't pick a topic that requires extensive specialized knowledge, such as how to reduce the trade deficit or the problems inherent in thermonuclear fusion. The issue you choose should be one you know a little something about and, to keep you interested, about which you have strong convictions. Also, it should be an issue you are willing to spend a reasonable amount of time exploring on your own or perhaps in the library. Aside from writing a convincing argument, a parallel goal of any project you research is to become better informed and more appreciative of the complexity of the issue. Therefore, select a topic on which you wish to be well informed and that you are willing to investigate and reflect on.

Formulating a Working Claim

Once you have decided on your topic and used some of the strategies we've discussed, you are ready to create a working claim. As we explained in Chapter 1, the claim is the heart of your essay. It functions as a thesis statement. It states what you believe or what action you'd like your readers to take. In Chapter 1 we provided examples of the different ways you can state your claim. However, at this early stage of your writing it would be difficult to create a claim that would be perfect for the paper you have yet to research and write. It's too early in the game to commit yourself. After all, your research may yield some surprising results, and you want to be open to all sides of the issue. At best, you can create a working claim—that is, a statement of your opinion or position on your topic that you can use temporarily to help you focus and organize your paper and limit your research.

After Rebecca, our first-year composition student, considered her subject of assisted suicide by clustering and freewriting, she realized what an enormous topic it was and that she needed to narrow it. She began by asking questions about assisted suicide. Should assisted suicide be legalized? Who should be allowed to commit suicide? anyone who wants to die? anyone in pain? just people who are terminally ill? For what reasons should assisted suicide be legalized? How can we determine when assisted suicide is appropriate? Who should make this decision? Is it morally wrong to end one's own life?

As Rebecca thought about the answers to these questions, she began to narrow the focus of her broad topic to one that she could explore in a paper of reasonable length. She decided that she would focus only on the issue of assisted suicide for the terminally ill. Her essay would consider the controversial issue of whether assisted suicide should be legalized. In particular, she was interested in the question of whether assisted suicide was morally wrong or a choice that each person had to make individually. Her working claim, then, both limited the range of her topic and very clearly expressed her point of view about it:

> Assisted suicide
>> Assisted suicide for the terminally ill
>>> Assisted suicide for the terminally ill should be legal.
>>>> Assisted suicide allows people to die with dignity.
>>>>> Dying with dignity is a basic human right.
> *Working claim:* Assisted suicide for the terminally ill should be legal because dying with dignity is a basic human right.

While Rebecca's views developed and changed as she investigated her topic further, her working claim helped her concentrate her research on those areas that pertained most directly to her ideas.

To arrive at a *working claim* for his paper on binge drinking, John also used some of the strategies illustrated earlier: brainstorming, freewriting, asking questions about the topic, and engaging in dialogue with others. When he sat down to create his working claim, he examined and reflected on his topic and decided on the following:

> Binge drinking is a serious problem on college campuses, and if we continue to ignore it or treat it as normal and acceptable student behavior, no one will ever find an effective way to eliminate it.

By creating a working claim early in his writing process John benefited in a number of ways. He clearly took a position about his topic and expressed his point of view. While he had the opportunity to change his viewpoint as he thought further about his topic, his working claim served as a baseline. John's working claim also helped him organize the reasons he needed to support his position.

Let's take a look at John's working claim to see how it is organized. His claim can be divided into three parts:

1. Binge drinking is a problem on college campuses.
2. It is ignored or simply accepted as normal student behavior.
3. No one has yet found an effective way to solve this problem.

All of these statements are arguable because, as we discussed in Chapter 1, they are based on judgment and interpretation, not on indisputable facts or personal opinion. As he developed his paper, John needed to decide on reasons to effectively convince his readers that these three parts of his working claim are true.

In addition, John's working claim helped him decide what he needed to investigate further. As John researched and became more knowledgeable about his topic, he revised his working claim to better reflect what he had learned. But at this stage of his paper, his working claim provided him with several specific areas that he needed to investigate in order to argue persuasively about them:

1. Is binge drinking really a problem on college campuses? How significant is it?
2. How is binge drinking ignored and by whom?
3. Is binge drinking regarded as normal student behavior and by whom?
4. What has been done to eliminate binge drinking?
5. What are some ways this problem can be dealt with?

In Chapter 8 we look at a number of ways available to John to research his topic. By using the questions suggested by his working claim as a guide, John had plenty of avenues to explore.

Thinking like a writer will help you make the jump from simply having an opinion on a subject to finding ways to express that opinion in an argument essay. In the next chapter we look at the way in which audience influences and affects the choices we make about what to include in an argument essay and how to present our arguments.

EXERCISES

1. Get together with a small group of students in your class and brainstorm possible topics for an argument essay concerning a controversial issue on your campus or in your community. Try to think of at least ten topics that are current and that most people in your group find interesting and arguable.
2. Make a visit to the periodicals section of your college library and look through current issues of periodicals and newspapers on the shelves to find out what issues and subjects are being debated in America and around the world. Find one or more topics that interest you and make copies of those articles for further reading and response in your journal.
3. Take some time to explore the Internet by doing a keyword search using a Web search engine (see page 185). In your journal, describe the results of your search. How many different sites devoted to your topic did you locate? What did you find surprising about the comments and opinions expressed by the participants?
4. Engage in a dialogue with other students, family members, friends, or people in the community who might have some interest and opinions on a potential topic. In your journal, record and respond to their diverse views.
5. Choose a topic that you might wish to investigate for an argument essay and use some of the strategies suggested in this chapter to get started: brainstorm, cluster, freewrite, question.
6. Formulate a list of questions about your potential topic.
7. After you have followed some of the strategies for exploring your topic, formulate a working claim. In your journal, identify which parts of your claim will need to be supported by reasons in your essay. Which parts of your claim will need to be investigated further?

chapter 4

ADDRESSING AUDIENCES

Thinking like a Reader

As we've discussed in previous chapters, the purpose of writing an argument is to prompt your listeners to consider seriously your point of view and for you to win their respect through the logic and skill of your thinking. When used productively, argument can be a way to resolve conflict and achieve common ground among adversaries. Thus, one of the primary ways to measure the success of your argument is to gauge how effectively it reaches and appeals to your audience. Knowing something about your audience will enable you to use that knowledge to make your arguments most effective.

Creating an argument would be a simple task if you could be guaranteed an audience of readers just like yourself. If everyone shared your cultural, educational, religious, and practical experiences, persuading them to accept your point of view would require very little effort. Clearly, however, this is not the case. A quick look around your classroom will reveal the many differences that make argument a challenging activity. Is everyone the same age? race? gender? ethnicity? Do you all listen to the same music? dress alike? live in the same neighborhood? vote for the same candidates? attend the same place of worship? Unless you attend a very unusual school, the answer to most of these questions will be a resounding "no." People are different; what interests you may bore the person behind you, whereas what puts you to sleep may inspire someone else to passionate activism. And what you see on the surface isn't the whole story about your classmates either. That rough-looking guy who works as a mechanic may write poetry in his spare time; that conservatively dressed woman may spend her weekends touring the countryside on a motorcycle. It's too easy to make assumptions about people's values and beliefs just by looking at them. If you want to persuade these people, you're going to have to assess them very carefully.

Knowing your audience will help you determine almost every aspect of the presentation of your case: the kind of language you use, the writing style (casual or formal, humorous or serious, technical or philosophical); the particular slant you take (appealing to the reader's reason, emotions, or ethics, or a combination of these); what emphasis to give the argument; the type of evidence you offer; and the kinds of authorities you cite. Also, this knowledge will let you better anticipate any objections to your position. In short, knowing your audience lets you adjust the shape of your argument the way you would refocus a camera after each photo you shoot.

If, for instance, you're writing for your economics professor, you would use technical vocabulary you would not use with your English professor. Likewise, in a newspaper article condemning alcohol abusers you would have to keep in mind that some of your readers or their family members might be recovering alcoholics; they may take exception to your opinions. A travel piece for an upscale international magazine would need to have a completely different slant and voice than one for the travel section of a small local newspaper.

Knowing your audience might make the difference between a convincing argument and a failing argument. Suppose, for instance, you decide to write an editorial for the student newspaper opposing a recently announced tuition hike. Chances are you would have a sympathetic audience in the student body because you share age, educational status, and interests. Most students do not like the idea of a higher tuition bill. That commonality might justify the blunt language and emotional slant of your appeal. It might even allow a few sarcastic comments directed at the administration. That same argument addressed to your school's board of trustees, however, would probably not win a round of applause. With them it would be wiser to adopt a more formal tone in painting a sympathetic picture of your financial strain; it's always smart to demonstrate an understanding of the opposition's needs, maybe even a compromise solution. In this case, your appeal to the trustees would be more credible if you acknowledged the university's plight while recommending alternative money-saving measures such as a new fund-raising program.

Or suppose you write an article with a religious thrust arguing against capital punishment. You argue that even in the case of confessed murderers, state execution is an immoral practice running counter to Christian doctrine; for supporting evidence you offer direct quotations from the New Testament. Were you to submit your article to a religious publication, your reliance on the authority of the scriptures would probably appeal to the editors. However, were you to submit that same article to the "My Turn" column for *Newsweek*, chances are it would be turned down, no matter how well written. The editors aren't necessarily an ungodly lot, but *Newsweek*, like most other large-circulation magazines, is published for an audience made up of people of every religious persuasion, as well as agnostics and atheists. *Newsweek* editors are not in the business of publishing material that excludes a large segment of its audience. Knowing your readers works in two ways: It helps you decide what materials to put into your argument, and it helps you decide where to publish your argument, whether it be on an electronic bulletin board, in a local paper, or on the op-ed page of the *Wall Street Journal*.

The Target Audience

The essays in this book come from a variety of publications, many of them magazines addressed to the "general" American readership. Others, however, come from publications directed to men or women, the political right or left, or from publications for people of particular ethnic, racial, and cultural identities. They're written for *target audiences.* When writers have a "target" audience in mind, particularly readers who share the same interests, opinions, and prejudices, they can take shortcuts with little risk of alienating anybody, because writer and readers have so many things in common. Consider the following excerpts concerning the use of animal testing in scientific research:

> Contrary to prevailing misperception, in vitro tests need not replace existing in vivo test procedures in order to be useful. They can contribute to chemical-safety evaluation right now. In vitro tests, for example, can be incorporated into the earliest stages of the risk-assessment process; they can be used to identify chemicals having the lowest probability of toxicity so that animals need be exposed only to less noxious chemicals.

It is clear from the technical terminology (e.g., *in vitro, in vivo, toxicity*), professional jargon (*test procedures, chemical-safety evaluation, risk-assessment process*), and the formal, detached tone, that the piece was intended for a scientifically educated readership. Not surprisingly, the article, "Alternatives to Animals in Toxicity Testing," was authored by two research scientists, Alan M. Goldberg and John M. Frazier, and published in *Scientific American* (August 1989). Contrast it with another approach to the topic:

> Almost 30 years ago, Queen had been a child herself, not quite two years old, living in Thailand under the care of her mother and another female elephant, the two who had tended to her needs every day since her birth. They taught her how to use her trunk, in work and play, and had given her a sense of family loyalty. But then Queen was captured, and her life was changed irrevocably by men with whips and guns. One man herded Queen by whipping and shouting at her while another shot her mother, who struggled after her baby until more bullets pulled her down forever.

What distinguishes this excerpt is the emotional appeal. This is not the kind of article you would find in *Scientific American* or most other scientific journals. Nor would you expect to see this kind of emotional appeal in a newsmagazine such as *Newsweek* or *Time*, or a general interest publication such as the Sunday magazine of many newspapers. The excerpt comes from an animal rights newsletter published by PETA, People for the Ethical Treatment of Animals. Given that particular audience, the writer safely assumes immediate audience sympathy with the plight of elephants. There is no need for the author to qualify or apologize for such sentimentalizing statements as "Queen had been a child herself" and "They taught her how to use her trunk, in work and play, and had given her a sense of family loyalty." In fact, given the context, the author is probably more interested in reminding readers of a shared cause than winning converts.

The General Audience

Unless you're convinced that your readers are in total agreement with you or share your philosophical or professional interests, you may have some trouble picturing just who you are persuading. It's tempting to say you're writing for a "general" audience; but, as we said at the beginning of this chapter, general audiences may include very different people with different backgrounds, expectations, and standards. Writing for such audiences, then, may put additional pressure on you.

In reality, of course, most of your college writing will be for your professors. This can be a little confusing because you may find yourself trying to determine just what audience your professor represents. You may even wonder why professors expect you to explain material with which they are familiar. You may feel that defining technical terms to your psychology instructor who covered them in class the week before, or summarizing a poem that you know your English professor can probably recite, is a waste of time. But they have a good reason: They assume the role of uninformed audience to let you show how much *you* know.

Of course, if you are arguing controversial issues you may find yourself in the awkward position of trying to second-guess your instructor's stand on an issue. You may even be tempted to tone down your presentation so as not to risk offense and, thus, an undesirable grade. However, most instructors try not to let their biases affect their evaluation of a student's work. Their main concern is how well a student argues a position.

For some assignments your instructor may specify an audience for you: members of the city council, the readers of the campus newspaper, Rush Limbaugh's radio listeners, and so on. But if no audience is specified, one of your earliest decisions about writing should be in choosing an audience. If you pick "readers of *The National Review*," for instance, you'll know you're writing for mostly male, conservative, middle-aged, middle-class whites; the expectations of these readers are very different than for readers of *Jet* or *Stereophile*. If you are constrained to (or want the challenge of) writing for the so-called general audience, construct a mental picture of who those people are so you'll be able to shape your argument accordingly. Here are some of the characteristics we think you might include in your definition.

The "general" audience includes those people who read *Newsweek, Time,* and your local newspaper. That means people whose average age is about 30, whose educational level is high school plus two years of college, who make up the vast middle class of America, who politically stand in the middle of the road, and whose racial and ethnic origins span the world. You can assume that they read the daily newspaper and watch the evening news and are generally informed about what is going on in the country. You can assume a good comprehension of language nuances and a sense of humor. They are people who recognize who Shakespeare was, though they may not be able to quote passages or name ten of his plays. Nor will they necessarily be experts in the latest theory of black holes or be able to explain how photo emulsions work. However, you can expect them to be open to technical explanations and willing to listen to arguments on birth control, gun control, weight control, and the issue of women and gays in the military. More importantly, you can look upon your audience members as people willing to hear what you have to say.

Guidelines for Knowing Your Audience

Before sitting down to write, think about your audience. Ask yourself the following questions: Will I be addressing other college students, or people of my parents' generation? Will my audience be of a particular political persuasion, or strongly identified with a specific cultural background? How might the age of my readers and their educational background influence the way they think about a given issue? On what criteria will they make their decisions about this issue? A good example of profiling your audience was evident in the 1996 presidential election. The Republicans gambled that "moral leadership" and "trust" were the chief criteria for voters. The Democrats, in a slogan made famous in the 1992 campaign, made the criterion "It's the economy, stupid." As the election results showed, the Democrats assessed their audience more accurately than did the Republicans.

As the example above illustrates, an effective argument essay takes into account the values, beliefs, interests, and experiences of its audience. If you simply choose to argue what you feel is important without regard to your audience, the only person you persuade may be yourself! An effective argument tries to establish common ground with the audience. While this may be difficult at times, recognizing what you have in common with your audience will enable you to argue most persuasively.

Before you can do this, however, you will need to create a profile of your audience. You may find the checklist on the next page helpful in assessing an audience. If you like visual prompts, write the answers to these questions on a card or a slip of paper that you can hang over your desk or display in a window on your computer screen while you're working on your argument. Looking at these questions and answers occasionally will remind you to focus your arguments on these particular people.

Using Debate and Dialogue

Debate and dialogue, two of the methods of developing arguments discussed in Chapter 1, can also be used to sharpen your awareness of audience. For an example of how this can happen, let's revisit John, our first-year composition student who had decided to write his argument essay on the topic of binge drinking. After reading critically in his subject area (Chapter 2) and formulating a working claim (Chapter 3), John turned his attention to the question of audience. He found that using debate and dialogue helped him answer some of the questions in the audience checklist and provided essential information about how his audience might respond to his ideas.

John decided that his audience would be a general one comprised of people of all ages. He anticipated that most people in his audience would not endorse excessive drinking, but with such a diverse group of people he was unsure whether they would have similar reasons for their concern and how strongly they would agree or

Audience Checklist

1. Who are the readers I will be addressing?
   a. What age group?
   b. Are they male, female, or both?
   c. What educational background?
   d. What socioeconomic status?
   e. What are their political, religious, occupational, or other affiliations?
   f. What values, assumptions, and prejudices do they have about life?
2. Where do my readers stand on the issue?
   a. Do they know anything about it?
   b. If so, how might they have learned about it?
   c. How do they interpret the issue?
   d. How does the issue affect them personally?
   e. Are they hostile to my stand on the issue?
3. How do I want my readers to view the issue?
   a. If they are hostile to my view, how can I persuade them to listen to me?
   b. If they are neutral, how can I persuade them to consider my viewpoint?
   c. If they are sympathetic to my views, what new light can I shed on the issue? How can I reinspire them to take action?
4. What do I have in common with my readers?
   a. What beliefs and values do we share?
   b. What concerns about the issue do we have in common?
   c. What common life experiences have we had?
   d. How can I make my readers aware of our connection?

disagree with his reasons. John found that using two strategies, a "Yes, but . . ." exchange and creating a dialogue among different perspectives, helped to answer questions 2 and 3 on the audience checklist: Where do my readers stand on the issue? and How do I want my readers to view the issue? He used this information to develop ways to engage his readers in the essay.

Working with classmates in small peer groups, John found that a "Yes, but . . ." exchange revealed specific points that his audience might use to oppose his reasons. For instance, John began with the following statement:

College administrators have a responsibility to deter binge drinking by their students.

He received several responses from his peer group:

Yes, college administrators have a responsibility to their students, but that responsibility should be limited to academic matters.

Yes, binge drinking by students should be a concern to college administrators, but college administrators shouldn't interfere with the private lives or habits of their students.

Yes, college administrators should try to deter binge drinking by students, but they will be ineffective unless they receive support from the community and parents.

Although each of John's classmates agreed that college administrators had a valid interest in student binge drinking, there was considerable disagreement over how far that interest should extend and how effective any action taken by administrators would be. The "Yes, but . . ." exchange gave John greater insight into the ways others might respond to his ideas. As he developed his argument, he was able to acknowledge and address such concerns by his potential audience.

In a similar fashion, John used dialogue to gain insight into question 4 on the audience checklist: What do I have in common with my readers? In particular, John wanted to discover any shared concerns and values among himself and those who took different positions on solving the problem of binge drinking. To create a dialogue John interviewed several of his classmates, his teachers, members of his family, and a few individuals from the community; he also read articles by health professionals concerned with alcohol abuse and young adults. His goal was to listen to a wide spectrum of views on the subject and to keep an open mind as he listened. He used his journal to record their comments and his own impressions. What emerged from this dialogue were several areas of shared concerns: Most agreed that binge drinking was an unhealthy practice that should be discouraged, and while there were many different suggestions about the measures that should be taken to eliminate it, all agreed that the students who engaged in binge drinking must ultimately accept responsibility for ending it. No solution would work, all agreed, unless the drinkers themselves were willing to stop. John found this information helpful because he knew that his audience would be more willing to listen to his argument if he could identify these shared values and concerns.

By engaging in both debate and dialogue, John gained knowledge that enabled him to appeal to his audience more effectively.

Adapting to Your Readers' Attitudes

Writing for a general audience is a challenge because in that faceless mass are three kinds of readers you'll be addressing:

1. people who agree with you
2. people who are neutral—those who are unconvinced or uninformed on the issue
3. people who don't share your views, and who might even be hostile to them

Each of these different subgroups will have different expectations of you and give you different obligations to meet if you are to present a convincing argument. Even readers sympathetic to your cause might not be familiar with special vocabulary, the latest developments around the issue, or some of the more subtle arguments from the opposition. Those hostile to your cause might be so committed to their own viewpoints that they might not take the time to discover that you share common concerns. And those neutral to the cause might simply need to be filled in on the issue and its background. If you're going to persuade your readers, you'll have to tailor your approach to suit their attitudes.

When addressing an audience, whether general or one of a particular persuasion, you must try to put yourself in its place. You must try to imagine the different needs and expectations these readers bring to your writing, always asking yourself what new information you can pass on and what new ways of viewing you can find for addressing the issue you're arguing. Let's look at some of the strategies you, as a writer, might use, depending on whether you anticipate a neutral, friendly, or unfriendly group of readers.

Addressing a Neutral Audience

Some writers think a neutral audience is the easiest to write for, but many others find this the most challenging group of readers. After all, they're *neutral*; you don't know which way they're leaning, or what may make them commit to your position. Your best role is the conveyor of knowledge: The information you bring, and the ways in which you present it, are the means by which you hope to persuade a neutral audience. Here are some of the ways to convey that information.

Fill in the Background

There are some issues about which few people are neutral: abortion, capital punishment, drug legalization, same-sex marriage, gun control. However, there are other issues about which some readers have not given a thought or made up their minds; or they may simply be uninformed. For instance, if you're part of a farming community, your concern about preserving good farmland might make you feel some urgency about unchecked industrial development in your area. To make a convincing case for readers from, say, Chicago or New York City, you first would have to tell them a little about the shortage of prime land for agriculture and why it is crucial to maintain the existing land. Similarly, as a resident of a large town you might need to explain to readers from rural Vermont or Iowa why you think their community should be concerned with mandatory recycling in large cities. In both cases your task would be to provide your readers with the information they need to evaluate the issue by relating some of the history and background behind the controversy. All the while, you need to encourage them to weigh with an open mind the evidence you present.

Present a Balanced Picture

Part of educating a neutral audience about your position involves presenting a balanced picture of the issue by presenting multiple perspectives about the issue, not just one. Even though you are trying to help your readers understand why your position has value, you will be more persuasive if you treat *all* views fairly, including opposing views. You should clearly and accurately lay out the key arguments of all sides; then demonstrate why your position is superior. Your readers need to feel that you have looked at the total picture and reached your position after carefully weighing all views, a process you hope your readers will engage in as well. Let your readers make their decisions based on their own analysis of the information you have provided. Don't be guilty of stacking the deck, a logical fallacy we discuss in Chapter 2. Not representing the other sides at all, or representing them unfairly and inaccurately, can leave you open to criticisms of distortion, and it may make your readers feel that you're misleading them.

Personalize the Issues

One sure way of gaining readers' attention is to speak their language—that is, address their personal needs, hopes, and fears. (It's what skillful politicians do all the time on the campaign trail.). If you want to engage your readers' attention, demonstrate how the problem will affect them personally. On the matter of farmland, explain why if nothing is done to prevent its loss, the prices of corn and beans will triple over the next three years. On the recycling issue, explain how unrestricted trash dumping will mean that city dwellers will try to dump more trash in rural areas. However, although personalizing the issue is an effective way to make your readers aware of the importance of your issue, you should avoid creating an ad misericordiam argument. To be fully credible you should be certain that the reasons and evidence you present to your readers are anchored in fact rather than emotion.

Show Respect

When you're an informed person talking about an issue to people with less knowledge than you, there's a dangerous tendency to speak down to them. Think how you feel when someone "talks down" to you. Do you like it? How persuasive do you think you can be if your readers think you're talking down to them? Don't condescend to or patronize them. Try not to simplify a complex issue so much that it is reduced to a false dilemma: "If we don't increase school taxes immediately, our children will no longer receive a quality education." Don't assume that your audience is so ill informed that it cannot envision a middle ground between the two alternatives. On the contrary, treat your readers as people who want to know what you know about the issue and who want you to demonstrate to them clearly and accurately why you think they should agree with you. Invite them into the discussion, encouraging them with sound reasons and strong evidence to consider the merits of your side. Although your audience may not be as informed as you, they are willing to listen and deserve respect.

Addressing a Friendly Audience

Writing an argument for the already converted is much easier than writing for a neutral audience or one that is hostile. In a sense, half the battle is won because no minds have to be changed. You need not brace yourself for opposing views or refutations. Your role is simply to provide readers with new information and to renew enthusiasm for and commitment to your shared position. Nonetheless, there are still steps you should take.

Avoid Appealing to Prejudices

One of the risks of addressing a sympathetic audience is appealing to prejudices rather than reasons and facts. Although it might be tempting to mock those who don't agree with you or to demean their views, don't. Stooping to that level only diminishes your own authority and undermines your credibility. Two of the logical fallacies we discuss in Chapter 2 address this problem. The first, an ad hominem argument, is a personal attack on those who disagree with your position. Unfortunately, this approach will reflect negatively on *you*. Use reason and hard evidence instead of insults and ridicule to underscore the weakness of other arguments while you make your readers aware of your mutual concerns. The second fallacy is an ad populum argument and involves using the presumed prejudices of your audience members to manipulate their responses to your argument. Once again, this approach will make you appear unreasonable and biased and may backfire if your audience does not share your prejudices. Instead, encourage your readers to respect different viewpoints, recognizing the merits of their arguments even though you ultimately disagree. It's simply a more reasonable approach, one that allows you and your readers to share informed agreement, and it will win the respect of friends and foes alike.

Offer New Information About the Issue

Even when your readers agree with you, they may need to have their memories refreshed regarding the history of the issue. In addition, you should provide readers with important new information on the issue. Such new developments might involve recent judiciary decisions, newly enacted legislation, or new scientific data that could serve to strengthen your position and their agreement or require a reconsideration of your views. Unless you are absolutely up-to-date about the progress of your issue, you will appear to be either ill informed or deliberately withholding information, seriously undermining your credibility with your audience, even a friendly one. Your willingness to share and educate your audience will enhance the persuasiveness of your views.

Addressing an Unfriendly Audience

As difficult as it may be to accept, some readers will be totally at odds with your views, even hostile to them. Writing for such a readership, of course, is especially challenging—far more than for neutral readers. So how do you present your argument to people you have little chance of winning over?

Seek Common Ground and Remind Your Audience About It

In this argumentative strategy, recommended by psychologist Carl Rogers, your goal is to find ways to connect with your audience through empathy and common experiences. For instance, let's say you are trying to persuade an audience of senior citizens to support a tax increase to fund local schools. After analyzing your audience you might conclude that many are living on limited incomes and are concerned about the financial burden of additional taxes. This factor might make them a hostile audience, one not easily receptive to your position. A good strategy, then, to begin your argument might be to let them know that you are well acquainted with the difficulties of living on limited means. You might even refer to relatives or friends who are in a similar position. If you let your audience know that you empathize with and understand their difficulties, they will be more willing to listen to you.

Remind your audience of the beliefs and values you have in common. While it is unlikely that many of the senior citizens still have children attending the local schools, nonetheless, they may value education and understand its importance. You can let them know that you share this value, one that underlies your support for additional public school funding.

Recognize the concerns of your audience as legitimate and worthy of attention; you will demonstrate that you are aware of and respect their views. This means, of course, finding out what their concerns are. For instance, if you are trying to persuade your audience to support a tax increase to fund new programs in the public schools in your district, do some reading to find out the reasons why people would choose not to support the tax increase. By addressing those concerns you will make your audience aware that you understand their position. This may make them more receptive to listening to yours.

Review: Addressing Audiences

A Neutral Audience
- Fill in the background
- Present a balanced picture
- Personalize the issues
- Show respect for your readers

A Friendly Audience
- Avoid appealing to prejudices
- Offer new information about the issue

An Unfriendly Audience
- Seek common ground
- Convey a positive attitude
- Remember the Golden Rule

To Improve Your Credibility with Your Audience, Avoid These Fallacies

Ad hominem argument	Leveling a personal attack against an opponent. A reliance on ad hominem arguments undercuts your credibility and may make you appear mean-spirited and desperate. Focus instead on the substance of an opponent's claim.

Ad misericordiam argument	Attempting to exploit the audience's emotions rather than appealing to logic and reason. Avoid using arguments that rely only on wrenching the reader's heart strings rather than logic and real evidence.
Ad populum argument	Appealing to the audience's presumed prejudices rather than proven facts. Even if you know the prejudices of your audience, such an appeal at best only persuades those already convinced. Rely on the force of logic and supporting evidence rather than bias and stereotyping.
Stacking the deck	Presenting only evidence that supports your points and withholding contrary evidence. Instead, acknowledge that conflicting evidence exists and respond to it.
False dilemma	Presenting an issue as an either-or-choice and ignoring the possibility of a middle ground. Treat your audience as intelligent equals who are aware that at least several thoughtful alternatives are likely to exist.

Convey a Positive Attitude

Whether or not they know it, your audience will benefit from seeing the issue from another side. In other words, approach a hostile audience as someone who can shed a different light on the problem. View them as people who are potentially interested in learning something new. Without being defensive, arrogant, or apologetic, make your claim, enumerate your reasons, and lay out the evidence for your readers to evaluate on their own. Regard them as intelligent people capable of drawing their own conclusions. You may not win converts, but you might at least lead some to recognize the merits of your side. You might even convince a few people to reconsider their views.

Remember the Golden Rule

Even though they may not agree with you, treat the opposition with respect. Look upon them as reasonable people who just happen to disagree with you. Demonstrate your understanding of their side of the issue. Show that you have made the effort to research the opposition. Give credit where credit is due. If some of their counterpoints make sense, say so. In short, treat those from the other side and their views as you would want to be treated. You may just win a few converts.

Sample Arguments for Analysis

How a writer appeals to his or her audience can have a positive or a negative effect on the way the writer's message is received. The following three articles are concerned with the controversy regarding regulations on smoking and the resulting treatment of smokers by society. The writers address the audience in notably different ways. For the first essay, by C. Everett Koop, we have used annotation to illustrate some of the strategies Koop uses to appeal to his audience and the assumptions he makes about them. As a class exercise, read each of these essays and then consider the following questions:

QUESTIONS FOR ANALYSIS AND DISCUSSION

1. Locate the claim or thesis statement and summarize the main ideas in each essay.
2. What kind of audience is each writer addressing? neutral? friendly? hostile? What evidence can you find to support this?
3. Which writers attempt to present a balanced picture to the audience? Provide examples.
4. Do the writers convey a positive attitude toward the audience? Do any of the writers antagonize the audience? How is this done?
5. Have these writers committed any of the logical fallacies we've discussed? Where do these errors occur and how would you correct them?
6. How well does each writer establish common ground with the audience?
7. What is the purpose of each essay? How effectively does each writer accomplish this purpose?

Don't Forget The Smokers
C. Everett Koop

Dr. C. Everett Koop served as Surgeon General of the United States from 1981 until 1989. His duties in office were to advise the public on matters such as smoking, diet and nutrition, environmental health hazards, and disease prevention. Since leaving office, Dr. Koop has been a spokesperson and activist on issues of public health. This article appeared in the *Washington Post* on March 8, 1998.

1   To date, most of the tobacco control efforts of this administration have focused on preventing young people from taking up smoking. Everyone can agree that teenagers and younger children should not smoke. Even the tobacco industry can safely join in that refrain, and frequently does, with characteristic and clamorous hypocrisy as it turns its marketing machines loose on the young. But at exactly what age does the plight of American smokers lose its poignancy?

Establishes common ground shared views

charged language

2   One-third of teenagers who experiment casually with cigarettes will become regular smokers, with one-half of these trying to quit, but failing, by age 18. In fact, the vast majority of
current smokers were hooked in their teens or earlier. During
the '80s, the tobacco industry mounted a public relations campaign maintaining that smoking was "an adult decision." It was
a model of reverse psychology, tempting teens at the same time
it offered false reassurance to their elders. The vast majority of
smokers are captive to their addiction, so that most who
"decide" to quit cannot—not without help or years of repeated
tries.

Assumes media-savvy reader familiar with ad campaigns

3   If we pretend that adult smoking is a consumer choice like
any other, we fall prey to the trap laid by Big Tobacco. Addiction makes the very notion of choice moot. Who would freely
choose sickness and suffering, lost productivity or 50 percent
chance of premature death? Yet cigarette smokers of all ages
continue to die prematurely at the rate of more than 400,000
per year. If not one single young person started smoking from
this day forward, these losses would still continue unabated for
30 years. Imagine 1,000 jumbo jets emblazoned with Marlboro
and Winston and Camel insignia crashing each year for the
next three decades. Should we accept such dramatic losses as
par for the course?

Allusion to Big Brother assumes reader has literary background

rhetorical question involves reader

4   We must not focus our efforts so narrowly on preventing
tobacco use by youth that we send smokers the message that we
have abandoned them—that their addiction is their own fault
and that we don't care about them. This is exactly what the tobacco industry wants them to hear. Forget quitting, hedge the
health bets instead. Responding to founded fears, tobacco
companies unleashed so-called "low-tar" brands in an effort to
hold on to their smokers and reduce the concerns of the unini-
tiated. But in their attempt to avoid becoming yet another statistic, smokers have only changed the form of their resultant
lung cancers from the squamous cell cancers of the upper lung
to the adenocarcinomas of the lower lung as they inhaled more
deeply to extract the nicotine their bodies craved from such
cigarettes. There is an alternative. We can combine tobacco
prevention initiatives with efforts to ensure that those who are
hooked can obtain effective treatments.

Addresses readers as adults who have power to shape public attitudes

Assumes readers are comfortable with medical terms

5   The facts are that quitting smoking at any age reduces the
risk of premature death; current treatments can substantially
increase the odds of quitting. It therefore seems logical that
each decision to smoke should present an equal opportunity
not to smoke and an equal opportunity to get help. The Food
and Drug Administration's actions in 1996 to restrict tobacco
marketing to minors and to approve over-the-counter marketing of nicotine gum and patches for adults were pioneering
steps in the right direction. So are several pieces of congres-

Uses facts and reasons, not emotions

Assumes broad general knowledge

sional legislation currently under discussion that include provisions for tobacco addiction treatments.

6   Nevertheless, much remains to be done if our nation is to
make tobacco dependence treatment as acceptable and as
readily available as tobacco itself. We must evaluate and approve potentially life-saving treatments for tobacco dependence at the level of priority we assign to treatments for diseases
such as AIDS and cancer. Signaling such a course could help
empower the private sector to meet these challenges in a way
that will contribute to the health of our nation in the short and
long run.

Suggests readers are in decision-making positions

7   Currently, the tobacco industry is lobbying Congress for
its own solution to the needs of smokers. Under the guise of
the new-found concern for the health of their consumers,
these companies want incentives to market products that they
claim will reduce the dangers of smoking. We do not want to
stifle development of such products. Indeed, we should require reduced toxicity of tobacco products, as we now understand that they are unnecessarily dangerous and addictive.
But such a course should not enable tobacco companies to
undermine our efforts to reduce overall tobacco use by allowing them to advertise their products with claims such as "low
tar" or "reduced delivery." Legitimate concern for the health
of tobacco users should balance efforts to reduce the toxicity
of tobacco products with the means to expedite the development of new treatments for those who are addicted. Under its
existing authorities, including its designation of cigarettes
and smokeless tobacco products as combination drug and device products, the FDA has many regulatory tools at its disposal to accomplish its goal of reducing the risk of death and disease in tobacco-addicted Americans. Congressional legislation
that weakens the FDA's authority over tobacco reduces its
ability to serve the public health.

Tone: serious

Sketches opposition's plan and shows weaknesses

Makes a direct appeal to knowledgeable readers

8   I strongly encourage any forthcoming congressional legislation or executive actions to strengthen, if not leave alone, the
FDA's authority over tobacco, and to support the FDA's ability
to evaluate new treatments and treatment approaches in a
manner that is consistent with the devastation wrought by un-
remitting tobacco use. Moreover, in our battle with Big Tobacco, we should not hide behind our children. Instead, as we take
every action to save our children from the ravages of tobacco,
we should demonstrate our commitment to those who are already addicted, and those who will yet become addicted, will
never expire.

Forceful language

Plays on connotation and denotation of word

What the Antismoking Zealots Really Crave
Jeff Jacoby

Jeff Jacoby, a founding director of the Pioneer Institute, a conservative public-policy think tank in Boston, writes a regular column for the *Boston Globe*, where this piece appeared on March 24, 1998.

1   A question for antitobacco militants: Why do you draw the line at private homes?

2   To protect nonsmokers, especially young ones, you've made it illegal to smoke in more and more places. You have banished smoking from tens of millions of private workplaces; from airplanes and buses; from most government buildings. You have gotten hundreds of cities—Boston is your latest conquest—to ban smoking in restaurants altogether. In California, you've even driven smokers from bars.

3   But smoking at home is OK.

4   Curious, no? You militants routinely justify your crusade by claiming to act for "the kids," yet in the one place a kid is likeliest to encounter cigarettes, smoking is wholly unregulated. Why? It can't be because you respect the rights of private property owners. After all, restaurants and bars are private property. And it can't be because the state never interferes in the way parents raise their children—the state interferes in everything from the commercials children see on television to the paint that goes on their walls. So why aren't you clamoring to take away parents' freedom to smoke at home?

5   Granted, that would just about outlaw *all* smoking. But isn't that what you want?

6   One of the nation's foremost antismoking activists, Stanton Glantz, compares cigarette manufacturers to Timothy McVeigh, the mass murderer of Oklahoma City. A *New York Times* reporter likens tobacco employees to "the guards and doctors in the Nazi death camps." Over a decade ago, the *Journal of the American Medical Association* was calling for "a declaration of all-out war" against the perpetrators of "the tobaccoism holocaust."

7   Such murderous rhetoric is typical. On taxpayer-funded billboards in California, a man about to light up asks, "Mind if I smoke?" The woman replies: "Care if I die?" Elizabeth Whelan of the American Council on Science and Health says smoking kills more people than "if every single day two filled-to-capacity jumbo jets crashed, killing all on board." A former director of the Centers for Disease Control has predicted that "the annual global death toll of tobacco will equal the total death toll of the Holocaust in Nazi Germany."

8   Such hysteria is more than repugnant, it is false. In *For Your Own Good* (Free Press), a lucid and superbly researched new book on the antitobacco jihad, journalist Jacob Sullum pinpoints the deceit:

9   "The rhetoric of tobacco's opponents implies a rough equivalence between a 65-year-old smoker who dies of lung cancer and a 40-year-old businessman killed in a plane crash, a 19-year-old soldier shot in the trenches of World War I, or a child murdered by the Nazis at Auschwitz. But there is a big difference between someone who dies suddenly at the hands of another person or in an accident and someone who dies as a result of a long-term, voluntarily assumed risk."

10   Maybe so, you antismoking activists might say, but the harm caused by smoking isn't limited to the smoker. His smoke poisons everyone he comes into contact with. They shouldn't be made to suffer because of his vile habit. Nonsmokers have a right to a smoke-free society.

11   In fact, the danger of secondhand smoke is more myth than science. Most epidemiological studies have found no statistically significant link between lung cancer and secondhand smoke. Exposure to cigarette fumes may not be *good* for your health, but the medical fact is that secondhand smoke is not likely to do lasting harm to anyone.

12   Still—what about those kids growing up in smokers' homes? How can you sworn enemies of tobacco be so intent on criminalizing the smoke in smoky jazz bars, yet do nothing about the millions of children whose parents light up with abandon? Why don't you demand that cigarettes be outlawed in any house with kids? In other words, why don't you demand that cigarettes be outlawed—period!

13   Maybe the answer is that even zealots like you realize it wouldn't work. Alcohol Prohibition in the 1920s was a hideous failure, drenching the country in corruption, crime, and oceans of impure alcohol. In a nation with 45 million smokers, Tobacco Prohibition would be no less a disaster and most of you know it.

14   Or maybe the answer is that you couldn't *afford* to end smoking entirely. Ban all tobacco, and there'd be no tobacco taxes or (legal) tobacco profits. No profits or taxes, no hundreds of billions of dollars to fund a settlement. No gusher of dollars for new "health care" programs. No bonanza for plaintiffs' lawyers. No lavish budgets for all your antitobacco outfits. No goose. No golden eggs.

15   But I think the real answer is that you don't think you can get away with it—yet. Already some of you *are* targeting smokers' homes. At least one law review article has claimed that parents who expose their children to tobacco smoke "should be viewed as committing child abuse." A Pennsylvania legislator has proposed a ban on smoking in any vehicle carrying a minor. More intrusion is on its way.

16   Nicotine may be pleasurable, but it's nothing like the high of forcing others to behave the way you want them to. Power over other people's pleasures is very addicting, isn't it? "The true nature of the crusade for a smoke-free society," Sullum writes, is "an attempt by one group of people to impose their tastes and preferences on another." It's illiberal, it's vindictive, it's intolerant. It's you.

Media Have Fallen for Misguided Antismoking Campaign
Robert J. Samuelson

Robert J. Samuelson, the recipient of numerous journalism awards, is a nationally known columnist who focuses on political, economic, and social issues. This article was published in the *Boston Globe* on September 30, 1997.

1   The media are deeply sensitive to the rights of those we consider minorities: the poor, the disabled, blacks, gays, and immigrants, among others. But there is one minority much larger than any of these (at least 25 percent of the population) whose rights we deny or ignore: smokers. The debate over cigarettes has been framed as if smokers are the unwitting victims of the tobacco industry. They lack free will and, therefore, their apparent desires and interests don't count. They are to be pitied and saved, not respected.

2   This is pack journalism run amok. We media types fancy ourselves independent thinkers. Just the opposite is often true: We're patsies for the latest crusade or fad. In this case, the major media have adopted the view of the public health community, which sees smoking as a scourge to be eradicated. The "story" is the crusade; the villain is the tobacco industry. Lost are issues that ought to inform this debate.

3   The simplest is whether, in trying to make Americans better off, the antismoking crusade would make many Americans worse off. Smokers would clearly suffer from huge price and tax increases. The cost of the $368.5 billion agreement between the tobacco industry and the state attorneys general is estimated at 62 cents a pack. President Clinton suggests raising that to $1.50 a pack—about six times today's federal tax (24 cents). The cost would hit the poor hardest. They smoke more than the rich.

4   Consider. About half (53 percent) of today's cigarette tax is paid by taxpayers with incomes of less than $30,000, estimates the congressional Joint Committee on Taxation. Higher prices will deter some people from smoking. But for the rest, would siphoning billions away from poorer people be good policy? Or fair?

5   The antismoking crusaders try to seem fair by arguing: (1) smoking has been increasing among teenagers who, once they try cigarettes, may become addicted for life; (2) tobacco ads cause much teenage smoking—teenagers are, therefore, victims; and (3) passive smoking (nonsmokers inhaling smoke) in public places is a serious health threat, justifying action against smokers. These assumptions permeate media coverage, but the first two are open to question and the third is untrue.

6   Start with teenage smoking. One survey from the University of Michigan does show a rise. In 1996, 34 percent of 12th-graders reported smoking in the past month—the highest since 1979 (34.4 percent). But the government's survey on drug abuse suggests the opposite: In 1996, only 18.3 percent of

teenagers between 12 and 17 had smoked in the past month, the lowest since 1985 (29 percent). It's hard to know which survey to believe, but neither depicts runaway teenage smoking.

7   As for ads, teenagers do a lot of dangerous things (drugs, early sex) that aren't advertised and are often illegal. The tobacco industry no doubt targets teenagers, but the ads may affect brand choices more than they do the decision to smoke. A new, comprehensive study—financed by the National Institutes of Health—suggests that teenagers' home environment is more important in determining who smokes. "Children who report feeling connected to a parent are protected against many different kinds of health risks including . . . cigarette, alcohol, and marijuana use," it says.

8   And even teenagers who smoke do not necessarily become lifetime smokers. Among 12th-graders, the percentage of those who once smoked (63 percent) is about twice as high as for those who currently do. The "addiction" isn't so great that millions haven't broken it.

9   Finally, passive smoking isn't a big public health risk, as many stories imply. The latest example of misreporting involved a study from Harvard Medical School. It purported to show that passive smoking doubled the risk of heart attacks, indicating a huge public health problem. That's how both the *New York Times* and *Washington Post* reported it. In fact, the study—at most—showed that passive smoking doubles a very tiny risk.

10   Here's why. The study followed 32,046 nonsmoking nurses between 1982 and 1992. Of these, four-fifths said they were exposed to passive smoking. But there were only 152 heart attacks (127 nonfatal) among all the nurses: a small number. Many heart attacks would have occurred even if no one was exposed to smoke. And most exposure to passive smoke is now private or voluntary, because public smoking has been barred in so many places. Will we outlaw husbands smoking in front of their wives—or vice versa?

11   You don't hear much of all this, because the press has an antismoking bias. The crusaders do have a case. Smoking is highly risky for smokers. But lots of things are risky, and don't smokers have a right to engage in behavior whose pleasures and pains are mainly theirs without being punished by the rest of society?

12   There is almost no one to make the smokers' case. They have been abandoned by the tobacco industry, politicians, and the press. Do smokers have rights? Apparently not.

Choosing Your Words

Whether addressing friends, foes, or the undecided, you must take care that your readers fully understand your case. In part this is accomplished by choosing your words carefully and by accurately defining any technical, unfamiliar, foreign, or abstract terms. Here are a few specific tips to follow to inform your readers without turning them off.

Distinguishing Denotation and Connotation

Many words, even the most common, carry special suggestions or associations, **connotations,** that differ from the precise dictionary definitions, **denotations.** For example, if you looked up the word *house* in the dictionary, one of the synonyms you'd find is *shelter.* Yet if you told people you live in a shelter, they would think that you live in a facility for the homeless or some kind of animal sanctuary. That is because *shelter* implies a covering or structure that protects those within from the elements or from danger. In other words, the term is not neutral, as is the word *house.* Likewise, dictionary synonyms for *horse* include *steed* and *nag,* but the former implies an elegant and high-spirited riding animal, while the latter suggests one that is old and worn out.

The denotations of words may be the same, but their connotations will almost always differ. And the reason is that dictionary denotations are essentially neutral and emotion free, while connotations are most often associated with attitudes or charged feelings that can influence readers' responses. Therefore, it is important to be aware of the shades of differences when choosing your words. Consider the different meanings the connotations of the bracketed choices lend these statements:

> By the time I got home I was _____ [sleepy, exhausted, weary, beat, dead].
> My boyfriend drives around in a red _____ [car, vehicle, buggy, clunker, jalopy].
> I could hear him _____ [shout, yell, bellow, scream, shriek].

Connotations can also be personal and, thus, powerful tools for shaping readers' responses to what you say. Consider the word *pig.* The dictionary definition, or denotation, would read something like this: "A domestic farm animal with a long, broad snout and a thick, fat body covered with coarse bristles." However, the connotation of *pig* is far more provocative, for it suggests someone who looks or acts like a pig; someone who is greedy or filthy; someone who is sexually immoral. (Most dictionaries list the connotations of words, although some connotations might only be found in a dictionary of slang—e.g., *The New Dictionary of American Slang,* edited by Robert L. Chapman, or *Slang!* by Paul Dickson.)

There is nothing wrong with using a word because of its connotations, but you must be aware that connotations will have an emotional impact on readers. You don't want to say something unplanned. You don't want to offend readers by using words loaded with unintentional associations. For instance, you wouldn't suggest to advertisers that they "should be more creative when hawking their products" unless you intended to insult them. Although the term *hawking* refers to selling, it is unflattering and misleading because it connotes somebody moving up and down the streets peddling goods by shouting. Linguistically the word comes from the same root as the word *huckster,* which refers to an aggressive merchant known for haggling and questionable practices.

Connotatively loaded language can be used to create favorable as well as unfavorable reactions. If you are arguing against the use of animals in medical research, you will get a stronger response if you decry the sacrifice of "puppies and kittens" rather than the cooler, scientific, and less charged "laboratory animals."

You can understand why politicians, newspaper columnists, and anyone advocating a cause use connotative language. The loaded word is like a bullet for a writer making a strong argument. Consider the connotative impact of the italicized terms in the following excerpts taken from essays in this text:

> Hidden cameras? That's the easiest call. Their growing use by TV news-magazine shows, including "Primetime Live" and NBC's "Dateline," is part of a ratings-driven descent by the major networks into the *swamp of tabloid journalism.* (Paul Starobin, *Why Those Hidden Cameras Hurt Journalism*)

> Such hysteria is more than repugnant, it is false. In *For Your Own Good* (Free Press), a lucid and superbly researched new book on the *antitobacco jihad,* journalist Jacob Sullum pinpoints the deceit . . . (Jeff Jacoby, *What the Anti-smoking Zealots Really Crave*)

> This year's list of would-be censors trying to *shoulder their way to the trough of celebrity* is hardly worth enumerating: Their 15 minutes might be up by the time I'm done. (Andrew Klavan, "In Praise of Gore")

Each of the italicized words was selected not for its denotations but its negative connotations. In the first example, Paul Starobin could have chosen a more neutral word such as *area* to convey his denotative meaning; however, he deliberately selects *swamp* to suggest a practice that is ethically murky, dark, and secretive. Similarly, Jeff Jacoby describes the organized effort against smoking as a *jihad,* which evokes the strong image of a fanatical group motivated by extreme religious fervor. The final example could have read as follows: "This year's list of would-be censors trying to *gain notoriety* is hardly worth enumerating: Their 15 minutes might be up by the time I'm done." However, Andrew Klavan clearly wanted to convey his disapproval of movie censors and, thus, selected words that create an image of them as aggressive and piglike, fighting their way to feed at fame.

Being Specific

To help readers better understand your argument, you need to use words that are precise enough to convey your exact meaning. If you simply say, "The weather last weekend was *terrible,*" your readers are left to come up with their own interpretations of what the weather was like. Was it hot and muggy? cold and rainy? overcast and very windy? some of each? Chances are your readers won't come up with the same weather conditions you had in mind. However, if you said, "Last weekend it rained day and night and never got above forty degrees," readers will have a more precise idea of the weekend's weather. And you will have accomplished your purpose of saying just what you meant.

The terms *general* and *specific* are opposites just as *abstract* and *concrete* are opposites. General words do not name individual things but classes or groups of things: animals, trees, women. Specific words refer to individuals in a group: your pet canary, the oak tree outside your bedroom window, the point guard. Of course, general and specific are themselves relative terms. Depending on the context or your frame of reference, a word that is specific in one context may be general in another. For instance, there is no need to warn a vegetarian that a restaurant serves veal Oscar and beef Wellington when simply *meat* will do. In other words, there are degrees of specificity appropriate to the situation. The following list illustrates just such a sliding scale, moving downward from the more general to the more specific.

General	Animal	Person	Book	Clothing	Food	Machine
	feline	female	novel	footwear	seafood	vehicle
	cat	singer	American	shoes	fish	fighter jet
Specific	Daisy, my pet	Sarah McLachlan	*The Great Gatsby*	her Nikes	tuna	F-117

General words are useful in ordinary conversation when the people you're addressing understand your meaning and usually don't ask for clarification. The same is true in writing when you are addressing an audience familiar with your subject. In such instances you can get away with occasional broad statements. For example, if you are running for class president, your campaign speeches would not require a great number of specifics as much as general statements of promise and principles:

> If elected, I intend to do what I can to ensure a comfortable classroom environment for each student at this college.

But when your audience is unfamiliar with your subject or when the context requires concrete details, generalities and abstract terms fall flat, leaving people wondering just exactly what you are trying to communicate. Let's say, for instance, you write a note to your dean explaining why you'd like to change the room where your English class meets. You wouldn't get very far on this appeal:

> Room 107 Richards is too small and uncomfortable for our class.

However, if you offer some specifics evoking a sense of the room's unpleasantness, you'd make a more persuasive case for changing the room:

> Room 107 Richards has 20 fixed seats for 27 students, leaving those who come in late to sit on windowsills or the floor. Worse still is the air quality. The radiators are fixed on high and the windows don't open. By the end of the hour it must be 90 degrees in there, leaving everybody sweaty and wilted including Prof. Hazzard.

What distinguishes this paragraph is the use of concrete details: "20 fixed seats for 27 students"; latecomers' forced to "sit on windowsills or on the floor"; radiators "fixed on high"; "the windows don't open"; "90 degrees"; and everybody was left "sweaty and wilted including Prof. Hazzard." But more than simply conjuring up a vivid impression of the room's shortcomings, these specifics add substance to your argument for a room change.

Concrete language is specific language—words that have definite meaning. Concrete language names persons, places and things: *Mother Teresa, Mark McGwire, New Zealand, Hartford, book, toothpaste.* Concrete terms conjure up vivid pictures in the minds of readers because they refer to particular things or qualities that can be perceived by the five senses—that is, they can be seen, smelled, tasted, felt, and heard. Abstract words, on the other hand, refer to qualities that do not have a definitive concrete meaning. They denote intangible qualities that cannot be perceived directly by the senses but are inferred from the senses—*powerful, foolish, talented, responsible, worthy.* Abstract words also denote concepts and ideas—*patriotism, beauty, victory, sorrow.* Although abstract terms can be useful depending on the context, writing that relies heavily on abstractions will fail to communicate clear meaning. Notice in the pairs below how concrete and specific details convert vague statements into vivid ones:

Abstract	He was very nicely dressed.
Concrete	He wore a dark gray Armani suit, white pinstriped shirt, and red paisley tie.
Abstract	Jim felt uncomfortable at Jean's celebration party.
Concrete	Jim's envy over Jean's promotion made him feel guilty.
Abstract	That was an incredible accident.
Concrete	A trailer truck jackknifed in the fog, causing seven cars to plow into each other, killing two, injuring eight, and leaving debris for a quarter mile along Route 17.

Abstract language is also relative. It depends on circumstances and the experience of the person using them. A *cold* December morning to someone living in Florida might mean temperatures in the forties or fifties. To residents of North Dakota, *cold* would designate air at subzero temperatures. It all depends on one's point of view. A *fair trial* might mean one thing to the prosecutor of a case, yet something completely different to the defense attorney. Likewise, what might be *offensive* language to your grandmother would probably not faze an average college student.

When employing abstract language you need to be aware that readers may not share your point of view. Consequently, you should be careful to clarify your terms or simply select concrete alternatives. Below is an excerpt from a student paper as it appeared in the first draft. As you can see, it is lacking in details and specifics and has a rather dull impact.

Vague: Last year my mother nearly died from medicine when she went to the hospital. The bad reaction sent her into a coma for weeks, requiring life-support systems around the clock. Thankfully, she came out of the coma and was released, but somebody should have at least asked what, if any, allergies she had.

Although the paragraph reads smoothly, it communicates very little of the dramatic crisis being described. Without specific details and concrete words, the reader misses both the trauma and the seriousness of the hospital staff's neglect, thus dulling the argument for stronger safeguards. What follows is the same paragraph revised with the intent of making it more concrete.

> **Revised:** Last year my mother nearly died from a codeine-based painkiller when she was rushed to the emergency room at Emerson Hospital. The severe allergic reaction sent her into a coma for six weeks, requiring daily blood transfusions, thrice weekly kidney dialysis, continuous intravenous medicines, a tracheotomy, and round-the-clock intensive care. Thankfully, she came out of the coma and was released, but the ER staff was negligent in not determining from her or her medical records that she was allergic to codeine.

Using Figurative Language

Words have their literal meaning, but they also can mean something beyond dictionary definitions, as we have seen. The sentence "Mrs. Jones is an angel" does not mean that Mrs. Jones is literally a supernatural winged creature, but a very kind and pleasant woman. What makes the literally impossible meaningful here is figurative language.

Figurative language (or a **figure of speech**) is comparative language. It is language that represents something in terms of something else—in figures, symbols, or likeness (Mrs. Jones and an angel). It functions to make the ordinary appear extraordinary and the unfamiliar appear familiar. It also adds richness and complexity to abstractions. Here, for instance, is a rather bland literal statement: "Yesterday it was 96 degrees and very humid." Here's that same sentence rendered in figurative language: "Yesterday the air was like warm glue." What this version does is equate yesterday's humid air to glue on a feature shared by each—stickiness. And the result is more interesting than the original statement.

The comparison of humid air to glue is linked by the words *like*. This example represents one of the most common figures of speech, the **simile.** Derived from the Latin *similis,* the term means similar. A simile makes an explicit comparison between dissimilar things (humid air and glue). It says that A is like B in one or more respects. The connectives used in similes are most often the words *like, as,* and *than:*

- A school of minnows shot by me like pelting rain.
- His arms are as big as hams.
- They're meaner than junkyard dogs.

When the connectives *like, as,* or *than* are omitted, then we have another common figure of speech, the **metaphor.** The term is from the Greek *meta* (over) + *pherin* ("to carry or ferry") meaning to carry over meaning from one thing to another. Instead of saying that A is like B, a metaphor equates them—A *is* B. For example, Mrs. Jones and an angel are said to be one and the same, although we all know that literally the two are separate entities.

- This calculus problem is a real pain in the neck.
- The crime in this city is a cancer out of control.
- The space shuttle was a flaming arrow in the sky.

Sometimes writers will carelessly combine metaphors that don't go with each other. Known as **mixed metaphors,** these often produce ludicrous results. For example:

- The heat of his expression froze them in their tracks.
- The experience left a bad taste in her eyes.
- The arm of the law has two strikes against it.

When a metaphor has lost its figurative value it is called a **dead metaphor:** the *mouth* of a river, the *eye* of a needle, the *face* of a clock. Originally these expressions functioned as figures of speech, but their usage has become so common in our language that many have become **clichés** ("golden opportunity," "dirt cheap," "a clinging vine"). More will be said about clichés below, but our best advice is to avoid them. Because they have lost their freshness, they're unimaginative and they dull your writing.

Another common figure of speech is **personification,** in which human or animal characteristics or qualities are attributed to inanimate things or ideas. We hear it all the time: trees *bow* in the wind; fear *grips* the heart; high pressure areas *sit* on the northeast. Such language is effective in making abstract concepts concrete and vivid and possibly more interesting:

- Graft and corruption walk hand in hand in this town.
- The state's new tax law threatens to gobble up our savings.
- Nature will give a sigh of relief the day they close down that factory.

As with other figures of speech, personification must be used appropriately and with restraint. If it's overdone it ends up calling undue attention to itself while leaving readers baffled:

Drugs have slouched their way into our schoolyards and playgrounds, laughing up their sleeves at the law and whispering vicious lies to innocent children.

For the sake of sounding literary, drugs here are personified as pushers slouching, laughing, and whispering. But such an exaggeration runs the risk of being rejected by readers as pretentious. If this happens, the vital message may well be lost. One must also be careful not to take shortcuts. Like dead metaphors, many once-imaginative personifications have become clichés: "justice is blind," "virtue triumphed," "walking death." While such may be handy catch phrases, they are trite and would probably be dismissed by critical readers as lazy writing.

Another figure of speech worth mentioning is the **euphemism,** which is a polite way of saying something blunt or offensive. Instead of toilets, restaurants have *restrooms.* Instead of a salesperson, furniture stores send us *mattress technicians.* Instead of false teeth, people in advertising wear *dentures.* The problem with euphemisms is that they conceal the true meaning of something. The result can be a kind of doubletalk—language inflated for the sake of deceiving the listener. Business and government are notorious for such practices. When workers are laid off, corporations talk about *restructuring* or *downsizing*. A few years ago the federal government announced *a revenue enhancement* when it really meant that taxes were going up; likewise, the Environmental Protection Agency referred to acid rain as *poorly buffered precipitation*; and when the CIA ordered a *nondiscernible microbinoculator* it got a poison dart. Not only are such concoctions pretentious, they are dishonest. Fancy-sounding language camouflages hard truths.

Fancy-sounding language also has no place in good writing. When euphemisms are overdone, the result is a lot of verbiage and little meaning. Consider the example below before the euphemisms and pretentious language are reduced:

> **Overdone:** In the event that gaming industry establishments be rendered legal, law enforcement official spokespersons have identified a potential crisis situation as the result of influence exerted by the regional career-offender cartel.

Readers may have to review this a few times before they understand what's being said. Even if they don't give up, a reader's job is not to rewrite your words. Writing with clarity and brevity shows respect for your audience. Here is the same paragraph with its pretentious wordiness and euphemisms edited down:

> **Revised:** Should casino gambling be legalized, police fear organized crime may take over.

Of course, not all euphemisms are double-talk concoctions. Some may be necessary to avoid sounding insensitive or causing pain. To show respect in a sympathy card to bereaved survivors, it might be more appropriate to use the expression *passed away* instead of the blunt *died*. Recently terms such as *handicapped* or *cripple* have given way to less derogatory replacements such as *a person with disabilities*. Likewise we hear *a person with AIDS* instead of "AIDS victim," which reduces the person to a disease or a label.

As with metaphors and personification, some euphemisms have passed into the language and become artifacts, making their usage potentially stale. People over age 65 are no longer "old" or "elderly," they're *senior citizens*; slums are *substandard housing*; the poor are *socially disadvantaged*. Although such euphemisms grew out of noble intentions, they tend to abstract reality. A Jules Feiffer cartoon from a few years ago captured the problem well. It showed a man talking to himself:

> I used to think I was poor. Then they told me I wasn't poor, I was needy. They told me it was self-defeating to think of myself as needy, I was deprived. Then they told me underprivileged was overused. I was disadvantaged. I still don't have a dime. But I have a great vocabulary.

Although euphemisms were created to take the bite off reality, they can also take the bite out of your writing if not used appropriately. As Feiffer implies, sometimes it's better to say it like it is; depending on the context, "poor" simply might have more bite than some sanitized cliché. Similarly, some old people resent being called "seniors" not just because the term is an overused label, but because it abstracts the condition of old age. Our advice regarding euphemisms is to know when they are appropriate and to use them sparingly. Good writing simply means knowing when the right expression will get the response you want.

Avoiding Clichés

A cliché (or trite expression) is a phrase that is old and overused to the point of being unoriginal and stale. At one time clichés were fresh and potent; overuse has left them flat. In speech we may resort to clichés for quick meaning. However, clichés can dull your writing and make you seem lazy for choosing a phrase on tap rather than trying to think of more original and colorful wording. Consider these familiar examples:

> apple of his eye
> bigger than both of us
> climbing the walls
> dead as a doornail
> head over heels
> last but not least
> mind over matter
> ripe old age
> short but sweet
> white as a ghost

The problem with clichés is that they fail to communicate anything unique. To say you were "climbing the walls," for example, is an expression that could fit a wide variety of contradictory meanings. Out of context, it could mean that you were in a state of high anxiety, anger, frustration, excitement, fear, happiness, or unhappiness. Even in context, the expression is dull. Furthermore, because such clichés are ready made and instantly handy, they blot out the exact detail you intended to convey to your reader.

Clichés are the refuge of writers who don't make the effort to come up with fresh and original expressions. To avoid them, we recommend being alert for any phrases you have heard many times before and coming up with fresh substitutes. Consider the brief paragraph below, which is full of clichés marked in italics, and its revision:

> **Trite:** *In this day and age* a university ought to be concerned with ensuring that its women students take courses that will strengthen their understanding of their own past achievements and future *hopes and dreams*. At the same time any school *worth its salt* should be *ready and able* to provide *hands-on experience*, activities, and courses that reflect a commitment to diversity and inclusiveness. Education must *seize the opportunity* of leading us *onward and up-*

ward so that we don't slide back to the male-only curriculum emphasis of the *days of old.*

Revised: A university today ought to be concerned with ensuring that its women students take courses that will strengthen their understanding of their own past achievements and future possibilities. At the same time any decent school should provide experience, activities, and courses that reflect a commitment to diversity and inclusiveness. Education must lead us forward so that we don't revert to the male-only curriculum emphasis of the past.

Defining Technical Terms

Special or technical vocabulary that is not clear from the context can function as an instant roadblock to freely flowing communication between you and your readers—sympathetic to your views or not. You cannot expect a novice in political science to know the meaning of *hegemony* or a nonmedical person to know exactly what you mean by *nephrological necrosis.* To avoid alienating nonexpert readers, you'll have to define such uncommon terms.

You can do so without being obtrusive or disrupting the flow of your writing with "time-outs" here and there to define terms. Notice how smoothly definitions have been slipped into the following passages.

> Judge Stephen Reinhardt of the Ninth Circuit Court of Appeals has deemed that a "dignified" death entails the right to have oneself killed, based upon the Constitution's 14th Amendment's "due process" clause. This passage has been held to protect personal liberty and privacy—as argued in previous decisions concerning abortion. (Kavanaugh, John F. "A Matter of Life and Death." *America* 15 Feb. 1997: 23.)

> As more Americans do business on line, Internet commerce has created new worries about the security of personal information. Many consider encryption—the technology used to encode information and keep it private—to be the solution. (Powers, Richard. "Losing Our Souls, Bit by Bit." *New York Times* 15 July 1998: A–19.)

> Recent school system initiatives to adopt policies based on recognition of indigenous black language patterns, referred to as "Black English" or "Ebonics," have been the focus of much animated and vigorous discussion. (Hall, Perry A. "The Ebonics Debate: Are We Speaking the Same Language?" *Black Scholar* 27 [Summer 1997]: 12.)

Clarifying Familiar Terms

Even some familiar terms can lead to misunderstanding because they are used in so many different ways with so many different meanings: *liberal, Native American, lifestyle, decent, active.* It all depends on who is using the word. For instance, to an environmentalist the expression *big business* might connote profit-hungry and sinister industrial conglomerates that pollute the elements; to a conservative, however, the phrase might mean the commercial and industrial establishment that drives our economy. Likewise, a *liberal* does not mean the same thing to a Democrat as it does to a Republican. Even if you're writing for a sympathetic audience, be as precise as you can about familiar terms. Remember the advice of novelist George Eliot: "We have all got to remain calm, and call things by the same names other people call them by."

Stipulating Definitions

For words that don't have a fixed or standard meaning, writers often offer a *stipulative* definition that explains what they mean by the term. For instance, in his essay "Regulating Racist Speech on Campus" (page 380), Charles R. Lawrence defines *racist language* as "injurious speech" aimed at making people feel inferior because of their race: "Assaultive racist speech functions as a preemptive strike. The invective is experienced as a blow, not as a proffered idea, and once the blow is struck, it is unlikely that a dialogue will follow." By stipulating language with the power to injure as opposed to language that simply insults, the author justifies his claim that such language does not deserve the protection of the First Amendment, since it falls under the category of "fighting words"—words exempt from such protection because "'their very utterance inflicts injury or intends to incite an immediate breach of the peace.'"

Similarly, although we have all heard about the controversy surrounding sexual harassment laws, a writer arguing for greater or lesser enforcement of these statutes must first supply a precise definition of sexual harassment. A stipulative definition of this key term will not only focus the argument; it will also ensure that the reader understands how the writer is using the term. For instance, in her essay "Sex Is the Least of It: Let's Focus Harassment Law on Work, Not Sex," Vicki Schultz defines sexual harassment as behavior that is intended to exclude women from the workplace rather than as sexual pursuit. She argues that "the problem we should be addressing isn't sex, it's the sexist failure to take women seriously as workers. Sex harassment is a means for men to claim work as masculine turf" (page 582). Such a stipulation is integral to her argument because it suggests that the determination of sexual harassment should be based on gender bias instead of overt sexual overtures.

Because we live in a multicultural society of shifting definitions and blurring categories, at times you may find it necessary to stipulate the ethnic and racial makeup of certain people. Suppose you are writing about *Hispanic people.* This term has been used to encompass millions of people of different countries, races, religious, and cultures—Cuban expatriots, Quiche Indians of Guatemala, Puerto Ricans of African blood, Mexican Americans, Jewish immigrants from Spain, and residents of Columbia. So as not to conflate disparate cultures and thereby cause misunderstanding and possible offense, it is necessary to offer a stipulative definition of the term. Depending on your purposes, it is reasonable to stipulate Hispanic as people with one or more Spanish parents. Or, you might write that you are referring to people raised in countries where Spanish is the primary language. Or you might stipulate people who simply have linguistic roots in Spanish-speaking Latin America. Some people might dispute your definition (or suggest you use a different term, such as *Latino*), but at least you will have clarified the people about whom you are writing.

In his essay "Youth Crime Has Changed—And So Must the Juvenile Justice System" (page 616), Tom Reilly argues that we must treat "juvenile killers . . . as the dangerous predators their own actions prove them to be." Realizing that this position may sound callous, Reilly is careful to distinguish these "juvenile killers" from "children who make poor choices, who need our help, and who can be turned around." By stipulating a precise definition, Reilly is careful to limit his argument to only those juvenile criminals who will not benefit from rehabilitation.

Stipulating your terms is like making a contract with your reader: You set down in black and white the important terms and their limits. The result is that you eliminate any misunderstanding and reduce your own vulnerability. And that can make the difference between a weak and a potent argument.

Avoiding Overdefinition

Where do you stop explaining and begin assuming your reader knows what you mean? What terms are "technical" or "specialized" or "important" enough to warrant definition? You certainly don't want to define terms unnecessarily or to oversimplify. In so doing, you run the risk of dulling the thrust of your claims while insulting the intelligence of your readers. Just how to strike a balance is a matter of good judgment about the needs and capabilities of your audience.

A good rule of thumb is to assume that your readers are almost as knowledgeable as you. This way, you minimize the risk of patronizing them. Another rule of thumb is the synonym test. If you can think of a word or short phrase that is an exact synonym for some specialized or important term in your argument, you probably don't need to define it. On the other hand, if you need a long phrase or sentence to paraphrase the term, you may want to work in a definition; it could be needed. And don't introduce your definitions with clauses like "As I'm sure you know" or "You don't need to be told that. . . ." If the audience didn't need to know it, you wouldn't be telling them, and if they do know what the terms mean, you may insult their intelligence with such condescending introductions.

Review: To Choose Your Words Carefully . . .

Consider both denotative and connotative meanings.

Be as specific and concrete as your context requires.

Use figurative language to add richness and complexity.

Check figurative language for precision and clarity.

Be alert for clichés and unnecessary euphemisms.

Define technical terms that are not clear from the context.

Define familiar terms and terms with multiple meanings.

Using Sarcasm and Humor Sparingly

Although we caution you against using sarcasm or humor too often, there are times when they can be very effective techniques of persuasion. Writers will often bring out their barbs for the sake of drawing blood from the opposition and snickers from the sympathetic. But artful sarcasm must be done with care. Too strong, and you run the risk of trivializing the issue or alienating your audience with a bad joke. Too vague or esoteric, and nobody will catch the joke. It's probably safest to use these touches when you are writing for a sympathetic audience; they're most likely to appreciate your wit. There is no rule of thumb here. Like any writer, you'll have to decide when to use these techniques and how to artfully work them in.

EXERCISES

1. Let's say you were assigned to write a position paper defending the construction of a nuclear power plant in your state. What special appeals would you make were you to address your paper to the governor? to residents living next to the site where the proposed plant is to be built? to prospective construction workers and general contractors? to local environmentalists?

2. Choose one of the following claims, then list in sentence form three reasons supporting the argument. When you've finished, list in sentence form three reasons in opposition to the claim:
   a. Snowboarders are a menace to skiers.
   b. To save lives, a 55-mile per hour speed limit should be enforced nationwide.
   c. Condoms should be advertised on television.
   d. Students with drug convictions should be denied federally subsidized student aid.

3. Let's assume you have made up your mind on gun control. Write a brief letter to the editor of your local newspaper stating your views on the issue. In your letter, fairly and accurately represent arguments of the opposition while pointing out any logical weaknesses, flaws, impracticalities, and other problems you see. What different emphasis would your letter have were it to appear in a gun owner's newsletter? in a pro-gun control newsletter?

4. Write a letter to your parents explaining why you need an extra hundred dollars of spending money this month.

5. Each of the sentences below will take on a different meaning depending on the connotations of the words in brackets. Explain how each choice colors the writer's attitude and the reader's reaction to the statement.
   a. Sally's style of dress is really _____ [weird, exotic, unusual].
   b. If a factory is _____ [polluting, stinking up, fouling] the air over your house, you have a right to sue.
   c. Anyone who thinks that such words have no effect is _____ [unaware, ignorant, unconscious] of political history.
   d. The anti-immigration passion being stirred up in this country has become _____ [popular, trendy, common].
   e. It was clear from the way she _____ [stomped, marched, stepped] out of the room how she felt about the decision.

6. Identify the figures of speech used in the following sentences from essays in this book. In each example note the two things being compared and explain why you think the comparisons are appropriate or not:

   a. "The rise of local news, the infotainment monster that ate the news industry, is a long and painful story about a key battlefront in the endless media war between capitalism and democracy, between the drive for profits and the constitutional responsibility of those licensed to use the airwaves to serve the public interest." (Elayne Rapping)

   b. "They squinted, and the skin of their faces was creased like the leather of old work gloves." (Scott Russell Sanders)

   c. "Baptized to English in school, at first I felt myself drowning—the ugly sounds forced down my throat—until slowly, slowly (held in the tender grip of my teachers), suddenly the conviction took: English was my language to use." (Richard Rodriquez)

   d. "Fiction lives or dies not on its messages, but on the depth and power of the emotional experience it provides." (Andrew Klavan)

   e. "We don't call the one *million* men who were killed or maimed *in one battle* in World War I (the Battle of the Somme) a holocaust, we call it 'serving the country.'" (Warren Farrell)

   f. "It is absurd to suggest that the government step in to censor viewing that parents have acquiesced in." (Robert Scheer)

   g. "Natural selection cannot push the buttons of behavior directly; it affects our behavior by endowing us with emotions that coax us toward adaptive choices." (Steven Pinker)

7. Rewrite the following paragraph to eliminate the clichés and trite expressions.

It is not that we don't care about what goes on up in space; it's that the vast majority of red-blooded Americans are hard put to see what these untold billions of dollars can do. While great strides have been made in space research, we ask ourselves: Is life any safer? Are material goods all the more abundant? Are we living to a ripe old age because of these vast expenditures? Beyond the shadow of a doubt the answer is a resounding no. Those in Congress with a vested interest need to be brought back to reality, for the nation's pressing problems of crime, homelessness, and unemployment are right here on Mother Earth. Nothing is sacred including the budget for NASA, which should follow the footsteps of other programs and be slashed across the board. Yes, that will be a rude awakening to some who will have to bite the bullet, but there are just so many tax dollars to go around. And in the total scheme of things, wasting it on exploring the depths of outer space is not the way it should be.

chapter 5

SHAPING ARGUMENTS

Thinking like an Architect

Just as there is no best way to build a house, there is no best structure for an argument. Some essays take an inductive approach. Such an essay begins with a specific circumstance and then presents reasons and evidence in support of or in opposition to that circumstance. Other essays adopt a deductive approach. These essays begin with an idea or philosophical principle, move to a specific circumstance, then conclude with why that circumstance is right and should be maintained, or wrong and should be changed. Some essays express their conclusions in the opening paragraphs. Others build up to them in the last paragraph. As an architect designing a blueprint will tell you, the structure of a building depends on the site, the construction crew, and the prospective owners. Arguments are the same. Depending on your topic, your goals, and your readers, you'll write very different kinds of arguments.

Although no two arguments look alike, every argument has three basic structural parts: a beginning, a middle, and an end. Each part performs certain basic functions. This isn't a simplistic definition. As in architecture, each part of a structure is there for a purpose; leave out one of the parts, and the whole collapses. So let's look at those parts and the jobs they do.

Components of an Argument

What follows is an organizational pattern for argument papers—a pattern to which, with some variations, most of the essays in this book conform. We offer it to help you plan your own argument papers. Although this model contains most of the components of arguments, it is not a formula written in stone. You should not feel bound to follow it every time you construct an argument. In fact, you might find it more effective to move blocks of writing around or to omit material. For instance, on issues unfamiliar to your readers, it might make sense to begin with background information so the context of your discussion will be understood. With familiar issues, it might be more persuasive to open with responses to opposing views. On especially controversial topics you might wish to reserve your responses for the main body of the paper. Or, for dramatic effect, you might decide to save them until the very end, thereby emphasizing your consideration of other perspectives. As a writer, you're free to modify this model any way you like; often you may want to try different models in different drafts of your paper to see which arrangement works best in each case. As with building houses, your choices in building arguments are numerous.

The Beginning

The beginning of your argument accomplishes, in a small space, three important goals.

- It introduces you, the writer. Here your audience meets you—senses your tone, your attitude toward your subject, and the general style of the piece.
- It appeals to your readers' reason, emotions, and/or sense of ethics. This can be done in a simple value statement, an anecdote, or some high-impact statistics intended to raise your readers' interest and concern.
- It identifies the topic and indicates your stand.

Depending on the issue and the audience, the beginning of an argument can be several paragraphs in length. In most arguments the beginning will end with a clear statement of the claim you are making—your thesis.

Although "Once upon a time . . . " is probably the most remembered introduction, it's not always the most effective; more ingenuity on your part is needed to "hook" your readers. For example, in *The Village Voice*, columnist Nat Hentoff began a column calling for eliminating duplication in the U.S. military by saying that he had telephoned the Pentagon press office for a comment on the subject. "Oh," said the officer with whom he spoke, "You want the *other* press office." As Hentoff remarked, he could have ended the column at that point; instead, he went on to develop his idea, confident that this introductory example would make his readers sympathetic to his point.

Composing good beginnings requires hard work. That's why many writers keep a journal in which they copy the strategies of writers they admire; that's how we happened to have a copy of Hentoff's introduction. As beginning arguers, you may want to develop your own repertoire of start-up strategies by copying strategies you admire into your own argument journal.

The Middle

The middle portion of your argument is where you do the argumentative work: presenting your information, responding to other views, making your case. If you think of it in terms of building construction, here's where you pour a foundation and lay the framework; put in all the walls, floors, and systems; and have the building inspector examine your work. There are a number of substages.

Provide Background Information

Before you can begin presenting your reasons, you want to be sure that your audience has the information necessary to understand the issue. Background information should answer any of the following questions depending on your topic:

- How significant is the issue? How many people are affected by it? Who are the people most affected?
- What facts, statistics, or information do your readers need to know to follow your reasons?
- What terminology or key words need to be defined so your readers will understand your meaning?
- What factors have caused the problem or situation to develop?
- What will be the consequences if the situation is not corrected?

If handled correctly, this part of your essay can be the most persuasive and convincing because it lets your readers know why you are concerned and the reasons behind that concern. Moreover, it gives your readers the opportunity to share your concern. For example, in "The Supreme Court and Physician-Assisted Suicide— The Ultimate Right" (page 500), Marcia Angell begins her essay with a review of recent and impending court decisions as well as voter initiatives on assisted suicide. She includes statistics that indicate widespread public support for the legalization of this practice. This information is not only informative; it creates a sense of urgency about the U.S. public's concern with the prospect of prolonged and painful terminal illness, and sets the stage for the argument she will develop in her essay.

Respond to Other Points of View

As we discussed in Chapter 4, it is important to let your audience know that you have seriously deliberated other points of view before reaching your own position. By doing this you appear informed and open minded. In this part of your essay you should briefly review a number of viewpoints that are different from your own. If you've engaged in debate and dialogue, as we suggested in Chapter 1, you should be aware of opposing views and common concerns. Now is your opportunity to identify them and respond. You might even acknowledge the sincerity of those holding contrary views and cite the merits of their positions. Such acknowledgments help establish your authority as a writer. They will also help you define your own position more specifically for your readers by contrasting it with others. For example, in the excerpt from his book *A Different Mirror* (page 338), Ronald Takaki demonstrates his awareness of the radically different perspectives on diversity held by Allan Bloom and E. D. Hirsch, two well-known cultural commentators. Takaki carefully quotes and paraphrases their writings to provide the reader with a brief account of their views before pointing out the ways in which he disagrees. By doing this, Takaki gains credibility and clarifies his own position.

Present Reasons in Support of Your Claim

The reasons supporting your claim comprise the heart of your essay and, therefore, its largest portion. Here you explain the reasons behind your claim and present supporting evidence—facts, statistics, data, testimony of authorities, examples—to convince your readers to agree with your position or take a particular course of action. Depending on the issue, this part of your essay usually takes several paragraphs, with each reason clearly delineated for your readers. Most of the essays in this book use this approach; Tom Reilly's "Youth Crime Has Changed—And So Must the Juvenile Justice System" (page 616) is a good example.

Anticipate Possible Objections to Your Reasons

Even with a friendly audience, readers will have questions and concerns about your reasons. If you ignore these objections and leave them unanswered, you will weaken the effectiveness of your argument. Therefore, it is always wise to anticipate possible objections so you can respond to them in a constructive fashion that will strengthen and clarify your ideas. The kind of objections you anticipate, of course, will depend on your familiarity with your audience—their interests, values, beliefs, experiences, and so on. If you have carefully analyzed your audience, as we suggest in Chapter 4, you will be more aware of the objections likely to surface in response to your reasons. Raising objections and responding to them will once again demonstrate your awareness of alternative viewpoints. It will also give you an opportunity to strengthen your reasons and increase your credibility. One good example of the successful response to objections is Gary Wills's "In Praise of Censure" (page 392).

The End

The end is usually a short paragraph or two in which you conclude your argument. Essentially, your ending summarizes your argument by reaffirming your stand on the issue. It might also make an appeal to your readers to take action. Some writers include an anecdote, a passionate summation, or even a quiet but resonant sentence. Lincoln's "Gettysburg Address," for example, ends with the quiet "government of the people, by the people, and for the people," which is one of the most memorable phrases in American political history. Looking over the essays in this book, you will find that no two end quite alike. As a writer, you have many choices; experimentation is usually the best way to decide what will work for you. Many writers copy effective conclusions into their journals so they can refresh their memories when writing their own arguments.

Sample Argument for Analysis

To illustrate this three-part argument structure we have included two sample argument essays for you to read. The first is "Indian Bones" by Clara Spotted Elk, a consultant for Native American interests. Although it is quite brief, the essay, published in the *New York Times* on March 8, 1989, contains all the essential components of an argument essay. It is followed by an analysis of its key structural features.

Review: The Structure of an Argument

The Beginning ...

Introduces you as a writer

States the problem

Establishes your position and appeal

Presents your claim (thesis)

The Middle ...

Provides background information

Responds to other points of view

Presents arguments supporting the claim

Anticipates possible objections

The End ...

Summarizes your position and implications

Invites readers to share your conclusion and/or take action

Indian Bones
Clara Spotted Elk

1   Millions of American Indians lived in this country when Columbus first landed on our shores. After the western expansion, only about 250,000 Indians survived. What happened to the remains of those people who were decimated by the advance of the white man? Many are gathering dust in American museums.

2   In 1985, I and some Northern Cheyenne chiefs visited the attic of the Smithsonian's Natural History Museum in Washington to review the inventory of their Cheyenne collection. After a chance inquiry, a curator pulled out a drawer in one of the scores of cabinets that line the attic. There were the jumbled bones of an Indian. "A Kiowa," he said.

3   Subsequently, we found that 18,500 Indian remains—some consisting of a handful of bones, but mostly full skeletons—are unceremoniously stored in the Smithsonian's nooks and crannies. Other museums, individuals and Federal agencies such as the National Park Service also collect the bones of Indian warriors, women, and children. Some are on display as roadside tourist attractions. It is estimated that another 600,000 Indian remains are secreted away in locations across the country.

4   The museum community and forensic scientists vigorously defend these grisly collections. With few exceptions, they refuse to return remains to the

tribes that wish to rebury them, even when grave robbing has been documented. They want to maintain adequate numbers of "specimens" for analysis and say they are dedicated to "the permanent curation of Indian skeletal remains."

5   Indian people are tired of being "specimens." The Northern Cheyenne word for ourselves is "tsistsistas"—human beings. Like people the world over, one of our greatest responsibilities is the proper care of the dead.

6   We are outraged that our religious views are not accepted by the scientific community and that the graves of our ancestors are desecrated. Many tribes are willing to accommodate some degree of study for a limited period of time—provided that it would help Indian people or mankind in general. But how many "specimens" are needed? We will not accept grave robbing and the continued hoarding of our ancestors' remains.

7   Would this nefarious collecting be tolerated if it were discovered that it affected other ethnic groups? (Incidentally, the Smithsonian also collects skeletons of blacks.) What would happen if the Smithsonian had 18,500 Holocaust victims in the attic? There would be a tremendous outcry in this country. Why is there no outcry about the Indian collection?

8   Indians are not exotic creatures for study. We are human begins who practice living religions. Our religion should be placed not only on a par with science when it comes to determining the disposition of our ancestors but on a par with every other religion practiced in this country.

9   To that end, Sen. Daniel K. Inouye will soon reintroduce the "Bones Bill" to aid Indians in retrieving the remains of their ancestors from museums. As in the past, the "Bones Bill" will most likely be staunchly resisted by the collectors of Indian skeletons—armed with slick lobbyists, lots of money and cloaked in the mystique of science.

10   Scientists have attempted to defuse this issue by characterizing their opponents as radical Indians, out of touch with the culture and with little appreciation of science. Armed only with a moral obligation to our ancestors, the Indians who support the bill have few resources and little money.

11   But, in my view, the issue should concern all Americans—for it raises very disturbing questions. American Indians want only to reclaim and rebury their dead. Is this too much to ask?

Analyzing the Structure

Now let's examine this essay according to the organizational features discussed so far.

The Beginning

Paragraph 1 clearly introduces the nature of the problem: The remains of the Indians "decimated by the advance of the white man" have wrongfully ended up "gathering dust in American museums." It isn't until paragraph 6 that Spotted Elk spells out her position: "We are outraged that our religious views are not accepted by the scientific community and that the graves of our ancestors are desecrated." (Because this essay was written for newspaper publication the paragraphs are shorter than they might be in a formal essay; you may not want to delay your thesis until the sixth paragraph in a longer essay.) Notice, too, that in the introduction the author's persona begins to assert itself in the brief and pointed summation of the American Indian's fate. When Spotted Elk mentions the staggering decline in the population of her ancestors, we sense a note of controlled but righteous anger in her voice. Citation of the gruesome facts of history also appeals to the reader's ethical sense by prompting reflection on the Indians' demise.

The Middle

- **Background Information** Paragraphs 2 and 3 establish the context of the author's complaint. Paragraph 2 is personal testimony to the problem—how she and other Native Americans viewed unceremonious "jumbled bones" in the museum drawer and were stunned by the representative insensitivity of their host curator, who treated the human remains as if they were a fossil. Paragraph 3 projects the problem to progressively larger contexts and magnitudes—from the single Kiowa in a drawer to the 18,500 in the Smithsonian at large; from that institution's collection to the estimated 600,000 remains in other museums, federal agencies and institutions, and "roadside tourist attractions." The broader scope of the problem is underscored here.

- **Response to Other Points of View** In paragraph 4, Spotted Elk tersely sums up the opposing position of the "museum community and forensic scientists": ". . . they refuse to return remains to the tribes." She also states their reasoning: "They want to maintain adequate numbers of 'specimens' for analysis and say they are dedicated to the 'permanent curation of Indian skeletal remains.'"

- **Reasons in Support of the Claim** Paragraphs 5 through 9 constitute the heart of Spotted Elk's argument. Here she most forcefully argues her objections and offers her reasons with supporting details: Indians resent being treated as specimens and want to bury their dead as do other religious people (paragraphs 5 and 6). She follows that with a concession that many Indians would accommodate some degree of anthropological study for a period of time, but do not approve of the huge permanent collections that now fill museums.

  In paragraph 7 the author continues to support her claim that American Indians have been discriminated against with regard to the disposition of ancestral remains. She writes that there would be a public outcry if the remains of other ethnic groups such as Holocaust victims were hoarded. Her proposal for change appears in paragraph 8: "Our religion should be placed not only on a par with science when it comes to determining the disposition of our ancestors but on a par with every other religion practiced in this country." This is the logical consequence of the problem she has addressed to this point. That proposal logically leads into paragraph 9, where she mentions efforts by Senator Daniel Inouye to see the "Bones Bill" passed into law. Throughout, Spotted Elk uses emotional words and phrases—*grisly, unceremoniously, slick lobbyists, cloaked in mystique*—to reinforce her points.

- **Anticipation of Possible Objections** In paragraph 10, the author addresses objections of the opposition, in this case those "[s]cientists [who] have attempted to defuse this issue by characterizing their opponents as radical Indians, out of touch with the culture and with little appreciation of science." She refutes all three charges (of being "radical," as well as out of touch with Indian culture and science) with the phrase "[a]rmed only with a moral obligation to our ancestors"—a phrase that reaffirms her strong connection with her culture. On the contrary, it is science that is out of touch with the "living religion" of Native Americans.

The End
The final paragraph brings closure to the argument. Briefly the author reaffirms her argument that Native Americans "want only to reclaim and rebury their dead." The question that makes up the final line of the essay is more than rhetorical, for it reminds us of the point introduced back in paragraph 5—that American Indians are no different than any other religious people with regard to the disposition of their ancestors. A powerful question brings the essay's conclusion into sharp focus.

As we stated in the beginning of this chapter, there is no best structure for an argument essay. As you develop your own essay, you may find it more effective to move certain structural features to locations that serve your purposes better. For instance, you may find that background information is more persuasive when you include it as support for a particular reason rather than provide it prior to your reasons. Possible objections might be raised along with each reason instead of saved for later. Ron Karpati's essay, "I Am the Enemy," provides a good example of a different approach to structuring an argument essay. Read the essay to see if you can pick out the structural elements he included and how he organized them. Following the essay, we've provided a brief analysis of its organization.

Sample Argument for Analysis

I Am the Enemy
Ron Karpati

Ron Karpati, a pediatrician and medical researcher of childhood illnesses, defends the use of animals in medical research. This article first appeared in *Newsweek*'s "My Turn" column in 1989.

1   I am the enemy! One of those vilified, inhumane physician-scientists involved in animal research. How strange, for I have never thought of myself as an evil person. I became a pediatrician because of my love for children and my desire to keep them healthy. During medical school and residency, however, I saw many children die of leukemia, prematurity and traumatic injury—circumstances against which medicine has made tremendous progress, but still has far to go. More important, I also saw children, alive and healthy, thanks to ad-

vances in medical science such as infant respirators, potent antibiotics, new surgical techniques and the entire field of organ transplantation. My desire to tip
the scales in favor of the healthy, happy children drew me to medical research.

2   My accusers claim that I inflict torture on animals for the sole purpose of
career advancement. My experiments supposedly have no relevance to medicine and are easily replaced by computer simulation. Meanwhile, an apathetic
public barely watches, convinced that the issue has no significance, and pub-
licity-conscious politicians increasingly give way to the demands of the activists.

3   We in medical research have also been unconscionably apathetic. We have
allowed the most extreme animal-rights protesters to seize the initiative and
frame the issue as one of "animal fraud." We have been complacent in our belief that a knowledgeable public would sense the importance of animal research to the public health. Perhaps we have been mistaken in not responding
to the emotional tone of the argument created by those sad posters of animals
by waving equally sad posters of children dying of leukemia or cystic fibrosis.

4   Much is made of the pain inflicted on these animals in the name of medical science. The animal-rights activists contend that this is evidence of our
malevolent and sadistic nature. A more reasonable argument, however, can be
advanced in our defense. Life is often cruel, both to animals and human beings. Teenagers get thrown from the back of a pickup truck and suffer severe
head injuries. Toddlers, barely able to walk, find themselves at the bottom of a
swimming pool while a parent checks the mail. Physicians hoping to alleviate
the pain and suffering these tragedies cause have but three choices: create an
animal model of the injury or disease and use that model to understand the
process and test new therapies; experiment on human beings—some experiments will succeed, most will fail—or finally, leave medical knowledge static,
hoping that accidental discoveries will lead us to the advances.

5   Some animal-rights activists would suggest a fourth choice, claiming that
computer models can simulate animal experiments, thus making the actual experiments unnecessary. Computers can simulate, reasonably well, the effects of
well-understood principles on complex systems, as in the application of the
laws of physics to airplane and automobile design. However, when the principles themselves are in question, as is the case with the complex biological systems under study, computer modeling alone is of little value.

6   One of the terrifying effects of the effort to restrict the use of animals in
medical research is that the impact will not be felt for years and decades: drugs
that might have been discovered will not be; surgical techniques that might
have been developed will not be, and fundamental biological processes that
might have been understood will remain mysteries. There is the danger that
politically expedient solutions will be found to placate a vocal minority, while
the consequences of these decisions will not be apparent until long after the
decisions are made and the decision making forgotten.

7   Fortunately, most of us enjoy good health, and the trauma of watching one's
child die has become a rare experience. Yet our good fortune should not make
us unappreciative of the health we enjoy or the advances that make it possible.
Vaccines, antibiotics, insulin and drugs to treat heart disease, hypertension and

stroke are all based on animal research. Most complex surgical procedures, such as coronary-artery bypass and organ transplantation, are initially developed in animals. Presently undergoing animal studies are techniques to insert genes in humans in order to replace the defective ones found to be the cause of so much disease. These studies will effectively end if animal research is severely restricted.

8   In America today, death has become an event isolated from our daily existence—out of the sight and thoughts of most of us. As a doctor who has watched many children die, and their parents grieve, I am particularly angered by people capable of so much compassion for a dog or a cat, but with seemingly so little for a dying human being. These people seem so insulated from the reality of human life and death and what it means.

9   Make no mistake, however: I am not advocating the needlessly cruel treatment of animals. To the extent that the animal-rights movement has made us more aware of the needs of these animals, and made us search harder for suitable alternatives, they have made a significant contribution. But if the more radical members of this movement are successful in limiting further research, their efforts will bring about a tragedy that will cost many lives. The real question is whether an apathetic majority can be aroused to protect its future against a vocal, but misdirected, minority.

Analyzing the Structure

The Beginning

In paragraph 1, Karpati introduces himself to the reader as a scientist and a pediatrician with a personal and professional interest in his topic. While his first sentence proclaims, "I am the enemy," Karpati almost immediately lets his readers know that he is only an enemy to those who oppose his work; he describes himself as a caring doctor who wishes to help children stay healthy. His second sentence informs the reader that his topic will be the use of animals as research subjects; in the next sentences he strongly implies that the advances made in medicine are the results of research using animals. His claim, stated in paragraph 3, is that animal research is important to public health. By using the example of ill or injured children who might benefit from this work, Karpati makes a strong emotional appeal to his readers.

The Middle

Background Information

This information appears in several places in the essay. Paragraph 1 includes a list of advances in medicine that have come about, the reader assumes, through animal research. Later, in paragraph 7, Karpati lists specific drugs and surgical procedures that have resulted from using animals as research subjects. However, Karpati seems more interested in informing readers how he, a scientist who uses animals to conduct his research, is characterized negatively by animal-rights supporters.

Response to Other Points of View

Because Karpati's essay is largely a defense of his position on animal research, he focuses heavily on the views of those who oppose his position. In paragraph 2 he briefly summarizes the accusations made about him by animal-rights supporters. In

paragraph 3 he suggests that these objections are voiced by extremists in that movement. Karpati goes on to indicate that he is aware of the reasons why others wish to
eliminate animal research. In paragraph 4 he acknowledges that "pain [is] inflicted
on these animals in the name of medical science." He agrees with the opposition
that "life is often cruel," but suggests through his examples that human suffering is
more compelling to physicians than is the suffering of animals. Later, in paragraph
9, Karpati refers back to this point and cites the contribution of the animal-rights
movement in making researchers more sensitive to the issue of animal suffering.

Reasons in Support of the Claim
In paragraphs 4 through 8 Karpati presents his reasons to support his claim that
medical research using animals should be continued for the benefit of human
health. In paragraphs 4 and 5 he explains that the alternatives to animal research—
experimenting on human subjects, relying on accidental discoveries, or using computer simulation—are not satisfactory. In paragraph 6 he warns that the impact of
restricting animal research will have a far-reaching and negative impact on medical
science. In paragraph 7 Karpati points to the results of animal research and its significant contributions to the healthy lives that most of his readers take for granted.
Finally, in paragraph 8, he reasserts the importance of human life over the well-
being of animals.

Possible Objections to Reasons
Karpati has included many of the objections to his reasons along with the reasons
themselves. For instance, in paragraphs 4 and 5 he anticipates that his readers
might wonder why humans and computers can't be substituted for animals in research. Karpati responds that experiments on humans will largely fail and computer
simulations cannot duplicate complex biological processes.

The End
In the last paragraph Karpati summarizes his main point: The efforts of radical
members of the animal-rights movement to limit the use of animals in research
"will bring about a tragedy that will cost many lives." He makes a strong appeal to
his readers to take action to prevent just that from happening.

Blueprints for Arguments
Our analysis of Karpati's essay gives some idea of its general organization, but it
does not reflect fine subdivisions or the way the various parts of the essay are logically connected. That can be done by making an outline. Think of an outline as a
blueprint of the argument you're building: It reveals structure and framework but
leaves out the materials that cover the frame.

   Opinions differ as to the value of making outlines before writing an essay.
Some writers need to make formal outlines to organize their thoughts. Others simply scratch down a few key ideas. Still others write essays spontaneously without
any preliminary writing. For the beginning writer an outline is a valuable aid because it demonstrates at a glance how the various parts of an essay are connected,

whether the organization is logical and complete, whether the evidence is sequenced properly, and whether there are any omissions or lack of proportion. Your outline need not be elaborate. You might simply jot down your key reasons in a hierarchy from strongest to weakest:

> Introduction
>
> Reason 1
>
> Reason 2
>
> Reason 3
>
> Reason 4
>
> Conclusion

This blueprint might be useful if you want to capture your readers' attention immediately with your most powerful appeal. Or you might use a reverse hierarchy, beginning with your weakest argument and proceeding to your strongest, in order to achieve a climactic effect for an audience sympathetic to your cause. The outline will help you build your case.

You might prefer, as do some writers, to construct an outline after, rather than before, writing a rough draft. This lets you create a draft without restricting the free flow of ideas and helps you rewrite by determining where you need to fill in, cut out, or reorganize. You may discover where your line of reasoning is not logical; you may also reconsider whether you should arrange your reasons from the most important to the least or vice versa in order to create a more persuasive effect. Ultimately, outlining after the first draft can prove useful in producing subsequent drafts and a polished final effort.

Outlines are also useful when evaluating somebody else's writing. Reducing the argument of the opposition to the bare bones exposes holes in the reasoning process, scanty evidence, and logical fallacies. In writing this book we used all three processes: We developed an outline to write the first draft and sway a publisher to accept it. Then experienced teachers read the draft and suggested changes to the outline to make it more effective. Finally, one of our collaborators took all the suggestions and her own ideas and created a new outline to help us revise the text. In our case, all three strategies were equally valuable.

The Formal Outline

Some teachers like students to submit *formal outlines* with their papers to show that the students have checked their structure carefully. This kind of outlining has several rules to follow:

- Identify main ideas with capital Roman numerals.
- Identify subsections of main ideas with capital letters, indented one set of spaces from the main ideas.
- Identify support for subsections with Arabic numerals indented two sets of spaces from the main ideas.

- Identify the parts of the support with lowercase Roman numerals, indented three sets of spaces from the main ideas.
- Identify further subdivisions with lowercase letters and then italic numbers, each indented one set of spaces to the right of the previous subdivision.
- Make sure all items have at least two points; it's considered improper informal outlining to have only one point under any subdivision.

To demonstrate what a formal outline can look like, we have outlined Clara Spotted Elk's essay, "Indian Bones":

    I. Hoarding of Indian remains
        A. At Smithsonian
            1. Single Kiowa at Smithsonian
            2. 18,500 others
        B. In other locations
   II. Authorities' defense of collections
        A. Refusal to return grave-robbed remains
        B. Maintainence of "specimens"
  III. Indians' response
        A. Outrage
            1. Desire to be seen as humans
            2. Desire to have religion accepted by science
            3. Nonacceptance of desecration of graves
            4. Resentment of lack of outcry by public
        B. Accommodation
            1. Limitation in time
            2. Service to Indians and mankind
        C. Demand equality with other religions
   IV. "Bones Bill" legislation
        A. Resistance from scientific community
            1. Slick lobbyists
            2. Money
            3. Scientific mystique
            4. Characterization of Indians
                i. Radicals
                ii. Out of touch with culture
                iii. Little appreciation of science
        B. Indian counter-resistance
            1. Few resources
            2. Little money
            3. Moral obligation to ancestors

Keep in mind that an outline should not force your writing to conform to a rigid pattern and, thus, turn your essay into something stilted and uninspired. Follow the model as a map, taking detours when necessary or inspired.

Two Basic Shapes for Arguments

Consider the following claims for arguments:

1. Watching television helps to eliminate some traditional family rituals.
2. Pornography poses a threat to women.
3. *Titanic* is an intelligent, sensitive movie.
4. Bilingual education programs fail to help non-English-speaking children become part of mainstream society.
5. Affirmative action is intended to reverse the longstanding tradition of unjust racial exclusion.
6. Cigarette advertising should be banned from billboards everywhere.
7. Medical doctors should not advertise.
8. Americans by law should be required to vote.
9. The production and sale of cigarettes ought to be outlawed.
10. Pass/fail grades have to be eliminated across the board if academic standards are to be maintained.

Looking over these statements, you might notice some patterns. The verbs in the first five are all in the present tense: *helps, poses, is, fail, is intended to.* However, each of the last five statements includes "should" words: *should, should not, ought to be, have to be.* These **obligation verbs** are found in almost all claims proposing solutions to a problem.

What distinguishes the first group from the second is more than the form of the verb. The first five claims are statements of the writer's stand on a controversial issue as it currently exists. The second group are proposals for what *should* be. Essentially, all the arguments in this book—and the ones you'll most likely write and read in your careers—fall into one of these two categories or a combination of each, for often a writer states his or her position on an issue, then follows it with proposals for changes. Later in this chapter we will discuss proposals. For the moment, let's take a look at position arguments.

Position Arguments

A *position argument* scrutinizes one side of a controversial issue. In such an argument the writer not only establishes his or her stand, but argues vigorously in defense of it. Position arguments are less likely to point to a solution to a problem. Instead, they are philosophical in nature—the kinds of arguments on which political and social principles are founded, laws are written, and business and government policies are established. Position papers also tend to address themselves to the ethical and moral aspects of a controversy. If, for instance, you were opposed to the university's policy of mandatory testing for the AIDS virus, you might write a position paper protesting your school's infringement of individual rights and invasion of privacy.

As indicated by the present tense of the verbs in the first five claims, the position argument deals with the status quo—the way things are, the current state of affairs. Such an argument reminds the audience that something *currently* is good or bad, better or worse, right or wrong. Like all arguments, they tend to be aimed at changing the audience's feelings about an issue—euthanasia, abortion, capital punishment, and so on. That is why many position papers tend to direct their appeals to the reader's sense of ethics rather than to reason.

By contrast, proposal arguments identify a problem and recommend a likely solution. That's why their claims contain verbs that *obligate* the readers to take some action. In this sense they are practical rather than philosophical. For instance, if you were concerned about the spread of AIDS among college students, you might write a paper proposing that condom machines be installed in all dormitories. When you offer a proposal, you're trying to affect the future.

What to Look for in Position Arguments

What follows are some key features of position arguments. As a checklist, they can help you evaluate someone's stand on an issue and help guide you in writing your own position papers.

The Writer Deals with a Controversial Issue. The best kind of position paper is one that focuses on a debatable issue, one in which there is clear disagreement: abortion, capital punishment, euthanasia, affirmative action, sex in advertising, freedom of speech, gay rights, homelessness, gun control. These are the issues about which people have many different perspectives.

The Writer Clearly States a Position. Readers should not be confused about where an author stands on an issue. Although the actual issue may be complex, the claim should be stated emphatically and straightforwardly. Don't waffle: "Using the death penalty in some situations and with some rights of appeal probably doesn't do much to lower crime anyway"; far better is an emphatic "Capital punishment is no deterrent to crime."

In formulating your claim, be certain that your word choice is not ambiguous. Otherwise the argument will be muddled and, ultimately, unconvincing. Ambiguity, however, should not be confused with ambivalence. Ambiguity is vagueness or lack of clarity; ambivalence means having simultaneously conflicting feelings. On particularly complex or difficult issues you can feel legitimate ambivalence. If you feel ambivalent about a position, you have two options: Choose another issue that you can argue more emphatically, or write a claim that clearly spells out your ambivalence and the conditions that determine your taking one side or the other on the issue. In his thoughtful essay "Free at Last? A Personal Perspective on Race and Identity" (page 326), Glenn C. Loury shares with his readers the conflict he experiences between his own definition of self and the racial identity that has been thrust upon him: "I have had to confront the problem of balancing my desire not to disappoint the expectations of others—both whites and blacks, but more especially blacks—with my conviction that one should strive to live life with integrity." His inability to choose sides becomes the focus of his essay.

The Writer Recognizes Other Positions and Potential Objections. For every argument there are bound to be a number of other perspectives. Such is the nature of controversy. As a writer representing a position, you cannot assume that your readers are fully aware of or understand all the disagreement surrounding the issue you're arguing. Nor can you make a persuasive case without anticipating challenges. So in your argument you must spell out accurately and fairly the main points of the opposition and objections that might arise. We offer six reasons for doing this:

1. *You reduce your own vulnerability.* You don't want to appear ill informed or naive on an issue. Therefore, it makes sense to acknowledge opposing points of view to show how well you've investigated the topic and how sensitive you are to it. Suppose, for instance, you are writing a paper arguing that "anyone who commits suicide is insane." To avoid criticism, you would have to be prepared to answer objections that fully rational people with terminal illnesses often choose to take their own lives so as to avoid a painful demise and curtail the suffering of loved ones. Even if you strongly disagree with your opposition, recognizing views from the other side demonstrates that you are a person of responsibility and tolerance—two qualities for which most writers of argument strive.

2. *You distinguish your own position.* By citing opposing views, you distinguish your own position from that of others. This not only helps clarify the differences, but lays out the specific points of the opposition to be refuted or discredited. Some writers do this at the outset of their arguments. Consider, for instance, how Ron Karpati sums up the views of the opposition in the opening paragraphs of his essay "I Am the Enemy."

3. *You can respond to opposing views.* A good response can challenge an opponent's ideas and examine the basis for the disagreement—whether personal, ideological, or moral. For instance, when Michael Kelley, in "Arguing for Infanticide" (page 171), responds to Steven Pinker's "Why They Kill Their Newborns" (page 162), he points out that Pinker's very logical argument for neonaticide ignores the moral and ethical values of our society regarding the relationship between mothers and their children. Kelley does not suggest that Pinker's reasons are incorrect; instead he challenges the basis for Pinker's argument.

4. *You might also challenge an opponent's logic, demonstrating where the reasoning suffers from flaws in logic.* For instance, the argument that Ms. Shazadi must be a wonderful mother because she's a great manager does not logically follow. While some qualities of a good manager might bear on successful motherhood, not all do. In fact, it can be argued that the very qualities that make a good manager—leadership, drive, ruthlessness, determination—might damage a parent-child relationship. This logical fallacy, called a false analogy, erroneously suggests that the two situations are comparable when they are not. An example of this can be found in Jeff Jacoby's "What the Antismoking Zealots Really Crave" (page 89) when he points out that a well-known antismoking activist has compared tobacco companies to mass murderers. While the dangers of cigarette smoking are widely accepted, the comparison between profit-driven corporations and murderous criminals cannot be supported with fact and reasonable evidence.

5. *You might challenge the evidence supporting an argument.* If possible, try to point out unreliable, unrealistic, or irrelevant evidence offered by the opposition; question the truth of counterarguments; or point to distortions. The realtor who boasts oceanside property is vulnerable to challenge if the house in question is actually half a mile from the beach. Look for instances of stacking the deck. For example, a writer might argue that supporting the building of a new sports complex will benefit the community by providing new jobs. However, if she fails to mention that workers at the old sports facility will then lose their jobs, she is misleading the audience about the benefits of this change. Challenge the evidence by looking for hasty generalizations. For example, a business degree from State U. may indeed guarantee a well-paying job after graduation, but the writer will need more than a few personal anecdotes to convince the reader that this is the case.

6. *You can gain strength through concessions.* Admitting weaknesses in your own stand shows that you are realistic, that you don't suffer from an inflated view of the virtues of your position. It also lends credibility to your argument while helping you project yourself as fair-minded. A successful example of this strategy is Ron Karpati's acknowledgment in paragraph 9 of "I Am the Enemy" (page 113) that the animal-rights movement has sensitized scientists to the needs of animals.

The Writer Offers a Well-Reasoned Argument to Support the Position. A position paper must do more than simply state your stand on an issue. It must try to persuade readers to accept your position as credible and convince them to adjust their thinking about the issue. Toward those ends, you should make every effort to demonstrate the best reasons for your beliefs and support the positions you hold. That means presenting honest and logically sound arguments.

Persuaders use three kinds of appeal: to *reason,* to *emotions,* and to readers' sense of *ethics.* You may have heard these described as the appeals of *logos, pathos,* and *ethos.* Although it is difficult to separate the emotional and ethical components from the rational or logical structure of an argument, the persuasive powers of a position argument may mean the proper combination of these three appeals. Not all arguments will cover all three appeals. Some will target logic alone and offer as support statistics and facts. Others centering around moral, religious, or personal values will appeal to a reader's emotions as well as reason. (These arguments are most successful for a readership that need not be convinced by force of reason alone.) Arguments based on emotion aim to reinforce and inspire followers to stand by their convictions. However, relying too heavily on an emotional appeal can result in an ad misericordiam argument, one that attempts to exploit the readers' pity. The most successful arguments are those that use multiple strategies to appeal to readers' hearts and minds.

When the issue centers on right-or-wrong or good-or-bad issues, position arguments make their appeals to the audience's ethical sense. In such papers your strategy has two intentions: one, to convince the reader that you are a person of goodwill and moral character and thus enhance your credibility; and, two, to suggest that any decent and moral readers will share your position.

The Writer's Supporting Evidence Is Convincing. A position paper does not end with an incontrovertible proof such as in a demonstration of a scientific law or mathematical theorem. No amount of logic can prove conclusively that your functional judgment is right or wrong; if that were the case, there would be few arguments. It is also impossible to prove that your aesthetic judgments are superior to another's or that a particular song, movie, or book is better than another. But your arguments have a greater chance of being persuasive if you can present evidence that convinces your readers that your argument is valid.

We'll say more about evidence in Chapter 6, but for now remember that a strong argument needs convincing evidence: facts, figures, personal observations, testimony of outside authorities, and specific examples. In general, the more facts supporting a position, the more reason there is for the reader to accept that position as valid. The same is true when refuting another position. An author needs to supply sound reasons and evidence to disprove or discredit an opponent's stand.

The Writer Projects a Reasonable Persona. Whenever we read an argument, we cannot help but be aware of the person behind the words. Whether it's in the choice of expressions, the tenacity of opinion, the kinds of examples, the force of the argument, the nature of the appeal, or the humor or sarcasm, we hear the author's voice and form an impression of the person. That impression, which is projected by the voice and tone of the writing, is the writer's *persona.*

Persona is communicated in a variety of ways: diction or the choice of words (formal, colloquial, slang, jargon, charged terms); the sentence style (long or short, simple or complex); and the kinds of evidence offered (from cool scientific data to inflammatory examples). As in face-to-face debates, a full range of feelings can be projected by the tone of a written argument: anger, irony, jest, sarcasm, seriousness.

Persona is the vital bond linking the writer to the reader. In fact, the success or failure of an argument might be measured by the extent to which the reader accepts the persona in an argument. If you like the voice you hear, then you have already begun to identify with the writer and are more likely to share in the writer's assumptions and opinions. If, however, that persona strikes you as harsh, distant, or arrogant, you might have difficulty subscribing to the author's argument even if it makes sense logically.

A good position argument projects a reasonable persona, one that is sincere and willing to consider opposing points of view. Steer clear of ad hominem arguments, which make personal attacks on those with whom you disagree rather than on their views. Although readers may not be convinced enough to change their stand or behavior, a writer with a reasonable persona can at least capture their respect and consideration. Remember, the success of your argument will largely depend on your audience's willingness to listen.

A word of warning. Not every persona has to be reasonable or pleasant, although for a beginner this works best. If an arrogant persona is fortified by wit and intelligence, readers may find it stimulating, even charming. A persona—whether outrageous, humorous, biting, or sarcastic—can be successful if it is executed with style and assurance. Some of the best arguments in Part 2 of this book have biting edges.

Checklist for Writing a Position Argument

Have you:
- chosen a controversial issue?
- clearly stated a position?
- recognized other positions and possible objections?
- developed a well-reasoned argument?
- provided convincing supporting evidence?
- projected a reasonable persona?

When you read an argument with a memorable persona, jot down in your argument journal the details of how the writer created it; that way, you can turn back to this information when you're trying to create personas for the arguments you write.

Sample Argument for Analysis

What follows is an example of a position argument written by Robert Wachbroit on the issue of cloning. Ever since scientists in Scotland cloned an adult sheep by using the DNA in her cells to produce an identical replica, the world has been both fascinated and horrified by the prospect of genetic cloning. While many see the advantages of cloning livestock and plants, the possibility of cloning human beings is strongly debated. Wachbroit is a research scholar at the Institute for Philosophy and Public Policy at the University of Maryland. This essay first appeared in the *Washington Post* on March 2, 1997. As you read, consider how Wachbroit incorporates the six key points of position arguments into his essay.

Should We Cut This Out? Human Cloning Is Not as Scary as It Sounds
Robert Wachbroit

1   The recent news of the successful cloning of an adult sheep—in which the sheep's DNA was inserted into an unfertilized sheep egg to produce a lamb with identical DNA—has generated an outpouring of ethical concerns. These concerns are not about Dolly, the now famous sheep, nor even about the considerable impact cloning may have on the animal breeding industry, but rather about the possibility of cloning humans. For the most part, however, the ethical concerns being raised are exaggerated and misplaced, because they are based on erroneous views about what genes are and what they can do. The danger, therefore, lies not in the power of the technology, but in the misunderstanding of its significance.

2   Producing a clone of a human being would not amount to creating a "carbon copy"—an automaton of the sort familiar from science fiction. It would be more like producing a delayed identical twin. And just as identical twins are two separate people—biologically, psychologically, morally and legally, though not genetically—so a clone is a separate person from his or her non-contemporaneous twin. To think otherwise is to embrace a belief in genetic determinism—the view that genes determine everything about us, and that environmental factors or the random events in human development are utterly insignificant. The overwhelming consensus among geneticists is that genetic determinism is false.

3   As geneticists have come to understand the ways in which genes operate, they have also become aware of the myriad ways in which the environment affects their "expression." The genetic contribution to the simplest physical traits, such as height and hair color, is significantly mediated by environmental factors. And the genetic contribution to the traits we value most deeply, from intelligence to compassion, is conceded by even the most enthusiastic genetic researchers to be limited and indirect. Indeed, we need only appeal to our ordinary experience with identical twins—that they are different people despite their similarities—to appreciate that genetic determinism is false.

4   Furthermore, because of the extra steps involved, cloning will probably always be riskier—that is, less likely to result in a live birth—than in vitro fertilization (IVF) and embryo transfer. (It took more than 275 attempts before the researchers were able to obtain a successful sheep clone. While cloning methods may improve, we should note that even standard IVF techniques typically have a success rate of less than 20 percent.) So why would anyone go to the trouble of cloning?

5   There are, of course, a few reasons people might go to the trouble, and so it's worth pondering what they think they might accomplish, and what sort of ethical quandaries they might engender. Consider the hypothetical example of the couple who wants to replace a child who has died. The couple doesn't seek to have another child the ordinary way because they feel that cloning would enable them to reproduce, as it were, the lost child. But the unavoidable truth is that they would be producing an entirely different person, a delayed identical twin of that child. Once they understood that, it is unlikely they would persist.

6   But suppose they were to persist? Of course we can't deny that possibility. But a couple so persistent in refusing to acknowledge the genetic facts is not likely to be daunted by ethical considerations or legal restrictions either. If our fear is that there could be many couples with that sort of psychology, then we have a great deal more than cloning to worry about.

7   Another disturbing possibility is the person who wants a clone in order to have acceptable "spare parts" in case he or she needs an organ transplant later in life. But regardless of the reason that someone has a clone produced, the result would nevertheless be a human being with all the rights and protections that accompany that status. It truly would be a disaster if the results of human cloning were seen as less than fully human. But there is certainly no moral jus-

tification for and little social danger of that happening; after all, we do not accord lesser status to children who have been created through IVF or embryo transfer.

8   There are other possibilities we could spin out. Suppose a couple wants a "designer child"—a clone of Cindy Crawford or Elizabeth Taylor—because they want a daughter who will grow up to be as attractive as those women. Indeed, suppose someone wants a clone, never mind of whom, simply to enjoy the notoriety of having one. We cannot rule out such cases as impossible. Some people produce children for all sorts of frivolous or contemptible reasons. But we must remember that cloning is not as easy as going to a video store or as engaging as the traditional way of making babies. Given the physical and emotional burdens that cloning would involve, it is likely that such cases would be exceedingly rare.

9   But if that is so, why object to a ban on human cloning? What is wrong with placing a legal barrier in the path of those with desires perverse enough or delusions recalcitrant enough to seek cloning despite its limited potential and formidable costs? For one thing, these are just the people that a legal ban would be least likely to deter. But more important, a legal barrier might well make cloning appear more promising than it is to a much larger group of people.

10   If there were significant interest in applying this technology to human beings, it would indicate a failure to educate people that genetic determinism is profoundly mistaken. Under those circumstances as well, however, a ban on human cloning would not only be ineffective but also most likely counterproductive. Ineffective because, as others have pointed out, the technology does not seem to require sophisticated and highly visible laboratory facilities; cloning could easily go underground. Counterproductive because a ban might encourage people to believe that there is a scientific basis for some of the popular fears associated with human cloning—that there is something to genetic determinism after all.

11   There is a consensus among both geneticists and those writing on ethical, legal and social aspects of genetic research, that genetic determinism is not only false, but pernicious; it invokes memories of pseudo-scientific racist and eugenic programs premised on the belief that what we value in people is entirely dependent on their genetic endowment or the color of their skin. Though most members of our society now eschew racial determinism, our culture still assumes that genes contain a person's destiny. It would be unfortunate if, by treating cloning as a terribly dangerous technology, we encouraged this cultural myth, even as we intrude on the broad freedom our society grants people regarding reproduction.

12   We should remember that most of us believe people should be allowed to decide with whom to reproduce, when to reproduce and how many children they should have. We do not criticize a woman who takes a fertility drug so that she can influence when she has children—or even how many. Why, then, would we object if a woman decides to give birth to a child who is, in effect, a non-contemporaneous identical twin of someone else?

13 By arguing against a ban, I am not claiming that there are no serious ethical concerns to the manipulation of human genes. Indeed there are. For example, if it turned out that certain desirable traits regarding intellectual abilities or character could be realized through the manipulation of human genes, which of these enhancements, if any, should be available? But such questions are about genetic engineering, which is a different issue than cloning. Cloning is a crude method of trait selection: It simply takes a pre-existing, unengineered genetic combination of traits and replicates it.

14 I do not wish to dismiss the ethical concerns people have raised regarding the broad range of assisted reproductive technologies. But we should acknowledge that those concerns will not be resolved by any determination we make regarding the specific acceptability of cloning.

Analysis of a Position Argument

The Writer Deals with a Controversial Issue. Ever since scientists announced they had cloned a sheep, the benefits and dangers of human cloning have been strongly debated by the general public, as well as by religious groups and scientists.

The Writer Clearly States a Position. In paragraph 1 Wachbroit explains his position that ethical concerns about cloning "are exaggerated and misplaced" because people misunderstand "what genes are and what they can do. The danger, therefore, lies not in the power of the technology, but in the misunderstanding of its significance."

The Writer Recognizes Other Positions and Possible Objections. Throughout his essay, Wachbroit considers other positions and responds to possible objections to his ideas. In paragraph 2 he discusses the theory of genetic determinism, whose proponents share "the view that genes determine everything about us." In paragraphs 7 and 8 Wachbroit presents and responds to concerns about the abuses that may result from an acceptance of cloning, from harvesting organs for "spare parts" to creating "designer children." In paragraph 9 he raises a major objection to his position—"Why object to a ban on human cloning?"—and answers his question in the paragraphs that follow. By acknowledging and discussing a number of perspectives, Wachbroit demonstrates he has seriously considered all sides. The reader has the impression that his position and reasons take these other concerns into account.

The Writer Offers Well-Developed Reasons to Support the Position. Each of Wachbroit's reasons addresses the central idea found in his claim: People fear cloning because they do not understand the limited power of genes to determine significant human qualities. As a result of this misunderstanding, cloning is seen as a potentially dangerous practice that should be banned. In particular, Wachbroit believes that once the myth of genetic determinism is revealed as unfounded, people will realize that cloning does not pose a threat to their ethical concerns.

  Wachbroit presents his first reason in paragraph 2 when he confronts the popular belief in genetic determinism—"the view that genes determine everything about us"—advanced by those critical of cloning. He explains that producing a clone would be much "like producing a delayed identical twin" and not a science fiction "automaton." Because we all know that identical twins are distinct individuals, Wachbroit reasons that a clone would be "biologically, psychologically, morally and legally, though not genetically . . . a separate person from his or her non-contemporaneous twin." In paragraph 3 Wachbroit works to disprove the theory of genetic determinism based on the scientific evidence that genes only control a limited number of human characteristics, such as hair color and height. According to Wachbroit, those human qualities "that we value most deeply, from intelligence to compassion" are only indirectly influenced by our genetic structure. Thus, Wachbroit insists, a clone could not be a "carbon copy" of another person because those essential qualities cannot be duplicated in humans, even with identical genes.

In paragraphs 5 through 8 Wachbroit directly addresses the "ethical quandaries" (paragraph 5) that might develop if cloning is used inappropriately. To those concerned that a clone will be created for "spare parts" for organ transplants, Wachbroit asserts that regardless of the reasons for creating a clone, "the result would nevertheless be a human being with all the rights and protections that accompany that status" (paragraph 7). In other words, an individual created through cloning would be protected from such bodily harm. Moreover, since "we do not accord lesser status to children who have been created through IVF or embryo transfer," Wachbroit argues that there is "no moral justification for and little social danger of that happening." In the case of couples who desire a "designer child" resembling a particular celebrity, Wachbroit suggests in paragraph 8 that the "physical and emotional burdens" that accompany the cloning process would deter those with such "frivolous" reasons for wanting a child. Therefore, according to Wachbroit, a legal ban is unnecessary.

Wachbroit further argues in paragraph 9 that such a ban would not deter the very people it is intended to stop: "those with desires perverse enough or delusions recalcitrant enough to seek cloning despite its limited potential and formidable costs." Moreover, Wachbroit warns in paragraph 10, a legal ban on cloning would drive it "underground," which would give the government even less control over it and allow greater opportunity for abuse. Referring back to his first reason, Wachbroit points out that a ban on cloning "might encourage people to believe that there is a scientific basis for some of the popular fears associated with cloning—that there is something to genetic determinism after all."

Finally, in paragraph 12 Wachbroit reminds his audience members of their shared belief in human reproductive freedom: "most of us believe people should be allowed to decide with whom to reproduce, when to reproduce and how many children they should have." If we support this freedom, Wachbroit argues, then we cannot deny people the right to clone themselves.

Although Wachbroit provides several strong reasons to support his position, some of his reasons and examples have their weaknesses. For instance, in paragraph 5 he concludes that the hypothetical couple who wish to replace a deceased child will abandon their efforts once they understand they cannot "reproduce" an actual replica of the lost child. However, this might not deter them; perhaps they would in fact be willing to settle for outer resemblance alone. Similarly, Wachbroit's assumption in paragraph 8, that the difficulties of cloning will deter people from employing it as a method of reproduction, may also be unconvincing. Many couples go through considerable difficulties to conceive children; Wachbroit does not demonstrate how cloning could be more difficult. Finally, Wachbroit's assumption in paragraph 12 that his audience agrees with his statements about reproductive freedom may rest on shaky ground. Contrary to his example, women have been criticized for taking fertility drugs and, as recent legal and criminal cases have demonstrated, society does have an interest in women's reproductive choices.

The Writer's Supporting Evidence is Convincing. Wachbroit supports his reasons with references to scientific research that indicates he is knowledgeable about cloning. These appear in paragraph 3 in his explanation of the way genes work; in paragraphs 4 and 7 in his discussion of in vitro fertilization and embryo transfer; and in his reference to geneticists in paragraph 11.

In addition, Wachbroit's hypothetical examples are familiar to most readers: the couple who might wish to replace a child who has died (paragraph 5), the individual who wishes to create "spare parts" in case of a need for organ transplant (paragraph 7), and the people who want to have a celebrity look alike child (paragraph 8). By focusing on examples that illustrate common concerns, Wachbroit's responses are targeted and convincing.

The Writer Projects a Reasonable Persona. The persona Wachbroit projects is that of a concerned and thoughtful scholar. He seriously considers the perspectives of others and treats their views respectfully even as he disagrees. For example, in paragraph 14 he states that he does not "wish to dismiss the ethical concerns people have raised" about cloning. Moreover, Wachbroit is careful to avoid appearing inflexible in his position. Even at the end of his essay, in paragraph 13, he acknowledges that people have raised "serious ethical concerns" about this new technology.

Proposal Arguments

Position arguments examine existing conditions. *Proposal arguments,* however, look to the future. They make recommendations for changes in the status quo—namely, changes in a policy, practice, or attitude. Essentially, what every proposal writer says is this: "Here is the problem, and this is what I think should be done about it." The hoped-for result is a new course of action or way of thinking.

Proposals are the most common kind of argument. We hear them all the time: "There ought to be a law against that"; "The government should do something about these conditions." We're always making proposals of some kind: "Van should work out more"; "You ought to see that movie"; "We should recycle more of our trash." As pointed out earlier in this chapter, because proposals are aimed at correcting problems, they almost always make their claims in obligation verbs such as *ought to, needs to be,* and *must.*

Sometimes proposal arguments take up local problems and make practical recommendations for immediate solutions. For instance, to reduce the long lines at the photocopy machines in your campus library, you might propose that the school invest in more copiers and station them throughout the building. Proposal arguments also seek to correct or improve conditions with more far-reaching consequences. If, for example, too many of your classmates smoke, you might write a proposal to your school's administration to remove all cigarette machines from campus buildings or to limit smoking areas on campus.

Still other proposals address perennial social issues in an effort to change public behavior and government policy. A group of physicians might recommend that marijuana be legalized for medical use. An organization of concerned parents might ask the federal government to ban toys that contain toxic or flammable materials. Everyone has ideas about things that should be changed; proposals are the means we use to make those changes happen.

What to Look for in Proposal Arguments

Proposals have two basic functions: (1) They inform readers that there is a problem; and (2) they make recommendations about how to correct those problems. To help you sharpen your own critical ability to build and analyze proposal arguments, we offer some guidelines.

The Writer States the Problem Clearly.   Because a proposal argument seeks to change the reader's mind and/or behavior, you first must demonstrate that a problem exists. You do this for several reasons. Your audience may not be aware that the problem exists or they may have forgotten it or think that it has already been solved. Sympathetic audiences may need to be reinspired to take action. It is crucial, therefore, that proposals clearly define the problem and the undesirable or dangerous consequences if matters are not corrected.

For both uninformed and sympathetic audiences, writers often try to demonstrate how the problem personally affects the reader. An argument for greater measures against shoplifting can be more convincing when you illustrate how petty thefts inevitably lead to higher prices. A paper proposing the elimination of pesticides might interest the everyday gardener by demonstrating how much carcinogenic chemicals can contaminate local drinking water. To make the problem even more convincing, the claim should be supported by solid evidence—statistics, historical data, examples, testimony of witnesses and experts, maybe even personal experience.

The Writer Clearly Proposes How to Solve the Problem.   After defining the problem clearly, you need to tell your readers how to solve it. This is the heart of the proposal, the writer's plan of action. Besides a detailed explanation of what should be done and how, the proposal should supply reliable supporting evidence for the plan: testimony of others, ideas from authorities, statistics from studies.

The Writer Argues Convincingly That This Proposal Will Solve the Problem.
Perhaps the first question readers ask is "How will this solution solve the problem?" Writers usually address this question by identifying the forces behind the problem and demonstrating how their plan will counter those forces. Suppose, for instance, you propose putting condom machines in all college dorms as a means of combat-

ing the spread of AIDS. To build a convincing case you would have to summon evidence documenting how condoms significantly reduce the spread of AIDS. To make the connection between the problem and your solution even stronger, you might go on to explain how readily available machines leave students little excuse for unsafe sex. Students cannot complain that they jeopardized their health because they couldn't make it to a drugstore.

The Writer Convincingly Explains How the Solution Will Work. Generally readers next ask how the plan will be put into action. Writers usually answer by detailing how their plan will work. They emphasize their plan's advantages and how efficiently (or cheaply, safely, conveniently) it can be carried out. For the condom machine proposal, that might mean explaining how and where the machines will be installed and how students can be encouraged to use them. You might cite advantages of your proposal, such as the easy installation of the machines and the low price of the contents.

The Writer Anticipates Objections to the Proposed Solution. Writers expect disagreement and objections to proposal arguments: Proposals are aimed at changing the status quo, and many people are opposed to or are fearful of change. If you want to persuade readers, especially hostile ones, you must show that you respect their sides of the argument too. Most proposal writers anticipate audience response to fortify their case and establish credibility. (See Chapter 4 for more discussion of audience response.)

The Writer Explains Why This Solution Is Better Than the Alternatives. Although you may believe that your solution to the problem is best, you cannot expect readers automatically to share that sentiment. Nor can you expect readers not to wonder about other solutions. Good proposal writers investigate other solutions that have been tried to solve this problem so they can weigh alternative possibilities and attempt to demonstrate the superiority of their plan and the disadvantages of others. If you are knowledgeable about ways the problem has been dealt with in the past, you might be able to show how your plan combines the best features of other, less successful solutions. For instance, in the condom machine proposal you might explain to your readers that universities have attempted to make students more aware that unsafe sex promotes the spread of AIDS; however, without the easy availability of condom machines, students are more likely to continue to engage in unsafe sex. The promotion of AIDS awareness and the presence of condom machines might significantly reduce that problem.

The Writer Projects a Reasonable Persona. As in position arguments, your persona is an important factor in proposals, for it conveys your attitude toward the subject and the audience. Because a proposal is intended to win readers to your side, the best strategy is to project a persona that is fair minded. Even if you dislike or are angry about somebody else's views on an issue, projecting a reasonable and knowledgeable tone will have a more persuasive effect than a tone of belligerence.

Checklist for Writing a Proposal Argument

Have you:
- clearly stated the problem?
- clearly proposed a solution?
- explained why the solution will work?
- demonstrated how the solution will work?
- addressed possible objections?
- shown why the solution is better than alternatives?
- projected a reasonable persona?

If you are arguing for condom machines in dormitories, you would be wise to recognize that some people might object to the proposal because availability might be interpreted as encouragement of sexual behavior. So as not to offend or antagonize such readers, adopting a serious, straightforward tone might be the best mode of presenting the case.

Sample Argument for Analysis

The following argument was written by Martha Balash, a first-year English composition student, whose assignment was to write a proposal argument. Read through Balash's essay and respond to the questions that follow. Note that Martha used research to support her ideas and documentation to acknowledge her sources. The style of documentation in this paper is MLA, which we discuss in detail in the Documentation Guide.

Schools Can Help to Prevent Teen Pregnancy
Martha Balash

1   The problem of teen pregnancy is one that has plagued our society for many years and continues to grow. According to research conducted by The National Campaign to Prevent Teen Pregnancy, over one million teenage girls in the United States between ages fourteen to nineteen will become pregnant this year. These numbers are astounding: it is estimated that every twenty-six seconds a teen becomes pregnant (Campaign).

2   Although teen pregnancy has been a problem for some time, no workable solution has had a major impact on reducing these overwhelming statistics. In the meantime, teenagers who become pregnant and have children are placing themselves at a higher risk for dropping out of high school and living in

poverty and on public assistance (Rolling and Burnett 142). This is a problem that affects us all, not just the individual teen mother and her family. The Center for Population Options reports that "53 percent of outlays for Aid to Families with Dependent Children (AFDC), food stamps, and Medicaid are attributable to households begun by teen births" (Sylvester). As a mother of two soon-to-be teenagers and a taxpayer, I am concerned that we find effective strategies for dealing with this situation.

3   The causes of teen pregnancy are numerous, but I feel that a major cause is a lack of education, not only for teens, but also for adults and parents as well. Teens are misinformed about many aspects of sex. They are not taught the importance of abstaining from sex nor, at the very least, the proper use of effective birth control and protection from sexually transmitted diseases. What makes this problem even worse is that often the adults who interact with teenagers are no better informed than the teens. They avoid discussing sexual issues with teens because they don't know what to advise or because they are uncomfortable with the subject. These adults need to be educated about correct information about sexual matters and about the importance of their role in their children's education. I think that the public schools could develop programs and services to help make this happen.

4   At present, the educational programs on sex in our schools are limited. Often the first time the subject is introduced formally is in a Family Living class during the last semester of fifth grade. In our school district a county health nurse came weekly for one hour to instruct the class over an eight-week period. Prior to the class, parents were invited to attend a meeting to hear about the program and to ask questions and voice concerns. This was a good start. However, after that initial meeting, parents were given no role to play. While students were encouraged to discuss the class at home with their parents, this kind of interaction could have been promoted more by having students complete homework assignments and projects which required parental participation. Detailed information about class topics could have been sent home to give parents and children an opportunity to communicate and become more aware of each others' ideas and attitudes about this important subject. By fostering open communication at this early age, the school could have helped to develop behaviors and habits that might continue into the teen years.

5   There are other ways that the schools can foster educational opportunities for parents and children. School districts need to have educators on their staffs who can be available for parents who seek information and guidance. Many parents don't know what is "normal" sexual behavior for children of a particular age. They may rely heavily on their memories of their own experiences when they were that age, and these may or may not be accurate or reliable. These educators could conduct regular workshops and parent discussion groups as well as be available for individual meetings with concerned parents.

6   There will be people who object to any interference from the schools regarding sex education. They feel strongly that children should learn about sex exclusively from their parents. I agree that this would be the ideal situation; sex

education must be more than just learning about the mechanics of sex. Important values and attitudes about love and relationships must be transmitted as well. However, the depressing statistics about teen pregnancy seem to indicate that some parents have not been successful at educating their children about this area of life. While schools certainly can't do the whole job, they can provide an opportunity for parents and children to begin a discussion about sex and life that can continue beyond the classroom.

7   There have been successful programs instituted throughout communities in the United States which have involved state education funding. One such program, Young Adults for Positive Achievement, was initiated in approximately fifty schools in California and resulted in a significant drop in the teen pregnancy rate in those areas. This program consisted of pregnancy education and prevention for teens (Vaz 50). My plan builds on their idea of using education to prevent teen pregnancy. By including parents and educators, my proposal attacks the problem from two fronts rather than just one.

8   It is essential for parents to remain involved in their children's lives throughout childhood and adolescence. Children need to know what their parents expect of them and how their parents feel about sex and dating. The schools need to take an active role in making this happen by providing educational programs and services to promote communication and understanding between parents and children.

WORKS CITED

Campaign For Our Children. *The National Teen Pregnancy Clock.* 21 Apr. 1998 <http://www.cfoc.org/clock.html>.

The National Campaign to Prevent Teen Pregnancy. *Facts and Stats.* 14 Oct. 1998 <http://www.teenpregnancy.org>.

Rolling, Peggy C., and Michael F. Burnett. "The Influence of Open-Mindedness and Knowledge on Attitudes Toward Teen Pregnancy Among Family and Consumer Services Teachers." *Family and Consumer Services Research Journal.* 26.2 (1997): 141–59.

Sylvester, Kathleen. "Preventable Calamity: How to Reduce Teenage Pregnancy." *USA Today* March 1997: 32[†]. Lexis-Nexis. 20 October 1998. <http://web.lexis-nexis.com/universe>.

Vaz, Valerie. "Programs That Work: Young Adults for Positive Achievement." *Essence* Oct. 1995: 50.

QUESTIONS FOR ANALYSIS AND DISCUSSION

Briefly summarize the main points of Martha Balash's essay. Then answer the following questions about the essay to see how it fulfills our guidelines for a proposal argument:

1. Where does Balash identify the problem? Explain how she demonstrates that the problem is significant. Does she explain how the problem might affect the reader? Where does she do this?
2. What does Balash propose to solve the problem? In what paragraph do you find the solution stated?

3. According to Balash's essay, how will her solution help to solve the problem? Where does she demonstrate this?

4. Does Balash explain how her solution will work? Where does she do this? Does she provide enough detail for you to understand how it will work?

5. Has Balash anticipated objections to her solution? in which paragraphs? Find an example of this. How does she respond to the objection? How does she acknowledge her audience's concerns?

6. Does Balash seem aware of other programs that have been tried to solve the problem? Where does she refer to them in her essay?

7. What attitude about her subject does Balash convey to her readers? Does she seem reasonable and balanced? If so, find some examples of how she conveys this.

EXERCISES

1. Look in several current issues of a local or national newspaper to find examples of essays written by columnists about controversial issues. You might find these in your college library or online through the Internet. Make a list in your journal of the strategies different writers use to begin their essays. Bring your examples to class and work in a group to share your findings. You may want to photocopy your examples so that each member has a "catalogue" of good introductions to consider.

2. Repeat exercise 1, but this time collect examples of conclusions from argument essays. Your goal here is to compile a catalogue of endings to consult for examples.

3. Construct a formal outline for one of the essays other than "Indian Bones" in this chapter. Compare it with another student's. If there are places where your outlines differ, analyze how your readings are different.

4. Go back to the examples you found for exercise 1. Divide the essays you and the members of your group found into position and proposal arguments.

5. In your journal, respond to the ideas in Ron Karpati's or Robert Wachbroit's essay. With which of their reasons do you agree? How would you refute any of their reasons? Make a pro/con checklist that lists their reasons and points you might use to debate them.

6. Through the Internet or your library resources, do some reading on either Karpati's or Wachbroit's subject to find out how others view the issue. Create a dialogue among the various positions on the issue and explore their points of view to find common or shared concerns or values. With this knowledge, deliberate about how you stand on the issue.

7. If you were to write an argument essay of your own on either subject, how would you begin your essay? Experiment with a few introductions.

8. Write a first draft of your own essay on either topic.

chapter **6**

USING EVIDENCE

Thinking like an Advocate

Because this is a democracy, there's a widespread conviction in our society that having opinions is our responsibility as citizens—a conviction supported by our fast-forward multimedia culture. You see it on the nightly news every time a reporter sticks a microphone in the face of somebody on the street, or whenever Oprah Winfrey or Montel Williams moves into the studio audience. It's the heart of talk radio and television programs. In newspapers and magazines it comes in the form of "opinion polls" that tally up our positions on all sorts of weighty issues:

"Should condoms be distributed in high schools?"
"Is the economy this year in better shape than it was last year at this time?"
"Do you think the American judicial system is just?"
"Can the government do more to prevent domestic terrorism?"
"Is capital punishment a deterrent to crime?"
"Is the president doing a good job running the country?"

All this on-the-spot opinion making encourages people to take an immediate stand on an issue, whether or not they have sufficient understanding and information about it. However, holding an opinion on a matter does not necessarily mean you have investigated the issue, or that you've carefully considered the views of others or that you've gathered enough information to support your position. If you want to make successful arguments you need more than a gut reaction or simple reliance on yourself for the "truth."

This means thinking of yourself as an *advocate*—a prosecutor or defense attorney, if you like. You need a case to present to the jury of your readers, one that convinces them that your interpretation is plausible. Like an advocate, when you're constructing an argument you look for support to put before your readers: facts, statistics, people's experiences—in a word, *evidence.* The jury judges your argument both on the evidence you bring forth and on the interpretation of that evidence that you present. So, like an advocate, to write successful arguments you need to be able to understand and weigh the value of the *supporting evidence* for your case.

How Much Evidence Is Enough?

Like any advocate, you need to decide *how much* evidence to present to your readers. Your decision will vary from case to case, although with more practice you'll find it easier to judge. Common sense is a good predictor: If the evidence is enough to persuade you, it's probably enough to persuade like-minded readers. Unsympathetic readers may need more proof. The more unexpected or unorthodox your claim, the more evidence you need to convince skeptical readers. It's often as much a case of the *right* evidence as it is the *right amount* of evidence. One fact or statistic, if it touches on your readers' most valued standards and principles, may be enough to swing an argument for a particular group. Here's where outlining (Chapter 5) can help; an outline helps you make sure you present evidence for every assertion you make.

It's easier to gather too much evidence and winnow out the least effective than to have too little and try to expand it. One of our teachers used to call this the "Cecil B. DeMille strategy," after the great Hollywood producer. DeMille's theory was that if audiences were impressed by five dancers, they'd really be overwhelmed by five hundred—but just to be sure, he'd hire a thousand. That's a good strategy to have when writing arguments; you can always use a sentence such as "Of the 116 explosions in GMC trucks with side-mounted fuel tanks, four cases are most frequently cited" and then go on to discuss those four. You've let your readers know that another 112 are on record so they can weigh this fact when considering the four you examine in particular. You may never need a thousand pieces of evidence—or dancers—in an argument, but there's no harm in thinking big!

Why Arguments Need Supporting Evidence

Evidence is composed of facts and their interpretations. As we said in Chapter 1, facts are pieces of information that can be verified—that is, statistics, examples, testimony, historical details. For instance, it is a fact that SAT verbal scores across the nation have gone up for the last three years. One interpretation might be that students today are spending more time reading and less time watching television than students in the last decade. Another interpretation might be that secondary schools are putting more emphasis on language skills. A third might be that changes in the test or the prevalence of test-preparation courses has contributed to the higher scores.

In everyday conversation we make claims without offering supporting evidence: "Poverty is the reason why there is so much crime"; The president is doing a poor job handling the economy"; "Foreign cars are better than American cars." Although we may have good reasons to back up such statements, we're not often called upon to do so, at least not in casual conversation. In written arguments, however, presenting evidence is critical, and a failure to do so is glaring. Without supporting data and examples, an argument is hollow. It will bore the reader, fail to convince, and collapse under criticism. Moreover, you'll be in danger of making a hasty generalization by drawing a conclusion with too little evidence, as the following paragraph illustrates.

Video games are a danger to the mental well-being of children. Some children play video games for hours on end, and the result is that their behavior and concentration are greatly affected. Many of them display bad behavior. Others have difficulty doing other, more important things. Parents with young children should be more strict about what video games their children play and how long they play them.

Chances are this paragraph has not convinced you that video games are a threat to children. The sample lacks the details that might persuade you. For instance, exactly what kind of bad behavior do children display? And what specific video games out of the hundreds on the market are the real culprits? How is concentration actually affected? What "more important things" does the author mean? And how many hours of video consumption need occur before signs of dangerous behavior begin to manifest themselves?

Consider how much sharper and more persuasive the following rewrite is with the addition of specific details, facts, and examples:

Video games may be fun for children, but they can have detrimental effects on their behavior. They encourage violent behavior. A steady dose of some of the more violent games clearly results in more aggressive behavior. One study by the Department of Psychology at State University has shown that after two hours of "Urban Guerrilla," 60 percent of the 12 boys and 20 percent of the 12 girls tested began to mimic the street-fighting gestures—punching, kicking, karate-chopping each other. It was also shown that such games negatively affect concentration. Even half an hour after their game playing had lapsed, the boys had difficulty settling down to read or draw. Since my parents restricted my little brother's game playing to weekends, he concentrates when completing his homework and has fewer fights with his best friend.

The statistics from the academic study, as well as the concrete case of the writer's own brother give readers something substantial to consider. Presenting supporting evidence puts meat on the bones of your argument. (In Chapter 8 we will go into greater depth about how to gather research evidence, particularly from the library.)

Forms of Evidence

We hope that when you begin to develop an argument, you utilize debate, dialogue, and deliberation, as we suggested in Chapter 1. As you do this, you need to expand and deepen your understanding of the issue by collecting useful evidence from both sides of the issue. Don't neglect this critical step: Remember, the bulk of your argument is composed of material supporting your claim.

Writers enlist four basic kinds of evidence to support their arguments: personal experience (theirs and others'), outside authorities, factual references and examples, and statistics. We'll examine each separately, but you'll probably want to use combinations of these kinds of evidence when building your arguments in order to convince a wide range of readers.

Personal Experience—Yours and Others'

The power of personal testimony cannot be underestimated. Think of the number of movies that have failed at the box office in spite of huge and expensive ad campaigns. Think of the number of times you've read a book on the recommendation of friends—or taken a certain course or shopped at a particular store. You might have chosen the college you're attending based on the recommendation of someone you know. Many people find the word-of-mouth judgments that make up personal testimony the most persuasive kind of evidence.

In written arguments, the personal testimony of other people is used to affirm facts and support your claim. Essentially, their experiences provide you with eyewitness accounts of events that are not available to you. Such accounts may prove crucial in winning over an audience. Suppose you are writing about the rising abuse of alcohol among college students. In addition to statistics and hard facts, your argument can gain strength from quoting the experience of a first-year student who nearly died one night from alcoholic poisoning. Or, in an essay decrying discrimination against minorities in hiring, consider the authenticity provided by an interview of neighborhood residents who felt they were passed over for a job because of race or ethnic identity.

Your own eyewitness testimony can be a powerful tool of persuasion. Suppose, for example, that you are writing a paper in which you argue that the big teaching hospital in the city provides far better care and has a lower death rate than the small rural hospital in your town. The hard facts and statistics on the quality of care and comparative mortality rates you provide will certainly have a stark persuasiveness. But consider the dramatic impact on those figures were you to recount how your own trip to the rural emergency room nearly cost you your life because of understaffing or the lack of critical but expensive diagnostic equipment.

Personal observation is useful and valuable in arguments. However, you should be careful not to draw hasty generalizations from such testimony. The fact that you and three of your friends are staunchly in favor of replacing letter grades with a pass/fail system does not support the claim that the entire student body at your school is in favor of the conversion. You need a much greater sample. Likewise, the dislike most people in your class feel for a certain professor does not justify the claim that the university tenure system should be abolished. On such complex issues, you need more than personal testimony to make a case.

You also have to remember the "multiple-perspective" rule. As any police officer can tell you, there are as many versions of the "truth" of an incident as there are people who saw it. The people involved in a car accident see it one way (or more), yet witnesses in a car heading in the other direction may interpret events differently, as will people in an apartment six stories above the street on which the accident took place. Your job is to sort out the different testimonies and make sense of them.

Personal experience—yours and that of people you know—is valuable. However, on bigger issues you need statistics and data, as well as the evidence provided by outside authorities.

Outside Authorities

Think of the number of times you've heard statements such as these:

> "Scientists have found that . . ."
>
> "Scholars inform us that . . ."
>
> "According to his biographer, President Lincoln decided that . . ."

What these statements have in common is the appeal to outside authorities—people recognized as experts in a given field, people who can speak knowledgeably about a subject. Because authoritative opinions are such powerful tools of persuasion, you hear them all the time in advertisements. Automobile manufacturers quote the opinions of professional race car drivers; the makers of toothpaste cite dentists' claims; famous basketball players push brand-name sneakers all the time. Similarly, a good trial lawyer will almost always rely on forensic experts or other such authorities to help sway a jury.

Outside authorities can provide convincing evidence to support your ideas. However, there are times when expert opinion can be used inappropriately. This faulty use of authority can undermine the effectiveness of your argument. For the most part, experts usually try to be objective and fair-minded when asked for opinions. But, an expert with a vested interest in an issue might slant the testimony in his or her favor. The dentist who has just purchased a huge number of shares in a new toothpaste company would not be an unbiased expert. You wouldn't turn for an unbiased opinion on lung cancer to scientists working for tobacco companies, or ask an employee facing the loss of his or her job to comment on the advisability of layoffs. When you cite authorities, you should be careful to note any possibility of bias so your readers can fairly weigh the contributions. (This is often done through *attribution*; see Chapter 8.) Knowing that Professor Brown's research will benefit from construction of the supercollider doesn't make her enthusiasm for its other potential benefits less credible, but it does help your readers see her contributions to your argument in their proper context.

Another faulty use of authority is the use of an expert to provide evidence in a subject area in which he or she possesses no expertise. If you are going to cite authorities, you must make sure that they are competent; they should have expertise in their fields. You wouldn't turn to a professional beekeeper for opinions on laser surgery any more that you would quote a civil engineer on macroeconomic theory. And yet, just that is done all the time in advertising. Although it makes better sense to ask a veterinarian for a professional opinion about what to feed your pet, advertisers hire known actors to push dog food (as well as yogurt and skin cream). Of course, in advertising, celebrity sells. But that's not the case in most written arguments. It would not impress a critical reader to cite Tom Cruise's views on the use of fetal tissue or the greenhouse effect. Again, think about the profile of your audience. Whose expertise would they respect on your topic? Those are the experts to cite.

Factual References and Examples

Facts do as much to inform as they do to persuade, as we mentioned in Chapter 1. If somebody wants to sell you something, they'll pour on the details. For instance, ask the used car salesperson about that red 1996 Ford Explorer in the lot and he or she will hold forth about what a "creampuff" it is: only 18,400 original miles, mint condition, five-speed transmission with overdrive, all-black leather interior, and loaded—AC, power brakes, cruise control, premium sound system, captain's chair, and so on. Or listen to how the cereal manufacturers inform you that their toasted Os now contain "all-natural oat bran, which has been found to prevent cancer." Information is not always neutral. The very selection process implies intent. By offering specific facts or examples about your claim, you can make a persuasive argument.

The strategy in using facts and examples is to get readers so absorbed in the information that they nearly forget they are being persuaded to buy or do something. So common is this strategy in television ads that some have been given the name "infomercials"—ads that give the impression of being a documentary on the benefits of a product. For instance, you might be familiar with the margarine commercial narrated by a man who announces that at thirty-three years of age he had a heart attack. He then recounts the advice of his doctor for avoiding coronary disease, beginning with the need for exercise and climaxing with the warning about cutting down on cholesterol. Not until the very end of the ad does the narrator inform us that, taking advantage of his second chance, the speaker has switched to a particular brand of margarine, which, of course, is cholesterol free.

In less blatant form, this "informational" strategy can be found in newspaper columns and editorials, where authors give the impression that they are simply presenting the facts surrounding particular issues when in reality they may be attempting to persuade readers to see things their way. For instance, suppose in an apparently objective commentary a writer discusses how history is replete with people wrongfully executed for first-degree murder. Throughout the piece the author cites several specific cases in which it was learned too late that the defendant had been framed or that the real killer had confessed. On the surface the piece may appear to be simply presenting historical facts, but the more subtle intention may be to convince people that capital punishment is morally wrong. The old tagline from *Dragnet,* "Just the facts, ma'am," isn't quite the whole picture. How those facts are used is also part of their persuasive impact.

Often facts and examples are used to establish cause-and-effect relationships. It's very important, when both writing and reading arguments, to test the links the facts forge. While one event may indeed follow another, you can't automatically assume a causal relationship. This can result in a logical fallacy, in this case post hoc, ergo propter hoc. For instance, it may rain the day after every launch of the space shuttle, but does that prove that shuttle launches affect the weather in Florida? Similarly, we are all familiar with politicians who claim credit for improvements in the economy that have little to do with the legislation they have proposed. They hope to gain votes by having the public believe that there is a direct causal relationship between their actions and the economic improvement. Often this strategy backfires when opponents point out the lack of any actual connection.

Sometimes even experts disagree; one might see the rise in prostate cancer rates for vasectomy patients as reason to abolish the surgery; another might point to other contributing causes (diet, lack of exercise, hormonal imbalance). If you don't have the expertise to determine which of the conflicting experts is correct, you'll probably decide based on the *weight of the evidence*—whichever side has the most people or the most plausible reasons supporting it. This, in fact, is how most juries decide cases.

Statistics

People are impressed by numbers. Saying that 77 percent of the student body at your school supports a woman's right to choose is far more persuasive than saying that a lot of people on campus are pro-choice. **Statistics** have a special no-nonsense authority. Batting averages, medical statistics, polling results (election and otherwise), economic indicators, the stock market index, unemployment figures, scientific ratings, FBI statistics, percentages, demographic data—they all are reported in numbers. If they're accurate, statistics are difficult to argue against, though a skillful manipulator can use them to mislead.

The demand for statistics has made market research a huge business in America. During an election year, weekly and daily results on voters' opinions of candidates are released from various news organizations and TV networks, as well as independent polling companies such as the Harris and Gallup organizations. Most of the brand-name products you buy, the TV shows and movies you watch, or the CDs you listen to were made available after somebody did test studies on sample populations to determine the potential success of these items. Those same statistics are then used in promotional ads. Think of the number of times you've heard claims such as these:

> "Nine out of ten doctors recommend Zappo aspirin."
>
> "Our new Speed King copier turns out 24 percent more copies per minute."
>
> "Sixty-eight percent of those polled approve of women in military combat roles."

Of course, these claims bear further examination. If you polled only ten doctors, nine of whom recommended Zappo, that's not a big enough sample to imply that 90 percent of *all* doctors do. To avoid drawing a hasty generalization from too small a sample, avoid using sweeping words such as *all, always, never,* or *none.* Either be straightforward about the statistics supporting your claim, or limit your claim with qualifiers such as *some, many, often,* or *few.* As Mark Twain once observed, "There are lies, damned lies, and statistics."

Numbers don't lie, but they can be manipulated. Sometimes, to sway an audience, claim makers will cite figures that are inaccurate or dated, or they will intentionally misuse accurate figures to make a case. If, for instance, somebody claims that 139 students and professors protested the invitation of a certain controversial guest to your campus, it would be a distortion of the truth not to mention that another 1500 attended the talk and gave the speaker a standing ovation. Providing only those numbers or statistics that support the writer's claim and ignoring or concealing figures that might indicate otherwise is one way of stacking the deck. While this practice might deceive—at least temporarily—an uninformed audience, the writer risks damaging his or her credibility once the true figures are revealed.

When you are reading statistics, it is always wise to be skeptical. Likewise, when quoting numbers, try to be accurate and honest. Be certain that your sources are themselves accurate. In the 1996 presidential campaign, the Republican party claimed that Bill Clinton had raised taxes 128 times while governor of Arkansas, trying to impress upon voters the notion that Clinton frequently raised taxes. When this claim was investigated, voters discovered that the "tax increases" included raising fees on fishing licenses, imposing court costs on convicted criminals, and counting some increases several times. As the Democratic party pointed out in rebuttal, under the Republican means of calculating "tax increases," former President George Bush, a Republican, had raised taxes nearly 350 times!

Be on guard for the misleading use of statistics, a technique used all too frequently in advertising. The manufacturer that claims its flaked corn cereal is 100 percent cholesterol free misleads the public because no breakfast cereal of any brand contains cholesterol (which is found only in animal fats). French fries prepared in pure vegetable oil are also cholesterol free, but that doesn't mean that they're the best food for your health. Manufacturers that use terms like *cholesterol free, light,* and *low fat* are trying to get you to buy their products without really examining the

Preview: To Evaluate Supporting Evidence, Ask . . .

- Is the evidence sufficient?
- Is the evidence detailed enough?
- Is the evidence relevant?
- Does the evidence fit the claim?
- Is the evidence up to date and verifiable?
- Is the evidence biased?
- Is the evidence balanced and fairly presented?

basis for their nutritional claims. Although it's tempting to use such crowd-pleasing statistics, it's a good idea to avoid them in your own arguments because they are deceptive. If your readers discover your deception, your chances of persuading them to accept your position or proposal become unlikely.

Some Tips About Supporting Evidence

Because, as argument writers, you'll be using evidence on a routine basis, it will help you to develop a systematic approach to testing the evidence you want to use. Here are some questions to ask yourself about the evidence you enlist in an argument.

Do You Have a Sufficient Number of Examples to Support Your Claim?

You don't want to jump to conclusions based on too little evidence. Suppose you want to make the case that electric cars would be better for the environment than motor vehicles. If all you offer as evidence is the fact that electric vehicles don't pollute the air, your argument would be somewhat thin. Your argument would be much more convincing if you offered the following evidence: that in addition to zero emission at the tailpipe—which is good for the atmosphere—electric cars do not use engine fluids or internal combustion parts, all of which constitute wastes that contaminate our landfills and water supplies. Furthermore, because electric vehicles don't use gasoline or oil, the hazards associated with storage of such fluids are eliminated.

Likewise, you should avoid making hasty generalizations based on your own experience as evidence. For instance, if your Acme Airlines flight to Chattanooga was delayed last week, you shouldn't conclude that Acme Airlines always leaves late. However, you would have a persuasive case were you to demonstrate that over the last six months 47 percent of the frequent flyers you interviewed complained that Acme flights left late.

Is Your Evidence Detailed Enough?

The more specific the details, the more persuasive your argument. Instead of generalizations, cite figures, dates, and facts; instead of paraphrases, offer quotations from experts. Remember that your readers are subconsciously saying, "Show me! Prove it!" If you want to tell people how to bake bread, you wouldn't write, "Mix some flour with some yeast and water"; you'd say, "Dissolve one packet of yeast in 1 cup of warm water and let it sit for ten minutes. Then slowly mix in 3 cups of sifted whole wheat flour." Or, as in our electric car example above, instead of simply asserting that there would be none of the fluid or solid wastes associated with internal combustion vehicles, specify that in electric vehicles there would be no motor oil, engine coolants, transmission fluid or filters, spark plugs, ignition wires, and gaskets to end up in landfills. What your readers want are specifics—and that's what you should give them.

Is Your Evidence Relevant to the Claim You Make or Conclusion You Reach?

Select evidence based on how well it supports the point you are arguing, not on how interesting, novel, or humorous it is or how hard you had to work to find it. Recall that using evidence that is unrelated or irrelevant is a logical fallacy called a non se-quitur. For instance, if you are arguing about whether John Lennon is the most influential songwriter in rock and roll history, you wouldn't mention that he had two sons or that he owned dairy cattle; those are facts, but they have nothing to do with the influence of his lyrics. Historian Barbara Tuchman relates that in writing *The Guns of August,* she discovered that the kaiser bought his wife the same birthday present every year: 12 hats of his choosing, which he required her to wear. Tuchman tried to use this detail in Chapter 1, then in Chapter 2, and so on, but was finally obligated to relegate the detail to a stack of notecards marked "Unused." It just didn't fit, even though for her it summarized his stubborn selfishness. (See did work it into a later essay, which is why we know about it.) Learn her lesson: Irrelevant evidence distracts an audience and weakens an argument's persuasive power.

Politicians have been known to deliberately use irrelevant evidence to distract the public attention away from the true issue. This is a logical fallacy called a **red herring.** For example, when Independent Counsel Kenneth Starr presented the results of a grand jury inquiry into the actions of President Bill Clinton, Clinton's defenders at first claimed that Starr was engaged in a right-wing conspiracy against the president; they did not respond directly to the charges in the report, hoping to use a red herring, namely the independent counsel's political associations, to deflect attention away from the serious charges leveled in the report. The tactic made it appear that they lacked an effective defense against the accusations.

Does Your Conclusion (or Claim) Exceed the Evidence?

Don't make generalizations about entire groups when your evidence points to select members. Baseball may be the national pastime, but it would be unwise to claim that *all* Americans love baseball. Experience tells you that some Americans prefer football or basketball, while others don't like any sports. Claims that are out of proportion to the evidence can result in a fallacy called the **bandwagon appeal.** The bandwagon appeal suggests to the audience that they should agree with the writer because everyone else does, rather than because the writer has supplied compelling evidence to support the reasons and claim. This is a favorite strategy of advertisers, who work to convince us that we should buy a certain product because everyone else is doing so. While this strategy is in itself fallacious, these salespeople are often unable to produce adequate evidence to support their sweeping claims of nationwide popularity for their product.

Is Your Evidence Up-to-Date and Verifiable?

You want to be sure that the evidence you enlist isn't so dated or vague that it fails to support your claim. For instance, figures demonstrating an increase in the rate of teen pregnancy will not persuade your audience if the numbers are ten years old. Similarly, it wouldn't be accurate to say that Candidate Oshawa fails to support the

American worker because fifteen years ago he purchased a foreign car. His recent and current actions are far more relevant.

When you're citing evidence, your readers will expect you to be specific enough for them to verify what you say. A writer supporting animal rights may cite the example of rabbits whose eyes were burned by pharmacological testing, but such tests have been outlawed in the United States for many years. Another writer may point to medical research that appears to abuse its human subjects, but not name the researchers, the place where the testing took place, or the year in which it occurred. The readers have no way of verifying the claim and may become suspicious of the entire argument because the factual claims are so difficult to confirm.

Is Your Evidence Slanted?

Sometimes writers select evidence that supports their case while ignoring evidence that does not. Often referred to as stacking the deck, this practice makes for an unfair argument, and one that could be disastrous for the arguer. Even though some of your evidence has merit, your argument will be dismissed if your audience discovers that you slanted or suppressed evidence.

For example, suppose you heard a friend make the following statements: "If I were you, I'd avoid taking a course with Professor Gorman at all costs. He gives surprise quizzes, he assigns fifty pages a night, and he refuses to grade on a curve." Even if these reasons are true, that may not be the whole truth. Suppose you learned that Professor Gorman is, in fact, a very dynamic and talented teacher whose classes successfully stimulate the learning process. By holding back that information, your friend's argument is suspect.

Sometimes writers will take advantage of their readers' lack of information on a topic and offer evidence that really doesn't support their claims. Recently several newspapers reported that a study written up in the *Archives of Internal Medicine* proved that eating nuts prevents heart attacks. According to the study, some thirty thousand Seventh-Day Adventists were asked to rate the frequency with which they ate certain foods. Those claiming to eat nuts five or more times a week reported fewer heart attacks. What the newspapers failed to report was that all Seventh-Day Adventists are vegetarians, and that those who ate more nuts also ate fewer dairy products (which are high in cholesterol and saturated fat, both of which contribute to heart disease) and eggs (also high in cholesterol) than others in the study. Newspapers have failed to report that all the subsequent pro-nut publicity was distributed by a nut growers' association.*

It is to your benefit to present all relevant evidence so that you clearly weigh both sides of an issue. As we discussed in Chapter 4, you want to demonstrate to your readers that you have made an effort to consider other perspectives and that your conclusions are fair and balanced. Otherwise your argument might not be

---

*Mirkin, Gabe and Diana Rich. *Fat Free Flavor Full,* Boston: Little, Brown, 1995: 51.

To Test Your Evidence for Logical Fallacies, Ask These Questions

Stacking the deck	Did I present evidence that only supports my point of view? Have I withheld evidence that might contradict it?
Non-sequitur	Is my evidence related and relevant to the reasons or claim it is supporting?
Hasty generalization	Have I provided sufficient evidence to support my conclusions?
Red herring	Does all of my evidence pertain to the true issue? Have I tried to distract my audience's attention with irrelevant concerns?
Bandwagon appeal	Can my evidence stand on its own? Have I argued that my audience should support my ideas because they reflect a popular viewpoint?
Faulty use of authority	Are the authorities I cite actually experts in my subject area? Could my authorities be biased because of their background or their professional or political associations?

taken seriously. Let's return to the argument that electric cars are more beneficial to the environment than cars with internal combustion engines. Your key evidence is the fact that electric cars do not use petroleum products and various motor parts that contribute to the pollution of air, land, and waterways. If you left your argument at that, you would be guilty of suppressing an important concern regarding electric vehicles: the disposal of the great amounts of lead in the huge electric vehicles' batteries. Failure to acknowledge that opposing point reduces your credibility as a writer. Readers would wonder either about your attempt at deception or about your ignorance. Either way they would dismiss your argument.

A much better strategy would be to confront this concern and then try to overcome it. While acknowledging that lead is a dangerous pollutant, you could point out that more than 95 percent of battery lead is recycled. You could also point out that progress is being made to improve battery technology and create alternatives such as the kinds of fuel cells used in spacecraft.* The result is a balanced presentation that makes your own case stronger.

---

*May, Thomas J. "Electric Cars Will Benefit the Environment and the Economy," *The Boston Globe* 10 Aug. 1994: 15.

In summary, using evidence means putting yourself in an advocate's place. You'll probably do this while building your argument, and certainly when you revise; then you should see yourself as an advocate for the other side and scrutinize your evidence as if you were going to challenge it in court. As a reader, you need to keep that Missouri "show me!" attitude in mind at all times. A little healthy skepticism will help you test the information you're asked to believe. The next chapter will help you do so.

Sample Argument for Analysis

The following is a paper written by a first-year student, Meg Kelley. Read it carefully and take notes about it in your argument journal. Then, either individually or in your peer group, answer the questions that follow.

RU 486: The French Abortion Pill and Its Benefits
Meg Kelley

1   For many years, abortion and women's rights have been heated issues in this country. The issue has always been which is more sacred, the right of Americans to choose, or the right of unborn human beings to live. In 1980, a new side to the conflict was introduced when French scientists developed a pill called RU 486.

2   According to a study published in the *New England Journal of Medicine* in April 1998, RU 486, often referred to as the "French abortion drug," is a steroid, mifipristone, which disrupts the implantation of a fertilized egg into the walls of the uterus. Taken in conjunction with misoprostol, a prostaglandin which causes uterine contractions, women can successfully abort a fetus without surgical intervention. Banned as illegal in the United States for the last decade, RU 486 has been tentatively approved by the U.S. Food and Drug Administration based upon the scientific evidence that it is "safe and effective" for women in the early stages of pregnancy (Spitz et al.; Maugh). However, RU 486 cannot receive full FDA approval until a manufacturer is willing to step forward and take responsibility for its production and distribution. As of today, no one has been willing to do this for fear of reprisals and boycotts from anti-abortion groups ("Safe Drug").

3   It is unfortunate that American women are still prevented from taking advantage of this alternative to surgical abortion because of the pressures being exerted by certain political groups in our country. This drug should be made available to the women who need it, both for idealistic reasons like the "certain inalienable rights" granted under the U.S. Constitution, and for the practical

reason that it offers a safe alternative to surgical abortion, with few side effects, and may offer further, undiscovered advantages.

4   There are hundreds of thousand of unwanted pregnancies in the United States every year. The unwanted pregnancy may be due to a rape in which the woman is helplessly victimized and left with the child of her attacker. A teenage girl who was never taught about effective contraception, or who was told myths about how to have "safe" sex ("You can't get pregnant the first time") may find herself in this situation. Contraceptives fail: a ripped condom, a wrongly used diaphragm. The birth control pill is only 99.9% safe; what about the other 0.1%? Or what about the woman who forgets to take the pill? Everyone makes stupid mistakes. Should she have to pay for hers for the rest of her life? Sure, many people will say, "You play, you pay." But we're not talking about making a bad bet on a horse; we're talking about a normal, biological human behavior.

5   Abortions are performed every day in the U.S. on women who find themselves in an unplanned pregnancy. For young girls constrained by parental consent laws in some states, illegal abortions are the route to salvation. Many of these abortions are unsafe, performed by non-doctors using unsterile instruments and risky procedures, which lead to tremendous complications, infection, illness, and sometimes death. Then there are the legal abortions. These are more sterile, performed by qualified medical professionals, and offer less danger to women's physical health. However, in these, as in any surgical procedure, there can be complications. The women are still scared, still have to "go under the knife" so to speak, and many have to fight their way through lines of people screaming "Don't kill your baby" in order even to get into the clinic. The women may have to travel long distances to gain access to the clinic, stay overnight because of legal waiting periods, take time off from work or school to have the surgery, and then recover afterwards.

6   However, for many, no amount of bed rest can heal the emotional pain in a situation like this. If you get rid of a part of you, your own flesh and blood, you will suffer, regardless of how you do it. Surgical abortion often leaves women feeling psychologically violated as well, and often they lose confidence in their sexuality, simply due to the nature of the surgery.

7   With RU 486, as Susan Jacoby points out, there are no incisions, no hospital stays, no absences from work, just the pill, pure and simple. The abortion pill has been found to have a few side effects. The study in the *New England Journal of Medicine* reported that some women experienced nausea, vomiting, and vaginal bleeding, which can be uncomfortable and inconvenient (Spitz et al.). However, these symptoms may not be any worse that those that result from a surgical abortion. The advantage of RU 486 is that women can take it easily and privately in their doctor's office. It does not involve an expensive clinic or hospital stay. Moreover, RU 486 is believed to have other useful uses. One particularly promising one is as a treatment for breast cancer. Breast cancer depends on progesterone to survive; the antiprogestins of RU 486 kill the cancer by attacking what it lives on (Jacoby). And scientists are still testing the drug for other productive uses.

8   Although the practical reasons for approving RU 486 to be marketed in the United States are many, there is one important matter that should be the ultimate reason for its approval, and that is principle. The Declaration of Independence, the blueprint of American freedom, states that "all men [and women] are created equal" and that every person has "certain unalienable rights" including "life, liberty, and the pursuit of happiness," which cannot be denied them by any government. Women in the United States should have the right to choose their fates themselves. Basically, by preventing availability of RU 486, these anti-abortion groups are limiting women's choices. Although abortion is now legal and RU 486 has been found to be "safe and effective," these groups are still trying to make RU 486 unavailable because that would make abortion less accessible. The citizens of the United States have not asked for such restrictions; what we have is a small group of people whose ideology is dictating what the general population can do. This is truly an issue that should be decided by the people most affected by it.

9   Many people who oppose RU 486 will cite the basic pro-life reasons why the pill should not be available. First, they feel that the unborn fetus has the right to the "life" in that "life, liberty, and the pursuit of happiness." Certainly, any child should have the right to all these things, but bringing an unwanted child into a more-than-likely single parent home with a low income and poor opportunities is not guaranteeing these rights, but almost surely destroying them. As Henry David Thoreau in *Walden* states, "And not, when I come to die, discover that I had not lived. I did not wish to live that what was not life, living is so dear" (257). "Life" in this case means more than heartbeats, breathing, walking, talking. It means being "alive," able to enjoy childhood without having to get a job at age ten to help support your family, or growing up in a bug-infested apartment where there is no heat or there are people being murdered outside your door, of continuing the vicious cycle of teen pregnancy by likely becoming a teen parent yourself. The life envisioned by the Founding Fathers [and Mothers] does not encompass being kicked out by your parents, dropping out of school, being forced to live on the streets, begging for change and scavenging food out of trash barrels. Isn't forcing a baby to live and make its way in the world under such miserable conditions much crueler than flushing a fertilized egg out of the body before it can develop into a baby?

10   The people who oppose RU 486 will also say that the abortion pill, if available on the U.S. market, will also be used as a means of birth control, since women won't bother to use contraception if they have access to such an easy way to abort a fetus. I personally don't feel that the majority of sexually active women in the U.S. are so ignorant or lazy as to prefer any kind of abortion to safe precautions. Besides, most women know that contraception is also used to prevent the spread of some sexually transmitted diseases. They aren't going to be more likely to expose themselves to infertility or death just because RU 486 is available. The final reason opponents give for banning RU 486 is that there could be yet-unknown side effects. Well, this is true of all drugs. No one is ever sure that the side effects that have already been discovered will be the only ones

for any drug. We allow the use of many experimental drugs in this country, including chemotherapy for cancer and AZT for AIDS, without outlawing them because they may have unknown side effects. As long as the women who take the drug are informed of the known side effects and the possibility of more, they should be allowed to use the drug under a physician's supervision.

11   I feel very strongly that the abortion pill should be released onto the U.S. market, in order to better the lives of many. We have so many impoverished, hopeless families out there, trapped in a cycle of poverty because of a mistake a man and woman make in a moment of time. We should give these women a chance to make something of their lives without these unplanned pregnancies, thus sparing the children as well. Why should we force these women to bear these unwanted babies when they are not ready or able to care for them, and consequently have two bitter, possibly impoverished people in the world, where there could have been one (sadder but) wiser person making something of her life and having children when she was prepared for that responsibility? RU 486 provides a safe alternative to all this misfortune, one in which everyone will benefit. Certainly allowing the distribution of RU 486 will not solve all the problems of poverty, homelessness, and inequality in this country, but it would relieve one of the worst consequences of those problems. The principle behind the right to choose is much too great to be jeopardized by a political group that does not like the idea of abortion.

WORKS CITED

Jacoby, Susan. "What You Thought: RU 486." *Glamour* Dec. 1992: 116.

Maugh, Thomas H., II. "U.S. Study of Abortion Drug Finds It to Be Safe." *Los Angeles Times* 30 April 1998: A1. *Lexis-Nexis.* 7 May 1998 <http://web.lexis-nexis.com/universe>.

"Safe Drug, No Sales." Editorial. *Washington Post* 18 May 1998: A16. Lexis-Nexis. 26 May 1998 <http://web.lexis-nexis.com/universe>.

Spitz, Irving et al. "Early Pregnancy Termination with Mifepristone and Misoprostol in the United States." *New England Journal of Medicine* 338 (1998): 1241–7.

Thoreau, Henry David. *Walden and Other Writings.* Ed. William Howarth. New York: Modern Library, 1981.

QUESTIONS FOR ANALYSIS AND DISCUSSION

1. What claim (Chapter 2) is Kelley arguing? What are the reasons for her claim? What do you think the pros and cons she listed in developing this argument might have been?

2. Who is Kelley's target audience? What clues does she give you? What values and prejudices might the readership hold?

3. What different forms of evidence (personal, outside authorities, factual references, statistics) does Kelley provide? Which form(s) of evidence does she rely on most?

4. Evaluate the supporting evidence Kelley provides. Is it relevant? Is it detailed enough? Does it seem dated and verifiable? Does her claim exceed her evidence? Does her evidence strike you as slanted? If you were her reader, would

you be persuaded by her reasons? What changes (if any) in evidence would you recommend to help her make her argument more persuasive.

5. Use debate, dialogue, and deliberation to respond to Kelley's essay in your journal (see Chapter 1 to review this process):

a. Make a pro/con checklist to identify the ideas with which you disagree.

b. Create a dialogue to help you understand and respond productively to Kelley's ideas.

c. Given what you've learned through debate and dialogue, write at least a page in which you deliberate about the conflicting issues that Kelley raises in her essay. How does your understanding of Kelley's position change or modify your own viewpoint? Is there a way to reconcile conflicting concerns about this subject?

chapter 7

ESTABLISHING CLAIMS

Thinking like a Skeptic

You have decided the issue you're going to argue. With the aid of debate and dialogue you've sharpened your ideas and considered alternative perspectives and common concerns. You've thought about your audience and determined what you have in common, where you might agree, and where you might disagree. After deliberating you have formulated a working claim, and you have gathered solid evidence to support it. Now it's time to establish the logical structure of your argument and decide how best to arrange this material to persuade your readers.

If you've ever tried handing in a paper made up of slapped-together evidence and first-draft organization, you've probably discovered a blueprint for disaster. Perhaps you didn't test your work, didn't revise it, or didn't think about how it would appeal to a reader. You assumed that because *you* understood how the parts fit together, your readers would as well. To help you detect and correct these problems, this chapter focuses on thinking like a *skeptic*—a skeptical building inspector, to be exact—because a skeptical attitude works best.

To construct a persuasive argument, one that has a chance of convincing your readers, you have to pay careful attention to the logical structure you are building. You can't take anything for granted; you have to question every step you take, every joist and joint. You have to ask yourself if you're using the right material for the right purpose, the right tool at the right time. In other words, you have to think like a building inspector examining a half-built two-story house—one whose builder is notoriously crafty at compromising quality. A healthy skepticism—and a logical system—help uncover flaws before they create a disaster.

The Toulmin Model

Stephen Toulmin, a British philosopher and logician, analyzed hundreds of arguments from various fields of politics and law.* He concluded that nearly every argument has certain patterns and parts. The best arguments, Toulmin found, are those

---

*Toulmin, Stephen, *The Uses of Argument.* Cambridge: Cambridge University Press, 1958.

addressed to skeptical audience, one eager to question the reasoning where it seems faulty, to demand support for wobbly assumptions, and to raise opposing reasons.

The slightly re-tooled version of the Toulmin model we describe below encourages you to become a skeptical audience. It provides useful everyday terms to help you unearth, weigh, and, if necessary, fix an argument's logical structures. It lets you verify that the major premises in your argument or those of your opposition are clear and accurate, helps you determine whether repairs to your claims are needed and whether counterarguments are addressed. It shows you where supporting evidence may be needed and helps you avoid logical fallacies. And, since Toulmin's terms are designed to be broadly practical, they allow you to present your case to a wide variety of readers.

Toulmin's Terms

According to Toulmin, a fully developed argument has six parts. They are the *claim,* the *grounds,* the *warrant,* the *backing,* the *qualifiers,* and the *rebuttals.*

The Claim

The **claim** is the assertion you are trying to prove. It is the position you take in your argument, often as a proposal with which you are asking your reader to agree. In a well-constructed argument, each part makes its ultimate claim, its conclusion, seem inevitable.

The Grounds

Just as every argument contains a claim, every claim needs supporting evidence. The **grounds** are the statistics, research studies, facts, and examples that bolster your claim and that your audience accepts without requiring further proof.

The Warrant

The claim is usually stated explicitly. However, underlying the claim are a number of assumptions and principles that are also critical to the success of your argument. These are the **warrants** that implicitly support your argument by connecting your claim to the grounds. They enable your audience to follow the reasoning in your argument. The success of your argument depends on whether the audience accepts the often half-buried assumptions, commonly held values, legal or moral principles, laws of nature, commonsense knowledge, or shared beliefs.

Visualizing how arguments are built and work can help you understand their structure. Imagine, then, an Amish barn raising—or the way a lot of very un-Amish suburban houses are constructed these days. After the foundation is dug and laid, prefabricated walls are put up. They're then stabilized by buttressing boards that are jammed diagonally between the walls and the ground. Think of the warrant as an argument's half-buried foundation. Everything is based on this foundation—including the argument's walls, its claims. The grounds are like those buttressing boards: they are lines of evidence that hold the walls up and together. The conclusion is the roof. The difference between arguments and buildings is that these buttressing boards, the grounds for your argument, aren't taken away when the argument's structure is complete.

The Backing

Because your warrant is an assumption, you cannot be certain that it will always be accepted by your readers. So you must provide reasons to back it up. These reasons, called *backing,* indicate that the warrant is reliable in a particular argument, though it doesn't have to be true in all cases at all times.

The Qualifiers

Qualifiers provide a way to indicate when, why, and how your claim and warrant are reliable. They're words or phrases such as *often, probably, possibly, almost always;* verbs like *may* and *might, can* and *could;* or adjectives and adverbs that yoke your claim to some condition. The subtlest kind of qualifier is an adjective that acknowledges that your claim is true to a degree: "Coming from a dysfunctional family *often* makes it *harder* to resist the angry lure of crime." The qualifiers *often* and *harder* imply that the statement is conditional and not absolute. They allow for exceptions.

You need to consider a few qualifications about using qualifiers; like antibiotics, they're too powerful to use unwisely. Using too few qualifiers can indicate that you're exaggerating your argument's validity. As we've mentioned in previous chapters, common fallacies, such as *hasty generalizations* are often potentially valid arguments that go astray by not qualifying their claims enough, if at all. Using *no* qualifiers can result in a claim that is too general and sweeping. Although many students think a qualified claim is a weak claim, in fact, the qualified claim is often the most persuasive. Few truths are *completely* true; few claims are *always* right. A well-qualified claim, then, shows that the writer respects both the difficulty of the issue and the intelligence of the reader.

Nevertheless, qualifiers alone cannot substitute for reasoning your way to the tough, subtle distinctions on which the most persuasive arguments depend. For example, look at the claim that "Innocent people have an inviolable right to life." It's wisely qualified with the word "innocent" since just saying "People have an inviolable right to life" wouldn't hold up. Hitler, after all, was a human. Did he too have "an inviolable right to life"? But even *innocent* is not qualification enough. It raises two many tough, troubling questions. "Innocent" of what? "Innocent" by whose judgment, and why? What if killing a few innocent people were the only way to end a war that is killing *many* innocent people?

Using a lot of qualifiers, therefore, is no guarantee that your argument is carefully reasoned. In fact, strongly qualifying your argument's claim may be a sign that you doubt your argument's validity. But such doubt can itself be encouraging. Misusing or overusing qualifiers can indicate that your instinct of anxiety is right—that you've discovered better reasons to doubt your initial argument than to defend it. In fact, acknowledging the appeal of a flawed claim—and describing how you only discovered its flaws once you tried trumpeting its strengths—is an effective way of earning the reader's respect. It shows you to be an honest arguer capable of learning from errors—and thus worth learning *from.*

Deciding what to state and what to imply is a large part of writing any good argument. Just as a building's cross-beams don't have to be visible to be working, not everything important in an argument has to be stated. For example, if someone were to claim that winters in Minnesota are "mostly long and cold," we probably wouldn't stop the flow of argument to ask him to define the qualifier *mostly.* We'd instead keep the qualifier in mind, and let the Minnesotan's definition of "mostly" emerge, implied, from the rest of the story. Similarly, it's sometimes wise to leave your argument's qualifiers implied.

Still, it's often better to risk belaboring the obvious. To minimize the chances that your reader will misunderstand (or altogether miss) your meaning, qualify your claims as clearly and explicitly as possible. "Reading" the argument you're writing like a skeptical reader will help you decide which qualifiers are needed, where they are needed, and how explicitly they need to be stated.

The Rebuttals

Reading your argument skeptically also allows you to participate, answer, and even preempt rebuttals. **Rebuttals** represent the exceptions to the claim. There are many different kinds of rebuttals, and any persuasive argument ought to acknowledge and incorporate the most important ones. Rebuttals are like large-scale qualifiers. They acknowledge and explain the conditions or situations in which your claim would not be true—while still proving how your claim *is* true under other conditions. It's wise, then, to anticipate such rebuttals by regularly acknowledging all your argument's limits. This acknowledgment will prompt you to craft your claims more carefully.

Let's say, for example, that a sportswriter argues that allowing big-market baseball teams to monopolize talent ruins competition by perpetuating dynasties. Your rebuttal might be to cite the overlooked grounds of ignored evidence—grounds that complicate, if not contradict, the writer's claim: "Then why have small-market teams won four of the last ten World Series?" Had the sportswriter anticipated and integrated this rebuttal, she could have improved the argument—from her warrant on up. Her argument could have taken into account this rebuttal in the form of more careful qualifications. "While the rule of money doesn't guarantee that the richer teams will always win the World Series, it does make it more difficult for hard-pressed teams to compete for available talent." This is now, of course, a less sweeping claim—and, therefore, more precise and persuasive.

Of course, no writer can anticipate their readers' every rebuttal, nor should the writer even try. But you should test your argument by trying to rebut it yourself or working with classmates in small groups. Then revise your arguments with those rebuttals in mind.

Review: Six Parts of an Argument

Claim	The assertion you are trying to prove
Grounds	The supporting evidence for the claim
Warrant	A generalization that explains why the evidence supports the claim
Backing	The reasons that show the warrant is reliable
Qualifiers	The words that show when, how, and why your claim is reliable
Rebuttal	The exceptions to the claim

Field Work: Excavating Warrants

Excavating your warrants in order to explicate your argument can help you in several ways: you persuade your reader more effectively, detect flaws in your own argument, and identify the cause of otherwise confusing debates more quickly.

For example, let's say you want to argue that all students in American schools should be taught in English rather than in the students' native or family languages. The grounds that you use to support this claim are that fluency in English is essential for success in American society. For your audience to accept the connection between your claim and your grounds, you and they must agree on several warrants that underlie it. The first might be the assumption that schools prepare students for success in U.S. society. Since one of the purposes of an education is to develop skills such as reading, writing, and thinking critically that are considered basic requirements for success, most of your audience would likely accept this assumption. Therefore, it can be left implied and unstated.

The next two warrants implied by your claim may not be as readily acceptable to your audience as the one above and will need to be explicitly supported in your essay. The first is that our English language skills affect whether we are successful. The second warrant, implied by the first, is that individuals who are not fluent in English will not be successful members of society. These warrants will need considerable backing to show that they are reliable. First of all, you will have to define *success*. Are you thinking of financial success, career success, or social success? Without a clear explanation of what you mean by success, your argument will be weakened. Second, once you have defined success you will need to provide backing to support your warrants. How do English language skills enable individuals to succeed, as you have defined it? How are individuals who lack fluency in English adversely affected? You will want to provide additional backing in the form of evidence, examples, and statistics to demonstrate that English language skills have a significant impact on an individual's chances for success.

Warrants

Notice the many layers of warrants that can underlie a single claim:

Claim	All students in American public schools should be taught in English-only classrooms.
Grounds	Fluency in English is essential for success in American society.
Warrant	Schools prepare students for success in our society.
Warrant	Success in American society can be determined by our English language skills.
Warrant	Individuals who are not fluent in English will not succeed in our society.
Warrant	Teaching classes only in the English language will ensure that students will be fluent in English.

Your last warrant is particularly important because it establishes a critical link between your claim that all students should be taught in English and the need for fluency to succeed. This warrant assumes non-native speaking students will achieve greater fluency in English in the English-only classroom. You will need additional backing to prove this warrant, especially when you take into account possible rebuttals. For instance, what about students who enter U.S. schools with no English skills at all? How can they learn the required curriculum with no fluency in English? Will English-only classrooms fail to teach them language skills as well as subject matter? Will this approach alienate them from the American educational system and, thus, from success in our society? Making your responses to these rebuttals explicit will strengthen your argument.

Using Toulmin's approach to analyze your argument allows you to dig beneath the surface of your claim to find the underlying assumptions that form its foundation. It also allows your audience to see that even if they disagree with your claim, they may agree with many of the principles and assumptions that support it. Revealing this common ground, however hidden it lies, can provide opportunities to begin a dialogue that emerges from the recognition of shared values and beliefs. For instance, take the notoriously divisive issue of capital punishment. Those who support capital punishment say, in essence, "A human life is so precious that anyone who is guilty of depriving another of it should forfeit his or her own life." The opposing side says, in effect, "Human life is so precious that we have no right to deprive another of it no matter what the cause." By digging down to the warrants that underlie these positions, we may be surprised to find that the two sides have much in common: a respect for and appreciation of the value of human life. This discovery, of course, is no guarantee that we can reconcile dramatically opposing views on a particular issue. But the recognition of

To Avoid Errors in Logic, Check for These Logical Fallacies

Post hoc, ergo propter hoc	Be certain to demonstrate a cause-effect relationship between events by uncovering all warrants that underlie your claim.
Slippery slope argument	Make explicit the chain of events that link a situation to its possible outcome. Provide proof that this progression will inevitably occur.

commonality might provide a first step toward increasing understanding—if not consensus—between opposing sides.

Digging deeply to excavate your warrants can also help you avoid two common logical fallacies: post hoc, ergo propter hoc and slippery slope arguments. A post hoc, ergo propter hoc fallacy occurs when the writer mistakenly draws a casual relationship between two or more events or situations that are unrelated or simply co-incidental. Similarly, a slippery slope argument is based on an assumption that a particular outcome is inevitable if certain events happen or if a situation is allowed to continue. In both cases, the writer fails to identify and support the underlying warrants that would create a convincing logical link.

Sample Arguments for Analysis

Now let's turn to three sample arguments to see how our version of the Toulmin model can help you test your own arguments more effectively. Our first argument essay was written by first-year student Melissa Spokas. Read through her essay carefully, making notes in your journal. Notice whether and how its parts work together—and where some of the parts need to be reworked. Then respond to the questions that follow.

For the Love of the Game
Melissa Spokas

1   Picture this. You're an Olympic-caliber swimmer. You're training hard every day. The Olympic Trials come and go. Before you know it, you're a member of the U.S. Olympic swim team. You're training longer and harder than ever before, for the major goal of your life is in your grasp. The Olympics come and you are favored to do well; some even pick you as a potential winner.

2   You step onto the starting blocks; the gun is fired. You dive into the cold still water and swim the fastest time of your life, only to be touched out at the wall by another swimmer. She's a relative unknown who's never before medalled in world-class competition. But suddenly she's taller, heavier, more muscular than you've ever seen her.

3   You suspect that she's been taking drugs, probably anabolic steroids. Her changed, more masculine appearance, as well as her markedly improved time suggest this. But drug test results taken right after the race show no signs of drugs in her system. Somehow, you're convinced that she cheated and beat the testing system. Bitterly you ask the question, "Shouldn't there be mandatory drug testing for all competitors, not just a few, and not just at pre-announced times?"

4   The intent of the Olympic drug testing program is to eliminate any competitive edge that results from the use of synthetic aids (Hainline and Wadler 197). Drug testing was introduced in 1968, but it wasn't until the 1976 Summer Games in Montreal that testing for anabolic steroids began. Since that time, nearly 100 athletes have tested positive for steroid use in Olympic competition.

5   Different athletic organizations have differing policies on drug testing. For example, the U.S. Olympic Committee publishes a banned substance list, then tests its top finishers and also randomly samples other team members (Hainline and Wadler 198). If an athlete tests positive, he or she is suspended for four years; in the realm of world class athletics, with its brief career length, this effectively ends an athlete's competitive career. The athletic federations of other countries have different policies; some, as in the former East Germany, devoted considerable ingenuity to helping their athletes "beat" the tests. Some other organizations use drug prevention education instead of mandatory drug testing; this is still primarily the case in high school athletics.

6   And who should be tested? That opinion varies; some say only the top finishers, while others argue for random testing of participants. There are four common options; the first is no testing at all. The second is "to test athletes for probable or reasonable cause" (Hainline and Wadler 197). Such testing is done when there is suspicion of the athlete using a substance on the banned list; however, sometimes prescribed or over-the-counter medications may cause positive tests. Female athletes taking birth control pills are particularly vulnerable to this trap. The third option is mandatory random testing of all participants, and the fourth is mandatory testing of top finishers at announced times, such as after a competition.

7   I believe that the third option is the only plausible one and that it should be adopted by all countries who send athletes to the Olympics. Testing should occur randomly: in training, at meets, or in the off-season. If athletes know when they are to be tested, they can "taper down" so that no trace of drugs will be found in their system on a particular date. Ben Johnson's famous disqualification from the 1988 Olympics as due to a miscalculation of when he should have started tapering down; this mathematical mistake stripped him of the title "World's Fastest Human." Random testing will make it impossible for athletes

and their trainers to cheat the intent of drug testing by tapering down. It will force them to reduce if not abandon taking anabolic steroids to enhance their performances, for the chance of losing their careers and potential earnings will be too great.

8   Drugs like anabolic steroids give an unfair advantage to athletes who use them; this isn't what sports, particularly Olympic sports, are supposed to be about. They're not supposed to be about winning at all costs, but about competition and love of the sport; these are the terms cited in the Olympic Creed each participant recites at the beginning of the Games. Anabolic steroids have also been proven physically harmful to human health, as victims like the late Lyle Alzado demonstrate. In the short term, steroids yield larger muscle mass and improved performance, but in the long term, steroid users face a number of debilitating, even potentially fatal, physical consequences from using the drug. Sports are supposed to improve your health and fitness, not destroy them. Steroid use is contrary to what sports are all about.

9   The Olympic goal isn't about winning, but about taking part, about being part of the "youth of the world" called together every four years. That's why they're called the Olympic *Games*. If random drug testing were mandatory, then this "win-at-all-costs" attitude would disappear, and the real meaning of the Olympic Creed would have a chance to make a comeback.

BIBLIOGRAPHY

Asken, Michael, *Dying to Win*. Washington: Acropolis, 1988.

Hainline, Brian, and Gary Wadler, *Drugs and the Athlete*. Philadelphia: F.A. Davis, 1989.

QUESTIONS FOR ANALYSIS AND DISCUSSION

1. Identify Spokas's claim. Where does she state it in her essay? Do you agree with her claim? Would instituting random mandatory drug testing of Olympic athletes reduce the "win-at-all-costs" attitude of athletes and provide cleaner competition? What disadvantages or problems might arise if this were put into effect?

2. On what grounds does Spokas base her claim? Find the specific evidence she presents to support her claim. Do you find it convincing and supportive? Do you agree with her interpretation of the Olympic ideal?

3. Spokas has several warrants, some of them stated explicitly and some implied. In paragraph 8 she states, "Drugs like anabolic steroids give an unfair advantage to athletes who use them; this isn't what sports, particularly Olympic sports, are supposed to be about." Do you agree with her warrant? On what commonly shared values or beliefs does she base this warrant? Are there any aspects of her warrant with which you disagree? What backing does Spokas provide to support her warrant? Is it sufficient?

4. What other warrants underlie Spokas's claim? In a small peer group, identify several layers of warrants and discuss whether these need additional backing to be convincing.

5. Notice the qualifiers Spokas uses in paragraph 6, when she states, "*Sometimes* prescribed or over-the-counter medications *may* cause positive tests" (emphasis added). What limitations do these qualifiers put on her statement? Do you think the possibility of false-positive test results should be a serious concern for anyone who institutes mandatory random testing? Could these tests violate the athlete's privacy?

6. Does Spokas acknowledge and answer anticipated rebuttals to her argument? Can you locate any in her essay? What rebuttals can you make in response to her argument?

Our next sample argument was published in the *New York Times Sunday Magazine* on November 2, 1997. It provides a very logical but highly provocative argument about a crime that has received considerable media attention: infanticide. The author, Steven Pinker, is the director of the Center for Cognitive Neuroscience at the Massachusetts Institute of Technology and author of *How the Mind Works* (1997) and *The Language Instinct* (1994). His essay explains his interpretation of why mothers kill their newborn babies and argues that society should reconsider its response to this crime.

Why They Kill Their Newborns
Steven Pinker

1 Killing your baby. What could be more depraved? For a woman to destroy the fruit of her womb would seem like an ultimate violation of the natural order. But every year, hundreds of women commit neonaticide: they kill their newborns or let them die. Most neonaticides remain undiscovered, but every once in a while a janitor follows a trail of blood to a tiny body in a trash bin, or a woman faints and doctors find the remains of a placenta inside her.

2 Two cases have recently riveted the American public. Last November, Amy Grossberg and Brian Peterson, 18-year-old college sweethearts, delivered their baby in a motel room and, according to prosecutors, killed him and left his body in a Dumpster. They will go on trial for murder next year and, if convicted, could be sentenced to death. In June, another 18-year-old, Melissa Drexler, arrived at her high-school prom, locked herself in a bathroom stall, gave birth to a boy and left him dead in a garbage can. Everyone knows what happened next: she touched herself up and returned to the dance floor. In September, a grand jury indicted her for murder.

3 How could they do it? Nothing melts the heart like a helpless baby. Even a biologist's cold calculations tell us that nurturing an offspring that carries our genes is the whole point of our existence. Neonaticide, many think, could be only a product of pathology. The psychiatrists uncover childhood trauma. The defense lawyers argue temporary psychosis. The pundits blame a throwaway society, permissive sex education and, of course, rock lyrics.

4 But it's hard to maintain that neonaticide is an illness when we learn that it has been practiced and accepted in most cultures throughout history. And that neonaticidal women do not commonly show signs of psychopathology. In a

classic 1970 study of statistics of child killing, a psychiatrist, Phillip Resnick, found that mothers who kill their *older* children are frequently psychotic, depressed or suicidal, but mothers who kill their newborns are usually not. (It was this difference that led Resnick to argue that the category infanticide be split into neonaticide, the killing of a baby on the day of its birth, and filicide, the killing of a child older than one day.)

5   Killing a baby is an immoral act, and we often express our outrage at the immoral by calling it a sickness. But normal human motives are not always moral, and neonaticide does not have to be a product of malfunctioning neural circuitry or a dysfunctional upbringing. We can try to understand what would lead a mother to kill her newborn, remembering that to understand is not necessarily to forgive.

6   Martin Daly and Margo Wilson, both psychologists, argue that a capacity for neonaticide is built into the biological design of our parental emotions. Mammals are extreme among animals in the amount of time, energy and food they invest in their young, and humans are extreme among mammals. Parental investment is a limited resource, and mammalian mothers must "decide" whether to allot it to their newborn or to their current and future offspring. If a newborn is sickly, or if its survival is not promising, they may cut their losses and favor the healthiest in the litter or try again later on.

7   In most cultures, neonaticide is a form of this triage. Until very recently in human evolutionary history, mothers nursed their children for two to four years before becoming fertile again. Many children died, especially in the perilous first year. Most women saw no more than two or three of their children survive to adulthood, and many did not see any survive. To become a grandmother, a woman had to make hard choices. In most societies documented by anthropologists, including those of hunter-gatherers (our best glimpse into our ancestors' way of life), a woman lets a newborn die when its prospects for survival to adulthood are poor. The forecast might be based on abnormal signs in the infant, or on bad circumstances for successful motherhood at the time— she might be burdened with older children, beset by war or famine or without a husband or social support. Moreover, she might be young enough to try again.

8   We are all descendants of women who made the difficult decisions that allowed them to become grandmothers in that unforgiving world, and we inherited that brain circuitry that led to those decisions. Daly and Wilson have shown that the statistics on neonaticide in contemporary North America parallel those in the anthropological literature. The women who sacrifice their offspring tend to be young, poor, unmarried and socially isolated.

9   Natural selection cannot push the buttons of behavior directly; it affects our behavior by endowing us with emotions that coax us toward adaptive choices. New mothers have always faced a choice between a definite tragedy now and the possibility of an even greater tragedy months or years later, and that choice is not to be taken lightly. Even today, the typical rumination of a depressed new mother—how will I cope with this burden?—is a legitimate concern. The emotional response called bonding is also far more complex than the

popular view, in which a woman is imprinted with a lifelong attachment to her baby if they interact in a critical period immediately following the baby's birth. A new mother will first coolly assess the infant and her current situation and only in the next few days begin to see it as a unique and wonderful individual. Her love will gradually deepen in ensuing years, in a trajectory that tracks the increasing biological value of a child (the chance that it will live to produce grandchildren) as the child proceeds through the mine field of early development.

10   Even when a mother in a hunter-gatherer society hardens her heart to sacrifice a newborn, her heart has not turned to stone. Anthropologists who interview these women (or their relatives, since the event is often too painful for the woman to discuss) discover that the women see the death as an unavoidable tragedy, grieve at the time and remember the child with pain all their lives. Even the supposedly callous Melissa Drexler agonized over a name for her dead son and wept at his funeral. (Initial reports that, after giving birth, she requested a Metallica song from the deejay and danced with her boyfriend turned out to be false.)

11   Many cultural practices are designed to distance people's emotions from a newborn until its survival seems probable. Full personhood is often not automatically granted at birth, as we see in our rituals of christening and the Jewish bris. And yet the recent neonaticides will seem puzzling. These are middle-class girls whose babies would have been kept far from starvation by the girl's parents or by any of thousands of eager adoptive couples. But our emotions, fashioned by the slow hand of natural selection, respond to the signals of the long-vanished tribal environment in which we spent 99 percent of our evolutionary history. Being young and single are two bad omens for successful motherhood, and the girl who conceals her pregnancy and procrastinates over its consequences will soon be disquieted by a third omen. She will give birth in circumstances that are particularly unpromising for a human mother: alone.

12   In hunter-gatherer societies, births are virtually always assisted because human anatomy makes birth (especially the first one) long, difficult and risky. Older women act as midwives, emotional supports and experienced appraisers who help decide whether the infant should live. Wenda Trevathan, an anthropologist and trained midwife, has studied pelvises of human fossils and concluded that childbirth has been physically tortuous, and therefore probably assisted, for millions of years. Maternal feelings may be adapted to a world in which a promising newborn is heralded with waves of cooing and clucking and congratulating. Those reassuring signals are absent from a secret birth in a motel room or a bathroom stall.

13   So what is the mental state of a teen-age mother who has kept her pregnancy secret? She is immature enough to have hoped that her pregnancy would go away by itself, her maternal feelings have been set at zero and she suddenly realizes she is in big trouble.

14   Sometimes she continues to procrastinate. In September, 17-year-old Shanta Clark gave birth to a premature boy and kept him hidden in her bedroom closet, as if he were E.T., for 17 days. She fed him before and after she

went to school until her mother discovered him. The weak cry of the preemie kept him from being discovered earlier. (In other cases, girls have panicked over the crying and, in stifling the cry, killed the baby.)

15   Most observers sense the desperation that drives a woman to neonaticide. Prosecutors sometimes don't prosecute; juries rarely convict; those found guilty almost never go to jail. Barbara Kirwin, a forensic psychologist, reports that in nearly 300 cases of women charged with neonaticide in the United States and Britain, no woman spent more than a night in jail. In Europe, the laws of several countries prescribed less-severe penalties for neonaticide than for adult homicides. The fascination with the Grossberg-Peterson case comes from the unusual threat of the death penalty. Even those in favor of capital punishment might shudder at the thought of two reportedly nice kids being strapped to gurneys and put to death.

16   But our compassion hinges on the child, not just on the mother. Killers of older children, no matter how desperate, evoke little mercy. Susan Smith, the South Carolina woman who sent her two sons, 14 months and 3 years old, to watery deaths, is in jail, unmourned, serving a life sentence. The leniency shown to neonaticidal mothers forces us to think the unthinkable and ask if we, like many societies and like the mothers themselves, are not completely sure whether a neonate is a full person.

17   It seems obvious that we need a clear boundary to confer personhood on a human being and grant it a right to life. Otherwise, we approach a slippery slope that ends in the disposal of inconvenient people or in grotesque deliberations on the value of individual lives. But the endless abortion debate shows how hard it is to locate the boundary. Anti-abortionists draw the line at conception, but that implies we should shed tears every time an invisible conceptus fails to implant in the uterus—and, to carry the argument to its logical conclusion, that we should prosecute for murder anyone who uses an IUD. Those in favor of abortion draw the line at viability, but viability is a fuzzy gradient that depends on how great a risk of an impaired child the parents are willing to tolerate. The only thing both sides agree on is that the line must be drawn at some point before birth.

18   Neonaticide forces us to examine even that boundary. To a biologist, birth is as arbitrary a milestone as any other. Many mammals bear offspring that see and walk as soon as they hit the ground. But the incomplete 9-month-old human fetus must be evicted from the womb before its outsize head gets too big to fit through its mother's pelvis. The usual primate assembly process spills into the first years in the world. And that complicates our definition of personhood.

19   What makes a living being a person with a right not to be killed? Animal-rights extremists would seem to have the easiest argument to make: that all sentient beings have a right to life. But champions of that argument must conclude that delousing a child is akin to mass murder; the rest of us must look for an argument that draws a small circle. Perhaps only the members of our own species, Homo sapiens, have a right to life? But that is simply chauvinism; a person of one race could just as easily say that people of another race have no right to life.

20   No, the right to life must come, the moral philosophers say, from morally significant traits that we humans happen to possess. One such trait is having a unique sequence of experiences that defines us as individuals and connects us to other people. Other traits include an ability to reflect upon ourselves as a continuous locus of consciousness, to form and savor plans for the future, to dread death and to express the choice not to die. And there's the rub: our immature neonates don't possess these traits any more than mice do.

21   Several moral philosophers have concluded that neonates are not persons, and thus neonaticide should not be classified as murder. Michael Tooley has gone so far as to say that neonaticide ought to be permitted during an interval after birth. Most philosophers (to say nothing of nonphilosophers) recoil from that last step, but the very fact that there can be a debate about the personhood of neonates, but no debate about the personhood of older children, makes it clearer why we feel more sympathy for an Amy Grossberg than for a Susan Smith

22   So how do you provide grounds for outlawing neonaticide? The facts don't make it easy. Some philosophers suggest that people intuitively see neonates as so similar to older babies that you couldn't allow neonaticide without coarsening the way people treat children and other people in general. Again, the facts say otherwise. Studies in both modern and hunter-gatherer societies have found that neonaticidal women don't kill anyone but their newborns, and when they give birth later under better conditions, they can be devoted, loving mothers.

23   The laws of biology were not kind to Amy Grossberg and Melissa Drexler, and they are not kind to us as we struggle to make moral sense of the teenagers' actions. One predicament is that our moral system needs a crisp inauguration of personhood, but the assembly process for Homo sapiens is gradual, piecemeal and uncertain. Another problem is that the emotional circuitry of mothers has evolved to cope with this uncertain process, so the baby killers turn out to be not moral monsters but nice, normal (and sometimes religious) young women. These are dilemmas we will probably never resolve, and any policy will leave us with uncomfortable cases. We will most likely muddle through, keeping birth as a conspicuous legal boundary but showing mercy to the anguished girls who feel they had no choice but to run afoul of it.

An Analysis Based on the Toulmin Model

Clearly Steven Pinker has taken a controversial stance on a disturbing social issue. In fact, in light of civilized society's attitudes toward the sacredness of the mother-infant bond, his position is one that many people might find shocking and repugnant. How could he propose that neonaticide, the murder of one's newborn infant, be viewed as an acceptable form of behavior, one that we have inherited from our evolutionary ancestors? As Pinker readily admits in the first three paragraphs of his essay, neonaticide seems alien to most of the values we as civilized people cherish.

Nevertheless, Pinker argues that while it may be regarded as immoral, neonaticide is not necessarily the act of a mentally deranged woman, but rather a difficult decision guided by an instinct for survival handed down to a mother by generations of women before her. While he does not condone or endorse this practice, Pinker urges his readers to try to understand a context that might drive women to commit such an act.

Your first reaction to Pinker's ideas may be to dismiss them as outrageous and unworthy of serious consideration. Yet by closely analyzing Pinker's argument using the Toulmin method, you will be able to see how carefully Pinker has crafted his argument to challenge many of our assumptions about human behavior and, in particular, motherhood.

Claims and Grounds

Pinker presents the first part of his claim in paragraph 4 of his essay: neonaticide is not an abnormal behavior but one that has been practiced "in most cultures throughout history." This statement seems to contradict the popular notion of neonaticide. Because our society regards neonaticide as an immoral act, many people likely assume that it is a rare occurrence. However, Pinker anticipates this assumption in paragraph 1 by reminding us that neonaticide *does* occur in our own society. It is, he claims, more common than we realize, since most murders of newborn babies go undetected. Only "every once in a while" do we discover that this act has taken place because some physical evidence is found. While Pinker offers no grounds for his assertion that "every year, hundreds of women commit neonaticide," his audience's familiarity with newspaper accounts of newborn's abandoned in dumpsters and public restrooms lends credibility to his statement. This point is important because it establishes a link between contemporary women's behavior and the practices of our "long vanished tribal environment."

Pinker develops this idea further in paragraphs 6 through 8 by suggesting that this behavior has been programmed into our "biological design" through human evolutionary development. He provides the grounds to support this part of his claim by citing two scholarly sources: Philip Resnick's study of child-killing statistics, which indicates that women who kill their newborn babies are typically not mentally ill, and research by Martin Daly and Margo Wilson that suggests neonaticide may be an intrinsic part of our "biological design," a necessity for human beings with limited resources to invest in their offspring. Relying on these grounds, Pinker goes on to argue in paragraph 9 that neonaticide is an "adaptive choice," one that is preferable to nurturing an infant whose continued survival is in doubt because of either the physical condition of the child or environmental difficulties for the mother.

So far, then, we have found two of the essential parts of the Toulmin model in Pinker's essay:

Claim Neonaticide is not a pathologic behavior but can be, rather, the result of evolutionary development.

Grounds   Various anthropological studies that indicate neonaticide is a common and accepted practice in many contemporary societies; studies by psychologists arguing that neonaticide is a normal part of our parenting emotions; research by psychologists demonstrating that women who commit neonaticide are not mentally ill

Warrants, Backing, and Rebuttals

Now let's move on to Pinker's warrants, which work to support his claim:

Pinker never directly states, yet he strongly implies as a *warrant,* that "biology is destiny." It is clear from his claim and the grounds used to support it that Pinker believes the biological impulses of a new mother who commits neonaticide may overwhelm her civilized sense of what is morally or even emotionally right. Human beings, according to Pinker, are at the mercy of their neurological programming. Pinker offers *backing* for this *warrant* in paragraph 10 when he relates interviews by anthropologists with women who have killed their newborn babies and who appear to grieve sincerely for their children, regarding their actions as "an unavoidable tragedy." These women, according to Pinker, were compelled to make a difficult choice, which each did in spite of her maternal feelings toward the newborn. Pinker reinforces this point later in the essay when he states in paragraph 23 that "the laws of biology were not kind to Amy Grossberg and Melissa Drexler," two young women who killed their infants just after birth. Pinker strongly implies that biological forces were at work when these women made their decisions.

Pinker's warrant provides plenty of opportunity for *rebuttal* because even if the reader accepts the idea that human beings, despite the teachings of civilized society, are still subject to the dictates of more primitive and instinctive urges, Pinker asserts that the urge to kill one's baby is stronger than, say, the maternal instinct to nurture that infant. We have all heard of situations in which a mother has risked or sacrificed her own life to save that of her child. Why, we might ask, wouldn't this emotion dominate the behavior of a new mother? Pinker acknowledges this rebuttal in paragraph 11 when he points out that the neonaticides we read about in newspapers are often committed by middle-class girls who have the resources to support a child or the option to give the baby up for adoption.

Pinker responds to this rebuttal in two ways: First, he reiterates his claim that the internal forces of our evolutionary background are stronger than the individual's own sense of right and wrong. These young women are responding to the "signals of the long-vanished tribal environment in which we spent 99 percent of our evolutionary history." Moreover, Pinker goes on to suggest, neonaticide is triggered by environmental and social factors, specifically, the age, marital status, and isolation of the new mother, that work to suppress more positive maternal responses. As he explains in paragraph 12, maternal feelings are more likely to emerge in an atmosphere of "cooing and clucking and congratulating" than in a "motel room or bathroom stall."

Pinker goes on to support his argument with several additional layers of warrants: If human behavior is controlled by deeply ingrained biological forces, then we can't be held legally responsible for these actions. In other words, while we may deeply deplore the act of neonaticide, we cannot fault these women for acting on an impulse they may not completely understand or feel able to control. In paragraph 15 Pinker provides backing for this claim by observing that few women in the United States are actually incarcerated for this crime and several European countries treat neonaticide less severely than other forms of homicide. Thus, although the killing of one's baby generates strong moral outrage in our society, we treat it less severely than most other offenses in the same category.

Logically, then, the next question must be "Why is this the case?" When older children are murdered by their mothers, as in Pinker's example of Susan Smith in paragraph 16, we waste little sympathy on the plight of the mother. We can agree with Pinker that "our compassion hinges on the child." Why do we react, according to Pinker, in a very different way to the death of a newborn? Pinker has very carefully brought us to his next warrant, which even he admits is the "unthinkable": Our reaction to the killing of a newborn and the killing of an older child is different because a newborn is not yet a "full person."

Pinker provides backing for his warrant in paragraphs 18 through 20. In paragraph 18 he points out a fact most readers would agree with: unlike other mammals, human babies are helpless at birth. They are "incomplete." It will take an infant several years to achieve the level of physical development that some mammals enjoy at birth. Thus, a newborn baby cannot claim its rights as a person based on its physical completeness. Then, Pinker asks, on what basis can a newborn be seen as possessing "a right not to be killed"? By what traits do we define a person with a right to life? In paragraph 20 Pinker calls on the *backing* of "moral philosophers" who describe the traits human beings must possess to be considered fully human. Pinker concludes that newborn babies "don't possess these traits any more than mice do."

Anticipating that most readers will have a strong negative response to these ideas, Pinker acknowledges several rebuttals to this warrant. In paragraph 17 he recognizes that neither side of the abortion debate would agree with his assertion that birth should not be a marker to determine when a human being is given a right to life. To anti-abortionists, who maintain that "personhood" begins at conception, Pinker responds that if we adopt this viewpoint, the destruction of any fertilized human egg would be considered murder. To those in favor of abortion rights, who consider personhood to begin when the baby is capable of living outside the protection of the mother's body, Pinker counters that this depends on the condition of the infant and the willingness of the parents to accept the risks inherent in a premature birth. In paragraph 19 Pinker also rejects the position that all life deserves to be preserved. If this were practiced, Pinker reasons, then "delousing a child is akin to mass murder." Pinker's stance forces us to reexamine how we define a "person" and how we can determine at what point the right to live unharmed begins.

We can briefly summarize Pinker's warrants and backing as follows:

Warrant 1   Biology is destiny. We are at the mercy of our neurological programming, which has been handed down from our evolutionary ancestors.

Backing   Examples of women who grieve for the newborns they killed; references to Melissa Drexler and Amy Grossberg, who killed their newborn infants.

Warrant 2   If human behavior is controlled by deeply ingrained biological forces, then women can't be held legally responsible for following their natural impulses.

Backing   Examples of lenient criminal treatment of women who commit neonaticide; examples of less severe penalties for women who kill newborns, as opposed to those given for the murder of older children or adults.

Warrant 3   A newborn infant is not a full person. Neonates do not yet possess those human qualities that bestow on them the right to life.

Backing   A description of a newborn infant's physical helplessness; a definition of a "full person" according to some moral philosophers; a comparison of the intellectual and moral awareness of a newborn infant with that of a mouse.

Qualifiers

Throughout his essay Pinker is careful to use *qualifiers* that limit and clarify his claim. There are many examples of these; we will point out a few that appear early in the essay along with our emphasis and comments:

Paragraph 4   "But it's *hard* [difficult but not impossible] to maintain that neonaticide is an illness when we learn that it has been practiced and accepted in *most* [but not all] cultures throughout history. And that neonaticidal women do not *commonly* [typical but not in all cases] show signs of psychopathology."

Paragraph 5   "But normal human motives are *not always* [happens some of the time] moral, and neonaticide *does not have to be* [but it could be] a product of malfunctioning neural circuitry or a dysfunctional upbringing."

By using qualifiers Pinker demonstrates his awareness that his claim may not always be true under all circumstances and accounts for the differing experiences of his audience.

As we stated at the beginning of this chapter, to construct a persuasive argument you must pay careful attention to the logical structure you are building. As the Toulmin method illustrates, unless your claim is supported by a firm foundation (your warrants) and well buttressed by convincing grounds and backing, your structure will not withstand the rebuttals that will test its strength.

Pinker's view on neonaticide is disturbing, to say the least. For his essay to be persuasive, the reader must be willing to accept each of his warrants and the backing he uses to support them. Four days after Pinker's essay appeared in the *New York Times,* the following article was published in the *Washington Post.* As you read the article, notice how author Michael Kelley, a senior writer at the *National Journal,* attacks Pinker's claim by questioning each of his warrants and their backing. Calling Pinker's premise one of the "most thoroughly dishonest constructs anyone has ever attempted to pass off as science," Kelley also levels severe criticism at one of Pinker's sources, Michael Tooley. Kelley comments that Pinker's citation of Tooley's radical views, even though he may not directly agree with them, makes him "guilty by association." Kelley's accusation demonstrates why you should choose your sources carefully. Your audience will associate your views with the company they keep.

Arguing for Infanticide
Michael Kelley

1   Of all the arguments advanced against the legalization of abortion, the one that always struck me as the most questionable is the most consequential: that the widespread acceptance of abortion would lead to a profound moral shift in our culture, a great devaluing of human life. This seemed to me dubious on general principle: Projections of this sort almost always turn out to be wrong because they fail to grasp that, in matters of human behavior, there is not really any such thing as a trendline. People change to meet new realities and thereby change reality.

2   Thus, for the environmental hysterics of the 1970s, the nuclear freezers of the 1980s and the Perovian budget doomsayers of the 1990s, the end that was nigh never came. So, with abortions, why should a tolerance for ending human life under one, very limited, set of conditions necessarily lead to an acceptance of ending human life under other, broader terms?

3   This time, it seems, the pessimists were right. On Sunday, Nov. 2, an article in the *New York Times,* the closest thing we have to the voice of the intellectual establishment, came out for killing babies. I am afraid that I am sensationalizing only slightly. The article by Steven Pinker in the *Times Magazine* did not go quite so far as to openly recommend the murder of infants, and printing the article did not constitute the *Times'* endorsement of the idea. But close enough, close enough.

4   What Pinker, a professor of psychology at the Massachusetts Institute of Technology, wrote and what the *Times* treated as a legitimate argument, was a thoroughly sympathetic treatment of this modest proposal: Mothers who kill their newborn infants should not be judged as harshly as people who take human life in its later stages because newborn infants are not persons in the full

sense of the word, and therefore do not enjoy a right to life. Who says that life begins at birth?

5   "To a biologist, birth is as arbitrary a milestone as any other," Pinker breezily writes. "No, the right to life must come, the moral philosophers say, from morally significant traits that we humans happen to possess. One such trait is having a unique sequence of experiences that defines us as individuals and connects us to other people. Other traits include an ability to reflect upon ourselves as a continuous locus of consciousness, to form and savor plans for the future, to dread death and to express the choice not to die. And there's the rub: our immature neonates don't possess these traits any more than mice do."

6   Pinker notes that "several moral philosophers have concluded that neonates are not persons, and thus neonaticide should not be classified as murder," and he suggests his acceptance of this view, arguing that "the facts don't make it easy" to legitimately outlaw the killing of infants.

7   Pinker's causally authoritative mention of "the facts" is important. Because Pinker is no mere ranter from the crackpot fringe but a scientist. He is, in fact, a respected explicator of the entirely mainstream and currently hot theory of evolutionary psychology, and the author of "How the Mind Works," a just-published, doubtlessly seminal, exceedingly fat book on the subject.

8   How the mind works, says Pinker, is that people are more or less hard-wired to behave as they do by the cumulative effects of the human experience. First cousins to the old Marxist economic determinists, the evolutionary psychologists are behavioral determinists. They believe in a sort of Popeye's theory of human behavior: I do what I do because I yam what I yam because I wuz what I wuz.

9   This view is radical; it seeks to supplant both traditional Judeo-Christian morality and liberal humanism with a new "scientific" philosophy that denies the idea that all humans are possessed of a quality that sets them apart from the lower species, and that this quality gives humans the capacity and responsibility to choose freely between right and wrong. And it is monstrous. And, judging from the writings of Pinker and his fellow determinists on the subject of infanticide, it may be the most thoroughly dishonest construct anyone has ever attempted to pass off as science.

10   Pinker's argument was a euphemized one. The more blunt argument is made by Michael Tooley, a philosophy professor at the University of Colorado, whom Pinker quotes. In this 1972 essay "Abortion and Infanticide," Tooley makes what he calls "an extremely plausible answer" to the question: "What makes it morally permissible to destroy a baby, but wrong to kill an adult?" Simple enough: Personhood does not begin at birth. Rather, "an organism possesses a serious right to life only if it possesses the concept of a self as a continuing subject of experiences and other mental states, and believes that it is itself such a continuing entity."

11   Some would permit the killing of infants "up to the time an organism learned how to use certain expressions," but Tooley finds this cumbersome and would simply establish "some period of time, such as a week after birth, as the interval during which infanticide will be permitted."

12   And Tooley does not bother with Pinker's pretense that what is under discussion here is only a rare act of desperation, the killing of an unwanted child by a frightened, troubled mother. No, no, no. If it is moral to kill a baby for one, it is moral for all. Indeed, the systematic, professionalized use of infanticide would be a great benefit to humanity. "Most people would prefer to raise children who do not suffer from gross deformities or from severe physical, emotional, or intellectual handicaps," writes eugenicist Tooley. "If it could be shown that there is no moral objection to infanticide the happiness of society could be significantly and justifiably increased."

13   To defend such an unnatural idea, the determinists argue that infanticide is in fact natural: In Pinker's words, "it has been practiced and accepted in most cultures throughout history." This surprising claim is critical to the argument that the act of a mother killing a child is a programmed response to signals that the child might not fare well in life (because of poverty, illegitimacy or other factors). And it is a lie.

14   In fact, although millions of mothers give birth every year under the sort of adverse conditions that Pinker says trigger the "natural" urge to kill the baby, infanticide is extremely rare in all modern societies, and is universally treated as a greatly aberrant act, the very definition of a moral horror. The only cultures that Pinker can point to in which infanticide is widely "practiced and accepted" are those that are outside the mores of Western civilization: ancient cultures and the remnants of ancient cultures today, tribal hunter-gatherer societies.

15   And so goes the entire argument, a great chain of dishonesty, palpable untruth piled upon palpable untruth. "A new mother," asserts Pinker, "will first coolly assess the infant and her situation and only in the next few days begin to see it as a unique and wonderful individual." Yes, that was my wife all over: cool as a cucumber as she assessed whether to keep her first-born child or toss him out the window. As George Orwell said once of another vast lie, "You have to be an intellectual to believe such nonsense. No ordinary man could be such a fool."

QUESTIONS FOR ANALYSIS AND DISCUSSION

1. Briefly outline the basic Toulmin components of Kelley's argument: What is his claim? What grounds does he use to support it? Then find and identify Kelley's warrants and the backing he provides to demonstrate their reliability.

2. To what aspects of Pinker's claim and warrants does Kelley object? On what grounds does he object?

3. Pinker limits his discussion of neonaticide to the behavior of "depressed new mothers" (paragraph 9). Does Kelley ignore this distinction in his response to Pinker? How does Kelley shift the discussion from Pinker's "anguished girls" (paragraph 23) to "millions of mothers" (paragraph 14 in Kelley)? Do you think this is a fair interpretation of Pinker's intent?

4. Kelley begins his essay with a reference to the legalization of abortion. On what basis does he suggest a link between the "widespread acceptance of abortion" and Pinker's theories about neonaticide?

5. In paragraph 3 of his essay Kelley states that Pinker "did not go quite so far as to openly recommend the murder of infants." Discuss the implications of Kelley's use of the qualifiers *quite* and *openly*. What do you think he intends to imply about Pinker's objectives?

6. In paragraph 10, what does Kelley mean by describing Pinker's argument as "euphemized"? What connection does Kelley make between Pinker's views and the theories expressed by Michael Tooley in his 1972 essay? Does your analysis of Pinker's claim and warrants lead you to believe that Pinker endorses Tooley's theories, as Kelley asserts?

7. In your journal, discuss your own response to Kelley's essay. Which reasons do you find particularly persuasive? With which reasons do you disagree, and why?

8. In paragraph 9, Kelley criticizes Pinker's attempt to take a "scientific" approach to a serious moral issue by suggesting that humans lack "the capacity and responsibility to choose freely between right and wrong." In your journal, consider how Pinker might respond to that statement. Would he agree with Kelley's interpretation of his ideas? How would Pinker suggest that society should deal with the problem of neonatacide?

chapter 8

RESEARCHING ARGUMENTS

Thinking like an Investigator

Most arguments derive their success from the evidence they contain, so good argumentative writers learn to find evidence in many sources and present the best evidence to support their claims. In the academic world, much of that evidence is gathered through *research,* either conducted in a lab or field or through examination of the previously published work of other investigators and scholars. The research paper you may be asked to write challenges you to learn how more experienced writers find and present evidence that meets the standards of the academic community.

When you walk through the library, you are surrounded with researched arguments. The book claiming that the Kennedy assassination was part of a CIA conspiracy is a researched argument. So are the journal articles asserting that Shakespeare's plays were written by Sir Francis Bacon, and the research report that claims AZT is an effective treatment for some AIDS patients. The article in *Fortune* on the need for changes in the capital gains tax is one too, as is the review claiming that Nirvana was the most important band of the 1990s. All of these arguments have something in common: To back up their claims, their authors have brought in supporting evidence that they gathered through a focused research effort. That evidence gives you and readers like you grounds by which to decide whether you will agree with the authors' claims. Libraries, then, aren't just storehouses for history; they provide good writers with valuable information to support their ideas.

In the previous chapters we've stressed the importance of finding evidence that will impress readers of your argument's merits. To review, researched evidence plays an important role in convincing readers of the following:

- Expert, unbiased authorities agree with your position in whole or in part, adding to your credibility.
- Your position or proposal is based on facts, statistics, and real-life examples, not mere personal opinion.
- You understand different viewpoints about your subject as well as your own.
- Your sources of information are verifiable, since researched evidence is always accompanied by documentation.

A good analogy to use, once again, is that of the lawyer presenting a case to a jury. When you write a researched argument, you're making a case to a group of people who will make a decision about a subject. Not only do you present your arguments in the case, but you call on witnesses to offer evidence and expert opinion, which you then interpret and clarify for the jury. In a researched argument, your sources are your witnesses.

Writing an argumentative research paper isn't different from writing any other kind of argument, except in scale. You will need more time to write the paper in order to conduct and assimilate your research, the paper is usually longer than nonresearched papers, and the formal presentation (including documentation) must be addressed in more detail. The argumentative research paper is an extension and refinement of the essays you've been writing. It's not a different species of argument.

Sources of Information

There are two basic kinds of research sources, and depending partly on the type of issue you've picked to research, one may prove more helpful than the other. The first kind is *primary sources,* which include firsthand accounts of events (interviews, diaries, court records, letters, manuscripts). The second is *secondary sources,* which interpret, comment on, critique, explain, or evaluate events or primary sources. Secondary sources include most reference works and any books or articles that expand on primary sources. Depending on whether you choose a local or a more global issue to write about, you may decide to focus more on primary or more on secondary sources; but in most research, you'll want to consider both.

Primary Sources

If you choose a topic of local concern to write about, your chief challenge will be finding enough research material; very current controversies or issues won't yet have books written about them, so you may have to rely more heavily on electronic databases, which you can access through a computer, or interviews and other primary research methods to find information. If you choose a local issue to argue, consider the following questions.

- Which experts on campus or in the community might you interview to find out the pros and cons of the debated issue? an administrator at your college? a professor? the town manager? Think of at least two local experts who could provide an overview of the issue from different angles or perspectives.
- What local resources—such as a local newspaper, radio station, TV station, or political group—are available for gathering printed or broadcast information? If one of your topics is a campus issue, for example, the student newspaper, student committees or groups, university on-line discussion groups, or the student government body might be places to search for information.

Once you determine that you have several possible sources of information available locally, your next step is to set up interviews or make arrangements to read

Preparing Interview Questions

Consider the following guidelines as you prepare questions for an interview.

- Find out as much information as you can about the issue and about the expert's stand on the issue before the interview. Then you won't waste interview time on general details you could have found in the newspaper or on the local TV news.
- Ask open-ended questions that allow the authority to respond freely, rather than questions requiring only "yes" or "no" answers.
- Prepare more questions than you think you need, and rank them in order of priority according to your purpose. Using the most important points as a guide, sequence the list in a logical progression.

or view related materials. Most students find that experts are eager to talk about local issues and have little problem setting up interviews. However, you'll need to allow plenty of time in your research schedule to gather background information, phone for interviews, prepare your questions, and write up your notes afterward. If you're depending on primary research for the bulk of your information, get started as soon as the paper is assigned.

Preparing for Interviews

A few common courtesies apply when preparing for interviews. First, be ready to discuss the purpose of your interview when setting up an appointment. Second, go into the interview with a list of questions that show you have already thought about the issue. Be on time, and have a notebook and pen to record important points. If you think you may want to quote someone directly, ask their permission to do so and read the quotation back to them to check it for accuracy.

Conducting Interviews

Be prepared to jot down only key words or ideas during the interview, reserving time afterward to take more detailed notes. Keep the interview on track by asking focused questions if the interviewee wanders while responding to your question. When you are leaving, ask if it would be okay to call if you find you have other questions later.

Writing Up Interviews

As soon as possible after the interview, review the notes you jotted down and flesh out the details of the conversation. Think about what you learned. How does the information you gathered relate to your main topic or question? Did you gather any information that surprised or intrigued you? What questions remain? Record the date of your interview in your notes as you may need this information to document your source when you write the paper.

Secondary Sources

Although many primary sources—published interviews, public documents, results of experiments, and first-person accounts of historical events, for example—are available in the college library, the library is also a vast repository of secondary source material. If your topic is regional, national, or international in scope, you'll want to consider both of these kinds of sources. For example, if your topic is proposed changes to the Social Security System, you might find information in the *Congressional Record* on committee deliberations, a primary source, and also read editorials on the op-ed page of the *New York Times* for interpretive commentary, a secondary source.

A Search Strategy

Because the sheer amount of information in the library can be daunting, plan how you will find information before you start your search. Always consult a reference librarian if you get stuck in planning your search or if you can't find the information you need.

Choosing Your Topic

Your argument journal may remind you of potential topics, and Chapter 3 covered how to develop a topic. But what if you still can't think of a topic? You might try browsing through two print sources that contain information on current issues:

> *Facts on File* (1940 to the present). A weekly digest of current news.
> *Editorials on File* (1970 to the present). Selected editorials from U.S. and Canadian newspapers reprinted in their entirety.

If you have access to the Internet, the *Political Junkie* Web site will provide you with ideas from the latest news stories in national and regional newspapers and

---

Preview: A Search Strategy

- Choose your topic.
- Get an overview of your topic.
- Compile a working bibliography.
- Locate sources.
- Evaluate sources.
- Take notes.

magazines, columnists' viewpoints on current issues, up-to-the-minute reports on public figures, and links to the Web sites of numerous political and social organizations. You can access this site at <http://www.politicaljunkie.com>. Also, think about which subjects you find interesting from the essays in Part 2 of this book. These four sources should give you a wealth of ideas to draw on.

Getting an Overview of Your Topic

If you know little about your topic, encyclopedias can give you general background information. Just as important, encyclopedia articles often end with bibliographies on their subjects—bibliographies prepared by experts in the field. Using such bibliographies can save you hours in the library.

If your library houses specialized encyclopedias, either in print or through computer, related to your topic, check them first. If not, go to the general encyclopedias. Following is a list of general and specialized encyclopedias you may find helpful.

General Encyclopedias

Academic American Encyclopedia. Written for high school and college students.

New Encyclopedia Britannica and *Britannica Online. Micropaedia* is a ten-volume index of the *New Encyclopedia Britannica.*

Encyclopedia Americana. Extensive coverage of science and technology and excellent on American history.

Specialized Encyclopedias

Encyclopedia of American Economic History (1980). Overview of U.S. economic history and aspects of American social history related to economics.

Encyclopedia of Bioethics (1995). Covers life sciences and health care.

Encyclopedia of Philosophy (1972). Scholarly articles on philosophy and philosophers.

Encyclopedia of Psychology (1994). Covers topics in the field of psychology.

Encyclopedia of Religion (1993). Covers theoretical, practical, and sociological aspects of religion worldwide.

Encyclopedia of Social Work (1995). Covers social work issues including minorities and women.

Encyclopedia of World Art (1959–1983). Covers artists and art works and contains many reproductions of art works.

McGraw-Hill Encyclopedia of Science and Technology (1997). Covers physical, natural, and applied sciences.

This is just a brief listing of the many encyclopedias available in areas that range from marriage and the family to folklore and social history. Your librarian can assist you in finding the encyclopedia you need. Be sure to check the dates of encyclopedias so you locate the most current information available.

Compiling a Working Bibliography

Because you don't know at the beginning of your search which sources will prove most relevant to your narrowed topic, keep track of every source you consult. Record complete publication information about each source in your notebook, on 3" × 5" index cards, or on printouts of on-line sources. The list that follows describes the information you'll need for particular kinds of sources.

For a Book

Authors' and/or editors' names

Full title, including subtitle

Place of publication (city, state, country)

Date of publication (from the copyright page)

Name of publisher

Volume or edition numbers

Library call number

For an Article

Authors' names

Title and subtitle of article

Title of periodical (magazine, journal, newspaper)

Volume number and issue number, if any

Date of the issue

All page numbers on which the article appears

Library location

For an Electronic Source

Authors' names, if given

Title of material accessed

Name of periodical (if applicable)

Volume and issue numbers (if applicable)

Date of material, if given

Page numbers or numbers of paragraphs (if indicated)

Title of the database

Publication medium (e.g., CD-ROM, diskette, microfiche, online)

Name of the vendor, if relevant

Electronic publication date

Date of access to the material, if relevant

Path specification for on-line media (e.g., FTP information; directory; file name)

Note that for electronic sources, which come in many different formats, you should record all the information that would allow another researcher to retrieve the documents you used. This will vary from source to source, but the important point is to give as much information as you can.

Your instructor may ask you to prepare an *annotated bibliography,* in which you briefly summarize the main ideas in each source and note its potential usefulness. You will also want to evaluate each source for accuracy, currency, or bias.

Jenny, a first-year composition student, decided to write her argument essay on book banning in the public schools. Here are some sample entries from her annotated bibliography:

Sample Entries for an Annotated Bibliography

> *Frequently Asked Questions: Parental Rights.* Family Research Council. 13 Oct. 1998 <http://www.frc.org:80/faq22.html>. This is a Web site created by a politically conservative organization that actively supports parental rights. This site provides the group's rationale for endorsing passage of a Parental Freedom of Information Act, which would give parents greater power over their children's education in the public schools. This site clearly states a political position against government interference in the exercise of parental rights, and it is not free of bias. However, it is informative and well supported and it provides persuasive information about this viewpoint.

> May, Timothy. "The Case for Not Letting Kids Read *Catcher in the Rye. Sacramento Bee* 4 May 1997: F-3. *Lexis-Nexis.* 28 Oct. 1998 <http://web.lexis-nexis.com/universe>. May agrees with a local high school district's decision to remove *Catcher in the Rye* from the approved reading list because he thinks it is too difficult for high school students to understand. He suggests that students should be assigned classic literature before reading contemporary fiction. May does not really address the issue for censorship; he is more concerned with proving that high school students lack sufficient background to appreciate *Catcher in the Rye.* Even though he claims that he does not approve of censorship, he supports the board's action. This does not seem to be a useful source for my paper.

> People for the American Way. *Attacks on the Freedom to Learn.* Washington: People for the American Way, 1996. This is an annual survey taken by a 300,000-member civil liberties organization that documents and analyzes national statistics on censorship attempts directed toward public education. It includes short descriptions of specific censorship incidents on a state-by-state basis. This survey is intended to demonstrate that censorship attempts are on the rise. There is a strong bias against any attempts to censor or limit educational materials, but the statistics seem reliable and they are supported by examples of actual attempts at censorship.

A working bibliography (as opposed to an annotated bibliography) would include the complete publication information for each source, but not the evaluation of its usefulness to the paper.

Locating Sources

Your college library offers a range of methods and materials for finding the precise information you need. Here is a brief guide to locating periodicals, books, and electronic sources.

Finding Periodicals

Instead of going to the periodicals room and leafing page by page through magazines, journals, and newspapers to find information pertinent to your topic, use periodical indexes to locate the articles you need. Your college library will have these indexes available in print, CD-ROM, or online databases. The form you choose will depend on what is available and how current your information must be. When deciding whether to use the printed or electronic versions, carefully note the dates of the material the indexes reference. For example, you cannot use the CD-ROM version of *The Reader's Guide to Periodical Literature* to find a source from 1979. However, for a more current source (from 1983 to present), use the CD-ROM version since it provides abstracts of articles. These will allow you to decide whether locating the full article is worth your time and effort. Here is a list of some of the periodical indexes often available in college libraries. If your library does not have these indexes, ask the reference librarian the best way to find periodical articles in your library.

Periodical Indexes
General

> *Reader's Guide to Periodical Literature.* 1915 to present. Print. Indexes popular journals and magazines and some reviews of movies, plays, books, and television.
>
> *Readers' Guide Abstracts.* 1983 to present. Same content as *Readers' Guide* but with abstracts.
>
> *Newspaper Abstracts.* 1985 to present. Abstracts to articles in national and regional newspapers.
>
> *New York Times.* 1851 to present. Extensive coverage is national and international.
>
> *Periodical Abstracts.* 1986 to present. Abstracts and full-text articles from more than 950 general periodicals.
>
> *ABI/Inform.* August 1971 to present. About eight hundred thousand citations to articles in 1,400 periodicals. Good source for business-related topics. Complete text of articles from 500 publications since 1991.
>
> *Lexis-Nexis Universe.* Full-text access to newspapers, magazines, directories, legal and financial publications, and medical journals.

Specialized

Applied Science and Technology Index/Applied Science and Technology Abstracts. 1913 to present. Covers all areas of science and technology.

Art Index/Art Abstracts. 1929 to present. Wide coverage of art and allied fields.

Business Periodicals Index. 1958 to present. Covers all areas of business.

Education Index/Education Abstracts. 1929 to present. June 1983 to present. Covers elementary, secondary, and higher education.

PAIS International in Print/PAIS Database (formerly *Public Affairs Information Service Bulletin*). 1915 to present. Excellent index to journals, books, and reports in economics, social conditions, government, and law.

Ethnic Newswatch. 1990 to present. Indexes news publications by various ethnic groups. Includes full texts of most articles.

Social Sciences Index (*International Index* 1907–1965; *Social Sciences and Humanities* 1965–1974; *Social Sciences Index* 1974 to present). 1907 to present. Indexes scholarly journals in political science, sociology, psychology, and related fields.

Humanities Index. (See *Social Sciences Index* entry for name changes.) 1907 to present. Covers scholarly journals in literature, history, philosophy, folklore, and other fields in the humanities.

America: History and Life. 1964 to present. Index and abstracts to articles in more than 2,000 journals. Covers the histories and cultures of the United States and Canada from prehistory to the present.

SPORT Discus. 1975 to present. Covers sports, physical education, physical fitness, and sports medicine.

Social Issues Researcher (*SIRS*). Full-text articles from newspapers, journals, and government publications related to the social sciences.

Congressional Universe. Offers a legislative perspective on congressional bills, hearings, public laws, and information on members of Congress.

Sociofile. 1974 to present. Coverage includes family and socialization, culture, social differentiation, social problems, and social psychology.

Essay and General Literature Index. 1900 to present. Indexes essays and chapters in collected works. Emphasis is on social sciences and humanities.

Finding Books

Your library catalog, whether available in printed (card), electronic, or microform format, indexes the books your library holds. (You may be able to access other kinds of sources using the catalog as well, for example, government documents or maps.) Every catalog provides access to books in three basic ways: by author, title, and general subject. If the catalog is electronic, you can also use keyword searching to locate books. In a keyword search on a computer terminal, you type in a word related to your topic, and the catalog lists all the sources that include that word in the title.

To make keyword searching more efficient, you can often combine two or more search terms. For example, if you know that you want information on "violence," and can narrow that to "violence and music not rap music," the catalog will give you a much shorter list of sources than if you had typed only "violence," which is a very broad topic. This is called Boolean searching, and the typical ways you can combine terms are to use "and" to combine search terms; "or" to substitute search terms (for example, "violent crime" or "assault"); and "not" to exclude terms. For example, suppose you are looking for information on cigarette smoking by teenagers. In a Boolean search, you could use the search phrase: *teenager or youth and smoking not marijuana.*

If you are searching by subject rather than author or title, it's useful to know that libraries organize subject headings according to the *Library of Congress Subject Headings (LCSH)*. These are large red books, usually located near the library's catalog. You will save time and be more successful if you look up your subject in the *LCSH*. For example, if you search the catalog using the term "movies," you won't find a single source. If you look up "movies" in the *LCSH,* it will tell you that the subject heading is "motion pictures." Type in "motion pictures," and you'll find the sources you need.

Listed below are other useful sources of information.

Biographies

There are so many different biographical sources it is difficult to know which one has the information you need. The following titles will save you a lot of time:

Biography and Genealogy Master Index. (Spans from B.C. to the present). Index to more than one million biographical sources.

Biographical Index. 1947 to present. International and all occupations. Guide to sources in books, periodicals, letters, diaries, etc.

Contemporary Authors. 1962 to present. Contains biographical information about authors and lists of their works.

Almanacs

World Almanac and Book of Facts. 1968 to present. Facts about government, business, society, etc. International in scope.

Statistical Abstract of the United States. 1879 to present. Published by the U.S. Bureau of the Census. Good source for statistics about all aspects of the United States including economics, education, society, and politics.

Statistical Masterfile. 1984 to present. State and national government statistics and private and international.

Reviews, Editorials

Book Review Digest. 1905 to present. Index to book reviews with excerpts from the reviews.

Book Review Index. 1965 to present. Indexes to more books than the above but doesn't have excerpts from reviews.

Bibliographies

Look for these in journal articles, books, encyclopedia articles, biographical sources, etc.

Finding Internet Sources

The Internet offers countless possibilities for research using government documents, newspapers and electronic journals, Web sites, business publications, and much more. You may have access to the Internet through either campus computer labs or your own computer. The easiest way to access the Net is by using the World Wide Web (WWW), a point-and-click system in which related documents are linked.

To make your search easier and more efficient, you can rely on several of the powerful search engines available for exploring the World Wide Web. Each of the search engines we've listed below uses keyword searches to find material on your topic. These words can specify your topic, supply the title of a book or article about your topic, name a person associated with your topic, and so on. It's important to try out a number of keyword combinations when you are searching for resources. For instance, if your topic is assisted suicide, you might also search under *euthanasia* and *physician-assisted suicide.* By adding additional terms such as *terminal illness, legalization,* and *patient's rights,* you may be able to both narrow your search and find material filed under different topic headings that is related to your subject.

Here is a list of the more popular search engines. You'll find them useful for locating information on the Internet:

Hotbot *<http://www.hotbot.com>*

This search engine will give you a lot of options. Keywords can be used for subject searches or to find a phrase that appears in the sources. You may also supply the name of a person or a title to prompt your search. It will search for each of your keywords separately or as a unit. You can also limit or expand the time parameters of your search from the current date to up to two years.

Yahoo! *<http://www.yahoo.com>*

Yahoo! works just like Hotbot. It will also expand your search by linking you to two other search engines, AltaVista and Infoseek, if you request them.

AltaVista *<http://www.altavista.com>*

AltaVista will give you the choice of searching the Web or Usenet groups, which are discussion groups on particular topics. Unlike Yahoo! and Hotbot, this engine will not give you the option of limiting your search to a certain time period.

Excite *<http://www.excite.com>*

> Excite has a unique feature that suggests a list of words related to your key-
> words to help you focus more specifically on your topic. It also supplies a
> list of newspaper articles about your topic.

Infoseek *<http://www.infoseek.com>*

> Infoseek can search the Web, news articles, newsgroups (personal essays by
> individuals), and information about private companies with services related
> to your topic. It also can supply maps and e-mail addresses.

Lycos *<http://www.lycos.com>*

> Lycos offers full texts of some journal and news articles, as well as access to
> Web sites, personal home pages, and a dictionary of keywords.

When you are using any search engine, be sure to check the instructions so you can
use it as effectively as possible. Also, don't rely on only one search engine. Use several to give yourself access to the broadest range of materials.

Three additional Web sites that may help you if you are searching for information related to government, politics, legislation, or statistics are the following:

Library of Congress *<http://www.loc.gov>*

> This Web site provides information about the U.S. Congress and the legisla-
> tive process. It will search for past legislative bills by topic, bill number, or
> title; allow you to read the *Congressional Record* from the current and past
> year's Congresses; find committee reports by topic or committee name; and
> provide full-text access to current bills under consideration in the House of
> Representatives and the Senate.

U.S. Census Bureau *<http://www.census.gov>*

> You can find facts, figures, and statistics derived from the last census at this
> site. There is also some information about world population.

White House *<http://www.whitehouse.gov>*

> At this site you can find current and past White House press briefings and
> news releases, as well as a full range of statistics and information produced
> by federal agencies for public use.

Remember that the Internet is constantly changing, so no book will be completely
up to date on how to access its information. Check to see if your college has workshops or courses on using the Internet—it's an important research tool and it's
worth your time to learn how to navigate in cyberspace.

Evaluating Sources

The first examination of your sources isn't intended to find the precise information
you'll use in your final paper; rather, it is a preliminary assessment to help you decide whether the material is *relevant* and *reliable* for your purposes.

Print Sources

You can often sense a print source's relevance by skimming its preface, introduction, table of contents, conclusion, and index (for books) or abstract and headings (for articles) to see whether your topic appears and how often. Many students mark their bibliography cards with numbers (1 = most relevant, 2 = somewhat relevant, 3 = not very relevant) to help them remember which sources they most want to examine. If a source contains no relevant material, mark the bibliography card "unusable" but don't discard it; if you refine your topic or claim later, you may want to go back to that source.

The reliability of a printed source is judged in a number of ways:

- Check the date: Is it recent or timely for your topic?
- Look at the citations: Is the author's evidence recent or timely?
- Is the author an expert in the field? To find out, use the biographical sources listed earlier in this chapter or find book reviews in the reference section.
- Where does the author work? A source's credentials may influence your readers. You may also find out what biases the author may have; for example, if the author is the founder of Scientists Against Animal Research, you'll have a good idea about his or her personal beliefs on that subject.

Electronic Sources

Using material that you find on the Internet will present special challenges in determining the value of a source. Unlike most printed journal and newspaper articles and books, Internet materials are not necessarily reviewed by editors or professional colleagues to determine whether the facts are correct and the conclusions reliable. Anyone who has (or knows someone who has) the technical skills can develop a Web site and post opinions for the world to read. Sometimes it's difficult to determine whether the information you find on the Web is worth using. While there are no hard-and-fast rules to indicate whether an Internet source is reliable, here are a few suggestions that will help you evaluate whether you have found a credible source:

- **Domain address.** Each Internet host computer is assigned a domain indicating the type of organization that created the site. This domain indicator appears at the end of the address. Most sites will be labeled one of the following:

    edu for an educational site
    gov for a government site
    com for a commercial site
    org for an organizational site

    While we can't vouch for the quality of all the material at these different domains, it is more likely that sites affiliated with an educational institution or a government office will provide information that has been carefully researched and prepared. Although commercial sites and sites sponsored by organizations may also provide valid information, it is important to check carefully for bias or misinformation that might be made available to further the interests of the business or organization.

- **Author of the site.** Try to identity the author or authors of the material published at the site. Is the author a professional or an authority in a field relevant to the topic? The director of a public health clinic may have opinions worth considering on the medical use of marijuana; he may or may not have the same level of credibility in a discussion about punishment for juvenile criminals.
- **Identity of the organization.** If the site is maintained by an organization, find out what interests, if any, the organization represents. Who created the organization? A government-appointed committee investigating public support of family planning will have a very different agenda from a committee organized by private interest groups. While both groups may be scrupulously honest in their presentation of the facts, each may interpret those facts with a particular bias. Your awareness of their "slant" will help you decide how to use the information. The reference section of most libraries can provide directories of associations and organizations.
- **Date of posting.** Check the date when the site was posted. Has the site been updated recently? If not, is the material still current and relevant?
- **Quality of references.** Are sources provided to support the information posted on the site? Most credible sites will document their facts, research studies, and statistics. Many articles and essays will be followed by a bibliography. It's always a good idea to double-check these references to determine whether the information is accurate. The absence of any references to support statements of fact and statistics may indicate that the site is unreliable.
- **Quality of material.** Look for indications that the material has been written or assembled by an educated, well-informed individual who offers a balanced and thoughtful perspective on the issue. Is the written text free of obvious grammatical mistakes, spelling errors, problems with sentence structure, and so on? Does the author indicate awareness and respect for other views even while disagreeing with them? Is the coverage of material thorough and well supported? Although poorly written and executed Web sites can be obvious indications of low reliability, don't be fooled by slick, attractive presentations either. You need to investigate beneath the surface to determine whether the content of the site meets academic standards of fairness and thoroughness.
- **Intended use.** Consider how you will use the material at the site. If you are looking for reliable statistics and factual information, then checking the author's credentials and the status of the organization or company will be important to maintaining your own credibility. However, there are times when personal examples and experiences of individuals who are not professionally qualified may still be of value. For example, a student writing a paper on Alzheimer's disease came across a site in which an Alzheimer's victim kept a diary of the progression of her illness. Even though she was not qualified to give expert medical opinion on the disease itself, her diary provided a unique insight into the feelings and perceptions of someone experiencing the loss of her intellectual capabilities. In her paper, the student writer was able to incorporate some of this compelling personal testimony.

Let's see how this advice works in practice. Jenny decided to do an Internet search to find background information for her argument essay on book banning in the public schools. (Sample entries from her annotated bibliography appear earlier in this chapter.) Using several search engines and a keyword search, Jenny had no trouble finding a large number of sites concerned with this subject. However, before relying on the information she found at the sites, Jenny had to determine which sites were reliable. To do this she examined several features of each site, as we've recommended above.

The first site Jenny found was called *The On-Line Books Page: Banned Books On-Line* <http://www.cs.cmu.edu/People/spok/banned-books.html>. Using the criteria from the list we've provided, Jenny made the following evaluation of the site (see Figure 8.1 on page 190):

- **Domain address.** Jenny noted that the domain address contained "edu," indicating an educational institution. As she read through the information on the Web site, she learned that the site was based at Carnegie Mellon University, a well-known and reputable school.
- **Author of the site.** At the end of the site, the author identified himself by name. Using the home page link (see Figure 8.2 on page 191), Jenny searched for additional information about him and found that he is a post-doctoral student in computer science at Carnegie Mellon University. Since this description didn't indicate any special expertise on the subject of banned books, Jenny needed to investigate more. An AltaVista key word search using the author's name produced more information about his recent Ph.D. from Carnegie Mellon in computer science and his other professional activities related to banned books.
- **Identity of the organization.** The links provided on the home page allowed Jenny to gather more information about *The On-Line Books Page* and its author. By clicking on The University Library Project link, Jenny found that the author was associated with a Carnegie Mellon project intended to make all authored works available on the Internet. She also learned that the Web space and computing support for the site were provided by the School of Computer Science at Carnegie Mellon. Another link specified the criteria used to determine which books were placed on the banned book list. Still other links provided further background information about the goals of the site and its association with the Library of Congress. This information and the support of well-known and credible organizations and projects made Jenny feel confident about the value of this site.
- **Date of posting.** Jenny noted that the material on the Web site was current, having last been updated in the very month in which she was doing her research. The site itself contained information about both recent attempts to limit public library Internet access and historical accounts of book banning.
- **Quality of references.** The author provided frequent references to other Web sites on banned books, as well as to printed books on censorship. Checking through the Internet and the college library, Jenny confirmed that these references were used reliably and even decided to incorporate some of them into her research.
- **Quality of material.** Jenny found the text well written and the entire site organized and thorough. To evaluate whether the author's perspective was well balanced, Jenny checked to see if books from all ends of the political spectrum were

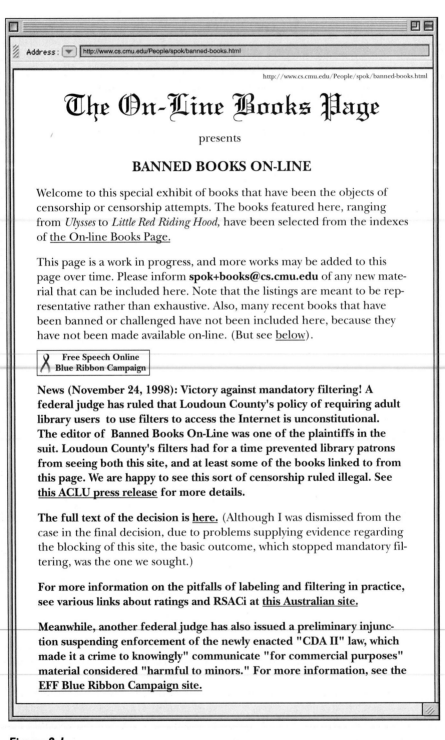

Figure 8.1

http://www.cs.cmu.edu/People/spok/aboutolbp.html

𝕿𝖍𝖊 𝕺𝖓-𝕷𝖎𝖓𝖊 𝕭𝖔𝖔𝖐𝖘 𝕻𝖆𝖌𝖊

ABOUT THE ON-LINE BOOKS PAGE

The On-Line Books Page is a directory of books that can be freely read right on the Internet. It includes:

- An index of thousands of on-line books on the Internet
- Pointers to significant directories and archives of on-line texts
- Special exhibits
- . . . and more!

The On-Line Books Page was founded in 1993 by John Mark Ockerbloom, formerly a graduate student (and now a postdoc) in computer science at Carnegie Mellon University. He remains the editor of the pages, and gladly accepts suggestions for new listings.

The index of individual titles includes books and definitive collections that meet these criteria. Starting in June 1998, it also lists major serial archive that meet these criteria. . . .

The On-Line Books Page, its sub-pages, and its compilation of listings are copyright 1993-1999 by John Mark Ockerbloom. Links to any point in these pages are welcome, and ordinary links do not require permission. However, if you want to redistribute or 'mirror' substantial portions of these listings or pages, or create derivative works or displays based on them (beyond what is clearly allowed by fair use), prior written permission is required.

Home – **About Us** – Get Involved! – In Progress / Requested – More Book Links

Books – News – Features – Archives – The Inside Story

Copyright 1993-1998 by John Mark Ockerbloom (spok+books@cs.cmu.edu)

Figure 8.2

included in the list. She discovered that the list included a group of diverse books, from the Bible to Qur'an to works of nineteenth-century poetry to contemporary books that had been criminalized under "hate speech" laws in other countries. Although it was clear to Jenny that the author of the site did not approve of book banning, this bias did not seem to distort the information he provided.

- **Intended use.** Jenny was interested in finding out the titles of books that were banned, those responsible for the banning, and the reasons behind the decisions.

She found The On-Line Books Page very useful. Jenny was particularly impressed by its range of titles. The site's list covered classic and historical works, as well as more modern ones. The explanations that accompanied each listing briefly explained the circumstances surrounding the book's censorship and provided specific dates and information about it.

After carefully evaluating *The On-Line Books Page: Banned Books On-Line,* Jenny concluded that it was a reliable source that might supply her with valuable information for her argument essay.

Jenny found three other Web sites that were also concerned with the issue of banned books. However, after using the criteria outlined above to evaluate the three, Jenny decided not to use them. Here are some of the reasons why:

- **Domain address.** Two of the sites had addresses that indicated that they had no association with any educational institution, government, business, or organization; the Web sites were developed by individuals for their own personal use. Jenny decided that the materials on these sites were more likely to reflect personal opinion than careful research. The third site was maintained by an organization that Jenny decided to investigate further.

- **Author of the site.** By using the links provided in each site, Jenny discovered that one author was a student writing a paper for an Internet course; another was an individual who supplied some personal information about his life (as well as family photographs), but nothing that indicated expertise on book banning; and the third was identified as a news editor for a newspaper published in California. Jenny needed more information before she could conclude that any of these authors was a reliable source.

- **Identity of the organization.** Only the site authored by the newspaper editor indicated an association with an organization. Using links in the site, Jenny found that he was affiliated with a religious group that strongly advocated the elimination of different races and religions in American life. After reading several articles on the group's Web site, Jenny concluded that the material contained strong political and racial bias that made her question the reliability of the newspaper editor.

- **Date of posting.** None of the sites had been updated within the past year. Although Jenny was interested in both historical and current information on book banning, she was concerned that the authors had made no attempts to keep the information in the sites current and timely.

- **Quality of references.** Only one site contained a list of related readings, and none of the sites used references to support statements of fact or opinion.

- **Quality of material.** Jenny immediately noticed the poor writing quality of the student paper. It was filled with misspellings and grammatical errors, and was poorly organized. The second site demonstrated better quality writing, but the author did not develop or support his ideas sufficiently. For instance, he based much of his claim on an "informal survey" without specifying the details of how the survey was conducted. The site authored by the newspaper editor did not reflect respect for other viewpoints or any attempt to present a balanced perspective on the issue of book banning.

- **Intended use.** Jenny wanted to be sure that the information she used in her argument essay was accurate. The absence of information about two of the authors and the political affiliations of the third caused her to doubt that any of these sites could be relied on for accuracy.

As Jenny discovered, the Internet can offer a wide array of source material to research, but it does take additional effort to determine which sources will meet the academic standards required for research. If you remember to think like an investigator and examine your findings carefully, you'll discover reliable and valuable information and ideas for your argument essays.

Taking Notes

There are as many different styles of note taking as there are writers. Some people like to use 4" × 6" cards, recording one idea on each card. This is useful because you can easily shift cards around as you change your outline; you don't have to recopy material as often. Other students take their notes in their argument journals or on sheets of wide computer paper so they can make notes or copy bibliographic references in the margins. If you decide to use note cards, we offer two words of advice: First, mark every note card in some way to identify the source. You might want to use the author's name, a short abbreviation of the title, or some kind of numbering system tying your note cards and bibliography together. Don't neglect this or you'll find yourself desperately searching for a reference at 2 A.M. on the day your paper is due, with no way to track it down. Second, on each note card indicate whether it's a summary, paraphrase, or direct quote; some people use different colored cards, pens, or highlighters to distinguish the three kinds of notes. Other people use the initials, *S, P,* and *Q* to make the cards. This designation proves useful when deciding on how and when to *document* your sources (see the Documentation Guide).

Most research notes fall into three categories: summary, paraphrase, and quotation.

Summary

Summary is most useful when you want to record the author's main idea without the background or supporting evidence. To summarize accurately, you condense an extended idea into a sentence or more in your own words. Your goal is to record the *essence* of the idea as accurately as possible in your own words.

Here's Jenny's summary of a passage from one of her sources.

Original

During the 1995–96 school year, there were more attempts to remove or restrict educational materials, censor school programs, stifle student expression, pass harmful, anti–public education legislation and inject coercive religious doctrine into the school day than ever before in the 14-year history of this report. Researchers confirmed 475 incidents in 44 states in all regions of the country. Those 475 incidents include both outright attempts to censor materials, as well as efforts to impose an ideological or sectarian agenda through other means. States with the highest number of incidents were California, Pennsylvania and Florida. No incidents, however, were reported in Arkansas, Delaware, Hawaii, North Dakota, Vermont, West Virginia, or Wyoming. (From People for the American Way, *Attacks on the Freedom to Learn,* p. 6.)

Jenny's Summary
People for the American Way reports that attempts to affect public school education through the censorship or control of educational materials or programs increased in 1995–6 more than any other year since their report was published. Four hundred and seventy-five incidents were recorded in 44 states across the country.

For more on writing summaries, see Chapter 2.

Paraphrase

Paraphrasing is useful when you want to preserve an author's line of reasoning or specific ideas, but don't want or need to use the original words. When you paraphrase, you restate the original in your own words and sentence structure as accurately as possible.

Here is an excerpt from another source that Jenny used in her paper:

Original
The past century has witnessed a subtle shift in the role of child-rearing from a private matter to a matter of increasingly public concern. Government bureaucrats display an arrogant, "we know best" attitude that manifests itself in such things as value-free sex education classes for elementary schoolchildren, education agendas that encourage children to question the authority of their parents, and the refusal to allow parents to view the curricula and testing materials used by their children's schools. (From Family Research Council, *Frequently Asked Questions: Parental Rights* <http://www.frc.org:80/faq22.html.>)

Jenny's Paraphrase
According to the Family Research Council, the responsibility of bringing up children has changed during this century from a reliance on the individual family unit to one in which the public plays an important part. The government thinks it knows better about child raising than a child's parents do. As a result, sex education classes in the schools ignore issues of morality, and schools teach children that their parents aren't always right. In addition, schools are unwilling to permit parents access to teaching and testing instruments.

Quotation

Direct quotation should be used only when the author's words are particularly memorable or succinct, or when the author presents factual or numerical evidence that can't be easily paraphrased. You must copy the author's *exact* wording, spelling, capitalization, and punctuation, *as you find it* (even if it contains an obvious mistake). Proofread every direct quotation at least twice; it's easier than you think to leave something out, change a verb tense, or add a word or two. If you want to add words for grammatical completeness or clarity, put them in square brackets such as these

[ ]. If you want to eliminate words, mark the omission with three spaced periods, called *ellipsis points* (if the omissions comes at the end of a sentence, the ellipsis is typed with four spaced periods). If you find a source you are certain to quote from, it might be worthwhile to photocopy it to avoid errors when rewriting the words.

Here is an example of the effective use of quotation, based on another of Jenny's sources:

Original

Congress shall make no law respecting an establishment of religion, or prohibiting the free exercise thereof; or abridging the freedom of speech, or of the press, or the right of the people peaceably to assemble, and to petition the government for a redress of grievances. (From the First Amendment of the Constitution of the United States.)

Jenny's Effective Use of Quotation

Most Americans agree with the rights granted by the First Amendment of the Constitution, which stipulates that "Congress shall make no law . . . abridging the freedom of speech, or of the press."

Drafting Your Paper

Sometimes the sheer size of a researched argument paper can be intimidating. As a result, some writers suffer from "writer's block" when they start composing the paper. Here are several strategies for starting your draft.

1. **Write a Five-Minute Summary.** The five-minute summary asks you to write a quick, one- or two-paragraph description of what your final paper will say. Basically you're creating a thumbnail sketch of the paper to clarify in your own mind how the paper will come together. The summary doesn't have to be formal; some people don't even use complete sentences. Almost always these summaries dispel writer's block and get your creativity flowing.

2. **Divide the Paper into Sections.** Dividing the paper into sections makes the task of writing a long paper more manageable. Most writers divided a paper, as we did in Chapter 5, into beginning, middle, and end, and further subdivide the middle.

3. **First Draft the Sections You're Confident About.** Drafting the sections you feel most confident about first builds momentum for drafting other parts of the paper. As reported by many students, this strategy might also lead you to alter the slant or emphasis of the final paper, thereby resulting in a better outcome.

4. **Use a Simple Code to Indicate Sources.** Using a simple code to indicate sources will save you a great deal of time in revising your paper. As you write your draft, you may not want to interrupt the flow of your ideas to copy quotations or summaries from note cards; instead, you can insert into your draft the author's or source's name and a quick reference to the content so that you'll know on a later draft what you intended to include. Here's an example of how Jenny used coded references in her first draft:

Attempts to ban books in public schools is on the rise. [People, Attacks 6] John Steinbeck's *Of Mice and Men* is a frequent target of protest for parents. [Mitchell, NYT B17]

Here you can see Jenny's code at work as she refers to notes from a report published by People for the American Way and an article from page B17 of the *New York Times.* Later she will have to incorporate these sources into the draft and provide parenthetical citations; for the time being she simply lists in shorthand the evidence to support her general statements.

Incorporating Your Research

Because the effort in finding sources and taking notes is so time-consuming, some writers think that their work will be "wasted" if they don't somehow cram all the notes they've taken into their final papers. Unfortunately, the results of such cramming often look less like a paper and more like note cards stapled together in a long string with an occasional sentence wedged between to provide transitions. Every successful writer ends up gathering more research data than is needed for a paper. But isn't it better to have plenty of material to pick and choose from than not have enough to make a persuasive case? The five tests we explained at the end of Chapter 6 (sufficiency, detail, relevance, avoidance of excess, and appropriateness) should determine which notes to incorporate into the final draft. Here, too, the flexibility of having one note per card may help you because you can shuffle and change the sequence of sources to see which order of presentation will have the most impact on your readers. If you're working with a computer, you may find yourself marking and moving blocks of text around as you judge the arrangement of your evidence. The first arrangement you come up with may not always be the best. Allow yourself some flexibility!

When incorporating sources into your paper, you don't want the "seams" to show between your own writing and the summaries, paraphrases, and quotations from your sources. So it's worth the effort to spend some time writing sentences and phrases that smoothly introduce sources into the text. Consider these two examples:

Awkward   The Anaheim school board decided to ban *Beloved,* and this was "not an example of censorship, but an isolated incident."

Revised   The school board in the Anaheim, California, school system stated that their decision to ban *Beloved* was "not an example of censorship, but an isolated incident."

Remember that while *you,* the writer, may understand how a particular source supports your points, your *readers* may miss the connections unless you provide them. "But I know what I meant!" isn't much of a defense when your readers can't follow your chain of thought. Again we fall back on the analogy of making a case to a jury: A good attorney not only presents a witness's testimony but helps the jury understand what that testimony means.

Attribution

Many students fail to understand the importance of introducing their sources when they incorporate them into a paper. This introduction is called **attribution,** and it is an important part of the process of documentation. Attribution shows your readers that your evidence comes from identifiable, reliable sources. When the attribution contains the name of a book or the author's professional affiliation or other credentials, it also suggests to your readers how reliable the source may be. For instance, if you present a statistic on divorce and attribute it to the book *How to Pick Up Women,* your readers are less likely to respect that statistic than if it came from the U.S. Census Bureau. Likewise, if you cite evidence that eating rutabagas prevents colon cancer, your readers will treat the evidence differently if it comes from an unbiased researcher at the Mayo Clinic rather than from one at the American Rutabaga Institute. In neither case is the evidence less likely to be true, but the attribution in both cases makes the difference in plausibility.

Attribution Verbs

Source Is Neutral

comments	observes	says
describes	points out	sees
explains	records	thinks
illustrates	reports	writes
notes		

Source Infers or Suggests, But Doesn't Actually Say So

analyzes	asks	assesses
concludes	considers	finds
predicts	proposes	reveals
shows	speculates	suggests
supposes	infers	implies

Source Argues

alleges	claims	contends
defends	disagrees	holds
insists	maintains	argues

Source Agrees with Someone/Something Else

admits	agrees	concedes
concurs	grants	allows

Source Is Uneasy or Disagrees

belittles	bemoans	complains
condemns	deplores	deprecates
derides	laments	warns

Many students have only one phrase in their repertoires for attribution: "According to. . . ." This works, but it is not very informative. By choosing a more connotative argumentative verb, as you do when you state a position or proposal, you can signal to your readers the source's attitude toward the statement. For instance, consider this sentence:

Senator Smith _____ that the change is needed.

Look how changing the verb can change the way your audience regards Smith's position (not all of these verbs will work in this sentence structure).

If you're not sure of the connotations of any of these verbs, or you're not sure that the sentence you created works with a particular choice, consult an unabridged dictionary or your instructor. Clumsy attribution can distract readers in the same way typos and grammatical errors can, so you want to make your attributions as smooth as possible. (For placement of a bibliographic reference after attributed material, see the next section on documentation.)

Revising and Editing Your Paper

After you have worked your source material into a draft, it's time to look at your writing skeptically, as your readers will. Start by testing all the parts of your argument. This may not be easy to do because you've been living with this topic for several weeks and may have lost your objectivity and ability to see the gaps. (If you're working in writing groups, ask another member to read your paper and offer you some feedback on it.) Then change, delete, add, or reorganize material to make your case more effectively.

To help you revise your argument, we recommend making an outline of the draft *as you've written it*—not as you intended to write it. This will serve as an x-ray of the paper, helping you detect any holes or imbalances. Moreover, it will show you the actual order in which points are presented so that you can consider reorganizing or changing your argumentative strategy. The strategies explained in Chapters 6 and 7 for assessing evidence and considering claims ought to help you at this stage; apply them as stringently to your own writing as you would to an essay you're reading.

If you made notes in your argument journal at an earlier date about connections you wanted to make in your final paper, now is the time to include those connections if, in fact, they fit into the paper's final shape. You might also consider other kinds of evidence to include. Can you think of personal experiences or those of other people to support the evidence of your outside authorities? Have you found facts and statistics to buttress the opinions you present? What are your readers' criteria for judging an issue? Have you presented claims that meet those criteria and phrased them in that manner? It's also time to make sure that all transitions between points are included and are accurate. For instance, if you switch points around, make sure that the point you can "second" is actually the second, not the third or fourth. Also, check to be sure you've included documentation for all your sources and that you have bibliographic note cards or other records of documentation information to prepare the notes in your final copy. Then polish your prose so that your sentences are smooth, your paragraphs are complete, and your grammar and punctuation are precise. Many students "let down" their efforts when they sense their papers are nearing completion; as a result, their final grades suffer. The revising and editing stage requires sharp attention. Don't undercut all your hard research efforts by presenting your argument in anything but its best form.

Preparing and Proofreading Your Final Manuscript

Once you have polished the draft to your satisfaction, it is time to attend to the presentation of your paper. Flawless presentation is important in research, not only because of the appreciation it will win from your instructor and readers, but also because it will reinforce your credibility with your readers. A sloppy paper with typographical or grammatical errors, missing documentation, or illegible print makes your readers think that your argument might be sloppy as well. A well-prepared paper suggests to your readers that you have taken extra care to ensure that everything is correct—not only the presentation, but the content as well. This good impression may make readers more inclined to accept your arguments.

Most instructors expect research papers to be neatly and legibly typed with clear titles, double spacing, standard margins (1-inch) and type sizes (10- or 12-point), and minimal handwritten corrections. Your last name and the page number should appear in the upper right-hand corner of every page after the title page. For English courses the standard guide to manuscript format is the *MLA Handbook for Writers of Research Papers*, 5th edition. MLA requirements are spelled out in most college composition handbooks and illustrated in Jenny's final paper (see the Documentation Guide). Before you submit your paper, proofread it carefully for typographical errors, misspellings, omitted words, and other minor errors. If possible, let several hours elapse before your final proofreading so you can see what you've actually typed instead of what you *think* you typed. Never let the pressure of a deadline keep you from proofreading your paper. Readers get annoyed by minor errors, and annoyed readers are less likely to be persuaded by the content of your argument.

Plagiarism

Plagiarism is a crime in the academic community. The scholarly world operates by exchanging information and acknowledging the sources of this information. If you fail to acknowledge your sources or make it appear that someone else's work is actually your own, you are sabotaging the exchange of scholarly information. You're blocking the channels. Perhaps it doesn't seem important to you now, but you should know that plagiarism has very serious consequences. It can earn you a failing grade on an assignment or for a course, a suspension or even expulsion from school, and/or a permanent notation on the transcripts that future employers and graduate schools will see. Even if you are never caught, you've still stolen ideas and words from someone.

Plagiarism falls into two categories: intentional and accidental. Intentional plagiarism includes copying a phrase, a sentence, or a longer passage from a source and passing it off as your own; summarizing or paraphrasing someone else's ideas without acknowledgment; and buying or borrowing a paper written by someone else and submitting it as your own. Accidental plagiarism includes forgetting to place quotation marks around someone else's words, and not acknowledging a source because you were ignorant of the need to document it. Carelessness and ignorance are not defenses against plagiarism.

Many questions about plagiarism involve the tricky subject of *common knowledge*—that is, standard information in a field of study, as well as commonsense observations and proverbial wisdom. Standard information includes the major facts in a discipline—for example, the chemical formula for water is H_2O or the Seneca Falls Convention for Women's Rights took place in 1848. If most of your sources accept such a fact without acknowledgment, you can assume it is common knowledge to readers in that field. However, if you're dealing with lesser-known facts (the numbers of soldiers at the Battle of Hastings), interpretations of those facts (assessments of the importance of the Seneca Falls meeting), or a specialist's observation (a scholar's analysis of Susan B. Anthony's rhetoric), you'll need to provide documentation.

Commonsense information, such as the notions that politicians are concerned with getting votes or that icy roads make driving dangerous, need not be documented. Proverbs and clichés don't need documentation either, although proverbs taken from recognized poems or literary works do. (Thus, "A stitch in time" needs no documentation, but "To be or not to be" should carry a reference to *Hamlet*).

Here are four simple rules to help you avoid plagiarism.

1. *Take your research notes carefully.* Write down (or print out) a full bibliographical reference for each source (the forms for these appear in the Documentation Guide). Also, note whether you are quoting, paraphrasing, or summarizing what you find in your source (see earlier discussion in this chapter). If your notes are clear and thorough, you'll never have to worry about which words and ideas are yours and which are your sources'.

2. *Always introduce your source carefully so that your audience knows to whom they're listening.* Proper attribution is a signal to your readers that you're switching from your own work to someone else's. It also is a signal to you to check that a source is represented accurately (with no exaggeration) and that a bibliographic citation appears in your list of Works Cited or References.

3. *When in doubt, document.* While it is possible to overdocument, it is not an intellectual crime to do so. Rather, it reveals a lack of self-confidence in your own argument or your determination to prove to your instructor and readers that you've seen every source ever published on your subject. However, overdocumenting is a less serious academic sin than plagiarizing!

4. *Enter the documentation right after the use of the source; it doesn't "carry over" between paragraphs or pages.* It is tempting, especially when using one source for an extended period, to leave all the documentation until the end of a large pas-

sage of text (which might be several paragraphs or several pages in length). But even if you weave attribution skillfully throughout the whole passage, the convention in academics is that you document a source in each paragraph in which you use it. If another source intervenes, it is twice as important that the main source be documented in every paragraph of use. So if you use the same article in four successive paragraphs, each of those paragraphs must have some parenthetical source reference. With skillful attribution the parenthetical reference can be reduced to a simple page number, which won't interrupt the "flow" of your text.

To understand how plagiarism works, let's look at some of the ways writers might handle, or mishandle, this passage from Dennis Baron's article "English in a Multicultural Society," which appeared in the Spring 1991 issue of *Social Policy*. Here's the original passage from page 8:

> The notion of a national language sometimes wears the disguise of inclusion: we must all speak English to participate meaningfully in the democratic process. Sometimes it argues unity: we must speak one language to understand one another and share both culture and country. Those who insist on English often equate bilingualism with lack of patriotism. Their intention to legislate official English often masks racism and certainly fails to appreciate cultural difference: it is a thinly veiled measure to disenfranchise anyone not like "us."

Plagiarized Use
Supporters of U.S. English argue we must all speak one language to understand one another and share both culture and country. But Dennis Baron argues that "[t]heir intention to legislate official English often masks racism and certainly fails to appreciate cultural difference" (8). English-only legislation really intends to exclude anyone who is not like "us."

This is plagiarism because the writer has copied Baron's words in the first sentence and paraphrased them in the last, but made it appear as though only the middle sentence were actually taken from Baron's article.

Plagiarized Use
Calls for a national language sometimes wear the disguise of inclusion, according to linguist Dennis Baron. When U.S. English argues that we must all speak English to participate meaningfully in the democratic process, or that we must speak one language to understand one another and share both culture and country, Baron says they are masking racism and failing to appreciate cultural difference (8).

Here the plagiarism comes in presenting Baron's actual words without quotation marks, so it looks as if the writer is paraphrasing rather than quoting. Even with the attribution and the citation of the source, this paragraph is still an example of plagiarism because the direct quotations are disguised as the writer's paraphrase.

Acceptable Use

Linguist Dennis Baron argues that supporters of official English legislation use the reasons of inclusions, unity, and patriotism to justify these laws, but that their efforts may hide racist and culturally intolerant positions. Baron says that sometimes English-only laws are "thinly-veiled measure[s] to disenfranchise anyone not like 'us.'" (8).

Here the source is properly handled. The writer paraphrases most of the original text in the first sentence, then skillfully incorporates a direct quotation in the second (note the use of square brackets to make the noun agree in number with the verb, and the conversion of double quotation marks from the original into single quotation marks in the quote). The attribution clearly says that both points are taken from Baron, but the quotation marks show where Baron's actual words, rather than the writer's, are used.

DOCUMENTATION GUIDE

MLA and APA Styles

Almost every academic discipline has developed its own system of *documentation,* a sort of code for indicating where the writer's evidence may be found. A good way to think of the rules of documentation is by analogy to a sport, for example, basketball: Academic readers expect you to play by the established rules (what to document, how to avoid plagiarism, how to attribute sources). If you want to play the game, you have to observe the rules. At the same time—as you probably know—there are accepted variations on the rules (e.g., 30- or 45-second shot clocks, the dimensions of the 3-point line) in certain basketball leagues. The various styles of documentation used in the humanities, social sciences, and natural sciences are the equivalent of these acceptable variations.

You must document any idea or words you *summarize, paraphrase,* or *quote directly* from a source. The two most common variations on documentation used in colleges and universities are the Modern Language Association (MLA) style, used widely in the humanities, and the American Psychological Association (APA) style, used widely in the social sciences. We will explain them in detail later in this chapter. (Some of your courses may also require you to use CBE [Council of Biology Editors] style; *The Chicago Manual of Style,* which you might know as Turabian style; or a journalistic style guide such as *The Associated Press Style Book.*) Think of these systems not as annoyances for you as a writer, but as rule books for playing the game of researched writing on different courts. Your instructor will tell you which rules to follow.

Where Does the Documentation Go?

Fortunately, both MLA and APA styles have abandoned footnotes in favor of parenthetical citations within the paper and a source list at the end of the paper, a much neater format to work with. In both styles you put a brief reference or attribution to your source in parentheses within the body of the paper, and a full bibliographical citation in a list of *Works Cited* (MLA) or *References* (APA). (These are the equivalents of what you probably called a "Bibliography" in high school.) Documenting your sources, if performed properly, will help you avoid plagiarism. The

203

shape that citations take in the two systems, however, is a little different, so make sure you observe the forms carefully.

Documentation Style

Let's look at how both systems handle documentation for some of the most commonly used information sources. Suppose you want to quote from Charles Siebert's article, "The DNA We've Been Dealt," which appeared in the September 17, 1995, issue of the *New York Times Magazine*. Here's how it would appear in your list of sources:

MLA   Siebert, Charles. "The DNA We've Been Dealt." *New York Times Magazine* 17 Sept. 1995: 50–64.

APA   Siebert, C. (1995, September 17). The DNA we've been dealt. *New York Times Magazine,* pp. 50–64.

As you can see, each style orders information differently.* Likewise, both styles use a parenthetical reference in the paper to show where the evidence comes from, but again they do it differently.

MLA   One author reports that "the Genome Project is expected to leave us with a complete readout of our biological blueprint by the year 2005 (at an estimated cost of $3 billion)" (Siebert 53).

If the author's name appears in your attribution, only the page number needs to go in the parentheses:

MLA   Charles Siebert reports that "the Genome Project is expected to leave us with a complete readout of our biological blueprint by the year 2005 (at an estimated cost of $3 billion)" (53).

Both references tell your readers that they can find this source in your Works Cited list, alphabetized by the last name, "Siebert." If you had more than one reference to Siebert in your Works Cited list, then you would add a shortened form of the title in the parentheses so readers would know to which Siebert article you were referring (Siebert, *DNA* 53).

The APA style references for the same situations would be

APA   One author reports that "the Genome Project is expected to leave us with a complete readout of our bio-

---

*Note that MLA begins the entry flush with the left margin; subsequent lines are indented 1/2" or five typewriter spaces. For APA, the first line of the entry is indented five spaces, and subsequent lines are flush with the margin. All entries should be double-spaced.

logical blueprint by the year 2005 (at an estimated cost of $3 billion)" (Siebert, 1995, p. 53).

or

APA   Charles Siebert (1995) reports that "the Genome Project is expected to leave us with a complete readout of our biological blueprint by the year 2005 (at an estimated cost of $3 billion)" (p. 53).

When you use more than one work by an author in your paper, APA style distinguishes them by date of publication. For example, if you cited two Siebert articles from 1995, the earlier one is designated 1995a, and the second is referred to as 1995b.

Using parenthetical citations for electronic sources can be much trickier because such sources typically have no page numbers. If your source uses paragraph numbers, provide the paragraph number preceded by *par.* or *pars.* If you need to include the author's name or a brief title, place a comma after the name or title. If another type of designation is used in the source to delineate its parts (such as *screens* or *Part II*), write out the word used for that part:

MLA   Between 1992 and 1996, the message delivered by political advertisements changed dramatically (Edwards, par. 15).

APA   Between 1992 and 1996, the message delivered by political advertisements changed dramatically (Edwards, 1998, par. 15).

If your source has no numbering, then no page or paragraph numbers should appear in your parenthetical reference unless your instructor indicates otherwise. Some instructors ask students to number the paragraphs of electronic sources to make references easier to locate.

A Brief Guide to MLA and APA Styles

The handbooks for MLA and APA documentation are available in most college libraries. If you don't find the information you need in the following brief guide, look for these books or Web sites:

MLA   Gibaldi, Joseph. *MLA Handbook for Writers of Research Papers.* 5th edition. New York: MLA, 1999.

The Web site of the Modern Language Association is: <http://www.mla.org>.

APA   *Publication manual of the American Psychological
                           Association (*4th ed.). (1994). Washington, D.C.: APA.

The American Psychological Association does not provide a guide to documentation
on its Web site; however, the Purdue University Online Writing Lab provides a useful
guide to APA documentation: <http://owl.english.purdue.edu/Files/34.html>.

General Format for Books

MLA   Author. *Title.* Edition. City of Publication: Publisher,
                           Year.

APA   Author. (Year of Publication). *Title.* City of Publi-
                           cation, State: Publisher.

One Author

MLA   Kozol, Jonathan. *Savage Inequalities: Children in Amer-
                           ica's Schools.* New York: Crown, 1991.

APA   Kozol, J. (1991). *Savage inequalities: Children in
                           America's schools.* New York: Crown.

MLA uses the author's full first name plus middle initial, whereas APA uses the
initial of the first name (unless more initials are needed to distinguish among people with the same initials). APA only capitalizes first words and proper nouns in titles and subtitles; MLA capitalizes all words except prepositions, conjunctions, and
particles. MLA lists only the city; APA lists the city but also includes the state if the
city is unfamiliar or could be confused with another. Finally, MLA permits the abbreviation of certain publishers' names, whereas APA drops unnecessary words such
as *Co., Inc.,* and *Publishers.*

Two or More Authors

MLA   Pyles, Thomas, and John Algeo. *History and Develop-
                           ment of the English Language.* 4th ed. Fort Worth:
                           Harcourt, 1993.

APA   Pyles, T., & Algeo, J. (1993). *History and develop-
                           ment of the English language* (4th ed.). Fort Worth, TX:
                           Harcourt, Brace, Jovanovich.

In MLA style, only the first author's name is given last name first. In APA style,
the ampersand (&) is used to join authors' names. The ampersand is also used in
parenthetical references (e.g., "[Pyles & Algeo 1993, p. 23]") but not in attribu-

tions (e.g., "According to Pyles and Algeo"). In MLA style, for works with four or more authors, you may replace all but the first author's name by the abbreviation *et al.* You may use that abbreviation in APA style if there are six or more authors.

More Than One Work by an Author

MLA   Baron, Dennis. *Grammar and Gender.* New Haven: Yale UP, 1986.

                         ---. *Grammar and Good Taste.* New Haven: Yale UP, 1982.

In MLA style, if you cite more than one work by a particular author, the individual works are listed in alphabetical order. For the second and any additional entries, type three hyphens and a period instead of the author's name; then skip a space and type the title, underlined.

In APA style, when citing more than one work by an author, the author's name is repeated and the entries are listed chronologically (first published to most recent) rather than in alphabetical order. If two works by one author are published in the same year, then the works are listed alphabetically by title.

Anthology with an Editor

MLA   Shapiro, Michael, ed. *Language and Politics.* New York: New York UP, 1984.

APA   Shapiro, M. (Ed.). (1984). *Language and politics.* New York: New York University Press.

Essay in a Collection or Anthology

MLA   Davis, Vivian I. "Paranoia in Language Politics." *Not Only English: Reaffirming America's Multilingual Heritage.* Ed. Harvey A. Daniels. Urbana: NCTE, 1990. 71–76.

APA   Davis, V. (1990). Paranoia in language politics. In H. Daniels (Ed.), *Not only English: Reaffirming America's multilingual heritage* (pp. 71–76). Urbana, IL: NCTE.

Book in a Later Edition

MLA   Zinn, Howard. *The Politics of History.* 2nd ed. Urbana: Illinois UP, 1990.

APA   Zinn, H. (1990). *The politics of history* (2nd ed.). Urbana, IL: University of Illinois Press.

Multivolume Work

MLA	Lincoln, Abraham. *The Collected Works of Abraham Lincoln.* Ed. Roy P. Basler. 5 vols. New Brunswick: Rutgers UP, 1953.
APA	Lincoln, A. (1953). *The collected works of Abraham Lincoln* (R. P. Basler, Ed.). (Vol. 5). New Brunswick, NJ: Rutgers University Press.

Book with a Group or Corporate Author

MLA	National Council of Teachers of English Committee on Classroom Practices. *Non-native and Nonstandard Dialect Students.* Urbana: NCTE, 1982.
APA	National Council of Teachers of English. Committee on Classroom Practices. (1982). *Non-native and nonstandard dialect students.* Urbana, IL: NCTE.

Begin the entry with the corporate or group name alphabetized by the first letter of the main word [not including *a, an,* or *the*].

Reference Works

MLA	Risanowsky, A. "Language." *The New Columbia Encyclopedia.* 1975 ed.
APA	Risanowsky, A. (1975). Language. In *The new Columbia encyclopedia* (Vol. 11, pp. 143–148). New York: Columbia.

If the reference book is widely available (such as a major encyclopedia or bibliography), a short bibliography form as shown here is acceptable in MLA; APA recommends including more information rather than less. For a less widely known reference book, MLA recommends using the form for a book, multiple-authored book, or series, depending on what the book is.

Editor's Preparation of a Previous Work

MLA	Austen, Jane. *Pride and Prejudice.* Ed. R. W. Chapman. Oxford: Oxford UP, 1988.
APA	Austen, J. (1988). *Pride and prejudice* (R. W. Chapman, Ed.). Oxford: Oxford University Press. (Original work published 1813).

Translated Work

MLA	Calvino, Italo. *Italian Folktales.* Trans. George Martin. New York: Harcourt, 1980.
APA	Calvino, I. (1980). *Italian folktales* (G. Martin, Trans.). New York: Harcourt. (Original work published 1956).

In APA style the date of the translation is placed after the author's name. The date of the original publication of the work appears in parentheses at the end of the citation. This text would be cited in an essay as (Calvino 1956/1980).

Anonymous Work

MLA	*Microsoft Windows.* Vers. 3.1. Belleville: Microsoft, 1992.
APA	*Microsoft Windows 3.1.* [Computer software]. (1992). Belleville, WA: Microsoft.

Articles

MLA format and APA format for articles are similar to the formats for books. One of the few differences concerns the "volume number" of each issue. Volume numbers for any magazine or journal found in a library or acquired by subscription (these usually appear six times a year or less frequently) should be included in your entry. If a journal appears monthly or more frequently, or can be acquired on newsstands, you can usually omit the volume number. If the journal has continuous pagination (i.e., if the January volume ends on page 88 and the February volume begins on page 89), you don't need to include the month or season of the issue in your citation. If the journal starts over with page 1 in each issue, then you must include the month or season in your citation.

Magazines and newspapers (unlike scholarly journals) often dispense articles over several pages (for instance pages 35–37, then continuing on 114–115). MLA and APA permit using the form "35+" instead of typing out all the pages on which such articles appear, except that in APA references to newspaper articles, all page numbers must be noted.

MLA	Author. "Article Title." *Journal or Magazine Title* volume number (Date): inclusive pages.
APA	Author. (Date). Article title. *Journal or Magazine Title, volume number,* inclusive pages.

Scholarly Journal with Continuous Pagination

MLA   Madrid, Arturo. "Official English: A False Policy Issue." *Annals of the American Association of Political and Social Sciences* 508 (1990): 62–65.

APA   Madrid, A. (1990). Official English: A false policy issue. *Annals of the American Association of Political and Social Sciences, 508,* 62–65.

Scholarly Journal with Each Issue Paged Separately

MLA   Baron, Dennis. "English in a Multicultural America." *Social Policy* 31 (Spring 1991): 5–14.

If this journal used issue numbers instead of seasons, the form would be *Social Policy* 31.1 (1991): 5–14.

APA   Baron, D. (1991). English in a multicultural America. *Social Policy, 31,* 5–14.

Magazine Article

MLA   Joelson, J. R. "English: The Language of Liberty." *The Humanist* July/Aug. 1989: 35+.

APA   Joelson, J. R. (1989, July/August). English: The language of liberty. *The Humanist,* 35+.

This is the form for a magazine that appears monthly. For a magazine that appears bimonthly or weekly, see the examples under "Anonymous Article."

Anonymous Article

MLA   "Lessons from the U.S. Army." *Fortune* 22 Mar. 1993: 68+.

APA   Lessons from the U.S. army. (1993, March 22). *Fortune,* 68+.

Review

MLA   Estrada, Alfred J. "Divided Over a Common Language." Rev. of *Hold Your Tongue: Bilingualism and the Politics of "English Only,"* by James Crawford. *Washington Post* 4 Oct. 1992: WBK4+.

APA   Estrada, A. (1992, October 4). Divided over a common language [Review of the book *Hold your tongue: Bilingualism and the politics of "English Only"*]. *The Washington Post,* pp. WBK4, WBK8.

When newspapers designate sections with identifying letters (e.g., A, B, or here, WBK), that information is included in the reference. The "4+" indicates that the review begins on page 4 and continues on other nonadjacent pages in the newspaper. APA includes initial particles such as "The" in a newspaper title; MLA omits them. If the reviewer's name does not appear, begin with "Rev. of *Title*" in the MLA system or [Review of the book *Title*]" in the APA system. If the reviewer's name does not appear, but the review has a title, begin with the title of the review in both systems.

Newspaper Article

MLA	Maliconico, Joseph. "New Influx of Immigrants." *New Jersey News-Tribune* 17 Mar. 1991: A1.
APA	Maliconico, J. (1991, March 17). New influx of immigrants. *The New Jersey News-Tribune,* p. A1.

Newspaper Editorial

MLA	Gilmar, Sybil T. "Language Foreign to U.S. Schools." Editorial. *Philadelphia Inquirer* 25 Apr. 1990: 17A.
APA	Gilmar, S. (1990, April 25). Language foreign to U.S. schools [Editorial]. *The Philadelphia Inquirer,* p. 17A.

Letter to the Editor of a Magazine or Newspaper

MLA	Shumway, Norman D. "Make English the Official Language." *Chicago Tribune* 30 Aug. 1992, sec. 4: 2.
APA	Shumway, N. (1992, August 30). Make English the official language [Letter to the editor]. *Chicago Tribune,* sec. 4, p. 2.

If the newspaper or magazine doesn't give a title to the letter, for MLA style add the word Letter followed by a period after the author's name. Do not underline or use quotation marks. For APA style skip that information and use the rest of the citation form.

Electronic Sources
Editorial or Letter to the Editor

MLA	Baker, Stewart. "The New Escape Censorship? Ha!" Editorial. *Wired* 3.09. 1 Apr. 1998 <http://www.wired.com/wired/3.09/departments/baker.if.html>.

If this were a letter to the editor, *Editorial* would be replaced by *Letter*.

APA	Baker, S. (1998, April 1). The net escape censorship? Ha! [25 paragraphs]. *Wired* [On-line serial], *3.09.*

Available: http://www.wired.com/wired/3.09/
departments/ baker.if.html

Electronic Mail

MLA	Mendez, Michael R. "Re: Solar power." E-mail to Edgar V. Atamian. 11 Sept. 1996.
APA	In APA, electronic correspondence via e-mail, listservs, and newsgroups typically does not appear in the reference list. It is cited only in an intext reference: (M. Mendez, personal communication, September 11, 1996).

Listserv

MLA	Kosten, Arthur. "Major Update of the WWWVL Migration and Ethnic Relations." Online posting. 7 Apr. 1998. ERCOMER News. 7 May 1998 <http://www.ercomer.org/archive/ercomernews/0002.html>.

Magazine Article

MLA	Pitta, Julie. "Un-Wired." *Forbes* 20 Apr. 1998. 6 Apr. 1998 <http://www.forbes.com/Forbes/98/020/6108045a.htm>.
APA	Pitta, J. (1998, April 20). Un-wired? [6 paragraphs]. *Forbes* [On-line serial]. Available: http://www.forbes. com/Forbes/98/0420/6108045a.htm

Note that MLA uses angle brackets to enclose the on-line address; APA does not.

Electronic Journal

MLA	Rumsey, Deborah J. "Cooperative Teaching Approach to Introductory Statistics." *Journal of Statistics Education* 6.1 (1998): 77 pars. 21 July 1998 <http://www. stat.ncsu.edu/info/jse/v6n1/rumsey.html>.
APA	Rumsey, D. (1998). A cooperative teaching approach to introductory statistics [77 paragraphs]. *Journal of Statistics Education* [On-line serial], 6(1). Available: http://www.stat.ncsu.edu/info/jse/v6n1/rumsey.html

CD-ROM

MLA	"Euthanasia." *The American Heritage Dictionary of the English Language.* 3rd ed. CD-ROM. Boston: Houghton-Mifflin, 1992.
APA	Euthanasia. (1992). In *The American heritage dictionary of the English language.* [CD-ROM]. Boston: Houghton-Mifflin.

Online Book

MLA	Clark, Rufus W. *The African Slave Trade.* Boston: American Tract Society: 1860. 19 June 1998 <http://moa.umdl.umich.edu/cgi/bin/moa/idx?notisid=AHL6707>.
APA	Clark, R. W. (1860). *The African slave trade* [Online]. Available: http://moa.umdl.umich.edu/cgi-bin/moa/idx?notisid=AHL6707

Web Page

MLA	*Using Modern Language Association (MLA) Format.* Purdue University Online Writing Lab. 1 August 1998 <http://owl.english.purdue.edu/files/33.html>.
APA	Using Modern Language Association (MLA) Format. (1998, 15 April). Purdue University Online Writing Lab. [Online]. Available: http://owl.english.purdue.edu/files/33.html. (1998, August 1).

For MLA, begin the entry with the name of the individual who created the Web site (last name first), if available, and then a period. Follow with the title of the site (underlined); the name of the organization associated with the site, if available; the date of access; and the electronic address.

For APA, begin with the last name of the author, then initials, then a period. Follow with the date of publication or latest update. If there is no individual author, then begin with the title of the site, then date of publication or update. Follow with the name of the organization associated with the site, if available; the medium; the electronic address; and the date of access.

Miscellaneous Sources
Film, Filmstrip, Slide Program, and Videotape

MLA	Lee, Spike, dir. *Do the Right Thing.* Perf. Lee, Danny Aiello, Ossie Davis, Ruby Dee, and Richard Edson. Paramount, 1989.

APA   Lee, S. (Director). (1989). *Do the right thing.* [Film].
Hollywood, CA: Paramount.

To cite a filmstrip, slide program, or videotape in MLA style, include the name
of the medium after the title without underlining (italicizing) or using quotation
marks, and add the running time to the end. If you are citing the work as a whole,
rather than the work of one of the creative artists involved in the project, start with
the title instead. For instance:

MLA   *Do the Right Thing.* Dir. Spike Lee. Videocassette. Paramount, 1989.

In APA style, substitute the name of the medium for *Film:* [Videotape].

Television or Radio Program

MLA   *The Bilingual Battle.* Dir. Steve Adubato, Jr. PBS, Secaucus. 25 March 1996.

APA   Adubato Jr., S. Director. (1996, March 25). *The
bilingual battle.* Secaucus, NJ: PBS.

Interview

MLA   Pennington, Professor Linda Beth. Personal interview.
20 April 1993.

APA   In APA, personal communications including interviews do not appear in the reference list. They are cited
only in an intext reference: (L. Pennington, personal interview, April 20, 1993).

The APA doesn't offer formal forms for "unrecoverable" materials such as personal letters or e-mail messages, lectures, and speeches, and in professional practice
these are not included in References listings. However, in collegiate writing assignments, most instructors will ask you to include them. You may, therefore, have to
design a hybrid citation form based on these more standard forms. Remember that
the APA encourages you to provide more, rather than less, information in your citations. The MLA has forms for almost any kind of communication, even nonrecov-
erable ones. Consult the *MLA Handbook for Writers of Research Papers,* 5th edition,
to find additional forms.

Sample Research Papers

Following are two sample student research papers, the first in MLA format and the
second in APA format. As you read them, notice the margins and other format requirements of the two different styles, such as the use of running heads, the placement of titles, and the different citation forms. We have added marginal annotations to highlight these special features and to demonstrate the structural elements
of the arguments.

Benson 1

Jenny Benson

Professor Johnson

English 112

November 22, 1998

Heading appears on first page

Censorship: A Threat to Public Education

Nearly fifty years ago, Ray Bradbury published the novel *Fahrenheit 451,* the story of a society so fearful of knowledge and uncensored thought that it chooses to burn all the books that exist. In this futuristic society, fire fighters no longer extinguish fires; they set them in a determined effort to control what people know and think. Books and the knowledge they hold are seen as evil and must be destroyed. While Bradbury's novel can be found in the science fiction section of most libraries, the plot of his book is not so farfetched as some people might believe. The danger of censorship continues to threaten our basic freedom to choose for ourselves what to read and to make our own judgments about its value.

Double-space between title and first line and throughout paper

1"

One inch margin on each side and at bottom

Introduces general topic and position

In recent years, the public schools have been the battleground upon which individuals who wish to limit our access to knowledge and information have focused their efforts. According to the 1996 People for the American Way annual survey of censorship challenges to public education, there were 300 attempts in 1995-96 to restrict or remove

Narrows topic to censorship in public schools

Provides background information

Last name and page number at right-hand corner of each page

1"

1/2"

Benson 2

books used in public school classrooms or libraries. The success rate for these challenges was 41% (6). Each successful challenge directly limited the rights of many school children. These incidents included attempts to censor health and history textbooks; literature collections, novels, and films; school newspapers and literary magazines; and numerous other types of publications (12). They occurred across the entire country; the survey documents forty-four states reporting censorship attempts (6).

Specific page number of source in parenthetical reference because author already cited in text

Most Americans agree with the rights granted by the First Amendment, which stipulates that "Congress shall make no law . . . abridging the freedom of speech, or of the press" ("Constitution"). A 1997 survey of 1,001 adults conducted by Market Shares Corporation for the *Chicago Tribune* confirmed that over half of those surveyed support the First Amendment rights guaranteed by the Constitution ("Speech Right"). However, recent controversies in public schools across the country over the choices of books for school reading and library use indicate that a small but vocal group of Americans think that censorship is appropriate when parents object to the subject matter of the books chosen for school use. In these cases, parents often demand that their son or daughter not be required to read a particular book or that the book be removed from the school reading list or library. As the statistics above

Ellipsis indicates words omitted from quotation

Abbreviated title of source in parenthetical reference; no page number because source is a single page

Benson 3

indicate, 41% of the time, they are effective. Statistics used
While parents do have the right to control   as evidence
the reading material of their own children,
the decision by school boards or school
administrators to remove a book from a school
in response to a protest by one or more
parents is wrong. Parents should not have the   Claim
right to censor or control the books used in
the public schools.

James L. Payne of the *National Review*   Acknowledges
correctly points out that parents have a   other positions
constitutional right to question the schools
about what their own children are reading
and learning (58). If they have a personal
objection to this material, they also have a
right to request that the school seriously
consider their complaints. It is important
for parents to become involved with their
children's education. As the Family Research
Council, a conservative political
organization, asserts in its position on
parental rights, parents should have the
right to "direct the upbringing and education   Direct quotation
of their children." However, this control   from electronic
should be limited to their own children. When   source with no
parents decide that the entire school   page numbers
curriculum should reflect their personal
values, they are affecting the education of
every child in the school, not just their   Re-states claim
own.

While schools need to be aware of the
concerns of parents in their district, this
should not be a primary consideration when

Benson 4

Reason supporting claim

they are deciding upon the books children should read as part of their studies. These choices should be based upon solid academic principles and established learning objectives rather than on the religious, social, or moral beliefs of particular individuals or groups. If the schools try to accommodate these narrow concerns, they will find that they are sacrificing great works of literature for minor and sometimes foolish reasons. For example, *The On-Line Books Page* Web site indicates that in 1996, Shakespeare's *Twelfth Night* was removed from

Specific evidence

the curriculum of a New Hampshire school district because some felt that it encouraged alternative lifestyle choices. In addition, "Little Red Riding Hood" was banned in two California school districts because the heroine is described as taking food and wine

Web site source. No page number.

to her grandmother (Ockerbloom). It is difficult to believe that any student would begin crossdressing after reading *Twelfth Night,* nor does it seem likely that children would be tempted to use alcohol after reading "Little Red Riding Hood." Yet, school districts banned these books as a result of these complaints.

Reason supporting claim

Even school boards may not be the best judges of the value or lack of value in a literary work. Sometimes these groups overreact to parents' complaints without having the knowledge needed to judge these books on their educational merits. In

Benson 5

Anaheim, California, the school board voted
4-1 to remove Toni Morrison's *Beloved* from
the Advanced Placement curriculum after one
anonymous individual in the community
objected to its contents. The board took this
action despite the recommendation of a joint
parent-school committee appointed to study
the book and the approval of an Instructional
Materials Review Committee. What is even more
revealing is that two of the four board
members who voted against the book did not
even read the entire text (Manfredi).

    Many parents want to protect their
children from ideas that they believe are
dangerous or frightening. While these
individuals are well-intentioned, their
concerns are misplaced. What these parents
fail to realize is that reading about these
ideas in the controlled setting of a
classroom gives children the opportunity
to ask questions and receive answers that
may help them better understand troubling
issues. Class discussion with their peers can
help them examine their own beliefs and
values. It may also reassure them that their
fears or fantasies are normal and shared by
others. For instance, *One Fat Summer,* a well-
respected book by Robert Lipsyte, was
assigned in a seventh grade developmental
reading class in Levittown, New York. It is
the story of an overweight boy who learns
how to deal with his tormentors and feel
self-confident. According to the teachers in
that district, students enjoyed reading and

Specific evidence

Acknowledges
possible
objection

Responds to
objection

Specific evidence

Benson 6

discussing this story because it was about the difficulties of growing up. However, this book was removed from the class because one parent complained about its treatment of adolescent sexuality (Vinciguerra) Now all of the children will be deprived of these discussions. Moreover, often these "dangerous" ideas are ones that children have encountered or will be exposed to at some point in their lives. Teen pregnancy, rape, child abuse, gangs, and drugs are all a part of our world. Trying to protect children from being exposed to them is futile and may make them unprepared to face these problems later in life.

Acknowledges possible objection and responds

It is fair for parents to expect the school district to establish clear academic guidelines for choosing the books used in the classroom. Books should be age-appropriate, possess literary merit, and relate to the rest of the curriculum. Parents have the right to question whether the school's choices fulfill these standards. But, especially in the case of library books, the school also has the right to expect parents to monitor their own children's reading. If parents do not wish their child to borrow a certain book from the school library, it is their responsibility to enforce this, not the school's. Removing the book from the school library because a parent finds it objectionable unfairly deprives other children of the opportunity to read it.

Benson 7

But the strongest reason to prevent the
banning of books in the public schools by
individuals or special interest groups is
that it undermines the basic reason for
public education: the free and open exchange
of ideas and access to knowledge and
information. By limiting students' exposure
to ideas, we limit their ability to think
critically, to make informed judgments based
on a broad range of information, and to
express those ideas as the First Amendment
guarantees. We prevent them from exercising
the full rights of their citizenship. By
catering to the concerns of a few, we violate
the freedom of the majority. In the United
States Supreme Court decision *Board of
Education v. Pico* in 1982, a case which
involved the banning of nine books from a
school library, the majority opinion stated:

> Just as access to ideas makes it
> possible for citizens . . . to exercise
> their right of free speech and press in
> a meaningful manner, such access
> prepares students for active and
> effective participation in the
> pluralistic, often contentious society
> in which they will soon be adult
> members. The special circumstances of
> the school library make that
> environment especially appropriate for
> the recognition of the First Amendment
> rights of students. (U.S. Supreme Court)

Reason
supporting claim

Use of authority

Long quotation
(more than four
lines). Left
margin indented
one inch
(10 spaces).
Double-spaced.

Parenthetical
reference
appears after
final
punctuation

Benson 8

This statement makes it clear that the Justices understood the connection between knowledge and freedom, and recognized that students are entitled to both.

Barbara Dority, an activist with the Washington Coalition Against Censorship, points out that even though attempts to censor public school materials are not successful most of the time, the threat of censorship negatively affects the choices that school personnel make. Teachers and librarians don't choose books that they might otherwise choose because they are afraid of stirring up controversy. School principals restrict student newspapers because they worry that students' ideas might offend others (52). Even the possibility of censorship is enough to stifle creativity and free thought.

There are always people, sometimes well-intentioned, who think that the suppression of ideas will result in a better, more moral environment. Unless we keep careful watch over these attempts to censor and limit the flow of knowledge, they will overwhelm and consume the rights of everyone else.

Benson 9

Works Cited

Bradbury, Ray. *Fahrenheit 451*. New York:
    Ballantine, 1953.

"Constitution of the United States."
    Britannica Online. Vers. 97.1.1. Mar. 1997.
    Encyclopedia Britannica. 14 Oct. 1998
    <http://www.eb.com:180>.

Dority, Barbara. "Public Education Under
    Siege." *The Humanist* July 1994: 36+.

"Frequently Asked Questions: Parental Rights."
    Family Research Council. 13 Oct. 1998
    <http://www.frc.org:80/faq22.html>.

Manfredi, Richard. "District Removes Morrison
    Novel." *Orange County Register* 16 May 1998:
    B-1.

Ockerbloom, John Mark. *The On-Line Books Page:*
    Banned Books On-Line. 11 Oct. 1998
    <http://www.cs.cmu.edu/People/spok/
    banned-books.html>.

Payne, James L. "Education Versus the American
    Way: People for the American Way's
    Censorship Allegations." *National Review*
    25 Sept. 1995: 58+.

People for the American Way. *Attacks on the*
    Freedom to Learn. Washington: People for
    the American Way, 1996.

"Speech Right Goes Too Far, Some Say." *Houston*
    Chronicle 5 July 1997: A-13.

U.S. Supreme Court: Board of Education v. Pico
    457 U.S. 853 (1982). Findlaw. 12 Nov. 1998
    <http://laws.findlaw.com/us/457/853.html>.

Vinciguerra, Thomas. "A 1977 Novel Comes Under
    Scrutiny." *New York Times* 8 June 1997,
    LI ed., sec. 13:8.

List is alphabetized by author's last name. Use title if no author. Double-space throughout.

Online encyclopedia.

Web sites are constantly updated. Include date of access. This Web address is no longer available.

Web site with individual author.

Titles of books, journals, and newspapers may be italicized or underlined.

1"

Television Desensitizes 1

Abbreviated title and page number appear on each page, including the title page

Television Desensitizes Children to Violence
Amber Sifritt
English 112
March 8, 1999

If your instructor requires an abstract of your paper, locate it on the second page of your paper

Television Desensitizes 2

Television Desensitizes Children to Violence

Double-space between title and first line and throughout paper

1"

Kids killing kids. It seems to be all over the news these days. The acts of violence have a depressing similarity: kids bring weapons to school and gun down classmates and teachers. The reasons behind these actions are shockingly simple: for instance, in Arkansas, one of the pre-teen murderers was upset because his girlfriend had ended their relationship. He took revenge by slaughtering four girls and a teacher, who used her body to shield another child. If this was a rare occurrence, we could attribute it to one disturbed child. But it's not. There have been incidents in Pennsylvania, Oregon, Kentucky, Colorado, and other communities all across the country. There is a problem occurring with this generation of children which we can't ignore. We must take action immediately to prevent any more child violence. Otherwise, our greatest fear will not be of wars or natural disasters; it will be of our own children.

Identifies issue and significance

There have been many theories advanced about the causes of these incidents. Some experts blame them on the availability of guns and the children's experience with firearms for target-shooting or hunting. Certainly, having relatively easy access to guns made these violent acts more likely to occur. But this theory does not explain *why* these children chose to commit these acts.

Presents other positions

Television Desensitizes 3

Many children, particularly in rural areas,
are familiar with guns from an early age;
this has been true since the early pioneer
days. But these children do not use guns to
fatally attack others. The question we must
ask goes deeper than this theory: what makes
it possible for a child to commit murder? I
think that one answer is that children have
become desensitized towards violence by
excessive television viewing. Parents need to   Claim
become aware of this potential danger and
begin to curtail the amount of time that
their children spend viewing television and
supervise the shows that they do watch.

     From early childhood on, children are   Reason
saturated with scenes of violence during   supporting claim
television viewing. According to Louise Brown
(1997), American children spend an average of
four hours a day glued to the television
screen. By the time they reach the age of
eighteen, they have watched 8,000 television   Statistics
murders. In Brown's article, she refers to
George Gerbner, an analyst who conducted a   Use of authority
thirty-year study of television violence.
Gerbner suggests that viewers who watch
television excessively develop a "Mean World
Syndrome." These individuals perceive the
world as more violent than it actually is.
For children this may result in the
expectation that difficulties in
relationships and everyday problems should
naturally be resolved by violent solutions.

     However, watching a daily dose of
violent murders and terrorism on the

Reason
supporting
claim

television screen may have additional
negative effects on children. Sissela Bok
(1998), a philosopher who studies the impact
of modern culture on our values and actions,
suggests that "desensitization in response to
media violence . . . actually helps to
counteract the fear and anxiety that such
violence might otherwise provoke" (p. 69). In
other words, rather than live in continual
fear of being the victim of a violent act,
children become numb to the violence they see
depicted on television, treating it casually
as part of their everyday world. Bok asks

Page number
cited
immediately
after quotation

whether this "numbing of feeling" (p. 69) may
make children less sensitive to the pain of
others. Given the casual way that the latest
child murderers have planned and executed
their crimes, it appears that these children
are quite insensitive to the suffering they
are causing.

> Penelope Leach (1994), a well-known
> child psychologist and expert on parenting,
> reinforces this point in her book *Children
> First:*

Long quotation
(over 40 words)
indented five
spaces from left
margin. No
quotation marks.
Page reference
appears at end,
outside final
puncuation.

> Two generations ago only a few
> unfortunate children ever saw any one
> hit over the head with a brick, shot,
> rammed by a car, blown up, immolated,
> raped or tortured. Now all children,
> along with their elders, see such
> images every day of their lives and
> are expected to enjoy them. . . . The
> seven-year-old who hides his eyes in
> the family cops-and-robbers drama is

> desensitized four years later to a
> point where he crunches potato chips
> through the latest video nasty.
> (p. 152)

Leach's point is that this is a gradual
process. One encounter with television
violence will not make a child grow callous
to the effects of violence; however, years of
repeated and constant exposure will have a
detrimental effect on a child's awareness of
the real consequences of a violent act.

Lt. Col. Dave Grossman, a former West
Point psychology professor and Army Ranger,
agrees that this repeated exposure to violent
acts can make them seem more acceptable. He
compares the exposure of children to violence
on television with basic training in the
military in which trainees are conditioned to
overcome their aversion to killing other
human beings by "psychological conditioning
techniques" (McCain, p. 37). While violence
is an unfortunate reality during times of
war, it is alarming that so many children
accept this as part of their daily lives
through their television viewing.

Words right from children's mouths
confirm the effect television has on them,
according to Louise Brown: "I like watching
shows with fights because I learn moves to
beat up my cousins," one child asserts.
Another child says, "Sometimes it might get
into your head that TV is your life." Still
another child is quoted as stating that she

Television Desensitizes 6

enjoys watching cartoons that show her how to

Author is not cited in text, so name and date appear in parenthetical citation

"kick butt" (Brown, 1997). As these
statements indicate, children take the
violence that they see on television quite
seriously. And, because children often can't
distinguish between make-believe and reality,
they are more likely to try to imitate the
violence they see in cartoons or other
programming, according to Barbara Wilson, a
senior researcher and professor of
communications at the University of
California at Santa Barbara (Stamper, 1998).
When children become comfortable with
violence, they aren't aware of its true
effect or outcome.

Statistics

Even more disturbing is the results of a
$3.5 million dollar study of over 6,000 hours
of television on twenty-three channels that
indicate that the "good guys" commit 40% of
the violence on television. This means that
children see their positive role models
engaging in violent behavior. Moreover, this
study finds that most of the violence
depicted on television "goes unpunished, is

Brackets are used to indicate insertion of word not found in source

unjustified, [and] has no lasting effect on
the victim" (Stamper, 1998). The consequence
of this is that children will emulate this
behavior and imitate it, thinking that it is
acceptable because of the way it is treated
on television.

Acknowledges possible objections and responds

While other forms of electronic media,
such as movies and rock music, may also be
responsible for desensitizing our children,

Television Desensitizes 7

television is a medium to which every child
has easy access. Children often need
transportation to go to the movies as well as
money to buy a ticket or CD; television,
however, is free and available in their own
homes. Unless parents make a special point of
supervising each and every television show
their children watch, children are free to
watch whatever looks interesting.
Unfortunately, violence and bloodshed often
attract young viewers. What makes this even
worse is that many of the talk shows and
cartoons containing violence are on at
convenient times for children to watch. For
instance, *The Jerry Springer Show, The Ricki*   Examples
Lake Show, X-Men, and *Spider-Man* are all
shown at times when children are home from
school. Since many parents work outside of
the home, children can spend the afternoon
watching and absorbing this violent material.

    Some people don't agree that television   Acknowledges
violence has a great impact on the young,   possible
impressionable minds of children. When they   objections and
see shows such as *The Jerry Springer Show* and   responds
South Park, they comment that these shows are
not any more violent than what children are
used to in the school yard or see on other
television programs. However, they are
missing the point. Just because violence is
seen regularly at school or on television
does not make it acceptable. And the more
often children see this, the more familiar it
becomes. We cannot use the current standards
for television to measure its acceptability.

Television Desensitizes 8

The most effective and universal solution to this problem would be to have the television industry establish a new set of rules and regulations regarding subject matter that is permitted on television shows designed for children and for those that will be aired at times when children will be watching. However, it seems unlikely that this will happen soon because unless pressure is applied by financial interests, such as corporate sponsors, television executives will not feel compelled to change. Television will probably not be cleaning up its act in the near future unless there is a powerful, organized effort on the part of the public to make it happen. We cannot wait for this to occur because we are paying too high a price in youth violence in the meantime.

Proposes solution

The responsibility to protect children from excessive television violence must rest with parents. Parents must assume an active role in monitoring their children's television consumption. It seems that too many parents fail to undertake this responsibility. Parents rely upon the television to be their children's baby-sitter, leaving them with free time to do other tasks. While this is reasonable for short periods of time, the four hours a day that the average child spends watching television indicates that many parents use the television to avoid interacting with their children. Parents need to sit down with their children during television viewing time and explain that what their children see on the screen is not real and that violence is not the best solution for a problem. Better yet, parents need to turn off the television and encourage their children to engage in other activities. Hobbies, sports, reading, chores around the house, and homework will be more productive uses of their children's intelligence and energies than staring passively at the television absorbing violent ways to deal with human relationships.

Turning off the television won't completely eliminate the terrible violence that children are committing. However, it will eliminate one of the ways that children become desensitized to violence and the pain that it causes others. It may restore some meaning to that Biblical admonition "Do unto others as you would have them do unto you."

Television Desensitizes 10

References

Indent first line of each citation five spaces from left margin. Begin all subsequent lines at the left margin

Bok, S. (1998). *Mayhem: Violence as public entertainment.* Reading, MA: Addison-Wesley.

Brown, L. (1997, December 13). The tube that rocks the cradle. *The Toronto Star,* p. SW6. Lexis-Nexis. [On-line]. Available: http://web.lexis-nexis.com/universe (1999, February 15).

Capitalize the first letter of title and subtitles

Leach, P. (1994). *Children first: What our society must do—and is not doing—for our children today.* New York: Alfred Knopf.

McCain, R. S. (1998, December 21). Television's bloody hands. *Insight on the News, 14,* 37.

Newspaper article from online database

Stamper, J. (1998, April 17). TV fantasy land warps children. *The Orlando Sentinel,* p. A1. Lexis-Nexis. [On-line]. Available: http://web.lexis-nexis.com/universe/ (1999, February 28).

As these research papers demonstrate, the researched argument is different from the other arguments you've written only in quantity and format, not in quality. You still must make a claim and find evidence to support it, tailor your presentation to your readers, and use a logical structure that considers the various sides of an issue. As you progress in your academic life and, later, in your professional life, you will find that variations on the researched argument can become successful senior projects, theses, sales proposals, journal articles, grant proposals—even books—so mastering the skills of argumentative writing will serve you well.

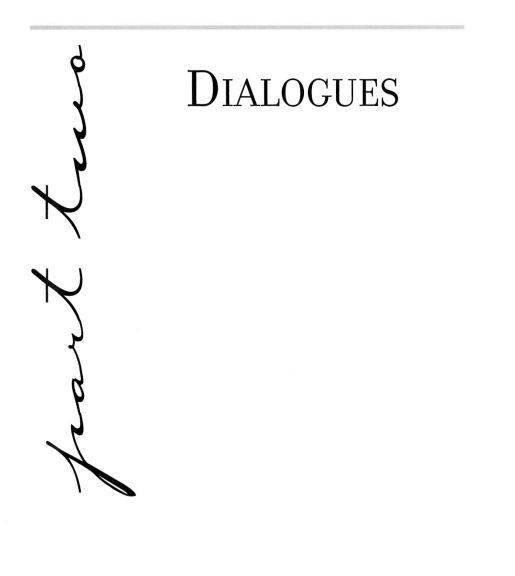

part two

DIALOGUES

chapter 9

GENDER MATTERS

What is it like to be a woman or a man at the beginning of the third millennium? In the past century we have witnessed enormous changes in the roles of both women and men at home, in the workplace, and in society. Traditional ways of defining the self in terms of gender have been challenged and irrevocably altered. The essays in this chapter examine how these changes have affected women and men as they continue to redefine themselves and their relationships with each other.

As a result of the feminist movement, today's young women do not face many of the barriers to educational opportunities and career advancement that women confronted not so long ago. Yet stereotypes about women's roles persist, creating conflicting messages that still prevent women from achieving their full potential. Mary Pipher discusses the trauma girls experience in early adolescence when they become aware that society values female passivity and physical attractiveness over independence and intelligence. According to Pipher, the cultural images of "women [who] have been sexualized and objectified, their bodies marketed to sell tractors and toothpaste" confuse and harm young women at a vulnerable stage in their development. Katie Roiphe explores how this conflict persists for women into adulthood. Even though she describes her life as "a model of modern female independence," with a well-paying job and a successful career, Roiphe secretly longs for a "Man in a Gray Flannel Suit" to take care of her financially and emotionally. These confusing messages about women's societal roles can have even more dangerous consequences, as Leslie Marmon Silko argues in "In the Combat Zone." She asserts that women are easy victims of male violence because they are "taught to be self-sacrificing, passive victims." Silko urges women to learn how to aggressively defend themselves.

As the essays in "Being Male" suggest, men don't have it any easier. Cultural myths about masculinity continue to oppress and limit men. William S. Pollack attributes the new "gender gap" in education, in which boys have fallen dramatically behind girls in measures of educational achievement, to a lack of responsiveness to the special educational needs of boys and a societal expectation about masculinity

238

that prevents boys from seeking help. In "The Men We Carry in Our Minds," Scott Russell Sanders challenges the widely held assumption that men are always powerful and privileged, arguing that many of the benefits automatically associated with manhood mask the pain and vulnerability of the ordinary man's life. Psychologist Warren Farrell also challenges the myth of male power with statistics and facts indicating how men are actually undervalued in U.S. society. In the final essay in this section, Bill Persky humorously describes an encounter with an intruder in his bedroom that revealed his true male identity: "an unlikely combination of Arnold Schwarzenegger and my mother."

The readings on "Gender Communications" explore how our sense of gender identity affects the way we communicate. In "Mr. Fix-It and the Home Improvement Committee," author John Gray examines the conflicts that arise from men's and women's approaches to problem solving. By understanding our gender differences, Gray suggests, we can learn to value and respect each other. Linguist Deborah Tannen's "I'm Sorry, I Won't Apologize" looks at why "real men don't say they're sorry," and the frustration this creates for the women in their lives. Finally, Anna Quindlen and Herbert Gold offer insights about the assumptions and understandings that underlie friendships within the genders.

BEING FEMALE: WHAT IS IT LIKE TO BE A WOMAN TODAY?

Saplings in the Storm
Mary Pipher

With the onset of adolescence children are faced with a multitude of gender-related issues. In addition to dealing with physical and emotional changes, many adolescents must try to adapt to shifting social roles. Changing social expectations can be overwhelming, says psychologist Mary Pipher, especially for girls. In this excerpt taken from the introduction to her bestselling *Reviving Ophelia,* Pipher is concerned that girls may be losing their true selves in an effort to conform.

Psychologist and family therapist Mary Pipher's most recent book is *Another Country: Navigating the Emotional Terrain of Our Elders* (1999), which examines the difficulties older adults face in American culture.

BEFORE YOU READ

Did the way you fit into your social groups change when you reached adolescence? If so, in what ways? What do you think accounts for such changes?

AS YOU READ

According to Pipher, what social constraints do girls alone face with the onset of adolescence? Why do these cultural pressures exist?

1   When my cousin Polly was a girl, she was energy in motion. She danced, did cartwheels and splits, played football, basketball and baseball with the neighborhood boys, wrestled with my brothers, biked, climbed trees and rode horses. She was as lithe and as resilient as a willow branch and as unrestrained as a lion cub. Polly talked as much as she moved. She yelled out orders and advice, shrieked for joy when she won a bet or heard a good joke, laughed with her mouth wide open, argued with kids and grown-ups and insulted her foes in the language of a construction worker.

2   We formed the Marauders, a secret club that met over her garage. Polly was the Tom Sawyer of the club. She planned the initiations, led the spying expeditions and hikes to haunted houses. She showed us the rituals to become blood "brothers" and taught us card tricks and how to smoke.

3   Then Polly had her first period and started junior high. She tried to keep up her old ways, but she was called a tomboy and chided for not acting more ladylike. She was excluded by her boy pals and by the girls, who were moving into makeup and romances.

4   This left Polly confused and shaky. She had temper tantrums and withdrew from both the boys' and girls' groups. Later she quieted down and reentered as Becky Thatcher. She wore stylish clothes and watched from the sidelines as the boys acted and spoke. Once again she was accepted and popular. She glided smoothly through our small society. No one spoke of the changes or mourned the loss of our town's most dynamic citizen. I was the only one who felt that a tragedy had transpired.

5   Girls in what Freud called the latency period, roughly age six or seven through puberty, are anything but latent. I think of my daughter Sara during those years—performing chemistry experiments and magic tricks, playing her violin, starring in her own plays, rescuing wild animals and biking all over town. I think of her friend Tamara, who wrote a 300-page novel the summer of her sixth-grade year. I remember myself, reading every children's book in the library of my town. One week I planned to be a great doctor like Albert Schweitzer. The next week I wanted to write like Louisa May Alcott or dance in Paris like Isadora Duncan. I have never since had as much confidence or ambition.

6   Most preadolescent girls are marvelous company because they are interested in everything—sports, nature, people, music and books. Almost all the heroines of girls' literature come from this age group—Anne of Green Gables, Heidi, Pippi Longstocking and Caddie Woodlawn. Girls this age bake pies, solve mysteries and go on quests. They can take care of themselves and are not yet burdened with caring for others. They have a brief respite from the female role and can be tomboys, a word that conveys courage, competency and irreverence.

7   They can be androgynous, having the ability to act adaptively in any situation regardless of gender role constraints. An androgynous person can comfort a baby or change a tire, cook a meal or chair a meeting. Research has shown that, since they are free to act without worrying if their behavior is feminine or masculine, androgynous adults are the most well adjusted.

8   Girls between seven and eleven rarely come to therapy. They don't need it. I can count on my fingers the girls this age whom I have seen: Coreen, who was physically abused; Anna, whose parents were divorcing; and Brenda, whose father killed himself. These girls were courageous and resilient. Brenda said, "If my father didn't want to stick around, that's his loss." Coreen and Anna were angry, not at themselves, but rather at the grown-ups, who they felt were making mistakes. It's amazing how little help these girls needed from me to heal and move on.

9   A horticulturist told me a revealing story. She led a tour of junior-high girls who were attending a math and science fair on her campus. She showed them side oats grama, bluestem, Indian grass and trees—redbud, maple, walnut and willow. The younger girls interrupted each other with their questions and tumbled forward to see, touch and smell everything. The older girls, the ninth-graders, were different. They hung back. They didn't touch plants or shout out questions. They stood primly to the side, looking bored and even a little disgusted by the enthusiasm of their younger classmates. My friend asked herself, What's happened to these girls? What's gone wrong? She told me, "I wanted to shake them, to say, 'Wake up, come back. Is anybody home at your house?' "

10   Recently I sat sunning on a bench outside my favorite ice-cream store. A mother and her teenage daughter stopped in front of me and waited for the light to change. I heard the mother say, "You have got to stop blackmailing your father and me. Every time you don't get what you want, you tell us that you want to run away from home or kill yourself. What's happened to you? You used to be able to handle not getting your way."

11   The daughter stared straight ahead, barely acknowledging her mother's words. The light changed. I licked my ice-cream cone. Another mother approached the same light with her preadolescent daughter in tow. They were holding hands. The daughter said to her mother, "This is fun. Let's do this all afternoon."

12   Something dramatic happens to girls in early adolescence. Just as planes and ships disappear mysteriously into the Bermuda Triangle, so do the selves of girls go down in droves. They crash and burn in a social and developmental Bermuda Triangle. In early adolescence, studies show that girls' IQ scores drop and their math and science scores plummet. They lose their resiliency and optimism and become less curious and inclined to take risks. They lose their assertive, energetic and "tomboyish" personalities and become more deferential, self-critical and depressed. They report great unhappiness with their own bodies.

13   Psychology documents but does not explain the crashes. Girls who rushed to drink in experiences in enormous gulps sit quietly in the corner. Writers such as Sylvia Plath, Margaret Atwood and Olive Schreiner have described the wreckage. Diderot, in writing to his young friend Sophie Volland, described his observations harshly: "You all die at 15."

14   Fairy tales capture the essence of this phenomenon. Young women eat poisoned apples or prick their fingers with poisoned needles and fall asleep for a hundred years. They wander away from home, encounter great dangers, are rescued by princes and are transformed into passive and docile creatures.

15   The story of Ophelia, from Shakespeare's *Hamlet,* shows the destructive forces that affect young women. As a girl, Ophelia is happy and free, but with adolescence she loses herself. When she falls in love with Hamlet, she lives only for his approval. She has no inner direction; rather she struggles to meet the demands of Hamlet and her father. Her value is determined utterly by their approval. Ophelia is torn apart by her efforts to please. When Hamlet spurns her because she is an obedient daughter, she goes mad with grief. Dressed in elegant clothes that weigh her down, she drowns in a stream filled with flowers.

16   Girls know they are losing themselves. One girl said, "Everything good in me died in junior high." Wholeness is shattered by the chaos of adolescence. Girls become fragmented, their selves split into mysterious contradictions. They are sensitive and tenderhearted, mean and competitive, superficial and idealistic. They are confident in the morning and overwhelmed with anxiety by nightfall. They rush through their days with wild energy and then collapse into lethargy. They try on new roles every week—this week the good student, next week the delinquent and the next, the artist. And they expect their families to keep up with these changes.

17   My clients in early adolescence are elusive and slow to trust adults. They are easily offended by a glance, a clearing of the throat, a silence, a lack of sufficient enthusiasm or a sentence that doesn't meet their immediate needs. Their voices have gone underground—their speech is more tentative and less articulate. Their moods swing widely. One week they love their world and their families, the next they are critical of everyone. Much of their behavior is unreadable. Their problems are complicated and metaphorical—eating disorders, school phobias and self-inflicted injuries. I need to ask again and again in a dozen different ways, "What are you trying to tell me?"

18   Michelle, for example, was a beautiful, intelligent seventeen-year-old. Her mother brought her in after she became pregnant for the third time in three years. I tried to talk about why this was happening. She smiled a Mona Lisa smile to all my questions. "No, I don't care all that much for sex." "No, I didn't plan this. It just happened." When Michelle left a session, I felt like I'd been talking in the wrong language to someone far away.

19   Holly was another mystery. She was shy, soft-spoken and slow-moving, pretty under all her makeup and teased red hair. She was a Prince fan and wore only purple. Her father brought her in after a suicide attempt. She wouldn't study, do chores, join any school activities or find a job. Holly answered questions in patient, polite monosyllables. She really talked only when the topic was Prince. For several weeks we talked about him. She played me his tapes. Prince somehow spoke for her and to her.

20   Gail burned and cut herself when she was unhappy. Dressed in black, thin as a straw, she sat silently before me, her hair a mess, her ears, lips and nose all

pierced with rings. She spoke about Bosnia and the hole in the ozone layer and asked me if I liked rave music. When I asked about her life, she fingered her earrings and sat silently.

21   My clients are not different from girls who are not seen in therapy. I teach at a small liberal arts college and the young women in my classes have essentially the same experiences as my therapy clients. One student worried about her best friend who'd been sexually assaulted. Another student missed class after being beaten by her boyfriend. Another asked what she should do about crank calls from a man threatening to rape her. When stressed, another student stabbed her hand with paper clips until she drew blood. Many students have wanted advice on eating disorders.

22   After I speak at high schools, girls approach me to say that they have been raped, or they want to run away from home, or that they have a friend who is anorexic or alcoholic. At first all this trauma surprised me. Now I expect it.

23   Psychology has a long history of ignoring girls this age. Until recently adolescent girls haven't been studied by academics, and they have long baffled therapists. Because they are secretive with adults and full of contradictions, they are difficult to study. So much is happening internally that's not communicated on the surface.

24   Simone de Beauvoir believed adolescence is when girls realize that men have the power and that their only power comes from consenting to become submissive adored objects. They do not suffer from the penis envy Freud postulated, but from power envy.

25   She described the Bermuda Triangle this way: Girls who were the subjects of their own lives become the objects of other's lives. "Young girls slowly bury their childhood, put away their independent and imperious selves and submissively enter adult existence." Adolescent girls experience a conflict between their autonomous selves and their need to be feminine, between their status as human beings and their vocation as females. De Beauvoir says, "Girls stop being and start seeming."

26   Girls become "female impersonators" who fit their whole selves into small, crowded spaces. Vibrant, confident girls become shy, doubting young women. Girls stop thinking, "Who am I? What do I want?" and start thinking, "What must I do to please others?"

27   This gap between girls' true selves and cultural prescriptions for what is properly female creates enormous problems. To paraphrase a Stevie Smith poem about swimming in the sea, "they are not waving, they are drowning." And just when they most need help, they are unable to take their parents' hands.

28   Olive Schreiner wrote of her experiences as a young girl in *The Story of an African Farm*. "The world tells us what we are to be and shapes us by the ends it sets before us. To men it says, work. To us, it says, seem. The less a woman has in her head the lighter she is for carrying." She described the finishing school that she attended in this way: "It was a machine for condensing the soul into the smallest possible area. I have seen some souls so compressed that they would have filled a small thimble."

29   Margaret Mead believed that the ideal culture is one in which there is a place for every human gift. By her standards, our Western culture is far from ideal for women. So many gifts are unused and unappreciated. So many voices are stilled. Stendhal wrote: "All geniuses born women are lost to the public good."

30   Alice Miller wrote of the pressures on some young children to deny their true selves and assume selves to please their parents. *Reviving Ophelia* suggests that adolescent girls experience a similar pressure to split into true and false selves, but this time the pressure comes not from parents but from the culture. Adolescence is when girls experience social pressure to put aside their authentic selves and to display only a small portion of their gifts.

31   This pressure disorients and depresses most girls. They sense the pressure to be someone they are not. They fight back, but they are fighting a "problem with no name." One girl put it this way: "I'm a perfectly good carrot that everyone is trying to turn into a rose. As a carrot, I have good color and a nice leafy top. When I'm carved into a rose, I turn brown and wither."

32   Adolescent girls are saplings in a hurricane. They are young and vulnerable trees that the winds blow with gale strength. Three factors make young women vulnerable to the hurricane. One is their developmental level. Everything is changing—body shape, hormones, skin and hair. Calmness is replaced by anxiety. Their way of thinking is changing. Far below the surface they are struggling with the most basic of human questions: What is my place in the universe, what is my meaning?

33   Second, American culture has always smacked girls on the head in early adolescence. This is when they move into a broader culture that is rife with girl-hurting "isms," such as sexism, capitalism and lookism, which is the evaluation of a person solely on the basis of appearance.

34   Third, American girls are expected to distance from parents just at the time when they most need their support. As they struggle with countless new pressures, they must relinquish the protection and closeness they've felt with their families in childhood. They turn to their none-too-constant peers for support.

35   Parents know only too well that something is happening to their daughters. Calm, considerate daughters grow moody, demanding and distant. Girls who loved to talk are sullen and secretive. Girls who liked to hug now bristle when touched. Mothers complain that they can do nothing right in the eyes of their daughters. Involved fathers bemoan their sudden banishment from their daughters' lives. But few parents realize how universal their experiences are. Their daughters are entering a new land, a dangerous place that parents can scarcely comprehend. Just when they most need a home base, they cut themselves loose without radio communications.

36   Most parents of adolescent girls have the goal of keeping their daughters safe while they grow up and explore the world. The parents' job is to protect. The daughters' job is to explore. Always these different tasks have created tension in parent-daughter relationships, but now it's even harder. Generally parents are more protective of their daughters than is corporate America. Parents aren't trying to make money off their daughters by selling them designer jeans or cigarettes, they just want them to be well adjusted. They don't see their

daughters as sex objects or consumers but as real people with talents and interests. But daughters turn away from their parents as they enter the new land. They befriend their peers, who are their fellow inhabitants of the strange country and who share a common language and set of customs. They often embrace the junk values of mass culture.

37   This turning away from parents is partly for developmental reasons. Early adolescence is a time of physical and psychological change, self-absorption, preoccupation with peer approval and identity formation. It's a time when girls focus inward on their own fascinating changes.

38   It's partly for cultural reasons. In America we define adulthood as a moving away from families into broader culture. Adolescence is the time for cutting bonds and breaking free. Adolescents may claim great independence from parents, but they are aware and ashamed of their parents' smallest deviation from the norm. They don't like to be seen with them and find their imperfections upsetting. A mother's haircut or a father's joke can ruin their day. Teenagers are furious at parents who say the wrong things or do not respond with perfect answers. Adolescents claim not to hear their parents, but with their friends they discuss endlessly all parental attitudes. With amazing acuity, they sense nuances, doubt, shades of ambiguity, discrepancy and hypocrisy.

39   Adolescents still have some of the magical thinking of childhood and believe that parents have the power to keep them safe and happy. They blame their parents for their misery, yet they make a point of not telling their parents how they think and feel; they have secrets, so things can get crazy. For example, girls who are raped may not tell their parents. Instead, they become hostile and rebellious. Parents bring girls in because of their anger and out-of-control behavior. When I hear about this unexplainable anger, I ask about rape. Ironically, girls are often angrier at their parents than at the rapists. They feel their parents should have known about the danger and been more protective; afterward, they should have sensed the pain and helped.

40   Most parents feel like failures during this time. They feel shut out, impotent and misunderstood. They often attribute the difficulties of this time to their daughters and their own failings. They don't understand that these problems go with the developmental stage, the culture and the times.

41   Parents experience an enormous sense of loss when their girls enter this new land. They miss the daughters who sang in the kitchen, who read them school papers, who accompanied them on fishing trips and to ball games. They miss the daughters who liked to bake cookies, play Pictionary and be kissed goodnight. In place of their lively, affectionate daughters they have changelings—new girls who are sadder, angrier and more complicated. Everyone is grieving.

42   Fortunately adolescence is time-limited. By late high school most girls are stronger and the winds are dying down. Some of the worst problems—cliques, a total focus on looks and struggles with parents—are on the wane. But the way girls handle the problems of adolescence can have implications for their adult lives. Without some help, the loss of wholeness, self-confidence and self-direction can last well into adulthood. Many adult clients struggle with the same issues that overwhelmed them as adolescent girls. Thirty-year-old accoun-

tants and realtors, forty-year-old homemakers and doctors, and thirty-five-year-old nurses and schoolteachers ask the same questions and struggle with the same problems as their teenage daughters.

43 Even sadder are the women who are not struggling, who have forgotten that they have selves worth defending. They have repressed the pain of their adolescence, the betrayals of self in order to be pleasing. These women come to therapy with the goal of becoming even more pleasing to others. They come to lose weight, to save their marriages or to rescue their children. When I ask them about their own needs, they are confused by the question.

44 Most women struggled alone with the trauma of adolescence and have led decades of adult life with their adolescent experiences unexamined. The lessons learned in adolescence are forgotten and their memories of pain are minimized. They come into therapy because their marriage is in trouble, or they hate their job, or their own daughter is giving them fits. Maybe their daughter's pain awakens their own pain. Some are depressed or chemically addicted or have stress-related illnesses—ulcers, colitis, migraines or psoriasis. Many have tried to be perfect women and failed. Even though they followed the rules and did as they were told, the world has not rewarded them. They feel angry and betrayed. They feel miserable and taken for granted, used rather than loved.

45 Women often know how everyone in their family thinks and feels except themselves. They are great at balancing the needs of their coworkers, husbands, children and friends, but they forget to put themselves into the equation. They struggle with adolescent questions still unresolved: How important are looks and popularity? How do I care for myself and not be selfish? How can I be honest and still be loved? How can I achieve and not threaten others? How can I be sexual and not a sex object? How can I be responsive but not responsible for everyone?

46 As we talk, the years fall away. We are back in junior high with the cliques, the shame, the embarrassment about bodies, the desire to be accepted and the doubts about ability. So many adult women think they are stupid and ugly. Many feel guilty if they take time for themselves. They do not express anger or ask for help.

47 We talk about childhood—what the woman was like at ten and at fifteen. We piece together a picture of childhood lost. We review her own particular story, her own time in the hurricane. Memories flood in. Often there are tears, angry outbursts, sadness for what has been lost. So much time has been wasted pretending to be who others wanted. But also, there's a new energy that comes from making connections, from choosing awareness over denial and from the telling of secrets.

48 We work now, twenty years behind schedule. We reestablish each woman as the subject of her life, not as the object of others' lives. We answer Freud's patronizing question "What do women want?" Each woman wants something different and particular and yet each woman wants the same thing—to be who she truly is, to become who she can become.

49   Many women regain their preadolescent authenticity with menopause. Because they are no longer beautiful objects occupied primarily with caring for others, they are free once again to become the subjects of their own lives. They become more confident, self-directed and energetic. Margaret Mead noticed this phenomenon in cultures all over the world and called it "pmz," postmenopausal zest. She noted that some cultures revere these older women. Others burn them at the stake.

50   Before I studied psychology, I studied cultural anthropology. I have always been interested in that place where culture and individual psychology intersect, in why cultures create certain personalities and not others, in how they pull for certain strengths in their members, in how certain talents are utilized while others atrophy from lack of attention. I'm interested in the role cultures play in the development of individual pathology.

51   For a student of culture and personality, adolescence is fascinating. It's an extraordinary time when individual, developmental and cultural factors combine in ways that shape adulthood. It's a time of marked internal development and massive cultural indoctrination.

52   I want to try in this book to connect each girl's story with larger cultural issues—to examine the intersection of the personal and the political. It's a murky place; the personal and political are intertwined in all of our lives. Our minds, which are shaped by the society in which we live, can oppress us. And yet our minds can also analyze and work to change the culture.

53   An analysis of the culture cannot ignore individual differences in women. Some women blossom and grow under the most hostile conditions while others wither after the smallest storms. And yet we are more alike than different in the issues that face us. The important question is, Under what conditions do most young women flower and grow?

54   Adolescent clients intrigue me as they struggle to sort themselves out. But I wouldn't have written this book had it not been for these last few years when my office has been filled with girls—girls with eating disorders, alcohol problems, posttraumatic stress reactions to sexual or physical assaults, sexually transmitted diseases (STDs), self-inflicted injuries and strange phobias, and girls who have tried to kill themselves or run away. A health department survey showed that 40 percent of all girls in my midwestern city considered suicide last year. The Centers for Disease Control in Atlanta reports that the suicide rate among children age ten to fourteen rose 75 percent between 1979 and 1988. Something dramatic is happening to adolescent girls in America, something unnoticed by those not on the front lines.

55   At first I was surprised that girls were having more trouble now. After all, we have had a consciousness-raising women's movement since the sixties. Women are working in traditionally male professions and going out for sports. Some fathers help with the housework and child care. It seems that these changes would count for something. And of course they do, but in some ways the progress is confusing. The Equal Rights Amendment was not ratified,

feminism is a pejorative term to many people and, while some women have high-powered jobs, most women work hard for low wages and do most of the "second shift" work. The lip service paid to equality makes the reality of discrimination even more confusing.

56   Many of the pressures girls have always faced are intensified in the 1990s. Many things contribute to this intensification: more divorced families, chemical addictions, casual sex and violence against women. Because of the media, which Clarence Page calls "electronic wallpaper," girls all live in one big town— a sleazy, dangerous tinsel town with lots of liquor stores and few protected spaces. Increasingly women have been sexualized and objectified, their bodies marketed to sell tractors and toothpaste. Soft- and hard-core pornography are everywhere. Sexual and physical assaults on girls are at an all-time high. Now girls are more vulnerable and fearful, more likely to have been traumatized and less free to roam about alone. This combination of old stresses and new is poison for our young women.

57   Parents have unprecedented stress as well. For the last half-century, parents worried about their sixteen-year-old daughters driving, but now, in a time of drive-by shootings and car-jackings, parents can be panicked. Parents have always worried about their daughters' sexual behavior, but now, in a time of date rapes, herpes and AIDS, they can be sex-phobic. Traditionally parents have wondered what their teens were doing, but now teens are much more likely to be doing things that can get them killed.

58   This book will tell stories from the front lines. It's about girls because I know about girls. I was one, I see them in therapy, I have a teenage daughter and I teach primarily young women. I am not writing about boys because I have limited experience with them. I'm not saying that girls and boys are radically different, only that they have different experiences.

59   I am saying that girls are having more trouble now than they had thirty years ago, when I was a girl, and more trouble than even ten years ago. Something new is happening. Adolescence has always been hard, but it's harder now because of cultural changes in the last decade. The protected place in space and time that we once called childhood has grown shorter. There is an African saying, "It takes a village to raise a child." Most girls no longer have a village.

60   Parents, teachers, counselors and nurses see that girls are in trouble, but they do not realize how universal and extreme the suffering is. This book is an attempt to share what I have seen and heard. It's a hurricane warning, a message to the culture that something important is happening. This is a National Weather Service bulletin from the storm center.

FOR ANALYSIS AND DISCUSSION

1. What does Pipher mean when she says that girls "disappear mysteriously into the Bermuda Triangle" in early adolescence? Why do you think she uses this analogy repeatedly?

2. How do girls change with the onset of adolescence? To what extent are these changes physical and to what extent are they cultural? Do you think girls must make sacrifices to "fit in"? Explain.

3. What is the benefit of androgyny to girls? Can the same benefits be applied to boys?

4. Pipher's essay focuses on what happens to girls when they reach adolescence. Do you think she feels boys face similar issues? Do you think Pipher thinks society is harder on girls than on boys? Explain.

5. Is audience important to the success of this essay? Why or why not? How could this essay apply to issues that face both men and women?

6. Place Pipher's essay in different historical contexts. For example, do you think the problems she describes faced girls in the 1930s or the 1950s? Are the underlying social pressures facing teenage girls the same today? Explain.

The Independent Woman
and Other Lies
Katie Roiphe

Although traditional gender roles have greatly changed over the past 30 years, some preconceived notions remain, especially concerning money, sending conflicting messages to both men and women, says writer Katie Roiphe. On the one hand, men are expected to view women as economic equals. On the other hand, they are still expected to pick up the check and earn more than their female companions.

Self-proclaimed "postfeminist" Katie Roiphe earned her Ph.D. in English from Princeton University and has contributed articles to *Harper's,* the *New York Times,* and *Esquire,* where this essay appeared in February of 1997. She is also the author of several books including *Last Night in Paradise: Sex and Morals at the Century's End* (1997), which explores Generation X's search for rules in the relationships between men and women.

BEFORE YOU READ

Who should pay for the date when a man and a woman go out? Does it matter? Do the circumstances change if they are married? Do you think that society as a whole feels that men should be the primary breadwinners?

AS YOU READ

What does Roiphe identify as "traditional" gender roles for men and women? Do you agree with her perspective?

1   I was out to drinks with a man I'd recently met. "I'll take care of that," he said, sweeping up the check, and as he said it, I felt a warm glow of security, as if everything in my life was suddenly going to be taken care of. As the pink cosmopolitans glided smoothly across the bar, I thought for a moment of how

nice it would be to live in an era when men always took care of the cosmopolitans. I pictured a lawyer with a creamy leather briefcase going off to
work in the mornings and coming back home in the evenings to the town-
house he has bought for me, where I have been ordering flowers, soaking in
the bath, reading a nineteenth-century novel, and working idly on my next
book. This fantasy of a Man in a Gray Flannel Suit is one that independent,
strong-minded women of the nineties are distinctly not supposed to have, but
I find myself having it all the same. And many of the women I know are having it also.

2   Seen from the outside, my life is the model of modern female independence. I live alone, pay my own bills, and fix my stereo when it breaks down.
But it sometimes seems like my independence is in part an elaborately constructed facade that hides a more traditional feminine desire to be protected
and provided for. I admitted this once to my mother, an ardent seventies feminist, over Caesar salads at lunch, and she was shocked. I saw it on her face: How
could a daughter of mine say something like this? I rushed to reassure her that
I wouldn't dream of giving up my career, and it's true that I wouldn't. But when
I think about marriage, somewhere deep in the irrational layers of my psyche, I
still think of the man as the breadwinner. I feel as though I am working for "fulfillment," for "reward," for the richness of life promised by feminism, and that
mundane things such as rent and mortgages and college tuitions are, ultimately, the man's responsibility—even though I know that they shouldn't be. "I
just don't want to have to think about money," one of my most competent female friends said to me recently, and I knew exactly what she meant. Our liber-
ated, postfeminist world seems to be filled with women who don't want to think
about money and men who feel that they have to.

3   There are plenty of well-adjusted, independent women who never fantasize
about the Man in the Gray Flannel Suit, but there are also a surprising number
who do. Of course, there is a well established tradition of women looking for
men to provide for them that spans from Edith Wharton's *The House of Mirth* to
Helen Gurley Brown's *Sex and the Single Girl* to Mona Simpson's *A Regular Guy*.
You could almost say that this is the American dream for women: Find a man
who can lift you out of your circumstances, whisk you away to Venice, and give
you a new life.

4   In my mother's generation, a woman felt she had to marry a man with a
successful career, whereas today she is supposed to focus on her own. Consider
that in 1990, women received 42 percent of law degrees (up from 2.5 percent
in 1960) and that as of 1992, women held 47 percent of lucrative jobs in the
professions and management. And now that American women are more economically independent than ever before, now that we don't need to attach ourselves to successful men, many of us still seem to want to. I don't think, in the
end, that this attraction is about bank accounts or trips to Paris or hundred dollar haircuts, I think it's about the reassuring feeling of being protected and provided for, a feeling that mingles with love and attraction on the deepest level.
It's strange to think of professional women in the nineties drinking cafe lattes

and talking about men in the same way as characters in Jane Austen novels, appraising their prospects and fortunes, but many of us actually do.

5   A friend of mine, an editor at a women's magazine, said about a recent breakup, "I just hated having to say, 'My boyfriend is a dog walker.' I hated the fact that he didn't have a job." And then immediately afterward, she said, "I feel really awful admitting all of this." It was as if she had just told me something shameful, as if she had confessed to some terrible perversion. And I understand why she felt guilty. She was admitting to a sort of 1950s worldview that seemed as odd and unfashionable as walking down the street in a poodle skirt. But she is struggling with what defines masculinity and femininity in a supposedly equal society, with what draws us to men, what attracts us, what keeps us interested. She has no more reason to feel guilty than a man who says he likes tall blonds.

6   I've heard many women say that they wouldn't want to go out with a man who is much less successful than they are because "he would feel uncomfortable." But, of course, he's not the only one who would feel uncomfortable. What most of these women are really saying is that they themselves would feel uncomfortable. But why? Why can't the magazine editor be happy with the dog walker? Why does the woman at Salomon Brothers feel unhappy with the banker who isn't doing as well as she is? Part of it may have to do with the way we were raised. Even though I grew up in a liberal household in the seventies, I perceived early on that my father was the one who actually paid for things. As a little girl, I watched my father put his credit card down in restaurants and write checks and go to work every morning in a suit and tie, and it may be that this model of masculinity is still imprinted in my mind. It may be that there is a picture of our fathers that many of us carry like silver lockets around our necks: Why shouldn't we find a man who will take care of us the way our fathers did?

7   I've seen the various destructive ways in which this expectation can affect people's lives. Sam and Anna met at Brown. After they graduated, Anna went to Hollywood and started making nearly a million dollars a year in television production, and Sam became an aspiring novelist who has never even filed a tax return. At first, the disparity in their styles of life manifested itself in trivial ways. "She would want to go to an expensive bistro," Sam, who is now twenty-seven, remembers, "and I would want to get a burrito for $4.25. We would go to the bistro, and either she'd pay, which was bad, or I'd just eat salad and lots of bread, which was also bad." In college, they had been the kind of couple who stayed up until three in the morning talking about art and beauty and *The Brothers Karamazov*, but now they seemed to be spending a lot of time arguing about money and burritos. One night, when they went out with some of Anna's Hollywood friends, she slipped him eighty dollars under the table so that he could pretend to pay for dinner. Anna felt guilty. Sam was confused. He had grown up with a feminist mother who'd drummed the ideal of strong, independent women into his head, but now that he'd fallen in love with Anna, probably the strongest and most independent woman he'd ever met, she wanted him to pay for her dinner so badly she gave him money to do it. Anna, I should say, is not a particularly materialistic person. She is not someone who cares about

Chanel suits and Prada bags. It's just that to her, money had become a luminous symbol of functionality and power.

8   The five-year relationship began to fall apart. Sam was not fulfilling the role of romantic lead in the script Anna had in her head. In a moment of desperation, Sam blurted out that he had made a lot of money on the stock market. He hadn't. Shortly afterward, they broke up. Anna started dating her boss, and she and Sam had agonizing long-distance phone calls about what had happened, "She kept telling me that she wanted me to be more of a man," Sam says. "She kept saying that she wanted to be taken care of." There was a certain irony to this situation, to this woman who was making almost a million dollars a year, sitting in her Santa Monica house, looking out at the ocean, saying that she just wanted a man who could take care of her.

9   There is also something appalling in this story, something cruel and hard and infinitely understandable. The strain of Anna's success and Sam's as of yet unrewarded talent was too much for the relationship. When Anna told Sam that she wanted him to be more masculine, part of what she was saying was that she wanted to feel more feminine. It's like the plight of the too-tall teenage girl who's anxiously scanning the dance floor for a fifteen-year-old boy who is taller than she is. A romantic might say, What about love? Love isn't supposed to be about dollars and cents and who puts their Visa card down at an expensive Beverly Hills restaurant. But this is a story about love in its more tarnished, worldly forms, it's about the balance of power, what men and women really want from one another, and the hidden mechanics of romance and attraction. In a way, what happened between my friends Sam and Anna is a parable of our times, of a generation of strong women who are looking for even stronger men.

10   I've said the same thing as Anna—"I need a man who can take care of me" —to more than one boyfriend, and I hear how it sounds. I recognize how shallow and unreasonable it seems. But I say it anyway. And, even worse, I actually feel it.

11   The mood passes. I realize that I can take care of myself. The relationship returns to normal, the boyfriend jokes that I should go to the bar at the plaza to meet bankers, and we both laugh because we know that I don't really want to, but there is an undercurrent of resentment, eddies of tension and disappointment that remain between us. This is a secret refrain that runs through conversations in bedrooms late at night, through phone wires, and in restaurants over drinks. One has to wonder, why, at a moment in history when women can so patently take care of themselves, do so many of us want so much to be taken care of?

12   The fantasy of a man who pays the bills, who works when you want to take time off to be with your kids or read *War and Peace,* who is in the end responsible, is one that many women have but fairly few admit to. It is one of those fantasies, like rape fantasies, that have been forbidden to us by our politics. But it's also deeply ingrained in our imaginations. All of girl culture tells us to find a man who will provide for us, a Prince Charming, a Mr. Rochester, a Mr. Darcy, a Rhett Butler. These are the objects of our earliest romantic yearnings, the pri-

vate desires of a whole country of little girls, the fairy tales that actually end up affecting our real lives. As the feminist film critic Molly Haskell says, "We never really escape the old-fashioned roles. They get inside our heads. Dependence has always been eroticized."

13   Many of the men I know seem understandably bewildered by the fact that women want to be independent only sometimes, only sort of, and only selectively. The same women who give eloquent speeches at dinner parties on the subject of "glass ceilings" still want men to pay for first dates, and this can be sort of perplexing for the men around them who are still trying to fit into the puzzle that the feminism of the seventies has created for them. For a long time, women have been saying that we don't want a double standard, but it sometimes seems that what many women want is simply a more subtle and refined version of a double standard: We want men to be the providers and to regard us as equals. This slightly unreasonable expectation is not exactly new. In 1963, a reporter asked Mary McCarthy what women really wanted, and she answered, "They want everything. That's the trouble—they can't have everything. They can't possibly have all the prerogatives of being a woman and the privileges of being a man at the same time."

14   "We're spoiled," says Helen Gurley Brown, one of the world's foremost theorists on dating. "We just don't want to give up any of the good stuff." And she may have a point. In a world in which women compete with men, in which all of us are feeling the same drive to succeed, there is something reassuring about falling—if only for the length of a dinner—into traditional sex roles. You can just relax. You can take a rest from yourself. You can let the pressures and ambitions melt away and give in to the archaic fantasy: For just half an hour, you are just a pretty girl smiling at a man over a drink. I think that old-fashioned rituals, such as men paying for dates, endure precisely because of how much has actually changed; they cover up the fact that men and women are equal and that equality is not always, in all contexts and situations, comfortable or even desirable.

15   This may explain why I have been so ungratefully day-dreaming about the Man in the Gray Flannel Suit thirty years after Betty Friedan published *The Feminine Mystique*. The truth is, the knowledge that I can take care of myself, that I don't really need a man, is not without its own accompanying terrors. The idea that I could make myself into a sleek, self-sufficient androgyne is not all that appealing. Now that we have all of the rooms of our own that we need, we begin to look for that shared and crowded space. And it is this fear of independence, this fear of not needing a man, that explains the voices of more competent, accomplished corporate types than me saying to the men around them, "Provide for me, protect me." It may be one of the bad jokes that history occasionally plays on us: that the independence my mother's generation wanted so much for their daughters was something we could not entirely appreciate or want. It was like a birthday present from a distant relative—wrong size, wrong color, wrong style. And so women are left struggling with the desire to submit and not submit, to be dependent and independent, to take care of ourselves and be

taken care of, and it's in the confusion of this struggle that most of us love and are loved.

16   For myself, I continue to go out with poets and novelists and writers, with men who don't pay for dates or buy me dresses at Bergdorf's or go off to their offices in the morning, but the Man in the Gray Flannel Suit lives on in my imagination, perplexing, irrational, revealing of some dark and unsettling truth.

FOR ANALYSIS AND DISCUSSION

1. What does Roiphe say is the "lie" of the independent woman? Why is it a "lie"? Do you agree with her perspective?

2. On what premises does Rophie base her argument? What evidence does she use to support it? Is her support sound? What assumptions, if any, does the argument make? Explain.

3. In paragraph 12 Roiphe likens the elicit nature of the "Man in the Gray Flannel Suit" fantasy to other fantasies women have including the "rape fantasy." What do you think she means by the "rape fantasy"? Does this analogy contribute to her argument? Why are these fantasies "forbidden to us by our politics"?

4. Have you ever experienced relationship difficulties stemming from earnings or income differences between the sexes? Explain.

5. In paragraph 13 Roiphe discusses what women really want. What do *you* think women really want? How does your analysis compare to Roiphe's conclusions?

In the Combat Zone
Leslie Marmon Silko

Safety experts warn women not to walk alone at night, to park where it is well-lit and to avoid areas that could conceal muggers or rapists. Self-defense classes for women stress avoidance tactics rather than ways to actively confront violence. This approach, says Leslie Marmon Silko, creates a cultural consciousness of women as targets. In this essay, published in 1995, Silko relates how her childhood hunting experiences helped empower her in a society that often views women as victims.

Leslie Marmon Silko is one of America's best-known Native-American writers. She is the author of several books, including the 1992 novel *Almanac of the Dead; Gardens in the Dunes* was released in April 1999.

BEFORE YOU READ

Have you ever found yourself planning your activities based on personal safety? For example, did you do without something because you were afraid of going to the store at night by yourself? Or have you skipped taking a shortcut when it was dark out? If not, why don't you fear these situations?

AS YOU READ

Note Silko's references to hunting throughout the essay. How does the theme of hunting unify the piece?

1   Women seldom discuss our wariness or the precautions we take after dark each time we leave the apartment, car, or office to go on the most brief errand. We take for granted that we are targeted as easy prey by muggers, rapists, and serial killers. This is our lot as women in the United States. We try to avoid going anywhere alone after dark, although economic necessity sends women out night after night. We do what must be done, but always we are alert, on guard and ready. We have to be aware of persons walking on the sidewalk behind us; we have to pay attention to others who board an elevator we're on. We try to avoid all staircases and deserted parking garages when we are alone. Constant vigilance requires considerable energy and concentration seldom required of men.

2   I used to assume that most men were aware of this fact of women's lives, but I was wrong. They may notice our reluctance to drive at night to the convenience store alone, but they don't know or don't want to know the experience of a woman out alone at night. Men who have been in combat know the feeling of being a predator's target, but it is difficult for men to admit that we women live our entire lives in a combat zone. Men have the power to end violence against women in the home, but they feel helpless to protect women from violent strangers. Because men feel guilt and anger at their inability to shoulder responsibility for the safety of their wives, sisters, and daughters, we don't often discuss random acts of violence against women.

3   When we were children, my sisters and I used to go to Albuquerque with my father. Sometimes strangers would tell my father it was too bad that he had three girls and no sons. My father, who has always preferred the company of women, used to reply that he was glad to have girls and not boys, because he might not get along as well with boys. Furthermore, he'd say, "My girls can do anything your boys can do, and my girls can do it better." He had in mind, of course, shooting and hunting.

4   When I was six years old, my father took me along as he hunted deer; he showed me how to walk quietly, to move along and then to stop and listen carefully before taking another step. A year later, he traded a pistol for a little single shot .22 rifle just my size.

5   He took me and my younger sisters down to the dump by the river and taught us how to shoot. We rummaged through the trash for bottles and glass jars; it was great fun to take aim at a pickle jar and watch it shatter. If the Rio San Jose had water running in it, we threw bottles for moving targets in the muddy current. My father told us that a .22 bullet can travel a mile, so we had to be careful where we aimed. The river was a good place because it was below the villages and away from the houses; the high clay riverbanks wouldn't let any bullets stray. Gun safety was drilled into us. We were cautioned about other

children whose parents might not teach them properly; if we ever saw another child with a gun, we knew to get away. Guns were not toys. My father did not approve of BB guns because they were classified as toys. I had a .22 rifle when I was seven years old. If I felt like shooting, all I had to do was tell my parents where I was going, take my rifle and a box of 12 shells and go. I was never tempted to shoot at birds or animals because whatever was killed had to be eaten. Now, I realize how odd this must seem; a seven-year-old with a little .22 rifle and a box of ammunition, target shooting alone at the river. But that was how people lived at Laguna when I was growing up; children were given responsibility from an early age.

6   Laguna Pueblo people hunted deer for winter meat. When I was thirteen I carried George Pearl's saddle carbine, a .30–30, and hunted deer for the first time. When I was fourteen, I killed my first mule deer buck with one shot through the heart.

7   Guns were for target shooting and guns were for hunting, but also I knew that Grandma Lily carried a little purse gun with her whenever she drove alone to Albuquerque or Los Lunas. One night my mother and my grandmother were driving the fifty miles from Albuquerque to Laguna down Route 66 when three men in a car tried to force my grandmother's car off the highway. Route 66 was not so heavily traveled as Interstate 40 is now, and there were many long stretches of highway where no other car passed for minutes on end. Payrolls at the Jackpile Uranium Mine were large in the 1950s, and my mother or my grandmother had to bring home thousands from the bank in Albuquerque to cash the miners' checks on paydays.

8   After that night, my father bought my mother a pink nickel-plated snub-nose .22 revolver with a white bone grip. Grandma Lily carried a tiny Beretta as black as her prayer book. As my sisters and I got older, my father taught us to handle and shoot handguns, revolvers mostly, because back then, semiautomatic pistols were not as reliable—they frequently jammed. I will never forget the day my father told us three girls that we never had to let a man hit us or terrorize us because no matter how big and strong the man was, a gun in our hand equalized all differences of size and strength.

9   Much has been written about violence in the home and spousal abuse. I wish to focus instead on violence from strangers toward women because this form of violence terrifies women more, despite the fact that most women are murdered by a spouse, relative, fellow employee, or next-door neighbor, not a stranger. Domestic violence kills many more women and children than strangers kill, but domestic violence also follows more predictable patterns and is more familiar—he comes home drunk and she knows what comes next. A good deal of the terror of a stranger's attack comes from its suddenness and unexpectedness. Attacks by strangers occur with enough frequency that battered women and children often cite their fears of such attacks as reasons for remaining in abusive

domestic situations. They fear the violence they imagine strangers will inflict upon them more than they fear the abusive home. More than one feminist has pointed out that rapists and serial killers help keep the patriarchy in place.

10   An individual woman may be terrorized by her spouse, but women are not sufficiently terrorized that we avoid marriage. Yet many women I know, including myself, try to avoid going outside of their homes alone after dark. Big deal, you say; well yes, it is a big deal since most lectures, performances, and films are presented at night; so are dinners and other social events. Women out alone at night who are assaulted by strangers are put on trial by public opinion: Any woman out alone after dark is asking for trouble. Presently, for millions of women of all socioeconomic backgrounds, sundown is lockdown. We are prisoners of violent strangers.

11   Daylight doesn't necessarily make the streets safe for women. In the early 1980s, a rapist operated in Tucson in the afternoon near the University of Arizona campus. He often accosted two women at once, forced them into residential alleys, then raped each one with a knife to her throat and forced the other to watch. Afterward the women said that part of the horror of their attack was that all around them, everything appeared normal. They could see people inside their houses and cars going down the street—all around them life was going on as usual while their lives were being changed forever.

12   The afternoon rapist was not the only rapist in Tucson at that time; there was the prime-time rapist, the potbellied rapist, and the apologetic rapist all operating in Tucson in the 1980s. The prime-time rapist was actually two men who invaded comfortable foothills homes during television prime time when residents were preoccupied with television and eating dinner. The prime-time rapists terrorized entire families; they raped the women and sometimes they raped the men. Family members were forced to go to automatic bank machines, to bring back cash to end the ordeal. Potbelly rapist and apologetic rapist need little comment, except to note that the apologetic rapist was good looking, well educated, and smart enough to break out of jail for one last rape followed by profuse apologies and his capture in the University of Arizona library. Local papers recounted details about Tucson's last notorious rapist, the red bandanna rapist. In the late 1970s this rapist attacked more than twenty women over a three-year period, and Tucson police were powerless to stop him. Then one night, the rapist broke into a midtown home where the lone resident, a woman, shot him four times in the chest with a .38 caliber revolver.

13   In midtown Tucson, on a weekday afternoon, I was driving down Campbell Avenue to the pet store. Suddenly the vehicle behind me began to weave into my lane, so I beeped the horn politely. The vehicle swerved back to its lane, but then in my rearview mirror I saw the small late-model truck change lanes and begin to follow my car very closely. I drove a few blocks without looking in the rearview mirror, but in my sideview mirror I saw the compact truck was right behind me. OK. Some motorists stay upset for two or three blocks, some require

ten blocks or more to recover their senses. Stoplight after stoplight, when I glanced into the rearview mirror I saw the man—in his early thirties, tall, white, brown hair, and dark glasses. This guy must not have a job if he has the time to follow me for miles—oh, ohhh! No beast more dangerous in the U.S.A. than an unemployed white man.

14   At this point I had to make a decision: do I forget about the trip to the pet store and head for the police station downtown, four miles away? Why should I have to let this stranger dictate my schedule for the afternoon? The man might dare to follow me to the police station, but by the time I reach the front door of the station, he'd be gone. No crime was committed; no Arizona law forbids tail-gating someone for miles or for turning into a parking lot behind them. What could the police do? I had no license plate number to report because Arizona requires only one license plate, on the rear bumper of the vehicle. Anyway, I was within a block of the pet store where I knew I could get help from the pet store owners. I would feel better about this incident if it was not allowed to ruin my trip to the pet store.

15   The guy was right on my rear bumper; if I'd had to stop suddenly for any reason, there'd have been a collision. I decide I will not stop even if he does ram into the rear of my car. I study this guy's face in my rearview mirror, six feet two inches tall, 175 pounds, medium complexion, short hair, trimmed moustache. He thinks he can intimidate me because I am a woman, five feet five inches tall, 140 pounds. But I am not afraid, I am furious. I refuse to be in-timidated. I won't play his game. I can tell by the face I see in the mirror this guy has done this before; he enjoys using his truck to menace lone women.

16   I keep thinking he will quit, or he will figure that he's scared me enough; but he seems to sense that I am not afraid. It's true. I am not afraid because years ago my father taught my sisters and me that we did not have to be afraid. He'll give up when I turn into the parking lot outside the Pet Store, I think. But I watch in my rearview mirror; he's right on my rear bumper. As his truck turns into the parking lot behind my car, I reach over and open the glove com-partment. I take out the holster with my .38 special and lay it on the car seat beside me.

17   I turned my car into a parking spot so quickly that I was facing my stalker who had momentarily stopped his truck and was watching me. I slide the .38 out of its holster onto my lap, I watched the stranger's face, trying to determine whether he would jump out of his truck with a baseball bat or gun and come af-ter me. I felt calm. No pounding heart or rapid breathing. My early experience deer hunting had prepared me well. I did not panic because I felt I could stop him if he tried to harm me. I was in no hurry. I sat in the car and waited to see what choice my stalker would make. I looked directly at him without fear be-cause I had my .38 and I was ready to use it. The expression on my face must have been unfamiliar to him; he was used to seeing terror in the eyes of the women he followed. The expression on my face communicated a warning: if he approached the car window, I'd kill him.

18   He took a last look at me and then sped away. I stayed in the car until his truck disappeared in the traffic of Campbell Avenue.

19   I walked into the pet store shaken. I had felt able to protect myself throughout the incident, but it left me emotionally drained and exhausted. The stranger had only pursued me—how much worse to be battered or raped.

20   Years before, I was unarmed the afternoon that two drunken deer hunters threatened to shoot me off my horse with razor-edged hunting crossbows. I was riding a colt on a national park trail near my home in the Tucson Mountains. These young white men in their late twenties were complete strangers who might have shot me if the colt had not galloped away erratically bucking and leaping—a moving target too difficult for the drunken bow hunters to aim at. The colt brought me to my ranch house where I called the country sheriff's office and the park ranger. I live in a sparsely populated area where my nearest neighbor is a quarter-mile away. I was afraid the men might have followed me back to my house so I took the .44 magnum out from under my pillow and strapped it around my waist until the sheriff or park ranger arrived. Forty-five minutes later, the park ranger arrived—the deputy sheriff arrived fifteen minutes after him. The drunken bow hunters were apprehended on the national park and arrested for illegally hunting; their bows and arrows were seized as evidence for the duration of bow hunting season. In southern Arizona that is enough punishment; I didn't want to take a chance of stirring up additional animosity with these men because I lived alone then; I chose not to make a complaint about their threatening words and gestures. I did not feel that I backed away by not pressing charges; I feared that if I pressed assault charges against these men, they would feel that I was challenging them to all-out war. I did not want to have to kill either of them if they came after me, as I thought they might. With my marksmanship and my .243 caliber hunting rifle from the old days, I am confident that I could stop idiots like these. But to have to take the life of another person is a terrible experience I will always try to avoid.

21   It isn't height or weight or strength that make women easy targets; from infancy women are taught to be self-sacrificing, passive victims. I was taught differently. Women have the right to protect themselves from death or bodily harm. By becoming strong and potentially lethal individuals, women destroy the fantasy that we are sitting ducks for predatory strangers.

22   In a great many cultures, women are taught to depend upon others, not themselves, for protection from bodily harm. Women are not taught to defend themselves from strangers because fathers and husbands fear the consequences themselves. In the United States, women depend upon the courts and the police; but as many women have learned the hard way, the police cannot be outside your house twenty-four hours a day. I don't want more police. More police on the street will not protect women. A few policemen are rapists and killers of women themselves; their uniforms and squad cars give them an advantage. No, I will be responsible for my own safety, thank you.

23   Women need to decide who has the primary responsibility for the health and safety of their bodies. We don't trust the State to manage our reproductive organs, yet most of us blindly trust that the State will protect us (and our reproductive organs) from predatory strangers. One look at the rape and murder statistics for women (excluding domestic incidents) and it is clear that the government FAILS to protect women from the violence of strangers. Some may cry out for a "stronger" State, more police, mandatory sentences, and swifter executions. Over the years we have seen the U.S. prison population become the largest in the world, executions take place every week now, inner-city communities are occupied by the National Guard, and people of color are harassed by police, but guess what? A woman out alone, night or day, is confronted with more danger of random violence from strangers than ever before. As the U.S. economy continues "to downsize," and the good jobs disappear forever, our urban and rural landscapes will include more desperate, angry men with nothing to lose.

24   Only women can put a stop to the "open season" on women by strangers. Women are TAUGHT to be easy targets by their mothers, aunts, and grandmothers who themselves were taught that "a women doesn't kill" or "a woman doesn't learn how to use a weapon." Women must learn how to take aggressive action individually, apart from the police and the courts.

25   Presently twenty-one states issue permits to carry concealed weapons; most states require lengthy gun safety courses and a police security check before issuing a permit. Inexpensive but excellent gun safety and self-defense courses designed for women are also available from every quality gun dealer who hopes to sell you a handgun at the end of the course. Those who object to firearms need trained companion dogs or collectives of six or more women to escort one another day and night. We must destroy the myth that women are born to be easy targets.

FOR ANALYSIS AND DISCUSSION

1. Why, according to Silko, do women live in a state of fear? What measures must they take to prevent personal harm? What effect does this mentality have on society as a whole?

2. How does a gun equalize the differences between men and women? Do you agree with Silko's father's comment that she and her sisters should never be afraid because a "gun equalized all differences in size and strength" (paragraph 8)?

3. Silko points out that "more than one feminist has pointed out that rapists and serial killers help keep the patriarchy in place" (paragraph 9). How do acts of violence against women maintain the "patriarchy"? What is the patriarchy?

4. Crime experts say that most rapes are motivated by a desire for power and not really for sex. Apply this fact to the rapists Silko describes in paragraphs 11 and 12.

5. In paragraph 22, Silko comments that in many cultures, women "are not taught to defend themselves from strangers because fathers and husbands fear the consequences themselves." What does she mean? Does this statement apply to American society? Explain.

6. How does Silko's story of her trip to the pet store support her argument? Explain.

7. Throughout the essay Silko makes references to hunting. Explore the multifaceted levels of this hunting theme.

WRITING ASSIGNMENTS: BEING FEMALE

1. Thirty years ago, the husband was naturally expected to be the primary breadwinner. If his wife worked at all, it was usually only to supplement the family's income. Do we still hold such beliefs, or has the cultural attitude in the United States changed with the times? Poll your classmates to find out their beliefs regarding income status. Should men be expected to have the greater income in a relationship? Ask your classmates to explain their views. For contrast, ask at least ten individuals over 40 years of age to answer the same question. Analyze your results and write an argument that draws some conclusions from your survey.

2. What does it mean to be a woman today? Write an essay explaining what you think it means to be female in today's society. What opportunities are or are not available to women in the United States today? How do women factor into the current social, intellectual, political, economic, and religious arenas? For men: Respond to this assignment from the male perspective. When you have completed your essay, create a dialogue together that explores these different perspectives.

3. Write an argument exploring the effects of the perception of women as victims in the media. Some areas of your exploration might draw from television, film, art, advertising, and other popular media. How do art and media representations of women enforce or refute the perception of women as victims and men as aggressors?

4. Pretend that you have been asked to write an article about male and female relationships in the 1990s for inclusion in a time capsule to be opened 100 years from now. Describe your own perception of male-female relationships and include examples drawn from popular culture. How do you think things will have changed in 100 years?

5. Several of the essays in this section comment that women must deal with the possibility of violence every time they leave their homes. Some feminists say that dwelling on violence against women in fact weakens them in today's society, that it allows terrorism to control women both physically and psychologically. Access the excerpt from Katie Roiphe's book *The Morning After: Sex, Fear, and Feminism on Campus* at <http://www.firstthings.com/ftissues/ft9404/elshtain .html>. Do you agree with her perspective of "co-responsibility?" Explain your view, drawing on personal experience, as well as on data from the article.

BEING MALE: WHAT IS IT LIKE TO BE A MAN TODAY?

How U.S. Schools Are Stifling Male Students
William S. Pollack

You have probably heard the statistic that boys score higher than girls in math and science. To rectify this situation many schools have implemented programs geared toward raising girls' scores in these subject areas. Such efforts seem to be working. However, in our effort to address the specific needs of girls, are we ignoring the boys? William Pollack believes we are doing just that, explaining that society holds boys to an unfair standard that sets them up for failure.

William S. Pollack is a professor of psychiatry at Harvard Medical School. He is the author of *Real Boys: Rescuing Our Sons from the Myths of Boyhood* (1998), from which this essay was adapted. Pollack is also the codirector of the Center for Men at McLean Hospital in Belmont, Massachusetts.

BEFORE YOU READ

Are there school subjects that we assume appeal more to one gender than to another? Do we presume that boys do better in some subjects than do girls, and vice versa? If so, which ones?

AS YOU READ

What do you think Pollack is advocating in this essay? Is his objective clear?

1   Boys are failing in school, and our schools are failing boys.

2   A spate of violent tragedies in schools across America—all perpetrated by young males—has thrust itself upon our cultural consciousness. These shocking incidents illustrate what has become a national crisis of boyhood.

3   Although this crisis has been largely invisible, journalists have begun to recognize elements of it: boys' perpetration of, and victimization by, violent crimes, their high suicide rates, their massively diminished self-esteem. Over 20 years of research and in my most recent study, "Listening to Boys' Voices," I have dug deeper to uncover its causes and manifestations. And I believe we can make practical changes—especially in schools—to rescue our sons from this downward spiral.

4   The silent crisis is rooted in the way boys are raised and treated by adults. Boys suffer emotionally without our being aware of it, and nowhere is this more evident than in our schools.

5   To the distress of teachers, administrators, parents and boys alike, coeducational public schools are some of the least comfortable, least friendly and least

productive environments in boys' lives. While it may still seem like a "man's world" from the perspective of power and wealth in adult society, on the whole, boys are falling terribly behind in our schools.

6   According to a University of Chicago study, which combined results of six major surveys on educational achievement spanning 30 years and involving thousands of children, there is a new "gender gap" in education—with boys falling to the bottom of the heap.

7   Due to our special efforts, girls have made steady gains in math and science, the study showed, while outperforming boys in reading and writing. The study found such large differences in boys' and girls' writing that, it concluded, "males are, on the average, at a rather profound disadvantage in the performance of this basic skill."

8   "The Condition of Education 1997," issued last year by the U.S. Department of Education, confirmed these findings. At all age levels, "females continue to outscore males in reading proficiency," it states. For the last 13 years, females of all ages "have outscored males in writing."

9   The report characterizes writing as a fundamental skill: for probing and understanding ideas and information, and for motivating others to do so. A deficiency in writing skills is likely to undermine one's academic success, self-esteem and career prospects. Secretary of Education Richard Riley called these basic reading and writing skills "make or break" points in education, career achievement and life choices.

10   "Teachers will tell you that . . . (poor readers) often get down on themselves . . . become frustrated, and often head down the road to truancy and dropping out," Riley said. Then things can get worse. "Some . . . begin to make the wrong choices about drugs."

11   Indeed, eighth-grade boys are 50 percent more likely to be held back a grade than girls. By high school, 67 percent of all special-education students are boys. Boys receive 71 percent of all school suspensions and are up to 10 times more likely than girls to be diagnosed with attention-deficit disorder.

12   What's more, the percentage of boys who attend college has dropped dramatically. Twenty years ago more boys went to college than girls. Today, only 58 percent of boys make it to college, compared with 67 percent of girls. Women earn about 55 percent of all bachelor's degrees, and the percentage continues to grow.

13   And overwhelmingly, recent research indicates that girls not only feel more confident about themselves as learners, but also are more ambitious in their career goals.

14   Perhaps worst of all, this educational crisis affects boys' self-esteem. By middle school, their self-esteem as learners is lower than girls'. While adolescent boys continue to show apparently average levels of self-regard, their scores on a measure called the "lie" scale—that is, their fabricated self-esteem or false bravado—skyrocket with age.

15   Such lowered self-view does more than lead to school failure. It creates a pathway to drugs, violence, depression and suicide.

16   How can such a national crisis remain so well concealed? How did things come to this? Most important, what must we do about it?

17   Many of the schools I visit are trying hard to do well. Many teachers and administrators care greatly about boys. But in general, our schools are failing boys in at least four major ways:

18   • Teachers simply do not appear to be doing a good job noticing the problems many boys have in certain academic subjects, namely reading and writing.

19   • Schools and teachers tend to be poorly versed in boys' specific emotional and social needs, and so they often handle these needs inappropriately or inadequately.

20   • Many schools do not provide warm or friendly environments for boys. When boys misbehave, rather than probing the misconduct to discover their emotional needs, educators tend to interpret the behavior solely as a discipline problem. Because the myth that "boys will be boys" is deeply entrenched, teachers and school administrators are often permitted to become punitive toward boys—thus pushing our sons even further toward academic failure, low self-esteem, conduct disorders and other emotional and behavioral problems.

21   • Schools generally do not have curricula and teaching methods designed to meet boys' specific needs and interests. Most schools have done little to make education stimulating for boys. Unlike their focused attention on girls' needs, schools have not developed boy-specific classroom materials. They have not been creative about making existing educational materials interesting for boys. They have not developed teaching methods that take into account boys' unique learning styles. And most elementary and middle schools have a dearth of male teachers, sending an early message to boys that education is primarily a female pursuit.

22   I firmly believe that—depending on how curricula are structured, how classrooms are run and what attitudes about boys prevail—a school can either shape boys positively or confuse them and lead them terribly astray. By addressing who a boy really is and what he really needs, a school can make a difference in helping him do well academically, feel positive about himself and develop a healthy sense of masculinity. A positive school experience, in short, can bolster a boy's self-esteem.

23   By contrast, a school that does not address boys' specific concerns can limit our sons' ability to realize their academic potential, their success at non-academic activities such as sports and the arts, and their chances for a fulfilling social life.

24   Worse, a difficult school experience may cause our sons to "act out" in class, suffer depression, become involved with drugs or alcohol, engage in inappropriate or unsafe sexual activities, or find themselves as victims or perpetrators of violence.

25   When we observe boys' emotional worlds more closely, we discover much quiet suffering under their outward bravado. We bring boys up according to a "code" that teaches them not to express vulnerable emotions, and shames them if they do.

26   One boy in my study, 14-year-old Kevin, explained how many boys fear speaking up: "I know that in many classes girls are supposedly intimidated by guys. But I think the opposite is true. Girls have an easier time opening up and communicating than guys do. . . . Many guys are afraid to speak up because they don't want to look stupid."

27   Boys' learning style requires a teacher's careful attention.

28   I've observed boys who are so resistant to reading books in class that they'll literally toss them aside to pursue more hands-on activities. Yet some of these same boys have been motivated to read on a computer, which allows them to have fun scrolling through the pages using the keyboard or mouse. I've also seen boys who, though identified as "lazy readers," became active, proficient readers when given material on subjects that interested them, such as sports, adventure stories and murder mysteries. One study found a correlation between boys' low reading skills and their association of reading with "feminine" skills.

29   Many classes simply aren't conducted in a way boys, with their naturally high energy levels, find captivating. When boys aren't engaged, they become discipline problems.

30   "Traditionally, classrooms are not organized to suit high-energy learners," says Maryland psychologist Gloria Van Derhorst. "In most classrooms, students are discouraged from getting out of their seats and are forced to learn by listening. This frustrates students who can learn better when they visualize concepts and physically move around."

31   Research suggests that whereas many girls may prefer to learn by watching or listening, boys generally prefer to learn by doing, by engaging in some action-oriented task. In learning environments biased against their strengths, boys may become frustrated and attempt to get their needs met by seeking negative attention.

32   This last-ditch rebellion completes the circle of failure, for now they are labeled "conduct-disordered" or "troublemakers," sent to the principal's office or the doctor's waiting room with a diagnosis of "hyperactivity."

33   Boys' classroom struggles have significant implications for society. In a 1997 health study, "Protecting Adolescents from Harm," researchers found that the second-largest factor shielding young people from emotional distress, drug abuse and violence—next to having close families—was their feeling of "school connectedness."

34   The more warmly a boy feels toward his school—connected, understood and treated fairly—the less likely he is to become suicidal, to abuse drugs and alcohol or to engage in impulsive sexual activities. A boy does best when he feels his teachers care, understand him and have high hopes for him academically.

FOR ANALYSIS AND DISCUSSION

1. On what evidence does Pollack base his argument that the nation's schools are failing boys? What type of logic does Pollack use to frame his view?

2. Pollack connects the recent rash of "violent tragedies" committed by young males to the failure of school systems to address the needs of boys. Do you agree with the connection? Explain your viewpoint.

3. What solutions does Pollack offer his readers? How can schools better serve boys? Can you offer any solutions of your own?

4. Pollack states that "[m]any classes simply aren't conducted in a way boys, with their naturally high energy levels, find captivating" (paragraph 29). What does this statement imply? Do you agree with this view?
5. Should classrooms be separated by gender in order to appeal to "boy learning styles" and "girl learning styles"? Explain.
6. Pollack points out that when boys lose interest in classwork, they are labeled as "troublemakers" and lazy. Do teachers hold boys to an unfair standard? Do girls enjoy more flexibility in the classroom?

The Men We Carry in Our Minds
Scott Russell Sanders

It is a statistical fact that men hold more positions of power and wealth than do women. Many women feel that simply being born male automatically confers status and power or, at the very least, makes life easier. Is it fair to stereotype men this way?

Scott Russell Sanders grew up in rural Tennessee and Ohio. He is the author of several award-winning books, including *Staying Put, Secrets of the Universe,* and *Paradise of Bombs* (1987), in which this essay appeared. Sanders's latest book, *Hunting for Hope: A Father's Journeys,* was released in 1998.

BEFORE YOU READ

Consider the stereotypical view that being male automatically grants one power, status, and privilege. Then think about three men you know well, such as your father, your brother, and a friend. Do their everyday life experiences bear out this generalization?

AS YOU READ

List the occupations and obligations of the men mentioned in the article. What socioeconomic segment of society is Sanders describing? What does this suggest about the relationship between gender and class?

1   "This must be a hard time for women," I say to my friend Anneke. "They have so many paths to choose from, and so many voices calling them."
2   "I think it's a lot harder for men," she replies.
3   "How do you figure that?"
4   "The women I know feel excited, innocent, like crusaders in a just cause. The men I know are eaten up with guilt."
5   "Women feel such pressure to be everything, do everything," I say. "Career, kids, art, politics. Have their babies and get back to the office a week later. It's as if they're trying to overcome a million years' worth of evolution in one lifetime."
6   "But we help one another. And we have this deep-down sense that we're in the *right*—we've been held back, passed over, used—while men feel they're in the wrong. Men are the ones who've been discredited, who have to search their souls."

7   I search my soul. I discover guilty feelings aplenty—toward the poor, the Vietnamese, Native Americans, the whales, an endless list of debts. But toward women I feel something more confused, a snarl of shame, envy, wary, tenderness, and amazement. This muddle troubles me. To hide my unease I say, "You're right, it's tough being a man these days."

8   "Don't laugh," Anneke frowns at me. "I wouldn't be a man for anything. It's much easier being the victim. All the victim has to do is break free. The persecutor has to live with his past."

9   How deep is that past? I find myself wondering. How much of an inheritance do I have to throw off?

10   When I was a boy growing up on the back roads of Tennessee and Ohio, the men I knew labored with their bodies. They were marginal farmers, just scraping by, or welders, steelworkers, carpenters; they swept floors, dug ditches, mined coal, or drove trucks, their forearms ropy with muscle; they trained horses, stoked furnaces, made tires, stood on assembly lines wrestling parts onto cars and refrigerators. They got up before light, worked all day long whatever the weather, and when they came home at night they looked as though somebody had been whipping them. In the evenings and on weekends they worked on their own places, tilling gardens that were lumpy with clay, fixing broken-down cars, hammering on houses that were always too drafty, too leaky, too small.

11   The bodies of the men I knew were twisted and maimed in ways visible and invisible. The nails of their hands were black and split, the hands tattooed with scars. Some had lost fingers. Heavy lifting had given many of them finicky backs and guts weak from hernias. Racing against conveyor belts had given them ulcers. Their ankles and knees ached from years of standing on concrete. Anyone who had worked for long around machines was hard of hearing. They squinted, and the skin of their faces was creased like the leather of old work gloves. There were times, studying them, when I dreaded growing up. Most of them coughed, from dust or cigarettes, and most of them drank cheap wine or whiskey, so their eyes looked bloodshot and bruised. The fathers of my friends always seemed older than the mothers. Men wore out sooner. Only women lived into old age.

12   As a boy I also knew another sort of men, who did not sweat and break down like mules. They were soldiers, and so far as I could tell they scarcely worked at all. But when the shooting started, many of them would die. This was what soldiers were *for,* just as a hammer was for driving nails.

13   Warriors and toilers: those seemed, in my boyhood vision, to be the chief destinies for men. They weren't the only destinies, as I learned from having a few male teachers, from reading books, and from watching television. But the men on television—the politicians, the astronauts, the generals, the savvy lawyers, the philosophical doctors, the bosses who gave orders to both soldiers and laborers—seemed as remote and unreal to me as the figures in Renaissance tapestries. I could no more imagine growing up to become one of these cool, potent creatures than I could imagine becoming a prince.

14   A nearer and more hopeful example was that of my father, who had escaped from a red-dirt farm to a tire factory, and from the assembly line to the

front office. Eventually he dressed in a white shirt and tie. He carried himself as if he had been born to work with his mind. But his body, remembering the earlier years of slogging work, began to give out on him in his fifties, and it quit on him entirely before he turned 65.

15   A scholarship enabled me not only to attend college, a rare enough feat in my circle, but even to study in a university meant for the children of the rich. Here I met for the first time young men who had assumed from birth that they would lead lives of comfort and power. And for the first time I met women who told me that men were guilty of having kept all the joys and privileges of the earth for themselves. I was baffled. What privileges? What joys? I thought about the maimed, dismal lives of most of the men back home. What had they stolen from their wives and daughters? The right to go five days a week, 12 months a year, for 30 or 40 years to a steel mill or a coal mine? The right to drop bombs and die in war? The right to feel every leak in the roof, every gap in the fence, every cough in the engine as a wound they must mend? The right to feel, when the layoff comes or the plant shuts down, not only afraid but ashamed?

16   I was slow to understand the deep grievances of women. This was because, as a boy, I had envied them. Before college, the only people I had ever known who were interested in art or music or literature, the only ones who read books, the only ones who ever seemed to enjoy a sense of ease and grace were the mothers and daughters. Like the menfolk, they fretted about money, they scrimped and made do. But, when the pay stopped coming in, they were not the ones who had failed. Nor did they have to go to war, and that seemed to me a blessed fact. By comparison with the narrow, ironclad days of fathers, there was an expansiveness, I thought, in the days of mothers. They went to see neighbors, to shop in town, to run errands at school, at the library, at church. No doubt, had I looked harder at their lives, I would have envied them less. It was not my fate to become a woman, so it was easier for me to see the graces. I didn't see, then, what a prison a house could be, since houses seemed to be brighter, handsomer places than any factory. I did not realize—because such things were never spoken of—how often women suffered from men's bullying. Even then I could see how exhausting it was for a mother to cater all day to the needs of young children. But if I had been asked, as a boy, to choose between tending a baby and tending a machine, I think I would have chosen the baby. (Having now tended both, I know I would choose the baby.)

17   So I was baffled when the women at college accused me and my sex of having cornered the world's pleasures. I think something like my bafflement has been felt by other boys (and by girls as well) who grew up in dirt-poor farm country, in mining country, in black ghettoes, in Hispanic barrios, in the shadows of factories, in Third World nations—any place where the fate of men is just as grim and bleak as the fate of women.

18   When the women I met at college thought about the joys and privileges of men, they did not carry in their minds the sort of men I had known in my child-

hood. They thought of their fathers, who were bankers, physicians, architects, stockholders, the big wheels of the big cities. They were never laid off, never short of cash at month's end, never lined up for welfare. These fathers made decisions that mattered. They ran the world.

19   The daughters of such men wanted to share in this power, this glory. So did I. They yearned for a say over their future, for jobs worthy of their abilities, for the right to live at peace, unmolested, whole. Yes, I thought, yes yes. The difference between me and these daughters was that they saw me, because of my sex, as destined from birth to become like their fathers, and therefore as an enemy to their desires. But I knew better. I wasn't an enemy, in fact or in feeling. I was an ally. If I had known, then, how to tell them so, would they have believed me? Would they now?

FOR ANALYSIS AND DISCUSSION

1. In paragraph 7 Sanders states that he has feelings of guilt toward a number of minority groups or social causes, but that his feelings toward women are more complicated. What do you think might be the reasons for his feelings? Can you identify with this perspective?

2. Do you think that Sanders feels women, not men, are the privileged class? Explain.

3. How do you think women from the different socioeconomic groups Sanders mentions would respond to the essay? For example, how would the educated daughters of the lawyers and bankers respond? How about the women from Sanders's hometown?

4. Sanders relates his argument entirely in the first person, using personal anecdotes to illustrate his point. How does this approach influence the reader? Would this essay be different if he told it from a third-person point of view? Explain.

5. In paragraph 8 Sanders's friend Anneke says that she "wouldn't be a man for anything. It's much easier being the victim." What does Anneke mean by this statement? Do you agree with her view? Why or why not?

6. What effect do you suppose Anneke's comments have on Sanders's audience? Why do you think he quotes her? How do her comments support his argument?

Is Male Power Really a Myth?
A First Glance
Warren Farrell

Like Scott Russell Sanders's essay, the following essay addresses the cultural stereotype of male power in today's society. In contrast to the narrative approach used by Sanders, however, Warren Farrell attempts, point for point, to debunk the many ideological conventions associated with male power. Farrell comments that many of the very things women associate with elite male power are actually very dangerous to men. Serving in the military, acting as "protector" in violent situations, and even working in high-stress jobs shorten men's lives.

Warren Farrell is a psychologist and author of the 1986 bestseller *Why Men Are the Way They Are.* The following article is an excerpt from his 1995 book *The Myth of Male Power: Why Men Are the Disposable Sex.*

BEFORE YOU READ

Consider the power structure in America today. Do you consider men or women to be the more powerful sex?

AS YOU READ

Make a list of the kinds of power Farrell describes in his article. After you read each one, write down whether you agree or disagree with his view. Do some arguments seem more reasonable than others?

The weakness of men is the façade of strength; the strength of women is the façade of weakness.[1]

1   There are many ways in which a woman experiences a greater sense of powerlessness than her male counterpart: the fears of pregnancy, aging, rape, date rape, and being physically overpowered; less socialization to take a career that pays enough to support a husband and children; less exposure to team sports and its blend of competitiveness and cooperation that is so helpful to career preparation; greater parental pressure to marry and interrupt career for children without regard for her own wishes; not being part of an "old boys" network; having less freedom to walk into a bar without being bothered. . . .

2   Fortunately, almost all industrialized nations have acknowledged these female experiences. Unfortunately, they have acknowledged only the female experiences—and concluded that women *have* the problem, men *are* the problem. Men, though, have a different experience. A man who has seen his marriage become alimony payments, his home become his wife's home, and his children become child-support payments for those who have been turned against him psychologically feels he is spending his life working for people who hate him. He feels desperate for someone to love but fears that another marriage might ultimately leave him with another mortgage payment, another set of children turned against him, and a deeper desperation. When he is called "commitment-phobic" he doesn't feel understood.

3   When a man tries to keep up with payments by working overtime and is told he is insensitive, or tries to handle the stress by drinking and is told he is a drunkard, he doesn't feel powerful, but powerless. When he fears a cry for help will be met with "stop whining," or that a plea to be heard will be met

with "yes, buts," he skips past *attempting* suicide as a cry for help, and just *commits* suicide. Thus men have remained the silent sex and increasingly become the suicide sex. . . .

A Man's Gotta Do What a Man's Gotta Do

4   ITEM. Imagine: Music is playing on your car radio. An announcer's voice interrupts: "We have a special bulletin from the president." (For some reason, you decide not to switch stations.) The president announces, "Since 1.2 million American men have been killed in war, as part of my new program for equality, we will draft only women until 1.2 million American women have been killed in war."

5   In post offices throughout the United States, Selective Service posters remind men that only they must register for the draft. If the post office had a poster saying "A Jew's Gotta Do What a Jew's Gotta Do" . . . Or if "A Woman's Gotta Do . . . " were written across the body of a pregnant woman . . .

6   The question is this: How is it that if any other group were singled out to register for the draft based merely on its characteristics at birth—be that group blacks, Jews, women, or gays—we would immediately recognize it as genocide, but when men are singled out based on their sex at birth, men call it power?

7   The single biggest barrier to getting men to look within is that what any other group would call powerlessness, men have been taught to call power. We don't call "male-killing" sexism; we call it "glory." We don't call the one *million* men who were killed or maimed *in one battle* in World War I (the Battle of the Somme[2]) a holocaust, we call it "serving the country." We don't call those who selected only men to die "murderers." We call them "voters."

8   Our slogan for women is "A Woman's Body, A Woman's Choice"; our slogan for men is "A Man's Gotta Do What a Man's Gotta Do."

The Power of Life

9   ITEM. In 1920 women in the United States lived *one* year longer than men.[3] Today women live *seven* years longer.[4] The male-female life-span gap increased 600 percent.

10   We acknowledge that blacks dying six years sooner than whites reflects the powerlessness of blacks in American society.[5] Yet men dying seven years sooner than women is rarely seen as a reflection of the powerlessness of men in American society.

11   Is the seven-year gap biological? If it is, it wouldn't have been just a one-year gap in 1920.

12   If men lived seven years *longer* than women, feminists would have helped us understand that life expectancy was the best measure of who had the power. And they would be right. Power is the ability to control one's life. Death tends to reduce control. Life expectancy is the bottom line—the ratio of our life's stresses to our life's rewards.

13   If power means having control over one's own life, then perhaps there is no better ranking of the impact of sex roles and racism on power over our lives than life expectancy. Here is the ranking:

Life Expectancy[6]
As a Way of Seeing
Who Has the Power

Females (white)	79
Females (black)	74
Males (white)	72
Males (black)	65

14   The white female outlives the black male by almost fourteen years. Imagine the support for affirmative action if a 49-year-old woman were expected to die sooner than a 62-year-old man. . . .

15   Just as life expectancy is one of the best indicators of power, suicide is one of the best indicators of powerlessness.

16   ITEM. Until boys and girls are 9, their suicide rates are identical;

- from 10 to 14, the boys' rate is twice as high as the girls';
- from 15 to 19, four times as high; and
- from 20 to 24, six times as high.[7]

17   ITEM. As boys experience the pressures of the male role, their suicide rate increases 25,000 percent.[8]

18   ITEM. The suicide rate for men over 85 is 1,350 percent higher than for women of the same age group.

19   Here is the breakdown:

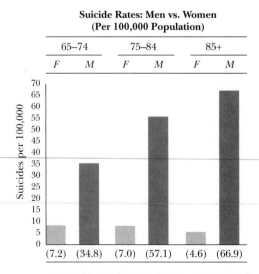

**Suicide Rates: Men vs. Women
(Per 100,000 Population)**

65–74		75–84		85+	
F	M	F	M	F	M
(7.2)	(34.8)	(7.0)	(57.1)	(4.6)	(66.9)

SOURCE: National Center for Health Statistics[9]

The Invisible Victims of Violence

20   ITEM. When Rodney King was beaten by police, we called it violence against blacks, not violence against men. Had *Regina* King been beaten, would no one have mentioned violence against women?

21   *Myth.* Elderly women are the most susceptible to violent crime.

22   ***Fact.*** Elderly women are the *least* susceptible to violent crime. The U.S. Department of Justice finds that a woman over 65 is less likely to be a victim of violent crime than anyone else in any other category. And she is less than half as vulnerable as a man her own age.[10]

23   *Myth.* Women are more likely than men to be victims of violence.

24   ***Fact.*** Men are almost twice as likely as women to be victims of violent crimes (even when rape is *included*).[11] Men are three times more likely to be victims of murder.[12]

25   When *Time* magazine ran a cover story of each of the 464 people shot in a single week, it concluded: "The victims were frequently those most vulnerable in society: the poor, the young, the abandoned, the ill, and the elderly."[13] When you read that, did you think of men? One had to count the pictures to discover that 84 percent of the faces behind the statistics were those of men and boys. In fact, the victims were mostly poor men, young men, abandoned men, ill men, and elderly men. Yet a woman—and only a woman—was featured on the cover. Men are the invisible victims of America's violence. . . .

Spending Power

26 A study of large shopping malls (including men's shops and sporting goods stores) found that seven times as much floor space is devoted to women's personal items as to men's.[14] *Both* sexes buy more for women. The key to wealth is not in what someone earns; it is in what is spent on ourselves, at our discretion—or in what is spent on us, at our hint.

27   Overall, women control consumer spending by a wide margin in virtually every consumer category.[15] With spending power comes other forms of power. Women's control over spending gives them control over TV programs because TV is dependent on sponsors. When this is combined with the fact that women watch more TV in every time slot,[16] shows can't afford to bite the hand that feeds them. Women are to TV what bosses are to employees. The result? Half of the 250 made-for-TV movies in 1991 depicted women as victims—subjected to "some form of physical or psychological mistreatment."[17]

28   In restaurants, men pay for women about ten times as frequently as women pay for men—the more expensive the restaurant, the more often the man pays.[18] Women often say, "Well, men earn more." But when two women go to a restaurant, they don't assume that the woman who earns more will pay the bill. The expectation on men to spend more on women creates the "Spending Obligation Gap."

29   I got a sense of this "Spending Obligation Gap" as soon as I thought about my first date. As a teenager, I loved baby-sitting. (I genuinely loved kids, but it was also the only way I could get paid for raiding a refrigerator!) But then I got to the dating age. Alas, baby-sitting paid only fifty cents an hour. Lawn mowing, though, paid two dollars an hour. I hated lawn mowing. (I lived in New Jersey, where bugs, humidity, and noonday sun made mowing a lawn less pleasant than raiding a refrigerator.) But as soon as I started dating, I started mowing lawns.

30   For boys, lawn mowing is a metaphor for the way we soon learn to take jobs we like less because they pay more. Around junior year of high school, boys begin to repress their interest in foreign languages, literature, art history, sociology, and anthropology because they know an art history major will make less than an engineer. Partially as a result of his different spending expectation (the possibility he might have to support a woman but cannot expect a woman to support him), more than 85 percent of students who take engineering as a college major are men; more than 80 percent of the art history majors are women.[19]

31   The difference in the earnings of the female art historian vs. the male engineer appears to be a measure of discrimination, when in fact both sexes knew ahead of time that engineering would pay more. In fact, the woman who enters engineering with the same lack of experience as the man averages $571 per year *more* than her male counterpart.[20]

32   In brief, the spending obligation that leads a man to choose a career he likes less that pays more is a sign of powerlessness, not power. But when he takes that job, women often assume he will pay because "after all, he earns more." Thus both sexes' expectations reinforce his powerlessness.

Influence Power

33   The Catholic church is often quoted as acknowledging, "Give us a child the first five years and we will shape its life." We acknowledge the influence power of the church over its youth; we often ignore the influence power of a mother over her children—including her sons. But it is the mother who can make the child's bedtime earlier, take away desserts, or ground the child if it doesn't obey. It is the hand that rocks the cradle that creates the child's everyday heaven or hell.

34   Few men have a comparable amount of influence. While theoretically the man was "the master of the house," most men felt they were visitors in their wives' castle in the same way a woman would have felt like a visitor had she entered her husband's place of work. From a woman's perspective, a man's home is his castle; from a man's perspective, a woman's home is his mortgage.

35   Almost every woman had a primary role in the "female-dominated" family structure; only a small percentage of men had a primary role in the "male-dominated" governmental and religious structures. Many mothers were, in a sense, the chair of the board of a small company—their family. Even in Japan, women are in charge of the family finances—a fact that was revealed to the average American only after the Japanese stock market crashed in 1992 and thousands of women lost billions of dollars that their husbands never knew they had

invested.[21] Conversely, most men were on their company's assembly line—either its physical assembly line or its psychological assembly line. . . .

36   Influence power, though, is not real power. If we told mothers, "The more children you have, the more power you will have," they would laugh. If we then said, "The more children you have, the more everyone will love you and respect you," the mother would feel pressured, not empowered. But when we tell men, "The more people you supervise, the more power you will have," they buy it. Real power does not come from caving in to pressure to expand obligations, it comes from controlling our own life.

37   Historically, a husband spent the bulk of his day under the eye of his boss—his source of income; a wife did not spend the bulk of her day under the eye of her husband—her source of income. She had more control over her work life than he had over his. . . .

38   The prohibition against divorce gave a woman security in her workplace. Nothing gave a man security in his workplace. His source of income could fire him; her source of income could not fire her. Even today, if he quits his job, he doesn't get severance pay; if she initiates divorce, she takes half the "corporate stock." . . .

39   In the 1990s, if a woman and man make love and she says she is using birth control but is not, she has the right to raise the child without his knowing he even has a child, and then to sue him for retroactive child support even ten to twenty years later (depending on the state). This forces him to take a job with more pay and more stress and therefore earlier death. Although it's his body, he has no choice. He has the option of being a slave (working for another without pay or choice) or being a criminal. *Roe* v. *Wade* gave women the vote over their bodies. Men still don't have the vote over theirs—whether in love or war. . . .

40   ITEM. The Mike Tyson trial. The hotel in which the jury is sequestered goes ablaze. Two firefighters die saving its occupants.

41   The trial of Mike Tyson made us increasingly aware of men-as-rapists. The firefighters' deaths did not make us increasingly aware of men-as-saviors. We were more aware of one man doing harm than of two men saving; of one man threatening one woman who is still physically alive than of dozens of men saving hundreds of people and two of those men being dead. In the United States, almost one million municipal firefighters *volunteer* to risk their lives to save strangers. Ninety-nine percent of them are men.[22] In exchange they ask only for appreciation. In exchange they are ignored.

The "Work Obligation Gap"

42 The media popularizes studies reporting women's greater amount of time spent on housework and child care, concluding, "Women work two jobs; men work one." But this is misleading. Women do work more hours inside the home, but men work more hours outside the home. And the average man commutes farther and spends more time doing yardwork, repairs, painting. . . .

What happens when all of these are combined? The University of Michigan's study (reported in the *Journal of Economic Literature* in 1991) found the average man worked sixty-one hours per week, the average woman fifty-six.[23]

43   Is this just a recent change in men? No. In 1975, the largest nationwide probability sampling of households found that when all child care, all housework, all work outside the home, commuting, and gardening were added together, husbands did 53 percent of the total work, wives 47 percent.[24]

The Unpaid Bodyguard

44   ITEM. Steve Petrix was a journalist who lived near me in San Diego. Every day he returned home to have lunch with his wife. Recently, as he got near his door, he heard his wife screaming. She was being attacked with a knife. Steve fought the assailant off his wife. His wife ran to call the police. The intruder killed Steve. Steve was 31.[25]

45   A friend of mine put it this way: "What would you pay someone who agreed that, if he was ever with you when you were attacked, he would intervene and try to get himself killed slowly enough to give you time to escape? What is the hourly wage for a bodyguard? You know that is your job as a man—every time you are with a woman . . . any woman, not just your wife."[26]

46   What do men as women's personal bodyguards and men as volunteer firefighters have in common besides being men? They are both unpaid. Men have not yet begun to investigate their unpaid roles. . . .

Man as "Nigger"?

47   In the early years of the women's movement, an article in *Psychology Today* called "Women as Nigger" quickly led to feminist activists (myself included) making parallels between the oppression of women and blacks.[27] Men were characterized as the oppressors, the "master," the "slaveholders." Black congresswoman Shirley Chisolm's statement that she faced far more discrimination as a woman than as a black was widely quoted.

48   The parallel allowed the hard-earned rights of the civil rights movement to be applied to women. The parallels themselves had more than a germ of truth. But what none of us realized was how each sex was the other's slave in different ways and therefore *neither* sex was the other's "nigger" ("nigger" implies a *one-sided* oppressiveness).

49   If "masculists" had made such a comparison, they would have had every bit as strong a case as feminists. The comparison is useful because it is not until we understand how men were *also* women's servants that we get a clear picture of the sexual *division* of labor and therefore the fallacy of comparing either sex to "nigger." For starters . . .

50   Blacks were forced, via slavery, to risk their lives in cotton fields so that whites might benefit economically while blacks died prematurely. Men were forced, via the draft, to risk their lives on battlefields so that everyone else might benefit economically while men died prematurely. The disproportionate numbers of blacks and males in war increases both blacks' and males' likeli-

hood of experiencing posttraumatic stress, of becoming killers in postwar civilian life as well, and of dying earlier. Both slaves and men died to make the world safe for freedom—someone else's.

51   Slaves had their own children involuntarily taken away from them; men have their own children involuntarily taken away from them. We tell women they have the right to children and tell men they have to fight for children.

52   Blacks were forced, via slavery, into society's most hazardous jobs; men are forced, via socialization, into society's most hazardous jobs. Both slaves and men constituted almost 100 percent of the "death professions." Men still do.

53   When slaves gave up their seats for whites, we called it subservience; when men give up their seats for women, we call it politeness. Similarly, we called it a symbol of subservience when slaves stood up as their master entered a room; but a symbol of politeness when men stand up as a woman enters the room. Slaves bowed before their masters; in traditional cultures, men still bow before women.[28] The slave helped the master put on his coat; the man helped the woman put on her coat. He still does. These symbols of deference and subservience are common with slaves to masters and with men to women.

54   Blacks are more likely than whites to be homeless; men are more likely than women to be homeless. Blacks are more likely than whites to be in prison; men are about twenty times more likely than women to be in prison. Blacks die earlier than whites; men die earlier than women. Blacks are less likely than whites to attend college or graduate from college. Men are less likely than women to attend college (46 percent versus 54 percent) and less likely to graduate from college (46 percent versus 55 percent).[29]

55   Apartheid forced blacks to mine diamonds for whites; socialization expected men to work in different mines to pay for diamonds for women. Nowhere in history has there been a ruling class working to afford diamonds they could give to the oppressed in hopes the oppressed would love them more.

56   Blacks are more likely than whites to volunteer for war in the hopes of earning money and gaining skills; men are more likely than women to volunteer for war for the same reasons. Blacks are more likely than whites to subject themselves to the child abuse of boxing and football in the hopes of earning money, respect, and love; men are more likely than women to subject themselves to the child abuse of boxing and football, with the same hopes.

57   Women are the only "oppressed" group to systematically grow up having their own private member of an "oppressor" class (called fathers) in the field, working for them. Traditionally, the ruling class had people in the field, working for them—called slaves.

58   Among slaves, the field slave was considered the second-class slave; the house slave, the first-class slave. The male role (out in the field) is akin to the field slave—or the second-class slave; the traditional female role (homemaker) is akin to the house slave—the first-class slave.

59   Blacks who are heads of households have a net worth much lower than heads of households who are white; men who are heads of households have a

net worth much lower than heads of households who are women.[30] No oppressed group has ever had a net worth higher than the oppressor.

60   It would be hard to find a single example in history in which a group that
cast more than 50 percent of the vote got away with calling itself the victim. Or
an example of an oppressed group which chooses to vote for their "oppressors"
more than it chooses to have its own members take responsibility for running.
Women are the only minority group that is a majority, the only group that calls
itself "oppressed" that is able to control who is elected to every office in virtually
every community in the country. Power is not in who holds the office, power is
in who chooses who holds the office. Blacks, Irish, and Jews never had more
than 50 percent of America's vote.

61   Women are the only "oppressed" group to share the same parents as the
"oppressor"; to be born into the middle class and upper class as frequently as
the "oppressor"; to own more of the culture's luxury items than the "oppressor"; the only "oppressed" group whose "unpaid labor" enables them to buy
most of the fifty billion dollars' worth of cosmetics sold each year; the only "oppressed" group that spends more on high fashion, brand-name clothing than
their "oppressors"; the only "oppressed" group that watches more TV during
every time category than their "oppressors."[31]

62   Feminists often compare marriage to slavery—with the female as slave. It
seems like an insult to women's intelligence to suggest that marriage is female
slavery when we know it is 25 million American females[32] who read an average
of *twenty* romance novels per *month,*[33] often with the fantasy of marriage. Are
feminists suggesting that 25 million American women have "enslavement" fantasies because they fantasize marriage? Is this the reason Danielle Steele is the
best-selling author in the world?

63   Never has there been a slave class that has spent a lot of time dreaming
about being a slave and purchasing books and magazines that told them "How
to Get a Slavemaster to Commit." Either marriage is something different from
slavery for women or feminists are suggesting that women are not very intelligent.

64   The difference between slaves and males is that African-American blacks
rarely thought of their slavery as "power," but men were taught to think of their
slavery as "power." If men were, in fact, slavemasters, and women slaves, then
why did men spend a lifetime supporting the "slaves" and the "slaves'" children? Why weren't the women supporting the men instead, the way kings were
supported by their subjects? Our understanding of blacks' powerlessness has allowed us to call what we did to blacks "immoral," yet we still call what we do to
males "patriotism" and "heroism" when they kill on our behalf, but "violence,"
"murder," and "greed" when they kill the wrong people the wrong way at the
wrong time.

65   By understanding that what we did to blacks was immoral, we were willing
to assuage our guilt via affirmative action programs and welfare. By thinking of
men as the dominant oppressors who do what they do for power and greed, we
feel little guilt when they die early in the process. By believing that women were

an oppressed slavelike class, we extended privileges and advantages to women that had originally been designed to compensate for our immorality to blacks. For women—and only women—to take advantage of this slavery compensation was its own brand of immorality. For men to cooperate was its own brand of ignorance. . . .

NOTES

1. Lawrence Diggs, *Transitions,* Nov./Dec. 1990, p. 10.

2. The Battle of the Somme was in 1916. British casualties were 420,000; French were 195,000; German were 650,000. See John Laffin, *Brassey's Battles: 3,500 Years of Conflict, Campaigns, and Wars from A-Z* (London: A. Wheaton & Co., 1986), p. 399.

3. 1920 statistics from the National Center for Health Statistics, *Monthly Vital Statistics Report,* vol. 38, no. 5, supplement, September 26, 1989, p. 4. In 1920, the life expectancy for men was 53.6 years; for women, 54.6 years.

4. Ibid., vol. 39, no. 13, August 28, 1991, p. 17. In 1990, women's average length of life was 78.8 years, men's, 72.0.

5. Ibid., vol. 38, no. 5, op. cit.

6. Ibid. The exact life span difference is 6.9 years between men and women. The life span for white females is 78.9; for black females, 73.6; for white males, 72.2; and for black males, 65.2.

7. U.S. Bureau of Health and Human Services, National Center for Health Statistics (hereinafter USBH&HS/NCHS), *Vital Statistics of the United States* (Washington, D.C.: USGPO, 1991), vol. 2, part A, "Mortality," p. 51, tables 1–9, "Death Rates for 72 Selected Causes by 5-Year Age Groups, Race, and Sex: U.S., 1988." The exact rates are:

Suicide Rates by Age and Sex per 100,000 Population

Age	Male	Female
5–9	0.1	0.0
10–14	2.1	0.8
15–19	18.0	4.4
20–24	25.8	4.1

8. The 25,000 percent figure is derived by comparing the 0.1 suicides per 100,000 boys under the age of nine to the 25.8 suicides per 100,000 boys between ages 20–24 in the table in the endnote above, from ibid.

9. Latest data available as of 1992. From USBH&HS/NCHS, *Vital Statistics of the United States,* vol. 2, "Mortality," part A, 1987.

10. Among those over the age of 65, 2.7 women per 1,000 and 6.2 men per 1,000 are victims of crimes of violence. U.S. Bureau of Justice Statistics, Office of Justice Programs, Bureau of Justice Statistics, *Criminal Victimization in the United States, 1988,* National Crime Survey Report NCJ–122024, December 1990, p. 18, table 5.

11. Ibid., *1987,* publication NCJ–115524, June, 1989, p. 16, table 3, "Personal Crimes, 1987."

12. Ibid.

13. "7 Deadly Days," *Time,* July 17, 1989, p. 31. . . .

14. Jacque Lynn Foltyn, "Feminine Beauty in American Culture" (Ph.D. diss., University of California at San Diego, 1987). Foltyn measured floor space of departments offering male versus female items in shopping malls and boutiques, on the assumption that if women's departments were not creating enough profit per square foot, they would be forced to give way to men's or general departments. Foltyn found seven times as much

floor space was devoted to female personal items as to male personal items. She also found the more valuable floor space was devoted to women's items (e.g., perfume counters immediately as we enter a department store).

15. See Diane Crispell, "The Brave New World," *American Demographic,* January 1992, p. 38. The article concludes that women dominate consumer spending in personal items, cleaning supplies and housewares, and food. In the category of furniture/cars, it is close to even—men have only a technical dominance.

16. A. C. Nielsen ratings, 1984.

17. Harry F. Waters, "Whip Me, Beat Me, and Give Me Great Ratings," *Newsweek,* November 11, 1991.

18. This is based on my own informal discussions with waiters in restaurants around the country in cities where I speak.

19. Also, 86 percent of engineering *graduates* are men; 83 percent of art history graduates are women. Unpublished information, U.S. Department of Education, Office of Educational Research and Improvement, National Center for Education Statistics, "IPEDS Completions Study," 1989, 1990. Interview on June 1, 1992, with Norman Brandt of the U.S. Office of Education.

20. The starting salary for a female engineer exceeds that for a man by $571 per year. See the Engineering Manpower Commission's *Women in Engineering* (Washington, D.C.: American Association of Engineering Society [AAES]), EMC Bulletin no. 99, December 1989, table 5.

21. Sonni Efron, "Honey, I Shrunk the Nest Egg," *Los Angeles Times,* June 20, 1992, front page.

22. In an interview on February 11, 1992, John Oddison of the government's United States Fire Administration reported that *99 percent of volunteer municipal firefighters are men.* Of all municipal firefighters, 964,000 are volunteers and 240,000 are career.

23. F. Thomas Juster and Frank P. Stafford, "The Allocation of Time: Empirical Findings, Behavioral Models, and Problems of Measurement," *Journal of Economic Literature,* vol. 29, June 1991, p. 477. Her average hours both inside and outside the home add up to fifty-six; his, to sixty-one.

24. Martha Hill, *Patterns of Time Use in Time, Goods, and Well-Being* (Ann Arbor: Institute for Social Research, University of Michigan, 1985), ed. F. Thomas Juster and Frank P. Stafford. See also Joseph H. Pleck, *Working Wives/Working Husbands* (Beverly Hills: Sage Publications, 1985), p. 41, table 2.3.

25. Carol J., Castañeda, *San Diego Union,* May 21, 1988.

26. Frederic Hayward, "The Male's Unpaid Role: Bodyguard and Protector," as reprinted in Francis Baumli, Ph.D., *Men Freeing Men* (Jersey City, N.J.: New Atlantis Press, 1985), p. 238.

27. Naomi Weisstein, "Women as Nigger," *Psychology Today,* vol. 3, no. 5, October, 1969, p. 20. This article is considered a classic of feminist literature. See, for example, Wendy Martin, *The American Sisterhood: Writings of the Feminist Movement from Colonial Times to the Present* (New York: Harper & Row, 1972), pp. 292–98.

28. Credit to Lawrence Diggs for some of these ideas related to symbols of deference, contained in his audiotape called "Introduction to Men's Issues" (P.O. Box 41, Roslyn, SD 57261).

29. U.S. Department of Education, National Center for Education Statistics, *Digest of Education Statistics 1991,* p. 167, table 161, "Total Enrollment in Institutions of Higher Education" shows that women are 54 percent of those enrolled in college; p. 234, table 228, "Earned

Degrees Conferred by Institutions of Higher Education," shows that women are 55 percent of those receiving bachelors' degrees from college.

30. Women who are heads of households have a net worth 141 percent greater than that of men who are heads of households. This is the latest data available from the Bureau of the Census as of 1992. See U.S. Department of Commerce, Bureau of the Census, *Statistical Abstracts of the US, 1989,* op. cit.

31. A. C. Nielsen ratings, 1984.

32. Interview, February 18, 1985, with John Markert, independent researcher and contributor to *Romantic Times* and author of "Marketing Love," dissertation in progress.

33. *Forbes* reports that the average romance novel buyer spent $1,200 in 1991. The average romance costs about $5 in 1991, leading to the purchase of approximately 240 books a year, or 20 books per month. For women who also read their friends' books, the number of books they read is more than 20 per month; for women who do not do this but buy some hardcovers, the figure is less than 20 per month. See Dana Wechsler Linden and Matt Rees, "I'm hungry. But not for food," *Forbes,* July 6, 1992, pp. 70–75.

FOR ANALYSIS AND DISCUSSION

1. In your own words, define "power." For example, is it control over others, financial stability, status, physical strength, decision-making ability? After determining your definition of power, make a chart in which you categorize who holds power in U.S. society. How does your definition compare to the points Farrell makes in his article?

2. In paragraph 7 Farrell comments that we "don't call the one *million* men who were killed or maimed *in one battle* in World War I . . . holocaust, we call it 'serving the country.'" Do you agree with this view? Is his conclusion logical? Explain.

3. Farrell's introduction presents a society in which males fear deeply the ramifications of divorce. The divorce cycle can lead men to alcoholism and even suicide. How does Farrell's portrayal of men's fears compare to the concerns and experiences of men you know?

4. How do you suppose Katie Roiphe would respond to Farrell's assertions? With which ones would she agree or disagree? What values or assumptions do Farrell and Roiphe share? Create a dialogue between the two writers, using specific ideas from each essay as well as responses you think likely, given each point of view.

5. Consider Farrell's story of journalist Steve Petrix, who was killed when he tried to fight off an intruder who had attacked his wife in their home. How does this story prove that "bodyguard power" is actually an antipower situation? What do you think Steve's wife would have done if the roles were reversed and she had been the one to discover an intruder attacking Steve?

Conan and Me
Bill Persky

Today's idealized image of men is more than the stoic and tough John Wayne stereotype of the past. Today's man must be also sensitive and caring: a sort of

Arnold Schwarzenegger with feelings. In the following essay Bill Persky uses his experience one fated night to argue that men can achieve their own ideal only by trusting and accepting themselves.

Bill Persky is a writer, director, and producer of television shows. The winner of five Emmy awards, with Sam Danoff he wrote and produced such hits as *The Dick Van Dyke Show, That Girl,* and *Kate & Allie.* The following essay first appeared in *Esquire* magazine in May 1989.

BEFORE YOU READ

Imagine a burglar breaks into a home or apartment. Would a man and a woman react the same way to this dangerous situation? Can you make such generalizations? Why or why not?

AS YOU READ

Note the strategies used to inject humor into this essay. List two forms of humor used and give examples of them.

1   Carl Reiner once said that he didn't believe Englishmen really had accents, they just all got together and agreed to talk that way to make the rest of us feel bad. The act was probably rooted in feelings of inadequacy dating back to their origin as druids who were still running around painted blue long after everyone else had moved on to cooked food and world conquest. Carl believed that if, at three in the morning, you crept into a room where an Englishman was sleeping and shouted "*Fire!*" he would wake in panic and say, "*Fire! Let's get the hell out of here!*" with no accent whatsoever.

2   Though I would gladly lose my New York accent under any circumstance, I have some images of myself that I'd like to think are real. And I have wondered how they would hold up if Carl crept into my room some night and sounded the alarm. I know who I would *like* to be in that rude awakening: I'd grab the kids and the cat and lead everyone in the building to safety, all with the calm, clear voice that I've already selected from several I've tried out in the shower. But I've always known that if that moment came, no matter what I may have hoped or planned, there would be only me, the real me, the one I doubt, question, and hide from the world and, with less success, from myself.

3   My moment came one morning last summer. It wasn't 3:00 A.M. but sometime after 5:00, and it wasn't Carl's shout of "Fire!" but the muffled thumping of a man climbing through my bedroom window. Instantly I found out who I was: an unlikely combination of Arnold Schwarzenegger and my mother.

4   I am still not sure who was the most effective as I leapt naked from my bed, grabbing the first weapon at hand, my pillow, and went on the attack, screaming, "*Get out! Get out!*" in a high-pitched voice. I resented my mother speaking for me at a time like that, and I consciously tried to get into a lower register, but it was her moment, and I couldn't take it away from her.

5   Schwarzenegger was doing a lot better, and I was pleased with him. He was actually engaged in hand-to-hand combat with an intruder who was three quarters of the way into my room. The window opened only a foot and a half, being held in place by a dowel I had inserted between the top and the frame to prevent anyone from climbing in. I made a note to get a longer pole if I lived.

6   The struggle raged as my burglar (we'd known each other long enough at this point for some familiarity) was pushing against a flower box to come the rest of the way in, and I was pushing and swinging my pillow to get him out. I needed a more formidable weapon. Actually, it was right there on the night table, but in my initial panic I had missed it—*The Bonfire of the Vanities*. Hitting him with that would have done major damage *and* made some kind of social comment.

7   Since the narrow opening was preventing either of us from making any headway, we were at a stalemate. My warrior self suddenly perceived with Zen clarity that if I removed the pole, I could open the window fully and my chances of getting him all the way out would improve. The thought that it would improve his chance of getting all the way in didn't occur to me. That's the trouble with Zen, it's so self-involved. I emitted a fierce yell borrowed from a sushi chef and yanked the pole free. Suddenly the tide of battle turned in my favor, as he was now up against a naked maniac with a pole instead of a pillow, and my mother switched from "Get out! Get out!" to a more macho "*You son of a bitch!*"

8   The combination must have been awesome, because he started to plead in what I am sure was his mother's voice, "*Don't hurt me! Don't hurt me!*" Don't hurt him? The thought never entered my mind, but as long as he brought it up, I considered it as an option. I could use the new upper-body strength I'd developed at the Vertical Club to knock him senseless. Originally I'd planned on using it to improve my serve. The struggle intensified until somehow his mother and my mother got to talking, as mothers will, and "Don't hurt me, Don't hurt me" seemed like a good idea all around. So I gave him a shove that wasn't needed to get him out and covered his escape over the wall with a hail of four-letter words, finally finding the voice I'd practiced for the occasion.

9   I closed and locked the window, drew the drapes, and stood waiting. I wasn't sure for what, probably to go into shock or some other reaction that comes when danger is past. This was only the second real fight I ever had. The first was fifty years ago in the third grade when Jerry Matz challenged me to meet him after school for reasons I can't for the life of me recall, but I think it was about who was going to marry Nina Yanoff. What I do remember is that I was nauseated all day and cried throughout the fight and even after I had won. Now here I was, not crying, not even breathing hard. I settled for calling the police. I felt it was the responsible thing to do, and I was dying to tell somebody.

10   My burglar and I are now just another crime statistic along with the other apartment on Sixty-second Street that was burglarized that night while the

occupants slept. The police are sure it was my burglar after he left me, so apparently our encounter had little impact on his life. But it's had a very profound effect on mine. I've made the obvious adjustments of sleeping in shorts, keeping the fireplace poker next to my bed, and getting bars for the windows. (That information is for my mother, whom I never told about the incident but who will probably read this, and I wouldn't want her to worry.)

11   On a less obvious but more meaningful level, the incident has changed the way I see myself in Carl's hypothesis. At the core I am tougher and braver than I knew. Even with the high-pitched voice, I really like the guy I turned out to be. I'd like to be that guy more often, and I think I know why I'm not. It isn't a question of courage but *clarity,* and the freedom that comes when you know you're right. In our daily lives things are never as clear-cut as someone coming through our bedroom window. They're vague or oblique, and our first instinct waits as we filter through too much information and conditioning. We lose that initial impulse that's pure us.

12   My burglar probably had a lousy childhood and was from a deprived racial or economic group. He might have been a terrific kid with all kinds of potential who never had a chance. In retrospect he might have been the real victim. But that night he was coming through my bedroom window, and one thing was crystal clear—he didn't belong there. So I was free to act as who I really am. It was a great feeling, one I would like to hold on to, trust, and go with. Every day there are less obvious intruders coming through the windows of my spirit and my soul, and they don't belong there either. So let them beware: Arnold and my mother are waiting.

FOR ANALYSIS AND DISCUSSION

1. In paragraph 2, Persky says that if ever faced with an urgent situation, "there would be only me, the real me, the one I doubt, question, and hide from the world and, with less success, from myself." What does this statement say about the kinds of behavior Persky attributes to men in dangerous situations? What kinds of demands and expectations are placed on men by society? How are these expectations reinforced?

2. If confronted with a dangerous situation, would your behavior be different if you were alone than if you faced it with a member of the opposite sex? If so, in what way? Do men and women hide their real selves? Explain.

3. Part of the point of this essay is that men are culturally conditioned to act in ways that match cultural sex-role stereotypes. What do you think Persky's personal cultural conditioning is? What clues does he offer to indicate his perspective? How do these clues influence the reader's response to the essay?

4. Can you relate to Persky's reaction when faced with a dangerous situation? Explain. Do you identify with his feelings? How does the incident, and his feelings about it, support his argument?

5. Why do you think Persky uses the quotation by Carl Reiner in his introduction? Does it help set the tone of the essay? What do you think the quotation means?

WRITING ASSIGNMENTS: BEING MALE

1. Write an essay in which you consider your own sense of cultural conditioning. Do you feel your behavior has been conditioned by sex-role expectations? In what ways? Is there a difference between the "real" you and the person you present to the world? If there is a difference, is it the result of cultural conditioning?

2. Write an essay explaining what you think it means to be male in today's society. How do men factor into current social, intellectual, political, economic, and religious arenas? What opportunities are available—or not available—to men? Do you think it is easier or better to be male in American culture? For women: Respond to this assignment from the female perspective. When you have completed your essay, create a dialogue together that explores these different perspectives.

3. One of the "myths of male power" cited by Warren Farrell is the fact that men and not women must register with the Selective Service. Read the editorial on "The Backlash" Web site by Rich Zubaty <http://www.backlash.com/1998/9-sept98/zubaty09.html> dealing with women and the draft. Do you agree with Zubaty's views? Should women be required to register for the draft? Poll your classmates for their opinions on the issue. Then explain your view in a well-supported argument drawing from the two essays, your polled results, and your own resources.

4. Write an essay in which you explore the terms "masculine" and "feminine." You might include library research as to the origins of the words, or research their changing implications over the years.

GENDER COMMUNICATIONS: ARE WE SPEAKING THE SAME LANGUAGE?

Mr. Fix-It and the Home Improvement Committee
John Gray

It is an often-repeated lament that men and women just don't understand each other. While some experts attribute the communication breakdown between the sexes to socialization, others ascribe it to biological differences. Men's and women's brains, say these experts, are wired differently; therefore, they communicate differently as well. John Gray takes this biological difference a few steps further and says men and women hail from separate planets. Martians and Venusians must learn each other's planetary languages to be able to communicate effectively.

John Gray is the author of the best-selling book *Men Are from Mars, Women Are from Venus,* from which this excerpt is taken. He holds a Ph.D. in psychology from Columbia Pacific University and has taught relationship seminars based on his Mars/Venus books throughout the world.

BEFORE YOU READ

Have you ever thought that a member of the opposite sex didn't understand you? When discussing an issue, have you ever experienced a gender-based "communication breakdown" that prevented you from arguing your point?

AS YOU READ

What evidence does Gray use to support his argument that men and women think differently?

1   The most frequently expressed complaint women have about men is that men don't listen. Either a man completely ignores her when she speaks to him, or he listens for a few beats, assesses what is bothering her, and then proudly puts on his Mr. Fix-It cap and offers her a solution to make her feel better. He is confused when she doesn't appreciate this gesture of love. No matter how many times she tells him that he's not listening, he doesn't get it and keeps doing the same thing. She wants empathy, but he thinks she wants solutions.

2   The most frequently expressed complaint men have about women is that women are always trying to change them. When a woman loves a man she feels responsible to assist him in growing and tries to help him improve the way he does things. She forms a home-improvement committee, and he becomes her primary focus. No matter how much he resists her help, she persists—waiting for any opportunity to help him or tell him what to do. She thinks she's nurturing him, while he feels he's being controlled. Instead, he wants her acceptance.

3   These two problems can finally be solved by first understanding why men offer solutions and why women seek to improve. Let's pretend to go back in time, where by observing life on Mars and Venus—before the planets discovered one another or came to Earth—we can gain some insights into men and women.

Life on Mars

4   Martians value power, competency, efficiency, and achievement. They are always doing things to prove themselves and develop their power and skills. Their sense of self is defined through their ability to achieve results. They experience fulfillment primarily through success and accomplishment.

5   Everything on Mars is a reflection of these values. Even their dress is designed to reflect their skills and competence. Police officers, soldiers, businessmen, scientists, cab drivers, technicians, and chefs all wear uniforms or at least hats to reflect their competence and power.

6   They don't read magazines like *Psychology Today, Self,* or *People.* They are more concerned with outdoor activities, like hunting, fishing, and racing cars. They are interested in the news, weather, and sports and couldn't care less about romance novels and self-help books.

7   They are more interested in "objects" and "things" rather than people and feelings. Even today on Earth, while women fantasize about romance, men fantasize about powerful cars, faster computers, gadgets, gizmos, and new more powerful technology. Men are preoccupied with the "things" that can help them express power by creating results and achieving their goals.

8   Achieving goals is very important to a Martian because it is a way for him to prove his competence and thus feel good about himself. And for him to feel good about himself he must achieve these goals by himself. Someone else can't achieve them for him. Martians pride themselves in doing things all by themselves. Autonomy is a symbol of efficiency, power, and competence.

9   Understanding this Martian characteristic can help women understand why men resist so much being corrected or being told what to do. To offer a man unsolicited advice is to presume that he doesn't know what to do or that he can't do it on his own. Men are very touchy about this, because the issue of competence is so very important to them.

10   Because he is handling his problems on his own, a Martian rarely talks about his problems unless he needs expert advice. He reasons: "Why involve someone else when I can do it by myself?" He keeps his problems to himself unless he requires help from another to find a solution. Asking for help when you can do it yourself is perceived as a sign of weakness.

11   However, if he truly does need help, then it is a sign of wisdom to get it. In this case, he will find someone he respects and then talk about his problem. Talking about a problem on Mars is an invitation for advice. Another Martian feels honored by the opportunity. Automatically he puts on his Mr. Fix-It hat, listens for a while, and then offers some jewels of advice.

12   This Martian custom is one of the reasons men instinctively offer solutions when women talk about problems. When a woman innocently shares upset feelings or explores out loud the problems of her day, a man mistakenly assumes she is looking for some expert advice. He puts on his Mr. Fix-It hat and begins giving advice; this is his way of showing love and of trying to help.

13   He wants to help her feel better by solving her problems. He wants to be useful to her. He feels he can be valued and thus worthy of her love when his abilities are used to solve her problems.

14   Once he has offered a solution, however, and she continues to be upset it becomes increasingly difficult for him to listen because his solution is being rejected and he feels increasingly useless.

15   He has no idea that by just listening with empathy and interest he can be supportive. He does not know that on Venus talking about problems is not an invitation to offer a solution.

Life on Venus

16 Venusians have different values. They value love, communication, beauty, and relationships. They spend a lot of time supporting, helping, and nurturing one another. Their sense of self is defined through their feelings and the quality of their relationships. They experience fulfillment through sharing and relating.

17   Everything on Venus reflects these values. Rather than building highways and tall buildings, the Venusians are more concerned with living together in harmony, community, and loving cooperation. Relationships are more important than work and technology. In most ways their world is the opposite of Mars.

18   They do not wear uniforms like the Martians (to reveal their competence). On the contrary, they enjoy wearing a different outfit every day, according to how they are feeling. Personal expression, especially of their feelings, is very important. They may even change outfits several times a day as their mood changes.

19   Communication is of primary importance. To share their personal feelings is much more important than achieving goals and success. Talking and relating to one another is a source of tremendous fulfillment.

20   This is hard for a man to comprehend. He can come close to understanding a woman's experience of sharing and relating by comparing it to the satisfaction he feels when he wins a race, achieves a goal, or solves a problem.

21   Instead of being goal oriented, women are relationship oriented; they are more concerned with expressing their goodness, love, and caring. Two Martians go to lunch to discuss a project or business goal; they have a problem to solve. In addition, Martians view going to a restaurant as an efficient way to approach food: no shopping, no cooking, and no washing dishes. For Venusians, going to lunch is an opportunity to nurture a relationship, for both giving support to and receiving support from a friend. Women's restaurant talk can be very open and intimate, almost like the dialogue that occurs between therapist and patient.

22   On Venus, everyone studies psychology and has at least a master's degree in counseling. They are very involved in personal growth, spirituality, and everything that can nurture life, healing, and growth. Venus is covered with parks, organic gardens, shopping centers, and restaurants.

23   Venusians are very intuitive. They have developed this ability through centuries of anticipating the needs of others. They pride themselves in being considerate of the needs and feelings of others. A sign of great love is to offer help and assistance to another Venusian without being asked.

24   Because proving one's competence is not as important to a Venusian, offering help is not offensive, and needing help is not a sign of weakness. A man, however, may feel offended because when a woman offers advice, he doesn't feel she trusts his ability to do it himself.

25   A woman has no conception of this male sensitivity because for her it is another feather in her hat if someone offers to help her. It makes her feel loved

and cherished. But offering help to a man can make him feel incompetent, weak, and even unloved.

26   On Venus it is a sign of caring to give advice and suggestions. Venusians firmly believe that when something is working it can always work better. Their nature is to want to improve things. When they care about someone, they freely point out what can be improved and suggest how to do it. Offering advice and constructive criticism is an act of love.

27   Mars is very different. Martians are more solution oriented. If something is working, their motto is don't change it. Their instinct is to leave it alone if it is working. "Don't fix it unless it is broken" is a common expression.

28   When a woman tries to improve a man, he feels she is trying to fix him. He receives the message that he is broken. She doesn't realize her caring attempts to help him may humiliate him. She mistakenly thinks she is just helping him to grow.

Give up Giving Advice

29   Without this insight into the nature of men, it's very easy for a woman unknowingly and unintentionally to hurt and offend the man she loves most.

30   For example, Tom and Mary were going to a party. Tom was driving. After about twenty minutes and going around the same block a few times, it was clear to Mary that Tom was lost. She finally suggested that he call for help. Tom became very silent. They eventually arrived at the party, but the tension from that moment persisted the whole evening. Mary had no idea of why he was so upset.

31   From her side she was saying "I love and care about you, so I am offering you this help."

32   From his side, he was offended. What he heard was, "I don't trust you to get us there. You are incompetent!"

33   Without knowing about life on Mars, Mary could not appreciate how important it was for Tom to accomplish his goal without help. Offering advice was the ultimate insult. As we have explored, Martians never offer advice unless asked. A way of honoring another Martian is *always* to assume he can solve his problem unless he is looking for help.

34   Mary had no idea that when Tom became lost and started circling the same block, it was a very special opportunity to love and support him. At that time he was particularly vulnerable and needed some extra love. To honor him by not offering advice would have been a gift equivalent to his buying her a beautiful bouquet of flowers or writing her a love note.

35   After learning about Martians and Venusians, Mary learned how to support Tom at such difficult times. The next time he was lost, instead of offering "help" she restrained herself from offering any advice, took a deep relaxing breath, and appreciated in her heart what Tom was trying to do for her. Tom greatly appreciated her warm acceptance and trust.

36   Generally speaking, when a woman offers unsolicited advice or tries to "help" a man, she has no idea of how critical and unloving she may sound to

him. Even though her intent is loving, her suggestions do offend and hurt. His reaction may be strong, especially if he felt criticized as a child or he experienced his father being criticized by his mother.

37   For many men, it is very important to prove that they can get to their goal, even if it is a small thing like driving to a restaurant or party. Ironically he may be more sensitive about the little things than the big. His feelings are like this: "If I can't be trusted to do a small thing like get us to a party, how can she trust me to do the bigger things?" Like their Martian ancestors, men pride themselves on being experts, especially when it comes to fixing mechanical things, getting places, or solving problems. These are the times when he needs her loving acceptance the most and not her advice or criticism.

Learning to Listen

38   Likewise, if a man does not understand how a woman is different, he can make things worse when he is trying to help. Men need to remember that women talk about problems to get close and not necessarily to get solutions.

39   So many times a woman just wants to share her feelings about her day, and her husband, thinking he is helping, interrupts her by offering a steady flow of solutions to her problems. He has no idea why she isn't pleased.

40   For example, Mary comes home from an exhausting day. She wants and needs to share her feelings about the day.

41   She says, "There is so much to do; I don't have any time for myself."

42   Tom says, "You should quit that job. You don't have to work so hard. Find something you like to do."

43   Mary says, "But I like my job. They just expect me to change everything at a moment's notice."

44   Tom says, "Don't listen to them. Just do what you can do."

45   Mary says, "I *am!* I can't believe I completely forgot to call my aunt today."

46   Tom says, "Don't worry about it, she'll understand."

47   Mary says, "Do you know what she is going through? She needs me."

48   Tom says, "You worry too much, that's why you're so unhappy."

49   Mary angrily says, "I am not always unhappy. Can't you just listen to me?"

50   Tom says, "I *am* listening."

51   Mary says, "Why do I even bother?"

52   After this conversation, Mary was more frustrated than when she arrived home seeking intimacy and companionship. Tom was also frustrated and had no idea what went wrong. He wanted to help, but his problem-solving tactics didn't work.

53   Without knowing about life on Venus, Tom didn't understand how important it was just to listen without offering solutions. His solutions only made things worse. You see, Venusians never offer solutions when someone is talking. A way of honoring another Venusian is to listen patiently with empathy, seeking truly to understand the other's feelings.

54   Tom had no idea that just listening with empathy to Mary express her feelings would bring her tremendous relief and fulfillment. When Tom heard

about the Venusians and how much they needed to talk, he gradually learned how to listen.

55   When Mary now comes home tired and exhausted their conversations are quite different. They sound like this:

56   Mary says, "There is so much to do. I have no time for me."

57   Tom takes a deep breath, relaxes on the exhale, and says, "Humph, sounds like you had a hard day."

58   Mary says, "They expect me to change everything at a moment's notice. I don't know what to do."

59   Tom pauses and then says, "Hmmm."

60   Mary says, "I even forgot to call my aunt."

61   Tom says with a slightly wrinkled brow, "Oh, no."

62   Mary says, "She needs me so much right now. I feel bad."

63   Tom says, "You are such a loving person. Come here, let me give you a hug."

64   Tom gives Mary a hug and she relaxes in his arms with a big sigh of relief. She then says, "I love talking with you. You make me really happy. Thanks for listening. I feel much better."

65   Not only Mary but also Tom felt better. He was amazed at how much happier his wife was when he finally learned to listen. With this new awareness of their differences, Tom learned the wisdom of listening without offering solutions while Mary learned the wisdom of letting go and accepting without offering unsolicited advice or criticism.

66   To summarize the two most common mistakes we make in relationships:

1. A man tries to change a woman's feelings when she is upset by becoming Mr. Fix-It and offering solutions to her problems that invalidate her feelings.

2. A woman tries to change a man's behavior when he makes mistakes by becoming the home-improvement committee and offering unsolicited advice or criticism.

In Defense of Mr. Fix-It and the Home-Improvement Committee

67   In pointing out these two major mistakes I do not mean that everything is wrong with Mr. Fix-It or the home-improvement committee. These are very positive Martian and Venusian attributes. The mistakes are only in timing and approach.

68   A woman greatly appreciates Mr. Fix-It, as long as he doesn't come out when she is upset. Men need to remember that when women seem upset and talk about problems is not the time to offer solutions; instead she needs to be heard, and gradually she will feel better on her own. She does not need to be fixed.

69   A man greatly appreciates the home-improvement committee, as long as it is requested. Women need to remember that unsolicited advice or criticism—especially if he has made a mistake—make him feel unloved and controlled.

He needs her acceptance more than her advice, in order to learn from his mistakes. When a man feels that a woman is not trying to improve him, he is much more likely to ask for her feedback and advice.

70   Understanding these differences makes it easier to respect our partner's sensitivities and be more supportive. In addition we recognize that when our partner resists us it is probably because we have made a mistake in our timing or approach.

FOR ANALYSIS AND DISCUSSION

1. What reason(s) does Gray give as responsible for the breakdown in communication between men and women? Do you agree with his conclusions?
2. How is Gray's essay an example of using consensus to solve an issue?
3. Consider the evidence Gray supplies to support his argument. How effectively does it help him make his point? Explain.
4. Describe, in your own words, the "planets" Mars and Venus as outlined by Gray. How do the people look? What features does each planet have? Finally, which planet would you prefer to live on, and why?
5. If you did not know the gender of the author of this article, could you guess? Why or why not? Does gender matter to the success of this article and the points it is trying to make? Explain.
6. Do you think the suggestions posed by Gray would work in real-life situations? Can you recall a scenario in which his techniques could have been applied? Explain, drawing from personal observation and experience, why you believe his suggestions would or would not work.

I'm Sorry, I Won't Apologize
Deborah Tannen

Do women apologize too much? Are men afraid to say "I'm sorry"? In this essay Tannen comments that even when men know they are wrong, they can't seem to bring themselves to honestly apologize, and even when women aren't wrong, they feel obliged to admit fault. Is this difficulty a result of socialization?

Deborah Tannen is a professor of linguistics at Georgetown University. She is the author of the bestsellers *You Just Don't Understand: Women and Men in Conversation* and *Talking from 9 to 5: Women and Men in the Workplace*. The following article appeared in the *New York Times* in July 1996.

BEFORE YOU READ

What do the words "I'm sorry" really mean? What motivates you to apologize? Do you think these two words can help avoid conflicts?

AS YOU READ

Have you ever wanted to say you were sorry for something but didn't because you were afraid to admit you were wrong? Did any difficulties arise because you didn't apologize?

1   Almost daily, news reports include accounts of public figures or heads of companies being forced to say they're sorry. In a recent case, Marge Schott, managing partner of the Cincinnati Reds, at first did not want to apologize for her remark that Hitler "was good at the beginning but he just went too far." Under pressure, she finally said that she regretted her remarks "offended many people." Predictably—and especially given her history with such comments—many were not satisfied with this response and successfully lobbied for her resignation.

2   This particular use of "I'm sorry" has a familiar ring. The other day my husband said to me, "I'm sorry I hurt your feelings." I knew he was really trying. He has learned, through our years together, that apologies are important to me. But he was grinning, because he also knew that "I'm sorry I hurt your feelings" left open the possibility—indeed, strongly suggested—that he regretted not what he did but my emotional reaction. It sometimes seems that he thinks the earth will open up and swallow him if he admits fault.

3   It may appear that insisting someone admit fault is like wanting him to humiliate himself. But I don't see it that way, since it's no big deal for me to say I made a mistake and apologize. The problem is that it becomes a big deal when he won't.

4   This turns out to be similar to the Japanese view. Following a fender bender, according to a Times article, the Japanese typically get out of their cars and bow, each claiming responsibility. In contrast, Americans are instructed by their insurance companies to avoid admitting fault. When an American living in Japan did just that—even though he knew he was to blame—the Japanese driver "was so incensed by the American's failure to show contrition that he took the highly unusual step of suing him."

5   The Japanese driver and I are not the only ones who are offended when someone obviously at fault doesn't just fess up and apologize. A woman who lives in the country told me of a similar reaction. One day she gave her husband something to mail when he went into town. She stressed that it was essential the letter be mailed that day, and he assured her it would. But the next day, when they left the house together, she found her unmailed letter in the car. He said, "Oh, I forgot to mail your letter." She was furious—not because he had forgotten, but because he didn't apologize. "If I had done that," she said, "I would have fallen all over myself saying how sorry I was. And if he had said he was sorry, I would have been upset about the letter, but I would have forgiven him. After all, anyone can forget something. But I couldn't stop being angry, because he didn't seem to care that much that he'd let me down. I know he felt

bad about it, but he wouldn't say so. Is that just him," she asked, "or is it something about men?"

6   I think it's something about men—not all men, of course. There are plenty of men who apologize easily and often, and plenty of women who—like Marge Schott—avoid it at all costs. But there are many women, seemingly more than men, who easily say they're sorry and can't understand why it's such a big deal for others. Indeed, many women say "I'm sorry" as a conversational ritual—an automatic tip of the verbal hat to acknowledge that something regrettable happened. And others sometimes take this too literally.

7   One woman, for example, was talking on the phone when she got an interrupting call that she had to take immediately. When she rang the first caller back, she began by acknowledging that she had inconvenienced him and possibly been rude. "This is Sharon," she said. "I'm sorry." He responded, "You're sorry you're Sharon?" He may well have intended this retort as a good-natured tease, but it irritated her because it implied there was something odd about what she had said, while she felt it was run-of-the-mill, even required. I suspect it struck him as odd because he would avoid saying "sorry" if he could. One C.E.O. found that he could avoid it entirely: his deputy told me that part of his job was to make the rounds after the boss had lost his temper and apologize for him.

8   It's as if there's a tenet that real men don't say they're sorry. Take the closing scene in "Crimson Tide." Gene Hackman plays an unyieldingly authoritarian Navy captain in charge of a submarine carrying nuclear warheads. When he gets an unconfirmed order to launch, he is determined to comply, but is thwarted by his lieutenant commander, played by Denzel Washington, who defies his commanding officer, sparks a mutiny and averts nuclear war. The order to launch turns out to have been an error. The final scene is one of those exhilarating, dramatic moments when justice is served. Standing at attention before a panel that has investigated the mutiny without hearing his side, the lieutenant commander expects to be court-martialed. Instead he is promoted—on the recommendation of his captain. As the film ends, the captain turns to his deputy and says, "You were right and I was wrong. . . . " The audience gasps: this icon of authoritarian rigidity is admitting error. Then he grins mischievously and finishes the sentence, ". . . about the horses—the Lipizzaners. They *are* from Spain, not Portugal." Never mind that they're really from Austria; the two men exchange a look of intense rapport, and the audience heaves a sigh of satisfying relief.

9   Not me. I felt frustrated. Why couldn't he just say it? "I made a mistake. You were right. I was wrong about starting that nuclear war."

10   And saying you're sorry isn't enough in itself. You have to seem sorry: your face should look dejected, your voice should sound apologetic. Describing how bad you feel is also a plus. Furthermore, the depth of remorse should be commensurate with the significance of the offense. An offhand "Sorry about that" might be fine for an insignificant error like dropping a piece of paper, but if you drop a glass of red wine on your host's brand new white couch, a fleeting "Sorry about that" will not suffice.

11   The same people who resist displaying contrition may be eager to see it in others. Nowhere is this more evident than in court. Judges and juries are widely believed to give milder sentences to defendants who seem contrite. Prisons used to be called "penitentiaries" because inmates were expected not only to serve their time but also to repent. Nowadays many offenders seem to regard prison sentences as contractual: I served my time, I paid my debt. No apologies.

12   Apologies seem to come most easily from those who know their error was not intentional. The Japanese Government, for example, quickly apologized for the obviously accidental downing of an American plane during joint military exercises. But they have been much more reluctant to apologize for offenses committed during World War II, like forcing Korean, Chinese, and Filipina girls to serve as "comfort women" to Japanese soldiers.

13   Sometimes, though, people react negatively to an apology from a public figure. The First Lady discovered this last year when she met with a group of female columnists—off the record, she thought—and talked about how she had been portrayed in the press. "I regret very much that the efforts on health care were badly misunderstood, taken out of context and used politically against the Administration. I take responsibility for that, and I'm very sorry for that," she said.

14   The first part of this quote clearly indicates that the fault was not with her actions—"the efforts on health care"—but rather with the way they were received and distorted by others. But because she went on to say the big, bad "S" word, all hell broke loose. One newspaper article quoted a political scientist as saying, "To apologize for substantive things you've done raises the white flag. There's a school of thought in politics that you never say you're sorry. The best defense is a good offense." A Republican woman in the Florida state cabinet was quoted as saying: "I've seen women who overapologize, but I don't do that. I believe you negotiate through strength."

15   And there's the rub—apologizing is seen as a sign of weakness. This explains why more men than women might resist apologizing, since most boys learn early on that their peers will take advantage of them if they appear weak. Girls, in contrast, tend to reward other girls who talk in ways that show they don't think they're better than their peers.

16   Hillary Clinton's experience also explains why those who resist saying "I apologize" may find it more palatable to say "I'm sorry," because I'm sorry is not necessarily an apology. It can be—and in the First Lady's statement it clearly was—an expression of regret. It means "I'm sorry that happened." Her experience shows how easily this expression of regret can be mistaken for an apology.

17   Given this ambiguity, shouldn't we all strike the phrase "I'm sorry" from our vocabularies? Not necessarily. I think we'd do better as a society if more people said "I'm sorry" rather than fewer. Instead of all the railing against Hillary Clinton for apologizing when she expressed regret, how come no one thought that either Newt Gingrich or his mother should apologize when the latter quoted her son as uttering an irrefutable insult against the First Lady? The problem seems to be not a surfeit of apologies but a dearth of them. One

business manager told me he has discovered that apologies can be a powerful tool: subordinates so appreciate his admitting fault that they not only forgive his errors but also become ever more loyal employees.

18   History includes many examples of apologies that were not weak but highly potent. Following the calamitous Bay of Pigs invasion, John F. Kennedy demonstrated the power not only of "taking responsibility" but also of actually taking blame. For someone that high up to admit fault was shocking—and effective. People forgave the President, and his Administration, for the colossal error.

19   I think those brave enough to admit fault would find a similar power at home: it's amazing how an apology, if it seems sincere, can dissipate another's anger, calm the roiling waters. Erich Segal got it exactly wrong. Love doesn't mean never having to say you're sorry. Love means being able to say you're sorry—and, like J.F.K., being strong enough to admit you were at fault.

FOR ANALYSIS AND DISCUSSION

1. In your own experience, which gender tends to apologize more often? Does your answer match Tannen's observations? What do you think accounts for the difference, if any?

2. Explore the culture of "no fault" in American society. Can American resistance to apology affect foreign relations? What does Tannen imply could be the far-reaching problems for our society if we don't learn to apologize more often?

3. In 1998 President Bill Clinton publicly admitted his role in the Monica Lewinsky scandal. Many people said he waited too long to apologize. Others stated that his apology didn't go far enough, and that it was insincere. Can you apply Clinton's apology to some of the points Tannen makes in her article? Explain.

4. Do you think apologizing means you are of weak character or encourages others to take advantage of you? Support your response with examples from your own experience.

5. What do you think writer Erich Segal meant when he said, "Love means never having to say you're sorry"? Do you agree? Do you approve of Tannen's revision of the phrase?

In Each Other's Company
Herbert Gold

In the fall of 1998 ABC introduced the short-lived sitcom *The Secret Lives of Men*, about what guys really talk about with each other behind closed doors. A female critic commented that the show was doomed to a short run because the writers would quickly run out of material. Did the critic have a point? Are men's friendships based more on action rather than on open communication? In this essay Herbert Gold explores his own friendships and what holds them together.

Herbert Gold is the author of many novels including *Bohemia* and *She Took My Arm as if She Loved Me.* The following article first appeared in the *New York Times Magazine*'s "About Men" column on August 19, 1984.

BEFORE YOU READ

Are men's friendships with each other different from women's with other women? If so, in what ways?

AS YOU READ

Note the adjectives Gold uses to describe different situations. How does his choice of words complement his essay and influence its tone?

1   These days, in California at least, the men I know seem to drink less and spend more time in coffeehouses telling each other how young they look. The child-custody fathers can bring their kids and find others of their species. The kids drink hot chocolate and eat oatmeal-raisin cookies. The fathers say: "Well, I didn't think it would work out like this. But it's working out okay." I sit there and guess that we are all in this thing together. Yes, we are getting older. No, we're not alone. We have our friendships.

2   Twisting and diving, loping and attacking—plainly grunting and sweating—a young textile tycoon and I play racquetball. With devout concentration, we hunt and roam in a closed arena. Evenly matched, we have learned not to be too cast down when we lose, although we chortle with joy when we win.

3   My partner's metabolism requires risk and the expense of inventive agility. I am struggling to understand why this fast play with a hard rubber ball and a short-handled racquet seems to rank with love, children and art as one of the great pleasures of life even if I lose—in fact, a pleasure without grief, which I can't say for love, children or art.

4   The tycoon and I are not intimate friends, but the game has made a bond between us. The racquet is a weapon, like the gun or the bow and arrow. Hunters also know this comradeship that springs up between men who share the ancient rituals of exertion, risk, competition. There are women in the club, but my partner and I share a bit of disdain for those who treat it merely as a singles' meeting spa. For the moment, we are content in each other's company.

5   A few years ago I was interviewed for a book about "male bonding," which is a pompous way to say "friendship between men." The writer and I discussed how old friends are the dearest, perhaps because of self-love: they have witnessed one's life. And then we speculated that sometimes new friends are the

best, because one is free to proclaim any self-inventions one likes, and the new infatuation makes credence easy and agreeable. So those occasional new friendships also imply self-love. You are whatever you seem to be at the moment, whatever the friend sees in you.

6   We were enjoying a meeting of minds about the deep matter of friendship, and I thought we understood each other. Then he asked, "Do you kiss your friend?"

7   "What?"

8   "On the lips?" he asked.

9   I began to laugh, and he looked hurt. I was laughing because I had thought we understood each other and we didn't; he was hurt because he had in mind a model for friendship based on a credo of his former wife's women's group, and evidently I didn't have that in mind.

10   So that other mode of association between men began to assert itself: hostile banter. I accused him of not attending to friendship, not listening to me, but merely going by the current politically correct feminist notion. He replied that women have a lot to teach men about friendship. We parted in mutual suspicion.

11   Now when we meet, a few years later, we recall the incident with a sense of the shared past, irritation and disappointment—emotions!—which amount to a curious friendship. We went through something together. Talk may not be as true as racquetball, but discussion can sometimes arrive at understanding.

12   My concert promoter friend, Bill, seems to live with telephones stuck in his ears. To get his attention, one must participate in his current deals, his angers, his frantic triumphs. Mostly this is a lonely sharing. Yet we are friends. I had the idea of hiking with him in the California woods and suggested to this obsessed talker that we take a vow of silence as we walked to the Tassajara Zen Monastery. He agreed, but before we could go he telephoned to say, "Something has come up."

13   "Something always comes up," I said.

14   Shamed, he put our hike back on his schedule. Our vow of silence lasted ten minutes, until the first bug bite. Then came his steady stream of cursing— un-broken-in boots, insect nips, poison oak for sure. So we talked. Then we were silent. We climbed and panted and forded streams. We learned something it was unnecessary to discuss: a difficult sharing affirms friendship. Planned and formal as a cross-country hike might be, fitted into a schedule, it nevertheless serves to define and establish the facts of feeling.

15   The great model for friendship is the lifeboat. Classically, war has occasioned these moments of unscheduled danger and sacrifice. No matter what good company I find in a man in a bar or on a commuter train, there remains that secret need to know: Will he pull me into the lifeboat when I am in danger of swamping at sea? Playing games, competing, confiding, long sharing of work or opinions, even the borrowing of money, provide only a shadow of the test. Is this a friendship that would survive the ship's going down, one of us in

the lifeboat, the other in the sea and reaching out? Will he carry me back to safety under fire? These urban palships of mind don't put this ultimate ideal to the test.

16   In Just Desserts, a San Francisco coffeehouse, there is, nevertheless, a sense of shared risk among single men—or men only delaying their return to the marital bed. Yes, finally the ship is going down. But meanwhile there are talk, compassion, jokes along the way.

17   And raising a child demands almost as much concentration as climbing into that half-swamped lifeboat. Now that my sons are old enough, they try and try to beat me at racquetball. One day soon they will. I'll try to take it good-naturedly, garrulous afterward, hoping they will be philosophical with me, as gentle in the ancient round of things, as the hunter appreciating the prey slung over his shoulders for the trek homeward.

FOR ANALYSIS AND DISCUSSION

1. What obvious differences, if any, can you think of between friendships within genders? Are these differences based on socialization or biology?
2. Consider Gold's story about his concert promoter friend Bill. He wants to spend time with Bill, but he comes up with the proposal that will prevent them from talking. Why does he do this? What do you think of his request? Would two women make a similar pact?
3. What evidence does Gold use to support his views? Do you think his evidence is solid? How might you dispute some of his views regarding male friendships?
4. What upsets Gold about the writer's question about kissing on the lips (paragraph 6)? Why do you think he is surprised by the question?
5. Why is talk not as "true as racquetball" (paragraph 11)?

The Comfort of Friends
Anna Quindlen

According to Anna Quindlen, despite the many social changes women have experienced this century in the spheres of family, career, education, and economics, their friendships are timeless. The things that bonded women together in the past still hold true for the present. For women's friendships, the more things change, the more they stay the same.

Anna Quindlen's nationally syndicated column, "Public and Private," appeared in the *New York Times* and other newspapers around the country. Her essays have been published in the collections *Living Out Loud* (1990) and *Thinking Out Loud* (1993). The recipient of a Pulitzer Prize, Quindlen has written seven books, including *Black and Blue* (1998).

BEFORE YOU READ

Think about the things that cement friendship. How can you tell your true friends from your acquaintances?

AS YOU READ

Consider Quindlen's analogy that women's friendships are like a quilt. How can a quilt represent friendship? How does this comparison set the tone for her essay?

1   I collect quilts not only because of their beauty but because of their history, or what I imagine their history to be. There is one here, lying on the couch, a satin crazy quilt with spiky silken stitches holding its parts together. In one corner is a flower and the initials EK in purple embroidery floss, in another a whimsical owl done in green crewel work, in another the name Sara in silky red script. When I look at it, I see a circle of women, building it bit by bit, block by block, and as they do so, talking to one another, about their days and their disappointments, their husbands and their children, the food they cook and the houses they furnish and the dreams they dream. There is a kind of quilt called a friendship quilt, but I imagine all of mine, no matter what their pattern, are emblems of female friendship, that essential thread that has so often kept the pieces of my own life together and from time to time kept me from falling apart.

2   I can imagine my own circle in these pieces of bright fabric. The striped patches are the West Coast friend who called today to ask about my work and to tell me about hers, to compare notes on our adolescent sons and our burgeoning books. The bits of deep purple represent the Washington friend who danced at my wedding and held my babies, as I did hers, and with whom I can always pick up as though we talk every day instead of every other month. That patch of bright color is my closest friend in elementary school, and that one my matron of honor, and another is my doctor friend, who checks in from her car phone, static punctuating our plans. And all through is my closest friend, to whom I talk every day. "Where were you?" she says if she gets my machine, and "Where were you?" I say if I get hers, and when we find one another, we move on to gossip and news, soul-searching and support. I can tell her anything, and she me, but most of the time we don't have to. Most of the time we already know everything we need to know.

3   "Write about what you and your friends are talking about on the telephone," an editor told me when I was given the assignment of writing a personal column a decade ago. That wasn't all I wrote about over the years, but I probably could have gotten a column out of nearly every phone conversation. On the other hand, if my husband had to rely on his phone conversations with friends for column ideas—well, you finish the sentence. Whenever I've used that particular comparison, whether I was talking to female friends at lunch or speaking to a group of women in public, they've always burst out laughing be-

fore I got to the end of the subordinate clause. It was an immediate, visceral recognition of what seems to be a central fact of human attachment: that what men call friendship is often skin deep, while what we women make of it is something probing and intimate, an emotional undressing, something akin to an essay every time we sit down to lunch or pick up the phone. As Anaïs Nin wrote, "Each friend represents a world in us, a world possibly not born until they arrive, and it is only by this meeting that a new world is born."

4   Simple gender distinctions are probably too broad a brush for these more egalitarian days, in which more men have intimate friendships, more women have less time for them, and more men and women have relationships that transcend both sex and romance. But the truth is that most of the women I know, in the midst of hectic, confusing and sometimes disappointing lives, find one of their greatest sources of strength in a circle of female friends. It's why the movies "Waiting To Exhale" and "The First Wives Club" did so well at the box office—not because they were about women trashing men but because they were about women finding their greatest solace in the love and support of other women.

5   Harvard professor Carol Gilligan, an authority on the behavior of girls, says that the emotional connections that make intimate friendships possible begin early. "People used to look out on the playground and say that the boys were playing soccer and the girls were doing nothing," Gilligan says. "But the girls weren't doing nothing—they were talking. They were talking about the world to one another. And they become very expert about that in a way the boys did not."

6   Naturally, this is not always so. There is a kind of woman, usually called a "man's woman," who always seems to see other women as competition or furniture, whose orientation is always toward the XY chromosomes in the room. Maybe all of us become that kind of woman for a time; I can certainly remember years, stretching from puberty until I knew better, when I would have blown off any of my girlfriends for a guy. And sometimes it is only maturity that allows us to be vulnerable, to trust and confide in the way real friendship requires; we can all remember the cruel vicissitudes of elementary school friendship, which often seemed like a game of musical chairs—four bars of tinny music and then suddenly no place for you in the magic circle.

7   Perhaps that's why, in the diary she received for her 13th birthday, Anne Frank wrote, "On the surface I seem to have everything, except my one true friend. All I think about when I'm with my friends is having a good time. I can't bring myself to talk about anything but ordinary everyday things." Instead, she told her diary what many of us tell our friends—about her romantic yearnings, her self-doubts, the differences with those closest to her. It's a model of female confidences, the immortal diary. "Dearest Kitty," begins one entry, "Mother and I had a so-called 'discussion' today." But there's a certain poignancy in the fact that Anne's closest confidant is paper and cardboard, incapable of reciprocal conversation. Of course, the diary is in many ways a vehicle, a way for Anne to know herself, which seems to be the end result of our closest friendships after all.

8   There were times, particularly when I found myself in a new and difficult role, when I practically went trolling for "one true friend": in the largely male newsrooms where I learned to be a reporter, the playgrounds where I first took my toddlers while trying to figure out how to be a mother, the hallways at school. Book groups and play groups: we cleave together. I only really understand myself, what I'm really thinking and feeling, when I've talked it over with my circle of female friends. When days go by without that connection, I feel like a radio playing in an empty room.

9   By circle of friends I don't mean a group of women all connected to each other—but all connected to me. It's the same with most of us, I think. Last month I went to a birthday lunch for one of my close friends; ranged around the table was a group of women, many of whom I'd never met before but all of whom I'd heard about many times. It was a meal of discovery—"Oh, that's her, and her, and her, too." They were friends of my friend from different times of her life, as I have mine, from school and work and my children's schools and my husband's work. In our constantly shifting lives, our female friends may be the greatest constant and the touchstone not only of who we are but who we once were, the people who, taken together, know us whole, from girlfriend to wife and mother and even to widow. Children grow and go; even beloved men sometimes seem to be beaming their perceptions and responses in from a different planet. But our female friends are forever.

10   Professor Gilligan says she thinks the women's movement had something to do with this, that it was when we began to value what it meant to us to be female that we were most able to be open with one another about our real lives, not the Hallmark card version, to reveal the aches beneath the apron, the bruises beneath the business suit. "For a long time our conversations focused on relationships with men," says Gilligan of her own circle. "But soon we were talking about everything: our love lives, our work, our angst. Times of crisis but also just ordinary times and good times. It's true closeness, true intimacy. The conversation lays the groundwork for a deeper connection."

11   But I suspect that sort of intimacy predates the newest wave of feminism, going back far further than we think. I remember my mother and her cousin Gloria, my grandmother and her friend Marion. I remember as a child thinking, seeing those women in conversation with one another, that it was like seeing an iceberg, knowing that so much was going on, had gone on beneath the surface of that moment, the years, the tears, the confidences. I read the letters of Victorian women, who, unencumbered by the sexual subtext that would accompany it today, spoke the language of love to one another and even shared the same bed in what was most often a gesture of emotional, not physical, intimacy. The historian Carroll Smith-Rosenberg says that close female friendships were taken for granted a century ago as a source of succor superior to the joining of two disparate parts in marriage. "Women," she wrote, "who had little status or power in the larger world of male concerns, possessed status and power in the lives of other women."

12   The first time I met Hillary Rodham Clinton, during the 1992 presidential campaign, she showed me a bracelet that she had just been given for her birthday. Her nine closest women friends had bought it for her, and the initials of each were engraved on the links. Later, during the president's first term, I asked how she managed to survive the maelstrom and continual scrutiny of life in the White House, and she showed me the bracelet once again. It was her circle of friends that kept her equilibrium constant. They were the people, she has said, to whom she sent the manuscript of her book to figure out how it could be improved. "Hillary," one said, "this is like a beautiful garden with some weeds." In a world in which she could never tell whom to trust, or how much, she knew her circle of friends would be honest. She also knew they would be kind. And she knew that when the going got rough and tough, she could call one of those women and get, not an instant analysis of how she should remake her image, but first and foremost a sympathetic ear.

13   Joanna Bull, who runs Gilda's Club, the support organization for people living with cancer and their families, says many of her support groups try to teach the men who participate to learn intimacy and openness in a way that is intuitive for many women and that comes from, and feeds, female friendships. "When I was diagnosed with leukemia," Bull recalls, "it meant everything in the world to me that there came from across the country 10 women who just nurtured me for the weekend. Some of them I rarely saw in person and mainly kept in touch with me by telephone. Most of them had never met one another. But all of them wanted to come right away, and they came to my house in California and we sat in the hot tub and we ate and drank and laughed and cried and talked and talked and talked. I don't think 10 men would do that. Which is sad for them."

14   As the mother of two sons, I wonder if our world of increasing gender equality will change that. My daughter has already begun to repeat the patterns I remember so well from my own girlhood: the little knot of girls in one corner of the schoolyard, trading sentences as though conversation were a contact sport; the cycle of best friends and betrayal, complete with tumultuous tears and favorite possessions gladly given away; the constant analysis of classroom personal relations, as though between math and reading she had also studied group dynamics. And my boys? Well, when the eldest is on the phone for a long, long time these days, chances are that he's talking to a girl friend. Maybe the friendship circles of years to come will be more polyglot than those of my friends. Maybe he will never say to his wife, "What do you two find to talk about every day?" because he will have learned what there is to talk about from his own circle of female friends.

15   What do we find to talk about? Well, let's see: Kids. Hormones. Living room drapes. O.J. Simpson. Madonna. Movies. Books. Clothes. Politics. Men. "Melrose Place." Sadness. Happiness. Aging. Loss. Breast cancer. Cosmetic surgery. Black bean soup. Pot pie. Love. Piece by piece, we stitch the world together into something we can work with, something with which we can cover

ourselves against the cold nights. I don't know what in the world I would do without them, for advice, for comfort, for simply knowing that there is someone out there who knows me as I am and loves me despite and because of it. I've never been in therapy, and maybe they are the reason why. We talk, therefore I am.

FOR ANALYSIS AND DISCUSSION

1. How important is verbal communication to the success of women's relationships? Do the things that bond women's friendships differ from those that link men?
2. Quindlen's editor told her, "Write about what you and your friends are talking about on the telephone." Write about a recent conversation you had on the phone with a friend and analyze its content. What could a transcript of your conversation tell others about your relationship with that person?
3. What is a "man's woman"? Explain.
4. Analyze Quindlen's "circle of friends." Are all her friendships the same? How do you think she feels about her friends? What do her friends provide her with?
5. Quindlen recalls the behaviors of boys and girls on the playground when she was a child. She ends her article with an observation of boys and girls on the playground today. What conclusions does she draw from her comparison? Do you agree?
6. What does Quindlen's friend say is "sad" about men's friendships (paragraph 13)? Why does she feel this way? Drawing from your own experience, do you agree or disagree with Quindlen's friend?

WRITING ASSIGNMENTS: GENDER COMMUNICATIONS

1. Much of this chapter focuses on communication differences between men and women. Do you think language itself can be gendered? For example, are there certain words that seem "male" and others that seem "female"? Review the essays by Gold and Quindlen and evaluate the words they use to convey their ideas. Write an argument essay that considers the idea of gendered language.
2. In the 1986 movie *When Harry Met Sally*, Harry (Billy Crystal) says to Sally (Meg Ryan) that men and women cannot be friends. Much of the movie is then spent trying to prove his statement wrong. Watch the movie. Support or refute Harry's statement. Can men and women be friends? Why or why not? Is there a middle ground? Support your view with examples from both the movie and your own experience.
3. Have you ever found yourself at an impasse with a member of the opposite sex because your communication styles were different? For example, did you think the person you were arguing with "just didn't get it" solely because of his or her gender? Explain what accounted for the miscommunication and how you resolved it.

4. Gender boundaries crumble in cyberspace. No one knows your identity unless you decide to tell them. Read Brenda Danet's article "Text as Mask: Gender and Identity on the Internet" at <http://atar.mscc.huji.ac.il/~msdanet/mask.html>. Danet points out that because we leave our bodies "behind" when we enter cyberspace, language itself is the only determiner of gender. Write an argument essay in which you address some of the points Danet makes in her article. You might try to research her points by joining an IRC (Internet Relay Chat) and assuming another "gender."

chapter **10**

RACE AND ETHNICITY

The United States is a union predicated on shared moral values, political and economic self-interest, and a common language. Yet it also is a nation of immigrants—people of different races, ethnic identities, religions, and languages. It is a nation whose motto *e pluribus unum* ("one out of many") bespeaks a pride in its multicultural heritage. In this chapter we explore some of the issues that arise from the diversity of our cultural and ethnic backgrounds.

By definition, stereotypes are fallacious assumptions about individuals or groups based on characteristics such as race, ethnic origin, social class, religion, gender, or physical appearance. In "Identity and Stereotypes" we examine the complex ways in which ethnic and racial stereotypes limit our relationships with others and distort how we define ourselves. Mary Crow Dog writes compellingly about the difficulties of retaining her identity as a Native American woman "surrounded by an alien, more powerful culture." The powerful damage that stereotypes can inflict on society is further examined by Alex Kotlowitz in his essay "Colorblind," in which he relates his experience in the towns of St. Joseph and Benton Harbor, Michigan, two communities divided by racial ignorance. Judith Ortiz Cofer explains that her Puerto Rican background causes others to make assumptions about her that are often negative and demeaning. However, it is not only negative stereotypes that can harm us; even stereotypes that attribute positive qualities to certain groups can deny individuals credit for their achievements, as Ted Gup points out about Asian Americans in "Who Is a Whiz Kid?" Finally, Glenn C. Loury confronts the tenuous nature of his own racial identity in "Free at Last?"

The next three readings in "Unity and Diversity" consider the ways in which our multiculturalism can both unify and divide us. Although America has been a multiethnic and multiracial society since its founding, in the last few decades different groups of Americans have reasserted their ethnic and racial identities. These Americans have looked with pride to their heritage as a way to distinguish themselves from the mainstream. While this attention to "roots" has created greater tolerance for differences, it has also challenged our definition of ourselves as Americans. Are we no longer the "great melting pot" that Arthur Schlesinger, Jr., extols in his essay "The Return to the Melting Pot"? Have we traded the goal of assimilation for the lure of ethnic identification? Ronald Takaki and Arturo Madrid also present perspectives on the ways that diversity can strengthen and threaten our sense of national unity.

The question of whether tolerance for difference undermines our national identity is brought into sharp focus in our last group of readings on the controversial issue of bilingual education. Should our schools provide students who are non-native speakers of English with education in their native language until they gain greater fluency in English? Will this impede or hasten their progress toward full assimilation into American culture? With the recent passage of state initiatives limiting established bilingual education programs, a reconsideration of the benefits and disadvantages of bilingual education has been thrust into the national spotlight. Richard Rodriguez and Glenn Garvin assert that teaching children in a language other than English deprives them of the opportunity to acquire strong English language skills and delays their entry into mainstream U.S. culture. On the other hand, Lourdes Rovira and Raul Yzaguirre argue strongly that bilingual education will enrich children's sense of their cultural heritage and ultimately ensure their social and educational success.

Social scientists predict that in the twenty-first century the United States will be a country in which today's ethnic and racial minorities will become the majority. It is critical, then, that we engage in a dialogue about the political, economic, and social impacts of these changes on our national identity as we work to live together as one nation. Use the readings in this chapter as an opportunity to begin this process.

IDENTITY AND STEREOTYPES: CAN WE MOVE BEYOND LABELS?

A Woman from He-Dog
Mary Crow Dog

Mary Brave Bird, formerly named Mary Crow Dog, was born in 1953 on the Rosebud reservation in South Dakota. A member of the Sioux, Brave Bird grew up in economic poverty, under the shadow of social inequality. In the 1960s she joined the tribal pride movement during a time of great violence and political upheaval.

With Richard Erdoes, Brave Bird has written two books, *Lakota Woman* (1990) and *Ohitika Woman* (1993). *Lakota Woman,* which won the 1991 American Book Award, details the hardships of reservation life and the American Indian Movement of the 1960s and 1970s. *Ohitika Woman* picks up where *Lakota Woman* leaves off, further exploring Brave Bird's life as a Native American. The following essay is an excerpt from *Lakota Woman.*

BEFORE YOU READ

What cultural images are associated with the racial labels "Native American" or "American Indian"? What do public schools teach about this segment of the American population? For example, what did you learn in school regarding Native American history, culture, and literature?

AS YOU READ

Note Brave Bird's style and tone. How does her use of style and tone contribute to her essay's message and affect her relationship with her audience?

> A nation is not conquered until
> the hearts of its women
> are on the ground.
> Then it is done, no matter
> how brave its warriors
> nor how strong their weapons.
> —Cheyenne proverb

1   I am Mary Brave Bird. After I had my baby during the siege of Wounded Knee they gave me a special name—Ohitika Win, Brave Woman, and fastened an eagle plume in my hair, singing brave-heart songs for me. I am a woman of the Red Nation, a Sioux woman. That is not easy.

2   I had my first baby during a firefight, with the bullets crashing through one wall and coming out through the other. When my newborn son was only a day old and the marshals really opened up upon us, I wrapped him in a blanket and ran for it. We had to hit the dirt a couple of times, I shielding the baby with my body, praying, "It's all right if I die, but please let him live."

3   When I came out of Wounded Knee I was not even healed up, but they put me in jail at Pine Ridge and took my baby away. I could not nurse. My breasts swelled up and grew hard as rocks, hurting badly. In 1975 the feds put the muzzles of their M–16s against my head, threatening to blow me away. It's hard being an Indian woman.

4   My best friend was Annie Mae Aquash, a young, strong-hearted woman from the Micmac Tribe with beautiful children. It is not always wise for an Indian woman to come on too strong. Annie Mae was found dead in the snow at the bottom of a ravine on the Pine Ridge Reservation. The police said that she had died of exposure, but there was a .38-caliber slug in her head. The FBI cut off her hands and sent them to Washington for fingerprint identification, hands that had helped my baby come into the world.

5   My sister-in-law, Delphine, a good woman who had lived a hard life, was also found dead in the snow, the tears frozen on her face. A drunken man had

beaten her, breaking one of her arms and legs, leaving her helpless in a blizzard to die.

6   My sister Barbara went to the government hospital in Rosebud to have her baby and when she came out of anesthesia found that she had been sterilized against her will. The baby lived only for two hours, and she had wanted so much to have children. No, it isn't easy.

7   When I was a small girl at the St. Francis Boarding School, the Catholic sisters would take a buggy whip to us for what they called "disobedience." At age ten I could drink and hold a pint of whiskey. At age twelve the nuns beat me for "being too free with my body." All I had been doing was holding hands with a boy. At age fifteen I was raped. If you plan to be born, make sure you are born white and male.

8   It is not the big, dramatic things so much that get us down, but just being Indian, trying to hang on to our way of life, language, and values while being surrounded by an alien, more powerful culture. It is being an iyeska, a half-blood, being looked down upon by whites and full-bloods alike. It is being a backwoods girl living in a city, having to rip off stores in order to survive. Most of all it is being a woman. Among Plains tribes, some men think that all a woman is good for is to crawl into the sack with them and mind the children. It compensates for what white society has done to them. They were famous warriors and hunters once, but the buffalo is gone and there is not much rep in putting a can of spam or an occasional rabbit on the table.

9   As for being warriors, the only way some men can count coup nowadays is knocking out another skin's teeth during a barroom fight. In the old days a man made a name for himself by being generous and wise, but now he has nothing to be generous with, no jobs, no money; and as far as our traditional wisdom is concerned, our men are being told by the white missionaries, teachers, and employers that it is merely savage superstition they should get rid of if they want to make it in this world. Men are forced to live away from their children, so that the family can get ADC—Aid to Dependent Children. So some warriors come home drunk and beat up their old ladies in order to work off their frustration. I know where they are coming from. I feel sorry for them, but I feel even sorrier for their women.

10   To start from the beginning, I am a Sioux from the Rosebud Reservation in South Dakota. I belong to the "Burned Thigh," the Brule Tribe, the Sicangu in our language. Long ago, so the legend goes, a small band of Sioux was surrounded by enemies who set fire to their tipis and the grass around them. They fought their way out of the trap but got their legs burned and in this way acquired their name. The Brules are part of the Seven Sacred Campfires, the seven tribes of the Western Sioux known collectively as Lakota. The Eastern Sioux are called Dakota. The difference between them is their language. It is the same except that where we Lakota pronounce an *L*, the Dakota pronounce a *D*. They cannot pronounce an *L* at all. In our tribe we have this joke: "What is a flat tire in Dakota?" Answer: "A b*d*owout."

11   The Brule, like all Sioux, were a horse people, fierce riders and raiders, great warriors. Between 1870 and 1880 all Sioux were driven into reservations, fenced in and forced to give up everything that had given meaning to their life—their horses, their hunting, their arms, everything. But under the long snows of despair the little spark of our ancient beliefs and pride kept glowing, just barely sometimes, waiting for a warm wind to blow that spark into a flame again.

12   My family was settled on the reservation in a small place called He-Dog, after a famous chief. There are still some He-Dogs living. One, an old lady I knew, lived to be over a hundred years old. Nobody knew when she had been born. She herself had no idea, except that when she came into the world there was no census yet, and Indians had not yet been given Christian first names. Her name was just He-Dog, nothing else. She always told me, "You should have seen me eighty years ago when I was pretty." I have never forgotten her face—nothing but deep cracks and gullies, but beautiful in its own way. At any rate very impressive.

13   On the Indian side my family was related to the Brave Birds and Fool Bulls. Old Grandpa Fool Bull was the last man to make flutes and play them, the old-style flutes in the shape of a bird's head which had the elk power, the power to lure a young girl into a man's blanket. Fool Bull lived a whole long century, dying in 1976, whittling his flutes almost until his last day. He took me to my first peyote meeting while I was still a kid.

14   He still remembered the first Wounded Knee, the massacre. He was a young boy at that time, traveling with his father, a well-known medicine man. They had gone to a place near Wounded Knee to take part in a Ghost Dance. They had on their painted ghost shirts which were supposed to make them bulletproof. When they got near Pine Ridge they were stopped by white soldiers, some of them from the Seventh Cavalry, George Custer's old regiment, who were hoping to kill themselves some Indians. The Fool Bull band had to give up their few old muzzle-loaders, bows, arrows, and even knives. They had to put their tipis in a tight circle, all bunched up, with the wagons on the outside and the soldiers surrounding their camp, watching them closely. It was cold, so cold that the trees were crackling with a loud noise as the frost was splitting their trunks. The people made a fire the following morning to warm themselves and make some coffee and then they noticed a sound beyond the crackling of the trees: rifle fire, salvos making a noise like the ripping apart of a giant blanket; the boom of cannon and the rattling of quick-firing Hotchkiss guns. Fool Bull remembered the grown-ups bursting into tears, the women keening: "They are killing our people, they are butchering them!" It was only two miles or so from where Grandfather Fool Bull stood that almost three hundred Sioux men, women, and children were slaughtered. Later grandpa saw the bodies of the slain, all frozen in ghostly attitudes, thrown into a ditch like dogs. And he saw a tiny baby sucking at his dead mother's breast.

15   I wish I could tell about the big deeds of some ancestors of mine who fought at the Little Big Horn, or the Rosebud, counting coup during the Grat-

tan or Fetterman battle, but little is known of my family's history before 1880. I hope some of my great-grandfathers counted coup on Custer's men, I like to imagine it, but I just do not know. Our Rosebud people did not play a big part in the battles against generals Crook or Custer. This was due to the policy of Spotted Tail, the all-powerful chief at the time. Spotted Tail had earned his eagle feathers as a warrior, but had been taken East as a prisoner and put in jail. Coming back years later, he said that he had seen the cities of the whites and that a single one of them contained more people than could be found in all the Plains tribes put together, and that every one of the wasičuns' factories could turn out more rifles and bullets in one day than were owned by all the Indians in the country. It was useless, he said to try to resist the wasičuns. During the critical year of 1876 he had his Indian police keep most of the young men on the reservation, preventing them from joining Sitting Bull, Gall, and Crazy Horse. Some of the young bucks, a few Brave Birds among them, managed to sneak out trying to get to Montana, but nothing much is known. After having been forced into reservations, it was not thought wise to recall such things. It might mean no rations, or worse. For the same reason many in my family turned Christian, letting themselves be "whitemanized." It took many years to reverse this process.

16   My sister Barbara, who is four years older than me, says she remembers the day when I was born. It was late at night and raining hard amid thunder and lightning. We had no electricity then, just the old-style kerosene lamps with the big reflectors. No bathroom, no tap water, no car. Only a few white teachers had cars. There was one phone in He-Dog, at the trading post. This was not so very long ago, come to think of it. Like most Sioux at that time my mother was supposed to give birth at home, I think, but something went wrong, I was pointing the wrong way, feet first or stuck sideways. My mother was in great pain, laboring for hours, until finally somebody ran to the trading post and called the ambulance. They took her—us—to Rosebud, but the hospital there was not yet equipped to handle a complicated birth, I don't think they had surgery then, so they had to drive mother all the way to Pine Ridge, some ninety miles distant, because there the tribal hospital was bigger. So it happened that I was born among Crazy Horse's people. After my sister Sandra was born the doctors there performed a hysterectomy on my mother, in fact sterilizing her without her permission, which was common at that time, and up to just a few years ago, so that it is hardly worth mentioning. In the opinion of some people, the fewer Indians there are, the better. As Colonel Chivington said to his soldiers: "Kill 'em all, big and small, nits make lice!"

17   I don't know whether I am a louse under the white man's skin. I hope I am. At any rate I survived the long hours of my mother's labor, the stormy drive to Pine Ridge, and the neglect of the doctors. I am an iyeska, a breed, that's what the white kids used to call me. When I grew bigger they stopped calling me that, because it would get them a bloody nose. I am a small woman, not much over five feet tall, but I can hold my own in a fight, and in a free-for-all with honkies I can become rather ornery and do real damage. I have white blood in

me. Often I have wished to be able to purge it out of me. As a young girl I used to look at myself in the mirror, trying to find a clue as to who and what I was. My face is very Indian, and so are my eyes and my hair, but my skin is very light. Always I wanted for the summer, for the prairie sun, the badlands sun, to tan me and make me into a real skin.

18   The Crow Dogs, the members of my husband's family, have no such problems of identity. They don't need the sun to tan them, they are full-bloods—the Sioux of the Sioux. Some Crow Dog men have faces which make the portrait of the buffalo Indian nickel look like a washed-out white man. They have no shortage of legends. Every Crow Dog seems to be a legend in himself, including the women. They became outcasts in their stronghold at Grass Mountain rather than being whitemanized. They could not be tamed, made to wear a necktie or go to a Christian church. All during the long years when practicing Indian beliefs was forbidden and could be punished with jail, they went right on having their ceremonies, their sweat baths and sacred dances. Whenever a Crow Dog got together with some relatives, such as those equally untamed, unregenerated Iron Shells, Good Lances, Two Strikes, Picket Pins, or Hollow Horn Bears, then you could hear the sound of the can gleska, the drum, telling all the world that a Sioux ceremony was in the making. It took courage and suffering to keep the flame alive, the little spark under the snow.

19   The first Crow Dog was a well-known chief. On his shield was the design of two circles and two arrowheads for wounds received in battle—two white man's bullets and two Pawnee arrow points. When this first Crow Dog was lying wounded in the snow, a coyote came to warm him and a crow flew ahead of him to show him the way home. His name should be Crow Coyote, but the white interpreter misunderstood it and so they became Crow Dogs. This Crow Dog of old became famous for killing a rival chief, the result of a feud over tribal politics, then driving voluntarily over a hundred miles to get himself hanged at Deadwood, his wife sitting beside him in his buggy; famous also for finding on his arrival that the Supreme Court had ordered him to be freed because the federal government had no jurisdiction over Indian reservations and also because it was no crime for one Indian to kill another. Later, Crow Dog became a leader of the Ghost Dancers, holding out for months in the frozen caves and ravines of the Badlands. So, if my own family lacks history, that of my husband more than makes up for it.

20   Our land itself is a legend, especially the area around Grass Mountain where I am living now. The fight for our land is at the core of our existence, as it has been for the last two hundred years. Once the land is gone, then we are gone too. The Sioux used to keep winter counts, picture writings on buffalo skin, which told our people's story from year to year. Well, the whole country is one vast winter count. You can't walk a mile without coming to some family's sacred vision hill, to an ancient Sun Dance circle, an old battleground, a place where something worth remembering happened. Mostly a death, a proud death or a drunken death. We are a great people for dying. "It's a good day to die!" that's our old battle cry. But the land with its tar paper shacks and out-

door privies, not one of them straight, but all leaning this way or that way, is also a land to live on, a land for good times and telling jokes and talking of great deeds done in the past. But you can't live forever off the deeds of Sitting Bull or Crazy Horse. You can't wear their eagle feathers, freeload off their legends. You have to make your own legends now. It isn't easy.

FOR ANALYSIS AND DISCUSSION

1. According to Brave Bird's account, what is it like to be an American Indian in the United States today? What difficulties seem to be particular to both her race and her gender?

2. Evaluate Brave Bird's statement in paragraph 7 that "if you plan to be born, make sure you are born white and male." What privileges does she associate with white males? What inequalities does she associate with Native Americans? Do you agree? Are white males indeed the privileged "race"?

3. Why does Brave Bird hope she is a "louse under the white man's skin" (paragraph 17)? Does this statement promote her argument or hinder it? Explain.

4. What do you think are Brave Bird's goals in writing this essay? What is she trying to achieve? Support your response with evidence from the essay.

5. Analyze the effect of Brave Bird's use of repeated phrases. For example, in what ways does she apply the term "it isn't easy"? To what situations does she attach this phrase?

6. In paragraph 8 Brave Bird states that the most difficult challenge facing Native Americans is hanging "on to [their] way of life, language, and values while being surrounded by an alien, more powerful culture." What is the definition of the word "alien"? Who represents this more powerful culture?

7. How does Brave Bird's recounting of her tribe's history support the points she is making? Specifically, how does her recounting of her struggles at the second Wounded Knee influence the audience? For further information about Wounded Knee II (1973) try the following Web sites: <http://www.dickshovel.com/lsa10.html> and <http://ctmmag.com/magazine/july98/julyctm3.html>.

Colorblind
Alex Kotlowitz

Do racial differences hinder effective communication? In this essay, Alex Kotlowitz states that "our personal and collective experiences are consistently informed by race." How can whites and blacks reach a consensus, asks Kotlowitz, when they can't even engage in a meaningful dialogue? The constant influence of race over our perceptions of both others and ourselves prevents us from seeing alternative perspectives.

Alex Kotlowitz is a reporter for the *Wall Street Journal*. His most recent book, *The Other Side of the River: A Story of Two Towns, a Death and America's Dilemma*, is a detailed account of the racially charged atmosphere surrounding a young boy's death in southwestern Michigan. The following essay first appeared in the January 11, 1998, issue of the *New York Times Magazine*.

BEFORE YOU READ

Have you ever experienced a communication barrier caused by racial differences? If so, how did you deal with the situation? Were you able to find an effective way to communicate and relate after all?

AS YOU READ

Notice Kotlowitz's use of quoted material to support his perspective. How effective is this material in conveying his message?

1   One Christmas day seven years ago, I'd gone over to the Henry Horner Homes in Chicago to visit with Lafeyette and Pharoah, the subjects of my book "There Are No Children Here." I had brought presents for the boys, as well as a gift for their friend Rickey, who lived on the other side of the housing complex, an area controlled by a rival gang. Lafeyette and Pharoah insisted on walking over with me. It was eerily quiet, since most everyone was inside, and so, bundled from the cold, we strolled toward the other end in silence. As we neared Damen Avenue, a kind of demilitarized zone, a uniformed police officer, a white woman, approached us. She looked first at the two boys, neither of whom reached my shoulder, and then directly at me. "Are you O.K.?" she asked.

2   About a year later, I was with Pharoah on the city's North Side, shopping for high-tops. We were walking down the busy street, my hand on Pharoah's shoulder, when a middle-aged black man approached. He looked at me, and then at Pharoah. "Son," he asked, "are you O.K.?"

3   Both this white police officer and middle-aged black man seemed certain of what they witnessed. The white woman saw a white man possibly in trouble; the black man saw a black boy possibly in trouble. It's all about perspective— which has everything to do with our personal and collective experiences, which are consistently informed by race. From those experiences, from our histories, we build myths, legends that both guide us and constrain us, legends that include both fact and fiction. This is not to say the truth doesn't matter. It does, in a big way. It's just that getting there may not be easy, in part because everyone is so quick to choose sides, to refute the other's myths and to pass on their own.

4   We'd do well to keep this in mind as we enter the yearlong dialogue on race convened by President Clinton. Yes, conversation is critical, but not without self-reflection, both individually and communally. While myths help us make sense of the incomprehensible, they can also confine us, confuse us and leave us prey to historical laziness. Moreover, truth is not always easily discernible—and even when it is, the prism, depending on which side of the river you reside on, may create a wholly different illusion. Many whites were quick to believe Susan Smith, the South Carolina mother who claimed that a black man had killed her children. And with the reawakening of the Tawana Brawley case, we learn that, although a grand jury has determined otherwise, many blacks

still believe she was brutally raped by a group of white men. We—blacks and whites—need to examine and question our own perspectives. Only then can we grasp each other's myths and grapple with the truths.

5   In 1992, I came across the story of a 16-year-old black boy, Eric McGinnis, whose body had been found a year earlier floating in the St. Joseph River in southwestern Michigan. The river flows between Benton Harbor and St. Joseph, two small towns whose only connections are two bridges and a powerful undertow of contrasts.

6   St. Joseph is a town of 9,000, and, with its quaint downtown and brick-paved streets, resembles a New England tourist haunt. But for those in Benton Harbor, St. Joseph's most defining characteristic is its racial makeup: it is 95 percent white. Benton Harbor, a town of 12,000 on the other side of the river, is 92 percent black and dirt poor. For years, the municipality so hurt for money that it could not afford to raze abandoned buildings.

7   Eric, a high-school sophomore whose passion was dancing, was last seen at the Club, a teen-age nightspot in St. Joseph, where weeks earlier he had met and started dating a white girl. The night Eric disappeared, a white man said he caught the boy trying to break into his car and chased him—away from the river, past an off-duty white deputy sheriff. That was the last known moment he was seen alive, and it was then that the myths began.

8   I became obsessed with Eric's death, and so for five years moved in and out of these two communities, searching for answers to both Eric's disappearance and to matters of race. People would often ask which side of the river I was staying on, wanting to gauge my allegiance. And they would often ask about the secrets of those across the way or, looking for affirmation, repeat myths passed on from one generation to the next.

9   Once, during an unusually bitter effort by white school-board members to fire Benton Harbor's black superintendent, one black woman asked me: "How do you know how to do this? Do you take lessons? How do you all stick together the way you do?" Of course, we don't. Neither community is as unified or monolithic as the other believes. Indeed, contrary to the impression of those in St. Joseph, the black community itself was deeply divided in its support for the superintendent, who was eventually fired.

10   On occasion, whites in St. Joseph would regale me with tales of families migrating to Benton Harbor from nearby states for the high welfare benefits. It is, they would tell me, the reason for the town's economic decline. While some single mothers indeed moved to Benton Harbor and other Michigan cities in the early 80's to receive public assistance, the truth is that in the 30's and 40's, factories recruited blacks from the South, and when those factories shut down, unemployment, particularly among blacks, skyrocketed.

11   But the question most often asked was: "Why us? Why write about St. Joseph and Benton Harbor?" I would tell them that while the contrasts between the towns seem unusually stark, they are, I believe, typical of how most of us live: physically and spiritually isolated from one another.

12   It's not that I didn't find individuals who crossed the river to spend time with their neighbors. One St. Joseph woman, Amy Johnson, devotes her waking hours to a Benton Harbor community center. And Eric McGinnis himself was among a handful of black teen-agers who spent weekend nights at the Club in St. Joseph. Nor is it that I didn't find racial animosity. One St. Joseph resident informed me that Eric got what he deserved: "That nigger came on the wrong side of the bridge," he said. And Benton Harbor's former schools superintendent, Sherwin Allen, made no effort to hide his contempt for the white power structure.

13   What I found in the main, though, were people who would like to do right but don't know where to begin. As was said of the South's politicians during Jim Crow, race diminishes us. It incites us to act as we wouldn't in other arenas: clumsily, cowardly and sometimes cruelly. We circle the wagons, watching out for our own.

14   That's what happened in the response to Eric's death. Most everyone in St. Joseph came to believe that Eric, knowing the police were looking for him, tried to swim the river to get home and drowned. Most everyone in Benton Harbor, with equal certitude, believes that Eric was killed—most likely by whites, most likely because he dated a white girl. I was struck by the disparity in perspective, the competing realities, but I was equally taken aback by the distance between the two towns—which, of course, accounts for the myths. Jim Reeves, the police lieutenant who headed the investigation into Eric's death, once confided that this teen-ager he'd never met had more impact on him than any other black person.

15   I'm often asked by whites, with some wonderment, how it is that I'm able to spend so much time in black communities without feeling misunderstood or unwelcomed or threatened. I find it much easier to talk to blacks about race than with fellow whites. While blacks often brave slights silently for fear that if they complain they won't be believed, when asked, they welcome the chance to relate their experiences. Among whites, there's a reluctance—or a lack of opportunity—to engage. Race for them poses no urgency; it does not impose on their daily routines. I once asked Ben Butzbaugh, a St. Joseph commissioner, how he felt the two towns got along. "I think we're pretty fair in this community," he said. "I don't know that I can say I know of any out-and-out racial-type things that occur. I just think people like their own better than others. I think that's pretty universal. Don't you? . . . We're not a bunch of racists. We're not anything America isn't." Butzbaugh proudly pointed to his friendship with Renée Williams, Benton Harbor's new school superintendent. "Renée was in our home three, four, five days a week," he noted. "Nice gal. Put herself through school. We'd talk all the time." Williams used to clean for Butzbaugh's family.

16   As I learned during the years in and out of these towns, the room for day-to-day dialogue doesn't present itself. We become buried in our myths, certain of our truths—and refuse to acknowledge what the historian Allan Nevins calls "the grains of stony reality" embedded in most legends. A quarter-century ago,

race was part of everyday public discourse; today it haunts us quietly, though on occasion—the Rodney King beating or the Simpson trial or Eric McGinnis's death—it erupts with jarring urgency. At these moments of crisis, during these squalls, we flail about, trying to find moral ballast. By then it is usually too late. The lines are drawn. Accusations are hurled across the river like cannon fire. And the cease-fires, when they occur, are just that, cease-fires, temporary and fragile. Even the best of people have already chosen sides.

FOR ANALYSIS AND DISCUSSION

1. Explore Kotlowitz's assertion that from our backgrounds we create racial concepts based on both fact and fiction. What kinds of "myths and legends" are created by race?
2. How do myths confine us? How do fabricated cultural perceptions of race prevent effective communication?
3. How does the story of Eric McGinnis support the points Kotlowitz is trying to make with his argument?
4. Explain what Kotlowitz means when he says that for whites race "poses no urgency" (paragraph 15). Do you agree with this view? What urgency does race pose for nonwhites?
5. What generalizations regarding whites and blacks does Kotlowitz make? How might these generalizations seem ironic, considering the content of the article?
6. How are whites portrayed in this article? How are blacks presented? Are the presentations equitable? Explain.

The Myth of the Latina Woman: I Just Met a Girl Named María
Judith Ortiz Cofer

Have you ever thought you could guess someone's ethnic background based on what he or she was wearing? Racial stereotypes are often based on misperceptions and a lack of understanding of other races. In this essay Judith Ortiz Cofer explores how racial stereotypes are created by cultural misunderstandings. She also describes how once stereotypes are established, they can be insulting and painful.

Born in Puerto Rico, Judith Ortiz Cofer moved to the United States when she was a young girl. Educated at both American and British universities, she is the author of several books, including the novel *The Line of the Sun* (1989), which was nominated for a Pulitzer Prize. Ortiz Cofer teaches literature and writing at the University of Georgia at Athens. The following essay is selected from her collection *The Latin Deli* (1993).

BEFORE YOU READ

Consider the ways the media perpetuate cultural stereotypes. Think about how various media, such as television and cinema, promote cultural cliches.

AS YOU READ

Ortiz Cofer comments that certain adjectives are often used to describe individuals from her ethnic background. What is the basis for these adjectives? What other words can you cite that are used to describe the personalities of women and men from certain ethnic backgrounds?

1   On a bus trip to London from Oxford University where I was earning some graduate credits one summer, a young man, obviously fresh from a pub, spotted me and as if struck by inspiration went down on his knees in the aisle. With both hands over his heart he broke into an Irish tenor's rendition of "María" from *West Side Story*. My politely amused fellow passengers gave his lovely voice the round of gentle applause it deserved. Though I was not quite as amused, I managed my version of an English smile: no show of teeth, no extreme contortions of the facial muscles—I was at this time of my life practicing reserve and cool. Oh, that British control, how I coveted it. But María had followed me to London, reminding me of a prime fact of my life: you can leave the Island, master the English language, and travel as far as you can, but if you are a Latina, especially one like me who so obviously belongs to Rita Moreno's gene pool, the Island travels with you.

2   This is sometimes a very good thing—it may win you that extra minute of someone's attention. But with some people, the same things can make *you* an island—not so much a tropical paradise as an Alcatraz, a place nobody wants to visit. As a Puerto Rican girl growing up in the United States and wanting like most children to "belong," I resented the stereotype that my Hispanic appearance called forth from many people I met.

3   Our family lived in a large urban center in New Jersey during the sixties, where life was designed as a microcosm of my parents' casas on the island. We spoke in Spanish, we ate Puerto Rican food bought at the bodega, and we practiced strict Catholicism complete with Saturday confession and Sunday mass at a church where our parents were accommodated into a one-hour Spanish mass slot, performed by a Chinese priest trained as a missionary for Latin America.

4   As a girl I was kept under strict surveillance, since virtue and modesty were, by cultural equation, the same as family honor. As a teenager I was instructed on how to behave as a proper señorita. But it was a conflicting message girls got, since the Puerto Rican mothers also encouraged their daughters to look and act like women and to dress in clothes our Anglo friends and their mothers found too "mature" for our age. It was, and is, cultural, yet I often felt humiliated when I appeared at an American friend's party wearing a dress more suitable to a semiformal than to a playroom birthday celebration. At Puerto Rican festivities, neither the music nor the colors we wore could be too loud. I still experience a vague sense of letdown when I'm invited to a "party" and it turns out to be a marathon conversation in hushed tones rather than a fiesta with salsa, laughter, and dancing—the kind of celebration I remember from my childhood.

5   I remember Career Day in our high school, when teachers told us to come dressed as if for a job interview. It quickly became obvious that to the barrio girls, "dressing up" sometimes meant wearing ornate jewelry and clothing that would be more appropriate (by mainstream standards) for the company Christmas party than as daily office attire. That morning I had agonized in front of my closet, trying to figure out what a "career girl" would wear because, essentially, except for Marlo Thomas on TV, I had no models on which to base my decision. I knew how to dress for school: At the Catholic school I attended we all wore uniforms; I knew how to dress for Sunday mass, and I knew what dresses to wear for parties at my relatives' homes. Though I do not recall the precise details of my Career Day outfit, it must have been a composite of the above choices. But I remember a comment my friend (an Italian-American) made in later years that coalesced my impressions of that day. She said that at the business school she was attending the Puerto Rican girls always stood out for wearing "everything at once." She meant, of course, too much jewelry, too many accessories. On that day at school, we were simply made the negative models by the nuns who were themselves not credible fashion experts to any of us. But it was painfully obvious to me that to the others, in their tailored skirts and silk blouses, we must have seemed "hopeless" and "vulgar." Though I now know that most adolescents feel out of step much of the time, I also know that for the Puerto Rican girls of my generation that sense was intensified. The way our teachers and classmates looked at us that day in school was just a taste of the cultural clash that awaited us in the real world, where prospective employers and men on the street would often misinterpret our tight skirts and jingling bracelets as a come-on.

6   Mixed cultural signals have perpetuated certain stereotypes—for example, that of the Hispanic woman as the "Hot Tamale" or sexual firebrand. It is a one-dimensional view that the media have found easy to promote. In their special vocabulary, advertisers have designated "sizzling" and "smoldering" as the adjectives of choice for describing not only the foods but also the women of Latin America. From conversations in my house I recall hearing about the harassment that Puerto Rican women endured in factories where the "boss men" talked to them as if sexual innuendo was all they understood and, worse, often gave them the choice of submitting to advances or being fired.

7   It is custom, however, not chromosomes, that leads us to choose scarlet over pale pink. As young girls, we were influenced in our decisions about clothes and colors by the women—older sisters and mothers who had grown up on a tropical island where the natural environment was a riot of primary colors, where showing your skin was one way to keep cool as well as to look sexy. Most important of all, on the Island, women perhaps felt freer to dress and move more provocatively, since, in most cases, they were protected by the traditions, mores, and laws of a Spanish/Catholic system of morality and machismo whose main rule was: *You may look at my sister, but if you touch her I will kill you.* The extended family and church structure could provide a young woman with a circle of safety in her small pueblo on the island; if a man "wronged" a girl, everyone would close in to save her family honor.

8   This is what I have gleaned from my discussions as an adult with older Puerto Rican women. They have told me about dressing in their best party clothes on Saturday nights and going to the town's plaza to promenade with their girlfriends in front of the boys they liked. The males were thus given an opportunity to admire the women and to express their admiration in the form of *piropos:* erotically charged street poems they composed on the spot. I have been subjected to a few piropos while visiting the Island, and they can be outrageous, although custom dictates that they must never cross into obscenity. This ritual, as I understand it, also entails a show of studied indifference on the woman's part; if she is "decent," she must not acknowledge the man's impassioned words. So I do understand how things can be lost in translation. When a Puerto Rican girl dressed in her idea of what is attractive meets a man from the mainstream culture who has been trained to react to certain types of clothing as a sexual signal, a clash is likely to take place. The line I first heard based on this aspect of the myth happened when the boy who took me to my first formal dance leaned over to plant a sloppy overeager kiss painfully on my mouth, and when I didn't respond with sufficient passion said in a resentful tone: "I thought you Latin girls were supposed to mature early"—my first instance of being thought of as a fruit or vegetable—I was supposed to *ripen,* not just grow into womanhood like other girls.

9   It is surprising to some of my professional friends that some people, including those who should know better, still put others "in their place." Though rarer, these incidents are still commonplace in my life. It happened to me most recently during a stay at a very classy metropolitan hotel favored by young professional couples for their weddings. Late one evening after the theater, as I walked toward my room with my new colleague (a woman with whom I was coordinating an arts program), a middle-aged man in a tuxedo, a young girl in satin and lace on his arm, stepped directly into our path. With his champagne glass extended toward me, he exclaimed, "Evita!"

10   Our way blocked, my companion and I listened as the man half-recited, half-bellowed "Don't Cry for Me, Argentina." When he finished, the young girl said: "How about a round of applause for my daddy?" We complied, hoping this would bring the silly spectacle to a close. I was becoming aware that our little group was attracting the attention of the other guests. "Daddy" must have perceived this too, and he once more barred the way as we tried to walk past him. He began to shout-sing a ditty to the tune of "La Bamba"—except the lyrics were about a girl named María whose exploits all rhymed with her name and gonorrhea. The girl kept saying "Oh, Daddy" and looking at me with pleading eyes. She wanted me to laugh along with the others. My companion and I stood silently waiting for the man to end his offensive song. When he finished, I looked not at him but at his daughter. I advised her calmly never to ask her father what he had done in the army. Then I walked between them and to my room. My friend complimented me on my cool handling of the situation. I confessed to her that I really had wanted to push the jerk into the swimming pool. I knew that this same man—probably a corporate executive, well educated, even worldly by most standards—would not have been likely to regale a

white woman with a dirty song in public. He would perhaps have checked his impulse by assuming that she could be somebody's wife or mother, or at least *somebody* who might take offense. But to him, I was just an Evita or a María: merely a character in his cartoon-populated universe.

11   Because of my education and my proficiency with the English language, I have acquired many mechanisms for dealing with the anger I experience. This was not true for my parents, nor is it true for the many Latin women working at menial jobs who must put up with stereotypes about our ethnic group such as: "They make good domestics." This is another facet of the myth of the Latin woman in the United States. Its origin is simple to deduce. Work as domestics, waitressing, and factory jobs are all that's available to women with little English and few skills. The myth of the Hispanic menial has been sustained by the same media phenomenon that made "Mammy" from *Gone with the Wind* America's idea of the black woman for generations; María, the housemaid or counter girl, is now indelibly etched into the national psyche. The big and the little screens have presented us with the picture of the funny Hispanic maid, mispronouncing words and cooking up a spicy storm in a shiny California kitchen.

12   This media-engendered image of the Latina in the United States has been documented by feminist Hispanic scholars, who claim that such portrayals are partially responsible for the denial of opportunities for upward mobility among Latinas in the professions. I have a Chicana friend working on a Ph.D. in philosophy at a major university. She says her doctor still shakes his head in puzzled amazement at all the "big words" she uses. Since I do not wear my diplomas around my neck for all to see, I too have on occasion been sent to that "kitchen," where some think I obviously belong.

13   One such incident that has stayed with me, though I recognize it as a minor offense, happened on the day of my first public poetry reading. It took place in Miami in a boat-restaurant where we were having lunch before the event. I was nervous and excited as I walked in with my notebook in my hand. An older woman motioned me to her table. Thinking (foolish me) that she wanted me to autograph a copy of my brand new slender volume of verse, I went over. She ordered a cup of coffee from me, assuming that I was the waitress. Easy enough to mistake my poems for menus, I suppose. I know that it wasn't an intentional act of cruelty, yet of all the good things that happened that day, I remember that scene most clearly, because it reminded me of what I had to overcome before anyone would take me seriously. In retrospect I understand that my anger gave my reading fire, that I have almost always taken doubts in my abilities as a challenge—and that the result is, most times, a feeling of satisfaction at having won a convert when I see the cold, appraising eyes warm to my words, the body language change, the smile that indicates that I have opened some avenue for communication. That day I read to that woman and her lowered eyes told me that she was embarrassed at her little faux pas, and when I willed her to look up at me, it was my victory, and she graciously allowed me to punish her with my full attention. We shook hands at the end of the reading, and I never saw her again. She has probably forgotten the whole thing but maybe not.

14   Yet I am one of the lucky ones. My parents made it possible for me to acquire a stronger footing in the mainstream culture by giving me the chance at
an education. And books and art have saved me from the harsher forms of ethnic and racial prejudice that many of my Hispanic *compañeras* have had to endure. I travel a lot around the United States, reading from my books of poetry
and my novel, and the reception I most often receive is one of positive interest
by people who want to know more about my culture. There are, however, thousands of Latinas without the privilege of an education or the entrée into society
that I have. For them life is a struggle against the misconceptions perpetuated
by the myth of the Latina as whore, domestic or criminal. We cannot change
this by legislating the way people look at us. The transformation, as I see it, has
to occur at a much more individual level. My personal goal in my public life is
to try to replace the old pervasive stereotypes and myths about Latinas with a
much more interesting set of realities. Every time I give a reading, I hope the
stories I tell, the dreams and fears I examine in my work, can achieve some universal truth which will get my audience past the particulars of my skin color, my
accent, or my clothes.

15   I once wrote a poem in which I called us Latinas "God's brown daughters."
This poem is really a prayer of sorts, offered upward, but also, through the hu-
man-to-human channel of art, outward. It is a prayer for communication, and
for respect. In it, Latin women pray "in Spanish to an Anglo God / with a Jewish heritage," and they are "fervently hoping / that if not omnipotent, / at least
He be bilingual."

FOR ANALYSIS AND DISCUSSION

1. How did Ortiz Cofer's cultural background prevent her from "fitting in"?
   What differences does she describe between Puerto Rican and "white" cultures?
2. How can cultural ideology and history hinder acceptance into "mainstream"
   corporate and social America? Explain.
3. How have the media promoted the image of the "Latina woman"? Evaluate
   Ortiz Cofer's analysis of why this stereotyping occurs. Do you agree?
4. What was the "island system" of morality for Puerto Ricans? How did it both
   liberate and restrain them? Analyze Ortiz Cofer's connection between the island system of life and the cultural misunderstandings she encountered in urban America.
5. Explain the connection between Ortiz Cofer's poem at the end of her essay and
   the points she makes earlier. Is this an effective way to end the essay?
6. Why does Ortiz Cofer consider herself to be "one of the lucky ones" (paragraph 14)?

Who Is a Whiz Kid?
Ted Gup

It is easy to spot negative and damaging racial stereotypes. In most cases, intolerance and even hate motivate such stereotypes. But what about so-called "good"

stereotypes, in which a particular race is dubbed smart, athletic, passionate, or musical? Are stereotypes permissible if they seem positive? How can "good" stereotypes in fact hurt?

Ted Gup is a former writer for the *Washington Post* and *Time*. His work has also appeared in *Gentlemen's Quarterly, Smithsonian, National Geographic, Mother Jones,* and *Sports Illustrated.* Gup is currently writing a history of the CIA and teaches journalism at Georgetown University. The following article appeared in the April 27, 1997, issue of *Newsweek.*

BEFORE YOU READ

In your experience, do you think society assumes that some races are inherently superior to others? What do you think accounts for such assumptions?

AS YOU READ

Is perpetuating a cultural stereotype acceptable if it promotes positive images? Are all stereotypes unacceptable?

1   Shortly after joining a national magazine some years ago as a writer, I found myself watching in horror as the week's cover story was prepared. The story was about "Asian-American whiz kids," and it featured a series of six student portraits, each face radiating with an intellectual brilliance. Being new to the enterprise, I was at first tentative in my criticism, cautioning that such a story was inherently biased and fueled racial and ethnic stereotypes. My criticism was dismissed. "This is something good we are saying about them," one top editor remarked. I reduced my criticism to writing. "What," I asked, "would be the response if the cover were about 'Jewish whiz kids'? Would anyone really dare to produce such an obviously offensive story?" My memo was ignored. Not long after, the cover appeared on the nation's newsstands, and the criticism began to fly. The editors were taken aback.

2   As a former Fulbright Scholar to China I have long taken a strong interest in the portrayal of Asian-Americans. But my interest went well beyond the academic. Even as the cover was being prepared, I was waiting to adopt my first son from Korea. His name was to be David. He was 5 months old when he arrived. That did not stop even some otherwise sophisticated friends from volunteering that he would no doubt be a good student. Probably a mathematician, they opined, with a tone that uncomfortably straddled jest and prediction. I tried to take it all with good humor, this idea that a 5-month-old who could not yet sit up, speak a word or control his bowels was already destined for academic greatness. Even his major seemed foreordained.

3   Many Asian-Americans seem to walk an uneasy line between taking pride in their remarkable achievements and needing to shake off stereotypes. The jokes abound. There is the apocryphal parent who asks "Where is the other point?" when his or her child scores a 99 on a test. Anther familiar refrain has the

young Asian-American student enumerating his or her hobbies: "studying, studying and more studying."

4 Several months after David arrived he and I entered a small mom-and-pop convenience store in our neighborhood. The owners were Korean. I noticed that the husband, standing behind the cash register, was eying my son. "Is he Korean?" he asked. "Yes," I nodded. He reached out for him and took him into his arms. "He'll be good in math," declared the man. "My God," I muttered. Not him, too!

5 It was preposterous. It was funny. And it was unnerving. Embedded in such elevated expectations were real threats to my son. Suppose, I wondered, he should turn out to be only a mediocre student, or, worse yet, not a student at all. I resented the stereotypes and saw them for what they were, the other side of the coin of racism. It is easy to delude one's self into thinking it harmless to offer racial compliments, but that is an inherent contradiction in terms. Such sweeping descriptives, be they negative or positive, deny the one thing most precious to all peoples—individuality. These stereotypes are pernicious for two reasons. First, such attributes are relative and tend to pit one race against another. Witness the seething enmity in many inner cities between Korean store owners and their African-American patrons. Stereotypes that hint at superiority in one race implicitly suggest inferiority in another. They are ultimately divisive, and in their most virulent form, even deadly. Who can forget the costs of the Aryan myth?

6 Many stereotypes also place a crushing burden on Asian-Americans. Few would deny that disproportionate numbers of Asian surnames appear each year among the winners of the Westinghouse science prizes or in the ranks of National Merit Scholars. But it might be a reflection of parental influences, personal commitment and cultural predilections, not genetic predisposition. A decade ago, as a Fulbright Lecturer in Beijing, I saw firsthand the staggering hours my Chinese students devoted to their studies. Were my students in the United States to invest similar time in their books I would have every reason to expect similar results.

7 I have often been told that Koreans are the "Jews of Asia," a reference to both their reported skills in business and their inherent intelligence. As a Jew, I cannot help but wince at such descriptions. I remember being one of the very few of my faith in a Midwest boarding school. There were many presumptions weighing on me, most of them grounded in my religion. My own classroom performance almost singlehandedly disabused my teachers of the myth that Jews were academically gifted. I barely made it through. Whether it was a lack of intelligence or simple rebellion against expectation, I do not know. I do know that more than once the fact that I was Jewish was raised as evidence that I could and should be doing better. Expectations based on race, be they raised or lowered, are no less galling.

8 David is now in the first grade. He is already taking math with the second graders and asking me about square roots and percentiles. I think back to the Korean merchant who took him in his arms and pronounced him a math whiz.

Was he right? Do Asian-Americans have it easier, endowed with some special strand of DNA? The answer is a resounding no. Especially in our house. My son David has learning disabilities to overcome and what progress he has made is individual in the purest and most heroic sense. No one can or should take that away from him, suggesting he is just another wunderkind belonging to a favored race.

9   A year after my first son arrived, we adopted his brother from Korea. His name is Matthew. Let it be known that Matthew couldn't care less about math. He's a bug man. Slugs and earthworms. I suspect he will never be featured on any cover stories about Asian-American whiz kids, but I will continue to resist anything and anyone who attempts to dictate either his interests or his abilities based on race or place of birth. Bugs are fine by me and should be more than fine by him.

FOR ANALYSIS AND DISCUSSION

1. When Gup questioned the decision to run a cover story on "Asian-American whiz kids" his editor dismissed his concerns with the comment "This is something good we are saying about them." What does this statement say about Gup's editor? Why do you think Gup mentions this comment?
2. What pressures do stereotypes place on children? How can stereotypes affect race relations?
3. How are stereotypes "the other side of the coin of racism"?
4. Analyze Gup's comment that stereotypes contribute to strained relationships between Koreans and blacks in inner cities. Do you agree?
5. What is the "Aryan myth"? What were its costs? Is the myth active today? If so, what is its continued impact?
6. Link some of the opinions and observations on racial stereotypes Gup makes in this article to a personal experience you had with racial stereotypes. How did stereotypes apply to the situation, and how did you handle the incident?

Free at Last? A Personal Perspective on Race and Identity in America
Glenn C. Loury

Establishing one's identity is a difficult task under the best of circumstances. The next essay examines the multifaceted issues of identity and race. Glenn Loury explores how identity can be shaped not so much by the individual but by external opinions and the ideology of the individual's social and ethnic groups.

Glenn Loury is a professor of economics at Boston University. His articles have appeared in the *New York Times,* the *Wall Street Journal,* and *The New Republic.* Loury is the author of *One by One and Inside Out: Essays and Reviews on Race and Responsibility in America* (1995). This article first appeared in *Commentary* in 1995.

BEFORE YOU READ

Have you ever felt it necessary to establish your ethnic background to a group of people in order to be accepted and heard by them?

AS YOU READ

Note Loury's use of the words "authentic," "passing," and "false." What do these words mean when applied to the various aspects of race?

1   A formative experience of my growing-up on the South Side of Chicago in the 1960s occurred during one of those heated, earnest political rallies so typical of the period. I was about eighteen at the time. Woody, who had been my best friend since Little League, suggested that we attend. Being political neophytes, neither of us knew many of the participants. The rally was called to galvanize our community's response to some pending infringement by the white power structure, the exact nature of which I no longer remember. But I can still vividly recall how very agitated about it we all were, determined to fight the good fight, even to the point of being arrested if it came to that. Judging by his demeanor, Woody was among the most zealous of those present.

2   Despite this zeal, it took courage for Woody to attend that meeting. Though he often proclaimed his blackness, and though he had a Negro grand-parent on each side of his family, he nevertheless looked to all the world like your typical white boy. Everyone, on first meeting him, assumed as much. I did, too, when we began to play together nearly a decade earlier, just after I had moved into the middle-class neighborhood called Park Manor, where Woody's family had been living for some time.

3   There were a number of white families on our block when we first arrived; within a couple of years they had all been replaced by aspiring black families like our own. I often wondered why Woody's parents never moved. Then I over-head his mother declare to one of her new neighbors, "We just wouldn't run from our own kind," a comment that befuddled me at the time. Somewhat later, while we were watching the movie *Imitation of Life* on television, my mother explained how someone could be black though he or she looked white. She told me about people like that in our own family—second cousins living in a fashionable suburb on whom one would never dare simply to drop in, because they were "passing for white." This was my earliest glimpse of the truth that racial identity in America is inherently a social and cultural, not simply a biolog-ical construct—that it necessarily involves an irreducible element of choice.

4   From the moment I learned of it I was at once intrigued and troubled by this idea of passing. I enjoyed imagining my racial brethren surreptitiously in-filtrating the citadels of white exclusivity. It allowed me to believe that, despite appearances and the white man's best efforts to the contrary, we blacks were nevertheless present, if unannounced, *everywhere* in American society. But I was

disturbed by an evident implication of the practice of passing—that denial of one's genuine self is a necessary concomitant of a black person's making it in this society. What "passing" seemed to say about the world was that if one were both black and ambitious it was necessary to choose between racial authenticity and personal success. Also, and ironically, it seemed grossly unfair to my adolescent mind that, however problematic it might be, this passing option was, because of my relatively dark complexion, not available to me!

5   It dawned on me after this conversation with my mother that Woody's parents must have been passing for white in preintegration Park Manor. The neighborhood's changing racial composition had confronted them with a moment of truth. They had elected to stay and to raise their children among "their own kind." This was a fateful decision for Woody, who, as he matured, became determined not simply to live among blacks but, perhaps in atonement for his parents' sins, unambiguously to become one. The young men in the neighborhood did not make this easy. Many delighted in picking fights with him, teasing him about being a "white boy," and refusing to credit his insistent, often repeated claim: "I'm a brother, too!"

6   The fact that some of his relatives were passing made Woody's racial-identity claims more urgent for him, but less compelling to others. He desperately wanted to be black, but his peers in the neighborhood would not let him. Because he had the option to be white—an option he radically rejected at the time—those without the option could not accept his claim to a shared racial experience. I knew Woody well. We became good friends, and I wanted to accept him on his own terms. But even I found myself doubting that he fully grasped the pain, frustration, anger, and self-doubt many of us felt upon encountering the intractability of American racism. However much he sympathized with our plight, he seemed to experience it only vicariously.

7   So there we were, at this boisterous, angry political rally. A critical moment came when the leaders interrupted their speech making to solicit input from "the people." Woody had an idea, and enthusiastically raised his voice above the murmur to be heard. He was cut short before finishing his first sentence by one of the dashiki-clad brothers-in-charge, who demanded to know how a "white boy" got the authority to have an opinion about what black people should be doing. That was one of our problems, the brother said, we were always letting white people "peep our hole card," while we were never privy to their deliberations in the same way.

8   A silence then fell over the room. The indignant brother asked if anyone could "vouch for the white boy." More excruciating silence ensued. Now was *my* moment of truth; Woody turned plaintively toward me, but I would not meet his eyes. To my eternal disgrace, I refused to speak up for him. He was asked to leave the meeting, and did so without uttering a word in his own defense. Subsequently, neither of us could bear to discuss the incident. I offered no apology or explanation, and he asked for none. However, though we continued to be friendly, our relationship was forever changed. I was never again to hear Woody exclaim: "I'm a brother, too."

9   I recall this story about Woody because his dilemma, and mine, tell us something important about race and personal identity in American society. His situation was made so difficult by the fact that he embraced a self-definition dramatically inconsistent with the identity reflexively and stubbornly imputed to him by others. This lack of social confirmation for his subjective sense of self left him uncertain, at a deep level, about who he really was. Ultimately there seemed to be no way for him to avoid living fraudulently—either as a black passing for white, or as a white trying (too hard) to be black. As his close friend and frequent companion I had become familiar with, and occasionally shared in, the pitfalls of this situation. People would assume when they saw us together both that he was white, and that I was "the kind of Negro who hangs out with white boys." I resented that assumption.

10   Since then, as a black intellectual making my living in the academic establishment during a period of growing racial conflict in our society, I have often experienced this dissonance between my self-concept and the socially imputed definition of who I am supposed to be. I have had to confront the problem of balancing my desire not to disappoint the expectations of others—both whites and blacks, but more especially blacks—with my conviction that one should strive to live life with integrity. This does not make me a heroic figure; I eschew the libertarian ideologue's rhetoric about the glorious individual who, though put upon by society, blazes his own path. I acknowledge that this opposition between individual and society is ambiguous, in view of the fact that the self is inevitably shaped by the objective world, and by other selves. I know that what one is being faithful to when resisting the temptation to conform to others' expectations by "living life with integrity" is always a socially determined, if subjectively experienced, vision of the self.

11   Still, I see this incident of a quarter-century ago as a kind of private metaphor for the ongoing problem of living in good faith, particularly as it relates to my personal identity as a black American. I have since lost contact with Woody. I suspect that, having tired of his struggle against society's presumptions about him, he is now passing. But that moment of truth in that South Side church basement, and my failure in the face of it, have helped me understand the depth of my own need to be seen by others as "black enough."

12   Upon reflection, my refusal to stand up for Woody exposed the tenuous quality of my personal sense of racial authenticity. The fact is, I willingly betrayed someone I had known for a decade, since we began to play stickball together in the alley that ran between our homes, a person whom I loved and who loved me, in order to avoid the risk of being rejected by strangers. In a way, at that moment and often again later in life, I was "passing" too—hoping to be mistaken for something I was not. I had feared that to proclaim before the black radicals in the audience that this "white boy" at my side was in fact our "brother" would have compromised my own chance of being received among them as a genuine colleague, too. Who, after all, was there to vouch for me, had I been dismissed by one of the "brothers" as an Uncle Tom?

13   This was not an unfounded concern, for at that meeting, as at so many others of the period, people with insufficiently militant views were berated as self-

hating, shuffle-along, "house nigger" types, complicit with whites in the perpetuation of racial oppression. Then, as now, blacks who befriended (or, heaven forbid, married) whites, who dressed or talked or wore their hair a certain way, who listened to certain kinds of music, read certain books, or expressed certain opinions were laughed at, ostracized and generally demeaned as inauthentic by other, more righteous (as in "self-righteous") blacks. The indignant brother who challenged Woody's right to speak at that rally was not merely imposing a racial test (only blacks are welcome here), he was mainly applying a loyalty test (are you truly with us or against us?) and this was a test that anyone present could fail through a lack of conformity to the collective definition of what is meant to be genuinely black. I feared that speaking up for Woody would have marked me as a disloyal Tom among the blacker-than-thou crowd. This was a fate, in those years, the thought of which I could not bear.

14   I now understand how this desire to be regarded as genuinely black, to be seen as a "regular brother," has dramatically altered my life. It narrowed the range of my earliest intellectual pursuits, distorted my relationships with other people, censored my political thought and expression, informed the way I dressed and spoke, and shaped my cultural interests. Some of this was inevitable and not all of it was bad, but in my experience the need to be affirmed by one's racial peers can take on a pathological dimension. Growing into intellectual maturity has been, for me, largely a process of becoming free of the need to have my choices validated by "the brothers." After many years I have come to understand that until I became willing to risk the derision of the crowd I had no chance to discover the most important truths about myself or about life—to know and accept my "calling," to perceive what I really value, what goals are most worth striving toward. In a perverse extension of the lesson from *Imitation of Life,* I have learned that one does not have to live surreptitiously as a Negro among whites in order to be engaged in a denial of one's genuine self for the sake of gaining social acceptance. This is a price that blacks often demand of each other as well.

15   I used to think about the irony in the idea of some blacks seeking to excommunicate others for crimes against the race, given that the external factors that affect us all are unaffected by the distinctions that so exercised the blacker-than-thou crowd. I would relish the seeming contradiction: I was still a "nigger" to the working-class toughs waiting to punish with their fists my trespass onto their white turf, yet I could not be a "brother" to the middle-class radicals with whom I shared so much history and circumstance. My racial identity in the larger white society was in no way conditional upon the espousal of particular beliefs or values (whatever my political views or cultural interests, I would always be black in white America), yet my standing among other blacks could be made conditional upon my fidelity to the prevailing party line of the moment. I would ponder this paradox, chafing at the restraint of an imposed racial uniformity, bemoaning the unfairness that I should have to face a threat of potential ostracism as punishment for the sin of being truthful to myself. In short, I would wallow in self-pity, which is always a waste of time. These days I am less given to, if not entirely free of, such inclinations.

16   Underlying my obsession with this paradox was a premise which I now believe to be mistaken—that being an authentic black person involves in some elemental way seeing oneself as an object of mistreatment by white people, while participating in a collective consciousness of that mistreatment with other black people. As long as I believed that my personal identity as a black American was necessarily connected to our country's history of racial violation, and derived much of its content from my sharing with other blacks in a recollection of and struggle against this violation, I was destined to be in a bind. For, as my evolving understanding of our history began to clash with the black consensus, and my definition of the struggle took on a different, more conservative form from that popular among other black intellectuals, I found myself cut off from the group, my racial bona fides in question. I was therefore forced to choose between my intellectual integrity and my access to that collective consciousness of racial violation and shared experience of struggle which I saw as essential to my black identity. Like Woody, lacking social confirmation of my subjective sense of self, I was left uncertain about who I really was.

17   I no longer believe that the camaraderie engendered among blacks by our collective experience of racism constitutes an adequate basis for any person's self-definition. Even if I restrict attention to the question "Who am I as a black American at the end of the twentieth century?," these considerations of historical victimization and struggle against injustice do not take me very far toward finding an answer. I am made "black" only in the most superficial way by virtue of being the object of a white racist's hate. The empathetic exchange of survivors' tales among "brothers," even the collective struggle against the clear wrong of racism, does not provide a tapestry sufficiently rich to give meaning and definition to the totality of my life. I am so much more than the one wronged, misunderstood, underestimated, derided, or ignored by whites. I am more than the one who has struggled against this oppression and indifference; more than a descendent of slaves now claiming freedom; more, that is, than either a "colored person" (as seen by the racist) or a "person of color" (as seen by the antiracist).

18   Who am I, then? Foremost, I am a child of God, created in this image, imbued with his spirit, endowed with his gifts, set free by his grace. The most important challenges and opportunities that confront me derive not from my racial condition, but rather from my human condition. I am a husband, a father, a son, a teacher, an intellectual, a Christian, a citizen. In none of these roles is my race irrelevant, but neither can racial identity alone provide much guidance for my quest to adequately discharge these responsibilities. The particular features of my social condition, the external givens, merely set the stage of my life, they do not provide a script. That script must be internally generated, it must be a product of a reflective deliberation about the meaning of this existence for which no political or ethnic program could ever substitute.

19   Or, to shift the metaphor slightly, the socially contingent features of my situation—my racial heritage and family background, the prevailing attitudes about race and class of those with whom I share this society—these are the building blocks, the raw materials, out of which I must construct the edifice of my life. The expression of my individual personality is to be found in the blue-

print that I employ to guide this project of construction. The problem of devising such a plan for one's life is a universal problem, which confronts all people, whatever their race, class, or ethnicity. By facing and solving this problem we grow as human beings, and give meaning and substance to our lives. In my view, a personal identity wholly dependent on racial contingency falls tragically short of its potential because it embraces too parochial a conception of what is possible, and of what is desirable.

20   Thus, and ironically, to the extent that we individual blacks see ourselves primarily through a racial lens, we sacrifice possibilities for the kind of personal development that would ultimately further our collective, racial interests. We cannot be truly free men and women while laboring under a definition of self derived from the perceptual view of our oppressor, confined to the contingent facts of our oppression. In *A Portrait of the Artist as a Young Man* James Joyce says of Irish nationalism: "When the soul of a man is born in this country there are nets flung at it to hold it back from flight. You talk to me of nationality, language, religion, I shall try to fly by these nets. . . . Do you know what Ireland is? . . . Ireland is the old sow that eats her farrow." It seems to me that, too often, a search for some mythic authentic blackness works similarly to hold back young black souls from flight into the open skies of American society. Of course there is the constraint of racism also holding us back. But the trick, as Joyce knew, is to turn such "nets" into wings, and thus to fly by them. One cannot do that if one refuses to see that ultimately it is neither external constraint nor expanded opportunity but rather an indwelling spirit that makes this flight possible.

21 Last winter, on a clear, cold Sunday afternoon, my three-year-old son and I were walking in the woods near our New England home. We happened upon a small pond, which, having frozen solid, made an ideal skating rink. Dozens of men, ranging in age from late teens to early thirties were distributed across the ice in clusters of ten or so, playing, or preparing to play hockey. They glided over the pond's surface effortlessly, skillfully passing and defending, stopping and turning on a dime, moving with such power, speed, and grace that we were spellbound as we watched them. Little Glenn would occasionally squeal with delight as he marveled at one astounding feat after another, straining against my grip, which alone prevented him from running out onto the ice to join in the fun.

22   All of these men were white—every last one of them. Few took notice of us at the pond's edge, and those who did were not particularly generous with their smiles, or, at least, it seemed to me. I sensed that we were interlopers, that if we had come with sticks and skates we would not necessarily have been welcome. But this may be wrong; I do not really know what they thought of our presence; no words were exchanged. I do know that my son very much enjoyed watching the game, and I thought to myself at the time that he would, someday too soon, come asking for a pair of skates, and for his dad to teach him how to use them. I found myself consciously dreading that day.

23   The thought of my son's playing hockey on that frozen pond did not sit well with me. I much preferred to think of him on a basketball court. Hockey, we all know, is a white man's game. Who was the last "brother" to play in the

NHL? Of course, I immediately sensed that this thought was silly and illegitimate, and attempted to banish it from my mind. But it kept coming back. I could not avoid the feeling that something important was at stake here. So I decided to discuss it with my wife, Linda.

24   We had carefully considered the implications for our children of our decision to buy a house in a predominantly white suburb. We joined and became active in a church with many black families like our own, in part so that our boys would be provided with suitable racial peers. We are committed to ensuring that their proper education about black history and culture, including their family history, is not left to chance. We are ever vigilant concerning the effect on their developing psyches of racial messages that come across on television, in their books, at their nursery school, and so on. On all of this Linda and I are in full accord. But she thought my concerns about hockey were taking things a bit too far.

25   I now believe she was right, and I think I have learned something important from our conversations about that issue. My aversion to the idea of my son's involvement in that Sunday-afternoon ritual we witnessed was rooted in my own sense of identity, as a black American man who grew up when and where I did, who has had the experiences I have had. Because *I* would not have felt comfortable there, I began to think that *he* should not want to be a part of that scene either. I was inclined to impose upon my son, in the name of preserving his authentic blackness, a limitation of his pursuits deriving from my life but not really relevant to his. It is as if I were to insist that he study Swahili instead of Swedish because I could not imagine myself being interested in speaking Swedish!

26   The fact is that, given the class background of our children and the community in which we have chosen to make our lives, it is inevitable that their racial sensibilities will be quite different from ours. Moreover, it is impossible to predict just what self-definition they will settle upon. This can be disquieting to contemplate for those of our generation concerned about retaining a "genuinely black" identity in the face of the social mobility we have experienced within our lifetimes. But it is not, I think, to be feared.

         The alternative seems much more frightening to me—stifling the development of our children's personalities by imposing upon them an invented ethnicity. I have no doubt that my sons will be black men of the twenty-first century, but not by their singing of racial anthems peculiar to our time. Theirs will be a blackness constructed yet again, out of the external givens of their lives, not mine, shaped by a cultural inheritance that I am responsible to transmit but expressed in their own voices, animated by a Spirit whose basis lies deeper than the color of any man's skin, and whose source is "no respecter of persons."

FOR ANALYSIS AND DISCUSSION

1. Loury comments that his friend Woody looked like a "typical white boy." What makes Woody "white"? If Woody has two grandparents who are black, presumably he must have two who are not black. Why, then, does he culturally identify himself as black, rather than white?

2. Evaluate Woody's desire to be one of the "brothers." How and why is it important to him to be seen as one?

3. How does Loury's story about the meeting and his actions at it contribute to his overall argument? Explain the connection between that story and the point Loury is making.

4. In paragraph 4 Loury comments that he was disturbed by the implications of "passing." Do you think he would have been more accepting of "passing" if it had been an option for him? Likewise, would his friend Woody have been so desperate to be accepted as black if he had not been so passably white? Explain.

5. According to Loury, what is the cost of accepting a socially constructed ethnic identity for oneself? Can race be self-limiting? Explain.

6. How important is group acceptance to dialogue, communication, and consensus? Is it a factor? Explain.

WRITING ASSIGNMENTS: IDENTITY AND STEREOTYPES

1. Think about the ways in which the social, intellectual, topographical, and religious histories of a race influence the creation of stereotypes. Identify current stereotypes that are active in this society. What are the origins of these stereotypes? Write an argument essay in which you dissect these stereotypes, and present ways to promote racial understanding beyond them.

2. Write an essay discussing your own family's sense of ethnic or racial identity. What are the origins of some of your family's values, practices, and customs? Have these customs met with prejudices? Write from the perspective that you are relaying this information to promote understanding to people of ethnic backgrounds different from your own.

3. Read the Web article "An Answer to America's 'Race Question'" by Reverend Earl W. Jackson of Boston at <http://www.nationalcenter.inter.net/NVJackson997.html>. Analyze Jackson's "answer." Write an essay in which you evaluate the feasibility of his answer. Or, if you wish, you may address why it may be right in principle but not in cultural reality.

UNITY AND DIVERSITY: CAN THEY EXIST TOGETHER?

The Return of the Melting Pot
Arthur Schlesinger, Jr.

What exactly is the "American melting pot?" At the turn of the century, most people felt it meant educating one's children in American schools, learning the English language, and blending into mainstream American society. But over the last 30 years or so, the concept of the melting pot has become threatening to some people.

To them it symbolizes the loss of individual cultures and beliefs at the expense of a blended ideal held by the status quo.

Arthur Schlesinger is a well-known historian and a columnist for the *New York Times*. The recipient of two Pulitzer Prizes for history, he is the author of *The Disuniting of America: Reflections on a Multicultural Society* (1992), in which he questions the rising popularity of radical multiculturalism. This essay appeared in the *Wall Street Journal* in 1990.

BEFORE YOU READ

Evaluate your feelings on multicultural education. Where do you stand on the issue?

AS YOU READ

How does Schlesinger use American history to support his argument? Is this an effective way to bolster his argument?

1   "What then is the American, this new man?" a French immigrant asked two centuries ago. Hector St. John de Crevecoeur gave the classic answer to his own question. "He is an American, who, leaving behind him all his ancient prejudices and manners, receives new ones from the new mode of life he has embraced, the new government he obeys, and the new rank he holds. . . . Here individuals of all nations are melted into a new race of man."

2   The conception of America as a transforming nation, banishing old identities and creating a new one, prevailed through most of American history. It was famously reformulated by Israel Zangwill, an English writer of Russian Jewish origin, when he called America "God's crucible, the great melting pot where all the faces of Europe are melting and re-forming." Most people who came to America expected to become Americans. They wanted to escape a horrid past and to embrace a hopeful future. Their goals were deliverance and assimilation.

3   Thus Crevecoeur wrote his "Letters from an American Farmer" in his acquired English, not in his native French. Thus immigrants reared in other tongues urged their children to learn English as speedily as possible. German immigrants tried for a moment to gain status for their language, but the effort got nowhere. The dominant culture was Anglo-Saxon and, with modification and enrichment, remained Anglo-Saxon.

Repudiation of the Melting Pot

4   The melting pot was one of those metaphors that turned out only to be partly true, and recent years have seen an astonishing repudiation of the whole conception. Many Americans today righteously reject the historic goal of "a new race of man." The contemporary ideal is not assimilation but ethnicity. The escape from origins has given way to the search for "roots." "Ancient prejudices

and manners" —the old-time religion, the old-time diet—have made a surprising comeback.

5   These developments portend a new turn in American life. Instead of a transformative nation with a new and distinctive identity, America increasingly sees itself as preservative of old identities. We used to say e pluribus unum. Now we glorify pluribus and belittle unum. The melting pot yields to the Tower of Babel.

6   The new turn has had marked impact on the universities. Very little agitates academia more these days than the demands of passionate minorities for revision of the curriculum: in history, the denunciation of Western civilization courses as cultural imperialism; in literature, the denunciation of the "canon," the list of essential books, as an instrumentality of the existing power structure.

7   A recent report by the New York State Commissioner of Education's task force on "Minorities: Equity and Excellence" luridly describes "African Americans, Asian Americans, Puerto Ricans/Latinos and Native Americans" as "victims of an intellectual and educational oppression." The "systematic bias toward European culture and its derivatives," the report claims, has "a terribly damaging effect on the psyche of young people of African, Asian, Latino and Native American descent" —a doubtful assertion for which no proof is vouch safed.

8   Of course teachers of history and literature should give due recognition to women, black Americans, Indians, Hispanics and other groups who were subordinated and ignored in the high noon of male Anglo-Saxon dominance. In recent years they have begun belatedly to do so. But the *cult of ethnicity,* pressed too far, exacts costs—as, for example, the current pressure to teach history and literature not as intellectual challenges but as psychological therapy.

9   There is nothing new, of course, about the yearnings of excluded groups for affirmations of their own historical and cultural dignity. When Irish-Americans were thought beyond the pale, their spokesmen responded much as spokesmen for blacks, Hispanics and others respond today. Professor John V. Kelleher, for many years Harvard's distinguished Irish scholar, once recalled his first exposure to Irish-American history—"turgid little essays on the fact that the Continental Army was 76 percent Irish, or that many of George Washington's closest friends were nuns and priests, or that Lincoln got the major ideas for the Second Inaugural Address from the Hon. Francis P. Mageghegan of Alpaca, New York, a pioneer manufacturer of cast-iron rosary beads." John Kelleher called this "the there's-always-an-Irishman-at-the-bottom-of-it-doing-the-real-work approach to American history."

10   Fortunately most Irish-Americans disregarded their spokesmen and absorbed the American tradition. About 1930, Kelleher said, those "turgid little essays began to vanish from Irish-American papers." He added, "I wonder whose is the major component in the Continental Army these days?" The answer, one fears, is getting to be blacks, Jews and Hispanics.

11   There is often artificiality about the attempts to use history to minister to psychological needs. When I encounter black insistence on inserting Africa into mainstream curricula, I recall the 1956 presidential campaign. Adlai Stevenson, for whom I was working, had a weak record on civil rights in America but was a

champion of African nationalism. I suggested to a group of sympathetic black leaders that maybe if Stevenson talked to black audiences about Africa, he could make up for his deficiencies on civil rights. My friends laughed and said that American blacks couldn't care less about Africa. That is no longer the case; but one can't escape the feeling that present emotions are more manufactured than organic.

12   Let us by all means teach women's history, black history, Hispanic history. But let us teach them as *history,* not as a means of *promoting group self-esteem.* I don't often agree with Gore Vidal, but I liked his remark the other day: "What I hate is good citizenship history. That has wrecked every history book. Now we're getting 'The Hispanics are warm and joyous and have brought such wonder into our lives,' you know, and before them the Jews, and before them the blacks. And the women. I mean, cut it out!"

13   Novelists, moralists, politicians, fabulators can go beyond the historical evidence to tell inspiring stories. But historians are custodians of professional standards. Their objective is critical analysis, accuracy and objectivity, not making people feel better about themselves.

14   Heaven knows how dismally historians fall short of their ideals; how sadly our interpretations are dominated and distorted by unconscious preconceptions; how obsessions of race and nation blind us to our own bias. All historians may in one way or another mythologize history. But the answer to bad history is not "good citizenship history"—more bad history written from a different viewpoint. The answer to bad history is better history.

15   The ideological assault in English departments on the "canon" as an instrument of political oppression implies the existence of a monolithic body of work designed to enforce the "hegemony" of a class or race or sex. In fact, most great literature and much good history are deeply subversive in their impact on orthodoxies. Consider the American canon: Emerson, Whitman, Melville, Hawthorne, Thoreau, Mark Twain, Henry Adams, William and Henry James, Holmes, Dreiser, Faulkner. Lackeys of the ruling class? Agents of American imperialism?

16   Let us by all means learn about other continents and other cultures. But, lamentable as some may think it, we inherit an American experience, as America inherits a European experience. To deny the essentially European origins of American culture is to falsify history.

17   We should take pride in our distinctive inheritance as other nations take pride in their distinctive inheritances. Certainly there is no need for Western civilization, the source of the ideas of individual freedom and political democracy to which most of the world now aspires, to apologize to cultures based on despotism, superstition, tribalism, and fanaticism. Let us abjure what Bertrand Russell called the fallacy of "the superior virtue of the oppressed."

18   Of course we must teach the Western democratic tradition in its true proportions—not as a fixed, final and complacent orthodoxy, intolerant of deviation and dissent, but as an ever-evolving creed fulfilling its ideals through debate, self-criticism, protest, disrespect and irreverence, a tradition in which all

groups have rights of heterodoxy and opportunities for self-assertion. It is a tradition that has empowered people of all nations and races. Little can have a more "terribly damaging effect on the psyche" than for educators to tell young blacks and Hispanics and Asians that it is not for them.

One Step at a Time

19   Belief in one's own culture does not mean disdain for other cultures. But one step at a time: No culture can hope to ingest other cultures all at once, certainly not before it ingests its own. After we have mastered our own culture, we can explore the world.

20   If we repudiate the quite marvelous inheritance that history has bestowed on us, we invite the fragmentation of our own culture into a quarrelsome spatter of enclaves, ghettos and tribes. The bonds of cohesion in our society are sufficiently fragile, or so it seems to me, that it makes no sense to strain them by encouraging and exalting cultural and linguistic apartheid. The rejection of the melting pot points the republic in the direction of incoherence and chaos.

21   In the 21st century, if present trends hold, non-whites in the U.S. will begin to outnumber whites. This will bring inevitable changes in the national ethos but not, one must hope, at the expense of national cohesion. Let the new Americans foreswear the cult of ghettoization and agree with Crevecoeur, as with most immigrants in the two centuries since, that in America "individuals of all nations are melted into a new race of man."

FOR ANALYSIS AND DISCUSSION

1. In paragraph 5 Schlesinger states that instead of working toward common goals and a common identity, we now "glorify pluribus and belittle unum." Explain what you think he means by that statement. How effective is his use of the "e pluribus unum" reference?

2. Schlesinger implies that multiculturalism isn't teaching history or literature as subjects in themselves, but as a means to promote "self-esteem." Analyze and formulate a response to this statement in which you support or refute Schelesinger's claim.

3. In paragraph 10 Schlesinger comments that it was fortunate that Irish Americans disregarded their "spokesman" and absorbed the American tradition". What is the "American tradition"? Why does Schlesinger think it was important that Irish Americans assimilated into mainstream culture? Do you agree?

4. How does Schlesinger support this statement: "[W]e inherit an American experience, as America inherits a European experience" (paragraph 16). Is it true? Explain.

5. How is the subject of multiculturalism approached in your school? How is American history taught in schools today? Compare the comments Schlesinger makes to your own educational experiences with multiculturalism.

A Different Mirror
Ronald Takaki

Are Americans who look "different" doomed to be forever taken as strangers in their own land? The author of this essay, Ronald Takaki, writes of his experiences as an American of Japanese heritage. Continually treated as a foreigner in his own country, Takaki draws from other minority sources to highlight many of the difficulties assimilation and nonacceptance present for those individuals who do not fit the status quo's definition of "American."

Ronald Takaki is considered to be among the nation's foremost spokespersons for multicultural education. He is a professor of ethnic studies at the University of California, Berkeley, and the author of *A Different Mirror: A History of Multicultural America* (1993), from which the following essay comes.

BEFORE YOU READ

Think about your own family's experience in the United States. How long did it take for them to be accepted by society? Was it an instant acceptance, or did it require generations before assimilation was complete?

AS YOU READ

How do the points made in the essay by Arthur Schlesinger, Jr., contrast with the issues addressed by Takaki? Who seems more credible, and why?

1   I had flown from San Francisco to Norfolk and was riding in a taxi to my hotel to attend a conference on multiculturalism. Hundreds of educators from across the country were meeting to discuss the need for greater cultural diversity in the curriculum. My driver and I chatted about the weather and the tourists. The sky was cloudy, and Virginia Beach was twenty minutes away. The rearview mirror reflected a white man in his forties. "How long have you been in this country?" he asked. "All my life," I replied, wincing. "I was born in the United States." With a strong southern drawl, he remarked: "I was wondering because your English is excellent!" Then, as I had many times before, I explained: "My grandfather came here from Japan in the 1880s. My family has been here, in America, for over a hundred years." He glanced at me in the mirror. Somehow I did not look "American" to him; my eyes and complexion looked foreign.

2   Suddenly, we both became uncomfortably conscious of a racial divide separating us. An awkward silence turned my gaze from the mirror to the passing landscape, the shore where the English and the Powhatan Indians first encountered each other. Our highway was on land that Sir Walter Raleigh had renamed "Virginia" in honor of Elizabeth I, the Virgin Queen. In the English cultural appropriation of America, the indigenous peoples themselves would become outsiders in their native land. Here, at the eastern edge of the conti-

nent, I mused, was the site of the beginning of multicultural America. Jamestown, the English settlement founded in 1607, was nearby: the first twenty Africans were brought here a year before the Pilgrims arrived at Plymouth Rock. Several hundred miles offshore was Burmuda, the "Bermoothes" where William Shakespeare's Prospero had landed and met the native Caliban in *The Tempest*. Earlier, another voyager had made an Atlantic crossing and unexpectedly bumped into some islands to the south. Thinking he had reached Asia, Christopher Columbus mistakenly identified one of the islands as "Cipango" (Japan). In the wake of the admiral, many peoples would come to America from different shores, not only from Europe but also Africa and Asia. One of them would be my grandfather. My mental wandering across terrain and time ended abruptly as we arrived at my destination. I said good-bye to my driver and went into the hotel, carrying a vivid reminder of why I was attending this conference.

3 Questions like the one my taxi driver asked me are always jarring, but I can understand why he could not see me as American. He had a narrow but widely shared sense of the past—a history that has viewed American as European in ancestry. "Race," Toni Morrison explained, has functioned as a "metaphor" necessary to the "construction of Americanness": in the creation of our national identity, "American" has been defined as "white."

4 But America has been racially diverse since our very beginning on the Virginia shore, and this reality is increasingly becoming viable and ubiquitous. Currently, one-third of the American people do not trace their origins to Europe; in California, minorities are fast becoming a majority. They already predominate in major cities across the country—New York, Chicago, Atlanta, Detroit, Philadelphia, San Francisco, and Los Angeles.

5 This emerging demographic diversity has raised fundamental questions about America's identity and culture. In 1990, *Time* published a cover story on "America's Changing Colors." "Someday soon," the magazine announced, "white Americans will become a minority group." How soon? By 2056, most Americans will trace their descent to "Africa, Asia, the Hispanic world, the Pacific Islands, Arabia—almost anywhere but white Europe." This dramatic change in our nation's ethnic composition is altering the way we think about ourselves. "The deeper significance of America's becoming a majority nonwhite society is what it means to the national psyche, to individuals' sense of themselves and their nation—their idea of what it is to be American."

6 Indeed, more than ever before, as we approach the time when whites become a minority, many of us are perplexed about our national identity and our future as one people. This uncertainty has provoked Allan Bloom to reaffirm the preeminence of Western civilization. Author of *The Closing of the American Mind*, he has emerged as a leader of an intellectual backlash against cultural diversity. In his view, students entering the university are "uncivilized," and the university has the responsibility to "civilize" them. Bloom claims he knows what their "hungers" are and "what they can digest." Eating is one of his favorite

opponents argument

metaphors. Noting the "large black presence" in major universities, he laments the "one failure" in race relations—black students have proven to be "indigestible." They do not "melt as have *all* other groups." The problem, he contends, is that "blacks have become blacks": they have become "ethnic." This separatism has been reinforced by an academic permissiveness that has befouled the curriculum with "Black Studies" along with "Learn Another Culture." The only solution, Bloom insists, is "the good old Great Books approach."

7   Similarly, E. D. Hirsch worries that America is becoming a "tower of Babel," and that this multiplicity of cultures is threatening to rend our social fabric. He, too, longs for a more cohesive culture and a more homogeneous America: "If we *had* to make a choice between the *one* and the *many,* most Americans would choose the principle of unity, since we cannot function as a nation without it." The way to correct this fragmentization, Hirsch argues, is to acculturate "disadvantaged children." What do they need to know? "Only by accumulating shared symbols, and the shared information that symbols represent," Hirsch answers, "can we learn to communicate effectively with one another in our national community." Though he concedes the value of multicultural education, he quickly dismisses it by insisting that it "should not be allowed to supplant or interfere with our schools' responsibility to ensure our children's mastery of American literate culture." In *Cultural Literacy: What Every American Needs to Know,* Hirsch offers a long list of terms that excludes much of the history of minority groups.

8   While Bloom and Hirsch are reacting defensively to what they regard as a vexatious balkanization of America, many other educators are responding to our diversity as an opportunity to open American minds. In 1990, the Task Force on Minorities for New York emphasized the importance of a culturally diverse education. "Essentially," the *New York Times* commented, "the issue is how to deal with both dimensions of the nation's motto: 'E pluribus unum'—'Out of many, one.'" Universities from New Hampshire to Berkeley have established American cultural diversity graduation requirements. "Every student needs to know," explained University of Wisconsin's chancellor Donna Shalala, "much more about the origins and history of the particular cultures which, as Americans, we will encounter during our lives." Even the University of Minnesota, located in a state that is 98 percent white, requires its students to take ethnic studies courses. Asked why multiculturalism is so important, Dean Fred Lukermann answered: As a national university, Minnesota has to offer a national curriculum—one that includes all of the peoples of America. He added that after graduation many students move to cities like Chicago and Los Angeles and thus need to know about racial diversity. Moreover, many educators stress, multiculturalism has an intellectual purpose. By allowing us to see events from the viewpoints of different groups, a multicultural curriculum enables us to reach toward a more comprehensive understanding of American history.

9   What is fueling this debate over our national identity and the content of our curriculum is America's intensifying racial crisis. The alarming signs and symptoms seem to be everywhere—the killing of Vincent Chin in Detroit, the black boycott of a Korean grocery store in Flatbush, the hysteria in Boston over

the Carol Stuart murder, the battle between white sportsmen and Indians over tribal fishing rights in Wisconsin, the Jewish-black clashes in Brooklyn's Crown Heights, the black-Hispanic competition for jobs and educational resources in Dallas, which *Newsweek* described as "a conflict of the have-nots," and the Willie Horton campaign commercials, which widened the divide between the suburbs and the inner cities.

10   This reality of racial tension rudely woke America like a fire bell in the night on April 29, 1992. Immediately after four Los Angeles police officers were found not guilty of brutality against Rodney King, rage exploded in Los Angeles. Race relations reached a new nadir. During the nightmarish rampage, scores of people were killed, over two thousand injured, twelve thousand arrested, and almost a billion dollars' worth of property destroyed. The live televised images mesmerized America. The rioting and the murderous melee on the streets resembled the fighting in Beirut and the West Bank. The thousands of fires burning out of control and the dark smoke filling the skies brought back images of the burning oil fields of Kuwait during Desert Storm. Entire sections of Los Angeles looked like a bombed city. "Is this America?" many shocked viewers asked. "Please, can we get along here," pleaded Rodney King, calling for calm. "We all can get along. I mean, we're all stuck here for a while. Let's try to work it out."

11   But how should "we" be defined? Who are the people "stuck here" in America? One of the lessons of the Los Angeles explosion is the recognition of the fact that we are a multiracial society and that race can no longer be defined in the binary terms of white and black. "We" will have to include Hispanics and Asians. While blacks currently constitute 13 percent of the Los Angeles population, Hispanics represent 40 percent. The 1990 census revealed that South Central Los Angeles, which was predominantly black in 1965 when the Watts rebellion occurred, is now 45 percent Hispanic. A majority of the first 5,438 people arrested were Hispanic, while 37 percent were black. Of the fifty-eight people who died in the riot, more than a third were Hispanic, and about 40 percent of the businesses destroyed were Hispanic-owned. Most of the other shops and stores were Korean-owned. The dreams of many Korean immigrants went up in smoke during the riot: two thousand Korean-owned businesses were damaged or demolished, totaling about $400 million in losses. There is evidence indicating they were targeted. "After all," explained a black gang member, "we didn't burn our community, just *their* stores."

12   "I don't feel like I'm in America anymore," said Denisse Bustamente as she watched the police protecting the firefighters. "I feel like I am far away." Indeed, Americans have been witnessing ethnic strife erupting around the world—the rise of neo-Nazism and the murder of Turks in Germany, the ugly "ethnic cleansing" in Bosnia, the terrible and bloody clashes between Muslims and Hindus in India. Is the situation here different, we have been nervously wondering, or do ethnic conflicts elsewhere represent a prologue for America? What is the nature of malevolence? Is there a deep, perhaps primordial, need for group identity rooted in hatred for the other? Is ethnic pluralism possible for

America? But answers have been limited. Television reports have been little more than thirty-second sound bites. Newspaper articles have been mostly superficial descriptions of racial antagonisms and the current urban malaise. What is lacking is historical context; consequently, we are left feeling bewildered.

13   How did we get to this point, Americans everywhere are anxiously asking. What does our diversity mean, and where is it leading us? *How* do we work it out in the post–Rodney King era?

14   Certainly one crucial way is for our society's various ethnic groups to develop a greater understanding of each other. For example, how can African Americans and Korean Americans work it out unless they learn about each other's cultures, histories, and also economic situations? This need to share knowledge about our ethnic diversity has acquired new importance and has given new urgency to the pursuit for a more accurate history.

Alternative

15   More than ever before, there is a growing realization that the established scholarship has tended to define America too narrowly. For example, in his prize-winning study *The Uprooted,* Harvard historian Oscar Handlin presented— to use the book's subtitle—"the Epic Story of the Great Migrations That Made the American People." But Handlin's "epic story" excluded the "uprooted" from Africa, Asia, and Latin America—the other "Great Migrations" that also helped to make "the American People." Similarly, in *The Age of Jackson,* Arthur M. Schlesinger, Jr., left out blacks and Indians. There is not even a mention of two marker events—the Nat Turner insurrection and Indian removal, which Andrew Jackson himself would have been surprised to find omitted from a history of his era.

Example

16   Still, Schlesinger and Handlin offered us a refreshing revisionism, paving the way for the study of common people rather than princes and presidents. They inspired the next generation of historians to examine groups such as the artisan laborers of Philadelphia and the Irish immigrants of Boston. "Once I thought to write a history of the immigrants in America," Handlin confided in his introduction to *The Uprooted.* "I discovered that the immigrants *were* American history." This door, once opened, led to the flowering of a more inclusive scholarship as we began to recognize that ethnic history was American history. Suddenly, there was a proliferation of seminal works such as Irving Howe's *World of Our Fathers: The Journey of the East European Jews to America,* Dee Brown's *Bury My Heart at Wounded Knee: An Indian History of the American West,* Albert Camarillo's *Chicanos in a Changing Society,* Lawrence Levine's *Black Culture and Black Consciousness,* Yuji Ichioka's *The Issei: The World of the First Generation Japanese Immigrants,* and Kerby Miller's *Emigrants and Exiles: Ireland and the Irish Exodus to North America.*

Scholarship

17   But even this new scholarship, while it has given us a more expanded understanding of the mosaic called America, does not address our needs in the post–Rodney King era. These books and others like them fragment American society, studying each group separately, in isolation from the other groups and the whole. While scrutinizing our specific pieces, we have to step back in order to see the rich and complex portrait they compose. What is needed is a fresh angle, a study of the American past from a comparative perspective. . . .

18   African Americans have been the central minority throughout our country's history. They were initially brought here on a slave ship in 1619. Actually, these first twenty Africans might not have been slaves; rather, like most of the white laborers, they were probably indentured servants. The transformation of Africans into slaves is the story of the "hidden" origins of slavery. How and when was it decided to institute a system of bonded black labor? What happened, while freighted with racial significance, was actually conditioned by class conflicts within white society. Once established, the "peculiar institution" would have consequences for centuries to come. During the nineteenth century, the political storm over slavery almost destroyed the nation. Since the Civil War and emancipation, race has continued to be largely defined in relation to African Americans—segregation, civil rights, the underclass, and affirmative action. Constituting the largest minority group in our society, they have been at the cutting edge of the Civil Rights Movement. Indeed, their struggle has been a constant reminder of America's moral vision as a country committed to the principle of liberty. Martin Luther King clearly understood this truth when he wrote from a jail cell: "We will reach the goal of freedom in Birmingham and all over the nation, because the goal of America is freedom. Abused and scorned though we may be, our destiny is tied up with America's destiny."

19   Asian Americans have been here for over one hundred and fifty years, before many European immigrant groups. But as "strangers" coming from a "different shore," they have been stereotyped as "heathen," exotic, and unassimilable. Seeking "Gold Mountain," the Chinese arrived first, and what happened to them influenced the reception of the Japanese, Koreans, Filipinos, and Asian Indians as well as the Southeast Asian refugees like the Vietnamese and the Hmong. The 1882 Chinese Exclusion Act was the first law that prohibited the entry of immigrants on the basis of nationality. The Chinese condemned this restriction as racist and tyrannical. "They call us 'Chink,'" complained a Chinese immigrant, cursing the "white demons." "They think we no good! America cuts us off. No more come now, too bad!" This precedent later provided a basis for the restriction of European immigrant groups such as Italians, Russians, Poles, and Greeks. The Japanese painfully discovered that their accomplishments in America did not lead to acceptance, for during World War II, unlike Italian Americans and German Americans, they were placed in internment camps. Two-thirds of them were citizens by birth. "How could I as a 6-month-old child born in this country," asked Congressman Robert Matsui years later, "be declared by my own Government to be an enemy alien?" Today, Asian Americans represent the fastest-growing ethnic group. They have also become the focus of much mass media attention as "the Model Minority" not only for blacks and Chicanos, but also for whites on welfare and even middle-class whites experiencing economic difficulties.

20   Chicanos represent the largest group among the Hispanic population, which is projected to outnumber African Americans. They have been in the United States for a long time, initially incorporated by the war against Mexico. The treaty had moved the border between the two countries, and the people of "occupied" Mexico suddenly found themselves "foreigners" in their "native

land." As historian Albert Camarillo pointed out, the Chicano past is an integral part of America's westward expansion, also known as "manifest destiny." But while the early Chicanos were a colonized people, most of them today have immigrant roots. Many began the trek to El Norte in the early twentieth century. "As I had heard a lot about the United States," Jesus Garza recalled, "it was my dream to come here." "We came to know families from Chihuahua, Sonora, Jalisco, and Durango," stated Ernesto Galarza. "Like ourselves, our Mexican neighbors had come this far moving step by step, working and waiting, as if they were feeling their way up a ladder." Nevertheless, the Chicano experience has been unique, for most of them have lived close to their homeland—a proximity that has helped reinforce their language, identity, and culture. This migration to El Norte has continued to the present. Los Angeles has more people of Mexican origin than any other city in the world, except Mexico City. A mostly mestizo people of Indian as well as African and Spanish ancestries, Chicanos currently represent the largest minority group in the Southwest, where they have been visibly transforming culture and society.

21   The Irish came here in greater numbers than most immigrant groups. Their history has been tied to America's past from the very beginning. Ireland represented the earliest English frontier: the conquest of Ireland occurred before the colonization of America, and the Irish were the first group that the English called "savages." In this context, the Irish past foreshadowed the Indian future. During the nineteenth century, the Irish, like the Chinese, were victims of British colonialism. While the Chinese fled from the ravages of the Opium Wars, the Irish were pushed from their homeland by "English tyranny." Here they become construction workers and factory operatives as well as the "maids" of America. Representing a Catholic group seeking to settle in a fiercely Protestant society, the Irish immigrants were targets of American nativist hostility. They were also what historian Lawrence J. McCaffrey called "the pioneers of the American urban ghetto," "previewing" experiences that would later be shared by the Italians, Poles, and other groups from southern and eastern Europe. Furthermore, they offer contrast to the immigrants from Asia. The Irish came about the same time as the Chinese, but they had a distinct advantage: the Naturalization Law of 1790 had reserved citizenship for "whites" only. Their compatible complexion allowed them to assimilate by blending into American society. In making their journey successfully into the mainstream, however, these immigrants from Erin pursued an Irish "ethnic" strategy: they promoted "Irish" solidarity in order to gain political power and also to dominate the skilled blue-collar occupations, often at the expense of the Chinese and blacks.

22   Fleeing pogroms and religious persecution in Russia, the Jews were driven from what John Cuddihy described as the "Middle Ages into the Anglo-American world of the *goyim* 'beyond the pale.'" To them, America represented the Promised Land. This vision led Jews to struggle not only for themselves but also for other oppressed groups, especially blacks. After the 1917 East St. Louis race riot, the Yiddish *Forward* of New York compared this anti-black violence to a 1903 pogrom in Russia: "Kishinev and St. Louis—the same soil, the same peo-

ple." Jews cheered when Jackie Robinson broke into the Brooklyn Dodgers in 1947. "He was adopted as the surrogate hero by many of us growing up at the time," recalled Jack Greenberg of the NAACP Legal Defense Fund. "He was the way we saw ourselves triumphing against the forces of bigotry and ignorance." Jews stood shoulder to shoulder with blacks in the Civil Rights Movement: two-thirds of the white volunteers who went south during the 1964 Freedom Summer were Jewish. Today Jews are considered a highly successful "ethnic" group. How did they make such great socioeconomic strides? This question is often re-framed by neoconservative intellectuals like Irving Kristol and Nathan Glazer to read: if Jewish immigrants were able to lift themselves from poverty into the mainstream through self-help and education without welfare and affirmative action, why can't blacks? But what this thinking overlooks is the unique history of Jewish immigrants, especially the initial advantages of many of them as liter-ate and skilled. Moreover, it minimizes the virulence of racial prejudice rooted in American slavery.

23   Indians represent a critical contrast, for theirs was not an immigrant experi-ence. The Wampanoags were on the shore as the first English strangers arrived in what would be called "New England." The encounters between Indians and whites not only shaped the course of race relations, but also influenced the very culture and identity of the general society. The architect of Indian removal, Pres-ident Andrew Jackson told Congress: "Our conduct toward these people is deeply interesting to the national character." Frederick Jackson Turner understood the meaning of this observation when he identified the frontier as our transforming crucible. At first, the European newcomers had to wear Indian moccasins and shout the war cry. "Little by little," as they subdued the wilderness, the pioneers became "a new product" that was "American." But Indians have had a different view of this entire process. "The white man," Luther Standing Bear of the Sioux explained, "does not understand the Indian for the reason that he does not un-derstand America." Continuing to be "troubled with primitive fears," he has "in his consciousness the perils of this frontier continent. . . . The man from Europe is still a foreigner and an alien. And he still hates the man who questioned his path across the continent." Indians questioned what Jackson and Turner trum-peted as "progress." For them, the frontier had a diffferent "significance": their history was how the West was lost. But their story has also been one of resistance. As Vine Deloria declared, "Custer died for your sins."

24   By looking at these groups from a multicultural perspective, we can com-paratively analyze their experiences in order to develop an understanding of their differences and similarities. Race, we will see, has been a social construc-tion that has historically set apart racial minorities from European immigrant groups. Contrary to the notions of scholars like Nathan Glazer and Thomas Sowell, race in America has not been the same as ethnicity. A broad compara-tive focus also allows us to see how the varied experiences of different racial and ethnic groups occurred within shared contexts.

25   During the nineteenth century, for example, the Market Revolution em-ployed Irish immigrant laborers in New England factories as it expanded

cotton fields worked by enslaved blacks across Indian lands toward Mexico. Like blacks, the Irish newcomers were stereotyped as "savages," ruled by passions rather than "civilized" virtues such as self-control and hard work. The Irish saw themselves as the "slaves" of British oppressors, and during a visit to Ireland in the 1840s, Frederick Douglass found that the "wailing notes" of the Irish ballads reminded him of the "wild notes" of slave songs. The United States annexation of California, while incorporating Mexicans, led to trade with Asia and the migration of "strangers" from Pacific shores. In 1870, Chinese immigrant laborers were transported to Massachusetts as scabs to break an Irish immigrant strike; in response, the Irish recognized the need for interethnic working-class solidarity and tried to organize a Chinese lodge of the Knights of St. Crispin. After the Civil War, Mississippi plants recruited Chinese immigrants to discipline the newly freed blacks. During the debate over an immigration exclusion bill in 1882, a senator asked: If Indians could be located on reservations, why not the Chinese?

26   Other instances of our connectedness abound. In 1903, Mexican and Japanese farm laborers went on strike together in California: their union officers had names like Yamaguchi and Lizarras, and strike meetings were conducted in Japanese and Spanish. The Mexican strikers declared that they were standing in solidarity with their "Japanese brothers" because the two groups had toiled together in the fields and were now fighting together for a fair wage. Speaking in impassioned Yiddish during the 1909 "uprising of twenty thousand" strikers in New York, the charismatic Clara Lemlich compared the abuse of Jewish female garment workers to the experience of blacks: "[The bosses] yell at the girls and 'call them down' even worse than I imagine the Negro slaves were in the South." During the 1920s, elite universities like Harvard worried about the increasing numbers of Jewish students, and new admissions criteria were instituted to curb their enrollment. Jewish students were scorned for their studiousness and criticized for their "clannishness." Recently, Asian-American students have been the targets of similar complaints: they have been called "nerds" and told there are "too many" of them on campus.

27   Indians were already here, while blacks were forcibly transported to America, and Mexicans were initially enclosed by America's expanding border. The other groups came here as immigrants: for them, America represented liminality—a new world where they could pursue extravagant urges and do things they had thought beyond their capabilities. Like the land itself, they found themselves "betwixt and between all fixed points of classification." No longer fastened as fiercely to their old countries, they felt a stirring to become new people in a society still being defined and formed.

28   These immigrants made bold and dangerous crossings, pushed by political events and economic hardships in their homelands and pulled by America's demand for labor as well as by their own dreams for a better life. "By all means let me go to America," a young man in Japan begged his parents. He had calculated that in one year as a laborer here he could save almost a thousand yen—an amount equal to the income of a governor in Japan. "My dear Father," wrote

an immigrant Irish girl living in New York, "Any man or woman without a family are fools that would not venture and come to this plentyful Country where no man or woman ever hungered." In the shtetls of Russia, the cry "To America!" roared like "wild-fire." "America was in everybody's mouth," a Jewish immigrant recalled. "Businessmen talked [about] it over their accounts; the market women made up their quarrels that they might discuss it from stall to stall; people who had relatives in the famous land went around reading their letters." Similarly, for Mexican immigrants crossing the border in the early twentieth century, El Norte became the stuff of overblown hopes. "If only you could see how nice the United States is," they said, "that is why the Mexicans are crazy about it."

29   The sight of America's ethnic diversity can be discerned across the continent—Ellis Island, Angel Island, Chinatown, Harlem, South Boston, the Lower East Side, places with Spanish names like Los Angeles and San Antonio or Indian names like Massachusetts and Iowa. Much of what is familiar in America's cultural landscape actually has ethnic origins. The Bing cherry was developed by an early Chinese immigrant named Ah Bing. American Indians were cultivating corn, tomatoes, and tobacco long before the arrival of Columbus. The term *okay* was derived from the Choctaw word *oke,* meaning "it is so." There is evidence indicating that the name *Yankee* came from Indian terms for the English—from *eankke* in Cherokee and *Yankwis* in Delaware. Jazz and blues as well as rock and roll have African-American origins. The "Forty-Niners" of the Gold Rush learned mining techniques from the Mexicans; American cowboys acquired herding skills from Mexican *vaqueros* and adopted their range terms—such as *lariat* from *la reata, lasso* from *lazo,* and *stampede* from *estampida.* Songs like "God Bless America," "Easter Parade," and "White Christmas" were written by a Russian-Jewish immigrant named Israel Baline, more popularly known as Irving Berlin.

30   Furthermore, many diverse ethnic groups have contributed to the building of the American economy, forming what Walt Whitman saluted as "a vast, surging, hopeful army of workers." They worked in the South's cotton fields, New England's textile mills, Hawaii's canefields, New York's garment factories, California's orchards, Washington's salmon canneries, and Arizona's copper mines. They built the railroad, the great symbol of America's industrial triumph. Laying railroad ties, black laborers sang:

> *Down the railrod, um-huh*
> *Well, raise the iron, um-huh*
> *Raise the iron, um-huh.*

Irish railroad workers shouted as they stretched an iron ribbon across the continent:

> *Then drill, my Paddies, drill—*
> *Drill, my heroes, drill,*
> *Drill all day, no sugar in your tay*
> *Workin' on the U.P. railway.*

Japanese laborers in the Northwest chorused as their bodies fought the fickle weather:

> *A railroad worker—*
> *That's me!*
> *I am great.*
> *Yes, I am a railroad worker.*
> *Complaining:*
> *"It is too hot!"*
> *"It is too cold!"*
> *"It rains too often!"*
> *"It snows too much!"*
> *They all ran off.*
> *I alone remained.*
> *I am a railroaxd worker!*

Chicano workers in the Southwest joined in as they swore at the punishing work:

> *Some unloaded rails*
> *Others unloaded ties,*
> *And others of my companions*
> *Threw out thousands of curses.*

31   Moreover, our diversity was tied to America's most serious crisis: the Civil War was fought over a racial issue—slavery. In his "First Inaugural Address," presented on March 4, 1861, President Abraham Lincoln declared: "One section of the country believes slavery is *right* and ought to be extended, while the other believes it is *wrong* and ought not to be extended." Southern secession, he argued would be anarchy. Lincoln sternly warned the South that he had a solemn oath to defend and preserve the Union. Americans were one people, he explained, bound together by "the mystic chords of memory, stretching from every battlefield and patriot grave to every living heart and hearthstone all over this broad land." The struggle and sacrifices of the War for Independence had enabled Americans to create a new nation out of thirteen separate colonies. But Lincoln's appeal for unity fell on deaf ears in the South. And the war came. Two and a half years later, at Gettysburg, President Lincoln declared that "brave men" had fought and "consecrated" the ground of this battlefield in order to preserve the Union. Among the brave were black men. Shortly after this bloody battle, Lincoln acknowledged the military contributions of blacks. "There will be some black men," he wrote in a letter to an old friend, James C. Conkling, "who can remember that with silent tongue, and clenched teeth, and steady eye, and well-poised bayonet, they have helped mankind on to this great consummation. . . . " Indeed, 186,000 blacks served in the Union Army, and one-third of them were listed

as missing or dead. Black men in blue, Frederick Douglass pointed out, were "on the battlefield mingling their blood with that of white men in one common effort to save the country." Now the mystic chords of memory stretched across the new battlefields of the Civil War, and black soldiers were buried in "patriot graves." They, too, had given their lives to ensure that the "government of the people, by the people, for the people shall not perish from the earth."

32   Like these black soldiers, the people in our study have been actors in history, not merely victims of discrimination and exploitation. They are entitled to be viewed as subjects—as men and women with minds, wills, and voices.

> *In the telling and retelling*
> *of their stories,*
> *They create communities*
> *of memory.*

They also re-vision history. "It is very natural that the history written by the victim," said a Mexican in 1874, "does not altogether chime with the story of the victor." Sometimes they are hesitant to speak, thinking they are only "little people." "I don't know why anybody wants to hear my history," an Irish maid said apologetically in 1900. "Nothing ever happened to me worth the tellin'."

33   But their stories are worthy. Through their stories, the people who have lived America's history can help all of us, including my taxi driver, understand that Americans originated from many shores, and that all of us are entitled to a dignity. "I hope this survey do a lot of good for Chinese people," an immigrant told an interviewer from Stanford University in the 1920s. "Make American people realize that Chinese people are humans. I think very few American people really know anything about Chinese." But the remembering is also for the sake of the children. "This story is dedicated to the descendants of Lazar and Goldie Glauberman," Jewish immigrant Minnie Miller wrote in her autobiography. "My history is bound up in their history and the generations that follow should know where they came from to know better who they are." Similarly, Tomo Shoji, an elderly Nisei woman, urged Asian Americans to learn more about their roots: "We got such good, fantastic stories to tell. All our stories are different." Seeking to know how they fit into America, many young people have become listeners; they are eager to learn about the hardships and humiliations experienced by their parents and grandparents. They want to hear their stories, unwilling to remain ignorant or ashamed of their identity and past.

34   The telling of stories liberates. By writing about the people on Mango Street, Sandra Cisneros explained, "the ghost does not ache so much." The place no longer holds her with "both arms. She sets me free." Indeed, stories may not be as innocent or simple as they seem to be. Native-American novelist Leslie Marmon Silko cautioned:

I will tell you something about stories . . .
They aren't just entertainment.
Don't be fooled.

Indeed, the accounts given by the people in this study vibrantly re-create moments, capturing the complexities of human emotions and thoughts. They also provide the authenticity of experience. After she escaped from slavery, Harriet Jacobs wrote in her autobiography: "[My purpose] is not to tell you what I have heard but what I have seen—and what I have suffered." In their sharing of memory, the people in this study offer us an opportunity to see ourselves reflected in a mirror called history.

35   In his recent study of Spain and the New World, *The Buried Mirror,* Carlos Fuentes points out that mirrors have been found in the tombs of ancient Mexico, placed there to guide the dead through the underworld. He also tells us about the legend of Quetzalcoatl, the Plumed Serpent: when this god was given a mirror by the Toltec deity Tezcatlipoca, he saw a man's face in the mirror and realized his own humanity. For us, the "mirror" of history can guide the living and also help us recognize who we have been and hence are. In *A Distant Mirror,* Barbara W. Tuchman finds "phenomenal parallels" between the "calamitous 14th century" of European society and our own era. We can, she observes, have "greater fellow-feeling for a distraught age" as we painfully recognize the "similar disarray," "collapsing assumptions," and "unusual discomfort."

36   But what is needed in our own perplexing times is not so much a "distant" mirror, as one that is "different." While the study of the past can provide collective self-knowledge, it often reflects the scholar's particular perspective or view of the world. What happens when historians leave out many of America's peoples? What happens, to borrow the words of Adrienne Rich, "when someone with the authority of a teacher" describes our society, and "you are not in it"? Such an experience can be disorienting—"a moment of psychic disequilibrium, as if you looked into a mirror and saw nothing."

37   Through their narratives about their lives and circumstances, the people of America's diverse groups are able to see themselves and each other in our common past. They celebrate what Ishmael Reed has described as a society "unique" in the world because "the world is here"—a place "where the cultures of the world crisscross." Much of America's past, they point out, has been riddled with racism. At the same time, these people offer hope, affirming the struggle for equality as a central theme in our country's history. At its conception, our nation was dedicated to the proposition of equality. What has given concreteness to this powerful national principle has been our coming together in the creation of a new society. "Stuck here" together, workers of different backgrounds have attempted to get along with each other.

People harvesting
Work together unaware
Of racial problems,

wrote a Japanese immigrant describing a lesson learned by Mexican and Asian farm laborers in California.

38   Finally, how do we see our prospects for "working out" America's racial crisis? Do we see it as through a glass darkly? Do the televised images of racial hatred and violence that riveted us in 1992 during the days of rage in Los Angeles frame a future of divisive race relations—what Arthur Schlesinger, Jr., has fearfully denounced as the "disuniting of America"? Or will Americans of diverse races and ethnicities be able to connect themselves to a larger narrative? Whatever happens, we can be certain that much of our society's future will be influenced by which "mirror" we choose to see ourselves. America does not belong to one race or one group, the people in this study remind us, and Americans have been constantly redefining their national identity from the moment of first contact on the Virginia shore. By sharing their stories, they invite us to see ourselves in a different mirror.

FOR ANALYSIS AND DISCUSSION

1. How does Takaki's story at the beginning of the essay prepare his audience for the argument to come? Is it an effective introduction? What does the story tell us about the author, his background, and his perspective?
2. What is America's "racial crisis"? What are the signs of this crisis and how do they compare to other racially motivated incidents in the past? Do you agree with Takaki's assertion that America is facing a racial crisis?
3. How does Takaki address the individual arguments made by Bloom and Hirsch? Does his argument seem balanced and fair? Explain.
4. How are certain ethnic groups labeled as continuously foreign? Why do they retain this social identifier? Why are some groups resisted while others are not? Explain.
5. How are races pitted against each other? Review Takaki's analysis of this situation when framing your response.
6. Takaki comments that Arthur Schlesinger, Jr.'s history book *The Age of Jackson* did not include blacks or Native Americans. Does this influence your opinion of Schlesinger's article earlier in the chapter? Explain.

Diversity and Its Discontents
Arturo Madrid

In this essay Arturo Madrid considers the ways people of many ethnic or racial backgrounds have been prevented from assimilating into mainstream U.S. society. Barred from sharing in the American experience, they have been denied both voice and recognition by many of America's powerful institutions.

Arturo Madrid is the Murchison Distinguished Professor of the Humanities at Trinity University, Texas, and a holder of the National Medal of the Humanities (1996). He was the founding president of The Tomas Rivera Center, a national institute for policy studies on Latino issues. The following essay was originally a speech he delivered to the American Association of Higher Education and was later published in *Academe.*

BEFORE YOU READ

What does diversity mean to you? In what ways do issues of diversity touch your daily life?

AS YOU READ

Evaluate the ways Madrid uses the words "exotic" and "other." What meanings do the words have in this context?

1   My name is Arturo Madrid. I am a citizen of the United States, as are my parents and as were my grandparents, and my great-grandparents. My ancestors' presence in what is now the United States antedates Plymouth Rock, even without taking into account any American Indian heritage I might have.

2   I do not, however, fit those mental sets that define America and Americans. My physical appearance, my speech patterns, my name, my profession (a professor of Spanish) create a text that confuses the reader. My normal experience is to be asked, "And where are *you* from?" My response depends on my mood. Passive-aggressive, I answer, "From here." Aggressive-passive, I ask, "Do you mean where am I originally from?" But ultimately my answer to these follow-up questions that ask about origins will be that we have always been from here.

3   Overcoming my resentment I will try to educate, knowing that nine times out of ten my words fall on inattentive ears. I have spent most of my adult life explaining who I am not. I am exotic, but—as Richard Rodriguez of *Hunger of Memory* fame so painfully found out—not exotic enough ... not Peruvian, or Pakistani, or Persian, or whatever. I am, however, very clearly the *other,* if only your everyday, garden-variety, domestic *other.* I will share with you another phenomenon that I have been a part of, that of being a missing person, and how I came late to that awareness. But I've always known that I was the *other,* even before I knew the vocabulary or understood the significance of otherness.

4   I grew up in an isolated and historically marginal part of the United States, a small mountain village in the state of New Mexico, the eldest child of parents native to that region and whose ancestors had always lived there. In those vast and empty spaces, people who look like me, speak as I do, and have names like mine predominate. But the *americanos* lived among us: the descendants of those nineteenth-century immigrants who dispossessed us of our lands; missionaries who came to convert us and stayed to live among us; artists who became enchanted with our land and humanscape and went native; refugees from unhealthy climes, crowded spaces, unpleasant circumstances; and, of course, the inhabitants of Los Alamos, whose socio-cultural distance from us was moreover accentuated by the fact that they occupied a space removed from and proscribed to us. More importantly, however, they—*los americanos*—were

omnipresent (and almost exclusively so) in newspapers, newsmagazines, books, on radio, in movies and, ultimately, on television.

5   Despite the operating myth of the day, school did not erase my otherness. It did try to deny it, and in doing so only accentuated it. To this day, schooling is more socialization than education, but when I was in elementary school—and given where I was—socialization was everything. School was where one became an American. Because there was a pervasive and systematic denial by the society that surrounded us that we were Americans. That denial was both explicit and implicit. My earliest memory of the former was that there two kinds of churches: theirs and ours. The more usual was the implicit denial, our absence from the larger cultural, economic, political and social spaces—the one that reminded us constantly that we were *the other*. And school was where we felt it most acutely.

6   Quite beyond saluting the flag and pledging allegiance to it (a very intense and meaningful action, given that the U.S. was involved in a war and our brothers, cousins, uncles, and fathers were on the front lines) becoming American was learning English and its corollary—not speaking Spanish. Until very recently ours was a proscribed language—either *de jure* (by rule, by policy, by law) or *de facto* (by practice, implicitly if not explicitly; through social and political and economic pressure). I do not argue that learning English was appropriate. On the contrary. Like it or not, and we had no basis to make any judgments on that matter, we were Americans by virtue of having been born Americans, and English was the common language of Americans. And there was a myth, a pervasive myth, that said that if we only learned to speak English well—and particularly without an accent—we would be welcomed into the American fellowship.

7   Sam Hayakawa and the official English movement folks notwithstanding, the true text was not our speech, but rather our names and our appearance, for we would always have an accent, however perfect our pronunciation, however excellent our enunciation, however divine our diction. That accent would be heard in our pigmentation, our physiognomy, our names. We were, in short, the *other*.

8   Being the *other* involves a contradictory phenomenon. On the one hand being the *other* frequently means being invisible. Ralph Ellison wrote eloquently about that experience in his magisterial novel *The Invisible Man*. On the other hand, being the *other* sometimes involves sticking out like a sore thumb. What is she/he doing here?

9   For some of us being the *other* is only annoying, for others it is debilitating; for still others it is damning. Many try to flee otherness by taking on protective colorations that provide invisibility, whether of dress or speech or manner or name. Only a fortunate few succeed. For the majority, otherness is permanently sealed by physical appearance. For the rest, otherness is betrayed by ways of being, speaking or of doing.

10   The first half of my life downplayed the significance and consequences of otherness. The second half has seen me wrestling to understand its complex and deeply ingrained realities; striving to fathom why otherness denies us a

voice or visibility or validity in American society and its institutions; struggling to make otherness familiar, reasonable, even normal to my fellow Americans.

11   I spoke earlier of another phenomenon that I am a part of: that of being a missing person. Growing up in northern New Mexico I had only a slight sense of our being missing persons. *Hispanos,* as we called (and call) ourselves in New Mexico, were very much a part of the fabric of the society, and there were *hispano* professionals everywhere about me: doctors, lawyers, school teachers, and administrators. My people owned businesses, ran organizations and were both appointed and elected public officials.

12   My awareness of our absence from the larger institutional life of society became sharper when I went off to college, but even then it was attenuated by the circumstances of history and geography. The demography of Albuquerque still strongly reflected its historical and cultural origins, despite the influx of Midwesterners and Easterners. Moreover, many of my classmates at the University of New Mexico in Albuquerque were Hispanos, and even some of my professors were. I thought that would obtain at UCLA, where I began graduate studies in 1960. Los Angeles already had a very large Mexican population, and that population was visible even in and around Westwood and on the campus. Many of the grounds-keepers and food-service personnel at UCLA were Mexican. But Mexican-American students were few and mostly invisible, and I do not recall seeing or knowing a single Mexican-American (or, for that matter, black, Asian, or American Indian) professional on the staff or faculty of that institution during the five years I was there. Needless to say, persons like me were not present in any capacity at Dartmouth College, the site of my first teaching appointment, and, of course were not even part of the institutional or individual mindset. I knew then that we—a we that had come to encompass American Indians, Asian-Americans, black Americans, Puerto Ricans, and women—were truly missing persons in American institutional life.

13   Over the past three decades, the *de jure* and *de facto* types of segregation that have historically characterized American institutions have been under assault. As a consequence, minorities and women have become part of American institutional life, and although there are still many areas where we are not to be found, the missing persons phenomenon is not as pervasive as it once was. However, the presence of the *other,* particularly minorities, in institutions and in institutional life, is, as we say in Spanish, a *flor de tierra* we are spare plants whose roots do not go deep, a surface phenomenon, vulnerable to inclemencies of an economic, political, or social nature.

14   Our entrance into and our status in institutional life is not unlike a scenario set forth by my grandmother's pastor when she informed him that she and her family were leaving their mountain village to relocate in the Rio Grande Valley. When he asked her to promise that she would remain true to the faith and continue to involve herself in the life of the church, she assured him that she would and asked him why he thought she would do otherwise. "Doña Trinida," he told her, "in the Valley there is no Spanish church. There is only an American church." "But," she protested, "I read and speak English and

would be able to worship there." The pastor responded, "It is possible that they will not admit you, and even if they do, they might not accept you. And that is why I want you to promise me that you are going to go to church. Because if they don't let you in through the front door, I want you to go in through the back door. And if you can't get in through the back door, go in the side door. And if you are unable to enter through the side door I want you to go in through the window. What is important is that you enter and that you stay."

15   Some of us entered institutional life through the front door; others through the back door; and still others through side doors. Many, if not most of us, came in through windows and continue to come in through windows. Of those who entered through the front door, some never made it past the lobby; others were ushered into corners and niches. Those who entered through back and side doors inevitably have remained in back and side rooms. And those who entered through windows found enclosures built around them. For, despite the lip service given to the goal of the integration of minorities into institutional life, what has frequently occurred instead is ghettoization, marginalization, isolation.

16   Not only have the entry points been limited, but in addition, the dynamics have been singularly conflictive. Gaining entry and its corollary, gaining space, have frequently come as a consequence of demands made on institutions and institutional officers. Rather than entering institutions more or less passively, minorities have of necessity entered them actively, even aggressively. Rather than waiting to receive, they have demanded. Institutional relations have thus been adversarial, infused with specific and generalized tensions.

17   The nature of the entrance and the nature of the space occupied have greatly influenced the view and attitudes of the majority population within those institutions. All of us are put into the same box; that is, no matter what the individual reality, the assessment of the individual is inevitably conditioned by a perception that is held of the class. Whatever our history, whatever our record, whatever our validations, whatever our accomplishments, by and large we are perceived unidimensionally and dealt with accordingly. I remember an experience I had in this regard, atypical only in its explicitness. A few years ago I allowed myself to be persuaded to seek the presidency of a well-known state university. I was invited for an interview and presented myself before the selection committee, which included members of the board of trustees. The opening question of the brief but memorable interview was directed at me by a member of that august body. "Dr. Madrid," he asked, "why does a one-dimensional person like you think he can be the president of a multi-dimensional institution like ours?"

18   Over the past four decades America's demography has undergone significant changes. Since 1965 the principal demographic growth we have experienced in the United States has been of peoples whose national origins are non-European. This population growth has occurred both through birth and through immigration. A few years ago discussion of the national birthrate had a scare dimension: the high—"inordinately high"—birthrate of the Hispanic population. The popular discourse was informed by words such as "breeding."

Several years later, as a consequence of careful tracking by government agencies, we now know that what has happened is that the birthrate of the majority population has decreased. When viewed historically and comparatively, the minority populations (for the most part) have also had a decline in birthrate, but not one as great as that of the majority.

19   There are additional demographic changes that should give us something to think about. African-Americans are now to be found in significant numbers in every major urban center in the nation. Hispanic-Americans now number over 15 million people, and although they are a regionally concentrated (and highly urbanized) population, there is a Hispanic community in almost every major urban center of the United States. American Indians, heretofore a small and rural population, are increasingly more numerous and urban. The Asian-American population, which has historically consisted of small and concentrated communities of Chinese-, Filipino-, and Japanese-Americans, has doubled over the past decade, its complexion changed by the addition of Cambodians, Koreans, Hmongs, Vietnamese, et al.

20   Prior to the Immigration Act of 1965, 69 percent of immigration was from Europe. By far the largest number of immigrants to the United States since 1965 have been from the Americas and from Asia: 34 percent are from Asia; another 34 percent are from Central and South America; 16 percent are from Europe; 10 percent are from the Caribbean; the remaining 6 percent are from other continents and Canada. As was the case with previous immigration waves, the current one consists principally of young people: 60 percent are between the ages of 16 and 44. Thus, for the next few decades, we will continue to see a growth in the percentage of non-European-origin Americans as compared to European-Americans.

21   To sum up, we now live in one of the most demographically diverse nations in the world, and one that is increasingly more so.

22   During the same period social and economic change seems to have accelerated. Who would have imagined at mid-century that the prototypical middle-class family (working husband, wife as homemaker, two children) would for all intents and purposes disappear? Who could have anticipated the rise in teenage pregnancies, children in poverty, drug use? Who among us understood the implications of an aging population?

23   We live in an age of continuous and intense change, a world in which what held true yesterday does not today, and certainly will not tomorrow. What change does, moreover, is bring about even more change. The only constant we have at this point in our national development is change. And change is threatening. The older we get the more likely we are to be anxious about change, and the greater our desire to maintain the status quo.

24   Evident in our public life is a fear of change, whether economic or moral. Some who fear change are responsive to the call of economic protectionism, others to the message of moral protectionism. Parenthetically, I have referred to the movement to require more of students without in turn giving them more as academic protectionism. And the pronouncements of E. D. Hirsch and Allan

Bloom are, I believe, informed by intellectual protectionism. Much more serious, however, is the dark side of the populism which underlies this evergoing protectionism—the resentment of the *other*. An excellent and fascinating example of that aspect of populism is the cry for linguistic protectionism—for making English the official language of the United States. And who among us is unaware of the tensions that underlie immigration reform, of the underside of the demographic protectionism?

25 A matter of increasing concern is whether this new protectionism, and the mistrust of the *other* which accompanies it, is not making more significant inroads than we have supposed in higher education. Specifically, I wish to discuss the question of whether a goal (quality) and a reality (demographic diversity) have been erroneously placed in conflict, and, if so, what problems this perception of conflict might present.

26 As part of my scholarship I turn to dictionaries for both origins and meanings of words. Quality, according to the *Oxford English Dictionary,* has multiple meanings. One set defines quality as being an essential character, a distinctive and inherent feature. A second describes it as a degree of excellence, of conformity to standards, as superiority in kind. A third makes reference to social status, particularly to persons of high social status. A fourth talks about quality as being a special or distinguishing attribute, as being a desirable trait. Quality is highly desirable in both principle and practice. We all aspire to it in our own person, in our experiences, in our acquisitions and products, and of course we all want to be associated with people and operations of quality.

27 But let us move away from the various dictionary meanings of the word and to our own sense of what it represents and of how we feel about it. First of all we consider quality to be finite; that is, it is limited with respect to quantity; it has very few manifestations; it is not widely distributed. I have it and you have it, but they don't. We associate quality with homogeneity, with uniformity, with standardization, with order, regularity, neatness. All too often we equate it with smoothness, glibness, slickness, elegance. Certainly it is always expensive. We tend to identify it with those who lead, with the rich and famous. And, when you come right down to it, it's inherent. Either you've got it or you ain't.

28 Diversity, from the Latin *divertere,* meaning to turn aside, to go different ways, to differ, is the condition of being different or having differences, is an instance of being different. Its companion word, diverse, means differing, unlike, distinct; having or capable of having various forms; composed of unlike or distinct elements. Diversity is lack of standardization, of regularity, of orderliness, homogeneity, conformity, uniformity. Diversity introduces complications, is difficult to organize, is troublesome to manage, is problematical. Diversity is irregular, disorderly, uneven, rough. The way we use the word diversity gives us away. Something is too diverse, is extremely diverse. We want a little diversity.

29 When we talk about diversity, we are talking about the *other,* whatever that other might be: someone of a different gender, race, class, national origin; somebody at a greater or lesser distance from the norm: someone outside the

set; someone who possesses a different set of characteristics, features, or attributes; someone who does not fall within the taxonomies we use daily and with which we are comfortable; someone who does not fit into the mental configurations that give our lives order and meaning.

30   In short, diversity is desirable only in principle, not in practice. Long live diversity . . . as long as it conforms to my standards, my mind set, my view of life, my sense of order. We desire, we like, we admire diversity, not unlike the way the French (and others) appreciate women; that is, *Vive la difference!*—as long as it stays in its place.

31   What I find paradoxical about and lacking in this debate is that diversity is the natural order of things. Evolution produces diversity. Margaret Visser, writing about food in her latest book, *Much Depends on Dinner,* makes an eloquent statement in this regard:

> Machines like, demand, and produce uniformity. But nature loathes it: her strength lies in multiplicity and in differences. Sameness in biology means fewer possibilities and therefore weakness.

32   The United States, by its very nature, by its very development, is the essence of diversity. It is diverse in its geography, population, institutions, technology; its social cultural, and intellectual modes. It is a society that at its best does not consider quality to be monolithic in form or finite in quantity, or to be inherent in class. Quality in our society proceeds in large measure out of the stimulus of diverse modes of thinking and acting; out of the creativity made possible by the different ways in which we approach things; out of diversion from paths or modes hallowed by tradition.

33   One of the principal strengths of our society is its ability to address, on a continuing and substantive basis, the real economic, political, and social problems that have faced and continue to face us. What makes the United States so attractive to immigrants is the protections and opportunities it offers; what keeps our society together is tolerance for cultural, religious social, political, and even linguistic difference; what makes us a unique, dynamic, and extraordinary nation is the power and creativity of our diversity.

34   The true history of the United States is one of struggle against intolerance, against oppression, against xenophobia, against those forces that have prohibited persons from participating in the larger life of the society on the basis of their race, their gender, their religion, their national origin, their linguistic and cultural background. These phenomena are not consigned to the past. They remain with us and frequently take on virulent dimensions.

35   If you believe, as I do, that the well-being of a society is directly related to the degree and extent to which all of its citizens participate in its institutions, then you will have to agree that we have a challenge before us. In view of the extraordinary changes that are taking place in our society we need to take up the struggle again, irritating, grating, troublesome, unfashionable, unpleasant as it is. As educated and educator members of this society we have a special responsibility for ensuring that all American institutions, not just our elementary and

secondary schools, our juvenile halls, or our jails, reflect the diversity of our society. Not to do so is to risk greater alienation on the part of a growing segment of our society; is to risk increased social tension in an already conflictive world; and, ultimately, is to risk the survival of a range of institutions that, for all their defects and deficiencies, provide us the opportunity and the freedom to improve our individual and collective lot.

36   Let me urge you to reflect on these two words—quality and diversity—and on the mental sets and behaviors that flow out of them. And let me urge you further to struggle against the notion that quality is finite in quantity, limited in its manifestations, or is restricted by considerations of class, gender, race, or national origin; or that quality manifests itself only in leaders and not in followers, in managers and not in workers, in breeders and not in drones; or that it has to be associated with verbal agility or elegance of personal style; or that it cannot be seeded, nurtured, or developed.

37   Because diversity—the *other*—is among us, will define and determine our lives in ways that we still do not fully appreciate, whether that other is women (no longer bound by tradition, house, and family); or Asians, African-Americans, Indians, and Hispanics (no longer invisible, regional, or marginal); or our newest immigrants (no longer distant, exotic, alien). Given the changing profile of America, will we come to terms with diversity in our personal and professional lives? Will we begin to recognize the diverse forms that quality can take? If so, we will thus initiate the process of making quality limitless in its manifestations, infinite in quantity, unrestricted with respect to its origins, and more importantly, virulently contagious.

38   I hope we will. And that we will further join together to expand—not to close—the circle.

FOR ANALYSIS AND DISCUSSION

1. What does Madrid mean when he says he was not "exotic enough" (paragraph 3)? Why does he identify himself as "other"?

2. Analyze Madrid's comment in paragraph 6 that "there was a myth, a pervasive myth, that said that if we only learned to speak English well—and particularly without an accent—we would be welcomed into the American fellowship." What do you think were the origins of this myth? Who created it? Why was it just a myth after all?

3. What is "intellectual protectionism" (paragraph 24)? How, according to Madrid, does it apply to universities? What impact does it have on students of all races and backgrounds?

4. In paragraph 14 Madrid relates the tale of his grandmother as she prepared to move to an area that did not have a Spanish church. Who is the "they" mentioned in the story? Why might this story be particularly disturbing?

5. Examine Madrid's exploration of the word "quality." Do you agree with his conclusions? Explain.

6. What does "diversity" mean to Madrid? To what extent do you agree or disagree with Madrid's argument concerning diversity?

WRITING ASSIGNMENTS: UNITY AND DIVERSITY

1. Universities embraced multiculturalism first. More recently, however, multiculturalism has experienced a backlash, at both the academic and the public levels. Investigate this issue and evaluate its causes. You may wish to interview faculty and students for their personal perspectives, as well as access the following Web resource maintained by the University of California, Berkeley, to help in your research: <http://ralph.berkeley.edu/postwar/multiculti.html>.

2. Access the Salon RoundTable discussion "Hanging Separately" at <http://salon1999.com/12nov1995/feature/race.html> regarding race relations between whites and blacks. Read the various commentaries about establishing a dialogue between races by well-known cultural critics including Shelby Steele and Stanley Crouch. Evaluate their answers to the questions "How can whites and blacks begin to talk? What should they talk about?" Then formulate your own responses, both to the questions presented by Salon and to the individual critics themselves.

3. Many of the essays in this section refer to the concept of a "mainstream" society. Write an essay in which you identify and describe "mainstream" society. Who is part of it, and how do they belong to it? Or, if you wish, you may argue that such an entity does not exist.

BILINGUAL EDUCATION: DOES IT ALIENATE OR ASSIMILATE?

Loco, Completamente Loco
Glenn Garvin

While always controversial, bilingual education is facing renewed scrutiny. Some Hispanic parents fear that their children are not adequately prepared to succeed in a primarily English-speaking United States. Other critics complain that bilingual education has become a "business," neglecting the needs of students as it pads school budgets and supports useless jobs. The next essay supports this view, claiming that Hispanic children are forced to speak Spanish at the expense of learning English.

Glenn Garvin is a reporter for the *Miami Herald* and author of *Everybody Had His Own Gringo: The CIA and the Contras* (1992). The following essay appeared in *Reason* magazine in January of 1998.

BEFORE YOU READ

You may not be aware that the United States does not have an official language. Do you think it should, and if so, should it be English?

AS YOU READ

What do you know about bilingual education? What do you think "bilingual education" means? Is your definition changed by the information presented in Garvin's article?

1   Rosa Torres had been dreading this call. Her daughter Angelica's first-grade teacher wanted to come over and talk. The teacher didn't say what she wanted to discuss, but Rosa knew. There had been a program on television, and the unfamiliar English words had rung in her head like a fire alarm: learning disorder. Surely that was what little Angelica had.

2   Every afternoon when she came home from school, Rosa asked the same question: What did you do in school today?

3   And every day Angelica gave the same answer: Nothing. She seemed bored, listless, maybe even—though Rosa didn't see how it was possible for a 6-year-old—depressed.

4   Rosa wondered how a child developed a learning disorder. Certainly there had been no sign of it a couple of years before, when Angelica started preschool at the YMCA. Rosa had been so worried, sending her little girl off without a word of English to spend a day among the American children. But everything had worked out just fine. Angelica rolled through there like a snowball, picking up more and more English every day. Soon she spoke it much better than Rosa, and after a while she spoke it much better than Spanish.

5   Of course, that wasn't surprising. After all, Angelica was an American, born just a few miles down the freeway from their home in Redwood City, a scruffy working-class town 30 miles south of San Francisco. It was her parents Rosa and Carlos who were the immigrants. They left Cuzco, the ancient Inca city in central Peru, with plans to study in America, learn English, get college degrees, live the good life.

6   Like most immigrants, they found out it wouldn't be all so easy as that—American landlords and shopkeepers wanted to be paid in cash, not dreams. Classes gave way to jobs, the kind you get when you can't speak English. Carlos was baking pizzas for a little more than minimum wage, Rosa babysitting for a little less. She spent her days with the children massaging the little bit of English she'd picked up in a couple of community college classes; the 3- and 4-year-olds were patient professors, never complaining about her fractured sentences, content to point at the big, white thing in the kitchen and repeat the word refrigerator a hundred times if that was what it took Rosa to get it. For adult company, she watched television while they napped, puzzling over Oprah's vocabulary as much as her ethos, smiling in secret delight whenever she got one of Regis and Kathie Lee's jokes.

7   The life, if not exactly the one she'd dreamed, wasn't a bad one. No one was sick, no one went to bed hungry. There was a roof over their heads. Little by little, they were adjusting to America. But now there was this trouble with

Angelica. Apprehensively, Rosa waited, tried to steel herself to hearing the words learning disorder not from a disembodied voice on TV but from the teacher's lips; not affixed to some unfortunate, not-quite-real children from another part of the planet, but to her own daughter, right here, right now.

8   The teacher turned out to be a Japanese lady (well, American, really; Rosa had to keep reminding herself how it worked here) with a manner that was at once kindly and intense. "I think you need to go talk to the principal at the school about Angelica," she said after they settled in.

9   "What about her?" asked Rosa, stomach churning, knowing the answer, dreading it.

10   "I think you need to get her into an English-speaking classroom," the teacher replied. "She understands English perfectly. And she doesn't like taking lessons in Spanish. I think it's really holding her back. It's damaging her."

11   "What do you mean, Spanish?" Rosa asked, silently cursing Oprah and Kathie Lee, who had obviously failed her, because this teacher wasn't making any sense.

12   "Spanish, that's what we're teaching her in," the teacher said. "Didn't anyone tell you? She's in a bilingual education program.

13   "Just go tell the principal she speaks English, and you want her out."

14   When the teacher left, Rosa still found it hard to believe the whole conversation hadn't been some horrendous translation glitch. The teacher had explained that Angelica, because she was Hispanic, had been swept into a class full of immigrant children from Mexico and El Salvador who spoke little or no English. OK, Rosa could understand how that might have happened. But why were the children being taught Spanish instead of English? How were they ever going to learn English if the school didn't teach it to them?

15   Nonetheless, a conversation with Angelica confirmed it. All day long, her teacher spoke Spanish. The books were in Spanish. Even the posters on the classroom wall were in Spanish. Only for a few minutes in the afternoon did the language switch to English. "And then we just learn some baby words like bread or paper," Angelica complained. Summoning the most malevolent curse in her 6-year-old vocabulary, she cried: "It's dumb!" Finally Rosa understood her daughter's moody shuffling of the past few months.

16   The solution, unfortunately, was not as simple as the teacher promised. When Rosa went in to see the school administrators a few days later, her request to transfer Angelica into an English-speaking class met with withering disapproval. "That's not in your daughter's best interests," one of the school officials said. They flashed incomprehensible charts around, used a lot of language Rosa did not understand, but the message came through loud and clear: We know better, we're the teachers.

17   Rosa was doubtful. The idea that kids would learn English by being taught in Spanish all day seemed, well, kind of nuts, especially for Angelica, whose best language was English. But . . . but . . . who was she to question them? An immigrant babysitter lady who spent her days in pathetic conversations with 4-year-

olds about who was smarter, Big Bird or the Cookie Monster? When Rosa left the office, her daughter was still enrolled in the Spanish class.

18   Each morning for the next two years, she watched Angelica mope off to a school that bored her nearly to tears. Each afternoon, when she checked the girl's homework, it was in Spanish. Rosa began to wonder why the program was called "bilingual." The principal had promised Rosa that the amount of English in the lessons would increase, but there was no sign of that happening.

19   And it never did. It wasn't until the family moved 20 miles south to Cupertino, a Silicon Valley suburb on the edge of San Jose, that Angelica got any English education. Then she had to have a lot of it. "Your daughter isn't reading anywhere near a third-grade level," the teacher told Rosa. "And she's behind in math and science, too." But Cupertino (fortunately, as far as Rosa was concerned) had no bilingual program. So Angelica stayed in the class, though all year she had to take special afterschool English lessons with newly arrived Chinese immigrant children.

20   This is what bilingual education did for my daughter, Rosa thought bitterly. It stole two years out of her life.

21   It was a hard fight, but Angelica won them back. Nobody in the house likes to recall that ugly year she spent in the third grade, but when it was over, she had caught up to the other kids. And as the years passed, her mother and father started catching up, too, to those immigrant dreams that, for a time, had faded into the distance. They became U.S. citizens. Carlos went to school, got a job as a graphic designer. Rosa stopped babysitting and started cleaning houses, which paid better. Her English blossomed. She began taking accounting courses at a community college. Two more babies arrived: Nathan and Joshua.

22   Nathan entered school without incident. But in 1996, when Joshua was ready for the first grade, school administrators called Rosa. They were starting this new bilingual program, and. . . .

23   As they talked, Rosa flashed back to that conversation nine years before, when a shy, frightened babysitter with a Peruvian passport let a bunch of school administrators overrule her common sense. She recalled the price her daughter paid. And she said: "No way."

24   Rosa Torres isn't alone. Bilingual education was born 30 years ago from a good-hearted but vague impulse by Congress to help Spanish speakers learn English. Instead, it has become a multi-billion-dollar hog trough that feeds arrogant education bureaucrats and militant Hispanic separatists. And now poor immigrant parents increasingly see it as the wall around a linguistic ghetto from which their children must escape if they want to be anything more than maids or dishwashers. Like Rosa Torres, they are starting to say no way:

25   • At 9th Street Elementary School in Los Angeles, located on the edge of the city's garment district, parents held about 90 children out of class for two weeks to force the school to start teaching English. "The only time they spoke English at the school was during lunch and recess," said Luisa

Hernandez, a sweatshop worker from Mexico whose 9-year-old daughter Yanira attends the school. "I want my daughter to learn English. All the exams for things like lawyers and doctors are in English. Without English, she would have to take a job like mine."

26   ● One hundred fifty Hispanic families in Brooklyn's Bushwick neighborhood sued the state of New York to force the release of their children from a bilingual program. Ada Jimenez, one of the plaintiffs, said her grandson spoke only English when he entered the Bushwick school system. "We were told that because my grandson has a Spanish last name, he should remain in bilingual classes," she said. Result: He flunked kingergarten. "He is now in seventh grade and cannot read in either English or Spanish," Jimenez said in an affidavit for the lawsuit.

27   ● Denver is considering a change that would limit students to three years in its bilingual program instead of the six that many of them have been staying. Leading the charge is school board member Rita Montero, who originally championed bilingual education—until her own son was enrolled. "The kids were doing work way below the regular grade level," she said. "I was furious." She yanked him from the program and enrolled him in another school across town: "I had to think, what is more important to me? To keep my child in a program where perhaps he'll learn some Spanish and that'll make me happy? Or do I want my child to be able to come out of public education with the ability to compete for scholarships, to be able to go to the college of his choice?"

28   ● An October 1997 poll by the *Los Angeles Times* showed that California voters favored a proposed ballot measure to limit bilingual education by an astonishing 4–1 margin. The support was greatest among Hispanics: 84 percent. "Wake up call for los Maestros . . . If you are into Bilingual Ed. your days are numbered," the bilingual paper *San Diego La Prensa* warned teachers. "We, los Chicanos, are responsible for putting you in . . . and you betrayed us. Bilingual Ed. has been turned into a full employment program for your own agenda that has nothing to with our kids . . . that's why 84 percent of la gente en Los Angeles voted against you . . . YOU BLEW THE PROGRAM."

29   ● In Los Lunas, New Mexico, high school students walked out to protest the lack of English tutoring. In Dearborn, Michigan, the school board junked a proposal for $5 million in federal money to begin a bilingual program after parents complained. In Princeton, New Jersey, immigrant parents raised so much hell about rules that made it difficult to get their children out of bilingual programs that the state legislature stepped in to change them.

30   Though usually poorly organized and often relatively powerless—they often aren't U.S. citizens and sometimes aren't even legal residents—the parents are starting to make themselves heard. Michigan has adopted reforms in its bilingual programs. Bethlehem, Pennsylvania, did away with its bilingual program altogether. So did Orange County and three smaller school districts in

California. In November, when Orange County voters were asked what they thought of the change, a crushing 86 percent approved. . . .

31   But the bilingual forces won't yield without a fight, certainly not to mere parents. When those buttinsky parents in Princeton were demanding the right to put their kids in English-speaking classrooms, Joseph Ramos, the co-chairman of the New Jersey Bilingual Council, advised the school board to tell them to mind their own business. "Why would we require parents unfamiliar with our educational system to make such monumental decisions," he asked, "when we as bilingual educators . . . are trained to make those decisions?" We know better, we're the teachers.

32   Some years ago, a newspaper sent me to interview S. I. Hayakawa, by then a retired senator from California. Hayakawa was legendarily combative: Asked once during a campaign stop what he thought about a local referendum on legalizing greyhound tracks, he snapped: "I'm running for the U.S. Senate. I don't give a goddamn about dog racing." When I spoke with him, he had recently lashed out at bilingual education. It seemed paradoxical, to say the very least: Hayakawa was a native of Canada whose parents were born in Japan; he grew up speaking Japanese. He had authored a widely used book on linguistics. "Senator," I began the interview, "why are you against people learning to speak two languages?" He looked at me as though I were daft. "Who said anything about that?" he demanded. "Only an idiot would be against speaking two languages. I'm against bilingual education."

33   That's still the biggest misconception among people who've never had a personal brush with bilingual education. It is not a program where two sets of children learn one another's language at the same time. That's called dual, or two-way, immersion. Only a few well-heeled school districts can afford to offer it, always as an elective, and the only complaint about it is that there usually aren't enough slots to go around. Another thing bilingual education is not is a program conducted mostly in English, where the teacher occasionally translates a particularly difficult concept, or offers extra language help to children with limited English skills. Known variously as English as a Second Language, sheltered English, or structured English immersion, these are all wrinkles in a technique that educators call immersion, because the students are expected to wade into English quickly.

34   As Hayakawa explained to me that day, when educators use the term bilingual education, it's shorthand for "transitional bilingual education," which is the other major technique for teaching languages. TBE, as it is often called, was originally structured around the idea that students would take the main curriculum in their native language while they learned English, so that they wouldn't fall behind in other subjects. But over the past two decades or so, most school districts have reshaped their TBE programs to reflect the ideas of the so-called "facilitation" theorists of language education. The facilitation theorists believe that children cannot effectively learn a second language until they are fully literate in the first one, a process that can take four to seven years.

(A new study from TBE advocates at the University of California at Riverside ups the ante to 10 years.)

35   During that time, a TBE student is supposed to be taught almost entirely in his native language, by a teacher fluent in that language, using books and films and tapes in that language. Gradually increasing bits of English are worked into the mix. At some point—bingo!—the child hits his "threshold" in the first language. Now he's ready to suck up English like a human vacuum cleaner.

36   The idea that a kid will learn English by being taught in Spanish does not usually strike people outside the education field as very plausible—"loco, completamente loco" was the reaction of Luisa Hernandez when the principal at 9th Street Elementary in Los Angeles explained it to her—but the theory is so inculcated in many teachers that they rarely question it. When they do, it can be a shattering experience. Rosalie Pedalino Porter, director of the Research in English Acquisition and Development Institute, taught Spanish bilingual classes in kindergarten and elementary school for five years in Springfield, Massachusetts. As a 6-year-old kid right off the boat from Sicily, Porter had done just fine without TBE, but education school had filled her with missionary zeal for the theory. She vividly remembers the day that she began to wonder if the bilingual god had failed.

37   It was a lesson in colors. "Juan, que color es este?" Porter asked one little boy, waving a box in her hand.

38   "Green," he replied.

39   "Verde," she corrected with the Spanish word.

40   "Green," Juan repeated.

41   "Verde," Porter corrected him again.

42   "Green," Juan answered again.

43   What in the hell am I doing? Porter wondered to herself. Why am I telling him not to speak English? Pretty soon, once her classroom door was closed, Porter was giving lessons in English. "I wasn't the only one, either," she says.

FOR ANALYSIS AND DISCUSSION

1. Evaluate Garvin's opening story about Rosa Torres and her daughter Angelica. Is it an effective opening? Is it credible?

2. Consider Garvin's list of "facts" detailing the atrocities of bilingual education. How effective is this list in supporting his argument? Analyze each fact in the list.

3. Garvin implies that bilingual education can not only hinder the academic performances of Hispanic elementary school age children, it also can actually force them to take on lower-paying jobs later in life. Do you agree?

4. Evaluate the tone Garvin uses in this essay. What effect does tone have on the audience's acceptance of his argument?

5. In paragraph 31 Garvin paraphrases the words of the cochairman of the New Jersey Bilingual Council, Joseph Ramos, regarding the role of parents in bilingual education. Is this a fair representation of Ramos? Explain.

6. What have you learned about bilingual education from reading this essay? Could you now present a balanced explanation of bilingual education to someone who had never heard of it?

Bilingualism: Outdated and Unrealistic
Richard Rodriguez

Does bilingual education really work? This essay reviews the origins and good intentions of bilingual education, and then explains why it is an outdated idea whose time has passed. Richard Rodriguez, a Mexican-American who struggled himself as a Spanish-speaking child in an English-speaking classroom, asserts bilingual education is "weighted at the bottom with Hispanic political grievances and with middle-class romanticism."

Richard Rodriguez is a contributing editor at the Pacific News Service. He is also the author of several books including *Days of Obligation* (1993) and *Hunger Of Memory* (1983), which details his journey as a "minority student" who pays the cost of social assimilation and academic success with a painful separation from his cultural past. The following essay appeared in November of 1985 in the *New York Times*.

BEFORE YOU READ

Assess the motivation behind the creation of bilingual programs. What social and political forces are involved in bilingual education?

AS YOU READ

What reasons does Rodriguez cite for the persistence of bilingual education, even though many studies indicate it isn't working? If it isn't consistently helping Hispanic children, why do so many such programs continue?

1 How shall we teach the dark-eyed child *ingles*? The debate continues much as it did two decades ago.

2 Bilingual education belongs to the 1960's, the years of the black civil rights movement. Bilingual education became the official Hispanic demand; as a symbol, the English-only classroom was intended to be analogous to the segregated lunch counter; the locked school door. Bilingual education was endorsed by judges and, of course, by politicians well before anyone knew the answer to the question: Does bilingual education work? Who knows? *Quien sabe?* The official drone over bilingual education is conducted by educationists with numbers and charts. Because bilingual education was never simply a matter of pedagogy, it is too much to expect educators to resolve the matter. Proclamations

concerning bilingual education are weighted at bottom with Hispanic political grievances and, too, with middle-class romanticism.

3   No one will say it in public; in private, Hispanics argue with me about bilingual education and every time it comes down to memory. Everyone remembers going to that grammar school where students were slapped for speaking Spanish. Childhood memory is offered as parable; the memory is meant to compress the gringo's long history of offenses against Spanish, Hispanic culture, Hispanics.

4   It is no coincidence that, although all of America's ethnic groups are implicated in the policy of bilingual education, Hispanics, particularly Mexican-Americans, have been its chief advocates. The English words used by Hispanics in support of bilingual education are words such as "dignity," "heritage," "culture." Bilingualism becomes a way of exacting from gringos a grudging admission of contrition—for the 19th-century theft of the Southwest, the relegation of Spanish to a foreign tongue, the injustice of history. At the extreme, Hispanic bilingual enthusiasts demand that public schools "maintain" a student's sense of separateness.

5   Hispanics may be among the last groups of Americans who still believe in the 1960's. Bilingual-education proposals still serve the romance of that decade, especially of the late 60's, when the heroic black civil rights movement grew paradoxically wedded to its opposite—the ethnic-revival movement. Integration and separatism merged into twin, possible goals.

6   With integration, the black movement inspired middle-class Americans to imitations—the Hispanic movement; the Gray Panthers; feminism; gay rights. Then there was withdrawal, with black glamour leading a romantic retreat from the anonymous crowd.

7   Americans came to want it both ways. They wanted in and they wanted out. Hispanics took to celebrating their diversity, joined other Americans in dancing rings around the melting pot.

Mythic Metaphors

8   More intently than most, Hispanics wanted the romance of their dual cultural allegiance backed up by law. Bilingualism became proof that one could have it both ways, could be a full member of public America and yet also separate, privately Hispanic. "Spanish" and "English" became mythic metaphors, like country and city, describing separate islands of private and public life.

9   Ballots, billboards and, of course, classrooms in Spanish. For nearly two decades now, middle-class Hispanics have had it their way. They have foisted a neat ideological scheme on working-class children. What they want to believe about themselves, they wait for the child to prove: that it is possible to be two, that one can assume the public language (the public life) of America, even while remaining what one was, existentially separate.

10   Adulthood is not so neatly balanced. The tension between public and private life is intrinsic to adulthood—certainly middle-class adulthood. Usually the city wins because the city pays. We are mass people for more of the day than we

are with our intimates. No Congressional mandate or Supreme Court decision can diminish the loss.

11   I was talking the other day to a carpenter from Riga, in the Soviet Republic of Latvia. He has been here six years. He told me of his having to force himself to relinquish the "luxury" of reading books in Russian or Latvian so he could begin to read books in English. And the books he was able to read in English were not of a complexity to satisfy him. But he was not going back to Riga.

12   Beyond any question of pedagogy there is the simple fact that a language gets learned as it gets used. One fills one's mouth, one's mind, with the new names for things.

13   The civil rights movement of the 1960's taught Americans to deal with forms of discrimination other than economic—racial, sexual. We forget class. We talk about bilingual education as an ethnic issue; we forget to notice that the program mainly touches the lives of working-class immigrant children. Foreign-language acquisition is one thing for the upper-class child in a convent school learning in French to curtsy. Language acquisition can only seem a loss for the ghetto child, for the new language is psychologically awesome, being, as it is, the language of the bus driver and Papa's employer. The child's difficulty will turn out to be psychological more than linguistic because what he gives up are symbols of home.

Pain and Guilt

14 I was that child! I faced the stranger's English with pain and guilt and fear. Baptized to English in school, at first I felt myself drowning—the ugly sounds forced down my throat—until slowly, slowly (held in the tender grip of my teachers), suddenly the conviction took: English was my language to use.

15   What I yearn for is some candor from those who speak about bilingual education. Which of its supporters dares speak of the price a child pays—the price of adulthood—to make the journey from a working-class home into a middle-class schoolroom? The real story, the silent story of the immigrant child's journey is one of embarrassments in public; betrayal of all that is private; silence at home; and at school the hand tentatively raised.

16   Bilingual enthusiasts bespeak an easier world. They seek a linguistic solution to a social dilemma. They seem to want to believe that there is an easy way for the child to balance private and public, in order to believe that there is some easy way for themselves.

17   Ten years ago I started writing about the ideological implications of bilingual education. Ten years from now some newspaper may well invite me to contribute another Sunday supplement essay on the subject. The debate is going to continue. The bilingual establishment is now inside the door. Jobs are at stake. Politicians can only count heads; growing numbers of Hispanics will insure the compliance of politicians.

18   Publicly, we will continue the fiction. We will solemnly address this issue as

an educational question, a matter of pedagogy. But privately, Hispanics will still seek from bilingual education an admission from the gringo that Spanish has value and presence. Hispanics of middle class will continue to seek the romantic assurance of separateness. Experts will argue. Dark-eyed children will sit in the classroom. Mute.

FOR ANALYSIS AND DISCUSSION

1. Consider Rodriguez's claim that "bilingualism becomes a way of exacting from gringos a grudging admission of contrition" (paragraph 4). What does Rodriguez mean by this statement? Explain.
2. According to Rodriguez, what price are Hispanic children paying for the results of bilingual education?
3. Both Rodriguez and Garvin quote the opinions of non-Hispanic immigrants regarding bilingual education. Why do they mention the opinions of these people? How do these opinions support their respective arguments?
4. According to Rodriguez, why is bilingualism a class issue? Do you think Garvin would agree?
5. What is the "dirty little secret" about bilingual education that Hispanics won't talk about?
6. Evaluate Rodriguez's closing paragraph. Is this an effective ending to his argument? Explain.

Let's Not Say Adios to Bilingual Education
Lourdes Rovira

In June 1998 California voters passed Proposition 227, effectively terminating bilingual education in that state. Although supporters of bilingual education blamed politicians, educators, and the white power structure for the decision, opinion polls indicated that a significant number of Hispanics themselves had doubts about bilingual education. In this article, Lourdes Rovira argues that denying students the option of bilingual education isn't simply a poor educational decision, it is an outright injustice.

Lourdes Rovira is the executive director for bilingual education for the Miami-Dade County school system. The following article first appeared in *U.S. Catholic* magazine in November 1998.

BEFORE YOU READ

Do you think bilingual education should be a right? Should it be a legally protected option for all children of Hispanic descent?

AS YOU READ

Consider how Rovira presents the facts of her argument. What support does she provide to buttress her points?

1   A great travesty occurred in California on June 2, 1998. By passing Proposition 227, California's voters elected to terminate bilingual education in their state. It was a sad day for our country because we allowed ill-informed politicians and xenophobic voters to dictate educational policy.

2   The United States is a country of immigrants—immigrants who have come seeking freedom and the pursuit of the American dream. Throughout history, English has been the common language that has united these immigrants from all over the world. English is the language of this great country. None of us who support bilingual education question the validity or the importance of the English language, as some would like the public to believe. Quality bilingual programs emphasize the acquisition of English. English is taught to all immigrant students; it is required, and we aim to perfect it in the school setting.

3   Yet to learn English, students need not forget the language they bring to school with them—be it Spanish, Vietnamese, or Urdu. Bilingual education is not like an antibiotic that we give to children who are sick, their illness being lack of English. As soon as the children are well, that is, as soon as they know English, the antibiotic—bilingual education—is removed. Good bilingual programs are not remedial but enrichment programs.

4   One common misunderstanding is that bilingual education is the exclusive domain of immigrant students. No, studying a second language is a right that belongs to all students—recently arrived refugees, African Americans, and, yes, white Americans. Languages expand a child's cognitive development. Knowing more than one language is not an impediment to intellectual capacity. If it were, the rest of the world's children outside of the United States would be intellectually inferior to ours. After all, the majority of them are bilingual.

5   Years ago, being bilingual was a privilege reserved for those who could afford to send their children to private tutors or to a finishing school in Europe. It was a privilege reserved for those who traveled and went to the opera. In today's global economy, being bilingual can no longer remain a privilege reserved for the elite. Today, being bilingual is a right that must transcend all socioeconomic strata. Denying all students that right is not only a mistake, it is an injustice.

6   Students are enabled—not disabled—by being bilingual; they are empowered by knowing more than one language. The American experience is strengthened, not weakened, by citizens who can cross languages and cultures. The United States can no longer afford to remain a monolingual country in a multilingual world. Being bilingual and biliterate not only gives people a political and economic advantage, it also allows them to be bridges between people of different cultures. For immigrant students, being bilingual means having the best of two worlds—their home culture and language and our nation's culture and

English language. For native speakers of English, knowing a second language means opening up their horizons to the richness of cultural diversity and becoming active participants in—and not merely spectators of—today's global society. In no way does it require supplanting one language and culture with another.

7   This may come as a surprise to many, but bilingual education is not a recent phenomenon in this country. It history in the U.S. falls into two distinct periods: the first from 1840 to 1920 and the second beginning in the early 1960s.

8   In 1840 a form of bilingual education originated in Cincinnati with a state law designed to draw German children into the American schools. Several other similar initiatives, which provided instruction in Dutch, Italian, and Polish, among others, took place during the latter part of the 19th century and the beginning of the 20th. During World War I, strong anti-German sentiments increased, and by the end of the war bilingual programs were terminated and "Americanism" and English-only instruction were promoted. Some states went so far as to impose restrictions on the instruction of foreign languages.

9   Instruction in and through two languages disappeared in the U.S. from 1920 until 1963, when thousands of Cuban refugees poured into the Miami area, opening up a second phase of bilingual schooling in this country. In an effort to meet the needs of the Cuban refugee children, the Miami-Dade County Public Schools organized a dual-language instructional program at Coral Way Elementary with a student population evenly divided between Spanish speakers and English speakers. Both groups spent half of their day being instructed in English and the other half in Spanish, thus immersing themselves in two languages and cultures.

10   Since then, federal and state laws and court decisions have not only allowed but directed local school districts to create special programs to meet the academic needs of non-English-speaking students. But almost 30 years after the passing of the Bilingual Education Act, the debate over the benefits of bilingual education continues to be politically and emotionally charged. Also lingering after 30 years seems to be a dreadful ignorance over the definition of bilingual education and its goals and practices. Those who make for themselves a political agenda over the issue attack bilingual education as a failure based on a very limited knowledge of one specific bilingual-education model while ignoring others that have been extremely successful, not only in this country but throughout the world.

11   Critics of bilingual education who regard it as a dismal failure claim that children enrolled in bilingual programs do not learn English and that the research regarding the benefits of bilingual programs is contradictory and inconsistent. They assert that immersion programs are superior to bilingual programs and believe that after one year of English immersion, non-English-speaking students will be ready to be mainstreamed into regular, English-speaking classes.

12   Much of educational policy, whether it is bilingual education or reading, stems from pendulum swings from one extreme to another. Unfortunately, immersion programs have failed to prove a successful track record. To wipe out

bilingual programs in favor of a sink-or-swim curriculum is a simplistic political solution to a complex educational issue. Moreover, it hardly seems fair to blame bilingual education for all the ills of California's 1.4 million limited-English-proficient students when less than 30 percent of them are enrolled in bilingual programs.

13   Those of us who have dedicated our professional lives to the promotion of bilingual education can assert that properly organized and executed bilingual programs not only work, they work extremely well. This does not mean that some bilingual models cannot be improved. However, there is ample research that demonstrates without a doubt that good bilingual programs are success-ful—and none that could claim such success for one-year immersion programs.

14   The school district I work for, Miami-Dade County Public Schools, the fourth largest in the country, has been in the forefront of bilingual education since the establishment of Coral Way Elementary in 1963. Our programs are recognized nationally and internationally as programs that promote excellence in English and another language for all students who want to avail themselves of that opportunity.

15   Bilingual programs in our district provide instruction in English for Speak-ers of Other Languages (ESOL) to students with limited English proficiency as soon as they enroll in school. Students are provided instruction in their home language for approximately 20 percent of the instructional time, but the pri-mary goal is the rapid acquisition of English. At the same time, Miami-Dade County Public Schools embrace diversity and offer all our students the oppor-tunity to enroll in quality programs that promote literacy in a language other than English. We promote high standards for all of our students whether the instruction is in English, Spanish, Haitian-Creole, or French. . . .

It is unfortunate that California's Proposition 227 passed. It is revolting that bilingual education has been killed at the hands of people who do not un-derstand its virtues. It is offensive that bilingual education continues to be solely associated with immigration. And it is shameful that we have forgotten that when this nation was founded, English was not the exclusive language of the country.

FOR ANALYSIS AND DISCUSSION

1. Compare the information presented in Rovira's opening paragraph to some of the statistics presented in Glenn Garvin's article. Do you agree that the Propo-sition 227 vote was driven by xenophobic motives? Explain.

2. In paragraph 3, Rovira states that students should not forget their native languages whether "Spanish, Vietnamese, or Urdu." Do you think she is ad-vocating that bilingual programs be established for languages other than Spanish?

3. Evaluate Rovira's comparison of the right to learn other languages in school to the principles of bilingual education. How do you think Senator Hayakawa (in Garvin's article) would respond to that statement?

4. How would Richard Rodriguez respond to Rovira's statement that "today, being bilingual is a right that must transcend all socioeconomic strata" (paragraph 5)? Would he find this a realistic viewpoint?

5. According to Rovira, who "killed" bilingual education in California? Does she adequately support this accusation? Explain.

What's Wrong with Bilingual Education? Is It "Lingual," or Is It "Education"?
Raul Yzaguirre

Educators who support bilingual education often cite poor teaching as the problem, rather than a faulty curriculum. Detractors attack the entire concept, maintaining that the best way to learn English is to use it exclusively in the classroom. The following essay evaluates some of the issues surrounding bilingual education as it pertains to educators and school systems.

Raul Yzaguirre is the president of the Washington-based National Council of La Raza, the nation's largest Hispanic civil rights organization. A frequent commentator on Latin issues, he has appeared on news programs on all major networks and contributed to publications including the *Wall Street Journal,* the *New York Times,* and *Newsweek.* Education policy analyst Raul Gonzalez assisted in the preparation of this essay, which appeared in the August 5, 1998, edition of *Education Week.*

BEFORE YOU READ

How do issues concerning bilingual education apply to "white ethnics"? How is their language acquisition process different from that of Hispanics?

AS YOU READ

What distinctions does Yzaguirre make regarding the words "lingual" and "education" as they pertain to "bilingual education"?

1 If someone had only read news coverage of the Ron Unz initiative that passed resoundingly on June 2 of this year (the so-called "English for the Children" California ballot proposition which all but mandates the end of bilingual education), one would think that bilingual education was an educationally unsound concept doomed to failure. Yet just in the last few months, three well-regarded reports were released that give a resounding educationally based endorsement of bilingual education.

2 The first was "Preventing Reading Difficulties in Young Children" by the National Research Council, a respected organization with unassailable research

standards that is not given to unfounded pronouncements. In the section on literacy, the NRC's carefully worded finding on bilingual education states:

3   "Schools have the responsibility to accommodate the linguistic needs of students with limited proficiency in English. . . . These children should be taught how to read in their native language while acquiring proficiency in spoken English, and then subsequently taught to extend their skills to reading in English."

4   Another recently released NRC study, "Educating Language-Minority Children," conducted in conjunction with the National Institute of Medicine, found:

5   "Bilingualism, far from impeding the child's overall cognitive or linguistic development, leads to positive growth in these areas. Programs whose goals are to promote bilingualism should do so without fear of negative consequences. English-language learners who develop their native-language proficiency do not compromise their acquisition of English."

6   Even more dramatic was the report from Jay P. Greene of the University of Texas at Austin, who did a meta-analysis of all the research done on bilingual education. Mr. Greene is not an educator and therefore has neither a predetermined agenda nor any claims to expertise on the subject. He is, however, an expert in the field of ensuring statistical and methodological validity in research. Using rigorous standards, Mr. Greene found that the research evidence was overwhelmingly in favor of bilingual education as the best way to educate limited-English-proficient, or LEP, children.

7   These three reports, taken together, should end any question about the effectiveness and worth of bilingual education, both as an educational strategy and as the best way to make sure that proficiency in English is achieved. But anybody who believes that this will end the debate is either uninformed, naive, or both.

8   Although I have been an observer of and a participant in this debate for years, it took me a long time to understand why there is so much passion and so little rational discussion on this issue. What I realized is that while I and other proponents of bilingual education were talking about education, others were really talking about language policy.

9   And while education philosophy is hardly emotion-free, language policy and practice affects us in a very personal way. It gets at the core of the kind of society we want or are likely to have. And since the debate on bilingual education should now be over, let us then have a discussion on *language*.

10   The debate over language has at least three aspects to it: language as a problem, language as a right, and language as a resource and/or a reality. For many years, educators saw language—or rather any language other than English as the primary or only language spoken by children attending school—as a problem. I use the term "problem" rather than challenge deliberately. It was not simply a question of the practicality of adding English to whatever language the child brought to the class to assure a common means of communication. Rather, it was a question of instilling in immigrant children, so far as it can be done, the objective of "absolute forgetfulness of all obligations, or connections

with other countries because of descent or birth," as the superintendent of schools in New York City noted in 1918.

11   Therefore, any language other than English was neither positive nor benign. It was a "problem" to be washed away, and led to a process which obliterated that other language because it represented a threat to the nation, or at least, to those who did not understand that language. And if the child failed to keep up with his or her peers, so be it; there were always factory and field jobs that did not require literacy but only the ability to understand the verbal commands of their bosses. At a time when universal literacy was only a dream even for native-born Americans and when there were a plentiful number of union factory jobs that allowed a hard-working person with drive and determination the opportunity to work, buy a home, and send his and her kids to college, this might have made some sense. It was the process by which millions of what we now call "white ethnics" assimilated into this society, and the process became a source of pride to them.

12   For others, particularly Native Americans and Hispanics whose roots in this country predated the British, the trade-off was not perceived to be so equitable. To those who had not gone through the psychological experience of crossing an ocean and leaving family and other ties behind them for greater opportunities, the idea of having to give up something so personal and so defining as language and culture for a society that did not accept them even when they did speak English, the trade-off was fraudulent and demeaning. Thus, intellectuals, activists, and other leaders from these groups and others reacted by raising the issue of language rights.

13   There are many ethnic Americans who lament that their ancestors were put through this pressure cooker that passed for a melting pot and that deprived them of their heritage. More vocal and more prominent, however, are Americans, particularly some white ethnic Americans, who are incensed with the idea of language as a "right," particularly if the notion is that this right should be paid for by their taxes. How many times have we heard, "My grandfather came to America not knowing a word of English and nobody helped him," or, "We were taught to learn English and nothing but English was spoken in front of us." Even some Hispanics, who had been forced to give up some of their birth language and heritage, became the staunchest supporters of this notion. Indeed, "contrarians" like the commentators Richard Rodriguez and Linda Chavez have been given far more publicity and coverage than mainstream Latino leaders for embracing this "philosophy." Mr. Rodriguez once went so far as to argue that it is great for non-Latinos to learn and speak Spanish but not Hispanics.

14   It is precisely folks who equate bilingual education with an effort to preserve, or worse, demand the right to, their own language that are most rabidly against bilingual education. Language as a right, or more precisely a minority language as a right, conjures up images of a Quebec-style divisiveness and the possible Balkanization of the country.

15   That, of course, is precisely the issue—the tendency to draw analogies that are familiar to us, which in the case of language are overwhelmingly about problems, controversies, and feuds. Even if the analogy does not apply, too many of us believe that it does. After talking to dozens of Canadians familiar with the Quebec separatist movement, I have yet to find one who believes that Hispanics in the United States are remotely like French-speaking Quebecers. For one thing, the Francophone separatists and the hard-line Anglo opponents of French-language rights are both opposed to bilingual education. It is the "One Canada" leadership that promotes bilingualism in the name of unity. But how often do you hear about countries where people speak different languages and enjoy peace and prosperity, as is the case in Switzerland and other countries? Peace and comity do not make the evening news.

16   Which brings us to a third way of understanding language: language as a powerful national resource. During World War II, America profited enormously from U.S. citizens who spoke other languages well. German-Americans, Italian-Americans, and even Japanese-Americans from our own internment camps served our country honorably and gallantly and were an asset in helping American forces understand the Axis powers. Navajo Indians known as the "code talkers" were assigned to different units to facilitate communications without fear of the enemy breaking the code. In fact, it was the only code not deciphered by the Axis powers.

17   There exists an enormous contradiction in this country. On the one hand, the National Governors' Association unanimously agreed last year that the United States should make foreign-language acquisition a priority in our schools, given the fact that we are the industrialized world's most linguistically ignorant nation. On the other hand, as a recent *Washington Post* headline summed it up: "California Rejection a Big Blow to Bilingualism." I believe this contradiction exists because the debate over bilingualism has been about language policy and not about education.

18   Let me be clear: I believe learning English is a must for every American. If anyone doubts my word, I would ask them to visit any of the 100 or so National Council of La Raza affiliates that provide English-language training to tens of thousands of Latinos each year. But it is equally unconscionable to allow the debate over bilingual education to lead our country into wasting such a valuable natural resource as a population that already speaks a multitude of languages. It is also wrong not to use the best method available to teach LEP children English, which research shows is bilingual education.

FOR ANALYSIS AND DISCUSSION

1. Yzaguirre makes several references to three "well-regarded reports" on bilingual education. What are the findings of these reports? How does he use the information from the reports to support his argument?

2. What does Yzaguirre say is the difference between education policy and language policy as it applies to bilingual education? Do you agree?

3. In paragraph 10 Yzaguirre reviews language assimilation policies in New York City in 1918. What does this policy say about America's cultural perspective at the time? Have things changed much? Do you think such a pronouncement could be made today? Explain.

4. Who are "white ethnic" Americans? What do many white ethnics find disturbing about bilingual education as a policy in many schools?

5. As analyzed by Yzaguirre, how is the Canadian bilingual system different from the American system? Do you agree with his assessment of the differences?

6. Many of the essays in this section make comparisons between bilingual education and the teaching of foreign languages in schools to nonbilingual students. Are they in fact the same? Review each author's perspective on this issue and evaluate it.

WRITING ASSIGNMENTS: BILINGUAL EDUCATION

1. Access the following Web site refuting Glenn Garvin's article on bilingual education: <http://www.physics.ucla.edu/~urrutia/chicano/CommentsGarvin.html>. Evaluate the online article's strengths and weaknesses. Which author seems more credible and why? If these two individuals were debating, based on the information written in both articles, whose argument would you accept? Write a paper analyzing the two articles and their arguments.

2. *Education Week on the Web* is an online magazine addressing the issues facing education today and the pedagogical concerns of teachers. Its creators have compiled a balance fact sheet on bilingual education, including links to online articles that explore the issue: <http://www.edweek.org/context/topics/biling .htm>. Access their Web site and, based on your research, write an essay in which you support your position on bilingual education. Strengthen your argument with facts and information from the Web site.

3. Interview a number of people that had to learn English as a second language. How did they do it? What difficulties did they encounter? What assistance were they given as they learned English? Encourage your interviewees to share stories of success as well as failure. Then present the information you gather in an argument essay.

4. Deliberate about the issue of bilingual education by analyzing the perspectives represented in the readings as well as in your own research. Then write a proposal essay in which you suggest a solution that addresses the concerns of critics and supporters of bilingual education.

chapter 11

FREEDOM OF EXPRESSION

The U.S. citizen's right to freedom of expression is based on a short passage in the First Amendment to the Constitution: "Congress shall make no law . . . abridging the freedom of speech, or of the press." With these simple words the writers of the Constitution created one of the pillars of our democratic system of government—a guarantee designed to encourage the free exchange of ideas, beliefs, and political debate. Most Americans passionately support their right to express themselves without fear of government reprisal. However, over the years questions have arisen about whether limits should be imposed on our right to freely express ourselves when the exercise of that right imposes hardship on or causes harm to others. What happens when the right of one person to state his or her beliefs conflicts with the right of others to be free from verbal abuse? What happens when free expression runs counter to community values? At what point does the perceived degree of offensiveness warrant censorship? And at what point does censorship threaten to undermine our constitutional rights? In this chapter we look at three areas that have generated debate and dialogue in recent times: censorship of campus speech, censorship of the Internet, and censorship of books.

The free and open exchange of ideas is critical to achieving the goals of higher education. However, when the ideas expressed are racist, sexist, or otherwise offensive toward specific groups on a college campus, does the university have the right to censor and punish that form of speech? In "Regulating Racist Speech on Campus," Charles R. Lawrence III argues that victims of harassing speech are alienated from the college community and denied the right to an education. Lawrence believes that universities must act to prevent this from happening by restricting this form of speech. At the same time, Alan Charles Kors finds this practice of censorship objectionable. Citing numerous examples of university "speech codes" and "harassment policies," Kors regards these efforts to control speech as forms of intimidation intended "to silence or to chill freedom of opinion and expression." Garry Wills responds to the challenge of dealing with unwanted speech by calling for measures that fall between pained tolerance and outright suppression. He recommends censure, the free expression of moral disapproval.

The drafters of the Constitution could not have envisioned that the words granting Americans the right to free speech would apply to the technology of cyberspace. However, the rapid growth of the information superhighway has sparked considerable discussion about whether roadblocks should be imposed to control the content of this new medium. Cathleen A. Cleaver voices her concern about the presence of pornography on the Internet and its accessibility to children. She urges greater regulation by government and industry to safeguard the public interest. On the other hand, Julia Watkins finds that the public's concern with the availability of pornography on the Internet is the result of exaggerated claims by the media and politicians and carefully examines the sources of this misleading information in her essay. Constitutional scholar William Bennett Turner points out that no new laws or regulations are needed for the Internet. The interpretations of the First Amendment that protect and restrict our written and verbal discourse can easily apply to digital communications as well.

The censorship of books challenges the rights guaranteed by the First Amendment on two fronts: the right to express ideas freely and the right to have access to the ideas of others. In "The Freedom to Read," the American Library Association and the Association of American Publishers explore the effects of censorship attempts on Americans' freedom to read and affirms the importance of making all viewpoints available for public scrutiny, even when the ideas are unpopular and offensive. Steve McKinzie looks at the efforts to censor published material differently, however. He views attempts to ban or censor reading materials as examples of citizens taking advantage of *their own* right to free speech. It would be wrong, he argues, to label them enemies of democracy for exercising their constitutional rights. Finally, science fiction author Ray Bradbury presents a writer's perspective on the question of editing literary works to accommodate popular notions of political correctness.

CENSORSHIP ON CAMPUS: SHOULD THERE BE LIMITS TO FREE SPEECH?

Regulating Racist Speech on Campus
Charles R. Lawrence III

The past few years have witnessed a disturbing rise in racist and sexist language on college campuses. Some administrators have dealt with the problem by banning offensive language on the grounds that racial slurs are violent verbal assaults that interfere with students' right to an education. Others fear that placing sanctions on racist speech violates the First Amendment guarantee of free expression. In the following essay, law professor Charles R. Lawrence III argues for the restriction of free speech by citing the U.S. Supreme Court's 1954 landmark decision in *Brown v. Board of Education.*

Charles R. Lawrence III teaches law at Georgetown University. *We Won't Go Back: Making the Case for Affirmative Action,* which he coauthored with his wife and fellow Georgetown professor Mari J. Matsuda, was published in 1997. Lawrence is best known for his work in antidiscrimination law, equal protection, and critical race theory. He is also a past president of the Society of American Law Teachers.

BEFORE YOU READ

Does the saying "Sticks and stones may break my bones, but names will never hurt me" apply to racist speech? Have you ever witnessed or experienced a verbal assault based on race? When such incidents occur on college campuses, should they be ignored, or dealt with formally?

AS YOU READ

Notice how the author cites and interprets the landmark case of *Brown v. Board of Education* to argue his point. For more information, read the excerpt from this case in Chapter 17, page 685.

1   I have spent the better part of my life as a dissenter. As a high-school student, I was threatened with suspension for my refusal to participate in a civil-defense drill, and I have been a conspicuous consumer of my First Amendment liberties ever since. There are very strong reasons for protecting even racist speech. Perhaps the most important of these is that such protection reinforces our society's commitment to tolerance as a value, and that by protecting bad speech from government regulation, we will be forced to combat it as a community.

2   But I also have a deeply felt apprehension about the resurgence of racial violence and the corresponding rise in the incidence of verbal and symbolic assault and harassment to which blacks and other traditionally subjugated and excluded groups are subjected. I am troubled by the way the debate has been framed in response to the recent surge of racist incidents on college and university campuses and in response to some universities' attempts to regulate harassing speech. The problem has been framed as one in which the liberty of free speech is in conflict with the elimination of racism. I believe this has placed the bigot on the moral high ground and fanned the rising flames of racism.

3   Above all, I am troubled that we have not listened to the real victims, that we have shown so little understanding of their injury, and that we have abandoned those whose race, gender, or sexual preference continues to make them second-class citizens. It seems to me a very sad irony that the first instinct of civil libertarians has been to challenge even the smallest, most narrowly framed efforts by universities to provide black and other minority students with the protection the Constitution guarantees them.

4   The landmark case of *Brown v. Board of Education* is not a case that we normally think of as a case about speech. But *Brown* can be broadly read as articulating the principle of equal citizenship. *Brown* held that segregated schools were inherently unequal because of the *message* that segregation conveyed—that black children were an untouchable caste, unfit to go to school with white children. If

we understand the necessity of eliminating the system of signs and symbols that signify the inferiority of blacks, then we should hesitate before proclaiming that all racist speech that stops short of physical violence must be defended.

5   University officials who have formulated policies to respond to incidents of racial harassment have been characterized in the press as "thought police," but such policies generally do nothing more than impose sanctions against intentional face-to-face insults. When racist speech takes the form of face-to-face insults, catcalls, or other assaultive speech aimed at an individual or small groups of persons, it falls directly within the "fighting words" exception to First Amendment protection. The Supreme Court has held that words which "by their very utterance inflict injury or tend to incite an immediate breach of the peace" are not protected by the First Amendment.

6   If the purpose of the First Amendment is to foster the greatest amount of speech, racial insults disserve that purpose. Assaultive racist speech functions as a preemptive strike. The invective is experienced as a blow, not as a proffered idea, and once the blow is struck it is unlikely that a dialogue will follow. Racial insults are particularly undeserving of First Amendment protection because the perpetrator's intention is not to discover truth or initiate dialogue but to injure the victim. In most situations, members of minority groups realize that they are likely to lose if they respond to epithets by fighting and are forced to remain silent and submissive.

7   Courts have held that offensive speech may not be regulated in public forums such as streets where the listener may avoid the speech by moving on, but the regulation of otherwise protected speech has been permitted when the speech invades the privacy of the unwilling listener's home or when the unwilling listener cannot avoid the speech. Racist posters, fliers, and graffiti in dormitories, bathrooms, and other common living spaces would seem to clearly fall within the reasoning of these cases. Minority students should not be required to remain in their rooms in order to avoid racial assault. Minimally, they should find a safe haven in their dorms and in all other common rooms that are a part of their daily routine.

8   I would also argue that the university's responsibility for insuring that these students receive an equal educational opportunity provides a compelling justification for regulations that insure them safe passage in all common areas. A minority student should not have to risk becoming the target of racially assaulting speech every time he or she chooses to walk across campus. Regulating vilifying speech that cannot be anticipated or avoided would not preclude announced speeches and rallies—situations that would give minority-group members and their allies the chance to organize counter-demonstrations or avoid the speech altogether.

9   The most commonly advanced argument against the regulation of racist speech proceeds something like this: we recognize that minority groups suffer pain and injury as the result of racist speech, but we must allow this hate mongering for the benefit of society as a whole. Freedom of speech is the lifeblood of our democratic system. It is especially important for minorities because often

it is their only vehicle for rallying support for the redress of their grievances. It will be impossible to formulate a prohibition so precise that it will prevent the racist speech you want to suppress without catching in the same net all kinds of speech that it would be unconscionable for a democratic society to suppress.

10   Whenever we make such arguments, we are striking a balance on the one hand between our concern for the continued free flow of ideas and the democratic process dependent on that flow, and, on the other, our desire to further the cause of equality. There can be no meaningful discussion of how we should reconcile our commitment to equality and our commitment to free speech until it is acknowledged that there is real harm inflicted by racist speech and that this harm is far from trivial.

11   To engage in a debate about the First Amendment and racist speech without a full understanding of the nature and extent of that harm is to risk making the First Amendment an instrument of domination rather than a vehicle of liberation. We have not known the experience of victimization by racist, misogynist, and homophobic speech, nor do we equally share the burden of the societal harm it inflicts. We are often quick to say that we have heard the cry of the victims when we have not.

12   The *Brown* case is again instructive because it speaks directly to the psychic injury inflicted by racist speech by noting that the symbolic message of segregation affected "the hearts and minds" of Negro children "in a way unlikely ever to be undone." Racial epithets and harassment often cause deep emotional scarring and feelings of anxiety and fear that pervade every aspect of a victim's life.

13   *Brown* also recognized that black children did not have an equal opportunity to learn and participate in the school community if they bore the additional burden of being subjected to the humiliation and psychic assault contained in the message of segregation. University students bear an analogous burden when they are forced to live and work in an environment where at any moment they may be subjected to denigrating verbal harassment and assault. The same injury was addressed by the Supreme Court when it held that sexual harassment that creates a hostile or abusive work environment violates the ban on sex discrimination in employment of Title VII of the Civil Rights Act of 1964.

14   Carefully drafted university regulations would bar the use of words as assault weapons and leave unregulated even the most heinous of ideas when those ideas are presented at times and places and in manners that provide an opportunity for reasoned rebuttal or escape from immediate injury. The history of the development of the right to free speech has been one of carefully evaluating the importance of free expression and its effects on other important societal interests. We have drawn the line between protected and unprotected speech before without dire results. (Courts have, for example, exempted from the protection of the First Amendment obscene speech and speech that disseminates official secrets, that defames or libels another person, or that is used to form a conspiracy or monopoly.)

15   Blacks and other people of color are skeptical about the argument that even the most injurious speech must remain unregulated because, in an unregulated marketplace of ideas, the best ones will rise to the top and gain

acceptance. Our experience tells us quite the opposite. We have seen too many good liberal politicians shy away from the issues that might brand them as being too closely allied with us.

16   Whenever we decide that racist speech must be tolerated because of the importance of maintaining societal tolerance for all unpopular speech, we are asking blacks and other subordinated groups to bear the burden for the good of all. We must be careful that the ease with which we strike the balance against the regulation of racist speech is in no way influenced by the fact that the cost will be borne by others. We must be certain that those who will pay that price are fairly represented in our deliberations and that they are heard.

17   At the core of the argument that we should resist all government regulation of speech is the ideal that the best cure for bad speech is good, that ideas that affirm equality and the worth of all individuals will ultimately prevail. This is an empty ideal unless those of us who would fight racism are vigilant and unequivocal in that fight. We must look for ways to offer assistance and support to students whose speech and political participation are chilled in a climate of racial harassment.

18   Civil rights lawyers might consider suing on behalf of blacks whose right to an equal education is denied by a university's failure to insure a nondiscriminatory educational climate or conditions of employment. We must embark upon the development of a First Amendment jurisprudence grounded in the reality of our history and our contemporary experience. We must think hard about how best to launch legal attacks against the most indefensible forms of hate speech. Good lawyers can create exceptions and narrow interpretations that limit the harm of hate speech without opening the floodgates of censorship.

19   Everyone concerned with these issues must find ways to engage actively in actions that resist and counter the racist ideas that we would have the First Amendment protect. If we fail in this, the victims of hate speech must rightly assume that we are on the oppressors' side.

FOR ANALYSIS AND DISCUSSION

1. What reasons does Lawrence offer for protecting racist speech from government restrictions? Do you agree? How are university restrictions different from those imposed by the government?

2. Lawrence opens his essay stating that he has a long history as a "dissenter." What is his strategy in saying this? What assumptions does he make about his audience? What does his refusal to participate in a civil defense drill have to do with the essay's central issues?

3. According to the author, in the debate over racist language, how does the fight against racism conflict with the fight for free speech? What fundamental problem does Lawrence have with this conflict? Are his reasons convincing?

4. Have you ever been the victim of abusive speech—speech that victimized you because of your race, gender, religion, ethnicity, or sexual preference? Do you agree with Lawrence's argument regarding "psychic injury"? Explain.

5. How convincingly does Lawrence argue that racist speech should not be protected by the First Amendment? What is the logic of his argument? What evidence does he offer as support?

6. Select one of Lawrence's arguments that you think is especially strong or especially weak and explain why you think so.

The Betrayal of Liberty on America's Campuses
Alan Charles Kors

In this essay Alan Charles Kors argues that instituting sanctions on speech is a direct violation of students' right to free expression. Exactly where should the line be drawn as to what constitutes "hate speech"? The ambiguity of many university codes, says Kors, leads to sanctioning students for ridiculous and outrageous reasons. When students must consider every word they say, and even how they say it, they are prevented from engaging in honest intellectual inquiry, debate, and dialogue.

Alan Charles Kors is a professor of history at the University of Pennsylvania. The following essay was a feature of the Bradley Lecture Series of the American Enterprise Institute for Public Policy Research in October 1998.

BEFORE YOU READ

If a member of the Ku Klux Klan, Louis Farrakhan, David Duke, or a member of a neo-Nazi group were invited to speak at your school, what would your reaction be? Would you hope that school authorities would act to rescind the invitation, or would you accept the presence of one of these speakers on campus, maybe even attending the talk? What do you think would be the reaction of the campus as a whole?

AS YOU READ

Evaluate the examples of racist and offensive speech Kors uses to support his point that free speech must be protected. How do these examples buttress his argument? Do you think they are effective in convincing his audience?

1   Those things that threaten free and open debate and those things that threaten academic freedom are the direct enemy of liberty. Such threats exist most dangerously at universities not in curriculum and scholarship, but in the new university *in loco parentis* (the university standing in the place of parents), where our nation's colleges and universities, across the board, are teaching contempt for liberty and its components: freedom of expression and inquiry; individual rights and responsibilities over group rights and entitlements; equal justice under law; and the rights of private conscience. *That* assault upon liberty is

occurring not in the sunlight of open decisions and advertised agendas, but in the shadows of an unaccountable middle-administration that has been given coercive authority over the lives, speech, consciences, and voluntary individuation and association of students.

2   Almost all colleges and universities, for example, have "harassment" policies that prohibit selective "verbal behavior" or "verbal conduct," but almost none has the honesty to call these "speech codes." These policies, adopted from employment law and catastrophic for universities, are applied to faculty and students, the latter not even being employees of a university, but, in fact, its clients. The core of these codes is the prohibition of the creation of "a hostile or offensive environment," with the remarkable variations and embellishments that follow from Hobbes's observation that to the learned it is given to be learnedly foolish. Within very recent times, Bowdoin College chose to outlaw jokes and ways of telling stories "experienced by others as harassing." Brown University banned verbal behavior that produced "feelings of impotence . . . anger . . . or disenfranchisement . . . [whether] intentional or unintentional." Colby prohibited speech that caused loss of "self-esteem." The University of Connecticut prohibited "inconsiderate jokes," "stereotyping," and even "inappropriately directed laughter." Indeed, a student at Sarah Lawrence College recently was convicted of laughing at something that someone else said, and was ordered as a condition of remaining in the college, for his laughter, to read a book entitled *Homophobia on Campus,* see a movie about "homophobia," and write a paper about "homophobia." Rutgers University included within the forbidden and "heinous act" of harassment, "communication" that is "in any manner likely to cause annoyance or alarm," which causes *me* a great deal of annoyance *and* alarm. The University of Maryland–College Park outlaws not only "idle chatter of a sexual nature" and "comments or questions about the sensuality of a person," but pointedly explains that these verbal behaviors "do not necessarily have to be specifically directed at an individual to constitute sexual harassment." Expression goes well beyond the verbal, however, because the University of Maryland also prohibits "gestures . . . that are expressive of an idea, opinion, or emotion," including "sexual looks such as leering and ogling with suggestive overtones; licking lips or teeth; holding or eating food provocatively."

3   At Carnegie Mellon University, a student called his female opponent in an election for the Graduate Student Organization a "megalomaniac." He was charged with sexual harassment. The Dean of Students explained the deeper meaning of calling a woman a megalomaniac, citing a vast body of what he termed feminist "victim theory" on the plaintiff's behalf, and the associate provost submitted a brief that stated, "I have no doubt that this has created a hostile environment which impacts Lara's productivity as a student leader and as a graduate student."

4   Many universities, such as Berkeley itself, no less, adopted speech codes that outlawed "fighting words." That term is taken from the U.S. Supreme Court decision of the 1940s, *Chaplinsky v. New Hampshire* (a decision surely mooted by later Supreme Court decisions), in which, leftists take note, the un-

protected fighting word was, of all things, "fascist." Many universities also leave the determination of whether something was a fighting word or created a hostile environment to the plaintiff. Thus, the University of Puget Sound states that harassment "depends on the point of view of the person to whom the conduct is unwelcome." The City University of New York warns that "sexual harassment is not defined by intentions, but by its impact on the subject." "No one," Bowdoin College warns, "is entitled to engage in behavior that is experienced by others as harassing." At the University of Connecticut, criticising someone's limits of tolerance toward the speech of others is itself harassment: its code bans "attributing objections to any of the above [instances of harassment] to 'hypersensitivity' of the targeted individual or group."

5   West Virginia University prohibited, among many other things, "insults, humor, jokes, and/anecdotes that belittle or demean an individual's or a group's sexuality or sex," and, try this one on for vagueness, "inappropriate displays of sexually suggestive objects or pictures which may include but are not limited to posters, pin-ups, and calendars." If applied equally, of course, such a policy would leave no sex or race safe in its conversations or humor, let alone in its artistic taste, but such policies never are applied equally. Thus, students at West Virginia received the official policies of the "Executive Officer for Social Justice," who stated the institutional orthodoxy about "homophobia" and "sexism." The Officer of Social Justice warned that "feelings" about gays and lesbians could not become "attitudes": "Regardless of how a person feels about others, negative actions or attitudes based on misconceptions and/or ignorance constitute prejudice, which contradicts everything for which an institution of higher learning stands." Among those prejudices it listed "heterosexism . . . the assumption that everyone is heterosexual, or, if they aren't, they should be." This, of course, outlawed specific religious inner convictions about sexuality. Because everyone had the right to be free from "harassment," the policy specified "behaviors to avoid." These prohibitions affected speech and voluntary associations based upon beliefs. Thus, "DO NOT [in capital letters] tolerate 'jokes' which are potentially injurious to gays, lesbians and bisexuals. . . . DO NOT determine whether you will interact with someone by virtue of his or her sexual orientation." The policy also commanded specific prescriptions: "value alternate lifestyles . . . challenge homophobic remarks . . . [and] use language that is not gender specific. . . . Instead of referring to anyone's romantic partner as 'girlfriend' or 'boyfriend,' use positive generic terms such as a 'friend,' 'lover,' or 'partner.' Speak of your own romantic partner similarly." The "homophobia" policy ended with the warning that "harassment" or "discrimination" based on sexual preference was subject to penalties that ranged "from reprimand . . . to expulsion and termination, and including public service and educational remediation." "Educational remediation," note well, is an academic euphemism for thought reform. Made aware of what their own university was doing, a coalition of faculty members threatened to expose West Virginia University for its obvious violations of the state and federal constitutions, and to sue the administration if need be. As I talk, the University has removed

the offending codes from its freshmen orientation packages and from its web-site. We shall see if it has removed them from its operational policies.

6   When federal courts struck down two codes restricting "verbal behavior" at public universities and colleges, namely, at the University of Michigan and the University of Wisconsin, other public colleges and universities—even in those jurisdictions where codes had been declared unconstitutional—did not seek to abolish their policies. Thus, Central Michigan University, after the University of Michigan code had been struck down, maintained a policy whose prohibitions included "any intentional, unintentional, physical, verbal, or nonverbal behavior that subjects an individual to an intimidating, hostile or offensive educational . . . environment by demeaning or slurring individuals through . . . written literature because of their racial or ethnic affiliation or using symbols, epitaphs [sic, we hope] or slogans that infer [sic] negative connotations about an individual's racial or ethnic affiliation."

7   In 1993, this policy was challenged, successfully, in Federal District Court. The Court noted that the code applied to "all possible human conduct," and, citing internal University documents, ruled that Central Michigan intended to apply it to speech "'which a person "feels" has affronted him or some group, predicated on race or ethnicity.'" The Court ruled that if the policy's words had meaning, it banned, precisely, protected speech. If someone's "treatise, term paper or even . . . cafeteria bull session" about the Middle East, the Court observed, blamed one group more than another on the basis of "some ancient ethnic traditions which give rise to barbarian combativeness or . . . inability to compromise," such speech, the Court found, "would seem to be a good fit with the policy language." In fact, the Court ruled, "Any behavior, even unintentional, that offends any individual is to be prohibited under the policy. . . . If the speech gives offense it is prohibited." When the President of Central Michigan University offered assurances that the policy was not intended to be enforced in such a way as to "interfere impermissibly with individuals' rights to free speech," the Court declared itself "emphatically unimpressed" by such a savings clause, and it observed: "The university . . . says in essence, 'trust us; we may interfere, but not impermissibly.' The Court is not willing to entrust . . . the First Amendment to the tender mercies of this institution's discriminatory harassment/affirmative action enforcer."

8   Many in the academy insist that the entire phenomenon labeled "political correctness" is the mythical fabrication of opponents of "progressive" change. The authors of an American Association of University Professors' special committee report, the "Statement on the 'Political Correctness' Controversy" (1991), insisted, without irony, that claims of "political correctness" were merely smokescreens to hide the true agenda of such critics—a racist and sexist desire to thwart the aspirations of minorities and women in the academic enterprise.

9   It is, in fact, almost inconceivable that anyone of good faith could live on a college campus unaware of the repression, legal inequality, intrusions into private conscience, and malignant double standards that hold sway there. In the Left's history of McCarthyism, the firing or dismissal of one professor or student,

the inquisition into the private beliefs of one individual, let alone the demands for a demonstration of fealty to community standards stand out as intolerable oppressions that coerced people into silence, hypocrisy, betrayal, and tyranny.

10   In fact, in today's assault on liberty on college campuses, there is not a small number of cases, speech codes, nor apparatuses of repression and thought reform. Number aside, however, a climate of repression succeeds not by statistical frequency, but by sapping the courage, autonomy, and conscience of individuals who otherwise might remember or revive what liberty could be.

11   Most students respect disagreement and difference, and they do not bring charges of harassment against those whose opinions or expressions "offend" them. The universities themselves, however, encourage such charges to be brought. At almost every college and university, students deemed members of "historically oppressed groups"—above all, women, blacks, gays, and Hispanics—are informed during orientations that their campuses are teeming with illegal or intolerable violations of their "right" not to be offended. To believe many new-student orientations would be to believe that there was a racial or sexual bigot, to borrow the mocking phrase of McCarthy's critics, "under every bed." At almost every college and university, students are presented with lists of a vast array of places to which they should submit charges of such verbal "harassment," and they are promised "victim support," "confidentiality," and sympathetic understanding when they file such complaints.

12   What an astonishing expectation to give to students: the belief that, if they belong to a protected category and have the correct beliefs, they have a right to four years of never being offended. What an extraordinary power to give to administrative tribunals: the prerogative to punish the free speech and expression of people to whom they assign the stains of historical oppression, while being free, themselves, to use whatever rhetoric they wish against the bearers of such stains. While the world looks at issues of curriculum and scholarship, above all, to analyze and evaluate American colleges and universities, it is, in fact, the silencing and punishment of belief, expression, and individuality that ought to concern yet more deeply those who care about what universities are and could be. Most cases never reach the public, because most individuals accused of "verbal" harassment sadly (but understandably) accept plea-bargains that diminish their freedom but spare them Draconian penalties, including expulsion. Those settlements almost invariably involve "sensitivity training," an appalling term, "training," to hear in matters of the human mind and spirit. Even so, the files on prosecutions under speech codes are, alas, overflowing.

13   "Settlements," by the way, are one of the best-kept and most frightening secrets of American academic life, almost always assigned with an insistence upon confidentiality. They are nothing less than an American version of thought reform from benighted offender into a politically correct bearer, in fact or in appearance, of an ideology that is the regnant orthodoxy of our universities *in loco parentis*.

14   From this perspective, American history is a tale of the oppression of all "others" by white, heterosexual, Eurocentric males, punctuated by the struggles

of the oppressed. "Beneficiaries" see their lives as good and as natural, and falsely view America as a boon to humankind. Worse, most "victims" of "oppression" accept the values of their oppressors. A central task of education, then, is to "demystify" such arbitrary power. Whites, males, and heterosexuals must recognize and renounce the injustice of their "privilege." Nonwhites, women, gays, and lesbians must recognize and struggle against their victimization, both in their beliefs and in their behaviors.

15   Such "demystification" has found a welcome home in a large number of courses in the humanities and social sciences, but for the true believers, this is insufficient, because most courses remain optional, many professors resist the temptation to proselytize, and students, for the most part, choose majors that take them far from oppression studies.

16   Indeed, students forever disappoint the ideologues. Men and women generally see themselves neither as oppressor nor oppressed, and, far from engaging in class warfare, often quite love each other. Most women refuse to identify themselves as "feminists." Group-identity centers—although they can rally support at moments of crisis—attract few students overall, because invitees busily go about the business of learning, making friends, pursuing interests, and seeking love—all the things that 18-to-22-year-olds have done from time immemorial. Attendance at group-identity organizations is often miniscule as a percentage of the intended population, and militant leaders complain endlessly about "apathy." Whites don't feel particularly guilty about being white, and almost no designated "victims" adopt truly radical politics. Most undergraduates unabashedly seek their portion of American freedom, legal equality, and bounty. What to do with such benighted students? Increasingly, the answer to that question is to use the *in loco parentis* apparatus of the university to reform their private consciences and minds. For the generation that once said, "Don't trust anyone *over* 30," the motto now is "Don't trust anyone *under* 30." Increasingly, Offices of Student Life, Residence Offices, and residence advisors have become agencies of progressive social engineering whose mission is to bring students to mandatory political enlightenment.

17   Such practices violate more than honest education. Recognition of the sanctity of conscience is the single most essential respect given to individual autonomy. There are purely practical arguments for the right to avoid self-incrimination or to choose religious (or other) creeds, but there is none deeper than restraining power from intruding upon the privacy of the self. Universities and colleges that commit the scandal of sentencing students (and faculty) to "sensitivity therapy" do not even permit individuals to choose their therapists. The Christian may not consult his or her chosen counselor, but must follow the regime of the social worker selected by the Women's Center or by the Office of Student Life. . . .

18   Imagine a campus on which being denounced for "irreligous bigotry" or "un-Americanism" carried the same stigma that being denounced for "racism," "sexism," and "homophobia" now carries in the academic world, so that in such hearings or trials, the burden of proof invariably fell upon the "offender." The

common sign at pro-choice rallies, "Keep your rosaries off our ovaries," would be prima facie evidence of language used as a weapon to degrade and marginalize, and the common term of abuse, "born-again bigot," would be compelling evidence of the choice to create a hostile environment for evangelicals. What panegyrics to liberty and free expression we would hear in opposition to any proposed code to protect the "religious" or the "patriotic" from "offense" and "incivility." Yet what deafening silence we have heard, in these times, in the campus acceptance of the speech provisions of so-called harassment codes.

19   The goal of a speech code, then, is to suppress speech one doesn't like. The goal of liberty and equal justice is to permit us to live in a complex but peaceful world of difference, disagreement, debate, moral witness, and efforts of persuasion—without coercion and violence. Liberty and legal equality are hard-won, precious, and, indeed—because the social world is often discomforting—profoundly complex and troublesome ways of being human. They require, for their sustenance, men and women who would abhor their own power of censorship and their own special legal privileges as much as they abhor those of others. In enacting and enforcing speech codes, universities, for their own partisan reasons, have chosen to betray the human vision of freedom and legal equality. It was malignant to impose or permit such speech codes; to deny their oppressive effects while living in the midst of those effects is beyond the moral pale.

20   On virtually any college campus, for all of its rules of "civility" and all of its prohibitions of "hostile environment," assimilationist black men and women live daily with the terms "Uncle Tom" and "Oreo" said with impunity, while their tormenters live with special protections from offense. White students daily hear themselves, their friends, and their parents denounced as "racists" and "oppressors," while their tormenters live with special protections from offense. Believing Christians hear their beliefs ridiculed and see their sacred symbols traduced—virtually nothing, in the name of freedom, may not be said against them in the classroom, at rallies, and in personal encounters—while their tormenters live with special protection from offense. Men hear their sex abused, find themselves blamed for all the evils of the world, and enter classrooms whose very goal is to make them feel discomfort, while their tormenters live with special protections from "a hostile environment."

21   It is our liberty, above all else, that defines us as human beings, capable of ethics and responsibility. The struggle for liberty on American campuses is one of the defining struggles of the age in which we find ourselves. A nation that does not educate in freedom will not survive in freedom, and will not even know when it has lost it. Individuals too often convince themselves that they are caught up in moments of history that they cannot affect. That history, however, is made by their will and moral choices. There is a moral crisis in higher education. It will not be resolved unless we choose and act to resolve it. . . .

22   It is easy, however, to identify the vulnerabilities of the bearers of this worst and, at the time, most marginal legacy of the '60s: they loathe the society that they believe should support them generously in their authority over its offspring; they are detached from the values of individual liberty, legal equality,

privacy, and the sanctity of conscience toward which Americans essentially are drawn; and, for both those reasons, they cannot bear the light of public scrutiny. Let the sunlight in.

FOR ANALYSIS AND DISCUSSION

1. Why does Kors believe racist and inflammatory speech should be protected by the First Amendment? What examples does he use to prove his point? Do you agree? Can you think of circumstances in which racist speech should not be protected?
2. How has this article affected your thinking on the subject of free speech and censorship? Has it changed your mind about the use of racially or sexually abusive language? Explain your perspective.
3. Consider the author's voice in this essay. What sense do you get of Kors as an individual? In a paragraph, try to characterize the author. Take into consideration his stand in the essay, his style and tone, and the examples he uses to support his view and how he presents them.
4. How are colleges and university administrators dealing with incidents of verbal abuse on American campuses? What is Kors's reaction to their handling of such problems? According to Kors, how are students being manipulated by university censorship rules?
5. Explain what Kors means when he says, "Many in the academy insist that the entire phenomenon labeled 'political correctness' is the mythical fabrication of opponents of 'progressive' change" (paragraph 8). Do you agree with this view?

In Praise of Censure
Garry Wills

When confronted with defamatory remarks, racial epithets, or offensive speech of any kind, what are our choices: censorship or tolerance? Are there any other choices between outright banning and First Amendment rights? Garry Wills thinks so. In this essay Wills argues that the open expression of moral disapproval—or censure—can be a powerful response to the objectionable. Censure does not repress ideas but holds them up for public scrutiny and examination. Such a mobilization of public opinion, Wills says, is more likely than legislation or repression to bring about social change.

Garry Wills is the Henry R. Luce Professor of American Culture and Public Policy at Northwestern University and a syndicated columnist. His most recent books are *Lincoln at Gettysburg* (1992) and *John Wayne's America: The Politics of Celebrity* (1997). This essay first appeared in *Time* magazine in July 1989.

BEFORE YOU READ

Do you think censure is an effective means of expressing disapproval of offensive material? How is censure carried out? Can you think of any recent examples of public censure that had an impact on the sale or promotion of something offensive?

AS YOU READ

As you read, determine what Wills means when he says, "It is a distortion to turn 'you can express any views' into the proposition 'I don't care what views you express.'"

1   Rarely have the denouncers of censorship been so eager to start practicing it. When a sense of moral disorientation overcomes a society, people from the least expected quarters begin to ask, "Is nothing sacred?" Feminists join reactionaries to denounce pornography as demeaning to women. Rock musician Frank Zappa declares that when Tipper Gore, the wife of Senator Albert Gore from Tennessee, asked music companies to label sexually explicit material, she launched an illegal "conspiracy to extort." A *Penthouse* editorialist says that housewife Terry Rakolta, who asked sponsors to withdraw support from a sitcom called *Married . . . With Children,* is "yelling fire in a crowded theater," a formula that says her speech is not protected by the First Amendment.

2   But the most interesting movement to limit speech is directed at defamatory utterances against blacks, homosexuals, Jews, women or other stigmatizable groups. It took no Terry Rakolta of the left to bring about the instant firing of Jimmy the Greek and Al Campanis from sports jobs when they made racially denigrating comments. Social pressure worked far more quickly on them than on *Married . . . With Children,* which is still on the air.

3   The rules being considered on college campuses to punish students for making racist and other defamatory remarks go beyond social and commercial pressure to actual legal muzzling. The rightwing *Dartmouth Review* and its imitators have understandably infuriated liberals who are beginning to take action against them and the racist expressions they have encouraged. The American Civil Liberties Union considered this movement important enough to make it the principal topic at its biennial meeting last month in Madison, Wis. Ironically, the regents of the University of Wisconsin had passed their own rules against defamation just before the ACLU members convened on the university's campus. Nadine Strossen, of New York University School of Law, who was defending the ACLU's traditional position on free speech, said of Wisconsin's new rules, "You can tell how bad they are by the fact that the regents had to make an amendment at the last minute exempting classroom discussion! What is surprising is that Donna Shalala [chancellor of the university] went along with it." So did constitutional lawyers on the faculty.

4   If a similar code were drawn up with right-wing imperatives in mind—one banning unpatriotic, irreligious or sexually explicit expressions on campus— the people framing Wisconsin-type rules would revert to their libertarian pasts. In this competition to suppress, is regard for freedom of expression just a matter of whose ox is getting gored at the moment? Does the left just get nervous about the Christian cross when Klansmen burn it, while the right will react only when Madonna flirts crucifixes between her thighs?

5   The cries of "un-American" are as genuine and as frequent on either side. Everyone is protecting the country. Zappa accuses Gore of undermining the

moral fiber of America with the "sexual neuroses of these vigilant ladies." He argues that she threatens our freedoms with "connubial insider trading" because her husband is a Senator. Apparently her marital status should deprive her of speaking privileges in public—an argument Westbrook Pegler used to make against Eleanor Roosevelt. *Penthouse* says Rakola is taking us down the path toward fascism. It attacks her for living in a rich suburb—the old "radical chic" argument that rich people cannot support moral causes.

6   There is a basic distinction that cuts through this free-for-all over freedom. It is the distinction, too often neglected, between censorship and censure (the free expression of moral disapproval). What the campuses are trying to do (at least those with state money) is to use the force of government to contain freedom of speech. What Donald Wildmon, the free-lance moralist from Tupelo, Miss., does when he gets Pepsi to cancel its Madonna ad is censure the ad by calling for a boycott. Advocating boycotts is a form of speech protected by the First Amendment. As Nat Hentoff, journalistic-custodian of the First Amendment, says, "I would hate to see boycotts outlawed. Think what that would do to Cesar Chavez." Or, for that matter, to Ralph Nader. If one disapproves of a social practice, whether it is racist speech or unjust hiring in lettuce fields, one is free to denounce that and to call on others to express their disapproval. Otherwise, there would be no form of persuasive speech except passing a law. This would make the law coterminous with morality.

7   Equating morality with legality is in effect what people do when they claim that anything tolerated by law must, in the name of freedom, be approved by citizens in all their dealings with one another. As Zappa says, "Masturbation is not illegal. If it is not illegal to do it, why should it be illegal to sing about it?" He thinks this proves that Gore, who is trying to make raunch in rock illegal, cannot even ask distributors to label it. Anything goes, as long as it's legal. The odd consequence of this argument would be a drastic narrowing of the freedom of speech. One could not call into question anything that was not against the law—including, for instance, racist speech.

8   A false ideal of tolerance has not only outlawed censorship but discouraged censoriousness (another word for censure). Most civilizations have expressed their moral values by mobilization of social opprobrium. That, rather than specific legislation, is what changed the treatment of minorities in films and TV over recent years. One can now draw opprobrious attention by gay bashing, as the Beastie Boys rock group found when their distributor told them to cut out remarks about "fags" for business reasons. Or by anti-Semitism, as the just disbanded rap group Public Enemy has discovered.

9   It is said that only the narrow-minded are intolerant or opprobrious. Most of those who limited the distribution of Martin Scorsese's movie *The Last Temptation of Christ* had not even seen the movie. So do we guarantee freedom of speech only for the broad-minded or the better educated? Can one speak only after studying whatever one has reason, from one's beliefs, to denounce? Then most of us would be doing a great deal less speaking than we do. If one has never seen any snuff movies, is that a bar to criticizing them?

10   Others argue that asking people not to buy lettuce is different from asking them not to buy a rocker's artistic expression. Ideas (carefully disguised) lurk somewhere in the lyrics. All the more reason to keep criticism of them free. If ideas are too important to suppress, they are also too important to ignore. The whole point of free speech is not to make ideas exempt from criticism but to expose them to it.

11   One of the great mistakes of liberals in recent decades has been the ceding of moral concern to right-wingers. Just because one opposes censorship, one need not be seen as agreeing with pornographers. Why should liberals, of all people, oppose Gore when she asks that labels be put on products meant for the young, to inform those entrusted by law with the care of the young? Liberals were the first to promote "healthy" television shows like *Sesame Street* and *The Electric Company*. In the 1950s and 1960s they were the leading critics of television, of its mindless violence, of the way it ravaged the attention span needed for reading. Who was keeping kids away from TV sets then? How did promoters of Big Bird let themselves be cast as champions of the Beastie Boys—not just of their *right* to perform but of their performance itself? Why should it be left to Gore to express moral disapproval of a group calling itself Dead Kennedys (sample lyric: "I kill children, I love to see them die")?

12   For that matter, who has been more insistent that parents should "interfere" in what their children are doing, Tipper Gore or Jesse Jackson? All through the 1970s, Jackson was traveling the high schools, telling parents to turn off TVs, make the kids finish their homework, check with teachers on their performance, get to know what the children are doing. This kind of "interference" used to be called education.

13   Belief in the First Amendment does not pre-empt other beliefs, making one a eunuch to the interplay of opinions. It is a distortion to turn "You can express any views" into the proposition "I don't care what views you express." If liberals keep equating equality with approval, they will be repeatedly forced into weak positions.

14   A case in point is the Corcoran Gallery's sudden cancellation of an exhibit of Robert Mapplethorpe's photographs. The whole matter was needlessly confused when the director, Christina Owr-Chall, claimed she was canceling the show to *protect it* from censorship. She meant that there might be pressure to remove certain pictures—the sadomasochistic ones or those verging on kiddie porn—if the show had gone on. But she had in mind, as well, the hope of future grants from the National Endowment for the Arts, which is under criticism for the Mapplethorpe show and for another show that contained Andres Serrano's *Piss Christ*, the photograph of a crucifix in what the title says is urine. Owr-Chall is said to be yielding to censorship, when she is clearly yielding to political and financial pressure, as Pepsi yielded to commercial pressure over the Madonna ad.

15   What is at issue here is not government suppression but government subsidy. Mapplethorpe's work is not banned, but showing it might have endangered federal grants to needy artists. The idea that what the government does

not support it represses is nonsensical, as one can see by reversing the statement to read: "No one is allowed to create anything without the government's
subvention." What pussycats our supposedly radical artists are. They not only
want the government's permission to create their artifacts, they want federal
authorities to supply the materials as well. Otherwise they feel "gagged." If they
are not given governmental approval (and money), they want to remain an
avant-garde while being bankrolled by the Old Guard.

16   What is easily forgotten in this argument is the right of citizen taxpayers.
They send representatives to Washington who are answerable for the expenditure of funds exacted from them. In general these voters want to favor their
own values if government is going to get into the culture-subsidizing area at all
(a proposition many find objectionable in itself). Politicians, insofar as they
support the arts, will tend to favor conventional art (certainly not masochistic
art). Anybody who doubts that has no understanding of a politician's legitimate
concern for his or her constituents' approval. Besides, it is quaint for those familiar with the politics of the art world to discover, with a shock, that there is
politics in politics.

17   Luckily, cancellation of the Mapplethorpe show forced some artists back to
the flair and cheekiness of unsubsidized art. Other results of pressure do not
turn out as well. Unfortunately, people in certain regions were deprived of the
chance to see *The Last Temptation of Christ* in the theater. Some, no doubt, considered it a loss that they could not buy lettuce or grapes during a Chavez boycott. Perhaps there was even a buyer perverse enough to miss driving the unsafe cars Nader helped pressure off the market. On the other hand, we do not
get sports analysis made by racists. These mobilizations of social opprobrium
are not examples of repression but of freedom of expression by committed
people who censured without censoring, who expressed the kinds of belief the
First Amendment guarantees. I do not, as a result, get whatever I approve of
subsidized, either by Pepsi or the government. But neither does the law come
in to silence Tipper Gore or Frank Zappa or even that filthy rag, the *Dartmouth
Review*.

FOR ANALYSIS AND DISCUSSION

1. How does Wills distinguish between censorship and censure? Which does he
   endorse in this essay? Cite specific examples from the essay to support your response.
2. Wills presents two sides to nearly all of the arguments discussed in his essay.
   What effect does having both sides of an argument available simultaneously
   have on you, the reader? How does this tactic affect Wills's own argument?
3. Evaluate Wills's introduction. How effective is it in drawing you into the topic?
   Does the first paragraph let you know from which position Wills will be arguing?
4. What does Wills think of Christina Owr-Chall's claim that she cancelled the
   Robert Mapplethorpe exhibit to protect it from censorship (paragraph 14)? Do
   you agree with Owr-Chall's decision? Why or why not?

5. In his conclusion Wills recounts nearly all of the censorship issues discussed in his essay. Do you find this an effective strategy for emphasizing his stand, or is it unnecessarily repetitive? Explain.

6. In the preceding essay Alan Charles Kors cites many examples that he believes prove that censorship rules have gone too far. Compare the examples in that essay to those presented by Wills. Do you think Kors and Wills would reach a consensus if they participated in a dialogue about this issue? What about Charles Lawrence? Explain.

WRITING ASSIGNMENTS: CENSORSHIP ON CAMPUS

1. In 1996 Robert B. Chatelle, cochair of the Political Issues Committee National Writers Union, wrote a letter to Wesleyan University President Douglas Bennet to express concern about a Wesleyan student who had been suspended by the university's student judicial board for violating the Wesleyan speech code. Read Chatelle's argument at <http://www.bethellutheran.org/~kyp/schools/bennet2.html>. Use a "Yes, but . . . " exchange and a dialogue to elucidate conflicting and shared concerns about this incident by all sides. Then, write an argument expressing your own views. Support your claim using information from the readings in this chapter, as well as from your own personal experience.

2. Many of the essays in this section discuss censorship codes limiting racist or hate speech. Write a code to be implemented at your university or college. Consider students' right to free speech, what constitutes hate speech, and what limits can be placed on hate speech. Write a prologue to your code explaining and supporting its tenets.

3. Imagine that as a condition of acceptance to your school you had to sign an agreement stating that you would refrain from using racist, sexist, or otherwise abusive language on campus. Weighing the social benefits of such a measure against the restrictions on freedom of expression, write a paper in which you explain why you would or would not sign such an agreement.

CENSORSHIP ON THE INTERNET: DOES THIS NEW MEDIUM CALL FOR NEW RULES?

The Internet: A Clear and Present Danger?
Cathleen A. Cleaver

Over the past ten years the Internet has had a major impact on American life. For many people the Internet is an educational tool, a marketplace, an intellectual and cultural forum, and a recreational outlet. Because the material on the Web is not regulated, the rule is often "anything goes." The issue of protecting children from offensive or pornographic material has motivated some parents and politicians to introduce legislation to control Internet content. Other groups fear that such control infringes on First Amendment rights. In the following essay Cathleen A. Cleaver argues that the Internet is a useful and necessary tool, but that people who use the Internet should be subject to the same "laws and regulations that govern their conduct elsewhere."

Cathleen A. Cleaver is director of legal policy at the Family Research Council, a Washington, D.C., research and advocacy organization. This essay was first delivered as a speech in a debate sponsored by Boston University's College of Communication on October 29, 1997.

BEFORE YOU READ

Do you think Internet content should be regulated? If so, who would control it? Is it even possible to regulate the Web?

AS YOU READ

Consider how Cleaver presents her argument in the context of protecting children. How effective is this tactic? What effect do you think it will have on her audience?

1   • Someone breaks through your firewall and steals proprietary information from your computer systems. You find out and contact a lawyer who says, "Man, you shouldn't have had your stuff on-line." The thief becomes a millionaire using your ideas, and you go broke, if laws against copyright violation don't protect material on the Internet.

2   • You visit the Antiques Anonymous Website and decide to pay their hefty subscription fee for a year's worth of exclusive estate sale previews in their private on-line monthly magazine. They never deliver, and, in fact, never intended to—they don't even have a magazine. You have no recourse, if laws against fraud don't apply to on-line transactions.

3   • Larry Flynt decides to branch out into the lucrative child porn market, and creates a Teen Hustler Web site, featuring nude adolescents and pre-teens. You find out and complain, but nothing can be done, if child pornography distribution laws don't apply to computer transmissions.

4   • A major computer software vendor who dominates the market develops his popular office software so that it works only with his browser. You're a small browser manufacturer who is completely squeezed out of the market, but you have to find a new line of work, if antitrust laws don't apply on-line.

5   • Finally, a pedophile e-mails your son, misrepresenting himself as a 12-year-old named Jenny. They develop an on-line relationship, and one day arrange to meet after school, where he intends to rape your son. Thankfully, you learn in advance about the meeting and go there yourself, where you find a 40-year-old man instead of Jenny. You flee to the police, who'll tell you there's nothing they can do, if child-stalking laws don't apply to the Internet.

The Issue

6 The awesome advances in interactive telecommunication that we've witnessed in just the last few years have changed the way in which many Americans communicate and interact. No one can doubt that the Internet is a technological revolution of enormous proportion, with outstanding possibilities for human advancement.

7 As lead speaker for the affirmative, I'm asked to argue that the Internet poses a "clear and present danger," but the Internet, as a whole, isn't dangerous. In fact, it continues to be a positive and highly beneficial tool, which will undoubtedly improve education, information exchange, and commerce in years to come. In other words, the Internet will enrich many aspects of our daily life. Thus, instead of defending this rather apocalyptic view of the Internet, I'll attempt to explain why some industry and government regulation of certain aspects of the Internet is necessary—or, stated another way, why people who use the Internet should not be exempt from many of the laws and regulations that govern their conduct elsewhere. My opening illustrations were meant to give examples of some illegal conduct which should not become legal simply because someone uses the Internet. In looking at whether Internet regulation is a good idea, I believe we should consider whether regulation is in the public interest. In order to do that, we have to ask the question: Who is the public? More specifically, does the "public" whose interests we care about tonight include children?

Children and the Internet

8 Dave Barry describes the Internet as a "worldwide network of university, government, business, and private computer systems, run by a 13-year old named Jason." This description draws a smile precisely because we acknowledge the highly advanced computer literacy of our children. Most children demonstrate computer proficiency that far surpasses that of their parents, and many parents know only what their children have taught them about the Internet, which gives new relevance to Wordsworth's insight: "The child is father of the man." In fact, one could go so far as to say that the Internet is as accessible to many children as it is inaccessible to many adults. This technological evolution is new in many ways, not the least of which is its accessibility to children, wholly independent of their parents.

9 When considering what's in the public interest, we must consider the whole public, including children as individual participants in this new medium.

Pornography and the Internet

10 This new medium is unique in another way. It provides, through a single avenue, the full spectrum of pornographic depictions, from the more familiar convenience store fare to pornography of such violence and depravity that it surpasses the worst excesses of the normal human imagination. Sites displaying this material are easily accessible, making pornography far more freely avail-

able via the Internet than from any other communications medium in the United States. Pornography is the third largest sector of sales on the Internet, generating $1 billion annually. There are an estimated 72,000 pornographic sites on the World Wide Web alone, with approximately 39 new explicit sex sites every day. Indeed, the *Washington Post* has called the Internet the largest pornography store in the history of mankind.

11   There is little restriction of pornography-related activity in cyberspace. While there are some porn-related laws, the specter of those laws does not loom large in cyberspace. There's an implicit license there that exists nowhere else with regard to pornography—an environment where people are free to exploit others for profit and be virtually untroubled by legal deterrent. Indeed, if we consider cyberspace to be a little world of its own, it's the type of world for which groups like the ACLU have long fought, but, so far, fought in vain.

12   I believe it will not remain this way, but until it changes, we should take the opportunity to see what this world looks like, if for no other reason than to reassure ourselves that our decades-old decisions to control pornography were good ones.

13   With a few clicks of the mouse, anyone, any child, can get graphic and often violent sexual images—the kind of stuff it used to be difficult to find without exceptional effort and some significant personal risk. Anyone with a computer and a modem can set up public sites featuring the perversion of their choice, whether it's mutilation of female genitals, eroticized urination and defecation, bestiality, or sites featuring depictions of incest. These pictures can be sold for profit, they can be sent to harass others, or posted to shock people. Anyone can describe the fantasy rape and murder of a specific person and display it for all to read. Anyone can meet children in chat rooms or via e-mail and send them pornography and find out where they live. An adult who signs onto an AOL chat room as a 13-year-old girl is hit on 30 times within the first half hour.

14   All this can be done from the seclusion of the home, with the feeling of near anonymity and with the comfort of knowing that there's little risk of legal sanction.

15   The phenomenon of this kind of pornography finding such a welcome home in this new medium presents abundant opportunities for social commentary. What does Internet pornography tell us about human sexuality? Photographs, videos, and virtual games that depict rape and the dehumanization of women in sexual scenes send powerful messages about human dignity and equality. Much of the pornography freely available without restriction on the Internet celebrates unhealthy and antisocial kinds of sexual activity, such as sadomasochism, abuse, and degradation. Of course, by its very nature, pornography encourages voyeurism.

16   Beyond the troubling social aspects of unrestricted porn, we face the reality that children are accessing it, and that predators are accessing children. We have got to start considering what kind of society we'll have when the next generation learns about human sexuality from what the Internet teaches. What does unrestricted Internet pornography teach children about relationships, about the equality of women? What does it teach little girls about themselves and their worth?

17   Opponents of restrictions are fond of saying that it's up to the parents to deal with the issue of children's exposure. Well, of course it is, but placing the burden solely on parents is illogical and ineffective. It's far easier for a distributor of pornography to control his material than it is for parents, who must, with the help of software, search for and find the pornographic sites, which change daily, and then attempt to block them. Any pornographer who wants to can easily subvert these efforts, and a recent Internet posting from a teenager wanting to know how to disable the filtering software on his computer received several effective answers. Moreover, it goes without saying that the most sophisticated software can only be effective where it's installed, and children will have access to many computers that don't have filtering software, such as those in libraries, schools, and at neighbors' houses.

Internet Transactions Should Not Be Exempt

18   Opponents of legal restrictions often argue simply that the laws just cannot apply in this new medium, but the argument that old laws can't apply to changing technology just doesn't hold. We saw this argument last in the early '80s with the advent of the videotape. Then, certain groups tried to argue that, since you can't view videotapes without a VCR, you can't make the sale of child porn videos illegal, because, after all, they're just plastic boxes with magnetic tape inside. Technological change mandates legal change only insofar as it affects the justification for a law. It just doesn't make sense that the government may take steps to restrict illegal material in *every* medium—video, television, radio, the private telephone, *and* print—but that it may do *nothing* where people distribute the material by the Internet. While old laws might need redefinition, the old principles generally stand firm.

19   The question of enforcement usually is raised here, and it often comes in the form of: "How are you going to stop people from doing it?" Well, no law stops people from doing things—a red light at an intersection doesn't force you to stop, but tells you that you should stop and that there could be legal consequences if you don't. Not everyone who runs a red light is caught, but that doesn't mean the law is futile. The same concept holds true for Internet laws. Government efforts to temper harmful conduct on-line will never be perfect, but that doesn't mean they shouldn't undertake the effort at all.

20   There's clearly a role for industry to play here. Search engines don't have to run ads for porn sites, or prioritize search results to highlight porn. One new search engine even has *sex* as the default search terms. Internet Service Providers can do something about unsolicited e-mail with hotlinks to porn, and they can and should carefully monitor any chat rooms designed for kids.

21   Some charge that industry standards or regulations that restrict explicit pornography will hinder the development of Internet technology. But that is to say that its advancement *depends upon* unrestricted exhibition of this material, and this cannot be true. The Internet does not belong to pornographers, and it's clearly in the public interest to see that they don't usurp this great new technology. We don't live in a perfect society, and the Internet is merely a reflection

of the larger social community. Without some mitigating influences, the strong will exploit the weak, whether a Bill Gates or a child predator.

Conclusion: Technology Must Serve Man

22 To argue that the strength of the Internet is chaos or that our liberty depends upon chaos is to misunderstand not only the Internet, but also the fundamental nature of our liberty. It's an illusion to claim social or moral neutrality in the application of technology, even if its development may be neutral. It can be a valuable resource only when placed at the service of humanity and when it promotes our integral development for the benefit of all.

23 Guiding principles simply cannot be inferred from mere technical efficiency, or from the usefulness accruing to some at the expense of others. Technology by its very nature requires unconditional respect for the fundamental interests of society.

24 Internet technology must be at the service of humanity and of our inalienable rights. It must respect the prerogatives of a civil society, among which is the protection of children.

FOR ANALYSIS AND DISCUSSION

1. In paragraph 8 Cleaver quotes comedian and writer Dave Barry. How does this quotation support her argument? Explain.
2. Cleaver comments that "[w]ith a few clicks of the mouse, anyone, any child, can get graphic and often violent sexual images (paragraph 13)." How easy is it to access pornography on the Web? Is it likely that children will unknowingly stumble on it? Address Cleaver's comment by drawing from your own personal experiences with the Internet.
3. In paragraph 16 Cleaver conjectures what the world will be like when the next generation of children matures, having learned about sexuality from the Internet. Discuss the validity of her fear.
4. Should laws that control the content and distribution of certain materials in print and in video also apply to the Web? Explain.
5. Cleaver implies that in the discussion of First Amendment rights and the Internet, an essential and significant audience—children—is left out of the debate. When activists argue in favor of unrestricted Internet content and freedom of speech, should they consider children? Explain.

Protecting Our Children from Internet Smut: Moral Duty or Moral Panic?

Julia Wilkins

The debate over government regulation of the Internet continues to be an active issue in today's political arena. Legislation controlling offensive material that was approved by President Clinton was later overruled by the Supreme Court as unconstitutional. Many magazines and newspapers have helped fuel the fire with reports of unchecked pornography running wild on the Web. But is pornography on the Web really as bad as the magazines imply? Julia Wilkins compares the panic over "Internet smut" to other social panics such as the McCarthy anticommunist witch-hunts of the 1950s.

Julia Wilkins is the author of several books on education. The following article first appeared in the September/October 1997 issue of *The Humanist.*

BEFORE YOU READ

How much have you heard about the issue of pornography and the Internet and what were the sources of the information? Is Internet pornography a legitimate problem that our society must address?

AS YOU READ

Wilkins opens her argument by comparing the current concern regarding Internet pornography with "moral panics" of the 1950s and 1980s. Are these incidents parallel? Do you agree with this analogy?

1   The term *moral panic* is one of the more useful concepts to have emerged from sociology in recent years. A moral panic is characterized by a wave of public concern, anxiety, and fervor about something, usually perceived as a threat to society. The distinguishing factors are a level of interest totally out of proportion to the real importance of the subject, some individuals building personal careers from the pursuit and magnification of the issue, and the replacement of reasoned debate with witchhunts and hysteria.

2   Moral panics of recent memory include the Joseph McCarthy anti-communist witchhunts of the 1950s and the satanic ritual abuse allegations of the 1980s. And, more recently, we have witnessed a full-blown moral panic about pornography on the Internet. Sparked by the July 3, 1995, *Time* cover article, "On a Screen Near You: Cyberporn," this moral panic has been perpetuated and intensified by a raft of subsequent media reports. As a result, there is now a widely held belief that pornography is easily accessible to all children using the Internet. This was also the judgment of Congress, which, proclaiming to be "protecting the children," voted overwhelmingly in 1996 for legislation to make it a criminal offense to send "indecent" material over the Internet into people's computers.

3   The original *Time* article was based on its exclusive access to Marty Rimm's *Georgetown University Law Journal* paper, "Marketing Pornography on the Information Superhighway." Although published, the article had not received peer review and was based on an undergraduate research project concerning descriptions of images on adult bulletin board systems in the United States. Using the information in this paper, *Time* discussed the type of pornography available

online, such as "pedophilia (nude pictures of children), hebephelia (youths) and . . . images of bondage, sadomasochism, urination, defecation, and sex acts with a barnyard full of animals." The article proposed that pornography of this nature is readily available to anyone who is even remotely computer literate and raised the stakes by offering quotes from worried parents who feared for their children's safety. It also presented the possibility that pornographic material could be mailed to children without their parents' knowledge. *Time*'s example was of a ten-year-old boy who supposedly received pornographic images in his e-mail showing "10 thumbnail size pictures showing couples engaged in various acts of sodomy, heterosexual intercourse and lesbian sex." Naturally, the boy's mother was shocked and concerned, saying, "Children should not be subject to these images." *Time* also quoted another mother who said that she wanted her children to benefit from the vast amount of knowledge available on the Internet but was inclined not to allow access, fearing that her children could be "bombarded with X-rated pornography and [she] would know nothing about it."

4   From the outset, Rimm's report generated a lot of excitement—not only because it was reportedly the first published study of online pornography but also because of the secrecy involved in the research and publication of the article. In fact, the *New York Times* reported on July 24, 1995, that Marty Rimm was being investigated by his university, Carnegie Mellon, for unethical research and, as a result, would not be giving testimony to a Senate hearing on Internet pornography. Two experts from *Time* reportedly discovered serious flaws in Rimm's study involving gross misrepresentation and erroneous methodology. His work was soon deemed flawed and inaccurate, and *Time* recanted in public. With Rimm's claims now apologetically retracted, his original suggestion that 83.5 percent of Internet graphics are pornographic was quietly withdrawn in favor of a figure less than 1 percent.

5   *Time* admitted that grievous errors had slipped past their editorial staff, as their normally thorough research succumbed to a combination of deadline pressure and exclusivity agreements that barred them from showing the unpublished study to possible critics. But, by then, the damage had been done: the study had found its way to the Senate.

Government Intervention

6 Senator Charles Grassley (Republican–Iowa) jumped on the pornography bandwagon by proposing a bill that would make it a criminal offense to supply or permit the supply of "indecent" material to minors over the Internet. Grassley introduced the entire *Time* article into the congressional record, despite the fact that the conceptual, logical, and methodological flaws in the report had already been acknowledged by the magazine.

7   On the Senate floor, Grassley referred to Marty Rimm's undergraduate research as "a remarkable study conducted by researchers at Carnegie Mellon University" and went on to say:

> The university surveyed 900,000 computer images. Of these 900,000 images, 83.5 percent of all computerized photographs available on the Inter-

net are pornographic. . . . With so many graphic images available on computer networks, I believe Congress must act and do so in a constitutional manner to help parents who are under assault in this day and age.

8   Under the Grassley bill, later known as the Protection of Children from Pornography Act of 1995, it would have been illegal for anyone to knowingly or recklessly transmit indecent material to minors. This bill marked the beginning of a stream of Internet censorship legislation at various levels of government in the United States and abroad.

9   The most extreme and fiercely opposed of these was the Communications Decency Act, sponsored by former Senator James Exon (Democrat–Nebraska) and Senator Dan Coats (Republican–Indiana). The CDA labeled the transmission of "obscene, lewd, lascivious, filthy, indecent, or patently offensive" pornography over the Internet a crime. It was attached to the Telecommunications Reform Act of 1996, which was then passed by Congress on February 1, 1996. One week later, it was signed into law by President Clinton. On the same day, the American Civil Liberties Union filed suit in Philadelphia against the U.S. Department of Justice and Attorney General Janet Reno, arguing that the statute would ban free speech protected by the First Amendment and subject Internet users to far greater restrictions than exist in any other medium. Later that month, the Citizens Internet Empowerment Coalition initiated a second legal challenge to the CDA, which formally consolidated with *ACLU v. Reno.* Government lawyers agreed not to prosecute "indecent" or "patently offensive" material until the three-judge court in Philadelphia ruled on the case.

10   Although the purpose of the CDA was to protect young children from accessing and viewing material of sexually explicit content on the Internet, the wording of the act was so broad and poorly defined that it could have deprived many adults of information they needed in the areas of health, art, news, and literature—information that is legal in print form. Specifically, certain medical information available on the Internet includes descriptions of sexual organs and activities which might have been considered "indecent" or "patently offensive" under the act—for example, information on breastfeeding, birth control, AIDS, and gynecological and urological information. Also, many museums and art galleries now have websites. Under the act, displaying art like the Sistine Chapel nudes could be cause for criminal prosecution. Online newspapers would not be permitted to report the same information as is available in the print media. Reports on combatants in war, at the scenes of crime, in the political arena, and outside abortion clinics often provoke images or language that could be constituted "offensive" and therefore illegal on the net. Furthermore, the CDA provided a legal basis for banning books which had been ruled unconstitutional to ban from school libraries. These include many of the classics as well as modern literature containing words that may be considered "indecent."

11   The act also expanded potential liability for employers, service providers, and carriers that transmit or otherwise make available restricted communications. According to the CDA, "knowingly" allowing obscene material to pass through one's computer system was a criminal offense. Given the nature of the

Internet, however, making service providers responsible for the content of the traffic they pass on to other Internet nodes is equivalent to holding a telephone carrier responsible for the content of the conversations going over that carrier's lines. So, under the terms of the act, if someone sent an indecent electronic comment from a workstation, the employer, the e-mail service provider, and the carrier all could be potentially held liable and subject to up to $100,000 in fines or two years in prison.

12   On June 12, 1996, after experiencing live tours of the Internet and hearing arguments about the technical and economical infeasibility of complying with the censorship law, the three federal judges in Philadelphia granted the request for a preliminary injunction against the CDA. The court determined that "there is no evidence that sexually oriented material is the primary type of content on this new medium" and proposed that "communications over the Internet do not 'invade' an individual's home or appear on one's computer screen unbidden. Users seldom encounter content 'by accident.' " In a unanimous decision, the judges ruled that the Communications Decency Act would constitutionally restrict free speech on the Internet.

13   The government appealed the judges' decision and, on March 19, 1997, the U.S. Supreme Court heard oral arguments in the legal challenge to the CDA, now known as *Reno v. ACLU*. Finally, on June 26, the decision came down. The Court voted unanimously that the act violated the First Amendment guarantee of freedom of speech and would have threatened "to torch a large segment of the Internet community."

14   Is the panic therefore over? Far from it. The July 7, 1997, *Newsweek*, picking up the frenzy where *Time* left off, reported the Supreme Court decision in a provocatively illustrated article featuring a color photo of a woman licking her lips and a warning message taken from the website of the House of Sin. Entitled "On the Net, Anything Goes," the opening words by Steven Levy read, "Born of a hysteria triggered by a genuine problem—the ease with which wired-up teenagers can get hold of nasty pictures on the Internet—the Communications Decency Act (CDA) was never really destined to be a companion piece to the Bill of Rights." At the announcement of the Court's decision, anti-porn protesters were on the street outside brandishing signs which read, "Child Molesters Are Looking for Victims on the Internet."

15   Meanwhile, government talk has shifted to the development of a universal Internet rating system and widespread hardware and software filtering. Referring to the latter, White House Senior Adviser Rahm Emanual declared, "We're going to get the V-chip for the Internet. Same goal, different means."

16   But it is important to bear in mind that children are still a minority of Internet users. A contract with an Internet service provider typically needs to be paid for by credit card or direct debit, therefore requiring the intervention of an adult. Children are also unlikely to be able to view any kind of porn online without a credit card.

17   In addition to this, there have been a variety of measures developed to protect children on the Internet. The National Center for Missing and Exploited Children has outlined protective guidelines for parents and children in its

pamphlet, *Child Safety on the Information Superhighway*. A number of companies now sell Internet newsfeeds and web proxy accesses that are vetted in accordance with a list of forbidden topics. And, of course, there remain those blunt software instruments that block access to sexually oriented sites by looking for keywords such as *sex, erotic,* and *X-rated*. But one of the easiest solutions is to keep the family computer in a well-traveled space, like a living room, so that parents can monitor what their children download.

Fact or Media Fiction?

18   In her 1995 *CMC* magazine article, "Journey to the Centre of Cybersmut," Lisa Schmeiser discusses her research into online pornography. After an exhaustive search, she was unable to find any pornography, apart from the occasional commercial site (requiring a credit card for access), and concluded that one would have to undertake extensive searching to find quantities of explicit pornography. She suggested that, if children were accessing pornography online, they would not have been doing it by accident. Schmeiser writes: "There will be children who circumvent passwords, Surfwatch software, and seemingly innocuous links to find the 'adult' material. But these are the same kids who would visit every convenience store in a five-mile radius to find the one stocking *Playboy*." Her argument is simply that, while there is a certain amount of pornography online, it is not freely and readily available. Contrary to what the media often report, pornography is not that easy to find.

19   There *is* pornography in cyberspace (including images, pictures, movies, sounds, and sex discussions) and several ways of receiving pornographic material on the Internet (such as through private bulletin board systems, the World Wide Web, newsgroups, and e-mail). However, many sites just contain reproduced images from hardcore magazines and videos available from other outlets, and registration fee restrictions make them inaccessible to children. And for the more contentious issue of pedophilia, a recent investigation by the *Guardian* newspaper in Britain revealed that the majority of pedophilic images distributed on the Internet are simply electronic reproductions of the small output of legitimate pedophile magazines, such as *Lolita,* published in the 1970s.

20   Clearly the issue of pornography on the Internet is a moral panic—an issue perpetuated by a sensationalistic style of reporting and misleading content in newspaper and magazine articles. And probably the text from which to base any examination of the possible link between media reporting and moral panics is Stanley Cohen's 1972 book, *Folk Devils and Moral Panic,* in which he proposes that the mass media are ultimately responsible for the creation of such panics. Cohen describes a moral panic as occurring when "a condition, episode, person or group of persons emerges to become a threat to societal values and interests; . . . the moral barricades are manned by editors . . . politicians and other 'right thinking' people." He feels that, while problematical elements of society can pose a threat to others, this threat is realistically far less than the perceived image generated by mass media reporting.

21   Cohen describes how the news we read is not necessarily the truth; editors have papers to sell, targets to meet, and competition from other publishers. It is

in their interest to make the story "a good read"—the sensationalist approach sells newspapers. The average person is likely to be drawn in with the promise of scandal and intrigue. This can be seen in the reporting of the *National Enquirer* and *People,* with their splashy pictures and sensationalistic headlines, helping them become two of the largest circulation magazines in the United States.

22   Cohen discusses the "inventory" as the set of criteria inherent in any reporting that may be deemed as fueling a moral panic. This inventory consists of the following:

23   ***Exaggeration in Reporting.***   Facts are often overblown to give the story a greater edge. Figures that are not necessarily incorrect but have been quoted out of context, or have been used incorrectly to shock, are two forms of this exaggeration.

24   Looking back at the original *Time* cover article, "On a Screen Near You: Cyberporn," this type of exaggeration is apparent. Headlines such as "The Carnegie Mellon researchers found 917,410 sexually explicit pictures, short stories and film clips online" make the reader think that there really is a problem with the quantity of pornography in cyberspace. It takes the reader a great deal of further exploration to find out how this figure was calculated. Also, standing alone and out of context, the oft-quoted figure that 83.5 percent of images found on Usenet Newsgroups are pornographic could be seen as cause for concern. However, if one looks at the math associated with this figure, one would find that this is a sampled percentage with a research leaning toward known areas of pornography.

25   ***The Repetition of Fallacies.***   This occurs when a writer reports information that seems perfectly believable to the general public, even though those who know the subject are aware it is wildly incorrect. In the case of pornography, the common fallacy is that the Internet is awash with nothing but pornography and that all you need to obtain it is a computer and a modem. Such misinformation is integral to the fueling of moral panics.

26   Take, for example, the October 18, 1995, *Scotland on Sunday,* which reports that, to obtain pornographic material, "all you need is a personal computer, a phone line with a modem attached and a connection via a specialist provider to the Internet." What the article fails to mention is that the majority of pornography is found on specific Usenet sites not readily available from the major Internet providers, such as America Online and Compuserve. It also fails to mention that this pornography needs to be downloaded and converted into a viewable form, which requires certain skills and can take considerable time.

27   ***Misleading Pictures and Snappy Titles.***   Media representation often exaggerates a story through provocative titles and flashy pictorials—all in the name of drawing in the reader. The titles set the tone for the rest of the article; the headline is the most noticeable and important part of any news item, attracting the reader's initial attention. The recent *Newsweek* article is a perfect example. Even

if the headline has little relevance to the article, it sways the reader's perception of the topic. The symbolization of images further increases the impact of the story. *Time*'s own images in its original coverage—showing a shocked little boy on the cover and, inside, a naked man hunched over a computer monitor—added to the article's ability to shock and to draw the reader into the story.

28   Through sensationalized reporting, certain forms of behavior become classified as *deviant*. Specifically, those who put pornography online or those who download it are seen as being deviant in nature. This style of reporting benefits the publication or broadcast by giving it the aura of "moral guardian" to the rest of society. It also increases revenue.

29   In exposing deviant behavior, newspapers and magazines have the ability to push for reform. So, by classifying a subject and its relevant activities as deviant, they can stand as crusaders for moral decency, championing the cause of "normal" people. They can report the subject and call for something to be done about it, but this power is easily abused. The *Time* cyberporn article called for reform on the basis of Rimm's findings, proclaiming, "A new study shows us how pervasive and wild [pornography on the Internet] really is. Can we protect our kids—and free speech?" These cries to protect our children affected the likes of Senators James Exon and Robert Dole, who took the *Time* article with its "shocking" revelations (as well as a sample of pornographic images) to the Senate floor, appealing for changes to the law. From this response it is clear how powerful a magazine article can be, regardless of the integrity and accuracy of its reporting.

30   The *Time* article had all of Cohen's elements relating to the fueling of a moral panic: exaggeration, fallacies, and misleading pictures and titles. Because certain publications are highly regarded and enjoy an important role in society, anything printed in their pages is consumed and believed by a large audience. People accept what they read because, to the best of their knowledge, it is the truth. So, even though the *Time* article was based on a report by an undergraduate student passing as "a research team from Carnegie Mellon," the status of the magazine was great enough to launch a panic that continues unabated—from the halls of Congress to the pulpits of churches, from public schools to the offices of software developers, from local communities to the global village.

FOR ANALYSIS AND DISCUSSION

1. In the first part of her essay, Wilkins discusses the flawed research techniques of the Rimm/Carnegie Mellon Internet pornography study. Does the fact that the study was flawed change the validity of the issues it addresses? How important are accurate data in an argument? What happens to a debate when data are discovered to be inaccurate or even deliberately skewed?

2. In paragraph 8 Wilkins discusses the 1995 Grassley bill. How does the author feel about this bill? How can you tell? Do you agree with her position?

3. What are the problems with the Communications Decency Act (CDA)? Is it possible to actually implement such legislation? Explain.
4. Wilkins comments in paragraph 17 that the easiest solution to protecting children from objectionable Internet material is to put the computer in a "well-traveled space, like a living room." Does this seem like a feasible solution to the problem?
5. Evaluate the feasibility of a V-chip for the Internet. Does such a solution seem workable? Would this solution help parents, while still protecting First Amendment rights?
6. Analyze Wilkins's method of uncovering skewed data and reports to support her argument. How effective is this technique?

What Part of "No Law" Don't You Understand?
William Bennett Turner

Given the fact that the First Amendment was written more than 200 years ago, some people do not believe that it addresses the new medium of cyberspace. William Bennett Turner disagrees. In this essay Turner defends the applicability of the First Amendment to digital communication, explaining that the First Amendment is flexible enough to protect our rights no matter what innovations in communication we develop, or what century we may be in.

William Bennett Turner is a San Francisco lawyer who specializes in constitutional law. He has argued three cases before the United States Supreme Court, including two First Amendment cases. He also teaches the First Amendment and the Press at the University of California, Berkeley. The following article was first published in *Wired* magazine in May 1998.

BEFORE YOU READ

Is an amendment written 200 years ago still applicable to modern U.S. society? What do you think the drafters of the Constitution would say about how we apply the First Amendment today?

AS YOU READ

How does Turner's "lesson" on First Amendment rights help support his argument? Would his argument be as effective if he had not given his readers this lesson first?

1   It's hard to imagine that our antique First Amendment, written in 1789, is up to the task of dealing with 21st-century digital communication. James Madison would have had a hard time getting his mind around instant worldwide electronic communication. The Supreme Court has said, ominously, that "differences in the characteristics of new media justify differences in the First Amend-

ment standards applied to them." In light of this, some thoughtful observers of new technology have proposed constitutional amendments to ensure that government does not censor, manage, or restrict electronic communications.

2   The truth, however, is that we don't need a new First Amendment for digital communication. All we need is adherence to the bedrock principles of First Amendment interpretation that have grown up with us over the first two centuries of the republic. Madison's 18th-century framework is flexible enough to protect our freedoms in any century.

Reality Check: Free Speech Is Not Absolute

3   The First Amendment speaks in seemingly absolute terms: "Congress shall make no law . . . abridging the freedom of speech or of the press." This has never meant, however, that people can say *whatever* they want *wherever* they want. Freedom of speech does not mean speech totally uninhibited by any legal restraint. It has always been true that some forms of speech can be outlawed or penalized—and many have been. Common examples include fraudulent advertising, child pornography, obscenity, "fighting words," help-wanted ads that discriminate on the basis of race, words used in a criminal transaction ("I'll kill your husband for US$10,000"), unkept promises, unlicensed broadcasts, libel, speech that infringes a copyright, and unauthorized disclosure of data used to make atomic weapons.

4   Correctly interpreted, the First Amendment does not prohibit all restrictions on speech. It doesn't prohibit private restrictions at all. Our constitution is a series of constraints on government, not on individuals or even powerful corporations. It is not a violation of the First Amendment for the Microsoft Network, if it so desired, to forbid postings that criticize Bill Gates. Microsoft is not the government, at least not yet. Similarly, CompuServe's censorship of sex newsgroups may offend freedom lovers but does not violate the First Amendment.

5   The amendment prohibits government restrictions on "the freedom of speech," not on all speech, and it's a mistake to argue that no speech can be restricted. In every case, the question is whether the particular "speech" is within the "freedom" comprehended by the amendment.

No Fine Print

6   The First Amendment means what the courts say it means. Since the amendment's words themselves don't tell us what falls within its "freedom," it is up to the courts, faced with the necessity of deciding particular cases, to spell out the rules for deciding exactly what speech is free, in the sense that it cannot legally be prohibited or penalized. While the courts sometimes go astray, it remains true that Americans have freer speech than any other people because our freedoms have been forthrightly defined and enforced by the courts.

7   In every case in which government tries to restrict speech, some high-minded—or at least plausible—reason is offered. When the Nixon Administration tried to suppress publication of the Pentagon Papers, it was argued that their publication would undermine national security. When Congress acted to

prohibit phone sex, it said that such action was necessary to protect children from exposure to indecent material. When state governments forbid publication of the names of rape victims, they say it is necessary to protect privacy and encourage the reporting of sex crimes. And so on. In each new case, a court has to decide whether the government's justification prevails over the interest in free speech.

Fundamental Free Speech Principles

8 In deciding free speech cases, the courts have elaborated some bedrock principles that inform First Amendment decision-making. What the First Amendment "freedom" means, in fact, is basically this set of principles. We should remind ourselves of them and ask whether they need adjustment for the 21st century. Here are some of them:

9 • Government may not restrict or penalize speech because of its content or its viewpoint. It must remain neutral in the marketplace of ideas.

10 • There is no such thing as a "false idea." This principle rests on the belief that bad ideas will be driven out not by censorship but by good ideas, that the remedy for offensive speech is not suppression, but more speech.

11 • Restrictions on speech must not be vague or uncertain but sufficiently precise so that everyone understands exactly what is unlawful. No overly broad meat-axe regulation is allowed—any restriction must be a sensitive tool that cuts no more than is necessary to serve the precise government interest involved.

12 • "Journalism" is not a licensed, credentialed profession. Under our legal system, the "lonely pamphleteer" has the same First Amendment rights as the publisher of the *New York Times*.

13 • The press cannot be ordered to print statements it does not wish to print.

14 • "Prior restraints" on speech—government orders that certain information not be published—are prohibited.

15 • Penalties (like damages in libel suits) may not be imposed for innocent mistakes that happen to defame someone.

16 • Advocacy—including advocacy of the overthrow of the government—cannot be outlawed, so long as it does not amount to inciting people to imminent lawless action. Speech short of incitement cannot be banned because of the anticipated adverse reaction of the audience.

17 • Punishment for "seditious libel"—scathing criticism of government—is not tolerated under the First Amendment.

18 • No one can own or control facts or ideas (though a person can copyright the unique way he or she expresses those facts or ideas).

19 These are all great protections that allow us to call ourselves free people. And these principles apply regardless of the means of communication: via big newspapers, small magazines, telephones, television, radio, or the street-corner orator. There is no reason to fear that these principles will not apply with full force to all forms of digital communication.

20   On the other hand, one must recognize that some of these principles—like the First Amendment itself—are not absolute. There can be exceptions. For example, government can restrict certain speech because of its content, if it proves that there's a "compelling" government interest (like protecting national security or shielding children from sexual exploitation) and there's no less onerous means of protecting the government interest. Even a "prior restraint" on certain speech may be warranted if the government proves, say, that disclosure of the locations of strategic missiles in wartime world sabotage the war effort or endanger troops.

21   The question, then, is whether anything about the nature of digital communication would justify exceptions to the basic principles of our longstanding First Amendment freedom.

New Media, New Rules?

22 The Supreme Court spoke too loosely when it said that differences in new media justify different First Amendment standards. The notion first surfaced in a 1949 case (*Kovacs v. Cooper*) involving restrictions on the use of sound trucks in congested cities. The court not surprisingly ruled that cities could keep the "new medium" from disrupting sleep and drowning out all conversation by blaring slogans at all hours and decibel levels. Such a regulation is a reasonable "time, place, and manner" restriction that does not forbid any speech based on its content. Government can more easily justify regulating the way the message is delivered rather than the message itself.

23   Unfortunately, the Supreme Court retrieved the thought about new media years later, reformulated it, and unthinkingly applied it to a case in which the issue was government regulation of content. In 1969, the court handed down *Red Lion,* the most important decision ever on broadcasting.

24   The Court upheld the FCC's "Fairness Doctrine," which required licensed broadcasters to cover important public issues and to give voice to contrasting views on the issues. In other words, broadcasters were required to air information they would otherwise have chosen not to air, including views with which they vehemently disagreed. For example, a broadcaster strongly in favor of constructing a nuclear power plant would have to air the anti-nuke point of view as well as his or her own.

25   The Court's rationale in *Red Lion* was that the airwaves were a public resource, and those licensed to monopolize one of the scarce frequencies could be required to use this government-bestowed benefit in the public interest. Scarcity of frequencies justified both government allocation of frequencies and regulation of content. The court said that requiring broadcasters to air diverse views enhanced rather than hobbled our First Amendment marketplace of ideas.

26   Just five years later, people concerned about the increasing concentration of media power in large corporations owning newspapers tried to get a similar concept applied to the world of print. They asked the Supreme Court to uphold a Florida law giving political candidates a "right of reply" to newspaper attacks against them during campaigns. The law was a lot like the FCC's

"personal attack" rule (part of the Fairness Doctrine), one that the court had enforced against broadcasters in Red Lion. But in the *Miami Herald* case, the Court rejected the argument as completely inconsistent with the First Amendment right of newspapers to exercise editorial discretion in deciding what to publish and what not to publish. The result left one rule for print and another for broadcast—the most prominent illustration to date of the different-media, different-standards rule.

27 Now that print is becoming electronic, will it lose its preferred status? Certainly not. There is far less need for a government-enforced right of reply regarding digital communication than there is for print. There is no "scarcity" problem. You can reply instantly without permission, and you don't have to worry about economic or license barriers to entry. Your ability to respond, virtually free of charge, makes it silly to think that government should strive for some kind of "fairness" or balance in digital communication.

28 Whatever the merits of the Fairness Doctrine (it was abandoned by the FCC in 1987, though the *Red Lion* precedent stands), the Supreme Court should not extend the broad statement that new media justify different First Amendment rules. Former Justice Robert Jackson's original statement in the sound-truck case was that "the moving picture screen, the radio, the newspaper, the handbill, the sound truck, and the street-corner orator have differing natures, values, abuses, and dangers. Each, in my view, is a law unto itself." In *Red Lion,* the Court gave too much emphasis to the "law unto itself" part. If all the Court meant to say is that the law must reflect the "differing natures, values, abuses, and dangers" of each medium, that's fine—the unique characteristics of computer-mediated communication favor greater freedom.

Not Broadcast, Not Print

29 Computer-mediated communication should have much greater freedom than, for example, broadcast. Instead of being one-way—from a broadcaster with a government license to a captive audience—it's interactive and from many to many. Its decentralization and user control are vastly different from the monopolistic control of scarce frequencies by powerful broadcasters.

30 Nor is the medium "intrusive" in the sense that our kids might be surprised and "assaulted" by hearing dirty words, such as when they scan radio stations. (This is what led the Court, in the 1978 *Pacifica* decision, to uphold the FCC prohibition of "indecency" on the radio.) User control means you need to work at it in a fairly sophisticated way to participate, and you have an incredible range of choice about exposing yourself to communication. Parental control should not be a thing of the past.

31 Of course, the fact that digital communication is cheap means anybody can become a publisher. There's no built-in preference for speech by the rich and powerful—those who own printing presses, tons of newsprint, or broadcast licenses—or for speech whose main appeal is to generate paid advertisements. It's far more democratic even than print.

32   Unfortunately, the Supreme Court has repeated the new-media new-rules statement in recent cases. In 1994, for example, the Court quoted the line from the *Red Lion* decision in deciding a case (*Turner Broadcasting v. FCC*) on whether cable television operators could be required to carry local broadcast and public television channels. I hope the Court, when it gets its first digital communication case, does not woodenly recite the same slogan.

33   The idea that there should be special First Amendment rules for new media makes little sense. The basic principles of First Amendment jurisprudence apply to all media. And, to the extent that digital communication is different—because it is fast, cheap, interactive, and controlled by decentralized users—the differences call for less regulation than traditional media, not more. The application of the basic principles should reflect these characteristics of the new technology.

New Wine into Old Vessels

34 So how would First Amendment principles established for older media apply to digital communication? Check out the bedrock principles already listed. They ought to resolve just about any restriction on digital communication that you can imagine.

35   Yes, the new technology will present different kinds of issues. It has occurred to many people that libel or "indecency" on the Internet presents novel problems, and that hate speech and the invasion of privacy will have to be dealt with. Cases involving the liability of access providers and bulletin board operators already have appeared in the lower courts. And issues about anonymous speech and encryption have been hotly debated, though not decided by the courts.

36   In my view, none of these problems requires alteration of any of the fundamental First Amendment principles. Deciding cases involving these new issues should be done the old-fashioned way: by looking to precedent, reasoning by analogy, and considering the policy implications of ruling one way or another.

37   The most immediate example is the impending telecommunications law prohibiting "obscene" or "indecent" speech on the Internet. Like it or not, this is a no-brainer. Material that is so gross as to fall within the Supreme Court's strict definition of obscenity, which is really hardcore material that has no artistic, political, or social value, is unprotected by the First Amendment regardless of the medium in which it appears. So, for better or for worse, we have to accept that Congress can make a law outlawing obscene speech on the Internet. To be sure, there are knotty issues involving whose "community standards" are being used to judge obscenity when an alleged dirty picture is uploaded in libertine San Francisco and downloaded in Logan, Utah, by a recipient with no geographic address.

38   This is a rule that could profit by reexamination in light of the new manner of communication. And maybe there should be a new, nongeographic definition of "community" that prevents federal prosecution of, for example, those who wish to discuss safe-sex options for preventing AIDS. But there's no basis

for arguing either that obscene speech is now legal because it's communicated by computer or that obscenity must now be judged by the standards of the most prudish community a prosecutor can find.

39   Indecent material—dirty words or pictures that the government can't prohibit adults from seeing but can keep from children—is treated differently from obscene material. The ban on "indecent" communications on the Internet is plainly invalid under the recognized principles that forbid vague, overly broad, content-based restrictions promoting interests that can be served by less restrictive means. The Supreme Court threw out, on those grounds, the comparable prohibition of "indecent" speech on the telephone in the Sable Communications case in 1989—it must do the same with the new law. The availability of less restrictive means, like filtering technology, will allow parents to control their children's access instead of reducing all communication to the level of what is fit for children.

40   Consider also what adjustments need to be made in the law of libel. More people will be "publishing" all over the country and presumably saying false and defamatory things about more people, and it won't be long before defamation cases work their way up the court system. Since *New York Times v. Sullivan* in 1964, all libel cases are governed, at least in part, by First Amendment rules. A public figure can't sue for an innocent mistake but basically has to prove that the publisher deliberately lied. Whether you are a public figure depends on whether you have ready access to the media to combat an untruth published about you, and whether you inject yourself into a particular controversy.

41   Well, if you are actively participating in a chat room or posting material on a bulletin board, you probably ought to be considered a "limited purpose" public figure and you will have to shrug off false—but not deliberately false—statements made about you in that forum. And because it's within your power to respond to statements instantaneously and to the very same audience that saw the falsehoods, any damages should be limited. Digital libel ought to be harder, not easier, to prove.

42   But what about the system operator, the one who allows "indecent" or libelous speech to be published on his or her system? The rule ought to be that the operator is not liabel as a "publisher" unless the operator actually knows that the system is being used for plainly unlawful speech. The operator cannot be a guarantor of the accuracy of all posted information. He or she cannot reasonably be expected to monitor all postings, to screen for possible torts or even dirty words. The analogy is to a bookstore owner, not a magazine publisher.

43   Hate speech and harassment can be found on the Internet, just as they can be found on college dormitory bulletin boards or over the telephone. They may wreck one's enjoyment of the digital conversation but they don't present any unique First Amendment problems that can't be dealt with by the established principles. Again, we have to remember that private regulation is not unconstitutional and there is no First Amendment prohibition against expelling those whose speech is abusive or unwelcome from your digital circle. If you want government to do it for you, you're asking that First Amendment princi-

ples be diluted. Remember, we don't protect speech because it can cause no harm but because we don't trust government to decide what expression is acceptable in our discourse.

FOR ANALYSIS AND DISCUSSION

1. Should there be different standards for different media? Explain.
2. In both Wilkins's and Turner's essays, the authors comment that the key to protecting children is "parental control." Evaluate how each author addresses the issue of parental control in the context of his or her argument. Do you agree with their perspectives?
3. Discuss the role of the "system operator" of Internet bulletin boards and chatrooms (paragraph 42). Should the system operator be responsible for Internet content? Explain.
4. Two of the articles in this section mention Bill Gates. In what context does his name come up? Why mention him at all?
5. In paragraph 43, Turner comments that hate speech doesn't "present any unique First Amendment problems that can't be dealt with by the established principles." What does he mean? What are the "established principles"? Explain.

WRITING ASSIGNMENTS: CENSORSHIP ON THE INTERNET

1. In her article on the "moral panic" regarding Internet pornography, Julia Wilkins cites the research of Lisa Schmeiser. Wilkins reports that "after an exhaustive search" Schmeiser was "unable to find any pornography, apart from the occasional commercial site (requiring a credit card for access)." Conduct your own research project on this issue. Assume you have the computer skills of a ten-year-old child. How difficult—or easy—is it to locate pornography on the Web? After researching, write a paper in which you support or refute Schmeiser's findings.
2. Both Wilkins and Bennett argue that parents should be responsible for what their children access on the Internet. This argument is often repeated for other forms of media, such as television, movies, and music. Write an argument supporting your position on the roles and responsibilities of parents in what their children see and hear.
3. Write an argument on your perspective regarding legislative control of Internet content. Before you write, use a pro/con checklist to explore the benefits and disadvantages of government control? What impact could it have? Conversely, what impact might a lack of restriction have on the Internet and its users?
4. Access the Justice on Campus Web site at <http://joc.mit.edu>. Read the list of recent news articles at the top of the site and access the pages that have been proposed for censure. Do you agree that these sites should be protected? What is controversial about them? Support your argument with information from the Web site and your own perspective.

Censorship of Books: What Constitutes Censorship?

The Freedom to Read
The American Library Association and the Association of American Publishers

The American Library Association, founded in 1876, is the oldest and largest national library association in the world. Addressing the needs of state, public, school, and academic libraries, it has over 55,000 members across the country. Dedicated to preserving the freedom of information distribution and assuring the access to information for all, the ALA and the AAP have even written their own "Bill of Rights." The following document was originally drafted and adopted in 1953. It was last revised in 1991 in response to increasing pressure from special interest groups to censure or limit the distribution of certain books in American libraries and schools.

BEFORE YOU READ
Is there a set of criteria that determines whether a book is "good" or "bad"? Who would set such standards?

AS YOU READ
Consider how this document is presented. How does the way the argument is delivered affect your impression of it? How do you think it will influence the audience?

1   The freedom to read is essential to our democracy. It is continuously under attack. Private groups and public authorities in various parts of the country are working to remove books from sale, to censor textbooks, to label "controversial" books, to distribute lists of "objectionable" books or authors, and to purge libraries. These actions apparently rise from a view that our national tradition of free expression is no longer valid; that censorship and suppression are needed to avoid the subversion of politics and the corruption of morals. We, as citizens devoted to the use of books and as librarians and publishers responsible for disseminating them, wish to assert the public interest in the preservation of the freedom to read.

2   We are deeply concerned about these attempts at suppression. Most such attempts rest on a denial of the fundamental premise of democracy: that the ordinary citizen, by exercising critical judgment, will accept the good and reject the bad. The censors, public and private, assume that they should determine what is good and what is bad for their fellow-citizens.

3   We trust Americans to recognize propaganda, and to reject it. We do not believe they need the help of censors to assist them in this task. We do not believe they are prepared to sacrifice their heritage of a free press in order to be

"protected" against what others think may be bad for them. We believe they still favor free enterprise in ideas and expression.

4   We are aware, of course, that books are not alone in being subjected to efforts at suppression. We are aware that these efforts are related to a larger pattern of pressures being brought against education, the press, films, radio and television. The problem is not only one of actual censorship. The shadow of fear cast by these pressures leads, we suspect, to an even larger voluntary curtailment of expression by those who seek to avoid controversy.

5   Such pressure toward conformity is perhaps natural to a time of uneasy change and pervading fear. Especially when so many of our apprehensions are directed against an ideology, the expression of a dissident idea becomes a thing feared in itself, and we tend to move against it as against a hostile deed, with suppression.

6   And yet suppression is never more dangerous than in such a time of social tension. Freedom has given the United States the elasticity to endure strain. Freedom keeps open the path of novel and creative solutions, and enables change to come by choice. Every silencing of a heresy, every enforcement of an orthodoxy, diminishes the toughness and resilience of our society and leaves it the less able to deal with stress.

7   Now as always in our history, books are among our greatest instruments of freedom. They are almost the only means for making generally available ideas or manners of expression that can initially command only a small audience. They are the natural medium for the new idea and the untried voice from which come the original contributions to social growth. They are essential to the extended discussion which serious thought requires, and to the accumulation of knowledge and ideas into organized collections.

8   We believe that free communication is essential to the preservation of a free society and a creative culture. We believe that these pressures towards conformity present the danger of limiting the range and variety of inquiry and expression on which our democracy and our culture depend. We believe that every American community must jealously guard the freedom to publish and to circulate, in order to preserve its own freedom to read. We believe that publishers and librarians have a profound responsibility to give validity to that freedom to read by making it possible for the readers to choose freely from a variety of offerings.

9   The freedom to read is guaranteed by the Constitution. Those with faith in free people will stand firm on these constitutional guarantees of essential rights and will exercise the responsibilities that accompany these rights.

10   We therefore affirm these propositions:

11   *1. It is in the public interest for publishers and librarians to make available the widest diversity of views and expressions, including those which are unorthodox or unpopular with the majority.* Creative thought is by definition new, and what is new is different. The bearer of every new thought is a rebel until that idea is refined and tested. Totalitarian systems attempt to maintain themselves in power by the ruthless suppression of any concept which challenges the established

orthodoxy. The power of a democratic system to adapt to change is vastly strengthened by the freedom of its citizens to choose widely from among conflicting opinions offered freely to them. To stifle every nonconformist idea at birth would mark the end of the democratic process. Furthermore, only through the constant activity of weighing and selecting can the democratic mind attain the strength demanded by times like these. We need to know not only what we believe but why we believe it.

12   *2. Publishers, librarians and booksellers do not need to endorse every idea or presentation contained in the books they make available. It would conflict with the public interest for them to establish their own political, moral or aesthetic views as a standard for determining what books should be published or circulated.* Publishers and librarians serve the educational process by helping to make available knowledge and ideas required for the growth of the mind and the increase of learning. They do not foster education by imposing as mentors the patterns of their own thought. The people should have the freedom to read and consider a broader range of ideas than those that may be held by any single librarian or publisher or government or church. It is wrong that what one can read should be confined to what another thinks proper.

13   *3. It is contrary to the public interest for publishers or librarians to determine the acceptability of a book on the basis of the personal history or political affiliations of the author.* A book should be judged as a book. No art or literature can flourish if it is to be measured by the political views or private lives of its creators. No society of free people can flourish which draws up lists of writers to whom it will not listen, whatever they may have to say.

14   *4. There is no place in our society for efforts to coerce the taste of others, to confine adults to the reading matter deemed suitable for adolescents, or to inhibit the efforts of writers to achieve artistic expression.* To some, much of modern literature is shocking. But is not much of life itself shocking? We cut off literature at the source if we prevent writers from dealing with the stuff of life. Parents and teachers have a responsibility to prepare the young to meet the diversity of experiences in life to which they will be exposed, as they have a responsibility to help them learn to think critically for themselves. These are affirmative responsibilities, not to be discharged simply by preventing them from reading works for which they are not yet prepared. In these matters taste differs, and taste cannot be legislated; nor can machinery be devised which will suit the demands of one group without limiting the freedom of others.

15   *5. It is not in the public interest to force a reader to accept with any book the prejudgment of a label characterizing the book or author as subversive or dangerous.* The ideal of labeling presupposes the existence of individuals or groups with wisdom to determine by authority what is good or bad for the citizen. It presupposes that individuals must be directed in making up their minds about the ideas they examine. But Americans do not need others to do their thinking for them.

16   *6. It is the responsibility of publishers and librarians, as guardians of the people's freedom to read, to contest encroachments upon that freedom by individuals or groups seeking to impose their own standards or tastes upon the community at large.* It is inevitable

in the give and take of the democratic process that the political, the moral, or the aesthetic concepts of an individual or group will occasionally collide with those of another individual or group. In a free society individuals are free to determine for themselves what they wish to read, and each group is free to determine what it will recommend to its freely associated members. But no group has the right to take the law into its own hands, and to impose its own concept of politics or morality upon other members of a democratic society. Freedom is no freedom if it is accorded only to the accepted and the inoffensive.

17   *7. It is the responsibility of publishers and librarians to give full meaning to the freedom to read by providing books that enrich the quality and diversity of thought and expression. By the exercise of this affirmative responsibility, they can demonstrate that the answer to a bad book is a good one, the answer to a bad idea is a good one.* The freedom to read is of little consequence when expended on the trivial; it is frustrated when the reader cannot obtain matter fit for that reader's purpose. What is needed is not only the absence of restraint, but the positive provision of opportunity for the people to read the best that has been thought and said. Books are the major channel by which the intellectual inheritance is handed down, and the principal means of its testing and growth. The defense of their freedom and integrity, and the enlargement of their service to society, requires of all publishers and librarians the utmost of their faculties, and deserves of all citizens the fullest of their support.

18   We state these propositions neither lightly nor as easy generalizations. We here stake out a lofty claim for the value of books. We do so because we believe that they are good, possessed of enormous variety and usefulness, worthy of cherishing and keeping free. We realize that the application of these propositions may mean the dissemination of ideas and manners of expression that are repugnant to many persons. We do not state these propositions in the comfortable belief that what people read is unimportant. We believe rather that what people read is deeply important, that ideas can be dangerous; but that the suppression of ideas is fatal to a democratic society. Freedom itself is a dangerous way of life, but it is ours.

FOR ANALYSIS AND DISCUSSION

1. What attempts at suppression of information are the ALA and the AAP concerned about? Do the authors provide any examples? Are examples necessary to support their argument? Explain.

2. In paragraph 6 the document states that "suppression is never more dangerous than in such a time of social tension." What do the authors mean by this statement? How do you think opponents to this declaration would respond?

3. Analyze the seven "declarations" of the ALA/AAP document and formulate a response to each. What questions do you have about them? What exceptions to these "declarations" can you anticipate?

4. How do the writers use the First Amendment and the Constitution to support their argument? Is this an effective means of persuasion?

5. Can you think of any attempts by certain groups to control the accessibility of written material (besides pornography) on the grounds that it is unacceptable? Explain the circumstances and reaction to their censorship attempt.

6. The writers mention the labeling of books. To what are they objecting? Are they against all types of labels? Explain.

Banned Books Week 1997:
A Case of Misrepresentation
Steve McKinzie

The fourth week of September 1997 was designated National Banned Book Week by the American Library Association. To promote dialogue on the issue of censorship and book banning, the ALA published a list of books that had been banned by various libraries and schools. Its goal was to raise national consciousness regarding what the association perceived to be an escalating problem nationwide, a view librarian Steve McKinzie refutes in the following essay.

Steve McKinzie is the head librarian for the Dickinson College Library. The following article was featured in the September 29, 1997 edition of the *Covenant Syndicate,* an online publication of the Center for the Advancement of Paleo Orthodoxy, which presents biblical perspectives on current issues.

BEFORE YOU READ

Is censorship of written materials ever permissible? If so, under what conditions? If not, why not?

AS YOU READ

Have you encountered or heard of the banning of books in schools? Who proposed the censorship and why was it enforced?

1   This week (September 21st–27th), the nation celebrates National Banned Book Week, a week-long propaganda fest and consciousness-raising extravaganza of the American Library Association's Office for Intellectual Freedom. The week's promoters parade a list of books that they charge have been banned in libraries and schools across the nation, talk about the importance of First Amendment Rights, and lament the rise of censorship from what they consider to be the ill-informed and malicious enemies of freedom and American democracy—a group that includes the usual conservatives of various flavors and, of course, that enemy of everything dear to the national consciousness, the Christian Right.

2   Now to begin with, most Americans have serious problems with the sort of radical libertarianism that the American Library Association (ALA) espouses. Most Americans don't buy into the notion that public libraries should buy anything no matter how pornographic, or that schools should teach anything, no

matter how controversial. The majority of Americans believe in community standards, and they stubbornly insist that schools, libraries, and other social institutions ought to support those standards. Even so, the real difficulty with the American Library Association's Banned Book week isn't its philosophy, however much people may question the ALA's anything-goes-approach to building a library collection and managing a school's curriculum.

3   No, the real problem is the dishonesty involved.

4   Banned Book Week isn't really what it says it is. The ALA has gone in for some serious mislabeling here. It has misleadingly categorized the week—a serious charge when you remember that librarians are supposed to be dispassionate and accurate catalogers or labelers of things.

5   In all honesty, what is the real state of censorship and book banning in America? Well, very few—if any—books in this country are currently banned. You can buy almost any title that you want, download tons of information from the Web that you need, and you can check out all sorts of things at your public library. Nor is censorship dangerously on the rise as the ALA is apt to insinuate.

6   The disparity between what actually is and what the week's promoters claim stems from their exaggerated notions of what constitutes censorship. In the eyes of the ALA and its Office for Intellectual Freedom, any kind of challenge to a book is to be considered an effort at banning and any kind of complaint about a title an attempt at unconscionable censorship. For a book to be labeled a banned book in their mind, someone needs only question its place in a given library's collection, or openly wonder if a specific title belongs in the children's section. To be reckoned a censor, one has only to suggest in public that a book may not be appropriate in a given high school English class.

7   Kathy Monteiro, a teacher in McClintock High School in Tempe, Arizona complained about her high schoolers' mandatory reading of *Huckleberry Finn*. She thought the book was racist. Parents in High Point, North Carolina questioned the appropriateness of Richard Wright's *Native Son* and Alice Walker's *Color Purple*. They thought the adult themes inappropriate for the grade level. Both these protests were officially recorded as examples of attempted censorship by ALA's Newsletter on Intellectual Freedom. All three titles were placed on the Banned Book List.

8   Let's get real. Such challenges are not attempts at censorship, and such complaints about books used in a classroom are not efforts to have certain titles banned. The people involved in these controversies about what students are required to read are merely speaking their minds, and no matter how much I disagree with their contentions (I enjoy anything by Mark Twain and think Richard Wright's *Native Son* to be something of a classic), they have a right to argue their point. They should be able to speak up without fear of being considered enemies of the Republic or being chastised as censors of great literature.

9   Parents who challenge the inclusion of a given text in a specific literature class and citizens who openly protest a library's collection development decision are only speaking out about things that they believe in. It is a grand American tradition and one that we should encourage as much as we can. We

shouldn't be trying to ban free speech in the name of free speech. Let people speak out about what they care about, without being branded a censor or labeled a book banner.

10   In short, the American Library Association needs to lighten up. At the very least, they should rename their week. As anyone can see, Banned Book Week isn't really about banned books. It is about people having differing opinions and caring enough to make those opinions known.

11   The nation could use a lot more of that, not less.

FOR ANALYSIS AND DISCUSSION

1. In the second paragraph McKinzie states that "most Americans have serious problems with the sort of radical libertarianism that the [ALA] espouses." What technique is McKinzie using to connect with his audience? Do you agree with this statement? How might this phraseology work for, or counter to, the aims of McKinzie's argument?

2. McKinzie cites some of the ALA examples of people wishing to censor books. What does he think is wrong with the ALA's examples? Do you agree?

3. How much do you learn about the ALA Banned Book List from McKinzie's article? What opinion can you formulate about the list from the information provided in his essay?

4. Evaluate McKinzie's closing statement that the ALA needs to "lighten up." How do you think the ALA would respond to this statement?

5. What is McKinzie's argument against the ALA? Does the fact that he is a librarian influence your perception of his argument?

Author's Afterword from
Fahrenheit 451
Ray Bradbury

First published in 1953, the classic novel *Fahrenheit 451* by Ray Bradbury depicts a future in which books forbidden by a totalitarian government are burned. In *Fahrenheit 451* firemen don't put out fires—they start them, burning books in giant bonfires. By controlling information the government creates a society in which the appearance of happiness is the highest goal—a place where trivial information is good, and knowledge and ideas are bad. The novel raises the question: What is the price of censorship "protection" and who decides what is acceptable to read?

Ray Bradbury is the author of more than 500 short stories, novels, plays, and poems, including *The Martian Chronicles* and *The Illustrated Man.* He has won many awards for his writing, including the Grand Master Award from the Science Fiction Writers of America.

BEFORE YOU READ

Imagine living in a country in which you could be arrested for reading the "wrong" books. What sort of world would it be if the police could enter your home and take your books away to be burned because the government had decided they were inappropriate for you to read?

AS YOU READ

How might the comments made to Bradbury regarding his books be considered ironic in light of the plot of *Fahrenheit 451*?

1   About two years ago, a letter arrived from a solemn young Vassar lady telling me how much she enjoyed reading my experiment in space mythology, *The Martian Chronicles*.

2   But, she added, wouldn't it be a good idea, this late in time, to rewrite the book inserting more women's characters and roles?

3   A few years before that I got a certain amount of mail concerning the same Martian book complaining that the blacks in the book were Uncle Toms and why didn't I "do them over"?

4   Along about then came a note from a Southern white suggesting that I was prejudiced in favor of the blacks and the entire story should be dropped.

5   Two weeks ago my mountain of mail delivered forth a pipsqueak mouse of a letter from a well-known publishing house that wanted to reprint my story "The Fog Horn" in a high school reader.

6   In my story, I had described a lighthouse as having, late at night, an illumination coming from it that was a "God-Light." Looking up at it from the viewpoint of any sea-creature one would have felt that one was in "the Presence."

7   The editors had deleted "God-Light" and "in the Presence."

8   Some five years back, the editors of yet another anthology for school readers put together a volume with some 400 (count 'em) short stories in it. How do you cram 400 short stories by Twain, Irving, Poe, Maupassant and Bierce into one book?

9   Simplicity itself. Skin, debone, demarrow, scarify, melt, render down and destroy. Every adjective that counted, every verb that moved, every metaphor that weighed more than a mosquito—out! Every simile that would have made a sub-moron's mouth twitch—gone! Any aside that explained the two-bit philosophy of a first-rate writer—lost!

10 Every story, slenderized, starved, bluepenciled, leeched and bled white, resembled every other story. Twain read like Poe read like Shakespeare read like Dostoevsky read like—in the finale—Edgar Guest. Every word of more than three syllables had been razored. Every image that demanded so much as one instant's attention—shot dead.

11 Do you begin to get the damned and incredible picture?

12 How did I react to all of the above?

13 By "firing" the whole lot.

14 By sending rejection slips to each and every one.

15 By ticketing the assembly of idiots to the far reaches of hell.

16   The point is obvious. There is more than one way to burn a book. And the world is full of people running about with lit matches. Every minority, be it Baptist/Unitarian, Irish/Italian/Octogenarian/Zen Buddhist, Zionist/Seventh-day Adventist, Women's Lib/Republican, Mattachine/Four Square Gospel feels it has the will, the right, the duty to douse the kerosene, light the fuse. Every dimwit editor who sees himself as the source of all dreary blanc-mange plain porridge unleavened literature, licks his guillotine and eyes the neck of any author who dares to speak above a whisper or write above a nursery rhyme.

17   Fire-Captain Beatty, in my novel *Fahrenheit 451,* described how the books were burned first by minorities, each ripping a page or a paragraph from this book, then that, until the day came when the books were empty and the minds shut and the libraries closed forever.

18   "Shut the door, they're coming through the window, shut the window, they're coming through the door," are the words to an old song. They fit my lifestyle with newly arriving butcher/censors every month. Only six weeks ago, I discovered that, over the years, some cubby-hole editors at Ballantine Books, fearful of contaminating the young, had, bit by bit, censored some 75 separate sections from the novel. Students, reading the novel which, after all, deals with censorship and book-burning in the future, wrote to tell me of this exquisite irony. Judy-Lynn Del Rey, one of the new Ballantine editors, is having the entire book reset and republished this summer with all the damns and hells back in place.

19   A final test for old Job II here: I sent a play, *Leviathan 99,* off to a university theater a month ago. My play is based on the "Moby Dick" mythology, dedicated to Melville, and concerns a rocket crew and a blind space captain who venture forth to encounter a Great White Comet and destroy the destroyer. My drama premiers as an opera in Paris this autumn. But, for now, the university wrote back that they hardly dared do my play—it had no women in it! And the ERA ladies on campus would descend with ballbats if the drama department even tried!

20   Grinding my bicuspids into powder, I suggested that would mean, from now on, no more productions of *Boys in the Band* (no women), or *The Women* (no men). Or, counting heads, male and female, a good lot of Shakespeare that would never be seen again, especially if you count lines and find that all the good stuff went to the males!

21   I wrote back maybe they should do my play one week, and *The Women* the next. They probably thought I was joking, and I'm not sure that I wasn't.

22   For it is a mad world and it will get madder if we allow the minorities, be they dwarf or giant, orangutan or dolphin, nuclear-head or water-conversationalist, pro-computerologist or Neo-Luddite, simpleton or sage, to interfere with aesthetics. The real world is the playing ground for each and every group, to make or unmake laws. But the tip of the nose of my book or stories or poems is where their rights end and my territorial imperatives begin, run and rule. If Mormons do not like my plays, let them write their own. If the Irish hate my Dublin stories, let them rent typewriters. If teachers and grammar school edi-

tors find my jawbreaker sentences shatter their mushmilk teeth, let them eat stale cake dunked in weak tea of their own ungodly manufacture. If the Chicano intellectuals wish to re-cut my "Wonderful Ice Cream Suit" so it shapes "Zoot," may the belt unravel and the pants fall.

23   For, let's face it, digression is the soul of wit. Take philosophic asides away from Dante, Milton or Hamlet's father's ghost and what stays is dry bones. Laurence Sterne said it once: Digressions, incontestably, are the sunshine, the life, the soul of reading! Take them out and one cold eternal winter would reign in every page. Restore them to the writer—he steps forth like a bridegroom, bids them all-hail, brings in variety and forbids the appetite to fail.

24   In sum, do not insult me with the beheadings, finger-choppings or the lung-deflations you plan for my works. I need my head to shake or nod, my hand to wave or make into a fist, my lungs to shout or whisper with. I will not go gently onto a shelf, degutted, to become a non-book.

25   All you umpires, back to the bleachers. Referees, hit the showers. It's my game. I pitch, I hit, I catch. I run the bases. At sunset I've won or lost. At sunrise, I'm out again, giving it the old try.

26   And no one can help me. Not even you.

FOR ANALYSIS AND DISCUSSION

1. Consider the tone Bradbury uses in this essay. Is he angry, defiant, sarcastic, resigned? How does his tone influence the audience's reception of his points? What does he hope to impress upon his audience?
2. According to Bradbury, what happens when books are edited to make them more "acceptable" to audiences? Explain.
3. What does Bradbury mean when he says, in paragraph 16, "There is more than one way to burn a book"?
4. Bradbury compares himself to Job. What is the effect of this comparison? Why does he use it? How might it be ironic?
5. What is the impact of Bradbury's final statement? Explain.

WRITING ASSIGNMENTS: CENSORSHIP OF BOOKS

1. In 1996 a publishing company printed the book *Hit Man: A Technical Manual for Independent Contractors,* which explained how to become a hit man to murder someone. Public outcry against the book resulted in its going out of publication, but the publishers defended their decision to print the book, citing the principles of freedom of speech and the First Amendment. Access the Northwestern University Web site, which addresses the issues of freedom of speech and the book at <http://faculty-web.at.nwu.edu/commstud/freespeech/cont/cases/hitman.html>. After accessing the page and exploring its contents, draft a response to the book's publishers. Support your response with information gathered from the site, as well as from your own perspective.

2. Access the ALA Web site listing the 1998 Banned Book List at <http://www.ala.org/bbooks/challeng.html>. How familiar are you with any of the books listed? Select a book you have read that is on the list and write an essay in which you either defend the book against censure or make a case for its banning.

3. Imagine that you are a parent. Write a letter in which you urge a teacher to remove certain books from the school's curriculum. Be specific about which books you want banned and why. Then exchange letters with a classmate. Assume the role of the teacher who receives the letter. Write a letter back to the "parent" defending the books, making sure to cite useful parts of the First Amendment, the ALA statement, and your own views.

chapter 12

MEDIA INFLUENCE

The clock radio wakes us, blaring advertisements for vitamins and fast foods, and tells us whether we'll need an umbrella or snow boots to get through the day. We glance at the headlines in the morning paper, then rush out the door, driving along a highway jammed with billboards displaying lounging vacationers soaking up the sun at exotic resorts. Our computer service provider intersperses e-mail and news flashes with promotions for life insurance bargains. At 6 and 11 P.M. our local TV anchors help us catch up on the day's tally of car accidents and house fires. If it's the weekend, we'll grab a tub of popcorn at the nearest movie theater while we laugh and sigh over the latest Julia Roberts or Brad Pitt romantic comedy. We rely heavily on the media to keep us in touch with world and local events, to inform us about consumer choices, to stimulate our imagination, and to entertain us. In this chapter we focus on three forms of media—advertising, television news, and movie and television violence—to examine the important and subtle ways the media influence our lives.

The first group of readings explores the language of advertising, one of the most pervasive forms of persuasion in American life. The language used in advertising is a special form of communication, one that combines words and fantasies for the sole purpose of separating consumers from their money. In "With These Words I Can Sell You Anything," language-watcher William Lutz demonstrates how advertisers manipulate simple English words so they appear to promise what the consumer desires. However, professional ad writer Charles A. O'Neill makes a persuasive argument that even though the language of ads can be appealing, no advertisement can force consumers to lay their money down. The last essay in this section, John Leo's "The Selling of Rebellion," examines how advertisers rely on popular cultural messages not necessarily related to their products to create consumer identification and interest. Sample advertisements then provide an opportunity to analyze how advertisers use language and visual images to sell their products.

More and more Americans rely on television news to find out what's happening in the world, in the nation, and in their communities. Television's unique ability to combine words, voices, and televised images makes its news programming distinctly different from print or radio journalism. Neil Postman and Steve Powers argue that television's primary function as an entertainment medium conflicts with its role as an objective source of news stories. According to Postman and Powers, television's strategy of dramatizing news events for the entertainment of viewers often results in a distortion of the actual facts. Elayne Rapping agrees that local television news stations "sugarcoat" serious and often tragic news stories, to the detriment of their viewers. She maintains that news organizations have a civic responsibility to keep the public informed, and television's creation of a "utopian fantasy of a better, kinder, more decent and meaningful world" undermines this objective. Paul Starobin expresses this same concern in his essay objecting to the growing use of hidden cameras by television news magazine shows to sensationalize their stories.

It seems that everyone agrees that violence dominates our movie and television screens, and many are convinced that viewing violence causes violent behavior. Yet no one can agree on a solution to this problem. In "Honey, I Warped the Kids" Carl M. Cannon surveys the thousands of studies conducted since 1954 on the relationship between screen violence and the real thing. In light of the overwhelming evidence linking the two, Cannon urges industry executives to self-regulate their shows. Robert Scheer looks at the same evidence and shares with Cannon the conviction that television violence and aggression are connected. But Scheer argues in "Violence Is Us" that it is the public's responsibility to voice its objections to violent programming and to monitor children's television viewing. In "In Praise of Gore" Andrew Klavan makes no apologies for violence on the screen. In fact, he celebrates it. But Klavan does argue that the relationship between fictional violence and actual violence is not as clear cut as some would have us believe. Eliminating violence in movie and television programming, Klavan asserts, will not resolve the problem of violence in our society.

ADVERTISING: HOW POWERFUL IS THE LANGUAGE OF PERSUASION?

With These Words, I Can Sell You Anything
William Lutz

In this essay, William Lutz analyzes the way words are used in ads—how they can misrepresent, mislead, and deceive consumers. Lutz alerts us to the special power of "weasel words"—those familiar and sneaky little critters that "appear to say one thing when in fact they say the opposite, or nothing at all." The real danger, Lutz argues, is how such language debases reality and the values of the consumer.

William Lutz has been called the "George Orwell of the 1990s." Chair of the Committee on Public Doublespeak of the National Council of Teachers of English, Lutz is the former editor of the *Quarterly Review of Doublespeak,* a magazine dedicated to the eradication of misleading official statements. The following essay is an excerpt from Lutz's book, *Doublespeak* (1990).

BEFORE YOU READ

Consider the phrase "like magic" as it might be used in an ad—for example, "Zappo dish detergent works like magic." What does the phrase suggest at a quick glance? What does it mean upon detailed analysis? Make a list of other such words used in advertising to make "big promises."

AS YOU READ

A "weasel word" is a word so hollow it has no meaning. As you read Lutz's article, consider your own reaction to such words when you hear them. Have they ever motivated you to make a purchase?

1   One problem advertisers have when they try to convince you that the product they are pushing is really different from other, similar products is that their claims are subject to some laws. Not a lot of laws, but there are some designed to prevent fraudulent or untruthful claims in advertising. Even during the happy years of nonregulation under President Ronald Reagan, the FTC did crack down on the more blatant abuses in advertising claims. Generally speaking, advertisers have to be careful in what they say in their ads, in the claims they make for the products they advertise. Parity claims are safe because they are legal and supported by a number of court decisions. But beyond parity claims there are weasel words.

2   Advertisers use weasel words to appear to be making a claim for a product when in fact they are making no claim at all. Weasel words get their name from the way weasels eat the eggs they find in the nests of other animals. A weasel will make a small hole in the egg, suck out the insides, then place the egg back in the nest. Only when the egg is examined closely is it found to be hollow. That's the way it is with weasel words in advertising: Examine weasel words closely and you'll find that they're as hollow as any egg sucked by a weasel. Weasel words appear to say one thing when in fact they say the opposite, or nothing at all.

"Help"—The Number One Weasel Word

3   The biggest weasel word used in advertising doublespeak is "help." Now "help" only means to aid or assist, nothing more. It does not mean to conquer, stop, eliminate, solve, heal, cure, or anything else. But once the ad says "help," it can say just about anything after that because "help" qualifies everything coming after it. The trick is that the claim that comes after the weasel word is usually so strong and so dramatic that you forget the word "help" and concentrate only on the dramatic claim. You read into the ad a message that the ad does not contain. More importantly, the advertiser is not responsible for the claim that you read into the ad, even though the advertiser wrote the ad so you would read that claim into it.

4   The next time you see an ad for a cold medicine that promises that it "helps relieve cold symptoms fast," don't rush out to buy it. Ask yourself what this claim is really saying. Remember, "helps" means only that the medicine will aid or assist. What will it aid or assist in doing? Why, "relieve" your cold "symptoms." "Relieve" only means to ease, alleviate, or mitigate, not to stop, end, or cure. Nor does the claim say how much relieving this medicine will do. Nowhere does this ad claim it *will cure anything*. In fact, the ad doesn't even claim it will *do* anything at all. The *ad only claims* that it will aid in relieving (not curing) your cold symptoms, which are probably a runny nose, watery eyes, and a headache. In other words, this medicine probably contains a standard decongestant and some aspirin. By the way, what does "fast" mean? Ten minutes, one hour, one day? What is fast to one person can be very slow to another. Fast is another weasel word.

5   Ad claims using "help" are among the most popular ads. One says, "Helps keep you young looking," but then a lot of things will help keep you young looking, including exercise, rest, good nutrition, and a facelift. More importantly, this ad doesn't say the product will keep you young, only "young *looking*." Someone may look young to one person and old to another.

6   A toothpaste ad says, "Helps prevent cavities," but it doesn't say it will actually prevent cavities. Brushing your teeth regularly, avoiding sugars in foods, and flossing daily will also help prevent cavities. A liquid cleaner ad says, "Helps keep your home germ free," but it doesn't say it actually kills germs, nor does it even specify which germs it might kill.

7   "Help" is such a useful weasel word that it is often combined with other action-verb weasel words such as "fight" and "control." Consider the claim, "Helps control dandruff symptoms with regular use." What does it really say? It will assist in controlling (not eliminating, stopping, ending, or curing) the *symptoms* of dandruff, not the cause of dandruff nor the dandruff itself. What are the symptoms of dandruff? The ad deliberately leaves that undefined, but assume that the symptoms referred to in the ad are the flaking and itching commonly associated with dandruff. But just shampooing with *any* shampoo will temporarily eliminate these symptoms, so this shampoo isn't any different from any other. Finally, in order to benefit from this product, you must use it regularly. What is "regular use"—daily, weekly, hourly? Using another shampoo "regularly" will have the same effect. Nowhere does this advertising claim say this particular shampoo stops, eliminates, or cures dandruff. In fact, this claim says nothing at all, thanks to all the weasel words.

8   Look at ads in magazines and newspapers, listen to ads on radio and television, and you'll find the word "help" in ads for all kinds of products. How often do you read or hear such phrases as "helps stop . . . ," "helps overcome . . . ," "helps eliminate . . . ," "helps you feel . . . ," or "helps you look . . . "? If you start looking for this weasel word in advertising, you'll be amazed at how often it occurs. Analyze the claims in the ads using "help," and you will discover that these ads are really saying nothing.

9   There are plenty of other weasel words used in advertising. In fact, there are so many that to list them all would fill the rest of this book. But, in order to identify the doublespeak of advertising and understand the real meaning of an ad, you have to be aware of the most popular weasel words in advertising today.

Virtually Spotless

10   One of the most powerful weasel words is "virtually," a word so innocent that most people don't pay any attention to it when it is used in an advertising claim. But watch out. "Virtually" is used in advertising claims that appear to make specific, definite promises when there is no promise. After all, what does "virtually" mean? It means "in essence of effect, although not in fact." Look at that definition again. "Virtually" means *not in fact*. It does *not* mean "almost" or "just about the same as," or anything else. And before you dismiss all this concern over such a small word, remember that small words can have big consequences.

11   In 1971 a federal court rendered its decision on a case brought by a woman who became pregnant while taking birth control pills. She sued the manufacturer, Eli Lilly and Company, for breach of warranty. The woman lost her case. Basing its ruling on a statement in the pamphlet accompanying the pills, which stated that, "When taken as directed, the tablets offer virtually 100 percent protection," the court ruled that there was no warranty, expressed or implied, that the pills were absolutely effective. In its ruling, the court pointed out that, according to *Webster's Third New International Dictionary,* "virtually" means "almost entirely" and clearly does not mean "absolute" (*Whittington* v. *Eli Lilly and Company,* 333 F. Supp. 98). In other words, the Eli Lilly company was really saying that its birth control pill, even when taken as directed, *did not in fact* provide 100 percent protection against pregnancy. But Eli Lilly didn't want to put it that way because then many women might not have bought Lilly's birth control pills.

12   The next time you see the ad that says that this dishwasher detergent "leaves dishes virtually spotless," just remember how advertisers twist the meaning of the weasel word "virtually." You can have lots of spots on your dishes after using this detergent and the ad claim will still be true, because what this claim really means is that this detergent does not *in fact* leave your dishes spotless. Whenever you see or hear an ad claim that uses the word "virtually," just translate that claim into its real meaning. So the television set that is "virtually trouble free" becomes the television set that is not in fact trouble free, the "virtually foolproof operation" of any appliance becomes an operation that is in fact not foolproof, and the product that "virtually never needs service" becomes the product that is not in fact service free.

New and Improved

13   If "new" is the most frequently used word on a product package, "improved" is the second most frequent. In fact, the two words are almost always used together. It seems just about everything sold these days is "new and improved." The next time you're in the supermarket, try counting the number of times you

see these words on products. But you'd better do it while you're walking down just one aisle, otherwise you'll need a calculator to keep track of your counting.

14   Just what do these words mean? The use of the word "new" is restricted by regulations, so an advertiser can't just use the word on a product or in an ad without meeting certain requirements. For example, a product is considered new for about six months during a national advertising campaign. If the product is being advertised only in a limited test market area, the word can be used longer, and in some instances has been used for as long as two years.

15   What makes a product "new"? Some products have been around for a long time, yet every once in a while you discover that they are being advertised as "new." Well, an advertiser can call a product new if there has been "a material functional change" in the product. What is "a material functional change," you ask? Good question. In fact it's such a good question it's being asked all the time. It's up to the manufacturer to prove that the product has undergone such a change. And if the manufacturer isn't challenged on the claim, then there's no one to stop it. Moreover, the change does not have to be an improvement in the product. One manufacturer added an artificial lemon scent to a cleaning product and called it "new and improved," even though the product did not clean any better than without the lemon scent. The manufacturer defended the use of the word "new" on the grounds that the artificial scent changed the chemical formula of the product and therefore constituted "a material functional change."

16   Which brings up the word "improved." When used in advertising, "improved" does not mean "made better." It only means "changed" or "different from before." So, if the detergent maker puts a plastic pour spout on the box of detergent, the product has been "improved," and away we go with a whole new advertising campaign. Or, if the cereal maker adds more fruit or a different kind of fruit to the cereal, there's an improved product. Now you know why manufacturers are constantly making little changes in their products. Whole new advertising campaigns, designed to convince you that the product has been changed for the better, are based on small changes in superficial aspects of a product. The next time you see an ad for an "improved" product, ask yourself what was wrong with the old one. Ask yourself just how "improved" the product is. Finally, you might check to see whether the "improved" version costs more than the unimproved one. After all, someone has to pay for the millions of dollars spent advertising the improved product.

17   Of course, advertisers really like to run ads that claim a product is "new and improved." While what constitutes a "new" product may be subject to some regulation, "improved" is a subjective judgment. A manufacturer changes the shape of its stick deodorant, but the shape doesn't improve the function of the deodorant. That is, changing the shape doesn't affect the deodorizing ability of the deodorant, so the manufacturer calls it "improved." Another manufacturer adds ammonia to its liquid cleaner and calls it "new and improved." Since adding ammonia does affect the cleaning ability of the product, there has been a "material functional change" in the product, and the manufacturer can now

call its cleaner "new," and "improved" as well. Now the weasel words, "new and improved" are plastered all over the package and are the basis for a multimillion-dollar ad campaign. But after six months the word "new" will have to go, until someone can dream up another change in the product. Perhaps it will be adding color to the liquid, or changing the shape of the package, or maybe adding a new dripless pour spout, or perhaps a——. The "improvements" are endless, and so are the new advertising claims and campaigns.

18   "New" is just too useful and powerful a word in advertising for advertisers to pass it up easily. So they use weasel words that say "new" without really saying it. One of their favorites is "introducing," as in, "Introducing improved Tide," or "Introducing the satin remover." The first is simply saying, here's our improved soap; the second, here's our new advertising campaign for our detergent. Another favorite is "now," as in "Now there's Sinex," which simply means that Sinex is available. Then there are phrases like "Today's Chevrolet," "Presenting Dristan," and "A fresh way to start the day." The list is really endless because advertisers are always finding new ways to say "new" without really saying it. If there is a second edition of this book, I'll just call it the "new and improved" edition. Wouldn't you really rather have a "new and improved" edition of this book rather than a "second" edition?

Acts Fast

19 "Acts" and "works" are two popular weasel words in advertising because they bring action to the product and to the advertising claim. When you see the ad for the cough syrup that "Acts on the cough control center," ask yourself what this cough syrup is claiming to do. Well, it's just claiming to "act," to do something, to perform an action. What is it that the cough syrup does? The ad doesn't say. It only claims to perform an action or do something on your "cough control center." By the way, what and where is our "cough control center"? I don't remember learning about that part of the body in human biology class.

20   Ads that use such phrases as "acts fast," "acts against," "acts to prevent," and the like are saying essentially nothing, because "act" is a word empty of any specific meaning. The ads are always careful not to specify exactly what "act" the product performs. Just because a brand of aspirin claims to "act fast" for headache relief doesn't mean this aspirin is any better than any other aspirin. What is the "act" that this aspirin performs? You're never told. Maybe it just dissolves quickly. Since aspirin is a parity product, all aspirin is the same and therefore functions the same.

Works Like Anything Else

21 If you don't find the word "acts" in an ad, you will probably find the weasel word "works." In fact, the two words are almost interchangeable in advertising. Watch out for ads that say a product "works against," "works like," "works for," or "works longer." As with "acts," "works" is the same meaningless verb used to make you think that this product really does something, and maybe even

something special or unique. But "works," like "acts," is basically a word empty of any specific meaning.

Like Magic

22   Whenever advertisers want you to stop thinking about the product and to start thinking about something bigger, better, or more attractive than the product, they use that very popular weasel word, "like." The word "like" is the advertiser's equivalent of a magician's use of misdirection. "Like" gets you to ignore the product and concentrate on the claim the advertiser is making about it. "For skin like peaches and cream" claims the ad for a skin cream. What is this ad really claiming? It doesn't say this cream will give you peaches-and-cream skin. There is no verb in this claim, so it doesn't even mention using the product. How is skin ever like "peaches and cream"? Remember, ads must be read literally and exactly, according to the dictionary definition of words. (Remember "virtually" in the Eli Lilly case.) The ad is making absolutely no promise or claim whatsoever for this skin cream. If you think this cream will give you soft, smooth, youthful-looking skin, you are the one who has read that meaning into the ad.

23   The wine that claims "It's like taking a trip to France" wants you to think about a romantic evening in Paris as you walk along the boulevard after a wonderful meal in an intimate little bistro. Of course, you don't really believe that a wine can take you to France, but the goal of the ad is to get you to think pleasant, romantic thoughts about France and not about how the wine tastes or how expensive it may be. That little word "like" has taken you away from crushed grapes into a world of your own imaginative making. Who knows, maybe the next time you buy wine, you'll think those pleasant thoughts when you see this brand of wine, and you'll buy it. Or, maybe you weren't even thinking about buying wine at all, but now you just might pick up a bottle the next time you're shopping. Ah, the power of "like" in advertising.

24   How about the most famous "like" claim of all, "Winston tastes good like a cigarette should"? Ignoring the grammatical error here, you might want to know what this claim is saying. Whether a cigarette tastes good or bad is a subjective judgment because what tastes good to one person may well taste horrible to another. Not everyone likes fried snails, even if they are called escargot. (*De gustibus non est disputandum,* which was probably the Roman rule for advertising as well as for defending the games in the Colosseum.) There are many people who say all cigarettes taste terrible, other people who say only some cigarettes taste all right, and still others who say all cigarettes taste good. Who's right? Everyone, because taste is a matter of personal judgment.

25   Moreover, note the use of the conditional, "should." The complete claim is, "Winston tastes good like a cigarette should taste." But should cigarettes taste good? Again, this is a matter of personal judgment and probably depends most on one's experiences with smoking. So, the Winston ad is simply saying that Winston cigarettes are just like any other cigarette: Some people like them and some people don't. On that statement, R. J. Reynolds conducted a very suc-

cessful multimillion-dollar advertising campaign that helped keep Winston the number-two-selling cigarette in the United States, close behind number one, Marlboro.

Can't It Be Up to the Claim?

26 Analyzing ads for doublespeak requires that you pay attention to every word in the ad and determine what each word really means. Advertisers try to wrap their claims in language that sounds concrete, specific, and objective, when in fact the language of advertising is anything but. Your job is to read carefully and listen critically so that when the announcer says that "Crest can be of significant value . . . ," you know immediately that this claim says absolutely nothing. Where is the doublespeak in this ad? Start with the second word.

27 Once again, you have to look at what words really mean, not what you think they mean or what the advertiser wants you to think they mean. The ad for Crest only says that using Crest "can be" of "significant value." What really throws you off in this ad is the brilliant use of "significant." It draws your attention to the word "value" and makes you forget that the ad only claims that Crest "can be." The ad doesn't say that Crest *is* of value, only that it is "able" or "possible" to be of value, because that's all that "can" means.

28 It's so easy to miss the importance of those little words, "can be." Almost as easy as missing the importance of the words "up to" in an ad. These words are very popular in sales ads. You know, the ones that say, "Up to 50 percent Off!" Now, what does that claim mean? Not much, because the store or manufacturer has to reduce the price of only a few items by 50 percent. Everything else can be reduced a lot less, or not even reduced. Moreover, don't you want to know 50 percent off of what? Is it 50 percent off the "manufacturer's suggested list price," which is the highest possible price? Was the price artificially inflated and then reduced? In other ads, "up to" expresses an ideal situation. The medicine that works "up to ten times faster," the battery that lasts "up to twice as long," and the soap that gets you "up to twice as clean" all are based on ideal situations for using these products, situations in which you can be sure you will never find yourself.

Unfinished Words

29 Unfinished words are a kind of "up to" claim in advertising. The claim that a battery lasts "up to twice as long" usually doesn't finish the comparison—twice as long as what? A birthday candle? A tank of gas? A cheap battery made in a country not noted for its technological achievements? The implication is that the battery lasts twice as long as batteries made by other battery makers, or twice as long as earlier model batteries made by the advertiser, but the ad doesn't really make these claims. You read these claims into the ad, aided by the visual images the advertiser so carefully provides.

30 Unfinished words depend on you to finish them, to provide the words the advertisers so thoughtfully left out of the ad. Pall Mall cigarettes were once advertised as "A longer, finer and milder smoke." The question is, longer, finer,

and milder than what? The aspirin that claims it contains "Twice as much of the pain reliever doctors recommend most" doesn't tell you what pain reliever it contains twice as much of. (By the way, it's aspirin. That's right; it just contains twice the amount of aspirin. And how much is twice the amount? Twice of what amount?) Panadol boasts that "nobody reduces fever faster," but, since Panadol is a parity product, this claim simply means that Panadol isn't any better than any other product in its parity class. "You can be sure if it's Westinghouse," you're told, but just exactly what it is you can be sure of is never mentioned. "Magnavox gives you more" doesn't tell you what you get more of. More value? More television? More than they gave you before? It sounds nice, but it means nothing, until you fill in the claim with your own words, the words the advertisers didn't use. Since each of us fills in the claim differently, the ad and the product can become all things to all people, and not promise a single thing.

31   Unfinished words abound in advertising because they appear to promise so much. More importantly, they can be joined with powerful visual images on television to appear to be making significant promises about a product's effectiveness without really making any promises. In a television ad, the aspirin product that claims fast relief can show a person with a headache taking the product and then, in what appears to be a matter of minutes, claiming complete relief. This visual image is far more powerful than any claim made in unfinished words. Indeed, the visual image completes the unfinished words for you, filling in with pictures what the words leave out. And you thought that ads didn't affect you. What brand of aspirin do you use?

32   Some years ago, Ford's advertisements proclaimed "Ford LTD—700 percent quieter." Now, what do you think Ford was claiming with these unfinished words? What was the Ford LTD quieter than? A Cadillac? A Mercedes Benz? A BMW? Well, when the FTC asked Ford to substantiate this unfinished claim, Ford replied that it meant that the inside of the LTD was 700 percent quieter than the outside. How did you finish those unfinished words when you first read them? Did you even come close to Ford's meaning?

Combining Weasel Words

33 A lot of ads don't fall neatly into one category or another because they use a variety of different devices and words. Different weasel words are often combined to make an ad claim. The claim, "Coffee-Mate gives coffee more body, more flavor," uses Unfinished Words ("more" than what?) and also uses words that have no specific meaning ("body" and "flavor"). Along with "taste" (remember the Winston ad and its claim to taste good), "body" and "flavor" mean nothing because their meaning is entirely subjective. To you, "body" in coffee might mean thick, black, almost bitter coffee, while I might take it to mean a light brown, delicate coffee. Now, if you think you understood that last sentence, read it again, because it said nothing of objective value; it was filled with weasel words of no specific meaning: "thick," "black," "bitter," "light brown," and "delicate." Each of those words has no specific, objective meaning, because each of us can interpret them differently.

34   Try this slogan: "Looks, smells, tastes like ground-roast coffee." So, are you now going to buy Taster's Choice instant coffee because of this ad? "Looks," "smells," and "tastes" are all words with no specific meaning and depend on your interpretation of them for any meaning. Then there's that great weasel word "like," which simply suggests a comparison but does not make the actual connection between the product and the quality. Besides, do you know what "ground-roast" coffee is? I don't, but it sure sounds good. So, out of seven words in this ad, four are definite weasel words, two are quite meaningless, and only one has any clear meaning.

35   Remember the Anacin ad—"Twice as much of the pain reliever doctors recommend most"? There's a whole lot of weaseling going on in this ad. First, what's the pain reliever they're talking about in this ad? Aspirin, of course. In fact, any time you see or hear an ad using those words "pain reliever," you can automatically substitute the word "aspirin" for them. (Makers of acetaminophen and ibuprofen pain relievers are careful in their advertising to identify their products as nonaspirin products.) So, now we know that Anacin has aspirin in it. Moreover, we know that Anacin has twice is much aspirin in it, but we don't know twice as much as what. Does it have twice as much aspirin as an ordinary aspirin tablet? If so, what is an ordinary aspirin tablet, and how much aspirin does it contain? Twice as much as Excedrin or Bufferin? Twice as much as a chocolate chip cookie? Remember those Unfinished Words and how they lead you on without saying anything.

36   Finally, what about those doctors who are doing all that recommending? Who are they? How many of them are there? What kind of doctors are they? What are their qualifications? Who asked them about recommending pain relievers? What other pain relievers did they recommend? And there are a whole lot more questions about this "poll" of doctors to which I'd like to know the answers, but you get the point. Sometimes, when I call my doctor, she tells me to take two aspirin and call her office in the morning. Is that where Anacin got this ad?

Read the Label, or the Brochure

37   Weasel words aren't just found on television, on the radio, or in newspaper and magazine ads. Just about any language associated with a product will contain the doublespeak of advertising. Remember the Eli Lilly case and the doublespeak on the information sheet that came with the birth control pills. Here's another example.

38   In 1983, the Estée Lauder cosmetics company announced a new product called "Night Repair." A small brochure distributed with the product stated that "Night Repair was scientifically formulated in Estée Lauder's U.S. laboratories as part of the Swiss Age-Controlling Skincare Program. Although only nature controls the aging process, this program helps control the signs of aging and encourages skin to look and feel younger." You might want to read these two sentences again, because they sound great but say nothing.

39   First, note that the product was "scientifically formulated" in the company's laboratories. What does that mean? What constitutes a scientific

formulation? You wouldn't expect the company to say that the product was casually, mechanically, or carelessly formulated, or just thrown together one day when the people in the white coats didn't have anything better to do. But the word "scientifically" lends an air of precision and promise that just isn't there.

40   It is the second sentence, however, that's really weasely, both syntactically and semantically. The only factual part of this sentence is the introductory dependent clause—"only nature controls the aging process." Thus, the only fact in the ad is relegated to a dependent clause, a clause dependent on the main clause, which contains no factual or definite information at all and indeed purports to contradict the independent clause. The new "skincare program" (notice it's not a skin cream but a "program") does not claim to stop or even retard the aging process. What, then, does Night Repair, at a price of over $35 (in 1983 dollars) for a .87-ounce bottle do? According to this brochure, nothing. It only "helps," and the brochure does not say how much it helps. Moreover, it only "helps control," and then it only helps control the "*signs* of aging," not the aging itself. Also, it "encourages" skin not to *be* younger but only to "look and feel" younger. The brochure does not say younger than what. Of the sixteen words in the main clause of this second sentence, nine are weasel words. So, before you spend all that money for Night Repair, or any other cosmetic product, read the words carefully, and then decide if you're getting what you think you're paying for.

Other Tricks of the Trade

41   Advertisers' use of doublespeak is endless. The best way advertisers can make something out of nothing is through words. Although there are a lot of visual images used on television and in magazines and newspapers, every advertiser wants to create that memorable line that will stick in the public consciousness. I am sure pure joy reigned in one advertising agency when a study found that children who were asked to spell the world "relief" promptly and proudly responded "r-o-l-a-i-d-s."

42   The variations, combinations, and permutations of doublespeak used in advertising go on and on, running from the use of rhetorical questions ("Wouldn't you really rather have a Buick?" "If you can't trust Prestone, who can you trust?") to flattering you with compliments ("The lady has taste." "We think a cigar smoker is someone special." "You've come a long way baby."). You know, of course, how you're *supposed* to answer those questions, and you know that those compliments are just leading up to the sales pitches for the products. Before you dismiss such tricks of the trade as obvious, however, just remember that all of these statements and questions were part of very successful advertising campaigns.

43   A more subtle approach is the ad that proclaims a supposedly unique quality for a product, a quality that really isn't unique. "If it doesn't say Goodyear, it can't be polyglas." Sounds good, doesn't it? Polyglas is available only from Goodyear because Goodyear copyrighted that trade name. Any other tire manufacturer could make exactly the same tire but could not call it "polyglas," be-

cause that would be copyright infringement. "Polyglas" is simply Goodyear's name for its fiberglass-reinforced tire.

44   Since we like to think of ourselves as living in a technologically advanced country, science and technology have a great appeal in selling products. Advertisers are quick to use scientific doublespeak to push their products. There are all kinds of elixirs, additives, scientific potions, and mysterious mixtures added to all kinds of products. Gasoline contains "HTA," "F–130," "Platformate," and other chemical-sounding additives, but nowhere does an advertisement give any real information about the additive.

45   Shampoo, deodorant, mouthwash, cold medicine, sleeping pills, and any number of other products all seem to contain some special chemical ingredient that allows them to work wonders. "Certs contains a sparkling drop of Retsyn." So what? What's "Retsyn"? What's it do? What's so special about it? When they don't have a secret ingredient in their product, advertisers still find a way to claim scientific validity. There's "Sinarest. Created by a research scientist who actually gets sinus headaches." Sounds nice, but what kind of research does this scientist do? How do you know if she is any kind of expert on sinus medicine? Besides, this ad doesn't tell you a thing about the medicine itself and what it does.

Advertising Doublespeak Quick Quiz

46   Now it's time to test your awareness of advertising doublespeak. (You didn't think I would just let you read this and forget it, did you?) The following is a list of statements from some recent ads. Your job is to figure out what each of these ads really says.

DOMINO'S PIZZA: "Because nobody delivers better."
SINUTAB: "It can stop the pain."
TUMS: "The stronger acid neutralizer."
MAXIMUM STRENGTH DRISTAN: "Strong medicine for tough sinus colds."
LISTERMINT: "Making your mouth a cleaner place."
CASCADE: "For virtually spotless dishes nothing beats Cascade."
NUPRIN: "Little. Yellow. Different. Better."
ANACIN: "Better relief."
SUDAFED: "Fast sinus relief that won't put you fast asleep."
ADVIL: "Better relief."
PONDS COLD CREAM: "Ponds cleans like no soap can."
MILLER LITE BEER: "Tastes great. Less filling."
PHILIPS MILK OF MAGNESIA: "Nobody treats you better than MOM (Philips Milk of Magnesia)."
BAYER: "The wonder drug that works wonders."
CRACKER BARREL: "Judged to be the best."
KNORR: "Where taste is everything."
ANUSOL: "Anusol is the word to remember for relief."
DIMETAPP: "It relieves kids as well as colds."

LIQUID DRÁNO: "The liquid strong enough to be called Dráno."

JOHNSON & JOHNSON BABY POWDER: "Like magic for your skin."

PURITAN: "Make it your oil for life."

PAM: "Pam, because how you cook is as important as what you cook."

IVORY SHAMPOO AND CONDITIONER: "Leave your hair feeling Ivory clean."

TYLENOL GEL-CAPS: "It's not a capsule. It's better."

ALKA-SELTZER PLUS: "Fast, effective relief for winter colds."

The World of Advertising

47   In the world of advertising, people wear "dentures," not false teeth; they suffer from "occasional irregularity," not constipation; they need deodorants for their "nervous wetness," not for sweat; they use "bathroom tissue," not toilet paper; and they don't dye their hair, they "tint" or "rinse" it. Advertisements offer "real counterfeit diamonds" without the slightest hint of embarrassment, or boast of goods made out of "genuine imitation leather" or "virgin vinyl."

48   In the world of advertising, the girdle becomes a "body shaper," "form per-suader," "control garment," "controller," "outerwear enhancer," "body gar-ment," or "anti-gravity panties," and is sold with such trade names as "The In-stead," "The Free Spirit," and "The Body Briefer."

49   A study some years ago found the following words to be among the most popular used in U.S. television advertisements: "new," "improved," "better," "ex-tra," "fresh," "clean," "beautiful," "free," "good," "great," and "light." At the same time, the following words were found to be among the most frequent on British television: "new," "good-better-best," "free," "fresh," "delicious," "full," "sure," "clean," "wonderful," and "special." While these words may occur most fre-quently in ads, and while ads may be filled with weasel words, you have to watch out for all the words used in advertising, not just the words mentioned here.

50   Every word in an ad is there for a reason; no word is wasted. Your job is to figure out exactly what each word is doing in an ad—what each word really means, not what the advertiser wants you to think it means. Remember, the ad is trying to get you to buy a product, so it will put the product in the best possi-ble light, using any device, trick, or means legally allowed. Your own defense against advertising (besides taking up permanent residence on the moon) is to develop and use a strong critical reading, listening, and looking ability. Always ask yourself what the ad is *really* saying. When you see ads on television, don't be misled by the pictures, the visual images. What does the ad say about the product? What does the ad *not* say? What information is missing from the ad? Only by becoming an active, critical consumer of the doublespeak of advertis-ing will you ever be able to cut through the doublespeak and discover what the ad is really saying.

51   Professor Del Kehl of Arizona State University has updated the Twenty-third Psalm to reflect the power of advertising to meet our needs and solve our problems. It seems fitting that this chapter close with this new Psalm.

The Adman's 23rd

The Adman is my shepherd;
I shall ever want.
He maketh me to walk a mile for a Camel;
He leadeth me beside Crystal Waters
    In the High Country of Coors;
He restoreth my soul with Perrier.
He guideth me in Marlboro Country
For Mammon's sake.
Yea, though I walk through the Valley of the
    Jolly Green Giant,
In the shadow of B.O., halitosis, indigestion,
    headache pain, and hemorrhoidal tissue,
I will fear no evil,
For I am in Good Hands with Allstate;
Thy Arid, Scope, Tums, Tylenol, and Preparation H—
They comfort me.
Stouffer's preparest a table before the TV
In the presence of all my appetites;
Thou anointest my head with Brylcream;
My Decaffeinated Cup runneth over.
Surely surfeit and security shall follow me
All the days of Metropolitan Life,
And I shall dwell in a Continental Home
With a mortgage forever and ever.

Amen.

FOR ANALYSIS AND DISCUSSION

1. How would a copywriter for an advertising agency respond to this article? Would he or she agree with the way Lutz characterizes all advertisements as trying to trick consumers with false claims into buying a product?

2. When you see the word "new" on a product, do you think twice about buying that product? What regulations restrict use of the word "new"? How can manufacturers make a product "new" to sidestep these regulations? Do these regulations serve the interest of the advertiser or the consumer?

3. Review Lutz's "Advertising Doublespeak Quick Quiz." Choose five items and analyze them using dictionary meanings to explain what the ads are really saying.

4. What tone does Lutz use throughout the article? Is his writing style humorous, informal, or academic? What strategies does he use to involve the reader in the piece?

5. What do you think of Lutz's ending his article with a parody of the Twenty-third Psalm? Do you find it appropriate or funny? Is it offensive? Does it suit the theme of the essay?

6. In paragraph 43 Lutz describes how manufacturers claim for their products unique properties that are not in fact unique after all. Could these claims be considered circular reasoning? Explain.

The Language of Advertising
Charles A. O'Neill

In this essay, marketing executive Charles A. O'Neill disputes William Lutz's criticism of advertising doublespeak. While admitting to some of the craftiness of his profession, O'Neill defends the huckster's language—both verbal and visual—against claims that it distorts reality. Examining some familiar television commercials and magazine ads, he explains why the language may be charming and seductive but far from brainwashing.

Charles O'Neill is an independent marketing and advertising consultant in Boston. This essay first appeared in the textbook *Exploring Language* in 1998.

BEFORE YOU READ

O'Neill makes several generalizations that characterize the language of advertising. Think about ads you have recently seen or read and make a list of your own generalizations about the language of advertising.

AS YOU READ

Does the fact that O'Neill is a professional advertising consultant influence your reception of his essay? Does it make his argument more or less persuasive?

1   The figure on the billboard and in the magazine ads looked like a rock singer, perhaps photographed in the midst of a music video taping session. He was poised, confident, shown leaning against a railing or playing pool with his friends. His personal geometry was always just right. He often wore a white suit, dark shirt, sunglasses. Cigarette in hand, wry smile on his lips, his attitude was distinctly confident, urbane.

2   He was so successful, this full-lipped, ubiquitous dromedary, that his success quite literally killed him. By mid-1997, with such people and agencies as President Clinton and the Federal Trade Commission harassing him at every turn, his masters had no choice. Camel market share reportedly climbed from 3.9 percent in 1989 to 4.4 percent by 1990. According to the FTC, six years after Joe was introduced, more than 13 percent of all smokers under the age of 18 chose Camels as their nicotine delivery system of choice. Finally, the president lent his weight to what had already become a raging debate. "Let's stop pretending that a cartoon camel in a funny costume is trying to sell to adults, not

children." New rules, introduced largely as a result of the debate about Joe, prohibit the use of cartoon characters in advertisements.

3   The obvious topic of the debate that finally killed Joe is cigarette advertising, but beneath the surface it signals something more interesting and broad based: the rather uncomfortable, tentative acceptance of advertising in our society. We recognize the legitimacy—even the value—of advertising, but on some level we can't quite fully embrace it as a "normal" part of our experience. At best, we view it as distracting. At worst, we view it as dangerous to our health and a pernicious threat to our social values. Also lending moral support to the debate about advertising is no less an authority than the Vatican. In 1997, the Vatican issued a document prepared by the Pontifical Council, titled "Ethics in Advertising." Along with acknowledgment of the positive contribution of advertising (e.g., provides information, supports worthy causes, encourages competition and innovation), the report states, as reported by the *Boston Globe*, "In the competition to attract ever larger audiences . . . communicators can find themselves pressured . . . to set aside high artistic and moral standards and lapse into superficiality, tawdriness and moral squalor."

4   How does advertising work? Why is it so powerful? Why does it raise such concern? What case can be made for and against the advertising business? In order to understand advertising, you must accept that it is not about truth, virtue, love, or positive social values. It is about money. Ads play a role in moving customers through the sales process. This process begins with an effort to build awareness of a product, typically achieved by tactics designed to break through the clutter of competitive messages. By presenting a description of product benefits, ads convince the customer to buy the product. Once prospects have become purchasers, advertising is used to sustain brand loyalty, reminding customers of all the good reasons for their original decision to buy.

5   But this does not sufficiently explain the ultimate, unique power of advertising. Whatever the product or creative strategy, advertisements derive their power from a purposeful, directed combination of images. Images can take the form of words, sounds, or visuals, used individually or together. The combination of images is the language of advertising, a language unlike any other.

6   Everyone who grows up in the Western world soon learns that advertising language is different from other languages. Most children would be unable to explain how such lines as "With Nice 'n Easy, it's color so natural, the closer he gets the better you look!" (the once-famous ad for Clairol's Nice 'n Easy hair coloring) differed from ordinary language, but they would say, "It sounds like an ad." Whether printed on a page, blended with music on the radio, or whispered on the sound track of a television commercial, advertising language is "different."

7   Over the years, the texture of advertising language has frequently changed. Styles and creative concepts come and go. But there are at least four distinct, general characteristics of the language of advertising that make it different from other languages. They lend advertising its persuasive power:

Engineered, Coded

Definite contradiction

> 1. The language of advertising is edited and purposeful.
> 2. The language of advertising is rich and arresting; it is specifically intended to attract and hold our attention.
> 3. The language of advertising involves us; in effect, *we* complete the message.
> 4. The language of advertising is a simple language; it holds no secrets from us.   *simple, no secrets*

Edited and Purposeful

Perhaps He forgot about the days of slavery

Walking down the street was and is a very social event.

What about a young single women 9 ? around men

8   In his famous book *Future Shock,* Alvin Toffler describes various types of messages we receive from the world around us each day. As he sees it, there is a difference between normal "coded" messages and "engineered" messages. Much of normal, human experience is "uncoded"; it is merely sensory. For example, Toffler describes a man walking down a street. Toffler notes that the man's sensory perceptions of this experience may form a mental image, but the message is not "designed by anyone to communicate anything, and the man's understanding of it does not depend directly on a social code—a set of agreed-upon signs and definitions."[1] In contrast, Toffler describes a talk show conversation as "coded"; the speaker's ability to exchange information with their host, and our ability to understand it, depend upon social conventions.

The language of advertising is coded. It is also a language of carefully engineered, ruthlessly purposeful messages. When Toffler wrote *Future Shock,* he estimated that the average adult was exposed to 560 advertising messages each day. Now, with the advent of 200-channel, direct-broadcast satellite television, the Internet, and other new forms of mass media Toffler could not have contemplated, this figure is surely exponentially higher today. None of these messages would reach us, to attract and hold our attention, if it were completely unstructured. Advertising messages have a clear purpose; they are intended to trigger a specific response.

Rich and Arresting

10   Advertisements—no matter how carefully "engineered"—cannot succeed unless they capture our attention. Of the hundreds of advertising messages in store for us each day, very few will actually command our conscious attention. The rest are screened out. The people who design and write ads know about this screening process; they anticipate and accept it as a premise of their business.

11   The classic, all-time favorite device used to breach the barrier is sex. The desire to be sexually attractive to others is an ancient instinct, and few drives are more powerful. A magazine ad for Ultima II, a line of cosmetics, invites readers to "find everything you need for the sexxxxiest look around. . . . " The ad goes on to offer other "Sexxxy goodies," including "Lipsexxxxy lip color, naked eye color . . . Sunsexxxy liquid bronzer." No one will accuse Ultima's marketing tacticians of subtlety. In fact, this ad is merely a current example of an approach that is as old as advertising. After countless years of using images of women in various stages of undress to sell products, ads are now displaying

men's bodies as well. A magazine ad for Brut, a men's cologne, declares in bold letters, "MEN ARE BACK"; in the background, a photograph shows a muscular, shirtless young man preparing to enter the boxing ring—a "manly" image indeed; an image of man as breeding stock.

12   Every successful advertisement uses a creative strategy based on an idea that will attract and hold the attention of the targeted consumer audience. The strategy may include strong creative execution or a straightforward presentation of product features and customer benefits.

- An ad for Clif Bars, an "energy bar," is clearly directed to people who want to snack but wouldn't be caught dead in a coffee house eating ginger spice cake with delicate frosting, much less ordinary energy bars—the kind often associated with the veggie and granola set: The central photograph shows a gristled cowboy-character, holding a Clif Bar, and asking, in the headline, "What 'n the hell's a carbohydrate?" Nosiree. This here energy bar is "bound to satisfy cantankerous folk like you."
- Recent cigar ads attract attention through the use of unexpected imagery. An ad for Don Diego cigars, for example, shows a bejeweled woman in an evening dress smoking a cigar, while through the half-open door her male companion asks, "Agnes, have you seen my Don Diegos?"
- A two-page ad for Diesel clothing includes a photo showing the principal participants in the famous Yalta conference in 1945 (Churchill, Roosevelt, and Stalin) with one important difference: Young models in Diesel clothing have been cleverly added and appear to be flirting with the dignitaries. The ad is presented as a "Diesel historical moment" and "the birth of the modern conference." This unexpected imagery is engaging and amusing, appealing to the product's youthful target audience.

Even if the text contains no incongruity and does not rely on a pun for its impact, ads typically use a creative strategy based on some striking concept or idea. In fact, the concept and execution are often so good that many successful ads entertain while they sell.

13   Consider, for example, the campaigns created for Federal Express. A campaign was developed to position Federal Express as the company that would deliver packages, not just "overnight," but "by 10:30 A.M." the next day. The plight of the junior executive in "Presentation," one TV ad in the campaign, is stretched for dramatic purposes, but it is, nonetheless, all too real: The young executive, who is presumably trying to climb his way up the corporate ladder, is shown calling another parcel delivery service and all but begging for assurance that he will have his slides in hand by 10:30 the next morning. "No slides, no presentation," he pleads. Only a viewer with a heart of stone can watch without feeling sympathetic as the next morning our junior executive struggles to make his presentation *sans* slides. He is so lost without them that he is reduced to using his hands to preform imitations of birds and animals in shadows on the

movie screen. What does the junior executive *viewer* think when he or she sees the ad?

1. Federal Express guarantees to deliver packages "absolutely, positively overnight."
2. Federal Express packages arrive early in the day.
3. What happened to that fellow in the commercial will absolutely not happen to me, now that I know what package delivery service to call.

14   A sound, creative strategy supporting an innovative service idea sold Federal Express. But the quality and objective "value" of execution doesn't matter. A magazine ad for Merit Ultra Lights made use of one word in its headline: "Yo!" This was, one hopes, not the single most powerful idea generated by the agency's creative team that particular month—but it probably sold cigarettes.

15   Soft drink and fast-foot companies often take another approach. "Slice of life" ads (so-called because they purport to show people in "real-life" situations) created to sell Coke or Pepsi have often placed their characters in Fourth of July parades or other family events. The archetypical version of this approach is filled-to-overflowing with babies frolicking with puppies in the sunlit foreground while their youthful parents play touch football. On the porch, Grandma and Pops are seen quietly smiling as they wait for all of this affection to transform itself in a climax of warmth, harmony, and joy. Beneath the veneer, these ads work through repetition: How-many-times-can-you-spot-the-logo-in-this-commercial?

16   More subtly, these ads seduce us into feeling that if we drink the right combination of sugar, preservatives, caramel coloring, and a few secret ingredients, we'll fulfill our yearning for a world where young folks and old folks live together in perfect bliss.

17   If you don't buy this version of the American Dream, search long enough and you are sure to find an ad designed to sell you what it takes to gain prestige within whatever posse you do happen to run with. As reported by *The Boston Globe*, "the malt liquor industry relies heavily on rap stars in delivering its message to inner-city youths, while Black Death Vodka, which features a top-hatted skull and a coffin on its label, has been using Guns N' Roses guitarist Slash to endorse the product in magazine advertising." A malt liquor company reportedly promotes its 40-ounce size with rapper King T singing, "I usually drink it when I'm just out clowning, me and the home boys, you know, be like downing it . . . I grab me a 40 when I want to act a fool." A recent ad for Sasson jeans is a long way from Black Death in execution, but a second cousin in spirit. A photograph of a young, blonde (they do have more fun, right?) actress appears with this text: "Baywatch actress Gena Lee Nolin Puts On Sasson. OO-LA-LA. Sasson. Don't put it on unless it's Sasson."

18   Ads do not often emerge like Botticelli's Venus from the sea, flawless and fully grown. Most often, the creative strategy is developed only after extensive research. "Who will be interested in our product? How old are they? Where do they live? How much money do they earn? What problem will our product

solve? Answers to these questions provide the foundation on which the creative strategy is built.

Involving

19   We have seen that the language of advertising is carefully engineered; we have discovered a few of the devices it uses to get our attention. R. J. Reynolds has us identifying with Joe in one of his many uptown poses. Coke and Pepsi have caught our eye with visions of peace and love. An actress offers a winsome smile. Now that they have our attention, advertisers present information intended to show us that their product fills a need and differs from the competition. It is the copywriter's responsibility to express, exploit, and intensify such product differences.

20   When product differences do not exist, the writer must glamorize the superficial differences—for example, differences in packaging. As long as the ad is trying to get our attention, the "action" is mostly in the ad itself, in the words and visual images. But as we read an ad or watch it on television, we become more deeply involved. The action starts to take place in us. Our imagination is set in motion, and our individual fears and aspirations, quirks, and insecurities, superimpose themselves on that tightly engineered, attractively packaged message.

21   Consider, once again, the running battle among the low-calorie soft drinks. The cola wars have spawned many "look-alike" advertisements, because the product features and consumer benefits are generic, applying to all products in the category. Substitute one cola brand name for another, and the messages are often identical, right down to the way the cans are photographed in the closing sequence. This strategy relies upon mass saturation and exposure for impact.

22   Some companies have set themselves apart from their competitors by making use of bold, even disturbing, themes and images. For example, it was not uncommon not long ago for advertisers in the fashion industry to make use of gaunt, languid models—models who, in the interpretation of some observers, displayed a certain form of "heroic chic." Something was most certainly unusual about the models appearing in ads for Prada and Calvin Klein products. A young woman in a Prada ad projects no emotion whatsoever; she is slightly hunched forward, her posture suggesting that she is in a trance or drug-induced stupor. In a Calvin Klein ad, a young man, like the woman in the Prada ad, is gaunt beyond reason. He is shirtless. As if to draw more attention to his peculiar posture and "zero body fat" status, he is shown pinching the skin next to his navel.

23   Just as he publicly attacked Joe Camel, President Clinton took an aggressive position against the depiction of heroin chic. In a speech in Washington, D.C., the president commented on the increasing use of heroin on college campuses, noting that "part of this has to do with the images that are finding their way to our young people." One industry observer agreed, asserting that "people got carried away by the glamour of decadence."

24   Do such advertisers as Prada and Calvin Klein bear responsibility—morally, if not legally—for the rise of heroin use on college campuses? Emergency room

visits connected with heroin use reportedly grew from 63,200 in 1993 to 76,000 by 1995, echoing a strong rise in heroin addiction. Is this a coincidence? Does heroin chic and its depiction of a decadent lifestyle exploit certain elements of our society—the young and uncertain, for example? Or did these ads, and others of their ilk, simply reflect profound bad taste? In fact, on one level, all advertising is about exploitation; the systematic, deliberate identification of our needs and wants, followed by the delivery of a carefully constructed promise that Brand X will satisfy them.

25   Symbols offer an important tool for involving consumers in advertisements. Symbols have become important elements in the language of advertising, not so much because they carry meanings of their own, but because we bring meaning to them. One example is provided by the campaign begun in 1978 by Somerset Importers for Johnnie Walker Red Scotch. Sales of Johnnie Walker Red had been trailing sales of Johnnie Walker Black, and Somerset Importers needed to position Red as a fine product in its own right. Their agency produced ads that made heavy use of the color red. One magazine ad, often printed as a two-page spread, is dominated by a close-up photo of red autumn leaves. At lower right, the copy reads, "When their work is done, even the leaves turn Red." Another ad—also suitably dominated by a photograph in the appropriate color—reads: "When it's time to quiet down at the end of the day, even a fire turns Red." Red. Warm. Experienced. Seductive.

26   As we have seen, advertisers make use of a great variety of techniques and devices to engage us in the delivery of their messages. Some are subtle, making use of warm, entertaining, or comforting images or symbols. Others, like Black Death Vodka and Ultima II, are about as subtle as MTV's "Beavis and Butt-head." Another common device used to engage our attention is old but still effective: the use of famous or notorious personalities as product spokespeople or models. Advertising writers did not invent the human tendency to admire or otherwise identify themselves with famous people. Once we have seen a famous person in an ad, we associate the product with the person: "Joe DiMaggio is a good guy. He likes Mr. Coffee. If I buy a Mr. Coffee coffee maker and I use it when I have the boss over for dinner, then maybe she'll think I'm a good guy, too." "Guns 'N Roses rule my world, so I will definitely make the scene with a bottle of Black Death stuck into the waistband of my sweat pants." "Gena Lee Nolin is totally sexy. She wears Sasson. If I wear Sasson, I'll be sexy, too." The logic is faulty, but we fall under the spell just the same. Advertising works, not because Joe DiMaggio is a coffee expert, Slash had discriminating taste, or Gena knows her jeans, but because we participate in it. In fact, we charge ads with most of their power.

A Simple Language

27   Advertising language differs from other types of language in another important respect; it is a simple language. To determine how the copy of a typical advertisement rates on a "simplicity index" in comparison with text in a magazine article, for example, try this exercise: Clip a typical story from the publication you

read most frequently. Calculate the number of words in an average sentence. Count the number of words of three or more syllables in a typical 100-word passage, omitting words that are capitalized, combinations of two simple words, or verb forms made into three-syllable words by the addition of *-ed* or *-es*. Add the two figures (the average number of words per sentence and the number of three-syllable words per 100 words), then multiply the result by .4. According to Robert Gunning, if the resulting number is 7, there is a good chance that you are reading *True Confessions.*[2] He developed this formula, the "Fog Index," to determine the comparative ease with which any given piece of written communication can be read. Here is the complex text of a typical cigarette endorsement:

> I demand two things from my cigarette. I want a cigarette with low tar and nicotine. But I also want taste. That's why I smoke Winston Lights. I get a lighter cigarette, but I still get a real taste. And real pleasure. Only one cigarette gives me that: Winston Lights.

The average sentence in this ad runs 7 words. *Cigarette* and *nicotine* are three syllable words, with *cigarette* appearing four times; *nicotine,* once. Consider *that's* as two words, the ad is exactly 50 words long, so the average number of three-syllable words per 100 is ten.

$$
\begin{array}{rl}
7 & \text{words per sentence} \\
+\,10 & \text{three-syllable words}/100 \\
\hline
17 & \\
\times\ .4 & \\
\hline
6.8 & \text{Fog Index}
\end{array}
$$

According to Gunning's scale, this ad—which has now been consigned to the dustbin of advertising history thanks to government regulations—is written at about the seventh-grade level, comparable to most of the ads found in mass-circulation magazines.

28   It's about as sophisticated as *True Confessions;* that is, harder to read than a comic book, but easier than *Ladies Home Journal.* Of course, the Fog Index cannot evaluate the visual aspect of an ad—another component of advertising language. The headline, "I demand two things from my cigarette," works with the picture (that of an attractive woman) to arouse consumer interest. The text reinforces the image. Old Joe's simple plea, "Try New Camel Lights," is too short to move the needle on the Fog Index meter, but in every respect it represents perhaps the simplest language possible, a not-distant cousin of Merit Ultra Lights' groundbreaking and succinct utterance, "Yo!"

29   Why do advertisers generally favor simple language? The answer lies with the consumer: Consider Toffler's speculation that the average American adult is subject to some 560 advertising or commercial messages each day. As a practical matter, we would not notice many of these messages if length or eloquence were counted among their virtues. Today's consumer cannot take the time to focus on anything for long, much less blatant advertising messages. In

Can not Pay attention long enough

effect, Toffler's "future" is here now, and it is perhaps more "shocking" than he could have foreseen at the time. Every aspect of modern life runs at an accelerated pace. Overnight mail has moved in less than ten years from a novelty to a common business necessity. Voice mail, pagers, cellular phones, e-mail, the Internet—the world is always awake, always switched on, and hungry for more information, now. Time generally, and TV-commercial time in particular, is now dissected into increasingly smaller segments. Fifteen-second commercials are no longer unusual.

30   Toffler views the evolution toward shorter language as a natural progression: three-syllable words are simply harder to read than one- or two-syllable words. Simple ideas are more readily transferred from one person to another than complex ideas. Therefore, advertising copy uses increasingly simple language, as does society at large. In *Future Shock,* Toffler speculates:

How does the length of the word determine or the simple complexity of the idea conveyed

> If the [English] language had the same number of words in Shakespeare's time as it does today, at least 200,000 words—perhaps several times that many—have dropped out and been replaced in the intervening four centuries. The high turnover rate reflects changes in things, processes, and qualities in the environment from the world of consumer products and technology.

It is no accident that the first terms Toffler uses to illustrate his point ("fastback," "wash-and-wear," and "flashcube") were invented not by engineers, or journalists, but by advertising copywriters.

31   Advertising language is simple language; in the ad's engineering process, difficult words or images—which in other forms of communication may be used to lend color or find shades of meaning—are edited out and replaced by simple words or images not open to misinterpretation. You don't have to ask whether King T likes to "grab a 40" when he wants to "act a fool," or whether Gena wears her Sassons when she wants to do whatever it is she does.

Who Is Responsible?

32   Some critics view the advertising business as a cranky, unwelcomed child of the free enterprise system—a noisy, whining, brash kid who must somehow be kept in line, but can't just yet be thrown out of the house. In reality, advertising mirrors the fears, quirks, and aspirations of the society that creates it (and is, in turn, sold by it). This factor alone exposes advertising to parody and ridicule. The overall level of acceptance and respect for advertising is also influenced by the varied quality of the ads themselves. Some ads, including a few of the examples cited here, seem deliberately designed to provoke controversy. For example, it is easy—as President Clinton and others charged—to conclude that Joe Camel represented a deliberate, calculated effort by R. J. Reynolds to encourage children to smoke cigarettes. But this is only one of the many charges frequently levied against advertising:

1. Advertising encourages unhealthy habits.
2. Advertising feeds on human weaknesses and exaggerates the importance of material things, encouraging "impure" emotions and vanities.
3. Advertising sells daydreams—distracting, purposeless visions of lifestyles beyond the reach of the majority of the people who are most exposed to advertising.
4. Advertising warps our vision of reality, implanting in us groundless fears and insecurities.
5. Advertising downgrades the intelligence of the public.
6. Advertising debases English.
7. Advertising perpetuates racial and sexual stereotypes.

33   What can be said in advertising's defense? Advertising is only a reflection of society. A case can be made for the concept that advertising language is an acceptable stimulus for the natural evolution of language. Is "proper English" the language most Americans actually speak and write, or is it the language we are told we should speak and write?

34   What about the charge that advertising debases the intelligence of the public? Those who support this particular criticism would do well to ask themselves another question: Exactly how intelligent is the public? Sadly, evidence abounds that "the public" at large is not particularly intelligent, after all. Johnny can't read. Susie can't write. And the entire family spends the night in front of the television, channel surfing for the latest scandal—hopefully, one involving a sports hero or political figure said to be a killer or a frequent participant in perverse sexual acts.

35   Ads are effective because they sell products. They would not succeed if they did not reflect the values and motivations of the real world. Advertising both reflects and shapes our perception of reality. Consider several brand names and the impressions they create: Ivory Snow is pure. Federal Express won't let you down. Absolut is cool. Sasson is sexxy. Mercedes represents quality. Our sense of what these brand names stand for may have as much to do with advertising as with the objective "truth."

36   Advertising shapes our perception of the world as surely as architecture shapes our impression of a city. Good, responsible advertising can serve as a positive influence for change, while generating profits. Of course, the problem is that the obverse is also true: Advertising, like any form of mass communication, can be a force for both "good" and "bad." It can just as readily reinforce or encourage irresponsible behavior, ageism, sexism, ethnocentrism, racism, homophobia, heterophobia—you name it—as it can encourage support for diversity and social progress. People living in society create advertising. Society isn't perfect. In the end, advertising simply attempts to change behavior. Do advertisements sell distracting, purposeless visions? Occasionally. But perhaps such visions are necessary components of the process through which our society changes and improves.

37   Joe's days as Camel's spokesman are over. His very success in reaching new smokers was the source of his undoing. But standing nearby and waiting to take his place is another campaign; another character, real or imagined; another product for sale. Perhaps, by learning how advertising works, we can become better equipped to sort out content from hype, product values from emotions, and salesmanship from propaganda.

NOTES

1. Alvin Toffler, *Future Shock* (New York: Random House, 1970), p. 146.
2. Curtis D. MacDougall, *Interpretive Reporting* (New York: Macmillan, 1968), p. 94.

FOR ANALYSIS AND DISCUSSION

1. O'Neill opens his essay with a discussion of the controversial figure Joe Camel. What are your views on the Joe Camel controversy? Do you think the FTC and the president were justified in expressing their concerns about the character? Should ads that target young people for products that are bad for them be outlawed? Explain.
2. Do you think it is ethical for advertisers to create a sense of product difference when there really isn't any? Consider advertisements for products such as gasoline, beer, or coffee.
3. In the last section of the essay O'Neill anticipates potential objections to his defense of advertising. What are some of these objections? What effect does his anticipation of these objections have on the essay as a whole?
4. In paragraph 25 O'Neill writes, "Symbols offer an important tool for involving consumers in advertisements." Can you think of specific symbols from the advertising world that you associate with your own life? Are they effective symbols for advertising?
5. O'Neill is an advertising professional. How does his writing style reflect the advertising techniques he describes? Cite examples to support your answer.
6. Can you think of any recent advertising campaigns that created controversy? What made them controversial?

The Selling of Rebellion
John Leo

What motivates a person to purchase one product over another? Sometimes it is simply the associations consumers make with a product that convince them to buy it. In this essay, John Leo examines the theme of rebellion in advertising. Why do people like to buy products that are associated with breaking rules? How do advertising gurus tap into this desire?

    Columnist John Leo is a contributing editor at *U.S. News & World Report* in which this essay appeared on October 12, 1998. His work has appeared in many major magazines and newspapers, including the *New York Times, McCall's, Newsweek,* and *Time*.

BEFORE YOU READ

Think of current ads that feature "rebellious" themes. What markets are these commercials targeting? How do such ads motivate their target markets to buy?

AS YOU READ

Consider what motivates you personally to purchase a product. What do you think are the chief advertising themes advertisers apply to your age group?

1   Most TV viewers turn off their brains when the commercials come on. But they're worth paying attention to. Some of the worst cultural propaganda is jammed into these 60-second and 30-second spots.

2   Consider the recent ad for the Isuzu Rodeo. A grotesque giant in a business suit stomps into a beautiful field, startling a deer and jamming skyscrapers, factories, and signs into the ground. (I get it: Nature is good; civilization and business are bad.) One of the giant's signs says "Obey," but the narrator says, "The world has boundaries. Ignore them." Trying to trample the Rodeo, the hapless giant trips over his own fence. The Isuzu zips past him, toppling a huge sign that says "Rules."

3   Presumably we are meant to react to this ad with a wink and a nudge, because the message is unusually flat-footed and self-satirical. After all, Isuzus are not manufactured in serene fields by adorable lower mammals. The maddened giant makes them in his factories. He also hires hip ad writers and stuffs them in his skyscrapers, forcing them to write drivel all day, when they really should be working on novels and frolicking with deer.

4   But the central message here is very serious and strongly antisocial: We should all rebel against authority, social order, propriety, and rules of any kind. "Obey" and "Rules" are bad. Breaking rules, with or without your Isuzu, is good. Auto makers have been pushing this idea in various ways since "The Dodge Rebellion" of the mid-1960s. Isuzu has worked the theme especially hard, including a TV ad showing a bald and repressive grade-school teacher barking at kids to "stay within the lines" while coloring pictures, because "the lines are our friends."

Away with Standards

5   A great many advertisers now routinely appeal to the so-called postmodern sensibility, which is heavy on irony (wink, nudge) and attuned to the message that rules, boundaries, standards, and authorities are either gone or should be gone. Foster Grant sunglasses has used the "no limits" refrain. So have Prince Matchabelli perfume ("Life without limits"), Showtime TV (its "No Limits" campaign) and AT&T's Olympics ads in 1996 ("Imagine a world without limits"). No Limits is an outdoor-adventure company, and No Limit is the name of a successful rap record label. Even the U.S. Army used the theme in a TV recruitment ad. "When I'm in this uniform I know no limits," says a soldier—a

scary thought if you remember Lt. William Calley in Vietnam or the Serbian Army today.

6   Among the ads that have used "no boundaries" almost as a mantra are Ralph Lauren's Safari cologne, Johnnie Walker scotch ("It's not trespassing when you cross your own boundaries"), Merrill Lynch ("Know no boundaries"), and the movie *The English Patient* ("In love, there are no boundaries").

7   Some "no boundaries" ads are legitimate—the Internet and financial markets, after all, aim at crossing or erasing old boundaries. The antisocial message is clearer in most of the "no rules" and "antirules" ads, starting with Burger King's "Sometimes, you gotta break the rules." These include Outback steakhouses ("No rules. Just right"), Don Q rum ("Break all the rules"), the theatrical troupe De La Guarda ("No rules"), Neiman Marcus ("No rules here"), Columbia House Music Club ("We broke the rules"), Comedy Central ("See comedy that breaks rules"), Red Kamel cigarettes ("This baby don't play by the rules"), and even Woolite (wool used to be associated with decorum, but now "All the rules have changed," an ad says under a photo of a young woman groping or being groped by two guys). "No rules" also turns up as the name of a book and a CD and a tag line for an NFL video game ("no refs, no rules, no mercy"). The message is everywhere—"the rules are for breaking," says a Spice Girls lyric.

8   What is this all about? Why is the ad industry working so hard to use rule-breaking as a way of selling cars, steaks, and Woolite? In his book *The Conquest of Cool,* Thomas Frank points to the Sixties counterculture. He says it has become "a more or less permanent part of the American scene, a symbolic and musical language for the endless cycles of rebellion and transgression that make up so much of our mass culture . . . rebellion is both the high- and mass-cultural motif of the age; order is its great bogeyman."

9   The pollster-analysts at Yankelovich Partners Inc. have a different view. In their book *Rocking the Ages: The Yankelovich Report in Generational Marketing,* J. Walker Smith and Ann Clurman say rule-breaking is simply a hallmark of the baby boom generation: "Boomers always have broken the rules. . . . The drugs, sex, and rock 'n roll of the '60s and '70s only foreshadowed the really radical rule-breaking to come in the consumer marketplace of the '80s and '90s."

10   This may pass—Smith says the post-boomers of generation X are much more likely to embrace traditional standards than boomers were at the same age. On the other hand, maybe it won't. Pop culture is dominated by in-your-face transgression now and the damage is severe. The peculiar thing is that so much of the rule-breaking propaganda is largely funded by businessmen who say they hate it, but can't resist promoting it in ads as a way of pushing their products. Isuzu, please come to your senses.

FOR ANALYSIS AND DISCUSSION

1. Summarize the argument Leo makes about the relationship between rebellion and American society. Do you agree with his argument? Explain.

2. Evaluate America's current obsession with rebellion. Is it indeed a new phenomenon, or is there a historical connection between Americans and the spirit of rebellion?

3. In paragraph 8 Leo quotes pollsters who say that "rule breaking is simply a hallmark of the baby boom generation." Do you agree? Are these advertisements targeting baby boomers' desire to keep breaking the rules? Is there a connection between the types of products using this theme and the target audience?

4. Leo mentions that advertisers are appealing to the "so-called postmodern sensibility." What is the "postmodern sensibility"? How does it connect to the concept of rule breaking? Do you agree with Leo's evaluation?

5. How might this "rule-breaking" approach to marketing backfire?

The general populace isn't merely lacking culture, it's lacking calcium. In fact, 60% of men and 90% of women don't get enough. The enlightened among us, however, drink 3 glasses of milk a day. A practice that can prevent a Freudian condition known as "calcium envy."

Milk: "Got Milk?"

1. In recent years, many of the advertisements promoting milk have featured famous actors, musicians, models, and athletes. Although the people change, certain visual cues are repeated in most of the ads. How do repetitive cues help sell a product? Would you know what this ad was selling if the words "got milk?" didn't appear in the copy?

2. How does the caption below the group complement both the people in the ad and the product they are promoting?

3. How does the glass each person is holding contribute to both the ad and its message? How is humor projected in the ad?

4. What is the image of milk? Who drinks milk? How might the ad influence public perception of the product? Do you think milk ads promote milk consumption?

5. Although the slogan has changed from simply "MILK" to "got milk?" the style of the advertising is little changed. What accounts for this continuity? Evaluate the effectiveness of changing the slogan. Is it better than the old one? Explain.

6. Apply the Fog Index from "The Language of Advertising" to the blurb at the bottom of the page. What is the grade level of the language? Why do you think the writing is at this level?

7. Who do you think is the target audience for this ad? How do you think a child would respond to it? a teenager? a young adult? Explain.

8. How are the print ads for the "got milk?" campaign different from the television commercials?

Diet Coke: "Laughter Is a Great Workout"

1. If you were leafing through a magazine and saw this ad, would you stop to read it? Why or why not?
2. Could you tell what this advertisement is selling strictly from the photograph? Does the fact that the subjects are not actually holding the product detract from the ad? If this is not an issue, explain why.
3. Who is the target audience for this advertisement? What values are expressed in the ad? How are those values conveyed to the audience?
4. Connect the slogan "Laughter is a great workout" to the promotion of the product. How do the slogan, the subjects, and the product come together?
5. Evaluate the three people in the ad. Would the impression of the ad be different if they were not wearing sunglasses or if they were all looking out of the picture? Explain.
6. Apply the Fog Index to this advertisement. What is the grade level of the text? Does it connect well to the target audience of the advertisement? Explain.
7. How does this ad reflect changing cultural attitudes? Using your library resources, check the diet drink ads from 20 years ago. How does this advertisement differ from those older ads? How have promotion styles changed to reflect modern values?

PREDATOR

How to avoid being the prey.

 You're being followed. Even after you turn, he's close behind. You're frightened. What do you do? Don't go home. You don't want to lead him to your loved ones. Instead, drive to a well-lighted place where there are lots of people. A store, service station, hospital or police station. Once there, make a scene. Lean on the horn; flash your lights. Draw attention. For more information about what to do when you're driving by yourself, get Alone Behind the Wheel, free from Shell. Pick one up at a station, visit us on the web at www.countonshell.com, or call 1-800-376-0200. **Count on Shell™**

Shell Gasoline: "Count on Shell"

1. Consider the setting for this advertisement. How does the setting help promote the product and the product's image? How would the advertisement's impact be different if the woman was driving during the day? What if it featured a man behind the wheel?
2. How does this ad target a particular audience? Is the audience gender-specific? Would women react to this advertisement differently than men? Explain.
3. Would you know what this ad was selling if the Shell symbol were not featured in the copy? How would you find out?
4. Shell, a gasoline company, is "selling" a free product in this advertisement—a safety guide. Thus, the actual product being sold is once removed from what is promoted in the ad. Is this an effective advertising technique for Shell? Explain.
5. How does the woman's expression promote the message of the ad? What effect does her expression have on the reader? Would this ad be less effective if it were not a dramatic photograph?
6. Apply the Fog Index to the words at the bottom of the advertisement. Who is the audience as determined by the Fog Index? Does it match Shell's probable target audience for the ad?

WRITING ASSIGNMENTS: ADVERTISING

1. Write an argument evaluating the ethics of advertising techniques in the twentieth century. Have ads changed over the last 50 or so years? What accounts for similarities or differences? Has advertising become more or less ethical? Be sure to explain your position and support it with examples from real advertisements.
2. You are an advertising executive. Invent a product and write an advertising campaign for it. Explain the reasons behind your campaign. Do you use "weasel words" or tap into a popular cultural consciousness? Do you use sex appeal to promote your product? Assume that you must defend the ad to your supervisors.
3. Access the Web sites for several popular soft drinks, including <http://www.coke.com> and <http://www.pepsi.com>. How does each site promote the product? Who are the sites' target audiences and how do they reflect that? What techniques do they use to sell? Write an essay analyzing the differences between online and paper advertising. Will the Web be the next great marketplace? What considerations are unique to this medium? In your essay, address the future of advertising products on the Web. Is it a passing fad or a medium that's here to stay?
4. Write a paper in which you consider advertising strategies. Support your evaluation with examples of advertising campaigns with which you are familiar. Make an argument for the appropriate or exploitativeness of such campaigns. You may draw support from the articles by William Lutz, Charles O'Neill, and John Leo.

TV NEWS: DO WE FIND IT CREDIBLE?

TV News: All the World in Pictures
Neil Postman and Steve Powers

It's 6:00 P.M. and you turn on the local evening news. You depend on it to keep you informed of the day's events both in your area and nationwide. But how much do you really learn from that nightly broadcast? According to Neil Postman and Steve Powers the answer is not very much. The nightly news, they argue, is really visual entertainment that only creates the illusion of keeping the public informed.

Neil Postman is chairman of the department of communication at New York University. He is the author of many books, including *Amusing Ourselves to Death* (1985), *The Disappearance of Childhood* (1994), and *The End of Education: Redefining the Value of School* (1995).

Steve Powers is an award-winning journalist with more than 30 years' experience in broadcast news. Postman and Powers are coauthors of *How to Watch TV News* (1992), from which this essay was taken.

BEFORE YOU READ

Think about your local television news broadcast. How much does it rely on video clips to tell the story? How are events narrated? How much information do you learn from each clip?

AS YOU READ

What is the authors' position on network news broadcasts? How can you tell?

1   When a television news show distorts the truth by altering or manufacturing facts (through re-creations), a television viewer is defenseless even if a re-creation is properly labeled. Viewers are still vulnerable to misinformation since they will not know (at least in the case of docudramas) what parts are fiction and what parts are not. But the problems of verisimilitude posed by re-creations pale to insignificance when compared to the problems viewers face when encountering a straight (no-monkey-business) show. All news shows, in a sense, are re-creations in that what we hear and see on them are attempts to represent actual events, and are not the events themselves. Perhaps, to avoid ambiguity, we might call all news shows "re-presentations" instead of "re-creations." These re-presentations come to us in two forms: language and pictures. The question then arises: what do viewers have to know about language and pictures in order to be properly armed to defend themselves against the seductions of eloquence (to use Bertrand Russell's apt phrase)? . . .

2   [Let us look at] the problem of pictures. It is often said that a picture is worth a thousand words. Maybe so. But it is probably equally true that one word

is worth a thousand pictures, at least sometimes—for example, when it comes to understanding the world we live in. Indeed, the whole problem with news on television comes down to this: all the words uttered in an hour of news coverage could be printed on one page of a newspaper. And the world cannot be understood in one page. Of course, there is a compensation: television offers pictures, and the pictures move. Moving pictures are a kind of language in themselves, but the language of pictures differs radically from oral and written language, and the differences are crucial for understanding television news.

3   To begin with, pictures, especially single pictures, speak only in particularities. Their vocabulary is limited to concrete representation. Unlike words and sentences, a picture does not present to us an idea or concept about the world, except as we use language itself to convert the image to idea. By itself, a picture cannot deal with the unseen, the remote, the internal, the abstract. It does not speak of "man," only of *a* man; not of "tree," only of *a* tree. You cannot produce an image of "nature," any more than an image of "the sea." You can only show a particular fragment of the here-and-now—a cliff of a certain terrain, in a certain condition of light; a wave at a moment in time, from a particular point of view. And just as "nature" and "the sea" cannot be photographed, such larger abstractions as truth, honor, love, and falsehood cannot be talked about in the lexicon of individual pictures. For "showing of" and "talking about" are two very different kinds of processes: individual pictures give us the world as object; language, the world as idea. There is no such thing in nature as "man" or "tree." The universe offers no such categories or simplifications; only flux and infinite variety. The picture documents and celebrates the particularities of the universe's infinite variety. Language makes them comprehensible.

4   Of course, moving pictures, video with sound, may bridge the gap by juxtaposing images, symbols, sound, and music. Such images can present emotions and rudimentary ideas. They can suggest the panorama of nature and the joys and miseries of humankind.

5   Picture—smoke pouring from the window, cut to people coughing, an ambulance racing to a hospital, a tombstone in a cemetery.

6   Picture—jet planes firing rockets, explosions, lines of foreign soldiers surrendering, the American flag waving in the wind.

7   Nonetheless, keep in mind that when terrorists want to prove to the world that their kidnap victims are still alive, they photograph them holding a copy of a recent newspaper. The dateline on the newspaper provides the proof that the photograph was taken on or after that date. Without the help of the written word, film and videotape cannot portray temporal dimensions with any precision. Consider a film clip showing an aircraft carrier at sea. One might be able to identify the ship as Soviet or American, but there would be no way of telling where in the world the carrier was, where it was headed, or when the pictures were taken. It is only through language—words spoken over the pictures or reproduced in them—that the image of the aircraft carrier takes on specific meaning.

8   Still, it is possible to enjoy the image of the carrier for its own sake. One might find the hugeness of the vessel interesting; it signifies military power on

the move. There is a certain drama in watching the planes come in at high speeds and skid to a stop on the deck. Suppose the ship were burning: that would be even more interesting. This leads to an important point about the language of pictures. Moving pictures favor images that change. That is why violence and dynamic destruction find their way onto television so often. When something is destroyed violently it is altered in a highly visible way; hence the entrancing power of fire. Fire gives visual form to the ideas of consumption, disappearance, death—the thing that burned is actually taken away by fire. It is at this very basic level that fires make a good subject for television news. Something was here, now it's gone, and the change is recorded on film.

9   Earthquakes and typhoons have the same power. Before the viewer's eyes the world is taken apart. If a television viewer has relatives in Mexico City and an earthquake occurs there, then he or she may take a special interest in the images of destruction as a report from a specific place and time; that is, one may look at television pictures for information about an important event. But film of an earthquake can be interesting even if the viewer cares nothing about the event itself. Which is only to say, as we noted earlier, that there is another way of participating in the news—as a spectator who desires to be entertained. Actually to see buildings topple is exciting, no matter where the buildings are. The world turns to dust before our eyes.

10   Those who produce television news in America know that their medium favors images that move. That is why they are wary of "talking heads," people who simply appear in front of a camera and speak. When talking heads appear on television, there is nothing to record or document, no change in process. In the cinema the situation is somewhat different. On a movie screen, closeups of a good actor speaking dramatically can sometimes be interesting to watch. When Clint Eastwood narrows his eyes and challenges his rival to shoot first, the spectator sees the cool rage of the Eastwood character take visual form, and the narrowing of the eyes is dramatic. But much of the effect of this small movement depends on the size of the movie screen and the darkness of the theater, which make Eastwood and his every action "larger than life."

11   The television screen is smaller than life. It occupies about 15 percent of the viewer's visual field (compared to about 70 percent for the movie screen). It is not set in a darkened theater closed off from the world but in the viewer's ordinary living space. This means that visual changes must be more extreme and more dramatic to be interesting on television. A narrowing of the eyes will not do. A car crash, an earthquake, a burning factory are much better.

12   With these principles in mind, let us examine more closely the structure of a typical newscast, and here we will include in the discussion not only the pictures but all the nonlinguistic symbols that make up a television news show. For example, in America, almost all news shows begin with music, the tone of which suggests important events about to unfold. The music is very important, for it equates the news with various forms of drama and ritual—the opera, for example, or a wedding procession—in which musical themes underscore the mean-

ing of the event. Music takes us immediately into the realm of the symbolic, a world that is not to be taken literally. After all, when events unfold in the real world, they do so without musical accompaniment. More symbolism follows. The sound of teletype machines can be heard in the studio, not because it is impossible to screen this noise out, but because the sound is a kind of music in itself. It tells us that data are pouring in from all corners of the globe, a sensation reinforced by the world map in the background (or clocks noting the time on different continents). The fact is that teletype machines are rarely used in TV news rooms, having been replaced by silent computer terminals. When seen, they have only a symbolic function.

13   Already, then, before a single news item is introduced, a great deal has been communicated. We know that we are in the presence of a symbolic event, a form of theater in which the day's events are to be dramatized. This theater takes the entire globe as its subject, although it may look at the world from the perspective of a single nation. A certain tension is present, like the atmosphere in a theater just before the curtain goes up. The tension is represented by the music, the staccato beat of the teletype machines, and often the sight of news workers scurrying around typing reports and answering phones. As a technical matter, it would be no problem to build a set in which the newsroom staff remained off camera, invisible to the viewer, but an important theatrical effect would be lost. By being busy on camera, the workers help communicate urgency about the events at hand, which suggests that situations are changing so rapidly that constant revision of the news is necessary.

14   The staff in the background also helps signal the importance of the person in the center, the anchor, "in command" of both the staff and the news. The anchor plays the role of host. He or she welcomes us to the newscast and welcomes us back from the different locations we visit during the filmed reports.

15   Many features of the newscast help the anchor to establish the impression of control. These are usually equated with production values in broadcasting. They include such things as graphics that tell the viewer what is being shown, or maps and charts that suddenly appear on the screen and disappear on cue, or the orderly progression from story to story. They also include the absence of gaps, or "dead time," during the broadcast, even the simple fact that the news starts and ends at a certain hour. These common features are thought of as pure technical matters, which a professional crew handles as a matter of course. But they are also symbols of a dominant theme of television news: the imposition of an orderly world—called "the news"—upon the disorderly flow of events.

16   While the form of a news broadcast emphasizes tidiness and control, its content can best be described as fragmented. Because time is so precious on television, because the nature of the medium favors dynamic visual images, and because the pressures of a commercial structure require the news to hold its audience above all else, there is rarely any attempt to explain issues in depth or place events in their proper context. The news moves nervously from a warehouse fire to a court decision, from a guerrilla war to a World Cup match, the

quality of the film most often determining the length of the story. Certain stories show up only because they offer dramatic pictures. Bleachers collapse in South America: hundreds of people are crushed—a perfect television news story, for the cameras can record the face of disaster in all its anguish. Back in Washington, a new budget is approved by Congress. Here there is nothing to photograph because a budget is not a physical event; it is a document full of language and numbers. So the producers of the news will show a photo of the document itself, focusing on the cover where it says "Budget of the United States of America." Or sometimes they will send a camera crew to the government printing plant where copies of the budget are produced. That evening, while the contents of the budget are summarized by a voice-over, the viewer sees stacks of documents being loaded into boxes at the government printing plant. Then a few of the budget's more important provisions will be flashed on the screen in written form, but this is such a time-consuming process—using television as a printed page—that the producers keep it to a minimum. In short, the budget is not televisable, and for that reason its time on the news must be brief. The bleacher collapse will get more time that evening.

17   While appearing somewhat chaotic, these disparate stories are not just dropped in the news program helter-skelter. The appearance of a scattershot story order is really orchestrated to draw the audience from one story to the next—through the commercial breaks to the end of the show. The story order is constructed to hold and build the viewership rather than place events in context or explain issues in depth.

18   Of course, it is a tendency of journalism in general to concentrate on the surface of events rather than underlying conditions; this is as true for the newspaper as it is for the newscast. But several features of television undermine whatever efforts journalists may make to give sense to the world. One is that a television broadcast is a series of events that occur in sequence, and the sequence is the same for all viewers. This is not true for a newspaper page, which displays many items simultaneously, allowing readers to choose the order in which they read them. If newspaper readers want only a summary of the latest tax bill, they can read the headline and the first paragraph of an article, and if they want more, they can keep reading. In a sense, then, everyone reads a different newspaper, for no two readers will read (or ignore) the same items.

19   But all television viewers see the same broadcast. They have no choices. A report is either in the broadcast or out, which means that anything which is of narrow interest is unlikely to be included. As NBC News executive Reuven Frank once explained:

> A newspaper, for example, can easily afford to print an item of conceivable interest to only a fraction of its readers. A television news program must be put together with the assumption that each item will be of some interest to everyone that watches. Every time a newspaper includes a feature which will attract a specialized group it can assume it is adding at least a little bit to its circulation. To the degree a television news program includes an item of this sort . . . it must assume that its audience will diminish.

20   The need to "include everyone," an identifying feature of commercial tele-vision in all its forms, prevents journalists from offering lengthy or complex ex-planations, or from tracing the sequence of events leading up to today's head-lines. One of the ironies of political life in modern democracies is that many problems which concern the "general welfare" are of interest only to special-ized groups. Arms control, for example, is an issue that literally concerns every-one in the world, and yet the language of arms control and the complexity of the subject are so daunting that only a minority of people can actually follow the issue from week to week and month to month. If it wants to act responsibly, a newspaper can at least make available more information about arms control than most people want. Commercial television cannot afford to do so.

21   But even if commercial television could afford to do so, it wouldn't. The fact that television news is principally made up of moving pictures prevents it from offering lengthy, coherent explanations of events. A television news show reveals the world as a series of unrelated, fragmentary moments. It does not—and cannot be expected to—offer a sense of coherence or meaning. What does this suggest to a TV viewer? That the viewer must come with a prepared mind—information, opinions, a sense of proportion, an articulate value system. To the TV viewer lacking such mental equipment, a news program is only a kind of rousing light show. Here a falling building, there a five-alarm fire, everywhere the world as an object, much without meaning, connections, or continuity.

FOR ANALYSIS AND DISCUSSION

1. According to Postman and Powers, what is wrong with news programs re-creating actual events? How does re-creation affect the viewer? How does it af-fect the story?
2. Consider the phrase "a picture is worth a thousand words." Is it true? How does it apply to television journalism?
3. Imagine that you are seeing each of these "pictures" in paragraphs 5 and 6 without any accompanying explanation. How many different ways could these pictures be interpreted? How important are words to the contexts of these pic-tures?
4. How do you think a broadcast journalist from your local network would re-spond to this essay? How argumentative is the essay? Explain.
5. What is the price viewers pay for fragmented video clips? Evaluate the benefits and costs of this style of journalism.
6. Consider the order in which news stories are presented during a broadcast. How do the stories control the audience? Does the fact that you are being ma-nipulated change your opinion of the nightly news? Explain.
7. Analyze the authors' last paragraph, which states that television news programs cannot offer a sense of coherence or meaning. Do you agree with this assess-ment? Why might this concept be ironic when you consider the reasons why people watch the news?

Watching the Eyewitless News
Elayne Rapping

Elayne Rapping argues that local news is anything but local. "Cookie-cutter" broadcast formulas make every local news broadcast alike, no matter what corner of America you are in. The anchors look alike, they speak the same, they follow the same formats, and they tell the same types of stories. Yet even more curious than this generic and mindless approach to news is the fact that most viewers like their news this way—safe and familiar.

Media analyst and film critic Elayne Rapping is professor of communications at Adelphi University. Her most recent book is *The Culture of Recovery: Making Sense of the Self-Help Movement in Women's Lives* (1997). This essay first appeared in the March 1995 issue of *The Progressive*.

BEFORE YOU READ

What is the difference between so-called "tabloid" television and news programming? What are the boundaries between the two? Are these boundaries blurring, and if so, in what ways?

AS YOU READ

Consider the adjectives Rapping uses to describe television news programs. Underline them as you read. How do these adjectives contribute to the overall tone of the essay?

1   Jimmy Cagney, the ultimate street-smart wise guy, used to snap, "Whadya hear? Whadya know?" in the days of black-and-white movies and Read All About It! headlines. But that was then and this is now. Today, when gangsta rap has replaced gangster movies, and television has replaced newsprint as the primary source of information (for two-thirds of us, the *only* source), Cagney's famous question is not only antiquated, it is beside the point. What we hear when we consume "the news" has only the most marginal relationship to what we *know* about anything.

2   I'm not referring here to CNN or the "evening news" on the national broadcast networks. I'm referring to what passes for news in the homes and minds of the vast majority of Americans today: the *Eyewitless, Happy Talk* local newscasts that run in many cities for as much as an hour and a half to two hours a day, on as many as seven or eight different channels.

3   The rise of local news, the infotainment monster that ate the news industry, is a long and painful story about a key battlefront in the endless media war between capitalism and democracy, between the drive for profits and the constitutional responsibility of those licensed to use the airwaves to serve the public interest. We know who's winning, of course. The game was rigged from the start.

4   To make sure it stays that way, most members of the Federal Communications Commission are appointed—no matter who's in the White House—from

the ranks of the industry itself. Indeed, if there is any phenomenon that gives dramatic support to Leonard Cohen's baleful lines, "Everybody knows the war is over/ Everybody knows the good guys lost," it's the specter of local news, slouching roughly across a wider and wider stretch of airwave time, planting its brainless images as it goes.

5   Local news as we know it was invented in 1970, the brainchild of a marketing research whiz hired by the industry to raise ratings by finding out what audiences "wanted to see." The Jeffersonian notion that public media should cover what citizens "need to know" was not a big consideration. Nor was it a concern to respect the audience's intelligence or diversity.

6   The researchers offered a limited, embarrassingly vapid list of choices of formats and subjects, while ignoring the possibility that different groups might want different kinds of information and analysis. More annoying still, they ignored the possibility that individual viewers, of all kinds, might want and need different things at different times for different reasons. Nope, said the marketing whizzes, this master model of "The News" will buy us the most overall-ratings bang per buck. Wrap it up and send it out.

7   And it worked. Their invention has conquered the TV world. The sets, the news lineups, the anchors, the weather maps, the sports features—all developed for a New York City market—quickly became a universal formula, sent out to every network affiliate and independent station in America, complete with fill-in-the-blanks guidelines for adaptation to any community, no matter how large or small, urban or rural. Local news today is the single most profitable form of nonfiction television programming in the country and, for most stations, the only thing they actually produce. Everything else comes from the networks. As time went by, this tendency toward cookie-cutter formulas, exported far and wide from a central media source, reached ever more depressing depths. The trend has led to ever more nationally produced, generic features exported to local stations to be passed off as "local."

8   So today we have a phenomenon euphemistically called "local news," although it is anything but, filled with images of a pseudo-community called "America," which is actually closer to Disney World in its representation of American life. But why should that surprise us, in a national landscape now filled, from coast to coast, with identical, mass-produced shopping malls that pass for town marketplaces, and hotels and airports that pass for village inns? In postmodern America, after all, this kind of brand-name synthetic familiarity appears to be the only thing that holds us—a nation of endlessly uprooted and mobile strangers—together.

9   When you turn on the news, whether at home or in an airport or Holiday Inn in some totally strange locale, you see a predictable, comforting spectacle. The town or city in question, whether Manhattan or Moose Hill, Montana, is presided over by a group of attractive, charming, well-dressed performers—whose agents, salaries, and movements up and down the ladder of media success, gauged by the size of the "market" they infiltrate, are chronicled each week in *Variety*. They seem to care endlessly for each other and us. "Tsk, tsk,"

they cluck at news of yet another gang rampage or Congressional scandal. "Ooh," they sigh, at news of earthquakes and plane crashes, far and near.

10   If it bleeds, it leads is the motto of the commercial news industry and local news. Its endless series of fires, shootouts, collapsing buildings, and babies beaten or abandoned or bitten by wild dogs is the state-of-the-art showcase for the industry. As Don Henley once put it, in a scathing song about the local-news phenomenon, "It's interesting when people die." And it's especially interesting when they die in bizarre or inhuman situations, when their loved ones are on camera to moan and wail, when a lot of them die at once. And since so much of our news is indeed personally terrifying and depressing, we need to have it delivered as cleverly and carefully as possible. And so we have the always smiling, always sympathetic, always confidently upbeat news teams to sugarcoat the bad news.

11   Not that local news ignores the politically important stories. Well, not entirely anyway. When wars are declared or covered, when elections are won or lost, when federal budgets and plant closings do away with jobs and services or threaten to put more and more of us in jail, for less and less cause, the local news teams are there to calm our jagged nerves and reassure us that we needn't worry.

12   This reassurance is sometimes subtle. National news items typically take up less than two minutes of a half-hour segment. And what's said and seen in that brief interlude is hardly enlightening. On the contrary, the hole for "hard news" is generally filled with sound bites and head shots, packaged and processed by the networks, from news conferences with the handful of movers and shakers considered "newsworthy"—the President and his key henchmen and adversaries, mostly.

13   But even local issues of serious import are given short shrift on these news-casts. Hard news affecting local communities takes up only a minute or two more airtime than national events. And local teams are obsessed with "man-on-the-street" spot interviews. Neighbors on local TV are forever gasping and wailing the most clichéd of reflex responses to actual local horrors, whether personal or social.

14   "It's so horrible," they say over and over again, like wind-up dolls with a limited repertoire of three-word phrases, when asked about a local disaster. And when the crisis affects them directly—a school budget cut or neighborhood hospital closing, for example—their on-air responses are equally vapid. "I don't know *what* we're going to do without any teachers or books," they say with puzzled, frenzied expressions as they try desperately to articulate some coherent reply to a complex issue they've just heard about.

15   I am not suggesting that the news should not feature community residents' views and experiences. Of course it should. But the local news teams' way of presenting such community responses is deliberately demeaning and fatuous. No one could say much worth saying in such a format. And if someone managed to come up with something serious and intelligent, rest assured it would be cut in favor of a more sensational, emotional response.

16   But real news, even about cats in trees or babies in wells, is hardly what takes up the most airtime. "Don't bother too much about that stuff," say the guys and gals in the anchor chairs. Here's Goofy Gil with the weather, or Snappy Sam with the sports—the two features which, on every local newscast, are given the longest time slots and the most elaborate and expensive props. The number and ornateness of the weather maps on local news, and the endlessly amazing developments in special-effects technology to observe climate changes and movements of impending "fronts" is truly mind-boggling.

17   Who needs this stuff? But we're forgetting that this is not the question to ask. "Who wants it?" is the criterion for news producers, and it is, understandably, the weather and sports that most people, most of the time, are likely to sit still for. If local news is meant to be a facsimile of a sunny Disneyesque community of happy, cozy campers, in which the bothersome bad guys and events of the day are quickly dealt with so that community harmony may once more reign, at least for the moment—and that *is* the intended fantasy—then what better, safer, kind of information than weather reports. Historically, after all, the weather is the standard small-talk item for people wishing to be pleasant and make contact without getting into anything controversial or heavy. It is the only kind of news we can all share in—no matter what our race, class, gender, or political differences—as members of a common community.

18   The researchers are not entirely wrong, after all, about what people in this kind of society want. They do want comfort, reassurance, and a community where they belong and feel safe. And why shouldn't they? They find precious little of those things in the streets and buildings they traverse and inhabit in their daily lives. In my urban neighborhood, parents warn children never to make eye contact with anyone on the street or subway; never to speak to anyone, even in case of tragedy or emergency; never to look at or listen to the pathetic souls who regularly beg for money or ramble incoherently in the hope that someone, anyone, will take pity and respond.

19   Remember when California was God's country, the Promised Land of Milk and Honey, to which people migrated for clean air, good jobs, and single-dwelling homes? Try to find these things in overpopulated, polluted, socially vexed and violent LA today. Don Henley, again, said it best some twenty years ago: "Call some place paradise/Kiss it good-bye."

20   But if we can't all dream of moving to sunny California anymore, there's always TV, where something resembling that innocent dream still exists. Eyewitness News and its various clones allow us to believe, just for a moment, that there really is a Santa Claus, a Mary Poppins, a Good Samaritan giving away fortunes to the needy, a spirit of Christmas Past to convert the most cold-hearted of corporate Scrooges. Indeed, this kind of "good news" is another staple of the genre. Charities, celebrations, instances of extraordinary good luck or good works by or for local residents are ever-present on local newscasts. Every day, in the midst of even the most dreadful and depressing news, there are legions of friends and neighbors to mourn and console each other, offering aid, bringing

soup and casseroles to the victims of natural and man-made disasters, stringing lights and hanging balloons for festive neighborhood gatherings.

21   The news teams themselves often play this role for us. They march at the head of holiday parades and shake hands and kiss babies at openings of malls and industrial parks. They are the neighbors—often thought of as friends by the loneliest among us—we wish we had in real life, there to do the right thing on every occasion. That is their primary function. They are not trained in journalism. They often cannot pronounce the local names and foreign words they read from teleprompters. But they sure can smile. And joke around. And let us in on the latest bargain to seek out or scam to avoid. In fact, the "Action Line" and "Shame on You" features, in which reporters hang out at local shopping centers trying out new gadgets, testing fabrics, and trapping shady shopkeepers in their nefarious efforts to sell us junk, poison, and instant death, are among the most popular and cheery things on the air.

22   The news teams also bring us gossip, at a time when more and more of us are lonely and scared of each other. The gossip is not about our actual neighbors of course, those suspicious, *different*-looking folks who just moved in. We don't open the door to them for fear they will shoot or rape us. No, no.

23   The news teams bring us word of our nice friends and neighbors, the celebrities we have come to know and love through their ever-present images on the TV screens that have become our virtual homes and communities. Marla and The Donald, Michael and Lisa Marie, Lyle and Julia, Richard and Cindy—we know and love these people and delight in sharing the latest bits of harmless scandal about them with co-workers and other semi-intimates.

24   Sociologist Joshua Gamson has suggested, in an insightful essay, that there is a lesson to be learned from the enormous popularity of tabloid television—a category in which I would certainly include local news. The lesson is not that people are stupid, venal, "addicted," or otherwise blameworthy for their fascinated interest in junk TV. On the contrary, it is those responsible for the quality of our public life who are more deserving of such terms of contempt and opprobrium. For it is, says Gamson, "Only when people perceive public life as inconsequential, as not their own, [that] they readily accept the invitation to turn news into play." And people most certainly do perceive public life as inconsequential and worse these days, whether outside their doors or in Washington or on Wall Street.

25   Only I don't think it is primarily the desire to "play" that drives people in droves to local newscasts, or even the trashier tabloid shows like *Hard Copy*. What people are getting from local newscasts—and here the researchers were right on the money, literally—is indeed *what they want*, in the most profound and sad sense of that phrase. They are getting what they always sought in fantasy and fiction, from *The Wizard of Oz* to *As the World Turns*. They are getting, for a brief moment, a utopian fantasy of a better, kinder, more decent and meaningful world than the one that entraps them.

26   It is not only that public life is inconsequential, after all. It is, far more tragically, that public and private life today are increasingly unjust, inhumane, painful, even hopeless, materially and spiritually, for many of us. And there is

no relief in sight except, ironically, on the local newscasts that are a respite from reality. Only, unlike the utopian villages of soap opera and fairy tale, these "imagined communities" are supposed to be, pretend to be, real and true. And for that reason they are more troubling than the trashiest or silliest of pop-culture fictions.

FOR ANALYSIS AND DISCUSSION

1. What problems does Rapping have with news features devoted to the views and experiences of community residents? Why does she find that segment of the local news lacking?
2. Analyze the relationship between the preestablished formula of local news broadcasts and their actual content. What is the relationship between form and function?
3. According to Rapping, what is "safe" news? Why do viewers prefer it? Do you agree?
4. Evaluate Rapping's tone. How does it likely influence the reader's reception of her argument? Is this an effective way to present her perspective? Explain.
5. If Rapping could restructure and reinvent the local television news program, what do you think her broadcast would be like? Support your response with points from the essay.

Why Those Hidden Cameras Hurt Journalism
Paul Starobin

Many prime-time news programs such as *60 Minutes, 20/20,* and *Dateline* feature "hidden camera" exposés designed to draw in viewers. In some cases the hidden camera can provide useful information and proof that a problem exists, but in other cases reporters go out of their way to trick individuals and businesses to expose dangerous or fraudulent activity. It is this type of entrapment journalism that Paul Starobin says is giving television journalism a bad name.

Paul Starobin writes for the *National Journal.* This essay appeared in the *New York Times* on January 28, 1997.

BEFORE YOU READ

Have you ever watched a prime-time news program that featured a hidden camera exposé? What did you think of the technique? Did you think the reporter was being sneaky? Did you feel any sympathy for the person thus being deceived?

AS YOU READ

As you read, assume you are part of the jury determining the integrity of the journalists in the stories Starobin discusses. For example, do you think a jury today would have ruled against Nellie Bly?

1   When a North Carolina jury took a swipe at hidden-camera television exposés last week, the press mostly circled the wagons and declared it a travesty. But what the Fourth Estate is defending is shoddy journalism, unworthy of the best tradition of investigative reporting.

2   The jury found ABC liable for $5.5 million in punitive damages for using deceptive research tactics, amounting to fraud, in a 1992 "Primetime Live" broadcast that accused the Food Lion supermarket chain of selling spoiled food. The show's producers faked résumés to get jobs at Food Lion stores and then used hidden cameras to catch workers prettying up tainted meat.

3   ABC's lawyer, Bill Jeffries, says the "Primetime" crew was punished "for being journalists." Nonsense. It was punished for trickery and deception.

4   Hidden cameras? That's the easiest call. Their growing use by TV news magazine shows, including "Primetime Live" and NBC's "Dateline," is part of a ratings-driven descent by the major networks into the swamp of tabloid journalism. Teaser promos for the programs hype concealed-camera feats to snag viewers who like to watch people who don't know they're being watched. But good journalism is not about sensationalizing how the story was obtained.

5   The more difficult issue is the use of undercover practices to get a story that might otherwise be difficult to report. So what if a few producers falsified their résumés to land jobs at Food Lion: Isn't this part and parcel of muckraking journalism?

6   Subterfuge does have a long tradition in investigative reporting, but it is a dubious one. The pioneer was Nellie Bly, who in 1887 feigned insanity to gain admission to the New York City Lunatic Asylum.

7   Bly's report in *The New York World* on her 10 days in the asylum exposed horrors that spurred needed reforms. But was that the only way to get the story? Probably not. The flamboyant Bly was an artful practitioner of what was known back then as "stunt journalism." She also posed as a prostitute and a thief and was regarded by some peers as a self-promoting sensationalizer and an embarrassment to the craft.

8   Broadsheet newspapers hyped derring-do disguised feats just as the TV news magazine shows now tout hidden-camera tricks. The headline for a front-page story on Bly's asylum exploit in the rival *New York Sun* blared "Playing Mad Woman," and the subhead declared, "Nellie Bly Too Sharp for the Island Doctors."

9   The greatest muckrakers shunned such ruses. Ida Tarbell brought down John D. Rockefeller's Standard Oil monopoly by the tireless bird-dogging of court records and other documents—a righteous tradition later upheld by I. F. Stone and honored these days by the crusaders who are following the money to expose the fund-raising practices of Newt Gingrich and Bill Clinton. And *Fortune* magazine didn't need to go undercover for its 1993 report on the exploitation of child labor in garment-industry sweatshops in New York City and Los Angeles.

10   Indeed, ABC could have done a devastating story on Food Lion without the tricks. Diane Sawyer, the "Primetime Live" anchor, said 70 current and former

employees of the chain had attested to unhealthful food-handling practices in on-the-record interviews with the show's researchers. But that wasn't sexy enough, so ABC went undercover to dramatize the tale. A commercial imperative, not a journalistic one, drove this piece.

11   Many news organizations ban undercover operations. Eager reporters can be tempted to entrap subjects or stage scenes to justify these ventures.

12   The *Chicago Sun-Times* and CBS's "60 Minutes" were appropriately criticized for a 1978 project that involved setting up a phony bar, the Mirage, to catch Chicago officials demanding bribes to overlook code violations.

13   A few years later, a television reporter for an NBC affiliate in Chicago took matters into his own hands when his hidden-camera crew failed to capture a real-life incident of police brutality. A cooperative cop helped him with a dramatization in which the reporter had himself handcuffed, locked into the back of a police wagon and filmed being violently tossed around as the vehicle sped away.

14   ABC points out that Food Lion sued for fraud, not libel, and so did not challenge the substance of the story. But news organizations should not be untruthful in their search for the truth. The North Carolina jury has fired a well-deserved warning shot. Stunt journalism saps the credibility of the press and makes life tougher for honest snoops.

FOR ANALYSIS AND DISCUSSION

1. Do you agree with the jury's decision to award Food Lion $5.5 million in punitive damages to punish ABC for using "deceptive research tactics, amounting to fraud"? How does this case compare to other programs that use hidden cameras to present their stories? Explain.

2. Research the story of Nellie Bly, the young reporter who posed as a victim of insanity to gain admittance to the New York City Lunatic Asylum. Bly uncovered many atrocities and her stories motivated changes in the system. Evaluate her tactics. Are her tactics just another example of deceitful journalism?

3. What effect does the use of hidden cameras have on the audience? Would the audience react the same way if the story was supported with interviews and documentation instead of hidden cameras? Why or why not?

4. Do you agree with Starobin that hidden camera journalism is ruining the profession? Explain.

5. Review the story in paragraph 13 about the reporter who failed to capture a real-life incidence of police brutality. Is there a difference between this story and the others in the article? What could have happened if viewers believed that the trumped-up video was actually real? Is this an example of news reporting serving the public interest?

6. How do you think a producer from one of the major prime-time news programs would respond to this essay? Explain.

WRITING ASSIGNMENTS: TV NEWS

1. Over the course of a week, watch several different local newscasts and consider the way in which they match Rapping's "cookie-cutter" model. What differences, if any, exist? If they are all basically the same, how does one show promote itself over another? Consider how the anchors dress, the set, any special news features, the commercials that air, and so on. Write an essay in which you describe what you see and analyze its relevance. Do you agree with Rapping's observations?

2. The Radio-Television News Director's Association (RTNDA) maintains a Web site covering its magazine *Communicator*. Read the online article by Bob Steele on the ethics of using hidden cameras at <http://www.rtnda.org/prodev/articles/hidden.htm>. How does Steele's opinion differ from Paul Starobin's? Write an argument in which you support your position on the use of hidden camera journalism, using information from Steele's and Starobin's articles, as well as from your own investigation of the issue.

3. You are a television news producer who must develop a local news broadcast. Conduct a survey on what people want to watch on television news. Consider your questions carefully. After gathering your information, design your newscast and explain in detail the reasons behind your design. How much does your broadcast resemble others already on the air? Do you rely on popular consciousness? Predict the success of your broadcast.

Movie and TV Violence: How Does It Affect Us?

Honey, I Warped the Kids
Carl M. Cannon

The debate over the relationship between television violence and actual violence is not new. Since 1954 as many as 3,000 studies on television and violence have been completed. In this essay, Carl M. Cannon calls on that large body of research to support his argument that because almost all experts agree that television can encourage aggressive behavior, it is reasonable to try to curb the amount of violence on television, especially programming for children.

Cannon is the White House correspondent for the *Baltimore Sun*. This article first appeared in *Mother Jones* in 1993.

BEFORE YOU READ

Slasher and murder films such as *Friday the 13th, Halloween, Scream,* and *Natural Born Killers* are seen by many to be causes of insensitivity, aggression, and violence among young viewers—particularly males. Is this an accurate judgment, according to your experience? Do you think such films encourage violent behavior?

AS YOU READ

Examine the author's comments on the studies he summarizes. Are these summaries adequate support for his argument? Evaluate the way Cannon uses this evidence to prove his case.

1 Tim Robbins and Susan Sarandon implore the nation to treat Haitians with AIDS more humanely. Robert Redford works for the environment. Harry Belafonte marches against the death penalty.

2 Actors and producers seem to be constantly speaking out for noble causes far removed from their lives. They seem even more vocal and visible now that there is a Democrat in the White House. But in the one area over which they have control—the excessive violence in the entertainment industry—Hollywood activists remain silent.

3 This summer, Washington was abuzz with talk about the movie *Dave*, in which Kevin Kline stars as the acting president. But every time I saw an ad featuring Kline, the movie I couldn't get out of my head was *Grand Canyon*. There are two scenes in it that explain much of what has gone wrong in America.

4 Kline's character has a friend, played by Steve Martin, who is a producer of the B-grade, violent movies that Hollywood euphemistically called "action" films. But after an armed robber shoots Martin's character in the leg, he has an epiphany.

5 "I can't make those movies any more," he decides. "I can't make another piece of art that glorifies violence and bloodshed and brutality. . . . No more exploding bodies, exploding buildings, exploding anything. I'm going to make the world a better place."

6 A month or two later, Kline calls on Martin at his Hollywood studio to congratulate him on the "new direction" his career has taken.

7 "What? Oh that," Martin says dismissively. "Fuck that. That's over. I must have been delirious for a few weeks there."

8 He then gins up every hoary excuse for Hollywood-generated violence you've ever heard, ending with: "<u>My movies reflect what's going on; they</u> don't <u>make what's going on.</u>"

9 This is Hollywood's last line of defense for why it shows murder and mayhem on the big screen and the little one, in prime time and early in the morning, to children, adolescents, and adults:

10 We don't cause violence, we just report it.

11 Four years ago, I joined the legion of writers, researchers, and parents who have tried to force Hollywood to confront the more disturbing truth. I wrote a series of newspaper articles on the massive body of evidence that establishes a direct cause-and-effect relationship between violence on television and violence in society.

12 The orchestrated response from the industry—a series of letters seeking to discredit me—was something to behold.

13 Because the fact is, on the <u>one issue over which they have</u> power, the liberals in <u>Hollywood don't act like progressive thinkers; they act like</u>, say, the National Rifle Association: Ad hominim

14   <u>Guns don't kill people, people kill people.</u>

15   <u>We don't cause violence in the world, we just reflect it.</u>

16   The first congressional hearings into the effects of television violence took place in 1954. Although television was still relatively new, its extraordinary marketing power was already evident. The tube was teaching Americans what to buy and how to act, not only in advertisements, but in dramatic shows, too.

17   Everybody from Hollywood producers to Madison Avenue ad men would boast about this power—and seek to utilize it on dual tracks: to make money and to remake society along better lines.

18   Because it seemed ludicrous to assert that there was only one area—the depiction of violence—where television did not influence behavior, the television industry came up with this theory: Watching violence is cathartic. A violent person might be sated by watching a murder.

19   The notion intrigued social scientists, and by 1956 they were studying it in earnest. Unfortunately, watching violence turned out to be anything but cathartic.

20   In the 1956 study, one dozen four-year-olds watched a "Woody Woodpecker" cartoon that was full of violent images. Twelve other preschoolers watched "Little Red Hen," a peaceful cartoon. Then the children were observed. The children who watched "Woody Woodpecker" were more likely to hit other children, verbally accost their classmates, break toys, be disruptive, and engage in destructive behavior during free play.

21   For the next thirty years, researchers in all walks of the social sciences studied the question of whether television causes violence. The results have been stunningly conclusive.

22   "There is more published research on this topic than on almost any other social issue of our time," University of Kansas Professor Aletha C. Huston, chairwoman of the American Psychological Association's Task Force on Television and Society, told Congress in 1988. "Virtually all independent scholars agree that there is evidence that television can cause aggressive behavior."

23   There have been some three thousand studies of this issue—eighty-five of them major research efforts—and they all say the same thing. Of the eighty-five major studies, the only one that failed to find a causal relationship between television violence and actual violence was paid for by NBC. When the study was subsequently reviewed by three independent social scientists, all three concluded that it actually did demonstrate a causal relationship.

24   Some highlights from the history of TV violence research:

25   • In 1973, when a town in mountainous western Canada was wired for television signals, University of British Columbia researchers observed first- and second-graders. Within two years, the incidence of hitting, biting, and shoving increased 160 percent in those classes.

26   • Two Chicago doctors, Leonard Eron and Rowell Huesmann, followed the viewing habits of a group of children for twenty-two years. They found that watching violence on television is the single best predictor of violent or ag-

gressive behavior later in life, ahead of such commonly accepted factors as parents' behavior, poverty, and race.

27   "Television violence affects youngsters of all ages, of both genders, at all socioeconomic levels and all levels of intelligence," they told Congress in 1992. "The effect is not limited to children who are already disposed to being aggressive and is not restricted to this country."

28 • Fascinated by an explosion of murder rates in the United States and Canada that began in 1955, after a generation of North Americans had come of age on television violence, University of Washington Professor Brandon Centerwall decided to see if the same phenomenon could be observed in South Africa, where the Afrikaner-dominated regime had banned television until 1975.

29   He found that eight years after TV was introduced—showing mostly Hollywood-produced fare—South Africa's murder rate skyrocketed. His most telling finding was that the crime rate increased first in the white communities. This mirrors U.S. crime statistics in the 1950s and especially points the finger at television, because whites were the first to get it in both countries.

30   Bolder than most researchers, Centerwall argues flatly that without violent television programming, there might be as many as ten thousand fewer murders in the United States each year.

31 • In 1983, University of California, San Diego, researcher David P. Phillips wanted to see if there was a correlation between televised boxing matches and violence in the streets of America.

32   Looking at crime rates after every televised heavyweight championship fight from 1973 to 1978, Phillips found that the homicide rate in the United States rose by an average of 11 percent for approximately one week. Phillips also found that the killers were likely to focus their aggression on victims similar to the losing fighter: if he was white, the increased number of victims were mostly white. The converse was true if the losing fighter was black.

33 • In 1988, researchers Daniel G. Linz and Edward Donnerstein of the University of California, Santa Barbara, and Steven Penrod of the University of Wisconsin studied the effects on young men of horror movies and "slasher" films.

34   They found that depictions of violence, not sex, are what desensitizes people.

35   They divided male students into four groups. One group watched no movies, a second watched nonviolent, X-rated movies, a third watched teenage sexual-innuendo movies, and a fourth watched the slasher films *Texas Chainsaw Massacre, Friday the 13th Part 2, Maniac,* and *Toolbox Murders.*

36   All the young men were placed on a mock jury panel and asked a series of questions designed to measure their empathy for an alleged female rape victim. Those in the fourth group measured lowest in empathy for the specific victim in the experiment—and for rape victims in general.

37   The anecdotal evidence is often more compelling than the scientific studies. Ask any homicide cop from London to Los Angeles to Bangkok if television violence induces real-life violence and listen carefully to the cynical, knowing laugh.

38   Ask David McCarthy, police chief in Greenfield, Massachusetts, why nineteen-year-old Mark Branch killed himself after stabbing an eighteen-year-old female college student to death. When cops searched his room they found ninety horror movies, as well as a machete and a goalie mask like those used by Jason, the grisly star of *Friday the 13th.*

39   Ask the families of thirty-five young men who committed suicide by playing Russian roulette after seeing the movie *The Deer Hunter.*

40   Ask George Gavito, a lieutenant in the Cameron County, Texas, sheriff's department, about a cult that sacrificed at least thirteen people on a ranch west of Matamoros, Mexico. The suspects kept mentioning a 1986 movie, *The Believers,* about rich families who engage in ritual sacrifice. "They talk about it like that had something to do with changing them," Gavito recalled later.

41   Ask LAPD lieutenant Mike Melton about Angel Regino of Los Angeles, who was picked up after a series of robberies and a murder in which he wore a blue bandanna and fedora identical to those worn by Freddy, the sadistic antihero of *Nightmare on Elm Street.* In case anybody missed the significance of his disguise, Regino told his victims that they would never forget him, because he was another Freddy Krueger.

42   Ask Britain Home Secretary Douglas Hurd, who called for further restrictions on U.S.-produced films after Michael Ryan of Hungerford committed Britain's worst mass murder in imitation of *Rambo,* massacring sixteen people while wearing a U.S. combat jacket and a bandoleer of ammunition.

43   Ask Sergeant John O'Malley of the New York Police Department about a nine-year-old boy who sprayed a Bronx office building with gunfire. The boy explained to the astonished sergeant how he learned to load his Uzi-like firearm: "I watch a lot of TV."

44   Or ask Manteca, California, police detective Jeff Boyd about thirteen-year-old Juan Valdez, who, with another teenager, went to a man's home, kicked him, stabbed him, beat him with a fireplace poker, and then choked him to death with a dog chain.

45   Why, Boyd wanted to know, had the boys poured salt in the victim's wounds?

46   "Oh, I don't know," the youth replied with a shrug. "I just seen it on TV."

47   Numerous groups have called, over the years, for curbing television violence: the National Commission on the Causes and Prevention of Violence (1969), the U.S. Surgeon General (1972), the Canadian Royal Commission (1976), the National Institute of Mental Health (1982), the U.S. Attorney General's Task Force on Family Violence (1984), the National Parents Teachers Association (1987), and the American Psychological Association (1992).

48   During that time, cable television and movie rentals have made violence more readily available while at the same time pushing the envelope for network TV. But even leaving aside cable and movie rentals, a study of television pro-

gramming from 1967 to 1989 showed only small ups and downs in violence, with the violent acts moving from one time slot to another but the overall violence rate remaining pretty steady—and pretty similar from network to network.

49   "The percent of prime-time programs using violence remains more than seven out of ten, as it has been for the entire twenty-two-year-period," researchers George Gerbner of the University of Pennsylvania Annenberg School for Communication and Nancy Signorielli of the University of Delaware wrote in 1990. For the past twenty-two years, they found, adults and children have been entertained by about sixteen violent acts, including two murders, in each evening's prime-time programming.

50   They also discovered that the rate of violence in children's programs is three times the rate in prime-time shows. By the age of eighteen, the average American child has witnessed at least eighteen thousand simulated murders on television.

51   By 1989, network executives were arguing that their violence was part of a larger context in which bad guys get their just desserts.

52   "We have never put any faith in mechanical measurements, such as counting punches or gunshots," said NBC's Alan Gerson. "Action and conflict must be evaluated within each specific dramatic context."

53   "Our policy," added Alfred R. Schneider of ABC, ". . . makes clear that when violence is portrayed [on TV], it must be reasonably related to plot development and character delineation."

54   Of course, what early-childhood experts could tell these executives is that children between the ages of four and seven simply make no connection between the murder at the beginning of a half-hour show and the man led away in handcuffs at the end. In fact, psychologists know that very young children do not even understand death to be a permanent condition.

55   But all of the scientific studies and reports, all of the wisdom of cops and grief of parents have run up against Congress's quite proper fear of censorship. For years, Democratic Congressman Peter Rodino of New Jersey chaired the House Judiciary Committee and looked at calls for some form of censorship with a jaundiced eye. At a hearing five years ago, Rodino told witnesses that Congress must be a "protector of commerce."

56   "Well, we have children that we need to protect," replied Frank M. Palumbo, a pediatrician at Georgetown University Hospital and a consultant to the American Academy of Pediatrics. "What we have here is a toxic substance in the environment that is harmful to children."

57   Arnold Fege of the national PTA added, "Clearly, this committee would not protect teachers who taught violence to children. Yet why would we condone children being exposed to a steady diet of TV violence year after year?"

58   Finally there is a reason to hope for progress.

59   Early this summer, Massachusetts Democrat Edward Markey, chair of the House Energy and Commerce subcommittee on telecommunications, said that

Congress may require manufacturers to build TV sets with a computer chip so that parents could block violent programs from those their children could select.

60   He joins the fight waged by Senator Paul Simon, a liberal Democrat from Illinois. Nine years ago, Simon flipped on a hotel television set hoping to catch the late news. "Instead," he has recalled many times, "I saw a man being sawed in half with a chainsaw, in living color."

61   Simon was unsettled by the image and even more unsettled when he wondered what repeatedly looking at such images would do to the mind of a fourteen-year-old.

62   When he found out, he called television executives, who told him that violence sells and that they would be at a competitive disadvantage if they acted responsibly.

63   Why not get together and adopt voluntary guidelines? Simon asked.

64   Oh, that would be a violation of antitrust law, they assured him.

65   Simon called their bluff in 1990 by pushing through Congress a law that allowed a three-year moratorium on antitrust considerations so that the industry could discuss ways to jointly reduce violence.

66   Halfway through that time, however, they had done nothing, and an angry Simon denounced the industry on the Senate floor. With a push from some prominent industry figures, a conference was set for this August 2 in Los Angeles.

67   This spring, CBS broadcast group president Howard Stringer said his network was looking for ways to cut back on violence in its entertainment, because he was troubled by the cost to society of continuing business-as-usual.

68   "We must admit we have a responsibility," he said.

69   Jack Valenti, the powerful head of the Motion Picture Association of America, wrote to producers urging them to participate in the August 2 conference. "I think it's more than a bunch of talk," Simon said. "I think this Conference will produce some results. I think the industry will adopt some standards."

70   The federal government, of course, possesses the power to regulate the airwaves through the FCC, and Simon and others believe that this latent power to control violence—never used—has put the fear of God in the producers. He also thinks some of them are starting to feel guilty.

71   "We now have more people in jail and prison per capita than any country that keeps records, including South Africa," Simon says. "We've spent billions putting people behind bars, and it's had no effect on the crime rate. None. People realize there have to be other answers, and as they've looked around, they have settled on television as one of them."

72   Maybe Simon is right. Maybe Hollywood executives will get together and make a difference.

73   Or maybe, like Steven Martin's character in *Grand Canyon,* producers and directors from New York to Beverly Hills will wake up after Simon's antitrust exemption expires December 1, shake off the effects of their holiday hangovers, and when asked about their new commitment to responsible film-making, answer:

74   "What? Oh that. Fuck that. That's over. We must have been delirious for a few weeks there."

FOR ANALYSIS AND DISCUSSION

1. Does Cannon convince you that a relationship exists between televised and real violence? If so, what was the most persuasive part of his argument? If not, why?
2. Summarize the television industry's response to calls for a decrease in media violence over the past 25 years. Have the attitudes of network executives toward the problem changed? Has violent programming changed? Explain.
3. What solution to the problem of media violence does Cannon support? What proposed solutions to the problem does he reject? How do you think television executives would react to his solutions?
4. Compare the evidence of the "scientific studies" Cannon cites in paragraphs 20–36 to the "anecdotal evidence" described in paragraphs 37–46. Which evidence do you find more compelling, and why?
5. Analyze the analogy Cannon makes in paragraph 13 between "the liberals in Hollywood" and the National Rifle Association. Do you find the comparison convincing? How are these two groups similar? How do they differ?
6. What assumptions does Cannon make about his audience, and how can you tell? To what extent is Cannon effective in addressing this audience?

Violence Is Us
Robert Scheer

Like Carl M. Cannon (previous essay) Robert Scheer believes that viewing violence desensitizes people, especially children, to the effects of violence. However, Scheer sees a different approach to the problem. Rather than seek government intervention, we should be governing ourselves. We can withdraw support of this market by "turning the damn thing off."

Award-winning journalist Robert Scheer is a contributing editor to the *Los Angeles Times* and the author of six books. This article first appeared in *The Nation* in 1993.

BEFORE YOU READ

Can a person's taste or predilection for viewing violence be changed, or is the viewing of violence the product of natural morbid curiosity? Is there any point in trying to make this change, or is it best to allow a passive outlet for it?

AS YOU READ

Scheer's tone is matter of fact. Find examples of cool, dispassionate statements that some readers might find startling or objectionable.

1 Once again Congressional committees are holding hearings on TV violence, and network executives, sincere visages firmly in place, are promising to clean up their act. Attorney General Janet Reno testified that if they don't, "government should respond."

2   There is something so beside the point about this handwringing, which has gone on since 1952, when the first Congressional hearing on TV violence was held. In 1968 a national commission headed by Milton Eisenhower warned: "We are deeply troubled by the television's constant portrayal of violence . . . in pandering to a public preoccupation with violence that television itself has helped to generate."

3   Of course, violence and base stupidity on TV and in the movies is excessive and getting worse. With the proliferation of cable channels, the market has become much more competitive, and violence sells. Hardly a night of channel-flipping goes by when my cable service doesn't offer up several truly grotesque chainsaw massacre–type films complete with dismembered parts and spurting blood.

4   Then, too, there are the cleaner assassinations presented on the networks both in their entertainment and local news hours. Remember the orgy of voyeurism, with three separate network movies devoted to the Amy Fisher–Joey Buttafuoco story? So-called news shows featuring real-life crime represent a major segment of entertainment scheduling. The fatal graveside shooting of a woman by her ex-spouse, captured by a television news camera, was gratuitously "teased" during the evening in many markets to get people to watch the news that night.

5   Nor do I deny the claims of most experts that viewing violence desensitizes people, particularly children, to the actual effects of violence, leaving them more likely to act out in antisocial ways. As the American Psychological Association reported to Congress in 1988, "Virtually all independent scholars agree that there is evidence that television can cause aggressive behavior."

6   More than 200 major studies support the common-sense suspicion that watching endless hours of violence is a public health menace. Those same studies demonstrate, although the pro-censorship prudes will never accept it, that the violent R-rated movies—not the sexually explicit X-rated ones—desensitize men to sexual violence. (As an example of this weirdly skewed double standard, wannabe censor Rev. Donald Wildmon took out full-page ads attacking *NYPD Blue*, not for its explicit violence—six homicides in the first episode—but rather because of a nude lovemaking scene, calling it "soft-core pornography.")

7   Another thing those studies show is that the poorer a family is, meaning the more vulnerable and desperate, the more hours they will spend in front of the television set. Children in poverty are most often left alone with the TV as the only available babysitter.

8   It can hardly be a good thing that children's shows two years ago reached an all-time high of thirty-two violent incidents per hour and that nine in ten children's programs involve violence. An authoritative study by George Gerbner of the University of Pennsylvania indicated that the average 16-year-old has witnessed 200,000 violent acts on TV, including 33,000 murders. Given the ease with which children can get guns in this society, there has to be some connection between the ease with which citizens are blown away by teenagers on television and in what passes for real life. And when they do it in real life they can be assured of their fifteen minutes of fame with top billing on the nightly local news.

9   Wayne LaPierre, vice president of the National Rifle Association, had a good point when he complained recently, "It galls us that every night we get lectured by ABC, NBC, and CBS News, and then they go to their entertainment programming and show all kinds of gratuitous violence." Hypocrites they are, and the voluntary labeling code that the network executives recently adopted in an effort to head off Congressional prohibitions on violent programming will change nothing. Although 72 percent of Americans polled by Times-Mirror say that we have too much violence on TV and it leads to higher crime rates, many of them must be tuning in, or the television moguls wouldn't be scheduling such fare.

10   Maybe it is time to face the fact that we have all this mayhem in our art and our lives because we like violence. Or if we don't actually like it, we need it. Why else would we favor local news programs that stress ambulance-chasing "action news"? Whether it's local or foreign news, our attention is grabbed completely only when death and destruction are at hand. That's what the endless focus groups conducted by news organizations report. It is true, as Steven Bochco, creator of *NYPD Blue*, has stated, that the violence issue on prime time is a "bogus issue," because "there's more violence on the 5 o'clock news than anything you'll see on the networks during prime time."

11   Anyway, how can you control it without putting decision-making into the hands of small-minded censors? What are the guidelines? Some reasonable ones, to cut the harmful effects on children, were suggested by University of Michigan psychology professor Leonard Eron, who is the dean of research in this area. "Gratuitous violence that is not necessary to the plot should be reduced or eliminated," is one that the networks say they accept. Another we all agree on is that the "devastating effects of violence, the permanence of its consequences . . . should be made clear," meaning you hurt or die from gunshot wounds. So far so good, but what about when he tells us, "Perpetrators of violence should not be rewarded for their violent acts," and that "those who act aggressively should be punished"? Those last two, while admirable goals, would distort a reality in which many criminals do get away with their crimes. Do we want television writers to lie to us? Don't we adults need to face up to the truth that crime is out of control?

12   Maybe adults should watch what they want, but should children, who are by definition impressionable, be exposed to a steady diet of mind-numbing violence laced with general stupidity? No, they shouldn't, but is this an issue the government or other would-be censors ought to get involved with?

13   The answer is, They are already involved, but despite endless guidelines for children's television, the fare is nastier than ever. The reason is that every regulation produces just that much more ingenuity on the part of the so-called creative people who make this junk. They are a crafty bunch and will always find some way of getting to the kids with the most primitive jolt.

14   Take the much-discussed *Beavis and Butt-Head* show, which now leads the race for the lowest common denominator. When a 5-year-old in Ohio burned the family trailer to the ground, his mother blamed the show, her son's favorite,

which had shown the two idiot characters setting fire to all sorts of objects. Hey, no problem, arson was taken out of the show in response to public outrage. There were the expected calls to ban *Beavis,* but no one stopped to ask the obvious question: Why had that mother let her 5-year-old watch endless hours of this repulsive show?

15   I asked the same question after reading a story in the *Los Angeles Times* about firefighters having to visit the schools of Orange County, California, to warn the kids that setting fires at home is a no-no. In one class, almost all the 12-year-olds said they watched *Beavis and Butt-Head* regularly and then began chanting the call of the show's lead, "Burn, burn, burn." That was in the conservative white upper-middle-class community of Mission Viejo, one of those planned paradises. Again, why did all those parents allow their kids to watch the show? It is absurd to suggest that the government step in to censor viewing that parents have acquiesced in.

16   The more important question is, Why do the children of paradise delight in this and other stupidities? I don't really know the full answer but it can't be, as Dan Quayle charged in the last election, that the cultural elite of Hollywood has seized their minds. Orange County voted overwhelmingly for Quayle and his running mate, the parents have thrown up the strongest defenses against Satan and his permissiveness, and church, Little League and Boy Scout attendance is very high.

17   One answer provided by the creators of this stuff is that it doesn't mean a thing. Kids have always tuned in to cartoons and movies in which characters are splattered or blown away. They concede that things are a bit wilder now, with far more blood and gore and nastier images, but that's modern technology for you. The demand is there and the supply will follow, but no harm is done—it's just a picture.

18   I don't buy this argument, because the impact of television and movies is too pervasive to be so easily dismissed. For many kids the electronic picture is their world, the result of an ever more technically effective medium having drowned out all other avenues of learning and stimulation.

19   It does desensitize and, yes, I don't think young kids should be watching *Beavis and Butt-Head* scenes featuring a poke in the eye with a pencil with blood spurting out, or a dog thrown into a washing machine followed by an insane giggle of approval. I doubt very much that *Beavis* creator Mike Judge will allow his little girls to watch the show.

20   But "we," collectively, can't and should not do anything about it. We can't because we live in a market economy in which blood lust and other primitive needs of people will be met one way or another, and trying to ban something just makes it more attractive and marketable. We shouldn't because it is the adults' right to flick on whatever they want on the increasingly responsive cable smorgasbord. And it is parents' responsibility to monitor what kids watch. The "we" as represented by the state should do nothing.

21   The alternative is for the public, or rather some segment of it, to demand something better on at least a few of the many channels that are opening up. There are plenty of good television programs and movies that aim higher and

do well at the box office. Since the market is master, people need not be passive about expressing their tastes. Where I live, for example, people have demanded successfully that the cable company carry the excellent Bravo channel, which it was threatening to drop.

22   "In the final analysis, it is still the law of supply and demand on all this stuff," says Norman Lear, whose *All in the Family* series first upped the ante for thoughtful prime-time programming. "It goes back to the advertisers; they are the people who pay for this stuff. If they didn't want it, it wouldn't be there. They are just dealing with product. They know from experience that something hard and outrageous will sell faster than something soft.

23   "It's no secret that there's a lot of baseness to human nature, but we don't always pander to it, and reasonable people don't wish to pander to it. But there is nothing reasonable about the bottom line and about needing to please Wall Street by the quarter—to find the instant rating successes that satisfy the bottom line.

24   "The network goes to someone to make a pilot, then they take it to Madison Avenue, and people look at it and say, 'That's a fucking hit!' They're the first people to look at it and say, 'I want in. I will spend my millions of dollars here because I think it will rate.' "

25   He adds that because no single sponsor is identified with a show, as was the case in the "Golden Age" of the *Philco Playhouse* and the *Alcoa Hour,* "no sponsor is seriously associated with the quality of the show."

26   That's what happened with *Beavis and Butt-Head*—its creator, Judge, had originally prepared it as a one-time entry for a festival of "sick and twisted" cartoons. He had no intention of turning his one-liner into a series, but MTV execs saw it and ordered up thirty-five episodes, and soon it was a multinational operation with teams of animators in New York and Korea frantically turning the stuff out.

27   The MTV execs were right. The demand was there. It's MTV's hottest show, and sixty-five more episodes are on the way for 1994 and worldwide distribution. If you don't like that because you think it represents the dumbing-down of American and world culture, then vote—by just turning the damn thing off. Don't beg Big Brother to do it for you.

FOR ANALYSIS AND DISCUSSION

1. Analyze the logic Scheer uses to support the claim that "we have all this mayhem in our art and our lives because we like violence" (paragraph 10). Does his reasoning persuade you? Explain your own perspective on this issue while addressing the author's.

2. What is Scheer's attitude toward television censorship? Consider the distinction Scheer makes between controlling material for children and controlling it for adults. What response do you think Cannon would have to this approach?

3. What does Scheer find so troubling about the program *Beavis and Butt-Head*? Why is he upset about the Orange County schoolchildren who like the show? What is your perspective on this issue?

4. How does Scheer propose to solve the problem of television violence? Does his seem to be a logical and effective solution? Which solution do you find more persuasive, Cannon's or Scheer's, and why?

5. In paragraphs 22–25 Scheer quotes television producer Norman Lear. What effect does his quoting Lear have on the essay? Does this authority add or detract from Scheer's argument?

6. Explain Scheer's references to the National Rifle Association in paragraph 9. How does it compare to references Cannon makes regarding the same organization? Why do both authors refer to the NRA?

In Praise of Gore
Andrew Klavan

Do you feel a dark and secret rush of pleasure when viewing a violent and blood-soaked scene from the latest slasher film? When the movie is over, are you already anticipating the sequel? According to Andrew Klavan, this response is natural and normal, even if we don't want to admit it, because individuals find pleasure in releasing their repressed violent impulses. Further, he argues, instead of making people more violent, the outlet of watching violence helps them *control* their violent impulses.

Andrew Klavan is a former newspaper and radio reporter and a two-time award winner of the Edgar Award for mystery fiction. His most recent novels include *True Crime* (1997), which was made into a 1998 movie starring Clint Eastwood, and *The Uncanny* (1998).

BEFORE YOU READ

Can you think of recent violent acts (suicide, murder, beatings) that were reported in the news media and said to be inspired by a film or television program? Are you convinced there is a direct link between the event and the film? Explain.

AS YOU READ

Klavan writes, "Pleasure that is unknowingly repressed is outwardly condemned." Find one or two examples of human behavior cited by Klavan to illustrate this point.

1   I love the sound of people screaming. Women screaming—with their clothes torn—as they run down endless hallways with some bogeyman in hot pursuit. Men, in their priapic cars, screaming as the road ends, as the fender plummets toward fiery oblivion under their wild eyes. Children? I'm a little squeamish about children, but okay, sure, I'll take screaming children too. And I get off on gunshots—machine gun shots goading a corpse into a posthumous jitter-bug; and the coital jerk and plunge of a butcher knife, and axes; even claws, if you happen to have them.

2   Yes, yes, yes, only in stories. Of course; in fiction only; novels, TV shows, films. I've loved the scary, gooey stuff since I was a child. I've loved monsters, shootouts, bluddy murther; women in jeopardy (as they say in Hollywood); the slasher in the closet; the intruder's shadow that spreads up the bedroom wall like a stain. And now, having grown to man's estate, I make a very good living writing these things: thriller novels like *Don't Say a Word,* which begins with a nice old lady getting dusted and ends with an assault on a child, the *The Animal Hour,* which features a woman's head being severed and stuffed into a commode.

3   Is it vicious? Disgusting? Sexist? Sick? Tough luck, it's my imagination—sometimes it is—and it's my readers' too—always, for all I know. And when they and I get together, when we dodge down that electric alleyway of the human skull where only murder is delight—well then, my friend, it's showtime.

4   But enough about me, let's talk about death. Cruel death, sexy death, exciting death: death, that is, on the page and on the screen. Because this is not a defense of violence in fiction; it's a celebration of it. And not a moment too soon either.

5   Hard as it is for a sane man to believe, fictional violence is under attack. Again. This year's list of would-be censors trying to shoulder their way to the trough of celebrity is hardly worth enumerating: Their 15 minutes might be up by the time I'm done. Film critic Michael Medved says cinematic violence is part of pop culture "war on traditional values"; Congressman Edward Markey says television violence should be reduced or regulated; some of our less thoughtful feminists tried to quash the novel *American Psycho* because of its descriptions of violence toward women and even some of the more thoughtful, like Catharine MacKinnon, have fought for censorship in law, claiming that written descriptions of "penises slamming into vaginas" deprive actual human beings of their civil rights.

6   It's nonsense mostly, but it has the appeal of glamour, of flash. Instead of trying to understand the sad, banal, ignorant souls who generally pull the trigger in our society, we get to discuss the urbane cannibal Hannibal Lecter from *The Silence of the Lambs,* Ice-T, penises, vaginas. It makes for good sound bites, anyway—the all-American diet of 15-second thoughts.

7   But Britain—where I've come to live because I loathe real guns and political correctness—is far from exempt. Indeed, perhaps nowhere has there been a more telling or emblematic attack on fictional violence than is going on here right now. It is a textbook example of how easily pundits and politicians can channel honest grief and rage at a true crime into a senseless assault on the innocent tellers of tales.

8   It began here this time with the killing of a child by two other children. On February 12, Jamie Bulger, a 2-year-old toddler, was led out of a Merseyside shopping mall by two 10-year-olds—two little boys. The boys prodded and carried and tugged the increasingly distraught baby past dozens of witnesses who did not understand what they were seeing. When they reached a deserted railroad embankment, the two boys tortured, mutilated, and finally killed their captive for no reasons that anyone has been able to explain.

9   The nation's effort to understand, its grief and disgust, its sense of social despair, did not resolve themselves upon a single issue until the trial judge pronounced sentence. "It is not for me to pass judgment on their upbringing," Mr. Justice Morland said of the boys. "But I suspect exposure to violent video films may in part be an explanation."

10   No one knew why he said such a thing. There had been speculation in some of the papers that *Child's Play 3* (with its devil doll, Chucky), which had been rented by one of the killers' fathers, had given the son ideas. But there was no testimony at the trial, no evidence presented showing that the boy had seen it or that it had had a contributing effect. It didn't matter. As far as journalists were concerned, as far as public debate was concerned, "video nasties," as they are called here, became the central issue of the case.

11   We finally know what we are seeing when we look upon the rampaging fire of violence in our society: We are seeing the effects of fiction on us. Got it? Our moral verities are crumbling by the hour. Our families are shattering. Our goals are dead. The best lack all conviction while the worst are full of passionate intensity.

12   And it's all Chucky's fault.

13   The instinct to censor is the tragic flaw of utopian minds. "Our first job," said Plato in his classic attack on the democratic system, "is to oversee the work of the story writers, and to accept any good stories they write, but reject the others." Because the perfectibility of human society is a fiction itself, it comes under threat from other, more believable fictions, especially those that document and imply the cruel, the chaotic, the Dionysian for their thrills.

14   For me to engage the latter-day Platos on their own materialistic, political terms would be to be sucked in to a form of dialogue that does not reflect the reality I know—and know I know. Because personally, I understand the world not through language but through an unfathomable spirit and an infinite mind. With language as a rude tool I try to convey a shadow of the world my imagination makes of the world at large. I do this for money and pleasure and to win the admiration of women. And when, in an uncertain hour, I crave the palliative of meaning, I remind myself that people's souls run opposite to their bodies and grow more childlike as they mature—and so I have built, in my work, little places where those souls can go to play.

15   The proper response to anyone who would shut these playgrounds down for any reason—to anyone who confuses these playgrounds with the real world—is not the specious language of theory or logic or even the law. It's the language of the spirit, of celebration and screed, of jeremiad and hallelujah. Of this.

16   Now, I would not say that my fictions—any fictions—have no effect on real life. Or that books, movies, and TV are mere regurgitations of what's going on in the society around them. These arguments strike me as disingenuous and self-defeating. Rather, the relationship between fiction and humanity's unconscious is so complex, so resonant, that it is impossible to isolate one from the other in terms of cause and effect. Fiction and reality do interact, but we don't know how, not at all. And since we don't understand the effect of one upon the

other—whence arises this magical certainty that violence in fiction begets violence in real life?

17   The answer seems to come straight out of Psychology 1A, but that doesn't negate the truth of it: Pleasure that is unknowingly repressed is outwardly condemned. The censor always attacks the images that secretly appeal to him or her the most. The assault on violent fiction is not really an attempt to root out the causes of violence—no one can seriously believe that. The attempt to censor fictional violence is a guilt-ridden slap at ourselves, in the guise of a mythical *them,* for taking such pleasure in make-believe acts that, in real life, would be reprehensible. How—we seem to be asking ourselves—how, in a world in which Jamie Bulger dies so young, can we kick back with a beer at night and enjoy a couple of hours of *Child's Play 3*?

18   How can we enjoy this stuff so much? So very much.

19   Not all of us, perhaps. I'm forever being told that there are people who'd rather not take violence with their fiction—although I wonder how many would say so if you included the delicate violence of an Agatha Christie or the "literary" violence of, say, Hemingway and Faulkner. But even if we accept the exceptions, even if we limit the field to real gore, it does seem to me that the numbers are incredible, the attraction truly profound.

20   Once I picked out what looked like a cheap horror novel by an author I'd never heard of. For months afterward, I asked the readers I knew if they had heard of the book, *'Salem's Lot,* or its author, Stephen King. None of them had. Later, the movie *Carrie* helped launch what has to be one of the most successful novelistic careers since Dickens. But even before that, readers were steadily discovering the nausea and mayhem and terror of the man's vision.

21   The moral, I mean, is this: To construct a bloodsoaked nightmare of unrelenting horror is not an easy thing. But if you build it, they will come. And so the maker of violent fiction—ho, ho—he walks among us in Nietzschean glee. He has bottled the Dionysian whirlwind and is selling it as a soft drink. Like deep-browed Homer, when he told of a spear protruding from a man's head with an eyeball fixed to the point, the violent storyteller knows that that gape of disgust on your respectable mug is really the look of love. You may denounce him, you may even censor him. You may just wrinkle your nose and walk away. But sooner or later, in one form or another, he knows you'll show up to see and listen to him. Fiction lives or dies not on its messages, but on the depth and power of the emotional experience it provides. An enormous amount of intellectual energy seems to have been expended in a failed attempt to suppress the central, disturbing, and irreducible fact of this experience: It's fun. Like sex: It's lots of fun. We watch fictional people love and die and screw and suffer and weep for our pleasure. It gives us joy.

22   And we watch them kill too. And this seems to give us as much joy as anything.

23   All right, I suppose you can talk about the catharsis of terror, or the harmless release of our violent impulses. Those are plausible excuses, I guess. It doesn't take a genius to notice how often—practically always—it's the villain of a successful piece of violent art who becomes its icon. Hannibal Lecter and

Leatherface, Freddy Krueger and Dracula—these are the posters that go up on the wall, the characters that we remember.

24   So I suppose, if you must, you could say these creatures represent our buried feelings. Where it's Medea or Jason (from *Friday the 13th*), the character who commits acts of savage violence always has the appeal of a Caliban: that thing of darkness that must be acknowledged as our own. Not that people are essentially violent, but that they are violent among other things and the violence has to be repressed. Some emotions must be repressed, and repressed emotions return via the imagination in distorted and inflated forms: That's the law of benevolent hypocrisy, the law of civilized life. It is an unstated underpinning of utopian thought that the repressed can be eliminated completely or denied or happily freed or remolded with the proper education. It can't. Forget about it. Cross it off your list of things to do. The monsters are always there in their cages. As Stephen King says, with engaging simplicity, his job is to take them out for a walk every now and then.

25   But again, this business of violent fiction as therapy—it's a defense, isn't it, as if these stories needed a reason for being. In order to celebrate violent fiction—I mean, *celebrate* it—it's the joy you've got to talk about. The joy of cruelty, the thrill of terror, the adrenaline of the hunter, the heartbeat of the deer—all reproduced in the safe playground of art. A joy indeed.

26   When it comes to our messier, unseemly pleasures like fictional gore, we are downright embarrassed by our delight. But delight it is. Nubile teens caught *in flagrante* by a nutcase in a hockey mask? You bet it's erotic. Whole families tortured to death by a madman who's traced them through their vacation photos? Ee-yewwww. Goblins who jump out of the toilet to devour you ass first? Delightful stuff.

27   And we've always been that way. The myths of our ancient gods, the lives of our medieval saints, the entertainments of our most civilized cultures have always included healthy doses of rape, cannibalism, evisceration, and general mayhem. Critics like Michael Medved complain that never before has it all been quite so graphic, especially on screen. We are becoming "desensitized" to bloodshed, he claims, and require more and more gore to excite our feelings. But when have human beings ever been particularly "sensitized" to fictional violence? The technology to create the illusion of bloodshed has certainly improved, but read *Titus Andronicus* with its wonderful stage direction, "Enter a messenger with two heads and a hand," read the orgasmic stalking of Lucy in *Dracula,* read de Sade, for crying out loud. There were always some pretty good indications of which way we'd go once we got our hands on the machinery.

28   Because we love it. It makes us do a little inner dance of excitement, tension, and release. Violent fiction with its graver purposes, if any, concealed—fiction unadorned with overt message or historical significance—rubs our noses in the fact that narratives of horror, murder, and gore are a blast, a gas. When knife-fingered Freddy Krueger of the *Nightmare on Elm Street* movies disembowels someone in a geyser of blood, when Hannibal Lecter washes down

his victim with a nice Chianti—the only possible reason for this nonreal, non-meaningful event to occur is that it's going to afford us pleasure. Which leaves that pleasure obvious, exposed. It's the exposure, not the thrill, the censors want to get rid of. Again: Celebration is the only defense.

29 And yet—I know—while I celebrate, the new not-very-much improved Rome is burning.

30 Last year sometime, I had a conversation with a highly intelligent Scottish filmmaker who had just returned from New York. Both of us had recently seen Sylvester Stallone's mountaineering action picture *Cliffhanger.* I'd seen it in a placid upper-class London neighborhood; he'd seen it in a theater in Times Square. I had been thrilled by the movie's special effects and found the hilariously dopey script sweetly reminiscent of the comic books I'd read as a child. My friend had found the picture grimly disturbing. The Times Square theater had been filled with rowdy youths. Every time the bad guys killed someone, the youths cheered—and when a woman was murdered, they howled with delight.

31 I freely confess that I would have been unable to enjoy the movie under these circumstances. Too damned noisy, for one thing. And, all right, yes, as a repression fan, I could only get off on the cruelty of the villains insofar as it fired my anticipation of the moment when Sly would cut those suckers down. Another audience could just as easily have been cheering the murder of Jews in *Schindler's List* or of blacks in *Mississippi Burning.* I understand that, and it would be upsetting and frightening to be surrounded by a crowd that seemed to have abandoned the nonnegotiable values.

32 Michael Medved believes—not that one film produces one vicious act—but that a ceaseless barrage of anti-religion, anti-family, slap-happy-gore films and fictions has contributed to the erosion of values so evident on 42nd Street. I don't know whether this is true or not—neither does he—but, as with the judge's remarks in the Bulger case, it strikes me as a very suspicious place to start. Surely, the Scotsman's story illustrates that the problem lies not on the screen but in the seats, in the lives that have produced that audience. Fiction cannot make of people what life has not, good or evil.

33 But more to the point: Though the Times Square crowd's reaction was scary—rude, too—it was not necessarily harmful in itself, either to them or to me. For all I know, it was a beneficial release of energy and hostility, good for the mental health. And in any case, it took place in the context of their experience of a fiction and so (outside of the unmannerly noise they made) was beyond my right to judge, approve, or condemn. Nobody has to explain his private pleasures to me.

34 Because fiction and reality are different. It seems appalling that anyone should have to say it, but it does need to be said. Fiction is not subject to the same moral restrictions as real life. It should remain absolutely free because, at whatever level, it is, like sex, a deeply personal experience engaged in by consent in the hope of anything from momentary release to satori. Like sex, it is available to fools and creeps and monsters, and that's life; that's tough. Because

fiction is, like sex, at the core of our individual humanity. Stories are the basic building blocks of spiritual maturity. No one has any business messing with them. No one at all.

35   Reality, on the other hand, needs its limits maintained by force if necessary, for the simple reason that there are actions that directly harm the safety and liberty of other people. They don't merely offend them; they don't just threaten their delicate sense of themselves; they *hurt* them—really, painfully, a lot. Again, it seems wildly improbable that this should be forgotten, but Americans' current cultural discussions show every evidence that it has been. Just as fictions are being discussed as if they were actions, actual crimes and atrocities are being discussed as if they were cultural events, subject to aesthetic considerations. Trial lawyers won a lesser conviction for lady-killer Robert Chambers by claiming his victim was promiscuous; columnists defended dick-chopper Lorena Bobbitt, saying it might be all right to mutilate a man in his sleep, provided he was a really nasty guy. The fellows who savaged Reginald Denny during the Los Angeles riots claim they were just part of the psychology of the mob. And the Menendez brothers based much of their defense on a portrayal of themselves as victims, a portrayal of their victims as abusers. These are all arguments appropriate to fiction only. Only in fiction are crimes mitigated by symbolism and individuals judged not for what they've done but because of what they represent. To say that the reaction to fiction and the reaction to reality are on a continuum is moral nonsense.

36   Fiction and real life must be distinguished from one another. The radical presumption of fiction is play, the radical presumption of real life is that Martin Amis called "the gentleness of human flesh." If we have lost the will to defend that gentleness, then God help us, because consigning Chucky to the flames is not going to bring it back.

37   One of the very best works of violent fiction to come along in the past few years is Thomas Harris' novel *The Silence of the Lambs.* The story, inspired, like *Psycho,* by the real-life case of murderer En Gein, concerns the hunt for the serial killer Jamie Gumb, a failed transsexual who strips his female victims' flesh in order to create a woman costume in which he can clothe himself.

38   When Harris introduces the killer's next victim—Catherine Martin—he presents us with a character we aren't meant to like very much. Rich, spoiled, arrogant, dissolute, Catherine is admirable only for the desperate cleverness she shows in her battle to stay alive. But for the rest of the novel—the attempt to rescue Catherine before it's too late—Harris depends on our fear of her, our identification with her, our deep desire to see her get out of this in one piece. He relies on our irrational—spiritual—conviction that Catherine, irritating though she may be, must not be killed because . . . for no good reason: because she Must Not. Harris knowingly taps in to the purely emotional imperative we share with the book's heroine, Clarice Starling, the FBI agent who's trying to crack the case: Like her, we won't be able to sleep until the screaming of innocent lambs is stopped. Harris makes pretty well sure of it.

39   At the end, in the only injection of auctorial opinion in the book, Harris wryly notes that the scholarly journals' articles on the Gumb case never use the words *crazy* or *evil* in their discussions of the killer. The intellectual world is uncomfortable with the inherent Must Not, the instinctive absolute, and the individual responsibility those words ultimately suggest. Harris, I think, is trying to argue that if we don't trust our mindless belief in the sanctity of human life, we produce monsters that the sleep of reason never dreamed of. *The Silence of the Lambs,* as the title suggests, is a dramatization of a world in which the spirit has lost its power to speak.

40   We live in that world, no question. With our culture atomizing, we think we can make up enough rules, impose enough restrictions, inject enough emptiness into our language to replace the shared moral conviction that's plainly gone. I think all stories—along with being fun—have the potential to humanize precisely because the richest fun of them is dependent on our identification with their characters. But stories can't do for us what experience hasn't. They're just not that powerful. And if some people are living lives in our society that make them unfit for even the most shallow thrills of fiction, you can't solve that problem by eliminating the fiction. By allowing politicians and pundits to turn our attention to "the problem of fictional violence," we are really allowing them to make us turn our backs on the problems of reality.

41   After a crime like the Jamie Bulger murder, we should be asking ourselves a million questions: about our abandonment of family life, about our approach to poverty and unemployment, about the failures of our educational systems— about who and what we are and the ways we treat each other, the things we do and omit to do. These are hard, sometimes boring questions. But when instead we let our discussions devolve, as they have, into this glamour-rotten debate on whether people should be able to enjoy whatever fiction they please, then we make meaningless the taking of an individual's life. And that's no fun at all.

FOR ANALYSIS AND DISCUSSION

1. Analyze Klavan's theory about the relationship between fiction, imagination, and reality (paragraph 14). Do you agree with this theory? How important is it to the success of Klavan's overall argument?
2. What is the theory of the "catharsis of terror" (paragraph 23)? Do you agree with it? Explain.
3. Summarize each of the seven sections of Klavan's essay in one complete sentence. Put the sentences together to view the essay's overall construction. How does the structure of the essay contribute to the effectiveness of Klavan's argument?
4. Compare and contrast Scheer's attitude toward the appeal of violent fiction with Klavan's. Which position do you agree with more, and why?
5. Evaluate Klavan's credibility. How does the fact that Klavan is a horror fiction writer contribute to the persuasiveness of his argument? In what ways might Klavan's profession detract from his credibility?

6. Analyze the rhetorical strategy of Klavan's opening paragraph. What effect does the opening have on the reader? What are the benefits and drawbacks of beginning an argument in this manner?

WRITING ASSIGNMENTS: MOVIE AND TV VIOLENCE

1. Access the Web site of the American Psychological Association (APA) at <http://www.apa.org/concept/children.html#television> and read a few of the articles concerning violent television programming and children. Many of the articles are concerned with cartoons and the fact that the long-term consequences of physical aggression are never addressed on these shows. Furthermore, the new TV rating system may actually encourage young children to watch shows labeled as appropriate for older children because such shows are considered "cool and forbidden." Write an argument essay in which you address the violence in television cartoons for children. Are cartoons too violent? Does portraying violence make children more aggressive? Try to find a solution that would satisfy children, parents, *and* the networks.

2. Over the course of a week, watch at least four major television networks, one per evening. Analyze the violent content on each network, and tabulate each violent act while evaluating its content. How responsibly does each network depict violence? Are the ramifications of violence addressed? Write an essay evaluating television violence on major networks.

3. A few years ago, several people convicted for murder cited the movie *Natural Born Killers* as their motivation for engaging in violent behavior. Write an argument essay in which you state a position about whether violent movies encourage violent behavior. Support your essay with information from the articles in this chapter, current events, and your own experience.

chapter 13

INDIVIDUAL RIGHTS

"It's a free country" is an expression that we often hear. Yet how "free" is it, really? What rights do ordinary citizens possess that cannot be limited by government regulation or control? Do we have the right to end our life if we are terminally ill? Are we entitled to the privacy of our homes and possessions? Do we have the right to refuse to submit to invasive testing of our bodily fluids? Many people would answer yes to these questions, yet the fact is that in each of these areas individual rights are nonexistent or in danger of extinction. The readings in this chapter examine the issue of individual rights in the contexts of physician-assisted suicide, privacy, and student drug testing.

The question of whether terminally ill individuals can choose to end their lives has been debated in the highest courts in this nation. Although the Supreme Court has ruled against legalizing physician-assisted suicide, some states, such as Oregon, have passed laws permitting it under special circumstances. Yet these legal actions have failed to reconcile the many moral, ethical, and religious concerns that continue to generate controversy about this issue. In our readings three physicians question the role of doctors in assisting terminally ill patients through this last and often painful period of their lives. Dr. Marcia Angell supports the right of dying patients to hasten their death with medical assistance. She argues that patients have the right to "self-determination" and that physicians have the responsibility to respond compassionately to human suffering. Dr. Timothy Quill relates the difficult choice he made when Diane, a terminally ill patient, requested and received his indirect help in ending her life. Quill, an advocate for informed patient choice, challenges a legal establishment that forces doctors and patients to exercise this choice in secrecy. However, Dr. Herbert Hendin, a psychiatrist, has strong reservations about legalizing assisted suicide. He is convinced that it is the fear of pain and the loss of control that motivates terminally ill people to choose suicide. Using the poignant example of Tim, a dying patient, Hendin demonstrates that once these anxieties are dealt with effectively, the patient can face impending death with dignity.

Most Americans assume their privacy is protected by the Fourth Amendment of the Bill of Rights, which ensures "the right of the people to be secure in their persons, houses, papers, and effects, against unreasonable searches and seizures." Yet according to some our privacy is being eroded by both the government and private industry. Gore Vidal looks at how unnecessary airport security, overzealous drug enforcement, and unrestrained police actions against innocent citizens violate the sanctity of our homes and personal possessions. Andrew Shapiro then reveals how private industry uses digital surveillance technology to spy on our electronic transactions, with the government's approval. Jonathan Franzen, on the other hand, finds the hysteria over the loss of privacy exaggerated. Americans have far more privacy today than they truly need, Franzen claims.

When the Vernonia, Oregon, school district required student athletes to submit to random drug testing, James Acton, a seventh grader who wanted to play football, protested that this requirement violated his Fourth Amendment right against "unreasonable searches" and refused to be tested. His legal case went all the way to the U.S. Supreme Court, which decided in a 6-3 vote to support the school district's policy. Here, four writers react to this decision. Conservative columnist George Will supports the court's ruling that students are not entitled to the same protection as adults under the Fourth Amendment and suggests that schools have the responsibility to protect students from the dangers of drug use. Gary Natriello then argues that the greatest harm from the court's decision is its interference with the relationship between students and teachers. For Claude Lewis the court's verdict is appropriate because the epidemic of illegal drugs in U.S. society supercedes the concern for violating the privacy of individual student athletes. Finally, David Rocah, of the American Civil Liberties Union, suggests that there are other ways to effectively address substance abuse by student athletes besides forcing them to submit to demeaning searches.

P<small>HYSICIAN</small>-A<small>SSISTED</small> S<small>UICIDE</small>: W<small>HO</small> H<small>AS THE</small> R<small>IGHT TO</small> C<small>HOOSE</small>?

The Supreme Court and Physician-Assisted Suicide—The Ultimate Right
Marcia Angell

Do terminally ill patients have the right to end their own lives? Do doctors have a moral obligation to help them? Marcia Angell writes in favor of permitting physician-assisted suicide for terminally ill patients who request it. Addressing the opposition's concerns one by one, Angell argues that respect for patient autonomy morally binds physicians to honor the requests of terminally ill patients. She explains why she hopes the Supreme Court will uphold recent rulings in several states that allow doctors to provide the means for terminally ill patients to die.

Marcia Angell is the executive editor of the *New England Journal of Medicine* in which this essay appeared in January of 1997. A pathologist, Dr. Angell writes on ethical issues in medicine and biomedical research.

BEFORE YOU READ

In your opinion, what are the rights of terminally ill patients? Is there a difference between a dying patient asking to be taken off a respirator and a dying patient asking for a lethal dose of a drug?

AS YOU READ

Consider how Angell frames her argument. Does her method of addressing the opposition's views help or hinder her discussion?

1   The U.S. Supreme Court will decide later this year whether to let stand decisions by two appeals courts permitting doctors to help terminally ill patients commit suicide.[1] The Ninth and Second Circuit Courts of Appeals last spring held that state laws in Washington and New York that ban assistance in suicide were unconstitutional as applied to doctors and their dying patients.[2,3] If the Supreme Court lets the decisions stand, physicians in 12 states, which include about half the population of the United States, would be allowed to provide the means for terminally ill patients to take their own lives, and the remaining states would rapidly follow suit. Not since *Roe v. Wade* has a Supreme Court decision been so fateful.

2   The decision will culminate several years of intense national debate, fueled by a number of highly publicized events. Perhaps most important among them is Dr. Jack Kevorkian's defiant assistance in some 44 suicides since 1990, to the dismay of many in the medical and legal establishments, but with substantial public support, as evidenced by the fact that three juries refused to convict him even in the face of a Michigan statute enacted for that purpose. Also since 1990, voters in three states have considered ballot initiatives that would legalize some form of physician-assisted dying, and in 1994 Oregon became the first state to approve such a measure.[4] (The Oregon law was stayed pending a court challenge.) Several surveys indicate that roughly two thirds of the American public now support physician-assisted suicide,[5,6] as do more than half the doctors in the United States,[6,7] despite the fact that influential physicians' organizations are opposed. It seems clear that many Americans are now so concerned about the possibility of a lingering, high-technology death that they are receptive to the idea of doctors' being allowed to help them die.

3   In this editorial I will explain why I believe the appeals courts were right and why I hope the Supreme Court will uphold their decisions. I am aware that this is a highly contentious issue, with good people and strong arguments on both sides. The American Medical Association (AMA) filed an amicus brief opposing the legalization of physician-assisted suicide,[8] and the Massachusetts Medical Society, which owns the *Journal*, was a signatory to it. But here I speak for myself, not the *Journal* or the Massachusetts Medical Society. The legal aspects of the case have been well discussed elsewhere, to me most compellingly in Ronald Dworkin's essay in the *New York Review of Books*.[9] I will focus primarily on the medical and ethical aspects.

4   I begin with the generally accepted premise that one of the most important ethical principles in medicine is respect for each patient's autonomy, and that when this principle conflicts with others, it should almost always take precedence. This premise is incorporated into our laws governing medical practice and research, including the requirement of informed consent to any treatment. In medicine, patients exercise their self-determination most dramatically when they ask that life-sustaining treatment be withdrawn. Although others may sometimes consider the request ill-founded, we are bound to honor it if the patient is mentally competent—that is, if the patient can understand the nature of the decision and its consequences.

5   A second starting point is the recognition that death is not fair and is often cruel. Some people die quickly, and others die slowly but peacefully. Some find personal or religious meaning in the process, as well as an opportunity for a final reconciliation with loved ones. But others, especially those with cancer, AIDS, or progressive neurologic disorders, may die by inches and in great anguish, despite every effort of their doctors and nurses. Although nearly all pain can be relieved, some cannot, and other symptoms, such as dyspnea, nausea, and weakness, are even more difficult to control. In addition, dying sometimes holds great indignities and existential suffering. Patients who happen to require some treatment to sustain their lives, such as assisted ventilation or dialysis, can hasten death by having the life-sustaining treatment withdrawn, but those who are not receiving life-sustaining treatment may desperately need help they cannot now get.

6   If the decisions of the appeals courts are upheld, states will not be able to prohibit doctors from helping such patients to die by prescribing a lethal dose of a drug and advising them on its use for suicide. State laws barring euthanasia (the administration of a lethal drug by a doctor) and assisted suicide for patients who are not terminally ill would not be affected. Furthermore, doctors would not be required to assist in suicide; they would simply have that option. Both appeals courts based their decisions on constitutional questions. This is important, because it shifted the focus of the debate from what the majority would approve through the political process, as exemplified by the Oregon initiative, to a matter of fundamental rights, which are largely immune from the political process. Indeed, the Ninth Circuit Court drew an explicit analogy between suicide and abortion, saying that both were personal choices protected by the Constitution and that forbidding doctors to assist would in effect nullify these rights. Although states could regulate assisted suicide, as they do abortion, they would not be permitted to regulate it out of existence.

7   It is hard to quarrel with the desire of a greatly suffering, dying patient for a quicker, more humane death or to disagree that it may be merciful to help bring that about. In those circumstances, loved ones are often relieved when death finally comes, as are the attending doctors and nurses. As the Second Circuit Court said, the state has no interest in prolonging such a life. Why, then, do so many people oppose legalizing physician-assisted suicide in these cases? There are a number of arguments against it, some stronger than others, but I believe none of them can offset the overriding duties of doctors to relieve suf-

fering and to respect their patients' autonomy. Below I list several of the more important arguments against physician-assisted suicide and discuss why I believe they are in the last analysis unpersuasive.

8   *Assisted suicide is a form of killing, which is always wrong. In contrast, withdrawing life-sustaining treatment simply allows the disease to take its course.* There are three methods of hastening the death of a dying patient: withdrawing life-sustaining treatment, assisting suicide, and euthanasia. The right to stop treatment has been recognized repeatedly since the 1976 case of Karen Ann Quinlan[10] and was affirmed by the U.S. Supreme Court in the 1990 *Cruzan* decision[11] and the U.S. Congress in its 1990 Patient Self-Determination Act.[12] Although the legal underpinning is the right to be free of unwanted bodily invasion, the purpose of hastening death was explicitly acknowledged. In contrast, assisted suicide and euthanasia have not been accepted; euthanasia is illegal in all states, and assisted suicide is illegal in most of them.

9   Why the distinctions? Most would say they turn on the doctor's role: whether it is passive or active. When life-sustaining treatment is withdrawn, the doctor's role is considered passive and the cause of death is the underlying disease, despite the fact that switching off the ventilator of a patient dependent on it looks anything but passive and would be considered homicide if done without the consent of the patient or a proxy. In contrast, euthanasia by the injection of a lethal drug is active and directly causes the patient's death. Assisting suicide by supplying the necessary drugs is considered somewhere in between, more active than switching off a ventilator but less active than injecting drugs, hence morally and legally more ambiguous.

10   I believe, however, that these distinctions are too doctor-centered and not sufficiently patient-centered. We should ask ourselves not so much whether the doctor's role is passive or active but whether the *patient's* role is passive or active. From that perspective, the three methods of hastening death line up quite differently. When life-sustaining treatment is withdrawn from an incompetent patient at the request of a proxy or when euthanasia is performed, the patient may be utterly passive. Indeed, either act can be performed even if the patient is unaware of the decision. In sharp contrast, assisted suicide, by definition, cannot occur without the patient's knowledge and participation. Therefore, it must be active—that is to say, voluntary. That is a crucial distinction, because it provides an inherent safeguard against abuse that is not present with the other two methods of hastening death. If the loaded term "kill" is to be used, it is not the doctor who kills, but the patient. Primarily because euthanasia can be performed without the patient's participation, I oppose its legalization in this country.

11   *Assisted suicide is not necessary. All suffering can be relieved if care givers are sufficiently skillful and compassionate, as illustrated by the hospice movement.* I have no doubt that if expert palliative care were available to everyone who needed it, there would be few requests for assisted suicide. Even under the best of circumstances, however, there will always be a few patients whose suffering simply cannot be adequately alleviated. And there will be some who would prefer suicide to any other measures available, including the withdrawal of life-sustaining treatment or the use of heavy sedation. Surely, every effort should be made to

improve palliative care, as I argued 15 years ago,[13] but when those efforts are unavailing and suffering patients desperately long to end their lives, physician-assisted suicide should be allowed. The argument that permitting it would divert us from redoubling our commitment to comfort care asks these patients to pay the penalty for our failings. It is also illogical. Good comfort care and the availability of physician-assisted suicide are no more mutually exclusive than good cardiologic care and the availability of heart transplantation.

12   *Permitting assisted suicide would put us on a moral "slippery slope." Although in itself assisted suicide might be acceptable, it would lead inexorably to involuntary euthanasia.* It is impossible to avoid slippery slopes in medicine (or in any aspect of life). The issue is how and where to find a purchase. For example, we accept the right of proxies to terminate life-sustaining treatment, despite the obvious potential for abuse, because the reasons for doing so outweigh the risks. We hope our procedures will safeguard patients. In the case of assisted suicide, its voluntary nature is the best protection against sliding down a slippery slope, but we also need to ensure that the request is thoughtful and freely made. Although it is possible that we may someday decide to legalize voluntary euthanasia under certain circumstances or assisted suicide for patients who are not terminally ill, legalizing assisted suicide for the dying does not in itself make these other decisions inevitable. Interestingly, recent reports from the Netherlands, where both euthanasia and physician-assisted suicide are permitted, indicate that fears about a slippery slope there have not been borne out.[14,15,16]

13   *Assisted suicide would be a threat to the economically and socially vulnerable. The poor, disabled, and elderly might be coerced to request it.* Admittedly, overburdened families or cost-conscious doctors might pressure vulnerable patients to request suicide, but similar wrongdoing is at least as likely in the case of withdrawing life-sustaining treatment, since that decision can be made by proxy. Yet, there is no evidence of widespread abuse. The Ninth Circuit Court recalled that it was feared *Roe v. Wade* would lead to coercion of poor and uneducated women to request abortions, but that did not happen. The concern that coercion is more likely in this era of managed care, although understandable, would hold suffering patients hostage to the deficiencies of our health care system. Unfortunately, no human endeavor is immune to abuses. The question is not whether a perfect system can be devised, but whether abuses are likely to be sufficiently rare to be offset by the benefits to patients who otherwise would be condemned to face the end of their lives in protracted agony.

14   *Depressed patients would seek physician-assisted suicide rather than help for their depression. Even in the terminally ill, a request for assisted suicide might signify treatable depression, not irreversible suffering.* Patients suffering greatly at the end of life may also be depressed, but the depression does not necessarily explain their decision to commit suicide or make it irrational. Nor is it simple to diagnose depression in terminally ill patients. Sadness is to be expected, and some of the vegetative symptoms of depression are similar to the symptoms of mental illness. The success of antidepressant treatment in these circumstances is also not ensured. Although there are anecdotes about patients who changed their minds about suicide after treatment,[17] we do not have good studies of how often that happens

or the relation to antidepressant treatment. Dying patients who request assisted suicide and seem depressed should certainly be strongly encouraged to accept psychiatric treatment, but I do not believe that competent patients should be required to accept it as a condition of receiving assistance with suicide. On the other hand, doctors would not be required to comply with all requests; they would be expected to use their judgment, just as they do in so many other types of life-and-death decisions in medical practice.

15   *Doctors should never participate in taking life. If there is to be assisted suicide, doctors must not be involved.* Although most doctors favor permitting assisted suicide under certain circumstances, many who favor it believe that doctors should not provide the assistance.[6,7] To them, doctors should be unambiguously committed to life (although most doctors who hold this view would readily honor a patient's decision to have life-sustaining treatment withdrawn). The AMA, too, seems to object to physician-assisted suicide primarily because it violates the profession's mission. Like others, I find that position too abstract.[18] The highest ethical imperative of doctors should be to provide care in whatever way best serves patients' interests, in accord with each patient's wishes, not with a theoretical commitment to preserve life no matter what the cost in suffering.[19] If a patient requests help with suicide and the doctor believes the request is appropriate, requiring someone else to provide the assistance would be a form of abandonment. Doctors who are opposed in principle need not assist, but they should make their patients aware of their position early in the relationship so that a patient who chooses to select another doctor can do so. The greatest harm we can do is to consign a desperate patient to unbearable suffering—or force the patient to seek out a stranger like Dr. Kevorkian. Contrary to the frequent assertion that permitting physician-assisted suicide would lead patients to distrust their doctors, I believe distrust is more likely to arise from uncertainty about whether a doctor will honor a patient's wishes.

16   *Physician-assisted suicide may occasionally be warranted, but it should remain illegal. If doctors risk prosecution, they will think twice before assisting with suicide.* This argument wrongly shifts the focus from the patient to the doctor. Instead of reflecting the condition and wishes of patients, assisted suicide would reflect the courage and compassion of their doctors. Thus, patients with doctors like Timothy Quill, who described in a 1991 *Journal* article how he helped a patient take her life,[20] would get the help they need and want, but similar patients with less steadfast doctors would not. That makes no sense.

17   *People do not need assistance to commit suicide. With enough determination, they can do it themselves.* This is perhaps the cruelest of the arguments against physician-assisted suicide. Many patients at the end of life are, in fact, physically unable to commit suicide on their own. Others lack the resources to do so. It has sometimes been suggested that they can simply stop eating and drinking and kill themselves that way. Although this method has been described as peaceful under certain conditions,[21] no one should count on that. The fact is that this argument leaves most patients to their suffering. Some, usually men, manage to commit suicide using violent methods. Percy Bridgman, a Nobel laureate in physics who in 1961 shot himself rather than die of metastatic cancer, said in

his suicide note, "It is not decent for Society to make a man do this to himself."[22]

18   My father, who knew nothing of Percy Bridgman, committed suicide under similar circumstances. He was 81 and had metastatic prostate cancer. The night before he was scheduled to be admitted to the hospital, he shot himself. Like Bridgman, he thought it might be his last chance. At the time, he was not in extreme pain, nor was he close to death (his life expectancy was probably longer than six months). But he was suffering nonetheless—from nausea and the side effects of antiemetic agents, weakness, incontinence, and hopelessness. Was he depressed? He would probably have freely admitted that he was, but he would have thought it beside the point. In any case, he was an intensely private man who would have refused psychiatric care. Was he overly concerned with maintaining control of the circumstances of his life and death? Many people would say so, but that was the way he was. It is the job of medicine to deal with patients as they are, not as we would like them to be.

19   I tell my father's story here because it makes an abstract issue very concrete. If physician-assisted suicide had been available, I have no doubt my father would have chosen it. He was protective of his family, and if he had felt he had the choice, he would have spared my mother the shock of finding his body. He did not tell her what he planned to do, because he knew she would stop him. I also believe my father would have waited if physician-assisted suicide had been available. If patients have access to drugs they can take when they choose, they will not feel they must commit suicide early, while they are still able to do it on their own. They would probably live longer and certainly more peacefully, and they might not even use the drugs.

20   Long before my father's death, I believed that physician-assisted suicide ought to be permissible under some circumstances, but his death strengthened my conviction that it is simply a part of good medical care—something to be done reluctantly and sadly, as a last resort, but done nonetheless. There should be safeguards to ensure that the decision is well considered and consistent, but they should not be so daunting or violative of privacy that they become obstacles instead of protections. In particular, they should be directed not toward reviewing the reasons for an autonomous decision, but only toward ensuring that the decision is indeed autonomous. If the Supreme Court upholds the decisions of the appeals courts, assisted suicide will not be forced on either patients or doctors, but it will be a choice for those patients who need it and those doctors willing to help. If, on the other hand, the Supreme Court overturns the lower courts' decisions, the issue will continue to be grappled with state by state, through the political process. But sooner or later, given the need and the widespread public support, physician-assisted suicide will be demanded of a compassionate profession.

REFERENCES

1. Greenhouse L. High court to say if the dying have a right to suicide help. *New York Times.* October 2, 1996:A1.

2. *Compassion in Dying v. Washington,* 79 F.3d 790 (9th Cir. 1996).

3. *Quill v. Vacco,* 80 F.3d 716 (2d Cir. 1996).

4. Annas GJ. Death by perscription—the Oregon initiative. *N Engl J Med* 1994;331:1240–3.

5. Blendon RJ, Szalay US, Knox RA. Should physicians aid their patients in dying? The public perspective. *JAMA* 1992;267:2658–62.

6. Bachman JG, Alcser KH, Doukas DJ, Lichtenstein RL, Corning AD, Brody H. Attitudes of Michigan physicians and the public toward legalizing physician-assisted suicide and voluntary euthanasia. *N Engl J Med* 1996;334:303–9.

7. Lee MA, Nelson HD, Tilden VP, Ganzini L, Schmidt TA, Tolle SW. Legalizing assisted suicide—views of physicians in Oregon. *N Engl J Med* 1996;334:310–5.

8. Gianelli DM. AMA to court: no suicide aid. *American Medical News.* November 25, 1996:1, 27, 28.

9. Dworkin R. Sex, death, and the courts. *New York Review of Books.* August 8, 1996.

10. *In re: Quinlan,* 70 N.J. 10, 355 A.2d 647 (1976).

11. *Cruzan v. Director, Missouri Department of Health,* 497 U.S. 261, 110 S. Ct. 2841 (1990).

12. Omnibus Budget Reconciliation Act of 1990, P.L. 101–508, sec. 4206 and 4751, 104 Stat. 1388, 1388–115, and 1388–204 (classified respectively at 42 U.S.C. 1395cc(f) (Medicare) and 1396a(w) (Medicaid) (1994).

13. Angell M. The quality of mercy. *N Engl J Med* 1982;306:98–9.

14. van der Maas PJ, van der Wal G, Haverkate I, et al. Euthanasia, physician-assisted suicide, and other medical practices involving the end of life in the Netherlands, 1990–1995. *N Engl J Med* 1996;335:1699–705.

15. van der Wal G, van der Maas PJ, Bosma JM, et al. Evaluation of the notification procedure for physician-assisted death in the Netherlands. *N Engl J Med* 1996;335:1706–11.

16. Angell M. Euthanasia in the Netherlands—good news or bad? *N Engl J Med* 1996;335:1676–8.

17. Chochinov HM, Wilson KG, Enns M, et al. Desire for death in the terminally ill. *Am J Psychiatry* 1995;152:1185–91.

18. Cassel CK, Meier DE. Morals and moralism in the debate over euthanasia and assisted suicide. *N Engl J Med* 1990;323:750–2.

19. Angell M. Doctors and assisted suicide. *Ann R Coll Physicians Surg Can* 1991;24:493–4.

20. Quill TE. Death and dignity—a case of individualized decision making. *N Engl J Med* 1991;324:691–4.

21. Lynn J, Childress JF. Must patients always be given food and water? *Hastings Cent Rep* 1983;13(5):17–21.

22. Nuland SB. *How we die.* New York: Alfred A. Knopf, 1994:152.

FOR ANALYSIS AND DISCUSSION

1. What does Angell mean when she states that the Supreme Court's decision will be as "fateful" as *Roe v. Wade*? What are the similarities between abortion and physician-assisted suicide? What are the differences? Why do you think Angell makes this connection?

2. What distinctions does Angell make in paragraphs 8 through 10 between physician-assisted suicide and euthanasia? Why does she feel that making a distinction is important? Do you agree or disagree with her distinctions?

3. In paragraph 12 Angell discusses the "slippery slope" argument held by her opponents that legalizing physician-assisted suicide will lead to its abuse. What are the abuses feared by opponents of physician-assisted suicide? Is Angell's statement that "no human endeavor is immune to abuses" (paragraph 13) a satisfactory response? Explain.
4. How does Angell's story about her own father's death influence her discussion? Is it persuasive? Does it help you understand her views?
5. Angell comments that physician-assisted suicide should be viewed from the perspective of the patient, and that doctors should act "in accord with each patient's wishes." Review paragraph 15. Is decision-making power truly in the patient's hands, or is it in the doctor's? Explain.

Death and Dignity—A Case of Individualized Decision Making
Timothy E. Quill

The Hippocratic Oath is a pledge that physicians recite when graduating from medical school in which they promise to help the sick. The oath includes phrases such as "I will not harm or injure" and "I will not give a fatal draught to anyone if I am asked." How, then, can doctors agree to help terminally ill patients to die? Quill's essay describes the difficult decisions physicians face when dealing with terminally ill patients who wish to end their suffering by ending their lives.

Timothy E. Quill was lead physician plaintiff in the case *Vacco v. Quill,* in which several New York physicians and three patients sued the states attorneys general, asserting that the ban on physician-assisted suicide was unconstitutional. Quill is a professor of medicine and psychiatry at the University of Rochester in New York and is the author of *A Midwife Through the Dying Process* (1996). This essay appeared in the *New England Journal of Medicine* on March 7, 1991.

BEFORE YOU READ

What obstacles does a terminally ill patient who wishes to commit suicide face in your state? What legal issues must the patient, the patient's family, and the physician consider?

AS YOU READ

What does it mean to "die with dignity"? What is dignity? Why is maintaining their dignity important to so many patients?

1   Diane was feeling tired and had a rash. A common scenario, though there was something subliminally worrisome that prompted me to check her blood count. Her hematocrit was 22, and the white-cell count was 4.3 with some metamyelocytes and unusual white cells. I wanted it to be viral, trying to deny

what was staring me in the face. Perhaps in a repeated count it would disappear. I called Diane and told her it might be more serious than I had initially thought—that the test needed to be repeated and that if she felt worse, we might have to move quickly. When she pressed for the possibilities, I reluctantly opened the door to leukemia. Hearing the word seemed to make it exist. "Oh, shit!" she said. "Don't tell me that." Oh, shit! I thought, I wish I didn't have to.

2   Diane was no ordinary person (although no one I have ever come to know has been really ordinary). She was raised in an alcoholic family and had felt alone for much of her life. She had vaginal cancer as a young woman. Through much of her adult life, she had struggled with depression and her own alcoholism. I had come to know, respect, and admire her over the previous eight years as she confronted these problems and gradually overcame them. She was an incredibly clear, at times brutally honest, thinker and communicator. As she took control of her life, she developed a strong sense of independence and confidence. In the previous 3 1/2 years, her hard work had paid off. She was completely abstinent from alcohol, she had established much deeper connections with her husband, college-age son, and several friends, and her business and her artistic work were blossoming. She felt she was really living fully for the first time.

3   Not surprisingly, the repeated blood count was abnormal, and detailed examination of the peripheral-blood smear showed myelocytes. I advised her to come into the hospital, explaining that we needed to do a bone marrow biopsy and make some decisions relatively rapidly. She came to the hospital knowing what we would find. She was terrified, angry, and sad. Although we knew the odds, we both clung to the thread of possibility that it might be something else.

4   The bone marrow confirmed the worst: acute myelomonocytic leukemia. In the face of this tragedy, we looked for signs of hope. This is an area of medicine in which technological intervention has been successful, with cures 25 percent of the time—long-term cures. As I probed the costs of these cures, I heard about induction chemotherapy (three weeks in the hospital, prolonged neutropenia, probable infectious complications, and hair loss; 75 percent of patients respond, 25 percent do not). For the survivors, this is followed by consolidation chemotherapy (with similar side effects; another 25 percent die, for a net survival of 50 percent). Those still alive, to have a reasonable chance of long-term survival, then need bone marrow transplantation (hospitalization for two months and whole-body irradiation, with complete killing of the bone marrow, infectious complications, and the possibility for graft-versus-host disease—with a survival of approximately 50 percent, or 25 percent of the original group). Though hematologists may argue over the exact percentages, they don't argue about the outcome of no treatment—certain death in days, weeks, or at most a few months.

5   Believing that delay was dangerous, our oncologist broke the news to Diane and began making plans to insert a Hickman catheter and begin induction chemotherapy that afternoon. When I saw her shortly thereafter, she was enraged at his presumption that she would want treatment, and devastated by

the finality of the diagnosis. All she wanted to do was go home and be with her family. She had no further questions about treatment and in fact had decided that she wanted none. Together we lamented her tragedy and the unfairness of life. Before she left, I felt the need to be sure that she and her husband understood that there was some risk in delay, that the problem was not going to go away, and that we needed to keep considering the options over the next several days. We agreed to meet in two days.

6   She returned in two days with her husband and son. They had talked extensively about the problem and the options. She remained very clear about her wish not to undergo chemotherapy and to live whatever time she had left outside the hospital. As we explored her thinking further, it became clear that she was convinced she would die during the period of treatment and would suffer unspeakably in the process (from hospitalization, from lack of control over her body, from the side effects of chemotherapy, and from pain and anguish). Although I could offer support and my best effort to minimize her suffering if she chose treatment, there was no way I could say any of this would not occur. In fact, the last four patients with acute leukemia at our hospital had died very painful deaths in the hospital during various stages of treatment (a fact I did not share with her). Her family wished she would choose treatment but sadly accepted her decision. She articulated very clearly that it was she who would be experiencing all the side effects of treatment and that odds of 25 percent were not good enough for her to undergo so toxic a course of therapy, given her expectations of chemotherapy and hospitalization and the absence of a closely matched bone marrow donor. I had her repeat her understanding of the treatment, the odds, and what to expect if there were no treatment. I clarified a few misunderstandings, but she had a remarkable grasp of the options and implications.

7   I had been a longtime advocate of active, informed patient choice of treatment or nontreatment, and of a patient's right to die with as much control and dignity as possible. Yet there was something about her giving up a 25 percent chance of long-term survival in favor of almost certain death that disturbed me. I had seen Diane fight and use her considerable inner resources to overcome alcoholism and depression, and I half expected her to change her mind over the next week. Since the window of time in which effective treatment can be initiated is rather narrow, we met several times that week. We obtained a second hematology consultation and talked at length about the meaning and implications of treatment and nontreatment. She talked to a psychologist she had seen in the past. I gradually understood the decision from her perspective and became convinced that it was the right decision for her. We arranged for home hospice care (although at that time Diane felt reasonably well, was active, and looked healthy), left the door open for her to change her mind, and tried to anticipate how to keep her comfortable in the time she had left.

8   Just as I was adjusting to her decision, she opened up another area that would stretch me profoundly. It was extraordinarily important to Diane to maintain control of herself and her own dignity during the time remaining to her. When this was no longer possible, she clearly wanted to die. As a former di-

rector of a hospice program, I know how to use pain medicines to keep patients comfortable and lessen suffering. I explained the philosophy of comfort care, which I strongly believe in. Although Diane understood and appreciated this, she had known of people lingering in what was called relative comfort, and she wanted no part of it. When the time came, she wanted to take her life in the least painful way possible. Knowing of her desire for independence and her decision to stay in control, I thought this request made perfect sense. I acknowledged and explored this wish but also thought that it was out of the realm of currently accepted medical practice and that it was more than I could offer or promise. In our discussion, it became clear that preoccupation with her fear of a lingering death would interfere with Diane's getting the most out of the time she had left until she found a safe way to ensure her death. I feared the effects of a violent death on her family, the consequences of an ineffective suicide that would leave her lingering in precisely the state she dreaded so much, and the possibility that a family member would be forced to assist her, with all the legal and personal repercussions that would follow. She discussed this at length with her family. They believed that they should respect her choice. With this in mind, I told Diane that information was available from the Hemlock Society that might be helpful to her.

9   A week later she phoned me with a request for barbiturates for sleep. Since I knew that this was an essential ingredient in a Hemlock Society suicide, I asked her to come to the office to talk things over. She was more than willing to protect me by participating in a superficial conversation about her insomnia, but it was important to me to know how she planned to use the drugs and to be sure that she was not in despair or overwhelmed in a way that might color her judgment. In our discussion, it was apparent that she was having trouble sleeping, but it was also evident that the security of having enough barbiturates available to commit suicide when and if the time came would leave her secure enough to live fully and concentrate on the present. It was clear that she was not despondent and that in fact she was making deep, personal connections with her family and close friends. I made sure that she knew how to use the barbiturates for sleep, and also that she knew the amount needed to commit suicide. We agreed to meet regularly, and she promised to meet with me before taking her life, to ensure that all other avenues had been exhausted. I wrote the prescription with an uneasy feeling about the boundaries I was exploring—spiritual, legal, professional, and personal. Yet I also felt strongly that I was setting her free to get the most out of the time she had left, and to maintain dignity and control on her own terms until her death.

10   The next several months were very intense and important for Diane. Her son stayed home from college, and they were able to be with one another and say much that had not been said earlier. Her husband did his work at home so that he and Diane could spend more time together. She spent time with her closest friends. I had her come into the hospital for a conference with our residents, at which she illustrated in a most profound and personal way the importance of informed decision making, the right to refuse treatment, and the ex-

traordinarily personal effects of illness and interaction with the medical system. There were emotional and physical hardships as well. She had periods of intense sadness and anger. Several times she became very weak, but she received transfusions as an outpatient and responded with marked improvement of symptoms. She had two serious infections that responded surprisingly well to empirical courses of oral antibiotics. After three tumultuous months, there were two weeks of relative calm and well-being, and fantasies of a miracle began to surface.

11   Unfortunately, we had no miracle. Bone pain, weakness, fatigue, and fevers began to dominate her life. Although the hospice workers, family members, and I tried our best to minimize the suffering and promote comfort, it was clear that the end was approaching. Diane's immediate future held what she feared the most—increasing discomfort, dependence, and hard choices between pain and sedation. She called up her closest friends and asked them to come over to say goodbye, telling them that she would be leaving soon. As we had agreed, she let me know as well. When we met, it was clear that she knew what she was doing, that she was sad and frightened to be leaving, but that she would be even more terrified to stay and suffer. In our tearful goodbye, she promised a reunion in the future at her favorite spot on the edge of Lake Geneva, with dragons swimming in the sunset.

12   Two days later her husband called to say that Diane had died. She had said her final goodbyes to her husband and son that morning, and asked them to leave her alone for an hour. After an hour, which must have seemed an eternity, they found her on the couch, lying very still and covered by her favorite shawl. There was no sign of struggle. She seemed to be at peace. They called me for advice about how to proceed. When I arrived at their house, Diane indeed seemed peaceful. Her husband and son were quiet. We talked about what a remarkable person she had been. They seemed to have no doubts about the course she had chosen or about their cooperation, although the unfairness of her illness and the finality of her death were overwhelming to us all.

13   I called the medical examiner to inform him that a hospice patient had died. When asked about the cause of death, I said, "acute leukemia." He said that was fine and that we should call a funeral director. Although acute leukemia was the truth, it was not the whole story. Yet any mention of suicide would have given rise to a police investigation and probably brought the arrival of an ambulance crew for resuscitation. Diane would have become a "coroner's case," and the decision to perform an autopsy would have been made at the discretion of the medical examiner. The family or I could have been subject to criminal prosecution, and I to professional review, for our roles in support of Diane's choices. Although I truly believe that the family and I gave her the best care possible, allowing her to define her limits and directions as much as possible, I am not sure the law, society, or the medical profession would agree. So I said "acute leukemia" to protect all of us, to protect Diane from an invasion into her past and her body, and to continue to shield society from the knowl-

edge of the degree of suffering that people often undergo in the process of dying. Suffering can be lessened to some extent, but in no way eliminated or made benign, by the careful intervention of a competent, caring physician, given current social constraints.

14   Diane taught me about the range of help I can provide if I know people well and if I allow them to say what they really want. She taught me about life, death, and honesty and about taking charge and facing tragedy squarely when it strikes. She taught me that I can take small risks for people that I really know and care about. Although I did not assist in her suicide directly, I helped indirectly to make it possible, successful, and relatively painless. Although I know we have measures to help control pain and lessen suffering, to think that people do not suffer in the process of dying is an illusion. Prolonged dying can occasionally be peaceful, but more often the role of the physician and family is limited to lessening but not eliminating severe suffering.

15   I wonder how many families and physicians secretly help patients over the edge into death in the face of such severe suffering. I wonder how many severely ill or dying patients secretly take their lives, dying alone in despair. I wonder whether the image of Diane's final aloneness will persist in the minds of her family, or if they will remember more the intense, meaningful months they had together before she died. I wonder whether Diane struggled in that last hour, and whether the Hemlock Society's way of death by suicide is the most benign. I wonder why Diane, who gave so much to so many of us, had to be alone for the last hour of her life. I wonder whether I will see Diane again, on the shore of Lake Geneva at sunset, with dragons swimming on the horizon.

FOR ANALYSIS AND DISCUSSION

1. Imagine that you have just been diagnosed with leukemia. You must make a decision to begin or refuse treatment. If you choose treatment, you face probable hair loss, extreme nausea, weakness, exhaustion, and opportunistic infections, but you have about a 25 percent chance of survival. If you refuse, you will certainly die within the year. What choice would you make? What conditions would influence your decision? Explain.

2. In paragraph 8 Quill states that "it was extraordinarily important to Diane to maintain control of herself and her own dignity." Do you think she accomplished this objective? Was assisted suicide the only way to maintain dignity and control? Explain.

3. Quill wonders why Diane had to be alone for the last hour of her life. How would the legalization of physician-assisted suicide change a patient's final hours?

4. Why do you think Quill states in paragraph 14 that he only *indirectly* made Diane's suicide possible? How does he stand on the issue of physician-assisted suicide? How can you tell?

Suicide, Assisted Suicide, and Medical Illness
Herbert Hendin

Is all the media attention on the issue of physician-assisted suicide detracting from larger issues, such as the need to better sensitize doctors to the dying process? Are some doctors supporting physician-assisted suicide out of a need to regain a sense of control over what are, essentially, uncontrollable situations. Herbert Hendin argues that patients often seek to end their lives because of feelings of fear and dread of what will happen to them as their illness progresses. He explains that the root of that fear is the loss of control, a fear many of their doctors feel as well. Euthanasia becomes the means for both patients and their doctors to deal with the frustration of terminal illness rather than the complications associated with the illness itself.

Herbert Hendin is the executive director of the American Suicide Foundation and professor of psychiatry at New York Medical College. He is the author of *Seduced by Death: Doctors, Patients and Assisted Suicide* (1998), from which this essay was taken.

BEFORE YOU READ

Imagine your reaction if confronted with the news that you had a terminal illness. Would the option of assisted suicide be important to you? Why or why not?

AS YOU READ

What does Hendin say are usually patients' greatest fears regarding terminal illnesses? What drives their desire to commit suicide?

1   A few years ago, a young professional in his early thirties who had acute myelocytic leukemia was referred to me for consultation. With medical treatment, Tim was given a 25 percent chance of survival; without it, he was told, he would die in a few months. Tim, an ambitious executive whose focus on career success had led him to neglect his relationships with his wife and family, was stunned. His immediate reaction was a desperate, angry preoccupation with suicide and a request for support in carrying it out. He was worried about becoming dependent and feared both the symptoms of his disease and the side effects of treatment.

2   Tim's request speaks directly to the question at the heart of assisted suicide and euthanasia: Does our need to care for people who are terminally ill and to reduce their suffering require us to give physicians the right to end their lives?

3   Asking this question, however, helps to make us aware that neither legalizing nor forbidding euthanasia addresses the much larger problem of providing humane care for those who are terminally ill. To some degree the call for legalization is a symptom of our failure to develop a better response to the problems

of dying and the fear of unbearable pain or artificial prolongation of life in intolerable circumstances.

4   People are apt to assume that seriously or terminally ill people who wish to end their lives are different from those who are otherwise suicidal. Yet the first reaction of many patients, like Tim, to the knowledge of serious illness and possible death is anxiety, depression, and a wish to die. Such patients are not significantly different from patients who react to other crises with the desire to end the crisis by ending their lives.

5   Patients rarely cite the fear of death itself as their reason for requesting assisted suicide or euthanasia, but clinicians often see such patients displace anxieties about death onto the circumstances of dying: pain, dependence, loss of dignity, and the unpleasant side effects of medical treatments. Focusing one's fear or rage onto these palpable events distracts from the fear of death itself. Tim's anxieties about the painful circumstances that would surround his death were not irrational, but all his fears about dying amplified them.

6   Once Tim and I could talk about the possibility or likelihood of his dying—what separation from his family and the destruction of his body meant to him—his desperation subsided. He accepted medical treatment and used the remaining months of his life to become closer to his wife and parents. At first, he would not talk to his wife about his illness because of his resentment that she was going on with her life while he would likely not be going on with his. A session with the two of them cleared the air and made it possible for them to talk openly with each other. Two days before he died, Tim talked about what he would have missed without the opportunity for a loving parting.[1]

7   The last days of most patients can be given such meaning if those treating them know how to engage them. Tim's need for communication with his wife, communication that was not possible until he voiced his envy and resentment over her going on with her life while he was probably not going to be doing so, finds parallels in the lives of most dying patients.

8   In a twist on conventional wisdom, the English palliative care specialist Robert Twycross has written, "where there is hope there is life," referring not to hope of a cure, but hope of doing something that gives meaning to life as long as it lasts.[2] Virtually everyone who is dying has unfinished business, even if only the need to share their life and their death with friends, family, a doctor, or a hospice worker. Without such purpose, terminally ill patients who are not in great physical distress may be tortured by the feeling that they are only waiting to die and may want to die at once.

9   If assisted suicide were legal, Tim probably would have asked a doctor's help in taking his own life. Because he was mentally competent, he would have qualified for assisted suicide and would surely have found a doctor who would agree to his request.

10   Since the Oregon law and similar laws being considered in other states do not require an independently referred doctor for a second opinion, Tim would likely have been referred by a physician supportive of assisted suicide to a colleague who was equally supportive; the evaluation would have been pro forma.

He could have been put to death in an unrecognized state of terror, unable to give himself the chance of getting well or of dying in the dignified way he did. The Oregon law is the latest example of how public frustration can lead to action that only compounds the problem; in the rush to legislate, advocates have failed to understand the problem they are claiming to solve.

11   Long before today's movement to legalize assisted suicide of patients who are seriously or terminally ill, we knew that physical illness contributes significantly to the motivation for suicide. Medical illness plays an important role in 25 percent of suicides, and this percentage rises with age: from 50 percent in suicides who are over fifty years old, to over 70 percent in suicides older than sixty.[3]

12   Most suicide attempts reflect a patient's ambivalence about dying, and those requesting assisted suicide show an equal ambivalence. The desire for death waxes and wanes in terminally ill patients, even among those who express a persistent wish to die.[4] Some patients may voice suicidal thoughts in response to transient depression or severe pain, but these patients usually find relief with treatment of their depressive illness or pain and are grateful to be alive.[5] Strikingly, the overwhelming majority of the patients who are terminally ill fight for life until the end; only 2 to 4 percent of suicides occur in the context of terminal illness.[6]

13   Like Tim, the vast majority of those who request assisted suicide or euthanasia are motivated primarily by dread of what will happen to them rather than by current pain or suffering.[7] Similarly, in several studies, more individuals, particularly elderly individuals, killed themselves because they feared or *mistakenly* believed they had cancer than killed themselves and actually had cancer.[8] In the same way, preoccupation with suicide is greater in those awaiting the results of tests for HIV antibodies than in those who know that they are HIV positive.[9]

14   Patients do not know what to expect and cannot foresee how their conditions will unfold as they decline toward death. Facing this ignorance, they fill the vacuum with their fantasies and fears. When these fears are dealt with by a caring and knowledgeable physician, the request for death usually disappears. . . .

15   Both patients who attempt suicide and those who request assisted suicide often test the affection and care of others, confiding feelings like "I don't want to be a burden to my family" or "My family would be better off without me." Such statements are classic indicators of suicidal depression.

16   Expressions of being a burden usually reflect depressed feelings of worthlessness or guilt, and may be pleas for reassurance. Whether physically healthy or terminally ill, these patients need assurance that they are still wanted; they also need treatment for depression. If the doctor does not recognize the ambivalence, anxiety, and depression that underlie a patient's request for death, the patient becomes trapped by that request and can die in a state of unrecognized terror. . . .

17   Patients are not alone in their inability to tolerate situations they cannot control. Lewis Thomas has written insightfully about the sense of failure and helplessness that doctors may experience in the face of death;[10] such feelings

may explain why doctors have such difficulty discussing terminal illness with patients. A majority of doctors avoid such discussions, while most patients would prefer frank talk.[11] These feelings might also explain both doctors' tendency to use excessive measures to maintain life and their need to make death a physician's decision. By deciding when patients die, by making death a medical decision, the physician preserves the illusion of mastery over the disease and the accompanying feelings of helplessness. The physician, not the illness, is responsible for the death. Assisting suicide and euthanasia become ways of dealing with the frustration of not being able to cure the disease.

REFERENCES

1. H. Hendin, *Suicide in America* (New York: Norton, 1995).

2. R. Twycross, "A View from the Hospice," in *Euthanasia Examined,* ed. J. Keown (Cambridge: Cambridge University Press, 1995).

3. T. B. MacKenzie and M. K. Popkin, "Medical Illness and Suicide," in *Suicide over the Life Cycle,* ed. S. J. Blumenthal and D. J. Kupfer (Washington, D.C.: American Psychiatric Press, 1990), 205–232.

4. E. J. Emanuel, D. L. Fairclough, E. R. Daniels, and B. R. Clarridge, "Euthanasia and Physician-Assisted Suicide: Attitudes and Experiences of Oncology Patients, Oncologists, and the Public, *Lancet,* 1996, 347:1,805–1,810.

5. H. Hendin and G. L. Klerman, "Physician-Assisted Suicide: The Dangers of Legalization," *American Journal of Psychiatry,* 1993, 150:143–145.

6. E. Robins, G. E. Murphy, R. H. Wilkinson Jr., S. Gassner, and J. Kayes, "Some Clinical Considerations in the Prevention of Suicide Based on a Study of 134 Successful Suicides," *American Journal of Public Health,* 1959, 49:888–889; P. Sainsbury, *Suicide in London: An Ecological Study* (New York: Basic Books, 1956); C. P. Seager and R. S. Flood, "Suicide in Bristol," *British Journal of Psychiatry,* 1965, 111:919–932.

7. H. Hendin, "Suicide and the Request for Assisted Suicide: Meaning and Motivation," *Duquesne Law Review,* 1996, 35:285–310.

8. Y. Conwell, E. D. Caine, and K. Olsen, "Suicide and Cancer in Late Life," *Hospital & Community Psychiatry,* 1990, 41:1334–1339, T. L. Dorpat, W. F. Anderson, and H. S. Ripley, "The Relationship of Physical Illness to Suicide," in *Suicidal Beaviors: Diagnosis and Management,* ed. H. L. P. Resnick (Boston: Little Brown, 1968).

9. S. Perry, "Suicidal Ideation and HIV Testing," *JAMA,* 1990, 263:679–682.

10. L. Thomas, "Dying as Failure?" *American Journal of Political Science,* 1984, 444: 1–4.

11. D. Hendin, *Death as a Fact of Life* (New York: Norton, 1973), citing Herman Feifel, "Physicians Consider Death," unpublished manuscript presented at 1967 meeting of the American Psychological Association.

FOR ANALYSIS AND DISCUSSION

1. Compare Tim's case to that of Timothy Quill's patient, Diane. What similarities do you see between the two patients? What differences? How soon after her diagnosis does Diane ask for "an essential ingredient in a Hemlock Society suicide"? Do you think that Hendin would feel the same about Diane's request for suicide assistance as he did about Tim's?

2. What kinds of fears and anxieties can prompt a patient to request assistance in committing suicide? How does Tim's case express Hendin's point about patient fears?

3. What does Hendin mean in paragraph 16 when he says patients' "expressions of being a burden . . . may be pleas for reassurance"? What are the needs of terminally ill patients besides pain control?

4. Hendin comments that some patients may seek to commit suicide because they fear the loss of control associated with terminal illness. He further comments that physicians may feel similar frustration because they are limited in their ability to help their patients. Why is the concept of control so important? What does Hendin imply is the real issue?

5. In paragraph 8 Hendin cites Robert Twycross's statement, "where there is hope there is life." How do you define "life"? Does this definition change when referring to the terminally ill? Explain.

WRITING ASSIGNMENTS: PHYSICIAN-ASSISTED SUICIDE

1. The patients in both Hendin's and Quill's essays were diagnosed with a form of leukemia. Imagine that a close friend has informed you that he or she has been diagnosed with this disease and is considering suicide. Write a letter to this friend in which you explain your position on suicide. Be sure to address your friend's emotions and fears about both the illness and the suicide.

2. Dr. Jack Kevorkian is perhaps the most notorious medical practitioner supporting physician-assisted suicide. Sometimes called "Dr. Death," Kevorkian made headlines after *60 Minutes* broadcast a video he provided documenting his direct involvement in the death of Thomas Youk, a patient suffering from Lou Gehrig's disease. He was found guilty of second degree murder and sentenced to seven to ten years in prison. Kevorkian recently stated that he was "moving beyond assisted suicide to euthanasia." Using resources available from the Internet <http://www.efn.org/~ergo/dr.k.html> and your library, sketch a profile of Kevorkian's activities over the past decade. What do you think of his actions and his subsequent conviction on charges of second degree murder? Make references to what you have learned from the three readings regarding physician-assisted suicide, including Angell's discussion of the difference between physician-assisted suicide and euthanasia.

3. The Hemlock Society is a nonprofit organization representing individuals who "firmly believe control over one's death is a fundamental right, and that the option of physician aid in dying is a fundamental choice." Access the Hemlock Society's Web site at <http://www.hemlock.org/> and examine its links, including its student page at <http://www.hemlock.org/hemlock/student.html>. How does the Web site present the Society's views on "good death"? Depending on how you stand on the issue of physician-assisted suicide, write an essay in which you evaluate the views expressed by the Hemlock Society.

The Right to Privacy: Is It Being Violated?

The War at Home
Gore Vidal

In this essay, Vidal explores how the U.S. government, under the pretense of protecting its citizens, is slowly eroding their right to privacy. At any time, police, if they believe there is probable cause, may break into our homes or tap our phones. Airport security guards may search our bags and even our persons. George Orwell's Big Brother state, says Vidal, is no longer the prediction of a novel; it is an American reality.

Gore Vidal is one of the most celebrated writers of the twentieth century. His most recent book is *1876: A Novel* (1998). The following article first appeared in the November 1998 issue of *Vanity Fair*.

BEFORE YOU READ

When were you last asked to produce identification? What were the circumstances? Did you resent the question or did you accept it as one of the realities of modern life?

AS YOU READ

How does Vidal use sarcasm to present his argument? How does this approach affect your overall response to the essay?

1   Most Americans of a certain age can recall exactly where they were and what they were doing on October 20, 1964, when word came that Herbert Hoover was dead. The heart and mind of a nation stopped. But how many recall when and how they first became aware that one or another of the Bill of Rights had expired? For me, it was sometime in 1960 at a party in Beverly Hills that I got the bad news from the constitutionally cheery actor Cary Grant. He had just flown in from New York. He had, he said, picked up his ticket at an airline counter at the magical old-world airport, Idlewild, whose very name reflected our condition. "There were these lovely girls behind the counter, and they were delighted to help me, or so they said. I signed some autographs. Then I asked one of them for my tickets. Suddenly she was very solemn. 'Do you have any identification?' she asked," (Worldly friends tell me that the "premise" of this story is now the basis of a series of TV commercials for Visa unseen by me.) I would be exaggerating if I felt the chill in the air that long-ago Beverly Hills evening. Actually, we simply laughed. But I did, for just an instant, wonder if the future had tapped a dainty foot on our mass grave.

2   Curiously enough, it was Grant again who bore, as lightly as ever, the news that privacy itself hangs by a gossamer thread. "A friend in London rang me this morning," he said. This was June 4, 1963. "Usually we have code names, but

this time he forgot. So after he asked for me I said into the receiver, 'All right. St. Louis, off the line. You, too, Milwaukee,' and so on. The operators love listening in. Anyway, after we talked business, he said, 'So what's the latest Hollywood gossip?' And I said, 'Well, Lana Turner is still having an affair with the black baseball pitcher.' One of the operators on the line gave a terrible cry. 'Oh, no!' "

3   Innocent days. Today, as media and Congress thunder their anthem, "Twinkle, twinkle, little Starr, how we wonder what you are," the current president is assumed to have no right at all to privacy because, you see, it's really about sex, not truth, a permanent nonstarter in political life. Where Grant's name assured him an admiring audience of telephone operators, the rest of us were usually ignored. That was then. Today, in the all-out, never-to-be-won twin wars on Drugs and Terrorism, two million telephone conversations a year are intercepted by law-enforcement officials. As for that famous "workplace" to which so many Americans are assigned by necessity, "the daily abuse of civil liberties . . . is a national disgrace," according to the American Civil Liberties Union in a 1996 report.

4   Among the report's findings, between 1990 and 1996, the number of workers under electronic surveillance increased from 8 million per year to more than 30 million. Simultaneously, employers eavesdrop on an estimated 400 million telephone conversations a year—something like 750 a minute. In 1990, major companies subjected 38 percent of their employees to urine tests for drugs. By 1996, more than 70 percent were thus interfered with. Recourse to law has not been encouraging. In fact, the California Supreme Court has upheld the right of public employers to drug-test not only those employees who have been entrusted with flying jet aircraft or protecting our borders from Panamanian imperialism but also those who simply mop the floors. The court also ruled that governments can screen applicants for drugs and alcohol. This was inspired by the actions of the city-state of Glendale, California, which wanted to test all employees due for promotion. Suit was brought against Glendale on the ground that it was violating the Fourth Amendment's protection against "unreasonable searches and seizures." Glendale's policy was upheld by the California Supreme Court, but Justice Stanley Mosk wrote a dissent: "Drug testing represents a significant additional invasion of those applicants' basic rights to privacy and dignity . . . and the city has not carried its considerable burden of showing that such an invasion is justified in the case of all applicants offered employment."

5   In the last year or so I have had two Cary Grant–like revelations, considerably grimmer than what went on in the good old days of relative freedom from the state. A well-known acting couple and their two small children came to see me one summer. Photos were taken of their four-year-old and six-year-old cavorting bare in the sea. When the couple got home to Manhattan, the father dropped the negatives off at a drugstore to be printed. Later, a frantic call from his fortunately friendly druggist: "If I print these I've got to report you and you could get five years in the slam-

mer for kiddie porn." The war on kiddie porn is now getting into high gear, though I was once assured by Wardell Pomeroy, Alfred Kinsey's colleague in sex research, that pedophilia was barely a blip on the statistical screen, somewhere down there with farm lads and their animal friends.

6   It has always been a mark of American freedom that unlike countries under constant Napoleonic surveillance, we are not obliged to carry identification to show to curious officials and pushy police. But now, due to Terrorism, every one of us is stopped at airports and obliged to show an ID which must include a mug shot (something, as Allah knows, no terrorist would ever dare fake). In Chicago after an interview with Studs Terkel, I complained that since I don't have a driver's license, I must carry a passport in my own country as if I were a citizen of the old Soviet Union. Terkel has had the same trouble. "I was asked for my ID—with photo—at this southern airport, and I said I didn't have anything except the local newspaper with a big picture of me on the front page, which I showed them, but they said that that was not an ID. Finally, they got tired of me and let me on the plane."

7   Lately, I have been going through statistics about terrorism (usually direct responses to crimes our government has committed against foreigners—although, recently, federal crimes against our own people are increasing). Only twice in 12 years have American commercial planes been destroyed in flight by terrorists; neither originated in the United States. To prevent, however, a repetition of these two crimes, hundreds of millions of travelers must now be subjected to searches, seizures, delays.

8   The state of the art of citizen-harassment is still in its infancy. Nevertheless, new devices, at ever greater expense, are coming onto the market—and, soon, to an airport near you—including the dream machine of every horny schoolboy. The "Body Search" Contraband Detection System, created by American Science and Engineering, can "X-ray" through clothing to reveal the naked body, whose enlarged image can then be cast onto a screen for prurient analysis. The proud manufacturer boasts that the picture is so clear that even navels, unless packed with cocaine and taped over, can be seen winking at the voyeurs. The system also has what is called, according to an A.C.L.U. report, "a joystick-driven Zoom Option" that allows the operator to enlarge interesting portions of the image. During all this, the victim remains, as AS&E proudly notes, fully clothed. Orders for this machine should be addressed to the Reverend Pat Robertson and will be filled on a first-come, first-served basis, while the proud new owner of "Body Search" will be automatically included in the F.B.I.'s database of Sexual Degenerates—Class B. Meanwhile, in February 1997, the "Al" Gore Commission called for the acquisition of 54 high-tech bomb-detection machines known as the CTX 5000, a baggage scanner that is a bargain at a million dollars and will cost only $100,000 a year to service. Unfortunately, the CTX 5000 scans baggage at the rate of 250 per hour, which would mean perhaps a thousand are needed to "protect" passengers at major airports from those two putative terrorists who might—or might not—strike again in the next

12 years, as they twice did in the last 12 years. Since the present scanning system seems fairly effective, why subject passengers to hours of delay, not to mention more than $54 million worth of equipment?

9   Presently, somewhat confused guidelines exist so that airline personnel can recognize at a glance someone who fits the "profile" of a potential terrorist. Obviously, anyone of mildly dusky hue who is wearing a fez gets busted on the spot. For those terrorists who do not seem to fit the "profile," relevant government agencies have come up with the following behavioral tips that should quickly reveal the evildoer. A devious drug smuggler is apt to be the very first person off the plane unless, of course, he is truly devious and chooses to be the last one off. Debonair master criminals often opt for a middle position. Single blonde young women are often used, unwittingly, to carry bombs or drugs given them by Omar Sharif look-alikes in sinister Casbahs. Upon arrival in freedom's land, great drug-sniffing dogs will be turned loose on them; unfortunately, these canine detectives often mistakenly target as drug carriers women that are undergoing their menstrual period: the sort of icebreaker that often leads to merry laughter all around the customs area. Apparently one absolutely sure behavioral giveaway is undue nervousness on the part of a passenger though, again, the master criminal will sometimes appear to be too much at ease. In any case, whatever mad rule of thumb is applied, a customs official has every right to treat anyone as a criminal on no evidence at all; to seize and to search without, of course, due process of law. . . .

10   Since the *Encyclopedia Britannica* is Britannica and not American, it is not surprising that its entry for "Bill of Rights, United States" is a mere column in length, the same as its neighbor on the page "Bill of Sale," obviously a more poignant document to the island compilers. Even so, they do tell us that the roots of our Rights are in Magna Carta and that the genesis of the Bill of Rights that was added as 10 amendments to our Constitution in 1791 was largely the handiwork of James Madison, who, in turn, echoed Virginia's 1776 Declaration of Rights. At first, these 10 amendments were applicable to American citizens only as citizens of the entire United States and not as Virginians or as New Yorkers, where state laws could take precedence according to "states' rights," as acknowledged in the 10th and last of the original amendments. It was not until 1868 that the 14th amendment forbade the states to make laws counter to the original bill. Thus every United States person, in his home state, was guaranteed freedom of "speech and press, and the right to assembly and to petition as well as freedom from a national religion." Apparently, it was Charlton Heston who brought the Second Amendment, along with handguns and child-friendly Uzis, down from Mount DeMille. Originally, the right for citizen militias to bear arms was meant to discourage a standing federal or state army and all the mischief that an armed state might cause people who wanted to live not under the shadow of a gun but peaceably on their own atop some sylvan Ruby Ridge.

11   Currently, the Fourth Amendment is in the process of disintegration, out of "military necessity"—the constitutional language used by Lincoln to wage civil war, suspend habeas corpus, shut down newspapers, and free southern

slaves. The Fourth Amendment guarantees "the right of the people to be se-cure in their persons, houses, papers, and effects, against unreasonable searches and seizures, shall not be violated, and no Warrants shall issue, but upon probable cause, supported by Oath or affirmation, and particularly de-scribing the place to be searched, and the persons or things to be seized." The Fourth is the people's principal defense against totalitarian government; it is a defense that is now daily breached both by deed and law.

12   In James Bovard's 1994 book, *Lost Rights,* the author has assembled a great deal of material on just what our law enforcers are up to in the never-to-be-won wars against Drugs and Terrorism, as they do daily battle with the American people in their homes and cars, on buses and planes, indeed, wherever they can get at them, by hook or by crook or by sting. Military necessity is a bit too highbrow a concept for today's federal and local officials to justify their mid-night smashing in of doors, usually without warning or warrant, in order to ter-rorize the unlucky residents. These unlawful attacks and seizures are often jus-tified by the possible existence of a flush toilet on the fingered premises. (If the warriors against drugs don't take drug fiends absolutely by surprise, the fiends will flush away the evidence.) This is intolerable for those eager to keep us sin-free and obedient. So in the great sign of Sir Thomas Crapper's homely inven-tion, they suspend the Fourth, and conquer.

13   Nineteen ninety-two. Bridgeport, Connecticut. *The Hartford Courant* re-ported that the local Tactical Narcotics Team routinely devastated homes and businesses they "searched." Plainclothes policemen burst in on a Jamaican gro-cer and restaurant owner with the cheery cry "Stick up, niggers. Don't move." Shelves were swept clear. Merchandise ruined. "They never identified them-selves as police," the *Courant* noted. Although they found nothing but a regis-tered gun, the owner was arrested and charged with "interfering with an arrest" and so booked. A judge later dismissed the case. Bovard reports, "In 1991, in Garland, Texas, police dressed in black and wearing black ski-masks burst into a trailer, waved guns in the air and kicked down the bedroom door when Ken-neth Baulch had been sleeping next to his seventeen-month-old son. A police-man claimed that Baulch posed a deadly threat because he held an ashtray in his left hand, which explained why he shot Baulch in the back and killed him. (A police internal investigation found no wrongdoing by the officer.) In March 1992, a police SWAT team killed Robin Pratt, an Everett, Washington, mother, in a no-knock raid carrying out an arrest warrant for her husband. (Her husband was later released after the allegations upon which the arrest warrant were based turned out to be false.)" Incidentally, this K.G.B. tactic—hold someone for a crime, but let him off if he then names someone else for a bigger crime, also known as Starr justice—often leads to false, even random allegations which ought not to be acted upon so murderously without a bit of homework first. *The Seattle Times* describes Robin Pratt's last moments. She was with her six-year-old daughter and five-year-old niece when the police broke in. As the bravest storm trooper, named Aston, approached her, gun drawn, the other police shouted, " 'Get down,' and she started to crouch onto her knees. She looked up at Aston

and said, 'Please don't hurt my children. . . . ' Aston had his gun pointed at her and fired, shooting her in the neck. According to [the Pratt family attorney John] Muenster, she was alive another one or two minutes but could not speak because her throat had been destroyed by the bullet. She was handcuffed, lying face down." Doubtless Aston was fearful of a divine resurrection; and vengeance. It is no secret that American police rarely observe the laws of the land when out wilding with each other, and as any candid criminal judge will tell you, perjury is often their native tongue in court. . . .

14   It is nicely apt that the word "terrorist" (according to the *O.E.D.*) should have been coined during the French Revolution to describe "an adherent or supporter of the Jacobins, who advocated and practiced methods of partisan repression and bloodshed in the propagation of the principles of democracy and equality." Although our rulers have revived the word to describe violent enemies of the United States, most of today's actual terrorists can be found within our own governments, federal, state, municipal. The Bureau of Alcohol, Tobacco, and Firearms (known as A.T.F.), the Drug Enforcement Agency, F.B.I., I.R.S., etc., are so many Jacobins at war against the lives, freedom, and property of our citizens.

FOR ANALYSIS AND DISCUSSION

1. Reread paragraph 9. What is the profile of a terrorist, according to Vidal's information? Explain Vidal's use of sarcasm to convey his point of view.
2. Evaluate Vidal's comments on the Second Amendment. What do you think are Vidal's views about the Second Amendment?
3. Analyze Vidal's tone. Did you find it engaging or off-putting? How does the tone influence the audience's reception of his argument?
4. Vidal states that "state-of-the-art citizen-harassment is in its infancy" (paragraph 8). What does he mean by this statement? What does he hope to accomplish by writing this essay?
5. What do you think is Gore Vidal's opinion about the so-called "war on drugs"? How can you tell? Explain.
6. Who, according to Vidal, are the real terrorists in America? Do you agree with his assessment?

Privacy for Sale: Peddling Data on the Internet
Andrew L. Shapiro

Did you know that every time you log on to the Internet, cyber-information gatherers might be monitoring you? Sometimes you are aware of their activities, when, for example, you fill out personal information in exchange for a service. But did you know that even when you do not consciously provide data, information engines can put "cookies" on your computer to track your movements? Is the loss of privacy the price we pay for the convenience of the Internet?

Attorney Andrew L. Shapiro is director of the Aspen Institute Internet Policy Project. One of the founders of a new school of thought called "technorealism," Shapiro is the author of *The Control Revolution: How New Technology Is Putting Individuals in Charge and Changing the World We Know* (1999). Shapiro also serves as a contributing editor for *The Nation,* in which the following article was published on June 23, 1997.

BEFORE YOU READ

How much do you value your privacy? Do you ever think about your right to privacy? How would you feel if you found out that personal information about you could be bought and sold?

AS YOU READ

What is Shapiro's position on the sale of personal information on the Internet? Is he against the practice? At what point in the essay do you find out his position?

1 I've got Ted Turner's Social Security number here, along with Rush Limbaugh's home address and a couple of phone numbers for Bob Dole in Kansas. I found this information for free on the Internet in about ten minutes. With a little money and some wily sleuthing, I could probably use this data to get their credit histories, financial records and maybe some confidential medical facts. I might even be able to screw around with their bank accounts.

2 It is this naked vulnerability that, quite justifiably, made Americans increasingly anxious about privacy over the past two decades. A 1995 Louis Harris poll found that 82 percent of respondents were concerned about their personal privacy, up from 64 percent in 1978. Over the same period, the proportion of those who were "very concerned" about privacy increased almost 50 percent. This new fear reflects the emergence of a sophisticated system of private surveillance—or dataveillance, as David Shenk calls it in his new book, *Data Smog*—that is rapidly overshadowing threats from the state.

3 It was once too expensive for anyone but the government to collect, store and coordinate data, creating profiles on hundreds of millions of citizens. But the creeping ubiquity of digital computer technology has ushered in a major industry of high-tech data pushers who are dedicated to gathering and selling personal information about practically everyone, mostly for marketing purposes. (Privacy experts estimate that the average American is profiled in at least twenty-five, and perhaps as many as 100, databases.) "Marketers can follow every aspect of our lives, from the first phone call we make in the morning to the time our security system says we have left the house, to the video camera at the toll booth and the charge slip we have for lunch," said President Clinton recently—a somewhat unexpected remark given his poor record on privacy. With

the rise of online commerce and communication, this collection increasingly happens imperceptibly and without the consent of the observed. The result is a broad and lucrative market for personal information that allows anyone with a buck to find out a whole lot about anyone else—often just by trolling around the Net. It's Orwell meets Adam Smith, introduced by Bill Gates.

4   Traditionally, privacy advocates have responded to this plight with calls for broad federal legislation to replace the current patchwork of state and federal law that leaves personal data woefully unprotected. Proposals usually require conspicuous notice of what information is being collected and for what purpose; meaningful and informed consent by consumers (for example, allowing them to "opt in" to data collection rather than having to "opt out"); the ability to access files about oneself and to correct inaccuracies; a scheme of redress for violations; and creation of an independent federal privacy protection agency to enforce compliance.

5   But in the current deregulatory climate, the Clinton Administration and some privacy defenders are taking a different approach. They're calling for the creation of a market for privacy to compete with or complement the growing market for personal information. (A report released in April by a presidential advisory panel, for example, mentioned "the intriguing possibility that privacy could emerge as a market commodity in the Information Age.") Just as there is demand for consumer data among profiteers, so there is a counterdemand on the part of individuals to keep that information private. The answer, say these advocates, is to have consumers bargain with vendors over acceptable rules for data collection and use.

6   For example, if I'm a real stickler for privacy, I may want to pay more to use an Internet service provider or a Web site that will guarantee me Level 5 privacy (on a hypothetical 1 to 5 scale where 5 represents a commitment not to gather any data). Someone else who doesn't care at all about privacy can pay less to use a Level 1 provider, the kind that sucks up data like a Dustbuster. From the company's standpoint, this makes sense because there is monetary value in that data. If they get it, they charge you less (or give you more); if they don't they charge more (or provide less).

7   This, in some sense, is how the World Wide Web works today. Web sites generally offer their material for free; in return, users give them personal information. This may mean typing your name, phone number or whatever in some blank registration field. But using something called "cookies," Web sites also surreptitiously collect data such as what Internet service provider you use, what site you most recently visited, what computer and browser you're using (for a demonstration, see www.cdt.org/privacy). Since the Net is already so geared toward information exchange, some privacy advocates figure they might as well formalize that process in an open market. That market would extend beyond cyberspace to every exchange of data—with the stores you shop at, your doctors, maybe even your friends.

8   Now, before you go postal about how your privacy rights are being sold down the river, consider some appealing features of the market for privacy:

Recognizing the value of information as an asset, it seeks to give consumers property rights in that information. Your data and sanctuary are your own; you sell them only if you choose—and you can, at least in theory, choose exactly who knows what about you. This would seem to be better than today's free-for-all, where the few rules that exist are vague and, even worse, our data are routinely stolen from us by invisible thieves.

9   Consider also that this market approach has received support not just from the Netscape-led business consortium looking into it but from many of the leading digital civil liberties organizations, including the Center for Democracy and Technology and the Electronic Frontier Foundation. C.D.T. is working with the World Wide Web Consortium, the Direct Marketing Association and others on the Platform for Privacy Preferences, a technical standard that will allow users to negotiate privacy practices with data collectors in a way similar to my Level 1 to 5 example. E.F.E. has teamed up with other industry players to create eTrust, a coalition that rewards privacy-friendly Web sites with a sort of Good Housekeeping seal of approval. Even stalwarts like Mark Rotenberg of the Electronic Privacy Information Center believe that consumers should start bargaining over the flow of their facts and figures. "There are already now markets for personal data," says Rotenberg. "The goal is to make them more fair, to give individuals more control."

10   The problem is, the data pushers will be fighting tooth and nail to see that this doesn't happen. And even if it does, the privatization of privacy will create as many dilemmas as it solves, if not more.

11   First, it may make privacy even more elusive than it is today, particularly online. For example, while dataveillance is the norm on the Net, cybersavvy privacy hawks have their ways of evading it. One trick is to use technologies that allow for anonymous Web surfing. Another is the ever popular low-tech option of providing false information when queried, which 34 percent of Net users admit they do, according to a Georgia Tech survey (you can bet the real number is higher). These renegade tactics will likely be unavailable in the world of formally established privacy markets. Users will have to contract with vendors in an above-board fashion and, as Pat Faley of the Direct Marketing Association sees it, "You're not going to be able to go to too many places if you want to be anonymous." That's the way the market works. You have to play by the rules, which may be different at every Web site you visit—not to mention noncyber data interactions (in a store, on the phone, etc.). This points to a bigger problem: All that time and effort spent dickering over various privacy arrangements adds up to what economists call high—even inefficiently high—transaction costs. In plain terms, it means more hassle for what may be less privacy.

12   Second, the privacy market will hit the poor particularly hard. As companies are able to charge increasingly higher rates for finer shades of privacy, poorer customers who can't afford these premiums will be left more exposed simply by dint of economic disadvantage. Even if the markups are small, a little added privacy may not seem worth it for those with little disposable income, especially since they are already likely to be monitored by the state if they receive

welfare or live in high-crime neighborhoods. (In fact, only 39 percent of Internet users expressed a willingness to pay a markup of more than half a cent on the dollar to assure their privacy, according to eTrust.) Do we really want to perpetuate such a system of first- and second-class privacy rights?

13   Third, the privacy market may create a false sense of comfort, blinding us to certain unforeseeable consequences of dealing in data. For example, though a company may faithfully notify me that it collects personal information for direct marketing, I may be exposed to more than just junk-mail annoyance. Inaccurate or incomplete information in databases is routinely used to determine whether someone should be hired, insured, rented to or given credit. The readily available nature of data can lead to discrimination, harassment and even physical danger—as a Los Angeles reporter demonstrated when he bought detailed information about 5,000 children from information broker Metromail using the name of Richard Allen Davis, who was convicted of murdering 12-year-old Polly Klaas. In the arm's length transactions of the market, vendors have "no incentive to have you think about these dangers," says Oscar Gandy Jr. of the University of Pennsylvania's Annenberg School for Communication. "We're not going to be fully informed."

14   Fourth, there is the problem of unequal bargaining power. While most companies are less interested in your data than in having you as a customer, certain powerful firms, such as the three major credit reporting agencies, are interested exclusively in your numbers. And these companies tend to be monopolistic, presenting consumers with little real choice in the market. If you don't like the terms of the deal they offer, there's really nowhere else you can go to establish a reputable credit report that will allow you to obtain, say, a checking account or a mortgage. And then there's the person who arrives at the hospital after a car accident: Is he supposed to haggle over use of his medical data before he's treated? What about kids browsing the Web who stumble upon, say, the Batman Forever site, which asks them to "help Commissioner Gordon with the Gotham census" by answering questions about what products they buy? (The site was recently changed after complaints from the Center for Media Education.) As Gandy argues in a recent article, "The fundamental asymmetry between individuals and bureaucratic organizations all but guarantees the failure of the market for personal information." Even a free-marketeer like E.F.F. chairwoman Esther Dyson says, "Where there is an element of coercion, you want some regulation."

15   Finally, looming over all of this is a commodification critique, which warns that privacy and personal information become debased when subjected to market pressures. "This is like asking people to pay to practice freedom of religion or free speech," says University of Washington professor Philip Bereano. "We do not buy and sell civil liberties. This is commodity fetishism. It is capitalism run amok." So it would seem. Yet Bereano is actually referring to well-established privacy rights, like the Fourth Amendment right to be free from unreasonable search and seizure and the due process right to make decisions about intimate matters such as contraception and abortion. These rights, one hopes,

cannot be peddled to the highest bidder. The situation is less clear, however, when it comes to personal information. In part, that's because privacy is not well defined or protected in our legal system (video rental records, for example, are protected but medical information is not). Privacy is not even mentioned in the Constitution, and our courts and legislatures have made it the somewhat insecure stepchild of legal rights.

16   Look, for example, at the compromised status of privacy in the ongoing debate over encryption, the text-scrambling technology that keeps electronic communications secure. Civil libertarians have argued strenuously and persuasively against law enforcement's attempts to tap encrypted messages—first with the Clipper Chip, now with an equally problematic "key recovery" scheme. But their arguments based on pure privacy principles have fallen on deaf ears. Instead, modest progress now seems likely because of complaints from high-tech giants in a tizzy over their inability to compete with the foreign software companies that are dominating the growing global market for encryption tools. Crypto supporters have every reason to cheer industry's armtwisting, since it may help secure passage of two pending bills in Congress lifting restrictions on this crucial technology. But a cynic would conclude that privacy is getting a boost just because profits—and perhaps some campaign donations—are at stake. What about the idea that privacy should be protected for its own sake?

17   Lately, it's an idea that has had more currency abroad than it has here. The Organization for Economic Cooperation and Development, for example, has rejected the Clinton Administration's attempts to hamstring encryption, and the European Union has enacted a strict directive limiting personal data transfer. Indeed, the E.U. will prod the United States during upcoming trade negotiations to beef up its lax standards. The Europeans can draw on any number of resources to chasten our leaders. Many instruments of international law recognize that privacy is a fundamental human right. It is also, according to scholars from various disciplines, a core value that protects dignity, autonomy, solitude and the way we present ourselves to the world.

18   While privacy can conceal scourges from scrutiny, it is more often a fulcrum of democracy preserving other basic freedoms, including rights of association and free speech, voting and the pursuit of liberty and happiness. As Justice William O. Douglas wrote in a 1952 dissent, echoing an idea expressed earlier by Justice Louis Brandeis, "The right to be let alone is indeed the beginning of all freedom." In this view, privacy attains special status: Just as we don't allow people to sell their vote, their body parts or themselves into slavery, we shouldn't allow them to sell their privacy.

19   But does this mean that I shouldn't be able to trade my own data for money or services? The market-failure problems noted above are certainly red flags. Stanford law professor Margaret Jane Radin, the author recently of *Contested Commodities,* points out that such concerns have led society to prevent other kinds of bargaining. A landlord, for example, is legally required to keep a rented apartment habitable; he can't ask the renter to waive that requirement in exchange for reduced rent. Similarly, a company can't sell a toaster at a $5

discount to a buyer who agrees not to sue in the event that a product defect causes her to be injured.

20   Perhaps, then, what this market needs is a safety net, a minimal level of personal information privacy that cannot be bartered away. This baseline should certainly prevent bargaining with kids. It might also include inalienable control over our most sensitive material, such as medical and financial information. Whatever its specific features, a safety net for privacy would help create an environment where personal information privacy is the norm, not the exception. The burden would be on data pushers to justify their practices rather than on hapless individuals trying to protect themselves in a perplexing new marketplace.

21   One more point: Some fans of the market for privacy, particularly those in industry, seem to think they've found a way to protect privacy that is an alternative to lawmaking and regulation—as if the choice was either the market or government. This is just wrong. As Phil Agre of the University of California, San Diego, notes, "Governments create markets—and the more intangible the commodity, the more that is true." To work efficiently and equitably, a privacy market will require a concrete legal regime to protect what's being traded and the integrity of that trading. Some sort of federal privacy agency will likely be necessary for enforcement—to protect against data theft, and to insure fair dealing and compliance. Whether or not we trust the self-regulatory efforts of groups like the Direct Marketing Association, they surely can't control the actions of fly-by-night companies that swoop down on the Net to pick up the trail of an unsuspecting mouse. "We'll see where the market will work and where it won't, and supplement that with government action," says Christine Varney, a Federal Trade Commissioner who will be leading an F.T.C. conference on these issues in mid-June.

22   What's clear is that the market for privacy won't do away with the need for new statutory protections and government oversight. It certainly won't give consumers the upper hand against the masterminds of dataveillance. If anything, it will further reduce privacy from an assumed right to the unceremonious status of a commodity. Folks like Ted Turner, Rush Limbaugh and Bob Dole will pay to keep meddlers from getting access to their confidential information. But what about the rest of us? If privacy is for sale, will we peddle our digits or save our data souls?

FOR ANALYSIS AND DISCUSSION

1. What does Shapiro mean when he says privacy defenders are calling for "the creation of a market for privacy to compete with the growing market for personal information" (paragraph 5)? How can there be a "market" for privacy? Is privacy something Americans should have to pay for? Explain.

2. What, according to Shapiro, is the price of privacy on the Internet? Do you agree? Explain.

3. Does privacy have boundaries? If so, what are they? For example, do you surrender your privacy when you log on to the Internet? Can you expect to have the same privacy rights in cyberspace that you have elsewhere?

4. Analyze each of Shapiro's points about the problems associated with the "privatization of privacy" (paragraphs 10–15). How does he support his evaluation of each of these points? Do you agree with his arguments?

5. According to Shapiro, what is the difference between the American and the European views of privacy rights? What do you think accounts for this difference?

6. What solution does Shapiro offer to solve the problem of peddling data on the Internet? How does this solution address both the needs of Internet users and the cyber-marketplace? Evaluate the feasibility of his solution.

Imperial Bedroom
Jonathan Franzen

What privacy rights do we surrender in the name of safety and health? Is it a fair exchange? In this essay Jonathan Franzen evaluates the current "privacy panic." Instead of having too little privacy, Franzen says, we have too much. And those rights we do give up are minor when we consider the benefits we gain in exchange.

Jonathan Franzen is the author of *Twenty-Seventh City* (1988) and *Strong Motion* (1992). A 1996 Guggenheim fellow, his essays have appeared in several magazines, including *Harper's* and the *New Yorker*. The following essay appeared in the October 12, 1998, edition of the *New Yorker*.

BEFORE YOU READ

Do you think individuals in the United States have more privacy now than they did 50 years ago? Consider your own level of privacy. Discuss with an older adult his or her perception of privacy 50 years ago and compare the two.

AS YOU READ

Franzen says, "On closer examination, privacy proved to be the Cheshire cat of values." What do you think he means by this statement? How does he support this statement throughout the essay?

1 Privacy, privacy, the new American obsession: espoused as the most fundamental of rights, marketed as the most desirable of commodities, and pronounced dead twice a week. Even before Linda Tripp pressed the "Record" button on her tape recorder, commentators were warning that "privacy is under siege," that "privacy is in a dreadful state," that "privacy as we now know it may not exist in the year 2000." Not just Big Brother but little brother, John Q. Public, too, is shadowing me through networks of computers. Security cameras no bigger than spiders watch from every shaded corner, dour feminists monitor bedroom behavior and water-cooler conversations, genetic sleuths decoct my entire being from a droplet of saliva, and voyeurs can retrofit ordinary camcorders with a filter that lets them *see through people's clothing*. Then comes the flood of dirty suds from the Office of the Independent Counsel, oozing forth through official and commercial channels to saturate the national consciousness. Lewinskygate

marks, in the words of the philosopher Thomas Nagel, "the culmination of a disastrous erosion" of privacy; it represents, in the words of the author Wendy Kaminer, "the utter disregard for privacy and individual autonomy that exists in totalitarian regimes." In the person of Kenneth Starr, "the public sphere" has finally overwhelmed—shredded, gored, trampled, invaded, run roughshod over—"the private."

2   The panic about privacy has all the finger-pointing and paranoia of a good old American scare, but it's missing one vital ingredient: a genuinely alarmed public. Americans care about privacy mainly in the abstract. Sometimes a well-informed community unites to defend itself, as when Net users bombarded the White House with E-mails against the "clipper chip," and sometimes an especially outrageous piece of news provokes national outcry, as when the Lotus Development Corporation tried to market a CD-ROM containing financial profiles of nearly half the people in the country. By and large, though, even in the face of wholesale infringements like the war on drugs, Americans remain curiously passive. I'm no exception. I read the editorials and try to get excited, but I can't. More often than not, I find myself feeling the opposite of what the commentators want me to. It's happened twice in the last month alone.

3   On the Saturday morning when the *Times* came carrying the complete text of the Starr report, what I felt as I sat alone in my apartment and tried to eat my breakfast was that my own privacy—not Clinton's, not Lewinsky's—was being violated. I love the distant pageant of public life, both the pageantry and the distance. Now a President was facing impeachment, and, as a good citizen, I had a duty to stay informed about the evidence; but the evidence here consisted of two people's groping, sucking, and mutual self-deception. What I felt, when this evidence landed beside my toast and coffee, wasn't a pretend revulsion to camouflage a secret interest in the dirt; I wasn't offended by the sex qua sex; I wasn't worrying about a potential future erosion of my own rights; I didn't feel the President's pain in the empathic way he'd once claimed to feel mine; I wasn't repelled by the revelation that public officials do bad things; and although I'm a registered Democrat, my disgust was of a different order from my partisan disgust at the news that the Giants had blown a fourth-quarter lead. What I felt I felt personally. I was being intruded on.

4   A couple of days later, I got a call from one of my credit-card providers, asking me to confirm two recent charges at a gas station and one at a hardware store. Such queries are common nowadays, but this one was my first, and for a moment I felt eerily exposed. At the same time, I was perversely flattered that someone, somewhere, had taken an interest in me and had bothered to phone. Not that the young male operator seemed to care about me personally. He sounded as if he were reading his lines from a laminated booklet. The strain of working hard at a job he almost certainly didn't enjoy seemed to thicken his tongue. He tried to rush his words out, to speed through them as if in embarrassment or vexation at how nearly worthless they were, but they kept bunching up in this teeth, and he had to stop and extract them with his lips, one by one. It was the computer, he said, the computer that routinely, ah, scans the, you

know, the pattern of charges . . . and was there something else he could help me with tonight? I decided that if this young person wanted to scroll through my charges and ponder the significance of my two fill-ups and my gallon of latex paint I was fine with it.

5   So here's the problem. On the Saturday morning the Starr report came out, my privacy was, in the classic liberal view, absolute. I was alone in my home and unobserved, unbothered by neighbors, unmentioned in the news, and prefectly free, if I chose, to ignore the report and do the pleasantly *al dente* Saturday crossword; yet the report's mere existence so offended my sense of privacy that I could hardly bring myself to touch the thing. Two days later, I was disturbed in my home by a ringing phone, asked to cough up my mother's maiden name, and made aware that the digitized minutiae of my daily life were being scrutinized by strangers; and within five minutes I'd put the entire episode out of my mind. I felt encroached on when I was ostensibly safe, and I felt safe when I was ostensibly encroached on. And I didn't know why.

6   The right to privacy—defined by Louis Brandeis and Samuel Warren, in 1890, as "the right to be let alone"—seems at first glance to be an elemental principle in American life. It's the rallying cry of activists fighting for reproductive rights, against stalkers, for the right to die, against a national health-care database, for stronger data-encryption standards, against paparazzi, for the sanctity of employee E-mail, and against employee drug testing. On closer examination, though, privacy proves to be the Cheshire cat of values: not much substance, but a very winning smile.

7   Legally, the concept is a mess. Privacy violation is the emotional core of many crimes, from stalking and rape to Peeping Tommery and trespass, but no criminal statute forbids it in the abstract. Civil law varies from state to state but generally follows a forty-year-old analysis by the legal scholar Dean William Prosser, who dissected the invasion of privacy into four torts: *intrusion* on my solitude; the publishing of *private facts* about me which are not of legitimate public concern; publicity that puts my character in a *false light;* and *appropriation* of my name or likeness without my consent. This is a crumbly set of torts. Intrusion looks like trespass, false light like defamation, and appropriation like theft; and the harm that remains when these extraneous offenses are subtracted is so admirably captured by the phrase "infliction of emotional distress" as to render the tort of private invasion all but superfluous. What really undergirds privacy is the classic liberal conception of personal autonomy. In the last few decades, many judges and scholars have chosen to speak of a "zone of privacy," rather than a "sphere of liberty," but this is a shift in emphasis, not in substance: not the making of a new doctrine but the remarketing of an old one.

8   Whatever you're trying to sell, whether it's luxury real estate or Esperanto lessons, it helps to have the smiling word "private" on your side. Last winter, as the owner of a Bank One Platinum Visa card, I was offered enrollment in a program called PrivacyGuard®, which, according to the literature promoting it, "*puts you in the know* about the very personal records available to your employer,

insurers, credit card companies and government agencies." The first three months of PrivacyGuard® were free, so I signed up. What came in the mail then was paperwork: envelopes and request forms for various record searches, also a disappointingly undeluxe logbook in which to jot down the search results. I realized immediately that I didn't care enough about, say, my driving records to wait a month to get them; it was only when I called PrivacyGuard® to cancel my membership, and was all but begged not to, that I realized the whole point of this "service" was to harness my time and energy to the task of reducing Bank One Visa's fraud losses.

9   Even issues that legitimately touch on privacy are rarely concerned with the actual emotional harm of unwanted exposure or intrusion. A proposed national Genetic Privacy Act, for example, is premised on the idea that my DNA reveals more about my identity and my future health than other medical data do. In fact, DNA is as yet no more intimately revealing than a heart murmur, a family history of diabetes, or an inordinate fondness for Buffalo chicken wings. As with any medical records, the potential for abuse of genetic information by employers and insurers is chilling, but this is only tangentially a privacy issue; the primary harm consists of things like job discrimination and higher insurance premiums. In a similar way, the problem of on-line security is mainly about nuts and bolts. What American activists call "electronic privacy" their European counterparts call "data protection." Our term is exciting; theirs is accurate. If someone is out to steal your Amex number and expiration date, or if an evil ex-boyfriend is looking for your new address, or if you're plotting a leveraged buyout of Texaco, you need the kind of hard-core secrecy that encryption seeks to guarantee. If you're talking to a friend on the phone about how much you hate "The English Patient," however, you need only a *feeling* of privacy (unless you work for Miramax).

10   The social drama of data protection goes something like this: a hacker or an insurance company or a telemarketer gains access to a sensitive database, public-interest watchdogs bark loudly, and few firewalls go up. Just as most people are moderately afraid of germs but leave virology to the Centers for Disease Control, most Americans take a reasonable interest in privacy issues but leave the serious custodial work to experts. Our problem now is that the custodians have started speaking a language of panic and treating privacy not as one of many competing values but as the one value that trumps all others.

11   The novelist Richard Powers recently declared in a *Times* Op-Ed piece that privacy is a "vanishing illusion" and that the struggle over the encryption of digital communications is therefore as "great with consequence" as the Cold War. Powers defines "the private" as "that part of life that goes unregistered," and he sees in the digital footprints we leave whenever we charge things the approach of "that moment when each person's every living day will become a Bloomsday, recorded in complete detail and reproducible with a few deft keystrokes." It is scary, of course, to think that the mystery of our identities might be reducible to finite data sequences. That Powers can seriously compare credit-card fraud and intercepted cell-phone calls to the threat of thermonuclear incineration, however, speaks mainly to the infectiousness of privacy panic. Where, after all, is it "registered" what Powers or anybody else is thinking, seeing, saying, wishing,

planning, dreaming, or feeling ashamed of? A digital "Ulysses" consisting of nothing but a list of its hero's purchases and other recordable transactions might run, at most, to four pages: was there really nothing more to Bloom's day?

12   When Americans do genuinely sacrifice privacy, moreover, they do so for tangible gains in health or safety or efficiency. Most legalized infringements— H.I.V. notification, airport X-rays, Megan's Law, Breathalyzer roadblocks, the drug-testing of student athletes, laws protecting fetuses, laws protecting the vegetative, remote monitoring of automobile emissions, county-jail strip searches, even Ken Starr's cleansing exposure of Presidential corruption—are essentially public-health measures. I resent the security cameras in Washington Square Park, but I appreciate the ones on a subway platform. The risk that someone is abusing my E-Z Pass toll records seems to me comfortably low in comparison with my gain in convenience. Ditto the risk that someone will make me a victim of the First Amendment; with two hundred and seventy million people in the country, my own chances of being nationally exposed are next to nil.

13   The legal scholar Lawrence Lessig has characterized Americans as "bovine" for making calculations like this and for thereby acquiescing in what he calls the "Sovietization" of personal life. The curious thing about privacy, though, is that simply by expecting it we can usually achieve it. One of my neighbors in the apartment building across the street spends a lot of time at her mirror examining her pores, and I can see her doing it, just as she can undoubtedly see me sometimes. But our respective privacies remain intact as long as neither of us *feels* seen. When I send a postcard through the U.S. mail, I'm aware in the abstract that mail handlers may be reading it, may be reading it aloud, may even be laughing at it, but I'm safe from all harm, unless, by sheer bad luck, the one handler in the country whom I actually know sees the postcard and slaps his forehead and says, "Oh, jeez, I know this guy."

14   Our privacy isn't merely exaggerated. It's founded on a fallacy. Ellen Alderman and Caroline Kennedy, in "The Right to Privacy," sum up the conventional wisdom of privacy advocates like this: "There is less privacy than there used to be." The claim has been made or implied so often, in so many books and editorials and talk-show dens, that Americans, no matter how passive they are in their behavior, now dutifully tell pollsters that they're very much worried about privacy. From almost any historical perspective, however, the claim seems bizarre.

15   In 1890, an American typically lived in a small town under conditions of near-panoptical surveillance. Not only did his every purchase "register" but it registered in the eyes and in the memory of shopkeepers who knew him, his parents, his wife, and his children. He couldn't so much as walk to the post office without having his movements tracked and analyzed by neighbors. Probably he grew up sleeping in a bed with his siblings and possibly with his parents, too. Unless he was well-off, his transportation—a train, a horse, his own two feet—either was communal or exposed him to the public eye.

16   In the suburbs and exurbs where the typical American lives today, tiny nuclear families inhabit enormous houses, in which each person has his or her own bedroom and, sometimes, bathroom. Compared even with suburbs in the

sixties and seventies, when I was growing up, the contemporary condominium development or gated community offers a striking degree of anonymity. It's no longer the rule that you know your neighbors. Communities increasingly tend to be virtual, the participants either faceless or firmly in control of the faces they present. Transportation is largely private: the latest S.U.V.s are the size of living rooms and come with onboard telephones, CD players, and TV screens; behind the tinted windows of one of these high-riding, I-see-you-but-you-can't-see-me mobile PrivacyGuard® units, a person can be wearing pajamas or a licorice bikini, for all anybody knows or cares. Maybe the government intrudes on the family a little more than it did a hundred years ago (social workers look in on the old and the poor, health officials require inoculations, the police inquire about spousal battery), but from a privacy perspective these intrusions don't begin to make up for the small-town snooping they've replaced.

17   "The right to be let alone"? Far from disappearing, it's exploding. It's the essence of modern American architecture, landscape, transportation, communications, and mainstream political philosophy. The real reason that Americans are passive about privacy is so big as to be almost invisible: we're flat-out *drowning* in privacy.

FOR ANALYSIS AND DISCUSSION

1. Why, according to Franzen, is privacy legally a "mess"? Cite examples that he gives to support this statement. Do you agree with him?
2. In paragraph 8, Franzen relates his experience with "PrivacyGuard®." Does PrivacyGuard® appear to really protect privacy? Do you have any experience with such a "credit protection" program? If so, compare your experience with Franzen's. How does this story support his overall argument?
3. Franzen comments that when Americans do sacrifice privacy, it is for good reason and for the public health. Evaluate this statement. Do you agree? How do you think Andrew Shapiro and Gore Vidal would respond to this comment?
4. In paragraph 10, Franzen states that people are so caught up with privacy issues that they are treating privacy "not as one of many competing values but as the one value that trumps all others." What might be the other values to which Franzen alludes? What values are important to you? Where does privacy appear on this list? Explain.
5. Why, according to Franzen, is our privacy panic founded on a fallacy (paragraph 15)? How does he support this statement? Do you agree?
6. "Bloomsday" (June 16) commemorates a day in the life of Leopold Bloom, the main character in Irish novelist James Joyce's masterwork, *Ulysses*. In the book, Joyce traces the journey Bloom takes through Dublin over a 19-hour period on June 16, 1904. Every place he stopped, whom he spoke with, and even where he ate and drank is documented in excruciating detail. Franzen relates novelist Richard Powers's fear that our lives are becoming Bloomsdays, in which we leave digital footprints everywhere. Do you agree with this assessment? How do we leave digital footprints?

WRITING ASSIGNMENTS: RIGHT TO PRIVACY

1. What are your privacy rights? Go to the Privacy Rights Clearinghouse Web site at <http://www.privacyrights.org> for fact sheets on privacy and your privacy rights. Write an argument essay in which you explore your views on privacy rights in American society.
2. While some authors in this section imply that we are subjected to more invasions of privacy than ever before, others infer that we are more anonymous now than we were a century ago. What are your impressions of this issue? Interview fellow students, parents, grandparents, and older relatives and ask them for their views on privacy. Assess whether we have more or less privacy today. Then, in an argument essay, address how Americans feel about privacy.
3. In the last essay in this section, Jonathan Franzen states that the infringements on our privacy are a small price to pay for the protections we enjoy. Compile a list of ways in which you sacrifice your privacy. You might include airport security checks, locker searchers, and even having to produce identification to pay with a check. Is this forfeiture of privacy rights justifiable? Write an argument essay in which you assess the costs and benefits of privacy loss.

STUDENTS AND DRUG TESTING: OFFENSE OR DEFENSE?

High Court Takes on School Athletes and Drug Testing
George Will

In 1991 James Acton tried out for his school's seventh-grade football team. His parents refused to sign a drug testing consent form for their son and he was banned from participating in any school sports. The Vernonia, Oregon, School District admitted there was no evidence that Acton had used drugs, but argued that the mandatory drug testing program for student athletes was necessary because drugs were causing major disciplinary problems at the school. The case was brought to the Supreme Court, which, at the time this article was written, upheld the right of the school to impose the drug testing. In this essay, George Will supports the court's decision, reasoning that such policies are necessary in today's culture, where drugs are closely connected to violent juvenile crime.

Pulitzer Prize-winning columnist George Will is the author, most recently, of *The Woven Figure: Conservatism and America's Fabric, 1994–1997* (1997) and *Bunts: Curt Flood, Camden Yards, Pete Rose and Other Reflections on Baseball* (1998). Will wrote this article for the Washington Post Writers Group in 1995.

BEFORE YOU READ

Should students have the same rights as adults? What message might be sent to students when they are randomly tested for drugs?

AS YOU READ

What constitutes a "reasonable" cause for implementing a drug-testing policy in a school? Is it the suspicion of a problem, discipline issues connected to the school's drug culture, protection of students who don't know better, or deterrent qualities associated with random drug testing?

1   The question before the Supreme Court was whether an appellate judge was correct when he said, "Children are compelled to attend school but nothing suggests that they lose their right to privacy in their excretory functions when they do so." By a 6–3 vote the court decided on Monday that the public school athletes voluntarily compromise that right in Vernonia, Ore.

2   In the late 1980s Vernonia teachers and administrators became alarmed by a boastful, flaunting embrace of drugs by students who became increasingly rude, profane and disruptive. Authorities noted that athletes, who often loom large in the lives of small towns, were leaders of the drug culture. And authorities worried about drug use increasing the risk of sports injuries. In addition to psychological effects on motivation, drugs can impair judgment, slow reaction time, mask pain, interfere with the body's normal fatigue responses, and increase heart rate and blood pressure.

3   So the school district instituted a policy of random urinalysis drug testing of all athletes. But James Acton, then a seventh-grader eager to play football, objected, arguing that the testing violates the Constitution's Fourth Amendment protection against "unreasonable searches."

4   So, what is "reasonable"? Vernonia's policy is, says the court. Speaking through Justice Scalia, whose opinion was joined by Justices Rehnquist, Kennedy, Thomas, Ginsburg and Breyer, the court noted that it is settled law that such testing constitutes a search. Reasonableness is judged by balancing the intrusiveness of a search against the promotion of a legitimate governmental interest, which the prevention of drug use by children surely is.

5   Unemancipated minors do not enjoy all the rights of adults, particularly in the context of a school acting somewhat in loco parentis, charged with inculcating civility. Students are routinely required to have vaccinations and physical examinations. And regarding non-compulsory participation in athletics, Scalia says: "School sports are not for the bashful." Athletes commonly submit to regulations and codes of conduct. So, "We find insufficient basis to contradict the judgment of Vernonia's parents, its school board, and the district court, as to what was reasonably in the interest of these children under the circumstances."

6   Justice O'Connor, dissenting and joined by Justices Stevens and Souter (appointees of Reagan, Ford and Bush, respectively), says the record in this case does not demonstrate that there was a drug problem at Acton's particular school. So much for trusting the judgment of the community and its institu-

tions. O'Connor says that Fourth Amendment law generally forbids broad "searches" of whole groups (in this case, athletes). Individualized suspicion is required to justify searches. She quotes a 1925 Supreme Court ruling:

7   "It would be intolerable and unreasonable if a prohibition agent were authorized to stop every automobile on the chance of finding liquor and thus subject all persons lawfully using the highways to the inconvenience and indignity of such a search."

8   But adult drivers have different rights than students, especially the subcategory of voluntary student athletes. Furthermore, O'Connor concedes that the record "demonstrates there was a drug-related discipline problem in Vernonia of 'epidemic proportions.' " The Oxford English Dictionary defines "epidemic" as "widely prevalent, universal." So what is wrong with a testing program that targets a category of persons—athletes—most identified with something "widely prevalent," persons who can avoid testing by avoiding non-compulsory athletic activity?

9   O'Connor would have the district deal with its drug problem, which she says the record showed to be "of epidemic proportions" (epidemic, but not proven to have touched Acton's school?), by focusing testing on students whose behavior is disruptive or otherwise suspicious. She says breezily that "any distress arising from what turns out to be a false accusation can be minimized by keeping the entire process confidential."

10   What America is she living in? The real America is full of people as litigious as Acton, people encouraged by court rulings to be exquisitely sensitive about their rights and dismissive of the judgments of local authorities. In this America, false accusations breed lawsuits, so O'Connor's suggestion is a recipe for causing the district to back off and live with its epidemic.

11   Time was when the discipline problems in American schools concerned running in the halls and cutting classes. But Vernonia is in today's America, where rights are trumps and seventh-graders get lawyers and local authorities get no respect. Which just may have something to do with the fact that the Vernonia school district, which is not unlike thousands of others, has a handbook in which the list of disciplinary "problem areas" includes "recklessly endangering," "weapons," "extortion," "arson" and "explosive devices."

FOR ANALYSIS AND DISCUSSION

1. What position does Will take on the drug-testing issue? What reasons does he use to support his position? Do you find them convincing? Explain.
2. Why do you think Will points out who appointed each of the dissenting Supreme Court Justices (paragraph 6)? Explain.
3. Is the comparison of testing students for drugs and stopping automobiles to check for liquor an equitable one? Is this comparison indeed parallel?
4. Answer the question Will raises in paragraph 8: "So what is wrong with a testing program that targets a category of persons—athletes . . . ?" Formulate your response as if you were responding directly to Will.
5. Does Vernonia represent "today's America"? Compare the situation in Vernonia as described by Will to your own school experience. Do you agree with Will's closing comments?

Testing for Drugs, Witches, and Leftover Milk
Gary Natriello

After the *Vernonia School District v. Acton* Supreme Court decision, many other school districts soon followed suit, requiring their athletes to consent to random drug testing. In this essay, educator and sociologist Gary Natriello questions this policy and the deeper issues it raises.

Gary Natriello teaches sociology and education at Teachers College, Columbia University. He is the author or coauthor of several books including *From Cashbox to Classroom: The Struggle for Fiscal Reform and Educational Change in New Jersey* (1997). The following article first appeared in the *Teachers College Record,* of which Natriello is an editor, in 1995.

BEFORE YOU READ

Is there a difference between random drug testing by lottery and selective drug testing of individuals suspected of using drugs? Is one method of testing more fair than the other? Explain.

AS YOU READ

Evaluate Natriello's comparison between witch hunting and drug testing. How does he use the concept of the witch hunt to support his argument against drug testing?

1   In its recent decision in the case of the *Vernonia School District* v. *Acton,* the U.S. Supreme Court upheld the right of a local school district to require student athletes to submit to random drug testing as a condition of being allowed to play interscholastic sports. The case involved a policy developed in response to teacher and administrator observations of a sharp increase in drug use in the late 1980s. The policy requires students participating in sports to sign a form consenting to the testing and to obtain the written consent of their parents. All athletes are tested at the beginning of the season, and once each week of the season 10 percent of the athletes are selected for testing by having their names blindly drawn from a "pool" by a student under the supervision of two adults.

2   Writing for the six-judge majority, Justice Antonin Scalia argued that the policy was reasonable and therefore constitutional. First, he argued that privacy rights were less for schoolchildren than for others and even less in the case of student athletes who by choosing to join a team voluntarily subject themselves to even more regulation than students in general. Second, he argued that the policy served the school district's important and perhaps compelling interest in deterring drug use. Writing for the minority, Justice Sandra Day O'Connor noted that mass searches conducted in the absence of particular suspicion have generally been deemed unreasonable and that the collection and testing of urine, compelled and monitored by the state, is both destructive of privacy and offensive to personal dignity.

3   In his recent book, *Testing Testing: Social Consequences of the Examined Life,* F. Allan Hanson describes the test for witches employed in the fifteenth, sixteenth, and seventeenth centuries.[1] The procedure, known as "swimming a witch," involved tying a suspect's right thumb to left big toe and left thumb to right big toe and then lowering the suspect into the water with a rope tied around the waist. The test was repeated three times, and floating was taken as proof of witchcraft, though Hanson notes that in southwest Germany in the 1640s, sinking was interpreted as the sign of guilt.

4   The two cases are not quite parallel. Although both are attempts to deal with threats to the community from agreed upon evils (drugs and witchcraft), both involve community participation (the blind drawing by a student and the escorting of the suspect to the water), and both are relatively intrusive (the collection of urine and the tying and dunking in water), there are differences. In the case of testing for witches the test was applied only to those suspected of practicing witchcraft. The Vernonia School District has adopted, and the U.S. Supreme Court has ruled constitutional, a policy which applies drug testing to all student athletes regardless of whether there is any prior reason to suspect them of drug use.

5   The policy upheld by the Supreme Court in the *Vernonia* case, if implemented in school districts more broadly, threatens to damage the very kind of community interests that the policy intends to reinforce. Such threats take a variety of forms. First, they involve the relationship between educators and those students in their care. Teachers and students can and often do form close working relationships as they pursue common interests. Such working relationships and the trust that they breed are a particular benefit of student and faculty participation in interscholastic athletics. But a policy that makes the school the venue for what is essentially a police action and educators enforcement agents for drug laws creates a climate in which the growth of trust is unlikely. Enactment of the policy demeans the student athletes who are tested without suspicion and diminishes the incentive for students to behave in ways that place them above suspicion. It also compromises the role of educators, preventing them from demonstrating to students that they can be deemed trustworthy.

6   Second, the policy of requiring parental consent to random drug testing as a condition of participation in interscholastic athletics poses a serious threat to the relationship between students and parents. Parents who refuse to grant their consent are cast as obstacles to student athletic participation, with immediate negative consequences for both students and parents. Perhaps more seriously, parents who grant their consent can only be viewed in the longer term as concurring in the school district lack of trust in their children. The policy of requiring parental consent to an act demeaning to the character of their children as the price for allowing students to participate in what might be very beneficial to school-sponsored activities places parents in an untenable situation. No matter what parents do, the outcome is likely to be a weakened relationship with their children.

7   The third relationship threatened by the implementation of the drug testing policy is the relationship between a student's deeds and word that is at the

very heart of the kind of personal integrity that parents and schools should try to instill and students should strive to develop. Drug testing elicits information on drug usage that students know and could be asked. Random drug testing in the absence of prior suspicion most assuredly does two things: it reveals whether a student has used drugs and it devalues the word of each student subjected to the testing. It is difficult to teach students the value of their word if no value is placed on it by the adults and institutions around them. The lesson of random drug testing without prior suspicion is the lesson of the insignificance of one's words, one's personal integrity. It is a lesson not easily forgotten.

8   In the spring of 1961 I was nearing the end of third grade, a year when I had the great good fortune to be taught by a wonderful creative and dynamic teacher who, even in hindsight it seems, must have invested a great deal of energy in preparing lessons. One day this third-grade class was confronted with a dilemma. Each day after our mid-morning snack we would dispose of our empty milk boxes in a large galvanized tub set out by the custodian only for these containers. Students were to drink all of their milk and place only empty boxes in the container. On this particular day the custodian reported to the teacher that someone had placed a container half-full of milk in the tub, and it had subsequently run from the box and dirtied the entire tub.

9   The teacher asked for the student who had left milk in the box to come forward, but no one did. After several more such requests, the teacher announced that she would conduct a test, a scientific procedure to identify the offender. She lined everyone up in front of the room. When we were all standing in a line, she began at one end checking pulses by placing her fingers against each student's wrist. As she checked the first few students she explained that the guilty student would have a fast pulse. Standing about in the middle of the line of students, I remember wondering whether the culprit was in front of me or behind me and really just wanting the event to be over. As the teacher moved down the line, student after student in front of me was exonerated and allowed to sit down. The teacher seemed to have no difficulty determining the innocence of these students. As my turn drew near I began to wonder which of the students after me in line would be caught. I never found out, because in another minute the teacher had checked my pulse, determined that it was fast, and concluded that I had left the half-full box in the tub. The test was over, those after me in line were never examined, and I was never directly asked if I had done the awful deed. I do not recall what happened next; I do not remember the punishment; apparently I will always remember the test.

10   Justice Scalia's opinion for the majority includes the argument that legitimate privacy expectations are less for student athletes than for other students because school sports, which require students to use public locker rooms to change and shower, are not notable for their privacy. But the issue of the violation of physical privacy by the collection of urine in the absence of prior suspicion is less important than the violation of the personal integrity of those not previously suspected of drug use entailed in rejecting their word, indeed in not even considering their word and previous deeds as legitimate sources of information.

11   The Supreme Court's decision is justified in part by the threat posed to student athletes, other students, and the entire educational process by drug use. Districts considering policies such as that of *Vernonia* should weigh the threat posed by the policy itself to the relations between students and staff, the relations between students and parents, and to the development of student personal integrity.

NOTES

1. F. Allan Hanson, *Testing Testing: Social Consequences of the Examined Life* (Berkeley: University of California Press, 1993), pp. 36–38.

FOR ANALYSIS AND DISCUSSION

1. Evaluate the title of this essay. How does it set up the reader's expectations for what is to follow? How well does the title connect to the actual content of the article?
2. In the *Vernonia School District v. Acton* decision, Supreme Court Justice Antonin Scalia argued that "privacy rights [are] less for schoolchildren" (paragraph 2). Consider the term "schoolchildren." Does it fit the profile of the students who face drug testing? Do you think Scalia's use of such terminology helped him argue his point? Explain.
3. What exactly is a "witch hunt?" What parallels exist between a witch hunt and random drug testing? Do you agree with Natriello's analogy?
4. How does Natriello support his argument? What details does he uncover for inspection? Consider, for example, the point he makes in paragraph 5, that drug testing forces educators to be police officers. Evaluate this point and the others that follow.
5. What is the objective behind drug testing of athletes (and all students in general)? Are athletes the right population to single out for testing for drug abuse?

Naïve Court Didn't Go Far Enough with Drug Testing
Claude Lewis

Most people will agree that teens and drugs are a bad mix. Drug use impairs academic and athletic performance, encourages antisocial behavior, and may even lead to crime. In response, some schools are turning to mandatory drug testing of athletes to curtail the problem. In this essay Claude Lewis says drug testing shouldn't be limited to athletes; all students should be randomly tested for drugs, for their own safety as well as that of the general population.

Claude Lewis has worked as a writer and editor for *Newsweek,* the *New York Herald Tribune,* and the *Philadelphia Inquirer* for more than 40 years. He is also the founder of the National Association of Black Journalists and the author of six books, including biographies of Adam Clayton Powell and Muhammad Ali. Now technically retired, he still writes a column twice a month for the *Philadelphia Inquirer.* The following article appeared in the *Sacramento Bee* on June 30, 1995.

BEFORE YOU READ

Would you sign a random drug testing agreement with your school's athletic department in order to play sports?

AS YOU READ

Consider the author's use of the first person in this essay. How does using the first person influence the audience's reception of his argument? Is this an effective way to reach his readers?

1   This nation has so badly botched the war on drugs that I find myself in painful agreement with a Supreme Court ruling that public schools can require students to take drug tests as a condition of playing sports.

2   Indeed, my concern for an end to the devastation of drug abuse and addiction is so great that I find myself wondering why such tests should be restricted to athletes. Why not apply the pain all at once and permit random testing of all students? If such draconian solutions are necessary, why single out those who play sports? What about the millions of other students who don't? Should they not be required to undergo random drug tests?

3   Random drug testing is the antithesis of a free society. Yet, I am persuaded that since the drug problem is so pervasive, destructive and corrupt, and since the government has failed so miserably for so long in ending its corrosive effects, we have few alternatives other than poking our noses in places where they don't belong.

4   When it comes to drugs, we have reached a point where the only cure may have to be worse than the disease. We "must" take the strongest possible action to protect the young and the unsuspecting.

5   Most Americans have never seen firsthand the powerful and depraved activity in the world of illicit drugs. I have talked with addicts for years and have witnessed the demise and deaths of countless young men and women who were unable to end their enslavement.

6   I have seen young people with old faces, the result of persistent experimenting with drugs. Because government has failed at containing addiction and our nation has no sure method of treating the army of addicts living among us, extreme measures must be adopted.

7   No longer is it possible, if it ever was, to accept the pathetic lie that drug addicts exist mainly in the inner city. The problem has grown so great that in almost any community, children and errant adults can locate drugs within a half-hour of their homes.

8   If the court's decision is, as some say, a victory, it is one of the saddest victories I can imagine. It is distressing that we must resort to limiting Fourth Amendment privacy rights to student athletes in order to protect them from the danger of drugs. Students spend more time in school than in any other institution outside their homes. And it is the school where initial exposure to illegal drugs often takes place.

9   The irony in all this is that it is not the students who have failed, but the adults who are responsible for them. In Washington, the court's ruling was met with wide acceptance among young athletes.

10   Others argue if there's no reason to suspect illegal drug use, students should not be subjected to random testing. Such notions were valid in another era. No more.

11   How else do we begin to get at the problem? Drug education is good but won't provide a total solution. Education must be a part of the solution along with other firm approaches. Few of us come new to this problem. America is one of the world's most drug-dependent nations and the problem threatens to grow worse.

12   An enormous number of crimes committed every year—from petty thefts to bank robberies to murders—are connected to addiction.

13   Supreme Court Justice Sandra Day O'Connor holds a naïve notion on the matter, calling the collection of urine samples "particularly destructive of privacy and offensive to personal dignity."

14   What could be more offensive to personal dignity than addiction itself? The court's ruling may contain some frightening implications, but not nearly as frightening as the growing new armies of addicts who will poison the future of many young people for generations.

FOR ANALYSIS AND DISCUSSION

1. Is drug testing a deterrent to drug use? If students knew they might be tested, would they think twice before using drugs? Explain.

2. In paragraph 4, Lewis says that drug testing is necessary to "protect the young and the unsuspecting." Do today's high school students fit this description? How would you respond to Lewis's statement?

3. If most Americans have "never seen" the world of illicit drugs (paragraph 5), is drug testing really needed? Or is it necessary only for some areas and some groups, such as athletes? How might Lewis's statement be used to argue *against* his point?

4. Evaluate Lewis's tone. Is it angry, militant, resigned, sad? How does his tone contribute to the message of his argument?

5. Why does Lewis think the Supreme Court's decision is "one of the saddest victories [he] can imagine (paragraph 8)? Do you agree? Explain your viewpoint.

6. In paragraph 11, Lewis asks, "How else do we begin to get at the drug problem?" Does he offer any solutions? Does he think drug testing is the solution?

7. What is your overall impression of this essay? Does it get its point across? If you were able to speak to Lewis, how would you respond to his comments?

Just Say No to Random Drug Testing
David Rocah

In 1997 the American Civil Liberties Union (ACLU) filed suit against the Ridge-field Park Board of Education on behalf of Bryan Wilson, a Ridgefield Park High School student. Wilson had played on the football team during his first two years of high school but was barred from continuing because he refused to agree to random drug testing. In the following essay David Rocah, representing the ACLU, explains why the ACLU felt compelled to defend this case, which was never tried. In 1998 the Ridgefield Park Board of Education agreed to rescind the policy following the opinion of Judge Sybil R. Moses, who found that the school district had no evidence of a more severe drug problem among student athletes, and thus had not demonstrated a sufficient need for the random drug testing program. The policy could be reimplemented, however, if a serious drug problem among students is ever demonstrated.

David Rocah is a staff attorney with the American Civil Liberties Union of New Jersey. The following article was published online in 1998 on the ACLU's Web site, *Voices of Liberty.*

BEFORE YOU READ

Is random drug testing an invasion of privacy? Does it involve a loss of dignity? Should it be tolerated as a necessary deterrent to drug use in today's society?

AS YOU READ

Does drug testing assume guilt until innocence is proven? How does drug testing apply to the rights guaranteed U.S. citizens by the Constitution? Does the Bill of Rights apply to the drug testing of students?

> In our system, state-operated schools may not be enclaves of total-itarianism. School officials do not possess absolute authority over their students. Students in school as well as out of school are "persons" under our Constitution.
> —Justice Abe Fortas, *Tinker v. Des Moines* (1969)

1   Ridgefield Park, like at least nine other school districts in New Jersey, recently decided that it would not permit its junior and senior high school students to participate in interscholastic sports unless they agreed to have their urine tested for traces of certain illicit drugs at random intervals during the athletic season. Because we believe that this intrusive and demeaning search of students' bodily fluids violates fundamental constitutional principles, the American Civil Liberties Union of New Jersey is representing a student and his parents in a legal challenge to the Ridgefield Park program.

2   One of the fundamental features of our legal system is that we are presumed innocent of any wrongdoing unless and until the government proves otherwise. Random drug testing of student athletes turns this presumption on its head, telling students that we assume they are using drugs until they prove to the contrary with a urine sample. The overwhelming majority of student athletes in Ridgefield Park, and throughout New Jersey, are law abiding citizens, and there is no basis in law or logic to presume otherwise or to treat them worse than accused criminals.

3   An equally cherished constitutional command is the rule that government officials may not search us without an adequate reason. Thus, for example, even though we know there is a drug problem in our society, we do not allow the police to randomly stop us on the street to see if we are carrying drugs.

4   The constitutional prohibition against "unreasonable" searches also embodies the principle that merely belonging to a certain group is not a sufficient reason for a search, even if many members of that group are suspected of illegal activity. Thus, for example, even if it were true that most men with long hair were drug users, the police would not be free to stop all long haired men and search them for drugs.

5   Unfortunately, many school officials concerned about drug use by students seem willing to ignore these principles. There is no doubt that the concern is well placed, and it is one that we share. Drug use is a scourge on our society, exacting a terrible toll in lost lives. And no one is arguing that we should tolerate students' use of illegal drugs. But zero tolerance for drugs should not lead us to have zero tolerance for constitutional limits. Sadly, that is exactly what is happening.

6   Parents and school officials currently have a wide variety of tools at their disposal to address drug use by students. Educating students about the dangers of drug use can be highly effective. A recent study by the Parent's Resource Institute for Drug Education shows that students who are warned about drugs by their parents use them 30 percent less often than those who are not, and students who said their parents set "clear rules" regarding drugs used them 57 percent less than those whose parents did not.

7   In addition, school officials currently have the power to require any student whom they reasonably suspect of using drugs to submit to a drug test. Indeed, if the affidavits submitted in court by the Ridgefield Park School Board are to be believed, school officials there have been grossly irresponsible in failing to act when they had reason to suspect particular students were using drugs. Not only did they not conduct drug tests, there is no indication that they even informed the parents of their suspicions.

8   Acting on the basis of individual suspicion ensures both that hundreds of innocent children are not subjected to a degrading search, and demonstrates that school officials care about all students who use drugs, not just student athletes. The Board also could have implemented a truly voluntary drug testing program, rather than coercing parents to consent by denying their children the opportunity to participate in interscholastic athletics. Had the Board done so, it is likely that no one would have objected, and the ACLU could not and would not have challenged it.

9   Given these tools, which, when employed vigorously can be an effective and constitutional means of dealing with drug use by the entire student body, why are school districts resorting to random drug testing of athletes? Because they improperly read a 1995 U.S. Supreme Court decision as giving them carte blanche. In a case involving a school district in Vernonia, Oregon, the Court decided that the district could constitutionally require student athletes to submit to random drug testing where officials testified that they were no longer able to maintain discipline in the school system because of a culture of pervasive drug use and disrespect for authority, and where student athletes were the leaders of the drug culture.

10   Are the parents and administrators in Ridgefield Park prepared to admit that they cannot maintain order and discipline in their schools? There is no evidence of this, and we would be surprised if it were so. Ridgefield Park has a fine school system, which sent 73 percent of its graduates to college last year.

11   Are student athletes leaders of the drug culture? Although the Ridgefield Park School Board's court papers scandalously attempted to portray its student athletes as a pack of drug addled alcoholics, these same athletes won state championships in football for the past two years. Nationally, student athletes have been found to have higher academic achievement and fewer disciplinary problems than non-athletes, due in large part to the tremendous discipline required to balance a full academic program and the time demanded by practice and competition schedules. Singling out athletes in New Jersey because of a problem in Vernonia, Oregon, is both ridiculous and unfair.

12   School officials argue that random drug testing will deter drug use. But students should not use drugs because they are harmful and illegal, not because they might get caught. Moreover, random drug testing simply encourages students to defer drug use until after the athletic season is completed, rather than completely refraining from drug use.

13   School officials also argue that participating in interscholastic athletics is a privilege, not a right, and that they may therefore impose any conditions on the exercise of that privilege that they see fit. This ignores the well established constitutional doctrine that the government may not condition the receipt of a governmental benefit on the waiver of constitutional rights. Just as a school could not condition participation in interscholastic athletics on students giving up their right to free speech, they also may not condition participation on students giving up their right to be free from unreasonable searches.

14   Some also argue that students who aren't doing anything wrong have nothing to fear. This ignores the fact that what they fear is not getting caught, but the loss of dignity and trust that the drug test represents. And we should all be afraid of government officials who believe that a righteous cause warrants setting aside bedrock constitutional protections. The lesson that our schools should be teaching is respect for the Constitution and for students' dignity and privacy, not a willingness to treat cherished constitutional principles as mere platitudes.

FOR ANALYSIS AND DISCUSSION

1. Rocah comments that the "overwhelming majority of student athletes . . . are law abiding citizens, and there is no basis . . . to presume otherwise" (paragraph 2). If this is true, why do you think Ridgefield Park decided to implement a drug-testing policy? If this statement were not true, would it then be permissible to test students for drug abuse?
2. Do Fourth Amendment rights apply to students under 18 years of age? How do you think the different players in this lawsuit would respond to this question?
3. Evaluate Rocah's argument in paragraph 8. Can Rocah project what people will and will not object to? Does he make other statements in his article in which he anticipates group opinions? What effect does this have on his overall argument?
4. In your experience, are student athletes the leaders of the drug culture in academic institutions?
5. Rocah points out that 73 percent of Ridgefield Park's graduates went on to college in 1996. He also claims that student athletes have higher academic achievement rates than do nonathletes. How might these statements be red herrings? Do they strengthen or weaken Rocah's argument? Explain.

WRITING ASSIGNMENTS: STUDENTS AND DRUG TESTING

1. Ridgefield Park dropped its drug-testing policy when faced with a lawsuit. The school's football, coach, Tony Gonzalez, said that he was "one thousand percent in favor" of mandatory drug screening because it gave student-athletes a way to counter peer pressure to drink alcohol or do drugs at parties. "It gives them an out . . . they can say, if I get tested I lose football" (The *Record Online* at <http://www.bergen.com/bse/testps199809252.htm)>. Write an argument essay in which you address your views of mandatory drug testing from a student's perspective. Consider Gonzalez's comment when framing your evaluation.
2. Access the Family Research Council's Web site on keeping kids drug free at <http://www.frc.org/insight/is95g1dr.html>. How effective are the solutions there? Evaluate the Council's position on drug testing. Do you agree with its approach to keeping students free from drugs? Is the plan realistic? Imagine you have been asked to evaluate the program. Write a report in which you appraise the positive and negative aspects of the Council's plan.
3. From the standpoint of a school administrator, write a letter to parents in which you explain why the school will be implementing a mandatory drug-testing program for student athletes. Frame your argument, drawing from information gathered from the essays in this section, as well as from personal experience. How do you address the controversial aspects of this issue? What approach would you take to avoid the most conflict?

REGULATING RELATIONSHIPS

Our social and professional lives depend on a complex network of relationships with others. Most of the time we can rely on common sense, good manners, and mutually shared assumptions to provide guidelines for these relationships. Occasionally, however, understandings break down or traditional rules no longer apply. In such situations we often turn to legal or legislative remedies to clarify the nature of these relationships and, if necessary, to impose regulations on them. But regulating human behavior is a tricky business. Sometimes these measures solve the problem, and sometimes they complicate it even more. In this chapter we look at the questions and conflicts that arise when legal institutions rather than individuals create rules for personal relationships.

The first three writers engage in a spirited dialogue about the controversial subject of same-sex marriage. Should couples of the same gender be legally allowed to marry? What problems and benefits might result? In "Virtually Normal," Andrew Sullivan challenges the prohibition against the marriages of gay couples by asserting that such unions will strengthen and support the institution of the family in our society. James Q. Wilson disagrees and expresses the conservative view that homosexual marriage will, instead, damage the "moral convictions" of the American family and should therefore not be legalized. However, when Jonathan Rauch joins the discussion in "For Better or Worse?" he uses Wilson's own arguments to conclude that same-sex marriage should be a cause supported by conservatives because of its stabilizing influence on the lives of gay people.

Can our legal system create laws to effectively regulate the complex relationships between men and women? Ever since the confirmation hearings of Clarence Thomas for his appointment to the Supreme Court, lawyers, feminists, legal scholars, and politicians have struggled over how to apply the 1980 Title VII Guidelines on Sexual Harassment to real-life conflicts between the sexes. The second set of readings focuses on this perplexing issue. Richard Dooling, an employment discrimination lawyer, suggests that our current interpretation of sexual harassment guidelines is too broad and proposes limiting them to workplace discrimination cases. Daphne Patai takes us from the workplace to the college campus and exam-

550

ines the ways in which sexual harassment laws have detrimentally affected the university learning environment. Finally, Vicki Schultz argues that as a result of the emphasis on protecting women from unwanted sexual advances our legal system has failed to recognize "non-sexual forms of harassment" that victimize both men and women.

Do laws permitting the opening of sealed adoption records threaten the privacy of birth mothers and adoptees or allow them access to valuable information about themselves? The readings in the section on adoption provide many different answers to this question. Elizabeth Bartholet, a lawyer and an adoptive parent, carefully examines all sides of the open record question and suggests that the exchange of information among the adopted child, the adoptive parents, and the birth parents would provide benefits for all. Using his own experience as an adopted child, Rev. Thomas F. Brosnan expresses his frustration at a system of closed records that denies adopted children their identities. However, not all adoptees feel Brosnan's sense of outrage. Online Forum participants Anne Harvey, Bill Pierce, and Anne Babb offer insights into the complications and heartache that can result when records are opened against the wishes of the adopted child and family. This view is shared by the National Committee for Adoption, which advocates the rights of the adoptive family to keep adoption records sealed. Finally, Carol Schaefer, an activist in adoption reform who searched for and found the son she gave up for adoption, presents the perspective of the birth mother.

SAME SEX MARRIAGE: IS CURRENT SOCIAL POLICY FAIR?

Virtually Normal
Andrew Sullivan

Many homosexual couples closely pattern heterosexual life. They live together, buy houses in the suburbs, and raise children. These couples maintain that the natural capstone of their commitment and lifestyle is to legalize their relationships through marriage. Opponents of same-sex marriage, including people who are tolerant of homosexuality, say that marriage is and should remain a uniquely heterosexual institution. In his essay, Andrew Sullivan argues that marriage should be a legal option for gay couples who want it.

Andrew Sullivan is a senior editor of *The New Republic* magazine and author of *Virtually Normal: An Argument About Homosexuality* (1995), from which this essay was taken. An active proponent of same-sex marriage, Sullivan is also the editor of *Same Sex Marriage: Pro and Con: A Reader* (1997), a collection of essays addressing the history of same-sex marriage, the legal issues surrounding it, and the "why marry?" debate.

BEFORE YOU READ

Do you think that gay couples should be allowed to marry? Why or why not?

AS YOU READ

Consider how Sullivan argues his case. What support does he use to buttress his ideas? What assumptions does Sullivan make regarding his audience and their shared set of values?

1   The most common conservative argument against same-sex marriage is that the public acceptance of homosexuality subverts the stability and self-understanding of the heterosexual family. But here the conservative position undermines itself somewhat. Since most conservatives concede the presence of a number of involuntarily homosexual persons, they must also concede that these persons are already part of "heterosexual" families. They are sons and daughters, brothers and sisters, even mothers and fathers, of heterosexuals. The distinction between "families" and "homosexuals" is, to begin with, empirically false; and the stability of existing families is closely linked to how homosexuals are treated within them. Presumably, it is against the interest of heterosexual families to force homosexuals into roles they are not equipped to play and may disastrously perform. This is not an abstract matter. It is quite common that homosexual fathers and mothers who are encouraged into heterosexual marriages subsequently find the charade and dishonesty too great to bear: spouses are betrayed, children are abandoned, families are broken, and lives are ruined. It is also common that homosexual sons and daughters who are denied the love and support of their families are liable to turn against the institution of the family, to wound and destroy it, out of hurt and rejection. And that parents, inculcated in the kind of disdain of homosexuality conservatives claim is necessary to protect the family, react to the existence of gay children with unconscionable anger and pain, and actually help destroy loving families.

2   Still, conservatives may concede this and still say that it's worth it. The threat to the stability of the family posed by public disapproval of homosexuality is not as great as the threat posed by public approval. How does this argument work? Largely by saying that the lives saved by preventing wavering straights from becoming gay are more numerous than the lives saved by keeping gay people out of heterosexual relationships and allowing greater tolerance of gay members of families themselves; that the stability of the society is better served by the former than by the latter. Now, recall that conservatives are not attempting to assert absolute moral truths here. They are making an argument about social goods, in this case, social and familial stability. They are saying that a homosexual life is, on the face of it, worse than a heterosexual life, as far as society is concerned. In Harvard psychologist E. L. Pattullo's words,

> Though we acknowledge some influences—social and biological—beyond their control, we do not accept the idea that people of bad character had

no choice. Further, we are concerned to maintain a social climate that will steer them in the direction of the good.

3   The issue here is bad character and the implied association of bad character with the life of homosexuals. Although many conservatives feel loath to articulate what they mean by this life, it's clear what lies behind it. So if they won't articulate it, allow me. They mean by "a homosexual life" one in which emotional commitments are fleeting, promiscuous sex is common, disease is rampant, social ostracism is common, and standards of public decency, propriety, and self-restraint are flaunted. They mean a way of life that deliberately subverts gender norms in order to unsettle the virtues that make family life possible, ridicules heterosexual life, and commits itself to an ethic of hedonism, loneliness, and deceit. They mean by all this "the other," against which any norm has to be defended and any cohesive society protected. So it is clear that whatever good might be served by preventing gay people from becoming parents or healing internal wounds within existing families, it is greatly outweighed by the dangers of unleashing this kind of ethic upon the society as a whole.

4   But the argument, of course, begs a question. Is this kind of life, according to conservatives, what a homosexual life *necessarily* is? Surely not. If homosexuality is often indeed involuntary, as conservatives believe, then homosexuals are not automatically the "other"; they are sprinkled randomly throughout society, into families that are very much like anybody else's, with characters and bodies and minds as varied as the rest of humanity. If all humans beings are, as conservatives believe, subject to social inducements to lead better or worse lives, then there is nothing inevitable at all about a homosexual leading a depraved life. In some cases, he might even be a paragon of virtue. Why then is the choice of a waverer to live a homosexual rather than a heterosexual life necessarily a bad one, from the point of view of society? Why does it lead to any necessary social harm at all?

5   Of course, if you simply define "homosexual" as "depraved," you have an answer; but it's essentially a tautologous one. And if you argue that in our society at this time, homosexual lives simply *are* more depraved, you are also begging a question. There are very few social incentives of the kind conservatives like for homosexuals *not* to be depraved: there's little social or familial support, no institution to encourage fidelity or monogamy, precious little religious or moral outreach to guide homosexuals into more virtuous living. This is not to say that homosexuals are not responsible for their actions, merely that in a large part of homosexual subculture there is much a conservative would predict, when human beings are abandoned with extremely few social incentives for good or socially responsible behavior. But the proper conservative response to this is surely not to infer that this behavior is inevitable, or to use it as a reason to deter others from engaging in a responsible homosexual existence, if that is what they want; but rather to construct social institutions and guidelines to modify and change that behavior for the better. But that is what conservatives resolutely refuse to do.

6   Why? Maybe for conservatives, there is something inherent even in the most virtuous homosexual life that renders it less desirable than the virtuous heterosexual life, and therefore merits social discouragement to deter the wa-verers. Let's assume, from a conservative perspective, the best-case scenario for such a waverer: he can choose between a loving, stable, and responsible same-sex relationship and a loving, stable, and responsible opposite-sex relationship. Why should society preference the latter?

7   The most common response is along the lines of Hadley Arkes, the conser-vative commentator, who has written on this subject on occasion. It is that the heterosexual relationship is good for men not simply because it forces them to cooperate and share with other human beings on a daily basis but because it forces them into daily contact and partnership with *women:*

> It is not marriage that domesticates men; it is women. Left to themselves, these forked creatures follow a way of life that George Gilder once re-counted in its precise, chilling measures: bachelors were twenty-two times more likely than married men to be committed to hospitals for mental dis-ease (and ten times more likely to suffer chronic diseases of all kinds). Sin-gle men had nearly double the mortality rate of married men and three times the mortality rate of single women. Divorced men were three times more likely than divorced women to commit suicide or die by murder, and they were six times more likely to die of heart disease.

I will leave aside the statistical difficulties here: it's perfectly possible that many of the problems Arkes recounts were reasons why the men didn't get married, rather than consequences of their failing to do so. Let's assume, for the sake of argu-ment, that Arkes is right: that marriage to a woman is clearly preferable to being single for an adult man; that such a man is more likely to be emotionally stable, physically healthy, psychologically in balance; and that this is good for the society as a whole. There is in this argument a belief that women are naturally more prone to be stable, nurturing, supportive of stability, fiscally prudent, and family-oriented than men, and that their connection to as many men as possible is there-fore clearly a social good. Let's assume also, for the sake of argument, that Arkes is right about that too. It's obvious, according to conservatives, that society should encourage a stable opposite-sex relationship over a stable same-sex relationship.

8   But the waverer has another option: *he can remain single.* Should society actu-ally encourage him to do this rather than involve himself in a stable, loving same-sex relationship? Surely, even conservatives who think women are essential to the successful socialization of men would not deny that the discipline of domesticity, of shared duties and lives, of the inevitable give-and-take of cohabitation and love with anyone, even of the same sex, tends to benefit men more than the option of constant, free-wheeling, etiolating bachelorhood. But this would mean creating a public moral and social climate which preferred stable gay relationships to gay or straight bachelorhood. And it would require generating a notion of homosexual responsibility that would destroy the delicately balanced conservative politics of private discretion and undiscriminating public disapproval. So conservatives are

stuck again: their refusal to embrace responsible public support for virtuous homosexuals runs counter to their entire social agenda.

9   Arkes's argument also leads to another (however ironic) possibility destabilizing to conservatism's delicate contemporary compromise on the homosexual question: that for a wavering woman, a lesbian relationship might actually be socially *preferable* to a heterosexual relationship. If the issue is not mere domesticity but the presence of women, why would two women not be better than one, for the sake of children's development and social stability? Since lesbianism seems to be more amenable to choice than male homosexuality in most studies and surveys, conservatism's emphasis on social encouragement of certain behaviors over others might be seen as even more relevant here. If conservatism is about the social benefits of feminizing society, there is no reason why it should not be an integral part of the movement for women to liberate themselves completely from men. Of course, I'm being facetious; conservatives would be terrified by all the single males such a society would leave rampaging around. But it's not inconceivable at all from conservative premises that, solely from the point of view of the wavering woman, the ascending priorities would be: remaining single, having a stable, loving opposite-sex relationship, and having a stable, loving same-sex relationship. And there is something deliciously ironic about the sensibility of Hadley Arkes and E. L. Pattullo finding its full fruition in a lesbian collective.

10   Still, the conservative has another option. He might argue that removing the taboo on homosexuality would unravel an entire fabric of self-understanding in the society at large that could potentially destabilize the whole system of incentives for stable family relationships. He might argue that now, of all times, when families are in an unprecedented state of collapse, is not the occasion for further tinkering with this system; that the pride of heterosexual men and women is at stake; that their self-esteem and self-understanding would be undermined if society saw them as equivalent to homosexuals. In this view, the stigmatization of homosexuals is the necessary corollary to the celebration of traditional family life.

11   Does this ring true? To begin with, it's not at all clear why, if public disapproval of homosexuals is indeed necessary to keep families together, homosexuals of all people should bear the primary brunt of the task. But it's also not clear why the corollary really works to start with. Those homosexuals who have no choice at all to be homosexual, whom conservatives do not want to be in a heterosexual family in the first place, are clearly no threat to the heterosexual family. Why would accepting that such people exist, encouraging them to live virtuous lives, incorporating their difference into society as a whole, necessarily devalue the traditional family? It is not a zero-sum game. Because they have no choice but to be homosexual, they are not choosing that option over heterosexual marriage; and so they are not sending any social signals that heterosexual family life should be denigrated.

12   The more difficult case, of course, pertains to Arkes's "waverers." Would allowing them the option of a stable same-sex relationship as a preferable social

option to being single really undermine the institution of the family? Is it inconceivable that a society can be subtle in its public indications of what is and what is not socially preferable? Surely, society can offer a hierarchy of choices, which, while preferencing one, does not necessarily denigrate the others, but accords them some degree of calibrated respect. It does this in many other areas. Why not in sexual arrangements?

13   You see this already in many families with homosexual members. While some parents are disappointed that their son or daughter will not marry someone of the opposite sex, provide grandchildren and sustain the family line for another generation, they still prefer to see that child find someone to love and live with and share his or her life with. That child's siblings, who may be heterosexual, need feel no disapproval attached to their own marriage by the simple fact of their sibling's difference. Why should society as a whole find it an impossible task to share in the same maturity? Even in the most homosexualized culture, conservatives would still expect over eighty percent of couples to be heterosexual: why is their self-esteem likely to be threatened by a paltry twenty percent—especially when, according to conservatives, the homosexual life is so self-evidently inferior?

14   In fact, it's perfectly possible to combine a celebration of the traditional family with the celebration of a stable homosexual relationship. The one, after all, is modeled on the other. If constructed carefully as a conservative social ideology, the notion of stable gay relationships might even serve to buttress the ethic of heterosexual marriage, by showing how even those excluded from it can wish to model themselves on its shape and structure. This very truth, of course, is why liberationists are so hostile to the entire notion. Rather than liberating society from asphyxiating conventions it actually harnesses one minority group—homosexuals—and enlists them in the conservative structures that liberationists find so inimical. One can indeed see the liberationists' reasons for opposing such a move. But why should conservatives oppose it?

FOR ANALYSIS AND DISCUSSION

1. Sullivan comments that conservatives fear homosexual marriage because it could "injure" the institution of the family. What is the basis of this concern? How does Sullivan address it? Which perspective do you support, and why?

2. Evaluate Sullivan's description of the conservative definition of sexuality in paragraph 3. Do you agree that this is a commonly held definition? How would you define "homosexual life"?

3. Sullivan expends a lot of effort addressing the views of conservatives, often referring collectively to his opposition as "they." What effect does this terminology have on the reader? Explain.

4. What is the reason, according to the author, for homosexual "depravity" (paragraphs 3 through 5)? Does his discussion of this issue strengthen or weaken the goals of his essay?

5. In paragraph 7, Sullivan introduces the arguments of conservative Hadley Arkes. How does Sullivan use Arkes's argument to support his own? Does he

accurately evaluate Arkes's points? Do you agree with Sullivan's summary of Arkes's argument, that "conservatism is about the social benefits of feminizing society" (paragraph 9)? Explain.

6. What are "waverers"? What options do they have, according to Sullivan? How do these options apply to gay marriage?

7. How would different audiences receive this argument in favor of gay marriage? For example, would it be as effective in addressing a college audience as it would an older or more conservative audience? What factors could influence the successful reception of Sullivan's essay?

Against Homosexual Marriage
James Q. Wilson

Opponents of same-sex marriage believe that our culture must preserve the virtue of the heterosexual family. They argue that homosexuality is not a "normal" lifestyle, and that to permit gays to marry would be to legitimize and morally accept homosexuality. They also fear that tampering with the institution of marriage will further weaken it. That is the position of James Q. Wilson, who believes that marriage is something that cannot be altered without severe ramifications to the overall culture.

Political scientist James Q. Wilson is the James Collins Professor of Management and Public Policy at UCLA. He is the author of many books, including *The Moral Sense,* in which he examines the link between traditional ideas of morality and biology and socialization. The following essay was first published in the March 1996 issue of *Commentary.*

BEFORE YOU READ

Ideology is the set of values inherent in a culture or a group of people. What is the current moral ideology of U.S. society regarding marriage? Which values do Americans, as a whole, embrace, and which do they reject?

AS YOU READ

Review the discussion of Toulmin logic in Chapter 7. As you read, try to identify where Wilson applies elements of Toulmin logic in the essay. What assumptions does Wilson make about his audience's prejudices?

1   Sullivan recounts three main arguments concerning homosexual marriage, two against and one for. He labels them prohibitionist, conservative, and liberal. I think it easier to grasp the origins of the three main arguments by referring to the principles on which they are based.

2   The prohibitionist argument is in fact a biblical one; the heart of it was stated by Dennis Prager in an essay reprinted in the *Public Interest* ("Homosexuality, the Bible, and Us," Summer 1993). When the first books of the Bible were

written, and for a long time thereafter, heterosexual love is what seemed at risk. In many cultures—not only in Egypt or among the Canaanite tribes surrounding ancient Israel but later in Greece, Rome, and the Arab world, to say nothing of large parts of China, Japan, and elsewhere—homosexual practices were common and widely tolerated or even exalted. The Torah reversed this, making the family the central unit of life, the obligation to marry one of the first responsibilities of man, and the linkage of sex to procreation the highest standard by which to judge sexual relations. Leviticus puts the matter sharply and apparently beyond quibble.

> Thou shalt not live with mankind as with womankind; it is an abomination. . . . If a man also lie with mankind, as he lieth with a woman, both of them have committed an abomination; they shall purely be put to death; their blood shall be upon them.

3   Sullivan acknowledges the power of Leviticus but deals with it by placing it in a relative context. What is the nature of this "abomination"? Is it like killing your mother or stealing a neighbor's bread, or is it more like refusing to eat shellfish or having sex during menstruation? Sullivan suggests that all of these injunctions were written on the same moral level and hence can be accepted or ignored *as a whole*. He does not fully sustain this view, and in fact a refutation of it can be found in Prager's essay. In Prager's opinion and mine, people at the time of Moses, and for centuries before him, understood that there was a fundamental difference between whom you killed and what you ate, and in all likelihood people then and for centuries earlier linked whom you could marry closer to the principles that defined life than they did to the rules that defined diets.

4   The New Testament contains an equally vigorous attack on homosexuality by St. Paul. Sullivan partially deflects it by noting Paul's conviction that the earth was about to end and the Second Coming was near; under these conditions, all forms of sex were suspect. But Sullivan cannot deny that Paul singled out homosexuality as deserving of special criticism. He seems to pass over this obstacle without effective retort.

5   Instead, he takes up a different theme, namely, that on grounds of consistency many heterosexual practices—adultery, sodomy, premarital sex, and divorce, among others—should be outlawed equally with homosexual acts of the same character. The difficulty with this is that it mistakes the distinction alive in most people's minds between marriage as an institution and marriage as a practice. As an institution, it deserves unqualified support: as a practice, we recognize that married people are as imperfect as anyone else. Sullivan's understanding of the prohibitionist argument suffers from his unwillingness to acknowledge this distinction.

6   The second argument against homosexual marriage—Sullivan's conservative category—is based on natural law as originally set forth by Aristotle and Thomas Aquinas and more recently restated by Hadley Arkes, John Finnis, Robert George, Harry V. Jaffa, and others. How it is phrased varies a bit, but in general its advocates support a position like the following: man cannot live

without the care and support of other people; natural law is the distillation of what thoughtful people have learned about the conditions of that care. The first thing they have learned is the supreme importance of marriage, for without it the newborn infant is unlikely to survive or, if he survives, to prosper. The necessary conditions of a decent family life are the acknowledgment by its members that a man will not sleep with his daughter or a woman with her son and that neither will openly choose sex outside marriage.

7   Now, some of these conditions are violated, but there is a penalty in each case that is supported by the moral convictions of almost all who witness the violation. On simple utilitarian grounds it may be hard to object to incest or adultery; if both parties to such an act welcome it and if it is secret, what difference does it make? But very few people, and then only ones among the overeducated, seem to care much about mounting a utilitarian assault on the family. To this assault, natural-law theorists respond much as would the average citizen—never mind "utility," what counts is what is right. In particular, homosexual uses of the reproductive organs violate the condition that sex serve solely as the basis of heterosexual marriage.

8   To Sullivan, what is defective about the natural-law thesis is that it assumes different purposes in heterosexual and homosexual love: moral consummation in the first case and pure utility or pleasure alone in the second. But in fact, Sullivan suggests, homosexual love can be as consummatory as heterosexual. He notes that as the Roman Catholic Church has deepened its understanding of the involuntary—that is, in some sense genetic—basis of homosexuality, it has attempted to keep homosexuals in the church as objects of affection and nurture, while banning homosexual acts as perverse.

9   But this, though better than nothing, will not work, Sullivan writes. To show why, he adduces an analogy to a sterile person. Such a person is permitted to serve in the military or enter an unproductive marriage; why not homosexuals? If homosexuals marry without procreation, they are no different (he suggests) from a sterile man or woman who marries without hope of procreation. Yet people, I think, want the form observed even when the practice varies; a sterile marriage, whether from choice or necessity, remains a marriage of a man and a woman. To this Sullivan offers essentially an aesthetic response. Just as albinos remind us of the brilliance of color and genius teaches us about moderation, homosexuals are a "natural foil" to the heterosexual union, "a variation that does not eclipse the theme." Moreover, the threat posed by the foil to the theme is slight as compared to the threats posed by adultery, divorce, and prostitution. To be consistent, Sullivan once again reminds us, society would have to ban adulterers from the military as it now bans confessed homosexuals.

10   But again this misses the point. It would make more sense to ask why an alternative to marriage should be invented and praised when we are having enough trouble maintaining the institution at all. Suppose that gay or lesbian marriage were authorized; rather than producing a "natural foil" that would "not eclipse the theme," I suspect such a move would call even more seriously into question the role of marriage at a time when the threats to it, ranging from

single-parent families to common divorces, have hit record highs. Kenneth Minogue recently wrote of Sullivan's book that support for homosexual marriage would strike most people as "mere parody," one that could further weaken an already strained institution.

11   To me, the chief limitation of Sullivan's view is that it presupposes that marriage would have the same, domesticating, effect on homosexual members as it has on heterosexuals, while leaving the latter largely unaffected. Those are very large assumptions that no modern society has ever tested.

12   Nor does it seem plausible to me that a modern society resists homosexual marriages entirely out of irrational prejudice. Marriage is a union, sacred to most, that unites a man and woman together for life. It is a sacrament of the Catholic Church and central to every other faith. Is it out of misinformation that every modern society has embraced this view and rejected the alternative? Societies differ greatly in their attitude toward the income people may have, the relations among their various races, and the distribution of political power. But they differ scarcely at all over the distinctions between heterosexual and homosexual couples. The former are overwhelmingly preferred over the latter. The reason, I believe, is that these distinctions involve the nature of marriage and thus the very meaning—even more, the very possibility—of society.

13   The final argument over homosexual marriage is the liberal one, based on civil rights.

14   As we have seen, the Hawaiian Supreme Court ruled that any state-imposed sexual distinction would have to meet the test of strict scrutiny, a term used by the U.S. Supreme Court only for racial and similar classifications. In doing this, the Hawaiian court distanced itself from every other state court decision—there are several—in this area so far. A variant of the suspect-class argument, though, has been suggested by some scholars who contend that denying access to a marriage license by two people of the same sex is no different from denying access to two people of different sexes but also different races. The Hawaiian Supreme Court embraced this argument as well, explicitly comparing its decision to that of the U.S. Supreme Court when it overturned state laws banning marriages involving miscegenation.

15   But the comparison with black-white marriages is itself suspect. Beginning around 1964, and no doubt powerfully affected by the passage of the Civil Rights Act of that year, public attitudes toward race began to change dramatically. Even allowing for exaggerated statements to pollsters, there is little doubt that people in fact acquired a new view of blacks. Not so with homosexuals. Though the campaign to aid them has been going on vigorously for about a quarter of a century, it has produced few, if any, gains in public acceptance, and the greatest resistance, I think, has been with respect to homosexual marriages.

16   Consider the difference. What has been at issue in race relations is not marriage among blacks (for over a century, that right has been universally granted) or even miscegenation (long before the civil-rights movement, many Southern states had repealed such laws). Rather, it has been the routine contact between the races in schools, jobs, and neighborhoods. Our own history, in

other words, has long made it clear that marriage is a different issue from the issue of social integration.

17   There is another way, too, in which the comparison with race is less than helpful, as Sullivan himself points out. Thanks to the changes in public attitudes I mentioned a moment ago, gradually race was held to be not central to decisions about hiring, firing, promoting, and schooling, and blacks began to make extraordinary advances in society. But then, in an effort to enforce this new view, liberals came to embrace affirmative action, a policy that said that race *was* central to just such issues, in order to ensure that *real* mixing occurred. This move crated a crisis, for liberalism had always been based on the proposition that a liberal political system should encourage, as John Stuart Mill put it, "experiments in living" free of religious or political direction. To contemporary liberals, however, being neutral about race was tantamount to being neutral about a set of human preferences that in such matters as neighborhood and schooling left groups largely (but not entirely) separate.

18   Sullivan, who wisely sees that hardly anybody is really prepared to ignore a political opportunity to change lives, is not disposed to have much of this either in the area of race or in that of sex. And he points out with great clarity that popular attitudes toward sexuality are anyway quite different from those about race, as is evident from the fact that wherever sexual orientation is subject to local regulations, such regulations are rarely invoked. Why? Because homosexuals can "pass" or not, as they wish; they can and do accumulate education and wealth; they exercise political power. The two things a homosexual cannot do are join the military as an avowed homosexual or marry another homosexual.

19   The result, Sullivan asserts, is a wrenching paradox. On the one hand, society has historically tolerated the brutalization inflicted on people because of the color of their skin, but freely allowed them to marry; on the other hand, it has given equal opportunity to homosexuals, while denying them the right to marry. This, indeed, is where Sullivan draws the line. A black or Hispanic child, if heterosexual, has many friends, he writes, but a gay child "generally has no one." And that is why the social stigma attached to homosexuality is different from that attached to race or ethnicity—"because it attacks the very heart of what makes a human being human: the ability to love and be loved." Here is the essence of Sullivan's case. It is a powerful one, even if (as I suspect) his pro-marriage sentiments are not shared by all homosexuals.

20   Let us assume for the moment that a chance to live openly and legally with another homosexual is desirable. To believe that, we must set aside biblical injunctions, a difficult matter in a profoundly religious nation. But suppose we manage the diversion, perhaps on the grounds that if most Americans skip church, they can as readily avoid other errors of (possibly) equal magnitude. Then we must ask on what terms the union shall be arranged. There are two alternatives—marriage or domestic partnership.

21   Sullivan acknowledges the choice, but disparages the domestic-partnership laws that have evolved in some foreign countries and in some American localities. His reasons, essentially conservative ones, are that domestic partnerships

are too easily formed and too easily broken. Only real marriages matter. But—
aside from the fact that marriage is in serious decline, and that only slightly
more than half of all marriages performed in the United States this year will be
between never-before-married heterosexuals—what is distinctive about marriage is that it is an institution created to sustain child-rearing. Whatever losses
it has suffered in *this* respect, its function remains what it has always been.

22   The role of raising children is entrusted in principle to married heterosexual couples because after much experimentation—several thousand years,
more or less—we have found nothing else that works as well. Neither a gay nor
a lesbian couple can of its own resources produce a child; another party must
be involved. What do we call this third party? A friend? A sperm or egg bank?
An anonymous donor? There is no settled language for even describing, much
less approving of, such persons.

23   Suppose we allowed homosexual couples to raise children who were created out of a prior heterosexual union or adopted from someone else's heterosexual contact. What would we think of this? There is very little research on the
matter. Charlotte Patterson's famous essay, "Children of Gay and Lesbian Parents" (*Journal of Child Development,* 1992), begins by conceding that the existing
studies focus on children born into a heterosexual union that ended in divorce
or that was transformed when the mother or father "came out" as a homosexual. Hardly any research has been done on children acquired at the outset by a
homosexual couple. We therefore have no way of knowing how they would behave. And even if we had such studies, they might tell us rather little unless they
were conducted over a very long period of time.

24   But it is one thing to be born into an apparently heterosexual family and
then many years later to learn that one of your parents is homosexual? It is
quite another to be acquired as an infant from an adoption agency or a parent-
for-hire and learn from the first years of life that you are, because of your family's position, radically different from almost all other children you will meet.
No one can now say how grievous this would be. We know that young children
tease one another unmercifully; adding this dimension does not seem to be a
step in the right direction.

25   Of course, homosexual "families," with or without children, might be
rather few in number. Just how few, it is hard to say. Perhaps Sullivan himself
would marry, but, given the great tendency of homosexual males to be promiscuous, many more like him would not, or if they did, would not marry with as
much seriousness. . . .

26   The courts in Hawaii and in the nation's capital must struggle with all these
issues under the added encumbrance of a contemporary outlook that makes
law the search for rights, and responsibility the recognition of rights. Indeed,
thinking of laws about marriage as documents that confer or withhold rights is
itself an error of fundamental importance—one that the highest court in
Hawaii has already committed. "Marriage," it wrote, "is a state-conferred legal-
partnership status, the existence of which gives rise to a multiplicity of rights
and benefits. . . . " A state-conferred legal partnership? To lawyers, perhaps; to

mankind, I think not. The Hawaiian court has thus set itself on the same course of action as the misguided Supreme Court in 1973 when it thought that laws about abortion were merely an assertion of the rights of a living mother and an unborn fetus.

27   I have few favorable things to say about the political systems of other modern nations, but on these fundamental matters—abortion, marriage, military service—they often do better by allowing legislatures to operate than we do by deferring to courts. Our challenge is to find a way of formulating a policy with respect to homosexual unions that is not the result of a reflexive act of judicial rights-conferring, but is instead a considered expression of the moral convictions of a people.

FOR ANALYSIS AND DISCUSSION

1. What is the effect of reprinting the passage on homosexuality from Leviticus? What does this passage mean to you? How does Wilson apply the passage to his argument?

2. How do the articles by Wilson and Sullivan differ in style and tone? How are they similar? If you had no opinion on this issue, which argument do you think you would find more persuasive, and why?

3. What is "natural law"? Apply the principles of the "natural law" argument (paragraph 6) to homosexuality. Can natural law exist in homosexual marriage? Explain.

4. Evaluate Wilson's argument against homosexual marriage on the premise that society is having a hard enough time maintaining the institution of marriage at all. Why does he think it vital that we not tamper with the current "system"? Do you agree?

5. In paragraph 15, Wilson contrasts the significant gains in the civil rights movement to the lack of gains in gay rights. He attributes this lack of progress to American society's unwillingness to accept homosexuality. Do you agree with his assessment? How do you think Andrew Sullivan would respond to this idea?

6. Consider Wilson's comment that it is possible that Sullivan might marry, but "the great tendency of homosexual males to be promiscuous" would most likely prevent others from doing so (paragraph 25). What is the purpose of this statement? How does it connect to Wilson's overall argument? Does it influence your opinion of the author? of Sullivan? Are homosexual males indeed more promiscuous than other "straight" male populations, such as college-age men? Explain.

For Better or Worse
Jonathan Rauch

Many opponents of same-sex marriage argue that heterosexual marriage must be preserved because it serves as the foundation of family life and the rearing of children. In the next essay, Jonathan Rauch questions this perspective. He points out that this definition would then also logically exclude sterile and older people from marriage, since they cannot, in fact, rear families. He also argues that as a morally driven institution, marriage would help to eliminate much of the dangerous behavior of homosexual males.

Jonathan Rauch serves as national correspondent for the *National Journal.* He is the author of *Kindly Inquisitors: The New Attacks on Free Thought* (1993) and *Demosclerosis: The Silent Killer of American Government* (1995). This essay is reprinted from the May 1996 issue of *The New Republic.*

BEFORE YOU READ

What are the "virtues" of marriage? Why do most people marry? What do they hope to gain by marrying? What does society expect from married couples as opposed to nonmarried couples?

AS YOU READ

Can you discern Rauch's position on homosexual marriage from the first paragraph? At what point in the article do you discover his position on the issue? Is this an effective strategy?

1   Whether gay marriage makes sense—and whether straight marriage makes sense—depends on what marriage is actually for. Current secular thinking on this question is shockingly sketchy. Gay activists say: marriage is for love, and we love each other, therefore we should be able to marry. Traditionalists say: marriage is for children, and homosexuals do not (or should not) have children, therefore you should not be able to marry. That, unfortunately, pretty well covers the spectrum. I say "unfortunately" because both views are wrong. They misunderstand and impoverish the social meaning of marriage.

2   So what is marriage for? Modern marriage is, of course, based upon traditions that religion helped to codify and enforce. But religious doctrine has no special standing in the world of secular law and policy (the "Christian nation" crowd notwithstanding). If we want to know what and whom marriage is for in modern America, we need a sensible secular doctrine.

3   At one point, marriage in secular society was largely a matter of business: cementing family ties, providing social status for men and economic support for women, conferring dowries, and so on. Marriages were typically arranged, and "love" in the modern sense was no prerequisite. In Japan, remnants of this system remain, and it works surprisingly well. Couples stay together because they view their marriage as a partnership: an investment in social stability for themselves and their children. Because Japanese couples don't expect as much emotional fulfillment as we do, they are less inclined to break up. They also take a somewhat more relaxed attitude toward adultery. What's a little ex-

tracurricular love provided that each partner is fulfilling his or her many other marital duties?

4   In the West, of course, love is a defining element. The notion of lifelong love is charming, if ambitious, and certainly love is a desirable element of marriage. In society's eyes, however, it cannot be the defining element. You may or may not love your husband, but the two of you are just as married either way. You may love your mistress, but that certainly doesn't make her your spouse. Love helps make sense of marriage emotionally, but it is not terribly important in making sense of marriage from the point of view of social policy.

5   If love does not define the purpose of secular marriage, what does? Neither the law nor secular thinking provides a clear answer. Today marriage is almost entirely a voluntary arrangement whose contents are up to the people making the deal. There are few if any behaviors that automatically end a marriage. If a man beats his wife, which is about the worst thing he can do to her, he may be convicted of assault, but his marriage is not automatically dissolved. Couples can be adulterous ("open") yet remain married. They can be celibate, too; consummation is not required. All in all, it is an impressive and also rather astonishing victory for modern individualism that so important an institution should be so bereft of formal social instruction as to what should go on inside of it.

6   Secular society tells us only a few things about marriage. First, marriage depends on the consent of the parties. Second, the parties are not children. Third, the number of parties is two. Fourth, one is a man and the other a woman. Within those rules a marriage is whatever anyone says it is.

7   Perhaps it is enough simply to say that marriage is as it is and should not be tampered with. This sounds like a crudely reactionary position. In fact, however, of all the arguments against reforming marriage, it is probably the most powerful.

8   Call it a Hayekian argument, after the great libertarian economist F. A. Hayek, who developed this line of thinking in his book *The Fatal Conceit.* In a market system, the prices generated by impersonal forces may not make sense from any one person's point of view, but they encode far more information than even the cleverest person could ever gather. In a similar fashion, human societies evolve rich and complicated webs of nonlegal rules in the form of customs, traditions and institutions. Like prices, they may seem irrational or arbitrary. But the very fact that they are the customs that have evolved implies that they embody a practical logic that may not be apparent to even a sophisticated analyst. And the web of custom cannot be torn apart and reordered at will because once its internal logic is violated it falls apart. Intellectuals, such as Marxists or feminists, who seek to deconstruct and rationally rebuild social traditions, will produce not better order but chaos.

9   So the Hayekian view argues strongly against gay marriage. It says that the current rules may not be best and may even be unfair. But they are all we have, and, once you say that marriage need not be male-female, soon marriage will stop being anything at all. You can't mess with the formula without causing unforeseen consequences, possibly including the implosion of the institution of marriage itself.

10   However, there are problems with the Hayekian position. It is untenable in its extreme form and unhelpful in its milder version. In its extreme form, it implies that no social reforms should ever be undertaken. Indeed, no laws should be passed, because they interfere with the natural evolution of social mores. How could Hayekians abolish slavery? They would probably note that slavery violates fundamental moral principles. But in so doing they would establish a moral platform from which to judge social rules, and thus acknowledge that abstracting social debate from moral concerns is not possible.

11   If the ban on gay marriage were only mildly unfair, and if the costs of changing it were certain to be enormous, then the ban could stand on Hayekian grounds. But, if there is any social policy today that has a fair claim to be scaldingly inhumane, it is the ban on gay marriage. As conservatives tirelessly and rightly point out, marriage is society's most fundamental institution. To bar any class of people from marrying as they choose is an extraordinary deprivation. When not so long ago it was illegal in parts of America for blacks to marry whites, no one could claim that this was a trivial disenfranchisement. Granted, gay marriage raises issues that interracial marriage does not; but no one can argue that the deprivation is a minor one.

12   To outweigh such a serious claim it is not enough to say that gay marriage might lead to bad things. Bad things happened as a result of legalizing contraception, but that did not make it the wrong thing to do. Besides, it seems doubtful that extending marriage to, say, another 3 or 5 percent of the population would have anything like the effects that no-fault divorce has had, to say nothing of contraception. By now, the "traditional" understanding of marriage has been sullied in all kinds of ways. It is hard to think of a bigger affront to tradition, for instance, than allowing married women to own property independently of their husbands or allowing them to charge their husbands with rape. Surely it is unfair to say that marriage may be reformed for the sake of anyone and everyone except homosexuals, who must respect the dictates of tradition.

13   Faced with these problems, the milder version of the Hayekian argument says not that social traditions shouldn't be tampered with at all, but that they shouldn't be tampered with lightly. Fine. In this case, no one is talking about casual messing around; both sides have marshaled their arguments with deadly seriousness. Hayekians surely have to recognize that appeals to blind tradition and to the risks inherent in social change do not, a priori, settle anything in this instance. They merely warn against frivolous change.

14   So we turn to what has become the standard view of marriage's purpose. Its proponents would probably like to call it a child-centered view, but it is actually an anti-gay view, as will become clear. Whatever you call it, it is the view of marriage that is heard most often, and in the context of the debate over gay marriage it is heard almost exclusively. In its most straightforward form it goes as follows (I quote from James Q. Wilson's fine book *The Moral Sense*):

> A family is not an association of independent people; it is a human commitment designed to make possible the rearing of moral and healthy children. Governments care—or ought to care—about families for this reason, and scarcely for any other.

15   Wilson speaks about "family" rather than "marriage" as such, but one may, I think, read him as speaking of marriage without doing any injustice to his meaning. The resulting proposition—government ought to care about marriage almost entirely because of children—seems reasonable. But there are problems. The first, obviously, is that gay couples may have children, whether through adoption, prior marriage or (for lesbians) artificial insemination. Leaving aside the thorny issue of gay adoption, the point is that if the mere presence of children is the test, then homosexual relationships can certainly pass it.

16   You might note, correctly, that heterosexual marriages are more likely to produce children than homosexual ones. When granting marriage licenses to heterosexuals, however, we do not ask how likely the couple is to have children. We assume that they are entitled to get married whether or not they end up with children. Understanding this, conservatives often make an interesting move. In seeking to justify the state's interest in marriage, they shift from the actual presence of children to the anatomical possibility of making them. Hadley Arkes, a political science professor and prominent opponent of homosexual marriage, makes the case this way:

> The traditional understanding of marriage is grounded in the "natural teleology of the body"—in the inescapable fact that only a man and a woman, and only two people, not three, can generate a child. Once marriage is detached from that natural teleology of the body, what ground of principle would thereafter confine marriage to two people rather than some larger grouping? That is, on what ground of principle would the law reject the claim of a gay couple that their love is not confined to a coupling of two, but that they are woven into a larger ensemble with yet another person or two?

17   What he seems to be saying is that, where the possibility of natural children is nil, the meaning of marriage is nil. If marriage is allowed between members of the same sex, then the concept of marriage has been emptied of content except to ask whether the parties love each other. Then anything goes, including polygamy. This reasoning presumably is what those opposed to gay marriage have in mind when they claim that, once gay marriage is legal, marriage to pets will follow close behind.

18   But Arkes and his sympathizers make two mistakes. To see them, break down the claim into two components: (1) Two-person marriage derives its special status from the anatomical possibility that the partners can create natural children; and (2) apart from (1), two-person marriage has no purpose sufficiently strong to justify its special status. That is, absent justification (1), anything goes.

19   The first proposition is wholly at odds with the way society actually views marriage. Leave aside the insistence that natural, as opposed to adopted, children define the importance of marriage. The deeper problem, apparent right away, is the issue of sterile heterosexual couples. Here the "anatomical possibility" crowd has a problem, for a homosexual union is, anatomically speaking, nothing but one variety of sterile union and no different even in principle: a

woman without a uterus has no more potential for giving birth than a man without a vagina.

20   It may sound like carping to stress the case of barren heterosexual marriage: the vast majority of newlywed heterosexual couples, after all, can have children and probably will. But the point here is fundamental. There are far more sterile heterosexual unions in America than homosexual ones. The "anatomical possibility" crowd cannot have it both ways. If the possibility of children is what gives meaning to marriage, then a postmenopausal woman who applies for a marriage license should be turned away at the courthouse door. What's more, she should be hooted at and condemned for stretching the meaning of marriage beyond its natural basis and so reducing the institution to frivolity. People at the Family Research Council or Concerned Women for America should point at her and say, "If she can marry, why not polygamy?"

21   Obviously, the "anatomical" conservatives do not say this, because they are sane. They instead flail around, saying that sterile men and women were at least born with the right-shaped parts for making children, and so on. Their position is really a nonposition. It says that the "natural children" rationale defines marriage when homosexuals are involved but not when heterosexuals are involved. When the parties to union are sterile heterosexuals, the justification for marriage must be something else. But what?

22   Now arises the oddest part of the "anatomical" argument. Look at proposition (2) above. It says that, absent the anatomical justification for marriage, anything goes. In other words, it dismisses the idea that there might be other good reasons for society to sanctify marriage above other kinds of relationships. Why would anybody make this move? I'll hazard a guess: to exclude homosexuals. Any rationale that justifies sterile heterosexual marriages can also apply to homosexual ones. For instance, marriage makes women more financially secure. Very nice, say the conservatives. But that rationale could be applied to lesbians, so it's definitely out.

23   The end result of this stratagem is perverse to the point of being funny. The attempt to ground marriage in children (or the anatomical possibility thereof) falls flat. But, having lost that reason for marriage, the antigay people can offer no other. In their fixation on excluding homosexuals, they leave themselves no consistent justification for the privileged status of *heterosexual* marriage. They thus tear away any coherent foundation that secular marriage might have, which is precisely the opposite of what they claim they want to do. If they have to undercut marriage to save it from homosexuals, so be it!

24   For the record, I would be the last to deny that children are one central reason for the privileged status of marriage. When men and women get together, children are a likely outcome; and, as we are learning in ever more unpleasant ways, when children grow up without two parents, trouble ensues. Children are not a trivial reason for marriage; they just cannot be the only reason.

25   What are the others? It seems to me that the two strongest candidates are these: domesticating men and providing reliable caregivers. Both purposes are critical to the functioning of a humane and stable society, and both are much

better served by marriage—that is, by one-to-one lifelong commitment—than by any other institution.

26   Civilizing young males is one of any society's biggest problems. Whenever unattached males gather in packs, you see no end of trouble; wildings in Central Park, gangs in Los Angeles, soccer hooligans in Britain, skinheads in Germany, fraternity hazings in universities, grope-lines in the military and, in a different but ultimately no less tragic way, the bathhouses and wanton sex of gay San Francisco or New York in the 1970s.

27   For taming men, marriage is unmatched. "Of all the institutions through which men may pass—schools, factories, the military—marriage has the largest effect," Wilson writes in *The Moral Sense*. (A token of the casualness of current thinking about marriage is that the man who wrote those words could, later in the very same book, say that government should care about fostering families for "scarcely any other" reason than children.) If marriage—that is, the binding of men into couples—did nothing else, its power to settle men, to keep them at home and out of trouble, would be ample justification for its special status.

28   Of course, women and older men don't generally travel in marauding or orgiastic packs. But in their case the second rationale comes into play. A second enormous problem for society is what to do when someone is beset by some sort of burdensome contingency. It could be cancer, a broken back, unemployment or depression; it could be exhaustion from work or stress under pressure. If marriage has any meaning at all, it is that, when you collapse from a stroke, there will be at least one other person whose "job" is to drop everything and come to your aid; or that when you come home after being fired by the postal service there will be someone to persuade you not to kill the supervisor.

29   Obviously, both rationales—the need to settle males and the need to have people looked after—apply to sterile people as well as fertile ones, and apply to childless couples as well as to ones with children. The first explains why everybody feels relieved when the town delinquent gets married, and the second explains why everybody feels happy when an aging widow takes a second husband. From a social point of view, it seems to me, both rationales are far more compelling as justifications of marriage's special status than, say, love. And both of them apply to homosexuals as well as to heterosexuals.

30   Take the matter of settling men. It is probably true that women and children, more than just the fact of marriage, help civilize men. But that hardly means that the settling effect of marriage on homosexual men is negligible. To the contrary, being tied to a committed relationship plainly helps stabilize gay men. Even without marriage, coupled gay men have steady sex partners and relationships that they value and therefore tend to be less wanton. Add marriage, and you bring a further array of stabilizing influences. One of the main benefits of publicly recognized marriage is that it binds couples together not only in their own eyes but also in the eyes of society at large. Around the partners is woven a web of expectations that they will spend nights together, go to parties together, take out mortgages together, buy furniture at Ikea together, and so on—all of which helps tie them together and keep them off the streets and at

home. Surely that is a very good thing, especially as compared to the closet-gay culture of furtive sex with innumerable partners in parks and bathhouses.

31   The other benefit of marriage—caretaking—clearly applies to homosexuals. One of the first things many people worry about when coming to terms with their homosexuality is: Who will take care of me when I'm ailing or old? Society needs to care about this, too, as the AIDS crisis has made horribly clear. If that crisis has shown anything, it is that homosexuals can and will take care of each other, sometimes with breathtaking devotion—and that no institution can begin to match the care of a devoted partner. Legally speaking, marriage creates kin. Surely society's interest in kin-creation is strongest of all for people who are unlikely to be supported by children in old age and who may well be rejected by their own parents in youth.

32   Gay marriage, then, is far from being a mere exercise in political point-making or rights-mongering. On the contrary, it serves two of the three social purposes that make marriage so indispensable and irreplaceable for heterosexuals. Two out of three may not be the whole ball of wax, but it is more than enough to give society a compelling interest in marrying off homosexuals.

33   There is no substitute. Marriage is the *only* institution that adequately serves these purposes. The power of marriage is not just legal but social. It seals its promise with the smiles and tears of family, friends and neighbors. It shrewdly exploits ceremony (big, public weddings) and money (expensive gifts, dowries) to deter casual commitment and to make bailing out embarrassing. Stag parties and bridal showers signal that what is beginning is not just a legal arrangement but a whole new stage of life. "Domestic partner' laws do none of these things.

34   I'll go further: far from being a substitute for the real thing, marriage-lite may undermine it. Marriage is a deal between a couple and society, not just between two people: society recognizes the sanctity and autonomy of the pair-bond, and in exchange each spouse commits to being the other's nurse, social worker and policeman of first resort. Each marriage is its own little society within society. Any step that weakens the deal by granting the legal benefits of marriage without also requiring the public commitment is begging for trouble.

35   So gay marriage makes sense for several of the same reasons that straight marriage makes sense. That would seem a natural place to stop. But the logic of the argument compels one to go a twist further. If it is good for society to have people attached, then it is not enough just to make marriage available. Marriage should also be *expected*. This, too, is just as true for homosexuals as for heterosexuals. So, if homosexuals are justified in expecting access to marriage, society is equally justified in expecting them to use it. I'm not saying that out-of-wedlock sex should be scandalous or that people should be coerced into marrying. The mechanisms of expectation are more subtle. When grandma cluck-clucks over a still-unmarried young man, or when mom says she wishes her little girl would settle down, she is expressing a strong and well-justified preference: one that is quietly echoed in a thousand ways throughout society and that produces subtle but important pressure to form and sustain unions.

This is a good and necessary thing, and it will be as necessary for homosexuals as heterosexuals. If gay marriage is recognized, single gay people over a certain age should not be surprised when they are disapproved of or pitied. This is a vital part of what makes marriage work. It's stigma as social policy.

If marriage is to work it cannot be merely a "lifestyle option." It must be privileged. That is, it must be understood to be better, on average, than other ways of living. Not mandatory, not good where everything else is bad, but better: a general norm, rather than a personal taste. The biggest worry about gay marriage, I think is, is that homosexuals might get it but then mostly not use it. Gay neglect of marriage wouldn't greatly erode the bonding power of heterosexual marriage (remember, homosexuals are only a tiny fraction of the population)—but it would certainly not help. And heterosexual society would rightly feel betrayed if, after legalization, homosexuals treated marriage as a minority taste rather than as a core institution of life. It is not enough, I think, for gay people to say we want the right to marry. If we do not use it, shame on us.

FOR ANALYSIS AND DISCUSSION

1. What is the American definition of what a marriage *should* be? How does it differ from the Japanese model Rauch describes? Would homosexual marriage be more accepted in Japanese society? Explain.
2. What, according to Rauch, is faulty with the Hayekian view of marriage? Is he effective in supporting his argument against Hayek? What is your view on Hayek's definition?
3. Evaluate Rauch's statement in paragraph 11 that "no one can argue that the deprivation [of gay marriage] is a minor one."
4. What issues are raised by the quotation by Hadley Arkes in paragraph 16? What other, less obvious issues are implicit in this quotation?
5. Analyze Rauch's comments in paragraph 26 that "unattached males" cause problems for society. Do you agree with this view? What support does he offer to back his argument? Is the example of gay males in bathhouses parallel to skinheads in Germany or gangs in Los Angeles? Explain.
6. How would the institution of gay marriage address the problem of "unattached" gay males? Why, according to Rauch, would gay marriage actually serve the principles of conservatives? Do you think conservatives would agree with his argument?
7. How do you think James Q. Wilson would respond to this essay? What points do you think he might concede, and with which would he completely disagree?

WRITING ASSIGNMENTS: SAME-SEX MARRIAGES

1. In your own words, define marriage. Then write an argument essay evaluating the definitions of marriage offered by the authors and how their definitions compare to the American reality of marriage. How does homosexual marriage fit into the current model? Does it have a place in today's society?

2. Select one of the articles in this section and write an argument essay in which you respond to its premise. As you deliberate about your ideas and the writer's views, look for values and concerns that you share with the writer and those with which you disagree. Address these elements in your essay.

3. The Family Research Council openly opposes homosexuality as "unhealthy, immoral and destructive to individuals, families, and societies." Read the transcript from the Council's program "Straight Talk" addressing the issue of homosexual marriage at <http://www.frc.org/net/st96d2.html> and its page on the Defense of Marriage Act at <http://www.frc.org/perspective/pv96h5hs.html>. Write an argument essay in which you address the Council's concerns regarding homosexual marriage's "threat" to the institution of the American family. Evaluate the argument and present your own view for comparison.

SEXUAL HARASSMENT: SHOULD WE ESTABLISH RULES OF BEHAVIOR?

Title VII Guidelines on Sexual Harassment
Equal Employment Opportunity Commission

The antidiscrimination policy of Title VII of the Civil Rights Act (1964) prohibits sex discrimination in the determination of wages, job classification, assignment, and promotion and training, and was amended in 1980 to include guidelines prohibiting forms of sexual harassment on the job. Enforced by the Equal Employment Opportunity Commission ((EEOC), § 1604.11 of Title VII continues to be the subject of much debate. In recent years, the cases of Anita Hill and Paula Jones have raised public sensitivity to and criticism of this piece of legislation. While the law is seemingly clear, courts' interpretations of it vary widely. What follows is the exact wording of § 1604.11 of Title VII's Guidelines on Sexual Harassment.

BEFORE YOU READ

What is "sexual harassment"? How does it affect the integrity of employment relationships?

AS YOU READ

Legal, corporate, and public interpretation of Title VII § 1604.11 has varied. As you read the law, consider whether the wording seems straightforward or ambiguous. What do you think accounts for the different interpretations of this legislation?

Part 1604—Guidelines on Discrimination Because of Sex

§ 1604.11 Sexual harassment.

1   (a) Harassment on the basis of sex is a violation of Sec. 703 of Title VII.[1] Unwelcome sexual advances, requests for sexual favors, and other verbal or physical conduct of a sexual nature constitute sexual harassment when (1) submission to such conduct is made either explicitly or implicitly a term or condition of an individual's employment, (2) submission to or rejection of such conduct by an individual is used as the basis for employment decisions affecting such individual, or (3) such conduct has the purpose or effect of unreasonably interfering with an individual's work performance or creating an intimidating, hostile, or offensive working environment.

2   (b) In determining whether alleged conduct constitutes sexual harassment, the Commission will look at the record as a whole and at the totality of the circumstances, such as the nature of the sexual advances and the context in which the alleged incidents occurred. The determination of the legality of a particular action will be made from the facts, on a case by case basis.

3   (c) Applying general Title VII principles, an employer, employment agency, joint apprenticeship committee, or labor organization (hereinafter collectively referred to as "employer") is responsible for its acts and those of its agents and supervisory employees with respect to sexual harassment regardless of whether the specific acts complained of were authorized or even forbidden by the employer and regardless of whether the employer knew or should have known of their occurrence. The Commission will examine the circumstances of the particular employment relationship and the job functions performed by the individual in determining whether an individual acts in either a supervisory or agency capacity.

4   (d) With respect to conduct between fellow employees, an employer is responsible for acts of sexual harassment in the workplace where the employer (or its agents or supervisory employees) knows or should have known of the conduct, unless it can show that it took immediate and appropriate corrective action.

5   (e) An employer may also be responsible for the acts of non-employees, with respect to sexual harassment of employees in the workplace, where the employer (or its agents or supervisory employees) knows or should have known of the conduct and fails to take immediate and appropriate corrective action. In reviewing these cases the Commission will consider the extent of the employer's control and any other legal responsibility which the employer may have with respect to the conduct of such non-employees.

6   (f) Prevention is the best tool for the elimination of sexual harassment. An employer should take all steps necessary to prevent sexual harassment from occurring, such as affirmatively raising the subject, expressing strong disapproval, developing appropriate sanctions, informing employees of their right to raise

---

[1]The principles involved here continue to apply to race, color, religion, or other origin. [Original note.]

and how to raise the issue of harassment under Title VII, and developing methods to sensitize all concerned.

7   (g) Other related practices: Where employment opportunities or benefits are granted because of an individual's submission to the employer's sexual advances or requests for sexual favors, the employer may be held liable for unlawful sex discrimination against other persons who were qualified for but denied that employment opportunity or benefit.

FOR ANALYSIS AND DISCUSSION

1. Compile a list of behaviors that would be considered sexual harassment according to Title VII § 1604.11. How has your understanding of what constitutes sexual harassment changed after reading the guidelines?
2. Analyze the wording of the guidelines. Is it clear, or is it open to interpretation? If you found parts of it unclear, explain where and why.
3. After reading § 1604.11, what is your opinion of recently publicized sexual harassment cases, such as the Paula Jones lawsuit against Bill Clinton?
4. If you had the authority, would you make any changes to Title VII § 1604.11? If so, what changes would you make, and why?

The End of Harassment
Richard Dooling

Has sexual harassment law gone too far? In this essay author Richard Dooling argues that sexual harassment lawsuits are "paralyzing companies all over America." Return Title VII to its "original plain language," says Dooling, and sexual harassment will take care of itself.

Richard Dooling is a lawyer and former editor of the *St. Louis University Law Journal.* He has written four books, including *Blue Streak: Swearing, Free Speech, and Sexual Harassment* (1996), a collection of essays on the First Amendment. His articles have appeared in many publications, including the *New Yorker, Wall Street Journal, George,* and *The National Review,* where this essay was published on May 4, 1998.

BEFORE YOU READ

Do you think men and women have different interpretations of what constitutes sexual harassment? Explain.

AS YOU READ

Evaluate Dooling's tone. What do his language and word choice reveal about his opinion on this subject? How do you think he feels about women, or can you tell?

1   Just as the O.J. trial was a public demonstration of the laws of evidence and procedure in criminal cases, so Paula Jones and her lawyers have provided the American public with an object lesson in the awesome scope and power of our current sexual-harassment laws. One woman's unsupported allegations are grounds for hauling even the President of the United States into a deposition where he can be forced to testify under oath about sexual encounters with former lovers, the size and shape of his penis, his shopping habits, and what books he gives as gifts.

2   It was not always so. As one pundit after another has reminded us, President Kennedy's escapades remained private, and the country was arguably better for it. Kennedy died in 1963, and Title VII of the Civil Rights Act was passed in 1964; before that there were no civil laws which pretended to referee the timeless scrimmage between men and women for power, money, sex, and influence—a contest which was fought by individuals in the marketplace and in the bedroom, until group rights and identity politics came into fashion.

3   Title VII began as a statute requiring employers to make decisions about the "terms and conditions of employment" without regard to race, color, religion, sex, or national origin. As any employment lawyer or line supervisor knows, the statute had precisely the opposite effect, because what the company lawyer now needs to know in order to assess hirings, firings, and promotions is the race, color, religion, sex, national origin, age, and disability of the employees involved. This is one of the many pernicious side effects itemized by Richard Epstein and other legal scholars who argue that Title VII is not only unnecessary but actively destructive.

4   Title VII and the other federal employment laws now protect so many minorities that they in effect confer a right to sue on a majority of employees. Still, to the extent that Title VII prohibits "discrimination" (that is, hiring or firing because of sex or race), it forbids an activity which, in theory, most people discriminated against can easily prove and most employers can easily avoid. Give similarly situated individuals the same pay for the same work. Hire and fire on the basis of objective, quantifiable criteria. Or get sued.

5   When Title VII acquired tremendous potential for abuse was when the courts decided it prohibited not just discrimination, but something vague called "harassment." As Justice Scalia noted in 1993, Title VII's "inherently vague statutory language . . . lets virtually unguided juries decide whether sex-related conduct engaged in (or permitted by) an employer is egregious enough to warrant an award of damages."

6   Amen. Any law that can be interpreted as forbidding lewd comments and dirty pictures in the workplace in one jurisdiction, and then as permitting dropping one's pants and saying "kiss it" in another, should be in constitutional-law lingo, void for vagueness. This is the major complaint of legal scholars like Eugene Volokh and Kingsley Browne, who have argued for years that Title VII's vagueness chills workplace speech and therefore violates the First Amendment. Employers instinctively prohibit any "sexual" speech for fear of punitive damages.

7   Ever since Title VII was interpreted as prohibiting "harassment," a parade of women—some arguably harassed, some merely annoyed—have come before the courts. After months, sometimes years, of costly discovery, juries are asked to determine whether she is more believable than he, whether the overture was "sexual," and whether it was "unwanted." And every year charges and suits paralyze companies all over America.

8   At the height of the Clinton scandal, every other pundit legitimately asked: "Is this how we want our President spending his time?" But this is precisely the question the stockholders ask when a secretary brings a global corporation to a halt by alleging that the CEO told her a dirty joke in the coffee room.

9   What would happen if Congress passed an amendment to Title VII, which simply confined its interpretation to its original plain language, namely, prohibiting discrimination in the terms and conditions of employment? Would boorish chauvinists have at unprotected women and minorities, who would suddenly be left with no legal remedy? Hardly. Many behaviors prohibited by the "harassment" components of Title VII are already prohibited by other civil and criminal laws. Any unauthorized touching is a battery. Abusive and threatening language may rise to the level of assault. Defamation prohibits injurious statements intended to harm a person's reputation. And so on. In short, what would happen if we simply allowed the same laws that protect us from one another on the street also to protect us in the workplace?

10   Unlike Title VII, which holds companies liable for their supervisors' behaviors, the tort and criminal laws make individuals liable for their own behaviors. How's that for deterrence? But of course, victimized plaintiffs need the employer's deep pockets—which should prompt us to ask ourselves whether it is more important to deter individual harassing behaviors, or to compensate victims with corporate checks under some construct of vicarious liability.

11   If it is too early in the season of public opinion to call for a repeal of Title VII, the time is ripe at least for pruning its most unworkable and unenforceable sections. Even the feminists quickly stopped talking about vague "power differentials" when the amorphous theory was about to be applied to their guy; maybe we could also do away with the equally vague admonition that all employees have "the right to work in an environment free from discriminatory intimidation, ridicule, and insult."

12   But above all, the nation should be asking itself: Do we really want to live under a law that pretends to be able to adduce evidence and settle a dispute between a man and a woman who went into a room alone together and came out with different stories?

FOR ANALYSIS AND DISCUSSION

1. In paragraph 2 Dooling comments that "group rights and identity politics" are a current "fashion." What does he mean by this? Do you agree with his assessment? Explain.

2. Based on this essay, what do you think is Dooling's definition of sexual harassment? How does it compare to your version and to that of Title VII § 1604.11?

3. In paragraph 9 Dooling wonders what would happen if Congress passed an amendment to Title VII. What type of amendment does he want passed? What does he think such an amendment would accomplish? Do you agree?

4. Is Dooling's use of the Paula Jones lawsuit an effective means of supporting his argument? How might his opposition respond to this example, and his comments regarding President Kennedy's personal life? Are the situations parallel?

5. Evaluate the overall effectiveness of Dooling's essay. Does he get his point across? Is his argument well reasoned and supported? Is it likely to persuade an audience? Explain.

6. Analyze Dooling's last paragraph. Is his final question an accurate assessment of the issue of sexual harassment in the workplace?

Heterophobia: Sexual Harassment and the Future
Daphne Patai

The following essay explores the impact of sexual harassment law on college campuses. Writing from the perspective of a woman who has experienced sexual harassment, Daphne Patai explains why she thinks sexual harassment rules are actually stifling the atmosphere of academic inquiry so vital to the university experience. While she concedes that some types of harassment are unacceptable, Patai fears the consequences that restrictive sexual harassment laws place on speech and expression.

Daphne Patai is professor of women's studies and Brazilian literature at the University of Massachusetts, Amherst. She is the author and editor of nine books including *Professing Feminism: Cautionary Tales from the Strange World of Women's Studies* (1994) and *Heterophobia: Sexual Harassment and the Future of Feminism* (1999). The following essay is an excerpt from the preface of *Heterophobia*.

BEFORE YOU READ

Have you experienced or witnessed sexual harassment on your college campus? If so, what were the circumstances surrounding it? For example, did it occur in a classroom or at a social event; was it instigated by a student or a faculty member; what happened? How did the school address the situation, if at all?

AS YOU READ

How does Patai's examples of her past personal experience with sexual harassment support the discussion that follows? Is this an effective way of framing her argument?

1   Like many women in our society, I have experienced what is now labeled "sexual harassment"—on the street, in school, and at work. In Paris, a man once grabbed my breast as he walked by me (I knew, as he approached me, that he was going to do something, but I didn't have the nerve to cross the street). In a

crowded subway in Rio de Janeiro, a man behind me masturbated while pressing up against me. In New York, a man whispered as he passed me, "Boy, would I like to eat that!" Before graduate school, when I worked as a secretary, one of my bosses was constantly irritated with me because I refused to date him. I finally complained to his superior, who rebuked us both: my immediate boss for pestering me, and me for being flirtatious. In another job, a boss said to me, "You must be horrible in bed—you're so efficient!" This same man asked me to count the steps up the Eiffel Tower (for the guidebook he was writing) and to do it on my own time. I refused; no, he did not fire me.

2   As a graduate student, I was pursued for two years by a professor from whom I nonetheless learned a great deal. When I went for a job interview after completing my Ph.D., an elderly male faculty member said, while shaking my hand, "She's pretty. Hire her!" (This didn't unnerve me nearly as much as did a female professor who sat filing her nails while I gave a public lecture as part of my interview.) Especially in the early years of my career as a teacher, I had male students occasionally make rude and arguably sexist comments to me. One wrote on my lectern, "Dafney, you are a feminist bitch!" Another, on a teaching evaluation form, advised me which of my hairstyles was sexiest. In class, when I was an assistant professor, a boy disagreed with a fact I had cited by saying out loud, "You know what you can do with your facts!" Still another borrowed books from me and repeatedly tried to come to my house to return them. And (in a reversal of my graduate school experience) an undergraduate student of mine, a young woman, declared herself to me and pursued me (in person, by mail, and by phone) for two years.

3   These episodes were not pleasant, but neither were they devastating. Least of all were they typical of my interactions with other human beings. Unlike many present-day commentators on the subject, I would feel exceedingly foolish if I were to refer to myself as a "survivor," or even a "victim," of sexual harassment. None of these experiences did me any real harm. But even if they had—and even if I grant that other women might react differently or have more disturbing experiences—I would have to weigh and measure the benefits of being spared this sort of behavior against the costs of preventing it. Certainly I cannot join forces with those activists who want to see all such events—even the pettiest street harassment that is not (yet) actionable in most places—become illegal.

4   There is, moreover, another side of the coin, which must also be acknowledged. True, I have never groped a strange man's crotch, but when I was a student, I did indeed aggressively pursue professors who interested me. So did many of my female friends. I used to find excuses to go to their offices and lead the conversation to personal subjects. Sometimes my girlfriends and I would follow a "favored" professor around in a car. Once I even trailed a man on foot for a block or two because his aftershave left an enticing fragrance in the air. (Was this "stalking"?) I have written "unwanted" letters of invitation to a professor-and-boss I found attractive. Rejection depressed me and made me angry. But I got over it.

5   From these incidents I take a simple lesson: that the experience of sexual interest and sexual play (which can indeed be obnoxious at times) is an ordinary part of human life, manifest in different ways in different societies but predictably present in one way or another, as it must have been since the Garden of Eden. It seems to me that except for egregious offenses such as assault, bribery, or extortion (whether sexual or not)—for which legal remedies have existed for many years—the petty annoyance of occasional misplaced sexual attentions or sexist putdowns has to be tolerated. Why? Because the type of vigilance necessary to inhibit it would create a social climate so unpleasant, and ultimately so repressive, that the cure would be much worse than the disease.

6   Would we really want to live in a sanitized world in which each of us is fully protected from any offensive or otherwise unwanted word or gesture? In which every interaction must be scrutinized for possible sexual implications or slights based on gender? In which a kind of paranoia poisons the very idea of sexual expression between people in situations containing that supposedly fatal element, a "power imbalance"? I don't think so. Yet from the very beginning, the subject of sexual harassment has been marked by definitions rooted in feminist assumptions about the relations between men and women, assumptions that are long overdue for questioning.

7   Today those with sensitivities heightened by feminist rhetoric are rewarded by being handed legal weapons to wield against their colleagues and teachers. A psychology professor at one school filed a grievance because someone in her department had put up a sprig of mistletoe. Result: a campus regulation stipulating that mistletoe has to be removed if anyone complains. Ironically, as story after story in the mounting literature on sexual harassment reveals, teachers who are most devoted to their classroom work, who are most ready to chat with students and to demystify the boundaries between teacher and student (as recommended by feminist pedagogy), are most often the ones who find themselves caught in the web of sexual harassment charges.

8   Consider the case of Michael Bullock, a popular forty-nine-year-old high school math instructor known for his devotion to teaching. A female student poked playfully at Bullock, in front of the class, commenting on his corpulence by saying that his chest was big. He replied that hers was small. This response led to his suspension from teaching. While waiting to hear whether he was to be reprimanded or transferred to an administrative job, Bullock killed himself. Now his students say, "He cared too much. That's what got him,"[1] In the emotional confusion that followed this event, a school spokeswoman defended the girl who had made the charge, expressing concern—and this is the most telling detail of the case—that the suicide would have the effect of discouraging other students from filing complaints.

9   At a California junior high school, in early 1998, all displays of affection were prohibited, including hugging, kissing, back-patting, and even "high fives." Some brave fourteen-year-old girls objected, insisting that they wanted to be able to hug their friends without fear of punishment. School officials replied that such rules have existed at many schools for years but have been enforced

only recently because "hugging" seems to have become a fad.[2] When interviewed on CNN, the principal of the school said with a straight face that long hugs between boys and girls were actually her target, but since she was unable to specify that, a blanket rule seemed the best alternative.[3] Evidently, fears of heterosexual touching, and efforts to reform the behavior of unregenerate adolescent girls, are far from over. These days we must be grateful for the occasional optimistic sign, such as the dropping of charges against a nine-year-old boy who was alleged to have rubbed himself against a girl of the same age in the lunch line.[4]

10   In the supposedly more adult universe of higher education, rational people are devising their own measures for warding off trouble. I have spoken to many colleagues who now say that they will not close their doors after a student enters their office. They watch their words and wonder whether it is wise to discuss "sensitive" issues in class, however germane these may be to their subject. Up and down the academic ranks, people are acutely aware of the dangers of doing something, however innocuous, however inadvertent, that another person, especially a subordinate, might possibly consider offensive or inappropriate. Lawsuits about matters that would have seemed ludicrous just a few years ago have now become commonplace. An offhand remark or misperceived gesture can threaten an entire career. A professor's encouraging words or practical help can be retroactively interpreted as "grooming" for sexual demands at a later time. On the other hand, criticism of students' classwork or disagreement with their ideas can be construed as contributing to an environment that impedes their full participation in academic life. A metaphor that happens to strike some student the wrong way can be claimed to have created a hostile environment in the classroom. A friendly hug may turn up months, or even years, later in a lawsuit, transformed into a "demand for a hug." These are not hypothetical situations. They are drawn from actual cases in recent years.

11   Senior professors and junior colleagues find themselves caught in a web of "power" and "hierarchy" that is viewed as precluding any kind of personal relationship. Many universities now have "consensual relations policies" regulating, or simply prohibiting, sexual relationships between people in "asymmetrical" positions. Yet despite the absence of "power differentials," student-to-student complaints are rapidly multiplying. In a particularly notorious response to this situation, Antioch College has adopted rules requiring students to seek explicit verbal permission for every step of sexual intimacy.

12   While such a policy will strike many as the sort of "solution" that any sane society would laugh out of existence, it is patently not enough to satisfy the sex regulators, whose main objective . . . is the dismantling of heterosexuality altogether. Meanwhile, unable to openly attempt to ban sex and thereby totally alienate their public, feminist reformers and their sympathizers have instead tried to set up an obstacle course in the relations between men and women.

13   This agenda is abetted by the frequent overreactions of college administrators fearful of lawsuits from alleged victims but not from alleged harassers. Thus it is that the former are given assistance, counseling, and support while

the latter are often suspended or otherwise punished at the mere threat of a sexual harassment charge and well in advance of any investigation. No one can be sure when the atmosphere around him (or, less often, her) will turn sour and charges will be made. Such an academic environment, I contend, is neither intellectually productive nor morally tolerable. That is why I now feel moved to speak my mind on an issue on which twelve or fifteen years ago I took the opposite position. Much has happened in the intervening years, and it has made the university a very different place from what it used to be.

14   . . . The current judicial, quasi-judicial, extra-legal, and administrative application of sexual harassment law, especially as manifested in the "hostile environment" doctrine and as practiced in colleges and universities, represents an unwelcome and dangerous shift in both law and custom. Hostile-environment actions are now based upon the subjective experience of "unwanted" or "offensive" conduct (including speech), as perceived by the accuser and tested by the "reasonable woman" standard, a concept I will discuss at length. It is becoming increasingly clear that this development transfers the burden of proof from the accuser to the accused, in violation of American due process. In addition, this shift has profound repercussions on the conduct of daily life. And such a consequence . . . is no accident. It is precisely what the proponents of sexual harassment regulations have in mind.

15   But university students are not children who need to be guarded against predatory adults. Nor are they mental health patients requiring tender care. Universities are, in fact, splendid places where mature and young adults—all postpubescent, most of them with the right to vote, to reproduce or not (through elective abortion), and to kill and be killed in military service—congregate, teach and learn, get to know one another, pursue intellectual and personal relationships (universities' "latent function," as Robert K. Merton called it, is to provide opportunities for people to seek romantic partners),[5] behave sensibly and foolishly, and generally get on with their interesting lives. Universities are, moreover, a unique domain in American life where academic theories are codified into policy and their effects are played out for all to see.

16   How did this admirable setting, in a remarkably short period of time, come to be redefined as a danger zone where abuse lurks in every corner, where "difference" must be unmasked as "power," which—to those trained in the rhetoric of sexual harassment—is logically tantamount to "abuse of power"? How did it happen that the notion of sexual harassment has with such apparent ease pervaded institutional and private life in contemporary America? . . . At this point, a short answer will suffice, simple and, alas, obvious: The mere allegation of "sexual harassment" now provides women with an extraordinarily effective weapon (albeit an altogether traditional one) to wield against men. Even women who reject the view that women's victimization is at the very heart of a society that is unrelentingly patriarchal have accepted the instrument handed to them by sexual harassment legislation. But a feminism that has latched onto sexual harassment as a means of bringing men to heel is, I believe, a feminism that will ultimately discredit women, too.

NOTES

1. Maria D. Vesperi, "A Sexual Harassment Charge, a Teacher's Suicide," *Sacramento Bee,* July 2, 1993, p. B7. For a troubling account of a comparable case in the workplace, see Christopher Byron's excellent article "The Joke That Killed," *Esquire* (January 1995): p. 84. Byron, in describing the suicide of an AT&T employee accused of sexual harassment, explains that the Department of Labor's Office of Federal Contract Compliance investigates approximately four thousand companies a year. If evidence is lacking that charges are being brought under Title VII, the company is suspected of being "soft on discrimination and harassment, which could lead to the revocation of contracts."

2. Mimi Ko Cruz, "No Hugs?" *Los Angeles Times,* February 12, 1998, p. B1.

3. CNN News, February 13, 1998.

4. Ann Gearan, "Sex Charges against Nine-Year-Old Dropped," *Daily Collegian* (Pennsylvania State University), June 26, 1997, p. 7.

5. Cited by Linda Vaden Gratch, "Recognizing Sexual Harassment," in *Sexual Harassment on Campus: A Guide for Administrators, Faculty, and Students,* ed. Bernice R. Sandler and Robert J. Shoop (Boston: Allyn & Bacon, 1997), p. 283.

FOR ANALYSIS AND DISCUSSION

1. In the introduction Patai describes some of her own experiences with sexual harassment. How do her experiences measure against the legislation of Title VII § 1604.11? Are these the types of encounters § 1604.11 is designed to protect against?

2. How would Patai's "pursuits" as a young graduate student, detailed in paragraph 4, be viewed today? Would we view them as benign if she were male? Do sexual harassment policies allow a double standard? Explain.

3. Evaluate the examples Patai uses to support her claim that sexual harassment laws are going too far. Are these cases typical of sexual harassment suits?

4. In paragraph 12, Patai states that "unable to openly attempt to ban sex and thereby totally alienate their public, feminist reformers . . . have instead tried to set up an obstacle course in the relations between men and women." Is this indeed the feminist agenda? Do you agree with Patai's assessment that this is the hidden agenda of sexual harassment legislation?

5. What measures have some professors taken to avoid the possibility of facing sexual harassment charges? Are the changes Patai describes extreme, or are they necessary in today's academic institutions? Explain.

6. What price, according to Patai, do academic institutions pay when a campus embraces sexual harassment legislation? Address her assertion that such an academic environment is "neither intellectually productive nor morally tolerable" (paragraph 13).

Sex Is the Least of It: Let's Focus on Harassment Law on Work, Not Sex
Vicki Schultz

For many people, sexual harassment means sexual overtures or inappropriate sexual references in the workplace. Yet Vicki Schultz argues that we have been focusing on the wrong issues. Schultz asserts that we face a far more dangerous form of sexual harassment—that of gender-based hostile behavior in which men ridicule the competence of female coworkers and seek to undermine their authority.

Vicki Schultz is a professor of law at Yale University. Her academic specialties include employment discrimination law, gender and work, and feminist theory. Schultz has been published by the *Yale Law Review, The Nation, Ms.,* and in many legal anthologies. The following article first appeared in *The Nation* in May 1998.

BEFORE YOU READ

Is there a difference between sexual harassment and "sexism" in the workplace? If so, what is the distinction?

AS YOU READ

Consider how the other authors featured in this section might respond to Schultz's argument. With what issues might they agree or disagree?

1   The Clarence Thomas hearings, the Tailhook incident, the Gene McKinney trial, the Clinton scandals—if these events spring to mind when you hear the words "sexual harassment," you are not alone. That such images of powerful men making sexual come-ons toward female subordinates should be the defining ones simply proves the power of the popular perception that harassment is first and foremost about sex. It's easy to see why: The media, the courts and some feminists have emphasized this to the exclusion of all else. But the real issue isn't sex, it's sexism on the job. The fact is, most harassment isn't about satisfying sexual desires. It's about protecting work—especially the most favored lines of work—as preserves of male competence and authority.

2   This term the Supreme Court heard three cases involving sex harassment in the workplace. Along with media coverage of current events, the Court's decisions will shape our understanding of this issue into the next century, for all these controversies raise the same fundamental question: Does sex harassment require a special body of law having to do with sexual relations, or should it be treated just like any other form of workplace discrimination?

3   If the Court decides that harassment is primarily a problem of sexual relations, it will be following the same misguided path some courts have taken since they first accepted that such behavior falls under the prohibitions of Title VII of the Civil Rights Act, the major federal statute forbidding sex discrimination in employment. Early decisions outlawed what is known as quid pro quo harassment—typically, a situation where a supervisor penalizes a subordinate who refuses to grant sexual favors. It was crucial for the courts to acknowledge that sexual advances and other interactions can be used in the service of discrimination. Yet their reasoning spelled trouble. The courts said harassment was sex bias because the advances were rooted in a sexual attraction that the ha-

rasser felt for a woman but would not have felt for another man. By locating the problem in the sexual character of the advances rather than in the workplace dynamics of which they were a part—for instance, the paternalistic prerogative of a male boss to punish an employee on the job for daring to step out of her "place" as a woman—the decisions threatened to equate sex harassment with sexual pursuits. From there it was a short step to the proposition that sex in the workplace, or at least sexual interactions between men and women in unequal jobs, is inherently suspect.

4   Yet the problem we should be addressing isn't sex, it's the sexist failure to take women seriously as workers. Sex harassment is a means for men to claim work as masculine turf. By driving women away or branding them inferior, men can insure the sex segregation of the workforce. We know that women who work in jobs traditionally held by men are more likely than other women to experience hostility and harassment at work. Much of the harassment they experience isn't "sexual" in content or design. Even where sexually explicit harassment occurs, it is typically part of a broader pattern of conduct intended to reinforce gender difference and to claim work as a domain of masculine mastery. As one experienced electrician put it in Molly Martin's Hard-Hatted Women, "[We] . . . face another pervasive and sinister kind of harassment which is gender-based, but may have nothing to do with sex. It is harassment aimed at us simply because we are women in a 'man's' job, and its function is to discourage us from staying in our trades."

5   This harassment can take a variety of forms, most of which involve undermining a woman on the job. In one case, male electricians stopped working rather than submit to the authority of a female subforeman. In another, Philadelphia policemen welcomed their new female colleagues by stealing their case files and lacing their uniforms with lime that burned their skin. Even more commonly, men withhold the training and assignments women need to learn to do the job well, or relegate them to menial duties that signal they are incompetent to perform the simplest tasks. Work sabotage is all too common.

6   Nor is this a purely blue-collar phenomenon. About one-third of female physicians recently surveyed said they had experienced sexual harassment, but almost half said they'd been subjected to harassment that had no sexual or physical component but was related simply to their being female in a traditionally male field. In one 1988 court case, a group of male surgical residents went so far as to falsify a patient's medical records to make it appear as though their female colleague had made an error.

7   Men do, of course, resort to sexualized forms of harassment. Sexual overtures may intimidate a woman or label her incompetent in settings where female sexuality is considered incompatible with professionalism. In one 1993 Supreme Court case, a company president suggested that a female manager must have had sex with a client to land an important account. Whether or not the harassment assumes a sexual form, however, what unites all these actions is that they create occupational environments that define womanhood as the opposite of what it takes to be a good worker.

8   From this starting point, it becomes clear that the popular view of harassment is both too narrow and too broad. Too narrow, because the focus on rooting out unwanted sexual activity has allowed us to feel good about protecting women from sexual abuse while leading us to overlook equally pernicious forms of gender-based mistreatment. Too broad, because the emphasis on sexual conduct has encouraged some companies to ban all forms of sexual interaction, even when these do not threaten women's equality on the job.

9   How has the law become too narrow? The picture of harassment-as-sex that developed out of the quid pro quo cases has overwhelmed the conception of the hostile work environment, leading most courts to exonerate seriously sexist misconduct if it does not resemble a sexual come-on. In *Turley v. Union Carbide Corp.*, a court dismissed the harassment claim of a woman whose foreman "pick[ed] on [her] all the time" and treated her worse than the men. Citing Catharine MacKinnon's definition of sexual harassment as "the unwanted imposition of sexual requirements in the context of a relationship of unequal power," the court concluded that the case did not involve actionable harassment because "the foreman did not demand sexual relations, he did not touch her or make sexual jokes."

10   By the same reasoning, in *Reynolds v. Atlantic City Convention Center*, the court ruled against a female electrical subforeman, Reynolds, whose men refused to work for her, made obscene gestures and stood around laughing while she unloaded heavy boxes. Not long before, the union's business agent had proclaimed, "[Now] is not the time, the place or the year, [nor] will it ever be the year for a women foreman." When the Miss America pageant came to town, an exhibitor asked that Reynolds be removed from the floor—apparently, the incongruity between the beauty contestants and the tradeswoman was too much to take—and Reynolds's boss replaced and eventually fired her. Yet the court concluded that none of this amounted to a hostile work environment: The obscene gestures that the court considered "sexual" were too trivial, and the rest of the conduct wasn't sufficiently sexual to characterize as gender-based.

11   These are not isolated occurrences. I recently surveyed hundreds of Title VII hostile work environment cases and found that the courts' disregard of nonsexual forms of harassment is an overwhelming trend. This definitely works against women in male-dominated job settings, but it has also hurt women in traditionally female jobs, who share the experience of harassment that denigrates their competence or intelligence as workers. They are often subjected to sexist forms of authority, humiliation and abuse—objectified not only as sexual commodities but as creatures too stupid or worthless to deserve respect, fit only to be controlled by others ("stupid women who have kids," "too fat to clean rooms," "dumb females who [can't] read or write").

12   Just as our obsession with sexual misconduct obscures many debilitating forms of harassment facing women, it also leads us to overlook some pernicious harassment confronting men on the job. If the legal cases provide any indication, the most common form of harassment men experience is not, as the film *Disclosure* suggests, a proposition from a female boss. It is, instead, hostility from male co-workers seeking to denigrate or drive away men who threaten the

work's masculine image. If a job is to confer manliness, it must be held by those who project the desired sense of manhood. It isn't only women who can detract from that image. In some work settings, men are threatened by the presence of any man perceived to be gay—for homosexuality is often seen as gender deviance—or any other man perceived to lack the manly competence considered suitable for those who hold the job. The case logs are filled with harassment against men who are not married, men who are not attractive to women, men who are seen as weak or slow, men who are openly supportive of women, men who wear earrings, and even young men or boys. Some men have taunted and tormented, battered and beaten other men in the name of purging the brotherhood of wimps and fags—not suitable to stand alongside them as workers.

13   We have been slow to name this problem sex-based harassment because it doesn't fit our top-down, male-female, sexual come-on image of harassment. In *Goluszek v. Smith,* the court ruled against an electronic maintenance mechanic who was disparaged and driven out by his fellow workers. They mocked him for not having a wife, saying a man had to be married to be a machinist. They used gender-based images to assault his competence, saying that if he couldn't fix a machine they'd send in his "daddy"—the supervisor—to do it. They drove jeeps at him and threatened to knock him off his ladder, and when he filed a grievance, his supervisor wrote him up for carelessness and eventually fired him. Not only did the court dismiss Goluszek's claim, the judge simply couldn't conceive that what happened to him was sexual harassment. "The 'sexual harassment' that is actionable under Title VII 'is the exploitation of a powerful position to impose sexual demands or pressures on an unwilling but less powerful person,' " the judge wrote. Perhaps lower courts will adopt a broader view now that the Supreme Court has ruled, in the recent *Oncale v. Sundowner Offshore Services* decision, that male-on-male harassment may be actionable even when it is not sexual in design.

14   Meanwhile, the traditional overemphasis on sex can lead to a repressive impulse to eliminate all hints of sexual expression from the workplace, however benign. Instead of envisioning harassment law as a tool to promote women's equality as workers, the popular understanding of harassment encourages courts and companies to "protect" women's sexual sensibilities. In *Fair v. Guiding Eyes for the Blind,* a heterosexual woman who was the associate director of a nonprofit organization claimed her gay male supervisor had created an offensive environment by making gossipy conversation and political remarks involving homosexuality. It is disturbing that current law inspired such a claim, even though the court correctly ruled that the supervisor's conduct was not sexual harassment.

15   Other men haven't fared so well. In *Pierce v. Commonwealth Life Insurance Co.,* a manager was disciplined for participating in an exchange of sexually explicit cards with a female office administrator. One of the cards Pierce had sent read, "Sex is a misdemeanor. De more I miss, de meanor I get." After thirty years with the company, he was summarily demoted and transferred to another office, with his pay slashed and his personal belongings dumped at a roadside

Hardee's. True, Pierce was a manager and he was responsible for enforcing the company's harassment policy. Still, the reasoning that led to his ouster is unsound—and dangerous. According to his superiors, he might as well have been a "murderer, rapist or child molester; that wouldn't be any worse [than what he had done]." This sort of thing gives feminism a bad name. If companies want to fire men like Pierce, let them do it without the pretense of protecting women from sexual abuse.

16   Equally alarming are reports that, in the name of preventing sexual harassment, some companies are adopting policies that prohibit a man and woman from traveling or staying at the same hotel together on business, or prevent a male supervisor from giving a performance evaluation to a female underling behind closed doors without a lawyer present. One firm has declared that its construction workers can't even look at a woman for more than five seconds. With such work rules, who will want to hire women? How will women obtain the training they need if their male bosses and colleagues can't interact with them as equals?

17   It's a mistake to try to outlaw sexual interaction in the workplace. The old Taylorist project of purging organizations of all sexual and other emotional dynamics was deeply flawed. Sexuality is part of the human experience, and so long as organizations still employ people rather than robots, it will continue to flourish in one form or another. And sexuality is not simply a tool of gender domination; it is also a potential source of empowerment and even pleasure for women on the job. Indeed, some research suggests that where men and women work as equals in integrated settings, sex harassment isn't a problem. Sexual talk and joking continues, but it isn't experienced as harassment. It's not impossible to imagine sexual banter as a form of playfulness, even solidarity, in a work world that is increasingly competitive and stressful.

18   Once we realize that the problem isn't sex but sexism, we can re-establish our concept of harassment on firmer ground. Title VII was never meant to police sexuality. It was meant to provide people the chance to pursue their life's work on equal terms—free of pressure to conform to prescribed notions of how women and men are supposed to behave in their work roles. Properly conceived, quid pro quo harassment is a form of discrimination because it involves men exercising the power to punish women, as workers, who have the temerity to say no, as women. Firing women who won't have sex on the job is no different from firing black women who refuse to perform cleaning work, or female technicians who refuse to do clerical work, that isn't part of their job descriptions.

19   So, too, hostile-work-environment harassment isn't about sexual relations; it's about how work relations engender inequality. The legal concept was created in the context of early race discrimination cases, when judges recognized that Jim Crow systems could be kept alive not just through company acts (such as hiring and firing) but also through company atmospheres that made African-American workers feel different and inferior. That discriminatory environments are sometimes created by "sexual" conduct is not the point. Sex

should be treated just like anything else in the workplace: Where it furthers sex discrimination, it should go. Where it doesn't, it's not the business of our civil rights laws.

20   It's too easy to allow corporate America to get away with banning sexual interaction without forcing it to attend to the larger structures of workplace gender discrimination in which both sexual and not-so-sexual forms of harassment flourish. Let's revitalize our understanding of harassment to demand a world in which all women and even the least powerful men can work together as equals in whatever endeavors their hearts and minds desire.

FOR ANALYSIS AND DISCUSSION

1. On what foundation does Schultz present her argument that sexual harassment is more about power and less about actual "sex"? How does she support this view?
2. How do you think Schultz would respond to Richard Dooling's commentary about sexual harassment? How do you think she would react to him personally? Are they discussing two entirely different things?
3. Why, according to Schultz, is sexism in the workplace far more dangerous than sexual advances or innuendoes? Do you agree?
4. Schultz mentions several lawsuits that were lost because sexual harassment precedent had focused on sexual advances rather than sexism. Apply her examples to Title VII § 1604.11. Should these cases have been protected by that section? Explain.
5. How can men, according to Schultz, suffer from sexual prejudice in the workplace?
6. Evaluate Schultz's overall argument. How balanced is it? How does it compare to the other arguments presented in this section? Explain.

WRITING ASSIGNMENTS: SEXUAL HARASSMENT

1. Evaluate the sexual harassment "climate" at your college or university. Does your school have a sexual harassment policy? Have any sexual harassment lawsuits been brought against faculty, staff, or students? In a well-supported and organized argument essay, explain why you think your college's sexual harassment policy is (a) inadequate, (b) sufficient, or (c) extreme.
2. Read the article by Cathy Young from the August/September online issue of *Reason Magazine,* "Why Bill Clinton Can't Handle the Truth," at <http://www.reason.com/9808/fe.young.html>. Using information gathered from the article, the essays in this section, and your own perspective, write an argument essay in which you address whether the Clinton scandals did or did not change the American perspective on sexual harassment.
3. Daphne Patai states that sexual harassment legislation is changing the intellectual climate on college campuses. Professor Matthew Dallek addresses the issue of sexual harassment on college campuses in his article "Harassment Backlash" in *Salon Magazine* at <http://www.salonmagazine.com/it/feature/

1998/12/14feature.html>. Write an argument essay addressing the phenomenon of "backlash" as it applies to sexual harassment on college campuses. What is causing it? What does this backlash mean for students and faculty? What is your opinion on this issue?

ADOPTION: DO SEALED RECORDS VIOLATE OR PROTECT OUR RIGHTS?

Adoption and the Sealed Record System
Elizabeth Bartholet

For most of the twentieth century, adoption severed all ties between birth parent and child. Records were sealed, preventing both birth parent and child from knowing anything about the other. Even today this system remains essentially intact, with records remaining confidential unless a court finds reasonable cause to release the information. However, recently this practice has come under fire, especially from adoptees who claim the right to their birth records. Moreover, they maintain that the secrecy surrounding adoption is morally wrong and psychologically damaging.

Elizabeth Bartholet is a professor of law at Harvard Law School. Her specialties include public interest law, adoption, reproductive technology, and employment discrimination. Bartholet's publications include "Beyond Biology: The Politics of Adoption and Reproduction" in the *Duke Journal of Gender Law and Policy* (1995) and *Family Bonds* (1993), from which the following was taken.

BEFORE YOU READ
Do adoptees have the right to see their original birth certificates? Why or why not?

AS YOU READ
What is the history of the adoption sealed record system? On what reasoning is it based? Why was it implemented in the United States?

1   The tradition[1] in this country through most of this century has been to sever all links with the birth family when the adoptive family is formed. The court creates a new parent-child relationship between the adoptive parents and the adoptee and simultaneously seals the records that document the transfer of the child from the birth to the adoptive family. The child is issued a new birth certificate, which reads as if he or she had been born to the adoptive parents. The original birth certificate goes into the sealed file. For legal purposes the child is effectively reborn, with all legal and relational links to the past destroyed. The sealed records are supposed to ensure against any reconnection with that past.

Members of the birth and adoptive families, along with the public, are denied access to them. The adoption agencies cooperate by keeping confidential any information that might enable birth families to figure out where their children have gone and adoptive families to figure out where their children come from. The records are sealed not simply for the duration of the adoptee's childhood but permanently, to be opened only on a showing of "good cause," which is generally defined as a demonstration of overwhelming necessity.

2   Societies in other times and places teach that adoption does not need to be constructed this way. The sealed record tradition is actually short-lived in the history of adoption as an institution. In early Roman times, adoption was for a period designed as an open relationship in which the adoptee knew and would inherit from both the biologic and the adoptive parents. In many societies to-day adoptions are arranged informally among the private parties, with the government taking no action to sever or to redefine parental links.[2] In the United States, adoptive arrangements were similarly informal until the latter part of the nineteenth century, and it was not until the 1920s that states began to pass laws designed to separate birth and adoptive families. Informal adoption continues to flourish in many communities in the United States today, as children are transferred on a temporary or long-term basis from one parental figure to another within a kinship or community network.[3]

3   The sealed record system stands in significant contrast to the manner in which our society structures other complex family relationships. It is no secret that relatively few families today fit the nuclear family image on which the adoptive family is modeled—the stable husband-wife couple raising their children on an ongoing basis to the exclusion of any other significant parental figures. Some children are raised in this kind of family, but most are raised by single mothers or divorced parents, either alone or in combination with some succession of mates. The legal system ordinarily makes no attempt to write out of existence, by sealing records or other such mechanisms, the various parental figures who walk out of their children's lives, such as the divorced parent who relinquishes custody. It is only in regulating adoptive families—families formed in the absence of any blood link—that the government feels that it has to seal records so as to figuratively destroy the existence of the family that *is* linked by blood.

4   The trend in this country is quite clearly in the direction of greater openness. The push for change is coming primarily from adult adoptees and birth parents—usually birth mothers, since birth fathers are rarely heard from. The openness proponents, together with their self-help and advocacy organizations, constitute what is known as the search movement. They have focused attention on the problems they see as inherent in the sealed record system and on the importance they attribute to the search that enables birth parents and adoptees to connect with each other.[4] The changing adoption market has also enabled many birth mothers who want openness to insist on it. The enormous demand for infants to adopt means that birth mothers can do a lot to establish the terms on which they will surrender their children, and many have been pushing for more openness.

5   This move has resulted in recent years in some changes in the legal framework governing adoption. A few states have enacted legislation that gives adult adoptees an absolute right to access their original birth records. Most states have enacted some kind of mutual consent system for releasing identifying information (naming the parties) to birth parents, adoptive parents, and adoptees, once the adoptees have reached the age of eighteen or twenty-one. As of 1991, more than thirty states had such legislation, with some states opting for passive registry systems, in which the various parties to the adoption can register their consent to or interest in contact, and others opting for active registry systems, in which the state facilitates a process for finding out whether the relevant parties will consent to a desired contact.

6   In addition, a significant amount of *de facto* openness has developed. Many birth mothers have been using their new bargaining power to obtain varying degrees of openness, ranging from a simple exchange of identifying information to elaborate agreements for ongoing correspondence and visitation. Also, search movement organizations have developed the search methodology to a fine art, enabling large numbers of adoptees and birth parents who want to locate each other to find their way through and around the sealed record rules.

7   A burning issue in today's adoption world is whether to move any further in this direction. Nearly everyone agrees on the importance of providing adoptive families with what is categorized as nonidentifying information about the birth family: health, genetic, and social information. But there is no consensus on where we should go from here with respect to identifying information. The National Committee for Adoption, an organization of adoption agencies that constitutes a powerful lobbying force, is adamantly opposed to any significant deviation from the sealed record system. It has gone along with proposals for passive mutual consent registries, but these registries have been notoriously ineffective in enabling adoptees who want to make contact with their birth families to do so.

8   The sealed record system continues to stand as a significant barrier between the birth and the adoptive family in most adoptive arrangements. Records continue to be sealed on a permanent basis as part of the adoption process. Almost all states deny the adult adoptee and the birth parent any access to the records unless the other party has consented, and some states require consent by the adoptive parents as well. Few states have created effective systems to assess whether birth parents or adoptees would consent if they knew their counterparts were interested in obtaining information or in arranging for a meeting. Most state and state-licensed agencies continue to arrange adoptions on a confidential basis and refuse to open up their records that would permit birth and adoptive families to get in touch with each other.

The Current Debate

9   The debate over the future of the sealed record system is fierce, with the opposing advocates at one another's throats. But the themes sounded on both sides of the debate are strangely similar: biologic links are of vital significance

to parenting; adoption is a flawed institution, and the families that it creates are both flawed and fragile.

10   For search movement advocates, the idea that biology is central to parenting is a reason for openness. They argue that adoptive families built on secrecy, on a denial of the birth family's existence, are sick at the core. They contend that adoptees who are cut off from knowledge of their biologic heritage suffer "genealogical bewilderment." They advocate the search for the birth family and what is called the reunion with that family as the road to recovery for today's adoptees and birth parents. They advocate elimination of the sealed record system and greater openness in communication between birth and adoptive families as the road to a healthy adoption system in the future. For many people in the search movement, openness is only a partial solution to the adoption "problem." They contend that the biologic link between parent and child is so important that the very institution of adoption should be eliminated or at least radically altered. They argue that birth mothers should not be put in situations that force them to surrender their children, and urge that society make greater efforts to preserve biologic families. In situations in which the birth family absolutely must relinquish day-to-day custody, they believe that guardianship arrangements should be substituted for adoption, so as to preserve a legal parenting link as well as an informational link with the birth family.[5]

11   For adoption traditionalists, the centrality of the biologic link is a reason to maintain the closed record system. They take a more positive view of adoption, arguing that it makes sense in many situations for birth parents to surrender their children for others to raise. But their claim that sealed records are essential to make adoption work reveals a similar sense of suspicion of the arrangement. They argue that sealed records are needed to protect the privacy of the birth parents, to enable the birth mother to put the past behind her and move on to a new life. They argue that sealed records are also needed to protect the privacy and integrity of the new adoptive family, preventing the confusion inherent in the existence of another set of parents and protecting the adoptee from unpleasant revelations about the circumstances surrounding his or her birth and surrender. Implicit in these arguments is the sense that there is something deeply shameful in giving birth to a child that one is not prepared to raise and in the decision to surrender, and that there is something very threatening to adoptive families about the existence of blood-linked relatives.

The Mixed Messages Inherent in a Move to Openness

12   For those who believe in adoption as a valid family form, the sealed record system should be deeply problematic. Sealed records and the creation of a new birth certificate mean that adoptive families are founded on a lie—a claim that the original birth never took place and that the adoptee was instead born into the adoptive family. Implicit in the lie is the assumption that the adoptive family is in fact a flawed and inferior family form. If it was as good as the biology-based family, there would be no need to lie. If it was permissible for birth mothers to relinquish children they felt unable to raise, there would be no need for them to seal off their past. If the parent-child relationship in the adoptive fam-

ily was as powerful and legitimate as other parenting relationships, there would be no need to seal the adoptive family off from threats that birth parents might appear on the scene to usurp the parenting role.

13   Greater openness seems a good move from this perspective. Adoption should be understood as a positive alternative to biologic parenting, not as a desperate last resort, either for birth parents or for the infertile. Adoptive families should be understood as healthy, functioning families, not as fragile entities that will fall apart if a "real" mother walks in the front door. The attempt to erase the birth family is destined to place adoptive families on the low end of a family hierarchy. Greater openness would free people to see that adoptive families are not simply viable but hold some special strengths as a family form.

14   Of course, greater openness might be thought to create a threatening sense of difference for adoptees as they grow up—a sense that there is something wrong with their family because, unlike other children, they have this other family to think about. But *most* children today grow up with a changing cast of characters playing various parenting roles as the years go by, with single parents living with some combination of relatives and friends and mates and with birth parents divorcing and moving out as stepparents move in to share or dispute parenting functions. In today's world, it is not at all clear that the sealed record system functions to reduce the adoptee's sense of difference. In fact, by treating the adoptee's extended family network so differently from other children's, the system seems to signal that there is something uniquely problematic and shameful about the particular complexity that has to do with adoptive status.

15   All this argues for reversing the current presumptions about identifying information. At present we seal adoption records and allow parties to the arrangement to obtain the information only upon a demonstration of good cause. We should move to a system of open records and allow the parties to request closure upon a demonstration of good cause.

16   While greater openness seems the appropriate move for the future, the politics of adoption today make decisions about what steps to take *now* very complicated. In the current context, a move to embrace openness might further denigrate rather than affirm adoption. The pressure for openness is coming from a movement that is profoundly hostile to adoption as a family form. In addition, today's world is one in which we are all bombarded on a regular basis with messages that reinforce the significance of biologically linked parenting. In this world birth parents *are* something of a threat to the viability of adoptive families. In a future world in which the stigma surrounding adoption and infertility has been eliminated or at least significantly reduced, opening records should send a signal that birth family links are real and relevant but not of necessary and central importance to an adoptee's personhood or to parenting relationships. The establishment of an open-record system today might send a very different signal.

17   Complicated issues also arise in thinking about just how powerful the connection between birth and adoptive families should be in any new regime of openness. It seems right to structure adoption as an independent family form

rather than as a poor imitation of the biological family in its idealized nuclear form. But freeing ourselves from the traditional model forces us to think about what should be central to the concept of family. We might want to embrace the idea of openness with respect to *information,* creating a system in which birth and adoptive families are free to know each other and to establish relationships throughout the adoptee's childhood as well as in adulthood. But we might reject any notion that birth and adoptive parents should share *control,* or attempt to divide the legal rights and responsibilities of parenting. By ridding ourselves of the notion that adoption should be designed to duplicate the biologic nuclear family, we would be forced to think about which aspects of that family model we want to appropriate and which we want to reject. We would be forced to think about the ways in which adoptive families should be similar, as well as the ways in which they should be different.

18   My idea of what an open regime would look like is quite different from the vision implicit in the claims of the search movement. If there were open access to birth records, I do not see most adoptees rushing to make contact with birth relatives. If identifying information were shared from the point of the adoption on, I do not imagine that there would be more than limited communication between adoptees and their birth relatives in most instances. But I may be wrong. Openness means that more ambiguity and contingency would be built into the adoptive situation. In some cases, the biologic relationship might prove important or even predominant. It might prove more generally important than I now think would be the case. But parenting should not imply that the parent owns the child's affections or has a right to exclude alternative relationships.

NOTES

1. On the issues discussed in this chapter, see Joan Hollinger, "Aftermath of Adoption," in Joan Hollinger, ed., *Adoption Law and Practice* (New York: Matthew Bender, 1988; supplement 1992); Lincoln Caplan, "Open Adoption," parts I and II, *New Yorker,* May 21 and 28, 1990.

2. See Carroll, *Adoption in Eastern Oceania.*

3. See Stack, *All Our Kin.*

4. Classic search movement texts include Arthur D. Sorosky, et al., *The Adoption Triangle: Sealed or Opened Records: How They Affect Adoptees, Birthparents, and Adoptive Parents* (Garden City, N.Y.: Anchor, 1984); Florence Fisher, *The Search for Anna Fisher* (New York: Fawcett Crest, 1974); Betty J. Lifton, *Twice Born: Memoirs of an Adopted Daughter* (New York: McGraw-Hill, 1975), and *Lost and Found: The Adoption Experience* (New York: Harper & Row, 1988); H. David Kirk, *Shared Fate* (New York: Free Press, 1964); and Ruthena H. Kittson (pseud.), *Orphan Voyage* (self-published, 1981).

5. See Annette Baran and Reuben Pannor, "It's Time for Sweeping Change," *American Adoption Congress Newsletter,* Summer 1990, p. 5.

FOR ANALYSIS AND DISCUSSION

1. Make a pro/con checklist of the arguments for and against the sealed record system. Evaluate which seem more compelling.

2. In paragraph 3, Bartholet comments that unlike in adoption procedures, the legal system does not "write out of existence" parents who walk out of their children's lives because of divorce. Evaluate this statement. Are the two situations parallel?

3. What is the "mutual consent system"? Why are search movement organizations pushing beyond the mutual consent system to completely open records? What is your position on this issue? Explain.

4. Evaluate the search movement's claim that "biology is central to parenting." What does this mean?

5. Analyze Bartholet's statement in paragraph 12 that "[s]ealed records and the creation of a new birth certificate mean adoptive families are founded on a lie."

6. What is Bartholet's position on adoption? What is her solution to this issue? Do you agree?

7. In her closing statements, Bartholet says that should adoption records be open, she does "not see most adoptees rushing to make contact with birth relatives." On what does she base this assertion? Does it strengthen her argument? Explain.

Strengthening Families
Rev. Thomas F. Brosnan

Many children of adoption experience a sense of loss and displacement, despite the best attempts of their adopted families to make them feel loved and truly included. This situation has nothing to do with the efforts of the adoptive family. Rather, says Reverend Thomas F. Brosnan, "it exists quite apart from the material well-being provided by the adoptive family." The desire to search for one's birth parents stems from a need to feel connected to one's "true" identity, a concept often difficult for nonadoptees to understand.

Reverend Thomas F. Brosnan is a Catholic priest of the Diocese of Brooklyn, New York, who works with families dealing with adoption issues. He is also an adoptee himself. The following essay was first delivered as a keynote speech at the 1996 National Maternity and Adoption Conference for Catholic Charities USA in San Antonio, Texas.

BEFORE YOU READ

How would you feel if your parents told you that you were adopted? Would you want to know? If you *are* adopted, how old were you when you found out and how did the knowledge affect you?

AS YOU READ

Why does Brosnan capitalize "Loss" and "Belong"? What impact does this make on the points he is trying to convey in his essay?

1   This presentation is entitled Strengthening Families. Through references to history, literature, film and personal experience I will attempt to offer some suggestions on how adoptive families might fight the subtle and not-so-subtle forces which seek to weaken and destabilize the family unit. I will suggest that strength is born of the acknowledgment of truth, specifically an acknowledgment of truth about the experience of Loss and the nature of Belonging.

2   By way of introduction my name is Tom Brosnan. I am a Roman Catholic Priest of the Diocese of Brooklyn, New York, where I presently live and work with Korean Catholics. I am no psychologist, pastoral counselor, or social worker; in other words, I'm no expert. My remarks come from my experience concerning my own adoption and that of other adopted persons, birth parents, and adoptive parents with whom I have worked over the past 15 years. This presentation is, I suppose a "confession" of sorts regarding my journey of discovering who I am; a process which, I would suggest, is the vocation of every human being, adopted or not.

3   Permit me to begin with a little background. In 1952 a young woman of 25 was living in a boarding house connected with the Peabody Conservatory of Music in Baltimore, Maryland. She was not a music student like her roommate or the rest of the inhabitants of the house, but was invited to stay there because there were few female boarders. She met a music student from Toronto, and they fell in love. She realized she was pregnant after her boyfriend had returned to Toronto at semester's end. She visited, she pleaded, but he said he could not, he would not marry her. Meanwhile another student from Peabody, a gallant young man from Virginia, who knew she was pregnant offered to marry her. The other students, not knowing she was pregnant, had a bridal shower for her in their boarding house. Within a few weeks however, she informed her friends that they decided not to marry. Becoming desperate the young woman told her older brother she was pregnant with no hope of marrying. The brother, a Jesuit priest, arranged for her to go to New York to deliver and relinquish the baby for adoption. The priest, the boyfriend, the gallant Southerner and her loyal roommate, Sophia, were the only ones who knew of her pregnancy. She delivered her child on January 10th 1953 at Misericordia Hospital, then located in Manhattan, and immediately relinquished the boy to adoption. He waited in a foster home for six months and was eventually adopted by a couple from Brooklyn where he lived with them and his adoptive mother's parents in a small row house in Flatbush.

4   My parents told me I was adopted when I was 12, though I can remember knowing since I was 5. We never talked about adoption, yet it seems to me these many years later that adoption, with all its cumbersome baggage, was the air we breathed. We never acknowledged to each other the truth about the loss each of us suffered. We were, I believe, victims of the closed adoption system which exerts an extraordinarily powerful hold on all members of the triad. It is a cruel task master and demands untold sacrifices. It is merciless in its destructive power. Like the razed Berlin Wall that divided a city for a generation, like the dismantled statues of Lenin across the Russias, I pray for the demise of the closed adoption system. And I offer these words in the hope to effect that out-

come by alerting you who are adoptive parents, adoption specialists, social workers and clergy to the dangers that secrecy and lies can wield on the family.

5   I love the movies. It's one of the few places I lose my self-control and permit myself to feel those difficult emotions which the experiences of Loss and Belonging evoke. One of my favorite films of all time is *Cinema Paradiso,* an Italian film of a few years ago about a fatherless young boy from a small Sicilian town who befriends the movie-house projectionist. The boy learns to love movies while learning to love the older man who teaches him so much. When he is 18 he joins the army and we see him standing with his mother and sister at the train station waiting for the good-byes to end. The old man is there too. He whispers in the boy's ear: "Go, and never, never come back." The boy obeys. He goes to Rome and becomes a famous film director. He calls his mother now and then but keeps his promise never to return to his hometown. Then, the old man dies, and the mother leaves a message on the son's answering machine telling him the day and time of the funeral. "You know he'll never come back," the skeptical sister tells the mother. But, he does.

6   On the day of his return the camera is focused on the mother as she sits in a rocker, nervously knitting. Slowly the camera closes in on the knitting needles, deftly moving back and forth twining yarn and space. The camera focuses on her wrinkled hands and the long needles when in the background we hear a car pull up on the gravel path. Suddenly the hands stop, the woman quickly stands, unconsciously catching a piece of yarn on her dress. The camera stays focused on the yarn as it unwinds with every step the mother takes toward the door. Then we hear the car door slam and the yarn ceases to unravel. We know without a word being spoken, or any visual image given besides the unraveling yarn, that mother and son have embraced after many lost years.

7   With this simple yet beautiful image I wish to remind you of something you already know: that the experience of Loss and the need to Belong are universal human experiences. But none of us likes to face the pain of Loss, and we don't like to be reminded of it in others. When we are reminded, our immediate reaction is to make it go away, to lessen its obvious import to the person, to hopelessly put a mere bandage on what is doubtless a gushing wound.

8   The Catholic Bishops of the United States have done just that in their recently published Book of Blessings. Among the many rituals is one entitled "Blessing for Parents and an Adopted Child." The prayer begins: "It has pleased God our heavenly Father to answer the earnest prayers of (this couple) for the gift of a child . . . " Despite the feeling of joy the words are meant to instill there remains the unasked question, have the events which preceded this adoption ritual, namely the relinquishment of the child by his mother, has that also pleased God? What is missing is any reference to what has had to have taken place in order for this joyful blessing to occur. There is no mention, no acknowledgment of Loss, of the relinquishment that had to have occurred in order for the adoption to have taken place.

9   Although difficult, it is essential to acknowledge this fundamental truth about the experience of Loss in adoption. It is not easy, however, and it is not a one-shot deal. It will have to be acknowledged at different times during the

adoptee's maturing process, but I believe it to be essential in the building of strong healthy families. Acknowledging truth about Loss means first of all to give up the lies about what actually happened. It means giving up myths like the chosen baby story so many adoptees were told. It means to accept the events as are known, not fabricating explanations which we think might lessen the blow. You know what I mean: like the "your parents were killed in a car crash" story, intended to save the adoptee from the truth which we presume to be far worse: a truth like "your parents weren't married; or, your mother was raped; or even, you're the product of incest." If the adoptive parents truly have the best interest of the child at heart, I would suggest that the truth is the only choice they really have in attempting to do what's best for their son or daughter.

10   "There is no truth existing which I fear," Thomas Jefferson once wrote, "or (that I) wish unknown to the whole world." Another Thomas, many centuries prior to Jefferson, placed truth at the heart of what it means to be a human being. "For (Thomas) Aquinas, the most decisive human trait is that human beings are truth-seeking animals, moved by love for the truth (come what may) . . . So inherent is this drive for the truth in human nature that it is an imperative . . . to address a human being in any lesser mode is to do his nature violence."

11   As H. David Kirk explained in his groundbreaking book on adoption, *Shared Fate*, published nearly 30 years ago, there is at least one condition that each member of the adoption triad shares, and that is the experience of Loss. Acknowledging the truth about Loss is the beginning of mutual respect and love. . . .

12   Not all, but many adoptive parents, come to the adoption process through the Loss we call infertility. Whether couples decide to adopt when they are first diagnosed, or whether they come to that decision only after they have endured the horrors and humiliations of the fertility clinics, once they decide to adopt they have acknowledged the terrible reality that they will never have their own children. The decision to adopt marks the moment they give up their dream of seeing "flesh of their flesh and bone of their bone." What the infertile couple needs to do is acknowledge that the choice to adopt is their second choice. To admit to themselves that if they had their way adoption would most likely not be a part of their lives. They choose to adopt because there is no other way to become parents.

13   Acknowledging the truth of Loss is also a part of the birth parents' lives, especially the mother. I believe there is no closer relationship than a mother and her unborn child. Perhaps you saw the moving *Losing Isaiah*. Whether or not you liked the scenario, perhaps you would agree with me that even a crack-addicted woman feels that powerful bond with her child. The act of relinquishment is so wrenching an event that young women have told me that they chose to abort their babies rather than relinquish them to adoption. Some of us may judge this to be the height of selfishness, but I wonder if there is not some instinctual response involved in making that drastic decision. No matter what the reasons for relinquishment might be, the emotional response to the act of relinquishment is analogous to abortion, an unbloody abortion if you will, but as one prominent psychiatrist has written, "a psychological abortion" nonetheless. . . .

14   In my biased opinion the greatest Loss is suffered by the adopted person. I want to make it very clear, however, that adoption may indeed be in many, many cases a wonderful blessing for all involved. It may indeed be the only merciful solution to a seemingly impossible situation. Adoption can be one of the noblest of human achievements, but for the adopted person it is always, always the result of a tragic loss. I am not suggesting that problems within the adoptive family are the result of any lack of love on the part of parents, but simply saying that we must acknowledge the truth and not believe the false premise, the myth, which suggests that love conquers all. Because love does not conquer all, love can not, love should not. "Love can neither eradicate biology," as one writer-adoptee has put it, nor can love alter events which have already occurred. Let's not pretend that love can or should.

15   Adoption is a life-long process and it is at times hard work. The adoptive parents must acknowledge the truth of their infertility not only when first adopting, but years later when their child enters puberty and they begin to witness his or her sexual awakening with all its potential fecundity. They must face it each time their adoptive children have children. Adoption can make an infertile couple into the greatest of parents, but it can never make them fertile.

16   Adoption as relinquishment is a life-long process for the birth mother. I've met a number of birth mothers who have never had any more children; and others, like my mother, who had one child every year, year after year. Some birth mothers feel so guilty, it has been observed they punish themselves by suppressing their fertility, while other seek to replace what was lost.

17   For the adoptee, life is adoption. I think this is true whether an adopted person admits it or not. There is always either an active curiosity about where you came from or a strong denial of any desire to know. If anyone asked me while I was in my teens or twenties if I wanted to know who my birth mother was I would have vehemently said "no, of course not." It took me over thirty years to realize what I needed to do. It is the adoptee's dilemma of belonging and not-belonging, struggling between the need to know and misguided feelings of loyalty and gratitude. I can never forget the experience I had when I began my search for my mother over ten years ago. Before I found her I discovered that her brother was a Jesuit priest who had died rather young at Georgetown University. One day I got in the car and drove down to Georgetown. I visited my uncle's grave and decided to ring the bell of the Jesuit residence. The priest who answered turned out to be not only my uncle's classmate but his best friend, having grown up with him in Philadelphia. Fr. Dineen was a very kind man and I spent the entire day with him listening to the many stories he longed to tell of my uncle and their friendship. After dinner he invited me to his room, "to see some old photos," he said. As we were about to open the album, it suddenly dawned on me that this would be the first time in my 33 years of life that I was to see someone related to me. Just last week I had a similar experience when I met with my mother's roommate, Sophia, the roommate she was living with when carrying me. This was our third meeting since my mother's death and Sophia said she had brought me a present. She took out a photograph she said

she found accidently. It was a picture of both my mother and father, cheek to cheek, posing in one of those quick-picture booths. I secretly wondered as I studied their faces whether I was there too, still unseen, but forever part of their lives. The losses suffered in adoption are also always there, whether we acknowledge them or not.

18   Those of you not adopted no doubt take for granted the importance of growing up with people related to you, who look and act like you. Adoptees miss that very primal experience. I would suggest it is at the heart of the dilemma of the adopted person who feels on some level that he does not belong in his adoptive family. This does not necessarily have anything to do with either the abundance of love within the adoptive family, or lack of it. It exists quite apart from the material well-being provided by the adoptive family. In adoption groups you often hear adoptees classify themselves as "good-adoptees" or "bad-adoptees." The good ones never searched while their parents were alive, the bad ones were always running away. But when the adopted person does decide to search, he is looking to belong. The adoptee feels himself to be a literal misfit, not quite fitting in, misplaced somehow, in another manner of speaking, he feels himself to be an exile. Belonging and identity are synonymous for the adoptee, but he must initiate his search, or at least acknowledge the desire to search for his identity, in order for the healing to begin. . . .

19   In the acknowledgment of the truth about Loss and the need to Belong a word must be said about Anger. The anger of the infertile couple at the loss of their dream: their intended children. The anger of the birth mother at the loss of her child: the relinquishment. In recent years we have seen, thank God, the anger of birth fathers whose rights are so often violated in the adoption process. And most significantly perhaps, the anger of the adopted person, who feels the extraordinary loss of parents, heritage and genetic connection.

20   For some adoptees, anger remains suppressed; for others, it becomes destructive and even violent. I can never forget the day I went to the Catholic Home Bureau in Manhattan to see if I could get any information regarding my adoption. The nun sat calmly behind the desk reading from the papers in front of her. She read me an account of my adoption and gave me the non-identifying information I had requested. I knew she was not supposed to tell me my mother's name but I asked just the same. She said, of course, she could not give me the name but then asked in a tone of voice that triggered in me a cascade of rage: "Why would you want to know, didn't you have a good adoption?" I realized that at that moment if I had had a gun I would have killed her. I am not exaggerating here, I know for certain I would have killed. Perhaps that's what happened to Moses the day he saw the Egyptian beating the Hebrew, an event which triggered in him a cascade of rage, an anger that had been welling up all his life, intimately connected with his struggle over identity and belonging, and absolutely pivotal in the history of salvation. . . .

21   A word of anger must be raised against what might be called the mark of illegitimacy. Society labels those born illegitimate, bastards. You may think it strange that I, as an illegitimately-born individual, am ambiguous about this designation. On the one hand I disdain the state and the church for creating

such a designation because of its repercussions. In order for me to be ordained a priest I had to request special dispensation because bastards could not receive Holy Orders. That has recently changed but the psychological effects of such a designation always remain. On the other hand, it is argued that the closed adoption system was created to protect the child from the mark of illegitimacy. If that is true (though I am not convinced it is the real reason for sealed records) then I would prefer to be labeled a bastard and be able to see my birth certificate, than continue to be denied that fundamental right. In any event my parents were not married, and so I am born in different status. But I am in good company, and feel a certain kindred spirit with other bastards of history. And there are many: Erasmus, Leonardo da Vinci, Pope Clement VII, to name a few. . . .

22   A word of anger must also be raised against the closed adoption system and sealed records. Closed records, while purporting to insure confidentiality for the birth mother, mean that I as an adopted person have no right to my own name. Sealed records rob me of my name, my heritage, my medical history, and any connection to those related to me by blood. My question is this: Is the practice of closed adoption which separates child from mother without the child's consent, which suppresses knowledge of family heritage and genetic connection, which refuses to reveal the child's name even to the child himself, are these any different from the methods employed by the institution of slavery? Who can honestly deny that it constitutes, at the very least, a psychological slavery; or as Dr. Leston Havens of Harvard put it, "a psychological possession of the human being"?

23   And a word of anger must be raised against the myth of confidentiality. Lawyers, social workers and church officials assert that confidentiality was promised to the birth mother, and a promise given can not be breached. But then, I ask, why was my name, that is, the name given to me at birth by my birth mother, that is, my mother's surname, why was that name printed on the very adoption papers given to my adoptive parents, if indeed the state wished to assure my birth mother of confidentiality? Why? Because confidentiality for the birth mother was not really ever intended. It is a myth. . . .

24   The adoption reform movement has attempted over the years to correct what seems to many members of the triad a terrible injustice. I would suggest that the injustice of closed adoption is based on a philosophy of life we call dualism. Dualism sees everything in black and white; everything is reduced to an either/or dichotomy. This virus of dualism invaded the psychology of adoption early on, and remains active yet: "Psychology emphasized environment rather than heredity as a more important factor in child development," Linda Burgess reminds us in her book *The Art of Adoption*. "Parents saw the chance to erase in their adopted children the hereditary components which, it was assumed, were of dubious quality . . . the personality and character of the child could be molded and their adopted children would become as if born to them."

25   Today, as near daily discoveries are made in genetic research, we are coming to appreciate the great impact of heredity in human development, not only in its obvious physical results but in the psychological and even emotional tem-

perament of the individual. And it becomes increasingly obvious that the human person is not the isolated product of either genetics or heredity, but rather the continuing result of a very complex interplay of inherited traits and environmental conditioning.

26   Dualist thinking invades our religious life and beliefs about human life. It undermines the proper relationship between body and soul, spirit and flesh. It distorts our vision and teaches us to disdain the body. It abhors the flesh; it loathes things sexual. And if adoption is about anything, it is about sex, about the uncontrollable urges of first love, or even the violent urges of adolescence. Dualist thinking teaches us to regard everything in the adoptees' history prior to the adoption as dark and dirty, to be forgotten and purged. Dualism is the preeminent denier of truth. True religion on the other hand seeks to embrace the tension between body and soul, spirit and flesh. Religion, according to the great Catholic theologian von Balthasar, is "the renewed bonding of previously separated parts." St. Teresa of Avila, the great Spanish mystic, put it this way: "For never, however exalted the soul may be, is anything else more fitting than self-knowledge . . . " The adopted person's search for his origins is then a religious experience. It is a spiritual journey, a pilgrimage of self-knowledge, a holy endeavor.

27   The search is undergone in order to gain the experience of integrity, of wholeness, of health. The Latin root of the word salvation is salus, meaning health. And the English words wholeness and holiness are more closely related than simply their shared sound. In the adopted person's search for origins, in his drive for the truth, and through his desire to belong, he becomes the paradigm, the sacrament if you will, of Everyman. "You have made us for Thyself, O Lord," St. Augustine wrote some 1500 years ago," and our hearts are restless until they rest in Thee." . . .

28   I began this presentation with a simple cinematic image, permit me to end with another from the film *Empire of the Sun*. It's about a British boy who is living in Shanghai with his parents when the Japanese are about to invade. In the mass confusion of the Europeans' exodus, the boy is separated from his parents, and spends his adolescence in a prisoner of war camp. It is the last scene of the movie which strikes a deep resonance within me. The war is over and parents of lost children have come to the Red Cross camp in the hope of finding their lost children. We see a group of youngsters huddled in a circle, adults moving slowly through them, desperate to find their missing children. The boy's father passes without recognizing him. His mother does the same, but then returns and studies the boy's haggard, weary face, and then she calls his name. The camera first focuses on the boy's face, then fixes solely on his eyes. The boy is so tired, he cannot even blink, he seems catatonic, his glassy eyes the windows to a worn and weary soul. The boy's mother embraces him. Then, and only then, the creased wrinkles around those eyes begin to relax and the boy finally, gratefully, slowly closes his eyes. The wandering, the worrying, the searching, is at an end. I wonder if this is what St. Augustine meant when he said "our hearts are restless until

they rest in Thee." I wonder if this is what that ancient prayer for the dead is meant to convey when we pray at burial: "Eternal rest grant unto them O Lord . . . "

29   And so permit me to conclude with a prayerful invocation of sorts, a plea to the Patron Saint of this beautiful city, St. Anthony of Padua. By what trick of grace are we all here today, I wonder, because you know St. Anthony is the Patron Saint of both the barren and the pregnant. Strengthening adoptive families is about acknowledging the permanence of infertility and the responsibility of an unwanted pregnancy.

30   And St. Anthony is, as all Catholics know, the founder of things lost. . . . St. Anthony, founder of the lost, can be a powerful ally to those of us who know what it means to lose something or someone. Strengthening adoptive families is about the acknowledgment of loss, the loss of children, the loss of parents, the loss of one's heritage and genetic connection.

31   St. Anthony is often pictured holding the Christ child in loving adoration. He adores Jesus as both divine and human, holding the tension of Jesus' true identity, his dual nature, without sacrificing the importance of one for the other. St. Anthony does not settle for an either/or solution. Perhaps St. Anthony is after all the best guide we could have to help us reject that dualism which forces us to think of adoption as an either/or dichotomy, having to choose between environment and heredity, and help us to embrace the creative tension found in each adopted person.

32   For in the adopted person is found a disquieting paradox that reminds all of us we are truly orphans. Adoption plays a mysterious trick on us, but I believe it a trick of grace. In the adopted person one may very well find the ground-of-being where sex and love have intercoursed; the sacrament, if you will, of the fusion of nature and grace.

FOR ANALYSIS AND DISCUSSION

1. Evaluate the effectiveness of Brosnan's connection between the concepts of loss and belonging, adoption, and *Cinema Paradiso*.
2. Brosnan claims that he is not an authority on the subject of adoption, yet he was adopted himself. What makes one an "authority" on adoption? Why do you think he says that he isn't an "expert"?
3. What is the myth of the "chosen baby" (paragraph 9)? What, according to Brosnan, is faulty with this story?
4. What are the types of loss discussed in this article? How does the concept of loss connect to adoption issues?
5. How is anger manifest in the lives of adoptees? Does Brosnan explain and provide supporting reasons for this anger? Explain.
6. How does Brosnan apply religious concepts to this essay? Do the religious references contribute to or detract from the effectiveness of his speech? Explain.

Erasing the Right to Privacy
Anne Harvey, Bill Pierce, and Anne Babb

In February 1997, PBS's *Online Forum* invited two respected authorities in adoption law to discuss the current adoption system and proposed changes to it. Bill Pierce believes that open records could severely harm the adoption process, and defends the right to privacy for the birth mother as well as the child. Anne Babb approaches the issue from a different perspective, arguing that open records would help millions of children find birth mothers who wouldn't mind being found. In the following discussion, Anne Harvey, an adoptee, asks them about her privacy rights.

Bill Pierce is the president of the National Council for Adoption and co-author of the *Encyclopedia of Adoption.* Dr. L. Anne Babb is the executive director of the nonprofit adoption advocacy center, the Family Tree Adoption and Counseling Center in Norman, Oklahoma. Babb is the author of *Adopting and Advocating for the Special Needs Child* (1997) and *Ethics in American Adoption* (1999).

BEFORE YOU READ

If adoption records were open, how would that fact impact the adoption process? Do mothers have the right to demand anonymity? Conversely, what about adoptees who do not want to be "found"?

AS YOU READ

Evaluate the responses by the two adoption authorities, Bill Pierce and Anne Babb. How do they phrase their responses? Does one seem more authoritative than the other? Do you find yourself agreeing more with one's responses than with the other's? If so, why?

1   Anne Harvey of Sacramento, CA, asks:

2   As an adoptee, I am infuriated that people are working to erase my right to privacy. Not all adoptees want or need to know about their biological mothers. Also, this intrusion causes great pain to my real mother, the woman who has raised me from birth. Who gives the "Adoption Council" the right to open up my life and my mother's life? How am I going to protect myself and her from people from a past I don't want or need?

3   Mr. Bill Pierce of the National Council for Adoption responds:

4   Anne, we strongly agree that no one has a right to erase your right to privacy. We know from speaking with many adopted persons over the years since NCFA was founded in 1980 that not all adoptees want or need to know about their biological parents. We are also aware that such intrusions can cause great pain to loving adoptive parents.

5   I do not know what "Adoption Council" you are referring to in your question, but it is certainly not our organization, the National Council for Adoption. We are for adoption. We are regularly attacked on the Internet—just visit

the sites that are open and know people monitor them like "Bastard Nation," for instance, to see what sorts of comments fly back and forth between people who otherwise are taken seriously because of their academic or personal histories with adoption.

6   It is sad that a country that venerates privacy and that has constitutional protections for people not to be violated in their own homes cannot rest easily, knowing that there are people lurking about, anxious to meet their own needs at the expense of intruding into others' lives. It is sadder still that many of the people who need protection are still minors and, I suspect, younger than you are. I think of the youngster whose biological mother bragged on the Internet about tricking a naïve archivist into giving her access to sensitive documents.

7   In that instance, the biological mother admitted stalking a minor child, even tracking the child to the child's classroom. Fortunately, it was possible to alert agency officials, who were aware of the biological parent's unwillingness to back off when the adoptive parents said no, and the family was told to take steps to protect their child from possible harm. Must of this incredible stalking goes on behind the scenes, where it cannot be monitored or reported to adoptive parents.

8   As an adult, you have relatively few options. You can contact an attorney and seek an injunction, once someone tries to contact you. But that is hardly preventive. And even then, there are times when biological parents will not back off, even when they are told that a meeting or a relationship of any kind is unwanted. I talked a few weeks ago to a young man who has had several encounters with a demanding, intrusive biological parent—and ten years later, he's still being harassed.

9   You can always write to the agency or attorney involved with arranging your adoption and say that you desire no contact and that if either the agency or attorney, either directly or indirectly, or by subterfuge, provides information leading to you being identified, you will take appropriate legal action. But even then, it is difficult to prove, as the case of Carol Sandusky, a young woman whose privacy was invaded by a public agency employee, demonstrates. That case is still in litigation, and Ms. Sandusky's attorney, Samuel Totaro, a Philadelphia lawyer who is also the current head of the American Academy of Adoption Attorneys, is pressing the issue as a civil rights matter.

10   It is quite a commentary on U.S. society that ordinary adopted individuals who desire privacy and to be left alone have to resort to the kind of defensive tactics, employing attorneys, that used to be reserved for the rich and famous like Jacqueline Kennedy. Those who want good legal advice on these issues must be careful in picking their attorneys, however—even some who are adoptive parents sometimes find themselves, for reasons I cannot imagine, siding with the anti-adoption snoopers and stalkers.

11   Dr. Anne Babb of the American Adoption Congress responds:

12   There is no state in the country that condones the unwelcome contact of adoptees by their birth parents or the unwanted contact of their birth parents by adoptees. Some states, like Tennessee, open adoption records and provide

for a "contact veto," allowing adoptees to allow or disallow actual contact from their birth families or relatives. All states protect their citizens from harassment and other unwanted interference with a person's privacy through provisions such as victim's protective orders or other legal means.

13   The American Adoption Congress supports the right of adult adoptees to obtain their original birth certificate and the right of adoptive parents, birth parents, and adoptees to decide what kind of contact, if any, they want to have with one another. Although the majority of adoptees do want their birth information and many seek contact with their birth families, some, like Ms. Harvey, do not. We certainly respect the right of all adoptees to decide for themselves whether or not they want to have their original birth records or to pursue contact with their birth parents or families. Our objection is to the action of states that would seek to hinder the self-determination of adoptees, birth parents, and adoptive parents in deciding the type and extent of contact they want. We also support the equal access of adoptees to their birth records.

14   With regard to Ms. Harvey's words about her "real" mother, I am reminded of the definitions of my friend, co-author, colleague and fellow adoptive mother Rita Laws, Ph.D., defining words commonly used in adoption:

> Natural child: Any child who is not artificial. Real Parent: Any parent who is not imaginary. Your own child: Any child who is yours to love. An adopted child is a natural child with real parents, who is loved.

15   This definition acknowledges all the parents in an adopted child's life without diminishing the role any parent played in the creation and nurturing of that child.

FOR ANALYSIS AND DISCUSSION

1. How do you think Bartholet and Brosnan would respond to Pierce's tales of birth parents "stalking" the children they gave up for adoption?
2. Are the rights of some adoptees and birth parents being sacrificed by the demands and needs of other adoptees and birth parents? What are the central issues, as discussed by Pierce and Babb, in this matter?
3. What does Pierce mean when he says it is sad that "there are people lurking about, anxious to meet their own needs at the expense of intruding into others' lives" (paragraph 6)? Who are the "lurking" people he mentions? How does this statement support his overall point?
4. Babb comments that the goal of open records is to allow "the self-determination of adoptees, birth parents, and adoptive parents [to determine] the type and extent of contract they want" (paragraph 13). Would open records indeed allow for a triad decision, or would they still create awkward and unwanted situations—or is this not even an issue? Explain.
5. Evaluate Babb's closing statement about the definition of "natural" children and "real" parents.

On the Confidentiality of Adoption Records
National Committee for Adoption

The National Committee for Adoption is a private, not-for-profit organization working "for adoption." The NCFA advocates the sealing of adoption records to protect the interests of birth parents, the adoptive family, and the adopted child. They do, however, advocate the full disclosure of all nonidentifying information such as medical histories as well as mutual consent registries that allow birth parents and children to contact each other if both parties so desire. They also believe that states should be more involved in assisting reunions if both parties are interested. The following reading is published and distributed by the NCFA.

BEFORE YOU READ

Make a list of the values and concerns shared by those for and against the release of all records pertaining to an individual's adoption. Can there by a consensus on this issue?

AS YOU READ

Evaluate the effectiveness of the question-and-answer format of this article. Does this style of argument strengthen the presentation of the NCFA's perspective?

1   *Why can't adopted adults and birthparents have access to all adoption records on demand?*

2   To answer this question, one needs to look at the reason for sealing adoption records and issuing amended birth certificates to adopted persons in the first place. Many will claim that the practice is outdated, but a review of the reasons shows that the rationale is as valid today as it was in the early part of this century when the practice began.

   1. To protect children born out-of-wedlock from public scrutiny;
   2. To protect women who bore children out-of-wedlock from public scrutiny;
   3. To protect the integrity of the adopted family as a legal family in the eyes of society;
   4. To be consistent with all other social services which hold confidentiality as a predominant principle of ethical practice;
   5. To protect all parties to an adoption from unsolicited or unwanted interference from other parties;
   6. To facilitate the grieving process for birthparents by providing closure.

3   Let's examine these reasons in today's society.

4   1. and 2. There are many in society today who say that the stigma of illegitimacy is no longer an issue in the U.S. Certainly this has not been the experience for many young women who are unmarried and pregnant and their offspring. While the public may be more tolerant, negative judgments are often

made about the individuals. It is not uncommon for adopted persons and adoptive parents to hear unkind comments from others about the adopted person's illegitimate beginnings and expectations of repeating his parents' "sins." Often when an adopted teen becomes pregnant, references are made to the fact that she was adopted and that the behavior is hereditary. No such connection is made of teens who become pregnant who were born inside of marriage.

5   From the perspective of birthparents, even today, many feel a need to conceal their pregnancy from the wider public. Many others who did not conceal their pregnancies wish they had because of the judgments that people have made about them upon hearing of an out-of-wedlock pregnancy and/or adoption.

6   But even if societal values had changed as significantly as many report and birthparents choosing adoption today were not affected by the stigma, that does not mean that birthparents of yesterday are still not affected. Many older birthmothers live in fear that their out-of-wedlock pregnancy will be disclosed without their consent. Many have not told subsequent spouses. Many have not told their children or in-laws or friends. Some may at some point choose to share this personal information with loved ones, but prefer to do it in their own way at the appropriate time. Many birthmothers who have been found must cling to elaborate stories they told to explain the adoption to preserve their sense of dignity. For example, it is not uncommon to hear a birthmother say that she thought the baby died at birth, implying unethical behavior on the part of the individual arranging the adoption. While there have been some abuses in adoption, some birthmothers have told NCFA that they created the story to explain the nonmarital pregnancy and subsequent adoption to family and friends.

7   3. The adoptive family is under increasing attack and the need to preserve its integrity is perhaps more important now than ever before. The vast media attention on "searches" have lead many Americans to see adoption as a temporary arrangement where adopted persons rejoin their biological families at the age of majority. Some individuals in the adoption field are advocating replacing traditional adoption which creates a new, permanent family with a form of guardianship where biological parents maintain parental relationships with the child without any of the legal or moral responsibilities to care for the child. The sealing of adoption records and amending the adopted person's birth certificate ensures that all public documents about relationships show that the adopted person is part of his new family. This prevents any question of parentage and allows the family and the adopted person to choose with whom they want to share this personal information.

8   4. All social service, medical, legal and mental health services are based on the principle of confidentiality. It is considered unethical by all professions to divulge any information to a third party about a client without the expressed, written permission of that client. Prior to consultation with another professional on an ongoing case, it is necessary for the counselor, doctor, attorney, etc. to get permission for the release of information to even discuss the case with another party. Adoption, because it contains aspects of all these different professions, operates the same way. All records kept by an attorney, an adop-

tion agency, or the courts about an adoption are confidential. As with any other confidential record, the information can only be released with the written permission of the person to whom the record belongs or a court order after a showing of just cause. In addition, most forms for the release of confidential information require a statement of what information will be released, to whom and for what purpose.

9   5. The correct understanding of both birthparents and adoptive parents when they choose adoption is that adoption creates in the legal and social sense new, permanent families and nullifies all rights, responsibilities and relationships with the family of origin. As such both parties have a right to go on with their lives without unsolicited or unwanted interference from the other parties. Adoptive parents need to feel secure in their role as parent so that they can provide the appropriate guidance to their child. By the same token, birthparents need to feel secure that they have fulfilled their responsibilities to the child and will not be called on later, to solve any problems the child may have as he grows.

10   In the extreme case, one of the reasons for sealing the records to begin with was to prevent birthparents from trying to reclaim the children they placed for adoption. Many people will say that this is not a valid concern in today's society. Yet, there are many cases of birthparents attempting to reestablish relationships with minor children they placed for adoption and while many "search" groups oppose this activity, many support and assist in it. There are also an increasing number of court cases brought against adoptive parents by birthparents who want visitation rights.

11   6. The sealing of adoption records represents unambiguously to birthparents and adoptive parents that their decision is final. In order for the decision for adoption to be truly informed every birthparent should understand the permanency of adoption. In order to come to peace with a loss, it is necessary to accept the loss and that includes accepting the permanency of the loss. Suggestions of possible "reunions" with the child they placed for adoption have encouraged fantasies for many birthmothers and as a result they have a very difficult time letting go of the child. Just as a divorcing woman would never be able to accept the end of her marriage if she had in the back of her mind that she may reconcile with her husband, neither can a birthmother let go of the end of her parenting relationship with the child if she kept the fantasy going that she would resume the relationship in 18 or 21 years.

12   *But shouldn't adopted persons' right to know about their past override these principles, particularly since they were unwilling participants in the adoption? I thought that the purpose of adoption is the best interest of the child.*

13   Adoption is supposed to focus on the best interest of the child and when the adopted person is a child, when it comes to a balancing of rights and needs, the child's rights and needs are given more weight than the other parties. However, when we are talking about adopted adults, we are talking about all parties being adults and therefore, the balance shifts so all parties are treated equally.

14   Secondly, this question assumes that the information in an adoption record is about the adopted person's past. In fact, most of the information in

the adoption record is about the birthparents' past and the adoptive parents' pasts. There is no "right" to know about someone else. Any "right" to know information is limited to information that directly affects an individual. In the case of adoption, the information pertaining to the adopted person is the medical and social history which may have an impact on the adopted person. This medical and social history can be shared without identifying information and without divulging personal information about the other parties' pasts.

15   For most birthparents, the period preceding and following an adoption is very traumatic. The records will contain very personal information on what was happening at the time in their lives with relationships with each other, their families and friends, and additional problems unrelated to the pregnancy, etc. Information in the home study on adoptive parents also may be very private and sensitive as they will be questioned about their marital relationships, including sexual relationship, their family histories including dysfunction, etc.

16   While children are involved in their parents' relationship and are affected by many of the choices made, they are not privy to every aspect of their parents' relationships and past. Children also do not necessarily have the right to know all the reasons for which parents make the choices they do. Parents may choose to share those reasons with them.

17   Children who were placed in adoptive homes should not be treated any differently than children born into a family. Making an adoption plan for a child or adopting a child does not forfeit one's right to privacy in personal relations for years to come.

18   *Should an adopted person be able to meet his or her grandparents, and vice versa?*

19   If adults (adopted persons and birthparents) wish to waive their right of privacy and meet each other, neither the state, or anyone else should prevent it. The more appropriate question would be, "What is the role of states in facilitating a meeting between adopted persons and birthparents and what is the appropriate mechanism for releasing confidential information that has been entrusted to the state?"

20   In general, a state has no role in exchanging the names, locations, and other identifying information about its citizens. However, since the state was involved in the adoption process and is the guardian of confidential information, it has a legitimate role in the exchange of information about persons affected by adoption.

21   Therefore, to answer the question of what the state's role is, it is necessary to work from the prevailing understanding of the nature of adoption (which was described in part above) and a state's participation in the adoption process.

22   States have a strong interest in protecting family life, and have, by law and regulation, set out the procedures by which permanent parental rights and responsibilities for a child are transferred from birthparents to adoptive parents in an ethical way that protects each party's rights and interests, particularly the child's.

23   Our society has long recognized that the family situation that best meets the developmental and emotional needs of children (even adult children) is one where there are two parents, a mother and a father, who enjoy a perma-

nent, stable marriage. Consequently, the goal in adoption is to place a child in a home which is not temporary, but to which she or he will belong as much as if that child were born into the family. Such a relationship, with its rights, privileges and obligations, lasts a lifetime.

24   It is clear from above that there is no right of an individual to compel a state to release identifying or other information on another person to whom their sole tie is biological, particularly since all rights, responsibilities, and relationships to the other party were legally terminated. Nevertheless, because of the unique role a state plays in adoption, all states have developed procedures whereby birthparents and adopted persons can waive their right of privacy and request to receive information about one another or try to establish contact. Underlying most of these laws is the understanding that the person being sought should give written consent before personal and identifying information is given to the searcher, unless a court orders otherwise.

25   To date 25 states have adopted some type of voluntary mutual consent adoption registry, which means that each party comes forward on his/her own, without a solicitation, and registers a desire to release identifying information about him/herself. Additionally, 14 states have processes in place which allow an intermediary to contact the second party at the request of the first party to gain consent for the release of identifying information. Nine states[1] and the District of Columbia maintain confidential records which can only be accessed by court order. Two states provide access to original birth certificates by adopted adults without the expressed permission of the birthparents. Hawaii makes an effort to locate the second party for 180 days before releasing the information in the sealed adoption record to the first party. . . .

26   NCFA will continue to advocate for the rights of all parties to an adoption. We will continue to advocate for the full disclosure of all known non-identifying information about a child's medical, abuse, treatment, and placement histories to all adoptive parents prior to a placement so that they can make informed decisions about meeting their child's needs. NCFA will advocate for mutual consent registries to give adults an opportunity to waive their right to privacy and exchange identifying information, and we will continue to oppose all attempts to destroy the rights of individuals involved in adoption.

27   It is important to note that only a small, but vocal, proportion of adopted persons are interested in contact with their biological parents. Using the numbers of the proponents of open adoption records, and giving them every benefit of the doubt for the largest possible estimate, the percentage of adopted persons interested in searching falls between one and five percent. A review of statistics from states with either mutual consent registries or search and consent systems shows far fewer adopted persons and birthparents searching. Most adopted persons and biological parents are content with their lives. Unfortunately, those who want to maintain their privacy cannot speak out for that right because their activism itself would violate that privacy.

28   The communications we have had from birthparents testify to how truly difficult it is for them to make this decision. And the aspects that make it so difficult are often the aspects that persuaded them to choose adoption: confiden-

tiality and permanence. They made a decision which they believed was for the good of themselves and their children. We do not believe the assurances they received should be taken away without the consent of the principal parties in the adoption plan: birthparent(s), adopted child, and adoptive parents.

29   Unfortunately, it must be said that not all reunions are happy ones, in the short or the long term. There are numerous horror stories of lives and families devastated by unauthorized contact. The circumstances surrounding the choice of a birthmother to make an adoption plan can be diverse and tragic. NCFA believes it is essential to look beyond the rhetoric of "happy family reunions" to the basic human rights involved in the debate.

FOR ANALYSIS AND DISCUSSION

1. How would the other authors featured in this section respond to the questions presented in this article? Explain.
2. Do you agree with the reasons the NCFA gives as to why records should be sealed? Do some of the reasons seem more compelling than others?
3. Evaluate the NCFA's position that adoption must be permanent for both the adoptive family's security and the birth parents' need for closure.
4. In paragraph 11, the NCFA states that adoptions must be final to impress on the birth parents the seriousness of the decision and to allow the birth mother to deal with the loss. Reverend Brosnan's essay also deals with issues of loss. How do you think he would respond to this statement?
5. Evaluate the NCFA's assertion in paragraphs 14 and 15 that adoptive children have no more right to information that their birth parents wish to keep private than do children raised with their birth parents. How does the NCFA support this claim? Do you agree?
6. The NCFA feels that the interests of a "small but vocal" group of adopted persons is driving the campaign for adoption reform. Birth parents who want to protect their privacy cannot be openly against reform because it would reveal their pasts. How is this issue addressed by the NCFA? How do you think Brosnan and Bartholet would respond?

The Promise of Confidentiality
Carol Schaefer

On November 3, 1998, the citizens of Oregon voted to pass Measure 58, which would allow people 21 and older who had been adopted in Oregon to obtain copies of their original birth certificates. The measure was scheduled to go into effect one month later, but Judge Albin W. Norblad granted an injunction halting its implementation in response to a lawsuit filed by a Portland attorney on behalf of four anonymous birth mothers. Many more women who claimed that the state had assured them confidentiality at the time they offered their children for adoption soon joined the suit.

Carol Schaefer is the author of the award-winning book *The Other Mother: A Woman's Love for the Child She Gave Up for Adoption* (1991), which chronicles her relinquishment, search, and eventual reunion with her son and was made into a movie featured on NBC in 1995. The letter that follows appeared in the *Washington Times* in October of 1998 and is Schaefer's response to Measure 58.

BEFORE YOU READ

Do adoptees have the right to contact their birth parents even when they know such contact is unwanted? Explain.

AS YOU READ

What support does Schaefer use to buttress her perspective? Does she speak—or imply that she speaks—for all birth mothers?

1   I have been involved with the adoption reform movement since searching for my son and since the publication of my book, "The Other Mother: A Woman's Love for the Child She Gave up for Adoption." NBC first aired the movie version of my book in 1995. Many, many lives were changed by it. NBC just aired the movie again on Oct. 3. Over the past 14 years, I have spoken in depth with countless birth mothers, adoptees and adoptive parents.

2   The major argument against Measure 58 is that we birth mothers were promised confidentiality. A distinction needs to be made between "secrecy and lies" and "confidentiality."

3   Many of us were not promised confidentiality, nor did we want it. During my day, the great majority of us were sent away, as pariahs, to the more than 200 homes for unwed mothers that existed in the United States. We were sequestered with friends, relatives or strangers. If we stayed at home, we hid in closets when guests came and ducked below the car window on the way to the doctor's office so as not to be seen by the neighbors. Many of us were treated by strangers in a punishing manner.

4   We submitted to these atrocities to protect our families from the shame of our unwed motherhood, to protect our children from the stigma of being born illegitimate and to ensure that we would remain wanted for marriage.

5   If we had stayed in our communities and tried to keep our babies, we would have been expelled from school. Few of us would have been hired for work, and many families would not have welcomed us back if we had brought our children home.

6   We were told we would be selfish if we kept our children and that we would be able to go on with our lives and pretend "it" had never happened. It may be difficult to imagine such advice in the 1990s. No one ever brought up the subject again.

7   Over the years, I have talked with mothers who do not want to be found or who have been found and are in shock, including women who have been raped. What I have discovered is that they are reliving the fears and the trauma of the original experience as if that part of themselves, frozen for so long, is

suddenly beginning to thaw. How can they trust that their husbands and children will support them now, when their families, their churches and their society did not offer support originally? Their fear of losing everyone's love all over again is a tragedy for all, Yet, when I have witnessed a mother face her fears and meet her child, it has been the most incredible blessing for all involved.

8   As we approach the new millennium, we must leave behind the archaic laws that enforce lies and secrets, that protect us from our truth and prevent us from experiencing our heritage and the bonds of love within our families of origin.

9   The humanitarian passage of Measure 58 will herald a great healing in this country. If we can't hold sacred the bond between a mother and her child, what can we hold sacred?

FOR ANALYSIS AND DISCUSSION

1. Evaluate Schaefer's use of the word "we" in her essay.
2. According to Schaefer, what is the difference between "secrecy and lies" and "confidentiality" (paragraphs 2 through 6). How do you think the women who are protesting the passage of Measure 58 would respond to this?
3. Assess Schaefer's comment that even women who gave up children resulting from rape would benefit from contact with their children (paragraph 7). Do you agree with her assessment? How does she support her argument?
4. Analyze the overall effectiveness of Schaefer's argument. Is she convincing? Explain.

WRITING ASSIGNMENTS: ADOPTION

1. You have been selected to develop an adoption policy to be implemented by your state. Write a proposal for your policy in which you explain the reasoning behind its design. Consider the multifaceted issues of adoption from the perspectives of birth parents, adoptive parents, and the adoptee.
2. Visit the Web site tracing the history of Oregon's Measure 58 at <http://www.plumsite.com/oregon/> and access the links that discuss the various perspectives on the issue. Then write an essay in which you defend or oppose the legislation. Use information gathered from the Web site to support your perspective.
3. You are a parent contemplating giving up your newborn for adoption. What are your reasons for offering your child for adoption? Would you agree to the release of your personal data, should your child want it or wish to contact you? Write an argument essay explaining the reasons behind your decision.
4. You are an adoptee. Would you want to find out more about your biological background? Where would you start? Access the Voices for Adoption homepage to learn more about adoption and searching for birth parents at <http://www.ibar.com/voices/articles/>. Drawing from information provided in the articles, as well as your own perspective on the issue, write an argument essay explaining why you would or would not seek out your birth parents.

chapter 15

CASEBOOK: JUVENILE CRIME, ADULT TIME?

Every week, it seems the newspaper headlines feature another murder or serious crime committed by individuals too young to vote or have a driver's license. This casebook on juvenile crime gives you the opportunity to become actively involved with this pressing and complex social problem. What is behind the surge in juvenile crime statistics? Why are juvenile crimes becoming more violent and deadly? Should juvenile offenders be treated differently than adult criminals if their crimes are the same? Are there ways to stop the cycle of poverty and youth crime before it becomes worse? These are questions that the writers in this casebook attempt to answer about the phenomenon of juvenile crime.

The ineffectiveness of the current juvenile justice system is the focus of several essays. Tom Reilly and Linda Collier argue that the current system is too "soft" in dealing with violent young offenders. They propose that children who commit particularly violent crimes must be held responsible for their actions and deserve to be tried and punished as adults under the law. Edward Humes instead urges an overhaul of the present justice system so that it can respond to the special needs of children who are in trouble to prevent them from becoming "hardened criminals." T. Markus Funk, however, sees little hope for the rehabilitation of juvenile delinquents. Because research indicates that juveniles with criminal records are "four times more likely to become adult offenders," he questions the practice of "sealing" or permanently erasing the criminal records of minors once they reach adulthood. While the policy of sealing records is intended to provide juvenile offenders with a "second chance," Funk argues that it endangers society by withholding information about an individual's criminal history from judges, law enforcement agencies, and future employers.

Why do juveniles commit violent crimes? Do social and economic factors contribute to this antisocial behavior? Mike Males and Faye Docuyanan analyze the relationship between juvenile crime and youth poverty. The growing indifference of the wealthy to the lack of opportunity for urban minority teens, they argue, has produced a generation of potentially violent young people who are alienated from traditional American values. Abbe Smith and Lael E. H. Chester agree that unless

we attack the source of juvenile crime, it will continue to grow. They urge us to focus on "community-based programs built on education, counseling, and job training" to provide young people with healthy alternatives to gangs and violence. In the
last reading, Geoffrey Canada discusses the need for responsible adults to protect
children from the dangers of the inner city and proposes his solutions to ending the
cycle of poverty, crime, and violence.

Extensive opportunities to conduct your own research on the subject of juvenile
crime appear after each reading and at the end of the chapter. You may wish to investigate the impact of juvenile crime on your community by visiting and interviewing
officials at law enforcement agencies, juvenile justice centers, halfway houses, and
other social and community organizations. For a look at how juvenile crime is dealt
with nationally, we recommend a number of Web sites that provide current facts and
statistics. Other Internet resources allow you to explore related issues such as gang culture or the relationship between the media and youth violence. Explore this issue in
depth to discover and argue for your own solutions to this critical social problem.

Youth Crime Has Changed—And So Must the Juvenile Justice System
Tom Reilly

Juvenile crime has risen at an alarming rate. In 1997, one quarter of those arrested
for weapons offenses were under the age of 18. And juvenile homicides have
quadrupled over the last ten years. As the juvenile crime rate rises, so does the number of violent crimes committed by young people. The severity of the crimes committed by juveniles has made both law enforcement officials and the general public
question the difference between "delinquent" and "criminal" behavior.

Tom Reilly wrote the following article, which originally appeared in the *Boston
Globe* in 1996, while serving as the district attorney for Middlesex County in the
state of Massachusetts. In 1998 he was elected state attorney general.

BEFORE YOU READ
Since you know that Tom Reilly was a district attorney when he wrote this article,
what perspective do you expect him to have on the issue of juvenile crime? If a
writer's perspective is predictable, does that make the argument less convincing?

AS YOU READ
What types of crimes do you associate with "juvenile delinquents"? What does the
term "juvenile delinquent" imply?

1   On July 1, 1899, the first juvenile court in the United States was established in
Cook County, Ill. It represented a dramatic shift in the way the criminal justice

system and all of American society dealt with wayward or criminally involved youth. The new court was founded on the principle of "parens patriae"—the idea that children should not be treated as criminals but as wards of the state.

2   Parens patriae encapsulated the view that children were not fully responsible for their conduct and were capable of being rehabilitated. It gave rise to the ongoing practice of terming youthful offenders "delinquents" and not criminals. Parens patriae remains the underlying philosophy of the juvenile justice system in Massachusetts and across the country. Then and now, juvenile court was designed more to protect the child than to punish bad behavior.

3   Until fairly recently, the juvenile justice system served our country and our children reasonably well. Beginning in the 1970s, however, the realities of juvenile crime began to change. Juvenile crime grew more violent and more common, and the system was unprepared. In recent years those changes have accelerated at an astonishing rate, and time and again the system has proven itself helpless under the crush.

4   Violent juvenile crime is increasing at double the rate of violent crime committed by adults. By the year 2005, the number of teen-agers between the ages of 14 and 17 will increase by 23 percent, and it appears likely that unless we change things now, those soon-to-be-teen-agers will be the most violence prone in history.

5   Our juvenile justice system is outdated, designed to address infractions like truancy and petty theft. These were serious problems a century ago, but they bear no resemblance to the "routine" infractions of the present day: everything from rape to crimes involving guns to cold-blooded murder. In 1996, juveniles are committing brutal crimes with such numbing regularity that it takes the most shocking failures of the juvenile justice system to respond to dramatize the out-of-touch mentality underlying it.

6   It makes no sense to change the system simply to navigate the current wave of public anger. We must instead reform the system to steer clear of the coming storm of violent juvenile crime. Parens patriae need not be fully abandoned. There are and will always be children who make poor choices, who need our help and who can be turned around. However, we cannot ignore reality. Crimes such as murder are serious; they cannot under any circumstances be excused or explained away. Here, hope for rehabilitation is a myth, and public protection must be the priority.

7   How can we possibly treat cold-blooded juvenile killers as "delinquents" and not as the dangerous predators their own actions prove them to be? When a person, any person, brings himself to a point where he deliberately murders another human being, there is no going back. A mere hope for rehabilitation is nothing but a gamble on other people's lives. The public has a right to expect that a killer will never, ever have the chance to kill again. Juveniles accused of murder should be tried as adults and, if convicted, sentenced as adults.

8   For other crimes, determining whether a juvenile can be rehabilitated is problematic under the current system, so conducting the trial first makes sense. Once a determination of guilt has been made and the court has a clear

view of the nature of the crime and whether or not a juvenile is dangerous or capable of rehabilitation, then a reasonable decision can be made whether to sentence as a juvenile or as an adult.

9   Even apart from these steps to hold juvenile offenders responsible, other aspects of the juvenile justice system must be reformed to achieve a proper balance between respect and sensitivity toward victims and a juvenile's due process rights. Eliminating "trial de novo" tops the list. Under de novo, a juvenile has the right to be tried first before a judge. If found guilty (or delinquent), the juvenile can simply demand a new trial before a jury, forcing victims to endure a painful ordeal not once, but twice. It's time to put an end to this unfair, wasteful system.

10   The juvenile justice system founded nearly a century ago was in many respects visionary, but ultimately it was a system designed to address the pressing issues of its day. That day is long past. It's time for us to craft a new vision for juvenile justice in Massachusetts, where compassion for the young and common sense about crime coexist. Our new vision should reflect our belief that the system does have a responsibility to protect a child's interests, but our system has an equally important responsibility to protect the public's safety interests.

FOR ANALYSIS AND DISCUSSION

1. Is our current juvenile justice system out of date? Why was the juvenile system created in the first place? What does Reilly believe needs to be done to update it? Do you agree?
2. What is the principle of "parens patriae"? Does it have a place in our criminal justice system today? Explain.
3. Reilly comments (paragraph 5) that in 1996, juveniles committed brutal crimes with "numbing" regularity. Is "numbing" an appropriate word choice? As the number of violent crimes committed by juveniles increases, are we indeed becoming numb to them?
4. Reilly points out that allowing juvenile killers to be rehabilitated at all is "nothing but a gamble on other people's lives" (paragraph 7). In your opinion, can individuals who commit calculated murder be rehabilitated? Does it make a difference if they are younger or older than 18?
5. In paragraph 7 Reilly asks, "How can we possibly treat cold-blooded juvenile killers as 'delinquents' and not as the dangerous predators their own actions prove them to be? How does Reilly's word choice affect you, the reader? How does it support his point of view?
6. What recommendations does Reilly make to hold juvenile offenders responsible for their actions? Do you agree with his recommendations? Explain.

FOR RESEARCH

1. Research the problem of juvenile crime in your community or state. Prepare a report in which you detail the different types and frequencies of crimes committed by juveniles in your area. How bad is the problem? Report your find-

ings to the class and make a recommendation that the current juvenile justice system is (1) too soft on youth, (2) too hard on youth, or (3) fine the way it is.

2. Interview at least 30 people from different age groups and ask them how they feel about juvenile crime (ten people under age 20, ten between 20 and 30, etc.). Do they think it is a problem? Is juvenile crime getting worse, and if so, in what ways? Should juveniles be treated as adults if they commit "adult crimes"? Ask any other questions you think might be helpful to your research. Then compile your data to determine unofficial public opinion regarding juvenile crime. Do all age groups seem to agree, or do they hold different opinions?

Adult Crime, Adult Time: Outdated Juvenile Laws Thwart Justice
Linda J. Collier

With juvenile crime increasing in both frequency and severity, many states are introducing tougher legislation for the prosecution of juvenile offenders. All but ten states have amended their laws to make it easier to try violent juvenile offenders as adults. And many states have adopted "blended sentencing" standards that allow judges to sentence juveniles as more than just "delinquents." However, some attorneys, like Linda J. Collier, contend that the new laws are still too flexible. They believe that adult crimes deserve adult punishment.

Linda Collier, a Pennsylvania lawyer who has worked in the juvenile courts, also teaches a course in juvenile delinquency at Cabrini College in Radnor, Pennsylvania. This article appeared in the *Washington Post* on April 6, 1998.

BEFORE YOU READ

What is an "adult" crime? How are "adult" crimes different from "juvenile" crimes? Can we make a distinction between them anymore?

AS YOU READ

Consider the types of crimes Collier cites as proof that the current juvenile justice system is outdated. Do you think these crimes are typical?

1   When prosecutor Brent Davis said he wasn't sure if he could charge 11-year-old Andrew Golden and 13-year-old Mitchell Johnson as adults after Tuesday afternoon's slaughter in Jonesboro, Ark., I cringed. But not for the reasons you might think.

2   I knew he was formulating a judgment based on laws that have not had a major overhaul for more than 100 years. I knew his hands were tied by the long-standing creed that juvenile offenders, generally defined as those under the age of 18, are to be treated rather than punished. I knew he would have to do legal cartwheels to get the case out of the juvenile system. But most of all, I

cringed because today's juvenile suspects—even those who are accused of committing the most violent crimes—are still regarded by the law as children first and criminals second.

3   As astonishing as the Jonesboro events were, this is hardly the first time that children with access to guns and other weapons have brought tragedy to a school. Only weeks before the Jonesboro shootings, three girls in Paducah, Ky., were killed in their school lobby when a 14-year-old classsmate allegedly opened fire on them. Authorities said he had several guns with him, and the alleged murder weapon was one of seven stolen from a neighbor's garage. And the day after the Jonesboro shootings, a 14-year-old in Daly City, Calif., was charged as a juvenile after he allegedly fired at his middle-school principal with a semiautomatic handgun.

4   It's not a new or unusual phenomenon for children to commit violent crimes at younger and younger ages, but it often takes a shocking incident to draw our attention to a trend already in progress. According to the U.S. Department of Justice, crimes committed by juveniles have increased by 60 percent since 1984. Where juvenile delinquency was once limited to truancy or vandalism, juveniles now are more likely to be the perpetrators of serious and deadly crimes such as arson, aggravated assault, rape and murder. And these violent offenders increasingly include those as young as the Jonesboro suspects. Since 1965, the number of 12-year-olds arrested for violent crimes has doubled and the number of 13- and 14-year-olds has tripled, according to government statistics.

5   Those statistics are a major reason why we need to revamp our antiquated juvenile justice system. Nearly every state, including Arkansas, has laws that send most youthful violent offenders to the juvenile courts, where they can only be found "delinquent" and confined in a juvenile facility (typically not past age 21). In recent years, many states have enacted changes in their juvenile crime laws, and some have lowered the age at which a juvenile can be tried as an adult for certain violent crimes. Virginia, for example, has reduced its minimum age to 14, and suspects accused of murder and aggravated malicious wounding are automatically waived to adult court. Illinois is now sending some 13-year-olds to adult court after a hearing in juvenile court. In Kansas, a 1996 law allows juveniles as young as 10 to be prosecuted as adults in some cases. These are steps in the right direction, but too many states still treat violent offenders under 16 as juveniles who belong in the juvenile system.

6   My views are not those of a frustrated prosecutor. I have represented children as a court-appointed *guardian ad litem,* or temporary guardian, in the Philadelphia juvenile justice system. Loosely defined, a guardian ad litem is responsible for looking after the best interest of a neglected or rebellious child who has come into the juvenile courts. It is often a humbling experience as I try to help children whose lives have gone awry, sometimes because of circumstances beyond their control.

7   My experience has made me believe that the system is doing a poor job at treatment as well as punishment. One of my "girls," a chronic truant, was a fos-

Changes in the Law

Many state legislatures have responded to the increased incidence of violent juvenile crime by enacting tougher legislation, according to a 1996 report from the federal government's Office of Juvenile Justice and Delinquency Prevention.

- Since 1992, all but 10 states have amended their laws to make it easier to prosecute some juveniles as adults.
- Since 1992, 16 states have adopted "blended sentencing" models that allow judges to impose a combination of juvenile and adult sanctions on some young offenders.
- Legislation has given prosecutors an expanded role in determining how violent juvenile offenders should be handled.

ter child who longed to be adopted. She often talked of how she wanted a pink room, a frilly bunk bed and sisters with whom she could share her dreams. She languished in foster care from ages 2 to 13 because her drug-ravaged mother would not relinquish her parental rights. Initially, the girl refused to tolerate the half-life that the state had maintained was in her best interest. But as it became clear that we would never convince her mother to give up her rights, the girl became a frequent runaway. Eventually she ended up pregnant, wandering from place to place and committing adult crimes to survive. No longer a child, not quite a woman, she is the kind of teenager offender for whom the juvenile system has little or nothing to offer.

8   A brief history: Proceedings in juvenile justice began in 1890 in Chicago, where the original mandate was to save wayward children and protect them from the ravages of society. The system called for children to be processed through an appendage of the family court. By design, juveniles were to be kept away from the court's criminal side, the district attorney and adult correctional institutions.

9   Typically, initial procedures are informal, non-threatening and not open to public scrutiny. A juvenile suspect is interviewed by an "intake" officer who determines the child's fate. The intake officer may issue a warning, lecture and release; he may detain the suspect; or, he may decide to file a petition, subjecting the child to juvenile "adjudication" proceedings. If the law allows, the intake officer may make a recommendation that the juvenile be transferred to adult criminal court.

10   An adjudication is similar to a hearing, rather than a trial, although the juvenile may be represented by counsel and a juvenile prosecutor will represent the interests of the community. It is important to note that throughout the pro-

ceedings, no matter which side of the fence the parties are on, the operating principle is that everyone is working in the best interests of the child. Juvenile court judges do not issue findings of guilt, but decide whether a child is delinquent. If delinquency is found, the judge must decide the child's fate. Should the child be sent back to the family—assuming there is one? Declare him or her "in need of supervision," which brings in the intense help of social services? Remove the child from the family and place him or her in foster care? Confine the child to a state institution for juvenile offenders?

11   This system was developed with truants, vandals and petty thieves in mind. But this model is not appropriate for the violent juvenile offender of today. Detaining a rapist or murderer in a juvenile facility until the age of 18 or 21 isn't even a slap on the hand. If a juvenile is accused of murdering, raping or assaulting someone with a deadly weapon, the suspect should automatically be sent to adult criminal court. What's to ponder?

12   With violent crime becoming more prevalent among the junior set, it's a mystery why there hasn't been a major overhaul of juvenile justice laws long before now. Will the Jonesboro shootings be the incident that makes us take a hard look at the current system? When it became evident that the early release of Jesse Timmendequas—whose murder of 7-year-old Megan Kanka in New Jersey sparked national outrage—had caused unwarranted tragedy, legislative action was swift. Now New Jersey has Megan's Law, which requires the advance notification of a sexual predator's release into a neighborhood. Other states have followed suit.

13   It is unequivocally clear that the same type of mandate is needed to establish a uniform minimum age for trying juveniles as adults. As it stands now, there is no consistency in state laws governing waivers to adult court. One reason for this lack of uniformity is the absence of direction from the federal government or Congress. The Bureau of Justice Statistics reports that adjacent states such as New York and Pennsylvania respond differently to 16-year-old criminals, with New York tending to treat offenders of that age as adults and Pennsylvania handling them in the juvenile justice system.

14   Federal prosecution of juveniles is not totally unheard of, but it is uncommon. The Bureau of Justice Statistics estimates that during 1994, at least 65 juveniles were referred to the attorney general for transfer to adult status. In such cases, the U.S. attorney's office must certify a substantial federal interest in the case and show that one of the following is true: The state does not have jurisdiction; the state refuses to assume jurisdiction or the state does not have adequate services for juvenile offenders; the offense is a violent felony, drug trafficking or firearm offense as defined by the U.S. Code.

15   Exacting hurdles, but not insurmountable. In the Jonesboro case, prosecutor Davis has been exploring ways to enlist the federal court's jurisdiction. Whatever happens, federal prosecutors of young offenders are clearly not the long-term answer. The states must act. So as far as I can see, the next step is clear: Children who knowingly engage in adult conduct and adult crimes should automatically be subject to adult rules and adult prison time.

FOR ANALYSIS AND DISCUSSION

1. What is the difference between "delinquent" and "criminal"? What do the terms mean socially? What do they mean when applied to the justice system?
2. How are juveniles processed through the juvenile court system? How does the process differ from what you know of the adult system? What accounts for the differences?
3. Collier comments (paragraphs 6 and 7) that the current system of using a guardian ad litem is failing. Does she provide a solution to its shortcomings? How does Collier's experience as a guardian ad litem support her argument that juveniles who commit adult crimes must be treated as adults? Are you convinced by her example?
4. What is "Megan's Law"? Why do you think Collier cites this law in her essay? How does it contribute to her argument?

FOR RESEACH

1. Review the way juveniles are processed through the court system. Although this system varies from state to state, try the Texas Youth Commission's Web site at <http://travis.tyc.state.tx.us/overview.html> for an overview of how juveniles are processed. Draw some conclusions from your research. For example, does the system seem logical and effective? If you were a district attorney for the state of Texas, would you find the Texas system of juvenile justice satisfactory? Explain.
2. Research some recent violent crimes committed by juveniles over the past few years. For example, you could review the Jonesboro, Arkansas, tragedy; the shootings in Paducah, Kentucky; and the shooting spree by Kip Kinkel at Thurston High School in Oregon at <http://www.oregonlive.com/todaysnews/shooting.html>. Do you think public opinion supports a change in juvenile justice? Has media exposure influenced public opinion?

Young and Arrestless: The Case Against Expunging Juvenile Arrest Records
T. Markus Funk

Many states allow or require the erasure of juvenile criminal records when a youth reaches the age of maturity (18 or 21). While "expungement" was originally designed to allow juveniles who engaged in petty crimes a clean slate, many states that mandate expungement include destroying records of even rape and murder convictions. In so doing, says T. Markus Funk, these states prevent the appropriate sentencing of young adult offenders, impede effective law enforcement, and put everyone at risk.

T. Markus Funk is a doctoral student in law at Oxford University. He wrote this article, which appeared in the February 1996 edition of the magazine *Reason,* while serving as a clerk for the United States District Court in St. Louis. He has written many articles on gun control, juvenile expungement policies, and recidivism rates.

BEFORE YOU READ

Expungement is the erasure of a juvenile's criminal record when he or she reaches the age of maturity (18 in some states, 21 in others). Could expungement encourage "borderline" juveniles to commit crimes?

AS YOU READ

Funk points out that, according to the statistics, juvenile offenders are likely to be adult offenders as well. How is expungement connected to this issue?

1   Daniel Doe (a pseudonym) is a violent man who, like most violent men, was also a violent teen. At age 12, police arrested him for vandalizing a neighbor's house—he had destroyed the furniture, spray-painted the walls, and drowned a caged pet bird in the bathtub. Two years later, he was burglarizing an apartment when the elderly occupant returned home and confronted him. In the scuffle that ensued, the old man broke his hip. When the man died from pneumonia several days later, Daniel was charged with and convicted of involuntary manslaughter.

2   Daniel's first "adult" arrest came at age 19, when he broke into an occupied home and severely beat the 45-year-old woman who lived there. By the time he was sentenced for that attack, however, his juvenile record, pursuant to Ohio law, had been "expunged"—destroyed. For the second time, Daniel was a first-time offender. Hence, a Cleveland judge, ignorant of Daniel's violent, extensive, felonious past, sentenced him to probation. Two months later, Daniel burglarized yet another house, this time beating the 81-year-old man who lived there to death.

3   Had the judge known of Daniel's violent criminal past and his demonstrated lack of any rehabilitative potential, there's little doubt that Daniel would have gone to the penitentiary before he had the opportunity to kill the old man.

4   But the judge didn't know because the law said that he *shouldn't* know.

5   Most states have statutory provisions that allow—or even mandate—the expungement of juvenile records once the juvenile turns a certain age. Sometimes the records are actually destroyed; sometimes they are merely "sealed." The practical effect of such legislation is to allow a minor who has committed criminal or, in the lingo of the juvenile courts, *delinquent* acts to permanently erase his or her record, usually at age 17 or 18. The stated goal of this policy is to allow the juvenile offender to enter adulthood with a proverbial clean slate, thereby shielding him (or, less likely, her) from the negative effects of having a criminal record.

6   Supporters say expungement is an enlightened practice that merely forgives youthful transgressions. But expungement is actually an astonishingly counterproductive policy that benefits only young criminals. The practice prevents society from acting on the simple fact that those who have committed crimes in the past are likely to commit crimes in the future and hence should be treated differently from true first-time offenders.

7   By making it virtually impossible to collect meaningful data about juvenile delinquents, expungement also makes it difficult to evaluate crime-prevention and rehabilitation programs. Outside of the criminal justice sphere, the policy has other deleterious effects. Employers, for instance, can't know whether potential employees are prone to stealing or other criminal behaviors. Given these various costs, it's not surprising that a number of states are seriously reevaluating the sealing of juvenile records.

8   Expungement laws hearken back to a simpler past. The practice "was designed to deal with delinquents who stole hubcaps, not those who mug old ladies," notes sociologist Rita Kramer in *At a Tender Age: Violent Youth and Juvenile Justice* (1988). Gargantuan increases in violent juvenile crime underscore the point. Today's juvenile offenders are generally distinguishable from their adult criminal counterparts only by their age—an arbitrary factor indeed. Juveniles are the fastest growing segment among violent offenders. Between 1983 and 1992, according to FBI estimates, violent crime committed by juveniles increased 57 percent. Murders and non-negligent manslaughter rates jumped 128 percent, aggravated assault 95 percent, and rape 25 percent. And cohort studies discussed in Neil A. Weiner and Marvin E. Wolfgang's *Violent Crime, Violent Criminals* (1989) show that juveniles account for up to 35 percent of all male police contacts.

9   The philosophy underlying expungement legislation can be traced to what is known as the Chicago School of Criminology, which, during the 1920s and '30s, championed environmental explanations of criminality. The Chicago School (the term refers to a broad-based intellectual movement that started at the University of Chicago) rejected traditional criminological theories that focused on issues of individual morality and volition and concentrated instead on factors external to the individual. This new model viewed America as a "criminogenic" society in which ghettos and slums taught the people who lived there how to become criminal by giving them deviant cultural values.

10   This environmental model reached its high-water mark in the early 1960s with Robert K. Merton's "Strain Theory," which posited that America's supposed obsession with ambition and economic success led to crime and deviance. Strain theory viewed delinquency as arising from the frustration felt by individuals who were unable to achieve culturally defined goals because they were denied the institutionalized means of doing so.

11   In the 1960s—the decade during which most expungement statutes currently in force were written—expungement advocates espoused what is known as the "labeling" or "social reaction" model. The labeling perspective is based on the premise that the very act of labeling those who are apprehended as "dif-

ferent" creates deviants who are different only because they have been "tagged" with the deviant label.

12   As criminologist Frank Tannenbaum, a prominent labeling-perspective theorist, argued in his 1983 book *Crime and the Community,* "The process of making the criminal . . . is a process of tagging, defining, identifying, segregating, describing, emphasizing, making conscious and self-conscious; it becomes a way of stimulating, suggesting, emphasizing, and evoking the very traits that are complained of." Hence, the only way to rehabilitate juvenile delinquents is to send them into adulthood with this label detached.

13   Aside from any philosophical and common-sense disagreements one may have with the labeling theorists, the major question regarding expungement is whether juvenile delinquents are "normal" kids who simply make youthful mistakes that are unlikely to be repeated in adulthood.

14   The answer is no. Delinquents are substantially different from non-delinquents. Research suggests that delinquents are more defiant, ambivalent about authority, emotionally unstable, extroverted, fearful of failure, resentful, hostile, suspicious, and defensive than non-delinquents. In their book *From Boy to Man, From Delinquency to Crime* (1987), University of Pennsylvania criminologist Marvin E. Wolfgang and his co-authors found that there is an extremely strong correlation between juvenile delinquency and adult crime, and that juvenile delinquency is the "best predictor of adult criminality." John Monahan, in his 1981 book *Predicting Violent Behavior,* has found that individuals with juvenile records are four times more likely to become adult offenders.

15   Similarly, a study tracing the criminal careers of 1,000 juvenile boys discussed in Sheldon and Eleanor Glueck's *Of Delinquency and Crime* (1974) found that 73.2 percent of those who could be located had been officially cataloged as repeat offenders within 10 years of their first appearance in juvenile court. An extensive FBI study discussed by Florida State University criminologist Gary Kleck, in *Point Blank* (1991), estimates that 74.7 percent of all murderers had arrests for violent felonies or burglaries, and murderers averaged four prior major felony arrests over a criminal career of at least six years. Those figures do not even begin to approximate the actual criminal histories of those individuals, since being arrested is itself a highly atypical consequence of violating the law. It is also worth noting that those figures would be even higher if juvenile expungement statutes did not artificially deflate them.

16   In fact, expungement statutes also make it virtually impossible to collect the kind of data that might lead to more effective crime prevention. In a 1992 article in the *Journal of Urban and Contemporary Law,* Carlton Snow, the former dean of Willamette University College of Law, argued that expungement statutes "impinge on a democratic society's ability to inform itself about all aspects of the criminal justice system. . . . Regardless of whether juvenile records are merely 'sealed' or actually destroyed, the data becomes less available for research purposes." The result: The general public is unable to evaluate the juvenile justice system accurately, and sociologists and criminologists are left less able to study important aspects of criminal behavior.

17   And, as the case of Daniel Doe illustrates, expungement often prevents the courts from adequately assessing the danger a younger criminal poses to society.

18   The functions that judges perform at sentencing—one of which is to determine the convict's rehabilitative potential, as evidenced by his response to prior convictions—are simply too important to allow incomplete information concerning the nature and seriousness of an individual's criminal past to interfere with the proper dispensation of punishment.

19   That's one of the major points in *United States v. Davis,* a 1995 case involving a convicted felon's due process challenge to the United States Sentencing Guidelines' directive to consider juvenile convictions in calculating a defendant's prior criminal history. Writing for the court, Judge William J. Bauer, of the Seventh Circuit Court of Appeals powerfully stated: "[I]t is imperative that the defendant's sentence account for his criminal history from the date of birth up to and including the moment of sentencing. The consideration of the defendant's juvenile record is essential, because it is clear that the 'magic age' of eighteen, seventeen, or sixteen, whatever it may be in a specific state, cannot wipe out all previous contacts with the law. The pubescent transgressions . . . help the sentencing judge to determine whether the defendant has simply taken one wrong turn from the straight and narrow or is a criminal recidivist."

20   Expungement similarly interferes with effective law enforcement, since police officers are impeded in their efforts to identify patterns of criminal conduct. There is voluminous case law stating that arrest records serve a valuable law-enforcement purpose, that the dissemination of criminal records promotes the public welfare, and that even "unresolved" arrest records provide significant information and aid in the resolution of criminal actions. When the police are investigating criminal activity, for instance, they routinely examine the prior criminal records of potential suspects to see if there is evidence of a modus operandi. Juvenile records are routinely withheld, making the police's job that much more difficult.

21   Expungement exacts costs beyond crime and punishment. It prevents employers from making fully informed hiring decisions, such as whether applicants are likely to pilfer. Compelling employers to hire individuals without full insight into their criminal propensities is a heavy penalty to force upon businesses. In *Privacy, Secrecy and Reputation,* Seventh Circuit Court of Appeals Judge Richard Posner says that arguments for expungement are "particularly weak in the context of employment, where competition exacts a heavy penalty from any firm that makes irrational employment decisions."

22   Perhaps more important, expungement forces employers into a very risky position from a workplace liability perspective. Under the common law, an employer has a duty to provide a safe work environment, and this duty has gradually been extended to hiring safe employees, since, in terms of legal analysis, a dangerous employee creates risks comparable to a defective machine. As Carlton Snow has pointed out, "Under the theory of vicarious liability, hiring applicants with expunged juvenile records is potentially hazardous for employers

and employees alike." Since an employer can be held liable for an employee's torts while on the job, says Snow, "complete knowledge about an applicant would allow an employer to take appropriate steps to decrease any liability resulting from an employee's subsequent conduct."

23   The explosion in juvenile crime and the growing intellectual disenchantment with expungement statutes are beginning to have an effect: A number of states are rethinking the policy of sealing or destroying juvenile records. This past spring, for instance, Connecticut passed a law that allows delinquency records to be disclosed to police, school officials, social service workers, and "anyone with a legitimate interest in the information." Republican Pennsylvania Gov. Tom Ridge is pushing to make "it harder to expunge juvenile records" and legislation passed last February lets judges review juvenile records before setting bail. Similar initiatives are underway in Louisiana, Texas, and Kentucky, where Democratic Gov. Paul Patton has announced a plan to "lift the secrecy of juvenile court proceedings for convictions of serious felony crimes."

24   At bottom, expungement statutes are attempts to lessen the penalty that public opinion places upon former offenders. But the "stigma" of having been a juvenile delinquent should only be of concern insofar as it *incorrectly* characterizes an individual who has been able to reform his life since his brief brush with the law as a juvenile. If a former delinquent remains engaged in criminal activity, then it is clear that the juvenile justice system has failed in its goal of rehabilitation, and concern for the offender should be replaced with concern for protecting society from a predatory recidivist.

25   And even if one accepts the notion that those who have committed a juvenile indiscretion will outgrow their reckless behavior, it remains necessary to differentiate between those who in fact can be rehabilitated and those whose rehabilitative potential is negligible—i.e., career criminals.

26   But current expungement statutes rarely make such a distinction, choosing instead to delete a teenager's criminal record upon reaching majority (or sooner), regardless of whether it consists of a one-time arrest for public urination or numerous convictions for assault, burglary, or rape. While expungement may be appropriate for the one-time child offender (who presumably has been rehabilitated), it is wholly inappropriate for a young chronic criminal who, based on numerous incidents of re-offending, shows no rehabilitative potential. As the number of offenses increases, the underlying delinquency becomes more troublesome, and it is likely that an anti-social pattern will continue throughout a criminal's adult years.

27   Given that adult criminality is often predicated upon juvenile delinquency, it follows that criminals have the most to gain, and that society has the most to lose, from any expungement scheme that allows individuals to start with a "clean slate"—or, more appropriately, a *cleaned* slate—upon reaching majority. That expungement is being challenged both intellectually and politically indicates that the costs may have finally become too much to bear.

FOR ANALYSIS AND DISCUSSION

1. What is "recidivism"? Why do current juvenile court policies make it difficult to determine just how common recidivism is?

2. Consider the labeling theorists' point that calling a criminal a criminal encourages the label's behavior. Does this theory make sense? Explain.

3. What is "strain theory"? What connection does strain theory have to current expungement policies?

4. According to Funk, how does expungement affect the ability of a judge to sentence an offender? How does it interfere with effective law enforcement?

5. Consider the way Funk formulates this essay. How does he frame his argument? Is it logical and effective? Is his introduction an effective way of drawing in his audience? Explain.

FOR RESEARCH

1. The Office of Juvenile Justice and Delinquency Prevention's Web site <http://www.ojjdp.ncjrs.org> provides a comprehensive look at the current state of juvenile crime. Read the articles on this site about strengthening the juvenile justice system. What factors influence juvenile crime? Can you make any connections between the OJJDP's findings and the theories described in Funk's article?

2. Make a list of the crimes committed by juvenile offenders in your state. To determine the kinds of crimes committed by youth today, access the Justice Information Center for statistical data on juvenile crime at <http://www.ncjrs.org/homepage.htm>. Ask 20 people of diverse ages to categorize which types of crimes they feel should be expunged when the offender reaches 18 and which should remain on the record. What can you conclude from your data? Did any of the people surveyed indicate that *all* offenses should be expunged, or did the people you polled seem to "rate" the crimes? Explain.

Giving Up on the Young
Mike Males and Faye Docuyanan

Participation in gangs among urban youth has reached epidemic proportions. Why are young people drawn to gangs? For some it is the feeling of belonging and a sense of purpose that motivates them to join. For others it is fear of violence in the streets. How can society help youths stay out of gangs and channel their energies more productively? The following article by Mike Males and Faye Docuyanan examines the issue of gangs. The authors are social ecology doctoral students at the University of California at Irvine. Mike Males is also author of *The Scapegoat Generation: America's War Against Adolescents* (1996). This essay first appeared in the February 1996 issue of *The Progressive*.

BEFORE YOU READ

What do you think of when you hear the word "gang"? What does the word mean?

AS YOU READ

Why are youths attracted to gangs? What do gangs offer them that the larger society does not?

1   Madness is the word Stephen Bruner uses to describe the summer of 1992. "The things I did, things I had done to me. . . . Madness." It was the summer after eighth grade. He and his gang Panic Zone hung out where the rural black community of Spencer intersects the southeast Oklahoma City suburb of Midwest City. He rattles off the names of a dozen gangs—Hoover Street, Westside, Candlewood, 6–0—that inhabit the district.

2   For his contribution to the madness, Bruner spent his ninth grade in an Oklahoma juvenile lockup. Now Bruner works as an intern for Wayne Thompson at the Oklahoma Health Care Project in Founder's Tower overlooking the city's opulent northwest side. Thompson himself spent three years in prison in the 1970s at Terminal Island and Lompoc for armed bank robbery on behalf of the San Francisco Black Panther chapter.

3   Madness, Thompson suggests, is "the natural, predictable reaction" of youths to the "larger, hostile adult culture that is anti-youth, particularly anti–African-American youth."

4   Twenty thousand more Oklahoma City children and teenagers live in poverty than a quarter of a century ago. "These kids are at risk of extinction if they depend upon adults to protect them," Thompson says. It is not just parents who fail them, but an adult society increasingly angry and punishing toward its youth. "That is the perception of the young people who are being ground up in this culture and the grinder of the juvenile-justice system. Their perception of their situation is very correct."

5   Today, state after state is imposing harsher penalties on juveniles who run afoul of the law. "The nationwide trend is to get tough on juvenile crime," says Gary Taylor of Legal Aid of Western Oklahoma. Rehabilitation and reintegration into the community are concepts that have already fallen out of fashion for adult criminals. Now they are fast becoming passé for juveniles, as well. Instead of prevention and rehabilitation programs, more prisons are being built to warehouse juveniles along with adults. The trend began in California; it is now sweeping the nation.

6   Juveniles are being waived into adult court at lower and lower ages. In Wisconsin, ten-year-olds can now be tried as adults for murder. Juveniles convicted of drug offenses in adult court receive lengthy mandatory sentences. In California, studies by the state corrections department show that youths serve sentences 60 percent longer than adults for the same crimes. Oklahoma wants to

try thirteen-year-olds as adults and petitioned the Supreme Court to allow executions of fourteen- and fifteen-year-olds.

7   And it's not just the states. It's the Clinton Administration, too. *The New York Times* reported in December that "proposals by the Administration would allow more access to juvenile records and give federal prosecutors discretion to charge serious juvenile offenders as adults."

8   In short, we are giving up on human beings at a younger and younger age.

9   Juvenile crime is on the rise. But the reason is not media violence, rap music, or gun availability—easy scapegoats that have little to do with the patterns of violence in real life. Rather, the reason is rising youth poverty.

10   Sensational press accounts make it seem as though juvenile crime is patternless. It is hardly that. Juvenile crime is closely tied to youth poverty and the growing opportunity gap between wealthier, older people and destitute, younger people. Of California's fifty-eight counties, thirty-one with a total of 2.5 million people recorded zero teenage murders in 1993. Central Los Angeles, which has roughly the same number of people, reported more than 200 teen murders.

11   In the thirty-one counties free of teenage killers, the same blood-soaked media and rock and rap music are readily available (more, since white suburban families over-subscribe to cable TV), and guns are easy to obtain. Nor can some "innate" teenage qualities be the cause, since by definition those qualities are as present in youths in areas where violent teenage crime is rare as in areas where it is common.

12   "We see kids from *all* walks of life," says Harry Hartmann, counselor with the L.A. Office of Education. But "the races are skewed to blacks and Hispanics," he acknowledges. Very skewed—six out of seven of those who are arrested for violent juvenile crimes are black or Hispanic. By strange coincidence, that is just about the proportion of the country's youths in poverty who are black or Hispanic.

13   "Poverty in a society of affluence, in which your self-esteem is tied to failure to achieve that affluence," is a more accurate explanation for our uniquely high level of violence, says Gilbert Geiss, a criminologist formerly with the University of California, Irvine. It's not just "poverty, per se."

14   L.A. County is a clear illustration. It's per-capita income is much higher, and its general poverty rate lower, than the United States as a whole. But its youth poverty rate is staggering: 200,000 impoverished adolescents live in the county.

15   L.A. County is home to one in fifteen teenage murderers in the United States. It's vast basin harbors such a bewildering array of gangs and posses that estimates of the number of youths allied with them at any one time are almost impossible to pin down.

16   Jennifer, seventeen, at the Search to Involve Philipino Americans (SIPA), a local community center, rattles off the names of twenty youth gangs, takes a breath, admits she has left some out. Los Angeles County (population 9 million) has more teen murders than the dozen largest industrial nations outside the United States combined. Of L.A.'s 459 teen murder arrestees in 1994, just

twenty-four were white. Blacks and Hispanics predominated, but Asian Americans comprise the fastest-rising group of violent juveniles.

17   "I tried to ask them, 'Why are you in it?' " Jennifer asks. "They don't know. A lot of people regret it after. 'Yeah, that was some stupid shit.' They thought it was so cool." But if stupid, confused kids were the whole problem, why are black kids in Los Angeles a dozen times stupider than white kids? Why are Asians getting stupider faster than anyone else?"

18   As youth poverty rises and becomes more concentrated in destitute urban neighborhoods, violence becomes more concentrated in younger age groups.

19   But today's reigning criminal-justice experts—UCLA's James Q. Wilson, Northeastern's James Alan Fox, Princeton's John D'Iulio, former Robert Kennedy aid Adam Walinsky—dismiss poverty as a cause of youth violence. Instead, they talk about an insidious culture of poverty, and they argue relentlessly that only more cops and more prisons will bring down juvenile crime. Instead of proposing more money for alleviating poverty or for crime prevention, they want more law enforcement—at a cost of tens of billion of dollars.

20   Writing in the September 1994 *Commentary,* Wilson calls the growing adolescent population "a cloud" that "lurks . . . just beyond the horizon." It will bring "30,000 more muggers, killers, and thieves than we have now." Wilson downplays poverty, racism, poor schools, and unemployment as "not . . . major causes of crime at all." The real problem, he writes, is "wrong behavior" by a fraction of the population (he pegs it at 6 percent) with bad temperament, concentrated in chaotic families and "disorderly neighborhoods."

21   If more prisons and surer sentences were the solutions to crime and delinquency, California should be a haven where citizens leave doors unlocked and stroll midnight streets unmenaced. California inaugurated the new era of imprisoning juvenile offenders in Ronald Reagan's second term as governor in 1971, and since then the state has incarcerated a higher percentage of its youths than any other state. By 1993, a state corrections study found teenagers served terms nearly a year longer than adults for equivalent offenses.

22   "I tell parents who want to release their kid to the [juvenile-justice] system: he might come out worse than when he went in," says Gilbert Aruyao of SIPA.

23   Eleven hundred new state laws passed during the 1980s set longer, more certain prison terms, especially for juveniles. California's forty-one-prison, 140,000-inmate system is the third-largest in the world; only the United States as a whole and China have larger inmate systems.

24   The Golden State's biggest growth industry is corrections. Seven new prisons opened in California from 1989 to 1994, at a cost of $1.3 billion, to accommodate 16,000 more prisoners; today, they confine 28,000 prisoners. From 1995 through 1996, four new prisons, costing $839 million, will open their doors. There's a new prison built every eight months. Each one is full upon opening.

25   "For that incorrigible 25 percent (of youth offenders), prisons may be the only way to go," says Harry Hartmann of the L.A. Office of Education. "It's really hard for them to change." In California in 1994, 140,000 persons under the age of twenty were arrested for felonies—including one out of five black males,

and one in ten Hispanic males ages sixteen through nineteen. If even one-tenth of that number must be imprisoned more or less permanently, the state's minority teenage male population will require four new prisons every year to contain them.

26   As youth poverty mushrooms and the attitudes of the large society become harsher, the traditional markers of race and class are sliding toward new re-alignments. "There's still a racial element, sure," says Thompson. "But this has gone beyond race now. "There's a larger madness."

27   Says Bruner: "There are white kids in black gangs, blacks in Mexican gangs, Mexicans in white gangs, blacks in white gangs, Asians in black gangs. We don't fight each other that way. It isn't a race thing. It's who's in the 'hood.' "

28   The *1995 Kids Count Factbook* lists 47,000 impoverished children and adolescents in the Oklahoma City metropolitan area—21,000 whites, 13,500 blacks, 4,500 Native Americans, 3,000 Asian Americans, 5,000 Latinos.

29   A November 1995 *Daily Oklahoma* series on the metropolis's exploding poverty reported that these adolescents are increasingly isolated, jammed together in a chain of destitute neighborhoods ringing downtown and extending eastward past the suburbs.

30   "You go to school with them, people ask of this guy you know, 'Is he OK with you,'cause if he's OK with you, he's OK with me,' " says Bruner. "If you're in a subcultural group, it's no different in society's eyes whether you're in a gang or not. Kids had no choice but to hang with us. Racism is here. You can't run away from it. [But] racism is not just black or white." Nonwhite youths, white youths on the wrong side, "we are all targets."

31   Bruner is training in office management and in television production and editing through Thompson's program. Enough of his friends remain trapped in the justice system. Bruner sees that as surrender. "They didn't get out like I did; now they're up for murder one."

32   Bruner says the system is rigged: "I believe they want to keep me and every other black male and minority male and poor kid in the system permanently, send us all to the penitentiary."

33   In 1988, Oklahoma petitioned the U.S. Supreme Court to execute four-teen- and fifteen-year-olds (and lost only on a 5–4 vote).

34   "Society wants to kill these kids," says Thompson. "The death penalty. Shooting them in the street. If it can't do that, then killing their spirit."

35   Gary Taylor, deputy director of Legal Aid of Western Oklahoma, recounts his agency's efforts to reform a juvenile prison system whose brutality and puni-tive excesses had been exposed nationally. "Beatings, sexual assaults, hog tying, extreme medical punishments, extreme isolation," said Taylor. "It was kid-kid; it was staff-kid."

36   There was no notion of rehabilitation. San Francisco lawyers for convicted murderer Freddy Lee Taylor investigated his incarceration in the Oklahoma ju-venile prison system and found "a concentration-camp environment," attorney Robert Rionda said.

37   Many of these youths were wrongly imprisoned: they had been removed from their homes because their parents were abusive or neglectful, or the

youths had committed minor offenses like curfew violations or truancy. Rionda's firm did not have to look hard to find Freddy Taylor's co-inmates: most were now in state prison serving terms for major felonies.

38   "There were many, many kids who were in the system because they were poor and in need of supervision, and they turned them into monsters," Rionda said.

39   In recent years, twice as many Oklahoma youths have been placed in the adult prison system as in the juvenile system. Oklahoma imprisons more of its citizens than any other state except Texas. If forcing youths into the adult prisons and administering harsh punishment is the remedy, Oklahoma, like California, should be a paradise of peace.

40   Yet arrest figures over the last decade show Oklahoma's juvenile violence growing at twice the already alarming national pace.

41   Los Angeles County and Oklahoma City officials stress prevention but note that it is underfunded. The most effective prevention effort by far is to raise fewer children in poverty. However, "reducing child poverty, much less eliminating it, is no longer a paramount priority for either political party," *U.S. News & World Report* pointed out in November 1995.

42   Wayne Thompson in Oklahoma City takes prevention seriously. "We approach juvenile crime as a public-health problem, not a law-enforcement problem," says Thompson. "Intervene, then trace the pathology back to its source." The source inevitably turns out to be "the low social, educational, and economic status of the families and communities" violent youths come from.

43   Thompson's program uses employment training and a variety of family services to reintegrate youths who have already been convicted back into their communities. "We want to empower these young people to change the social and economic circumstances of their lives," he says.

44   An initial evaluation showed that Thompson's program was more effective than law-enforcement approaches in preventing recidivism among delinquent youths as well as preventing younger members of their families from following in their older siblings' footsteps. The clientele served by the program is small— fewer than 100 youths per year.

45   The adults most responsive to Thompson's approach are in the business community, Republicans more than Democrats, he notes. "That's frightening," he says. "The social services, academia, are bound like serfs to the status quo."

46   When he talks to Oklahoma City's business groups, Thompson finds growing concern over the costs of more prisons and "alarm in the white community because the gangs are becoming more integrated." He doesn't push charity or altruism.

47   "I tell them, 'You're going to die in fifteen or twenty years, and you have grandchildren. They're going to have to live with the environment we've created. And we've created a hellacious environment.' This is not just some teenage rite-of-passage problem. The alienation of young people from the traditional institutions is profound. This is the legacy we're leaving: armed camps. If we don't learn how to share with the people who are now powerless, this culture is ultimately going to acquire the means to bring our society to an end."

FOR ANALYSIS AND DISCUSSION

1. Males and Docuyanan comment that juvenile criminal offenders are being "ground up" in a system that is "increasingly angry and punishing toward its youth" (paragraph 4). How do the opinions of Males and Docuyanan contrast with those of Funk, Collier, and Reilly? In your journal, create a "Yes, but . . . " exchange among these writers to explore their different perspectives.

2. According to Males and Docuyanan, what is the reason for the rise in juvenile crime? Can you link their opinions to any of the theories expressed in the Funk article? Explain.

3. How do Males and Docuyanan use statistical data to support their argument? Is their use of statistics successful? Can you think of ways to argue against these statistics?

4. What accounts for the appeal of gangs? Why are teens drawn into gangs? What do they hope to gain from gang membership? What racial and economic factors influence teens to join gangs?

5. In paragraph 42, Wayne Thompson, a former prison inmate now active in juvenile crime prevention, comments, "We approach juvenile crime as a public-health problem, not a law-enforcement problem." How can juvenile crime be defined as a "public health problem"? Does our perspective on the issue change if we view it this way? Explain.

FOR RESEARCH

1. This essay uses statistical data to support its argument. Isolate the data from the text. Write an argument essay in which you discuss your view on juvenile crime using just the data gathered from this article.

2. Are there any gangs in your area? Research local gang activities as documented in newspapers and local publications. Contact your police department for information about gang activities. Are gangs a problem in your area? If so, based on your research analyze what you think may be the cause. If not, explain why gangs are not a concern for your community.

Cruel Punishment for Juveniles
Abbe Smith and Lael E. H. Chester

According to the authors of this essay, treating juveniles as adults only helps society to forget that they are really still kids. Instead of giving up on troubled kids, which the authors say is the easy way out, we should instead be focusing on how to help them. Yet the answer isn't to throw the current system out. Rather, the current system must be improved with funding and social commitment. Drawing from their personal experiences in dealing with young offenders, Abbe Smith and Lael E. H. Chester claim that punishing juveniles in the adult system is fundamentally and morally wrong.

Abbe Smith is a visiting associate professor of law at Georgetown University and coauthor of *Beyond the Rodney King Story: An Investigation of Police Conduct in*

Minority Communities (1995). The following article was first published in the *Boston Globe* in 1996, when Lael E. H. Chester was a fellow at the Criminal Justice Institute at Harvard Law School.

BEFORE YOU READ

Is punishing juveniles *as* adults the same thing as punishing juveniles *with* adults? Why or why not?

AS YOU READ

Smith and Chester are opposing a pending piece of legislation in this article. Why are they opposed to it?

1   The first time we saw Frankie was in the lock-up of the Cambridge District Court. He was barely 17, baby-faced, nothing but skin and bones, his scrawniness exaggerated by baggy pants.

2   Frankie had spent the night in jail, an adult jail. In Massachusetts, 17 is the age of adulthood for purposes of criminal prosecution. He had been arrested for breaking into the basement of the house from which his best friend's family had just been evicted. His friend wanted to retrieve his punching bag.

3   Frankie didn't know us, but boy was he glad to see us. He managed to hold back tears—there were guys in the cell who were old enough to be his father, and crying was the last thing he wanted to do—but his eyes held a mix of worry, fear and exhaustion. You're my lawyers? he asked. Wow, that's good news. And both of my parents are out there in the court room? Gee, I wasn't sure I'd ever see them again.

4   His parents were relieved and furious when the police called the night before, nearly an hour after Frankie was due home. With mixed feelings, they decided that Frankie should spend the night in jail. Maybe it'd teach him a lesson.

5   Maybe.

6   In recent years, there has been an increasing call in the commonwealth and the country to stop "coddling" juveniles in a separate justice system and punish them like adults. Now the call has gone further. We should punish kids with adults.

7   A bill recently introduced by Rep. Bill McCollum, chairman of the House Judiciary Subcommittee on Crime, seeks to end the jailhouse separation of juvenile and adult offenders and allow kids to serve time in adult prisons. Notwithstanding the powerful political rhetoric accompanying its introduction, the strategically entitled "Violent Youth Predator Act of 1996," is not sound social policy.

8   It is wrong to suggest that young offenders are being "coddled" in the juvenile institutions to which more and more are sent. There is simply no funding for small, community-based youth programs built on education, counseling

and job training. Whether we call them locked rooms or locked cells, juvenile offenders are already spending time in prison.

9   Subjecting children to punishment with adults defines cruel and unusual punishment. Sexual and physical assault are already prevalent in adult prisons. One can imagine the scale of these offenses if we send in a fresh crop of younger and more vulnerable prey. Given the number of prisoners with HIV (the Journal of the American Medical Association reports the rate of AIDS among incarcerated adults is six times that of the general population), sending children into adult prisons might as well be a death sentence.

10   The truth is that the get-tough approach is being driven by a few highly publicized cases that do not reflect the reality of most juvenile crime. In Massachusetts, juvenile homicides are a tiny percentage of juvenile arrests (there were 14 homicide cases out of 22,000 juvenile arraignments this year). The increased rate of homicides by juveniles nationally is largely due to the proliferation of guns in this country, not the changed nature of children.

11   And yet instead of pushing for a ban on all firearms, Massachusetts lawmakers prefer to increase mandatory minimum sentences for gun-related offenses by adults and juveniles. Instead of banning guns, we banish kids.

12   The federal government has also been in danger of embracing punishment over prevention. Along with doing away with federal and state mandates separating children from adult prisoners, the bill would abolish the Office of Juvenile Justice and Delinquency Prevention, the only federal agency that sponsors research on juvenile violence prevention.

13   We know that the problem of juvenile crime and violence is much more complicated than this angry antichild bill suggests. In the ravaged urban neighborhoods where most violent juvenile crime occurs, there are no clear lines between "good" and "bad" kids. As John Silva, director of safety and security for the Cambridge public schools, has observed: "Good kids have guns . . . there's so much fear. Good kids who want to go to school and do the right thing—they're afraid of the gangs and the drug dealers; they want to protect themselves and their families. Good kids, bad kids—the categories don't apply anymore."

14   We know much more about the causes of juvenile crime and how to prevent it than a policy which would raze juvenile institutions and send youngsters into adult prisons for more sophisticated training in violent crime and victimization.

15   We also know that, as Robert J. Sampson and John H. Laub pointed out in their groundbreaking 1993 book on juvenile delinquency, "Crime in the Making: Pathways and Turning Points Through Life," most youthful wrongdoers do not become adult criminals. There are important turning points—quality education, well-paid work, stable marriage—that help young offenders become law-abiding adults.

16   The juvenile justice programs that have been shown to work—community-based programs that deal with kids on an individual basis—are hanging by a financial thread. We seem to prefer to make fun of "midnight basketball," the much maligned program in the Clinton crime bill, than acknowledging it makes sense to provide kids with alternatives to the street.

17   Why do we appear to hate our most troubled kids? When we call young lawbreakers "superpredators" and "violent youth predators," we stop thinking of them as kids, or as people. Race and racism help to fuel the anticrime hysteria sweeping the land. When most people think of juvenile crime, they think of young, African-American males, the ones we see hiding their faces on the TV news.

18   By arguing against punishing kids with adults, we are not demeaning the seriousness of violent juvenile crime. Violence perpetrated by juveniles has the same devastating effect on victims as violence perpetrated by adults. Youth violence contributes to community breakdown and causes despair for the families of both victims and perpetrators.

19   But we are talking about kids, many of whom have barely had a childhood on the mean streets of our cities. We are talking about kids, most of whom have been badly hurt themselves.

20   Frankie, the hapless burglar, is a juvenile wrongdoer. The burglary charge makes him a serious juvenile wrongdoer, an accused felon. He is more like most juvenile offenders than these "predators" the politicians are railing about. But if the politicians have their way, children like Frankie could be locked up with experienced adult inmates.

21   His parents regretted leaving Frankie in jail for the night, even though it was only one night and nothing really happened to him. When he was led out into the courtroom for arraignment, he was shackled to an adult detainee. He was held in the dock with seasoned criminals. His parents think that one night in jail killed something in Frankie. Maybe his childhood.

FOR ANALYSIS AND DISCUSSION

1. How does the case of Frankie in this article support Smith and Chester's argument? Why do you think they chose his case for this article?
2. Frankie's parents deliberately left him in jail overnight to "teach him a lesson." Did Frankie's crime merit this punishment? Could there be more to this story we don't know? Do you think Frankie learned his lesson?
3. Why is punishing juveniles with adult criminals "cruel and unusual punishment"? Create a pro/con checklist to examine different perspectives about this view.
4. According to the authors, how do current handgun laws promote juvenile crime? What do the authors think Massachusetts legislators should be doing with regard to handgun laws? Do you agree with their view? Why or why not?
5. The authors repeatedly employ the phrase "we know" throughout their essay. Does this phrase support their perspective? Who is "we"?
6. How does racism promote the "anticrime" sentiment in today's criminal courts? Is it true that the typical image people conjure up when they think of juvenile offenders is of a "young, African-American male"? Explain.

FOR RESEARCH

1. Smith and Chester comment that there is an "anticrime hysteria" sweeping the nation. Racism and ignorance, they say, fuel this hysteria. Interview 20 people

from different age groups and ask each to describe his or her "typical" juvenile offender and a typical juvenile crime. Ask each to explain on what he or she bases those descriptions. Research actual juvenile offender profiles and their crimes at <http://www.ncjrs.org/txtfiles/delc94.txt> and compare your findings with the opinions expressed in your survey.

2. What do young offenders themselves think about juvenile crime? A survey conducted by the California Bar Association and reported by Leslie Goldberg in the *Houston Chronicle,* May 2, 1996, entitled "Half of Youths Surveyed Have Broken the Law," indicated that "many of the children [surveyed] saw no connection between breaking the law and consequences." Access the "Crime is a Choice" Web site at <http://www.ncpa.org/hotlines/juvcrm/tcc1.html>. Are the young offenders profiled in Goldberg's survey "cold blooded," as Reilly describes them, or "hapless" children, as Smith and Chester see them? Explain.

Tough Justice for Juveniles
Edward Humes

Much of the media attention devoted to juvenile crime details the horror stories: youngsters with guns shooting classmates or angry youths taking out misguided frustration by shooting a store clerk during a robbery. For all the attention these crimes receive, statistics indicate that they do not represent the typical juvenile offense. In the effort to get tough on crime, some people inside the system say we are ignoring the real problem: How do we help the *average* juvenile offender?

Edward Humes, a Pulitzer Prize–winning journalist, spent a year in the juvenile courts of Los Angeles as a substitute teacher in the juvenile detention hall. While there he encouraged his pupils to write about their lives, and published some of their stories in *No Matter How Loud I Shout: A Year in the Life of Juvenile Court.* The following article appeared in the May 29, 1996, edition of the *New York Times.*

BEFORE YOU READ

Is punishing juveniles as adults for typical juvenile offenses a good idea? Should the severity of the crime be considered when determining how a juvenile offender should be prosecuted?

AS YOU READ

Humes comments that in the debate of juvenile crime, we are asking all the wrong questions. What does he say are the right ones? Does he provide the answers to his questions?

1 Should we combat the problem of youth violence by sending more children to adult prison? The answer is simple: We're asking the wrong question.

2 Our national fixation with meting out adult punishments to young criminals has blinded us to the underlying crisis—the juvenile system's shocking in-

ability to impose meaningful penalties, or even supervision, on offenders *before* they become the "predators" we so fear.

3   Consider two young offenders I met in the Los Angeles Juvenile Court, the nation's largest.

4   Ronald was charged with killing his employers at an ice cream store after they mildly criticized his tardiness. As the husband and wife drove him home one night, Ronald pulled a saw-off shotgun from his book bag, shot them both in the head and stole the day's receipts.

5   Because Ronald committed the murders nine days before his 16th birthday, he could not be tried as an adult. Now in a California youth prison, he must be freed—without supervision or even a criminal record—by the time he is 25, the age at which the state loses jurisdiction over people imprisoned as juveniles. (In many states, that age is 21.)

6   George entered the system at the age of 5 as a victim of abuse. The juvenile court raised him—and a poor parent it was, shunting him from one foster home to another and entrusting him to drug-abusing guardians. He roamed the streets and joined a gang while under the court's supervision. His crimes—a joy ride in a stolen car, a burglary—carried no punishment, just an occasional phone call from an overworked probation officer with 200 other children to monitor.

7   "They never gave me a reason to straighten out," George told me. "It was like they were daring me to do more crimes." Only after an adult criminal gave him the attention he craved by recruiting him for a robbery did the system notice George. By then, he had reached 16. He was sent to adult court.

8   During the long wait to be tried, he lived and went to school in a juvenile detention hall, his first stable home in years. He advanced three grades and received his high school diploma, earned praise as a tutor for other teen-agers and won a citywide essay contest for students. Yet he received a 12-year prison sentence, longer than Ronald's murder term.

9   Still, it is the Ronald's of the world we hear about, not the Georges, even though Ronald is an aberration and George's experience is repeated daily in juvenile courts. Indeed, Ronald's case became a cause célèbre in California, leading to new laws to send 14-year-olds to adult court.

10   Thus, an insignificant number of children who beat the system are driving the general direction of juvenile criminal justice. Murders committed by children younger than 16 in Los Angeles, for example, account for just five-hundredths of 1 percent of youth crime.

11   We can keep tinkering with laws so we can ship more and younger children to adult court, but this does nothing to return juvenile courts to their original mission: to deal with young people before they become hardened criminals. Instead, our courts wait until something serious happens, scoop up the child, brand him or her an adult and throw away the key on another "predator." Too late for the child, too late for his victim, too late for us all, as we shell out $25,000 a year for a cell.

12   Fixing all this isn't so much a matter of money as it is of attitude. The courts we have created for children are the lowest rung of our justice system; they are far less prestigious for judges and lawyers than forums reserved for contract disputes and whiplash claims. Many judges consider service in these

courts a punishment. Often, the least experienced prosecutors and defenders walk its halls. Caseloads are enormous. Frustration is rampant, given a system that goes easy on a Ronald while destroying a George.

13   The right questions in the debate about youth and crime are: How do we save first-time offenders from lives of crime? How do we turn the best of our legal profession toward saving children? Only when we deal with these issues will we start to "crack down" on juvenile crime. Along the way, we just might find that the notion of treating children differently from adults, simply because they are children, is not so outdated after all.

FOR ANALYSIS AND DISCUSSION

1. Humes repeats the word "predator" several times in his essay. Why does he put the word in quotation marks? What are the connotations of "predator"? Why is it important that he use this word in his argument?
2. The author uses the real-life cases of two young men to support his argument. Why did he choose these cases? How much does he tell us about Ronald, and how much about George? Are their cases different? Explain.
3. Humes mentions how much it costs to imprison a felon for a year. How could this information further help his argument?
4. According to Humes, what is the current attitude of officials in the juvenile courts? How does this attitude contribute to the overall problem?
5. Are you swayed to Humes's point of view after reading this article? What are the article's strengths and weaknesses? Explain.

FOR RESEARCH

1. Read the excerpt from Humes's book, *No Matter How Loud I Shout: A Year in the Life of Juvenile Court,* detailing what happens when a young offender is brought to lock-up at <http://www.tncrimlaw.com/pdconf/forum/v8_n2_p4.html>. After reading some of the profiles detailed by Humes, do you think there are different degrees of criminal responsibility? Would it solve the problem if current laws were changed to allow courts to punish juveniles as adults? How would you rewrite the law if you had the power to do so? Explain the basis behind your decisions.
2. Contact some prisons in your state and find out how much it costs the state (and the taxpayers) to incarcerate a person for one year. In the case of juveniles, would it make sense to increase the number of prisons to hold them as adult offenders, or could the money be spent in another way? Explain.

Peace in the Streets
Geoffrey Canada

Young people become criminals when they have neither hope nor heroes. Such is the claim of Geoffrey Canada who draws from his experience working with young people in Harlem. In the essay below, he argues that instead of focusing on punishment, society should concentrate on preventing the circumstances that contribute to youth violence. He advocates reducing violence as a whole—in the media, on television, and on the streets. By making a safer world for our children, we make a safer world for all of us.

Geoffrey Canada is President and CEO of Harlem's Rheedlen Center for Children and Families. He is also responsible for the Beacon Schools and the Peacemakers program in Harlem, and serves as the east coast coordinator for the Children's Defense Fund's Black Community Crusade for Children. The article below is an excerpt from his 1995 book *Fist, Stick, Knife, Gun: A Personal History of Violence in America.*

BEFORE YOU READ

Who are your heroes? What do you think makes someone a hero? Is there a discrepancy between "real" heroes and the ones created by popular culture?

AS YOU READ

How does Canada position himself at the center of the solution to the problem of youth violence? Is this an effective way to present his argument?

1   It's a Wednesday night in October and I'm early for my martial arts class in Harlem. I walk into the brightly lit gym and all eyes turn toward me. I'm walking with purpose, quickly and silently. A little boy begins to run over to me and an older student grabs his arm. I see him whispering in the younger boy's ear. I'm sure he's telling him, "You can't talk to him before class." And he's right. I stand in front of my class, looking unhappy and displeased. Everyone wonders who is out of place or not standing up straight. This is part of my act. Finally I begin the class and then I'm lost in the teaching. I'm trying to bring magic into the lives of these kids. To bring a sense of wonder and amazement. I can feel the students losing themselves and focusing on me. They are finally mine. I have them all to myself. I have crowded all the bad things out of their minds: The test they failed, the father who won't come by to see them, the dinner that won't be on the stove when they get home. I've pushed it all away by force of will and magic.

2   This is my time and I know all the tricks. I yell, I scream, I fly through the air with the greatest of ease. And by the time the class is ending my students' eyes are wide with amazement and respect, and they look at me differently. I line them up and I talk to them. I talk to them about values, violence, and hope. I try to build within each one a reservoir of strength that they can draw from as they face the countless tribulations small and large that poor children face every day. And I try to convince each one that I know their true value, their worth as human beings, their special gift that God gave to them. And I hope they will make it to the next class with something left in that reservoir for me to add to week by week. It is from that reservoir that they will draw the strength to resist the drugs, the guns, the violence.

3   My two best students usually walk with me after class and stay with me until I catch a cab. I tell them it's not necessary, but they are there to make sure I get home all right. What a world. So dangerous that children feel that a second-degree black belt needs an escort to get home safely.

4   This community, like many across this country, is not safe for children, and they usually walk home at night filled with fear and apprehension. But when I walk with them after class they are carefree, as children ought to be. They have no fear. They believe that if anything happens they'll be safe because I'm there. I'll fly through the air and with my magic karate I'll dispatch whatever evil threatens them. When these children see me standing on the corner watching them walk into their buildings they believe what children used to believe, that there are adults who can protect them. And I let them believe this even if my older students and I know different. Because in a world that is so cold and so harsh, children need heroes. Heroes give hope, and if these children have no hope they will have no future. And so I play the role of hero for them even if I have to resort to cheap tricks and theatrics.

5   If I could get the mayors, the governors, and the president to look into the eyes of the 5-year-olds of this nation, dressed in old raggedy clothes, whose jacket zippers are broken but whose dreams are still alive, they would know what I know—that children need people to fight for them. To stand with them on the most dangerous streets, in the dirtiest hallways, in their darkest hours. We as a country have been too willing to take from our weakest when times get hard. People who allow this to happen must be educated, must be challenged, must be turned around.

6   If we are to save our children we must become people they will look up to. We must stand up and be visible heroes. I want people to understand the crisis and I want people to act: Either we address the murder and mayhem in our country or we simply won't be able to continue to have the kind of democratic society that we as Americans cherish. Violence is not just a problem of the inner cities or of the minorities in this country. This is a national crisis and the nation must mobilize differently if we are to solve it.

7   Part of what we must do is change the way we think about violence. Trying to catch and punish people after they have committed a violent act won't deter violence in the least. In life on the street, it's better to go to jail than be killed, better to act quickly and decisively even if you risk being caught.

8   There are, however, things that governments could and should do right away to begin to end the violence on our streets. They include the following:

9   **Create a Peace Officer Corps.** Peace officers would not be police; they would not carry guns and would not be charged with making arrests. Instead they would be local men and women hired to work with children in their own neighborhoods. They would try to settle "beefs" and mediate disputes. They would not be the eyes and ears of the regular police force. Their job would be to try to get these young people jobs, to get them back into school, and most importantly, to be at the emergency rooms and funerals where young people

come together to grieve and plot revenge, in order to keep them from killing one another.

10 **Reduce the Demand for Drugs.**   Any real effort at diverting the next generation of kids from selling drugs *must* include plans to find employment for these children when they become teenagers. While that will require a significant expenditure of public funds, the savings from reduced hospitalization and reduced incarceration will more than offset the costs of employment.

11   And don't be fooled by those who say that these teenagers will never work for five dollars an hour when they can make thousands of dollars a week. I have found little evidence of this in my years of working with young people. Most of them, given the opportunity to make even the minimum wage, will do so gladly. The problem for many young people has been that they have looked for work year after year without ever finding a job. In some cities more than 40 percent of minority youth who want to work can't find employment.

12 **Reduce the Prevalence of Domestic Violence and Child Abuse and Neglect.** Too many children learn to act violently by experiencing violence in their homes. Our society has turned a blind eye to domestic violence for so long that the smacking, punching, and beating of women has become almost routine. And in many of the same homes where women are being beaten, the children are being beaten also. Our response as a society has been to wait until the violence has gotten so bad that the woman has to go to a battered-women's shelter (often losing the only place she has to live), or we have to take the abused child from the family. In both cases we break up a family, and common sense tells us this ends up costing us more money than it would have if we had intervened early and kept the family together.

13   The best mode of early intervention for really troubled families is family preservation services—intensive, short-term interventions designed to teach families new coping skills. The family preservation worker spends as much time as needed with a family to ensure that it gets the type of support and skills that it needs to function as a supportive unit rather than a destructive one.

14 **Reduce the Amount of Violence on Television and in the Movies.**   Violence in the media is ever more graphic, and the justification for acting violently is deeply implanted in young people's minds. The movie industry promotes the message that power is determined not merely by carrying a gun, but by carrying a big gun that is an automatic and has a big clip containing many bullets.

15   What about rap music, and especially "gangsta rap"? It is my opinion that people have concentrated too much attention on this one source of media violence. Many rap songs are positive, and some are neither positive nor negative—just kids telling their stories. But there are some rap singers who have decided that their niche in the music industry will be the most violent and vile. I

would love to see the record industry show some restraint in limiting these rappers' access to fame and fortune.

16   But by singling out one part of the entertainment industry as violent and ignoring others that are equally if not more violent (how many people have been killed in movies starring Arnold Schwarzenegger, Sylvester Stallone, and Clint Eastwood?) we will have no impact on reducing violence in this country. The television, movie, and record industries must all reduce the amount of violence they sell to Americans.

17   **Reduce and Regulate the Possession of Handguns.**   I believe all handgun sales should be banned in this country. Recognizing, however, that other Americans may not be ready to accept a ban on handguns, I believe there are still some things we must do.

18   *Licensing.* Every person who wants to buy a handgun should have to pass both a written test and a field test. The cost for these new procedures should be paid by those who make, sell, and buy handguns.

19   *Insurance.* Gun manufacturers and dealers should be required to register every handgun they manufacture and sell. This registration would be used to trace guns that wind up being used for crimes, and the manufacturers and dealers should be held liable for damages caused by any gun they manufacture and sell. Individual citizens would be required to carry insurance policies for liability and theft on their handguns, which would increase the pressure on citizens to make sure that their guns were safely locked away.

20   *Ammunition identification.* While we are beginning to bring some sane regulations to the handgun industry, we must also begin to make the killing of Americans with handguns less anonymous than it is today. One way to do this is to make all handgun ammunition identifiable. Gun owners should have to sign for specially coded ammunition, the purchase of which would then be logged into a computer. The codes should be etched into the shell casing as well as the bullet itself, and the codes should be designed so that even when a bullet breaks into fragments it can still be identified.

21   *Gun buy-backs.* The federal government, which recently passed a $32 billion crime bill, needs to invest billions of dollars over the next ten years buying guns back from citizens. We now have more than 200 million guns in circulation in our country. A properly cared-for gun can last for decades. There is no way we can deal with handgun violence until we reduce the number of guns currently in circulation. We know that young people won't give up their guns readily, but we have to keep in mind that this is a long-term problem. We have to begin to plan now to get the guns currently in the hands of children out of circulation permanently.

22   The truth of the matter is that reducing the escalating violence will be complicated and costly. If we were fighting an outside enemy that was killing our children at a rate of more than 5,000 a year, we would spare no expense. What

happens when the enemy is us? What happens when those Americans' children are mostly black and brown? Do we still have the will to invest the time and resources in saving their lives? The answer must be yes, because the impact and fear of violence has overrun the boundaries of our ghettos and has both its hands firmly around the neck of our whole country. And while you may not yet have been visited by the spectre of death and fear of this new national cancer, just give it time. Sooner or later, unless we act, you will. We all will.

FOR ANALYSIS AND DISCUSSION

1. According to Canada, what accounts for the lack of heroes in American society? What impact does this lack of heroes have on today's youth? Do you agree with his connection between America's lack of real heroes and the increase in youth crime?
2. What is Canada's tone in this essay? What effect does the tone have on his audience? Does his tone influence the reader to accept his views?
3. How does Canada's use of personal experience support his perspective? Is this an effective strategy? Does personal experience make an author more credible? Explain your view.
4. Address each of Canada's solutions concerning the problem of violence. Are his solutions feasible?
5. In paragraph 22, Canada comments that if Americans were "fighting an outside enemy" we would spare no expense to protect our children. Who is Canada's implied *inside* enemy?
6. What evidence does Canada use to support his claims? Is his evidence sound and his conclusions logical?

FOR RESEARCH

1. Evaluate the qualities and values American culture attributes to heroes. Who are the American heroes? Review the following analysis on what makes someone a hero by radio host Rick Minyard at <http://www.morningexpress.com/heroes.htm>. How does Minyard's list compare to popular "heroes" in our culture?
2. Geoffrey Canada is president and CEO of the Rheedlen Center for Children and Families in Harlem. Learn more about this organization, its goals and its methods for achieving these goals at <http://www.ncbn.org/docs/Resources/R_ncbnpubs/confs/conf_s98/s98_Plen/index.htm>. Apply the Center's goals to some of the points made in this chapter regarding addressing youth crime. Do you think the Center is targeting the right issues? Explain.

WRITING AND RESEARCH ASSIGNMENTS: JUVENILE CRIME, ADULT PUNISHMENT?

1. Steve Nawojczyk, a nationally recognized gang researcher and educator, has developed an excellent Web site devoted to information about gangs at <http://www.gangwar.com>. Access his link on gang dynamics. Based on research you gather from this site, describe gang dynamics and propose some measures communities might take to discourage or eliminate gangs.

2. In his article, Tom Reilly comments that rehabilitation of violent youth does not work. How are youth rehabilitated? Research the juvenile rehabilitation practices of your state's justice system. Are they working? Based on the incidences of youth crime and recidivism rates, defend or challenge the current system. Recommend changes that address any problems you have found.

3. T. Markus Funk states that "if there is anything approaching a truism in criminal law, it is that violent men most likely were violent teens." Expungement of juvenile criminal records, he believes, only contributes to the problem. Should expungement of juvenile records be disallowed? What is your state's policy regarding expungement? Use a pro/con checklist to become aware of opposing viewpoints and create a dialogue to explore how each might respond to the other's concerns. Then, rewrite the law or defend the current one.

4. You have been hired as a consultant to research the current juvenile justice system. You are asked to evaluate some of the prevention programs proposed by various juvenile justice organizations. Access the juvenile justice evaluation Web site prepared by Randy Nalor and research crime prevention programs at <http://www.fsu.edu/~crimdo/jjclearinghouse/jj10.html>. Pick one or several that you think make sense and then write about why you think they could work. Likewise, you may select one or several current programs and explain why you think they would *not* work.

5. Many of the articles in this casebook use statistics to support their arguments. Drawing on the opinions expressed in the chapter, as well as your own, write an argument evaluating current trends in juvenile justice. Does juvenile crime *seem* to be getting worse because of media attention, or is the rise in juvenile crime really a problem? Access the National Center for Policy Analysis Web site for current crime statistics at <http://www.ncpa.org/hotlines/juvcrm/tcc3a.html>.

6. Several of the authors in this chapter mention media violence as fueling the current increase in juvenile crime. Does the media influence juvenile crime? Research the following Web sites for information about media violence: <http://www.fsu.edu/~crimdo/jjclearinghouse/jj10.html> and <http://www.fsu/edu/~crimdo/jjclearinghouse/jj11.html>. Does your research indicate that there is a connection between juvenile crime and the media? Link your explanation to your Internet research, as well as to your personal experience.

7. Mike Males and Faye Docuyanan present an argument against the more popular opinion that we need to be tougher on juvenile offenders—build more prisons, try juveniles as adults, and exact longer sentences. Supporting the more popular view are Tom Reilly, Linda Collier, and T. Markus Funk. Create a dialogue among these writers to discover if they share any of the same values and assumptions about juvenile crime and youthful offenders..

8. How does youth poverty contribute to crime? Research the connection between poverty and crime. Is one a logical extension of the other? Why or why not? From the information collected by the National Criminal Justice Reference Service at <http://www.ncjrs.org/jjfact.htm>, what connections can you make between poverty and crime? Are most juvenile offenders poor? Does poverty influence the type and severity of crimes committed by youth? Present your conclusions in a well-supported argument.

9. Several authors in this chapter point out that the current juvenile justice system was developed one hundred years ago and is now outdated. What was criminal justice like in the eighteenth and nineteenth centuries? How was the system different? Write a short essay on the history of criminal justice in America. Try the "Basics of Juvenile Justice" Web site at <http://www.uaa.alaska.edu/just/just110/intro2.html> and the Colonial Williamsburg "Justice in the 18th Century" Web site at <http://www.pbs.org/williamsburg/jjustice.html> for information about the history of criminal justice.

10. Northeastern University criminal justice professor James A. Fox predicts that youth crime will reach an unprecedented high in the next ten years. Review his report to the U.S. attorney general (1995) at <http://www.ojp.usdoj.gov/bjs/abstract/tjvfox.htm>. What are the implications of Fox's survey? Do you agree with his predictions? Write an essay in which you defend or challenge Fox's conclusions.

11. Many of the articles in this chapter profile young adolescent males as juvenile offenders. There is little mention of female juvenile offenders. Why are girls mentioned so infrequently in discussions of juvenile justice? When politicians talk of restructuring juvenile laws along more adult lines, are they also considering female offenders? Should it matter?

Write an essay in which you profile female offenders and discuss why they seem to be largely left out of the "discussion" about juvenile crime. The following Web sites listed below discuss girls in the juvenile justice system:

Girls in the Juvenile Justice System: <http://statlab.stat.yale.edu/cityroom/kidslink2/justice/texts/9701-02.html>.

Females in Juvenile Justice: <http://www.ojp.usdoj/gov/Reports/98Guides/wcjs98/chap2.htm>.

Profile of a Female Offender: <http://www.ojp.usdoj.gov/Reports/98Guides/wcjs98/chap1.htm>.

What About Girls?: <http://ncjrs.org/txtfiles/fs-9884.txt>.

chapter **16**

CASEBOOK: TEEN PARENTS: CHILDREN HAVING CHILDREN?

Accarding to the popular media, teen parents are to blame for most of society's ills: drug use, crime, poverty, child abuse, homelessness, violence—the list is long. Teen parents themselves are portrayed as lazy, immoral, greedy, and ignorant. Are these stereotypes true, or have teen parents become the scapegoat of politicians and government bureaucrats who want to place the responsibility for the failure of numerous social programs on anyone but themselves? Are teen parents the perpetrators of societal problems or the victims? And, if teen pregnancy is a real problem, what can we do about it? This casebook gives you the opportunity to investigate the facts about teen parents and to arrive at your own conclusions. The writers go beyond simplistic stereotypes to explore whether teen pregnancy is a critical concern, the reasons why unmarried teens become parents, and the ways society can assist them.

Has teen pregnancy really reached epidemic proportions? Kathy Sylvester and Kristin Luker present differing views in response to this question. Each employs statistics to reach a very different conclusion. Sylvester regards the current rate of teen pregnancy as cause for alarm. She cites numerous studies that indicate that the number of unmarried teenage girls who are getting pregnant has risen, to the detriment of children and families. Kristin Luker, on the other hand, questions the hysteria about teen births, pointing out that the number actually peaked during the 1950s and has declined and stabilized since then. In her essay Luker suggests that pointing to "heedless, irresponsible teenagers" is a way to explain a host of unrelated and "dismaying social phenomena."

Who are teen mothers, and with the widespread availability of contraception, why are teens even getting pregnant? In "Teenage Childbearing and Personal Responsibility" Arline Geronimus provides insights into the lives of teen mothers and the difficult decisions they face. She points out the discrepancy between the widely accepted image of a teen mother and the social and economic realities that define her life. Geronimus uses her research to reveal the complicated and compelling factors that may actually make motherhood a reasonable choice for a disadvantaged teen girl.

How can society effectively address the problem of unwanted teen pregnancy and the problems it creates for the children produced? The solutions differ widely, depending on whether the writer sees teen parenting as a practical problem or as the failure of conventional morality. Margaret P. Battin ignores the moral issue of unmarried teenagers having babies and instead recommends a highly controversial strategy: the contraceptive "immunization" of all adolescents. If this practice were done as a matter of course when children reach adolescence, she reasons, the problem of unwanted pregnancy would become moot. James Q. Wilson, however, views the problem of teenagers becoming parents as the failure of U.S. society to enforce and sustain moral guidelines in which "custom and shame" would deter unmarried people from having babies. Wilson believes that teen parents are capable neither of instilling these values in their children nor of acting as responsible parents. Therefore, he proposes that young, unmarried pregnant girls who wish to receive public support be required to live in a family shelter or group home, which can provide guidance and instruction in parenting.

The readings in this casebook represent only a small sample of the diverse perspectives on this subject. Use these ideas to begin your own in-depth exploration of the issue of teen parenting through research, debate, dialogue, and deliberation. Try to go beyond the ready-made myths and stereotypes about teenagers having babies to a fuller understanding of the real causes and effects that underlie this problem, and come up with some solutions of your own.

Teenage Pregnancy: A Preventable Calamity
Kathy Sylvester

With unmarried teenage mothers accounting for nearly one-third of the births in America in 1995, social commentators, health officials, and educators are searching for a deterrent to unwanted and unplanned pregnancies. A commonly held view is that teenage mothers are responsible for many social ills, including welfare abuse, crime, child neglect, poor scholastic achievement, and perpetuation of the cycle of poverty. Some social commentators such as Kathy Sylvester locate the problem of teenage pregnancy in America's current moral deficiencies. Until America stops coddling teen parents and allowing this "unacceptable social choice" of children having children, teen pregnancy, and all the ills that accompany it, will simply get worse.

Kathy Sylvester is vice president for domestic policy at the Progressive Policy Institute in Washington, D.C. This excerpt from her policy report on teenage pregnancy for the Institute was published in 1996.

BEFORE YOU READ

List the factors you believe are responsible for the large number of unplanned pregnancies among teens. What change in policy, attitude, or practice would be most effective in reducing these numbers?

AS YOU READ

What does the word "calamity" mean? Why does Sylvester apply it to the issue of teen pregnancy? As you read the article, apply this word to the points she makes regarding teen pregnancy?

1   A preventable calamity is taking place in communities all across America: Young women who are still children themselves are bearing children of their own.

2   It is a calamity for these young mothers because early motherhood denies them opportunities and choices. It is a calamity for their children because most will grow up poor and fatherless. And it is a calamity for this nation because these children are likely to repeat the tragic cycle of poverty and dysfunction into which they were born.

3   Compelling evidence now supports what most Americans have long understood intuitively. Family structure and lifestyle, as well as economics, influence how children turn out. Children of young, unmarried mothers fare badly, and society pays the cost. The equation is straightforward: As poverty is the most accurate predictor of teen pregnancy, teen pregnancy is a near certain predictor of poverty. And in this country, two-thirds of never-married mothers now raise their child in poverty.

4   Beyond these statistics are stories of personal tragedy—stories of children who begin life with disadvantages from which they may never recover. Children of unmarried teen mothers are far more likely than the children of older, two-parent families to fall behind and drop out of school, to get into trouble with the law, to abuse drugs and join gangs, to have children of their own out of wedlock, and to become dependent on welfare.

5   The problem is urgent. There are now nine million children living in welfare families (Committee 1993). As those nine million children reach adolescence, many are "scripted" to repeat the lives of their parents. We must intervene and break the cycle before those children, too, become parents too soon and create a new generation of disadvantaged.[1]

6   To reverse this cycle requires nothing less than a categorical declaration by our nation's civic, moral, and community leaders that it is wrong not simply foolish or impractical for women and men to make babies they cannot support emotionally and financially. We must reject moral relativism and reassert our common values.

7   It is also time to challenge the complacent view that having babies out of wedlock is simply a lifestyle choice, and that since all lifestyle choices are equally valid, no behavior should be condemned. This stance is untenable in the face of compelling evidence that not all choices are equal in terms of their impact on children, and that children need fathers as well as mothers.

8   Massive federal spending on remedial programs will not solve the problem. Neither will castigating teen mothers, cutting off their welfare checks, and moving their children into orphanages. Government's role is not to insulate indi-

viduals from the consequences of their behavior. Nor should government insulate individuals from the values of their own communities.

9   The role of government must shift radically. Government must be the catalyst for strategies to change public perceptions about teen pregnancy as well as public perceptions about who is responsible for it, and how it should be solved.

10   All parents must be held accountable for supporting their children, and those who accept government help must also accept reciprocal obligations. At the same time, society must recognize its obligation to young parents and young people who are not yet parents. We must offer them real opportunities to create better lives for themselves and their children and a great deal of help along the way.

11   If we choose to ignore the problem, this self-perpetuating cycle will continue to create a separate society of single mothers and fatherless children. It will continue to deepen the social and economic divide between two-parent and single-parent families. It will continue to deepen resentments between rich and poor, and between black and white. And all of these divisions will further penetrate our culture.

12   What was once a socially unacceptable choice is now commonplace. In 1993, 6.3 million U.S. children were living with a single parent who had never married: 21 percent of white children, 32 percent of Hispanic children, and 57 percent of African-American children (Saluter 1994).[2]

13   Unmarried motherhood is not limited only to teenagers. Out-of-wedlock births are increasing more rapidly, in fact, among women in their 30s than among teens, among whites than among minorities. But society has a particular interest in and responsibility for preventing unwed teenage childbearing.

14   First, teenage mothers who enter the welfare system early are the most likely welfare recipients to get "stuck" in the system: Nearly half of long-term welfare recipients are women who gave birth before age 17. Teenage mothers are far more likely than older mothers to rely on government to support their children.

15   But government in the form of an army of social workers and counselors is no substitute for a missing parent. Bureaucratic compassion is a poor substitute for the nurturance, moral guidance, and kinship that strong families can offer children.

16   When an older woman chooses single parenthood, she may be creating a serious disadvantage for her child by denying that child a life with two adult parents. When a teenager makes that same choice, she creates an even graver disadvantage for her child: denying her child a life with even one adult parent. Teenage mothers, who often have little adult support, face the nearly impossible task of trying to raise children while growing up themselves. No amount of welfare, no social support system, can lift that enormous burden.

17   Finally, we must acknowledge that while older women may consciously choose unwed motherhood, teenage motherhood is not always such a conscious choice. In many communities, teen childbearing is commonplace while marriage is uncommon (Moore 1994).[3] For young women whose mothers and sisters and schoolmates all are unmarried mothers, teen childbearing seems in-

evitable. We owe it to these young women to insist that it is not inevitable. We must insist that they delay motherhood until they are able to understand its consequences. Then we must offer them other choices.

18   Each year, more than one million American teenage girls become pregnant—one in nine. Before the end of their teenage years, 43 percent of teenage girls become pregnant once (Forrest 1987). The United States has one of the highest teen pregnancy rates of any western industrialized nation. About half of these young women give birth; the majority do not marry. By 1991, 69 percent of teen mothers were unmarried—a rate that doubled in just one generation (Moore 1994; Simons 1991).[4,5]

19   For too long, policymakers have chosen an easy path providing a marginal existence for teenage mothers and their children and consigning them to impoverished lives in a separate welfare society. It has been more convenient to declare preventing teen pregnancy "beyond the capacity of government" than to take an unequivocal moral position against it and take steps to reverse the trend.

20   Instead of debating the critical question how to reverse the trends and reinstate the presumption that all children deserve to be born into stable and nurturing families politicians have been arguing over peripheral issues. Should we give out condoms in high schools? Is it politically incorrect to use the term "illegitimate"? And was the decision of an unmarried fictional television character to have a child a moral one? Debate on these issues diverts attention from the lives of real children.

21   Now we must pay attention to the lives of real people and acknowledge our urgent and compelling national interest in preventing pregnancies by young women unprepared to be mothers. To do that, we must change both the culture of acceptance and the context in which teenagers make decisions about sex and childbearing. Only then can we begin to arrest the trend.

22   This paper proposes a four-part strategy to accomplish those objectives:

23   1. Launching a national campaign to end the moral relativism that has characterized discussions of teen pregnancy. The campaign must begin with the unequivocal assertion that unmarried teen childbearing is morally wrong because of its costs for children and society. We must cast single motherhood as a selfish act because it harms children; we must resurrect the notion that it is dishonorable for a man to father a child he does not support.

24   2. Shifting government's role to that of catalyst. Government can no longer insulate those responsible for teen pregnancy from the consequences of their actions. Public policy must discourage, rather than support, decisions to bear or father children out of wedlock. This shift includes ending unqualified public assistance for unmarried teen mothers, requiring accountability for all fathers, and punishing sexual predators. At the same time, government must become a catalyst for solutions designed at the community level—solutions that strengthen and support families and reinforce community values.

25   3. Redefining responsible sexual behavior. That definition should be based on this simple premise: While many in our society now accept sex outside of marriage, we must reassert that children belong inside marriage.

26   4. Creating new opportunities and incentives for young women and men at risk of becoming parents too soon. We must stop rewarding the wrong behavior and instead offer rewards for disadvantaged young women and men who finish school and delay parenting. To help them, we must offer the support of caring adults, the chance to do well in school and go on to good jobs, and the reinforcement along the way of tangible and meaningful incentives, such as Individual Development Accounts.

NOTES

1. In 1987, there were 7.2 million children living in AFDC families; by 1993, that number had risen 31 percent to 9.5 million.

2. In 1983, there were 3.7 million, and in 1960, there were only 243,000.

3. In 1991, 95 percent of Atlanta's teen mothers were unmarried; the rate was 88 percent in Baltimore, 90 percent in Cleveland, 71 percent in Oklahoma City, 92 percent in Milwaukee, and 93 percent in Richmond.

4. The rate of unmarried teenagers in 1970 was 30 percent.

5. In 1950, 14 percent of births to teenagers were to unmarried mothers.

REFERENCES

Committee on Ways and Means: US House of Representatives. July 7, 1993. Overview of Entitlement Programs 1993 Green Book. Washington, DC: US Government Printing Office.

Forrest, J. D. 1987. "Proportion of Girls Ever Pregnant Before Age 20." Cited in Cheryl Hayes (ed.) Risking the Future: Adolescent Sexuality, Pregnancy and Childbearing, Vol. I. Washington, DC: National Academy Press. Vol. 1: 50–51.

Moore, Kristin A., Ph.D., and Nancy O. Snyder. January 1994. Facts at a Glance. Washington, DC: Child Trends, Inc.

Saluter, Arlene F. 1994. Marital Status and Living Arrangements: March 1993. US Bureau of the Census, Current Population Reports. Washington, DC: US Government Printing Office. Series P20–478:: VII.

Simons, Janet M, Belva Finlay and Alice Yang. 1991. The Adolescent and Young Adult Fact Book. Washington, DC: Children's Defense Fund.

FOR ANALYSIS AND DISCUSSION

1. What, according to Sylvester, is wrong about teenage pregnancy? Do you agree with her views? What other moral issues does teenage pregnancy raise for you, your friends, or adults you know?

2. Based on your own experience, do you agree with Sylvester's claim (paragraph 7) that America holds the "complacent view" that bearing a child out of wedlock is okay?

3. What is "moral relativism"? How does it apply to teen pregnancy?

4. Sylvester comments that Americans must "reassert our common values." What are those common values? Who decides what they are? Are "common values" indeed common? Explain.

5. In paragraph 17 Sylvester says that we must insist that young women delay motherhood. How would "insisting" solve the problem of teen pregnancy? Analyze this aspect of Sylvester's solution.

6. What is Sylvester advocating in this article? Review her solutions (paragraphs 22–26) and address the feasibility of each.

FOR RESEARCH

1. Access the following article on teen pregnancy by Melissa Lauber: <http://www.villagelife.org/news/archives/pregoverview.html>. How prevalent is the problem? Read the related stories featured at the end of Lauber's article about some programs designed to reduce teen pregnancy. Compare these other programs to the solutions offered by Sylvester.

2. Interview at least 20 individuals regarding their views on teen pregnancy and its causes. Try to interview a cross-section of the population. What causes teen pregnancy? Is it a grave social problem? Based on the results of this research write an essay on how people in your area feel about teen pregnancy. Is it indeed a "calamity"?

Constructing an Epidemic
Kristin Luker

Many politicians and the media would have us believe that the problem of teen pregnancy has reached extensive proportions. President Clinton himself has called teenage pregnancy "one of our most pressing social problems." But is adolescent pregnancy, in fact, a social epidemic? According to sociologist and law professor Kristin Luker, the problem is highly overrated. In the following essay Luker questions the validity of the statistics and challenges some of the cultural assumptions regarding the issue of teen pregnancy.

Kristin Luker is a professor of sociology at UC–Berkeley, in whose law school she also teaches. She is the author of several books including *Dubious Conceptions: The Politics of Teenage Pregnancy* (1996), from which this excerpt is drawn.

BEFORE YOU READ

How could the issue of teen pregnancy be a socially constructed epidemic? What does the word "epidemic" mean, and what impact does it have when coupled with the words "teen pregnancy"?

AS YOU READ

How does Lukas address the statistics concerning teenage pregnancy? What does her version of the situation reveal about the problem of teen pregnancy? Is her version more believable than Kathy Sylvester's? Why or why not?

1   By the early 1980s Americans had come to believe that teenagers were becoming pregnant in epidemic numbers, and the issue occupied a prominent place on the national agenda. "Teenage pregnancy," along with crack-addicted mothers, drive-by shootings, and the failing educational system, was beginning to be used as a form of shorthand for the country's social ills.[1] Everyone now agreed that it was a serious problem, and solutions were proposed across the ideological spectrum. Conservatives (members of the New Right, in particular) wanted to give parents more control over their daughters, including the right to determine whether they should have access to sex education and contraception.[2] Liberals, doubting that a "just say no" strategy would do much to curtail sexual activity among teenagers, continued to urge that young men and women be granted the same legal access to abortion and contraception that their elders had. Scholars debated the exact costs of early pregnancy to the individuals involved and to society, foundations targeted it for funding and investigation, government at all levels instituted programs to reduce it, and the media gave it a great deal of scrutiny.[3] In the early 1970s the phrase "teenage pregnancy" was just not part of the public lexicon. By 1978, however, a dozen articles per year were being published on the topic; by the mid-1980s the number had increased to two dozen; and by 1990 there were more than two hundred, including cover stories in both *Time* and *Newsweek*.[4]

2   Ironically (in view of all this media attention), births to teenagers actually *declined* in the 1970s and 1980s. During the baby boom years (1946–1964), teenagers, like older women, increased their childbearing dramatically: their birthrates almost doubled, reaching a peak in 1957. Subsequently, the rates drifted back to their earlier levels, where they have pretty much stayed since 1975.[5] The real "epidemic" occurred when Dwight Eisenhower was in the White House and poodle skirts were the height of fashion.[6] But although birthrates among teenagers were declining, other aspects of their behavior were changing in ways that many people saw as disturbing. From the vantage point of the 1970s, the relevant statistics could have been used to tell any one of a number of stories. For example, when abortion was legalized in 1973, experts began to refer to a new demographic measure, the "pregnancy rate," which combined the rate of abortion and the rate of live births. In the case of teenagers an increasing abortion rate meant that, despite a declining birthrate, the pregnancy rate was going up, and dramatically so.[7]

3   Since the rise in the pregnancy rate among teenagers (and among older women as well) was entirely due to the increase in abortions, it is curious that professionals and the public identified pregnancy, rather than abortion, as the problem. It is likewise curious that although the abortion rate increased for all women, most observers limited their attention to teenagers, who have always accounted for fewer than a third of the abortions performed. Teenagers *are* proportionately overrepresented in the ranks of women having abortions. But to pay attention almost exclusively to them, while neglecting the other groups that account for 70 percent of all abortions, does not make sense.

4   A similar misdirection characterized the issue of illegitimacy. In the 1970s teenagers were having fewer babies overall than in previous decades, but they—like older women—were having more babies out of wedlock. Compared to other women, teenagers have relatively few babies, and a very high proportion of these are born to unmarried parents (about 30 percent in 1970, 50 percent in 1980, and 70 percent in 1995). But although most babies born to teenagers are born out of wedlock, most babies born out of wedlock are *not* born to teens. In 1975 teens accounted for just under a half of all babies born out of wedlock; in 1980 they accounted for 40 percent; and in 1990 they accounted for fewer than a third.[8] Obviously, teens should hardly be the only population of interest.

5   Thus, in the 1970s and early 1980s the data revealed a number of disquieting trends, and teenagers became the focus of the public's worry about these trends. More single women were having sex, more women were having abortions, more women were having babies out of wedlock, and—contrary to prevailing stereotypes—older women and white women were slowly replacing African Americans and teens as the largest groups within the population of unwed mothers. These trends bespeak a number of social changes worth looking at closely. Sex and pregnancy had been decoupled by the contraception revolution of the 1960s; pregnancy and birth had been decoupled by the legalization of abortion in the 1970s; and more and more children were growing up in "postmodern" families—that is, without their biological mother and father—in part because divorce rates were rising and in part because more children were being born out of wedlock. But these broad demographic changes, which impinged on women and men of all ages, were seen as problems that primarily concerned *teenagers*. The teenage mother—in particular, the black teenage mother—came to personify the social, economic, and sexual trends that in one way or another affected almost everyone in America.

6   A number of different responses might have been devised to meet the challenge of these new trends. It would have been logical, for example, to focus on the problem of abortion, since more than a million abortions were performed each year despite the fact that people presumably had access to effective contraception. Or the problem might have been defined as the increase in out-of-wedlock births, since more and more couples were starting families without being married.[9] Or policymakers could have responded to the way in which sexual activity and childbearing were, to an ever greater extent, taking place outside marriage (in 1975 about three-fourths of all abortions were performed on single women).[10] Yet American society has never framed the problem in any of these broader terms. The widest perspective was perhaps that of the antiabortion activists, who saw the problem as abortion in general. A careful reading of the specialist and nonspecialist media suggests that, with a few exceptions, professionals and the general public paid scant attention to abortion and out-of-wedlock childbearing among older women, while agreeing that abortion and illegitimate births among teenagers constituted a major social and public-health problem. Why did Americans narrow their vision to such an

extent? How did professionals, Congress, and the public come to agree that there was an "epidemic" of pregnancy among teenagers and that teenagers were the main (if not the only) population worth worrying about?[11]

A Story That Fits the Data

7   . . . Advocates for young people had used Congress and the media to publicize an account of teenagers and their circumstances that seemed to make sense of the emerging demographic data and that was extremely persuasive. In essence, they claimed that teenagers, like older women, were increasingly likely to have sex and that their sexual activity was increasingly likely to take place outside marriage. Teens, however, like poor women of earlier generations, had been left out of the contraceptive revolution that had so changed the lives of other American women. They were having babies they did not want and could not support. Many of them were too inexperienced to know how to avoid conception, to appreciate the difficulties of childrearing, or to obtain an abortion (besides, abortion was expensive). And most gave birth without the support of the partner who had impregnated them. Unless they were granted access to affordable contraception and abortion, they would continue to have babies out of wedlock and would be mired in a life of poverty. Advocates noted that most babies born to teenagers were born out of wedlock, and that babies who lived with one parent were obviously less well off than those who lived with two. Moreover, black teenagers, who have always been disadvantaged in American society, had much higher rates of childbearing and illegitimacy than whites, although the reproductive behavior of white teenagers was beginning to resemble that of blacks. And in this account, teens who gave birth were much more likely to drop out of school than those who did not, so that as adults they were less well educated and hence poorer than women who postponed their childbearing.

8   Taken together, the data added up to a story that made sense to many people. It convinced Americans that young mothers like Michelle Brown—those who gave birth while still in high school and who were not married—were a serious social problem that brought a host of other problems in its wake. It explained why babies like David were born prematurely, why infant mortality rates in the United States were so high compared to those in other countries, why so many American students were dropping out of high school, and why AFDC costs were skyrocketing. Some people even believed that if teenagers in the United States maintained their high birthrates, the nation would not be able to compete internationally in the coming century. Others argued that distressing racial inequalities in education, income, and social standing were in large part due to the marked difference in the birthrates of white and black teenagers.

9   Yet this story, which fed both on itself and on diffuse social anxiety, was incomplete; the data it was based on were true, but only partial. Evidence that did not fit the argument was left out, or mentioned only in passing. Largely ignored, for example, was the fact that a substantial and growing proportion of all unmarried mothers were not teenagers. And on those rare occasions when older unwed mothers were discussed, they were not seen as a cause for con-

cern.[12] Likewise, although the substantially higher rates of out-of-wedlock childbearing among African Americans were often remarked upon, few observers pointed out that illegitimacy rates among blacks were falling or stable while rates among whites were increasing. Few noted that most of the teenagers giving birth were eighteen- and nineteen-year-olds, or that teens under fifteen had been having babies throughout much of the century.[13]

10   This story, as it emerged in the media and in policy circles in the 1970s and 1980s, fulfilled the public's need to identify the cause of a spreading social malaise. It led Americans to think that teenagers were the only ones being buffeted by social changes, whereas these changes were in fact pervasive; it led them to think that heedless, promiscuous teenagers were responsible for a great many disturbing social trends; and it led them to think that teenagers were doing these things unwittingly and despite themselves. When people spoke of "children having children" or of "babies having babies," their very choice of words revealed their belief that teenage mothers, because of their youth, should not be held morally responsible for their actions. "Babies" who had babies were themselves victims; they needed protection from their own ungovernable impulses.

11   In another sense, limiting the issue to teenagers gave it a deceptive air of universality; after all, everyone has been or will be a teenager. Yet the large-scale changes that were taking place in American life did not affect all teenagers equally. The types of behavior that led teenagers to get pregnant and become unwed mothers (engaging in premarital sex, and bearing and keeping illegitimate children) were traditionally much more common among African Americans than among whites, and more common among the poor than among the privileged.

12   For average Americans in the 1970s, life had undergone profound changes in just a few short years. Unmarried couples were engaging more readily in sex, and doing so much more openly. Many of them were even living together, instead of settling for furtive sex in the back seats of cars. When an unmarried woman got pregnant, she no longer made a sudden marriage or a hasty visit to a distant aunt; now she either terminated her pregnancy or openly—even proudly—had her baby. Often she chose to live as a single parent or to set up housekeeping with her partner, rather than allowing her child to be adopted by a proper, married middle-class couple. In the 1970s people of all ages began to follow this way of life, but the inchoate fears of the public coalesced in large part exclusively around teenagers. The new patterns of sexual behavior and new family structures were simply more visible among younger people, who had not committed themselves to the older set of choices. At the same time, teenagers, especially those who had children, were defined as people who were embarking on a lifetime of poverty. The debate, in centering on teenagers in general, thus combined two contrasting features of American society: it permitted people to talk about African Americans and poor women (categories that often overlapped) without mentioning race or class; but it also reflected the fact that the sexual behavior and reproductive patterns of white teenagers were beginning to

resemble those of African Americans and poor women—that is, more and more whites were postponing marriage and having babies out of wedlock.

13   The myriad congressional hearings, newspaper stories, and technical reports on the "epidemic" of pregnancy among teenagers could not have convinced the public to subscribe to this view if other factors in American life had not made the story plausible. The social sciences abound with theories suggesting that the public is subject to "moral panics" which are in large part irrational, but in this case people were responding to a particular account because it helped them make sense of some very real and rapidly changing conditions in their world.[14] It appeared to explain a number of dismaying social phenomena, such as spreading signs of poverty, persistent racial inequalities, illegitimacy, freer sexual mores, and new family structures.[15] It was and continues to be a resonant issue because of the profound changes that have taken place in the meanings and practices associated with sexuality and reproduction, in the relations among sex, marriage, and childbearing, and in the national and global economies. Through the story of "teenage pregnancy," these revolutionary changes acquired a logic and a human face.[16]

NOTES

1. For example, see William Bennett, *The Index of Leading Cultural Indicators: Facts and Figures on the State of American Society* (New York: Simon and Schuster, 1994).

2. Although much of the rhetoric on the Right is about "children," conservatives and even many liberals think of pregnancy among teenagers as something fundamentally affecting "girls" or young women. The issue is usually framed in such a way that half of the people involved—namely, young men—are excluded, and this selectivity is an enormous handicap in the effort to find a solution. As we will see, thinking about the problem in terms of two sexes rather than one opens up a number of new possible solutions.

3. For an overview, see U.S. House of Representatives, 99th Congress, Select Committee on Children, Youth and Families, "Teen Pregnancy: What Is Being Done? A State-by-State Look" (Washington, D.C.: Government Printing Office, 1986); Charles Stewart Mott Foundation, *A State-by-State Look at Teenage Childbearing in the United States* (Flint, Mich.: Charles Stewart Mott Foundation, 1991); Gloria Magat, ed., *Adolescent Pregnancy: Still News in 1989* (New York: Grantmakers Concerned with Adolescent Pregnancy, Women and Foundations/Corporate Philanthropy, 1989); Junior League, *Teenage Pregnancy: Developing Life Options* (New York: Association of Junior Leagues, 1988). For the National Urban League's program with Kappa Alpha Psi, see Cheryl Hayes, ed., *Risking the Future: Adolescent Sexuality, Pregnancy, and Childbearing* (Washington, D.C.: National Academy Press, 1987), vol. 1, p. 178.

4. Prior to the mid 1970s, pregnant teenagers were treated by the media as a subset of "school-age mothers" or of the larger set of "unwed mothers." See *Reader's Guide to Periodic Literature*, 1968–1994. A tabulation of these stories by title and content has been compiled by Kristin Luker.

5. In 1955, out of every thousand adolescent women of all races, 90 gave birth. By 1975 the rate had fallen until it was approximately equal to that of 1915: 60 per thousand. And by 1985 it had declined even further, to only 50 per thousand. Interestingly, the fertility of teenagers has always been remarkably similar to that of

older women; the birthrates for both groups rise and fall in tandem. (The similarities are most marked, of course, between the rates for teens and the rates for women who are just a little older—twenty to twenty-four.) Clearly, the fertility of American women tends to respond to large, society-wide forces. See National Center for Health Statistics, *Advance Report of Final Natality Statistics* (Hyattsville, Md.: Public Health Service, various years).

6. Robert L. Heuser, *Fertility Tables for Birth Cohorts by Color: United States, 1917–1973,* DHEW Publication no. (HRA) 76–11182 (Rockville, Md.: National Center for Health Statistics, 1976); National Center for Health Statistics, *Advance Report of Final Natality Statistics, 1987* (Rockville, Md.: National Center for Health Statistics, 1989), vol. 38, no. 3. Even the post-1988 upturn in birthrates among teenagers is still within the range of historical fluctuation, although whether this will continue to be so is uncertain.

7. In 1973, among teenage women of all races, 60 out of every thousand gave birth and 21 per thousand had abortions; thus, a total of 81 out of every thousand were becoming pregnant. In 1980, in contrast, the rate of live births was 52 per thousand and the abortion rate had more than doubled, to 44 per thousand; the pregnancy rate had thus increased to 96 per thousand.

8. For an overview, see *Statistical Abstract of the United States* (Washington, D.C.: Government Printing Office, 1993), Table 101, "Births to Unmarried Women, by Race of Child and Age of Mother, 1970–1990"; U.S. Center for Health Statistics, *Vital Statistics of the United States,* various years; idem, *Monthly Vital Statistics,* various years.

9. This has led to a set of new social practices unanticipated by Emily Post. People now speak of "my baby's father" or "my baby's mother." One proud father even placed a notice in his local paper announcing that his fiancée had just given birth to their baby (I am indebted to Sheldon Messinger for this information). In the late 1980s commentators did begin to take note of the rising rate of out-of-wedlock births in general; but even within this broader context, experts and the media still focused on teenage mothers.

10. Larry Bumpass and James A. Sweet, "Children's Experience in Single-Parent Families: Implications of Cohabitation and Marital Transition," *Family Planning Perspectives* 21 (November–December): 256–260.

11. In 1986 polls revealed that more than 84 percent of Americans considered pregnancy among teenagers a "major" problem facing the country. Harris poll for PPFA, 1985. See also Roper Report 86-3, 1986 R37XE.

12. Some people, among them demographers such as Phillips Cutwright and polemicists such as Charles Murray, argue that the proportion or ratio of out-of-wedlock births is much more important than the rate. In demographic terms, a "rate" is an event that is standardized over a specified population for a particular period of time. Thus, the birthrate is defined as the number of births (the numerator) per thousand women aged fifteen to forty-four (the denominator) in a year. But many commentators speak of the "illegitimacy rate" or the "abortion rate" when what they really have in mind is a proportion or ratio, a figure that compares two sets of *events* rather than an event to a population. What many people call the "illegitimacy rate" is really a measure that compares the number of out-of-wedlock births (the numerator) to the total number of births (the denominator). The problem here is that there can be wide fluctuations in *both* of the events being charted, and these fluctuations can lead to dramatic changes in the measure. (Populations fluctuate, too, of course, but much less sharply.) The illegitimacy *rate* (the number of out-of-wedlock births per thousand unmarried women aged fifteen to forty-four) went from 25.4 in 1970 to 43.8 in 1990, an increase of about 70 percent, while the illegitimacy *ratio*

(the proportion of out-of-wedlock births to legitimate births) went from 11 percent to 28 percent of all births during that same period, an increase of more than 250 percent. The dramatically larger increase in the ratio, compared to the increase in the rate, was due to an increase in the propensity of American women to bear children out of wedlock, and simultaneously, a declining propensity to bear children in wedlock. Among African Americans, virtually all of the increase in the illegitimacy ratio was due to declining marital fertility (the denominator), and in fact illegitimacy rates for African American women declined for most of the 1970–1990 period. As Cutright says, what the majority of a cohort is doing matters. Still, commentators tended to emphasize troubling statistics (changes in the proportion of babies born out of wedlock) over more comforting ones (such as the decreases in the incidence of pregnancy per sexually experienced woman and in the rate of out-of-wedlock births among African Americans).

13. One could make the case that this *was* the real story: the fact that birthrates among very young women had not changed much. Since the period of childhood had gradually lengthened in the course of the nineteenth and twentieth centuries, one would have expected a reduction in births to very young women. Birthrates among fourteen-year-olds for the calendar years 1925–1990 were as follows

1925	3.9 per thousand
1930	3.8
1935	3.7
1940	3.8
1945	3.9
1950	5.8
1955	6.1
1960	6.0
1965	5.2
1970	6.6
1975	7.1
1980	6.5
1985	6.2
1990	7.8

Source for 1925–1970: Heuser, *Fertility Tables for Birth Cohorts by Color*, "Central Birth Rates for All Women during Each Year 1917–73 by Age and Live-Birth Order for Each Cohort from 1888 to 1959," p. 37, Table 4a. Source for 1975–1990: *Vital Statistics of the United States: Natality*, "Central Birth Rates by Live-Birth Order, Current Age of Mother, and Color for Women in Each Cohort," p. 1–32, Table 1–16 (1975): p. 1–142, Table 1.18 (1980); p. 1–36, Table 1–18 (1985); p. 1–45, Table 1–19 (1990).

14. The classic example is Stanley Cohen, *Folk Devils and Moral Panics* (Oxford: Basil Blackwell, 1987). For another view, one that is more in line with the position presented here, see John Kingdon, *Agendas, Alternatives, and Public Policies* (Boston: Little, Brown, 1984).

15. This does not imply that stories told by advocates are necessarily right. Indeed, as in this case, advocates typically confront contradictory data and must strive to make sense of them long before the whole pattern of the phenomenon is clear. On the issue of pregnancy among teenagers, advocates and policymakers were wrong in several important respects, and their errors had profound implications for social policy.

16. Rosalind Petchesky has made the astute point that social scientists often speak of "revolutions" when only white and middle-class behavior has changed. See Petchesky, *Abortion and Women's Choice: The State, Sexuality and Reproductive Freedom* (Boston: Northeastern University Press, 1990).

FOR ANALYSIS AND DISCUSSION

1. When, according to Luker, did the real "epidemic" of teen pregnancy occur? How did society react to the problem? What differences exist between it (the real epidemic) and the current teen pregnancy situation?
2. What accounts for the apparent rise in pregnancy rates? Why is citing this rise presenting a skewed perspective of the problem?
3. What is the typical profile of teenage motherhood? Who does society have as a scapegoat? Is this profile accurate, based on the statistics?
4. Luker comments that media attention is also to blame for presenting teen pregnancy as a widespread problem. What do you think accounts for all the attention the media devote to this topic? Is there a difference between the ways the news media and popular culture present the situation? Explain.
5. How did teens become the scapegoat for so many of society's ills in the 1970s and 1980s? What problems have been blamed on youths? Are they still commonly held responsible for social problems today?

FOR RESEARCH

1. Using Web resources, personal interviews, journal sources, and examples from popular culture, research teenage sexuality over the past 40 years. How has teen sexuality changed? What did teens do if they became pregnant 30 years ago? What options are available to pregnant teens today?
2. Luker comments that during the 1970s and 1980s the media publicized extensively the issue of teen pregnancy. How is teen pregnancy presented today? Draw from all forms of media, including television, movies, music, advertising, magazines and journals, and newspapers. What messages are sent to teens by the various media? From your research, develop a profile of different social perspectives on teen pregnancy.

Teenage Childbearing and Personal Responsibility: An Alternative View
Arline T. Geronimus

It is a common assumption not only that teenage pregnancy is a problem, but that most teen pregnancies are unwanted and unplanned. Yet more than half of all teen pregnancies are carried to term. Would this number be so high if pregnancies were indeed unwanted? Arline T. Geronimus offers a unique perspective on teen pregnancy and presents various alternatives as to why young women get pregnant.

Arline Geronimus is an associate professor in the department of health behavior and health education at the University of Michigan. This article first appeared in the *Political Science Quarterly* in the fall of 1997.

BEFORE YOU READ

What is your definition of a family unit? Is there only one acceptable definition, or is there a variety of configurations that can make up a family? Is teen pregnancy more acceptable if there is a strong family network established to support the young mother and her baby?

AS YOU READ

What support does Geronimus provide to back up her assertion that teen pregnancy may occur more by choice than by chance?

1   The nature and scope of the welfare reform debate resulting in the Personal Responsibility and Work Opportunity Reconciliation Act of 1996 (PRWORA) reflect a growing convergence toward the position that poverty is the result of poor people's values and behaviors. Among examples of this convergence is a perspective on teenage childbearing that informed some provisions of PRWORA, "Teenage childbearing" operates as a uniquely effective symbol of the failure to act responsibly. At first glance, everyone can agree that teenage childbearing is a "bad thing," unambiguously harmful to all involved—the young parents, the innocent children, and the larger society. Because of its perceived social costs and the fact that children are involved, the invocation of incentives and punishments to alter this behavior is now considered to be within the legitimate purview of public policy. This particular form of social engineering garners enthusiastic support from representatives of different political persuasions. To the extent that it represents concern for the well-being of vulnerable children it appeals to those with the desire to help the needy. And because to many it represents extramarital sexuality it ignites the interests of those who seek to reaffirm social order. But if this apparent consensus siphons energy and resources away from searching debate about the nature of poverty, it presents a definite social danger. . . .

Family Support

2   The dominant cultural ideal in the United States is for a baby to be born into an intact nuclear family. A critical reason teenage childbearing has been problematized is its perceived link to single parenting. Senator Specter observed that, "It may well be the most important problem as we grapple with teenage pregnancy where we have a family coming into existence without any family structure at all." Sociological and anthropological evidence suggest that categorizing families as either nuclear or nonexistent is overly simplistic, as I discuss below. However, the tendency to do so in the case of teen mothers has been re-enforced by overdrawn popularized images. Because a teen mother is more likely to be unmarried now

than in the past, the popularized image of teen parenthood is of an absent father and an immature, problem-prone girl raising her (unwanted) child alone. Given this image, common sense suggests that teen childbearing must jeopardize the health and well-being of children and be costly to society.

3   These nagging doubts might be assuaged by reconstructing this image to be more consistent with the literature. Teen mothers in the United States tend to be older (two-thirds of teen mothers are 18–19 years old; only 2 percent are under age 15), are more likely to be married (about 40 percent are married and teens constitute less than one-third of all unmarried mothers), or, if not married, to benefit from the support and guidance of others than the popularized image suggests. That is, welfare policy makers—along with many middle class Americans—fail to distinguish between the function of providing stability, care, and economic support to children that is most often provided by married couples in the United States from the form of marriage itself.

4   Within the United States, population-variation in family structure is well-documented, both for the current period and historically. Some scholarly theories to explain this variation take non-nuclear family structures as deficient, prima facie, while others attempt to appraise their strengths, weaknesses, and origins without prejudgement. This latter academic tradition was ignored in the welfare reform debate. Yet, consistent with this tradition, some research suggests it may be more accurate to think of a poor teen mother (at least in African American communities that have been studied the most extensively) as an emerging adult participant in active multigenerational social networks than as a rebellious adolescent set apart from her elders, raising her baby alone.

5   Ethnographic observation and analyses of survey data provide evidence in African American communities that mothers, fathers (or father surrogates), grandmothers, aunts, uncles, and others from both maternal and paternal sides (regardless of parental marital status) actively contribute to the support and nurturance of the young. This approach to shared childrearing, in effect, pools risk among poor families, providing social insurance against common risks. These include risks of severe income shortfall due to the unpredictability of wages, employment (or welfare benefits); risks of hunger, homelessness, or early adult disability; and risks of physical separation between children and any specific individual adult (for example, inflexible work requirements, incarceration, or premature death). If we concern ourselves with family functioning rather than form, it is possible that in some circumstances greater stability, care, and economic support for children may be realized through family systems and forms of union that are not nuclear and that do not place high value on legal marriage, per se. . . .

6   The tendency to categorize poor teens in terms of their adolescent status instead of their socioeconomic group may also be misleading if it conceptually sets the individual teenager (or teenager and her boyfriend) as having impulses opposed to the viewpoints of more mature elders, taking risks and making pregnancy resolution decisions in a vacuum apart from mature guidance. Yet, at least in specific socioeconomically disadvantaged local settings, there is evidence to suggest that teens generally decide how to resolve unplanned pregnancies in collaboration with elders. In some instances, teens are encouraged to become

mothers by elders who speak from life experience. In these instances, ethnographers interpret the elders as drawing on their socially-suited knowledge that poor families must rely on each other for caretaking as well as for economic support. As poor families configure themselves, elders may make judgments about which teens are promising economic providers and which ones are better at caretaking. They may recruit teens for whichever aspects of kinwork are currently required. In communities where babies are highly valued, longevity is in question, and the experience of grandparenthood is longed for, elders may also encourage early childbearing. More speculatively, if as the research suggests in extremely disadvantaged communities, early childbearing maximizes the health and well-being of infants, a caring elder might encourage it.

Poor Teens and Life Prospects

7   Middle-class teens have opportunities stretching well beyond age 18 or 19 to become better educated, better skilled, and thus eventually more employable. If they bore children as teenagers, their childcare obligations might well conflict dramatically with their ability to utilize these opportunities. And, given such opportunities, middle-class youth have every reason to believe that they will be better providers for their children if they delay parenthood. But this is not true for the young women most likely to become teen mothers. Poor youth and minority youth in general, as well as those who have suffered early school failure, in particular, face more restricted educational or labor market opportunities. Poor families do appear to mobilize to support those teenagers believed to possess the skills necessary to overcome chronic barriers to achievement and upward mobility, including discouraging them from engaging in the dating activities of their peers. But other poor teens may have less to gain from postponing childbearing. Meanwhile, to the extent they have access to kin support for childcare the trade-offs between school, work and childcare may be diminished. In targeting policy to address unequal opportunity among American youth, it is likely that social forces other than early childbearing constitute the major impediments to labor market success among poor teen mothers.

8   Differences in life prospects between poor and better-off teenagers are evident at their most basic and literal level. The most profound inappropriate assumption that leads us to believe that postponing childbearing well beyond the teen years is always in children's best interests is the assumption that teens from all social classes face a predictable future with death far off in its "logical position . . . at the close of a long life." Yet, in the United States, one of the most disturbing expressions of social inequality is the variation across socioeconomic groups in rates of premature adult mortality. For example, the following table shows the probability that a 15-year-old male or female will survive to age 45, 55, or 65 for U.S. whites and for African American residents of two poor communities: Harlem and Chicago's south side. 95 percent of white women, but less than 80 percent of Harlem or Chicago women, survive to their 55th birthday. More than one-third of Harlem or Chicago women die by age 65. For men, the statistics are more grim. Less than three-quarters of Harlem or Chicago

TABLE: *Percent Surviving to Age X Conditional on Survival to Age 15 in Selected Populations, 1990*

Age	U.S. Whites	Harlem	Chicago
WOMEN			
45	98	87	88
55	95	78	79
65	87	65	63
MEN			
45	94	71	73
55	89	55	55
65	77	37	37

Notes: Harlem refers to African American residents of the Central Harlem Health Center District in New York City. Chicago refers to African American residents of highly impoverished southside Community Areas of Near Southside, Douglas, Oakland, Fuller Park, Grand Boulevard, and Washington Park. Mortality calculations based on data from the 1990 Census of the Population (adjusted for coverage error) and from death certificates for 1989–1991. See Geronimus et al., "Excess Mortality Among Blacks and Whites in the United States" for general methods.

men survive to age 45, compared to 94 percent of U.S. whites. Little more than half of Harlem or Chicago men can expect to survive to age 55, and almost two-thirds who reach their 15th birthday will not live to see their 65th. (This represents less than half the probability that the typical white 15-year-old-male nationwide will survive to age 65.) In Harlem and Chicago, 15 year old men have less chance of surviving to age 45 than the typical white 15 year old nationwide has of surviving to age 65. Deaths from chronic diseases, rather than the more publicized instances of homicide, are the primary reason.

9   Lower, but still strikingly high rates of early adult mortality for women and men have been described for other urban areas such as Watts in Los Angeles or Central City Detroit. In predominantly African American poor urban populations—some of the same populations where early childbearing is common and engenders the most concern in the general population—the probability of premature mortality appears sufficiently high that, unlike the average American teenager, teens in these areas cannot confidently expect to survive through or even to middle adulthood.

10   Without such confidence, to postpone central goals such as childbearing is to risk forgoing them. And if one believes that responsible parenthood includes maximizing the chance that a parent will survive to see and help her child grow up, then insecurity about one's own longevity would be a serious consideration when contemplating whether to defer parenthood.

11   When these aspects of the life experience of the poor are ignored and teen mothers are viewed merely as youth, the state may appear justified in moving in, in loco parentis, to regulate the behavior of poor teens, whether through the "tough love" approaches advocated by conservatives or the paternalistically supportive approaches suggested by liberals. As Representative Linda Smith (R-WA) argued on March 23, 1995: "The most compassionate thing we can do for these little kids and their kids is to not give them cash grants, to not go on and reward the wrong decisions, to not reward sometimes their mothers who encourage them in some tenement house to go get pregnant so they can get the welfare that they have learned to live on." But if compassion is what we aim for, then this approach of constructing all sexually active teenage women as unsupervised adolescents and using that image to justify government policy as surrogate parent is deeply problematic. It pathologizes the role of elders in the decisions of poor teens. It definitionally attributes the same psychosocial developmental trajectories, opportunities, and human resources for helping to rear children (now or in the future) to all teenagers. But, as we have seen, there are marked variations across social groupings in all of these factors. Generalizing from middle class to poor teens may lead to mistaken characterization of the motivations of unmarried, sexually active teens who are poor and of the opportunities and resources dependably available to them for realizing more socially approved goals than early childbearing. It is not only incorrect in its premise that every teen, by definition, is unprepared to be a responsible mother, but also in its implications that every teen, by definition, will be in a better position to be one at a later date.

An Alternative View: The Rationality of Childbearing

12   The perspective on teen childbearing that helped to inform the PRWORA is not only inconsistent with important empirical evidence, but it is also only one among several theoretical perspectives on the relationship of teenage childbearing to socioeconomic disadvantage. Here I outline one alternative perspective that is consistent with existing empirical evidence, but leads to a different conclusion regarding the rationality or "responsibility" of early fertility timing, at least among an important subset of teen mothers. I focus on poor, urban African Americans for two reasons. First, there is more research evidence about this subset of the disadvantaged. Second, insofar as public concern about teen childbearing is now racialized, teenage childbearing is construed as one in a constellation of pathological behaviors particularly engaged in by an urban, African American "underclass." I argue instead that the generally earlier fertility exhibited in these communities relative to the national average has a quite different meaning. It does not represent the abandonment by teens or their elders of the mainstream "family value" that responsible parents strive to bring children into the world when they are most prepared to provide for their children's well-being, broadly defined. Instead, it expresses attempts to embrace

this view of the appropriate time for childbearing within extremely adverse circumstances that constrain and qualitatively alter the routes available for achieving this goal.

13   What if a poor, African American teen wants the following: to have two or three healthy children who will continue to thrive and will be provided for materially and emotionally until they reach adulthood. Moreover, she (or he) wants to achieve this result, while minimizing the chance of needing government assistance in order to do so. If this is what she values, what age would she or the elders who advise her think would be the most appropriate to begin childbearing?

14   What if, as the literature suggests, in pursuing these goals, there are complicating factors? The poor teen might die at any time, might well not survive through middle age, and is likely to suffer from a chronic disease or disability starting at even younger ages. If she delays childbearing, this early health deterioration will jeopardize her chances of bearing normal-weight infants who survive infancy. If she does bear a low birthweight baby, that child is at increased risk of long-term developmental deficits. If she has a "special needs" child, that will be a drain on family resources and may depress the child's school performance and future economic prospects. The possibility of early death or disability also characterizes the people a poor mother depends on to support and care for her children—be they her baby's father or members of a broader social network. And a child with a disabled family member is more likely to exhibit behavior problems. The research findings suggest that a poor mother faces particular uncertainty if she follows the nuclear family model and depends primarily on a husband for economic, practical or emotional support. His chance of early death is distressingly high. Meanwhile, his earnings potential is likely to be low and unreliable.

15   In fact, whether or not she marries before her first birth, a poor mother must expect to contribute substantially to the financial support of her children. But her chances for labor market attachment are also unreliable. If she finds employment, the wages and benefits she can command may not offset the costs of being a working mother. She cannot expect paid maternity leave; nor is accessible or affordable daycare available that would free her from reliance on kin for childcare once she does return to work. Moreover, she faces the social expectations that she help care for her kin as their health falters. Postponing childbearing increases the chance that her young children compete with ailing elders for her energies and decreases the chance that their father will survive through much of their childhood. Her greatest chance of long-term labor force attachment will be if her children's pre-school years coincide with her years of peak access to social and practical support provided by relatively healthy kin. Her best chance of achieving her stated goals is by becoming a mother at a young age. Note that, the kin-network approach to childrearing is motivated, among other reasons, by the community-level social expectations that adults work whenever they can, however they can, and that others pitch in to make this possible. Put another way, if the poor place value on economic self-suffi-

ciency through gainful employment then they often must accept jobs that separate them from their children, sometimes for long periods. Low-skill jobs provide income and other practical and psychological rewards, but they may also exacerbate disease risk and the chance of early disability or mortality. Working-poor parents may experience legitimate worries of becoming compromised in their capacity to provide for their children or of leaving them orphaned. If along with their work ethic, parents also value providing consistent emotional and material support for their children, then they must develop, invest in, and rely on informal social capital. By doing so they do their best to insure their children caring adults willing and able to supplement or even substitute for parental support.

16   In sum, one need not assume the abandonment of personal responsibility to explain persistently high rates of early childbearing in poor communities. Instead, the scenario described here suggests the possibility that poor teens in collaboration with their elders may be making rational and responsible decisions. Instead of being a sign that their values place them apart from the mainstream, the behavior of teen mothers can be read as representing mainstream values whose phenotypic manifestations take different forms as suits the environmental contingencies that must be addressed. Of course, it is not being assumed that poor teens or their elders know the precise statistical odds they face of restricted opportunities, early death and disability, or infant mortality. But it is equally unreasonable to assume that their life experiences do not impress some version of these facts upon them.

17   The perspective that teenage childbearing represents trade-offs made in order to maximize children's well-being in hard circumstances may also explain why early childbearing has persisted in extremely disadvantaged communities, despite increased access to contraceptive technology and abortion and in the face of very public disapproval of the behavior. It would suggest that it may continue to persist in the face of welfare reform. . . .

18   Despite two decades of active attempts to reduce teenage childbearing in poor communities, there has been little evidence of a successful targeted program. Meanwhile teen childbearing rates have fallen and risen along with secular trends in childbearing obtaining to greater or lesser extent among mothers of all ages. Trends in nonmarital childbearing rates among teens also appear to mimic more general trends in nonmarital childbearing rather than be particularly responsive to expansions or retrenchments in welfare generosity. Nonmarital birth rates did begin rising in the 1960s when AFDC was relatively generous but they continued to rise through the 1970s and 1980s when eligibility requirements became more stringent and the real value of benefits declined.

19   Like everyone else, poor teens and their elders respond to incentives when making fertility-related decisions. But the most important incentives to them may not be narrow carrot-and-stick incentives of the kind envisioned and manipulated by welfare reformers. Instead, they may derive from larger, more enduring aspects of their life experience. For example, faced with this trade-off, a

woman might accept reduced welfare benefits, if by early childbearing she increases the chance that her child will be born healthy and have able-bodied caretakers who survive through his childhood.

20   I argue that the motivations underlying high rates of teenage childbearing in poor communities may be versions of exactly those values that many now believe the poor, generally, and African American residents of central cities, in particular, lack. These motivations can be understood in light of the problems that together form the larger context in which teen childbearing takes place. These problems merit policy attention. They include problems in educational systems, labor market opportunities, child care, housing, and health that impede the productivity and shorten the lives of young through middle-aged adults in some poor communities, making it difficult for them to escape the anxieties that accompany the profound uncertainties they face. These anxieties, in turn, may move responsible future-oriented, and caring adults to arrange and invest in elaborate systems of social insurance, which in turn exert pressure towards earlier childbearing and away from marriage.

21   Through PRWORA, President Clinton and the 104th Congress have set policies in motion that are likely to exacerbate anxiety among the poor, perhaps providing indirect incentives toward early childbearing. Meanwhile, the Congress did little to improve job or educational prospects for the poor and appeared to be set on dismantling the public health service. Increasingly stringent Medicaid and Food Stamps eligibility criteria included in provisions of PRWORA threaten the health and longevity of the poor and may effectively deny the option of nursing home care to some segments of the poor population. In turn, young adults in these segments may be increasingly called upon to care for ailing elderly. If early childbearing reduces the stress of juggling this obligation with work and child care responsibilities, and if ailing elders long to be grandparents, social expectation in these communities may move in the direction of teenage childbearing. . . .

22   When the crusade against teen childbearing fails, will that failure be interpreted as evidence that the poor are morally even more far removed from the mainstream than they are already thought to be? Will that failure provide further ammunition for those who argue that public spending on social programs is wasteful? Or will we take the opportunity to learn that the poor continue to suffer from many compelling problems, problems that could be reduced by public intervention? Rather than being a cause of public problems, teenage childbearing may be emblematic of the price paid by the poor themselves—not by the larger society—as they work actively to fulfill the values of self-sufficiency, hard work, and responsibility to children and elders in a hostile environment that wears away their health and limits their life chances.

FOR ANALYSIS AND DISCUSSION

1. Does society assume that most teen pregnancies are unwanted? How do you think sociologists and politicians would react to Geronimus's assertion that many teen pregnancies, especially among those from low-income backgrounds, may in fact be planned and wanted?

2. If it were true that certain segments of the population had statistically shorter life spans, would teen pregnancy be more socially acceptable? Explain.

3. Drawing from your own experience and those of your peers, do you think teens consider the factors Geronimus presents in her article when they get pregnant? Evaluate Geronimus's views and the logic of her assertions.

4. Consider Geronimus's statement regarding teen motherhood at the end of paragraph 11. What does she mean when she says that teens who wait to have children may not be in a better position to provide for them later, when they are adults? Do you agree?

5. Do you agree with the feasibility of the scenario Geronimus proposes in paragraph 15? How would you address the validity of her scenario if you were debating the causes of teen pregnancy in a public forum?

6. In paragraph 16 Geronimus implies that teen pregnancies in poorer communities are in fact planned with the help of elders. Does this assertion make sense? On what evidence does she base her view? Analyze her perspective.

FOR RESEARCH

1. Why do American teenagers become pregnant? Explore this question by interviewing three people in your community who work with young people. You could interview school psychologists, youth counselors, clergy, or other social work professionals. If you know a teen parent, interview her or him for a more personal perspective. Drawing from the evidence you gather from your interviews, write an argument essay in which you evaluate the basic points Geronimus makes.

2. The fact that some teens deliberately get pregnant by choice has been addressed on many television programs, including *Oprah*. Teens say their reasons range from an effort to keep a boyfriend to simply wanting "something of their own" to give them the love they crave. To impress upon teens the consequences of pregnancy and parenthood, a group of educators developed the "Baby Think It Over" program. Access their Web site at <http://www.btio.com/btioprov.htm>. Analyze the effectiveness of the BTIO program. Do you think the rate of teen pregnancies would decrease if the BTIO program were required in junior high schools?

A Better Way of Approaching Adolescent Pregnancy
Margaret P. Battin

Many people consider adolescent pregnancy a major social problem. The disadvantages for both mother and child can be tremendous. One in three teen mothers drops out of school. Children of teen mothers are statistically more likely to be teen parents themselves. And one study has even indicated that as many as nine out of ten prison inmates are products of teen pregnancies.

Many social scientists agree that current policies are failing to curtail adolescent pregnancy. Margaret Battin, a professor of philosophy at the University of Utah, proposes a controversial solution to the problem that sidesteps issues of teenage morality and sex education: pharmacologically preventing teens from conceiving in the first place.

Battin is the author or coauthor of more than a dozen books on ethical questions facing modern America. Her most recent book, *Physician Assisted Suicide: Expanding the Debate (Reflective Bioethics)* was published in 1998. The following essay was published in the journal *Reproductive Health Matters* in November of 1996.

BEFORE YOU READ

What would American society be like if all teens were pharmaceutically prevented from getting pregnant? What would you do if such a bill were proposed by the government?

AS YOU READ

If pregnancy education works reasonably well in countries such as the Netherlands and Sweden, what is wrong with the American system? To what does the author attribute the United States' failure to prevent teen pregnancy?

1   For all young women, pregnancy and childbearing is physiologically riskier in the earliest postpubescent years than later. Very early pregnancy is associated with higher rates of both maternal and infant morbidity and mortality. In many cultures, pregnancy in early adolescence is regarded as socially disruptive, especially when no father is known or present and the young mother is the child's sole means of support; it is seen as perpetuating a cycle of poverty. Early pregnancy is often associated with higher rates of malnourishment and inadequate schooling for the child, less education and less economic independence for the mother and higher rates of disturbance in the home.

2   . . . The individual, social and global risks of very early childbearing are substantial. Given the very large number of adolescent pregnancies that occur annually and the multiple grounds on which postponement of them may seem desirable, we must ask whether there may not be a better strategy for prevention or reduction of unplanned adolescent pregnancy. I would like to propose a thought-experiment—a conjecture—about a better way of approaching the matter of adolescent pregnancy. This may seem outrageous; but because it reveals so much about our current attitudes, I think it is important to have it carefully considered.

3   Clearly, what is done now does not work, at least not everywhere. The prevention of teenage pregnancy, at least in those countries which attempt it, is currently approached mainly by education: adolescent girls are informed of the benefits of avoiding pregnancy and warned of its risks, and are provided

with information about the behavioural and contraceptive means of doing so. . . . If education about pregnancy prevention is adequate, it is assumed, teenagers will remain abstinent, or provide themselves with contraceptives or insist that their partners do so.

4   In some countries, this works well: in the Netherlands and Sweden for example, the rate of teenage pregnancy is very low. In other countries, such as the United States, it is less successful: the rate of teenage pregnancy is high, the highest in the developed world. This is often attributed to differences in sex education: in the United States, unlike the northern European countries formal sex education is often grossly inadequate . . . and cultural pressures . . . often favour rather than discourage teenage pregnancy.

5   In some countries, adolescent pregnancy is effectively prevented not by education but by rigid sex-segregation and severe sanctions if it occurs. In other countries, especially in the developing world, pregnancy during adolescence is common.

6   In many cultures in sub-Saharan Africa, for instance, traditional cultural patterns encourage very early marriage and immediate childbearing. . . . Pregnancy during adolescence varies widely among cultures but it is nevertheless frequent on a global scale. . . .

7   Is there a better way to approach adolescent pregnancy, given its consequences, its risks and its ubiquitousness—a better way than ineffectual reliance on education or rigid sex segregation? . . . What if it were arranged that adolescent girls, from puberty through 17 (or, in most places, legal adulthood), could not become pregnant unless they made a deliberate, conscious choice to do so? How would this change their prospects, their offspring's prospects and the prospects of their families, societies and the world?

8   This is conjecture only in one sense: we are probably politically incapable of making it happen. But it is not merely a thought-experiment in another sense: after all, we already have the technology available now that would make this possible. This technology, not usually distinguished from its predecessors, involves long-term contraception which is "automatic" in its function: it works all the time regardless of what the user does. Unlike short term modalities such as the condom, the diaphragm, the sponge, and various herbal potions and powders, true "automatic" long-term contraception provides continuous pregnancy prevention without any further action on the part of the user: without having to obtain it, store it, apply it or activate it, ingest it or insert it, either beforehand or at the time of sex—indeed, without having to do anything at all. (It is this feature of user-independence that makes true long-term contraception ideal for young or inexperienced users.)

9   Such a strategy would be like immunising youngsters against other health risks: tetanus, diphtheria, pertussis, polio—except that long-term contraception is not permanent and can be immediately reversed when the user wishes. Nor does such contraception in any way interfere with adult reproductive capacity; it is just that adolescents do not become pregnant unless they actively choose to do so. . . .

10   At the moment, there are just two contraceptives for women which are sufficiently long-term to remain effective throughout adolescence but nevertheless permit a complete and immediate return to fertility if the user wishes—the
subdermal, levonorgestrel implant (Norplant) and the intra-uterine device
(IUD). . . . Norplant is effective for years; the contemporary IUD is effective for
eight to ten years. Both have excellent reliability and safety records, though
both involve some disadvantages, including side effects and culturally unacceptable consequences like altered bleeding patterns or invasion of modesty.
There are no reliable, safe, long-term contraceptive technologies yet available
for males. . . . Other long-acting female contraceptives now on the market, such
as Depo-Provera and, when taken continuously, the Pill, still require user cooperation: this means remembering and obtaining repeat applications, not a
foolproof expectation for teenagers.

11   But this conjecture . . . is not limited to the currently available technologies. Improvements in the two current truly "automatic" technologies, Norplant and the IUD, and only newly developing modalities allow us to imagine a
world in which reliance on educational strategies of variable (but generally
low) effectiveness for preventing teen pregnancy is no longer necessary. . . .
Every adolescent has [protection], just as every adolescent is immunised
against polio whether they expect to be exposed or not. Indeed, the use of such
contraception would be entirely independent of sex: initiated at puberty, it
would simply be a basic protective feature of their lives. Of course, sexually active adolescents would still need to concern themselves about sexually transmitted diseases, and use condoms if appropriate in addition, but they would not
need to worry about unwanted pregnancy.

12   Of course, adolescents could still have children if they wished to do so.
Pregnancy would simply require a positive choice to have the contraceptive device neutralised or removed. Nevertheless, up to the time of legal adulthood,
adolescents would be protected from incurring pregnancy in involuntary, inadequately informed, impulsive or unthinking ways—just the ways in which many,
perhaps most, adolescent pregnancies occur.

13   Think about this conjecture carefully. Consider the physical and psychological costs of unwanted, unplanned adolescent pregnancy to the young girls
themselves, to their partners, families, and social groupings; then consider the
larger social costs to their societies, and finally consider the strains in terms of
global population and resource pressures. Of course there are often benefits to
early pregnancy. But if it were routine that young girls were reliably protected
against pregnancy they did not intend, many of the costs would disappear, the
benefits could be maintained for those who chose them, and in general, young
women would reach legal adulthood prepared to make their own reproductive
choices in a more mature way. This would have incalculable repercussions for
gender equality; it could alleviate social friction over the issue of abortion,
since pregnancy would all be by choice; and it would have a very favourable impact on poverty-perpetuating and population pressures—all without violating
any woman's right to have the number of children she wished.

14   Too bad we aren't developing fully reliable, perfectly safe, side-effect-free long term contraceptive technologies for both women and men at a faster rate. This would permit a change in human reproduction control from reliance on short-term methods to the routine use of long-term "automatic" contraception: it would, so to speak, change the default mode in human reproduction—choices about reproduction would no longer be negative choices to avoid children, but positive choices to have them. This simple change—from negative choice to prevent pregnancy (which is what our sex-education programmes ask of teenagers now) to a positive choice to seek pregnancy—may seem a very minor change in decisional structure, based on a small difference in contraceptive technology, but it is one with incalculable consequences for women, men and the world.

FOR ANALYSIS AND DISCUSSION

1. In paragraph 8 Battin comments that we are "politically incapable" of chemically preventing teen pregnancy. What does Battin mean by this statement? Do you think this political incapacity is good or bad?
2. Consider Battin's comparison of forced teen contraception to immunizing against other diseases of childhood. Is this a sensible comparison? What does this comparison imply about teen pregnancy overall? Explain your perspective.
3. On what logic does Battin base her proposal? Is her reasoning sound?
4. Hypothetically, if Battin's proposal were enforced in America, do you think teens would in fact be allowed to get pregnant if they so wished (paragraph 12)? Explain.
5. Battin's proposal targets females for contraceptive control. Is it fair to reserve this measure only for girls? What far-reaching implications could this idea have on women's health in general?
6. Battin's argument addresses the possible benefits of forced contraception. What are some of the negative aspects? For example, research indicates that less than half of all sexually active teens use condoms during intercourse. How could you connect this statistic to Battin's proposal?

FOR RESEARCH

1. In paragraph 13 Battin conjectures that her solution could "alleviate social friction over the issue of abortion." Are teenagers responsible for most abortions? Are abortions widely available to teens? Research this issue and evaluate Battin's speculation.
2. Should teenagers have reproductive rights? Conduct a survey and distribute it to at least 20 teenagers between the ages of 13 and 19, as well as to at least 20 adults. In your survey, encourage respondents to explain their views. Then form a group of at least four students and discuss your results. Is the issue clear cut, or are the answers more complex? With your group, formulate a response to Battin's proposal, based on the surveys and group discussion.

"Charter Families": Hope for the Children of Illegitimacy?

James Q. Wilson

Several of the articles in this casebook address the expense teen parenthood places on the social welfare system. Most point out that teen parents and the children of teen parents are more likely to remain on welfare for long periods of time. During a keynote speech at the Pioneer Institute for Public Policy Research, James Q. Wilson addressed the problems of teenage pregnancy and its connection to the welfare system. He proposed that if teenage mothers want to establish a "household" on public monies, they should do so under the supervision of an established family shelter or group home.

A commentator on politics and society for more than four decades, James Q. Wilson is the author of several books including *The Moral Sense,* which addresses the understanding of complex social structures and individual behavior. Wilson is currently a professor emeritus in the political science department at the University of California, Los Angeles.

BEFORE YOU READ

Create a sketch of the typical teenage mother. Include background details including socioeconomic level, home life, education, age, motive for pregnancy, and means of financial support. After reading Wilson's essay, how do you think his proposal would affect your portrait of the typical teenage mother?

AS YOU READ

Do you think Wilson's plan is a solution, a deterrent, or both? Explain.

1   Three key words are associated with Pioneer Institute's work: community, choice, and competition. Now I would like to add a fourth "c" —character.

2   The American political regime as envisioned by its founders was not supposed to have anything to do with character. It was supposed to enable people living in villages and towns to compose their differences at the national level sufficient to secure a more perfect union and ensure domestic tranquillity and justice.

3   It was assumed, as Tocqueville remarked a few decades later, that it was in private associations (family, neighborhood, and peer groups) and small political institutions (village and town governments) that character could be formed, so the national government could take character for granted. "Men," Madison wrote, "are presumed to have sufficient virtue to constitute and maintain a free republic."

4   Today, by contrast, we are properly concerned with the issue of character and it has been placed on the national agenda by both political parties. Why is it that the assumptions that influenced the men who gathered in Philadelphia

in 1787 are no longer the assumptions we bring to contemplating the true purpose of our national polity?

5   One reason is that government has gotten bigger. As government gets bigger, it touches all aspects of our lives. As it touches all aspects of our lives, we increasingly put our concerns back on the government. The price of big government is an ever-expanding agenda.

6   Forty years ago, when I began studying politics, it was inconceivable that the federal government would ever be held responsible for crime, drug abuse, illegitimacy, welfare, civil rights, clean air, or clean water. Today it is responsible for all those things.

7   Not only have our aspirations and the size of the federal government changed, but so has our culture. In many spheres of our lives we are no longer confident that local private institutions like families, churches, and neighborhoods are sufficient to form a culture that will sustain and enrich a free society.

8   One of the areas in which this concern has become most sharply focused is illegitimacy. An illegitimacy crisis that affects both black and white has been growing without let-up since the early 1960s. It has shaped the profound debate now unfolding in Washington about the relationship between federal welfare programs and the very formation and maintenance of families.

9   When Title IV, which created the program now known as Aid to Families with Dependent Children (AFDC), was added to the Social Security Act of 1935, it was the least controversial part of that landmark legislation. For years after its enactment, it caused scarcely a national political ripple. The reason was that it gave federal support to a few state programs designed to provide short-term compensation to women who had been widowed due to the First World War, coal mining disasters, or had been divorced or deserted by husbands. It nationalized these programs by extending them to the other states.

10   No one expected it would become a way of life and no one ever expected teenagers would apply for it. All that has changed. Today, the average new AFDC enrollee spends only two or three years on welfare and then moves on. It acts as a stop-gap measure to provide for the needs of women and children during a particularly difficult time in their lives. This is the group for whom AFDC was originally intended.

11   But if you look at the total number of welfare recipients, as opposed to those who enter the roles in any given year, you notice that the typical recipient has been on welfare for ten years. Increasingly, this has extended into second and third generations. Many come and leave quickly, but a few remain. And the number who remain now constitute the largest share of the whole.

12   There is a spirited debate about why this should be so. I think it is fair to say that no one can confidently claim to know the answer to this question. It is difficult to sustain the argument that the existence of welfare causes dependency if it did not do so during the first 30 years of its history. Evidence about the effect of state differences in welfare payments on rates of welfare participation is inconclusive.

13   There has probably been a profound cultural shift that has de-stigmatized illegitimacy and removed barriers that once inhibited people from remaining on AFDC for long periods of time. Even if we assume that the system of public payments did not cause this phenomenon, it certainly makes it possible. If the system did not exist, the current degree of dependency would not exist.

14   Even if you disagree with that assertion, the system has surely not cured its own defects. Rates of illegitimacy and single parenthood among black and white Americans have risen steadily since the early 1960s and that trend shows little sign of tapering off.

15   The harms associated with single parenthood and illegitimacy are now so well documented that the evidence need not be reviewed. But let me give you one example gathered by the government itself. A few years ago, the Department of Health and Human Services selected over 30,000 households across the country, designed to represent a statistical cross section. They interviewed the mother, father, or both about the welfare of their children. Except for the very highest income level, children raised in single parent households are materially worse off, irrespective of race. They are worse off in terms of educational achievement, social well-being, aggressiveness, and difficulty with the law.

16   It should not take massive studies to establish this phenomenon. It is evident to many who confront life in hospital emergency rooms, police stations, juvenile courts, or welfare offices on a daily basis. The problem has crystallized in the form of our concern about the unmarried teenage mother.

17   If you survey the history of families around the world, every culture has had teenage mothers. Indeed, what is striking today is how long many women wait before having children. But what was different in the past is that those girls gave birth as part of an embedded structure; with a husband, grandmothers, aunts, uncles, and siblings. They were part of an extended family or a village in which there were many people who not only helped take care of the child, but taught the mother to be a mother and required that the father be a father. The debate I hear in Washington about reforming the current system is remarkably inattentive to the core fact that young girls living apart from other adults cannot expect much success at raising children alone.

18   Instead, the debate is posing questions like how do we save money on the welfare budget? How soon can we require recipients to work? How can we use modern technology to go after deadbeat dads? These may all be worthwhile concerns, but they should be viewed as subordinate to the central goal of saving the children whose lives are being destroyed as a consequence of growing up in this environment.

19   To solve this problem, we must ask all levels of government and the private sector to do something American government has never had to do before: constitute and support a viable alternative to the traditional family for the children and young women most at risk. One trembles even to utter this phrase because in the Anglo-Saxon legal tradition, the king with all his legions stops at the threshold of the hut of the very poorest peasant.

20   We all understand that government cannot raise children. But there is something out there that is not working and government must change its allocation of incentives to give us a fighting chance to solve the problem. Let me suggest a strategy and then indicate how I think Pioneer Institute and all of you can help implement it.

21   We must get young, unmarried, pregnant girls embedded in a social structure under adult supervision. This not only provides an opportunity to give their children a good start in life, but teaches them how to be a parent and protect themselves from the desperate conditions of gangs, drugs, and crime that often exist around them.

22   I therefore propose that if young, pregnant, unmarried women wish to establish an independent household at public expense, they should be given this support only on the condition that they live in some kind of family shelter or group home managed under private auspices, including religious groups. Part of the welfare reform debate currently raging in Washington focuses on the so-called Ashcroft Amendment, sponsored by Senator John Ashcroft of Missouri. The amendment states that nothing in the proposed welfare reform bill shall prevent religious groups from providing social services to welfare recipients on an equal basis with secular groups.

23   It is not clear what is meant by "services," or how funds would be transferred to these groups. But it is sending the message to young women that the character of the children they are raising is so important to this society that we insist they raise them in a truly adult setting provided by one of a variety of private organizations. And we will reinforce this by saying your check cannot be cashed unless it is co-signed by the person who manages the program. You are free to choose the program—secular or religious—you wish to join. But we will not fund you to set up an independent household, given what we know about the harm it does to the children.

24   Up to this point I have said nothing about the other half of the equation—the men involved. I have learned from talking to audiences across the country that the riskiest policy for a male speaker is to act as if this were a problem created by women that could be solved by placing more constraints on women. But let me clarify a few points from the perspective of someone who has been researching the history of families and fatherhood around the world. Men and women differ in their willingness to make a commitment to the welfare of a child. This can be established by the simple fact that in any culture where there are single parent families, more than 90 percent of them are headed by women. This cannot happen by accident. If it were simply a matter of cultural convention, you would find places where half or more of single parent families were headed by men. But you do not.

25   Men and women differ due to evolution, biology, and a variety of other factors. But since women care for children when men will not, much of civilization has been devoted to the problem of disciplining males. Society in all cultures has invented a few techniques to get males to play their role. When I was growing up, young unmarried women who got pregnant had a couple of choices.

They either went away to live with relatives, had the child, then returned while the relatives raised the child, or they told their fathers and brothers who the father of the child was. The father and brothers then told the boy, "either you marry the girl or we will beat you to death." The other option for the boy was to run away and join the navy.

26   None of these options seem to work anymore. The force of custom and shame is no longer as powerful as it once was. The law once played a role in forcing men to take responsibility by requiring that paternity be clarified. Women once played a role by denying sexual access to men unwilling to make a commitment.

27   If you want to summarize in hyperbolic and exaggerated terms what the core problem of character formation is today, it is that the only one of these forces that still operates is the woman's willingness to say "no." In place of law, we have no-fault divorce. In place of custom and shame, we have created a sense that everyone should "do his own thing." And fathers and brothers, far from beating up someone who has impregnated a daughter without marrying her, are themselves busy with other people's daughters.

28   Unfortunately, this leaves the burden with women. But women should not bear the burden alone; the state should be on their side. To the extent it can, it is desirable for the state to enforce the obligations of paternity.

29   This has proven to be extremely difficult. For several years, particularly since Congress passed the Family Support Act in 1988, programs have been in place to get states to devise ways of collecting child support payments from absent fathers. Many states have vigorously pursued the fathers, but have not collected much money.

30   But again we are moving away from the core problem. The key is not to supply dollars, but to supply the father. It is his presence, not just his money, that has been lost. The average child raised by a mother only sees his father a few times a year.

31   The problem of re-constituting this character forming institution cannot be solved by government. But I would suggest that just as we have formed and are encouraging charter schools, we should form and encourage charter families. Groups from the private sector who are willing to accept government money to provide long-term shelters for young girls who cannot or will not live with their own parents and who have children with no fathers to take care of them.

32   I have no idea whether this will work. It is the task of Pioneer Institute and organizations like it to encourage this type of experimentation.

33   Money is going to flow from Washington to the states in the form of block grants. With some degree of restriction, states will have the opportunity to design and implement their own welfare programs. Most states will reproduce less expensive forms of the current system.

34   But I hope Massachusetts will be among the states that use this opportunity to tear up the old script. Leave the existing system intact for women who need it as a bridge to get through death, desertion, or divorce, and will leave welfare in two or three years. But provide a radically different option, privately-run and

with a built-in social structure, for those young girls who are now raising the next generation of our children.

FOR ANALYSIS AND DISCUSSION

1. What is the AFDC? What was its original purpose? Has the AFDC truly become "a way of life" for people? What proof does Wilson provide to support his statements regarding the AFDC?

2. Has illegitimacy become "destigmatized"? What was the stigma of illegitimacy in the past? What is our common cultural view of it now? Do you think Wilson approves of the new attitude toward illegitimacy? What is your view?

3. How does Wilson hope to implement his charter home plan? What agencies in government would have to work together to establish his plan? Do you think Republicans, Democrats, both, or neither would embrace his solution? Why? What consensus is needed for his plan to work?

4. Like Battin's proposal, Wilson's plan is aimed at controlling young women. Whereas Battin proposed governing girls' reproductive organs, Wilson suggests we physically supervise mother and child in a controlled environment. Do these proposals "punish" young women, or are they simply situations in which the end justifies the means?

5. Do you find Wilson a credible writer? What assumptions does he make about his audience's values and concerns? Do you think the audience's reaction would be less receptive if he were addressing a group of high school students? Explain.

FOR RESEARCH

1. Access the "National Strategy to Prevent Teen Pregnancy's Annual Report," developed by the U.S. Department of Health and Human Services at <http://aspe.os.dhhs.gov/hsp/teenp/97-98rpt.htm>. What trends does the DHHS report regarding teen pregnancy? How do group homes factor into the DHHS plan to address teen pregnancy? How does the DHHS report compare to the information presented in the readings?

2. Many of the solutions proposed by the authors in this casebook target teenage mothers. Why are teenage fathers largely left out of the debate? Should they be included? In a group investigation, discuss the stereotype of teen fatherhood. How is it different from that of teen motherhood? Develop a profile and share it with the class. Then, as a class, discuss the issues facing teen fathers.

WRITING AND RESEARCH ASSIGNMENTS: TEEN PARENTS

1. If you are not now a parent, imagine how your life would change if you suddenly became one. Consider the impact on all areas of your life: school, work, social life, home life, and so on. Write an essay that addresses what your life would be like as a teen parent as opposed to an adult parent. Would the outcome be different or the same? Do adults make better parents? Why or why not?

2. Write an argument essay in which you evaluate one of the pregnancy "solutions" proposed in this casebook. You could address Battin's contraceptive control of teenagers, Sylvester's moral campaign, or Wilson's group homes for welfare mothers. Support your essay with evidence from the readings, your own experience, and information gathered from some of the Web sites provided in the chapter.

3. Write an argument essay exploring the extent to which popular culture influences attitudes about teenage sexuality. Is there a contradiction between how the media portray teenage sex and how they present teen pregnancy? Analyze the discrepancy, if one exists.

4. Is teen pregnancy a moral issue? Does it have its roots in moral complacency and irresponsible social attitudes? Write an argument essay in which you address the moral aspects of teen pregnancy. If teen pregnancy is indeed a moral issue, what has caused the breakdown of traditional morality? Can morality be retaught? Explain.

5. Access the National Campaign to Prevent Teen Pregnancy's Web site at <http://www.teenpregnancy.org>. Drawing from the information the site provides, assess the effectiveness of the campaign. What are its strengths and weaknesses? Can you make any suggestions for improvement?

6. Most of the articles in this casebook address teenage motherhood. Is teen pregnancy a "women's issue"? Are politicians and sociologists neglecting the other half of the picture? Write an essay addressing the issue of teen fatherhood. Why do you think teen fathers are left out of the debate?

7. The Alan Guttmacher Institute reports that more than half the 17-year-olds in the United States have had sexual intercourse. Access the Guttmacher Institute Web site at <http://www.agi-usa.org/pubs/fb_teen_sex.html>, and review its 1998 statistics regarding teen sexuality and pregnancy. Use the information provided by the Guttmacher Institute to write an argument essay in which you evaluate one of the essays in this casebook. Supplement your essay's points with your own personal experience and that of your peers.

chapter **17**

THE BLACK FREEDOM STRUGGLE: ARGUMENTS THAT SHAPED HISTORY

The Black Freedom Struggle was a defining movement in twentieth century American history. Efforts by African Americans to secure greater civil rights began long before the start of this century through the activism of Booker T. Washington and W. E. B. DuBois; however, it was not until the Supreme Court decision in *Brown v. Board of Education of Topeka* in 1954 that all of America became acutely aware of the deprivations that African Americans endured. The conflict that began in the South between African Americans who demanded basic freedoms and the white bureaucracy that withheld those freedoms erupted into a battle that forever changed the social, economic, and political content of American life. It is the voices of citizens who took part in this struggle that we have attempted to capture in the readings of this chapter, voices that emerge from many segments of the political and social spectrum.

Here you will find the arguments not only of those who supported the fight for freedom but also those who opposed it. Tom Brady, the leader of the white Citizens Council movement, presents the case for white supremacy in "Black Monday: Segregation or Amalgamation . . . America Has Its Choice." "The Southern Manifesto" expresses the outrage of southern members of the U.S. Congress at the Supreme Court's decision to end segregated schools. But the South was not the only area in the country that deprived black children of equal education. Jonathan Kozol's evocative description of the conditions in the school where he taught in a predominantly black neighborhood in Boston reminds us that this form of discrimination was practiced across the nation.

Even among supporters of equal rights, activists promoted very different strategies. Martin Luther King, Jr., argues compellingly for the power of nonviolent protest against hatred and bigotry. However, Jan Howard's analysis suggests that the use of nonviolence may have been calculated to actually provoke violence and gain sympathy from the rest of the country. Malcolm X responds to both of these arguments in "Message to the Grass Roots" as he urges his supporters to respond to violence with violence of their own.

684

In our readings on equal opportunity, James Baldwin provides insight into the limitations that black youths faced in the early 1960s. John F. Kennedy's 1963 speech, supporting his use of federal troops to escort black students to classes at the University of Alabama, sadly confirms the truth of Baldwin's assertions. Even the right to vote was not permitted to black citizens of the South without a fight, as Fannie Lou Hamer recalls in "From Sharecropper to Lobbyist." It was often at the grassroots level that the most symbolic victories were won. Edgar French's dramatic account of the Montgomery, Alabama, bus boycott argues persuasively for the power of the common people to overcome overwhelming odds through their determination and courage.

"Reflections on the Struggle" looks back on the Black Freedom Struggle from today's vantage point. Tamar Jacoby's "The Next Reconstruction" considers whether integration of institutions, such as schools and businesses, has mitigated or increased the racial tensions in our society. Gregory Kane questions the wisdom of providing black children with an education devoid of black role models. Finally, Nell Irvin Painter and Shelby Steele engage in a dialogue about affirmative action's effect on the way African Americans define themselves.

Consider the many larger questions raised by these writers: How can we best bring about significant social change: through the courts or through protest and demonstrations? How can we recognize the needs of those who lack political power? Did the Black Freedom Struggle accomplish its goals of African American equality? Have programs such as affirmative action contributed to or delayed the full acceptance of black Americans in our society? The essays that you will read in this chapter are arguments that truly changed history, but the long-term effects of those changes are constantly being reevaluated. We invite you to join the discussion.

EDUCATION: OPENING THE SCHOOLHOUSE DOORS

Brown v. Board of Education of Topeka

The following is an excerpt from the Supreme Court's decision in *Brown v. Board of Education of Topeka* (1954). Chief Justice Earl Warren wrote the decision that overturned the 1896 ruling of *Plessy v. Ferguson,* which permitted the racial segregation of schools, provided that educational facilities were equal in quality. This doctrine had become known as "separate but equal." The *Brown* decision concluded that racially segregated schools were, in fact, not equal. It accounted for social and psychological factors that made segregation harmful despite the actual physical "equality" of the schools.

Warren, the fourteenth chief justice of the United States, was serving his first term when the *Brown v. Board of Education of Topeka* decision was rendered. Speaking for a unanimous court, he declared the separation of public school children by race unconstitutional. Warren served on the Supreme Court until his retirement in 1969.

BEFORE YOU READ

What makes "quality" education? For example, is it the building, the curriculum, the teachers, the composition of students? Or is it a balance of all these factors?

AS YOU READ

Consider how Warren's statement is framed. How does he support his statement that "in the field of public education the doctrine of 'separate but equal' has no place"?

1   Today, education is perhaps the most important function of state and local governments. Compulsory school attendance laws and the great expenditures for education both demonstrate our recognition of the importance of education to our democratic society. It is required in the performance of our most basic pub-

"The crowd moved in closer and then began to follow me, calling me names . . . My knees started to shake all of a sudden and I wondered whether I could make it to the center entrance a block away. It was the longest block I ever walked in my life . . . [The crowd] moved closer and closer. Somebody started yelling, "Lynch her! Lynch her!" (Excerpts from Elizabeth Eckford's "Don't Let Them See You Cry")

lic responsibilities, even service in the armed forces. It is the very foundation of good citizenship. Today it is a principal instrument in awakening the child to cultural values, in preparing him for later professional training, and in helping him to adjust normally to his environment. In these days, it is doubtful that any child may reasonably be expected to succeed in life if he is denied the opportunity of an education. Such an opportunity, where the state has undertaken to provide it, is a right which must be made available to all on equal terms.

2   We come to the question presented: Does segregation of children in public schools solely on the basis of race, even though the physical facilities and other "tangible" factors may be equal, deprive the children of the minority group of equal education opportunities? We believe that it does.

3   In *Sweatt v. Painter, supra,* in finding that a segregated law school for Negroes could not provide them equal educational opportunities, this Court relied in larger part on "those qualities which are incapable of objective measurement but which make for greatness in a law school." In *McLaurin v. Oklahoma State Regents, supra,* the Court, in requiring that a Negro admitted to a white graduate school be treated like all other students, again resorted to intangible considerations: ". . . his ability to study, to engage in discussions and exchange views with other students, and, in general, to learn his profession." Such considerations apply with added force to children in grade and high schools. To separate them from others of similar age and qualifications solely because of their race generates a feeling of inferiority as to their status in the community that may affect their hearts and minds in a way unlikely to ever be undone. . . .

4   We conclude that in the field of public education the doctrine of "separate but equal" has no place. Therefore, we hold that the plaintiffs and others similarly situated for whom the actions have been brought are, by reason of the segregation complained of, deprived of equal protection of the laws guaranteed by the Fourteenth Amendment. This disposition makes unnecessary any discussion whether such segregation also violates the Due Process Clause of the Fourteenth Amendment.

5   Because these are class actions, because of the wide applicability of this decision, and because of the great variety of local conditions, the formulation of decrees in these cases presents problems of considerable complexity. On reargument, the consideration of appropriate relief was necessarily subordinated to the primary question—the constitutionality of segregation in public education. We have now announced that such segregation is a denial of the equal protection of the laws. . . .

6   *It is so ordered.*

FOR ANALYSIS AND DISCUSSION

1. What does the Supreme Court list as the important functions of education in our society? Considering that this decision was rendered in 1954, do you believe education fulfills these same roles and functions today? Explain your perspective.

2. The *Sweatt v. Painter* decision found that a separate law school for African Americans deprived students of the opportunity to exchange ideas and learn their profession. In essence it deprived them of a "real world" education. How does this decision regarding a law school apply to students in elementary and secondary schools? Why do you think the Supreme Court made this analogy?

3. The *Brown* decision required that schools be desegregated. Do you believe schools are truly desegregated more than 40 years later? Did the court's decision achieve its objective? Explain your view, drawing on your own educational experiences.

4. Reread the final, carefully worded paragraph. What was the Supreme Court saying? What obstacles did this decision face in 1954?

5. What do you think "separate but equal" was supposed to mean? Can racially segregated schools be equal? What do you think was the basis for the "separate but equal" decision in 1896?

Black Monday: Segregation or Amalgamation . . . America Has a Choice
Tom P. Brady

The following article is an excerpt from a 92-page booklet that was widely distributed throughout the South in 1955. The booklet was expanded from a speech delivered by Judge Tom P. Brady of Brookhaven, Mississippi, to the Sons of the American Revolution. Brady was dubbed the "intellectual leader" of the Citizens Council movement of Mississippi, and his views represented those of many other whites living in the South during that time. Educated at Princeton, Brady was among the most respected individuals in the Mississippi white resistance. He later served as a Mississippi Supreme Court justice.

BEFORE YOU READ

Consider the impact the *Brown* decision made in 1954 America. Whom did it affect the most? Is the impact of the decision still felt today?

AS YOU READ

Think about how Brady presents his argument. Is Brady's "evidence" supporting his perspective logical? Why do you think he formulates his essay this way?

Foreword

1   "Black Monday" is the name coined by Representative John Bell Williams of Mississippi to designate Monday, May 17th, 1954, a date long to be remembered throughout this nation. This is the date upon which the Supreme Court of the United States handed down its socialistic decision in the Segregation cases on appeal from the States of Kansas, South Carolina, Virginia and

Delaware. "Black Monday" is indeed symbolic of the date. Black denoting darkness and terror. Black signifying the absence of light and wisdom. Black embodying grief, destruction and death. Should Representative Williams accomplish nothing more during his membership in Congress he has more than justified his years in office by the creating of this epithet, the originating of this watchword, the shouting of this battle cry.

2   Black Monday ranks in importance with July 4th, 1776, the date upon which our Declaration of Independence was signed. May 17th, 1954, is the date upon which the declaration of socialistic doctrine was officially proclaimed throughout the nation. It was on Black Monday that the judicial branch of our government usurped the sacred privilege and right of the respective states of this union to educate their youth. This usurpation constitutes the greatest travesty of the American Constitution and jurisprudence in the history of this nation.

3   Denunciation and abuse are the favorite weapons of the clumsy, frustrated and uncontrolled. I shall strive to proceed without them, but impartial frankness and truth should not be confused with bitter criticism and reproach.

4   "Black Monday" is not written primarily in behalf of the white people of the seventeen States affected by the Segregation decision, though it is hoped it will be beneficial to them. It is, however, written with the fervent desire that it will be of material benefit to both the white and colored people of this country, wheresoever situated. It is written to alert and encourage every American, irrespective of race, who loves our Constitution, our Government and our God-given American way of life. It is composed for the average American who firmly believes that the legislative, judicial and executive branches of our Federal Government should remain separate and distinct; who maintains that the Federal Government was constructed by the States for the benefit of the States, and that the States were not created for the establishment and advancement of a paternalistic or totalitarian Government. It is dedicated to those who firmly believe that socialism and communism are lethal messes of porridge for which our sacred birthright shall not be sold.

America Comes of Age

5 The years from 1620 to 1936 were miraculous. The whole gamut of American experience can be found in this interim. Thirteen pathetically weak colonies oppose the greatest military power on earth, Great Britain. They were not without assistance, and after almost seven trying, bloody years, victory is won at Yorktown, and a nation is born. Certain figures stand out from the crowd: Washington, Jefferson, Franklin, Patrick Henry, Wayne, Randolph, Paine, Adams, Greene, Morgan and Hamilton. It is ridiculous to assume that the American negro played any part in this struggle, though he had been in this country approximately one hundred and fifty years. He made no contribution whatsoever.

6   After 1782, when peace was signed with England, the colonies began to recuperate from the devastating experience. Expansion took place and com-

merce came into being. The trek southward had begun and the cry of "Westward Ho!" was first being faintly heard. England, smarting under her previous defeat and irked by the Yankee merchant ships which were importing and exporting goods from all over the world, precipitated the War of 1812. Again certain men are conspicuous—John Marshall, who had already given us his inestimable genius; Stephen Decatur, Paul Jones, Lawrence, Hull, Bainbridge, Francis Scott Key and Andrew Jackson. Like the war of 1776, the War of 1812 was a just war, and the United States emerged victorious. It is ridiculous to assume that the American negro played any part in this struggle, though he had been in this country almost two hundred years.

7   The Louisiana purchase and then the conquering of the West began. The "Forty Niners"—the Indian wars, the liberation of Texas. No American negroes were massacred with Custer, or died in the sacred Alamo. In the struggle for development, in the expansion and growth which was taking place—in the laying of the solid foundation of our nation, it is ridiculous to assume that the American negro played any part except as a body servant or hostler.

8   Then came the bloodiest of all wars—the most destructive to the white genius and ability of this country—the Civil War. The negro was the fundamental cause of this war—never forget this fact—and it is ridiculous to assume that he played any part in it except as a servant to those unable to fight. And then the saddest and most terrible of all American dramas was enacted—the Reconstruction period—the pious greed of the New England slave trader had brought the negro to our shores and now his insatiable hatred and envy was to be placated. Military governments were established, the face of the Southern white soldier who had survived the war was ground in the dust by the foot of his conqueror with the aid of the carpetbagger from the North—the scalawag of the South, and the negro. Yes, you are correct in assuming a small segment of the negro race played a part in this rapine. It was as thorough as Sherman's "March to the Sea." In truth, the South has not yet fully recovered from this scorched earth policy, pillage and the bitter hatred which blazed and still smolders against it. Let us briefly review a few significant events of this tragic era.

9   The true and succinct words of Charles Wallace Collins, found in his remarkable book, "Whither Solid South," best outlines the situation and problem:

10   **"Immediately after the Civil War, Amendments 13 and 15, which prohibited slavery and provided that the power to vote should not be denied on account of race or color,** [here as elsewhere, emphasis in original] were submitted to the States for ratification. They attracted little attention. **But when the 14th Amendment came along it was filled with dynamite.** The Radical Republicans were in control of Congress and they intended to enact legislation under this Amendment which would weaken the States and set up a strong central Government in Washington which would take over jurisdiction of the civil rights of individuals and thereby dominate the South through carpetbagger-negro rule.

11   **"On June 16, 1866, Congress submitted the Fourteenth Amendment** to the States for ratification. This required the approval of **three-fourths of the States.** Each of the former Confederate States, except Tennessee, voted to reject the

Amendment, and ratification was thereby defeated. **The Amendment had been lawfully submitted and the rejection was lawful under the procedure provided by the Constitution. That should have been the end of the matter. But Congress became infuriated at the failure of the Amendment to be ratified and from thenceforth adopted high-handed measures. It took over the Southern States by military occupation, disfranchised the white people and put the ballot into the hands of the negro—coached by the carpetbaggers.**"

12   **Now hear this, oh, High Priests of Washington:**

13   **"In 1868 the Fourteenth Amendment was resubmitted to the States for ratification, and this time it was ratified almost unanimously by the Southern States. The United States Army attended to the details. This last ratification was unlawful and in violation of the Constitution.** That is why, in so far as the negro is concerned, the Fourteenth Amendment has never been of any moral force in the South." (See Chapter VI of "Whither Solid South.")

14   Congress next proceeded to enact legislation to enforce the Amendment. There went to the statute books at this time **the Enforcement Act of 1870, the Ku Klux Act of 1871 and the Civil Rights Act of 1875. The first case to reach the Supreme Court in a test of these Acts was U.S. vs. Cruikshank.** This case arose in Louisiana. Cruikshank and a number of other white men broke up by violent means a negro political meeting. Cruikshank and other whites were arrested, tried in the Federal Court and convicted of the violation of the Enforcement Act of 1870.

15   The case reached the Supreme Court of the United States in 1876 on appeal. **The Court held that Congress of itself had no power, and derived no power from the Fourteenth Amendment to legislate in respect to the acts of individual persons; that the restrictions of the Amendment ran only against action by the State.** In this case the State of Louisiana had taken no action. It held that whatever crime which may have been committed could only be a violation of the law of the State, in respect to which the State courts were open. The Court said:

16   "The very highest duty of the States, when they entered into the Union under the Constitution, was to protect all persons within their boundaries in the enjoyment of these inalienable rights."

17   The Cruikshank case saved the South and, furthermore, **saved our Republican form of Government.** It was strongly and completely confirmed by the **Supreme Court in 1883 in the Civil Rights Case,** which held that Congress gained 'no countenance of authority' from the Fourteenth Amendment to enact laws governing the civil rights of individuals.

18   From the time of these decisions until 1936—a period of sixty years—there was peace in the South between the two races. However, during the latter part of this period, large numbers of negroes moved north to such cities as Chicago, Detroit, Philadelphia and New York. Here they gradually developed political power under the simple qualification of the age of manhood for voting. They developed local leadership. **The National Association for the Advancement of the Colored People was organized in New York.** It became a nationwide orga-

nization, with chapters all over the country, including the South. It entered politics. The Association and all of its subsidiaries and affiliates went over to the Democratic Party in 1936, and there, with the support of Northern Democrats, successfully—although indirectly—challenged the South. **The Convention's two-thirds rule was abolished, the South thereby losing its traditional veto over the nomination.** The South was thereafter unable to make any show of strength to recover its former position.

19   As a result of this development, the negro leaders began to agitate for a reversal of the Supreme Court's position on civil rights. They planned to ask for new civil rights legislation by Congress with a view to having it confirmed by the Supreme Court. The core of this movement was the Truman Civil Rights Program, which has now been reintroduced in the 83rd Congress as a somewhat obverse side to the segregation cases.

20   It is interesting to note that the Attorney General in his appearance for the Eisenhower Administration in the segregation cases, in effect, refused to support these civil rights bills. **He advised the Court against legislation by Congress in this field. He warned that great confusion would be caused if the long line of precedents stemming from the Cruikshank case were to be reversed.**

21   [Attorney General Herbert] Brownell advised the Court **that it had the judicial power in itself to decree that segregation in the public school violates the Fourteenth Amendment by the State concerned.** The question then arises: by what means could the Court enforce its decree? The Federal judiciary in the South has no equipment, personnel or any sort of organization to enforce such a decree in the face of a solid adverse public opinion, against one-third of the population of the United States.

22   Such decree has been promulgated, and when the States refuse to abolish segregation and the doctrine in the Cruikshank case remains inviolate, the decree will be frustrated.

23   The Supreme Court does not possess the legislative power. When a case comes before the Court, as does a case before any court, the issue is joined, arguments are made and a decision rendered. That decision binds the parties to that particular case. The legislative power of the Federal Government is vested in the Congress of the United States. **The Supreme Court has no power to make a decree which could have the effect of an Act of Congress.** The Supreme Court can, of course, exceed its powers and violate the Constitution and invade the province of Congress and that of the state legislatures—as has frequently been the case. Has the Supreme Court the power to establish by decree a national segregation policy which would bind all of the forty-eight states—a power which Congress itself does not possess?

24   This is the true question which "Black Monday" actually decided.

FOR ANALYSIS AND DISCUSSION

1. In the first paragraph Brady states that "Black Monday" symbolizes darkness, terror, grief, destruction, and death. What other meaning of "Black Monday" has he left out? Why do you think he deliberately omits this obvious connotation?

2. Review Brady's account of American history (paragraphs 5 through 8). Is his account accurate? Does his rendition of history support his argument? Explain.

3. Brady seems to justify the segregation of blacks from the white population by suggesting that African Americans did not have any meaningful influence and involvement in U.S. history. Is his argument valid? Could it apply to other immigrant groups?

4. How does Brady feel about the National Association for the Advancement of Colored People (NAACP)? Are his feelings based on reason? How might his opinions be viewed as hypocritical, based on his essay's own words?

5. According to Brady, what is the "true question Black Monday actually decided"? Why does he feel the Supreme Court's decision has no foundation?

The Southern Manifesto

The "Southern Manifesto" was introduced into the *Congressional Record* on March 12, 1956. The "Manifesto" was signed by 96 politicians from the Senate and the House of Representatives who represented eleven southern states. None of the politicians were African American. The purpose of the "Manifesto" was to demonstrate the widespread determination on the part of the South to resist the Supreme Court's 1954 decision to racially desegregate public schools (see *Brown v. Topeka Board of Education*).

BEFORE YOU READ

We tend to think of disagreements between the North and South as something from the nineteenth century. Do today's social and political disagreements still have roots in the geographical boundaries "north" and "south"?

AS YOU READ

How valid is the claim in the "Manifesto" that because the Constitution does not mention education, there was no intention "that it should affect the system of education maintained by the United States"?

Declaration of Constitutional Principles

1   The unwarranted decision of the Supreme Court in the public school cases is now bearing the fruit always produced when men substitute naked power for established law.

2   The Founding Fathers gave us a Constitution of checks and balances because they realized the inescapable lesson of history that no man or group of men can be safely entrusted with unlimited power. They framed this Constitution with its provisions for change by amendment in order to secure the fundamentals of government against the dangers of temporary popular passion or the personal predilections of public officeholders.

3   We regard the decision of the Supreme Court in the school cases as a clear abuse of judicial power. It climaxes a trend in the Federal Judiciary undertak-

ing to legislate, in derogation of the authority of Congress, and to encroach upon the reserved rights of the States and the people.

4   The original Constitution does not mention education. Neither does the 14th amendment nor any other amendment. The debates preceding the submission of the 14th amendment clearly show that there was no intent that it should affect the system of education maintained by the States.

5   The very Congress which proposed the amendment subsequently provided for segregated schools in the District of Columbia.

6   When the amendment was adopted in 1868, there were 37 States of the Union. Every one of the 26 States that had any substantial racial differences among its people, either approved the operation of segregated schools already in existence or subsequently established such schools by action of the same lawmaking body which considered the 14th amendment.

7   As admitted by the Supreme Court in the public school case *(Brown v. Board of Education)*, the doctrine of separate by equal schools "apparently originated in *Roberts v. City of Boston* (1849), upholding school segregation against attack as being violative of a State constitutional guarantee of equality." This constitutional doctrine began in the North, not in the South, and it was followed not only in Massachusetts, but in Connecticut, New York, Illinois, Indiana, Michigan, Minnesota, New Jersey, Ohio, Pennsylvania and other northern States until they, exercising their rights as States through the constitutional processes of local self-government, changed their school systems.

8   In the case of *Plessy v. Ferguson* in 1896 the Supreme Court expressly declared that under the 14th amendment no person was denied any of his rights if the States provided separate but equal public facilities. This decision has been followed in many other cases. It is notable that the Supreme Court, speaking through Chief Justice Taft, a former President of the United States, unanimously declined in 1927 in *Lum v. Rice* that the "separate but equal" principle is "within the discretion of the State in regulating its public schools and does not conflict with the 14th amendment."

9   This interpretation, restated time and again, became a part of the life of the people of many of the States and confirmed their habits, customs, traditions, and way of life. It is founded on elemental humanity and commonsense, for parents should not be deprived by Government of the right to direct the lives and education of their own children.

10   Though there has been no constitutional amendment or act of Congress changing this established legal principle almost a century old, the Supreme Court of the United States, with no legal basis for such action, undertook to exercise their naked judicial power and substituted their personal political and social ideas for the established law of the land.

11   This unwarranted exercise of power by the Court, contrary to the Constitution, is creating chaos and confusion in the States principally affected. It is destroying the amicable relations between the white and Negro races that have been created through 90 years of patient effort by the good people of both races. It has planted hatred and suspicion where there has been heretofore friendship and understanding.

12   Without regard to the consent of the governed, outside agitators are threatening immediate and revolutionary changes in our public-school systems. If done, this is certain to destroy the system of public education in some of the States.

13   With the gravest concern for the explosive and dangerous condition created by this decision and inflamed by outside meddlers:

14   We reaffirm our reliance on the Constitution as the fundamental law of the land.

15   We decry the Supreme Court's encroachments on rights reserved to the States and to the people, contrary to established law, and to the Constitution.

16   We commend the motives of those States which have declared the intention to resist forced integration by any lawful means.

17   We appeal to the States and people who are not directly affected by those decisions to consider the constitutional principles involved against the time when they too, on issues vital to them, may be the victims of judicial encroachment.

18   Even though we constitute a minority in the present Congress, we have full faith that a majority of the American people believe in the dual system of government which has enabled us to achieve our greatness and will in time demand that the reserved rights of the States and of the people be made secure against judicial usurpation.

19   We pledge ourselves to use all lawful means to bring about a reversal of this decision which is contrary to the Constitution and to prevent the use of force in its implementation.

20   In this trying period, as we all seek to right this wrong, we appeal to our people not to be provoked by the agitators and troublemakers invading our States and to scrupulously refrain from disorder and lawless acts.

FOR ANALYSIS AND DISCUSSION

1. Why do you think the "Southern Manifesto" claims the Constitution was framed "against the dangers of temporary popular passion"? Was the *Brown* decision based on "popular passion"? Explain.
2. This document is called the "Southern Manifesto." What are the social and political implications of this title?
3. In paragraph 11 the "Manifesto" states that the *Brown* decision is destroying relations between the "white and Negro races." Based on your reading, who is upset by the decision? Are both races indeed against the decision, as the statement seems to imply?
4. Is the "Southern Manifesto" framed as a well-constructed and logical argument? Detail its strengths and weaknesses. What is the key message in the "Manifesto"? Is it based on constitutional or social issues?

Death at an Early Age
Jonathan Kozol

For many people the term "classroom" conjures images of book-lined walls, colorful artwork on bulletin boards, and neat rows of desks facing a blackboard. In the following essay, however, we are confronted with just the opposite reality. Jonathan Kozol describes his experience teaching in a classroom in the predominately black neighborhood of Roxbury, Massachusetts. He would later be fired from this position for reading the work of the black poet Langston Hughes to his students.

Jonathan Kozol graduated from Harvard University and later attended Oxford University in England on a Rhodes Scholarship. His book detailing his Roxbury teaching experience, *Death at an Early Age,* received the 1968 National Book Award. He has since written eight other books, including the 1996 national best-seller, *Amazing Grace: The Lives of Children and the Conscience of a Nation.*

BEFORE YOU READ

Think back to when you were in elementary school. What was your classroom like? How important is the classroom environment to children's learning ability?

AS YOU READ

What emotions do you feel when reading this essay? For whom do you feel sympathy? Do you find yourself getting angry? at whom?

1   The room in which I taught my Fourth Grade was not a room at all, but the corner of an auditorium. The first time I approached that corner, I noticed only a huge torn stage curtain, a couple of broken windows, a badly listing blackboard and about thirty-five bewildered-looking children, most of whom were Negro. White was overcome in black among them, but white and black together were overcome in chaos. They had desks and a teacher, but they did not really have a class. What they had was about one quarter of the auditorium. Three or four blackboards, two of them broken, made them seem a little bit set apart. Over at the other end of the auditorium there was another Fourth Grade class. Not much was happening at the other side at that minute so that for the moment the noise did not seem so bad. But it became a real nightmare of conflicting noises a little later on. Generally it was not until ten o'clock that the bad cross-fire started. By ten-thirty it would have attained such a crescendo that the children in the back rows of my section often couldn't hear my questions and I could not hear their answers. There were no carpetings or sound-absorbers of any kind. The room, being large, and echoing, and wooden, added resonance to every sound. Sometimes the other teacher and I would stagger the lessons in which our classes would have to speak aloud, but this was a makeshift method and it also meant that our classes had to be induced to maintain an unnatural and otherwise unnecessary rule of silence during the rest of the time. We couldn't always do it anyway, and usually the only way out was to try to outshout each other so that both of us often left school hoarse or wheezing. While her class was reciting in unison you could not hear very much in mine. When she was talking alone I could be hard above her but the trouble then was that little

bits of her talk got overheard by my class. Suddenly in the middle of our geography you could hear her saying:

2   "AFTER YOU COMPARE, YOU HAVE GOT TO BRING DOWN."

3   Or "PLEASE GIVE THAT PENCIL BACK TO HENRIETTA!"

4   Neither my class nor I could help but be distracted for a moment of sudden curiosity about exactly what was going on. Hours were lost in this way. Yet that was not the worst. More troublesome still was the fact that we did not ever *feel* apart. We were tucked in the corner and anybody who wanted could peek in or walk in or walk past. I never minded an intruder or observer, but to notice and to stare at any casual passer-by grew to be an irresistible temptation for the class. On repeated occasions I had to say to the children: "The class is still going. Let them have their discussion. Let them walk by if they have to. You should still be paying attention over here."

5   Soon after I came into that auditorium, I discovered that it was not only our two Fourth Grades that were going to have their classes here. We were to share the space also with the glee club, with play rehearsals, special reading, special arithmetic, and also at certain times a Third or Fourth Grade phonics class. I began to make head-counts of numbers of pupils and I started jotting them down:

6   Seventy children from the two regular Fourth Grades before the invasion.

7   Then ninety one day with the glee club and remedial arithmetic.

8   One hundred and seven with the play rehearsal.

9   One day the sewing class came in with their sewing machines and then that seemed to become a regular practice in the hall. Once I counted one hundred and twenty people. All in the one room. All talking, singing, yelling, laughing, reciting—and all at the same time. Before the Christmas break it become apocalyptic. Not more than one half of the classroom lessons I had planned took place throughout that time.

10   "Mr. Kozol—I can't hear you."

11   "Mr. Kozol—what's going on out there?"

12   "Mr. Kozol—couldn't we sing with them?"

13   One day something happened to dramatize to me, even more powerfully than anything yet, just what a desperate situation we were really in. What happened was that a window whose frame had rotted was blown right out of its sashes by a strong gust of wind and began to fall into the auditorium, just above my children's heads. I had noticed that window several times before and I had seen that its frame was rotting, but there were so many other things equally rotted or broken in the school building that it didn't occur to me to say anything about it. The feeling I had was that the Principal and custodians and Reading Teacher and other people had been in that building for a long time before me and they must have seen the condition of the windows. If anything could be done, if there were any way to get it corrected, I assumed they would have done it by this time. Thus, by not complaining and by not pointing it out to anyone, in a sense I went along with the rest of them and accepted it as something inevitable. One of the most grim things about teaching in such a school and such

a system is that you do not like to be an incessant barb and irritation to every-body else, so you come under a rather strong compulsion to keep quiet. But after you have been quiet for a while there is an equally strong temptation to begin to accept the conditions of your work or of the children's plight as natural. This, in a sense, is what had happened to me during that period and that, I suppose, is why I didn't say anything about the rotting window. Now one day it caved in.

14   First there was a cracking sound, then a burst of icy air. The next thing I knew, a child was saying: "Mr. Kozol—look at the window!" I turned and looked and saw that it was starting to fall in. It was maybe four or five feet tall and it came straight inward out of its sashes toward the heads of the children. I was standing, by coincidence, only about four or five feet off and was able to catch it with my hand. But the wind was so strong that it nearly blew right out of my hands. A couple of seconds of good luck—for it was a matter of chance that I was standing there—kept glass from the desks of six or seven children and very possibly preserved the original shape of half a dozen of their heads. The ones who had been under the glass were terrified but the thing that I noticed with most wonder was that they tried very hard to hide their fear in order to help me get over my own sense of embarrassment and guilt. I soon realized I was not going to be able to hold the thing up myself and I was obliged to ask one of the stronger boys in the class to come over and give me a hand. Meanwhile, as the children beneath us shivered with the icy wind and as the two of us now shivered also since it was a day when the mercury was hovering all morning close to freezing, I asked one of the children in the front row to run down and fetch the janitor.

15   When he asked me what he should tell him, I said: "Tell him the house is falling in." The children laughed. It was the first time I had ever come out and said anything like that when the children could hear me. I am sure my reluctance to speak out like that more often must seem odd to many readers, for at this perspective it seems odd to me as well. Certainly there were plenty of things wrong within that school building and there was enough we could have joked about. The truth, however, is that I did not often talk like that, nor did many of the other teachers, and there was a practical reason for this. Unless you were ready to buck the system utterly, it would become far too difficult to teach in an atmosphere of that kind of honesty. It generally seemed a great deal easier to pretend as well as you could that everything was normal and okay. Some teachers carried out this posture with so much eagerness, in fact, that their defense of the school ended up as something like a hymn of praise and adoration. "You children should thank God and feel blessed with good luck for all you've got. There are so many little children in the world who have been given so much less." The books are junk, the paint peels, the cellar stinks, the teachers call you nigger, and the windows fall in on your heads. "Thank God that you don't live in Russia or Africa! Thank God for all the blessings that you've got!" Once, finally, the day after the window blew in, I said to a friend of mine in the evening after school: "I guess that the building I teach in is not in very good condition." But to state a condition of dilapidation and ugliness and physical danger in

words as mild and indirect as those is almost worse than not saying anything at all. I had a hard time with that problem—the problem of being honest and of confronting openly the extent to which I was compromised by going along with things that were abhorrent and by accepting as moderately reasonable or unavoidably troublesome things which, if they were inflicted on children of my own, I would have condemned savagely.

16   A friend of mine to whom I have confided some of these things has not been able to keep from criticizing me for what he thinks of as a kind of quiet collusion. When I said to him, for example, that the Reading Teacher was trying to do the right thing and that she was a very forceful teacher, he replied to me that from what I had described to him she might have been a very forceful teacher but she was not a good teacher but a very dangerous one and that whether she was *trying* to do the right thing or not did not impress him since what she *did* do was the wrong thing. Other people I know have said the same thing to me about this and I am certain, looking back, that it is only the sheer accident of the unexpected events which took place in my school during the last weeks of the spring that prompted me suddenly to speak out and to take some forthright action. I am also convinced that it is that, and that alone, that has spared me the highly specialized and generally richly deserved contempt which is otherwise reserved by Negro people for their well-intending but inconsistent liberal friends.

17   After the windows blew in on us that time, the janitor finally came up and hammered it shut with nails so that it would not fall in again but also so that it could not open. It was a month before anything was done about the large gap left by a missing pane. Children shivered a few feet away from it. The Principal walked by frequently and saw us. So did supervisors from the School Department. So of course did the various lady experts who traveled all day from room to room within our school. No one can say that dozens of people did not know that children were sitting within the range of freezing air. At last one day the janitor came up with a piece of cardboard or pasteboard and covered over about a quarter of that lower window so that there was no more wind coming in but just that much less sunshine too. I remember wondering what a piece of glass could cost in Boston and I had the idea of going out and buying some and trying to put it in myself. That rectangle of cardboard over our nailed-shut window was not removed for a quarter of the year. When it was removed, it was only because a television station was going to come and visit in the building and the School Department wanted to make the room look more attractive. But it was winter when the window broke, and the repairs did not take place until the middle of the spring.

18   In case a reader imagines that my school may have been unusual and that some of the other schools in Roxbury must have been in better shape, I think it's worthwhile to point out that the exact opposite seems to have been the case. The conditions in my school were said by many people to be considerably better than those in several of the other ghetto schools. One of the worst, according to those who made comparisons, was the Endicott, also situated in the Ne-

gro neighborhood and, like my own school, heavily imbalanced. At Endicott, I learned, it had become so overcrowded that there were actually some classes in which the number of pupils exceeded the number of desks and in which the extra pupils had to sit in chairs behind the teacher. A child absent one day commonly came back the next day and found someone else sitting at his desk. These facts had been brought out in the newspapers, pretty well documented, and they were not denied by the School Department. Despite this, however, as in most cases like this, nothing had been done. When the parents of the Endicott children pressed the School Department to do something about it, a series of events transpired which told a large part of the story of segregation in a very few words.

19   The School Department offered, in order to resolve the problem, to buy a deserted forty-year-old Hebrew school and then allot about seven thousand dollars to furnish it with desks and chairs. Aside from the indignity of getting everybody else's castoffs (the Negroes already lived in former Jewish tenements and bought in former Jewish stores), there also was the telling fact that to buy and staff this old Hebrew school with about a dozen teachers was going to cost quite a lot of money and that to send the children down the street a couple of miles to a white school which had space would have saved quite a lot. The Hebrew school was going to cost over $180,000. To staff it, supply it with books and so forth would cost about $100,000 more. To send the children into available seats in nearby white classrooms (no new teachers needed) would have cost $40,000 to $60,000 for the year. The School Department, it seemed, was willing to spend something in the area of an extra $240,000 in order to put the Negro children into another segregated school. It was hard for me to believe, even after all I had seen and heard, that it could really be worth a quarter of a million dollars to anyone to keep the Negro children separate. As it happened, the School Committee dragged its heels so long and debated the issue in so many directions that most of the school year passed before anything of a final nature was decided. Meanwhile the real children in the real Endicott classrooms had lost another real year from their real lives.

FOR ANALYSIS AND DISCUSSION

1. Does the term "separate but equal" (see *Brown v. Topeka Board of Education*) seem ironic when applied to Kozol's classroom? Explain.

2. Could a "classroom" environment such as the one Kozol describes exist today? Why or why not? Have education and society changed in the last 30 years to prevent such a situation from happening today? Explain.

3. In paragraph 19, Kozol details to what extent the school department would go to "keep the Negro children separate." This essay describes a situation from 1964, ten years after the *Brown* decision was rendered. Is this classroom situation related to the *Brown* decision? Why or why not? Explain your view.

4. What do we expect from our public school system? How do we expect schools to achieve our expectations? How does the school where Kozol taught measure

up to our expectations? Who is ultimately responsible for the condition and quality of schools?

5. A friend accuses Kozol of participating in a "quiet collusion" (paragraph 16). What does the friend mean by this statement? Does the knowledge that Kozol was fired for "curriculum deviation" because he taught a Langston Hughes poem influence your view of his situation?

WRITING ASSIGNMENTS: EDUCATION

1. Discuss with your parents or other family members old enough to remember the impact of the *Brown* decision about how it affected them. What memories do they have of the decision? The Supreme Court realized that its ruling would not be welcome in some areas of the country. Research the ruling and its immediate aftermath. In a well-constructed argument, explain why the *Brown* ruling was or was not successful.

2. The "Southern Manifesto" argues that the *Brown* decision is unconstitutional because the Constitution does not mention education. How well do we know our Constitution? What rights and privileges does it protect, or do we expect it to protect? Are there other rights not mentioned in the Constitution that we expect our government to protect? Can the Constitution be flexible and malleable? Was the *Brown* ruling constitutional? Explain your view using specific examples from the U.S. Constitution and current laws.

3. More than 40 years have passed since the *Brown v. Topeka Board of Education* decision. However, the issue it dealt with has remained a current one. In 1995 the Institute on Race and Poverty held a forum called "In Pursuit of a Dream Deferred: Linking Housing and Education" in which it examined the persistence of racial segregation in schools and its possible relationship to housing segregation. Read some of the forum's essays presented on the Institute's Web site at <http://www1.umn.edu/irp>, including the essay by the forum's coordinator, Dr. Kenneth B. Clark. Does where we live affect the quality of our education? If so, in what ways? Drawing from both information on the Web site and your own experiences, write an essay detailing the connection between education and housing.

NON-VIOLENCE/VIOLENCE: FIGHTING FOR EQUALITY

Letter from Birmingham Jail
Martin Luther King, Jr.

Martin Luther King Jr. (1929–1968) was one of the most prominent and charismatic leaders for black civil rights in America. An ordained minister with a doctorate in theology, King organized the Southern Christian Leadership Conference in

1957 to promote justice and equality for African Americans. Under King's leadership, the civil rights movement eventually eliminated racist laws that prohibited blacks from using restaurants, public swimming pools, and seats in the forward sections of buses. For his efforts King was awarded the Nobel Peace Prize in 1964. Four years later, while supporting striking sanitation workers in Memphis, King was assassinated.

In 1963 King was arrested at a sit-in demonstration in Birmingham, Alabama. Written from a jail cell, the famous letter reprinted here was addressed to King's fellow clergy, who were critical of his activities in the name of social justice. However, the letter also addresses the collective conscience of the American people.

BEFORE YOU READ

In this letter King justifies his civil disobedience by arguing that the established laws are unjust. What laws seem unjust to you? Would you demonstrate to protest an unjust law?

AS YOU READ

Note King's response to his critics. What different strategies does he use to win them over to his point of view? Also notice how King logically analyzes each point of their criticism.

My Dear Fellow Clergymen:

1   While confined here in the Birmingham city jail, I came across your recent statement calling my present activities "unwise and untimely." Seldom do I pause to answer criticism of my work and ideas. If I sought to answer all the criticisms that cross my desk, my secretaries would have little time for anything other than such correspondence in the course of the day, and I would have no time for constructive work. But since I feel that you are men of genuine good will and that your criticisms are sincerely set forth, I want to try to answer your statement in what I hope will be patient and reasonable terms.

2   I think I should indicate why I am here in Birmingham, since you have been influenced by the view which argues against "outsiders coming in." I have the honor of serving as president of the Southern Christian Leadership Conference, an organization operating in every southern state, with headquarters in Atlanta, Georgia. We have some eighty-five affiliated organizations across the South, and one of them is the Alabama Christian Movement for Human Rights. Frequently we share staff, educational and financial resources with our affiliates. Several months ago the affiliate here in Birmingham asked us to be on call to engage in a nonviolent direct-action program if such were deemed necessary. We readily consented, and when the hour came we lived up to our promise. So I, along with several members of my staff, am here because I was invited here, I am here because I have organizational ties here.

"When your first name becomes "nigger," your middle name becomes "boy" (however old you are) and your last name becomes "John," and your wife and mother are never given the respected title "Mrs.";... when you are forever fighting a degenerating sense of "nobodiness"—then you will understand why we find it difficult to wait." (Excerpt from Martin Luther King, Jr.'s "Letter From Birmingham Jail")

3   But more basically, I am in Birmingham because injustice is here. Just as the prophets of the eighth century B.C. left their villages and carried their "thus saith the Lord" far beyond the boundaries of their home towns, and just as the Apostle Paul left his village of Tarsus and carried the gospel of Jesus Christ to the far corners of the Greco-Roman world, so am I compelled to carry the gospel of freedom beyond my own home town. Like Paul, I must constantly respond to the Macedonian call for aid.

4   Moreover, I am cognizant of the interrelatedness of all communities and states. I cannot sit idly by in Atlanta and not be concerned about what happens in Birmingham. Injustice anywhere is a threat to justice everywhere. We are caught in an inescapable network of mutuality, tied in a single garment of destiny. Whatever affects one directly, affects all indirectly. Never again can we afford to live with the narrow, provincial "outside agitator" idea. Anyone who lives inside the United States can never be considered an outsider anywhere within its bounds.

5   You deplore the demonstrations taking place in Birmingham. But your statement, I am sorry to say, fails to express a similar concern for the conditions that

brought about the demonstrations. I am sure that none of you would want to rest content with the superficial kind of social analysis that deals merely with effects and does not grapple with underlying causes. It is unfortunate that demonstrations are taking place in Birmingham, but it is even more unfortunate that the city's white power structure left the Negro community with no alternative.

6 　　In any nonviolent campaign there are four basic steps: collection of the facts to determine whether injustices exist; negotiation; self-purification; and direct action. We have gone through all these steps in Birmingham. There can be no gainsaying the fact that racial injustice engulfs this community. Birmingham is probably the most thoroughly segregated city in the United States. Its ugly record of brutality is widely known. Negroes have experienced grossly unjust treatment in the courts. There have been more unsolved bombings of Negro homes and churches in Birmingham than in any other city in the nation. These are the hard, brutal facts of the case. On the basis of these conditions, Negro leaders sought to negotiate with the city fathers. But the latter consistently refused to engage in good-faith negotiation.

7 　　Then, last September, came the opportunity to talk with leaders of Birmingham's economic community. In the course of the negotiations, certain promises were made by the merchants—for example, to remove the stores' humiliating racial signs. On the basis of these promises, the Reverend Fred Shuttlesworth and the leaders of the Alabama Christian Movement for Human Rights agreed to a moratorium on all demonstrations. As the weeks and months went by, we realized that we were the victims of a broken promise. A few signs, briefly removed, returned; the others remained.

8 　　As in so many past experiences, our hopes had been blasted, and the shadow of deep disappointment settled upon us. We had no alternative except to prepare for direct action, whereby we would present our very bodies as a means of laying our case before the conscience of the local and the national community. Mindful of the difficulties involved, we decided to undertake a process of self-purification. We began a series of workshops on nonviolence, and we repeatedly asked ourselves: "Are you able to accept blows without retaliating?" "Are you able to endure the ordeal of jail?" We decided to schedule our direct-action program for the Easter season, realizing that except for Christmas, this is the main shopping period of the year. Knowing that a strong economic-withdrawal program would be the by-product of direct action, we felt that this would be the best time to bring pressure to bear on the merchants for the needed change.

9 　　Then it occurred to us that Birmingham's mayoralty election was coming up in March, and we speedily decided to postpone action until after election day. When we discovered that the Commissioner of Public Safety, Eugene "Bull" Connor, had piled up enough votes to be in the run-off, we decided again to postpone action until the day after the run-off so that the demonstrations could not be used to cloud the issues. Like many others, we waited to see Mr. Connor defeated, and to this end we endured postponement after postponement. Having aided in this community need, we felt that our direct-action program could be delayed no longer.

10   You may well ask: "Why direct action? Why sit-ins, marches and so forth? Isn't negotiation a better path?" You are quite right in calling for negotiation. Indeed, this is the very purpose of direct action. Nonviolent direct action seeks to create such a crisis and foster such a tension that a community which has constantly refused to negotiate is forced to confront the issue. It seeks so to dramatize the issue that it can no longer be ignored. My citing the creation of tension as part of the work of the nonviolent-resister may sound rather shocking. But I must confess that I am not afraid of the word "tension." I have earnestly opposed violent tension, but there is a type of constructive, nonviolent tension which is necessary for growth. Just as Socrates felt that it was necessary to create a tension in the mind so that individuals could rise from the bondage of myths and half-truths to the unfettered realm of creative analysis and objective appraisal, so must we see the need for nonviolent gadflies to create the kind of tension in society that will help men rise from the dark depths of prejudice and racism to the majestic heights of understanding and brotherhood.

11   The purpose of our direct-action program is to create a situation so crisis-packed that it will inevitably open the door to negotiation. I therefore concur with you in your call for negotiation. Too long has our beloved Southland been bogged down in a tragic effort to live in monologue rather than dialogue.

12   One of the basic points in your statement is that the action that I and my associates have taken in Birmingham is untimely. Some have asked: "Why didn't you give the new city administration time to act?" The only answer that I can give to this query is that the new Birmingham administration must be prodded about as much as the outgoing one, before it will act. We are sadly mistaken if we feel that the election of Albert Boutwell as mayor will bring the millennium to Birmingham. While Mr. Boutwell is a much more gentle person than Mr. Connor, they are both segregationists, dedicated to maintenance of the status quo. I have hope that Mr. Boutwell will be reasonable enough to see the futility of massive resistance to desegregation. But he will not see this without pressure from devotees of civil rights. My friends, I must say to you that we have not made a single gain in civil rights without determined legal and nonviolent pressure. Lamentably, it is an historical fact that privileged groups seldom give up their privileges voluntarily. Individuals may see the moral light and voluntarily given up their unjust posture; but, as Reinhold Niebuhr has reminded us, groups tend to be more immoral than individuals.

13   We know through painful experience that freedom is never voluntarily given by the oppressor; it must be demanded by the oppressed. Frankly, I have yet to engage in a direct-action campaign that was "well timed" in the view of those who have not suffered unduly from the disease of segregation. For years now I have heard the word "Wait!" It rings in the ear of every Negro with piercing familiarity. This "Wait" has almost always meant "Never." We must come to see, with one of our distinguished jurists, that "justice too long delayed is justice denied."

14   We have waited for more than 340 years for our constitutional and God-given rights. The nations of Asia and Africa are moving with jet-like speed toward gaining political independence, but we still creep at horse-and-buggy pace toward gaining a cup of coffee at a lunch counter. Perhaps it is easy for those who

have never felt the stinging darts of segregation to say, "Wait." But when you have seen vicious mobs lynch your mothers and fathers at will and drown your sisters and brothers at whim; when you have seen hate-filled policemen curse, kick, and even kill your black brothers and sisters; when you see the vast majority of your twenty million Negro brothers smothering in an airtight cage of poverty in the midst of an affluent society; when you suddenly find your tongue twisted and your speech stammering as you seek to explain to your six-year-old daughter why she can't go the public amusement that has just been advertised on television, and see tears welling up in her eyes when she is told that Funtown is closed to colored children, and see ominous clouds of inferiority beginning to form in her little mental sky, and see her beginning to distort her personality by developing an unconscious bitterness toward white people; when you have to concoct an answer for a five-year-old son who is asking: "Daddy, why do white people treat colored people so mean?"; when you take a cross-country drive and find it necessary to sleep night after night in the uncomfortable corners of your automobile because no motel will accept you; when you are humiliated day in and day out by nagging signs reading "white" and "colored"; when your first name becomes "nigger," your middle name becomes "boy" (however old you are) and your last name becomes "John," and your wife and mother are never given the respected title "Mrs."; when you are harried by day and haunted by night by the fact that you are Negro, living constantly at tiptoe stance, never quite knowing what to expect next, and are plagued with inner fears and outer resentments; when you are forever fighting a degenerating sense of "nobodiness"—then you will understand why we find it difficult to wait. There comes a time when the cup of endurance runs over, and men are no longer willing to be plunged into the abyss of despair. I hope, sirs, you can understand our legitimate and unavoidable impatience.

15   You express a great deal of anxiety over our willingness to break laws. This is certainly a legitimate concern. Since we so diligently urge people to obey the Supreme Court's decision of 1954 outlawing segregation in the public schools, at first glance it may seem rather paradoxical for us consciously to break laws. One may well ask: "How can you advocate breaking some laws and obeying others?" The answer lies in the fact that there are two types of laws: just and unjust. I would be the first to advocate obeying just laws. One has not only a legal but a moral responsibility to obey just laws. Conversely, one has a moral responsibility to disobey unjust laws. I would agree with St. Augustine that "an unjust law is no law at all."

16   Now, what is the difference between the two? How does one determine whether a law is just or unjust? A just law is a man-made code that squares with the moral law or the law of God. An unjust law is a code that is out of harmony with the moral law. To put it in the terms of St. Thomas Aquinas: An unjust law is a human law that is not rooted in eternal law and natural law. Any law that uplifts human personality is just. Any law that degrades human personality is unjust. All segregation statutes are unjust because segregation distorts the soul and damages the personality. It gives the segregator a false sense of superiority and the segregated a false sense of inferiority. Segregation, to use the terminology of the Jewish philosopher Martin Buber, substitutes an "I-it" relationship for an "I-thou" relationship and ends up relegating persons to the status of

things. Hence segregation is not only politically, economically and sociologically unsound, it is morally wrong and sinful. Paul Tillich has said that sin is separation. Is not segregation an existential expression of man's tragic separation, his awful estrangement, his terrible sinfulness? Thus it is that I can urge men to obey the 1954 decision of the Supreme Court, for it is morally right; and I can urge them to disobey segregation ordinances, for they are morally wrong.

17   Let us consider a more concrete example of just and unjust laws. An unjust law is a code that a numerical or power majority group compels a minority group to obey but does not make binding on itself. This is *difference* made legal. By the same token, a just law is a code that a majority compels a minority to follow and that it is willing to follow itself. This is *sameness* made legal.

18   Let me give another explanation. A law is unjust if it is inflicted on a minority that, as a result of being denied the right to vote, had no part in enacting or devising the law. Who can say that the legislature of Alabama which set up that state's segregation laws was democratically elected? Throughout Alabama all sorts of devious methods are used to prevent Negroes from becoming registered voters, and there are some counties in which, even though Negroes constitute a majority of the population, not a single Negro is registered. Can any law enacted under such circumstances be considered democratically structured?

19   Sometimes a law is just on its face and unjust in its application. For instance, I have been arrested on a charge of parading without a permit. Now, there is nothing wrong in having an ordinance which requires a permit for a parade. But such an ordinance becomes unjust when it is used to maintain segregation and to deny citizens the First-Amendment privilege of peaceful assembly and protest.

20   I hope you are able to see the distinction I am trying to point out. In no sense do I advocate evading or defying the law, as would the rabid segregationist. That would lead to anarchy. One who breaks an unjust law must do so openly, lovingly, and with a willingness to accept the penalty. I submit that an individual who breaks a law that conscience tells him is unjust, and who willingly accepts the penalty of imprisonment in order to arouse the conscience of the community over its injustice, is in reality expressing the highest respect for law.

21   Of course, there is nothing new about this kind of civil disobedience. It was evidenced sublimely in the refusal of Shadrach, Meshach and Abednego to obey the laws of Nebuchadnezzar, on the ground that a higher moral law was at stake. It was practiced superbly by the early Christians, who were willing to face hungry lions and the excruciating pain of chopping blocks rather than submit to certain unjust laws of the Roman Empire. To a degree, academic freedom is a reality today because Socrates practiced civil disobedience. In our own nation, the Boston Tea Party represented a massive act of civil disobedience.

22   We should never forget that everything Adolf Hitler did in Germany was "legal" and everything the Hungarian freedom fighters did in Hungary was "illegal." It was "illegal" to aid and comfort a Jew in Hitler's Germany. Even so, I am sure that, had I lived in Germany at the time, I would have aided and comforted my Jewish brothers. If today I lived in a Communist country where certain principles dear to the Christian faith are suppressed, I would openly advocate disobeying that country's antireligious laws.

23   I must make two honest confessions to you, my Christian and Jewish brothers. First, I must confess that over the past few years I have been gravely disappointed with the white moderate. I have almost reached the regrettable conclusion that the Negro's great stumbling block in his stride toward freedom is not the White Citizen's Counciler or the Ku Klux Klanner, but the white moderate, who is more devoted to "order" than to justice; who prefers a negative peace which is the absence of tension to a positive peace which is the presence of justice; who constantly says: "I agree with you in the goal you seek, but I cannot agree with your methods of direct action"; who paternalistically believes he can set the timetable for another man's freedom; who lives by a mythical concept of time and who constantly advises the Negro to wait for a "more convenient season." Shallow misunderstanding from people of good will is more frustrating than absolute misunderstanding from people of ill will. Lukewarm acceptance is much more bewildering than outright rejection.

24   I had hoped that the white moderate would understand that law and order exist for the purpose of establishing justice and that when they fail in this purpose they become the dangerously structured dams that block the flow of social progress. I had hoped that the white moderate would understand that the present tension in the South is a necessary phase of the transition from an obnoxious negative peace, in which the Negro passively accepted his unjust plight, to a substantive and positive peace, in which all men will respect the dignity and worth of human personality. Actually, we who engage in nonviolent direct action are not the creators of tension. We merely bring to the surface the hidden tension that is already alive. We bring it out in the open, where it can be seen and dealt with. Like a boil that can never be cured so long as it is covered up but must be opened with all its ugliness to the natural medicines of air and light, injustice must be exposed, with all the tension its exposure creates, to the light of human conscience and the air of national opinion before it can be cured.

25   In your statement you assert that our actions, even though peaceful, must be condemned because they precipitate violence. But is this a logical assertion? Isn't this like condemning a robbed man because his possession of money precipitated the evil act of robbery? Isn't this like condemning Socrates because his unswerving commitment to truth and his philosophical inquiries precipitated the act by the misguided populace in which they made him drink hemlock? Isn't this like condemning Jesus because his unique God-consciousness and never-ceasing devotion to God's will precipitated the evil act of crucifixion? We must come to see that, as the federal courts have consistently affirmed, it is wrong to urge an individual to cease his efforts to gain his basic constitutional rights because the quest may precipitate violence. Society must protect the robbed and punish the robber.

26   I had also hoped that the white moderate would reject the myth concerning time in relation to the struggle for freedom. I have just received a letter from a white brother in Texas. He writes: "All Christians know that the colored people will receive equal rights eventually, but it is possible that you are in too great a religious hurry. It has taken Christianity almost two thousand years to accomplish what it has. The teachings of Christ take time to come to earth." Such an attitude stems from a tragic misconception of time, from the strangely irra-

tional notion that there is something in the very flow of time that will inevitably cure all ills. Actually, time itself is neutral; it can be used either destructively or constructively. More and more I feel that the people of ill will have used time much more effectively than have the people of good will. We will have to repent in this generation not merely for the hateful words and actions of the bad people but for the appalling silence of the good people. Human progress never rolls in on wheels of inevitability; it comes through the tireless efforts of men willing to be co-workers with God, and without this hard work, time itself becomes an ally of the forces of social stagnation. We must use time creatively, in the knowledge that the time is always ripe to do right. Now is the time to make real the promise of democracy and transform our pending national elegy into a creative psalm of brotherhood. Now is the time to lift our national policy from the quicksand of racial injustice to the solid rock of human dignity.

27   You speak of our activity in Birmingham as extreme. At first I was rather disappointed that fellow clergymen would see my nonviolent efforts as those of an extremist. I began thinking about the fact that I stand in the middle of two opposing forces in the Negro Community. One is a force of complacency, made up in part of Negroes who, as a result of long years of oppression, are so drained of self-respect and a sense of "somebodiness" that they have adjusted to segregation; and in part of a few middle-class Negroes who, because of a degree of academic and economic security and because in some ways they profit by segregation, have become insensitive to the problems of the masses. The other force is one of bitterness and hatred, and it comes perilously close to advocating violence. It is expressed in the various black nationalist groups that are springing up across the nation, the largest and best known being Elijah Muhammad's Muslim movement. Nourished by the Negro's frustration over the continued existence of racial discrimination, this movement is made up of people who have lost faith in America, who have absolutely repudiated Christianity, and who have concluded that the white man is an incorrigible "devil."

28   I have tried to stand between these two forces, saying that we need emulate neither the "do-nothingism" of the complacent nor the hatred and despair of the black nationalist. For there is the more excellent way of love and nonviolent protest. I am grateful to God that, through the influence of the Negro church, the way of nonviolence became an integral part of our struggle.

29   If this philosophy had not emerged, by now many streets of the South would, I am convinced, be flowing with blood. And I am further convinced that if our white brothers dismiss as "rabble-rousers" and "outside agitators" those of us who employ nonviolent direct action, and if they refuse to support our nonviolent efforts, millions of Negroes will, out of frustration and despair, seek solace and security in black-nationalist ideologies—a development that would inevitably lead to a frightening racial nightmare.

30   Oppressed people cannot remain oppressed forever. The yearning for freedom eventually manifests itself, and that is what has happened to the American Negro. Something within has reminded him of his birthright of freedom, and something without has reminded him that it can be gained. Consciously or unconsciously, he has been caught up by the *Zeitgeist,* and with his black broth-

ers of Africa and his brown and yellow brothers of Asia, South America and the Caribbean, the United States Negro is moving with a sense of great urgency toward the promised land of racial justice. If one recognizes this vital urge that has engulfed the Negro community, one should readily understand why public demonstrations are taking place. The Negro has many pent-up resentments and latent frustrations, and he must release them. So let him march; let him make prayer pilgrimages to the city hall; let him go on freedom rides—and try to understand why he must do so. If his repressed emotions are not released in nonviolent ways, they will seek expression through violence; this is not a threat but a fact of history. So I have not said to my people: "Get rid of your discontent." Rather, I have tried to say that this normal and healthy discontent can be channeled into the creative outlet of nonviolent direction action. And now this approach is being termed extremist.

31   But though I was initially disappointed at being categorized as an extremist, as I continue to think about the matter I gradually gained a measure of satisfaction from the label. Was not Jesus an extremist for love: "Love your enemies, bless them that curse you, do good to them that hate you, and pray for them which despitefully use you, and persecute you." Was not Amos an extremist for justice: "Let justice roll down like waters and righteousness like an everflowing stream." Was not Paul an extremist for the Christian gospel: "I bear in my body the marks of the Lord Jesus." Was not Martin Luther an extremist: "Here I stand; I cannot do otherwise, so help me God." And John Bunyan: "I will stay in jail to the end of my days before I make a butchery of my conscience." And Abraham Lincoln: "This nation cannot survive half slave and half free." And Thomas Jefferson: "We hold these truths to be self-evidence, that all men are created equal . . . " So the question is not whether we will be extremists, but what kind of extremists we will be. Will we be extremists for hate or for love? Will we be extremists for the preservation of injustice or for the existence of justice? In that dramatic scene on Calvary's hill three men were crucified. We must never forget that all three were crucified for the same crime—the crime of extremism. Two were extremists for immorality, and thus fell below their environment. The other, Jesus Christ, was an extremist for love, truth and goodness, and thereby rose above his environment. Perhaps the South, the nation and the world are in dire need of creative extremists. . . .

32   If I have said anything in this letter that overstates the truth and indicates an unreasonable impatience, I beg you to forgive me. If I have said anything that understates the truth and indicates my having a patience that allows me to settle for anything less than brotherhood, I beg God to forgive me.

33   I hope this letter finds you strong in the faith. I also hope that circumstances will soon make it possible for me to meet each of you, not as an integrationist or a civil-rights leader but as a fellow clergyman and a Christian brother. Let us all hope that the dark clouds of racial prejudice will soon pass away and the deep fog of misunderstanding will be lifted from our fear-drenched communities, and in some not too distant tomorrow the radiant stars of love and brotherhood will shine over our great nation with all their scintillating beauty.

Yours for the cause of Peace and Brotherhood,
Martin Luther King, Jr.

FOR ANALYSIS AND DISCUSSION

1. King states: "We will have to repent in this generation not merely for the hateful words and actions of the bad people but for the appalling silence of the good people" (paragraph 26). What does this statement mean to you? Do you agree? In what situations might silence be "appalling"? Explain.

2. Describe King's voice in this letter? What does his voice reveal about King's personality, and how does it affect his argument? How does King establish credibility, authority, and personality in his letter?

3. In paragraph 12 King states that the Birmingham officials at the time were "dedicated to maintenance of the status quo." What was the status quo in 1963 Birmingham? What is the status quo today?

4. In paragraph 14 King provides a "catalogue" of reasons why the civil rights movement cannot "wait" any longer. Analyze this technique in terms of King's argument. What effect does this cataloging have on the reader?

5. Martin Luther King, Jr. was first and foremost a preacher. Does the writing style in his letter indicate his profession? If so, in what ways? How effective would this letter be if delivered as a speech? Is it as effective in letter form? Explain.

6. In paragraphs 15 through 20 King provides proof regarding the differences between just and unjust laws. Examine this section and decide whether his logic is effective.

The Provocation of Violence: A Civil Rights Tactic?

Jan Howard

The powerful images of unarmed protestors being clubbed by southern police officers; the bombed church in Birmingham, Alabama, where four young black girls died; and the faces of James Chaney, Michael Schwerner, and Andrew Goodman, murdered civil rights activists, were burned into the consciousness of America during the 1960s. It was the sight of this violence and hatred that provoked the American public and its leaders to take long overdue action on behalf of African American civil rights. In her essay, Jan Howard raises the provocative question of whether the nonviolence urged by Dr. King and his followers was itself a deliberate strategy intended to provoke violence and win sympathy for the cause of civil rights.

Jan Howard received her Ph.D. from Stanford University in 1961 and was active in the civil rights movement, participating in the Mississippi Summer Project, Freedom Summer, to register Black voters. Currently, Dr. Howard is Chief of the Prevention Research Branch in the National Institute on Alcohol Abuse and Alcoholism, working to enhance studies of minority issues. This essay appeared in *Dissent* magazine in 1966.

BEFORE YOU READ

How do you feel when you hear of an act of violence against an innocent person related on the evening news or in a newspaper? Does it make you want to take action? If so, in what way?

AS YOU READ

After reading Howard's essay, are you convinced that the provocation of violence is indeed a latent tactic employed to incite change? How convincing is Howard's argument?

1   The civil rights movement is pledged to nonviolence. It is commonly assumed by those of us involved in it that the provocation of violence is alien to its strategy and that violence is simply a calculated risk in trying to achieve its goals. But the facts compel me to question this assumption and to suggest that the provocation of violence is often used as a latent tactic.

2   This contention is difficult to prove. I am certain many of us working for civil rights are unconscious of the way we exploit violence. And since the whole ideology of the movement implies an abhorrence of violence, none of us wants to admit that violence is more than a calculated risk. In the South violence against civil rights workers often occurs spontaneously, without any attempt to invite it; so it is hard to know where provocation as risk leaves off and provocation as tactic begins.

3   Yet the record suggests that in many situations the provocation of violence has become more than a calculated risk of the movement. It has the earmarks of a strategy.

4   Consider what happened in the 1964 Mississippi Summer Project. Its purposes were to register Negroes to vote; to teach them in Freedom Schools; and to expose white college students to the rigors of Southern poverty and repression. I understand still another goal was expressed by leaders of the project long before it actually began—getting federal troops to Mississippi to protect the voter registration drive. The fulfillment of this goal hinged on violence, and the leaders knew it. They also knew something else—that the government was reluctant to provide protection. For several years a seasoned cadre of Negro civil rights workers had been waging the voter registration drive under conditions of open brutality and terror. When they asked for federal protection, the government was uncooperative.

5   Leaders of the movement anticipated that bringing hundreds of outsiders to Mississippi would trigger violence, but this time the violence would be against students from white, affluent, influential families, and the federal government would be forced to protect them. The prophecy was largely correct. The project had only begun when three of the workers were murdered. This single act gave the program more publicity than any other kind of action would have. It did not bring federal troops, but it brought FBI agents and federal mar-

shals in large numbers, and by their presence they reduced the likelihood of violence against the civil rights workers.*

6   The chain of events in this and similar situations forces us to consider this question: when is the provocation of violence more than a calculated risk of the movement? I suggest an answer: when the movement adopts a goal which it believes can be fulfilled only through violence. It is then, in effect, relying on violence to achieve some end. Violence is not simply a calculated risk; it is part of an over-all plan. And the instrumental value of violence is a built-in impetus for actions that will provide it.

7   Because the Summer Project had so many goals, one can always argue that the goal of getting federal troops had no special effect on the actions of the movement. It would have brought the students South anyway. This argument begs the question. With respect to achieving one goal, the provocation of violence can be merely a calculated risk; but with respect to achieving another, it can be a latent tactic.

8   Selma, Alabama, provides another illustration of what I have in mind. In discussing the rationale behind the Selma protest, Dr. Martin Luther King clearly suggests that the movement in Selma, like the movement in Mississippi, was relying on violence to achieve some goal.†

> The goal of the demonstrations in Selma, as elsewhere, is to dramatize the existence of injustice and to bring about the presence of justice. . . . Long years of experience indicate to us that Negroes can achieve this goal when four things occur:
>
>   1. Nonviolent demonstrators go into the streets to exercise their constitutional rights.
>   2. *Racists resist by unleashing violence against them.*
>   3. Americans of conscience in the name of decency demand federal intervention and legislation.
>   4. The Administration, under mass pressure, initiates measures of immediate intervention and remedial legislation.[2]

9   When nonviolent protest does provoke violent retaliation, civil rights leaders know how to capitalize on the situation and turn it to our advantage. But when nonviolence begets nonviolent opposition, this can really frustrate the movement, as I learned firsthand at Selma in the days immediately following the march that turned around. The police then blocked us from marching to the county courthouse. And King's aides followed his example, leading us to the barricades but no further.

---

*Federal agents did not define their role as protective, but as "investigative." Still their presence served as a deterrent to violence.

†King, of course, turned the second march around but not until we went to the brink and in his words "made our point, revealing the continued presence of violence, and showing clearly who are the oppressed and who the oppressors."[1]

10   We were gripped by a tremendous sense of frustration and futility. I believe this reaction was caused in large part by the failure of the nonviolent technique to provoke violence. Safety Director Baker headed the police, and they were on their best behavior. They refused to be provoked into violence even when a group of Negro youths broke ranks and charged their line, and Baker readily approved all forms of nonviolent protest such as speeches and prayers. Thus, demonstrators found it impossible to make the police initiate action that the movement could capitalize on. We were forced either to be violent ourselves or to bear the burden of seemingly ineffective nonviolence. And for many this burden was shame—shame because we were just standing there, not getting through, not pushing through, not being beaten, not being arrested, just standing there.

11   The obvious sign of failure was that we were not getting through to the courthouse. But I think participants also sensed a more subtle sign of failure: the lack of violence. When you turn the other cheek and nobody bothers to slap it, it's hard to believe you are a threat to anyone. Both kinds of failure were articulated by spokesmen for the movement when they announced on the evening of the all-night vigil: "We will tell the police: You must let us through, or you must beat us, tear gas us, or jail us." In essence they were imploring: "You must let nonviolence work, or you must be violent. Give us some sense of effectiveness."

12   I am not suggesting participants in the movement are attracted to violence for its own sake. But I am suggesting we are consciously and unconsciously drawn toward violence because violence pays dividends for the movement.

13   First and foremost, it is a powerful catalyst to arouse public opinion. If the 600 Negroes who were tear gassed and beaten in Selma had walked all the way to Montgomery without a violent incident, we would still be awaiting a voting bill. Nor is Selma an isolated case. It was the bombings in Birmingham that forced President Kennedy to submit the historic Civil Rights Bill. The bared fangs of Bull Connor's police dogs—the burning bus of the Freedom Riders—the tear-stained face of Medgar Evers' widow: these are the alarms that awaken the conscience of America.

14   When bigotry erupts into violence, this dramatizes the everyday plight of the Negro and shows the righteousness of the movement's cause. In the words of Dr. King, the murder of the three civil rights workers was "a grisly and eloquent demonstration to the whole nation of the moral degeneracy upon which segregation rests."[3] Can nonviolence pay such "eloquent" dividends?

15   Violence is dramatic, and Americans like the dramatic. Mass media will give extensive coverage to violence and threats of violence while they ignore more subtle injustices against the Negro and more subtle attempts to remedy injustice. And the federal government can be forced to intervene in situations of violence while it turns its back on less inflammatory brutality.

16   But there is more to the attraction of violence than its power to arouse the public at large. Civil rights leaders have other audiences in mind when they march into battle. They are trying to arouse the apathetic Negro by showing

him that other Negroes would rather stand up in battle than be bent by the yoke of submission. And they are trying to bolster the nerve of the active Negro as well. To quote Dr. King:

> Those who have lived under the corrosive humiliation of daily intimida-
> tion are imbued by demonstrations with a sense of courage and dignity
> that strengthens their personalities. Through demonstrations, Negroes
> learn that unity and militance have more force than bullets. They find that
> the bruises of clubs, electric cattle prods and fists hurt less than the scars of
> submission.[4]

17   The enemy constitutes still another audience. According to King, "segregationists learn from demonstrations that Negroes who have been taught to fear
can also be taught to be fearless."[5]

18   A further attraction of violence for participants in a nonviolent movement
inheres in the fact that violence is the antithesis of nonviolence. Thus, the
moral superiority of nonviolence is most graphically displayed in a violent setting.* Nonviolence reaches the height of its legitimacy when it is counterposed
with the illegitimacy of naked violence.

19   Finally, we should recognize that not all participants in the movement are
philosophically committed to nonviolence. There is division in the ranks, and
this is another pressure toward violence. A sizable number scattered throughout the movement do not believe in nonviolence, either as a principle or a tactic. Even the group that subscribes to nonviolence is divided. Some are committed to it as an end in itself; others view it simply as an expedient tactic. Since
the latter have no philosophical attachment to nonviolence, they are more vulnerable to the appeal of violence as a strategy than the committed are. This
group and the nonbelievers are constantly pressuring the committed to prove
that nonviolence works. Sometimes this pressure forces the committed to exploit violence as a means of gaining symbolic victories for nonviolence. They
may hastily involve the movement in a dramatic protest because they know
drama has a quick pay-off. Or they may try other means of winning laurels for
nonviolence even if they have to throw caution and some principles to the
winds. As they are forced to take more and more chances, violence as risk becomes violence as certainty.

20   I felt the pressure on the leaders in Selma when nonviolence appeared to
be ineffective. The situation was so tense and the youngsters were so eager to
take on the police that King's aides had to respond to the dissatisfaction. They
made several frantic attempts to show that nonviolence works. On at least two
occasions they sent small groups to the courthouse by evasive routes to stage a

---

*Some participants in the movement may be drawn into battle for more personal reasons: to prove to them-
selves and others that they are pacifists out of principle rather than fear or to prove they are truly committed
to nonviolence. Thus, Charles Mauldin, a teen-age leader, wants a chance to be tested. He says, "It's easy to
talk about non-violence, but in a lot of cases you've got to be tested, and reinspire yourself."[6]
    The movement actually increases the attraction of violence by reserving the greatest acclaim for those
who have braved it.

demonstration. One venture came within a hair of triggering mob violence. But the leaders could say to their critics that they had succeeded in getting past the police nonviolently.

21   I am not suggesting that the violence of white segregationists always pays dividends for the movement. The impact on the public at large depends in part on the character of the victim. The brutalizing of whites arouses much more attention and anger than the brutalizing of Negroes. Violence which rallies national sentiment behind the movement can tear a local community apart and freeze positions, so that it becomes more difficult to win localized demands. Even on a national level, a given type of violence seems to pay diminishing returns. Tear gas in Selma outraged the nation, but only three weeks later smoke bombs in Camden went practically unnoticed. Does the American public have a rising degree of tolerance for violence? If so, there must be an escalation of violence to get the same effect. This may be an unforeseen consequence of using the dramatic protest to arouse public opinion.

22   The strategy of the movement in this country raises a very important question: Does a movement which is dedicated to nonviolence as *the* means of action and reaction inherently need violence to sustain it? The evidence suggests that it does. I remember what Reverend Andrew Young, one of King's top aides, said in Browns Chapel as he reflected on the fact that Safety Director Baker was a nonviolent police chief. He said that the Bakers really thwart the movement but that the Bull Connors and Jim Clarks play into the hands and give it momentum.

23   The philosophy of nonviolent struggle seems in part to be predicated on the idea that there will be violence against the movement. The success of nonviolent struggle may require that this prophecy be fulfilled. Thus, we who are involved may be captives of a social dynamic, without necessarily being aware of the forces acting upon us. I still hear the words of the parade captain I spoke to in the march that turned around. As we followed the leaders back to Selma, he vociferously declared:

> "We should have kept marching right through the troopers!"
>   "And what price are you willing to pay to keep marching?" I asked.
> "One life? Ten lives? A hundred?"
>   "No lives," he replied. "No lives."

24   Did he really mean "no lives?" Or was he refusing to admit even to himself that the nonviolent movement often thrives on violence? Perhaps he was refusing to admit something even more important—that he is disillusioned with the nonviolent approach to winning battles.

25   The violence of white segregationists may be necessary to sustain the nonviolent movement, but it may not be sufficient. If the public and the government do not respond to that violence, and what it represents, with enough indignation and power to change the Negro's inhuman condition to a human one—then the Negro and his white allies will totally abandon nonviolence as a principle and strategy. Already we see the emergence of the Deacons, an armed league of Negroes pledged to using violence in self-defense. And we see the

nonviolent movement wrestling with its conscience and struggling to cope with the attitudes represented by the Deacons. Pressured by the reality of life, the movement has already embraced the tactic of capitalizing on violence and the tactic of provoking it. To sustain itself, will it now be forced to sanction the use of violence in self-defense? What is the next step?

NOTES

1. King, Martin Luther, Jr. "Behind the Selma March," *Saturday Review,* April 3, 1965, p. 17.
2. *Ibid.,* p. 16. (Italics added)
3. King, Martin Luther, Jr. "Let Justice Roll Down," *The Nation,* March 15, 1965, p. 271.
4. *Ibid.,* p. 270.
5. *Ibid.*
6. Adler, Renata. "Letter From Selma," *The New Yorker,* April 10, 1965, p. 138.

FOR ANALYSIS AND DISCUSSION

1. How can violence be employed to promote a cause? Does violence succeed in changing the opposition's point of view? Explain.
2. In what ways does the line between provocation of violence as a risk blur with the provocation of violence as a direct tactic? Why would activists openly dedicated to nonviolent protest subtly employ provocation as a tactic? What do they hope to gain for their cause?
3. In paragraph 10 Howard states that the inability of the demonstrators in Selma, Alabama, to provoke the police to violence resulted in a sense of "shame." What caused this feeling of shame? Why were nonviolent protesters upset that their protest was just that—nonviolent?
4. How does Howard's "list" of reasons why we are drawn to violence (beginning in paragraph 13) support her argument? Is her reasoning sound and logical? Explain.
5. How can the provocation of violence backfire? Is there a saturation point at which we become desensitized to violence?
6. Consider Howard's tone in this essay. Can you tell how she feels about the use of violence to incite change? Does she support the tactics used by the demonstrators? How can you tell?

Message to the Grass Roots
Malcolm X

Malcolm X was born Malcolm Little in 1925 in Omaha, Nebraska. Although he graduated from junior high school at the top of his class, Malcolm was discouraged from continuing his schooling because of his race. He moved to Roxbury, Massachusetts, with his sister Ella, where he took a job as a shoeshine boy. He became involved in several crime rings and was eventually arrested and convicted of robbery in 1946. While in prison, Malcolm became a follower of Elijah Muhammad, the leader of the

Nation of Islam (which was sometimes called the Black Muslim Movement); re-scinded his "slave name," Little; and was assigned the new name "X." He quickly rose through the ranks of the Nation of Islam and became one of its top administrators.

In 1964, Malcolm X left the Nation of Islam to form his own organization, the Muslim Mosque, which articulated a more secular black nationalism. After a trip to Mecca, however, he began to change his view toward whites, considering the possi-bility that some whites could contribute to the struggle for racial equality. A year later, on February 21, 1965, Malcolm X was assassinated in the Audubon Ballroom in Harlem, New York, while addressing a full house. The following speech was de-livered to an almost entirely black audience on November 1963 in Detroit while Malcolm X was still a member of the Nation of Islam.

BEFORE YOU READ

Have you ever been excluded from something because of your race, gender, color, or religious or sexual orientation? If so, how did it make you feel?

AS YOU READ

Consider the author's voice as you read his speech. Does his tone engage you or alienate you?

1   We want to have just an off-the-cuff chat between you and me, us. We want to talk right down to earth in a language that everybody here can easily under-stand. We all agree tonight, all of the speakers have agreed, that America has a very serious problem. Not only does America have a very serious problem, but our people have a very serious problem. The only reason she has a problem is she doesn't want us here. And every time you look at yourself, be you black, brown, red or yellow, a so-called Negro, you represent a person who poses such a serious problem for America because you're not wanted. Once you face this as a fact, then you can start plotting a course that will make you appear intelli-gent, instead of unintelligent.

2   What you and I need to do is learn to forget our differences. When we come together, we don't come together as Baptists or Methodists. You don't catch hell because you're a Baptist, and you don't catch hell because you're a Methodist. You don't catch hell because you're a Methodist or Baptist, you don't catch hell because you're a Democrat or Republican, you don't catch hell because you're a Mason or an Elk, and your sure don't catch hell because you're an American; because if you were an American, you wouldn't catch hell. You catch hell because you're a black man. You catch hell, all of us catch hell, for the same reason.

3   So we're all black people, so-called Negroes, second-class citizens, ex-slaves. You're nothing but an ex-slave. You don't like to be told that. But what else are you? You are ex-slaves. You didn't come here on the "Mayflower." You came here on a slave ship. In chains, like a horse, or a cow, or a chicken. And you

were brought here by people who came here on the "Mayflower," you were brought here by the so-called Pilgrims, or Founding Fathers. They were the ones who brought you here.

4   We have a common enemy. We have this in common: We have a common oppressor, a common exploiter, and a common discriminator. But once we all realize that we have a common enemy, then we unite—on the basis of what we have in common. And what we have foremost in common is the enemy—the white man. He's an enemy to all of us. I know some of you all think that some of them aren't enemies. Time will tell.

5   In Bandung back in, I think, 1954, was the first unity meeting in centuries of black people. And once you study what happened at the Bandung conference, and the results of the Bandung conference, it actually serves as a model for the same procedure you and I can use to get our problems solved. At Bandung all the nations came together, the dark nations from Africa and Asia. Some of them were Buddhists, some of them were Muslims, some of them were Christians, some were Confucianists, some were atheists. Despite their religious differences, they came together. Some were communists, some were socialists, some were capitalists—despite their economic and political differences, they came together. All of them were black, brown, red or yellow.

6   The number-one thing that was not allowed to attend the Bandung conference was the white man. He couldn't come. Once they excluded the white man, they found that they could get together. Once they kept him out, everybody else fell right in and fell in line. This is the thing that you and I have to understand. And these people who came together didn't have nuclear weapons, they didn't have jet planes, they didn't have all of the heavy armaments that the white man has. But they had unity.

7   They were able to submerge their little petty differences and agree on one thing: That one African came from Kenya and was being colonized by the Englishman, and another African came from the Congo and was being colonized by the Belgian, and another African came from Guinea and was being colonized by the French, and another came from Angola and was being colonized by the Portuguese. When they came to the Bandung conference, they looked at the Portuguese, and at the Frenchman, and at the Englishman, and at the Dutchman, and learned or realized the one thing that all of them had in common—they were all from Europe, they were all Europeans, blond, blue-eyed and white skins. They began to recognize who their enemy was. The same man that was colonizing our people in Kenya was colonizing our people in the Congo. The same one in the Congo was colonizing our people in South Africa, and in Southern Rhodesia, and in Burma, and in India, and in Afghanistan, and in Pakistan. They realized all over the world where the dark man was being oppressed, he was being oppressed by the white man; where the dark man was being exploited, he was being exploited by the white man. So they got together on this basis—that they had a common enemy.

8   And when you and I here in Detroit and in Michigan and in America who have been awakened today look around us, we too realize here in America we

all have a common enemy, whether he's in Georgia or Michigan, whether he's in California or New York. He's the same man—blue eyes and blond hair and pale skin—the same man. So what we have to do is what they did. They agreed to stop quarreling among themselves. Any little spat that they had, they'd settle it among themselves, go into a huddle—don't let the enemy know that you've got a disagreement.

9   Instead of airing our differences in public, we have to realize we're all the same family. And when you have a family squabble, you don't get out on the sidewalk. If you do, everybody calls you uncouth, unrefined, uncivilized, savage. If you don't make it at home, you settle it at home; you get in the closet, argue it out behind closed doors, and then when you come out on the street, you pose a common front, a united front. And this is what we need to do in the community, and in the city, and in the state. We need to stop airing our differences in front of the white man, put the white man out of our meetings, and then sit down and talk shop with each other. That's what we've got to do.

10   I would like to make a few comments concerning the difference between the black revolution and the Negro revolution. Are they both the same? And if they're not, what is the difference? What is the difference between a black revolution and a Negro revolution? First, what is a revolution? Sometimes I'm inclined to believe that many of our people are using this word "revolution" loosely, without taking careful consideration of what this word actually means, and what its historic characteristics are. When you study the historic nature of revolutions, the motive of a revolution, the objective of a revolution, the result of a revolution, and the methods used in a revolution, you may change words. You may devise another program, you may change your goal and you may change your mind.

11   Look at the American Revolution in 1776. That revolution was for what? For land. Why did they want land? Independence. How was it carried out? Bloodshed. Number one, it was based on land, the basis of independence. And the only way they could get it was bloodshed. The French Revolution—what was it based on? The landless against the landlord. What was it for? Land. How did they get it? Bloodshed. Was no love lost, was no compromise, was no negotiation. I'm telling you—you don't know what a revolution is. Because when you find out what it is, you'll get back in the alley, you'll get out of the way.

12   The Russian Revolution—what was it based on? Land; the landless against the landlord. How did they bring it about? Bloodshed. You haven't got a revolution that doesn't involve bloodshed. And you're afraid to bleed. I said, you're afraid to bleed.

13   As long as the white man sent you to Korea, you bled. He sent you to Germany, you bled. He sent you to the South Pacific to fight the Japanese, you bled. You bleed for white people, but when it comes to seeing your own churches being bombed and little black girls murdered, you haven't got any blood. You bleed when the white man says bleed; you bite when the white man says bite; and you bark when the white man says bark. I hate to say this about us, but it's true. How are you going to be nonviolent in Mississippi, as violent as you were in Korea? How can you justify being nonviolent in Mississippi and Al-

abama, when your churches are being bombed, and your little girls are being murdered, and at the same time you are going to get violent with Hitler, and Tōjō, and somebody else you don't even know?

14   If violence is wrong in America, violence is wrong abroad. If it is wrong to be violent defending black women and black children and black babies and black men, then it is wrong for America to draft us and make us violent abroad in defense of her. And if it is right for America to draft us, and teach us how to be violent in defense of her, then it is right for you and me to do whatever is necessary to defend our own people right here in this country.

15   The Chinese Revolution—they wanted land. They threw the British out, along with the Uncle Tom Chinese. Yes, they did. They set a good example. When I was in prison, I read an article—don't be shocked when I say that I was in prison. You're still in prison. That's what America means: prison. When I was in prison, I read an article in *Life* magazine showing a little Chinese girl, nine years old; her father was on his hands and knees and she was pulling the trigger because he was an Uncle Tom Chinaman. When they had the revolution over there, they took a whole generation of Uncle Toms and just wiped them out. And within ten years that little girl became a full-grown woman. No more Toms in China. And today it's one of the toughest, roughest, most feared countries on this earth—by the white man. Because there are no Uncle Toms over there.

16   Of all our studies, history is best qualified to reward our research. And when you see that you've got problems, all you have to do is examine the historic method used all over the world by others who have problems similar to yours. Once you see how they got theirs straight, then you know how you can get yours straight. There's been a revolution, a black revolution, going on in Africa. In Kenya, the Mau Mau were revolutionary; they were the ones who brought the word "Uhuru" to the fore. The Mau Mau, they were revolutionary, they believed in scorched earth, they knocked everything aside that got in their way, and their revolution also was based on land, a desire for land. In Algeria, the northern part of Africa, a revolution took place. The Algerians were revolutionists, they wanted land. France offered to let them be integrated into France. They told France, to hell with France, they wanted some land, not some France. And they engaged in a bloody battle.

17   So I cite these various revolutions, brothers and sisters, to show you that you don't have a peaceful revolution. You don't have a turn-the-other-cheek revolution. There's no such thing as a nonviolent revolution. The only kind of revolution that is nonviolent is the Negro revolution. The only revolution in which the goal is loving your enemy is the Negro revolution. It's the only revolution in which the goal is a desegregated lunch counter, a desegregated theater, a desegregated park, and a desegregated public toilet; you can sit down next to white folks—on the toilet. That's no revolution. Revolution is based on land. Land is the basis of all independence. Land is the basis of freedom, justice, and equality.

18   The white man knows what a revolution is. He knows that the black revolution is world-wide in scope and in nature. The black revolution is sweeping Asia, is sweeping Africa, is rearing its head in Latin America. The Cuban Revo-

lution—that's a revolution. They overturned the system. Revolution is in Asia, revolution is in Africa, and the white man is screaming because he sees revolution in Latin America. How do you think he'll react to you when you learn what a real revolution is? You don't know what a revolution is. If you did, you wouldn't use that word.

19   Revolution is bloody, revolution is hostile, revolution knows no compromise, revolution overturns and destroys everything that gets in its way. And you, sitting around here like knot on the wall, saying, "I'm going to love these folks no matter how much they hate me." No, you need a revolution. Whoever heard of a revolution where they lock arms, as Rev. Cleage was pointing out beautifully, singing "We Shall Overcome"? You don't do that in a revolution. You don't do any singing, you're too busy swinging. It's based on land. A revolutionary wants land so he can set up his own nation, an independent nation. These Negroes aren't asking for any nation—they're trying to crawl back on the plantation.

20   When you want a nation, that's called nationalism. When the white man become involved in a revolution in this country against England, what was it for? He wanted this land so he could set up another white nation. That's white nationalism. The American Revolution was white nationalism. The French Revolution was white nationalism. The Russian Revolution too—yes, it was—white nationalism. You don't think so? Why do you think Khrushchev and Mao can't get their heads together? White nationalism. All the revolutions that are going on in Asia and Africa today are based on what? —black nationalism. A revolutionary is a black nationalist. He wants a nation. I was reading some beautiful words by Rev. Cleage, pointing out why he couldn't get together with someone else in the city because all of them were afraid of being identified with black nationalism. If you're afraid of black nationalism, you're afraid of revolution. And if you love revolution, you love black nationalism.

21   To understand this, you have to go back to what the young brother here referred to as the house Negro and the field Negro back during slavery. There were two kinds of slaves, the house Negro and the field Negro. The house Negroes—they lived in the house with the master, they dressed pretty good, they ate good because they ate his food—what he left. They lived in the attic or the basement, but still they lived near the master; and they loved the master more than the master loved himself. They would give their life to save the master's house—quicker than the master would. If the master said, "We got a good house here," the house Negro would say, "Yeah, we got a good house here." Whenever the master said "we," he said "we." That's how you can tell a house Negro.

22   If the master's house caught on fire, the house Negro would fight harder to put the blaze out than the master would. If the master got sick, the house Negro would say, "What's the matter, boss, *we* sick?" *We* sick! He identified himself with his master, more than his master identified with himself. And if you came to the house Negro and said, "Let's run away, let's escape, let's separate," the house Negro would look at you and say, "Man, you crazy. What you mean, separate? Where is there a better house than this? Where can I wear better clothes than this? Where can I eat better food than this?" That was that house Negro.

In those days he was called a "house nigger." And that's what we call them to-day, because we've still got some house niggers running around here.

23   This modern house Negro loves his master. He wants to live near him. He'll pay three times as much as the house is worth just to live near his master, and then brag about "I'm the only Negro out here." "I'm the only one on my job." "I'm the only one in this school." You're nothing but a house Negro. And if someone comes to you right now and says, "Let's separate," you say the same thing that the house Negro said on the plantation. "What you mean, separate? From America, this good white man? Where you going to get a better job than you get here?" I mean, this is what you say. "I ain't left nothing in Africa," that's what you say. Why, you left your mind in Africa.

24   On that same plantation, there was the field Negro. The field Negroes— those were the masses. There were always more Negroes in the field than there were Negroes in the house. The Negro in the field caught hell. He ate leftovers. In the house they ate high up on the hog. The Negro in the field didn't get any-thing but what was left of the insides of the hog. They call it "chitt'lings" nowa-days. In those days they called them what they were—guts. That's what you were—gut-eaters. And some of you are still gut-eaters.

25   The field Negro was beaten from morning to night; he lived in a shack, in a hut; he wore old, castoff clothes. He hated his master. I say he hated his master. He was intelligent. That house Negro loved his master, but the field Negro—re-member, they were in the majority, and they hated the master. When the house caught on fire, he didn't try to put it out; that field Negro prayed for a wind, for a breeze. When the master got sick, the field Negro prayed that he'd die. If someone came to the field Negro and said, "Let's separate, let's run," he didn't say, "Where we going?" He'd say, "Any place is better than here." You've got field Negroes in America today. I'm a field Negro. The masses are the field Ne-groes. When you see this man's house on fire, you don't hear the little Negroes talking about "*our* government is in trouble." They say, "*The* government is in trouble." Imagine a Negro: "*Our* government"! I even heard one say "*our* astro-nauts!" They won't even let him near the plant—and "our astronauts"! "*Our* Navy" —that's a Negro that is out of his mind, a Negro that is out of his mind.

26   Just as the slavemaster of that day used Tom, the house Negro, to keep the field Negroes in check, the same old slavemaster today has Negroes who are nothing but modern Uncle Toms, twentieth-century Uncle Toms, to keep you and me in check, to keep us under control, keep us passive and peaceful and nonviolent. That's Tom making you nonviolent. It's like when you go to the dentist, and the man's going to take your tooth. You're going to fight him when he starts pulling. So he squirts some stuff in your jaw called novocaine, to make you think they're not doing anything to you. So you sit there and because you've got all that novocaine in your jaw, you suffer—peacefully. Blood run-ning down your jaw, and you don't know what's happening. Because someone has taught you to suffer—peacefully.

27   The white man does the same thing to you in the street, when he wants to put knots on your head and take advantage of you and not have to be afraid of your fighting back. To keep you from fighting back, he gets these old religious

Uncle Toms to teach you and me, just like novocaine, to suffer peacefully. Don't stop suffering—just suffer peacefully. As Rev. Cleage pointed out, they say you should let your blood flow in the streets. This is a shame. You know he's a Christian preacher. If it's a shame to him, you know what it is to me.

28   There is nothing in our book, the Koran, that teaches us to suffer peacefully. Our religion teaches us to be intelligent. Be peaceful, be courteous, obey the law, respect everyone; but if someone puts his hand on you, send him to the cemetery. That's a good religion. In fact, that's that old-time religion. That's the one that Ma and Pa used to talk about: an eye for an eye, and a tooth for a tooth, and a head for a head, and a life for a life. That's a good religion. And nobody resents that kind of religion being taught but a wolf, who intends to make you his meal.

29   This is the way it is with the white man in America. He's a wolf—and you're sheep. Any time a shepherd, a pastor, teaches you and me not to run from the white man and, at the same time, teaches us not to fight the white man, he's a traitor to you and me. Don't lay down a life all by itself. No, preserve your life, it's the best thing you've got. And if you've got to give it up, let it be even-steven.

FOR ANALYSIS AND DISCUSSION

1. Who does Malcolm X identify as the "common enemy"? Who does he include or exclude from his definition of the "common enemy"? What does he hope to achieve by identifying this common enemy to his audience?
2. Several times during his speech, Malcolm X comments on the variety of "black people" in the world: "black, brown, red, yellow." Yet in paragraphs 7 and 8, Malcolm X classifies all white people as blond and blue-eyed. Why do you think he defines the races this way? What effect do you think it provokes in the audience? Is there any irony in his classification? Explain.
3. Why do you think Malcolm X lists great revolutions for freedom in his speech? What is the point he is trying to make by citing these revolutions? How does his message differ from that of Martin Luther King, Jr.?
4. What term does Malcolm X use to describe African Americans who work within the established social system? What does he compare them to? What effect do you think this comparison has on his audience? Why is audience important to the success of this speech?
5. How would Malcolm X react to Jan Howard's theory about the uses of violence? Support your response with specific examples from his speech and Howard's essay.

WRITING ASSIGNMENTS: NONVIOLENCE/VIOLENCE

1. Reread the letter by Martin Luther King, Jr. and the speech by Malcolm X. What are the similarities and differences between King's and Malcolm X's strategies for achieving equality for African Americans? In a well-organized argument, explain why you believe one method has been more effective in the struggle for civil rights or why neither was. Support your essay with informa-

tion from the articles, as well as outside research. For more information about Malcolm X, try the CMG Web site at <http://www.cmgww.com/historic/malcolm/malcolm.html>. The University of Oregon maintains a comprehensive archive dedicated to Web resources on Martin Luther King, Jr. at <http://darkwing.uoregon.edu/~holman/mlk/mlk.html>. There are also numerous books and journal articles about these two historical figures.

2. Using the techniques employed in King's letter from the Birmingham jail, write a letter directed toward people you respect protesting an injustice that you feel they may not entirely understand. Take care to take the concerns of your audience into account as you explain the nature of the injustice, the reasons for the injustice, and the reasons why your argument should be accepted.

3. In 1960, four college freshmen sat down at a lunch counter in Greensboro, North Carolina, and ordered sodas, coffee, and doughnuts. They were not served, but then again, they did not expect to be. These four young men, who later came to be known as the "Greensboro Four," were staging a "sit-in." Research the situation at Greensboro at <http://www.greensboro.com/sitins>. What role did sit-ins play in the fight for civil rights? Were they effective in promoting change? Were these four young men, or the students who followed them, that different from you? With a group of four or five students, discuss how you would stage a sit-in today. What would you protest? How would you try to effect change?

EQUAL OPPORTUNITY: OUTLAWING DISCRIMINATION

My Dungeon Shook: Letter to My Nephew on the One Hundredth Anniversary of the Emancipation
James Baldwin

Racism, many people would agree, is still alive in America today. The following essay presents an African American perspective on racism. In it, James Baldwin asks his nephew to look beyond the expectations of the white establishment and to succeed despite the boundaries society has tried to place on him.

James Baldwin was born and educated in New York City. In 1948 he moved to Paris to pursue a career as a writer, but he returned to the United States in 1957 to help fight in the civil rights movement. Considered one of America's foremost African American writers, Baldwin's works include *Another Country, Nobody Knows My Name,* and the play *Blues for Mister Charlie.* He died in 1987. At the time of this death, Baldwin was working on a biography of Martin Luther King, Jr.

BEFORE YOU READ

In what ways is racism apparent where you live? How do geography and location influence racism?

AS YOU READ

What is Baldwin's tone in this essay? Consider how his tone might influence audiences of different races.

Dear James:

1   I have begun this letter five times and torn it up five times. I keep seeing your face, which is also the face of your father and my brother. Like him, you are tough, dark, vulnerable, moody—with a very definite tendency to sound truculent because you want no one to think you are soft. You may be like your grandfather in this, I don't know, but certainly both you and your father resemble him very much physically. Well, he is dead, he never saw you, and he had a terrible life; he was defeated long before he died because, at the bottom of his heart, he

On May 28, 1963, African American students and a white professor staged a sit-in at a Woolworth's lunch counter in Jackson, Mississippi, to protest its segregation. White youths sprayed them with ketchup, mustard, sugar, soda, and even spray paint; then the angry crowd beat them.

really believed what white people said about him. This is one of the reasons that he became so holy. I am sure that your father has told you something about all that. Neither you nor your father exhibit any tendency towards holiness: you really *are* of another era, part of what happened when the Negro left the land and came into what the late E. Franklin Frazier called "the cities of destruction." You can only be destroyed by believing that you really are what the white world calls a *nigger*. I tell you this because I love you, and please don't you ever forget it.

2   I have known both of you all your lives, have carried your Daddy in my arms and on my shoulders, kissed and spanked him and watched him learn to walk. I don't know if you've known anybody from that far back; if you've loved anybody that long, first as an infant, then as a child, then as a man, you gain a strange perspective on time and human pain and effort. Other people cannot see what I see whenever I look into your father's face, for behind your father's face as it is today are all those other faces which were his. Let him laugh and I see a cellar your father does not remember and a house he does not remember and I hear in his present laughter his laughter as a child. Let him curse and I remember him falling down the cellar steps, and howling, and I remember, with pain, his tears, which my hand or your grandmother's so easily wiped away. But no one's hand can wipe away those tears he sheds invisibly today, which one hears in his laughter and in his speech and in his songs. I know what the world has done to my brother and how narrowly he has survived it. And I know, which is much worse, and this is the crime of which I accuse my country and my countrymen, and for which neither I nor time nor history will ever forgive them, that they have destroyed and are destroying hundreds of thousands of lives and do not know it and do not want to know it. One can be, indeed one must strive to become, tough and philosophical concerning destruction and death, for this is what most of mankind has been best at since we have heard of man. (But remember: *most* of mankind is not *all* of mankind.) But it is not permissible that the authors of devastation should also be innocent. It is the innocence which constitutes the crime.

3   Now, my dear namesake, these innocent and well-meaning people, your countrymen, have caused you to be born under conditions not very far removed from those described for us by Charles Dickens in the London of more than a hundred years ago. (I hear the chorus of the innocents screaming, "No! This is not true! How *bitter* you are!" —but I am writing this letter to *you*, to try to tell you something about how to handle *them*, for most of them do not yet really know that you exist. I *know* the conditions under which you were born, for I was there. Your countrymen were *not* there, and haven't made it yet. Your grandmother was also there, and no one has ever accused her of being bitter. I suggest that the innocents check with her. She isn't hard to find. Your countrymen don't know that *she* exists, either, though she has been working for them all their lives.)

4   Well, you were born, here you came, something like fifteen years ago; and though your father and mother and grandmother, looking about the streets through which they were carrying you, staring at the walls into which they brought you, had every reason to be heavyhearted, yet they were not. For here you were, Big James, named for me—you were a big baby, I was not—here you

were: to be loved. To be loved, baby, hard, at once, and forever, to strengthen
you against the loveless world. Remember that: I know how black it looks today,
for you. It looked bad that day, too, yes, we were trembling. We have not
stopped trembling yet, but if we had not loved each other none of us would
have survived. And now you must survive because we love you, and for the sake
of your children and your children's children.

5   This innocent country set you down in a ghetto in which, in fact, it intended
that you should perish. Let me spell out precisely what I mean by that, for the
heart of the matter is here, and the root of my dispute with my country. You
were born where you were born and faced the future that you faced because you
were black and *for no other reason*. The limits of your ambition were, thus, expected to be set forever. You were born into a society which spelled out with brutal clarity, and in as many ways as possible, that you were a worthless human being. You were not expected to aspire to excellence: you were expected to make
peace with mediocrity. Wherever you have turned, James, in your short time on
this earth, you have been told where you could go and what you could do (and
how you could do it) and where you could live and whom you could marry. I
know your countrymen do not agree with about this, and I hear them saying,
"You exaggerate." They do not know Harlem, and I do. So do you. Take no
one's word for anything, including mine—but trust your experience. Know
whence you came. If you know whence you came, there is really no limit to
where you can go. The details and symbols of your life have been deliberately
constructed to make you believe what white people say about you. Please try to
remember that what they believe, as well as what they do and cause you to endure, does not testify to your inferiority but to their inhumanity and fear. Please
try to be clear, dear James, through the storm which rages about your youthful
head today, about the reality which lies behind the words *acceptance* and *integration*. There is no reason for you to try to become like white people and there is
no basis whatever for their impertinent assumption that *they* must accept *you*.
The really terrible thing, old buddy, is that *you* must accept *them*. And I mean
that very seriously. You must accept them and accept them with love. For these
innocent people have no other hope. They are, in effect, still trapped in a history which they do not understand; and until they understand it, they cannot be
released from it. They have had to believe for many years, and for innumerable
reasons, that black men are inferior to white men. Many of them, indeed, know
better, but, as you will discover, people find it very difficult to act on what they
know. To act is to be committed, and to be committed is to be in danger. In this
case, the danger, in the minds of most white Americans, is the loss of their identity. Try to imagine how you would feel if you woke up one morning to find the
sun shining and all the stars aflame. You would be frightened because it is out of
the order of nature. Any upheaval in the universe is terrifying because it so profoundly attacks one's sense of one's own reality. Well, the black man has functioned in the white man's world as a fixed star, as an immovable pillar: and as he
moves out of his place, heaven and earth are shaken to their foundations. You,
don't be afraid. I said that it was intended that you should perish in the ghetto,
perish by never being allowed to go behind the white man's definitions, by

never being allowed to spell your proper name. You have, and many of us have, defeated this intention; and, by a terrible law, a terrible paradox, those innocents who believed that your imprisonment made them safe are losing their grasp of reality. But these men are your brothers—your lost, younger brothers. And if the word *integration* means anything, this is what it means: that we, with love, shall force our brothers to see themselves as they are, to cease fleeing from reality and begin to change it. For this is your home, my friend, do not be driven from it; great men have done great things here, and will again, and we can make America what America must become. It will be hard, James, but you come from sturdy, peasant stock, men who picked cotton and dammed rivers and built railroads, and, in the teeth of the most terrifying odds, achieved an unassailable and monumental dignity. You come from a long line of great poets, some of the greatest poets since Homer. One of them said, *The very time I thought I was lost, My dungeon shook and my chains fell off.*

6   You know, and I know, that the country is celebrating one hundred years of freedom one hundred years too soon. We cannot be free until they are free. God bless you, James, and Godspeed.

Your uncle,

James

FOR ANALYSIS AND DISCUSSION

1. What limitations, according to Baldwin, does society place on African Americans? Who is "society" in this essay? How are society's limitations expressed?
2. Who is presented as morally and intellectually superior in Baldwin's essay? On what evidence does he base his view? How are whites deluded and "trapped by their history"?
3. Baldwin states that his goal is to "force our brothers to see themselves as they are, [and] to cease fleeing from reality." Who are these brothers? What is the reality that they must see and face? Do you agree with Baldwin's concept of reality? Explain.
4. This letter was written to Baldwin's nephew on the one hundredth anniversary of emancipation. Why do you think Baldwin chose this date? How do the sentiments expressed in his letter connect to this historical event?
5. How effective is Baldwin's title? How does it complement the content of his essay? What attitude does it convey?

President's Speech: June 11, 1963
John F. Kennedy

In 1963 several protests—the most famous being in Birmingham, Alabama—were staged against racial segregation. Several weeks after the Alabama protests, Alabama governor George C. Wallace tried to block the registration of two black students into the University of Alabama. President Kennedy deployed the National Guard to the university to ensure the peaceful admission of the students. The evening of this event, Kennedy made a nationally televised speech commenting on his actions and calling for Americans to support the equality of all races. Within hours of Kennedy's speech Mississippi NAACP leader Medgar Evers was shot outside his home in Jackson, a victim of racial hatred.

BEFORE YOU READ

Imagine that you could be barred from attending a university based solely on your skin color. How would you react?

AS YOU READ

How does Kennedy explain his decision to deploy the National Guard? Consider what he says—and does not say—in his speech. What significance does he ascribe to the events at the University of Alabama?

1 This nation was founded by men of many nations and backgrounds. It was founded on the principle that all men are created equal; and that the rights of every man are diminished when the rights of one man are threatened.

2 It ought to be possible, therefore, for American students of any color to attend any public institution they select without having to be backed up by troops. It ought to be possible for American consumers of any color to receive equal service in places of public accommodation, such as hotels and restaurants, and theaters and retail stores, without being forced to resort to demonstrations in the street.

3 And it ought to be possible for American citizens of any color to register and to vote in a free election without interference or fear of reprisal.

4 It ought to be possible, in short, for every American to enjoy the privileges of being American without regard to his race or his color.

5 This is not a sectional issue. Difficulties over segregation and discrimination exist in every city, in every state of the Union, producing in many cities a rising tide of discontent that threatens the public safety.

6 Nor is this a partisan issue. In a time of domestic crisis, men of goodwill and generosity should be able to unite regardless of party or politics.

7 This is not even a legal or legislative issue alone. It is better to settle these matters in the courts than on the streets, and new laws are needed at every level. But law alone cannot make men see right.

8 We are confronted primarily with a moral issue. It is as old as the Scriptures and is as clear as the American Constitution. The heart of the question is whether all Americans are to be afforded equal rights and equal opportunities; whether we are going to treat our fellow Americans as we want to be treated.

9 If an American, because his skin is dark, cannot eat lunch in a restaurant open to the public; if he cannot send his children to the best public schools available; if he cannot vote for the public officials who represent him; if, in short, he cannot enjoy the full and free life which all of us want, then who

among us would be content to have the color of his skin changed and stand in his place?

10   Who among us would then be content with the counsels of patience and delay? One hundred years of delay have passed since President Lincoln freed the slaves, yet their heirs, their grandsons, are not fully free. They are not yet freed from the bonds of injustice; they are not yet freed from social and economic oppression.

11   And this nation, for all its hopes and all its boasts, will not be fully free until all its citizens are free.

12   Now the time has come for this nation to fulfill its promise. The events in Birmingham and elsewhere have so increased the cries for equality that no city or state or legislative body can prudently choose to ignore them.

13   The fires of frustration and discord are burning in every city, North and South. Where legal remedies are not at hand, redress is sought in the streets in demonstrations, parades and protests, which create tensions and threaten violence—and threaten lives.

14   We face, therefore, a moral crisis as a country and a people. It cannot be met by repressive police action. It cannot be left to increased demonstrations in the streets. It cannot be quieted by token moves or talk. It is a time to act in the Congress, in your state and local legislative body, and, above all, in all of our daily lives.

15   I am, therefore, asking the Congress to enact legislation giving all Americans the right to be served in facilities which are open to the public—hotels, restaurants and theaters, retail stores and similar establishments. This seems to me to be an elementary right.

16   I'm also asking Congress to authorize the Federal Government to participate more fully in lawsuits designed to end segregation in public education. We have succeeded in persuading many districts to desegregate voluntarily. Dozens have admitted Negroes without violence.

17   Other features will also be requested, including greater protection for the right to vote.

18   But legislation, I repeat, cannot solve this problem alone. It must be solved in the homes of every American in every community across our country.

19   In this respect, I want to pay tribute to those citizens, North and South, who've been working in their communities to make life better for all.

20   They are acting not out of a sense of legal duty but out of a sense of human decency. Like our soldiers and sailors in all parts of the world, they are meeting freedom's challenge on the firing line, and I salute them for their honor—their courage.

FOR ANALYSIS AND DISCUSSION

1. Kennedy claims that the American people are confronted with a "moral issue." Explain what he means. Why do you think he cites both the Constitution *and* the Scriptures? To what scriptural reference is he referring? How does this reference support his view?

2. What is the "promise" Kennedy states the nation must now fulfill? When was this promise made? How is it to be achieved? Use references from the speech to support your response.

3. Can you draw any parallels between the situation in Alabama in 1963 and contemporary U.S. society? For example, the admission of female students into some military institutions has met with resistance in recent years. Do any similarities exist between the two situations? Explain.

4. To whom is Kennedy's speech directed? Can you determine his audience? Why is it important that Kennedy consider his audience when delivering this speech?

5. Do you think this is an effective speech? Is it logical and well constructed? Does it appeal to reason or emotion? Explain.

From Sharecropper to Lobbyist: The Political Awakening of Fannie Lou Hamer
Fannie Lou Hamer

Fannie Lou Hamer was born in 1917 in Montgomery County, Mississippi, the granddaughter of a slave and the child of sharecroppers. In 1962 she tried to register to vote at the courthouse in Indianola, Mississippi. She and eleven other blacks were arrested because their bus was "the wrong color." A year later, after being arrested for participating in a civil rights event, Hamer was severely beaten in Montgomery County Jail, a beating orchestrated by the police. In 1964 she traveled to Atlantic City to tell the Democratic Party's national convention about the atrocities occurring in the Mississippi Delta. She challenged the all-white Mississippi delegation on the grounds that it did not fairly represent the state because most blacks were illegally prevented from voting. As a direct result, the Democrats agreed that in the future no delegation would be allowed into a convention from a state where anyone was illegally denied the vote. A year later, President Johnson signed the Voting Rights Act. A civil rights activist for many years, Fannie Lou Hamer died in 1977. The following excerpt is taken from Hamer's autobiography, *To Praise Our Bridges*.

BEFORE YOU READ

Imagine trying to register to vote, only to be arrested for driving a car that was the wrong color. Who would you turn to for help?

AS YOU READ

Consider the extreme poverty in which Hamer grew up. How did whites use this poverty to control blacks? Remember these events occurred in the South only 40 years ago.

1   . . . My parents were sharecroppers and they had a big family. Twenty children. Fourteen boys and six girls. I'm the twentieth child. All of us worked in the fields, of course, but we never did get anything out of sharecropping. We'd make fifty and sixty bales and end up with nothing.

2   I was about six years old when I first went to the fields to pick cotton. I can remember very well the landowner telling me one day that if I would pick thirty pounds he would give me something out of the commissary: some Cracker-Jacks, Daddy Wide-Legs, and some sardines. These were things that he knew I loved and never had a chance to have. So I picked my thirty pounds that day. Well, the next week I had to pick sixty and by the time I was thirteen I was picking two and three hundred pounds.

3   . . . Well, after the white man killed off our mules, my parents never did get a chance to get up again. We went back to sharecropping, halving, it's called. You split the cotton half and half with the plantation owner. But the seed, fertilizer, cost of hired hands, everything is paid out of the cropper's half. My parents tried so hard to do what they could to keep us in school, but school didn't last but four months out of the year and most of the time we didn't have clothes to wear. I dropped out of school and cut corn stalks to help the family.

4   . . . I married in 1944 and stayed on the plantation until 1962, when I went down to the courthouse in Indianola to register to vote. That happened because I went to a mass meeting one night.

5   Until then I'd never heard of no mass meeting and I didn't know that a Negro could register and vote. Bob Moses, Reggie Robinson, Jim Bevel, and James Forman were some of the SNCC workers who ran that meeting. When they asked for those to raise their hands who'd go down to the courthouse the next day, I raised mine. Had it up high as I could get it. I guess if I'd had any sense I'd-a-been a little scared, but what was the point of being scared. The only thing they could do to me was kill me and it seemed like they'd been trying to do that a little bit at a time since I could remember.

6   . . . Well, there was eighteen of us who went down to the courthouse that day and all of us were arrested. Police said the bus was painted the wrong color—said it was too yellow. After I got bailed out I went back to the plantation where Pap and I had lived for eighteen years. My oldest girl met me and told me that Mr. Marlow, the plantation owner, was mad and raising sand. He had heard that I had tried to register. That night he called on us and said, "We're not going to have this in Mississippi and you will have to withdraw. I am looking for your answer, yea or nay?" I just looked. He said, "I will give you until tomorrow morning. And if you don't withdraw, you will have to leave. If you do go withdraw, it's only how I feel, you might still have to leave." So I left the same night. Pap had to stay on till work on the plantation was through. Ten days later they fired into Mrs. Tucker's house where I was staying. They also shot two girls at Mr. Sissel's.

7   . . . What I really feel is necessary is that the black people in this country will have to upset this applecart. We can no longer ignore the fact that America is NOT the ". . . land of the free and the home of the brave." I used to question this

for years—what did our kids actually fight for? They would go in the service and go through all of that and come right out to be drowned in the river in Mississippi.

8   . . . I've work on voter registration here ever since I went to that first mass meeting. In 1964, we registered 63,000 black people from Mississippi into the Freedom Democratic Party. We formed our own party because the whites wouldn't even let us register. We decided to challenge the white Mississippi Democratic Party at the National Convention. We followed all the laws the white people themselves made. We tried to attend the precinct meetings and they locked the doors on us or moved the meetings and that's against the law they made for their own selves. So we were the ones that held the real precinct meetings. At all these meetings across the state we elected our representatives to go to the National Democratic Convention in Atlantic City. But we learned the hard way that even though we had all the law and all the righteousness on our side, that white man is not going to give up his power to us.

9   We have to build our own power. We have to win every single political office we can, where we have a majority of black people. . . . The question for black people is not, when is the white man going to give us our rights, or when is he going to give us good education for our children, or when is he going to give us jobs—if the white man gives you anything—just remember when he gets ready he will take it right back. We have to take for ourselves.

10   . . . I went to Africa in 1964 and I learned that I sure didn't have anything to be ashamed of from being black. Being from the South we never was taught much about our African heritage. The way everybody talked to us, everybody in Africa was savages and really stupid people. But I've seen more savage white folks here in America than I seen in Africa. I saw black men flying the airplanes, driving buses, sitting behind the big desks in the bank and just doing everything that I was used to seeing white people do. I saw, for the first time in my life, a black stewardess walking through the plane and that was quite an inspiration for me.

11   . . . I was treated much better in Africa than I was treated in America. I often get letters that say, "Go back to Africa." Now I have just as much if not more right to stay in America as whoever wrote those letters. . . . It is our right to stay here and we stay and fight for what belongs to us.

FOR ANALYSIS AND DISCUSSION

1. What is the tone of Hamer's essay? Is it bitter, resigned, controlled, or triumphant? How does her tone influence her message?
2. In what ways was the condition of poverty used to keep African Americans politically impotent? What other tactics were employed to keep blacks out of the political arena? How does Hamer feel about this strategy? How does she hope to overcome this control?
3. Who is Hamer trying to reach in this essay? What is she trying to accomplish? Is her essay effective? Does it achieve her objective? Explain why or why not.
4. What message does Hamer have for those whites that tell her to "go back to Africa"? How does Africa compare to the America of Hamer's experience? Is

Hamer's America the only one? Do you think Hamer's experience would have been different had she been born in Detroit or Boston?

The Beginnings of a New Age
Edgar N. French

On December 1, 1955, Rosa Parks, a black woman, was arrested in Montgomery, Alabama, for refusing to surrender her seat on a bus to a white man. On December 5 she was found guilty and fined for the offense. That same day, blacks began to boycott the buses of Montgomery. The year-long boycott marked the beginning of many other unified civil rights actions protesting the injustices facing African Americans.

Several months into the bus boycott, black citizens held a mass meeting and voted unanimously to quit the boycott. Edgar N. French, a minister of the A.M.E. Zion Church in Montgomery and the secretary of the Montgomery Improvement Association, which directed the boycott, stood before the crowd and preached so powerfully that all were persuaded to continue the protest. In the following essay French reflects on the hardships and meaning of this pivotal event for the civil rights movement.

BEFORE YOU READ

What would you do if you were denied rights that were guaranteed you under the U.S. Constitution? What if the police and local politicians refused to hear your complaints?

AS YOU READ

Consider how French describes the political and social situations in Montgomery in 1955–1956. What would it have been like to be living in Montgomery during that time?

1   The ground-swell of social unrest erupted like a great volcano in the city of Montgomery, State of Alabama, December 5, 1955. The city, the state, the nation, and the world were stuck dumb by the unusual, unexpected, and un-dreamed of phenomenon which followed the arrest, trial and conviction of what might have been "just another Negro citizen." Newspapers, radio, and television spread the news: "Negroes Boycott Buses in Montgomery, Alabama." While this message was relayed around the world, the white City Fathers asked, "Where are our Negroes? These are strange people, far different from the Negroes we have known." Little did they realize that a combination of conditions and circumstances which had existed for many years had, slowly but surely, cast a new Negro to replace the old Negro in the South.

2   The State of Alabama is proud of its geographical location. The license plate on every motor vehicle in the state bears the inscription "Heart of Dixie."

Likewise the city of Montgomery takes pride in its history, boasting of the fact that it is the cradle of the Confederacy. Even though the guns of the Civil War were silenced almost a hundred years ago and the breach in the union was declared mended, the freedom for which the war was waged and won had not been fully realized by the southern blacks or whites in 1955, nor fully realized even to this date.

3   What precipitated the Montgomery crisis? This is a question many people have asked, but only the over-zealous, over-confident or foolish dare to offer a conclusive answer. After years of reflection on the movement, or "boycott," as it was called, this writer can offer only his personal view, as a participant, of the circumstances and conditions which precipitated the breakthrough, a breakthrough that crystallized the attitudes of the Negro people into a mass protest against local customs.

4   The conditions existing in other cities and states which were causing the oppressed people to seek relief through the courts were also to be found in Montgomery, Alabama. Here, too, the white citizens were of the opinion that the Negro had no rights which the white man was bound to respect. Here, too, the gospel of the Fatherhood of God and the Brotherhood of Man was proclaimed from pulpits, as the voices of Negroes and whites, separately assembled in their respective churches on opposite sides of Dexter Avenue, blended in the air to the pleasure of passers-by as each group sang, "Jesus, Lover of My Soul, Let Me to Thy Bosom Fly."

5   The laws of the white worshippers made mandatory some line of demarcation whenever whites and Negroes assembled. The *Plessy vs. Ferguson* decision, which gave legal sanction to the dual system of education under the doctrine of separate but equal, also gave sanction to the denial of educational opportunity for Negro children. Denial of educational opportunity led to denial of job opportunity, and economic inequality to social inequality.

6   It would be a mistake to assert that the Negro citizens of this southern metropolis had not tried to free themselves from the shackles which had bound them through the years prior to the Supreme Court decision of 1954. The desire for freedom and first-class citizenship had become the obsession of every man and woman of color who had felt the piercing pangs of oppression. But every effort put forth to break segregation and discrimination was met by double and sometimes triple counter-attack by the white citizens.

7   By 1953, there was a peculiar kind of social unrest. The common people were voluntarily discussing their desire to exercise fully and freely their rights as citizens and to be treated and respected as human beings. It was not at all uncommon to hear a colored citizen say, "We have been in *this* all of our lives! WE are tired of *this!* We want somebody to lead us out of *this!* We are willing to do whatever is necessary. We want somebody to tell us what to do and show us how to do it . . . " In order to understand fully what the people meant by "this," one would have had to live in Montgomery prior to December, 1955. But some understanding can be gained by taking a look at the circumstances which gave rise to an historic movement.

8   There are two means of public conveyance in Montgomery: taxi and bus. It is unlawful as well as improper for a white cab operator to pick up a Negro passenger, unless the passenger is a Negro woman and the cab driver has immoral designs. It is next to impossible to describe to the average American citizen the internal turmoil that seizes an individual when he is refused a needed service because of his color or race.

9   A line of demarcation separated the racial groups on the Montgomery buses which carried thousands of people to their destinations daily. The dividing line sometimes took the form of a sign designating the area for Negroes and the area for whites. More often than no, on predominantly Negro streets, separation of races was declared in terms of a number of seats reserved for "whites only." This, Negroes had learned, was the ideal; in reality, the line of demarcation was an imaginary line which existed only in the mind of the bus operator. Wherever his whims dictated, the dividing line was located. The determining factor of his whims was the number of white passengers boarding the bus at each stop. The flexibility of the line became apparent at stop number two, number three, and so on.

10   It was also not uncommon for bus drivers to pass by Negroes waiting at bus stops, because they knew whites were waiting several blocks ahead. Often, since Negroes could not easily pass whites who were standing in the front of crowded busses, they were forced to pay their fares and proceed to the rear for boarding. Many a Negro passenger was left standing without his fare, as the operator, failing to open the rear door, drove away.

11   Since the Civil War, Negroes have sought legal redress from the magistrates to the State Supreme Court, although they could easily foretell what the verdict would be. Case after case was squashed, thrown out, or, when tried and appealed, the verdict of lower courts was sustained. The Supreme Court decision of 1954 restored hope to a people who had come to feel themselves helpless victims of outrageous and inhuman treatment.

12   This new-found hope expressed itself in the events surrounding the arrest and conviction of Mrs. Rosa Parks, a Negro seamstress. On December 1, 1955, after working and shopping, Mrs. Park boarded a bus, paid the fare and took a seat in what was designated at that point as the area for Negroes. Soon the line of demarcation shifted to the rear of Mrs. Parks and she was ordered by the driver to move accordingly. A white man was standing by, awaiting her seat. She refused to move. Officers were summoned and Mrs. Parks was placed in jail.

13   Mrs. Rosa Parks was a typical American housewife who shared in the support of her household by working as a seamstress in a downtown department store. As a member of the Methodist Church, she was held in high esteem by her fellow parishioners. Although mild-mannered and soft-spoken, the warmth and radiance of her personality bespoke her presence in almost any setting. The reason given by Mrs. Parks for her refusal to move when ordered to do so was, "My feet were hurting. I'd been working and shopping all day and I was tired."

14   The news of the arrest of Mrs. Parks was immediately seized upon as a means of giving united expression to the new-found hope which had stemmed

from the Supreme Court decision. The Negro Interdenominational Ministerial Alliance was called into immediate session, and to this meeting came other prominent civic and social leaders. In every heart and mind was the thought that now we must register our protest against the inhuman, unchristian, unlawful, and unethical indignities which we have suffered through the years.

15   A strange sense of community and group consciousness seized each person present. This same attitude would soon be realized in many places. Not only was Mrs. Rosa Parks arrested but every Negro in Montgomery felt arrested. The penalties which were soon to be pronounced on her, also awaited all other people of color, who dared to defy the "beasts of Ephesus." Group consciousness did not exclude from its consideration the whites, who later were to be referred to sympathetically and with various degrees of affection as "our white brethren." The group was mindful of the difficulty of holding another in a pit without actually restricting the holder's freedom. The action decided upon to gain our freedom had to be of such a nature as would point up the thoughtlessness of our oppressors.

16   The meeting opened on the note of the denial of our civil rights. It closed with the decision that we should register our protest against the arrest and trial of the latest victim of "cock-crowing White Supremacy" in Montgomery. No Negro was to ride a bus to work or to town, not even to the hospital, on Monday, December 5, 1955.

17   There were approximately three dozen people present at this meeting on Saturday, December 3rd, a number that was to multiply itself more than a thousandfold, two days later, on the evening of the fifth. This small group set itself the mammoth task of getting their protest decision over to the 50,000 Negroes who lived in the various sections of the large city. They divided the city into sections and assigned individuals to cover each section. The assignees were responsible for notifying everyone in their area. It was important that not one family should be missed. This seemed like a staggering, if not an impossible, assignment, but the self-appointed mailmen began their deliveries the same night. A prepared statement was to be placed under as many doors and in as many mail boxes as possible by late Saturday night. All Negro ministers were asked to announce the protest plan to their congregations on Sunday. All sermons were to be concerned with some aspect of social justice with emphasis upon what was happening in Montgomery—a wonderful challenge during Advent.

18   The Saturday night check-up revealed that much had been accomplished, through many women had twisted shoe heels, several had developed bunions, and all had tired legs. Overweight ministers assured themselves that walking was good for the waistline. Although there was not time for pastoral visits, ministers had been closer to the realities of living in slum areas than ever before. They had really been among poorly clad and undernourished children, alcoholics, and many other forms of human deprivation they hardly realized existed. The stark evils of social and economic injustices experienced in these few hours made it easy for many of the ministers to discard their well-prepared manuscripts at the Sunday Worship hour, and to speak concerning the evils of

their day. Many of the school teachers involved laid aside their economic and sociology text books the following Monday and taught absolute reality instead of superficial idealism.

19   A few brokenhearted, unpaid postmen reported at the end of that Saturday, that their area was too broad to cover. Some families had been missed. Some would call it fate, others might say luck, but for this hard-working group, God was on their side! One of the notices intended only for Negroes fell into the hands of a reporter for the local newspaper, *The Montgomery Advertiser.* With comments appropriate to inform every reader of the intention of the Negroes, the paper carried the words of the circular exactly as it was printed:

> Another Negro has been arrested and thrown in jail because she refused to give up her seat on a bus . . . Trial will be held Monday, December 5 . . . No Negro will ride any city bus on Monday to work, to town or any place . . . Don't ride the bus Monday! Report to Holt Street Baptist Church, Monday night for further instruction.

The group gave a sigh of relief Sunday morning as they read this notice on the front page of a paper which reached almost every family in the city. Now *everyone* had the message. But would they respond?

20   The morning of December 5th found ministers out of bed at an hour unusual for most men of the cloth; they had to know if the message had really been understood. Buses were checked from 5 a.m. until the hour for the trial. No Negroes were riding! Really a few Negroes who were hard-pressed to get to their jobs might have ridden, but again providence came to the aid of those who were struggling for justice.

21   The white City Fathers felt confident that the group leading the protest was a "goon squad" designed to prevent, by force, Negroes from riding the buses. Arrangements were made for two police motorcycles to lead, and two squad cars to follow each bus into the Negro sections, presumably to haul in anyone deemed an interferer. The less-informed Negroes regarded this unusual spectacle as a plan to keep Negroes *off* the buses. Therefore, the plan of the City Fathers worked in reverse. The few colored people who went to the bus stops as usual, upon seeing the unusual spectacle of a police escort, were frightened away.

22   This first phase of the beginning of a new age for an oppressed people in the "Heart of Dixie" bore an outward sign of victory, although a long, hard struggle lay ahead. There was almost complete consensus that this was the time the Negroes should take a firm stand for their freedom. "We have proven to ourselves that we can stick together. We have shown the white people that we can stick together. Let us stand firmly until they know we mean business." Such statements were on the lips of the colored citizens milling about the streets. Many of these people took a holiday, their only reason being, "We want to celebrate!" . . .

23   Many southern whites regard themselves as masters, and Negroes as servants who are to obey their every command. Such was the case with the authorities of Montgomery. They *commanded* the Negroes to return to the buses, after

which, they promised, they would give consideration to their grievances. "Negroes cannot force us to do anything," they said. "We have the economic and
political power. We can crush you at will. We have laws you must obey. If we do
not have a law on the books for the crime you are committing, we will make a
law. Return to the buses and then we will talk with your leaders. Return or we
will crush you!"

24   When this ultimatum was not obeyed, every conceivable attempt was made
to deprive the Negro of even the third class citizenship which was reluctantly
accorded him. The city police force was expanded to ensure that the job be
well done. Colored drivers stopping to pick up their wives in the downtown
area were given tickets for blocking traffic. Responsible drivers, followed by pa-
trols, were given tickets for speeding, reckless driving, or whatever charge could
be dreamed up at the moment. Negroes on the streets were attacked by groups
of white men and beaten mercilessly. Negroes at home and in offices were harassed day and night by paid white telephone operators. Homes and churches
were bombed. But an enlarged police force could "catch" nothing but innocent Negro drivers! . . .

25   The beginning of this "get-tough policy," as the city officials called it,
proved to be trying for the Negro citizens. We had preached, "Love your enemies," "Do good to those who hate you," "Render not evil for evil, but overcome evil with good." The time had come for the real test of these preachments. Were our people prepared to practice what they had been taught? Had
we reached the point where our faith in the ultimate triumph of justice over injustice would enable us to stand firmly for what we knew to be right? We were
mindful of the claims of those who had held that they were the controllers of
the wealth and power of the state. But we could not forget the ancient writer
who said, "The earth is the Lord's, the fullness thereof, the world and they that
dwell therein." We would stand with the ancient writer.

26   The mass arrest of nearly one hundred people in one day followed. The
firmness and passion of the struggling group came to the front. For the first
time, police officers were confronted by Negroes who acted like men. Some informed the officers to expect them to report to jail at a certain hour. One retired colored widow instructed an arresting officer to return to his post, saying,
"My chauffeur will drive me to jail." Many, who knew their names were on the
list, reported to the jail voluntarily. Others went calmly, and sat chatting
leisurely in the cells long after bonds had been arranged, doors had been
opened, and they were free to go. Some, like myself, do not even know who
signed their bonds.

27   This was strange and unusual behavior for Negroes. Less than a year prior
to this event, they thought themselves defenseless against the unlawful cruelties
of their oppressors. The swinging of a "headache stick," the flashing of a gun by
a cop, or the threat of imprisonment had silenced thousands of voices that
might have cried out for justice. All of the threats which had been used to suppress the Negro had lost their potency. Iron bars and the prison cell could be a
pleasant sight if such meant freedom and first-class citizenship for all unborn

generations of American children. The thirst for freedom had pushed all fears into the background. The desire for full-fledged citizenship had rendered null and void any acceptance of second-class citizenship. The aspiration, resolve, and determination expressed by Patrick Henry in the statement, "I know not what course others may take, but as for me, give me liberty or give me death," obsessed these people who had been denied. There was no room for doubt that they would ever again accept anything less than first-class citizenship. It was a hard decision to make after years of compromise and complacency during which the better educated Negroes in Montgomery, as well as in many other places in the South, knew they were not allowed participation in government. For them, the claim that democracy is "government of the people, by the people, and for the people," was in fact a false claim, for if it were not false, then they were not people. But it was sheer folly to think of registering and voting, even though they paid their taxes and respected all laws.

28   Their decision to act confronted the group with a larger problem: *How* to win the rights guaranteed by the Constitution of the United States? We all knew we would have to fight hard and long. We knew the enemy was strong, but we had to be stronger. To a great extent we were outnumbered; but this could be balanced by strategy. The oppressors were experts in inflicting physical harm, but we would not raise a hand to harm a hair on anyone's head. We all believed that love is stronger than hate. If we were to help those who were persecuting us, we had to win them by firmness and love. We would respect them, respect ourselves, and consequently demand respect from them. . . .

29   Going to and from work without riding buses presented a great challenge. To lessen the hardship, all who owned cars were asked to pick up their neighbors on their way to work. Voluntary car pools formed quickly. Those who had reasonable distances to go were encouraged to walk. Many walked five to seven miles daily. Business and professional men and women, as well as housewives, who owned cars, cruised the streets and picked up people who were walking in the rain and cold, and drove them without pay to their jobs. . . .

30   As the days grew into weeks and the weeks into months, the signs of strain were on every face. The novelty of the protest was over. There were no indications that consideration would be given any of the proposals that had been made. Instead, there were loud, strong statements denouncing our actions and promising that more hardships would be heaped upon us if we continued our rebellious actions.

31   By this time the tires were well worn on the cars. Many of the family cars had broken down and there were not enough funds to repair them. And, as in the beginning of the movement, all local communication media remained closed to us. We could not even buy space in the local newspaper for a statement to the general public. Not only was "freedom of the press" denied us, but "freedom of speech" as well. When the association contacted the radio and television stations asking to pay for the privilege of making a statement to the nation, the request was denied. To the Negro leaders it seemed that the white man had created a monster of which the white man, himself, was deathly

afraid. They believed, as did the great President who said, "There is nothing to fear but fear itself."

32   The faith of the Negro in the unforeseen and the eternal had brought him through many seemingly impossible situations. This was, therefore, no exception. The word of the struggle did reach the outside world. Not many Negroes in the city asked for an explanation of how this publicity came about, nor did they try to explain the response of people everywhere whose generous contributions swelled the treasury from a few dollars to thousands. Their prayers and hopes were based on the belief that "God would make a way." When the way was opened they thanked God and walked in it.

33   The funds which came in abundance made possible the enlarging of the car pools, the purchasing of station wagons, the renting of a parking area downtown as a pickup station, the hiring of dispatchers, and the repairing of some of the cars which had been used in the early days of the struggle. This is not to say that these funds brought an end to sacrifice and suffering. Such would be far from the truth. There were many who never rode a car; until the end, they walked. But the contributions which came from so many people in many different places gave all renewed courage. The pain of the criticisms and insults hurled at them by the local whites was completely overcome by the expression of thousands who said by their actions, "We are with you to the end."

34   The new sense of dignity and worth of the individual conceived by the minority group in this Southern city expressed itself in many ways. The Negroes ceased to think of themselves as mere servants of their employers. They began to see themselves as important contributors to the economic, social, political, and spiritual progress of a great nation. The tremendous loss of revenue by the bus company in Montgomery focused the attention of the Negro upon the large part he played in the economic life of the city. The cooks, maids, and butlers gained new insights into their worth.

35   The Citizens' Council, in retaliation, recommended the firing of Negro help who refused to ride the buses. When thoughtless whites began to carry out this recommendation, important discoveries were made. The mistresses who turned their help away discovered, to their surprise, when the hour came for them to go to their business or social affairs that there was no one to care for little Betty and Paul; there were a thousand chores to be done about the house but there was no butler nor maid. Some maids, who were fired because they refused to pay for insults and for the privilege of standing over empty seats, found employment, either next door or further down the block in which they had worked for years. . . .

36   One morning a very old lady was seen approaching a bus stop. It was obvious that she was walking with severe difficulty. Her destination was her doctor's office. The hour of her appointment was near. There was not a car belonging to the car pool in sight. A long wait for one to return proved to be in vain. As she started on her way, a bus approached. The dispatchers at the post prevailed upon her to take the bus. "Everyone would understand. We will be happy to explain the circumstances at the mass meeting," they assured her. "We think you

are too tired to go on walking." The frail body, heavily taxed by years of hardship, moved slowly away, and to those who were encouraging her to ride the bus, she said, "I'll walk! I'll walk so someday all of God's children can ride in peace. Yes, my body is tired, but my soul is rested!" And she went on her way.

37   One bus driver told of an experience he had with a group of school children. It was a rainy day, and the weather was cold. Seeing the poorly-clad children walking in the rain and knowing they were not responsible for the boycott was more than he wanted to have on his conscience. Since there were no passengers on the bus, he stopped and invited them aboard, out of the rain. The response the children gave was indicative both of their involvement in the crisis and of the inadequacy of their training in the neglected segregated schools. "Us ain't ridin' no bus today," cried one child. "Us boycotting," said another. And turning, they walked proudly on in the rain.

38   What was it that provoked this uprising and set 50,000 Negroes solidly against the status quo? There is much to be said for "the straw which broke the camel's back." The deprivations and inhuman injustices heaped upon the Afro-Americans in the South for generations had left their mark. The racial group has been so welded together by wholesale injustices that what happened to one happened to all. There had been years and years when Negroes were lynched in Montgomery, one or more at a time. Little had been said about the lynchings and nothing had been done at all. Some Negroes bemoaned the situation, but for the most part nurtured their anxieties and fears in their bosoms. The year 1955 stood in marked contrast to this long-ago period. Somehow people had finally found courage in the midst of adversities. No longer would they be silent. No longer would they fail to act.

39   Those who hold that the Negro was a coward and afraid to speak out for himself may be able to find some justification for their claim. It is not difficult for the intelligent person to understand that there is not much left when manhood is taken from a man, no matter what his race. Anyone who has been reduced to the status of a slave, bound by the legal and social customs of his society, and brow-beaten and indoctrinated by false ideas of White Supremacy from his infancy does well to stand at all on his feet. But this is not the whole story. For years the Negroes in Montgomery, as elsewhere, had been crying, but their voices had been unheard, except by God, and their tears had not been seen. Many brave souls had dared to stand up against the "beasts of Ephesus," only to be hanged, shot, or driven from the city. But now there were too many to kill, or drive away.

40   Most of the Negroes recognized their legitimate claim to the rights and privileges accorded the citizens of Alabama, and the city of Montgomery, including access to all public facilities. They knew, from as far back as they could trace their families, that they had split rails, cleared forests, planted and harvested crops, dug ditches, paved roads and built the city. The pay received for their labor hardly provided them with the bare necessities of life. But they had planned well and spent wisely the little they had earned. Many had been on foreign soil defending a nation and a people which had given only lip service to

their rights in the democracy they were fighting to preserve. Those who returned brought back with them the desire to be respected for the services they had rendered and the sacrifices they had made. The newspapers, radio, and television brought into the homes of Negroes reports of current happenings from all over the world. The struggles of oppressed peoples for freedom everywhere evoked sympathetic response from companions in tribulation.

41   One must never underestimate the impact of the historic Supreme Court decision of May 17, 1954 on the Negroes throughout the South. However, history refutes any claim that this date marked the beginning of their struggle. The stony road leading to the decision bears the marks of disappointments, hardships, and setbacks. Legal battles were fought in courts where injustice seemed to triumph. Negro families had had their homes bombed, mortgages foreclosed, and had suffered other types of economic and social pressure, because they dared to demand equal educational opportunity for their children.

42   In spite of the agony and the heartache, parents in Southern States brought suits, and the legal staff of the N.A.A.C.P. continued to plead the cause of justice, citizenship, and constitutional rights for all Americans regardless of race or creed. The reward for these efforts and sacrifices came when the High Court decreed that separate, as it relates to school and similar institutions, is inherently unequal. The mandate that separation based on race is unconstitutional was the greatest pronouncement the Negro had heard since the Emancipation Proclamation and the Fourteenth Amendment. If the statement made by a doctor is representative of the thinking of others of his group, many southern whites looked with favor upon the decision. Said the doctor, "The Emancipation Proclamation freed the Negro physically; the Supreme Court decision of 1954 freed the white man's conscience. Many of us have never felt that what we have been doing has been right, but we had no good excuse to change."

43   If this man, and possibly others like him, viewed the Supreme Court decision as an excuse for agreeing to change, more can be said for those who suffered. For the Negro felt that the Court had finally opened a way to the land of freedom and opportunity for which he had longed and fought for some time. He knew that he had reluctantly obeyed state laws and city ordinances which deprived him of his constitutional rights. This, he had been told, is the duty and responsibility of all good citizens. Surely those who had preached obedience to the law should, themselves, be good examples of their preachments. Now that it was made very clear what the law was, would the changes be forthcoming?

44   It was not long before the intention of southern lawmakers was made unmistakably clear. The only law the white citizens of Alabama would obey was that made on their own Capitol Hill by their own state legislature. And the Negroes had come to realize that the Court would not and could not fight their battles for them. They did understand that they could use the legal arm to help secure the rights the courts said belonged to them.

45   The court decision outlawing segregation based on race in public education was pregnant with implications for the dawning of a new age and new hori-

zons for people of color in the South. The reactions of the southern whites was a clear demonstration of the fact that they intended no changes, whatsoever, in the *status quo*. They were set on maintaining what they called "our Southern way of life." The Negroes, on the other hand, were definitely looking for change. They were determined to change some of the social patterns of the South. In order that this might be done they would have to develop the courage, the skill, and the understanding to bring about such changes in the patterns which are consistent only in their inconsistencies. For example, movie houses which admit whites only, may be attended by a Negro maid if she is escorting "Mr. Charlie's little Johnny." Negroes with bandannas on their heads and faking a peculiar accent have been admitted to "white-only" places under the disguise of Indians, Arabians, or some other nationality. Anyone, except an American Negro, is permitted to enter.

46   These social practices on the part of whites are generally thought of as being carry-overs from the days of slavery. Three hundred years would seem long enough for the race which claims superiority to all others to have discovered its grave error. But some have closed their eyes to reality, and have denied the obvious truth: given an equal opportunity, Negroes are capable of standing, head and shoulder, with representatives of any racial group. The Montgomery strugglers accepted the challenge of forcing their oppressors to recognize and respect this truth. A gradual process, yes, but a continuous process as well.

47   The bus boycott ended officially on December 20, 1956; it was on that date that the Supreme Court's mandate reached Montgomery. On December 21st, 1956, more than a year after Mrs. Rosa Parks' arrest, integrated buses operated for the first time in the history of the city. Even before the bus boycott case had reached the Supreme Court, Negroes were already thinking of other areas to be attacked. The fact that court cases concerning the rights of Negroes had been lost in the past was no deterrent to the determination of the people at this time. They would continue to use the strong arm of federal law to break the yoke of unconstitutional state laws. The dream of a way of life of which the Negroes had had only a taste was adequate to sustain them in their strivings.

48   The boycott was a decided victory for the people of Montgomery and for the whole of humanity. It was never regarded by the Negroes as a struggle of blacks against whites. Rather it was thought of as a struggle of justice against injustice. Those who possessed faith in humanity and faith in God believed that justice would triumph. Sustained by such a faith and fortified by a visible sign of assurance, the people of color would continue to press their claim for first-class citizenship. Discrimination in city and state-owned parks, playgrounds, swimming pools and golf courses would be attacked with renewed and intensified vigor. All first class citizens participate in state and Federal government. This meant that Negroes would have to demand the right to register and vote. They walked to gain the privilege of riding; by standing in line they would gain their opportunity of registering and voting. And finally, the most glaring of all types of segregation, segregation in Christian worship, could never escape severe crit-

icism and firm attempts to correct the error. The fact that the eleven o'clock hour on Sunday morning is the most segregated hour of the week is of great concern to all who believe in the brotherhood of man.

49   When the boycott had ended, the next point of attack and the exact procedure to be followed were not specifically known. All only knew that the end of the boycott was the beginning of what was to be. The movement for freedom had gained such momentum that nothing could stop it. Even if the leaders of the movement had to fill an untimely grave, the volcano of social unrest would continue its eruptions, and the lava of love and nonviolent action would continue to force its way into the American conscience.

FOR ANALYSIS AND DISCUSSION

1. Who is the "new Negro" described by French in the first paragraph? How does this "new Negro" differ from the old? Why are the "white city fathers" concerned about this emerging kind of person?

2. Edgar comments that "every effort to break segregation and discrimination was met with double and sometimes triple counter-attack by the white people" (paragraph 6). Who are the "white people"? How did whites try to thwart black efforts for justice?

3. What did the arrest of Rosa Parks incite the black citizens of Montgomery to do? What did her action set in motion? If necessary, research Rosa Parks and the Montgomery bus boycott for more information about this event.

4. How did the bus boycott unify the black population of Montgomery? How did it, according to French, "restore dignity" to them?

5. French explains that the bus boycott was never meant to be an action of blacks against whites, but rather of justice against injustice. Explain, in your own words, what you think French means by this statement.

WRITING ASSIGNMENTS: EQUAL OPPORTUNITY

1. Research the civil rights movement of the 1950s and 1960s. How was U.S. society different 40 years ago? In what ways has it changed? Has racial inequality been eradicated? In a well-reasoned argument, support your view by drawing from your research and your personal experience. Access the *Seattle Times* photo archive at <http://www.seattletimes.com/mlk/movement/PT/phototour .html> for a visual perspective of the era.

2. Describe an experience you had with racism. The experience could have happened to you personally, or it could be one that you witnessed. How did you react to it? With the advantage of hindsight, would you have reacted differently now?

3. What does it mean to be racially defined in today's society? Do racial boundaries still prevent people from enjoying the rights granted and protected under the Constitution? Support your perspective with personal experiences and by citing current events.

4. In 1955 Rosa Parks, perhaps unknowingly, started a revolution. Access the Hall of Public Service's Web site at <http://www.achievement.org/autodoc/

page/par0int-1> and read about Rosa Parks. Why is she dubbed the "mother of the civil rights movement"? What did her action do for the people of Montgomery, Alabama? Do you think her act was courageous? Write about your impressions of this remarkable woman and her place in history.

REFLECTIONS ON THE STRUGGLE: LOOKING BACK, MOVING FORWARD

The Next Reconstruction
Tamar Jacoby

Compared to their status 30 years ago, it would seem that race relations have come a long way. Yet despite their professed efforts at integrating, blacks and whites still move largely in separate spheres. If current public policy strategies remain unaltered, experts fear that prevailing attitudes toward race relations will remain unchanged.

Tamar Jacoby is a senior fellow at the Manhattan Institute for Policy Research. Her latest book, *Someone Else's House,* examines America's integration policies since the 1960s. The following article appeared in the June 22, 1998, issue of the *New Republic.*

BEFORE YOU READ

Think about your friends and the group of people with whom you regularly socialize. Do they represent a variety of ethnic and racial backgrounds?

AS YOU READ

As the century comes to a close, many people believe integration has come a long way since the 1960s. Has America progressed that much? Is America truly "color blind"?

1   Sometimes, there is nothing more discouraging than a glimpse of the best we can do, and, when it comes to race relations, you see it in Atlanta. I spent a lot of time there recently reporting a book about race, and what I found was that the conventional wisdom is right: Blacks and whites get along better in Atlanta than just about anywhere else in America. It's a majority-black city and a well-known mecca for black professionals. But unlike whites in many urban areas with majority-black populations—Detroit, for example—Atlanta's middle-class whites have stayed in town. The economy is flourishing. The city's public life, in restaurants, theaters, parks, and shopping malls, is encouragingly integrated, and both blacks and whites feel they have a stake in the booming future.

2   Still, for all that, Martin Luther King's dream—a single community in which both blacks and whites would feel truly at home—is as elusive in Atlanta

"Peaceful coexistence is easier than forging new, more respectful and equitable ways to live together. Peaceful coexistence allows everyone to hold on to stereotypes: we never get close enough, after all, to disabuse ourselves." (Excerpt from Tamar Jacoby's "The Next Reconstruction")

as anywhere in America. The problem is different from what it used to be and is sometimes hard to define. Impoverished blacks are as alienated in Atlanta as anywhere in the country; most whites are just as indifferent to black poverty. But, even among the middle class, there is something missing in Atlanta. Whites live on one side of town, blacks on the other, their tree-lined streets and private schools and clubs often indistinguishable but still color-coded—now voluntarily so. Almost everyone in the city has occasion to work with someone of the other race, but very few have made real friendships across the color line. I asked one white man, a well-known journalist who has been covering the city's black establishment for more than 25 years, whether he did much socializing with black colleagues after office hours. "I can count the number of times I've been in a black home on the fingers of one hand," he told me. "Race relations?" asked another white man, a longtime liberal who had also spent his life working alongside blacks. "We don't have race relations in Atlanta anymore."

3   Unfortunately, when it comes to race, Atlanta is typical. Abigail and Stephan Thernstrom, Orlando Patterson, and others who remind us how much race relations have changed for the better are right. But we still haven't achieved the ideal of the 1960s. Comfortable and prosperous a life as it is, what prevails in Atlanta isn't racial harmony. It's peaceful coexistence—a wary truce between two groups who believe they are fundamentally different and will always live separately.

4   How did this happen? It's not just that we're tired or defeated or settling for this. On the contrary. We've let it happen, even caused it to happen, by deciding that this is all we're aiming for. In the years since the civil rights era, we've concluded that it doesn't make sense to think of ourselves as one community. We talk now about the "African American community" and the "Asian community" —and we think what makes us different from one another is more important than what we have in common. Blacks and whites assume that the other group was formed by a different culture, that "they" want to be different—and they're part of another America.

5   Partly, of course, this is a product of the mistrust and alienation built up over centuries. But, in the last 35 years, instead of figuring out how to move beyond those habits, we've embraced them, and, today, in the wake of California's Proposition 209, we are about to make the same mistake again. Faced with the results of repealing affirmative action, many analysts—most notably the social scientist Nathan Glazer writing in TNR's pages some weeks ago . . . —have argued that it's worth reinstating preferences in order to preserve what little integration we have. But to settle for that would be to miss the opportunity to achieve much more.

6   Of course, it's easy to see the attraction of the status quo. Peaceful coexistence is easier than forging new, more respectful and equitable ways to live together. Peaceful coexistence allows everyone to hold on to stereotypes: we never get close enough, after all, to disabuse ourselves. It lets whites go on thinking that they've done enough to help, even as it spares blacks the need to put aside old grudges. We glory in the small particulars that set us and ours apart and shrug off the challenge of figuring out who we are as individuals or, more important still, what it is we all have in common. As with any skewed relationship, creating this standoff has been a joint effort, but, after centuries of unfulfilled promises, it's hard to blame blacks for the alienation. What's harder to justify is the way that whites—usually well-meaning whites in positions of power—have chosen to meet the challenge of black inequality by effectively fostering a separate black America.

7   This pattern began in the mid-1960s, when the Malcolm-X–inspired ideal of Black Power began to eclipse King's integrationist credo. Black Power argued that the country was inherently racist, that blacks were fundamentally different from whites, that they would never be fully at home here, and that they were right to be angry at what the system had done to them. Well into the '60s, polls showed black America deeply divided on these issues: drawn to the showy anger of the Stokely Carmichaels and H. Rap Browns but still hopeful and largely intent on inclusion. Yet, in the name of racial peace, well-meaning liberals encouraged the Black Power movement, even glamorized it, rather than committing the nation to the hard work of addressing the discontent that gave rise to black demagogues.

8   The same phenomenon repeated itself in the later '60s when black youths took to the streets, looting and burning their own broken-down communities. There were no short-cut answers to the frustration that drove these kids to vio-

lence: Once the most obvious barriers had been leveled by the great civil rights laws, the much more intractable problem was mainly one of social inequality. But, instead of counseling education and job training and work, well-meaning whites on the Kerner Commission and elsewhere endorsed the rioter's impatience and scrambled to find easy ways to address it. The War on Poverty, with its substantive emphasis on schooling and work habits, was abandoned by Republicans and Democrats alike, and in its place Americans resorted to a host of quick-fix solutions: color-coded electoral districts instead of real political power; racial preferences to create the appearance of equality; guilty deference masquerading as respect; symbolic gestures; and cash grants.

9   In the cultural realm, too, whites have opted again and again to encourage quick fixes instead of hard work—in this case, the difficult and ever more elusive challenge of forging a real interracial community. Like hiring preferences and electoral apportionment to insure that black voters are represented by black officials, identity politics makes life easier for everyone. Black students live in black dorms—and life goes on as usual elsewhere on campus. Black scholars celebrate Africa, and we all honor Black History Month. But almost no one gives any serious thought to how to move beyond this tokenism. Meanwhile, in the name of multiculturalism, we've encouraged a generation of young blacks to believe that the main thing they bring to school and work is not their talents or skills but their "black point of view." We accept, even preach, the doctrine that the races are fundamentally different and that the best we can hope for is an edgy meeting across the gulf we approvingly label "diversity." Well-intentioned as such deference may be, it will not lead to inclusion. On the contrary, it can only delay the kind of push that is still needed to bridge the gap, particularly for the poorest blacks with the fewest changes and most meager skills.

10   After more than 30 years of short-cut answers, there is much damage to undo. And yet we are about to make the same mistake again. Proposition 209 in California has shown just how little preferences really achieved. Racial outreach brought black students to public campuses, but it did nothing to prepare them for the challenges they would meet there. And now that preferences have been dropped many blacks cannot get in. The number of black freshmen in the University of California system will drop by 18 percent this fall, the number at the elite Berkeley campus by 57 percent—from 5.6 percent of the freshman class to 2.4 percent. Most Americans are appalled by these numbers, but, instead of recognizing our error, many well-meaning whites are urging us to restore some version of the old preferences.

11   Of course, tackling the underlying causes of black academic underachievement would be much harder and much more expensive. It would mean overhauling the public school system. It would mean an extensive public relations effort to reverse the widespread sense among young African Americans that doing well in school is "acting white." It would mean making the streets of the inner city safe enough for children to get to school and study without fear. And all of that together would only take care of kindergarten through twelfth grade,

leaving us the still-harder tasks of pre-college preparation and job training—not to mention improving the education at second-tier colleges like the University of California Riverside campus, where the number of black freshmen has jumped, in the wake of Prop 209, by 34 percent.

12   This is the task we started with the War on Poverty and then gave up abruptly when we grasped just how big a chore it was. What we know now is that it probably isn't a job for government or, at least, government alone. It will take a concerted effort by the private and public sectors, blacks and whites, religious institutions, and a broad range of leaders at the grassroots and higher up. But slapping the Band-Aid of preferences back on will not replace the work that's needed—only defer it yet again and prolong the divided way we live.

13   Those who argue for reinstating affirmative action cite mostly pragmatic reasons. "The painful facts make it necessary," Glazer writes. The facts he cites are certainly discouraging: not just next year's U.C. admissions rates but also the persistent gap between black and white SAT scores, the distressingly high black college dropout rate, the continued unraveling of the black family, and more. Glazer and others don't quite say so, but what they conclude from these figures is that there's little point in a national effort to improve life chances for blacks. We haven't been able to raise black academic performance yet, they reason. Why should the future be different?

14   The problem with this reasoning is that America hasn't really tried yet. More than 30 years after the launching of the War on Poverty, we're only beginning to zero in on the kinds of development programs that work. Most of us have only recently grasped just how small a part government can play in stimulating the slow, hard personal transformation that economist Glenn Loury describes with the phrase, "One by one from the inside out." The nation as a whole has never mustered anything like the collective will to push government and business to do what they can; in fact, for reasons of racial sensitivity, we've hardly been able to talk about the nature of the push that's needed. And not even our best pilot efforts, many of them mounted by the inner-city churches, have been tried on a scale commensurate with the problem. Social and cultural development is a long, slow process, and, even under the best of circumstances, it can take several generations. But surely it would be wrong to give up without trying.

15   Part of the reason the challenge is so daunting is that much of it has to do with attitudes—attitudes toward school and work but also toward one's place in the larger culture—and here is where the mainstream has been sending all the wrong signals. The idea that blacks and whites are basically different, that we can never escape the past, that peaceful coexistence between two mistrustful groups is as good as it gets—all of this trickles down through the culture and poisons attitudes. The message is repeated and reinforced daily in countless ways, some of them explicit—some as innocuous as the idea that only black adults can be role models for black kids. No wonder many black students hesitate to make an effort in school; they've learned to see school as training for life in an alien civilization. No wonder ghetto youth are more likely to disobey the law; to them, the law is the arm of an age-old enemy. No wonder even middle-

class blacks making their way into the system are often demoralized, convinced that the "white world" will never be fair to them.

16   Well-meaning whites didn't create this alienation; it's been three centuries in the making. But, instead of getting better with the progress of the last few decades, if anything, black estrangement is getting worse. The first step to reverse this trend is a sustained program of acculturation and education for the poorest and most alienated blacks, but it will have to come twinned with a new, more hopeful message about community. What we have in common is more important than our differences. Martin Luther King wasn't wrong about America or blacks' place in it, and there is all the reason in the world for trying—at school, at work, in getting along, and at doing what has to be done to heal the ghetto. This is a demanding agenda, but it is the only antidote to the weary peaceful coexistence that passes for race relations in America today.

FOR ANALYSIS AND DISCUSSION

1. What type of segregation exists in Atlanta today? Why does Jacoby feel the peaceful coexistence of Atlanta's black and white populations is not acceptable? Do you agree with her perspective?
2. According to Jacoby, ethnic individualism prevents social unity. What impact does the author feel Malcolm X had on American society? What does she think are the drawbacks of cultural identity?
3. Jacoby makes the interesting observation that "once obvious racial barriers had been leveled by the great civil rights laws" (paragraph 8) blacks were faced with a more difficult enemy—social inequality. What does Jacoby mean by "social inequality"? Why did that pose a greater challenge than the "obvious racial barriers" of the civil rights movement? How did blacks confront this new "enemy"?
4. Describe your experiences with multiculturalism in school. What is multiculturalism? How is it addressed in public schools today? Do you agree with Jacoby that multiculturalism downplays the talents of blacks in favor of emphasizing their race alone? Explain.

Maybe Segregation Wasn't So Damaging
Gregory P. Kane

In 1954 the Supreme Court handed down the now-famous decision of *Brown v. Board of Education,* which called for the desegregation of public schools. Previously segregation of blacks and whites had been permitted, provided the schools were "equal in quality." The Supreme Court determined that segregated schools were by their very nature inherently unequal. Despite the decision, however, the demographic make-up of many schools remained basically unchanged.

Gregory Kane, a columnist for the *Baltimore Sun* who focuses on the city's African American community, grew up in Baltimore and attended Baltimore schools in the aftermath of the famous ruling. He attended a largely black school—a school the Supreme Court would consider "inherently unequal." However, Kane feels that he enjoyed a fulfilling and complete education. Perhaps, says Kane, integrated education is not the answer for all black children. The following article appeared in the May 17, 1994, issue of the *Baltimore Sun.*

BEFORE YOU READ

Consider the demographics of your university or college. Is the population diversity different from that of your high school or elementary school?

AS YOU READ

What impact did the knowledge that their school was inherently unequal have on the children in Kane's Baltimore schools? Did it adversely affect their education?

1   I was not quite 29 months old the day in 1954 that the Supreme Court outlawed school segregation in its famous Brown vs. Board of Education decision. I entered kindergarten in the fall of 1956 and spent all but 3 of the next 13 years in Baltimore schools that were considered segregated and "inherently unequal" by the Supreme Court.

2   That "inherently unequal" education did not seem to do me any harm. I suspect the same could be said of many other black Americans who were educated during that same period and before. We should all dwell on this before we lament the continued segregation of America's schools on the 40th anniversary of the Brown decision.

3   Instead of wringing our hands, maybe we should ask ourselves whether the NAACP was operating under the wrong assumption when it advocated desegregation. Maybe black children need good education, not necessarily integrated education. And maybe the two are not synonymous.

4   W. E. B. DuBois, a co-founder of the NAACP and the editor of its magazine, *The Crisis,* for many years, said as much in an editorial in January of 1934. The NAACP leadership thought he had lost his mind, but it seems in retrospect that DuBois may have come to his senses.

5   DuBois was not alone. The African-American writer Zora Neale Hurston had nothing but contempt for the Brown decision. Growing up in a black town in Florida may have given Hurston the curious notion that black schools were anything but "inherently inferior." She wrote in the *Orlando Sentinel* in the wake of the high court's decision:

> I had promised God, and some other responsible characters, including a bunch of bishops, that I was not going to part my lips concerning the United States Supreme Court decision on ending segregation in the public schools of the South . . . I break my silence just this once . . . The whole matter revolves around the self-respect of my people. How much satisfaction can I get from a court order for somebody to associate with me who

does not wish me near them? . . . I regard the ruling of the United States Supreme Court as insulting rather than honoring my race.

6   I didn't get my first dose of integrated education until January of 1962—eight years after Brown—when I spent the second semester of the fifth grade and all of the sixth grade at Mordecai Gist International School in Northwest Baltimore. From kindergarten through the first semester of the fifth grade, the teachers at the inherently inferior segregated schools of West Baltimore educated me as best they could.

7   The other years of my integrated education were spent at Baltimore City College from 1967 to 1969. I managed to graduate seventh in my class, but it was my teachers at the segregated Harlem Park Junior High School who prepared me for City.

8   My seventh-grade social studies teacher was Mr. Golden—a thin rail of a man whose standards were nearly as austere as his appearance. He opened our eyes to the world around us, telling us of the burgeoning civil rights movement and all the protagonists and antagonists therein—the NAACP, the Congress of Racial Equality, the Black Muslims (as the Nation of Islam was incorrectly called then) and the Ku Klux Klan.

9   It was in Mr. Golden's class that I first learned of the 178,000 black soldiers who fought on the Union side in the Civil War. On some days he would divide the class into two sides, and we would have a Jeopardy-like contest with one side pitting its knowledge against the other. Separately and unequally, we learned much and had fun doing it. Would integrated education have been significantly more rewarding?

10   My other teachers were just as effective. Mrs. Tilly handled seventh-grade English. Mrs. Davidson took care of French for two years in a row. Mr. Drain taught a superb ninth-grade world history class. Mrs. Holmes was an excellent ninth-grade math teacher until she took a job in private industry. The best of the lot may have been Mr. Scott, who taught ninth-grade English. Back then, an E was the equivalent of an A. He didn't give out E's, this Mr. Scott. No student was worthy of them. He assured the entire class constantly that we "weren't ready," that we had to meet higher standards consistently if we were to succeed. He put me on a debating team in which I and a partner had to argue for the establishment of a teen curfew. I didn't think I could do it, but we won the debate. After wading through Charles Dickens' "Great Expectations" for a class project and memorizing several passages from Shakespeare's "Julius Caesar," I got my E. But I had to work for it.

11   As we look back on Brown today, we may rightfully regret the academic performance of predominantly black schools across the country. But let us not delude ourselves into thinking that students in those schools aren't achieving them because they don't have white students sitting next to them.

FOR ANALYSIS AND DISCUSSION

1. In paragraph 3 Kane questions whether the NAACP was operating under the wrong assumption when it advocated desegregation. What do you think this

assumption was? Why does Kane think the NAACP may have been wrong? Do you agree? Explain.

2. What made Mordecai Gist Elementary School different from Kane's other schools? How does Kane feel about his education in the "inferior" segregated schools in Baltimore? How did he feel about Mordecai Gist Elementary?

3. What did Mr. Golden teach Kane's social studies class? Do you think a similar curriculum was taught in the less segregated schools in the 1960s? Explain.

4. Is there a certain amount of arrogance attached to the belief that desegregated schools are better than "segregated" ones? Why or why not?

5. What is Kane's tone in his article? How does he use voice to convey his message to the reader?

6. Kane often draws from the actual wording of the Supreme Court decision in *Brown v. Board of Education*. Why do you think he does this? What tone does he use when employing these words?

Whites Say I Must Be on Easy Street
Nell Irvin Painter

Affirmative action is an outgrowth of the 1964 Civil Rights Act and, later, the establishment of the Equal Employment Opportunity Commission ((EEOC). Its policies were developed to guarantee equal opportunity to all regardless of race, color, gender, religion, or national origin. In particular, its aim was to compensate African Americans for a long tradition of discrimination in employment. However, some critics—many white and some black—view affirmative action as unfair. Claiming that affirmative action gives preferential treatment to less qualified individuals, detractors sometimes call affirmative action "reverse racism." Historian Nell Irvin Painter points out that affirmative action policies have given some whites the impression that it is easy to get a professional job if you are black.

Nell Irvin Painter is currently Edwards Professor of American History at Princeton University, where she teaches the history of the American South. Her most recent work is *Sojourner Truth: A Life, A Symbol.* The following article appeared in the *New York Times* in 1981.

BEFORE YOU READ

Do you associate affirmative action with "equal opportunity" or "preferential treatment"? Explain your answer with reference to a specific case, if you can.

AS YOU READ

Painter says that the man's comments at the lecture embarrassed her. What do you think was the motivation behind his comments? Was he merely making conversation, or did he have a direct purpose in mind?

1 I've always thought affirmative action made a lot of sense, because discrimination against black people and women was prolonged and thorough. But I've

been hearing talk in the last several years that lets me know that not everyone shares my views. The first time I noticed it was shortly after I had moved to Philadelphia, where I used to live. One evening I attended a lecture—I no longer remember the topic—but I recall that I arrived early and was doing what I did often that fall. I worked at polishing my dissertation. In those days I regularly carried chapters and a nicely sharpened pencil around with me. I sat with pencil and typescript, scratching out awkward phrases and trying out new ones.

2   Next to me sat a white man of about 35, whose absorption in my work increased steadily. He watched me intently—kindly—for several moments. "Is that your dissertation?" I said yes, it was. "Good luck in getting it accepted," he said. I said that it had already been accepted, thank you.

3   Still friendly, he wished me luck in finding a job. I appreciated his concern, but I already had a job. Where? At Penn, for I was then a beginning assistant professor at the University of Pennsylvania. "Aren't you lucky," said the man, a little less generously, "you got a job at a good university." I agreed. Jobs in history were, still are, hard to find.

4   While cognizant of the job squeeze, I never questioned the justice of my position. I should have a job, and a good one. I had worked hard as a graduate student and had written a decent dissertation. I knew foreign languages, had traveled widely and had taught and published. I thought I had been hired because I was a promising young historian. Unlike the man beside me, I didn't think my teaching at a first-rate university required an extraordinary explanation.

5   "I have a doctorate in history," he resumed, "but I couldn't get an academic job." With regret he added that he worked in school administration. I said I was sorry he hadn't been able to find the job he wanted. He said: "It must be great to be black and female, because of affirmative action. You count twice." I couldn't think of an appropriate response to that line of reasoning, for this was the first time I'd met it face to face. I wished the lecture would start. I was embarrassed. Did this man really mean to imply that I had my job at his expense? The edge of competition in his voice made me squirm.

6   He said that he had received his doctorate from Temple, and yet he had no teaching job, and where was my degree from? "Harvard," I said. It was his time not to reply. I waited a moment for his answer, then returned to my chapter.

7   Now I live in North Carolina, but I still hear contradictory talk about affirmative action. Last spring I was having lunch with some black Carolina undergraduates. One young woman surprised me by deploring affirmative action. I wondered why. "White students and professors think we only got into the University of North Carolina because we're black," she complained, "and they don't believe we're truly qualified." She said that she knew that *she* was qualified and fully deserved to be at Carolina. She fulfilled all the regular admissions requirements. It was the stigma of affirmative action that bothered her; without it other students wouldn't assume she was unqualified.

8   Another student said that the stigma of affirmative action extended to black faculty as well. She had heard white students doubting the abilities of black professors. Indeed, she herself tended to wait for black professors to disprove her assumption that they did not know their fields. She was convinced

that without affirmative action, students would assume black faculty to be as good as white.

9   That's what I've been hearing from whites and blacks. White people tell me I must be on easy street because I'm black and female. (I do not believe I've ever heard that from a black person, although some blacks believe that black women have an easier time in the white world than black men. I don't think so.) White people tell me, "You're a twofer." On the one side of the color line, every black student knows that he or she is fully qualified—I once thought that way myself. It is just the other black people who need affirmative action to get in. No one, not blacks, not whites, benefits from affirmative action, or so it would seem.

10   Well, I have, but not in early 1960s, when I was an undergraduate in a large state university. Back then, there was no affirmative action. We applied for admission to the university like everyone else; we were accepted or rejected like everyone else. Graduate and undergraduate students together, we numbered about 200 in a student body of nearly 30,000. No preferential treatment there.

11   Yet we all knew what the rest of the university thought of us, professors especially. They thought we were stupid because we were black. Further, white women were considered frivolous students; they were only supposed to be in school to get husbands. (I doubt that we few black women even rated a stereotype. We were the ultimate outsiders.) Black students, the whole atmosphere said, would not attend graduate or professional school because their grades must be poor. Women had no business in postgraduate education because they would waste their training by dropping out of careers when they married or became pregnant. No one said out loud that women and minorities were simply and naturally inferior to white men, but the assumptions were as clear as day: whites are better than blacks; men are better than women.

12   I am one of the few people I know who will admit to having been helped by affirmative action. To do so is usually tantamount to admitting deficiency. To hear people talk, affirmative action exists only to employ and promote the otherwise unqualified, but I don't see it that way at all. I'm black and I'm female, yet I was hired by two history departments that had no black members before the late 60's, never mind females. Affirmative action cleared the way.

13   Thirty-five years ago, John Hope Franklin, then a star student, now a giant in the field of American history, received a doctorate in history from Harvard. He went to teach in a black college. In those days, black men taught in black colleges. White women taught in white women's colleges. Black women taught in black women's colleges. None taught at the University of Pennsylvania or the University of North Carolina. It was the way things were.

14   Since then, the civil rights movement and the feminist movement have created a new climate that permitted affirmative action, which, in turn, opened areas previously reserved for white men. Skirts and dark skins appeared in new settings in the 1970s, but in significant numbers only after affirmative action mandated the changes and made them thinkable. Without affirmative action, it never would have occurred to any large, white research university to consider me for professional employment, despite my degree, languages, publications, charm, grace, *despite* my qualifications.

15   My Philadelphia white man and my Carolina black women would be surprised to discover the convergence of their views. I doubt that they know that
their convictions are older than affirmative action. I wish I could take them
back to the early 60's and let them see that they're reciting the same old white-
male–superiority line, fixed up to fit conditions that include a policy called affirmative action. Actually, I will not have to take those people back in time at
all, for the dismantling of affirmative action fuses the future and the past. If it
achieves its stated goals, we will have the same old discrimination, unneedful of
new clothes.

FOR ANALYSIS AND DISCUSSION

1. What is the "stigma" of affirmation action Painter's students mention in their
   lunch conversation with her? How wide is its scope? Can minority students
   avoid this stigma?
2. What is Painter's opinion of affirmative action? Does Painter's admission of the
   negative aspects of affirmative action detract from her argument? Explain.
3. Has Painter's essay changed or reinforced your thinking about affirmative action? If so, in what ways? Which points of her essay do you find particularly
   convincing?
4. In paragraph 12 Painter comments that few people she knows will admit to
   having been helped by affirmative action. Why is this the case? Do you think
   these same people would openly criticize affirmative action?
5. Painter, as a historian, draws from lessons from the past to predict the future. What does Painter believe will happen if affirmative action policies are
   dismantled?

Ghettoized by Black Unity
Shelby Steele

America has long been called the "land of opportunity." Yet until recently, African
Americans were barred from the opportunities America offered its other citizens.
The following essay by Shelby Steele calls for African Americans to move beyond
"black identity" to seize the opportunities before them. According to Steele, black
power reinforces a victim-focused identity.

Shelby Steele is a professor of English at San Jose State University and a leading
figure in national debates regarding black issues. He is the author of several books,
including the widely acclaimed *The Content of Our Character: A New Vision of Race
in America* (1990), in which this essay appeared.

BEFORE YOU READ

How do you identify yourself? Is your ethnic background a part of your identity? If
so, how significant is it?

AS YOU READ

What racial stereotypes does Steele battle in his daily life? What racial stereotypes existed in the region or country where you grew up? What were these stereotypes based on?

1   There are many profound problems facing black America today: a swelling black underclass; a black middle class that declined slightly in size during the Eighties; a declining number of black college students; an epidemic of teenage pregnancy, drug use, and gang violence; continuing chronic unemployment; astoundingly high college and high school dropout rates; an increasing number of single-parent families; a disproportionately high infant mortality rate; and so on. Against this despair it might seem almost esoteric for me to talk about the importance of individual identity and possibility. Yet I have come to believe that despite the existing racism in today's America, opportunity is the single most constant but unexploited aspect of the black condition. The only way we will see the advancement of black people in this country is for us to focus on developing ourselves as individuals and embracing opportunity.

2   I have come to this conclusion over time. In the late Sixties, I was caught up in the new spirit of black power and pride that swept over black America like one of these storms that change the landscape. I will always believe this storm was inevitable and, therefore, positive in many ways. What I gained from it was the power to be racially unapologetic, no mean benefit considering the long trial of patience that blacks were subjected to during the civil rights movement. But after a while, by the early Seventies, it became clear that black power did not offer much of a blueprint for how to move my life forward; it told me virtually nothing about who I was as an individual or how I might live in the world as myself. Of course, it was my mistake to think it could. But in the late Sixties, "blackness" was an invasive form of collective identity that cut so deeply into one's individual space that it seemed also to *be* an individual identity. It came as something of a disappointment to realize that the two were not the same, that being "black" in no way spared me the necessity of being myself.

3   In the early Seventies, without realizing it, I made a sort of bargain with the prevailing black identity—I subscribed in a general way to its point of view so that I could be free to get on with my life. Many blacks I knew did the same.

4   And what were we subscribing to? Generally, I think it was a form of black identity grounded in the spirit of black power. It carried a righteous anger at and mistrust of American society; it believed that blacks continued to be the victims of institutional racism, that we would have to maintain an adversarial stance toward society, and that a tight racial unity was necessary both for survival and advancement. This identity was, and is, predicated on the notion that those who burned you once will burn you again, and it presupposes a deep racist reflex in American life that will forever try to limit black possibility.

5   I think it was the space I cleared for myself by loosely subscribing to this identity that ultimately put me in conflict with it. It is in the day-to-day struggle

of living on the floor of a society, so to speak, that one gains a measure of what is possible in that society. And by simply living as an individual in America—with my racial-identity struggle suspended temporarily—I discovered that American society offered me, and blacks in general, a remarkable range of opportunity if we were willing to pursue it.

6   In my daily life I continue to experience racial indignities and slights: This morning I was told that blacks had too much musical feeling (soul, I suppose) to be good classical musicians; yesterday I passed two houses with gnomish black lawn jockeys on their front porches; my children have been called "nigger," as have I; I wear a tie and carry a briefcase so that my students on the first day of class will know I'm the professor; and so on. I also know that actual racial discrimination persists in many areas of American life. I have been the victor in one housing-discrimination suit, as were my parents before me. My life is not immune to any of this, and I will never endure it with élan. Yet I have also come to realize that, in this same society, I have been more in charge of my fate than I ever wanted to believe and that though I have been limited by many things, my race was not foremost among them.

7   The point is that both realities exist simultaneously. There is still racial insensitivity and some racial discrimination against blacks in this society, but there is also much opportunity. What brought me into conflict with the prevailing black identity was that it was almost entirely preoccupied with the former to the exclusion of the latter. The black identity I was subscribing to in the Seventies—and that still prevails today—was essentially a "wartime" identity shaped in the confrontational Sixties. It saw blacks as victims even as new possibilities for advancement opened all around.

8   Why do we cling to an adversarial, victim-focused identity and remain preoccupied with white racism? Part of the reason, I think, is that we carry an inferiority anxiety—an unconscious fear that the notion that we are inferior may, in fact, be true—that makes the seizing of opportunity more risky for us, since setbacks and failures may seem to confirm our worst fears. To avoid this risk we hold a victim-focused identity that tells us there is less opportunity than there actually is. And, in fact, our victimization itself has been our primary source of power in society—the basis of our demands for redress. The paradoxical result of relying on this source of power is that it rewards us for continuing to see ourselves as victims of a racist society and implies that opportunity itself is something to be given instead of taken.

9   This leaves us with an identity that is at war with our best interests, that magnifies our oppression and diminishes our sense of possibility. I think this identity is a burden for blacks, because it is built around our collective insecurity rather than a faith in our human capacity to seize opportunity as individuals. It amounts to a self-protective collectivism that focuses on black unity instead of individual initiative. To be "black" in this identity, one need only manifest the symbols, postures, and rhetoric of black unity. Not only is personal initiative unnecessary for being "black" but the successful exercise of initia-

tive—working one's way into the middle class, becoming well-off, gaining an important position—may, in fact, jeopardize one's "blackness," make one somehow less black.

10 This sort of identity is never effective and never translates into the actual uplift of black people. Though it espouses black pride, it is actually a repressive identity that generates a victimized self-image, curbs individualism and initiative, diminishes our sense of possibility, and contributes to our demoralization and inertia. Uplift can only come when many millions of blacks seize the possibilities inside the sphere of their personal lives and use them to move themselves forward. Collectively we can resist oppression, but racial development will always be, as Ralph Ellison once put it, "the gift" of individuals.

11 There have been numerous government attempts at remedying the list of problems I mentioned earlier. Here and there a program has worked; many more have been failures. Clearly, we should find the ones that do work and have more of them. But my deepest feeling is that, in a society of increasingly limited resources, there will never be enough programs to meet the need. We black Americans will never be saved or even assisted terribly much by others, never be repaid for our suffering, and never find that symmetrical, historical justice that we cannot help but long for.

12 As Jean-Paul Sartre once said, we are the true "existential people." We have always had to create ourselves out of whole cloth and find our own means for survival. I believe that black leadership must recognize the importance of this individual initiative. They must preach it, tell it, sell it, and demand it. Our leadership has looked at government and white society very critically. Now they must help us look at ourselves. We need our real problems named and explained, otherwise we have no chance to overcome them. The impulse of our leaders is to be "political," to keep the society at large on edge, to keep them feeling as though they have not done enough for blacks. And, clearly, they have not. But the price these leaders pay for this form of "politics" is to keep blacks focused on an illusion of deliverance by others, and no illusion weakens us more. Our leaders must take a risk. They must tell us the truth, tell us of the freedom and opportunity they have discovered in their own lives. They must tell us what they tell their own children when they go home at night; to study hard, to pursue their dreams with discipline and effort, to be responsible for themselves, to have concern for others, to cherish their race and at the same time build their own lives as Americans. When our leaders put a spotlight on our victimization and seize upon our suffering to gain us ineffectual concessions, they inadvertently turn themselves into enemies of the truth, not to mention enemies of their own people.

13 I believe that black Americans are freer today than ever before. This is not a hope; this is a reality. Racial hatred has not left the American landscape. Who knows how or when this will occur. And yet the American black, supported by a massive body of law and, for the most part, the goodwill of his fellow citizens, is basically as free as he or she wants to be. For every white I have met who is a

racist, I have met twenty more who have seen me as an individual. This, I am not ashamed to say, has been my experience. I believe it is time for blacks to begin the shift from a wartime to a peacetime identity, from fighting for opportunity to seizing it. The immutable fact of late–twentieth-century American life is that it *is* there for blacks to seize. Martin Luther King did not live to experience this. But then, of course, on the night before he died, he seemed to know that he would not. From the mountaintop he had looked over and seen the promised land, but he said, "I may not get there with you . . ." I won't say we are snuggled deep in the promised valley he saw beyond the mountain; everyday things remind me that we are not. But I also know we have it better than our greatest leader. We are on the other side of his mountaintop, on the downward slope toward the valley he saw. This is something we ought to know. But what we must know even more clearly is that nothing on this earth can be promised except a chance. The promised land guarantees nothing. It is only an opportunity, not a deliverance.

FOR ANALYSIS AND DISCUSSION

1. Steele mentions that many African Americans in the seventies "made a sort of bargain with the prevailing black identity" (paragraph 3). What was this prevailing identity? How did it develop? Can a movement define the identify of an entire race of people? Explain.

2. According to Steele, the black power movement of the seventies prevented African Americans from moving their lives forward. What does he mean by this statement? How can pride in one's heritage and ethnic identity prevent progress? Or does it?

3. Why does Steele think it is easier for African Americans to remain resentful and angry victims of society? What reasons does he give for this prevailing anger? Is such resentment justified? Explain.

4. What did Martin Luther King, Jr. say about the "promised land"? What do you think the promised land was to King? What do you think it is for Steele?

WRITING ASSIGNMENTS: REFLECTIONS ON THE STRUGGLE

1. Racetalks Initiatives is an ongoing interdisciplinary project conducted by University of Pennsylvania law professors Lani Guinier and Susan Sturm that examines racial and gender issues. Access the Racetalks Web site at <http://www.law.upenn.edu/racetalk/> and read some of the student papers there. Then find out the affirmative action policy of your own school's admissions department. Are there numerical quotas? Write an argument in which you defend or criticize your policy. Support your essay with information from the Racetalks Web site.

2. Evaluate the diversity of employees at three institutions in your area: a school, a bank, and a successful local business. What is the racial distribution of the different types of positions at each institution? For example, who are the tellers,

the service people, and the officers of the bank? Evaluate the information you collect and discuss it with the class. Is opportunity available to all? After merging your data with those of other members of your class, write an essay evaluating employment diversity in the area.

3. Imagine that Martin Luther King, Jr. and Malcolm X were put in a time machine from 1965 and moved forward 35 years. Interview each leader for his opinion on race relations in the 1990s. What do you think each would say? Do you think the two would be satisfied or discouraged? Organize your paper as if it were a real interview.

credits

Note: Page numbers followed by *italicized* letter *f* indicate material presented in figures.